Moors /MDA/   Sahara ~~more~~ morocco
Eur. med. fr. Fr. zone.

100 YRS WAR - 1337-1453

The Pocket Oxford Dictionary of

ALGERIA

1830 - Fr Territory → 1954 Front de
libe-ration Nationale started 8 yr. reb →
independence July 5, 1962 - Ahmed ~~Beela~~
Ben Bella, president. → Pieds noirs
(Eur, Fr,) left country → 60° + 70° soc.
State → 1965 coup. ~~19 th~~ Boume-
dienne president - Chadli, in 79 when
he died → vowed reforms, liberalization,
affirm Arab, islamic culture → to 90° →
1999 Bouteflika pres - Islamic
Salvation Army AIS ~~su~~ surrendered
→ political roller coaster → ↑ 70's + 80s
west. Sahara struggle made Algeria mad
at France, who supported Morocco → lefer,
↑ gas export prices from Algeria → 86/88
peace, french assets frozen since ind.
released in return for fin. aid →
92 mil. coup. → rumours Fr. knew →
93 Balladur PM of France, eco. +
pol. support increased. → 94 so

Much terrorism against french → GIA
declared war → Morroco/Algeria border
dispute after tourist killing in Morocco →
95 neg. commenced → King HASSAN of
Morocco → pissed that Algeria sup. ind. for
West. siah. → Zeroual
- GIA - Groupe Islamic Arm
- MIA - Armed Islamic Movement.

CHECHNYA - obtained ceium-137 - radioactive isotope.
- Leb pres - Lahhoud
- 2nd Crusade & soldirs - Kurd -1187 recaptured
  chr. lost, then
  Jerusalem →3rd Crusade - King Richard of
  England → truce, mus. had holy land)
  but chr. could visit shrines → mus. had
  all of holy land by 1291 - stories of
  crusades led to exploration, led to renaissance
- 1932 Iraq became fully independant
- 1958 overthrow of King Faisal → Left wing
  → 1959 - withdrew from bagdhad pact.
- 79 - hussein
- Russia Afgan - 79-89
- Camb. 75-79 - ind. from frs in '53 - Prince
  Sihanouk stayed neutral through V-N - 1970
  overthrown By U.S backed Lon Nol → R.W →
  Sihanouk formed resistence w-Pol Pot
  V-N. intervened - left 1990 -93 elections

The Pocket Oxford Dictionary of
Biography

Edited by
ANGUS STEVENSON

Oxford

OXFORD UNIVERSITY PRESS

Oxford University Press, Great Clarendon Street, Oxford OX2 6DP

Oxford New York
Athens Auckland Bangkok Bogota Bombay
Buenos Aires Calcutta Cape Town Dar es Salaam
Delhi Florence Hong Kong Istanbul Karachi
Kuala Lumpur Madras Madrid Melbourne
Mexico City Nairobi Paris Singapore
Taipei Tokyo Toronto Warsaw

and associated companies in
Berlin Ibadan

Oxford is a registered trade mark of Oxford University Press

Published in the United States by
Oxford University Press Inc., New York

© *Oxford University Press 1997*

First published 1997
Reprinted with corrections 1998

British Library Cataloguing in Publication Data
Data available

Library of Congress Cataloging in Publication Data
The Pocket Oxford Dictionary of Biography | edited by Angus Stevenson.
1. Biography—Dictionaries. I. Stevenson, Angus.
CT103.P63 1997 920'.003—dc20 96-30696
ISBN 0-19-860062-3

10 9 8 7 6 5 4 3

Designed in Swift and Frutiger by Jane Stevenson
Typeset by Interactive Sciences Ltd
Printed in Great Britain by
Mackays PLC, Chatham, Kent

Contents

Acknowledgements

Chief Editor, Current English Dictionaries
Patrick Hanks

Managing Editor, Encyclopedic Dictionaries
Judy Pearsall

Editor
Angus Stevenson

Senior Editors
Catherine Soanes, David Shirt

Assistant Editors
Michael Lacewing, Tom Penn, Rachel Unsworth

Pronunciation Editor
Judith Scott

Introduction

This is the first edition of the *Pocket Oxford Dictionary of Biography*. The book is intended as a handy, inexpensive reference work providing concise and accessible information on a great number of figures of international importance, both historical and contemporary. The dictionary contains some 4,350 biographies in a simple A–Z format and represents a wide-ranging selection of figures from all periods, countries, and spheres of activity.

As well as giving the important facts about a person's life and work, the entries provide information which puts in a wider context the life and achievements of the subject and his or her overall importance within a particular field or historical period. The entries are presented in a straightforward, readable style with a minimum of symbols and abbreviations.

The text is based on the biographical entries of the *Oxford English Reference Dictionary* (1995). The entries have been updated or rewritten as necessary, and in addition some 500 new biographies have been written: many of these are for figures from the worlds of film, sport, contemporary politics, and popular culture.

A particular feature of the *Pocket Oxford Dictionary of Biography* is its coverage of scientists, from world-famous pioneers such as Albert Einstein to inventors like Rudolf Diesel, computer pioneers like Bill Gates, and popular or 'alternative' scientists such as James Lovelock, originator of the Gaia hypothesis.

The appendices offer information that is more usefully presented in tabular form, giving lists for the Prime Ministers of the United Kingdom, New Zealand, Canada, and Australia, Presidents of the US, and kings and queens of England and the United Kingdom.

Selecting which entries to include in a reference work of this kind is not a straightforward task, and given the limitations of space the final selection will almost certainly prove controversial. Throughout the book the aim has been to cover as broad a spectrum as possible in order to be of maximum help and interest to readers.

Pronunciation

Guidance on the pronunciation of a headword will be found in most cases immediately after the headword, enclosed in oblique strokes / /, and is based on the standard pronunciation associated especially with southern England (sometimes referred to as 'received pronunciation').

■ In some cases, more than one pronunciation is given: that given first is generally the preferred pronunciation.

■ Pronunciations for variant forms are given at the main entry; those for alternative names are given at the alternative name (cross-reference) entry.

■ The first pronunciation given is always the standard pronunciation in English, even if the entry relates to a foreign name. A second pronunciation reflecting that used in the original language may be given where this is substantially different from the English pronunciation.

The International Phonetic Alphabet

Pronunciations are given using the International Phonetic Alphabet (IPA). The symbols used, with their values, are as follows:

Consonants

$b, d, f, h, k, l, m, n, p, r, s, t, v, w,$ and z have their usual English values. Other symbols are used as follows:

g	(get)	ŋ	(ring)	ʃ	(she)
tʃ	(chip)	θ	(thin)	ʒ	(decision)
dʒ	(jar)	ð	(this)	j	(yes)
x	(loch)				

Vowels

short vowels		long vowels		diphthongs	
æ	(cat)	ɑː	(arm)	eɪ	(day)
e	(bed)	iː	(see)	aɪ	(my)
ə	(ago)	ɔː	(saw)	ɔɪ	(boy)
ɪ	(sit)	ɜː	(her)	əʊ	(no)
ɒ	(hot)	uː	(too)	aʊ	(how)
ʌ	(run)			ɪə	(near)
ʊ	(put)			eə	(hair)
				ʊə	(poor)
				aɪə	(fire)
				aʊə	(sour)

■ (ə) signifies the indeterminate sound as in garden, carnal, and altruism.

■ (r) at the end of a word indicates an r that is sounded when a word beginning with a vowel follows, as in *clutter up* and *an acre of land*.

The main or primary stress of a word is shown by ' preceding the relevant syllable; any secondary stress in words of three or more syllables is shown by , preceding the relevant syllable.

■ In addition the following IPA symbols are used in the representation of foreign pronunciations:

Consonants

ç
β
ʎ
ɬ
ɣ
ɲ

Vowels

short vowels	long vowels	nasalized vowels
a	a:	
ɑ		ɑ̃
ɛ	e:	ɛ̃
i		
o	o:	
u		
œ		œ̃
ɔ		ɔ̃
ø	ø:	
		ə̃
y	y:	
ɥ		

A

Aalto /'ɑːltəʊ/, (Hugo) Alvar (Henrik) (1898–1976), Finnish architect and designer. His early work was in the neoclassical style, but in the late 1920s he adopted the 'international style', in such buildings as the Viipuri (Vyborg, now in Russia) Library (1927–35) and the Paimio convalescent home (1929–33). In Finland he often used mixed materials such as brick, copper, and timber in his designs to blend with the landscape. Outside Finland his best-known work is the Baker House hall of residence at Massachusetts Institute of Technology, where he taught 1945–9. As a designer he is known as the inventor of bent plywood furniture.

Abbas /ə'bæs/, Ferhat (1899–1989), Algerian nationalist leader. After attempting to cooperate with the French in setting up an Algerian state, he became disenchanted and in 1956 joined the revolutionary Front de Libération Nationale (FLN). He was elected President of the provisional government of the Algerian republic (based in Tunisia) in 1958 and President of the constituent assembly of independent Algeria in 1962. In 1963 he was detained for opposing the FLN's proposed constitution, but was released the following year.

Abbe /'æbɪ/, Ernst (1840–1905), German physicist. He worked with Carl Zeiss from 1866, and in 1868 invented the apochromatic lens. He also designed several optical instruments, including a light condenser for use in microscopes and a refractometer. He became sole owner of the Zeiss company in 1888.

Abduh /'æbduː/, Muhammad (1849–1905), Egyptian Islamic scholar, jurist, and liberal reformer. As Grand Mufti of Egypt from 1899, he introduced reforms in Islamic law and education and is best known for his *Treatise on the Oneness of God*.

Abdul Hamid II /ˌæbdʊl 'hæmɪd/ (known as 'the Great Assassin') (1842–1918), the last sultan of Turkey 1876–1909. An autocratic ruler, he suspended Parliament and the constitution and is remembered for the brutal massacres of Christian Armenians in 1894–6. In 1909 he was deposed after the revolt in the previous year of the Young Turks.

Abdullah /æb'dʊlə/, Sheikh Muhammad (known as 'the Lion of Kashmir') (1905–82), Kashmiri Muslim leader. In the 1930s he actively opposed the rule of the Hindu maharajah of Kashmir. After accepting Indian sovereignty (1947), he eventually won for Kashmir a form of autonomy within India, although he was imprisoned for much of the time between 1953 and 1968 on suspicion of seeking its full independence.

Abdullah ibn Hussein /æbˌdʊlə ˌɪb(ə)n hʊ'seɪn/ (1882–1951), king of Jordan 1946–51. He served as emir of Transjordan 1921–46, and was Jordan's first king when it became independent in 1946. He was assassinated in 1951.

Abdul Rahman /ˌæbdʊl 'rɑːmən/, Tunku (1903–90), Malayan statesman, Prime Minister of Malaya 1957–63 and of Malaysia 1963–70. A skilled negotiator, he secured Malayan independence from Britain (1957) and was one of the architects of the federation of Malaysia (1963).

Abel /'ɑːb(ə)l/, Niels Henrik (1802–29), Norwegian mathematician. He proved that equations of the fifth degree cannot be solved by conventional algebraic methods, and made advances in the fields of power series and elliptic functions. He died in poverty of tuberculosis at the age of 26.

Abelard /'æbɪˌlɑːd/, Peter (1079–1142), French scholar, theologian, and philosopher. His independence of mind, particularly his application of philosophical principles to theological questions, impressed his contemporaries but brought him into frequent conflict with the authorities and led to his being twice condemned for heresy. He lectured in Paris until his academic career was cut short in 1118 by his tragic love affair with his pupil Héloïse, niece of Fulbert, a canon of Notre-Dame. Abelard was castrated at Fulbert's instigation; he entered a monastery, and made Héloïse become a nun. Abelard continued his controversial teaching, applying reason

to questions of faith, notably to the doctrine of the Trinity. In the early 1130s he and Héloïse put together a collection of their love letters and other correspondence, which was published in 1616. Abelard and Héloïse are buried together in Paris.

Aberdeen /ˌæbəˈdiːn/, 4th Earl of (title of George Hamilton Gordon) (1784–1860), British Conservative statesman, Prime Minister 1852–5. He reluctantly involved his country in the Crimean War (1853–6) and was subsequently blamed for its mismanagement and obliged to resign.

Abiola /ˌæbɪˈəʊlə/, Moshood (Kashimawo Olawale) (born 1937), Nigerian politician. The leader of the Social Democratic Party, he declared himself President-elect in June 1993 after election results showed him to be on the way to a comfortable victory. The election was annulled by the ruling military regime; a year later Abiola again declared himself President, but was placed under house arrest.

Abrahams /ˈeɪbrəˌhæmz/, Harold (Maurice) (1899–1978), English athlete. In 1924 he became the first Englishman to win the 100 metres in the Olympic Games. His story was the subject of the film *Chariots of Fire* (1981).

Achebe /əˈtʃeɪbɪ/, Chinua (born Albert Chinualumgu) (born 1930), Nigerian novelist, poet, short-story writer, and essayist. His novels, all written in English, show traditional African society in confrontation with European customs and values. They include *Things Fall Apart* (1958) and *A Man of the People* (1966). In 1989 Achebe won the Nobel Prize for literature.

Acheson /ˈeɪtʃɪs(ə)n/, Dean Gooderham (1893–1971), American statesman. In 1949 he became Secretary of State to President Truman. He urged international control of nuclear power, was instrumental in the formation of NATO, and implemented the Marshall Plan and the Truman Doctrine.

Adam /ˈædəm/, Robert (1728–92), Scottish architect. He undertook a grand tour of Europe, starting in 1754, mainly in France and Italy, which gave him knowledge of ancient buildings and modern neoclassical theory. Robert and his brother James (1730–94) set up in business in London in 1758 and in the course of the next forty years initiated the 'Adam Revolution', introducing a lighter, more decorative

style than the Palladianism favoured by the British architecture of the previous half-century. Typical examples of their work include Home House in Portland Square, London, and Register House in Edinburgh.

Adams[1] /ˈædəmz/, Ansel (Easton) (1902–84), American photographer. In the 1930s he developed the use of large-format cameras and small apertures to produce sharp images with maximum depth of field, very different from the fashionable soft-focus work of the time. Many of Adams's collections, such as *My Camera in the National Parks* (1950) and *This is the American Earth* (1960), depict the American wilderness and reflect his interest in conservation.

Adams[2] /ˈædəmz/, John (1735–1826), American Federalist statesman, 2nd President of the US 1797–1801. He was a key figure in the drafting of the Declaration of Independence (1776), and was minister to Britain 1785–8.

Adams[3] /ˈædəmz/, John Couch (1819–92), English astronomer. In 1843 he postulated the existence of an eighth planet from perturbations in the orbit of Uranus. Similar calculations performed almost simultaneously by Le Verrier resulted in the discovery of Neptune three years later. Adams carried out numerous advanced mathematical calculations, including improved figures for the moon's parallax and motion.

Adams[4] /ˈædəmz/, John Quincy (1767–1848), American statesman, 6th President of the US 1825–9. The eldest son of President John Adams, he was minister to Britain 1809–14. As Secretary of State (1817–24) he helped to shape the Monroe doctrine, the principle of US foreign policy that any intervention by external powers in the politics of the Americas is a potentially hostile act against the US. After leaving office he was prominent in the campaign against slavery.

Addams /ˈædəmz/, Jane (1860–1935), American social reformer and feminist. Inspired by Toynbee Hall in London, she founded Hull House, a social settlement, in Chicago in 1889; this became a national model for the combat of urban poverty and the treatment of young offenders. She was prominent in the suffrage movement, serving as president of the National American Woman Suffrage Association (1911–14); also a pacifist, she presided over the first

Women's Peace Congress at The Hague in 1915. She shared the Nobel Peace Prize with the educationist Nicholas Butler (1862–1947) in 1931.

Addington /'ædɪŋtən/, Henry, 1st Viscount Sidmouth (1757–1844), British Tory statesman, Prime Minister 1801–4. As Home Secretary (1812–21), he introduced harsh legislation to suppress the Luddites and other protest groups.

Addison[1] /'ædɪs(ə)n/, Joseph (1672–1719), English poet, dramatist, essayist, and Whig politician. In 1711 he founded the *Spectator* with Sir Richard Steele. His tragedy *Cato* (1713) was an immediate success. In the history of English literature he is notable for his simple unornamented prose style, which marked the end of the more mannered and florid writing of the 17th century.

Addison[2] /'ædɪs(ə)n/, Thomas (1793–1860), English physician. He described the disease now named after him, ascribing it correctly to defective functioning of the adrenal glands. Distinguished for his zeal in the investigation of disease, Addison had a great reputation as a clinical teacher, and Guy's Hospital in London attained fame as a school of medicine during the time of his connection with it.

Adenauer /'ædɪˌnaʊə(r)/, Konrad (1876–1967), German statesman, first Chancellor of the Federal Republic of Germany 1949–63. He co-founded the Christian Democratic Union in 1945. As Chancellor, he is remembered for the political and economic transformation of his country. He secured the friendship of the US and was an advocate of strengthening political and economic ties with Western countries through NATO and the European Community.

Adler /'ædlə(r)/, Alfred (1870–1937), Austrian psychologist and psychiatrist. At first a disciple of Sigmund Freud, he came to disagree with Freud's idea that mental illness was caused by sexual conflicts in infancy, arguing that society and culture were equally, if not more, significant factors. In 1907 he introduced the concept of the inferiority complex, asserting that the key to understanding both personal and mass problems was the sense of inferiority and the individual's striving to compensate for this. In 1911 he and his followers formed their own school to develop the ideas of individual psychology, and in 1921

he founded the first child guidance clinic, in Vienna.

Adorno /ə'dɔːnəʊ/, Theodor Wiesengrund (born Theodor Wiesengrund) (1903–69), German philosopher, sociologist, and musicologist. Director of the Frankfurt Institute for Social Research 1958–69, he was a leading figure in the Frankfurt School of philosophy, which reappraised Marxism in terms of modern industrial society. He is known for such works as *Dialectic of Enlightenment* (1947, written with Max Horkheimer) and *Negative Dialectics* (1966). In these works Adorno develops his concept of reason as a key factor of social control, concluding that philosophical authoritarianism is inevitably oppressive and all theories should be systematically and consciously rejected.

Adrian IV /'eɪdrɪən/ (born Nicholas Breakspear) (*c*.1100–59), pope 1154–9. The only Englishman to have held this office, he assisted Henry II of England to gain control of Ireland and opposed Frederick I's (Barbarossa's) claims to power.

Aelfric /'ælfrɪk/ (*c*.955–*c*.1020) Anglo-Saxon monk, writer, and grammarian. His chief works are the *Catholic Homilies* (990–2) and the *Lives of the Saints* (993–6), both written in Old English. He also wrote a Latin grammar, which earned him the name 'Grammaticus'.

Aeschines /'iːskɪˌniːz/ (*c*.390–*c*.314 BC), Athenian orator and statesman. He opposed Demosthenes' efforts to unite the Greek city-states against Macedon, with which he attempted to make peace. Aeschines was tried for treason in 343 but acquitted, and left Athens for Rhodes in 330 after failing to defeat Demosthenes.

Aeschylus /'iːskɪləs/ (*c*.525–*c*.456 BC), Greek dramatist. The earliest writer of Greek tragic drama whose works survive, he is best known for his trilogy the *Oresteia* (458 BC), consisting of *Agamemnon*, *Choephoroe*, and *Eumenides*. These tell the story of Agamemnon's murder at the hands of his wife Clytemnestra and the vengeance of their son Orestes. Aeschylus is distinguished by the scale and grandeur of his conceptions. He departed from tradition by giving more weight to dialogue than to choral song and in adding a second actor to the existing one plus chorus.

Aesop /'iːsɒp/ (6th century BC), Greek storyteller. The moral animal fables associated

with him were probably collected from many sources, and initially communicated orally; they were later popularized by the Roman poet Phaedrus (1st century BC), who translated some of them into Latin. Aesop is said to have lived as a slave on the island of Samos.

Aga Khan /ˌɑːgə ˈkɑːn/ the title of the imam or leader of the Nizari sect of Ismaili Muslims. The first Aga Khan was given his title in 1818 by the shah of Persia, subsequently moving with the majority of the Nizaris to the Indian subcontinent. The present (4th) Aga Khan (Karim Al-Hussain Shah, born 1937 in Geneva) inherited the title from his grandfather in 1957. The title of Aga Khan (which comes from the Turkish words for master and ruler) carries with it responsibility for various services and welfare provisions for members of the Nizari community.

Agassi /ˈægəsɪ/, André (born 1970), American tennis player. Agassi was a precocious tennis talent and by the age of 18 was ranked third in the world. Noted for his unconventional on-court appearance and impetuous behaviour, early in his career Agassi clashed repeatedly with the tennis establishment. He won the Wimbledon men's singles title in 1992, successive grand slam titles in 1994 and 1995, and a gold medal in the 1996 Olympics.

Agassiz /ˈægəsɪ/, Jean Louis Rodolphe (1807–73), Swiss-born zoologist, geologist, and palaeontologist. In 1837 Agassiz was the first to propose that much of Europe had once been in the grip of an ice age. He lived in America from 1846 onwards and became an influential teacher and writer on many aspects of natural history. He was an opponent of Darwin's theory of evolution, holding that organisms were immutable and independent of each other.

Agnes, St[1] /ˈægnɪs/ (died c.304), Roman martyr. Said to have been a Christian virgin who refused to marry, she was martyred during the reign of Diocletian. She is the patron saint of virgins and her emblem is a lamb (Latin *agnus*). Feast day, 21 January.

Agnes, St[2] /ˈægnɪs/ (c.1211–82), patron saint of Bohemia. She was canonized in 1989. Feast day, 2 March.

Agnesi /æˈnjeɪʒɪ/, Maria Gaetana (1718–99), Italian mathematician and philosopher. She is regarded as the first female mathematician of the Western world, though she worked on a variety of scientific subjects. Her major work, which appeared in two volumes in 1748, was a comprehensive treatment of algebra and analysis, of which perhaps the most important part was concerned with differential calculus.

Agostini /ˌægəˈstiːnɪ/, Giacomo (born 1944), Italian racing motorcyclist. Between 1966 and 1975 he won a record fifteen world titles, and held the 500 cc. title eight times, also a record. Among his other wins were the Isle of Man TT (ten times, between 1966 and 1975). He retired in 1975 and subsequently became manager of the Yamaha racing team.

Agricola /əˈgrɪkələ/, Gnaeus Julius (AD 40–93), Roman general and governor of Britain 78–84. As governor he completed the subjugation of Wales, advanced into Scotland, and defeated the Caledonian Highland tribes at the battle of Mons Graupius.

Agrippa /əˈgrɪpə/, Marcus Vipsanius (63–12 BC), Roman general. Augustus' adviser and son-in-law, he played an important part in the naval victories over Mark Antony, and held commands in western and eastern provinces of the empire.

Aidan, St /ˈeɪd(ə)n/ (died AD 651), Irish missionary. While a monk in the monastery at Iona, he was assigned the mission of Christianizing Northumbria by the Northumbrian king Oswald (c.604–41). Aidan founded a church and monastery at Lindisfarne in 635 and became its first bishop; he also established a school for training missionaries of the Celtic Church. He later founded further churches and monasteries in Northumbria.

Airy /ˈeərɪ/, Sir George Biddell (1801–92), English astronomer and geophysicist. He investigated the diffraction pattern of a point source of light and devised cylindrical lenses to correct for astigmatism. In geophysics, he proposed the concept of isostasy to account for the gravitational anomalies associated with mountain masses, and gave an improved estimate of the earth's density. Airy was Astronomer Royal for forty-six years.

Aitken /ˈeɪtkɪn/, William Maxwell, see BEA-VERBROOK.

Akbar /ˈækbɑː(r)/, Jalaludin Muhammad (known as Akbar the Great) (1542–1605), Mogul emperor of India 1556–1605. Akbar expanded the Mogul empire to incorporate northern India, and established admin-

istrative efficiency and a coherent commercial system. He was the first ruler of India to promote religious and racial toleration. Akbar abolished slavery, prohibited the practice of suttee, legitimized the remarriage of widows, and banned polygamy except in cases of infertility.

Akhenaten /ˌækəˈnɑːt(ə)n/ (also **Akhenaton, Ikhnaton** /ɪkˈnɑːt(ə)n/) (14th century BC), Egyptian pharaoh of the 18th dynasty, reigned 1379–1362 BC. The husband of Nefertiti, he came to the throne as Amenhotep IV, and after six years introduced the monotheistic solar cult of Aten, the sun disc, with the king as sole intermediary, changing his name to Akhenaten. The capital of Egypt was moved from Thebes to his newly built city of Akhetaten (now Tell el-Amarna). He was succeeded by his son-in-law, Tutankhamen, who abandoned the new religion early in his reign.

Akhmatova /ækˈmɑːtəvə/, Anna (pseudonym of Anna Andreevna Gorenko) (1889–1966), Russian poet. A member of the Acmeist group of poets with Osip Mandelstam, Akhmatova favoured concrete detail, direct expression, and precision of language as a reaction against the mysticism of contemporary symbolist poetry. The personal and Christian tone of *Anno Domini* (1922), however, contributed to her official disfavour, which was to last for over thirty years. Her works include *Poem without a Hero* (1940–62) and *Requiem* (1940).

Alain-Fournier /ˌælænˈfʊənɪˌeɪ/ (pseudonym of Henri-Alban Fournier) (1886–1914), French novelist. A literary columnist, he completed only one novel before he was killed in action in the First World War. The book, *Le Grand Meaulnes* (1913), is a lyrical semi-autobiographical narrative set in the countryside of Alain-Fournier's adolescence. His early poems and short stories were published as *Miracles* in 1924.

Alarcón /ˌæləˈkɒn/, Pedro Antonio de (1833–91), Spanish novelist and short-story writer. His best-known work, the humorous short story *The Three-Cornered Hat* (1874), was the source for Manuel de Falla's ballet and Hugo Wolf's opera, both of the same name.

Alarcón y Mendoza see RUIZ DE ALARCÓN Y MENDOZA.

Alaric /ˈælərɪk/ (c.370–410), king of the Visigoths 395–410. Alaric invaded Greece (395–6) and then Italy (400–3), but was checked on each occasion by the Roman general Stilicho (c.365–408). He invaded Italy again in 408 and in 410 captured Rome.

Alban, St /ˈɔːlbən/ (3rd century), the first British Christian martyr. A pagan of Verulamium (now St Albans, Herts.), he was converted and baptized by a fugitive priest whom he sheltered. When soldiers searched his house, he put on the priest's cloak and was arrested and condemned to death. Feast day, 22 June.

Albee /ˈɔːlbiː, ˈæl-/, Edward Franklin (born 1928), American dramatist. He was initially associated with the Theatre of the Absurd; *Who's Afraid of Virginia Woolf* (1962) marked a more naturalistic departure and showed an interest in closely observed human relationships. Later plays, such as *Tiny Alice* (1965) and *A Delicate Balance* (1966), demonstrate his increasing preoccupation with abstract issues.

Albers /ˈælbəz/, Josef (1888–1976), German-born American artist, designer, and teacher. He was a teacher at the Bauhaus until 1933, and his work was strongly influenced by constructivism. His designs are characterized by intellectual calculation and the use of simple geometric shapes, as in his furniture design (including the first laminated chair for mass production) and pictures made with pieces of coloured glass. He experimented with colour juxtapositions in his *Homage to the Square* series (begun in 1950). As a teacher at Black Mountain College in North Carolina (1934–50), he was instrumental in disseminating Bauhaus principles throughout the US.

Albert, Prince /ˈælbət/ (1819–61), consort to Queen Victoria. First cousin of the queen and prince of Saxe-Coburg-Gotha, he revitalized the British court in the first twenty years of his wife's reign. He was one of the driving forces behind the Great Exhibition of 1851; its profits allowed the construction of the Royal Albert Hall (1871) and of museum buildings in South Kensington. In 1861, just before his premature death from typhoid fever, his moderating influence was crucial in keeping Britain out of the American Civil War.

Alberti /ælˈbeətɪ/, Leon Battista (1404–72), Italian architect, humanist, painter, and art critic. He wrote the first account of the theory of perspective in the Renaissance in his *Della Pittura* (1435). He is also credited

with reawakening interest in Roman architecture, after the publication of his *De Re
Aedificatoria* (1485). His own architecture,
classical in style, includes the façades of
the churches of Santa Maria Novella in
Florence and of San Francesco in Rimini.

Albertus Magnus, St /ˈælˌbɜːtəs ˈmægnəs/
(known as 'Doctor Universalis') (*c.*1200–80),
Dominican theologian, philosopher, and
scientist. A teacher of St Thomas Aquinas,
he was a pioneer in the study of Aristotle
and contributed significantly to the com-
parison of Christian theology and pagan
philosophy. His particular interest in the
physical sciences, including alchemy,
earned him a reputation for magical
powers. Feast day, 15 November.

Albinoni /ˌælbɪˈnəʊnɪ/, Tomaso (1671–1751),
Italian composer. He wrote more than fifty
operas, but is now best known for his
melodic instrumental music. Several of his
many concertos have seen a revival, but the
Adagio in G with which he is popularly
associated was in fact composed by the
Italian musicologist Remo Giazotto (born
1910), based on a manuscript fragment by
Albinoni.

Albinus see ALCUIN.

Albuquerque /ˈælbəˌkɜːkɪ/, Alfonso de
(known as Albuquerque the Great) (1453–
1515), Portuguese colonial statesman. He
first travelled east in 1502, and, after being
appointed viceroy of the Portuguese Indies
four years later, conquered Goa and made
it the capital of the Portuguese empire in
the east. Albuquerque made further conquests in Ceylon, Malacca, Ormuz, the
Sunda Islands, and the Malabar Coast, but
was relieved of office as a result of a court
intrigue at home and died on the passage
back to Portugal.

Alcaeus /ælˈsiːəs/ (*c.*620–*c.*580 BC), Greek
lyric poet. His most important contribution was a new form of lyric metre in four-
line stanzas, the alcaic; he also wrote
political odes, drinking-songs, and love-
-songs. His works were an important model
for the Roman poet Horace as well as for
French and English verse of the Renaissance.

Alcibiades /ˌælsɪˈbaɪəˌdiːz/ (*c.*450–404 BC),
Athenian general and statesman. Educated
in the household of Pericles, he became the
pupil and friend of Socrates. In the Peloponnesian War he sponsored the unsuccessful Athenian expedition against Sicily,

but fled to Sparta after being recalled for
trial on a charge of sacrilege. He later held
commands for Athens against Sparta and
Persia, before his enemies finally forced
him from Athens and had him murdered
in Phrygia.

Alcock /ˈɔːlkɒk/, Sir John William (1892–
1919), English aviator. Together with Sir
Arthur Whitten Brown, he made the first
non-stop transatlantic flight (16 hours 27
minutes) on 14–15 June 1919, from Newfoundland to Clifden, Ireland, in a converted Vickers Vimy bomber.

Alcott /ˈɔːlkɒt/, Louisa May (1832–88),
American novelist. From an early age she
published sketches and stories to support
her family, including *Hospital Sketches*
(1863), which recounted her experiences as
a nurse in the Civil War. Her most popular
novel was *Little Women* (1868–9), a largely
autobiographical work about a New England family, written for adolescent girls.
She wrote a number of sequels to this as
well as novels for adults. Alcott was involved in diverse reform movements, including women's suffrage.

Alcuin /ˈælkwɪn/ (*c.*735–804) (also **Albinus**
/ælˈbiːnəs/), English scholar, theologian,
and adviser to Charlemagne. While attached to the court of the Frankish leader,
he improved the palace library and transformed the court into a cultural centre for
Charlemagne's empire (a period referred to
as the Carolingian Renaissance). On becoming abbot of Tours in 796, he established an
important library and school there. He
developed the type of script known as
Carolingian minuscule, which influenced
the development of the roman type now
used in printed books.

Aldiss /ˈɔːldɪs/, Brian W(ilson) (born 1925),
English novelist and critic. Known primarily for his works of science fiction such as
Frankenstein Unbound (1973) and *Moreau's
Other Island* (1980), he has done much to
promote the cause of science fiction as a
literary genre, including writing a history
of the subject, *Billion Year Spree* (1973).

Aldrin /ˈɔːldrɪn/, Edwin Eugene (known as
'Buzz') (born 1930), American astronaut.
Originally an air-force pilot, he became an
astronaut in 1963, and walked in space for
5 hours 37 minutes during the 1966 Gem-
ini 12 mission. In 1969 he took part in the
first moon landing, the Apollo 11 mission,
becoming the second person to set foot on
the moon, after Neil Armstrong.

Aldus Manutius /ˌɔːldəs məˈnjuːʃɪəs/ (Latinized name of Teobaldo Manucci; also known as Aldo Manuzio) (1450–1515), Italian scholar, printer, and publisher. He is remembered for the fine first editions of many Greek and Latin classics which were printed at his press in Venice. Aldus Manutius pioneered the widespread use of italic type, which he used as a text type in many of his printed books.

Alekhine /ˈælɪˌkiːn, ˈæljəkɪn/, Alexander (born Aleksandr Aleksandrovich Alyokhin) (1892–1946), Russian-born French chess player. Notorious for his multiple strategies of attack, he was world champion 1927–35 and from 1937 until his death.

Alembert /ˈæləmˌbeə(r)/, Jean le Rond d' (1717–83), French mathematician, physicist, and philosopher. His most famous work was the *Traité de dynamique* (1743), in which he developed his own laws of motion. From 1746 to 1758 he was Diderot's chief collaborator on the *Encyclopédie*, a seminal text of the Age of Enlightenment.

Alexander[1] /ˌælɪgˈzɑːndə(r)/ (known as Alexander the Great) (356–323 BC), son of Philip II, king of Macedon 336–323. He was a pupil of Aristotle. After his succession he invaded Persia, liberating the Greek cities in Asia Minor, and then defeating the Persians in Egypt, Syria, and Mesopotamia. While in Egypt he founded Alexandria (332 BC), his first and greatest city. He went on to extend his conquests eastwards, taking Bactria and the Punjab. He died of a fever at Babylon, and his empire quickly fell apart after his death. Regarded as a god in his lifetime, he became a model for many subsequent imperialist conquerors of antiquity, and the subject of many fantastic legends.

Alexander[2] /ˌælɪgˈzɑːndə(r)/ the name of three kings of Scotland:
Alexander I (c.1077–1124), son of Malcolm III, reigned 1107–24. During his reign he paid homage to King Henry I of England as his overlord. Nevertheless, he maintained the independence of the Scottish Church from the English Church.
Alexander II (1198–1249), son of William I of Scotland, reigned 1214–49. He generally restored friendly relations with England, negotiating a treaty with King Henry III. He extended royal authority within his own realm, particularly in the western Highlands and the south-west.
Alexander III (1241–86), son of Alexander

II, reigned 1249–86. He built up a strong, united, and prosperous kingdom, and succeeded in annexing the Hebrides and the Isle of Man in 1266. His death in a riding accident left Scotland without a male heir to the throne, and plunged the country into three decades of dynastic upheaval and struggle against English domination.

Alexander[3] /ˌælɪgˈzɑːndə(r)/ the name of three tsars of Russia:
Alexander I (1777–1825), reigned 1801–25. Alexander came to the throne after the murder of his tyrannical father Paul, and pursued reforming policies in education, science, administration, and the system of serfdom. The first half of his reign was dominated by the military struggle with Napoleon, which culminated in the French emperor's unsuccessful invasion of Russia in 1812. In the latter part of his reign Alexander became disillusioned by the failure of the Holy Alliance (a loose alliance of European powers proclaimed 1814–15 to uphold the principles of Christianity) and less interested in reforms at home.
Alexander II (known as Alexander the Liberator) (1818–81), son of Nicholas I, reigned 1855–81. He introduced a programme of modernization and political and economic reforms, including limited emancipation of the serfs (1861), nationwide construction of railways and schools, and the creation of local government in the provinces (1864). Alexander's harsh suppression of peasant revolts and revolutionary movements led, however, to the hardening of radical opposition in the form of terrorist groups, such as the People's Will, a group of which succeeded in assassinating the tsar with a bomb in March 1881.
Alexander III (1845–94), son of Alexander II, reigned 1881–94. Ascending the throne after his father's assassination, Alexander III fell back on repressive conservatism, heavily centralizing the imperial administration, weakening local government, abolishing autonomous peasant administrations, and persecuting Jews. Although his reign witnessed considerable economic development, his social policies produced a dangerous situation in Russia, which he bequeathed to his doomed son and successor Nicholas II.

Alexander[4] /ˌælɪgˈzɑːndə(r)/, Harold (Rupert Leofric George), 1st Earl Alexander of Tunis (1891–1969), British Field Marshal and Conservative statesman. In the Second

World War he supervised the evacuation from Dunkirk, the withdrawal from Burma, and the victorious campaigns in North Africa (1943), Sicily, and Italy (1943–5). After the war he became Governor-General of Canada (1946–52) and British Minister of Defence (1952–4).

Alexander Nevsky /'njefskɪ/ (also **Nevski**) (canonized as St Alexander Nevsky) (c.1220–63), Russian national hero. Born Aleksandr Yaroslavich, he was elected prince of Novgorod in 1236, ruling it until 1263. He was called 'Nevsky' after the River Neva, on whose banks he defeated the Swedes in 1240. In 1242 he defeated the powerful German order the Teutonic Knights on the frozen Lake Peipus. Feast day, 30 August or 23 November.

Alfonso XIII /æl'fɒnsəʊ/ (1886–1941), king of Spain 1886–1931. Alfonso ruled under the regency of his mother until 1902, during which time Spain lost her colonial possessions in the Philippines and Cuba to the US. In 1923 he supported Miguel Primo de Rivera's assumption of dictatorial powers, but by 1931 Alfonso had agreed to elections. When these indicated the Spanish electorate's clear preference for a republic, the king was forced to abdicate.

Alfred /'ælfrɪd/ (known as Alfred the Great) (849–99), king of Wessex 871–99. Alfred's military resistance saved SW England from Viking occupation. He negotiated the treaty giving the Danelaw to the Norsemen (886). A great reformer, he reorganized his land-based garrisons, founded the English navy, issued a new code of laws, introduced administrative and financial changes, revived learning, and promoted the use of English for literature and education.

Alfvén /'ælven/, Hannes Olof Gösta (1908–95), Swedish theoretical physicist. He worked mainly in plasma physics, and pioneered the study of magnetohydrodynamics. His contributions have proved important for studies of plasmas in stars and in controlled thermonuclear fusion, though he opposed the development of nuclear reactors and weapons. Alfvén shared the Nobel Prize for physics in 1970.

Algren /'ɔːlgrən/, Nelson (Abraham) (1909–81), American novelist. He drew on his childhood experiences in the slums of Chicago for his vivid, realistic novels, the first of which was *Somebody in Boots* (1935). Other works include *The Man with the Golden Arm* (1949) and *Walk on the Wild Side* (1956).

Ali, Muhammad, see MUHAMMAD ALI[1], MUHAMMAD ALI[2].

Alighieri /ˌælɪ'ɡjeərɪ/, Dante, see DANTE.

Allen[1] /'ælən/, Ethan (1738–89), American soldier. He tried to obtain independence for the state of Vermont, commanding the irregular force the Green Mountain Boys 1770–5. In 1775, during the War of Independence, he seized the British Fort Ticanderoga, but the same year was captured at Montreal. On his release in 1778 he presented to Congress Vermont's claims to independence, which was achieved the following year.

Allen[2] /'ælən/, Woody (born Allen Stewart Konigsberg) (born 1935), American film director, writer, and actor. Allen stars in most of his own films, which humorously explore themes of neurosis and sexual inadequacy. Zany early comedies such as *Play it Again, Sam* (1972) and *Love and Death* (1975) were followed by the slightly graver *Annie Hall* (1977), for which he won three Oscars. His later films include the Oscar-winning *Hannah and her Sisters* (1986) and *Husbands and Wives* (1992). In 1993 he was involved in a much-publicized court case with his former partner Mia Farrow (born 1945) over custody of their children, after he had embarked on an affair with Farrow's adopted daughter.

Allenby /'ælənbɪ/, Edmund Henry Hynman, 1st Viscount (1861–1936), British soldier. A veteran of the Boer War, during the First World War he commanded the First Cavalry Division and later the Third Army on the Western Front. In 1917 he was sent to the Middle East to lead the Egyptian Expeditionary Force. Having captured Jerusalem in December 1917, he went on to defeat the Turkish forces in Palestine in 1918. He was promoted to Field Marshal and later served as High Commissioner in Egypt (1919–25).

Allende /æ'jendɪ/, Salvador (1908–73), Chilean statesman, President 1970–3. Co-founder of the Chilean Socialist Party (1933) and the first avowed Marxist to become president after a free election, Allende used his term to introduce socialist measures, including the nationalization of several industries, the redistribution of land, and the opening of diplomatic relations with Communist countries. Soon

faced with a severe economic crisis, industrial unrest, and the withdrawal of foreign investment, he was overthrown and killed in 1973 in a military coup led by General Pinochet.

Allston /'ɔːlstən/, Washington (1779–1843), American landscape painter. He was the first major artist of the American romantic movement; his early works (for example *The Deluge*, 1804, and his vast unfinished canvas, *Belshazzar's Feast*, 1817–43) exhibit a taste for the monumental, apocalyptic, and melodramatic, in the same vein as the English painters J. M. W. Turner and John Martin. More influential in America, however, were his later visionary and dreamlike paintings such as *Moonlit Landscape* (1819).

Alma-Tadema /ˌælmə'tædɪmə/, Sir Lawrence (1836–1912), Dutch-born British painter. Influenced by a trip to Naples and Pompeii in 1863, he turned to lush genre scenes set in the ancient world, which earned him many imitators. His major paintings include *Pyrrhic Dance* (1869) and *Roses of Heliogabalus* (1888).

Almodóvar /ˌælmə'dəʊvɑː(r)/, Pedro (born 1951), Spanish film director. His films are outlandishly inventive and deal outrageously with sexual matters. *Women on the Verge of a Nervous Breakdown* (1988) is one of his most successful works, merging gaiety, violence, and tragedy. His other films include *Tie Me Up, Tie Me Down!* (1990), *High Heels* (1991), and *Kika* (1993).

Altdorfer /'æltdɔːfə(r)/, Albrecht (c.1485–1538), German painter and engraver. Inspired by travels along the Danube and in the Austrian Alps in 1511, he emerged as one of the first European landscape painters of modern history and principal artist of the Danube School. His romantic treatment of landscape and the emotional harmony of landscape and human action (as in *Saint George in the Forest*) epitomize the methods and sentiments of the school.

Althusser /'æltuˌseə(r)/, Louis (1918–90), French philosopher. His work in reinterpreting traditional Marxism in the light of structuralist theories had a significant influence on literary and cultural theory from the 1970s. He sought to reassert an anti-humanist approach to Marxism and develop it into a structural analysis of society. His most important works include *For Marx* (1965) and *Reading Capital* (1970).

Found guilty of the murder of his wife, he spent his last years in a mental asylum.

Altman /'ɔːltm(ə)n, 'ɒl-/, Robert (born 1925), American film director. He made his name with *MASH* (1970), a black comedy about an army surgical hospital at the front in the Korean war. He has been nominated for an Oscar for best director four times, for *MASH*, *Nashville* (1975), *The Player* (1992), and *Short Cuts* (1993), which he also co-wrote.

Alvarez /æl'vɑːrez/, Luis Walter (1911–88), American physicist. In particle physics, he discovered the phenomenon whereby an atomic nucleus can capture an orbiting electron, and made (with F. Bloch) the first measurement of the neutron's magnetic moment. He also developed the bubble chamber for detecting charged particles, for which he received the Nobel Prize for physics in 1968. In 1980 Alvarez and his son Walter, a geologist, discovered iridium in sediment from the Cretaceous–Tertiary boundary and proposed that this resulted from a catastrophic meteorite impact which caused a drastic climate change and resulted in the extinction of the dinosaurs.

Amati /ə'mɑːtɪ/ a family of Italian violinmakers. The three generations, all based in Cremona, included Andrea (c.1520–c.1580), his sons Antonio (1550–1638) and Girolamo (1551–1635), and, most notably, the latter's son Nicolò (1596–1684). From Nicolò's workshop came the violin-makers Antonio Stradivari and Andrea Guarneri (c.1626–98), uncle of Giuseppe Guarneri 'del Gesù'. The Amatis developed the basic proportions of the violin, viola, and cello, refining the body outlines, sound-holes, purfling, and scroll.

Ambrose, St /'æmbrəʊz/ (c.339–97), Doctor of the Church. He was a Roman governor at Milan and a converted Christian, though not yet baptized, when he was elected bishop of Milan (374) and became a champion of orthodoxy. He was partly responsible for the conversion of St Augustine of Hippo. His knowledge of Greek enabled him to introduce much Eastern theology and liturgical practice into the West; Ambrosian (antiphonal) plainsong is associated with his name, and the Athanasian Creed has been attributed to him. Feast day, 7 December.

Amenhotep /ˌɑːmen'həʊtep/ (Greek name Amenophis) the name of four Egyptian pharaohs of the 18th dynasty:

Amenhotep I (16th century BC), son of Ahmose I (founder of the 18th dynasty), reigned 1546–1526. He fought wars in Nubia and raided Libya.

Amenhotep II (15th century BC), son of Hatshepsut and Tuthmosis III, reigned 1450–1425. Brought up as a warrior, he fought successful campaigns in Syria and the Middle East; he completed some of the buildings begun by his father.

Amenhotep III (15th–14th centuries BC), son of Tuthmosis IV, reigned 1417–1379. After early military campaigns, his reign was generally peaceful and prosperous; he embarked on an extensive building programme centred on his capital, Thebes, including the colossi of Memnon and the Luxor temple.

Amenhotep IV see AKHENATEN.

Amin /æˈmiːn/, Idi (full name Idi Amin Dada) (born 1925), Ugandan soldier and head of state 1971–9. Having risen through the ranks of the army to become its commander, in 1971 he overthrew President Obote and seized power. His rule was characterized by the advancing of narrow tribal interests, expulsion of non-Africans (most notably the Ugandan Asians), and the murder of thousands of his political opponents. With Tanzanian assistance he was overthrown in 1979.

Amis[1] /ˈeɪmɪs/, Sir Kingsley (1922–95), English novelist and poet. He achieved popular success with his first novel *Lucky Jim* (1954), a satire on middle-class and academic aspirations set in a provincial university and seen through the eyes of its anti-Establishment hero. Amis's later novels show a more sombre tendency, exemplified in works such as *The Folks that Live on the Hill* (1990). He won the Booker Prize for his novel *The Old Devils* (1986). He also published four volumes of poetry.

Amis[2] /ˈeɪmɪs/, Martin (Louis) (born 1949), English novelist. Son of Kingsley Amis, he published his first novel, *The Rachel Papers*, in 1973. His other novels include *Money* (1984) and *Time's Arrow* (1991). Chiefly set against a background of contemporary urban life, his works are notable for their black humour and inventive use of language, especially slang and dialect.

Ampère /ˈæmpeə(r), French ɑ̃pɛr/, André-Marie (1775–1836), French physicist, mathematician, and philosopher. He was a child prodigy who became one of the founders of electromagnetism and electrodynamics, and is best known for his analysis of the relationship between magnetic force and electric current. Ampère also developed a precursor of the galvanometer.

Amundsen /ˈɑːmʊnds(ə)n/, Roald (1872–1928), Norwegian explorer. Amundsen made his name as a polar explorer when he became the first to navigate the Northwest Passage in the small sailing vessel *Gjöa* (1903–6), during which expedition he also travelled over the ice by sledge and located the site of the magnetic North Pole. In 1911 he beat the British explorer Robert F. Scott in the race to be the first to reach the South Pole. In the 1920s Amundsen devoted himself to aerial exploration of the polar regions, eventually disappearing on a search for the missing Italian airship expedition led by Umberto Nobile (1885–1978).

Anacreon /əˈnækrɪən/ (c.570–478 BC), Greek lyric poet. The surviving fragments of his work include iambic invectives and elegiac epitaphs, but he is most famous for his poetry written in celebration of love and wine.

Anaxagoras /ˌænækˈsægərəs/ (c.500–c.428 BC), Greek philosopher. He taught in Athens, where his pupils included Pericles. He believed that all matter was infinitely divisible and initially held together in a motionless, uniform mixture until put into a system of circulation directed by Spirit or Intelligence, which created the sky and earth, from which the sun, moon, and stars were formed. His concept of an independent moving cause prepared the way for a fully teleological view of nature.

Anaximander /æˌnæksɪˈmændə(r)/ (c.610–c.545 BC), Greek scientist, who lived at Miletus. He is reputed to have drawn the earliest map of the inhabited world, to have introduced the sundial into Greece, and to have taught that life began in water and that man originated from fish. He believed that all phenomena result from vortical motion in the primordial substance, and that the earth is cylindrical and poised in space.

Anaximenes /ˌænækˈsɪmɪˌniːz/ (c.546 BC), Greek philosopher and scientist, who lived at Miletus. Anaximenes believed the earth to be flat and shallow, and his view of astronomy was a retrograde step from that of Anaximander. He also proposed a theory of condensation and rarefaction, as a means of change from the basic form of

matter to the diversity of natural substances.

Andersen /'ændəs(ə)n/, Hans Christian (1805–75), Danish writer. The son of a poor shoemaker, he published several volumes of poetry and was acknowledged in Scandinavia as a novelist and travel writer before publishing the first of his fairy tales. These appeared from 1835 and include 'The Snow Queen', 'The Ugly Duckling', and 'The Little Match Girl'. Although deeply rooted in Danish folklore, the stories were also shaped by Andersen's own psychological alienation. His clear, simple prose set a new style of writing for both children and adults.

Anderson[1] /'ændəs(ə)n/, Carl David (1905–91), American physicist. In 1932, while using a cloud chamber to investigate cosmic rays, he accidentally discovered the positron — the first antiparticle known. He shared the Nobel Prize for physics for this in 1936, and also discovered the muon later the same year.

Anderson[2] /'ændəs(ə)n/, Elizabeth Garrett (1836–1917), English physician. Debarred from entry to medical courses because of her sex, she studied privately and in 1865 obtained a licence to practise from the Society of Apothecaries. In 1866 she opened a dispensary for women and children in London, which later became a hospital; it was renamed the Elizabeth Garrett Anderson Hospital in 1918. In 1870 she received the degree of MD from Paris University, and in 1873 she became the first woman to be elected to the BMA. Her influence was considerable in securing the admission of women to professional medical bodies.

Anderson[3] /'ændəs(ə)n/, Lindsay (Gordon) (1923–94), English film director. He made a number of documentary films during the 1950s, and won an Oscar for *Thursday's Children* (1955). His first feature film, the fiercely satirical *This Sporting Life* (1963), established him as a leading director in Britain. He went on to produce the bleak but blackly humorous trilogy *If . . .* (1968), *O Lucky Man* (1973), and *Britannia Hospital* (1982) and the more sentimental *The Whales of August* (1987).

Anderson[4] /'ændəs(ə)n/, Marian (1902–93), American operatic contralto. Despite early recognition of her singing talents, racial discrimination meant that she was initially unable to give concerts in her native land. She gained international success from several European tours between 1925 and 1935, but it was not until after her New York début in 1936 that her American career flourished. In 1955 she became the first black singer to perform at the New York Metropolitan Opera.

Anderson[5] /'ændəs(ə)n/, Philip Warren (born 1923), American physicist. He made contributions to the study of solid-state physics, and research on molecular interactions has been facilitated by his work on the spectroscopy of gases. He also investigated magnetism and superconductivity, and his work is of fundamental importance for modern solid-state electronics. He shared the Nobel Prize for physics in 1977.

Andre /'ɑːndreɪ/, Carl (born 1935), American minimalist sculptor. His most famous works are installations created by stacking or arranging ready-made units such as bricks, cement blocks, or metal plates according to a mathematically imposed modular system and without adhesives or joints. Andre's *Equivalent VIII* (1966), which consists of 120 bricks arranged two deep in a rectangle, was the subject of protests in Britain at the alleged waste of public money when it was purchased by the Tate Gallery.

Andretti /æn'dretɪ/, Mario (Gabriele) (born 1940), Italian-born American motor-racing driver. In the 1960s he won the Indy car championship three times (1965, 1966, 1969) and won the Indianapolis 500 in 1969. In 1968 he began Formula One racing, and won the world championship in 1978 before retiring from Formula One in 1982 and returning to Indy car racing; he won that sport's championship again in 1984.

Andrew, Prince /'ændruː/, Andrew Albert Christian Edward, Duke of York (born 1960), second son of Elizabeth II. Educated at Gordonstoun School, Scotland, and the Royal Naval College, Dartmouth, he gained a commission in the Royal Marines and in 1982 served as a helicopter pilot in the Falklands War. He married Sarah Ferguson (known as 'Fergie', born 1959) in 1986; the couple formally separated in 1993 and were divorced in 1996. They have two children, Princess Beatrice Elizabeth Mary (born 1988) and Princess Eugenie Victoria Helena (born 1990).

Andrew, St /'ændruː/, an Apostle, the brother of St Peter. An apocryphal work dating probably from the 3rd century describes his death by crucifixion; the X-shaped cross became associated with his name during the Middle Ages. Since *c.*750 he has been regarded as the patron saint of Scotland; he is also a patron saint of Russia. Feast day, 30 November.

Andrews[1] /'ændruːz/, Julie (born Julia Elizabeth Wells) (born 1935), English actress and singer. Early success in the British and American theatre, including her creation of the role of Eliza Doolittle in *My Fair Lady* on Broadway (1956), was followed by her film début in *Mary Poppins* (1964), for which she won an Oscar. Her wholesome appeal and talents as a singer were further displayed in *The Sound of Music* (1965). In her later films, such as *10* (1979), she moved away from her typecast prim image to play more diverse roles.

Andrews[2] /'ændruːz/, Thomas (1813–85), Irish physical chemist. He is best known for his work on the continuity of the gaseous and liquid states. His discovery of the critical temperature of carbon dioxide suggested that any gas could be liquefied if the temperature was sufficiently low, and he also showed that ozone is an allotrope of oxygen.

Andrić /'ændrɪtʃ/, Ivo (1892–1975), Yugoslav novelist, essayist, and short-story writer. A diplomat turned writer, he wrote his best-known novels while living under voluntary house arrest in German-occupied Belgrade. Set in his native Bosnia, these include *The Bridge on the Drina* (1945), whose narrative symbolically bridges past and present, as well as Western and Eastern cultures, and *Bosnian Chronicle* (1945). He was awarded the Nobel Prize for literature in 1961.

Andropov /æn'drɒpɒf/, Yuri (Vladimirovich) (1914–84), Soviet statesman, General Secretary of the Communist Party of the USSR 1982–4 and President 1983–4. Born in Russia, he served as ambassador to Hungary 1954–7, playing a significant role in the crushing of that country's uprising in 1956. He was appointed chairman of the KGB in 1967; its suppression of dissidents enhanced Andropov's standing within the Communist Party, and he gained the presidency on Brezhnev's death. While in office, he initiated the reform process carried through by Mikhail Gorbachev, his chosen successor.

Angelic Doctor the nickname of St Thomas Aquinas.

Angelico /æn'dʒelɪˌkəʊ/, Fra (born Guido di Pietro, monastic name Fra Giovanni da Fiesole) (*c.*1400–55), Italian painter. He was a Dominican friar and his work was intended chiefly for contemplation and instruction. His simple and direct, mature style shows an awareness and understanding of contemporary developments in Renaissance painting, especially in his mastery of new ideas such as perspective. His most celebrated works are the frescos in the convent of San Marco, Florence (*c.*1438–47), and the *Scenes from the Lives of SS Stephen and Lawrence* (1447–9) in the private chapel of Pope Nicholas V in the Vatican.

Angelou /'ændʒəˌluː/, Maya (born 1928), American novelist and poet. After working variously as a waitress, actress, teacher, and night-club singer, she became involved in the black civil-rights movement in the 1950s and 1960s. She received critical acclaim as a writer with the first volume of her autobiography, *I Know Why the Caged Bird Sings* (1970), which recounts her harrowing childhood experiences. More volumes of autobiography followed, as well as several volumes of poetry, including *Oh Pray My Wings Are Gonna Fit Me Well* (1975).

Ångström /'æŋstrəm/, Anders Jonas (1814–74), Swedish physicist. He wrote on terrestrial magnetism and the conduction of heat, but his most important work was in spectroscopy. He proposed a relationship between the emission and absorption spectra of chemical elements, discovered hydrogen in the sun's atmosphere, and published an atlas of the solar spectrum. He measured optical wavelengths in the unit later named in his honour.

Anne /æn/ (1665–1714), queen of England and Scotland (known as Great Britain from 1707) and Ireland 1702–14. The last of the Stuart monarchs, daughter of the Catholic James II (but herself a Protestant), she succeeded her brother-in-law William III to the throne, there presiding over the Act of Union, which completed the unification of Scotland and England. None of the many children she bore survived into adulthood, and by the Act of Settlement (1701) the throne passed to the House of Hanover on her death.

Anne, Princess, Anne Elizabeth Alice Louise, the Princess Royal (born 1950), daughter of Elizabeth II. A skilled horsewoman,

she rode for Great Britain in the 1976 Olympics. She has also been involved in the work of charitable organizations, notably in her capacity as president of Save the Children Fund, a position she has held since 1971. She was married to Captain Mark Philips (born 1948) 1973–92. In December 1992 she married Commander Timothy Laurence. She has two children, Peter Mark Andrew Philips (born 1977) and Zara Anne Elizabeth Philips (born 1981).

Anne, St, traditionally the mother of the Virgin Mary, first mentioned by name in the apocryphal gospel of James (2nd century). The extreme veneration of St Anne in the late Middle Ages was attacked by Martin Luther and other reformers. She is the patron saint of Brittany and the province of Quebec in Canada. Feast day, 26 July.

Anne Boleyn see BOLEYN.

Anne of Cleves /kliːvz/ (1515–57), fourth wife of Henry VIII. Henry's marriage to her (1540) was the product of his minister Thomas Cromwell's attempt to forge a dynastic alliance with one of the Protestant German states. Henry, initially deceived by a flattering portrait of Anne painted by Holbein, took an instant dislike to his new wife and dissolved the marriage after six months.

Annigoni /ˌænɪˈgəʊnɪ/, Pietro (1910–88), Italian painter. One of the few 20th-century artists to practise the techniques of the Old Masters, he painted mainly in tempera, and his religious paintings include altarpieces and frescos. However, he is most famous for his portraits of Queen Elizabeth II (1955, 1970), President Kennedy (1961), and other prominent figures.

Anouilh /ˈɒnwiː, French anuj/, Jean (1910–87), French dramatist. Anouilh's first success was *Traveller without Luggage* (1937), and he soon achieved widespread popularity. His characters typically struggle for personal integrity against the constraints of society and family background. Works include romantic comedies such as *Ring Round the Moon* (1947), fantasies (*Thieves' Carnival*, 1932), historical dramas (*Beckett or The Honour of God*, 1959), and *Antigone* (1944), a reworking of the Greek myth with undertones of the contemporary situation in Nazi-occupied Paris.

Anselm, St /ˈænselm/ (c.1033–1109), Italian-born philosopher and theologian, Archbishop of Canterbury 1093–1109. A

distinguished theologian and reformer who worked to free the Church from secular control, he preferred to defend the faith by intellectual reasoning rather than by basing arguments on scriptural and other written authorities. The most famous of his writings is a mystical study on the Atonement (*Cur Deus Homo?*). Feast day, 21 April.

Antall /ˈæntæl/, Jozsef (1933–93), Hungarian statesman, Prime Minister 1990–3. In 1990 he became leader of the Hungarian Democratic Forum and was elected Premier in the country's first free elections for more than forty years.

Anthemius /ænˈθiːmɪəs/ (known as Anthemius of Tralles) (6th century AD), Greek mathematician, engineer, and artist. His experiments included study of the effects of compressed steam, and he had a high reputation for both these and his artistic pursuits. In 532 he was chosen by Justinian to design the church of St Sophia in Constantinople.

Anthony, St /ˈæntənɪ/ (also **Antony**) (c.251–356), Egyptian hermit, the founder of monasticism. At the age of 20 he gave away his possessions and went to live as a hermit in the Egyptian desert, attracting a colony of followers. These he organized into a community which became the first to live under a monastic rule. Shortly before his death he used his influence in association with Athanasius against the Arians. During the Middle Ages the belief arose that praying to St Anthony would effect a cure for ergotism. Feast day, 17 January.

Anthony of Padua, St /ˈpædjʊə/ (also **Antony**) (1195–1231), Portuguese Franciscan friar. His charismatic preaching in the south of France and Italy made many converts. His devotion to the poor is commemorated by the alms known as St Anthony's bread; he is invoked to find lost articles. Feast day, 13 June.

Antiochus /ænˈtaɪəkəs/ the name of eight Seleucid kings, notably:
Antiochus III (known as Antiochus the Great) (c.242–187 BC), reigned 223–187 BC. He restored and expanded the Seleucid empire, regaining the vassal kingdoms of Parthia and Bactria and conquering Armenia, Syria, and Palestine. When he invaded Europe he came into conflict with the Romans, who defeated him on land and sea and severely limited his power.

Antiochus IV Epiphanes (c.215–163 BC), son of Antiochus III, reigned 175–163 BC. His firm control of Judaea and his attempt to Hellenize the Jews resulted in the revival of Jewish nationalism and the Maccabean revolt.

Antoninus Pius /ˌæntəˌnaməs 'paɪəs/ (86–161), Roman emperor 138–61. The adopted son and successor of Hadrian, he was the first of the Antonine emperors. His reign was generally peaceful and he ruled in harmony with the Senate, pursuing a policy of moderation and liberality. Although no great conqueror, he extended the empire; the frontier of Britain was temporarily advanced to the Antonine Wall.

Antonioni /ænˌtəʊnɪ'əʊnɪ/, Michelangelo (born 1912), Italian film director. He won international acclaim with *L'avventura* (1960), and made his first colour film, *Il deserto rosso*, in 1964. His films concentrate on the study of character and illuminate such themes as suicide and humankind's alienation from the environment. His other films include *Blow-Up* (1966), *Zabriskie Point* (1970), and *The Passenger* (1975).

Antony /'æntənɪ/, Mark (Latin name Marcus Antonius) (c.83–30 BC), Roman general and triumvir. A supporter of Julius Caesar, in 43 he was appointed one of the triumvirate with Octavian and Lepidus after Caesar's murder the previous year. Following the battle of Philippi he took charge of the Eastern Empire, where he established his association with Cleopatra. Quarrels with Octavian led finally to his defeat at the sea battle of Actium in NW Greece in 31 and to his suicide the following year.

Antony, St see ANTHONY, ST.

Antony of Padua, St see ANTHONY OF PADUA, ST.

Anyaoku /ˌænjə'əʊkuː/, Eleazar Chukwuemeka (born 1933), Nigerian diplomat. After holding posts in the Commonwealth Secretariat in the 1970s and 1980s, he was appointed Commonwealth Secretary-General in 1989, the first African to hold this position.

Apelles /ə'peliːz/ (4th century BC), Greek painter. The court painter to Alexander the Great, Apelles is now only known from written sources, but was highly acclaimed throughout the ancient world. Among his recorded pictures was a depiction of Aphrodite rising from the sea and a work entitled *Calumny*; both of these were emulated by Botticelli in the 15th century.

Apollinaire /ə,pɒlɪ'neə(r)/, Guillaume (pseudonym of Wilhelm Apollinaris de Kostrowitzki) (1880–1918), French poet. He was born in Rome of Polish descent. In 1900 he moved to Paris and began writing collections of poetry, including *Les Alcools* (1913) and *Calligrammes* (1918). His poems, which are written without punctuation, are a conscious attempt to be resolutely modern. He coined the term *surrealist* and was acknowledged by the surrealist poets as their precursor.

Apollinaris /ə,pɒlɪ'neərɪs/ (c.310–c.390), bishop of Laodicea in Asia Minor. He upheld the heretical doctrine, condemned at the Council of Constantinople (381), which asserted that Christ had a human body and soul but no human spirit, this being replaced by the divine Logos.

Apollonius [1] /ˌæpə'ləʊnɪəs/ (known as Apollonius of Perga) (c.260–190 BC), Greek mathematician. In his principal surviving work, *Conics*, he examined and redefined the various conic sections, and was the first to use the terms *ellipse*, *parabola*, and *hyperbola* for these classes of curve. He also dealt with other aspects of higher geometry, and from his astronomical studies he probably originated the concept of epicycles to account for the retrograde motion of the outer planets.

Apollonius [2] /ˌæpə'ləʊnɪəs/ (known as Apollonius of Rhodes) (3rd century BC), Greek poet. The librarian at Alexandria, he was the author of many works on grammar. He is chiefly known for his epic poem *Argonautica*; written in Homeric style and dealing with the expedition of the Argonauts, it was the first such poem to place love (Medea's love for Jason) in the foreground of the action.

Appel /'ɑːp(ə)l/, Karel (born 1921), Dutch painter, sculptor, and graphic artist. An exponent of abstract expressionism, he is best known for his paintings, executed in impasto and bright colours and characteristically depicting swirling abstract images suggestive of human and animal forms or fantasy figures. He has also produced polychrome aluminium sculptures.

Appleton /'æp(ə)ltən/, Sir Edward Victor (1892–1965), English physicist. His investigation of the Heaviside or E layer of the atmosphere led him to the discovery of a

higher region of ionized gases (the Appleton layer, now resolved into two layers, F1 and F2), from which short-wave radio waves are reflected back to earth. This work, for which he was awarded the Nobel Prize for physics in 1947, was important for long-range radio transmission and radar.

Apuleius /ˌæpjʊˈliːəs/ (born AD c.123), Roman writer, born in Africa. Renowned as an orator, he wrote a variety of rhetorical and philosophical works, but is best known as the author of the *Metamorphoses (The Golden Ass)*, a picaresque novel which recounts the adventures of a man who is transformed into an ass. Apuleius' writings are characterized by an exuberant and bizarre use of language.

Aquinas, St Thomas /əˈkwaɪnəs/ (known as 'the Angelic Doctor') (1225–74), Italian philosopher, theologian, and Dominican friar. Regarded as the greatest figure of scholasticism, he also devised the official Roman Catholic tenets as declared by Pope Leo XIII. His works include many commentaries on Aristotle as well as the *Summa Contra Gentiles* (intended as a manual for those disputing with Spanish Muslims and Jews). His principal achievement was to make the work of Aristotle acceptable in Christian western Europe; his own metaphysics, his account of the human mind, and his moral philosophy were a development of Aristotle's, and in his famous arguments for the existence of God ('the Five Ways') he was indebted to Aristotle and to Islamic philosophers. Feast day, 28 January.

Aquitaine, Eleanor of, see ELEANOR OF AQUITAINE.

Arafat /ˈærəˌfæt/, Yasser (born 1929), Palestinian leader, chairman of the Palestine Liberation Organization from 1968. In 1956 he co-founded Al Fatah, the Arab group which came to dominate the PLO from 1967. In 1974 he became the first representative of a non-governmental organization to address the United Nations General Assembly. Despite challenges to his authority within the PLO, he has remained its leader. After the signing of a PLO–Israeli peace accord providing for limited Palestinian autonomy in the West Bank and the Gaza Strip, in July 1994 Arafat became leader of the new Palestine National Authority. The same year he shared the Nobel Peace Prize with Yitzhak Rabin and Shimon Peres. Arafat won a landslide victory in the first Palestinian presidential elections (1996).

Aragon, Catherine of, see CATHERINE OF ARAGON.

Arbus /ˈɑːbəs/, Diane (1923–71), American photographer. Her early career was spent in the world of traditional fashion photography, but she is best known for her sometimes disturbing images of people on the streets of New York and other US cities. She began to take these in 1958, often showing the poor or depicting unusual individuals such as transvestites.

Arbuthnot /ɑːˈbʌθnət/, John (1667–1735), Scottish physician and writer. He was the physician to Queen Anne and is known as the author of medical works as well as for his satirical writings. A friend of Jonathan Swift and acquainted with Alexander Pope and John Gay, he was the principal author of a satirical work entitled *Memoirs of Martinus Scriblerus* (c.1714). His *History of John Bull* (1712), a collection of pamphlets advocating the termination of the war with France, was the origin of John Bull, the personification of the typical Englishman.

Archer /ˈɑːtʃə(r)/, Jeffrey (Howard), Baron Archer of Weston-super-Mare (born 1940), British writer and Conservative politician. Conservative MP for Louth from 1969 to 1974, he resigned his seat after being declared bankrupt. To pay his debts, he embarked on a career as a novelist, *Not a Penny More, Not a Penny Less* (1975) becoming the first of many best sellers. He was deputy chairman of the Conservative Party 1985–6, resigning after a libel case, and was created a life peer in 1992.

Archilochus /ɑːˈkɪləkəs/ (8th or 7th century BC), Greek poet. Acclaimed in his day as equal in stature to Homer and Pindar, he wrote satirical verse and fables and is credited with the invention of iambic metre.

Archimedes /ˌɑːkɪˈmiːdiːz/ (c.287–212 BC), Greek mathematician and inventor, of Syracuse. He is known as the inventor of the Archimedean screw and other devices, for his boast 'give me a place to stand on and I will move the earth', and for his discovery of Archimedes' principle (legend has it that he made this discovery while taking a bath, and ran through the streets shouting 'Eureka!'). Among his mathematical discoveries are the ratio of the radius of a circle to its circumference, and formulas for the surface area and volume of a sphere and of

a cylinder. He devised weapons for use against the Roman fleet during the siege of Syracuse, but was killed during the attack.

Archipenko /ˌɑːkɪˈpjeŋkəʊ/, Aleksandr (Porfirevich) (1887–1964), Russian-born American sculptor. He adapted cubist techniques to sculpture and attempted to unite form and colour in a mixed medium. He introduced the idiom of 'negative form' into modern sculpture in works such as *Walking Woman* (1912), opening parts of it with holes and concavities to create a contrast of solid and void. From c.1946 he experimented with 'light' sculpture, making structures of plastic lit from within.

Arden /ˈɑːd(ə)n/, Elizabeth (born Florence Nightingale Graham) (c.1880–1966), Canadian-born American businesswoman. She trained as a nurse before going to New York, where she opened her own beauty salon on Fifth Avenue in 1909. An effective use of advertising gave her brand a select and elegant image and contributed to the success of her business; she ultimately owned in excess of 100 beauty salons in America and Europe and her range of cosmetics comprised more than 300 products.

Arendt /ˈɑːrənt/, Hannah (1906–75), German-born American philosopher and political theorist. A pupil of Martin Heidegger, she established her reputation as a political thinker with *The Origins of Totalitarianism* (1951), one of the first works to propose that Nazism and Stalinism had common roots in the 19th century, sharing anti-Semitic, imperialist, and nationalist elements. *Eichmann in Jerusalem* (1963) aroused controversy with its suggestion that the lack of a political tradition among Jews contributed in part to their own genocide. In 1959 she became the first woman professor at Princeton University.

Ariosto /ˌærɪˈɒstəʊ/, Ludovico (1474–1533), Italian poet. His *Orlando Furioso* (final version 1532), about the exploits of Roland (Orlando) and other knights of Charlemagne, was the greatest of the Italian romantic epics; Spenser used its narrative form as a model for his *Faerie Queene*.

Aristarchus[1] /ˌærɪˈstɑːkəs/ (known as Aristarchus of Samos) (3rd century BC), Greek astronomer. Founder of an important school of Hellenic astronomy, he was aware of the rotation of the earth and, by placing the sun at the centre of the universe, was able to account for the seasons. He knew that the sun must be larger than the earth and that the stars must be very distant. Many of his theories were more accurate than those of Ptolemy, which replaced them.

Aristarchus[2] /ˌærɪˈstɑːkəs/ (known as Aristarchus of Samothrace) (c.217–145 BC), Greek scholar. The librarian at Alexandria, he is regarded as the originator of scientific literary scholarship, and is noted for his editions of the writings of Homer and other Greek authors, as well as for commentaries and treatises on their works.

Aristides /ˌærɪˈstaɪdiːz/ (known as Aristides the Just) (5th century BC), Athenian statesman and general. In the Persian Wars he commanded the Athenian army at the battle of Plataea in 479 BC, and was subsequently prominent in founding the Delian League, an alliance of Greek city-states that joined against Persians between 478 and 447 BC and constituted the Athenian empire.

Aristippus /æˈrɪstɪpəs/ (known as Aristippus the Elder) (late 5th century BC), Greek philosopher. He was a native of Cyrene and pupil of Socrates, and is generally considered the founder of the Cyrenaic school, holding that pleasure is the highest good and that virtue is to be equated with the ability to enjoy. His grandson Aristippus the Younger further developed his philosophy.

Aristophanes /ˌærɪˈstɒfəˌniːz/ (c.450–c.385 BC), Greek dramatist. His eleven surviving comedies, characterized by inventive situations and exuberant language, are largely occupied with topical themes; Aristophanes satirizes politicians and intellectuals (such as Socrates), and parodies contemporary poets such as Aeschylus and Euripides. Much use is made of political and social fantasy, as exemplified by the city of the birds ('Cloud-cuckoo-land') in the *Birds*, and by the women's sex-strike for peace in *Lysistrata*.

Aristotle /ˈærɪˌstɒt(ə)l/ (384–322 BC), Greek philosopher and scientist. A pupil of Plato and tutor to Alexander the Great, in 335 BC he founded a school and library (the Lyceum) outside Athens. His surviving written works constitute a vast system of analysis, including logic, physical science, zoology, psychology, metaphysics, ethics, politics, and rhetoric. In reasoning, he established the inductive method. In metaphysics, he rejected Plato's doctrine of forms or ideals; for him form and matter

were the inseparable constituents of all existing things. His empirical approach to science is most notable in the field of biology, where he analysed and described the stomach of ruminants and the development of the chick embryo. His work on the classification of animals by means of a scale ascending to man (without implying evolution) was not fully appreciated until the 19th century: Darwin acknowledged a debt to him. The influence of Aristotle in all fields has been considerable: from the 9th century it pervaded Islamic philosophy, theology, and science, and, after being lost to the West for some centuries, became the basis of scholasticism in medieval Christian thought. In astronomy, his proposal that the stars and the planets are composed of a perfect incorruptible element (ether), carried on revolving spheres centred on the earth, was a serious handicap to later thinking.

Arkwright /'ɑːkraɪt/, Sir Richard (1732–92), English inventor and industrialist. A pioneer of mechanical cotton-spinning, in 1767 he patented a water-powered spinning machine (known as a 'water frame'), the first such machine to produce yarn strong enough to be used as warp. He also improved the preparatory processes, including carding. He established spinning mills in Lancashire, Derbyshire, and Scotland, and became rich and powerful, despite disputes with rivals over patents and opposition to his mechanization of the industry.

Armani /ɑːˈmɑːnɪ/, Giorgio (born 1935), Italian fashion designer. After studying medicine at university he worked as a window-dresser before becoming a designer for Nino Cerruti in 1961. He then worked for several designers until 1975, when he established his own company and rapidly became one of Italy's best-known ready-to-wear designers for both men and women.

Armstrong [1] /'ɑːmstrɒŋ/, Edwin Howard (1890–1954), American electrical engineer. He was the inventor of the superheterodyne radio receiver and the frequency modulation (FM) system in radio. The former involved him in bitter legal wrangles with Lee De Forest. During the 1930s Armstrong developed the FM system, which removed the static that had ruined much early broadcasting, but the radio industry was very slow to accept it. After the war

Armstrong was again involved in legal battles to protect his patent, eventually committing suicide.

Armstrong [2] /'ɑːmstrɒŋ/, (Daniel) Louis (known as 'Satchmo', an abbreviation of 'Satchelmouth') (1900–71), American jazz musician. He learned the cornet in the Waifs' Home in New Orleans, later switching to the trumpet. He played on Mississippi river-boats before forming his own small groups, with which he made some sixty recordings in 1925–8. He later led various big bands, toured internationally, and appeared in many films, including *The Birth of the Blues* (1941). A major influence on Dixieland jazz, he was a distinctive singer as well as a trumpet player and was noted for his talent for improvisation.

Armstrong [3] /'ɑːmstrɒŋ/, Neil (Alden) (born 1930), American astronaut. A former fighter pilot and test pilot, he began training as an astronaut in 1962, being appointed to command the Apollo 11 mission, during which he became the first man to set foot on the moon (20 July 1969).

Arne /ɑːn/, Thomas (1710–78), English composer. He is remembered for his distinctive contribution to 18th-century theatrical music, especially with his settings of Shakespearian songs such as 'Blow, Blow Thou Winter Wind', and for his operas *Artaxerxes* (1762) and *Love in a Village* (1762). His famous song 'Rule, Britannia' (with words attributed to James Thomson) was composed for the masque *Alfred* (1740).

Arnold [1] /'ɑːn(ə)ld/, Sir Malcolm (Henry) (born 1921), English composer and trumpeter. Arnold's style as a composer is characterized by an adventurous and colourful use of traditional tunefulness and form, eschewing the atonality of many of his contemporaries. His prolific output is evident in his many film scores, including that for *Bridge over the River Kwai*, for which he received an Oscar in 1957. His oeuvre also includes eight symphonies and eighteen concertos: among his best-known works is the overture *Tam O'Shanter* (1955).

Arnold [2] /'ɑːn(ə)ld/, Matthew (1822–88), English poet, essayist, and social critic. Author of 'The Scholar Gipsy' (1853), 'Dover Beach' (1867) and 'Thyrsis' (1867), he held the post of professor of poetry at Oxford (1857–67) and published several works of literary and

social criticism, including *Culture and Anarchy* (1869). This established him as an influential social and cultural critic, who, in his views on religion, education, and the arts, criticized the Victorian age in terms of its materialism, philistinism, and complacency.

Arp /ɑːp/, Jean (also known as Hans Arp) (1887–1966), French painter, sculptor, and poet. An associate of many leading avant-garde artists of the early 20th century, he exhibited with Wassily Kandinsky's *Blaue Reiter* group in 1912, the German expressionists in 1913, and the surrealists in France in the 1920s. He co-founded the Dada movement in Zurich in 1916. His sculpture includes painted wood reliefs such as *Constellation in Five White Forms and Two Black* (1932). In the 1930s he worked in marble and bronze, making three-dimensional abstract curvilinear sculptures suggestive of organic forms.

Arrau /æ'raʊ/, Claudio (1903–91), Chilean pianist. A child prodigy whose first public performance was at the age of 5, he became a renowned interpreter of the works of Chopin, Liszt, Beethoven, Mozart, Schumann, and Brahms. An unostentatious pianist, he built his reputation largely on the meticulous musicianship and intellectual penetration which accompanied his virtuoso technique.

Arrhenius /ə'reɪnɪəs, ə'riːn-/, Svante August (1859–1927), Swedish chemist. One of the founders of modern physical chemistry, he was the first Swede to win the Nobel Prize for chemistry, which was awarded in 1903 for his work on electrolytes.

Arrow /'ærəʊ/, Kenneth Joseph (born 1921), American economist. He is chiefly noted for his work on general economic equilibrium and for his contribution to the study of social choice. His most startling theory, expounded in *Social Choices and Individual Values* (1951), showed the impossibility of aggregating the preferences of individuals into a single combined order of priorities for society as a whole. He shared the Nobel Prize for economics in 1972.

Artaud /ɑː'təʊ/, Antonin (1896–1948), French actor, director, and poet. Influenced by Balinese dancing and oriental drama, he sought to return drama to its symbolic and ritualistic roots, developing the concept of the non-verbal Theatre of Cruelty, which concentrated on the use of sound, mime, and lighting. He expounded

his theory in a series of essays published as *Le Théâtre et son double* (1938), but his only play to be based on it was *Les Cenci* (1935). He was a significant influence on postwar experimental theatre.

Artaxerxes /ˌɑːtə'zɜːksiːz/ the name of three kings of ancient Persia:
Artaxerxes I son of Xerxes I, reigned 464–424 BC.
Artaxerxes II son of Darius II, reigned 404–358 BC.
Artaxerxes III son of Artaxerxes II, reigned 358–338 BC.

Arthur[1] /'ɑːθə(r)/ traditionally king of Britain, historically perhaps a 5th or 6th-century Romano-British chieftain or general. His life and court have become the focus for many romantic legends in various languages, including the exploits of adventurous knights and the quest for the Holy Grail. The stories were developed and recounted by Malory, Chrétien de Troyes, and others; the Norman writer Wace (12th century) mentions the 'Round Table', which enabled the knights to be seated in such a way that none had precedence. Arthur's court was at Camelot, a place variously located by writers and historians in Wales, Somerset, Cornwall, and Winchester.

Arthur[2] /'ɑːθə(r)/, Chester Alan (1830–86), American Republican statesman, 21st President of the US 1881–5. He was appointed Garfield's Vice-President in 1881 and became President after Garfield's assassination. During his term of office, he was responsible for improving the strength of the US navy.

Aryabhata I /ˌærɪə'bɑːtə/, (476–c.550), Indian astronomer and mathematician. He wrote two works, one of which is now lost. The surviving work, the *Aryabhatiya* (499), has sections dealing with mathematics, the measurement of time, planetary models, the sphere, and eclipses. India's first space satellite was named after him.

Ascham /'æskəm/, Roger (c.1515–68), English humanist scholar and writer. His posts included that of tutor to the future Elizabeth I and Latin secretary to Queen Mary and later to Elizabeth. He is noted for his treatise on archery, *Toxophilus* (1545), and *The Scholemaster* (1570), a practical and influential treatise on education.

Ashcroft /'æʃkrɒft/, Dame Peggy (Edith Margaret Emily) (1907–91), English actress.

She played a number of Shakespearian roles including Desdemona to Paul Robeson's Othello (1930) and Juliet in John Gielgud's production of *Romeo and Juliet* (1935). Other outstanding performances included the title role in Ibsen's *Hedda Gabler* (1954), for which she received a royal award. She won an Oscar for best supporting actress in the film *A Passage to India* (1984).

Ashdown /'æʃdaʊn/, Jeremy John Durham ('Paddy') (born 1941), British Liberal Democrat politician, born in India. Formerly a Liberal MP (1983–8), he became the first leader of the Liberal Democrats (originally the Social and Liberal Democrats) in 1988.

Ashe /æʃ/, Arthur (Robert) (1943–93), American tennis player. He won the US Open championship in 1968 and Wimbledon in 1975, and was the first black male player to achieve world rankings. He died of AIDS, having contracted HIV from a blood transfusion.

Ashkenazy /ˌæʃkə'nɑːzɪ/, Vladimir (Davidovich) (born 1937), Russian-born pianist and conductor. A child prodigy, he made his Moscow début in 1945 and went on to win several international awards, including sharing the first prize in the 1962 Moscow Tchaikovsky Piano Competition with John Ogdon (1937–89). Ashkenazy left the Soviet Union the following year, settling in Iceland and then Switzerland. He has been acclaimed for his interpretations of composers such as Mozart, Rachmaninov, Chopin, Beethoven, and Schubert.

Ashley /'æʃlɪ/, Laura (1925–85), Welsh fashion and textile designer. In the 1960s her clothes, in traditional floral patterns and reflecting romantic Victorian and Edwardian styles, became highly popular, as did the range of furnishing fabrics and wallpapers which her company (founded with her husband Bernard) introduced. The chain of shops under Laura Ashley's name spread through Britain and later to Europe, America, Australia, and Japan.

Ashmole /'æʃməʊl/, Elias (1617–92), English antiquary. Ashmole showed an insatiable desire for knowledge, studying such diverse topics as alchemy, astrology, Hebrew, and mathematics. In 1677 he presented to Oxford University his collection of rarities, which he had inherited from John Tradescant and which formed the nucleus of the Ashmolean Museum.

Ashton /'æʃtən/, Sir Frederick (William Mallandaine) (1904–88), British ballet-dancer, choreographer, and director. He became chief choreographer and principal dancer of the Vic-Wells Ballet in 1935, remaining with the company when it became the Sadler's Wells and finally the Royal Ballet, of which he was director 1963–70. As a choreographer, Ashton established a lyrical and fluid style of classical ballet, creating successful new works as well as making popular adaptations of historical ballets.

Ashurbanipal /ˌæʃʊə'bɑːnɪp(ə)l/, king of Assyria *c.*668–627 BC. The grandson of Sennacherib, he was responsible for the sacking of the Elamite capital Susa and the suppression of a revolt in Babylon. However, he is chiefly recognized for his patronage of the arts; he established a library of more than 20,000 clay tablets at Nineveh, which included literary, religious, scientific, and administrative documents.

Asimov /'æzɪˌmɒf/, Isaac (1920–92), Russian-born American writer and scientist. He was a distinguished biochemist, but is more widely known as the author of many works of science fiction, books on science for non-scientists, and essays on a wide variety of subjects. Among his best-known science fiction is *I, Robot* (1950) and the *Foundation* trilogy (1951–3). Building on Karel Čapek's concept of the robot, in 1941 Asimov coined the term *robotics*.

Askey /'æskɪ/, Arthur (Bowden) (1900–82), English comedian and actor. Having made his professional début in 1924, he was always in demand after the success of his radio show *Band Waggon* (1938–9), and appeared in a great number of pantomimes, West End musicals, and films. Askey used his smallness of stature to great effect in his exuberant comedy act.

Asoka /ə'səʊkə, ə'ʃəʊ-/ (died *c.*232 BC), emperor of India *c.*269–232 BC. He embarked on a campaign of conquest, but after his conversion to Buddhism (which he established as the state religion) he renounced war and sent out missionaries as far afield as Syria and Ceylon to spread his new faith.

Asquith /'æskwɪθ/, Herbert Henry, 1st Earl of Oxford and Asquith (1852–1928), British Liberal statesman, Prime Minister 1908–16. In the years before the First World War he introduced the third bill for Irish Home

Rule, while also contending with the challenge posed by the women's suffrage movement and outrage from the House of Lords over Lloyd George's People's Budget (1909). In 1915 Asquith brought the Conservatives into a coalition government, but his failure to consult his colleagues divided the Liberals; he was displaced as Prime Minister by Lloyd George the following year, but retained the party leadership.

Assad /'æsæd/, Hafiz al- (born 1928), Syrian Baath statesman, President since 1971. While in office he has ensured the strengthening of Syria's oil-based economy and suppressed political opposition such as the uprising of Muslim extremists (1979–82). He supported the coalition forces during the 1991 Gulf War.

Assisi, Clare of, see CLARE OF ASSISI, ST.

Assisi, Francis of, see FRANCIS OF ASSISI, ST.

Astaire /ə'steə(r)/, Fred (born Frederick Austerlitz) (1899–1987), American dancer, singer, and actor. He danced in music-halls from an early age, before starring in a number of film musicals, including *Top Hat* (1935), *Follow the Fleet* (1936), and *Shall We Dance?* (1937), in a successful partnership with Ginger Rogers. After his partnership with Rogers ended he continued to appear in films such as *Easter Parade* (1948) with Judy Garland.

Aston /'æstən/, Francis William (1877–1945), English physicist. Aston worked in Cambridge with J. J. Thomson, inventing the mass spectrograph. With this he eventually discovered many of the 287 naturally occurring isotopes of non-radioactive elements, announcing in 1919 the whole-number rule governing their masses. He was awarded the Nobel Prize for chemistry in 1922.

Astor /'æstə(r)/, Nancy Witcher Langhorne, Viscountess (1879–1964), American-born British Conservative politician. She became the first woman to sit in the House of Commons when she succeeded her husband as MP for Plymouth in 1919. She supported causes about which she had deep convictions, such as temperance and women's rights, rather than following the party line.

Asturias /æ'stʊərɪˌæs/, Miguel Ángel (1899–1974), Guatemalan novelist and poet. He is best known for his experimental novel *The President* (1946), which deals with the disintegration of human relationships under a repressive dictatorship. Later novels, such as *Mulata* (1963), draw more extensively on his knowledge of Mayan myth and history. He was awarded the Nobel Prize for literature in 1967.

Atatürk /'ætəˌtɜːk/, Kemal (born Mustafa Kemal; also called Kemal Pasha) (1881–1938), Turkish general and statesman, President 1923–38. Leader of the postwar Turkish Nationalist Party, he was elected President of a provisional government in 1920. With the official establishment of the Turkish republic in 1923, he was elected its first President, taking the name of Atatürk (Turkish for 'father of the Turks') in 1934. During his presidency he introduced many political and social reforms, including the abolition of the caliphate, the adoption of the Roman alphabet for writing Turkish, and other policies designed to make Turkey a modern secular state.

Athanasius, St /ˌæθə'neɪʃəs/ (c.296–373), Greek theologian. As bishop of Alexandria he was a consistent upholder of Christian orthodoxy, especially against Arianism. He aided the ascetic movement in Egypt and introduced knowledge of monasticism to the West. Feast day, 2 May.

Athelstan /'æθəlstən/ (895–939), king of England 925–39. Effectively the first king of all England, Athelstan came to the thrones of Wessex and Mercia in 924 before becoming king of all England a year later. He successfully invaded both Scotland and Wales and inflicted a heavy defeat on an invading Danish army.

Atkinson /'ætkɪns(ə)n/, Sir Harry (Albert) (1831–92), New Zealand statesman, Prime Minister 1876–7, 1883–4, and 1887–91. Born in Britain, he emigrated to New Zealand in 1853 and became a member of the House of Representatives in 1861, also serving as a commander in the Maori Wars in the early 1860s. During his first term as Prime Minister he passed a bill abolishing the colony's provincial governments. He later served as colonial treasurer (1879–82; 1882–3) and is chiefly remembered for the austere economic policy that he pursued throughout the 1880s to boost New Zealand's recovery from economic depression.

Attenborough[1] /'æt(ə)nbərə/, Sir David (Frederick) (born 1926), English naturalist and broadcaster. In 1952 he joined the BBC, where he developed the concept of filming

animals in their natural habitats for the series *Zoo Quest* (1954–64). He became a household name with his documentary film series *Life on Earth* (1979), *The Living Planet* (1983), and *The Trials of Life* (1990). He is the brother of Richard Attenborough.

Attenborough² /ˈæt(ə)nbərə/, Richard (Samuel), Baron Attenborough of Richmond-upon-Thames (born 1923), English film actor, producer, and director. From 1942 onwards he appeared in a number of war films and comedies, and extended his repertoire into character roles such as that of Pinkie in *Brighton Rock* (1947). The films he has directed include *Oh! What a Lovely War* (1969), *Gandhi* (1982, for which he won an Oscar), *Cry Freedom* (1987), and *Shadowlands* (1993). He is the brother of David Attenborough.

Attila /əˈtɪlə/ (406–53), king of the Huns 434–53. From his base in Hungary he ravaged vast areas between the Rhine and the Caspian Sea between 445 and 450, inflicting great devastation on the Eastern Roman Empire. Attila then invaded the Western Empire but was defeated by the joint forces of the Roman army and the Visigoths at Châlons in 451. He and his army were the terror of Europe during his lifetime, and he earned the nickname 'Scourge of God'.

Attlee /ˈætlɪ/, Clement Richard, 1st Earl Attlee (1883–1967), British Labour statesman, Prime Minister 1945–51. He became Labour Party leader in 1935, and deputy Prime Minister in 1942 in Churchill's coalition government. Following his party's landslide election victory in 1945, Attlee became the first Labour Prime Minister to command an absolute majority in the House of Commons. His term saw the creation of the modern welfare state and a wide programme of nationalization of major industries (including coal, gas, and electricity). Foreign policy initiatives included a progressive withdrawal from colonies and support for NATO.

Atwood /ˈætwʊd/, Margaret (Eleanor) (born 1939), Canadian novelist, poet, critic, and short-story writer. She made her name with the novel *The Edible Woman* (1969), which was championed by the resurgent women's movement of the time. Her novels explore the question of women finding and asserting their identities, and include *The Handmaid's Tale* (1986), her dystopian vision of a patriarchal state, and *Cat's Eye* (1989).

Aubrey /ˈɔːbrɪ/, John (1626–97), English antiquarian and author. He was a pioneer of field archaeology, most of his researches being centred on the earthworks and monuments in Wiltshire (particularly Avebury and Stonehenge), and became one of the first Fellows of the Royal Society in 1663. With regard to his written works, he is chiefly remembered for the lively and anecdotal collection of biographies of eminent persons such as John Milton and Francis Bacon known as *Brief Lives*, a bowdlerized edition of which was first published in 1813.

Auden /ˈɔːd(ə)n/, W(ystan) H(ugh) (1907–73), British-born poet. *Look, Stranger!* (1936) is the collection of poems that secured his position as a leading left-wing poet. He supported the Republicans in the Spanish Civil War, and wrote *Spain* (1937). Auden also collaborated with Christopher Isherwood on several Brechtian verse dramas, notably *The Ascent of F6* (1936). After emigrating to America in 1939, he continued to publish volumes of poetry, including *The Age of Anxiety* (1947), which was awarded the Pulitzer Prize. He also worked on several opera libretti, such as Stravinsky's *The Rake's Progress* (1951).

Audubon /ˈɔːdəb(ə)n/, John James (1785–1851), American naturalist and artist. He is chiefly remembered for his great illustrated work *The Birds of America* (1827–38), which was compiled during his travels through America. He portrayed even the largest birds life-size, and painted them not in conventionally formal postures but in dramatic and sometimes violent action. Eventually published in Britain, the book had lasting success, both artistically and as a major contribution to natural history. The National Audubon Society is a North American organization for the study and protection of birds, founded in 1886.

Auer /ˈaʊə(r)/, Carl, Baron von Welsbach (1858–1929), Austrian chemist. Working at Heidelberg, under Bunsen, he discovered in 1885 that the so-called element didymium was actually a mixture of two rare-earth elements, neodymium and praseodymium. In the same year Auer patented the incandescent gas mantle for which he is remembered today. He also discovered the cerium–iron alloy that is used for flints in cigarette and gas lighters.

Auerbach /'ɔ:bæk/, Frank (born 1931), German-born British painter. He came to Britain in 1939 and studied at the Royal College of Art (1952–5). His work (characteristically nudes, portraits, and townscapes) is in oil, and is noted for its use of impasto, the paint at times seeming more modelled than brushed.

Augustine, St[1] /ɔ:'gʌstɪn/ (known as St Augustine of Canterbury) (died c.604), Italian churchman. Sent from Rome by Pope Gregory the Great to refound the Church in England, he and his party landed in Kent in 597 and were favourably received by King Ethelbert (whose wife was a Christian), who was afterwards converted. Augustine founded the first church and a monastery at Canterbury, and was consecrated as its first archbishop, but failed to reach agreement with representatives of the existing Celtic Church, which still survived in Britain on bases at Iona and Lindisfarne and was at variance with Rome on questions of discipline and practice. Feast day, 26 May.

Augustine, St[2] /ɔ:'gʌstɪn/ (known as St Augustine of Hippo) (354–430), Doctor of the Church. Born in North Africa of a pagan father and a Christian mother, he underwent a series of spiritual crises in his early life, described in his *Confessions*. While in Milan he was influenced by the bishop, Ambrose, adopting his Neoplatonic understanding of Christianity and being baptized by him in 386. Augustine henceforth lived a monastic life, becoming bishop of Hippo in North Africa in 396. His episcopate was marked by his continual opposition to the heresies of the Pelagians, Donatists, and Manichees. Of his extensive writings, perhaps his best-known work is the *City of God*. His theology has dominated all later Western theology, with its psychological insight, its sense of man's utter dependence on grace (expressed in his doctrine of predestination), and its conception of the Church and the sacraments. Feast day, 28 August.

Augustus /ɔ:'gʌstəs/ (born Gaius Octavianus; also called (until 27 BC) Octavian) (63 BC–AD 14), the first Roman emperor. Originally called Gaius Octavianus, he took the name Gaius Julius Caesar Octavianus when he was adopted by the will of his great-uncle Julius Caesar in 44 BC. He established his position as one of the triumvirate of 43 BC, gaining supreme power by his defeat of

Antony in 31 BC. A constitutional settlement in 27 BC in theory restored the republic but in practice regularized his sovereignty; in the same year he was given the title Augustus (Latin for 'venerable'). His rule was marked abroad by a series of expansionist military campaigns and at home by moral and religious reforms intended to restore earlier Roman values disrupted during previous civil wars.

Aung San /aʊŋ 'sæn/ (1914–47), Burmese nationalist leader. A leader of the radicals from his student days, during the Second World War he accepted Japanese assistance and secret military training for his supporters. Returning to Burma in 1942 he became leader of the Japanese-sponsored Burma National Army, which defected to the Allies in the closing weeks of the war in the Pacific. As leader of the postwar Council of Ministers, in January 1947 he negotiated a promise of full self-government from the British; in July of that year he and six of his colleagues were assassinated by political rivals during a meeting of the Council.

Aung San Suu Kyi /aʊŋ ˌsæn su: 'tʃi:/ (born 1945), Burmese political leader. Daughter of Aung San, she became the co-founder and leader of the National League for Democracy (NLD), the country's main opposition party, in 1988. Although she was placed under house arrest in 1989 and not allowed to stand as a candidate, the NLD won 80 per cent of the seats in the democratic elections of 1990; the ruling military government refused to recognize the NLD's victory. A supporter of political reform through non-violent public protest and democratic processes, she was awarded the Nobel Peace Prize in 1991. She was released from house arrest in 1995.

Aurangzeb /'ɔ:rəŋˌzeb, 'aʊərəŋ-/ (1618–1707), Mogul emperor of Hindustan 1658–1707. Having usurped the throne from his father, Aurangzeb assumed the title Alamgir (Conqueror of the World). His expansionist policies increased the Mogul empire to its widest extent, and it experienced a period of great wealth and splendour, but constant rebellions and wars greatly weakened the empire and it declined sharply after his death.

Aurelian /ɔ:'ri:liən/ (Latin name Lucius Domitius Aurelianus) (c.215–75), Roman emperor 270–5. Originally a common soldier, he rose through the ranks and was

elected emperor by the army. By a series of military campaigns, including the defeat of Queen Zenobia at Palmyra (272), he successfully quelled rebellions and repelled barbarian invaders; he also built new walls round Rome, and established the state worship of the sun. He was assassinated by his own army officers.

Aurelius /ɔːˈriːlɪəs/, Marcus (full name Caesar Marcus Aurelius Antoninus Augustus) (121–80), Roman emperor 161–80. The adopted successor of Antoninus Pius, he was occupied for much of his reign with wars against Germanic tribes invading the empire from the north. He was by nature a philosophical contemplative; his *Meditations* are a collection of aphorisms and reflections based on a Stoic outlook and written down for his own guidance.

Auric /ˈɔːrɪk/, Georges (1899–1983), French composer. While studying music in Paris, he met Erik Satie and Jean Cocteau, under whose influence he and five other composers formed the anti-romantic group Les Six. His works include operas, ballets (notably Diaghilev's *Les Matelots*, 1925), orchestral works, and songs, but he is probably best known for film music such as the scores for *The Lavender Hill Mob* (1951) and *Moulin Rouge* (1952).

Austen /ˈɒstɪn/, Jane (1775–1817), English novelist. The youngest of seven children of a Hampshire rector, she was greatly stimulated by her extended and affectionate family. Her major novels are *Sense and Sensibility* (1811), *Pride and Prejudice* (1813), *Mansfield Park* (1814), *Emma* (1815), *Northanger Abbey* (1818), and *Persuasion* (1818). They are notable for skilful characterization and penetrating social observation; Austen brings a dry wit and satirical eye to her portrayal of middle and upper-class life, capturing contemporary values and moral dilemmas.

Austin[1] /ˈɒstɪn/, Herbert, 1st Baron Austin of Longbridge (1866–1941), British motor manufacturer. Having joined the Wolseley Sheep Shearing Machine Company in 1893, Austin persuaded the company to embark on the manufacture of cars. He produced vehicles with them until 1905, when he opened his own works near Birmingham. The output of the factory steadily increased, especially following the launch of the Austin Seven (known as 'the Baby Austin') in 1921; 300,000 models of this car were produced before 1939.

Austin[2] /ˈɒstɪn/, John (1790–1859), English jurist. Regarded as the founder of analytical jurisprudence, he was greatly influenced by the utilitarianism of his friend Jeremy Bentham, as can be seen from his work *The Province of Jurisprudence Determined* (1832). An important influence on the English legal system, Austin is significant for his strict delimitation of the sphere of law and its distinction from that of morality, as well as his examination of the connotations of such common legal terms and ideas as right, duty, liberty, injury, and punishment.

Austin[3] /ˈɒstɪn/, John Langshaw (1911–60), English philosopher. A lecturer and later professor of moral philosophy at Oxford University (1952–60), he was a careful and witty exponent of the linguistic school of philosophy, seeking to elucidate philosophical problems by analysis of the words in which they are expressed. Two of his courses of lectures were published posthumously in 1962: *Sense and Sensibilia* discusses perception, while *How to Do Things with Words* distinguishes 'performative' utterances (in which something is done, such as promising or making marriage vows) from utterances that convey information.

Averroës /əˈverəʊˌiːz/ (Arabic name ibn-Rushd) (c.1126–98), Spanish-born Islamic philosopher, judge, and physician. His extensive body of work includes writings on jurisprudence, science, philosophy, and religion. His most significant works were his commentaries on Aristotle, which, through a reliance on Neoplatonism, interpreted Aristotle's writings in such a way as to make them consistent with Plato's, and sought to reconcile the Greek and Islamic philosophical traditions. These commentaries exercised a strong and controversial influence on the succeeding centuries of Western philosophy and science.

Avicenna /ˌævɪˈsenə/ (Arabic name ibn-Sina) (980–1037), Persian-born Islamic philosopher and physician. His surviving works include treatises on philosophy, medicine, and religion. His philosophical system, while drawing heavily on Aristotle, is closer to Neoplatonism, and was the major influence on the development of 13th-century scholasticism. His *Canon of Medicine*, which combined his own knowledge with Roman and Islamic medicine, was a standard medical text in the medieval world.

He also produced a philosophical encyclopedia, *The Recovery*.

Ávila, Teresa of see TERESA OF ÁVILA, ST.

Avogadro /ˌævəˈɡɑːdrəʊ/, Amedeo (1776–1856), Italian chemist and physicist. He is best known for his hypothesis (formulated in 1811), from which it became relatively simple to derive both molecular weights and a system of atomic weights.

Awdry /ˈɔːdrɪ/, Reverend W(ilbert) V(ere) (1911–97), English writer of children's stories. He began to tell his railway stories to his three-year-old son when the boy had measles, and then went on to write them down. His wife persuaded him to offer the stories for publication, and they developed into the immensely popular *Thomas the Tank Engine* series, of which the first book, *The Three Railway Engines*, appeared in 1945. He also wrote several books for adults on steam railways and industrial archaeology.

Ayatollah Khomeini see KHOMEINI.

Ayckbourn /ˈeɪkbɔːn/, Sir Alan (born 1939), English dramatist. *Relatively Speaking* (1967) was his first major success, and was followed by the domestic farce *Absurd Person Singular* (1973) and the trilogy *The Norman Conquests* (1974). A prolific and successful writer of comedies dealing with suburban and middle-class life, in his later plays he often explores darker themes and blurs the distinction between farce and tragedy. Other works include *Way Upstream* (1982) and *A Chorus of Disapproval* (1985). Most of his plays are premièred at Scarborough's Stephen Joseph Theatre in the Round, where he became artistic director in 1971.

Ayer /eə(r)/, Sir A(lfred) J(ules) (1910–89), English philosopher. In Vienna in 1932, he attended the meetings of the group of philosophers, scientists, and mathematicians known as the Vienna Circle, becoming a notable proponent of logical positivism; his book *Language, Truth, and Logic* (1936) was one of the most successful philosophical works of the 20th century. In moral philosophy he was disinclined to defend any specific theory of moral judgement, holding that for all practical purposes a tolerant utilitarianism was the soundest basis for private conduct and public morality.

Aylward /ˈeɪlwəd/, Gladys (May) (1902–70), English missionary. In 1932 she bought a railway ticket to northern China with her savings, and helped found an inn in Yangsheng (later portrayed in the 1959 film *The Inn of the Sixth Happiness*). During the Sino-Japanese war she made a perilous journey to lead a hundred children to safety, and in 1949 returned to England to great acclaim. She later settled in Taiwan as head of an orphanage.

Ayub Khan /ˌaɪjuːb ˈkɑːn/, Muhammad (1907–74), Pakistani soldier and statesman, President 1958–69. After independence he became the first Commander-in-Chief of the country's army (1951–8) and served as Minister of Defence 1954–5, taking over the presidency shortly after the declaration of martial law. His term of office saw the introduction of a new constitution and the lifting of martial law in 1962, but civil liberties were curtailed. Opposition to his foreign policy with regard to India and his increasingly repressive style of government led to widespread disorder and he was ultimately forced to resign.

Azikiwe /ˌɑːzɪˈkiːweɪ/, (Benjamin) Nnamdi (1904–96), Nigerian statesman, President 1963–6. In 1944 Azikiwe founded the anti-colonial National Council of Nigeria and the Cameroons, a gathering of forty political, labour, and educational groups. He was the first Governor-General of an independent Nigeria (1960–3) and its first President when it became a republic. When his civilian government was ousted by a military coup in 1966, Azikiwe joined the Biafran secessionist government. In 1978, after the reunification of Nigeria, he founded the Nigerian People's Party and was its leader until 1983.

B

Baade /ˈbɑːdə/ (Wilhelm Heinrich) Walter (1893–1960), German-born American astronomer. Using cepheid variable stars, he proved that the Andromeda galaxy was much further away than had been thought, which implied that the universe was much older and more extensive than had been earlier supposed. Baade also contributed to the understanding of the life cycles of stars, identifying several radio sources optically.

Babbage /ˈbæbɪdʒ/, Charles (1791–1871), English mathematician, inventor, and pioneer of machine computing. His interest in the compilation of accurate mathematical and astronomical tables led to his design for a mechanical computer or 'difference engine' (in which he was assisted by Byron's daughter, Ada Lovelace), which would both perform calculations and print the results. Because of practical and financial difficulties neither this machine nor a subsequent analytical engine was finished in Babbage's lifetime (although a difference engine was constructed in London for the double centenary of Babbage's birth). His analysis of the postal service led to the introduction of the penny post; he also invented the heliograph and the ophthalmoscope.

Babbitt /ˈbæbɪt/, Milton (Byron) (born 1916), American composer and mathematician. His compositions developed from the twelve-note system of Schoenberg and Webern; his first twelve-note work was *Composition for Orchestra* (1941). He later pioneered the use of synthesizers in composition; his works using synthesizers include *Philomel* (1964) and *Canonic Form* (1983).

Babur /ˈbɑːbʊə(r)/ (born Zahir al-Din Muhammad) (1483–1530), descendant of Tamerlane and the first Mogul emperor of India c.1525–30. He invaded India c.1525 and conquered the territory from the Oxus to Patna. A Muslim, he instigated the policy of religious toleration towards his non-Muslim subjects which was continued by later Mogul emperors.

Bacall /bəˈkɔːl/, Lauren (born 1924), American actress. After little success on stage, Bacall concentrated on her film career,

playing opposite Humphrey Bogart in *To Have or Have Not* (1944). The partnership proved compelling; the pair married in 1945 and co-starred in a succession of box-office hits, including *The Big Sleep* (1946) and *Key Largo* (1948). After a less active period, she made a stage comeback in 1967 and returned to films with *Murder on the Orient Express* (1974).

Bach /bɑːx/, Johann Sebastian (1685–1750), German composer. An exceptional and prolific composer, he was known in his own lifetime chiefly as an organist; it was not until almost a century after his death that his position as an outstanding representative of the German musical baroque was fully appreciated. His compositions range from violin concertos, suites, and the six Brandenburg Concertos (1720–1) to many clavier works and more than 250 sacred cantatas. His large-scale choral works include *The Passion according to St John* (1723), *The Passion according to St Matthew* (1729), and the *Mass in B minor* (1733–8); through these and other liturgical works Bach expressed his devout Protestant faith in the Lutheran tradition. Of his twenty children, his eldest son Wilhelm Friedemann Bach (1710–84) became an organist and composer, Carl Philipp Emanuel Bach (1714–88) wrote much church music, more than 200 keyboard sonatas, and a celebrated treatise on clavier-playing, and Johann Christian Bach (1735–82) became music-master to the British royal family and composed thirteen operas and many instrumental works.

Bacharach /ˈbækəˌræk/, Burt (born 1929), American writer of popular songs. After studying classical music Bacharach went into pop music as a conductor, arranger, and accompanist for a number of musicians, notably Marlene Dietrich. With lyricist Hal David (born 1921) he became an acclaimed songwriter in the 1960s with songs like 'Walk On By' (1961), 'Alfie' (1966), and 'Do You Know the Way to San Jose?' (1968), many of which were performed by the singer Dionne Warwick. Bacharach also composed scores for several films, notably *Casino Royale* (1967) and *Butch Cassidy*

and the Sundance Kid (which included 'Raindrops Keep Falling on my Head', 1969).

Bacon[1] /'beɪkən/, Francis, Baron Verulam and Viscount St Albans (1561–1626), English statesman and philosopher. The preeminent legal figure of the late Elizabethan and early Stuart periods, he eventually rose to become Lord Chancellor under James I before falling from favour after impeachment on charges of corruption. His radical philosophical beliefs, especially as expounded in *The Advancement of Learning* (1605) and *Novum Organum* (1620), proved very influential, dominating the field for a century after his death. He advocated the inductive method and rejected the formulation of a priori hypotheses; his views were instrumental in the founding of the Royal Society in 1660.

Bacon[2] /'beɪkən/, Francis (1909–92), Irish painter. Having settled permanently in England in 1928, he first came to public prominence with the triptych *Three Studies for Figures at the Base of a Crucifixion* (1944), which depicts the Furies as monstrous semi-human figures. He often drew inspiration from photographs, film stills, or from other paintings; from the late 1950s his work chiefly depicted human figures in grotesquely distorted postures, their features blurred or erased, and set in confined interior spaces.

Bacon[3] /'beɪkən/, Roger (c.1214–94), English philosopher, scientist, and Franciscan monk. Bacon taught at Oxford and Paris; although widely acclaimed in scholarly circles he fell foul of his own order, which eventually imprisoned him as a heretic because of his interest in science. Bacon is most notable for his work in the field of optics and for emphasizing the need for an empirical approach to scientific study. He is also said to have prophesied flying machines and described the manufacture of gunpowder.

Baden-Powell /ˌbeɪd(ə)n'pəʊəl/, Robert (Stephenson Smyth), 1st Baron Baden-Powell of Gilwell, English soldier and founder of the Boy Scout movement. He became a national hero after his successful defence of Mafeking (1899–1900) in the Boer War. The Boy Scout movement, which he founded in 1908, and the Girl Guide movement, which he founded together with his sister Agnes and his wife Olave in 1910, grew to become important international youth movements.

Bader /'bɑːdə(r)/, Sir Douglas (Robert Steuart) (1910–82), British airman. Despite having lost both legs in a flying accident in 1931, he rejoined the RAF in 1939 and saw action as a fighter pilot during the evacuation from Dunkirk (1940) and in the Battle of Britain (1940–1), becoming a national hero. After the war he was noted for his work on behalf of disabled people.

Baedeker /'beɪdɪkə(r)/, Karl (1801–59), German publisher. In 1827 he started his own publishing firm in Koblenz. He is remembered chiefly for the series of guidebooks to which he gave his name and which are still published today.

Baer /beə(r)/, Karl Ernest von (1792–1876), German biologist. His discovery that ova were particles within the ovarian follicles was his chief contribution to embryology. He also formulated the principle that in the developing embryo general characters appear before special ones, and his studies were used by Darwin in the theory of evolution.

Baeyer /'baɪə(r)/, Adolph Johann Friedrich Wilhelm von (1835–1917), German organic chemist. An able experimental chemist, he prepared the first barbiturates, and investigated dyes, synthesizing indigo and determining its structural formula. His work pioneered the study of ring structures and stimulated the synthetic dye industry. He was awarded the Nobel Prize for chemistry in 1905.

Baez /'baɪez/, Joan (born 1941), American folk-singer. From the late 1950s she was a prominent figure in the American folk revival; she is best known for her performances at civil-rights demonstrations of the early 1960s. Albums include *Any Day Now* (1968) and *Diamonds and Rust* (1975).

Baffin /'bæfɪn/, William (c.1584–1622), English navigator and explorer. The pilot of several expeditions in search of the Northwest Passage (1612–16), he discovered the largest island of the Canadian Arctic in 1616; this and the strait between it and Greenland are named after him. The record he established for attaining the most northerly latitude was not broken until the mid-19th century.

Bagehot /'bædʒət/, Walter (1826–77), English economist and journalist. He worked as a banker before becoming editor of the *Economist* in 1860, a post which he held until his death. His insight into economic

and political questions is shown in his books *The English Constitution* (1867), *Lombard Street* (1873), and *Economic Studies* (1880).

Bailey /'beɪlɪ/, David (born 1938), English photographer. His career began with *Vogue* magazine in 1960, where, using a 35-mm camera and outdoor locations, he brought a new look to fashion features. He was a prominent figure of the 1960s pop culture; his idiosyncratic, jokey portraits of fellow celebrities were included in *Goodbye Baby and Amen* (1969). More recently, his subjects have included the Vietnamese boat-people and the townscape of his north London neighbourhood, contained in *David Bailey's NW1* (1982).

Baird /beəd/, John Logie (1888–1946), Scottish pioneer of television. He started his work in the early 1920s, gave a demonstration in London in 1926, and made the first transatlantic transmission and demonstration of colour television in 1928. Baird used a mechanical system of picture scanning, which was soon displaced in television development by an electronic system developed by V. K. Zworykin and others in the 1930s.

Baker[1] /'beɪkə(r)/, Dame Janet (Abbott) (born 1933), English operatic mezzo-soprano. From 1957 onwards she made regular appearances in opera and on the concert platform; her Covent Garden début was in 1966 in Britten's *A Midsummer Night's Dream*. Noted for her role as Dido in Purcell's *Dido and Aeneas*, she also includes in her wide repertoire interpretations of Mahler's song cycles and Bach's oratorios. She retired from the operatic stage in 1982.

Baker[2] /'beɪkə(r)/, Josephine (1906–75), American dancer. Appearing with the Revue Nègre in Paris at the age of 19, she caused a stir with her exotic dancing, risqué clothing, and remarkable entrances. She was a star of the Folies-Bergère in the 1930s, and became a screen idol in such films as *La Sirène des tropiques* (1927). She was awarded the Legion of Honour for her work with the French resistance during the Second World War. Experience of racial discrimination in the US led her to join the campaign for black civil rights in the 1950s.

Bakewell /'beɪkwel/, Robert (1725–95), English pioneer in scientific methods of livestock breeding and husbandry. He produced pedigree herds of sheep and cattle from his Leicestershire farm; his irrigation of the grassland gave four cuts a year, and

feeding and selective breeding greatly increased the meat production from his animals.

Bakker /'bækə(r)/, Robert T. (born 1945), American palaeontologist. He proposed, and vigorously defends, the controversial idea that dinosaurs were both active and warm-blooded, citing three lines of supporting evidence: the ability to live in cold climates, the lack of growth rings in bone, and the low ratios of predator to prey. Bakker wrote *The Dinosaur Heresies* in 1986, and *Raptor Red* (a novel about a dinosaur) in 1995.

Bakst /bækst/, Léon (born Lev Samuilovich Rozenberg) (1866–1924), Russian painter and designer. Associated with Diaghilev's magazine *The World of Art* from 1899, he became one of the most influential members of the Diaghilev circle and the Ballets Russes. He designed the decor for such Diaghilev productions as *Scheherazade* (1910), *L'Après-midi d'un faune* (1912), and *The Sleeping Princess* (1921). His use of rich, luxuriant colour and often exotic set designs and costumes had a significant influence on fashion and the development of art deco.

Bakunin /bæ'ku:nɪn/, Mikhail (Aleksandrovich) (1814–76), Russian anarchist. After taking part in the revolutions of 1848 in France, Germany, and Poland he was exiled to Siberia, but escaped in 1861 and went to London. He participated in the First International, founded in 1864, but as a leading exponent of anarchism came into conflict with Karl Marx by calling for violent means to destroy the existing political and social order. He was expelled from the First International in 1872.

Balanchine /'bælən,tʃi:n, -,ʃi:n/, George (born Georgi Melitonovich Balanchivadze) (1904–83), Russian-born American ballet-dancer and choreographer. He worked as chief choreographer of Diaghilev's Ballets Russes during the 1920s. In 1934 he co-founded the company which later became the New York City Ballet, where he choreographed many ballets and revivals. Notable works include *The Firebird* (1949) and *A Midsummer Night's Dream* (1962).

Balboa /bæl'bəʊə/, Vasco Núñez de (1475–1519), Spanish explorer. Having settled in the new Spanish colony of Hispaniola in 1501, in 1511 Balboa joined an expedition

to Darien (in Panama) as a stowaway, but rose to command it after a mutiny. He founded a colony in Darien and continued to make expeditions into the surrounding areas. In 1513 he reached the western coast of the isthmus after an epic twenty-five-day march, thereby becoming the first European to see the Pacific Ocean.

Balcon /'bɔːlkən/, Sir Michael (1896–1977), English film producer. He was responsible for several early Hitchcock films but is mainly remembered for his long association with Ealing Studios, during which he produced such famous comedies as *Kind Hearts and Coronets* and *Whisky Galore* (both 1949), and *The Man in the White Suit* and *The Lavender Hill Mob* (both 1952).

Baldwin[1] /'bɔːldwɪn/, James (Arthur) (1924–87), American novelist. His first novel, *Go Tell it on the Mountain* (1953), telling of one day in the lives of members of a Harlem church, launched Baldwin as a leading writer. *Giovanni's Room* (1956), set in Paris, dealt with sexual (especially homosexual) and racial relationships, subjects further explored in *Another Country* (1962). A civil-rights activist in the 1950s, he subsequently published several collections of essays on racial questions, including *Nobody Knows My Name* (1961) and *No Name in the Street* (1972).

Baldwin[2] /'bɔːldwɪn/, Stanley, 1st Earl Baldwin of Bewdley (1867–1947), British Conservative statesman, Prime Minister 1923–4, 1924–9, and 1935–7. His second term was marked by the return to the gold standard, the General Strike of 1926, and the annexation of Ethiopia by Fascist Italy; his last included the abdication of King Edward VIII, which he handled skilfully. Although international relations continued to deteriorate with the German occupation of the Rhineland (1936) and the outbreak of the Spanish Civil War (1936), Baldwin opposed demands for rearmament, believing that the public would not support it.

Balenciaga /bæˌlensɪ'ɑːgə/, Cristóbal (1895–1972), Spanish couturier. He established his own business in Madrid in 1932, moving to Paris in 1937. His garments were noted for their simplicity, elegance, and boldness of design. In the 1950s he contributed to the move away from the tight-waisted New Look originated by Christian Dior to a looser, semi-fitted style, which culminated in 1955 with the introduction

of a tunic dress, and in 1957 with a chemise ('the sack').

Balfour /'bælfə(r)/, Arthur James, 1st Earl of Balfour (1848–1930), British Conservative statesman, Prime Minister 1902–5. His premiership saw the formation of the Committee of Imperial Defence and the creation of the *entente cordiale* with France (1904), but the party split over the issue of tariff reform, forcing Balfour's resignation, although he remained as party leader until 1911. In 1917, in his capacity as Foreign Secretary during the First World War, Balfour issued the declaration in favour of a Jewish national home in Palestine that came to be known as the Balfour Declaration.

Ball[1] /bɔːl/, John (died 1381), English rebel. Ball was a Wycliffite priest who preached an egalitarian social message. He was excommunicated and imprisoned for heresy, but released in June 1381 during the Peasants' Revolt. He was later captured, tried, and hanged as a traitor.

Ball[2] /bɔːl/, Lucille (1911–89), American comedienne. In 1949 she won recognition in the film *Miss Grant Takes Richmond* (in Britain *Innocence is Bliss*), using her expressive features, grating voice, and faultless timing to great comic effect. Her other screen successes include *Fancy Pants* (1950) and the enormously popular television series *I Love Lucy* (1951–5).

Ballantyne /'bælənˌtaɪn/, R(obert) M(ichael) (1825–94), Scottish writer. In 1856 he published his first adventure story, *The Young Fur Traders*. This and other early stories draw on his experiences in North Canada, where he worked as a clerk before returning to Edinburgh in 1848. After the success of *The Coral Island* (1857), his best-known work, he became an acclaimed writer of stories for boys.

Ballard /'bælɑːd/, J(ames) G(raham) (born 1930), British novelist and short-story writer, born in China. Ballard was born in Shanghai and educated at Cambridge. His early work consists of dystopian science-fiction novels and stories such as his first novel, *The Drowned World* (1962). In 1984 he published the autobiographical novel *Empire of the Sun*, which heralded a movement away from science fiction and was made into a film by Steven Spielberg in 1988.

Ballesteros /ˌbælə'steərɒs/, Severiano ('Sevvy') (born 1957), Spanish golfer. Balles-

teros continually set golfing records. In 1979 he became the youngest player in the 20th century to win the British Open (also taking the title in 1984 and 1988), and the following year was the youngest-ever winner of the US Masters, being only the second European to win the event.

Balzac /'bælzæk/, Honoré de (1799–1850), French novelist. He is chiefly remembered for his series of ninety-one coordinated and interconnected novels and stories known collectively as *La Comédie humaine*, which appeared in a collected edition 1842–8, and includes *Eugénie Grandet* (1833) and *Le Père Goriot* (1835). The fulfilment of his project to create an authentic and comprehensive representation of French society during the late 18th and early 19th centuries, it is a significant work of 19th-century realism. Balzac's panorama of society deals with all aspects of public and personal experience, located in rural and urban settings; recurrent themes include the role of money in shaping personal and social relations and the extent to which environment determines the individual.

Banda /'bændə/, Hastings Kamuzu (1906–97), Malawian statesman, Prime Minister 1964–94 and President 1966–94. He studied medicine in the US and practised in Britain before returning to lead his country (formerly Nyasaland) to independence. As the first President of the Republic of Malawi he created an autocratic and paternalistic one-party state; a pragmatist, he was the first black African leader to visit South Africa (1970) and later established trading links with it. Banda was defeated in Malawi's first multi-party elections in 1994; the following year he was acquitted on charges of murdering four political opponents.

Bandaranaike /ˌbændərəˈnaɪkə/, Sirimavo Ratwatte Dias (born 1916), Sinhalese stateswoman, Prime Minister of Sri Lanka 1960–5, 1970–7, and since 1994. The world's first woman Prime Minister, she succeeded her husband, S. W. R. D. Bandaranaike (1899–1959), after his assassination. Opposition to her policies and continuing ethnic conflict resulted in an overwhelming defeat in the 1977 elections. She was charged with misuse of power in 1980, stripped of her civil rights for six years, and expelled from Parliament. Her daughter, Chandrika Bandaranaike Kumaratunga, became Prime Minister and then President in 1994, being succeeded as Prime Minister by her mother.

Bankhead /'bæŋkhed/, Tallulah (1903–68), American actress. Making her stage début in New York in 1918, Bankhead became noted for her uninhibited public persona, rich laugh, and harsh drawl. Her most successful film appearance was in Alfred Hitchcock's *Lifeboat* (1944).

Banks[1] /bæŋks/, Gordon (born 1937), English footballer. Banks was an outstanding goalkeeper who, after making his England début in 1963, performed excellently in the 1966 World Cup, letting in only three goals during the tournament. He also played in the 1970 World Cup, but in 1972 a serious eye injury sustained in a car crash effectively ended his playing career.

Banks[2] /bæŋks/, Sir Joseph (1743–1820), English botanist. Banks accompanied Captain James Cook on his first voyage to the Pacific. He was president of the Royal Society for more than forty years and helped to establish the Royal Botanic Gardens at Kew, both as a repository of living specimens from all over the world and as a centre for the introduction of plants to new regions. Banks also imported merino sheep from Spain and sent them on to Australia. His herbarium and library became a centre of taxonomic research, later becoming part of the British Museum.

Bannister /'bænɪstə(r)/, Sir Roger (Gilbert) (born 1929), British middle-distance runner and neurologist. While still a medical student, in May 1954 he became the first man to run a mile in under 4 minutes, with a time of 3 minutes 59.4 seconds. He retired from athletics in the same year and went on to a distinguished medical career.

Banting /'bæntɪŋ/, Sir Frederick Grant (1891–1941), Canadian physiologist and surgeon. Banting initiated research into the secretion of the pancreas in a laboratory provided by J. J. R. Macleod. A series of experiments with dogs, carried out with C. H. Best's assistance, led to the discovery of insulin in 1921–2. They then purified the extracts of insulin and used them to treat diabetes, which had previously been an incurable and fatal disease. Banting and Macleod shared a Nobel Prize in 1923; an institute named after Banting was later opened in Toronto.

Barbarossa[1] /ˌbɑːbəˈrɒsə/ see FREDERICK I.

Barbarossa[2] /ˌbɑːbəˈrʊsə/, (born Khair ad-Din) (c.1483–1546), Barbary pirate. In conjunction with his brothers he became notorious for his successes against Christian vessels in the eastern Mediterranean. He served as viceroy to the Ottoman sultan until 1533, when he was made grand admiral. He conquered Tunisia the same year, but was expelled by the Holy Roman emperor Charles V in 1535.

Barber /ˈbɑːbə(r)/, Samuel (1910–81), American composer. He travelled extensively in Europe and developed a style based on romanticism allied to classical forms; his music includes operas, ballets, choral works, and orchestral and chamber music. His best-known works include the *Adagio for Strings* (1936) and the opera *Vanessa* (1958).

Barbirolli /ˌbɑːbɪˈrɒlɪ/, Sir John (Giovanni Battista) (1899–1970), English conductor, of Franco-Italian descent. Originally a cellist, he began his conducting career in 1924. He subsequently became conductor of several major opera companies and orchestras, including Covent Garden in Britain and the New York Philharmonic in the US. In 1943 he returned to England as conductor of the Hallé Orchestra, Manchester, where he was responsible for rebuilding the orchestra's reputation; he was appointed conductor laureate there for life in 1968 in recognition of his contribution.

Barbour /ˈbɑːbə(r)/, John (c.1320–95), Scottish poet and prelate. He was Archdeacon of Aberdeen (1357–95), and probably taught at Oxford and Paris. The only poem ascribed to him with certainty is *The Bruce*, a verse chronicle relating the deeds of Robert the Bruce and his follower James Douglas, and including an account of the Battle of Bannockburn.

Bar-Cochba /bɑːˈkɒkbə/ the Jewish leader of a rebellion in AD 132. He led the Jewish rebellion against Hadrian's intention to rebuild Jerusalem as a non-Jewish city, and claimed to be, and was accepted by some of his Jewish contemporaries as, the Messiah. A number of letters in his handwriting have been found in archaeological excavations near the Dead Sea in Israel. He was designated as Bar-Cochba (from Aramaic, meaning 'son of a star') only in Christian sources; Jewish sources call him Simeon.

Bardot /bɑːˈdəʊ/, Brigitte (born Camille Javal) (born 1934), French actress. She made her film début in 1952, but it was *And God Created Woman* in 1956 that established her reputation as an international sex symbol. Subsequent films include *Love is My Profession* (1959) and *A Very Private Affair* (1962). After retiring from acting she became an active supporter of animal welfare.

Barenboim /ˈbærənˌbɔɪm/, Daniel (born 1942), Israeli pianist and conductor, born in Argentina. He quickly gained a reputation in his youth, making his piano début in 1953 and playing with the Royal Philharmonic Orchestra three years later. Barenboim was musical director of the Orchestre de Paris 1975–88 and then of the Chicago Symphony Orchestra (from 1991). In 1967 he married the cellist Jacqueline du Pré.

Barents /ˈbærənts/, Willem (died 1597), Dutch explorer. The leader of several expeditions in search of the North-east Passage to Asia, Barents discovered Spitsbergen and reached Novaya Zemlya, off the coast of which he died.

Barker /ˈbɑːkə(r)/, George (Granville) (1913–91), English poet. A self-styled 'Augustinian anarchist', he displays in his works a penchant for puns, distortion, and abrupt changes of tone. In his *True Confession of George Barker* (1950, augmented 1965), he presented himself as both irreverent and guilt-ridden.

Barnabas, St /ˈbɑːnəbəs/ a Cypriot Levite and Apostle. He introduced St Paul to the Apostles and accompanied him on the first missionary journey to Cyprus and Asia Minor, returning to Cyprus after they disagreed and separated (Acts 4–15). The traditional founder of the Cypriot Church, he is said to have been martyred in Cyprus in AD 61. Feast day, 11 June.

Barnard /ˈbɑːnɑːd/, Christiaan Neethling (born 1922), South African surgeon. A pioneer in the field of human heart transplantation, he performed the first operation of this kind in December 1967.

Barnardo /bəˈnɑːdəʊ/, Thomas John (1845–1905), Irish-born doctor and philanthropist. He went to London in 1866 and while still a student of medicine, he founded the East End Mission for destitute children (1867), the first of many such homes. Now known as Dr Barnardo's Homes, they cater chiefly for those with physical and mental disabilities.

Barnum /'bɑ:nəm/, P(hineas) T(aylor) (1810–91), American showman. He became famous in the mid-19th century for his extravagant advertising and exhibition of freaks at his American Museum in New York. He billed his circus, opened in 1871, as 'The Greatest Show on Earth'; ten years later he joined forces with his former rival Anthony Bailey (1847–1906) to found the Barnum and Bailey circus.

Barrault /bæ'rəʊ/, Jean-Louis (1910–94), French actor and director. He left the Comédie française in 1946 to found his own company with his wife, the actress Madeleine Renaud. The company worked together until 1956, performing a mixed classical and modern repertoire that included works by Molière and Eugène Ionesco. Barrault directed a number of acclaimed films, including *Les Enfants du paradis* (1945) and *The Longest Day* (1962).

Barrett /'bærət/, Elizabeth, see BROWNING[1].

Barrie /'bærɪ/, Sir J(ames) M(atthew) (1860–1937), Scottish dramatist and novelist. His Scottish background provided the setting for several novels, including *The Little Minister* (1891). He abandoned fiction for the theatre in the early 1900s, gaining success with comedies such as *The Admirable Crichton* (1902) and *Dear Brutus* (1917). However, Barrie's most famous play is *Peter Pan* (1904), a fantasy for children about a boy who would not grow up. Barrie bequeathed the copyright of this to the Great Ormond Street Children's Hospital in London.

Barry /'bærɪ/, Sir Charles (1795–1860), English architect. Having studied architecture during visits to Italy, France, and Greece (1817–20), he established his reputation with his Italianate design of the Travellers' Club in Pall Mall, London (1830–2). In 1836 he won a competition to design the new Houses of Parliament after the old buildings had been destroyed by fire; it was designed in the Perpendicular style, with most of the detail and internal fittings contributed by A. W. N. Pugin. Work on the building began in 1840 and continued after Charles Barry's death, his son Edward Middleton Barry (1830–80) completing the project.

Barrymore /'bærɪ,mɔ:(r)/ an American family of actors. Lionel (1878–1954) withdrew from a successful career in the theatre in 1925 and devoted himself to films; these included *A Free Soul* (1931), for which he won an Oscar, and *Grand Hotel* (1932). His sister, Ethel (1879–1959), was also an actress; she gave notable stage performances in *The Second Mrs Tanqueray* (1924) and *The Corn is Green* (1942), and won an Oscar for her part in the film *None But the Lonely Heart* (1944). Their brother, John (1882–1942), was a light comedian as well as a serious actor; his most celebrated role was on stage as Hamlet, both in New York (1922) and in London (1925).

Bart /bɑ:t/, Lionel (born 1930), English composer and lyricist. Bart wrote the music and lyrics for *Fings Ain't Wot They Used T'Be* (1959), which together with *Lock Up Your Daughters* (1959) contributed to the revival of the English musical. *Oliver!* (1960) achieved 2,618 performances, setting a new record for a musical. *Twang!* (1965), however, was an expensive failure and seriously harmed Bart's career in the theatre.

Barth[1] /bɑ:θ/, John (Simmons) (born 1930), American novelist and short-story writer. He is known as a writer of complex, elaborate, experimental novels, including *The Sot-Weed Factor* (1960), a fantastic parody of an 18th-century picaresque tale, and *Giles Goat-Boy* (1966), a satirical allegory of the modern world conceived in terms of a university campus; *Letters* (1979) consists of correspondence exchanged by characters from his previous novels.

Barth[2] /bɑ:t, bɑ:θ/, Karl (1886–1968), Swiss Protestant theologian. Under the shadow of the First World War he was led to a radical questioning of contemporary religious thought and in 1919 published his seminal work *Epistle to the Romans*. A rebuttal of liberal 19th-century Protestant theology, the book established a neoorthodox or theocentric approach. He emphasized the supremacy and transcendence of God and the dependence of man on divine grace, and stressed that the teachings of Christ as related in the Bible were the only route to an understanding of God. His work had its greatest impact in the 1930s, but it exerts a continuing influence on Protestant theology today.

Barthes /bɑ:t/, Roland (1915–80), French writer and critic. Barthes was a leading exponent of structuralism in literary criticism and cultural analysis. In the 1950s and 1960s, he spearheaded the *nouvelle critique*, which challenged the traditional

approach of literary criticism. His iconoclastic work *On Racine* (1963) is still a subject of controversy amongst literary critics. Barthes was increasingly drawn to the theory of semiotics after *Mythologies* (1957), his critique of contemporary culture, proceeding to define the theory in further detail in *Elements of Semiology* (1964). Later works, such as the essay 'The Death of the Author' (1968) and *S/Z* (1970), which stress the role of the reader in constructing a text, were influential in the development of deconstruction and post-structuralism.

Bartholdi /bɑːˈtɒldɪ, -ˈθɒldɪ/, Frédéric-Auguste (1834–1904), French sculptor. He is known especially for his colossal figures, such as the *Statue of Liberty* (*Liberty Enlightening the World*), which was presented to the US in 1886, and is located on an island in New York harbour.

Bartholomew, St /bɑːˈθɒləˌmjuː/ an Apostle. He is said to have been flayed alive in Armenia, and is hence regarded as the patron saint of tanners. Feast day, 24 August.

Bartók /ˈbɑːtɒk/, Béla (1881–1945), Hungarian composer. While his early work reflects the influence of Liszt, Wagner, Brahms, and Richard Strauss, he later developed an original musical language; basically homophonic and harmonically adventurous, his music is often percussive and owes much to Hungarian folk music, which he began to record, notate, and classify in 1904. His work includes six string quartets (1908–39), three piano concertos (1926; 1930–1; 1945), *Concerto for Orchestra* (1943), and an opera, *Duke Bluebeard's Castle* (1911). He emigrated to America in 1940 because of political pressures in Hungary.

Bartolommeo /ˌbɑːtɒləˈmeɪəʊ/, Fra (born Baccio della Porta) (*c.*1472–1517), Italian painter. A Dominican friar, he worked chiefly in Florence and made visits to Venice and Rome, where he was much impressed with the work of Raphael and Michelangelo. His work particularly displays the influence of the former, as is demonstrated in the balance of his compositions and the use of rapt expressions and significant gestures. Notable works are *The Vision of St Bernard* (1507) and *The Mystic Marriage of St Catherine* (1511).

Barton /ˈbɑːt(ə)n/, Sir Edmund (1849–1920), Australian statesman and jurist, first Prime Minister of Australia 1901–3. He led the Australian federation movement from

1891. He helped draft the proposed Commonwealth constitution and went to England in 1900 (accompanied by Alfred Deakin) to see the bill through Parliament. He resigned as Prime Minister in 1903 to become a senior judge in the High Court of Australia, serving until 1920.

Baryshnikov /bəˈriːʃnɪˌkɒf/, Mikhail (Nikolaevich) (born 1948), American ballet-dancer, born in Latvia of Russian parents. In 1974 he defected to the West while touring with the Kirov Ballet. He then danced with the American Theater Ballet and the New York City Ballet, where roles were devised for him by Jerome Robbins (*Opus 191/The Dreamer*, 1979) and Sir Frederick Ashton (*Rhapsody*, 1980). He was artistic director of the American Theater Ballet 1980–90.

Basie /ˈbeɪsɪ/, Count (born William Basie) (1904–84), American jazz pianist, organist, and band-leader. He took up the piano at an early age and had lessons with Fats Waller. In 1935 he formed his own big band, which became known as the Count Basie Orchestra. One of the best-known bands of the swing era, with its strong rhythm section and employment of some of the top instrumentalists and vocalists of the day, it enjoyed great success for many years.

Basil, St /ˈbæz(ə)l/ (known as St Basil the Great) (*c.*330–79), Doctor of the Church. The brother of St Gregory of Nyssa, he was a staunch opponent of the heresy of Arianism, which denied Christ's divinity. He lived as a hermit until 370, when he was appointed bishop of Caesarea in Cappadocia. He put forward a monastic rule which is still the basis of monasticism in the Eastern Church. Feast day, 14 June.

Baskerville /ˈbæskəˌvɪl/, John (1706–75), English printer. He designed the typeface that bears his name, and from 1757 onwards produced editions of authors such as Virgil, Milton, and Horace which were notable for their quality of type and paper.

Bateman /ˈbeɪtmən/, H(enry) M(ayo) (1887–1970), Australian-born British cartoonist. From 1904 Bateman developed an exclusively visual style of cartoon strip which was used in several periodicals, including *Tatler* and *Punch*. His best-known series of cartoons, entitled 'The Man Who . . .', ran from 1912 and illustrated social gaffes resulting from snobbery.

Bates[1] /beɪts/, Henry Walter (1825–92), English naturalist. He travelled with A. R. Wallace in Brazil, writing *The Naturalist on the River Amazons* (1863). He described the phenomenon now known as Batesian mimicry, suggesting that, by natural selection, animals which use mimicry in this way are more likely to survive.

Bates[2] /beɪts/, H(erbert) E(rnest) (1905–74), English novelist and short-story writer. His many short stories appeared in several collected volumes, including *The Beauty of the Dead* (1940). Of his novels, perhaps his best known is *The Darling Buds of May* (1958), which gained wide popularity in Britain when dramatized for television (1990–2).

Bateson /'beɪts(ə)n/, William (1861–1926), English geneticist and coiner of the term *genetics* in its current sense. He decided that variation is discontinuous, publicizing Mendel's work when he came across it many years later. Bateson found that some genes were not independent of one another, though he explained this as being caused by the reduplication of gametes and did not accept the idea of chromosomes.

Batista /bə'tiːstə/, Fulgencio (full name Fulgencio Batista y Zaldívar) (1901–73), Cuban soldier and statesman, President 1940–4 and 1952–9. He was instrumental in the military coup which overthrew the existing Cuban regime in 1933, and ruled Cuba indirectly through a succession of Presidents until his own election as President in 1940. He regained power after a coup in 1952; his second government was supported by the US but was notoriously corrupt and ruthless. Facing increased opposition from the guerrillas led by Fidel Castro, he was finally overthrown and fled to the Dominican Republic in 1959.

Batten /'bæt(ə)n/, Jean (1909–82), New Zealand aviator. She was the first woman to fly from England to Australia and back (1934–5), breaking Amy Johnson's record for the England to Australia journey by nearly five days. In 1936, she made the first direct solo flight from England to New Zealand in a time of 11 days 45 minutes.

Baudelaire /'bəʊdə,leə(r)/, Charles (Pierre) (1821–67), French poet and critic. An associate and champion of the painters Manet and Delacroix, he began his literary career writing art criticism and reviews, but is now largely known for *Les Fleurs du mal* (1857), a series of 101 lyrics in a variety of

metres. In these he explores his sense of isolation, exile, sin, boredom, and melancholy, as well as the attraction of evil and vice and the fascination and degradation of Parisian life. He died in poverty and obscurity, and it was only in the later years of the 19th century that his importance to the symbolist movement was recognized.

Baudrillard /'bəʊdrɪ,jɑː(r)/, Jean (born 1929), French sociologist and cultural critic. Baudrillard combined the translation and criticism of left-wing literature with a career as a sociologist, which culminated in a chair at Nanterre University. His membership of the 'New Left' *Tel Quel* group helped extend his criticism of the prevailing capitalist ideologies to encompass Marxist doctrines. Often associated with postmodernism, Baudrillard's writing (for example *America*, 1986) both castigates and celebrates the social and intellectual fragmentation that it describes.

Bax /bæks/, Sir Arnold (Edward Trevor) (1883–1953), English composer. A lasting sympathy for the Celtic revival, particularly of Irish literature, fostered in him an enduring love of Ireland's scenery and folksong. This is expressed musically in works such as *An Irish Elegy* (1917) for English horn, harp, and strings. *Tintagel* (1917) and his other tone poems are the best known of his works today, but he also composed seven symphonies, chamber works, songs, and choral music.

Baxter /'bækstə(r)/, James K(eir) (1926–72), New Zealand poet, dramatist, and critic. He published more than thirty books of poems; his early lyric poetry focuses on the New Zealand landscape and its influence on its inhabitants. A convert to Roman Catholicism, in *Jerusalem Sonnets* (1970) he develops a fluid sonnet form to express his spirituality; *Autumn Testament* (1972) reflects his humanistic socialism. His criticism includes *Aspects of Poetry in New Zealand* (1967).

Bayard /'beɪɑːd/, Pierre du Terrail, Chevalier de (1473–1524), French soldier. He served under several French monarchs, including Louis XII, and became known as the knight 'sans peur et sans reproche' (fearless and above reproach).

Baylis /'beɪlɪs/, Lilian Mary (1874–1937), English theatre manager. She assisted in the running of the Royal Victoria Coffee Music Hall, a temperance hall housed in the Royal Victoria Theatre (the Old Vic).

Under her management from 1912, the Old Vic acquired a reputation as the world's leading house for Shakespearian productions. Her initiative in reopening the old Sadler's Wells Theatre in 1931 led to the development of the Royal Ballet and the English National Opera.

Beale /biːl/, Dorothea (1831–1906), English educationist. With her friend and fellow educationist Frances Buss she pioneered women's higher education in Britain. From 1858 until her death she was principal of Cheltenham Ladies' College, where she introduced a curriculum similar to that used in public schools for boys. She founded St Hilda's College in Cheltenham (1885) as the first English training college for women teachers, and established St Hilda's Hall in Oxford for women teachers in 1893. She was also a strong supporter of women's suffrage.

Beamon /ˈbiːmən/, Robert ('Bob'), (born 1946), American athlete. He set a world record of 8.90 metres (29 ft 2^1/$_2$in.) in the long jump at the 1968 Olympic Games in Mexico City; this was not beaten until 1991.

Beardsley /ˈbɪədzlɪ/, Aubrey (Vincent) (1872–98), English artist and illustrator. His work, which was influenced by the Pre-Raphaelites and Japanese prints, first came to public notice with his illustrations for Thomas Malory's *Morte d'Arthur* (1893); in 1894 he became artistic editor of the quarterly periodical *The Yellow Book*. He produced notable illustrations for Oscar Wilde's *Salome* (1894) and for Alexander Pope's *The Rape of the Lock* (1896). He is regarded as the chief English representative of the Aesthetic Movement in art; his illustrations are characterized by linear arabesque and an emphasis on flat areas of black and white, and typify the stylistic and aesthetic considerations of art nouveau.

Beaton /ˈbiːt(ə)n/, Sir Cecil (Walter Hardy) (1904–80), English photographer. During the 1930s he worked with *Vogue* magazine and quickly earned international fame for his fashion features and portraits of celebrities; he is especially remembered today for his many portraits of the British royal family. His approach to photography was essentially theatrical, with subjects often posed amid elaborate settings to create tableaux. After the Second World War he diversified into costume and set design for films, ballet, and the theatre; he won two Oscars for his design and costumes for the film *My Fair Lady* (1964).

Beatty[1] /ˈbiːtɪ/, David, 1st Earl Beatty of the North Sea and of Brooksby (1871–1936), British admiral. As commander of battle-cruiser squadrons during the First World War he gained victories over German cruisers off Heligoland (1914) and the Dogger Bank (1915) and played a major role in the Battle of Jutland. He was Commander-in-Chief of the Grand Fleet from 1916 and received the German naval surrender in 1918. He was First Sea Lord 1919–27 and supervised the postwar reorganization of the navy.

Beatty[2] /ˈbeɪtɪ, ˈbiːtɪ/, Warren (born Henry Warren Beaty) (born 1937), American actor, film director, and screenwriter. Beatty gained a reputation as a suave, handsome leading man, but made considerable efforts to diversify and became involved in film production. He starred in and produced *Bonnie and Clyde* (1967), co-directed *Heaven Can Wait* (1978), and was producer, co-writer, star, and Oscar-winning director of *Reds* (1981). His later films include *Dick Tracy* (1990).

Beau Brummell see BRUMMELL.

Beaumarchais /ˈbəʊmɑːˌʃeɪ/, Pierre Augustin Caron de (1732–99), French dramatist. An important comic dramatist, he is chiefly remembered for his comedies *The Barber of Seville* (1775) and *The Marriage of Figaro* (1784); although still popular in France, they are best known in Britain as the inspiration for operas by Rossini and Mozart.

Beaumont /ˈbəʊmɒnt/, Francis (1584–1616), English dramatist. He was educated at Oxford and entered the Inner Temple in 1600. He became an associate of Ben Jonson and John Fletcher, and collaborated with the latter in *Philaster* (1609), *The Maid's Tragedy* (1610–11), and many other plays. *The Knight of the Burning Pestle* (c.1607) is attributed to Beaumont alone.

Beau Nash see NASH[4].

Beauvoir, Simone de, see DE BEAUVOIR.

Beaverbrook /ˈbiːvəˌbrʊk/, (William) Max (-well) Aitken, 1st Baron (1879–1964), Canadian-born British Conservative politician and newspaper proprietor. He made his fortune in Canadian business before coming to Britain and winning election to

Parliament in 1910. However, it is for his activities as a newspaper proprietor that he is best known; he bought the *Daily Express* in 1916 and made it the daily newspaper with the world's largest circulation. He launched the *Sunday Express* in 1918 and acquired the *Evening Standard* in 1923, thus consolidating his substantial newspaper empire. As Minister of Aircraft Production in Churchill's Cabinet (1940), Beaverbrook made an important contribution to victory in the Battle of Britain.

Bechstein /'bekstaɪn/, Friedrich Wilhelm Carl (1826–1900), German piano-builder. His name is used to designate a piano manufactured by him or by the firm which he founded in 1856.

Beckenbauer /'bekən‚baʊə(r)/, Franz (born 1945), German footballer and manager. Under his captaincy Bayern Munich won a number of championships and West Germany won the World Cup in 1974. After a spell in the US (1976–80) he returned to West Germany, where he was manager of the national team that won the World Cup again in 1990.

Becker /'bekə(r)/, Boris (born 1967), German tennis player. He became the youngest man to win the men's singles championship at Wimbledon in 1985, the first time that the title had been won by an unseeded player. He won at Wimbledon again in 1986 and 1989 and also won the US Open (1989) and the Australian Open (1991).

Becket, St Thomas à /'bekɪt/ (c.1118–70), English prelate and statesman. A close and influential friend of Henry II, he served as his Chancellor and in 1162 became Archbishop of Canterbury, a position Becket accepted with reluctance, foreseeing the inevitable conflict of interests between the king and the Church. He soon found himself in open opposition to Henry, first on a matter of taxation and later over the coronation of Henry's son, and the king in anger uttered words which led four knights to assassinate Becket in his cathedral on 29 December. The murder aroused indignation throughout Europe, miracles were soon reported at his tomb, and Henry was obliged to do public penance there. The shrine became a major centre of pilgrimage until its destruction under Henry VIII (1538). Feast day, 29 December.

Beckett /'bekɪt/, Samuel (Barclay) (1906–89), Irish dramatist, novelist, and poet. A permanent resident in France from the mid-1930s, he is best known for his plays, especially *Waiting for Godot* (1952). A seminal work in the Theatre of the Absurd, the play was highly influential during the postwar period, especially because of Beckett's use of dramatic narrative and symbolism. His later works were increasingly short and enigmatic. Beckett was awarded the Nobel Prize for literature in 1969.

Beckford /'bekfəd/, William (1759–1844), English writer and collector. He inherited a large fortune from his father, which he spent lavishly. He travelled in Europe, collected works of art and curios, and commissioned the building of Fonthill Abbey in Wiltshire, a Gothic folly, where he lived in seclusion 1796–1822. He is remembered as the author of the fantastic oriental romance *Vathek* (1786, originally written in French).

Beckmann[1] /'bekmən/, Ernst Otto (1853–1923), German chemist. Beckmann devised a method of determining a compound's molecular weight by measuring the rise in boiling-point of a solvent containing the compound. For this he designed an accurate thermometer with an adjustable range. He also discovered a rearrangement reaction important in organic synthesis.

Beckmann[2] /'bekmən/, Max (1884–1950), German painter and graphic artist. Beckmann was an expressionist and his paintings typically reflect his first-hand experience of human evil during the First World War; a characteristic work is *The Night* (1919), a torture scene in which contemporary social conditions are portrayed with powerful symbolism. Beckmann was dismissed from his teaching post in Frankfurt by the Nazis in 1933; the same year he painted *Robbery of Europe*. In 1937 his work was denounced as 'degenerate' and he fled to Holland, before going to the US in 1947.

Becquerel /'bekə‚rel/, Antoine-Henri (1852–1908), French physicist. He shared the 1903 Nobel Prize for physics with Marie and Pierre Curie for his discovery of natural radioactivity in uranium salts, which he proceeded to investigate. Initially, the rays emitted by radioactive substances were named after him.

Bede, St /biːd/ (known as the Venerable Bede) (c.673–735), English monk, theologian, and historian. He lived and worked at the monastery in Jarrow, on Tyneside. Often regarded as 'the Father of English

History', he wrote a number of historical works including *The Ecclesiastical History of the English People* (completed in 731). This is considered a primary source for early English history; it has vivid descriptions and is based on careful research, separating fact from hearsay and tradition. Feast day, 27 May.

Beecham /'biːtʃəm/, Sir Thomas (1879–1961), English conductor and impresario. He was associated with most of the leading British orchestras, founding the London Philharmonic in 1932 and the Royal Philharmonic in 1947; he was also artistic director of the Royal Opera House in the 1930s. He did much to stimulate interest in new and neglected music; a champion of Delius, he was also responsible for introducing Diaghilev's Ballets Russes and the work of Sibelius and Richard Strauss to the public.

Beecher /'biːtʃə(r)/, Henry Ward (1813–87), American clergyman, orator, and writer. He was ordained as a Congregationalist in 1837 and ten years later accepted the pulpit of the Plymouth Church of Brooklyn. There he won fame as one of the greatest orators of his day, attacking political corruption and slavery in an emotional, florid style.

Beeching /'biːtʃɪŋ/, Richard, Baron (1913–85), English businessman and engineer. Chairman of the British Railways Board (1963–5), Beeching is best remembered for the 'Beeching axe', the plan which proposed the closure of a substantial proportion of the British rail network. Much of the plan was rapidly carried out, although a change of government prevented its completion. Beeching was created a life peer in 1965 and became deputy chairman of ICI the same year.

Beerbohm /'bɪəbəʊm/, Sir Henry Maximilian ('Max') (1872–1956), English caricaturist, essayist, and critic. A central figure of the Aesthetic Movement, from 1894 he contributed to the quarterly periodical *The Yellow Book*. He was well placed to comment on the avant-garde tendencies of the period, which he did in collections of essays and caricatures. His one completed novel, *Zuleika Dobson* (1911), is a fantasized distillation of the atmosphere of *fin-de-siècle* Oxford. From 1935 onwards he achieved success in the new medium of radio; some of his broadcasts were published in *Mainly on the Air* (1946).

Beethoven /'beɪtəʊv(ə)n, 'beɪt,həʊ-/, Ludwig van (1770–1827), German composer. Pre-eminently an instrumental composer, he reinvigorated the forms of sonata, symphony, and concerto that had matured during the latter part of the 18th century, reshaping them and expanding their terms of reference. Despite increasing deafness, he was responsible for a prodigious musical output; his work includes nine symphonies (such as the *Eroica* of 1804, originally dedicated to his hero Napoleon), thirty-two piano sonatas, sixteen string quartets, the opera *Fidelio* (1814), and the Mass in D (the *Missa Solemnis* of 1823). In the piano sonatas of 1816–22 and the string quartets of 1824–6 the old structural forms are merely implicit; in his Ninth Symphony (1824) he broke with precedent altogether in the finale by introducing voices to sing Schiller's *Ode to Joy*. With his expansion of 18th-century forms and techniques in his earlier work, and the personal emotion and individuality of his later works, he is often seen as bridging the classical and romantic movements.

Beeton /'biːt(ə)n/, Mrs Isabella Mary (1836–65), English writer on cookery. Her bestselling *Book of Cookery and Household Management* (1861), first published serially in a women's magazine, contained over 3,000 recipes and articles, as well as sections giving advice on legal and medical matters.

Begin /'begɪn/, Menachem (1913–92), Israeli statesman, Prime Minister 1977–84. A member of the Zionist organization Irgun 1943–8, following Israel's independence he founded the Herut Party (which evolved from Irgun) and served as leader of the opposition 1948–67. In 1973 he took up the position of joint chairman of the Likud coalition, becoming Prime Minister in 1977, when the Likud party was successful at the polls. His hard line on Arab–Israeli relations, particularly with regard to retaining territories occupied by Israel during the Arab–Israeli War (1967), softened in a series of meetings with President Sadat of Egypt. The result was a peace treaty between Egypt and Israel; the two leaders shared the Nobel Peace Prize in 1978.

Behan /'biːən/, Brendan (Francis) (1923–64), Irish dramatist and poet. A committed supporter of Irish nationalism, he spent periods in Borstal and in prison for his involvement in terrorist activities; his

period of Borstal training is described in his autobiographical novel *Borstal Boy* (1958). His play *The Quare Fellow* (1956), set in an Irish prison and evoking the horror and humour prevailing on the eve of a hanging, is based on the time he spent in Dublin's Mountjoy prison (1942–6); the work became a key text in the contemporary anti-hanging debate.

Behn /beɪn/, Aphra (1640–89), English novelist and dramatist. Regarded as the first professional woman writer in England, she is best known for her philosophical novel *Oroonoko, or the History of the Royal Slave* (1688). Based on her trip to Suriname in 1663, the novel deplores the slave trade and Christian attitudes towards it, and encourages respect for its African hero. Of her fifteen plays, perhaps the best known is her Restoration comedy *The Rover* (1678).

Behrens /'beərənz/, Peter (1868–1940), German architect and designer. As architect and chief designer for the electrical combine AEG from 1907, his brief included the design of the company's products and stationery in addition to their buildings, and his work was a significant influence in the development of modern architecture and industrial design. His architectural work is notable for its functional employment of modern materials such as steel and glass. Behrens was also an influential teacher and trained leading architects such as Walter Gropius and Le Corbusier.

Behring /'beərɪŋ/, Emil Adolf von (1854–1917), German bacteriologist and one of the founders of immunology. He discovered in 1890 that animals can produce substances in the blood which counteract the effects of bacterial toxins. Behring applied this knowledge to the curing of diphtheria and tetanus, injecting patients with blood serum taken from animals previously exposed to the disease. He was awarded a Nobel Prize in 1901.

Beiderbecke /'baɪdə,bek/, Bix (born Leon Bismarck Beiderbecke) (1903–31), American jazz musician and composer. A self-taught cornettist and pianist, he was one of a handful of white musicians who profoundly influenced the development of jazz. His bell-like tone and lyrical improvisations on the cornet were his hallmarks. During a career abruptly terminated by his death from alcoholism, Beiderbecke played with Louis Armstrong and American bandleader Paul Whiteman (1890–1967).

Béjart /beɪˈʒɑː(r)/, Maurice (born Maurice Jean Berger) (born 1927), French choreographer. He is chiefly identified with The Ballet of the 20th Century, the company which he founded in Brussels in 1959. His choreography is noted for its fusion of classic and modern dance. The first choreographer to stage ballet performances in a sports arena, he is remembered for his innovative productions of *The Firebird* (1970) and *Notre Faust* (1975).

Bell[1] /bel/ Alexander Graham (1847–1922), Scottish-born American scientist and inventor. Bell studied sound waves, the mechanics of speech, and speech therapy. Having moved to the US in the early 1870s, he developed his ideas for transmitting speech electrically, and gave the first public demonstration of the telephone in 1876; he founded the Bell Telephone Company the following year. He also invented the gramophone (1897) as a successful rival to Thomas Edison's phonograph. He later carried out research in a number of other areas, including hydrofoil speedboats and aeronautics.

Bell[2] /bel/, Currer, Ellis, and Acton, the pseudonyms used by Charlotte, Emily, and Anne Brontë.

Bell[3] /bel/, Gertrude (Margaret Lowthian) (1868–1926), English archaeologist and traveller. She travelled widely as a field archaeologist in the Middle East, acquiring an extensive knowledge of the desert Arabs and local politics, and undertook liaison work with the Arabs for the British government in 1915. A supporter of Arab independence, she assisted in the negotiations for Iraq's independence (1920–1) in her capacity as Oriental Secretary to the British High Commissioner. Her writings include a description of her travels in Syria, *The Desert and the Sown* (1907).

Bell[4] /bel/, Vanessa (1879–1961), English painter and designer. She was a prominent member of the Bloomsbury Group, together with her younger sister Virginia Woolf. In 1913 she left her husband Clive Bell to live with fellow artist Duncan Grant. She was a regular contributor to Roger Fry's Omega workshops (1913–19), and built a reputation as one of the most gifted English artists of her time.

Bellini[1] /beˈliːnɪ/ a family of Italian painters. Jacopo (c.1400–70) was trained by Gentile da Fabriano: his elder son Gentile

(c.1429–1507) was prominent as a portrait-ist and narrative painter. Jacopo's younger son Giovanni (c.1430–1516) is the most famous of the family; he had a large workshop of pupils and assistants and transformed the family's native Venice into a major centre of Renaissance painting. Stylistically he was influenced by his brother-in-law Mantegna, although his painting is less severe than Mantegna's and has a serene contemplative quality. Giovanni Bellini's work in the 15th and early 16th centuries is dominated by madonnas and other sacred subjects (such as *The San Giobbe Altarpiece*, 1480). In works such as *The Agony in the Garden* (c.1460), Giovanni Bellini also made a significant contribution to-wards the treatment of figures within a landscape. He continued to develop as an artist, in later life painting the newly fash-ionable pagan themes (such as *Feast of the Gods*, 1514) and mysterious allegories, his work reflecting the influence of his pupils Giorgione and Titian.

Bellini[2] /beˈliːnɪ/, Vincenzo (1801–35), Ital-ian composer. Of his eleven operas, the most famous are *La Sonnambula* (1831), *Norma* (1831), and *I Puritani* (1835). His work is typically dramatic and lyrical, displays a close relationship between the music and libretto, and is characterized by long, ele-gant melodies, such as 'Casta Diva' from *Norma*.

Belloc /ˈbelɒk/ (Joseph) Hilaire (Pierre René) (1870–1953), French-born British writer, historian, and poet, of French–British des-cent. A devout Roman Catholic, he collab-orated with his friend G. K. Chesterton in works often critical of modern industrial society and socialism, notably in *The Servile State* (1912). His writings include biog-raphies of Napoleon and Oliver Cromwell, but he is now best known for his light verse, such as *The Bad Child's Book of Beasts* (1896) and *Cautionary Tales* (1907).

Bellow /ˈbeləʊ/, Saul (born 1915), Canadian-born American novelist, of Russian Jewish descent. A leading figure in mid-20th-cen-tury American fiction, he has written nov-els as diverse as the comic *The Adventures of Augie March* (1953) and the more sombre and semi-autobiographical *Herzog* (1964). His other works include the collection of short stories *Him with His Foot in His Mouth* (1984). His fiction is both ironic and opti-mistic in its treatment of the human condi-tion. He was awarded the Nobel Prize for literature in 1976.

Belshazzar /belˈʃæzə(r)/ (6th century BC), son of Nebuchadnezzar and last king of Babylon. According to Dan. 5, he was killed in the sack of the city and his doom was foretold by writing which appeared on the walls of his palace at a great banquet. In inscriptions and documents from Ur, how-ever, he was perhaps the grandson of Ne-buchadnezzar and the son of Nabonidos, last king of Babylon, and did not himself reign.

Ben Bella /ben ˈbelə/, (Muhammad) Ahmed (born 1916), Algerian statesman, Prime Minister 1962–3 and President 1963–5. In 1952 he founded the Front de Libération Nationale (FLN), which instigated the Al-gerian War of Independence (1954–62). He was elected Prime Minister of a provisional government shortly before the end of the war, becoming the first President of an independent Algeria the following year. As President he initiated social and economic reform and encouraged closer links with other Arab nations. Overthrown in a mili-tary coup, he was kept under house arrest until 1979 and lived in exile until 1990, when he returned to Algeria to lead the opposition to the ruling regime.

Benedict, St /ˈbenɪdɪkt/ (c.480–c.550), Ital-ian hermit. A hermit from the age of 14, he attracted many followers by his piety; of these he chose the most devoted to form twelve small monastic communities, ultimately establishing a monastery at Monte Cassino (c.540). His *Regula Mona-chorum* (known as the Rule of St Benedict), austere but tempered by moderation, formed the basis of Western monasticism. Feast day, 11 July (formerly 21 March).

Beneš /ˈbeneʃ/, Edvard (1884–1948), Czecho-slovak statesman, Prime Minister 1921–2, President 1935–8 and 1945–8. A founder (with Tomáš Masaryk) of modern Czecho-slovakia, he served as Masaryk's Minister of Foreign Affairs 1919–35, during which time he championed the League of Nations (he served as its chairman six times) and established close ties with France and the Soviet Union. He resigned as President over the Munich Agreement, and during the Second World War came to London as head of the Czechoslovakian government in exile (1941–5). In 1945 he returned to his country to regain the presidency, but re-signed after the 1948 Communist coup.

Benetton /'benɪ,tɒn/, Luciano (born 1935), Italian businessman, and his sister Giuliana (born 1938), Italian designer and businesswoman. Luciano established the original Benetton company with his brothers in 1965; Giuliana began by making sweaters which Luciano sold to shops in their home town of Treviso, opening the company's first shop in 1968. By the mid-1980s the firm had become a multinational clothing company with thousands of retail outlets worldwide.

Ben-Gurion /ben'guəriən/, David (1886–1973), Israeli statesman, Prime Minister 1948–53 and 1955–63. Born in Poland, he emigrated to Palestine in 1906, where he became an active Zionist. He was elected leader of the predominant socialist faction (the Mapai Party) of the Zionist movement in 1930. When the state of Israel was established in 1948, he became the country's first Prime Minister and Minister of Defence. After expulsion from the Labour Party in 1965 he formed a new party with Moshe Dayan.

Benn /ben/, Anthony (Neil Wedgwood) ('Tony') (born 1925), British Labour politician. He became a Labour MP in 1950, but was debarred from the House of Commons on succeeding to the title of Viscount Stansgate in 1960. He renounced his title in 1963 and was re-elected the same year, going on to hold several government posts, including Secretary of State for Industry (1974–5) and Secretary for Energy (1975–9). He made unsuccessful bids for the party leadership in 1976 and 1988, and continued to be active on the left of the party.

Bennett[1] /'benɪt/, Alan (born 1934), English dramatist and actor. He achieved fame with the revue *Beyond the Fringe* (1960) and the satirical comedy *Forty Years On* (1969), lampooning the Bloomsbury Group and other cult figures. Other plays in the same vein followed, including *Getting On* (1972), a political satire about a Labour MP. He has also written for television, for example, the monologue series *Talking Heads* (1987) and the play *A Question of Attribution* (1991).

Bennett[2] /'benɪt/, (Enoch) Arnold (1867–1931), English novelist, dramatist, and critic. He began his literary career in London writing stories for periodicals and editing the journal *Woman*; in Paris (1902–12) he was greatly influenced by the French realists and wrote several successful plays.

However, his fame rests on the novels and stories set in the Potteries ('the Five Towns') of his youth, notably *Anna of the Five Towns* (1902), *The Old Wives' Tale* (1908), and the *Clayhanger* series (1902–8), in which he portrays provincial life and culture in documentary detail.

Bennett[3] /'benɪt/, Richard Rodney (born 1936), English composer. He studied in Paris with Pierre Boulez (1956–8), then settled in London. He is known for his film scores, notably those for *Far from the Madding Crowd* (1967) and *Murder on the Orient Express* (1974). His concert works include operas, such as *The Mines of Sulphur* (1965), concertos, and chamber pieces, and his later work pays increasing attention to internal rhythmic structure.

Benny /'benɪ/, Jack (born Benjamin Kubelsky) (1894–1974), American comedian and actor. Benny made his radio début in 1931 on *The Ed Sullivan Show* and launched his own series in 1932. *The Jack Benny Show* was successfully transplanted to television in 1950 and ran until 1965, attracting a mass audience. Often the butt of his own mordant humour, Benny was a self-effacing figure renowned for his timing and delivery.

Bentham /'benθəm/, Jeremy (1748–1832), English philosopher and jurist. The first major proponent of utilitarianism, as put forward in *A Fragment on Government* (1776) and more fully in his *Introduction to the Principles of Morals and Legislation* (1789), he argued that the proper object of all legislation and conduct was to secure 'the greatest happiness of the greatest number', and was concerned to reform the law by giving it a clear theoretical justification. With John Stuart Mill he co-founded the organ of the philosophical radicals, *The Westminster Review*, in 1824. Bentham exercised a decisive influence on 19th-century British thought, particularly in the field of political reform.

Bentley /'bentlɪ/, Edmund Clerihew (1875–1956), English journalist and novelist. Examples of his comic verse-form, the clerihew, were first published along with some sketches by his friend G. K. Chesterton in *Biography for Beginners* (1905). More clerihews appeared in volumes such as *Clerihews Complete* (1951). He was a successful journalist, and is also remembered for his detective novel *Trent's Last Case* (1913).

Benz /benz, German bɛnts/, Karl Friedrich (1844–1929), German engineer and motor manufacturer. One of the pioneers of the motor car, in 1883 he formed a company to develop the internal-combustion engine, and in 1885 he built the first vehicle to be driven by such an engine. Benz's company was merged with Daimler in 1926.

Berenice /ˌberɪˈnaɪsɪ/ (3rd century BC), Egyptian queen, wife of Ptolemy III. She dedicated her hair as a votive offering for the safe return of her husband from an expedition. The hair was stolen and (according to legend) placed in the heavens. She is commemorated in the name of the constellation Coma Berenices (*Berenice's hair*).

Berg /beəg/, Alban (Maria Johannes) (1885–1935), Austrian composer. A pupil of Schoenberg, he was one of the leading exponents of twelve-note composition. He is best known for the Violin Concerto (1935), composed as a memorial after the death of the eighteen-year-old daughter of Alma and Walter Gropius, and for his two operas, *Wozzeck* (1914–21) and *Lulu* (1928–35).

Berger /ˈbɜːgə(r)/, Hans (1873–1941), German psychiatrist. He attempted to correlate mental activity with brain physiology, detecting electric currents in the exposed cortex in 1924. Finding that these could also be detected through the intact skull, Berger went on to develop encephalography, which has since been used extensively to diagnose neurological conditions.

Bergerac see CYRANO DE BERGERAC.

Bergius /ˈbɜːgɪəs/, Friedrich Karl Rudolf (1884–1949), German industrial chemist. He is best known for his process for producing petroleum and other hydrocarbons from coal dust, using hydrogen and a catalyst under high pressure. He also made a type of coal by carbonizing peat, achieved the complete hydrolysis of cellulose, and developed industrial processes for synthesizing phenol and ethylene glycol. Bergius shared the Nobel Prize for chemistry in 1931.

Bergman[1] /ˈbɜːgmən/, (Ernst) Ingmar (born 1918), Swedish film and theatre director. His work is characterized by his use of haunting imagery and a symbolism often derived from Jungian dream analysis. He came to international fame with the film *Smiles of a Summer Night* (1955) and achieved further worldwide success with *The Seventh Seal* (1956) and *Wild Strawberries* (1957). An important theatre director, he has directed many of his players in both media.

Bergman[2] /ˈbɜːgmən/, Ingrid (1915–82), Swedish actress. She made her name on stage and screen in Sweden before embarking on an international career in Hollywood in the 1930s. Although her film career was a long one, it is probably for her romantic role opposite Humphrey Bogart in *Casablanca* (1942) that she is best known. Other notable films include *For Whom the Bell Tolls* (1943) and *Anastasia* (1956); she received an Oscar for the latter, as well as for her role in *Murder on the Orient Express* (1974).

Bergson /ˈbɜːgs(ə)n, French berksɔn/, Henri (Louis) (1859–1941), French philosopher. His philosophy is dualistic, dividing the world into life (or consciousness) and matter. In his most famous work, *Creative Evolution* (1907), he attacked scientific materialism and rejected the Darwinian theory of evolution. He proposed instead that life possesses an inherent creative impulse (*élan vital*), the continuous operation of which as it seeks to impose itself upon matter leads to the production of new forms. Bergson's work influenced writers such as Marcel Proust and George Bernard Shaw; he was awarded the Nobel Prize for literature in 1927.

Beria /ˈberɪə/, Lavrenti (Pavlovich) (1899–1953), Soviet politician and head of the secret police (NKVD and MVD) 1938–53. Born in Georgia, he rose to prominence within the Soviet Communist Party under Stalin's patronage. As head of the secret police Beria was directly involved in the infamous 'purge trials' in which Stalin's opponents were eliminated; he was also responsible for the deportation of thousands to forced labour camps. After Stalin's death he was rumoured to be planning to seize power; feared by rival politicians, he was arrested. Although his fate is not certain, it was officially announced that he had been tried and shot as a traitor.

Bering /ˈbeərɪŋ/, Vitus (Jonassen) (1681–1741), Danish navigator and explorer. At the instigation of Peter the Great he led several Russian expeditions aimed at discovering whether Asia and North America were connected by land. He sailed along the coast of Siberia and in 1741 reached Alaska from the east. On the return jour-

ney his ship was wrecked and he died on an island which now bears his name. Also named after him are the Bering Sea and Bering Strait.

Berio /ˈberɪəʊ/, Luciano (born 1925), Italian composer. A serialist, he has often adopted an experimental approach to groupings of instruments and singers, the use of electronic sound, and the combination of live and pre-recorded music. His works include *Circles* (1960), for singer, harp, and percussion, a series of *Sequences* (1958–75) for virtuoso solo instruments, and the opera *Un Re in Ascolto* (1984).

Berkeley[1] /ˈbɜːklɪ/, Busby (born William Berkeley Enos) (1895–1976), American choreographer and film director. As a leading Broadway dance director, he was introduced to films by Samuel Goldwyn, for whom he choreographed *Whoopee* (1930). In films such as the *Gold Diggers* series (1922–37) and *Babes in Arms* (1939), he quickly became famous for his spectacular and dazzling sequences in which huge casts of rhythmically moving dancers formed kaleidoscopic patterns on the screen.

Berkeley[2] /ˈbɑːklɪ/, George (1685–1753), Irish philosopher and bishop. His idealist philosophy is set out in his major works *A Treatise Concerning the Principles of Human Knowledge* (1710) and *Three Dialogues between Hylas and Philonous* (1713). He denied the existence of matter, holding that there are only minds and mental events; material objects exist solely by being perceived. To the objection that objects would leap in and out of existence according to whether they were being looked at, he replied that God perceives everything, and that this gives objects — ideas in the mind of God — a continuous existence. He held this to be a sound argument for the existence of God.

Berkeley[3] /ˈbɑːklɪ/, Sir Lennox (Randall Francis) (1903–89), English composer. He studied in Paris 1927–32, and his compositions display a distinct French influence. His works, which are noted for their intensity of feeling and technical elegance, include four operas, among them *Nelson* (1953) and *Ruth* (1956), four symphonies, music for ballet and film, and sacred choral music.

Berkoff /ˈbɜːkɒf/, Steven (born 1937), English dramatist, director, and actor. Much of Berkoff's work is politically radical in content and shocking and aggressive in style,

parodying established dramatic styles and showing the influence of Antonin Artaud and Franz Kafka. His first original play, *East*, a work in blank verse about his East End boyhood, was presented at the 1975 Edinburgh Festival. Among Berkoff's other plays are *Greek* (1979), a modern version of the Oedipus myth, and *The Murder of Jesus Christ* (1981).

Berlin[1] /bɜːˈlɪn/, Irving (born Israel Baline) (1888–1989), Russian-born American songwriter. He had no formal musical training, but began writing songs when he was 16; in 1911 he had a hit with 'Alexander's Ragtime Band'. Thereafter he contributed to many musical shows, revues, and films, including *Annie Get Your Gun* (1946) and *Holiday Inn* (1942); the latter contained the song 'White Christmas', sung by Bing Crosby, which proved to be one of the best-selling records of all time. Berlin also wrote 'God Bless America' (1939), which became the unofficial national anthem of the US.

Berlin[2] /bɜːˈlɪn/, Sir Isaiah (1909–97), Latvian-born British philosopher. He spent his academic career at Oxford University, becoming professor of Social and Political Theory in 1957 and subsequently Master of Wolfson College (1966–75) and emeritus professor at All Souls. He devoted his career to the history of ideas, which he discusses in books such as *Karl Marx* (1939), *Four Essays on Liberty* (1959), and *Vico and Herder* (1976).

Berlioz /ˈbeəlɪˌəʊz/, (Louis-)Hector (1803–69), French composer. He was one of the most original composers of his time and a major exponent of 19th-century programme music. His *Symphonie fantastique* (1830) reflects his unhappy passion for Harriet Smithson, an Irish actress. His other major works include the five-act opera *Les Troyens* (1856–9) and the cantata *La Damnation de Faust* (1846).

Bernadette, St /ˌbɜːnəˈdet/ (born Marie Bernarde Soubirous) (1844–79), French peasant girl. Her visions of the Virgin Mary in Lourdes in 1858 led to the town's establishment as a centre of pilgrimage. Bernadette later became a nun and she was canonized in 1933. Feast day, 18 February.

Bernadotte[1] /ˌbɜːnəˈdɒt/, Folke, Count (1895–1948), Swedish statesman. A member of the Swedish royal family, Bernadotte gained a reputation as a neutral arbiter in international disputes. As vice-president of the Swedish Red Cross during the Second

World War, he arranged the exchange of prisoners of war, and in 1945 acted as an intermediary between Himmler and the Allies, conveying a German offer of capitulation. Charged with the role of UN mediator in Palestine in 1948, he was assassinated by the militant Zionist organization the Stern Gang.

Bernadotte[2] /ˌbɜːnəˈdɒt/, Jean Baptiste Jules (1763–1844), French soldier, king of Sweden (as Charles XIV) 1818–44. One of Napoleon's marshals, he was adopted by Charles XIII of Sweden in 1810 and became king in 1818, thus founding Sweden's present royal house.

Bernard /beəˈnɑː(r)/, Claude (1813–78), French physiologist. Bernard used animal experiments to show the role of the pancreas in digestion, the method of regulation of body temperature, and the function of nerves supplying the internal organs. He realized that the constant composition of the body fluids was essential for the optimal functioning of the body, discovered the biological importance of glycogen, and investigated the action of curare.

Bernard, St /ˈbɜːnəd/ (c.996–c.1081), French monk. He founded two hospices to aid travellers in the Alps. The St Bernard passes, where the hospices were situated, and St Bernard dogs, once kept by the monks and trained to aid travellers, are named after him. Feast day, 28 May.

Bernard of Clairvaux, St /ˈbɜːnəd, kleəˈvəʊ/ (1090–1153), French theologian and abbot. He was the first abbot of Clairvaux in France; his monastery there became one of the chief centres of the Cistercian order. Enjoying papal favour, he was an important religious force in Europe, and the Cistercian order grew rapidly under his influence. He was noted for his asceticism, severity, and eloquence; his preaching at the council of Vézelay in 1146 instigated the Second Crusade; he had the French theologian Peter Abelard condemned for heresy. Feast day, 20 August.

Bernhardt /ˈbɜːnhɑːt/, Sarah (born Henriette Rosine Bernard) (1844–1923), French actress. Internationally acclaimed and regarded as the greatest tragic actress of her day, she gained her first major successes in 1872, playing Cordelia in *King Lear* and the queen in Victor Hugo's *Ruy Blas*. She was noted for her clear voice, magnetic personality, and great beauty; of all her performances, she is probably best known for her portrayal of Marguerite in *La Dame aux camélias* by Alexandre Dumas *fils*. The amputation of a leg in 1915 after an accident did not diminish her activity and she continued to act in seated roles.

Bernini /beəˈniːnɪ/, Gian Lorenzo (1598–1680), Italian sculptor, painter, and architect. An outstanding figure of the Italian baroque, Bernini is notable for the vigour, movement, and dramatic and emotional power of his works. Using a variety of materials, including stucco, stone, and marble, he fused sculpture, architecture, and painting into a decorative whole. Working chiefly in Rome, he became architect to St Peter's in 1629, for which his work included the great canopy over the high altar and the colonnade round the piazza in front of the church. One of his most famous sculptures is *The Vision of St Teresa* (1644–67) in the church of Santa Maria della Vittoria in Rome.

Bernoulli /bɜːˈnuːɪ/ a Swiss family that produced many eminent mathematicians and scientists. Jakob (Jacques or James) Bernoulli (1654–1705) made discoveries in calculus, which he used to solve minimization problems, and he contributed to geometry and the theory of probabilities. His brother Johann (Jean or John, 1667–1748) also contributed to differential and integral calculus. Both were professors of mathematics at Basle. Daniel Bernoulli (1700–82), son of Johann, was professor of mathematics at St Petersburg and then held successively the chairs of botany, physiology, and physics at Basle. Although his original studies were in medicine, his greatest contributions were to hydrodynamics and mathematical physics.

Bernstein /ˈbɜːnstiːn, -stam/, Leonard (1918–90), American composer, conductor, and pianist. As a conductor, he worked with the New York Philharmonic Orchestra (1945–8 and 1957–69) and toured extensively. As a composer, he encompassed a wide range of forms and styles in his music; his large instrumental and choral works often juxtapose a romantic intensity with jazz and Latin American elements. His best-known compositions include the symphony *The Age of Anxiety* (1947–9), the musical *West Side Story* (1957), and film music such as that for *On the Waterfront* (1954).

Berra /ˈberə/, Yogi (born Lawrence Peter Berra) (born 1925), American baseball player. He was especially famous as a

catcher with the New York Yankees in the 1950s and early 1960s, setting the record for the most home runs (313) by a catcher in the American League. He became known in the US for his pithy sayings such as (on baseball) 'You can't think and hit at the same time'. The cartoon character Yogi Bear (1958) is popularly believed to have been named after Berra, though the animators deny that this was their intention.

Berry /'berɪ/, Chuck (born Charles Edward Berry) (born 1931), American rock and roll singer, guitarist, and songwriter. One of the first great rock and roll stars with a large teenage following, he first had a hit with 'Maybellene' (1955); this was followed by 'Johnny B Goode' and 'Sweet Little Sixteen' (both 1958). His recording career was interrupted by a period of imprisonment (1962–4); although he continued to release albums throughout the 1970s and 1980s, his only major hit single during that time was 'My Ding A Ling' (1972). His music had a significant influence on the development of rock music; British pop and rock groups such as the Beatles and the Rolling Stones are particularly indebted to him.

Bertillon /'beəti:ˌjɒn/, Alphonse (1853–1914), French criminologist. He devised a system of body-measurements for the identification of criminals, which was widely used in France and other countries until superseded by the technique of fingerprinting at the beginning of the 20th century.

Bertolucci /ˌbeətə'lu:tʃɪ/, Bernardo (born 1940), Italian film director. He made his début as a director in 1962. Critical acclaim came in 1964 with *Before the Revolution* and later with *The Spider's Stratagem* (1970), but it was with the box-office success of the sexually explicit *Last Tango in Paris* (1972) that he first gained a wide audience. His film *The Last Emperor* (1988), which dealt with the fall of the imperial dynasty in China, won nine Oscars.

Berzelius /bɜːˈziːlɪəs/, Jöns Jakob (1779–1848), Swedish analytical chemist. Berzelius studied about 2,000 compounds and by 1818 had determined the atomic weights of most of the then known elements. He discovered three new elements (cerium, selenium, and thorium), suggested the basic principles of modern chemical notation, and introduced the terms *isomerism*, *polymer*, *protein*, and *catalysis*.

Besant /'bez(ə)nt, bɪ'zænt/, Annie (1847–1933), English theosophist, writer, and politician. An atheist, socialist, and advocate of birth control, she became an active member of the Fabian Society in 1885. In 1889, after meeting Helena Blavatsky, she converted to theosophy. Besant was the president of the Theosophical Society from 1907 until her death, and settled in the society's headquarters in Madras in India, where she became involved in politics and pressed for Indian self-government. She established and directed the Home Rule India League (1916) and served as president of the Indian National Congress (1917–23).

Bessel /'bes(ə)l/, Friedrich Wilhelm (1784–1846), German astronomer and mathematician. Self-taught in navigation and astronomy, he rose to become director of the new observatory in Königsberg. He determined the positions of some 75,000 stars, and was the first to obtain accurate measurements of stellar distances using the parallax resulting from the earth's changing position. Bessel worked intensively on the orbits of planets and binary stars, developing mathematical functions that are named after him. Following a study of the orbit of Uranus he predicted the existence of an eighth planet.

Bessemer /'besɪmə(r)/, Sir Henry (1813–98), English engineer and inventor. Bessemer is best known for the steel-making process that bears his name. At the time of the Crimean War in the 1850s, his proposals for the redesign of guns received little encouragement in Britain but a great deal from Napoleon III. The material available for gun construction was inadequate, however, so Bessemer then worked on a series of experiments and patents in the search for stronger material.

Best[1] /best/, Charles Herbert (1899–1978), American-born Canadian physiologist. His employer, Professor J. J. R. Macleod, placed him with F. G. Banting to assist in his research on pancreatic extracts. The research team announced the discovery of insulin in 1922. Unlike the others, Best was not awarded a Nobel Prize in 1923, but Banting shared half the prize money with him. He succeeded Banting as director of the Banting and Best Department of Medical Research at the University of Toronto in 1941, a post which he retained until 1967.

Best² /best/, George (born 1946), Northern Irish footballer. He joined Manchester United soon after leaving school and later played for Northern Ireland. An attacking winger with exceptional ball control, he was the leading scorer in the First Division in the 1967–8 season; he won a European Cup winners' medal and was named European Footballer of the Year in 1968. Unable to overcome a succession of personal and other problems in the late 1960s, his career as a top footballer came to a premature end soon after.

Bethune /be'θju:n/, Henry Norman (1890–1939), Canadian surgeon. He invented or improved a number of surgical instruments, but became disillusioned with medicine in Canada following his experiences of the surgical treatment of tuberculosis in his country. Bethune joined the Communist Party in 1935 and served in the Spanish Civil War against the Fascists, organizing the first mobile blood-transfusion service. Finally, he joined the Chinese army in their war against Japan as a surgeon, becoming a hero in the People's Republic; he died from septicaemia while in China.

Betjeman /'betʃəmən/, Sir John (1906–84), English poet. His poems, as seen in collections such as *New Bats in Old Belfries* (1945), are self-deprecating, witty, and gently satirical; using traditional verse forms, they capture the spirit of his age. He also published a verse autobiography, *Summoned by Bells*, in 1960. His collection of architectural essays *In Ghastly Good Taste* (1933) reflects his interest in the preservation of Victorian and Edwardian buildings; he did much to raise public awareness of the merits of such architecture. He was appointed Poet Laureate in 1972.

Betterton /'betət(ə)n/, Thomas (1635–1710), English actor. A leading actor of the Restoration period, he played a variety of roles including the tragic parts of Hamlet and Macbeth, and comic roles such as Sir Toby Belch in *Twelfth Night*. He also adapted the plays of John Webster, Molière, and Beaumont and Fletcher for his own productions.

Betti /'betɪ/, Ugo (1892–1953), Italian dramatist, poet, and short-story writer. He practised as a judge in Rome (1930–43); his writing did not gain wide recognition until just before his death, when *Crime on Goat Island* (1950) was produced in Paris. This and his other most widely produced plays, including *Corruption in the Palace of Justice* (1949), take the form of harrowing legal examinations that result in the exposure of the real motives, evil, and guilt that lie beneath the social surfaces of the characters.

Beuys /bɔɪs/, Joseph (1921–86), German artist. He is regarded as one of the most influential figures of avant-garde art in Europe in the 1970s and 1980s. His work consisted of 'assemblages' of various articles of rubbish, and he also directed a number of 'happenings'. In 1979 he co-founded the German Green Party.

Bevan /'bev(ə)n/, Aneurin ('Nye') (1897–1960), British Labour politician. A brilliant though often abrasive orator, he was MP for Ebbw Vale 1929–60. His most notable contribution was the creation of the National Health Service (1948) during his time as Minister of Health 1945–51. He resigned from the government in protest against the introduction of health-service charges. The leader of the left wing of the Labour Party, he was defeated by Hugh Gaitskell in the contest for the party leadership in 1955.

Beveridge /'bevərɪdʒ/, William Henry, 1st Baron (1879–1963), British economist and social reformer, born in India. As director of the London School of Economics (1919–37), Beveridge transformed it into an institution of international repute. His most notable achievement was as chairman of the committee which prepared the Beveridge Report (Report on Social Insurance and Allied Services, 1942); this recommended the establishment of a comprehensive scheme of social insurance and formed the basis of much subsequent social legislation establishing the welfare state in the UK.

Bevin /'bevɪn/, Ernest (1881–1951), British Labour statesman and trade unionist. He was one of the founders of the Transport and General Workers' Union, serving as its first General Secretary (1921–40), and was a leading organizer of the General Strike (1926). He later entered Parliament, serving as Minister of Labour in Churchill's war Cabinet. As Foreign Secretary (1945–51), he helped form the Organization for European Economic Cooperation (1948) and NATO (1949). Unable to find a solution to the problem of Palestine, he surrendered

the British mandate to the United Nations in 1947.

Bewick /'bjuːɪk/, Thomas (1753–1828), English artist and wood engraver. His best works are the shrewdly observed and expressive animal studies which illustrate such books as *A History of British Birds* (1797, 1804).

Bhutto[1] /'buːtəʊ/, Benazir (born 1953), Pakistani stateswoman, Prime Minister 1988–90 and 1993–6. The daughter of Zulfikar Ali Bhutto and an opponent of the existing regime, she became joint leader in exile of the Pakistan People's Party (1984), returning to Pakistan in 1986 to campaign for open democratic elections. Following President Zia ul-Haq's death she became the first woman Prime Minister of a Muslim country. She took her country back into the Commonwealth and promised radical social reform, but failed to win widespread support from other parties. She was dismissed as Prime Minister and defeated in the ensuing election, re-elected as head of a coalition government in 1993, and dismissed again in 1996.

Bhutto[2] /'buːtəʊ/, Zulfikar Ali (1928–79), Pakistani statesman, President 1971–3 and Prime Minister 1973–7. As Pakistan's Foreign Minister (1963–6) he instigated a rapprochement with China and became known as an outspoken defender of his country's interests. He formed the Pakistan People's Party in 1967, coming to power as Pakistan's first civilian President in 1971 and later (after constitutional changes) serving as Prime Minister. While in office, he did much to strengthen national morale and introduced social, constitutional, and economic reforms. He was ousted by a military coup and executed for conspiring to murder a political rival.

Bierce /bɪəs/, Ambrose (Gwinnett) (1842–c.1914), American writer. He served in the American Civil War (1861–5) and later became a prominent journalist in California, London, and Washington. He is best known for his realistic and sardonic short stories, strongly influenced by Edgar Allan Poe and including *Cobwebs from an Empty Skull* (1874) and *In the Midst of Life* (1898), and for the wickedly witty *The Devil's Dictionary* (1911). In 1913 he travelled to Mexico and mysteriously disappeared.

Biko /'biːkəʊ/, Stephen ('Steve') (1946–77), South African radical leader. While a medical student, he founded and became president of the South African Students Organization (1968). In 1972 he co-founded the Black People's Convention, a coalition of organizations which aimed to raise awareness of oppression in the black community and develop a sense of pride. He was banned from political activity in 1973 and his freedom of speech and association were severely restricted; detained several times in the last years of his life, he died in police custody, becoming a symbol of heroic resistance to apartheid in black townships and beyond.

Billy the Kid see BONNEY.

Binet /'biːneɪ/, Alfred (1857–1911), French psychologist and pioneer of modern intelligence testing. He was requested to devise a test which would detect intellectually slow schoolchildren, and together with the psychiatrist Théodore Simon (1873–1961) he produced tests (now known as *Binet* or *Binet–Simon tests*) intended to examine general reasoning capacities rather than perceptual-motor skills. Believing that bright and dull schoolchildren were simply advanced or retarded in their mental growth, Binet devised a mental age scale which described performance in relation to the average performance of students of the same physical age.

Birdseye /'bɜːdzaɪ/, Clarence (1886–1956), American businessman and inventor. A former fur-trader, he had observed food preservation techniques practised by local people in Labrador; this led him to develop a process of rapid freezing of foods in small packages suitable for retail selling, creating a revolution in eating habits.

Birgitta, St see BRIDGET, ST[2].

Birtwistle /'bɜːtˌwɪs(ə)l/, Sir Harrison (Paul) (born 1934), English composer and clarinettist. In 1967 he was a co-founder of the Pierrot Players and wrote much of his work for them and for the English Opera Group. His early work was influenced by Stravinsky; later compositions are more experimental.

Bishop /'bɪʃəp/, Elizabeth (1911–79), American poet. Bishop's first two collections, *North and South* (1946) and *A Cold Spring* (1955), received the Pulitzer Prize when published as a combined edition in 1955. She lived in Brazil from 1952 to 1967 and her formal, structured poetry contrasts her experiences in South America with her

New England origins. Her *Complete Poems* (1969) was followed by *Geography III* (1976).

Bismarck /'bɪzmɑːk/, Otto (Eduard Leopold) von, Prince of Bismarck, Duke of Lauenburg (known as 'the Iron Chancellor') (1815–98), German statesman. As Minister-President and Foreign Minister of Prussia under Wilhelm I from 1862, Bismarck was the driving force behind the unification of Germany, orchestrating wars with Denmark (1864), Austria (1866), and France (1870–1) in order to achieve this end. As Chancellor of the new German Empire (1871–90), he continued to dominate the political scene, passing legislation intended to break the influence of the Catholic Church at home and consolidating Germany's position as a European power by creating a system of alliances. Bismarck was forced to resign in 1890 after a policy disagreement with Wilhelm II.

Bizet /'biːzeɪ/, Georges (born Alexandre César Léopold Bizet) (1838–75), French composer. Although his first major work was the Symphony in C major (1855), this was not performed until 1933, and it was as an operatic composer that he strove to make his reputation. Critical acclaim was largely unforthcoming during his lifetime, but *The Pearl Fishers* (1863) and *Carmen* (1875) have since gained considerable popularity; the latter, based on a story by the French novelist Prosper Mérimée (1803–70), is regarded as Bizet's masterpiece.

Bjerknes /'bjɜːknəs/, Vilhelm Frimann Koren (1862–1951), Norwegian geophysicist and meteorologist. His studies of circulation and vortices led to his theory of physical hydrodynamics for atmospheric and oceanic circulation, and he developed mathematical models for weather prediction. With colleagues, he later formulated a theory which accounted for the generation of cyclones and introduced the term *front* to meteorology.

Black /blæk/, Joseph (1728–99), Scottish chemist. Black studied the chemistry of gases and formulated the concepts of latent heat and thermal capacity. He developed accurate techniques for following chemical reactions by weighing reactants and products. In studying the chemistry of alkalis he isolated the gas carbon dioxide, going on to investigate its chemistry in turn.

Blackett /'blækɪt/, Patrick Maynard Stuart, Baron (1897–1974), English physicist. During the Second World War he was involved in operational research in the U-boat war and was a member of the Maud Committee, which dealt with the development of the atom bomb. He modified the cloud chamber for the study of cosmic rays, and was awarded the Nobel Prize for physics in 1948.

Blackmore /'blækmɔː(r)/, R(ichard) D(oddridge) (1825–1900), English novelist and poet. He published several collections of poetry before turning to fiction; his fame rests almost entirely on his popular romantic novel *Lorna Doone* (1869), set on 17th-century Exmoor.

Black Prince (name given to Edward, Prince of Wales and Duke of Cornwall) (1330–76), eldest son of Edward III of England. A soldier of considerable ability, he was responsible for a number of English victories during the early years of the Hundred Years War, most notably that at Poitiers in 1356. His health failed at a relatively early age and he predeceased his father; his own son eventually came to the throne as Richard II. The name Black Prince apparently derives from the black armour he wore when fighting.

Blackstone /'blækstəʊn/, Sir William (1723–80), English jurist. His major work was the *Commentaries on the Laws of England* (1765–9), based on lectures given at Oxford University; setting out English legal structure and principles, it became a highly influential exposition of English law, forming the basis of legal education in England and the US.

Blackwood /'blækwʊd/, Algernon (Henry) (1869–1951), English writer. He was sent to Canada by his parents at the age of 20, and his ten struggling years spent there and in the US were later described in his vivid autobiography *Episodes Before Thirty* (1923). He then worked as a journalist before returning to England and devoting himself to writing. He became known for novels of fantasy and the macabre such as *The Centaur* (1911) and short-story collections like *Pan's Garden* (1912).

Blair /bleə(r)/, Anthony Charles Lynton ('Tony') (born 1953), Scottish Labour statesman, Prime Minister since 1997. His victory made him the youngest Prime Minister since Lord Liverpool in 1812. He became MP for Sedgefield in 1983 and was elected leader of the Labour Party in 1994,

following the death of the former leader John Smith (1938–94).

Blake[1] /bleɪk/, Peter (born 1932), English painter. In the late 1950s and early 1960s he was prominent in the pop art movement in the UK. His work is characterized by a nostalgia for the popular culture of the 1930s and 1940s and a combination of sophistication and naivety; it often features collages in which painted images are juxtaposed with real objects. One of his most famous creations is the cover design for the Beatles album *Sergeant Pepper's Lonely Hearts Club Band* (1967).

Blake[2] /bleɪk/, William (1757–1827), English artist and poet. His poems mark the beginning of romanticism and a rejection of the Age of Enlightenment; they include *Songs of Innocence* (1789) and *Songs of Experience* (1794). The short poem known as 'Jerusalem', which later became a popular hymn, appears in *Milton* (1804–8). His major prose work, *The Marriage of Heaven and Hell* (c.1790–3), is a collection of paradoxical and revolutionary aphorisms. His watercolours and engravings, like his writings, were only fully appreciated after his death.

Blakey /'bleɪkɪ/, Arthur ('Art') (1919–90), American jazz drummer. In 1955 Blakey formed the influential jazz group the Jazz Messengers. Blakey was a pioneer in the early days of the bebop movement and he continued to hold a leading position in the jazz world throughout his subsequent career.

Blanchard /'blænʃɑːd/, Jean Pierre François (1753–1809), French balloonist. Together with American John Jeffries (1744–1819) he made the first crossing of the English Channel by air, flying by balloon from Dover to Calais on 7 January 1785, and was the first to fly a balloon in the US. Blanchard was among the earliest to experiment with parachuting, using animals in his demonstrations; he was killed making practice jumps by parachute from a balloon.

Blavatsky /blæ'vætskɪ/, Helena (Petrovna) (known as Madame Blavatsky; née Hahn) (1831–91), Russian spiritualist, born in Ukraine. She went to the US in 1873, and in 1875 founded the Theosophical Society in New York together with the American Henry Steel Olcott (1832–1907). The movement was based on Hindu and Buddhist teachings and taught of the transmigration of souls and universal fellowship; in 1878 Blavatsky and Olcott transferred the society's headquarters to India.

Blériot /'bleriəʊ/, Louis (1872–1936), French aviation pioneer. Trained as an engineer, he built one of the first successful monoplanes in 1907. On 25 July 1909 he became the first to fly the English Channel (Calais to Dover) in a monoplane. Later he became an aircraft manufacturer, building more than 800 aeroplanes of forty different types between 1909 and 1914.

Blessed Virgin Mary, the mother of Jesus (see **Mary**[1]).

Bligh /blaɪ/, William (1754–1817), British naval officer. In 1787 he was appointed captain of HMS *Bounty* on a voyage to the West Indies. Two years later part of his crew mutinied, led by the first mate Fletcher Christian, and Bligh was set adrift in an open boat, arriving safely at Timor in the East Indies a few weeks later. Bligh later took command of the *Glatton* under Admiral Nelson in the battle of Copenhagen (1801). While serving as governor of New South Wales (1805–8), he was deposed by disaffected officers, but was subsequently exonerated of blame and promoted to vice-admiral.

Bliss /blɪs/, Sir Arthur (Edward Drummond) (1891–1975), English composer. In his earlier work he showed an interest in avant-garde music, particularly that of Schoenberg and Stravinsky, composing at Elgar's behest *A Colour Symphony* (1922). In later years, however, he tended more to traditional forms, as in his symphony for orator, chorus, and orchestra *Morning Heroes* (1930), composed as a memorial to the victims of the First World War. He also wrote ballet and film scores, including the powerful music for Alexander Korda's *Things to Come* (1934–5).

Blixen /'blɪks(ə)n/, Karen (Christentze), Baroness Blixen-Finecke (née Dinesen; also known by the pseudonym of Isak Dinesen) (1885–1962), Danish novelist and short-story writer. Blixen married her second cousin in 1914 and moved to Kenya. Despite divorcing in 1921 she stayed on to run their coffee plantation, becoming deeply involved with the country and people. She returned to Denmark in 1931 and published her first major work, *Seven Gothic Tales*, in 1934. Her autobiography *Out of Africa* (1937) was made into a successful film in 1985.

Bloch /blɒx/, Ernest (1880–1959), Swiss-born American composer, of Jewish descent. Before he settled in the US in 1916, his opera *Macbeth* (1910) was produced in Paris to great acclaim. His musical language derives from the late 19th-century romanticism of Liszt and Richard Strauss; the influence of Jewish musical forms can be seen in the *Israel Symphony* (1912–16), *Solomon* (1916), and numerous other orchestral compositions.

Blondin /'blɒndɪn/, Charles (born Jean-François Gravelet) (1824–97), French acrobat. He is renowned for walking across a tightrope suspended over Niagara Falls in 1859; on subsequent occasions he performed the same feat blindfold, with a wheelbarrow, and carrying a man on his back.

Bloody Mary the nickname of Mary I of England (see MARY[2]).

Bloomfield /'bluːmfiːld/, Leonard (1887–1949), American linguist. One of the founders of American structural linguistics, his primary aim was to establish linguistics as an autonomous and scientific discipline; his most important work was the influential *Language* (1933).

Blum /bluːm/, Léon (1872–1950), French statesman, Prime Minister 1936–7, 1938, 1946–7. A lawyer and literary critic, he was drawn into politics by the Dreyfus affair of 1894; he joined the Socialist Party in 1902 and became its leader in opposition in 1925. During the 1930s he led the Popular Front, being elected France's first socialist and Jewish Prime Minister in 1936. He introduced significant labour reforms, but was forced to resign the following year. Interned in Germany during the Second World War, he returned to France to head a socialist caretaker Cabinet, and retained the party leadership until his death.

Blumenbach /'bluːmənˌbɑːx/, Johann Friedrich (1752–1840), German physiologist and anatomist. He is regarded as the founder of physical anthropology, though his approach has since been much modified. He classified modern humans into five broad categories (Caucasian, Mongoloid, Malayan, Ethiopian, and American), based mainly on cranial measurements.

Blunden /'blʌndən/, Edmund (Charles) (1896–1974), English poet and critic. His prose work *Undertones of War* (1928) is a sensitive account of his experiences in the First World War. His poetry reveals his deep love of the English countryside, as can be seen in *Pastorals* (1916) and *The Waggoner and Other Poems* (1920).

Blunt /blʌnt/, Anthony (Frederick) (1907–83), British art historian, Foreign Office official, and Soviet spy. He was director of the Courtauld Institute of Art (1947–74), Surveyor of the King's (later Queen's) Pictures (1945–72), and one of the leading figures in establishing art history as an academic discipline in Britain. In 1965 he confessed that he had been a Soviet agent since the 1930s and had facilitated the escape of the spies Guy Burgess and Donald Maclean in 1951. These facts were made public in 1979, and he was subsequently stripped of the knighthood that he had been awarded in 1956.

Blyton /'blaɪt(ə)n/, Enid (1897–1968), English writer of children's fiction. Her best-known creation for young children was the character Noddy, who first appeared in 1949; her books for older children included the series of *Famous Five* and *Secret Seven* adventure stories. In all she wrote more than 400 books, many of which were translated into other languages.

Boadicea see BOUDICCA.

Boas /'bəʊæz/, Franz (1858–1942), German-born American anthropologist. A pioneer of modern anthropology, he developed the linguistic and cultural components of ethnology. Against the trend of contemporary theory he drew attention to the subjective nature of previous studies, pointing out how they were based on a Western cultural viewpoint. Instead he insisted that cultural development must be explored by means of field studies reconstructing histories of particular cultures. He did much to overturn the theory that Nordic peoples constitute an essentially superior race; his writings were burnt by the Nazis. His works include *Race, Language, and Culture* (1940).

Boccaccio /bəˈkɑːtʃɪˌəʊ/, Giovanni (1313–75), Italian writer, poet, and humanist. His most famous work, the *Decameron* (1348–58), is a collection of 100 tales told by a group of ten young people living in the country to escape the Black Death. Boccaccio collected the stories, which range from the serious to the light-hearted and the bawdy, from contemporary popular fiction and transformed them into a narrative whole. He is an important figure in the

history of narrative fiction and influenced many later writers, including Chaucer, Shakespeare, and Tennyson.

Boccherini /ˌbɒkə'riːnɪ/, Luigi (1743–1805), Italian composer and cellist. A prolific composer, chiefly of chamber music, he is especially known for his cello concertos and sonatas.

Bodley /'bɒdlɪ/, Sir Thomas (1545–1613), English scholar and diplomat. In 1558 he was entered at Magdalen College, Oxford, and became a fellow of Merton College in 1564, lecturing in Greek. He spent many years travelling and in 1585 became an ambassador to Queen Elizabeth I. He expended a great amount of money enlarging the Oxford University library, which was opened in 1602, being renamed the Bodleian by King James I in 1604.

Bodoni /bə'dəʊnɪ/, Giambattista (1740–1813), Italian printer. The typeface which he designed (characterized by extreme contrast between uprights and diagonals), and others based on it, are named after him.

Boethius /bəʊ'iːθɪəs/, Anicius Manlius Severinus (c.480–524), Roman statesman and philosopher. He is best known for *The Consolation of Philosophy*, a work written in a mixture of prose and verse while he was in prison for treason. In this he argued that the soul can attain happiness in affliction by realizing the value of goodness and meditating on the reality of God. While drawing upon Stoicism and Neoplatonism, his work echoed Christian sentiments and exercised considerable influence throughout the Middle Ages.

Bogarde /'bəʊgɑːd/, Sir Dirk (born Derek Niven van den Bogaerde) (born 1921), British actor and writer, of Dutch descent. He became famous in the 'Doctor' series of comedy films (including *Doctor in the House*, 1953). His later films include *The Servant* (1963), *Death in Venice* (1971), and *A Bridge Too Far* (1977). He has also published a number of volumes of autobiography and several novels.

Bogart /'bəʊgɑːt/, Humphrey (DeForest) (1899–1957), American actor. His acting career began on the stage in 1922; his success as a ruthless gangster in the play *The Petrified Forest* was repeated in the screen version of 1936. Many memorable gangster films followed, including *They Drive by Night* (1940). His best-known films are probably *Casablanca* (1942), *The Big Sleep*

(1946, in which he played opposite his fourth wife Lauren Bacall), and *The African Queen* (1951).

Bohr /bɔː(r)/, Niels Hendrik David (1885–1962), Danish physicist and pioneer in quantum physics. Bohr's theory of the structure of the atom incorporated quantum theory for the first time and is the basis for present-day quantum-mechanical models. In 1927 he proposed the principle of complementarity, which accounted for the paradox of regarding subatomic particles both as waves and as particles. In the 1930s Bohr fled from Nazi persecution, escaping from German-occupied Denmark in 1943 and helping to develop the atom bomb, first in Britain and then in the US. He later became concerned about the implications of atomic weapons and stressed the need to study the peaceful applications of atomic energy. Niels Bohr was awarded the 1922 Nobel Prize for physics; his son, Aage Niels Bohr (born 1922), shared the 1975 prize for his studies of the physics of the atomic nucleus.

Boileau /'bwʌləʊ/, Nicholas (full surname Boileau-Despréaux) (1636–1711), French critic and poet. Boileau is considered particularly important as one of the founders of French literary criticism, a field in which his influence has been profound. He gained wide recognition as the legislator and model for French neoclassicism with his didactic poem *Art poétique* (1674); based on Horace's *Ars Poetica*, it establishes canons of taste and defines principles of composition and criticism.

Bokassa /bə'kæsə/, Jean Bédel (1921–96), Central African Republic statesman and military leader, President 1972–6, emperor 1976–9. He led a successful coup in 1966, from which time he steadily increased his personal power, becoming President for life and later self-styled emperor of his country, which he renamed the Central African Empire. He was held responsible for many deaths and was ousted in 1979; in 1987 he was tried for his crimes and sentenced to death, but the sentence was eventually commuted.

Boldrewood /'bəʊldəˌwʊd/, Rolf (pseudonym of Thomas Alexander Browne) (1826–1915), Australian novelist. His most enduring work was *Robbery Under Arms* (first published as a serial in 1882–3), a narration of the life and crimes of a bushranger under sentence of death.

Boleyn /bəˈlɪn/, Anne (1507–36), second wife of Henry VIII and mother of Elizabeth I. Although the king had fallen in love with Anne, and had divorced Catherine of Aragon in order to marry her (1533), she fell from favour when she failed to provide him with a male heir. She was eventually executed because of alleged infidelities.

Bolger /ˈbʊldʒə(r)/, James B(rendan) (born 1935), New Zealand National Party statesman, Prime Minister since 1990.

Bolingbroke /ˈbʊlɪŋbrʊk/, the surname of Henry IV of England (see HENRY¹).

Bolívar /ˈbʊlɪˌvɑː(r), Spanish boˈliβar/, Simón (known as 'the Liberator') (1783–1830), Venezuelan patriot and statesman. Bolívar was active in the Latin-American independence movement from 1808 onwards. Although his military career was not without its failures, and although his dream of a South American federation was never realized, he succeeded in driving the Spanish from Venezuela, Colombia, Peru, and Ecuador; Upper Peru was named Bolivia in his honour.

Böll /bɜːl/, Heinrich (Theodor) (1917–85), German novelist and short-story writer. His years in the German army (1938–44) provided the material for his earliest work, including the novel *Adam, Where Art Thou?* (1951). His later work concerns aspects of postwar German society and is frequently critical of the prevailing political and business ethos; it differs stylistically from the realism of his early writing in that it uses symbolism and narrative devices such as flashback. Significant works include *Billiards at Half Past Nine* (1959) and *The Lost Honour of Katharina Blum* (1974). He was awarded the Nobel Prize for literature in 1972.

Bolt /bəʊlt/, Robert (Oxton) (1924–95), English dramatist and screenwriter. He taught in Somerset 1950–8 before devoting himself to writing after the success of his first play, *Flowering Cherry* (1958). His other plays include his acclaimed *A Man for All Seasons* (1960), which was filmed in 1967. His screenplay for this won an Oscar, as did that for *Dr Zhivago* (1965). He also wrote screenplays for *Lawrence of Arabia* (1962) and *The Mission* (1986).

Boltzmann /ˈbʊltsmən/, Ludwig (1844–1906), Austrian physicist. Boltzmann made contributions to the kinetic theory of gases, statistical mechanics, and thermodynamics. He recognized the importance of the electromagnetic theory of J. C. Maxwell, but had difficulty in getting his own work on statistical mechanics accepted until the discoveries in atomic physics at the turn of the century. He derived the Maxwell–Boltzmann equation for the distribution of energy among colliding atoms, correlating entropy with probability when he brought thermodynamics and molecular physics together.

Bonaparte /ˈbəʊnəˌpɑːt/ (Italian **Buonaparte** /ˌbwonaˈparte/) a Corsican family including the three French rulers named Napoleon.

Bonaventura, St /ˌbʊnəvenˈtjʊərə/ (born Giovanni di Fidanza; known as 'the Seraphic Doctor') (1221–74), Franciscan theologian. Appointed minister general of his order in 1257, he was made cardinal bishop of Albano in 1273. He wrote the official biography of St Francis and had a lasting influence as a spiritual writer. Feast day, 15 (formerly 14) July.

Bond /bɒnd/, Edward (born 1934), English dramatist. His first play, *The Pope's Wedding* (1962), was followed by *Saved* (1965), which attracted controversy over a scene depicting the stoning to death of a baby. His plays continued to include scenes of violence and cruelty while exploring socio-historical themes and contemporary issues. Notable works include *Narrow Road to the Deep North* (1968), *Restoration* (1981), and *September* (1990).

Bonhoeffer /ˈbʊnˌhɜːfə(r)/, Dietrich (1906–45), German Lutheran theologian and pastor. Originally influenced by the neo-orthodox theology of Karl Barth, in his later writings he moved away from biblical orthodoxy and concentrated on a Christianity informed by contemporary social and political issues. He was an active opponent of Nazism both before and during the Second World War, becoming involved in the German resistance movement. Arrested in 1943, he was sent to Buchenwald concentration camp and later executed.

Boniface, St /ˈbʊnɪˌfeɪs/ (born Wynfrith; known as 'the Apostle of Germany') (680–754), Anglo-Saxon missionary. Sent to Frisia and Germany to spread the Christian faith, he laid the foundations of a settled ecclesiastical organization there and made many converts. He was appointed Primate of Germany in 732, and in 741 was given authority to reform the whole Frankish

history of narrative fiction and influenced many later writers, including Chaucer, Shakespeare, and Tennyson.

Boccherini /ˌbɒkəˈriːnɪ/, Luigi (1743–1805), Italian composer and cellist. A prolific composer, chiefly of chamber music, he is especially known for his cello concertos and sonatas.

Bodley /ˈbɒdlɪ/, Sir Thomas (1545–1613), English scholar and diplomat. In 1558 he was entered at Magdalen College, Oxford, and became a fellow of Merton College in 1564, lecturing in Greek. He spent many years travelling and in 1585 became an ambassador to Queen Elizabeth I. He expended a great amount of money enlarging the Oxford University library, which was opened in 1602, being renamed the Bodleian by King James I in 1604.

Bodoni /bəˈdəʊnɪ/, Giambattista (1740–1813), Italian printer. The typeface which he designed (characterized by extreme contrast between uprights and diagonals), and others based on it, are named after him.

Boethius /bəʊˈiːθɪəs/, Anicius Manlius Severinus (c.480–524), Roman statesman and philosopher. He is best known for *The Consolation of Philosophy*, a work written in a mixture of prose and verse while he was in prison for treason. In this he argued that the soul can attain happiness in affliction by realizing the value of goodness and meditating on the reality of God. While drawing upon Stoicism and Neoplatonism, his work echoed Christian sentiments and exercised considerable influence throughout the Middle Ages.

Bogarde /ˈbəʊɡɑːd/, Sir Dirk (born Derek Niven van den Bogaerde) (born 1921), British actor and writer, of Dutch descent. He became famous in the 'Doctor' series of comedy films (including *Doctor in the House*, 1953). His later films include *The Servant* (1963), *Death in Venice* (1971), and *A Bridge Too Far* (1977). He has also published a number of volumes of autobiography and several novels.

Bogart /ˈbəʊɡɑːt/, Humphrey (DeForest) (1899–1957), American actor. His acting career began on the stage in 1922; his success as a ruthless gangster in the play *The Petrified Forest* was repeated in the screen version of 1936. Many memorable gangster films followed, including *They Drive by Night* (1940). His best-known films are probably *Casablanca* (1942), *The Big Sleep*

(1946, in which he played opposite his fourth wife Lauren Bacall), and *The African Queen* (1951).

Bohr /bɔː(r)/, Niels Hendrik David (1885–1962), Danish physicist and pioneer in quantum physics. Bohr's theory of the structure of the atom incorporated quantum theory for the first time and is the basis for present-day quantum-mechanical models. In 1927 he proposed the principle of complementarity, which accounted for the paradox of regarding subatomic particles both as waves and as particles. In the 1930s Bohr fled from Nazi persecution, escaping from German-occupied Denmark in 1943 and helping to develop the atom bomb, first in Britain and then in the US. He later became concerned about the implications of atomic weapons and stressed the need to study the peaceful applications of atomic energy. Niels Bohr was awarded the 1922 Nobel Prize for physics; his son, Aage Niels Bohr (born 1922), shared the 1975 prize for his studies of the physics of the atomic nucleus.

Boileau /ˈbwʌləʊ/, Nicholas (full surname Boileau-Despréaux) (1636–1711), French critic and poet. Boileau is considered particularly important as one of the founders of French literary criticism, a field in which his influence has been profound. He gained wide recognition as the legislator and model for French neoclassicism with his didactic poem *Art poétique* (1674); based on Horace's *Ars Poetica*, it establishes canons of taste and defines principles of composition and criticism.

Bokassa /bəˈkæsə/, Jean Bédel (1921–96), Central African Republic statesman and military leader, President 1972–6, emperor 1976–9. He led a successful coup in 1966, from which time he steadily increased his personal power, becoming President for life and later self-styled emperor of his country, which he renamed the Central African Empire. He was held responsible for many deaths and was ousted in 1979; in 1987 he was tried for his crimes and sentenced to death, but the sentence was eventually commuted.

Boldrewood /ˈbəʊldəˌwʊd/, Rolf (pseudonym of Thomas Alexander Browne) (1826–1915), Australian novelist. His most enduring work was *Robbery Under Arms* (first published as a serial in 1882–3), a narration of the life and crimes of a bushranger under sentence of death.

Boleyn /bə'lɪn/, Anne (1507–36), second wife of Henry VIII and mother of Elizabeth I. Although the king had fallen in love with Anne, and had divorced Catherine of Aragon in order to marry her (1533), she fell from favour when she failed to provide him with a male heir. She was eventually executed because of alleged infidelities.

Bolger /'bɒldʒə(r)/, James B(rendan) (born 1935), New Zealand National Party statesman, Prime Minister since 1990.

Bolingbroke /'bɒlɪŋ,brʊk/, the surname of Henry IV of England (see HENRY¹).

Bolívar /'bɒlɪ,vɑ:(r), Spanish bo'liβar/, Simón (known as 'the Liberator') (1783–1830), Venezuelan patriot and statesman. Bolívar was active in the Latin-American independence movement from 1808 onwards. Although his military career was not without its failures, and although his dream of a South American federation was never realized, he succeeded in driving the Spanish from Venezuela, Colombia, Peru, and Ecuador; Upper Peru was named Bolivia in his honour.

Böll /bɜ:l/, Heinrich (Theodor) (1917–85), German novelist and short-story writer. His years in the German army (1938–44) provided the material for his earliest work, including the novel *Adam, Where Art Thou?* (1951). His later work concerns aspects of postwar German society and is frequently critical of the prevailing political and business ethos; it differs stylistically from the realism of his early writing in that it uses symbolism and narrative devices such as flashback. Significant works include *Billiards at Half Past Nine* (1959) and *The Lost Honour of Katharina Blum* (1974). He was awarded the Nobel Prize for literature in 1972.

Bolt /bəʊlt/, Robert (Oxton) (1924–95), English dramatist and screenwriter. He taught in Somerset 1950–8 before devoting himself to writing after the success of his first play, *Flowering Cherry* (1958). His other plays include his acclaimed *A Man for All Seasons* (1960), which was filmed in 1967. His screenplay for this won an Oscar, as did that for *Dr Zhivago* (1965). He also wrote screenplays for *Lawrence of Arabia* (1962) and *The Mission* (1986).

Boltzmann /'bɒltsmən/, Ludwig (1844–1906), Austrian physicist. Boltzmann made contributions to the kinetic theory of gases, statistical mechanics, and thermodynamics. He recognized the importance of the electromagnetic theory of J. C. Maxwell, but had difficulty in getting his own work on statistical mechanics accepted until the discoveries in atomic physics at the turn of the century. He derived the Maxwell–Boltzmann equation for the distribution of energy among colliding atoms, correlating entropy with probability when he brought thermodynamics and molecular physics together.

Bonaparte /'bəʊnə,pɑ:t/ (Italian **Buonaparte** /,bwona'parte/) a Corsican family including the three French rulers named Napoleon.

Bonaventura, St /,bɒnəven'tjʊərə/ (born Giovanni di Fidanza; known as 'the Seraphic Doctor') (1221–74), Franciscan theologian. Appointed minister general of his order in 1257, he was made cardinal bishop of Albano in 1273. He wrote the official biography of St Francis and had a lasting influence as a spiritual writer. Feast day, 15 (formerly 14) July.

Bond /bɒnd/, Edward (born 1934), English dramatist. His first play, *The Pope's Wedding* (1962), was followed by *Saved* (1965), which attracted controversy over a scene depicting the stoning to death of a baby. His plays continued to include scenes of violence and cruelty while exploring socio-historical themes and contemporary issues. Notable works include *Narrow Road to the Deep North* (1968), *Restoration* (1981), and *September* (1990).

Bonhoeffer /'bɒn,hɜ:fə(r)/, Dietrich (1906–45), German Lutheran theologian and pastor. Originally influenced by the neo-orthodox theology of Karl Barth, in his later writings he moved away from biblical orthodoxy and concentrated on a Christianity informed by contemporary social and political issues. He was an active opponent of Nazism both before and during the Second World War, becoming involved in the German resistance movement. Arrested in 1943, he was sent to Buchenwald concentration camp and later executed.

Boniface, St /'bɒnɪ,feɪs/ (born Wynfrith; known as 'the Apostle of Germany') (680–754), Anglo-Saxon missionary. Sent to Frisia and Germany to spread the Christian faith, he laid the foundations of a settled ecclesiastical organization there and made many converts. He was appointed Primate of Germany in 732, and in 741 was given authority to reform the whole Frankish

Church. The first papal legate north of the Alps, Boniface greatly assisted the spread of papal influence. He was martyred in Frisia. Feast day, 5 June.

Bonington /'bɒnɪŋtən/, Christian John Storey ('Chris') (born 1934), English mountaineer. He made the first British ascent of the north face of the Eiger in 1962. He was the leader of two expeditions to Mount Everest: one by a hitherto unclimbed route in 1975 and the other in 1985, when he reached the summit.

Bonnard /'bɒnɑ:(r)/, Pierre (1867–1947), French painter and graphic artist. A member of a group of painters called the Nabi Group, he produced ornamental screens and lithographs before concentrating on painting from about 1905. His works continue and develop the impressionist tradition; notable for their rich, glowing colour harmonies, they mostly depict domestic interior scenes, nudes, and landscapes.

Bonney /'bɒnɪ/, William H. (known as 'Billy the Kid'; born Henry McCarty) (1859–81), American outlaw. In 1868 his family moved from New York City to New Mexico, where he killed a man when only 12 years old and subsequently became a notorious robber and murderer. Sheriff Pat Garrett captured him in 1880, but he escaped, only to be shot by Garrett at Fort Sumner, New Mexico.

Bonnie Prince Charlie see STUART[1].

Boole /bu:l/, George (1815–64), English mathematician. Professor at Cork in Ireland from 1849, Boole wrote important works on differential equations and other branches of mathematics, but is remembered chiefly for the algebraic description of reasoning now known as Boolean algebra. The study of mathematical or symbolic logic developed mainly from his ideas.

Boone /bu:n/, Daniel (c.1734–1820), American pioneer. Moving west from his native Pennsylvania, Boone made trips into the unexplored area of Kentucky from 1767 onwards, organizing settlements and successfully defending them against hostile Indians. He later moved further west to Missouri, being granted land there in 1799. As a hunter, trail-blazer, and fighter against the Indians he became a legend in his own lifetime.

Booth /bu:ð/, William (1829–1912), English religious leader, founder and first general of the Salvation Army. A Methodist revivalist preacher, he worked actively to improve the condition of the poor, attending to both their physical and spiritual needs. In 1865, assisted by his wife Catherine (1829–90), he established a mission in the East End of London which became the Salvation Army in 1878. Booth's family had a close involvement with the movement, which continued into the 20th century; his eldest son, William Branwell Booth (1856–1929), succeeded his father as general in 1912, while a granddaughter, Catherine Branwell Booth (1884–1987), was a commissioner in the Army.

Border /'bɔ:də(r)/, Allan (Robert) (born 1955), Australian cricketer. A batsman and occasional spin bowler, he first played for his country in 1978 and became captain six years later. At the time of his retirement from international cricket in 1994 he had made 156 test match appearances (93 as captain) and scored 11,174 runs (all three figures being world records).

Bordet /'bɔ:deɪ/, Jules (1870–1961), Belgian bacteriologist and immunologist. He discovered the heat-sensitive complement system found in blood serum, and demonstrated its role in antibody–antigen reactions and bacterial lysis. He also isolated a number of pathogenic bacteria, and developed a vaccine for whooping cough. Bordet was awarded a Nobel Prize in 1919.

Borg /bɔ:g/, Björn (Rune) (born 1956), Swedish tennis player. His first major titles were the Italian and French championships (1974); he then went on to win five consecutive men's singles titles at Wimbledon (1976–80), beating the record of three consecutive wins held by Fred Perry.

Borges /'bɔ:xes/, Jorge Luis (1899–1986), Argentinian poet, short-story writer, and essayist. His first three collections of poetry (1923–9) explore the themes of time and identity that are later treated in his fiction. His first volume of short stories, *A Universal History of Infamy* (1935, revised 1954), recounting the lives of real and fictitious criminals and exploring the relationships between fiction, truth, and identity, is regarded as a founding work of magic realism. His fiction also includes *The Aleph and Other Stories* (1949).

Borgia[1] /'bɔ:ʒə/, Cesare (c.1476–1507), Italian statesman. The illegitimate son of Cardinal Rodrigo Borgia (later Pope Alexander

VI) and brother of Lucrezia Borgia, he became a cardinal in 1493. He succeeded his brother Juan, possibly through murder, as captain-general of the papal army in 1499. Through two campaigns he became master of a large portion of central Italy, but after the death of his father (1502) his enemies rallied and he was defeated at Naples in 1504.

Borgia[2] /'bɔːʒə/, Lucrezia (1480–1519), Italian noblewoman. The illegitimate daughter of Cardinal Rodrigo Borgia (later Pope Alexander VI), she married three times, according to the political alliances useful to her father and to her brother, Cesare Borgia. Always associated with the scandals of her birth and marriages, after her third marriage in 1501 she established herself as a patron of the arts and became increasingly religious.

Boris Godunov see GODUNOV.

Bormann /'bɔːmən/, Martin (1900–c.1945), German Nazi politician. Bormann was appointed to Hitler's personal staff in 1928 and succeeded Hess as Party chancellor in 1941. Bormann was considered to be Hitler's closest collaborator, but remained the most obscure of the top Nazis and disappeared at the end of the Second World War. He was sentenced to death *in absentia* at the Nuremberg trials in 1945 and was formally pronounced dead in 1973 after identification of a skeleton exhumed in Berlin.

Born /bɔːn/, Max (1882–1970), German theoretical physicist and a founder of quantum mechanics. In 1921 he was appointed professor of theoretical physics at Göttingen, but in 1933 he had to flee the Nazi regime and settled in Britain. After retirement from Edinburgh University he returned to Göttingen to write mainly on the philosophy of physics and the social responsibility of scientists. He provided a link between wave mechanics and quantum theory by postulating a probabilistic interpretation of Schrödinger's wave equation, for which he was awarded the Nobel Prize for physics in 1954. He also wrote popular textbooks on optics and atomic physics.

Borodin /'bɒrədɪn/, Aleksandr (Porfirevich) (1833–87), Russian composer. He began to compose music at the age of 9, but trained as a chemist before undertaking formal musical studies in 1862. A member of the group known as 'The Five' or 'The Mighty Handful' (the others were Mily (Alekseevich) Balakirev (1837–1910), César (Antonovich) Cui (1835–1918), Mussorgsky, and Rimsky-Korsakov), he composed symphonies, string quartets, songs, and piano music, but is best known for the epic opera *Prince Igor* (completed after his death by Rimsky-Korsakov and Glazunov).

Borromini /,bɒrə'miːnɪ/, Francesco (1599–1667), Italian architect. He worked in Rome for most of his life, first as a mason at St Peter's and subsequently on the Palazzo Barberini (1620–31) as the chief assistant to his rival Bernini. Borromini's own buildings include the churches of San Carlo alle Quattro Fontane (1641) and San Ivo della Sapienza (1643–60). A leading figure of the Italian baroque, he used subtle architectural forms, innovative spatial composition, and much sculptural decoration. His work was central to the development of the baroque in Italy and an important influence on architecture in Austria and southern Germany.

Borrow /'bɒrəʊ/, George (Henry) (1803–81), English writer. His travels in England, Europe, Russia, and the Far East, sometimes in the company of gypsies, provided material for his picaresque narrative *Lavengro* (1851) and its sequel *The Romany Rye* (1857). In these books he combines fiction with a factual account of his travels. He also wrote *Wild Wales* (1862).

Bosanquet /'bəʊz(ə)n,ket/, Bernard James Tindall (1877–1936), English all-round cricketer. As a bowler for Middlesex and England he is credited with inventing the googly (an off-break bowled with apparent leg-break action), which in Australia was named the bosie after him.

Bosch /bɒʃ/, Hieronymus (c.1450–1516), Dutch painter. His highly detailed works are typically crowded with creatures of fantasy, half-human half-animal, and grotesque demons, and are interspersed with human figures in non-realistic settings that are often representations of sin and folly. His style is distinctly unlike that of mainstream Dutch painting of the period, and the elements of the grotesque and fantasy in his work prefigure the style of the surrealists.

Bose[1] /bəʊs/, Sir Jagdis Chandra (1858–1937), Indian physicist and plant physiologist. He investigated the properties of very short radio waves, wireless telegraphy, and radiation-induced fatigue in inorganic materials. His physiological work involved

comparative measurements of the responses of plants exposed to stress.

Bose[2] /bəʊs/, Satyendra Nath (1894–1974), Indian physicist. He contributed to statistical mechanics, quantum statistics, and unified field theory, and derived Planck's black-body radiation law without reference to classical electrodynamics. With Einstein, he described fundamental particles which later came to be known as bosons. Bose also worked on X-ray crystallography and the electromagnetic properties of the ionosphere.

Boswell /'bɒzwəl/, James (1740–95), Scottish author and biographer. After travels in Europe, where he met Jean-Jacques Rousseau and Voltaire, he practised law, although his ambitions were directed towards literature and politics. He first met Samuel Johnson in London (1763) and Boswell's *Journal of a Tour to the Hebrides* (1785) describes their travels together in 1773. He is now best known for his celebrated biography *The Life of Samuel Johnson* (1791), which gives a vivid and intimate portrait of Johnson and an invaluable panorama of the age and its personalities.

Botha[1] /'bəʊtə/, Louis (1862–1919), South African soldier and statesman, first Prime Minister of the Union of South Africa 1910–19. One of the most successful Boer leaders in the Boer War, Botha became Commander-in-Chief in 1900 and waged guerrilla warfare against the British forces. As Transvaal's first Prime Minister he played a leading role in the National Convention (1908–9), which was responsible for drafting the constitution for the Union of South Africa; he became its Prime Minister a year later. Botha supported the Allies in the First World War, gaining recognition for his annexation of German South West Africa in 1915.

Botha[2] /'bəʊtə/, P(ieter) W(illem) (born 1916), South African statesman, Prime Minister 1978–84, State President 1984–9. He joined the National Party in 1936 and was involved in party organization, particularly in Cape Province, until his election as Prime Minister in 1978. He abolished the office of Prime Minister in 1984, replacing it with that of State President. An authoritarian leader, he continued to enforce apartheid, but in response to pressure introduced limited reforms, including a new constitution (1984) giving certain classes of non-whites a degree of political representation. His resistance to more radical change ultimately led to his fall from power.

Botham /'bəʊθəm/, Ian (Terence) (born 1955), English all-round cricketer. He made his county début for Somerset in 1974 and his test début against Australia in 1977 and was admired for his bold attacking style of batting and skill as a medium-fast bowler. In 1978 he became the first player to score 100 runs and take eight wickets in a single test match; in 1982 he also achieved the record of 3,000 runs and 250 wickets in test matches overall. He retired from first-class cricket in 1993.

Bothwell /'bɒθwel/, 4th Earl of (title of James Hepburn) (c.1536–78), Scottish nobleman and third husband of Mary, Queen of Scots. Mary's chief adviser, he was implicated in the murder of Lord Darnley (1567). He was tried for the crime but acquitted, and he married Mary later the same year. The marriage was annulled in 1570 and Bothwell, facing opposition from other nobles, fled to Denmark, where he died in prison.

Botticelli /ˌbɒtɪ'tʃelɪ/, Sandro (born Alessandro di Mariano Filipepi) (1445–1510), Italian painter. A pupil of Filippo Lippi, he had his own studio in Florence and enjoyed the patronage of the Medici. His reputation rests largely on his mythological paintings such as *Primavera* (c.1478) and *The Birth of Venus* (c.1480). His work was neglected until the second half of the 19th century, when it was re-evaluated and championed by John Ruskin and Walter Pater; it had a significant influence on the Pre-Raphaelites, especially Edward Burne-Jones.

Boucher /'bu:ʃeɪ/, François (1703–70), French painter and decorative artist. One of the foremost artists of the rococo style in France, Boucher reflected the elegant social life of the period in his work, and enjoyed both royal and aristocratic patronage. His output ranged from large decorative paintings of mythological scenes to popular engravings, *fêtes galantes*, and tapestry design. Significant paintings include *The Rising of the Sun* (1753) and *Summer Pastoral* (1749).

Boucher de Perthes /ˌbu:ʃeɪ də 'peət/, Jacques (1788–1868), French archaeologist. He discovered some of the first evidence of man-made stone tools near the bones of extinct (Pleistocene) animals in the valley of the River Somme in northern France. In the decade following 1837 he argued that

these tools (and their makers) belonged to a remote pre-Celtic 'antediluvian' age, but it was not until the 1850s, when geologists supported his claims, that his findings were accepted.

Boudicca /bəʊˈdɪkə, ˈbuːdɪkə/ (also **Boadicea** /ˌbəʊdɪˈsiːə/) (died AD 62), a queen of the Britons, ruler of the Iceni tribe in eastern England. When Rome broke the treaty made with King Prasutagus (her husband) after his death in AD 60, Boudicca led her forces in revolt against the Romans and sacked Colchester, St Albans, and London before being completely defeated by the Roman governor Suetonius Paulinus. She committed suicide soon after her defeat, but her name became a symbol of native resistance to the Roman occupation.

Bougainville /ˈbuːgənˌvɪl/, Louis Antoine de (1729–1811), French explorer. After a distinguished early military career, Bougainville joined the French navy and led the first successful French circumnavigation of the globe 1766–9, visiting many of the islands of the South Pacific and compiling an invaluable scientific record of his findings. The island of Bougainville is named after him, as is the plant bougainvillea.

Boulez /ˈbuːlez/, Pierre (born 1925), French composer and conductor. His first publicly acclaimed work was *Le Marteau sans maître* (1954, revised 1957); other more recent compositions include *Répons* (1981–6). He was principal conductor with the New York Philharmonic Orchestra (1971–8). His works explore and develop serialism and aleatory music, making use of traditional, and, in particular, electronic instruments.

Boult /bəʊlt/, Sir Adrian (Cedric) (1889–1983), English conductor. Noted especially for his championship of English composers, he was music director of the BBC (1930–49) and trained and conducted the BBC Symphony Orchestra (1931–50). He was also principal conductor of the London Philharmonic Orchestra (1950–7) and continued to conduct until 1981.

Boulting /ˈbəʊltɪŋ/, John (1913–85) and Roy (born 1913), English film producers and directors. Twin brothers, they worked together, interchanging responsibilities as film producer and director. They made a number of memorable films, including *Brighton Rock* (1947) and *Seven Days to Noon* (1950). From the late 1950s their main output was comedy and farce, including *Private's Progress* (1956) and *I'm All Right Jack* (1959).

Boulton /ˈbəʊlt(ə)n/, Matthew (1728–1809), English engineer and manufacturer. With his partner James Watt he pioneered the manufacture of steam engines, which they began to produce in 1774. Under Boulton's influence the engines began to enjoy widespread commercial success.

Bourguiba /bʊəˈgiːbə/, Habib ibn Ali (born 1903), Tunisian nationalist and statesman, President 1957–87. Having negotiated the settlement that led to his country's autonomy, he was its first Prime Minister after independence in 1956 and was chosen as its first President when the country became a republic in 1957. A moderate socialist, he embarked on a reform programme intended to improve Tunisia's economy and to establish democratic government. He was deposed following continuing political unrest.

Bourke-White /bɜːkˈwaɪt/, Margaret (1906–71), American photojournalist. As a staff photographer with *Life* magazine in 1937 she took photographs of the effects of the Depression among the rural poor in the southern US. During the Second World War she was the first female photographer to be attached to the US armed forces, at the end of the war accompanying the Allied forces when they entered the concentration camps. Later assignments included the Korean War (1950–3) and work in India and South Africa.

Boutros-Ghali /ˌbuːtrɒsˈgɑːlɪ/, Boutros (born 1922), Egyptian diplomat and politician, Secretary-General of the United Nations (1992–6).

Bow /bəʊ/, Clara (1905–65), American actress. One of the most popular stars and sex symbols of the 1920s, she was known as the 'It Girl'; her best-known roles were in the silent films *It* (1927) and *The Wild Party* (1929).

Bowen /ˈbəʊɪn/, Elizabeth (Dorothea Cole) (1899–1973), British novelist and short-story writer, born in Ireland. Her writing is distinguished by delicate characterization and acute observation, especially of emotions and the relationships between her chiefly upper-middle-class characters. Among her best-known novels are *The Death of the Heart* (1938) and *The Heat of the Day* (1949).

Bowie[1] /'bəʊɪ/, David (born David Robert Jones) (born 1947), English rock singer, songwriter, and actor. His first hit single, 'Space Oddity' (1969), was followed by a number of other hit singles and albums such as *Hunky Dory* (1971), *Ziggy Stardust* (1972), and *Aladdin Sane* (1973); later albums include *Let's Dance* (1983). He became known for his theatrical performances and unconventional stage personae, involving the use of elaborate costumes and make-up. He also acted in a number of films, especially in the 1980s.

Bowie[2] /'bəʊɪ/, James ('Jim') (1799–1836), American frontiersman. In 1828 he moved from Georgia to Texas and became a leader among the American settlers who opposed Mexican rule. He shared command of the garrison that resisted the attack on the Alamo, where he died.

Bowles /bəʊlz/, Paul (Frederick) (born 1910), American writer and composer. In the 1930s he lived in Europe and North Africa, studying music and working as a music critic and composer; in 1941 he was funded to write the opera *The Wind Remains*. Bowles's first novel, *The Sheltering Sky* (1949), was published to widespread acclaim. His novels concern westerners in the Arab world and deal with isolation, loneliness, and the loss of tradition. Bowles became a resident of Tangier in 1952. His other books include *Let It Come Down* (1952) and *The Spider's House* (1966).

Boyce /bɔɪs/, William (1711–79), English composer and organist. His compositions include songs, overtures, church anthems and services, and eight symphonies; one of his most famous songs is 'Hearts of Oak'. He is noted also for his *Cathedral Music* (1760–73), an anthology of English sacred music of the 16th to 18th centuries.

Boycott /'bɔɪkɒt/, Geoffrey (born 1940), English cricketer. His career with Yorkshire began in 1962 and he first played for England two years later. Often controversial, he was an opening batsman of great concentration. He was captain of his county 1971–5, and had scored more than 150 centuries by the time he retired from first-class cricket in 1986.

Boyd /bɔɪd/, Arthur (Merric Bloomfield) (born 1920), Australian painter, potter, etcher, and ceramic artist. His first paintings were influenced by expressionism and surrealism; later works, such as *The Mockers* (1945), show the influence of Rembrandt,

Bosch, and Bruegel. He became famous for his large ceramic totem pole erected in Melbourne and for his series of twenty pictures inspired by his travels among the Aboriginals of central Australia.

Boyer /'bɔɪeɪ/, Charles (1897–1977), French-born American actor. Before going to Hollywood in the 1930s, he enjoyed a successful stage career in France. He played romantic leading roles in films such as *Mayerling* (1936); his other memorable films include *Gaslight* (1944) and *Barefoot in the Park* (1968).

Boyle /bɔɪl/, Robert (1627–91), Irish-born scientist. A founder member of the Royal Society, Boyle advanced a corpuscular view of matter which was a precursor of the modern theory of chemical elements and a cornerstone of his mechanical philosophy which became very influential. He is best known for his experiments with the air pump, assisted initially by Robert Hooke, which led to the law named after him: this states that the pressure of a given mass of gas is inversely proportional to its volume at constant temperature.

Boz /bɒz/ the pseudonym used by Charles Dickens in his *Pickwick Papers* and contributions to the *Morning Chronicle*.

Brabham /'bræbəm/, Sir John Arthur ('Jack') (born 1926), Australian motor-racing driver. After making his Grand Prix début in Australia, he moved to the UK, where he won his first Formula One world championship in 1959, repeating his success again in 1960 and in 1966.

Bradbury[1] /'brædbəri/, Malcolm (Stanley) (born 1932), English novelist, critic, and academic. His first three novels (including *The History Man*, 1975) are satires of university campus life; *Rates of Exchange* (1983) recounts the experiences of an academic on a lecture tour of an eastern European country. His critical works include studies of Evelyn Waugh (1962) and Saul Bellow (1982).

Bradbury[2] /'brædbəri/, Ray (Douglas) (born 1920), American writer of science fiction. He is best known for his collections of short stories, such as *The Martian Chronicles* (1950) and *The Golden Apples of the Sun* (1953). His novels include *Fahrenheit 451* (1951), a depiction of a future totalitarian state.

Bradley /'brædlɪ/, James (1693–1762), English astronomer. Bradley was appointed Savilian professor of astronomy at Oxford

in 1721 and Astronomer Royal in 1742. His attempt to measure the distance of stars from the earth by means of stellar parallax resulted in his discovery of the aberration of light, which he ascribed correctly to the combined effect of the velocity of light and the earth's annual orbital motion. He also observed the oscillation of the earth's axis, which he termed *nutation*. His star catalogue was published posthumously.

Bradman /'brædmən/, Sir Donald George ('Don') (born 1908), Australian cricketer. An outstanding batsman who dominated the sport in his day, he began his career in 1927 with New South Wales and played for his country from 1928 until his retirement in 1948. He scored 117 centuries in first-class cricket, twenty-nine of them in test matches; he holds the record for the highest Australian test score against England (334 at Leeds in 1930). His test-match batting average of 99.94 is well above that of any other cricketer of any era.

Bragg /bræg/, Sir William Henry (1862–1942), English physicist, a founder of solid-state physics. His early work was concerned with X-rays and ionizing radiation, but in 1912 he began to collaborate with his son, Sir (William) Lawrence Bragg (1890–1971), in developing the technique of X-ray diffraction for determining the atomic structure of crystals; for this they shared the 1915 Nobel Prize for physics. He later established a research school for crystallography at University College, London, and became director of the Royal Institution in 1923. His son was appointed head of the same establishment in 1953. Their diffraction studies of organic crystals were of fundamental importance in molecular biology.

Brahe /'brɑːhɪ, 'brɑːə/, Tycho (1546–1601), Danish astronomer. A nobleman, he built his own observatory, which he equipped with new instruments for determining planetary motions and star positions with great precision, making due allowance for atmospheric refraction. He was regarded as the leading observational astronomer of his day; his observations of comets, published in the book *De Nova Stella* (1577), demonstrated that they followed regular sun-centred paths, but despite this he adhered to a geocentric picture of the orbits of the planets. A 'new star' which he observed in 1572 is now known to have been a supernova. From the 1590s he corresponded with Kepler, who later assisted him in his work.

Brahms /brɑːmz/, Johannes (1833–97), German composer and pianist. He lived for most of the last thirty-five years of his life in Vienna and owed much of his early success to the friendship and patronage of Schumann, whom he first met in 1853. Firmly opposed to the 'New German' school of Liszt and the young Wagner, he eschewed programme music and opera and concentrated his energies on 'pure' and traditional forms. He wrote four symphonies, two piano concertos, a violin concerto (1879) and the Double Concerto (1887), chamber and piano music, choral works including the *German Requiem* (1857–68), and nearly 200 songs.

Braille /breɪl/, Louis (1809–52), French educationist. In 1819 he entered the Institute des Jeunes Aveugles in Paris, having been blind from the age of 3. By the age of 15 he had developed his own system of raised-point reading and writing, which was immediately accepted by his fellow students, although it was not officially adopted until two years after his death.

Brain /breɪn/, Dennis (1921–57), English French-horn player. His mastery of the instrument's entire range, together with his subtleties of phrasing and variety of tone, inspired many composers, including Benjamin Britten and Paul Hindemith, to write works for him. He was killed in a car accident.

Braine /breɪn/, John (Gerard) (1922–86), English novelist. His first novel, *Room at the Top* (1957), was an instant success, its opportunistic hero being hailed as a representative example of an 'angry young man'. Braine's later novels express less radical views and include *Finger of Fire* (1977) and *One and Last Love* (1981).

Bramah /'brɑːmə/, Joseph (1748–1814), English inventor. One of the most influential engineers of the Industrial Revolution, Bramah is best known for his hydraulic press, used for heavy forging; he also patented a successful lock. His other inventions included milling and planing machines and other machine tools, a beer-engine, a machine for numbering banknotes, and a water-closet.

Bramante /bræ'mæntɪ/, Donato (di Angelo) (1444–1514), Italian architect. Strongly influenced by the architecture of ancient

Rome, his work often typifies the Renaissance spirit striving for the ideal of classical perfection as exemplified by the Tempietto in the cloister of San Pietro in Montorio (1502). As architect to Pope Julius II he designed works at the Vatican as well as the new St. Peter's (begun in 1506); his floor-plan for the latter, in the form of a Greek cross crowned with a central dome, was the starting-point for subsequent work on the basilica.

Branagh /'brænə/, Kenneth (Charles) (born 1960), English actor, producer, and director. In 1984 he joined the Royal Shakespeare Company, where he attracted critical acclaim for roles such as Henry V; in 1989 he played the same part in the film of *Henry V*, which he also directed. He has starred in and directed several other films, such as *Peter's Friends* (1992) and *Mary Shelley's Frankenstein* (1994). He married Emma Thompson in 1989; the couple separated in 1995.

Brancusi /bræŋ'kuːzɪ/, Constantin (1876–1957), Romanian sculptor, who spent much of his working life in France. His sculpture represents an attempt to move away from a representational art and to capture the essence of forms by reducing them to their ultimate, almost abstract, simplicity. His subjects, often executed in marble and polished bronze, were frequently repeated and refined several times in his quest for simplicity, as can be seen in his series of twenty-eight 'bird' sculptures (c.1911–36). Brancusi's influence on modern sculpture is particularly apparent in the work of Jacob Epstein and Barbara Hepworth.

Brando /'brændəʊ/, Marlon (born 1924), American actor. An exponent of method acting, he first attracted critical acclaim in the stage production of *A Streetcar Named Desire* (1947); he starred in the film version four years later. Other notable early films included *The Wild One* (1953) and *On the Waterfront* (1954), for which he won an Oscar. His later career included memorable roles in *The Godfather* (1972) and *Apocalypse Now* (1979).

Brandt[1] /brænt/, Hermann Wilhelm ('Bill') (1904–83), German-born British photographer. He studied in Paris with Man Ray before moving to London in 1932. He portrayed English social conditions in several books and journals, and was commissioned by the government to record conditions in the London Blitz during the Second World War. He is best known for his almost abstract treatment of the nude, on which he published a number of books, including *Perspectives of Nudes* (1961).

Brandt[2] /brænt/, Willy (born Karl Herbert Frahm) (1913–92), German statesman, Chancellor of West Germany 1969–74. He was mayor of West Berlin 1957–66 and in 1964 he became chairman of the West German Social Democratic Party. He achieved international recognition for his policy of détente and the opening of relations with the former Communist countries of the Eastern bloc in the 1960s. A pragmatist, he encouraged the negotiation of joint economic projects and a policy of non-aggression. He also chaired the Brandt Commission on the state of the world economy, whose report was published in 1980. He was awarded the Nobel Peace Prize in 1971.

Branson /'bræns(ə)n/, Richard (born 1950), English businessman. He set up his own record company, Virgin Records, in 1969, and later influenced the opening up of air routes with his company Virgin Atlantic Airways, established in 1984. He is also famous for making the fastest transatlantic crossing by boat in 1986 and the first by hot-air balloon in 1987.

Braque /bræk/, Georges (1882–1963), French painter. A co-founder of the cubist movement with Picasso in 1908, Braque was influenced by Cézanne's geometrical simplification of forms. His collages, which introduced commercial lettering and fragmented objects into pictures to contrast the real with the 'illusory' painted image, were the first stage in the development of synthetic cubism. He continued to paint during the postwar period in an essentially cubist style, gradually introducing brighter colours into his work, and becoming noted for his treatment of still life.

Brassey /'bræsɪ/, Thomas (1805–70), English engineer and railway contractor. He built his first railway in England in the 1830s and went on to contract work for railways in Europe, India, South America, and Australia. He built more than 10,000 km (6,500 miles) of railways worldwide and during one period employed an estimated 75,000 workers.

Braun[1] /braʊn/, Eva (1910–45), German mistress of Adolf Hitler. Secretary to Hitler's staff photographer, Braun became Hitler's

mistress in the 1930s. Hitler and Braun are thought to have married during the fall of Berlin, shortly before committing suicide together in the air-raid shelter of his Berlin headquarters.

Braun[2] /braʊn/, Karl Ferdinand (1850–1918), German physicist. Braun contributed to wireless telegraphy and to the development of the cathode ray tube. He discovered the rectification properties of certain crystals and invented the coupled system of radio transmission. His demonstration that a beam of electrons could be deflected by a voltage difference between deflector plates in an evacuated tube, or by a magnetic field, led to the development of the Braun tube, the forerunner of the cathode ray tube. He shared the Nobel Prize for physics in 1909.

Braun[3] /braʊn/, Wernher Magnus Maximilian von (1912–77), German-born American rocket engineer. An enthusiast for space travel from boyhood, Braun began to develop rockets in the 1930s. His work received support from the German army, his team being responsible for the V-2 rockets used by Germany in the Second World War. After the war he moved to the US, leading the efforts which eventually resulted in successful launches of satellites, interplanetary missions, and the landing of men on the moon in 1969.

Breakspear /'breɪkspɪə(r)/, Nicholas, see ADRIAN IV.

Bream /briːm/, Julian (Alexander) (born 1933), English guitarist and lute-player. He made his London début in 1950 and benefited from an early involvement with Andrés Segovia. He formed the Julian Bream Consort for the performance of early consort music and has revived and edited much early music. Britten, Walton, and others composed works for him.

Brecht /brext/, (Eugen) Bertolt (Friedrich) (1898–1956), German dramatist, producer, and poet. His interest in combining music and drama led to a number of successful collaborations with Kurt Weill, the first of these being *The Threepenny Opera* (1928), an adaptation of John Gay's *The Beggar's Opera*. In his later drama, which was written in exile after Hitler's rise to power and includes *Mother Courage* (1941) and *The Caucasian Chalk Circle* (1948), Brecht experimented with his ideas of a Marxist 'epic theatre' with its 'alienation effect', whereby theatrical illusion is controlled

and the audience is confronted with the real political issues at stake.

Brel /brel/, Jacques (1929–78), Belgian singer and composer. Brel gained a reputation in Paris, where he first appeared in 1954, as an original songwriter whose satirical wit was balanced by his idealism and hope. He became a cult figure, and his cabaret-revue at the Village Gate in New York, which opened in 1968, ran for 1,847 performances. His last album, *Brel* (1977), sold more than 2 million copies.

Brendan, St /'brendən/ (c.486–c.575), Irish abbot. The legend of the 'Navigation of St Brendan' (c.1050), describing his voyage with a band of monks to a promised land (possibly Orkney or the Hebrides), was widely popular in the Middle Ages. Feast day, 16 May.

Bresson /'bresɒn/, Robert (born 1907), French film director. An influential though not a prolific director, he is noted for his austere intellectual style and meticulous attention to detail. His most notable films, most of which feature unknown actors, include *Diary of a Country Priest* (1951), *The Trial of Joan of Arc* (1962), and *The Devil, Probably* (1977).

Breton /'bret(ə)n, French brətɔ̃/, André (1896–1966), French poet, essayist, and critic. Influenced by the work of Sigmund Freud and the poet Paul Valéry, Breton was first involved with Dadaism, co-founding the movement's review *Littérature* in 1919. When Dada collapsed in the early 1920s, Breton launched the surrealist movement; its chief theorist, he first outlined the movement's philosophy in his manifesto of 1924. His creative writing is characterized by surrealist techniques such as 'automatic' writing and the startling juxtaposition of images, as in his famous poetic novel *Nadja* (1928).

Breughel see BRUEGEL.

Breuil /'brɜːɪ/, Henri (Édouard Prosper) (1877–1961), French archaeologist. He is noted for his work on palaeolithic cave-paintings, in particular those at Altamira in Spain, which he was able to authenticate. He also made detailed studies of examples in the Dordogne region of France and in southern Africa.

Brewster /'bruːstə(r)/, Sir David (1781–1868), Scottish physicist. He is best known for his work on the laws governing the polarization of light, and for his invention

of the kaleidoscope. Brewster also worked extensively on the optical classification of crystals and minerals, and on the use of spectroscopy for chemical analysis.

Brezhnev /'breʒnef/, Leonid (Ilich) (1906–82), Soviet statesman, General Secretary of the Communist Party of the USSR 1966–82 and President 1977–82. Born in Russia, he held offices within the Soviet Communist Party (CPSU) before and after the Second World War, rising to become Chairman of the Presidium in 1960. In 1964 he and Aleksei Kosygin forced Nikita Khrushchev to resign and Brezhnev eventually became General Secretary of the Party. His period in power was marked by intensified persecution of dissidents at home and by attempted détente followed by renewed cold war in 1968. He was largely responsible for the decision to invade Czechoslovakia in 1968.

Bride, St see BRIDGET, ST[1].

Bridge /brɪdʒ/, Frank (1879–1941), English composer, conductor, and violist. His compositions include chamber music, songs, and orchestral works, among them *The Sea* (1910–11). His later works, such as the string trio *Rhapsody* (1928) and *Oration* (for cello and orchestra, 1930), show stylistic elements akin to those of Schoenberg. Benjamin Britten was one of his pupils.

Bridges /'brɪdʒɪz/, Robert (Seymour) (1844–1930), English poet and literary critic. His long philosophical poem *The Testament of Beauty* (1929), written in the Victorian tradition, was instantly popular; he was Poet Laureate 1913–30. He also wrote two important critical essays, *Milton's Prosody* (1893) and *John Keats* (1895). He made an important contribution to literature in publishing his friend Gerard Manley Hopkins's poems in 1918.

Bridget, St[1] /'brɪdʒɪt/ (known as St Bridget of Ireland) (also **Bride** /'briːdə, braɪd/, **Brigid** /'brɪdʒɪd/) (6th century), Irish abbess. She was venerated in Ireland as a virgin saint and noted in miracle stories for her compassion; her cult soon spread over most of western Europe. It has been suggested that she may represent the Irish goddess Brig. Feast day, 1 February.

Bridget, St[2] /'brɪdʒɪt/ (known as St Bridget of Sweden) (also **Birgitta** /bɪə'ɡɪtə/) (c.1303–73), Swedish nun and visionary. She experienced her first vision of the Virgin Mary at the age of 7. After her husband's death she was inspired by further visions to devote herself to religion and she founded the Order of Bridgettines (c.1346) at Vadstena in Sweden. Feast day, 23 July.

Bridgman /'brɪdʒmən/, Percy Williams (1882–1961), American physicist. He worked mainly on the properties of liquids and solids under very high pressures, and designed an apparatus that achieved a fluid pressure of 30,000 atmospheres. His techniques were later used in making artificial diamonds and other minerals, and he became involved in the Manhattan Project, which was set up in 1942 to develop an atom bomb. Bridgman also published several major contributions to the philosophy of science, including *The Logic of Modern Physics* (1927). He was awarded the Nobel Prize for physics in 1946.

Briggs /brɪɡz/, Henry (1561–1630), English mathematician. He was renowned for his work on logarithms, in which he introduced the decimal base, made the thousands of calculations necessary for the tables, and popularized their use. Briggs also devised the usual method used for long division.

Bright /braɪt/, John (1811–89), English Liberal politician and reformer. A noted orator, Bright was the leader, along with Richard Cobden, of the campaign to repeal the Corn Laws. He was also a vociferous opponent of the Crimean War (1854) and was closely identified with the 1867 Reform Act.

Brigid, St see BRIDGET, ST[1].

Brindley /'brɪndlɪ/, James (1716–72), pioneer British canal builder. He began with the Bridgwater canal near Manchester, which included an aqueduct that was a wonder of the age. He designed some 600 km (375 miles) of waterway, connecting most of the major rivers of England. Brindley believed in building contour canals with the minimum of locks, embankments, cuttings, or tunnels, at the expense of greater lengths, and such canals have proved to be the longest to survive.

Brink /brɪŋk/, André (born 1935), South African novelist, short-story writer, and dramatist. Brink, who writes in Afrikaans and translates his work into English, gained international recognition with his seventh novel *Looking on Darkness* (1973), an open criticism of apartheid which became the first novel in Afrikaans to be banned by

the South African government. Subsequent novels include *A Dry White Season* (1979) and *A Chain of Voices* (1982).

Brisbane /'brɪzbən/, Sir Thomas Makdougall (1773–1860), Scottish soldier and astronomer. In 1790 he joined the army and served with distinction, becoming majorgeneral in 1813. From 1821 until 1825 he was appointed governor of New South Wales. He became an acclaimed astronomer, and honorary degrees were conferred upon him by Edinburgh, Oxford, and Cambridge universities. Brisbane, the capital of Queensland, was named after him.

Britten /'brɪt(ə)n/, (Edward) Benjamin, Lord Britten of Aldeburgh (1913–76), English composer, pianist, and conductor. Chiefly known for his operas, he made settings of the work of a varied range of writers, including George Crabbe (*Peter Grimes*, 1945), Shakespeare (*A Midsummer Night's Dream*, 1960), and Thomas Mann (*Death in Venice*, 1973). His many choral works include the *War Requiem* (1962), based on Wilfred Owen's war poems. In 1948, with the tenor Peter Pears, he founded the Aldeburgh Festival, which became one of Britain's major music festivals. He was made a life peer in 1976, the first composer to be so honoured.

Brodsky /'brɒdskɪ/, Joseph (born Iosif Aleksandrovich Brodsky) (1940–96), Russianborn American poet. He wrote in both Russian and English, and his poetry is preoccupied with themes of loss and exile. Brodsky is most famous for his collection *The End of a Beautiful Era* (1977). He was awarded the Nobel Prize for literature in 1987.

Bronowski /brə'nɒfskɪ/, Jacob (1908–74), Polish-born British scientist, writer, and broadcaster. Bronowski qualified in mathematics, worked from 1942 to 1963 with various UK government bodies, and spent the last ten years of his life in a research post in California. He was a great popularizer of science and the history of intellectual thought, writing such books as *The Common Sense of Science* (1951) and *The Western Intellectual Tradition* (1960) and presenting the 1970s television documentary series *The Ascent of Man*.

Brontë /'brɒnteɪ/, Charlotte (1816–55), Emily (1818–48), and Anne (1820–49), English novelists. Motherless and largely educated at home, the three sisters led a lonely childhood in the village of Haworth in a remote part of Yorkshire. Apart from work as governesses and, for Emily and Charlotte, a visit to Brussels, their experience of the outside world was unusually limited. All died young, Emily of tuberculosis after the publication (but before the success) of her masterpiece *Wuthering Heights* (1847). Anne also died of tuberculosis, after publishing *Agnes Grey* (1845) and *The Tenant of Wildfell Hall* (1847). Charlotte died during pregnancy, when she was already famous for her romantic tour-de-force *Jane Eyre* (1847) and for *Shirley* (1849) and *Villette* (1853). Their works were published under the pseudonyms Currer, Ellis, and Acton Bell. Of their early poetry, collected in *Poems by Currer, Ellis and Acton Bell* (1846), Emily's has been the most highly regarded.

Bronzino /brɒn'ziːnəʊ/, Agnolo (born Agnolo di Cosimo) (1503–72), Italian painter. A pupil of Pontormo, who adopted him, Bronzino spent most of his career in Florence as court painter to Cosimo de' Medici. Bronzino's mannerist work influenced the course of European court portraiture for a century. His paintings include the allegorical *Venus, Cupid, Folly, and Time* (c.1546).

Brook /brʊk/, Peter (Stephen Paul) (born 1925), English theatre director. Appointed co-director of the Royal Shakespeare Company in 1962, he earned critical acclaim with *King Lear* (1963) and *A Midsummer Night's Dream* (1970). In 1971 he founded the International Centre for Theatre Research in Paris, developing new acting techniques drawn from mime and other cultures.

Brooke /brʊk/, Rupert (Chawner) (1887–1915), English poet. His works include 'Tiara Tahiti' and other poems, but he is most famous for his wartime poetry *1914 and Other Poems* (1915) and for his lighter verse, such as 'The Old Vicarage, Grantchester'. He died of blood-poisoning while on naval service in the Mediterranean.

Brookner /'brʊknə(r)/, Anita (born 1928), English novelist and art historian. She has written studies of Jacques-Louis David (1981) and Watteau (1968). Her career as a novelist began in 1981 with *A Start in Life*; three years later she won the Booker Prize for *Hotel du Lac* (1984). Her novels are characterized by their pervading atmosphere of melancholy and their use of allusion.

Brooks[1] /brʊks/, Cleanth (1906–94), American teacher and critic. A leading proponent of the New Criticism movement, he

edited *The Southern Review*, a journal that advanced the movement's ideas, from 1935 to 1942. He taught at Yale University 1947–75 and wrote a number of critical works such as *Modern Poetry and Tradition* (1939) and *The Well-Wrought Urn* (1947). He was cultural attaché at the US Embassy in London between 1964 and 1966.

Brooks[2] /brʊks/, Mel (born Melvin Kaminsky) (born 1927), American film director and actor. After some years as a television comic and joke-writer Brooks began directing his own zany film scripts, often acting in his own productions. His début *The Producers* (1967) was followed by the spoofs *Blazing Saddles* (1974) and *Silent Movie* (1976), which established Brooks's characteristic style. Later films include *Spaceballs* (1987), a parody of George Lucas's *Star Wars* films.

Brouwer /'braʊə(r)/, Adriaen (c.1605–38), Flemish painter. He was based in Haarlem, where he probably studied with Frans Hals; he provides an important link between Dutch and Flemish genre painting. His most typical works represent peasant scenes in taverns; they are characterized by a delicate use of colour, which contrasts with the coarseness of the subject-matter.

Brown[1] /braʊn/, Sir Arthur Whitten (1886–1948), Scottish aviator. He made the first transatlantic flight in 1919 with Sir John William Alcock.

Brown[2] /braʊn/, Ford Madox (1821–93), English painter. He became a friend of and influence on the Pre-Raphaelites, and a number of his paintings, including *Chaucer at the Court of Edward III* (1851) and *The Last of England* (1855), were inspired by the ideals of the Brotherhood. In 1861 he became a founder member of William Morris's company, for which he designed stained glass and furniture. In later life he designed a cycle of twelve frescos in Manchester Town Hall (1878–93).

Brown[3] /braʊn/, James (born 1928), American soul and funk singer and songwriter. Influenced by gospel and early rhythm and blues, he became known as 'Soul Brother Number One' in the 1960s, playing a leading role in the development of funk and having a significant influence on many other areas of popular music. His many hits include 'Papa's Got a Brand New Bag' (1965) and 'Sex Machine' (1970).

Brown[4] /braʊn/, John (1800–59), American abolitionist. The leader of an unsuccessful uprising in Virginia in 1859, he was captured and executed after raiding the government arsenal at Harpers Ferry, intending to arm runaway black slaves and start a revolt. Although the revolt never materialized, Brown became a hero of the American abolitionists in the subsequent American Civil War. He is commemorated in the popular marching-song 'John Brown's Body'.

Brown[5] /braʊn/, Lancelot (known as Capability Brown) (1716–83), English landscape gardener. He evolved an English style of landscape parks, made to look natural by serpentine waters, clumps of trees, and other artifices. Famous examples of his work are to be found at Blenheim Palace in Oxfordshire, Chatsworth House in Derbyshire, and Kew Gardens. He earned his nickname by telling his patrons that their estates had 'great capabilities'.

Browne /braʊn/, Sir Thomas (1605–82), English author and physician. He achieved prominence with his *Religio Medici* (1642), a confession of Christian faith, drawing together a collection of imaginative and erudite opinions on a vast number of subjects more or less connected with religion. *Hydriotaphia; Urn Burial* (1658), a study of burial customs, is a notable example of Browne's elaborately ornate language.

Browning[1] /'braʊnɪŋ/, Elizabeth Barrett (1806–61), English poet. After first becoming known with *The Seraphim* (1838), she established her reputation with *Poems* (1844), which was so well received that she was seriously considered as a possible successor to William Wordsworth as Poet Laureate. In 1845 Robert Browning began his passionate correspondence with her. The pair met and were secretly married the following year, eloping to Italy to escape the wrath of Barrett's domineering father. She is best known for the love poems *Sonnets from the Portuguese* (1850), the experimental verse novel *Aurora Leigh* (1857), and the posthumous *Last Poems* (1862).

Browning[2] /'braʊnɪŋ/, Robert (1812–89), English poet. In 1842 he established his name as a poet with the publication of *Dramatic Lyrics*, containing such poems as 'The Pied Piper of Hamelin' and 'My Last Duchess'. *Dramatic Romances and Lyrics* (1845), which included 'Home Thoughts from Abroad', built on this success. In 1846

he eloped to Italy with Elizabeth Barrett, and a highly creative period followed: *Men and Women* (1855) and *The Ring and the Book* (1868–9), a series of dramatic monologues, were among the important works completed during this time.

Brubeck /'bruːbek/, David Warren ('Dave') (born 1920), American jazz pianist, composer, and band-leader. Brubeck studied composition under Arnold Schoenberg and Darius Milhaud before forming the Dave Brubeck Quartet in 1951. He gained a reputation as an experimental musician and won international recognition with the album *Time Out*, which included the immensely popular 'Take Five' (1959). Brubeck continued to record with small groups throughout the 1980s and 1990s.

Bruce[1] /bruːs/, Robert the, see ROBERT.

Bruce[2] /bruːs/, James ('the Abyssinian') (1730–94), Scottish explorer. After serving as consul-general at Algiers 1763–5, Bruce set off from Cairo in 1768 on an expedition to Ethiopia, becoming the first European to discover the source of the Blue Nile in 1770. His *Travels to Discover the Sources of the Nile* (1790), containing an account of his expedition, was dismissed by his contemporaries as fabrication.

Bruce[3] /bruːs/, Lenny (born Leonard Alfred Schneider) (1925–66), American comedian. Bruce gained notoriety as a nightclub comedian whose satire and 'sick' humour flouted the bounds of respectability. Bruce was imprisoned for obscenity in 1961 and in 1963 was refused entry to Britain and banned in Australia. He was convicted of illegal possession of drugs the same year and in 1966 was found dead in Hollywood following an accidental drugs overdose.

Bruckner /'brʊknə(r)/, Anton (1824–96), Austrian composer and organist. After dividing his time for several years between teaching and organ-playing, he turned to composition, writing ten symphonies between 1863 and his death, together with four masses and a *Te Deum* (1884). Bruckner was often persuaded by well-meaning friends to alter his scores; for the most part, though, editors have been able to trace his original intentions.

Bruegel /'brɔɪg(ə)l/ (also **Breughel**, **Brueghel**), a family of Flemish artists. Pieter (*c.*1525–69, known as Pieter Bruegel the Elder) joined the Antwerp guild in 1551, but produced the bulk of his famous work in Brussels, where he moved in 1563. He worked successfully in a variety of genres, including landscapes, religious allegories, and satires of peasant life. His major works include *The Procession to Calvary* (1564), *The Blind Leading the Blind* (1568), and *The Peasant Dance* (1568). Both of his sons also worked as painters, chiefly in Antwerp. Pieter ('Hell') Bruegel the Younger (1564–1638) is known primarily as a very able copyist of his father's work; he is also noted for his paintings of devils (hence his diabolic nickname). Jan ('Velvet') Bruegel (1568–1623) was a celebrated painter of flower, landscape, and mythological pictures.

Brummell /'brʌm(ə)l/, George Bryan (known as Beau Brummell) (1778–1840), English dandy. He was the arbiter of British fashion for the first decade and a half of the 19th century, owing his social position to his close friendship with the Prince of Wales (later George IV). Brummell quarrelled with his patron and fled to France to avoid his creditors in 1816, eventually dying penniless in a mental asylum in Caen.

Brundtland /'brʌntlænd/, Gro Harlem (born 1939), Norwegian Labour stateswoman. After serving as Environment Minister in the Labour government, in February 1981 she became Norway's first woman Prime Minister, but only held office until October of that year. During her second premiership (1986–9) she chaired the World Commission on Environment and Development (known as the Brundtland Commission), which produced the report *Our Common Future* in 1987. In 1992, during her third term of office (1990–6), Norway's application to join the EU was accepted by Europe but voted down in a referendum (1994).

Brunel[1] /brʊ'nel/, Isambard Kingdom (1806–59), English engineer. Son of Sir Marc Isambard Brunel, he was equally versatile, designing the famous Clifton suspension bridge in Bristol (1829–30), then in 1833 becoming chief engineer of the Great Western Railway, for which he surveyed more than a thousand miles of line (originally laid with broad gauge track, which he favoured) and designed many engineering works. He turned to steamship construction with the *Great Western* (1838), the first successful transatlantic steamship. His *Great Eastern* (1858) remained the world's largest ship until 1899. A little-known but

remarkable achievement was Brunel's design in 1855 for a prefabricated hospital for the Crimean War.

Brunel[2] /bruˈnel/, Sir Marc Isambard (1769–1849), French-born British engineer. He came to England in 1799 and persuaded the government to adopt his designs for mass-production machinery at Portsmouth dockyard, an early example of automation. He also designed other machines for woodworking, boot-making, knitting, and printing. A versatile civil engineer, he built bridges, landing stages, and the first tunnelling shield, which he used to construct the first tunnel under the Thames (1825–43).

Brunelleschi /ˌbruːnəˈleskɪ/, Filippo (born Filippo di Ser Brunellesco) (1377–1446), Italian architect. The most famous Florentine architect of the 15th century, he is especially noted for the dome of Florence cathedral (1420–61), which he raised, after the fashion of ancient Roman construction, without the use of temporary supports. It is the largest dome in the world in diameter and inspired Michelangelo's design for St Peter's in Rome. Brunelleschi revived Roman architectural forms and is also often credited with the Renaissance 'discovery' of perspective.

Bruno[1] /ˈbruːnəʊ/, Frank(lin Ray) (born 1961), English boxer. He turned professional in 1982, and won thirty-seven out of forty fights over the next thirteen years. In 1995 Bruno became the WBC world heavyweight champion; by this time he was a popular media personality in Britain. The following year he was defeated by Mike Tyson, whom he had first fought in 1989, and announced his retirement.

Bruno[2] /ˈbruːnəʊ/, Giordano (1548–1600), Italian philosopher. After a period in the Dominican order, he became a follower of the magical tradition of Hermes Trismegistus. He was a supporter of the heliocentric Copernican view of the solar system, envisaging an infinite universe of numerous worlds moving in space. He was tried by the Inquisition for heresy and later burned at the stake.

Bruno, St /ˈbruːnəʊ/ (c.1032–1101), German-born French churchman. After withdrawing to the mountains of Chartreuse in 1084, he founded the Carthusian order at La Grande Chartreuse in SE France in the same year. Feast day, 6 October.

Bruton /ˈbruːt(ə)n/, John (Gerard) (born 1947), Irish Fine Gael statesman, Taoiseach (Prime Minister) since 1994.

Brutus /ˈbruːtəs/, Marcus Junius (85–42 BC), Roman senator. With Cassius he was a leader of the conspirators who assassinated Julius Caesar in the name of the Republic in 44. He and Cassius were defeated by Caesar's supporters Antony and Octavian at the battle of Philippi in 42, after which he committed suicide.

Buber /ˈbuːbə(r)/, Martin (1878–1965), Israeli religious philosopher, born in Austria. A supporter of Hasidism and a committed Zionist, he settled in Palestine in 1938 after fleeing the Nazis. His most famous work I and Thou (1923) sums up much of his religious philosophy, comparing mutual and reciprocal relationships with objective or utilitarian ones. His other important publications include Between Man and Man (1946) and Eclipse of God (1952).

Buchan[1] /ˈbʌkən/, Alexander (1829–1907), Scottish meteorologist. He proposed that at certain times of the year the temperature regularly deviated from the normal, though it is now thought that such cold spells are probably distributed at random. As well as writing a standard textbook on meteorology, he produced maps and tables of atmospheric circulation, and of ocean currents and temperatures, based largely on information gathered on the voyage of HMS Challenger in 1872–6.

Buchan[2] /ˈbʌkən/, John, 1st Baron Tweedsmuir (1875–1940), Scottish novelist. Although he wrote several non-fictional works, he is remembered for his adventure stories, which often feature recurring heroes such as Richard Hannay. These include The Thirty-Nine Steps (1915), Greenmantle (1916), and The Three Hostages (1924). Buchan was also active in public life, serving as MP for the Scottish Universities (1927–35) and as Governor-General of Canada (1935–40).

Buchanan /bjuːˈkænən/, James (1791–1868), American Democratic statesman, 15th President of the US 1857–61. He consistently leaned towards the pro-slavery side in the developing dispute over slavery. Towards the end of his term the issue grew more fraught and he retired from politics in 1861.

Buchner /ˈbʌknə(r), ˈbuːxnə(r)/, Eduard (1860–1917), German organic chemist. He

discovered that intact yeast cells were not necessary for alcoholic fermentation, which could be carried out by an active extract that he called *zymase*. Buchner investigated the chain of reactions involved in fermentation, identifying various other enzymes. He won the Nobel Prize for chemistry in 1907.

Buck /bʌk/, Pearl S(ydenstricker) (1892–1973), American writer. Her earliest novels, including the Pulitzer Prize-winning *The Good Earth* (1931), were inspired by her experiences in China, where she was brought up and worked as a missionary and teacher. She continued to write on her return to America in 1935, producing novels such as *Dragon Seed* (1942) as well as several short stories, children's books, and essays. She won the Nobel Prize for literature in 1938.

Buckland /'bʌklənd/, William (1784–1856), English geologist. He taught at Oxford, later becoming dean of Westminster. He helped to redefine geology, linking type of deposit with local dynamic conditions and using the associated fossils to establish former habitats and climate. He was the first to describe and name a dinosaur (*Megalosaurus*), in 1824. Buckland supported the idea of a past catastrophic event, first interpreting this as being the biblical flood and later moving to the idea of an ice age.

Buddha /'bʊdə/ a title given to successive teachers (past and future) of Buddhism, although it usually denotes the founder of Buddhism, Siddhartha Gautama (c.563 BC–c.480 BC). Although born an Indian prince (in what is now Nepal), he renounced his kingdom, wife, and child to become an ascetic, taking religious instruction until he attained enlightenment (nirvana) through meditation beneath a bo tree in the village of Bodhgaya. He then taught all who wanted to learn, regardless of sex, class, or caste, until his death. 'Buddha' means 'enlightened' in Sanskrit.

Budge /bʌdʒ/, John Donald ('Don') (born 1915), American tennis player. He was the first to win the four major singles championships — Australian, French, British, and US — in one year (1938). In both 1937 and 1938 he won the Wimbledon singles, men's doubles, and mixed doubles.

Buffalo Bill (born William Frederick Cody) (1846–1917), American showman. A former US army scout and dispatch-bearer, Cody gained his nickname for killing 4,280 buffalo in eight months to feed the Union Pacific Railroad workers. He subsequently devoted his life to show business, particularly his Wild West Show, which travelled all over Europe and the US. These dramatics more than any real frontier exploits made Cody a national figure; his death in 1917 was widely seen as symbolizing the end of an era.

Buffon /'buːfɒn/, Georges-Louis Leclerc, Comte de (1707–88), French naturalist. He was one of the founders of palaeontology and suggested that the earth was much older than was generally accepted. Buffon saw all life as the physical property of matter, thereby stressing the unity of all living species and minimizing the apparent differences between animals and plants. He produced a remarkable compilation of the animal kingdom, the *Histoire Naturelle*, which was begun in 1749 and had reached thirty-six volumes by the time of his death.

Bukharin /bʊ'kɑːrɪn/, Nikolai (Ivanovich) (1888–1938), Russian revolutionary activist and theorist. Editor of *Pravda* (1918–29), a member of the Politburo (1924–9), and chairman of Comintern from 1926, he initially supported Stalin but was later denounced by him and expelled from the Politburo. After working as editor of the official government newspaper *Izvestia* (1934–7), he became one of the victims of Stalin's purges and was arrested, convicted, and shot. Bukharin was a model for Rubashov, hero of Arthur Koestler's novel *Darkness at Noon* (1940).

Bulganin /bʊl'gɑːnɪn/, Nikolai (Aleksandrovich) (1895–1975), Soviet statesman, Chairman of the Council of Ministers (Premier) 1955–8. Born in Russia, he succeeded Stalin as Minister of Defence in 1946, and was appointed Vice-Premier in the government of Georgi Malenkov in 1953. Following Malenkov's resignation in 1955, Bulganin became Premier, sharing power with Nikita Khrushchev, who replaced him.

Bultmann /'bʊltmən/, Rudolf (Karl) (1884–1976), German Lutheran theologian. He held that the Gospels were a patchwork of traditional elements and insisted on the need for demythologizing the whole Gospel story. He emphasized what he saw as its 'existential' rather than its historical significance, asserting that faith in Christ rather than belief in him was the key. His important works include *The History of the*

Synoptic Tradition (1921), *Jesus Christ and Mythology* (1960), and *Existence and Faith* (1964).

Bulwer-Lytton /ˌbʊlwə'lɪt(ə)n/ see LYTTON.

Bunin /'buːnɪn/, Ivan (Alekseevich) (1870–1953), Russian poet and prose-writer. An opponent of modernism, he made peasant life and love the most prominent themes in his prose works, which include the novel *The Village* (1910), the short-story collection *The Gentleman from San Francisco* (1914), and an autobiography, *The Well of Days* (1910). He opposed the October Revolution and left Russia in 1918, eventually reaching France and remaining in permanent exile. In 1933 he became the first Russian to be awarded the Nobel Prize for literature.

Bunsen /'bʌns(ə)n, German 'bʊnz(ə)n/, Robert Wilhelm Eberhard (1811–99), German chemist. Bunsen was a pioneer of chemical spectroscopy and photochemistry. During his early research he lost the use of his right eye in an explosion. With G. Kirchhoff he developed spectroscopy, using it to detect new elements (caesium and rubidium) and to determine the composition of substances and of the sun and stars. Bunsen designed numerous items of chemical apparatus, besides the burner (developed in 1855) for which he is best known.

Bunting /'bʌntɪŋ/, Basil (1900–85), English poet and journalist. In 1923 he went to Paris, where he started a career as a journalist. He met, and was much influenced by, leading modernists including Ezra Pound and T. S. Eliot. Bunting published his early work abroad and returned to Northumberland in 1952, remaining largely unacknowledged as a poet until he gained recognition with *Briggflatts* (1966).

Buñuel /buː'nwel/, Luis (1900–83), Spanish film director. Profoundly influenced by surrealism, he wrote and directed his first film *Un Chien andalou* (1928) jointly with Salvador Dali. Remarkable for their shocking and terrifying images, his films often attacked the Establishment (in particular the Church); after the banning of his early work, he left Spain and worked on dubbing American films for fifteen years before re-establishing his reputation in Mexico with *Los Olvidados* (1950). Among the notable films that followed were *Belle de jour* (1967) and *The Discreet Charm of the Bourgeoisie* (1972).

Bunyan /'bʌnjən/, John (1628–88), English writer. He served with the Parliamentary army during the Civil War, an experience which possibly inspired his allegory *The Holy War* (1682). In 1653 he joined the Nonconformist Church at Bedford, where he preached and clashed with the Quakers. He was put under arrest in 1660 for unlicensed preaching and spent most of the next twelve years in prison, where he wrote his spiritual autobiography *Grace Abounding* (1666) and a number of other works; during a later period of imprisonment, he began his major work *The Pilgrim's Progress* (1678–84), an allegory recounting the spiritual journey of its hero Pilgrim.

Buonaparte see BONAPARTE.

Buonarroti /ˌbwɒnə'rɒti/, Michelangelo, see MICHELANGELO.

Burbage /'bɜːbɪdʒ/, Richard (c.1567–1619), English actor. He was the creator of most of Shakespeare's great tragic roles — Hamlet, Othello, Lear, and Richard III. He was also associated with the building of the Globe Theatre.

Burgess[1] /'bɜːdʒɪs/, Anthony (pseudonym of John Anthony Burgess Wilson) (1917–93), English novelist and critic. His experiences as an education officer in Malaya and Borneo (1954–60) inspired his first novels *The Malayan Trilogy* (1956–9). One of his best-known novels is *A Clockwork Orange* (1962), a disturbing, futuristic vision of juvenile delinquency, violence, and high technology. His many other works include the best-selling novel *Earthly Powers* (1980).

Burgess[2] /'bɜːdʒɪs/, Guy (Francis de Moncy) (1911–63), British Foreign Office official and spy. Acting as a Soviet agent from the 1930s, he worked for MI5 while ostensibly employed by the BBC. After the war, he served the Foreign Office and became Second Secretary at the British Embassy in Washington, DC, under Kim Philby. Charged with espionage in 1951, he fled to the USSR with Donald Maclean.

Burghley /'bɜːlɪ/, William Cecil, 1st Baron (1520–98), English statesman. Secretary of State to Queen Elizabeth I 1558–72 and Lord High Treasurer 1572–98, Burghley was the queen's most trusted councillor and minister and the driving force behind many of her government's policies.

Burgoyne /bɜː'gɔɪn/, John ('Gentleman Johnny') (1722–92), English general and dramatist. He is largely remembered for

surrendering to the Americans at Saratoga (1777) in the War of American Independence. His plays include the comedies *The Maid of the Oaks* (1774) and *The Heiress* (1786).

Burke[1] /bɜːk/, Edmund (1729–97), British man of letters and Whig politician. Burke was a prolific writer on the issues of political emancipation and moderation, supporting proposals for relaxing the laws against Roman Catholics in Britain and protesting against the harsh handling of the American colonies. He was a fierce opponent of the radical excesses of the French Revolution, calling on European leaders to resist the new regime in the influential *Reflections on the Revolution in France* (1790).

Burke[2] /bɜːk/, John (1787–1848), Irish genealogical and heraldic writer. He compiled *Burke's Peerage* (1826), the first reference guide of peers and baronets in alphabetical order.

Burke[3] /bɜːk/, Robert O'Hara (1820–61), Irish explorer. He emigrated to Australia in 1853 and led a successful expedition from south to north across Australia in the company of William Wills and two other men — the first white men to make this journey. On the return journey, however, Burke, Wills, and a third companion died of starvation.

Burke[4] /bɜːk/, William (1792–1829), Irish murderer. A notorious body-snatcher operating in Edinburgh, he was hanged for a series of fifteen or more murders carried out for profit. His accomplice, fellow-Irishman William Hare (*fl.*1820s), gave King's evidence and was never heard of again.

Burne-Jones /bɜːnˈdʒəʊnz/, Sir Edward (Coley) (1833–98), English painter and designer. A founder member of William Morris's business venture, he created many tapestry and stained-glass window designs for Morris & Company. He was preoccupied by medieval and literary themes, and invented an escapist, dreamlike world in his paintings; his work is regarded, with that of Morris, as typical of the later Pre-Raphaelite style. Major works include the tapestry *The Adoration of the Magi* in Exeter College Chapel, Oxford, and the paintings *The Golden Stairs* (1880) and *The Mirror of Venus* (1898–9).

Burnett /bɜːˈnet/, Frances (Eliza) Hodgson (1849–1924), British-born American novel-

ist. She is remembered chiefly for her novels for children, including *Little Lord Fauntleroy* (1886), *The Little Princess* (1905), and *The Secret Garden* (1911).

Burney /ˈbɜːnɪ/, Frances ('Fanny') (1752–1840), English novelist. Her first novel, the satire *Evelina* (1778), brought her fame and the patronage of Dr Johnson. Her second novel, *Cecilia* (1782), was also a success. However, her father exhorted her to accept a post serving Queen Charlotte at court in 1786. Unhappy, Burney sought permission to retire in 1791. Two years later she married General Alexandre d'Arblay (1753–1818), with whom she was interned in France by Napoleon, finally returning in 1812. Her *Letters and Diaries* were published in 1846.

Burns[1] /bɜːnz/, George (born Nathan Birnbaum) (1896–1996), American comedian. In 1922 he paired up in vaudeville with the comedienne Gracie Allen (1902–64), whom he married in 1926. They had shows on radio until the 1950s, when they moved to television, Burns playing the straight man to Allen's childlike daftness. He retired on her death, but reappeared in films from 1975, winning an Oscar for *The Sunshine Boys* that year.

Burns[2] /bɜːnz/, Robert (1759–96), Scottish poet. He developed an inclination for literature at an early age; his *Poems, Chiefly in the Scottish Dialect* (1786) was an immediate success. The satire 'The Jolly Beggars' (1786) and the narrative poem 'Tam o' Shanter' (1791) are among his most important poems. Approached in 1786 to collect old Scottish songs for *The Scots Musical Museum* (1787–1803), he responded with over 200 songs, including the famous lyrics 'Auld Lang Syne' and 'Ye Banks and Braes'. Burns was a firm patriot, and his popularity with the Scots is reaffirmed annually in the Burns Night celebrations held worldwide on his birthday, 25 January.

Burr /bɜː(r)/, Aaron (1756–1836), American Democratic Republican statesman. After losing the presidential election to Jefferson in 1800, Burr was elected Vice-President. He was defeated in the contest for the governorship of New York in 1804, largely through the campaign of his rival Alexander Hamilton. Later the same year Burr killed Hamilton in a duel. He subsequently plotted to invade Mexico in order to form an independent administration there; it was also alleged that he intended to annex

Mexico to the western US and establish a separate empire. Burr was tried for treason and acquitted in 1807.

Burra /'bʌrə/, Edward (1905–76), English painter. He was fascinated by low-life and seedy subjects, as paintings such as *Harlem* (1934) attest. Usually he worked in water-colour, but on a large scale and using layers of pigment. In the mid-1930s he became fascinated with the bizarre and fantastic (*Dancing Skeletons*, 1934), and in the 1950s and 1960s he turned to land-scape.

Burroughs[1] /'bʌrəʊz/, Edgar Rice (1875–1950), American novelist and writer of sci-ence fiction. He is remembered principally for his adventure stories about Tarzan, who first featured in *Tarzan of the Apes* (1914).

Burroughs[2] /'bʌrəʊz/, William S(eward) (1914–97), American novelist. In the 1940s he became addicted to heroin and also became associated with figures who were later prominent members of the beat gen-eration. His best-known writing deals in a unique, surreal style with life as a drug ad-dict (*Junkie*, 1953; *The Naked Lunch*, 1959).

Burt /bɜːt/, Cyril Lodowic (1883–1971), Eng-lish psychologist. Burt spent most of his working life in London, including eighteen years as professor of psychology at Uni-versity College. He worked chiefly on the study of intelligence and attempted to de-termine whether it is inherited. Burt claimed to show a high degree of correl-ation between pairs of identical twins, but subsequent accusations that some of his data was fabricated have caused his work to remain controversial.

Burton[1] /'bɜːt(ə)n/, Richard (born Richard Jenkins) (1925–84), Welsh actor. He played a number of Shakespearian roles and per-formed in the radio adaptation of Dylan Thomas's *Under Milk Wood* (1954), before becoming well known in films such as *The Spy Who Came in from the Cold* (1966) and *Who's Afraid of Virginia Woolf* (1966). He often co-starred with Elizabeth Taylor (to whom he was twice married).

Burton[2] /'bɜːt(ə)n/, Sir Richard (Francis) (1821–90), English explorer, anthropolo-gist, and translator. He joined the Indian Army in 1842; subsequent travels took him to Mecca disguised as a Pathan, and to Brazil, Damascus, and Trieste as consul. With John Hanning Speke, he became the

first European to discover Lake Tanganyika (1858). As a translator, he is best known for his unexpurgated versions of the *Kama Sutra* (1883), the *Arabian Nights* (1885–8), *The Perfumed Garden* (1886), and other works of Arabian erotica. His interest in sexual be-haviour and deviance, as well as his de-tailed ethnographical notes, led him to risk prosecution many times under the Obscene Publications Act of 1857.

Busby /'bʌzbɪ/, Sir Matt(hew) (1909–94), Scottish-born footballer and football man-ager. Busby became manager of Manches-ter United in 1945, leading them on to win the 1948 FA Cup and two League Cham-pionships. Busby was fashioning a new, young team which seemed destined for European success when an air crash at Munich airport in 1958 killed most of the side and left Busby himself severely in-jured. He reconstructed the team and won two more League Championships and in 1968 the European Cup.

Bush /bʊʃ/, George (Herbert Walter) (born 1924), American Republican statesman, 41st President of the US 1989–93. He was director of the CIA from 1976 to 1977, and President Reagan's Vice-President from 1981 to 1988. In 1989 Bush was elected President. While in office he negotiated further arms reductions with the Soviet Union and organized international action to liberate Kuwait following the Iraqi inva-sion in 1990.

Busoni /bu:'səʊnɪ/, Ferruccio (Benvenuto) (1866–1924), Italian composer, conductor, and pianist. A child prodigy, Busoni began performing at the age of 9 and went on to become an international concert pianist. As a composer he is best known for his works for piano, and for his unfinished opera *Doktor Faust* (1925). His later music anticipated some of the harmonic and rhythmic developments of Webern, Bartók, and Messiaen.

Buss /bʌs/, Frances Mary (1827–94), English educationist. At the age of 18 she was in charge of her own school, which in 1850 became known as the North London Colle-giate School for Ladies. She was to remain headmistress there until 1894 and was the first to use the title headmistress. In 1886 she co-founded a training college for women teachers in Cambridge. With her

friend Dorothea Beale, she also campaigned for higher education for women.

Bute /bjuːt/, 3rd Earl of (title of John Stuart) (1713–92), Scottish courtier and Tory statesman, Prime Minister 1762–3. His influence with George III ensured his appointment as Premier, but he was widely disliked and soon fell out of favour with the king.

Buthelezi /ˌbuːtəˈleɪzɪ/, Chief Mangosuthu (Gatsha) (born 1928), South African politician. In 1953 he was appointed assistant to the Zulu king Cyprian, a position he held until 1968. He was elected leader of Zululand (later KwaZulu) in 1970 and was responsible for the revival of the Inkatha movement, of which he became leader in 1975. He was appointed Minister of Home Affairs in Nelson Mandela's Cabinet (1994).

Butler[1] /ˈbʌtlə(r)/, Reginald Cotterell ('Reg') (1913–81), English sculptor. As a conscientious objector, he worked as a blacksmith during the Second World War. In 1947 he took up sculpture as an assistant to Henry Moore, working mainly in forged or cast metal. Butler suddenly became prominent in 1953, when he won an international competition for a monument (never built) to the Unknown Political Prisoner.

Butler[2] /ˈbʌtlə(r)/, Samuel ('Hudibras') (1612–80), English poet. His reputation rests on his three-part satirical poem *Hudibras* (1663–78), a mock romance parodying the Puritan sects and the Civil War, which rapidly became the most popular poem in England at the time. It was highly approved by Charles II, who granted the author a pension, although Butler is said to have died in penury.

Butler[3] /ˈbʌtlə(r)/, Samuel (1835–1902), English novelist. Emigrating in 1859, he became a successful sheep farmer in New Zealand, before returning to England in 1864. Turning to literature, he published his satirical anti-utopian novel *Erewhon* (1872) and its sequel *Erewhon Revisited* (1901), both of which challenged aspects of Darwinism. His semi-autobiographical *The Way of All Flesh* (1903) parodies child–parent relations and the effects of inherited family traits.

Butterfield /ˈbʌtəˌfiːld/, William (1814–1900), English architect. Butterfield was one of the most individual exponents of the Gothic revival. Associated with the Oxford Movement, he was a deeply reli-

gious man who mainly designed churches. His mature style uses hard, angular forms and patterned, coloured brickwork, thereby breaking with the historicist approach of contemporaries such as Pugin. Among his designs are All Saints', Margaret Street, London (1850–9), and Keble College, Oxford (1867–83).

Buxtehude /ˈbʊkstəˌhuːdə/, Dietrich (c.1637–1707), Danish organist and composer. He worked as an organist in Lübeck from 1668 until his death, turning the traditional Sunday evening concerts there into celebrated occasions for the performance of his vocal, organ, and chamber music. His skill as an organist inspired Bach to walk more than 200 miles from Anstadt to hear him play. His toccatas, preludes, fugues, and choral variations give some idea of his mastery of the instrument as well as of his gifts as a composer.

Byatt /ˈbaɪət/, A(ntonia) S(usan) (born 1936), English novelist and literary critic. Her fiction is noted for its use of literary and historical allusion and pastiche. Major novels include *The Virgin in the Garden* (1978), set largely in the coronation year of 1953, with complex allegorical references to Spenser, Shakespeare, and Raleigh, and *Possession* (1990), a satire of the literary biography industry, which won the Booker Prize. She is the elder sister of the novelist Margaret Drabble.

Byrd[1] /bɜːd/, Richard E(velyn) (1888–1957), American explorer, naval officer, and aviator. He claimed to have made the first aeroplane flight over the North Pole in 1926, although his actual course has been disputed. He was the first to fly over the South Pole in 1929 and led further scientific expeditions to the Antarctic in 1933–4 and 1939–41.

Byrd[2] /bɜːd/, William (1543–1623), English composer. Joint organist of the Chapel Royal with Tallis, he is often held to be one of the finest Tudor composers. As a Roman Catholic under the Anglican Elizabeth I, he wrote for both Churches and is most famous for his Latin masses for three, four, and five voices and his Anglican Great Service. He composed a great quantity of music for virginals in addition to much consort music, including more than forty consort songs.

Byron /ˈbaɪərən/, George Gordon, 6th Baron (1788–1824), English poet. His first literary success was *Childe Harold's Pilgrimage* (1812–

18). In 1815 there were rumours of an incestuous relationship with his half-sister, his wife left him, and debts associated with his ancestral home increased. Ostracized and embittered, he left England permanently and stayed with Shelley in Geneva, finally settling in Italy. In *Beppo* (1818) he found a new ironic colloquial voice, which he fully developed in his epic satire *Don Juan* (1819–24). Though criticized on moral grounds, Byron's poetry exerted considerable influence on the romantic movement, particularly on the Continent. In 1824 he joined the fight for Greek independence, but died of malaria before seeing serious battle.

C

Caballé /ˌkæbəˈljeɪ, Spanish ˌkaβaˈʎʎe/, Montserrat (born 1933), Spanish operatic soprano. Caballé made her operatic début in 1956. In addition to her concert repertoire, for which she has won acclaim, Caballé has earned an international reputation in a wide variety of stage roles, especially in operas by Donizetti and Verdi.

Cabot /'kæbət/, John (Italian name Giovanni Caboto) (c.1450–c.1498), Italian explorer and navigator. He and his son Sebastian (c.1475–1557) sailed from Bristol in 1497 with letters patent from Henry VII of England in search of Asia, but in fact discovered the mainland of North America. The site of their arrival is uncertain (it may have been Cape Breton Island, Newfoundland, or Labrador). John Cabot returned to Bristol and undertook a second expedition in 1498. Sebastian made further voyages of exploration after his father's death, most notably to Brazil and the River Plate (1526).

Cadbury /'kædbərɪ/, George (1839–1922), English cocoa and chocolate manufacturer and social reformer. He and his brother Richard (1835–99) took over their father's business in 1861 and established Cadbury Brothers. Committed Quakers, they greatly improved working conditions and in 1879 George Cadbury moved the works to a new factory on a rural site (which he called Bournville) outside Birmingham, where he subsequently built a housing estate intended primarily for his workers.

Cade /keɪd/, John ('Jack') (died 1450), Irish rebel. In 1450 he assumed the name of Mortimer and led the Kentish rebels against Henry VI. They occupied London for three days and executed both the treasurer of England and the sheriff of Kent. When many of the rebels accepted an offer of pardon, Cade fled, but died of a wound received in an attempt to capture him.

Caedmon /'kædmən/ (7th century), English poet and monk. According to Bede he was an illiterate herdsman, who received in a vision the power of song and was called to sing in praise of the Creation. He then joined the monastery at Whitby and later wrote English poetry inspired by biblical themes. The only authentic fragment of his work is a song in praise of the Creation, quoted by Bede.

Caesar see JULIUS CAESAR.

Cage /keɪdʒ/, John (Milton) (1912–92), American composer, pianist, and writer. A pupil of Schoenberg, he is notable for his experimental approach to music, including the use of silence and the role of chance. He was a pioneer of aleatory music, in which the composition or performance is randomly determined, for example by use of a computer or dice. Cage experimented with musical instruments, inventing the 'prepared piano' (with pieces of metal, rubber, etc., inserted between the strings to alter the tone), and also used electronic instruments and various sound-effects.

Cagney /'kægnɪ/, James (1899–1986), American actor. He is chiefly remembered for his parts as a gangster in films such as The Public Enemy (1931) and Angels with Dirty Faces (1938). Also a skilled dancer and comedian, he received an Oscar for his part in the musical Yankee Doodle Dandy (1942).

Caine /keɪn/, Sir Michael (born Maurice Micklewhite) (born 1933), English film actor. He had his first major role in Zulu (1963), and soon established a reputation for laconic, anti-heroic roles, for example as a spy in The Ipcress File (1965) and as a streetwise cockney in Alfie (1966). Since then, he has appeared in a wide variety of films, such as Educating Rita (1983) and Hannah and Her Sisters (1986), for which he won an Oscar.

Calamity Jane (born Martha Jane Cannary) (c.1852–1903), American frontierswoman. A colourful character noted for her skill at shooting and riding, she dressed as a man and lived for a time in Wyoming, where she became known for her wild behaviour and heavy drinking. She later joined Buffalo Bill's Wild West Show.

Caldecott /'kɔːldɪˌkɒt/, Randolph (1846–86), English graphic artist and watercolour painter. He is best known for his illustrations for children's books, such as those for The House that Jack Built (1878). A medal awarded annually for the illustration of

American children's books is named after him.

Calder /ˈkɔːldə(r)/, Alexander (1898–1976), American sculptor and painter. He was one of the first artists to introduce movement into sculpture, from the early 1930s, making mobiles incorporating abstract forms and often using wire. His static sculptures (such as *The Red Crab*, 1962) are known by contrast as 'stabiles'.

Calderón de la Barca /ˌkɔːldəˌrɒn deɪ læ ˈbɑːkə, ˌkɒl-/, Pedro (1600–81), Spanish dramatist and poet. He wrote some 120 plays, more than 70 of them religious dramas for outdoor performance on the festival of Corpus Christi. His secular dramas include *El Alcalde de Zalamea* (*c*.1643).

Caldwell /ˈkɔːldwel/, Erskine (Preston) (1903–87), American novelist and short-story writer. Caldwell worked in a variety of jobs in every southern state and reproduced the dialect of the poor whites in his realistic, earthy, and popular novels. *Tobacco Road* (1932), his best-known work, was adapted for the stage and ran for more than seven years on Broadway. His other books include *God's Little Acre* (1933), *Georgia Boy* (1943), and *Close to Home* (1962).

Caligula /kəˈlɪɡjʊlə/ (born Gaius Julius Caesar Germanicus) (AD 12–41), Roman emperor 37–41. Brought up in a military camp, he gained the nickname Caligula (Latin for 'little boot') as an infant on account of the miniature military boots he wore. Caligula's brief reign as emperor, which began when he succeeded Tiberius and ended with his assassination, became notorious for its tyrannical excesses.

Callaghan /ˈkæləhən/, (Leonard) James, Baron Callaghan of Cardiff (born 1912), British Labour statesman, Prime Minister 1976–9. He became Prime Minister following Harold Wilson's resignation; the leader of a minority government, he was forced in 1977 to negotiate an agreement with the Liberal Party (known as the Lib–Lab Pact) to stay in power. After widespread strikes in the so-called 'winter of discontent' (1978–9), Callaghan received a vote of no confidence; the Labour Party was defeated by the Conservatives in the subsequent election.

Callas /ˈkæləs/, Maria (born Maria Cecilia Anna Kalageropoulos) (1923–77), American-born operatic soprano, of Greek parentage. She was a coloratura soprano whose bel canto style of singing especially suited her to early Italian opera; a number of works by Rossini, Bellini, and Donizetti were revived for her.

Callicrates /kəˈlɪkrəˌtiːz/ (5th century BC), Greek architect. He was the leading architect in Periclean Athens, and with Ictinus designed the Parthenon (447–438 BC). Many other structures are attributed to him, including the Ionic temple of Athena Nike on the Acropolis (448–after 421 BC).

Callil /kəˈlɪl/, Carmen (Thérèse) (born 1938), Australian publisher. She settled in Britain and worked with various publishers before founding her own feminist publishing house, Virago, in 1972. Virago books, with their distinctive jacket design, soon established a strong market identity, bringing overlooked women writers of the past to a wider public and also publishing new female authors.

Callimachus /kəˈlɪməkəs/ (*c*.305–*c*.240 BC), Greek poet and scholar. As head of the library at Alexandria, he compiled a critical catalogue of the existing Greek literature of his day. As a poet he is best known for his short or episodic poetry, especially hymns and epigrams.

Calloway /ˈkæləˌweɪ/, Cab(ell) (1907–94), American jazz singer and band-leader. He led a succession of outstanding big bands between 1928 and 1953. He was famous for his style of scat singing, for his flamboyant appearance, and for songs such as 'Minnie the Moocher' (1931) and 'Jumpin' Jive' (1939). He appeared in several films, including *Stormy Weather* (1943), *The Cincinnati Kid* (1965), and *The Blues Brothers* (1980).

Calvin[1] /ˈkælvɪn/, John (1509–64), French Protestant theologian and reformer. He began his theological career in France, but was forced to flee to Basle in Switzerland after embracing Protestantism in the early 1530s. At Basle he published (1536) the first edition of his *Institutes of the Christian Religion*, the first systematic account of reformed Christian doctrine and a work which he continued to revise and extend throughout his lifetime. He attempted a re-ordering of society on reformed Christian principles, with strong and sometimes ruthless control over the private lives of citizens. From 1541 he lived in Geneva, where he established the first Presbyterian government. Through his *Institutes* and an extensive body of commentary on the

Scriptures, he exerted an important influence on the development of Protestant thought; his theological system, Calvinism, was further developed by his followers, notably Theodore Beza (1519–1605).

Calvin[2] /'kælvm/, Melvin (1911–97), American biochemist. He investigated the metabolic pathways involved in photosynthesis, discovering the cycle of reactions which is named after him, and attempting to duplicate them synthetically. He was awarded the Nobel Prize for chemistry in 1961.

Calvino /kæl'vi:nəʊ/, Italo (1923–87), Italian novelist and short-story writer, born in Cuba. His first novel *The Path to the Nest of Spiders* (1947) is considered a significant example of neo-realism, whereas his later works increasingly use fantasy, allegory, and innovative narrative structures and have been associated with magic realism; his later novels include *Invisible Cities* (1972) and *If on a Winter's Night a Traveller* (1979).

Cambyses /kæm'baɪsi:z/ (died 522 BC), son of Cyrus, king of Persia 529–522 BC. He is chiefly remembered for his conquest of Egypt in 525 BC.

Cameron /'kæmərən/, Julia Margaret (1815–79), English photographer. Although she did not take up photography until the age of 48, she quickly gained acclaim for her portraits of prominent figures such as Alfred Tennyson, Charles Darwin, and Thomas Carlyle. She is credited with being the first to use soft-focus techniques; her work often reflects the influence of contemporary painting, especially that of the Pre-Raphaelites.

Camões /kæ'mɔɪnʃ/, Luis (Vaz) de (also **Camoëns** /'kæməʊˌens/) (c.1524–80), Portuguese poet. Little is known of his early life; in 1553 he travelled to India and the Far East, returning to Portugal in 1570. His most famous work, *The Lusiads* (1572), describes Vasco da Gama's voyage and discovery of the sea route to India and celebrates the golden age of Portuguese discovery; combining classical elements with a strong sense of Portuguese history and identity, it became established from the 17th century as Portugal's national epic.

Campbell[1] /'kæmb(ə)l/, Donald (Malcolm) (1921–67), English motor-racing driver and holder of world speed records. Following in the footsteps of his father Sir Malcolm Campbell, he broke a number of world speed records in boats and cars named *Bluebird*. In 1964 he achieved a speed of 276.33 m.p.h. (445 k.p.h.) on water and 403 m.p.h. (649 k.p.h.) on land, both in Australia. He was killed in an attempt to achieve a water speed of 300 m.p.h. (483 k.p.h.) on Coniston Water in England.

Campbell[2] /'kæmb(ə)l/, Sir Malcolm (1885–1948), English motor-racing driver and holder of world speed records. In 1935 he became the first man to exceed a land speed of 300 m.p.h. (483 k.p.h.), driving his car *Bluebird* on Bonneville Flats in Utah in the US, a record which was not broken until 1950. He also achieved a water-speed record of 141.74 m.p.h. (228 k.p.h.) in his boat of the same name in 1939.

Campbell[3] /'kæmb(ə)l/, Mrs Patrick (née Beatrice Stella Tanner) (1865–1940), English actress. Renowned for her wit and beauty, she created the part of Paula in Pinero's *The Second Mrs Tanqueray* (1893) and also gave notable performances in roles ranging from Shakespeare to Ibsen. George Bernard Shaw wrote the part of Eliza Doolittle in *Pygmalion* (1914) for her and they exchanged letters over a long period.

Campbell[4] /'kæmb(ə)l/, (Ignatius) Roy(ston Dunnachie) (1901–57), South African poet. His works include *The Flaming Terrapin* (1924), an allegorical narrative of the Flood, and *The Wayzgoose* (1928), a satire on South African life. His first autobiography *Broken Record* (1934) and the long poem *Flowering Rifle* (1939) show strong right-wing sympathies; he fought on Franco's side in the Spanish Civil War.

Campbell[5] /'kæmb(ə)l/, Thomas (1777–1844), Scottish poet. He published *The Pleasures of Hope* (1799) and *Gertrude of Wyoming* (1809) among other volumes of verse, and is now chiefly remembered for his patriotic lyrics such as 'The Battle of Hohenlinden' and 'Ye Mariners of England'.

Campbell-Bannerman
/ˌkæmb(ə)l'bænəmən/, Sir Henry (1836–1908), British Liberal statesman, Prime Minister 1905–8. He was first elected to Parliament as MP for the Stirling burghs in 1868 and became leader of his party in 1899. His premiership, which ended with his resignation only a few days before his death, saw the grant of self-government to the defeated Boer republics of Transvaal (1906) and the Orange River Colony (1907), the passing of the important Trade Disputes Act (1906), which exempted trade

unions from certain liabilities in connection with strikes, and the entente with Russia (1907).

Campion /ˈkæmpɪən/, Jane (born 1954), New Zealand film director and screenwriter. Campion's films reflect her interest in awkward, shy, or marginalized young women who possess great strength of character and inner tranquillity. Among them are *An Angel at My Table* (1990) and especially *The Piano* (1993), for which Campion received an Oscar for best screenplay.

Campion, St Edmund /ˈkæmpɪən/ (1540–81), English Jesuit priest and martyr. He was ordained a deacon in the Church of England in 1569 but because of his Roman Catholic sympathies he went abroad, becoming a Catholic and a Jesuit priest (1573). He was a member of the first Jesuit mission to England (1580). In 1581 he was arrested, charged with conspiracy against the Crown, tortured, and executed. Feast day, 1 December.

Camus /ˈkæmjuː/, Albert (1913–60), French novelist, dramatist, and essayist. He joined the French resistance during the Second World War and became co-editor (with Jean-Paul Sartre) of the left-wing daily *Combat* (1944–7). His essay *The Myth of Sisyphus* (1942) and his first novel *The Outsider* (1942) gained him international respect; each conveys his conception of the absurdity of human existence and aligns him closely with Sartre's existentialism. Other notable works include the novel *The Plague* (1947) and the essay *The Rebel* (1951). He was awarded the Nobel Prize for literature in 1957.

Canaletto /ˌkænəˈletəʊ/ (born Giovanni Antonio Canale) (1697–1768), Italian painter. Working chiefly in his native city of Venice, he was especially popular with the English aristocracy, who commissioned his paintings of Venetian festivals and scenery as mementoes of their grand tour. His early work is dramatic and freely handled, reflecting his training as a theatrical scene painter, but from *c.*1730 he changed to the more topographically precise style for which he is mainly remembered, aided by his use of the camera obscura. His works include *Scene in Venice: The Piazzetta Entrance to the Grand Canal* (c.1726–8).

Candolle /kænˈdɒl/, Augustin Pyrame de (1778–1841), Swiss botanist. His prolific writings in taxonomy and botany were highly influential, particularly his belief that taxonomy should be based on morphological characters, and his scheme of classification prevailed for many years. Candolle also contributed to agronomy, and was a pioneer in plant geography and the linking of soil type with vegetation.

Canetti /kəˈnetɪ/, Elias (born 1905), Bulgarian-born British writer. Although he lived in England from 1938, he continued to write in German. His novel *Auto-da-Fé* (1936) concentrates on the doomed attempt of the aloof, narrow-minded intellectual to avoid contamination by the material world. *Crowds and Power* (1960), a behavioural study of crowds and dictators, is his other most important work. He was awarded the Nobel Prize for literature in 1981.

Canmore /ˈkænmɔː(r)/, the nickname of Malcolm III of Scotland (see MALCOLM).

Canning /ˈkænɪŋ/, George (1770–1827), British Tory statesman, Prime Minister 1827. Foreign Secretary from 1807, he resigned in 1809 after a disagreement with his rival Castlereagh over a disastrous expedition in the Napoleonic Wars, but returned to office following Castlereagh's suicide in 1822. During this ministry he presided over a reversal of Britain's hitherto conservative foreign policy, being particularly responsible for the support of nationalist movements in various parts of Europe. He succeeded Lord Liverpool as Prime Minister in 1827, but died shortly afterwards.

Cannizzaro /ˌkænɪˈzɑːrəʊ/, Stanislao (1826–1910), Italian chemist. He is chiefly remembered for his revival of Avogadro's hypothesis, using it to distinguish clearly between atoms and molecules, and introducing the unified system of atomic and molecular weights. Cannizzaro also discovered a reaction (named after him) in which an aldehyde is converted into an acid and an alcohol in the presence of a strong alkali.

Canova /kəˈnəʊvə/, Antonio (1757–1822), Italian sculptor. Canova's inventive approach to classical models has led to him being regarded as a leading exponent of neoclassicism. His most famous works range from classical subjects such as *Cupid and Psyche* (1792) and *The Three Graces* (1813–16) to funeral monuments and life-size busts; highly regarded in his day, he executed commissions for papal and royal monuments and for Napoleon and his family.

Cantona /'kæntə,nɑː/, Eric (born 1966), French footballer. He played for Marseille and other French clubs and for the French national side before joining Leeds United in 1992. He won the League Championship with them that year and then won it in 1993, 1994, 1996, and 1997 with Manchester United. A gifted but volatile forward, he was fined and suspended in 1995 for a flying kick against a spectator who had insulted him during a match. He announced his retirement from the game in 1997.

Cantor /'kæntɔː(r)/, Georg (1845–1918), Russian-born German mathematician. Cantor's work on numbers laid the foundations of the theory of sets. He introduced the concept of transfinite numbers, and his work stimulated 20th-century exploration of number theory and the logical foundation of mathematics.

Canute /kə'njuːt/ (also **Cnut**, **Knut**) (died 1035), son of Sweyn I, Danish king of England 1017–35, Denmark 1018–35, and Norway 1028–35. After Edmund Ironside's murder in 1016, Canute became king of England, ending a prolonged struggle for the throne. As king, he presided over a period of relative peace. He is most commonly remembered for demonstrating to fawning courtiers his inability to stop the rising tide; this demonstration of the limited powers of human beings, even if they be kings, has become distorted in folklore so as to suggest that Canute really expected to succeed in turning back the tide.

Capability Brown see BROWN[5].

Capablanca /ˌkæpə'blæŋkə/, José Raúl (1888–1942), Cuban chess player. As world champion 1921–7 he made a considerable impact on the game, particularly on opening theory.

Čapek /'tʃæpek/, Karel (1890–1938), Czech novelist and dramatist. He wrote several plays with his brother Josef (1887–1945), including The Insect Play (1921), a satire on human society and totalitarianism. Čapek's best-known independent work was R.U.R. (Rossum's Universal Robots) (1920), a cautionary drama about the dangers of mechanization set 'on a remote island in 1950–60'. The title introduced the word robot to the English language.

Capet /'kæpɪt, kæ'pet, French kapɛ/, Hugh (or Hugo) (938–96), king of France 987–96. His election as king in 987 marked the foundation of the Capetian dynasty, which survived until 1328.

Capone /kə'pəʊn/, Alphonse ('Al') (1899–1947), American gangster, of Italian descent. He was notorious for his domination of organized crime in Chicago in the 1920s; his earnings from liquor, prostitution, gambling, and other rackets were estimated to be $30 million per year. Although indirectly responsible for many murders, including those of the St Valentine's Day Massacre (1929), he was never tried for any of them; it was for federal income-tax evasion that he was eventually imprisoned in 1931.

Capote /kə'pəʊtɪ/, Truman (born Truman Streckfus Persons) (1924–84), American writer. His works range from the light-hearted novella Breakfast at Tiffany's (1958) to the grim and meticulous re-creation of a brutal multiple murder in In Cold Blood (1966).

Capp /kæp/, Al (born Alfred Gerald Caplin) (1909–79), American cartoonist. He began his career as an assistant on a number of cartoon strips for the Associated Press. In 1934 his own comic strip 'Li'l Abner' appeared in the New York Mirror. The strip featured a number of social caricatures including the protagonist, Li'l Abner, a shy and awkward rustic. The strip was hugely popular and ran until Capp's retirement in 1977.

Capra /'kæprə/, Frank (1897–1991), Italian-born American film director. His reputation rests on the film comedies which he made in the 1930s and early 1940s, such as It Happened One Night (1934), Mr Deeds Goes to Town (1936), and Arsenic and Old Lace (1944). He won six Oscars for his films.

Caracalla /ˌkærə'kælə/ (born Septimius Bassanius; later called Marcus Aurelius Severus Antoninus Augustus) (188–217), Roman emperor 211–17. He spent much of his reign campaigning in Germany and in the East, where he hoped to repeat the conquests of Alexander the Great, but was assassinated in Mesopotamia. By an edict of 212 he granted Roman citizenship to all free inhabitants of the Roman Empire. His name was derived from that of a kind of tunic he characteristically wore.

Caratacus /kə'rætəkəs/ (also **Caractacus** /-'ræktəkəs/) (1st century AD), British chieftain, son of Cunobelinus. He took part in the resistance to the Roman invasion of

AD 43, and when defeated fled to Yorkshire, where he was handed over to the Romans in AD 51.

Caravaggio /ˌkærəˈvædʒɪˌəʊ/, Michelangelo Merisi da (c.1571–1610), Italian painter. An important figure in the transition from late mannerism to baroque, he reinvigorated religious art and had a far-reaching influence on later artists. The characteristic features of his work include naturalistic realism (achieved partly by the use of ordinary people as models for biblical characters) and dramatic use of light and shade.

Cardin /ˈkɑːdæn/, Pierre (born 1922), French couturier. He was the first designer in the field of *haute couture* to show a collection of clothes for men as well as women (1960). He is also noted for his ready-to-wear clothes and accessories.

Carey /ˈkeərɪ/, George (Leonard) (born 1935), English Anglican churchman, Archbishop of Canterbury since 1991. He was formerly a theology lecturer and comes from a broadly evangelical background. The controversial introduction of women priests into the Church of England was finally approved under his leadership.

Carling /ˈkɑːlɪŋ/, Will(iam David Charles) (born 1965), English Rugby Union player. He made his England début in 1988 and was appointed captain the same year. He led England to the Five Nations championship in 1991, 1992, 1994, and 1996, and to the World Cup Final in 1990. He is the most-capped England centre and holds the world record for international appearances as captain, a position he retired from in 1996.

Carlyle /kɑːˈlaɪl/, Thomas (1795–1881), Scottish historian and political philosopher. He worked as a teacher before starting to write articles for the *Edinburgh Encyclopedia* and critical works on German literature in the 1820s. His first major philosophical work was *Sartor Resartus* (1833–4), which dealt with social values and is written in a mannered prose style. He established his reputation as a historian with his history of the French Revolution (1837), the first volume of which he was forced to rewrite after the manuscript was accidentally burnt. Many of his works on history, politics, and social philosophy advocate a benevolent autocracy rather than democracy; *On Heroes, Hero Worship, and the Heroic in History* (1841) was the starting-point for his development of these ideas. Carlyle's influence on the development of social and political ideas in Britain during the 19th century was considerable.

Carmichael /kɑːˈmaɪk(ə)l/, Hoagy (born Howard Hoagland Carmichael) (1899–1981), American jazz pianist, composer, and singer. His best-known songs include 'Stardust' (1929), 'Two Sleepy People' (1938), and 'In the Cool, Cool, Cool of the Evening' (1951).

Carnap /ˈkɑːnæp/, Rudolf (1891–1970), German-born American philosopher. One of the originators of logical positivism, he was a founder and the most influential member of the Vienna Circle and was noted for his contributions to logic, the analysis of language, the theory of probability, and the philosophy of science. His emphasis on scientific method in philosophy and the need to verify statements through observation marked a turning-point in philosophical enquiry and the rejection of traditional metaphysics. His major works include *The Logical Structure of the World* (1928) and *The Logical Foundations of Probability* (1950).

Carné /kɑːˈneɪ/, Marcel (1909–96), French film director. He held a dominant position among film-makers of the 1930s and 1940s, gaining his reputation in particular for the films which he made with the poet and scriptwriter Jacques Prévert (1900–77). Characterized by a fatalistic outlook and a masterly evocation of atmosphere, they include *Quai des brumes* (1938), *Le Jour se lève* (1939), and *Les Enfants du paradis* (1945).

Carnegie /kɑːˈneɪgɪ, ˈkɑːnəgɪ/, Andrew (1835–1919), Scottish-born American industrialist and philanthropist. He built up a considerable fortune in the steel industry in the US, then retired from business in 1901 and devoted his wealth to charitable purposes on both sides of the Atlantic, supporting many educational institutions, libraries, and the arts. One of his most notable achievements was the creation of the Carnegie Peace Fund to promote international peace.

Carnot /ˈkɑːnəʊ/, Nicolas Léonard Sadi (1796–1832), French scientist. An army officer for most of his life, Carnot became interested in the principles of operation of steam engines, and analysed the efficiency of such engines using the notion of a cycle of reversible temperature and pressure changes of the gases. Carnot's work was

recognized after his death as being of crucial importance to the theory of thermodynamics.

Carothers /kəˈrʌðəz/, Wallace Hume (1896–1937), American industrial chemist. He took up the study of long-chain molecules, now called polymers, and developed the first successful synthetic rubber, neoprene, and the first synthetic fibre able to be spun from a melt, Nylon 6.6. He committed suicide at the age of 41 before nylon had been commercially exploited.

Carpaccio /kɑːˈpætʃɪˌəʊ/, Vittore (c.1455–1525), Italian painter. He is noted especially for his paintings of Venice and for his lively narrative cycle of paintings *Scenes from the Life of St Ursula* (1490–5).

Carr /kɑː(r)/, Emily (1871–1945), Canadian painter and writer. Her paintings, inspired by the wilderness of British Columbia, often drew on the motifs of American Indian folk art. From 1927 she came into contact with the group of Canadian landscape painters known as the Group of Seven and produced such expressionist works as *Forest Landscape II* and *Sky* (both 1934–5).

Carracci /kəˈrɑːtʃɪ/ a family of Italian painters. Ludovico (1555–1619) is remembered chiefly as a distinguished teacher; with his cousins he established an academy at Bologna which was responsible for training many important painters. His cousin Annibale (1560–1609) is the most famous of the family, especially for his work in Rome, such as the ceiling of the Farnese Gallery (1597–1600). Taking the art of Raphael and Michelangelo as a starting-point, he developed a style which proved to be a foundation of the Italian baroque. He is also remembered for his invention of the caricature. Annibale's brother Agostino (1557–1602) was chiefly an engraver, but he also worked with his brother in the Farnese Gallery.

Carrel /kəˈrel, ˈkærəl/, Alexis (1873–1944), French surgeon and biologist. He developed improved techniques for suturing arteries and veins, and carried out some of the first organ transplants. He also succeeded in keeping organs alive outside the body by perfusion, using a glass pump devised with the aid of Charles Lindbergh. Carrel, who spent much of his career in the US, received a Nobel Prize in 1912.

Carreras /kəˈreərəs/, José (born 1946), Spanish operatic tenor. Since his operatic début in his native city of Barcelona (1970), he has given many performances in opera houses worldwide. Noted for his soft voice in the upper register, he has had great success in the operas of Verdi, Puccini, and Donizetti; his repertoire also includes traditional Catalan songs and popular light music, such as the musical *West Side Story*.

Carrington /ˈkærɪŋtən/, Dora (de Houghton) (1893–1932), English painter. Carrington studied at the Slade School of Art in London between 1910 and 1914. She became involved with the Bloomsbury Group and in particular Lytton Strachey, with whom she continued a relationship despite her marriage in 1921. When he died in 1932 she committed suicide, shooting herself at Hungerford in Berkshire.

Carroll /ˈkærəl/, Lewis (pseudonym of Charles Lutwidge Dodgson) (1832–98), English writer. He worked as a mathematics lecturer at Oxford University 1855–81; after a boat trip with Alice Liddell, the daughter of the dean of his college, he was inspired to write *Alice's Adventures in Wonderland* (1865) and *Through the Looking Glass* (1871). Both books tell the story of a child's fantastic dream adventures; illustrated by John Tenniel, they became classics of children's literature. Carroll also wrote nonsense verse, notably *The Hunting of the Snark* (1876), and experimented in portrait photography.

Carson[1] /ˈkɑːs(ə)n/, John William ('Johnny') (born 1925), American television personality. Carson's monologues on the daytime *The Johnny Carson Show* convinced NBC executives to engage him as permanent host of *The Tonight Show* in 1962. Carson's sharp quips and impish image proved popular with late-night audiences, so much so that Carson termed himself 'America's most effective birth-control device'. He retired from the show in 1992.

Carson[2] /ˈkɑːs(ə)n/, Rachel (Louise) (1907–64), American zoologist. Remembered as a pioneer ecologist and popularizer of science, she wrote *The Sea Around Us* (1951) and *Silent Spring* (1963), an attack on the indiscriminate use of pesticides and weedkillers.

Carson[3] /ˈkɑːs(ə)n/, William Hunter Fisher ('Willie') (born 1942), Scottish jockey. In 1972 he became the first Scotsman to be champion jockey and also had his first

Classic success in the 2,000 Guineas. His first Derby win came seven years later, and he won again in 1980 and 1989.

Carter[1] /'kɑ:tə(r)/, Angela (1940–92), English novelist and short-story writer. Her fiction is characterized by fantasy, black humour, and eroticism, while her second novel *The Magic Toyshop* (1967) established her as a major exponent of magic realism. Later novels, such as *The Passion of New Eve* (1977), offer a strong feminist perspective on capitalism and Western society. Her exploration of the symbolic function of myth and folklore in the unconscious is reflected in short stories such as 'The Company of Wolves' (1979), which formed the basis for a film in 1984.

Carter[2] /'kɑ:tə(r)/, Elliott (Cook) (born 1908), American composer. He is noted for his innovative approach to metre and eclectic choice of sources as diverse as modern jazz and Renaissance madrigals.

Carter[3] /'kɑ:tə(r)/, Howard (1874–1939), English archaeologist. In 1922 he achieved fame when, studying the Valley of the Kings at Thebes, he discovered the tomb of Tutankhamen. His work, under the patronage of Lord Carnarvon, gave a great boost to public interest in archaeology.

Carter[4] /'kɑ:tə(r)/, James Earl ('Jimmy') (born 1924), American Democratic statesman, 39th President of the US 1977–81. A progressive and reformist governor of Georgia (1970–4), he was elected President on a manifesto of civil rights and economic reform. Although his administration was notable for achieving the Panama Canal Treaty (1977) and the Camp David agreements (1978), it was dogged in the last few years by Carter's inability to resolve the crisis caused by the seizure of American hostages in Iran.

Cartier /'kɑ:tɪˌeɪ/, Jacques (1491–1557), French explorer. The first to establish France's claim to North America, he made three voyages to Canada between 1534 and 1541, sailing up the St Lawrence River as far as present-day Montreal and building a fort at Cap Rouge (a few miles upstream of what is now Quebec City).

Cartier-Bresson /ˌkɑ:tɪeɪˈbresɒn/, Henri (born 1908), French photographer and film director. Intent on capturing the 'decisive moment' of a scene or event, he travelled widely, recording the lives of ordinary people without artificial composition and

establishing a reputation as a humane and perceptive observer. His collections of photographs include *The Decisive Moment* (1952). Between 1936 and 1939 he worked as assistant to the film director Jean Renoir, also making his own documentary film about the Spanish Civil War, *Return to Life* (1937).

Cartland /'kɑ:tlənd/, Dame (Mary) Barbara (Hamilton) (born 1901), English writer. A prolific author, she specializes in light romantic fiction; her popular romances include *Bride to a Brigand* (1983) and *A Secret Passage to Love* (1992).

Cartwright /'kɑ:traɪt/, Edmund (1743–1823), English engineer, inventor of the power loom. Initially a clergyman, he became interested in textile machinery, and despite financial failures continued to innovate, developing machines for wool-combing and rope-making and an engine which used alcohol rather than steam. His achievements were recognized eventually in 1809 by the government, which voted him an award of £10,000.

Caruso /kəˈru:səʊ/, Enrico (1873–1921), Italian operatic tenor. His voice combined a brilliant upper register with a baritone-like warmth. He appeared in both French and Italian opera and had his greatest successes in operas by Verdi, Puccini, and Jules Massenet (1842–1912). The first major tenor to be recorded on gramophone records, he became a household name even among those who never attended operatic performances.

Cary /'keərɪ/, (Arthur) Joyce (Lunel) (1888–1957), English novelist. A number of his novels are set in Africa, where he had served briefly in the colonial service. His major works constitute two trilogies; the first is concerned with art and includes *The Horse's Mouth* (1944), a memorable portrait of an outrageous artist, while the second deals with political life and includes *Not Honour More* (1955).

Casals /kəˈsælz/, Pablo (also called Pau Casals) (1876–1973), Spanish cellist, conductor, and composer. The foremost cellist of his time, he was noted especially for his performances of Bach suites and the Dvořák Cello Concerto. He refused to perform in Hitler's Germany and went into voluntary exile in 1939 during the Franco regime, living first in the French Pyrenees and then in Puerto Rico. His compositions include the oratorio *The Manger* (1943–60).

Casanova /ˌkæsə'nəʊvə/, Giovanni Jacopo (full surname Casanova de Seingalt) (1725–98), Italian adventurer. He is famous for his memoirs (first published in French 1828–38), describing his adventures in Europe and especially his sexual encounters.

Casement /'keɪsmənt/, Sir Roger (David) (1864–1916), Irish nationalist. He served with the British consular service in Africa until his retirement in 1912, when he joined the Irish nationalist cause. Shortly after the outbreak of the First World War he visited Germany to seek support for an Irish uprising. He was captured on his return to Ireland before the Easter Rising of 1916, and subsequently hanged by the British for treason. His diaries reveal his homosexuality and were used to discredit a campaign for his reprieve; they were not made available to the public until 1959.

Cash /kæʃ/, Johnny (born 1932), American country music singer and songwriter. The poverty and hardship of his childhood are reflected in his early songs, which tend to feature outlaws, prisoners, or characters who are unlucky in life or love. He formed a brief association with Bob Dylan in the 1960s; during the 1970s he turned increasingly to gospel music. His most famous hits include 'I Walk the Line' (1956) and 'A Boy Named Sue' (1969).

Caslon /'kæzlən/, William (1692–1766), English typographer. He established a type foundry (continued by his son William, 1720–78) which supplied printers on the Continent as well as in England. His name is applied to the types cut by the Caslons or to later type styles modelled on the same characteristics.

Cassatt /kə'sæt/, Mary (1844–1926), American painter. Cassatt worked mostly in Paris and was persuaded to exhibit with the impressionists by Degas. She was noted for her draughtsmanship, etching, and drypoint studies. Her paintings, including *Lady at the Tea Table* (1885), display a close interest in everyday subject matter.

Cassini /kə'si:nɪ/, Giovanni Domenico (1625–1712), Italian-born French astronomer. He helped to establish the Paris Observatory and became its director, specializing in the solar system. He determined the rotational periods of Jupiter and Saturn, calculated the movements of the Galilean moons of Jupiter, discovered four of the moons of Saturn, and described a gap in the rings of Saturn (now known as Cassini's division). Cassini also contributed to geodesy, but wrongly believed the shape of the earth to be a prolate spheroid, a theory supported by the three generations of his descendants who succeeded him at the Paris Observatory.

Cassius /'kæsɪəs/, Gaius (full name Gaius Cassius Longinus) (died 42 BC), Roman general. With Brutus he was one of the leaders of the conspiracy in 44 BC to assassinate Julius Caesar. He and Brutus were defeated by Caesar's supporters Antony and Octavian at the battle of Philippi in 42 BC, in the course of which he committed suicide.

Casson /'kæs(ə)n/, Sir Hugh (Maxwell) (born 1910), English architect. Casson was professor of Interior Design at the Royal College of Art (1953–75). His directorship of architecture at the Festival of Britain (1948–51) ensured the site's success as a piece of organized townscape. Casson was president of the Royal Academy from 1976 to 1984.

Castle /'kɑːs(ə)l/, Barbara (Anne), Baroness Castle of Blackburn (born 1911), British Labour politician. Castle became Labour MP for Blackburn in 1945 and remained in the House for thirty-four years. She held a number of government posts, including chairman of the Labour Party (1958–9) and, controversially, Minister of Transport (1965–8), introducing the 70 m.p.h. speed limit and the breathalyser test. Castle was elected to the European Parliament in 1979, and was created a life peer in 1990.

Castlereagh /'kɑːs(ə)l,reɪ/, Robert Stewart, Viscount (1769–1822), British Tory statesman. Born in Ulster, he began his political career as a Whig in the Irish Parliament and continued to concern himself with Irish affairs after becoming a Tory in 1795. He became Foreign Secretary in 1812, and in this capacity represented his country at the Congress of Vienna (1814–15), playing a central part in reviving the Quadruple Alliance (whereby Britain, Russia, Austria, and Prussia united to defeat Napoleon). He committed suicide, apparently as a result of mental strain owing to pressure of work.

Castro /'kæstrəʊ/, Fidel (born 1927), Cuban statesman, Prime Minister 1959–76 and President since 1976. He forced President Batista from power in 1959, setting up a Communist regime which he has led ever since. The abortive US-backed invasion at-

tempt by Cuban exiles at the Bay of Pigs in 1961 boosted his popularity, as did his successful survival of the Cuban Missile Crisis of 1962. He became leader of the Non-Aligned Movement in 1979, in spite of Cuba's reliance on the USSR for economic aid. Since the collapse of the Soviet bloc Castro has strictly maintained Communism in Cuba.

Cather /'kæðə(r)/, Willa (Sibert) (1876–1974), American novelist and short-story writer. The state of Nebraska, where she was brought up, provides the setting for some of her best writing; early major novels include *O Pioneers!* (1913), *The Song of the Lark* (1915), and *My Antonia* (1918), while among later works is the best-selling *Death Comes for the Archbishop* (1927), a celebration of the Catholic Church in New Mexico.

Catherine II /'kæθrɪn/ (known as Catherine the Great) (1729–96), empress of Russia, reigned 1762–96. A German princess, she was made empress following a plot which deposed her husband Peter III (1728–62). Her attempted social and political reforms were impeded by entrenched aristocratic interests, and in later years her reign became increasingly conservative. Under Catherine Russia played an important part in European affairs, participating in the three partitions of Poland and forming close links with Prussia and Austria, while to the south and east further territorial advances were made at the expense of the Turks and Tartars.

Catherine, St (known as St Catherine of Alexandria) (died c.307), early Christian martyr. Traditionally, she opposed the persecution of Christians under the Roman emperor Maxentius, debated with fifty scholars sent to undermine her position, and refused to recant or to marry the emperor. She is then said to have been tortured on a spiked wheel and beheaded when it broke. The Catherine wheel subsequently became her emblem. Feast day, 25 November.

Catherine de' Medici /də 'medɪtʃɪ, mə-'diːtʃɪ/ (1519–89), queen of France. The wife of Henry II of France, Catherine ruled as regent 1560–74 during the minority reigns of their three sons, Francis II (reigned 1559–60), Charles IX (reigned 1560–74), and Henry III (reigned 1574–89). She proved unable or unwilling to control the confused situation during the French Wars

of Religion, and it was on her instigation that Huguenots were killed in the Massacre of St Bartholomew (1572).

Catherine of Aragon /'ærəgən/ (1485–1536), first wife of Henry VIII, youngest daughter of Ferdinand and Isabella of Castile, mother of Mary I. Originally married to Henry's elder brother Arthur in 1501, she was widowed six months later, and married Henry in 1509. She gave birth to five children, but all except her daughter Mary died in infancy. Concerned about Catherine's failure to produce a male heir, and attracted to Anne Boleyn, Henry attempted to divorce his wife on the debatable grounds that her marriage to his brother made the marriage illegal. Catherine was sent into retirement, but neither she nor the pope accepted the annulment of the marriage, a fact which led eventually to England's break with the Roman Catholic Church.

Catiline /'kætɪˌlaɪn/ (Latin name Lucius Sergius Catilina) (c.108–62 BC), Roman nobleman and conspirator. Repeatedly thwarted in his ambition to be elected consul, in 63 BC he planned an uprising in Italy. His fellow-conspirators in Rome were successfully suppressed and executed on the initiative of the consul Cicero, and Catiline died in a battle in Etruria.

Cato /'keɪtəʊ/, Marcus Porcius (known as Cato the Elder or Cato the Censor) (234–149 BC), Roman statesman, orator, and writer. An implacable enemy of Carthage, he fought in the second Punic War as a young man and continually warned against the Carthaginian threat when a senator. As censor in 184 BC he engaged in a vigorous programme of moral and social reform, and attempted to stem the growing influence of Greek culture on Roman life. His many writings include a lost history of Rome and an extant work on agriculture. His great-grandson, Cato the Younger (95–46 BC), was an opponent of the dictatorial ambitions of Julius Caesar.

Catullus /kə'tʌləs/, Gaius Valerius (c.84–c.54 BC), Roman poet. His one book of verse contains poems in a variety of metres on a range of subjects; he is best known for his poems to a married woman addressed as 'Lesbia', although he also wrote a number of longer mythological pieces. His importance for later Latin poetry lies both in the impetus he gave to the development of the

love-elegy and in his cultivation of an Alexandrian refinement and learning.

Cauchy /'kaʊʃɪ, French koʃi/, Augustin Louis, Baron (1789–1857), French mathematician. His numerous textbooks and writings introduced new standards of criticism and rigorous argument in calculus, from which grew the field of mathematics known as analysis. He transformed the theory of complex functions by discovering his integral theorems and introducing the calculus of residues. Cauchy also founded the modern theory of elasticity, produced fundamental new ideas about the solution of differential equations, and contributed substantially to the founding of group theory.

Cavafy /kə'vɑːfɪ/, Constantine (Peter) (born Konstantinos Petrou Kavafis) (1863–1933), Greek poet. Cavafy's poems refer mainly to the Hellenistic and Graeco-Roman period of his native Alexandria, and are suffused with an ironic awareness of the instability of life and the limits of human knowledge. His first volume of poems was privately printed in 1904. Cavafy's posthumous reputation grew rapidly and his poetry has exerted a considerable influence on modern Greek verse.

Cavell /'kæv(ə)l/, Edith (Louisa) (1865–1915), English nurse. In charge of the Berkendael Medical Institute in Brussels during the First World War, she helped many Allied soldiers to escape from occupied Belgium. She was arrested by the Germans and brought before a military tribunal, where she openly admitted her actions and was sentenced to death. Her execution provoked widespread condemnation and she became famous as a heroine of the Allied cause.

Cavendish /'kæv(ə)ndɪʃ/, Henry (1731–1810), English chemist and physicist. Pursuing his research in his own private laboratory, Cavendish identified hydrogen as a separate gas, studied carbon dioxide, and determined their densities relative to atmospheric air. He also established that water was a compound, and determined the density of the earth. The full extent of his discoveries in electrostatics was not known until his manuscripts were published in 1879: he had anticipated Coulomb, Ohm, and Faraday, deduced the inverse square law of electrical attraction and repulsion, and discovered specific inductive capacity. The Cavendish Laboratory at Cambridge was named after him.

Cavour /kə'vʊə(r)/, Camillo Benso, Conte di (1810–61), Italian statesman. He was the driving force behind the unification of Italy under Victor Emmanuel II, king of the kingdom of Sardinia. In 1847 Cavour founded the newspaper *Il Risorgimento* to further the cause of unification. As Premier of Piedmont (1852–59; 1860–1), he obtained international support by forming an alliance with France and participating in the Crimean and Franco-Austrian wars. In 1861 he saw Victor Emmanuel crowned king of a united Italy, and became Italy's first Premier.

Cawley /'kɔːlɪ/, Evonne (Fay) (née Goolagong) (born 1951), Australian tennis player. She won two Wimbledon singles titles (1971; 1980) and was three times Australian singles champion (1974–6).

Caxton /'kækstən/, William (c.1422–91), the first English printer. Having learned the art of printing on the Continent, Caxton printed his first English text in 1474 and went on to produce about eighty other texts, including editions of Malory's *Le Morte d'Arthur*, Chaucer's *Canterbury Tales*, and his own translations of French romances.

Cayley[1] /'keɪlɪ/, Arthur (1821–95), English mathematician and barrister. Cayley wrote almost a thousand mathematical papers in algebra and geometry. These include articles on determinants, the newly developing group theory, and the algebra of matrices. He also studied dynamics and physical astronomy. The Cayley numbers, a generalization of complex numbers, are named after him.

Cayley[2] /'keɪlɪ/, Sir George (1773–1857), British engineer, the father of British aeronautics. He is best known for his understanding of the principles of flight, his model gliders, and the first man-carrying glider flight in 1853. Cayley's research, inventions, and designs covered schemes and devices for land reclamation, artificial limbs, theatre architecture, railways, lifeboats, finned projectiles, optics, electricity, hot-air engines, and what was later called the Caterpillar tractor. He was a founder of the original Polytechnic Institution (1838), and was an MP for a time.

Ceaușescu /tʃaʊ'ʃesku:/, Nicolae (1918–89), Romanian Communist statesman, first

President of the Socialist Republic of Romania 1974–89. Noted for his independence of the USSR, for many years he fostered his own personality cult, making his wife Elena his deputy and appointing many other members of his family to high office. His regime became increasingly totalitarian, repressive, and corrupt; a popular uprising in December 1989 resulted in its downfall and in the arrest, summary trial, and execution of Ceauşescu and his wife.

Cecil /'ses(ə)l, 'sɪs-/, William, see BURGHLEY.

Cecilia, St /sɪ'siːljə/ (2nd or 3rd century), Roman martyr. According to legend, she took a vow of celibacy but was forced to marry a young Roman; she converted her husband to Christianity and both were martyred. She is frequently pictured playing the organ and is the patron saint of church music. Feast day, 22 November.

Céline /seɪ'liːn/, Louis-Ferdinand (pseudonym of Louis-Ferdinand Destouches) (1894–1961), French novelist. He was a doctor by profession whose autobiographical novel, the truculent satire *Voyage au bout de la nuit*, aroused considerable and often hostile comment on its publication in 1932. In 1944 he was forced to flee to Germany and Denmark owing to his professed anti-Semitism, but returned to Paris after the Second World War.

Cellini /tʃɪ'liːnɪ/, Benvenuto (1500–71), Italian goldsmith and sculptor. His work is characterized by its elaborate virtuosity; the salt-cellar of gold and enamel which he made while working for Francis I of France is an outstanding example and typifies the late Renaissance style. The latter part of his life was spent in Florence, where he cast the bronze *Perseus* (1545–54), regarded as his masterpiece. His autobiography is famous for its racy style and its vivid picture of Italian Renaissance life.

Celsius /'selsɪəs/, Anders (1701–44), Swedish astronomer, best known for his thermometer scale. He was professor of astronomy at Uppsala, and joined an expedition to measure a meridian in the north, which verified Newton's theory that the earth is flattened at the poles. In 1742 he advocated a metric temperature scale with 100° as the freezing-point of water and 0° as the boiling-point; however, the thermometer which was actually introduced at the Uppsala Observatory had its scale reversed.

Cerenkov see CHERENKOV.

Cervantes /sɜ:'vænti:z/, Miguel de (1547–1616) (full surname Cervantes Saavedra), Spanish novelist and dramatist. His most famous work is *Don Quixote* (1605–15), a satire on chivalric romances. It tells the story of an amiable knight who imagines himself called upon to roam the world in search of adventure on his horse Rosinante, accompanied by the shrewd squire Sancho Panza. The character of Don Quixote had widespread appeal in many other countries and continues to inspire innumerable imitations; his name has passed into the English language as the adjective *quixotic*.

Cetshwayo /se'tʃweɪəʊ/ (also **Cetewayo** /ˌsetɪ'weɪəʊ/) (c.1826–84), Zulu king. Cetshwayo became ruler of Zululand in 1873. He increased his army to defend his territory against the Boers and defeated the British at Isandhlwana in 1879. His capital, Ulundi, was captured eight months later, whereupon he was deposed and sent to London. In 1883 British efforts to restore him failed and he was driven out by an anti-royalist faction.

Cézanne /seɪ'zæn/, Paul (1839–1906), French painter. Although his early work is associated with impressionism, it is with post-impressionism that he is most closely identified. From the 1880s his work is dominated by the increasing use of simplified geometrical forms (the cylinder, the sphere, and the cone), which he regarded as being the structural basis of nature; this later work was an important influence on the development of cubism. He is especially known for his landscapes, many of which depict the Mont Sainte-Victoire in Provence, for still lifes such as *Still Life with Cupid* (1895), and for his *Bathers* paintings (1890–1905).

Chabrol /ʃæ'brɒl/, Claude (born 1930), French film director. He gained recognition in the late 1950s as one of the directors of the *nouvelle vague*, making his directorial début with *Le Beau serge* (1958). An admirer of the work of Alfred Hitchcock, he has directed many films that combine mystery and suspense with studies of personal relationships and social situations. Notable films include *Les Biches* (1968) and *Le Boucher* (1970).

Chadwick /'tʃædwɪk/, Sir James (1891–1974), English physicist. He became assistant director at the Cavendish Laboratory, Cambridge, where he studied the artificial

disintegration of elements such as beryllium when bombarded by alpha particles. This led to the discovery of the neutron, for which he received the 1935 Nobel Prize for physics. During World War Two he was involved with the atom bomb project, and afterwards stressed the importance of university research into nuclear physics.

Chagall /ʃəˈgɑːl/, Marc (1887–1985), Russian-born French painter and graphic artist. Working chiefly in Paris, he was associated with the avant-garde circle of Delaunay, Modigliani, and Chaim Soutine. Inspired by fauvism and Russian folk art, he used rich emotive colour and dream imagery, as can be seen in paintings such as *Maternity* (1913); his early work had a significant influence on the development of surrealism. Other achievements came within theatre design (the costumes and decor for Stravinsky's *The Firebird*, 1945), stained-glass windows, and murals.

Chain /tʃeɪn/, Sir Ernst Boris (1906–79), German-born British biochemist. (See FLOREY.)

Chaka see SHAKA.

Chaliapin /ʃæˈljɑːpɪn/, Fyodor (Ivanovich) (1873–1938), Russian operatic bass. He made his début in St Petersburg, later going to Moscow, where he excelled in Russian opera, most notably in the title role of Mussorgsky's *Boris Godunov*. He left Russia after the Revolution and developed a successful international career, appearing in a wide range of operas in many different countries.

Chamberlain[1] /ˈtʃeɪmbəlɪn/, Joseph (1836–1914), British Liberal statesman. He became a Liberal MP in 1876, but left the party in 1886 because of Gladstone's support of Irish Home Rule. The leader of the Liberal Unionists from 1891, in the coalition government of 1895 he served as Colonial Secretary, in which post he played a leading role in the handling of the Second Boer War.

Chamberlain[2] /ˈtʃeɪmbəlɪn/, (Arthur) Neville (1869–1940), British Conservative statesman, Prime Minister 1937–40. The son of Joseph Chamberlain, as Prime Minister of a coalition government he pursued a policy of appeasement towards Germany, Italy, and Japan; in 1938 he signed the Munich Agreement ceding the Sudetenland to Germany, which he claimed would mean 'peace in our time'. Although the policy was primarily intended to postpone

war until Britain had rearmed, it caused increasing discontent in his own party; he was forced to abandon it and prepare for war when Hitler invaded the rest of Czechoslovakia in 1939. Chamberlain's war leadership proved inadequate and he was replaced by Winston Churchill.

Chamberlain[3] /ˈtʃeɪmbəlɪn/, Owen (born 1920), American physicist. He worked on the Manhattan Project for the development of the atom bomb during the Second World War, after which he investigated subatomic particles using a bevatron accelerator. He and E. G. Segrè discovered the antiproton in 1955, and four years later they shared the Nobel Prize for physics.

Chambers /ˈtʃeɪmbəz/, Sir William (1723–96), Scottish architect. Travels in the Far East and studies in France and Italy helped to mould his eclectic but conservative neo-classical style. His most notable buildings include Somerset House in London (1776) and the pagoda in Kew Gardens (1757–62).

Champlain /ʃæmˈpleɪn/, Samuel de (1567–1635), French explorer and colonial statesman. He made his first voyage to Canada in 1603, and between 1604 and 1607 explored the eastern coast of North America. In 1608 he was sent to establish a settlement at Quebec, where he developed alliances with the native peoples for trade and defence. He was appointed Lieutenant-Governor in 1612; much of his subsequent career was spent exploring the Canadian interior. After capture and imprisonment by the English (1629–32), he returned to Canada for a final spell as governor (1633–5).

Champollion /ʃɒmˈpɒljɒn/, Jean-François (1790–1832), French Egyptologist. A pioneer in the study of ancient Egypt, he is best known for his success in deciphering some of the hieroglyphic inscriptions on the Rosetta Stone in 1822.

Chandler /ˈtʃɑːndlə(r)/, Raymond (Thornton) (1888–1959), American novelist. Of British descent and educated largely in England (1896–1912), Chandler is particularly remembered as the creator of the private detective Philip Marlowe and as one of the exponents of the tough, realistic style of hard-boiled detective fiction. His novels, which include *The Big Sleep* (1939), *Farewell, My Lovely* (1940), and *The Long Goodbye* (1953), are written in an ironic, terse, and fast-moving style; many were made into films, especially of the *film noir* genre,

and Chandler himself worked on the screenplays.

Chandragupta Maurya /ˌtʃʌndrəˈɡʊptə ˈmaʊrɪə/ (c.325–297 BC), Indian emperor. He founded the Mauryan empire, the first empire in India to extend over most of the subcontinent. From his capital at Paliputra he expanded westwards across the River Indus, annexing provinces deep into Afghanistan from Alexander's Greek successors. The empire continued to expand after his death, but ended in 185 BC.

Chandrasekhar /ˌtʃʌndrəˈsiːkə(r), -ˈseɪkə(r)/, Subrahmanyan (1910–95), Indian-born American astronomer. He worked on stellar evolution, suggesting the process whereby some stars eventually collapse to form a dense white dwarf. He demonstrated that for this to happen the star's mass must not exceed 1.44 solar masses (the Chandrasekhar limit): stars above this mass collapse further to form neutron stars.

Chanel /ʃəˈnel/, Coco (born Gabrielle Bonheur Chanel) (1883–1971), French couturière. She opened her first Paris couture house in 1924, quickly achieving success with her simple but sophisticated designs. Loose and comfortable, her garments were a radical departure from the dominant stiff corseted styles of the day. She also manufactured her own range of perfumes, costume jewellery, and textiles.

Chaney /ˈtʃeɪnɪ/, Lon (full name Alonso Chaney) (1883–1930), American actor. In a career which began in 1913 Chaney played a wide variety of deformed villains and macabre characters in more than 150 films. He attracted the soubriquet 'the Man of a Thousand Faces' both for his versatility and for his skill in make-up. Chaney was especially known for his sympathetic portrayal of grotesques, such as Quasimodo in The Hunchback of Notre Dame (1923) and the musician in The Phantom of the Opera (1925).

Chanute /tʃəˈnuːt/, Octave (1832–1910), French-born American aviation pioneer. Educated as a railway engineer, he built his first glider in 1896 and later produced others, of which the most successful was a biplane which made over 700 flights. His encouragement of the Wright brothers and of the serious study of aeronautics greatly assisted them in making the world's first controlled powered flight.

Chaplin /ˈtʃæplɪn/, Sir Charles Spencer ('Charlie') (1889–1977), English film actor and director. Moving to Hollywood in 1914 he made many short comedies, mostly playing a little bowler-hatted tramp, a character which remained his trademark for more than twenty-five years. A master of mime who combined pathos with slapstick clowning, he was best suited to the silent medium; his most successful films include The Kid (1921) and The Gold Rush (1925). The director of all his films, he combined speech and mime in Modern Times (1936), while The Great Dictator (1940), a satire on Hitler, was his first proper sound film and his last appearance in his familiar bowler-hatted role.

Chapman /ˈtʃæpmən/, George (c.1560–1634), English poet and dramatist. Although acclaimed as a dramatist in his day, he is now chiefly known for his translations of Homer; twelve books of the Iliad were published in 1611 and the complete Iliad and Odyssey in 1616. They are commemorated in Keats's sonnet 'On First Looking into Chapman's Homer' (1817).

Chappell /ˈtʃæp(ə)l/, Gregory Stephen ('Greg') (born 1948), Australian cricketer. After making his first-class début for South Australia in 1966, he played county cricket in England in 1968 and 1969, and was first selected to play for his country in 1970. He captained Australia from 1975 to 1984, becoming the first Australian to score more than 7,000 runs in test matches.

Charcot /ˈʃɑːkəʊ/, Jean-Martin (1825–93), French neurologist. Working at the Salpêtrière clinic in Paris, he established links between various neurological conditions and particular lesions in the central nervous system. He described several such diseases, some of which are named after him, and he is regarded as one of the founders of modern neurology. Charcot's work on hysteria was taken up by his pupil Sigmund Freud.

Charlemagne /ˈʃɑːləˌmeɪn/ (Latin Carolus Magnus Charles the Great) (742–814), king of the Franks 768–814 and Holy Roman emperor (as Charles I) 800–14. He created an empire by conquering and Christianizing the Saxons (772–7; 782–5), Lombards (774), and Avars (791–9), and restoring areas of Italy to the pope. His coronation by Pope Leo III in Rome on Christmas Day, 800, is taken as having inaugurated the Holy Roman Empire. He gave government

new moral drive and religious responsibility, and encouraged commerce and agriculture. A well-educated man, he promoted the arts and education, and under Alcuin his principal court at Aachen became a major centre of learning. The political cohesion of his empire did not last, but the influence of his scholars persisted in the Carolingian Renaissance.

Charles[1] /tʃɑːlz/ the name of two kings of England, Scotland, and Ireland:

Charles I (1600–49), son of James I, reigned 1625–49. His reign was dominated by the deepening religious and constitutional crisis that eventually resulted in the English Civil War. His attempt to rule without Parliament (1629–40) eventually failed when he was obliged to recall Parliament to fund his war with Scotland; disputes with the new Parliament led to civil war in 1642. Charles surrendered to the Scots in 1646 and was handed over to Parliament in 1647. He escaped and made an alliance with the Scots in return for religious concessions, but the Royalist forces were defeated in 1648 and the Parliamentary army demanded Charles's death. He was tried by a special Parliamentary court and beheaded.

Charles II (1630–85), son of Charles I, reigned 1660–85. After his father's execution in 1649 Charles was declared king in Scotland and then crowned there in 1651, but was forced into exile the same year, when his army attempted to invade England and was defeated by Cromwell's forces at Worcester. He remained in exile on the Continent for nine years before he was restored after the collapse of Cromwell's regime. Charles displayed considerable adroitness in handling the difficult constitutional situation, but continuing religious and political strife dogged his reign. Although he failed to produce a legitimate heir, he moved to ensure the Protestant succession by arranging the marriage of his niece Mary to William of Orange.

Charles[2] /tʃɑːlz/ the name of four kings of Spain:

Charles I (1500–58), son of Philip I, reigned 1516–56, Holy Roman emperor (as Charles V) 1519–56. He united the Spanish and imperial thrones when he inherited the latter in 1519. His reign was characterized by the struggle against Protestantism in Germany, by rebellion in Castile, and by war with France (1521–44). Exhausted by these struggles, Charles handed

Naples, the Netherlands, and Spain over to his son Philip II and the imperial crown (1556) to his brother Ferdinand, and retired to a monastery in Spain.

Charles II (1661–1700), reigned 1665–1700. The last Habsburg to be king of Spain, he inherited a kingdom already in a decline which he was unable to halt. Childless, he chose Philip of Anjou, grandson of Louis XIV of France, as his successor; this ultimately gave rise to the War of the Spanish Succession.

Charles III (1716–88), reigned 1759–88. He tried with some success to restore Spain's position as an international power through an increase in foreign trade, while at home his reforms brought Spain a brief cultural and economic revival.

Charles IV (1748–1819), reigned 1788–1808. He was dominated by his wife Maria Luisa and her lover Manuel de Godoy (Prime Minister from 1792). During the Napoleonic Wars he suffered the loss of the Spanish fleet, destroyed along with that of France at Trafalgar in 1805. Following the French invasion of Spain in 1807, Charles was forced to abdicate. He died in exile in Rome.

Charles[3] /tʃɑːlz/ the name of seven Holy Roman emperors:

Charles I see CHARLEMAGNE.

Charles II (823–77), reigned 875–7.

Charles III (839–88), reigned 881–7.

Charles IV (1316–78), reigned 1355–78.

Charles V Charles I of Spain (see CHARLES[2]).

Charles VI (1685–1740), reigned 1711–40. His claim to the Spanish throne instigated the War of the Spanish Succession, but he was ultimately unsuccessful. He became emperor on the death of his elder brother; with no surviving male heirs, he drafted the Pragmatic Sanction in an attempt to ensure that his daughter Maria Theresa succeeded to the Habsburg dominions. The failure of this to be accepted by the whole of Europe triggered a struggle for power on Charles's death and the War of the Austrian Succession.

Charles VII (1697–1745), reigned 1742–5.

Charles[4] /tʃɑːlz/, Ray (born Ray Charles Robinson) (born 1930), American pianist and singer. Despite becoming totally blind at the age of 6, he persevered with a musical career. He drew on blues, jazz, and country music for his inspiration and

achieved stardom with songs such as 'What'd I Say' (1959), 'Georgia On My Mind' (1960), and 'Busted' (1963).

Charles VII /tʃɑːlz, French ʃarl/ (1403–61), king of France 1422–61. At the time of his accession to the throne, much of northern France was under English occupation, including Reims, where he should have been crowned. After the intervention of Joan of Arc, however, the French experienced a dramatic military revival. Charles was crowned at Reims, and his reign eventually saw the defeat of the English and the end of the Hundred Years War. He modernized the administration of the army and did much to lay the foundations of French power in the following decades.

Charles XII /tʃɑːlz/ (also **Karl XII** /kɑːl/) (1682–1718), king of Sweden 1697–1718. Three years after his succession, he embarked on the Great Northern War against the encircling powers of Denmark, Poland-Saxony, and Russia. In the early years he won a series of victories, but in 1709 he embarked on an expedition deep into Russia which ended in the destruction of his army at Poltava and the internment of Charles until 1715. He resumed his military career after his return but was killed while besieging a fortress in Norway.

Charles, Prince /tʃɑːlz/, Charles Philip Arthur George, Prince of Wales (born 1948), heir apparent to Elizabeth II. Educated at Gordonstoun School in Scotland and Trinity College, Cambridge, he was invested as Prince of Wales in 1969. He served in the Royal Navy 1971–6, and married Lady Diana Spencer (see DIANA, PRINCESS) in 1981; the couple publicly announced their separation in 1993 and divorced in 1996. They have two children, Prince William Arthur Philip Louis (born 1982) and Prince Henry Charles Albert David ('Harry', born 1984).

Charles Martel /mɑːˈtel/ (c.688–741), Frankish ruler of the eastern part of the Frankish kingdom from 715 and the whole kingdom from 719. He earned his nickname *Martel* ('the hammer') from his victory at Poitiers in 732, which effectively checked the Muslim advance into Europe. His rule marked the beginning of Carolingian power; Charlemagne was his grandson.

Charlton[1] /tʃɑːlt(ə)n/, John ('Jack') (born 1935), English footballer and manager, brother of Bobby Charlton. A rugged defender, he played for Leeds United (1952–

73) and was a member of the England side that won the World Cup in 1966. He later managed Middlesbrough, Sheffield Wednesday, and Newcastle United before taking over the management of the Republic of Ireland national team (1986–95).

Charlton[2] /tʃɑːlt(ə)n/, Sir Robert ('Bobby') (born 1937), English footballer, brother of Jack Charlton. An outstanding striker, he played for Manchester United 1954–73, appearing 751 times and scoring 245 goals, and for England (1957–73); he scored forty-nine goals for his country (a record for an England player) and was a member of the side that won the World Cup in 1966. After retiring as a player he managed Preston North End (1973–5) and became a director of Manchester United (from 1984).

Chateaubriand /ˌʃætəʊˈbriːɒn/, François-René, Vicomte de (1768–1848), French writer and diplomat. An important figure in early French romanticism, he established his literary reputation with *Atala* (1801), but *Le Génie du christianisme* (1802), which contributed to the post-Revolution religious revival in France, won him his greatest fame. A supporter of the royalist cause during the French Revolution, he lived in exile in England (1793–1800), where he published his *Essai sur les révolutions* (1797). His autobiography, *Mémoires d'outre-tombe* (1849–50), gives an eloquent account of his life against a background of political upheaval.

Chatham /tʃætəm/, 1st Earl of, see PITT[1].

Chatterton /tʃætət(ə)n/, Thomas (1752–70), English poet. He is chiefly remembered for his fabricated poems professing to be the work of Thomas Rowley, an imaginary 15th-century monk. Poverty and lack of recognition drove Chatterton to suicide at the age of 17. First published in 1777, the Rowley poems were eventually proved spurious in the philologist W. W. Skeat's 1871 edition. Chatterton's tragic life was much romanticized by Keats and Wordsworth.

Chaucer /tʃɔːsə(r)/, Geoffrey (c.1342–1400), English poet. Born in London, he served at court and in a number of official posts before going on a series of diplomatic missions to Spain, Italy, France, and Flanders in the 1370s. From the late 1380s, particularly with the death of his wife in 1387, he suffered a number of periods of misfortune and financial insecurity. His early work (including *The Book of the Duchess*,

1369) shows the influence of French literature; he also translated part of the *Roman de la rose* during this period. During the middle period of his career, in which he wrote the long narrative poem *Troilus and Criseyde* (1385) and *The Parlement of Fowles*, his work was particularly influenced by Italian poets of his day, such as Petrarch and Boccaccio. It was not until the later part of his life that he wrote his most famous work, the *Canterbury Tales* (*c*.1387–1400), a cycle of linked tales told by a group of pilgrims who meet in a London tavern before their pilgrimage to the shrine of St Thomas à Becket in Canterbury. In this work in particular Chaucer demonstrated skills of characterization, humour, versatility, and a distinctive narrative style that established him as the traditional starting-point for English literature and as the first great English poet; in addition Chaucer's vernacular work helped to establish the East Midland dialect of English of his day as the standard literary language.

Chauliac /'ʃəʊlɪˌæk/, Guy de (*c*.1300–68), French physician. Probably the most influential surgeon of the Middle Ages, he was private physician to three successive popes in Avignon from 1342. In his *Chirurgia Magna* (1363) Chauliac was the first to describe many surgical techniques, and it remained the standard work in Europe until at least the 17th century.

Cheever /'tʃiːvə(r)/, John (1912–82), American short-story writer and novelist. He was contributing short stories regularly for the *New Yorker* by the age of 22. His stories frequently deal satirically with affluent New Englanders living in suburbia, and have been collected in volumes such as *The Housebreaker of Shady Hill* (1958). His novels include *The Wapshot Chronicle* (1957) and its sequel, *The Wapshot Scandal* (1964).

Chekhov /'tʃekɒf/, Anton (Pavlovich) (1860–1904), Russian dramatist and short-story writer. Chekhov studied medicine in Moscow, and combined his medical practice with writing short humorous stories for journals. He is best known as the author of such plays as *The Seagull* (1895), *Uncle Vanya* (1900), *The Three Sisters* (1901), and *The Cherry Orchard* (1904). First produced at the Moscow Art Theatre under Konstantin Stanislavsky, they established the theatre's reputation and style. Chekhov's work portrays upper-class life in pre-revolutionary Russia with a blend of naturalism and symbolism and almost imperceptible shifts from comedy to tragedy. He had a considerable influence on 20th-century drama; George Bernard Shaw paid tribute to him in *Heartbreak House* (1919).

Cheops /'kiːɒps/ (Egyptian name Khufu) (*fl.* early 26th century BC), Egyptian pharaoh of the 4th dynasty. He commissioned the building of the Great Pyramid at Giza.

Cherenkov /tʃɪ'reŋkɒf/, Pavel (Alekseevich) (also **Cerenkov**) (1904–90), Soviet physicist. From the 1930s he investigated the effects of high-energy particles, in particular the blue light emitted from water containing a radioactive substance. He suggested the cause of this radiation (an example of what is now called *Cerenkov radiation*), and shared the 1958 Nobel Prize for physics for this discovery.

Chernenko /tʃə'njeŋkəʊ/, Konstantin (Ustinovich) (1911–85), Soviet statesman, General Secretary of the Communist Party of the USSR and President 1984–5. Born in Siberia, he became a full member of the Politburo in 1978 and was a close associate of Brezhnev from this time. Chernenko succeeded Yuri Andropov to the presidency, but died after only thirteen months in office. He was succeeded by Mikhail Gorbachev.

Cherubini /ˌkerʊ'biːnɪ/, (Maria) Luigi (Carlo Zenobio Salvatore) (1760–1842), Italian composer. Born in Florence, he spent most of his composing career in Paris (where he became director of the Conservatoire) and is principally known for his church music and operas. He is now chiefly remembered for his opera *The Water-Carrier* (1800), of which the overture is sometimes still performed.

Cherwell /'tʃɑːwel/, Frederick Alexander Lindemann, 1st Viscount (1886–1957), German-born British physicist. He studied a wide variety of subjects, and a number of theories and items are named after him. These include a theory of specific heat, a theory of the upper atmosphere, a formula concerning the melting-point of crystals, an electrometer, and a glass for transmitting X-rays. He was Churchill's adviser on scientific and aeronautical matters during the war.

Cheshire /'tʃeʃə(r)/, (Geoffrey) Leonard (1917–92), British airman and philanthropist. He served as a fighter pilot in the Second World War, was awarded the VC in

1944 for his one hundred bombing missions, and was an official observer of the atom bomb dropped on Nagasaki in 1945. From the late 1940s he founded the Cheshire Foundation Homes for the disabled and incurably sick; these spread to forty-five countries. Cheshire married the philanthropist Sue Ryder in 1959.

Chesterton /ˈtʃestət(ə)n/, G(ilbert) K(eith) (1874–1936), English essayist, novelist, and critic. He first came to prominence as a journalist for *The Speaker*, in which, with Hilaire Belloc, he took an anti-imperialist platform on the Boer War question. His best-known novel is his 'Merry England' fantasy *The Napoleon of Notting Hill* (1904), but he is also widely remembered for his creation of the character Father Brown, a priest with a talent for crime detection, who first appears in *The Innocence of Father Brown* (1911). Chesterton became a Roman Catholic in 1922; his other writings include biographies of St Francis of Assisi and St Thomas Aquinas.

Chevalier /ʃəˈvælɪˌeɪ/, Maurice (1888–1972), French singer and actor. He gained an international reputation in the Paris music-halls of the 1920s, particularly in the Folies-Bergère, where he regularly partnered the French dancer Mistinguett (1874–1956). He went on to star in successful Hollywood musicals such as *Innocents of Paris* (1929), *Love Me Tonight* (1932), and *Gigi* (1958).

Chiang Kai-shek /ˌtʃjæŋ kaɪˈʃek/ (also **Jiang Jie Shi** /ˌdʒjæŋ dʒi: ˈʃi:/) (1887–1975), Chinese statesman and general, President of China 1928–31 and 1943–9 and of Taiwan 1950–75. A prominent general in the army of Sun Yat-sen, in 1925 he became leader of the Kuomintang when Sun Yatsen died, and launched a military campaign to unite China. In the 1930s he concentrated more on defeating the Chinese Communists than on resisting the invading Japanese, but he proved unable to establish order and was defeated by the Communists after the end of the Second World War. Forced to abandon mainland China in 1949, he set up a separate Nationalist Chinese State in Taiwan.

Chichester[2] /ˈtʃɪtʃɪstə(r)/, Sir Francis (Charles) (1901–72), English yachtsman. In 1960 he won the first solo transatlantic yacht race in his boat *Gipsy Moth III*. In 1966–7 he sailed alone round the world in *Gipsy Moth IV*, taking 107 days to sail from Plymouth to Sydney, and 119 days to make the return voyage. He was knighted on his return.

Chifley /ˈtʃɪflɪ/, Joseph Benedict (1885–1951), Australian Labor statesman, Prime Minister 1945–9. He entered Parliament in 1928; after the Second World War he became Prime Minister on the death of John Curtin. During his term of office he continued to fulfil Labor's nationalization and welfare programme; he also initiated Australia's immigration policy and the Snowy Mountains hydroelectric scheme. He was defeated in the 1949 election but remained leader of the Labor Party until his death.

Childers /ˈtʃɪldəz/, (Robert) Erskine (1870–1922), Irish writer and political activist, born in England. His fame as a writer stems from his novel *The Riddle of the Sands* (1903), in which two amateur yachtsmen discover German preparations for an invasion of England. A supporter of Irish Home Rule from 1910, he settled in Ireland in 1920, became a Sinn Fein MP in 1921, and, in the same year, Minister of Propaganda. In 1922 he was court-martialled and shot for his involvement in the civil war following the establishment of the Irish Free State. His son Erskine Hamilton Childers (1905–74) was President of Ireland 1973–4.

Chippendale /ˈtʃɪp(ə)n̩ˌdeɪl/, Thomas (1718–79), English furniture-maker and designer. He is one of the most famous names in the history of British furniture, mainly on account of his book *The Gentleman and Cabinetmaker's Director* (1754). This was the first comprehensive book of furniture designs and was immensely influential in Britain and the US. Many of the designs are in a neoclassical vein, with elements of the French rococo, chinoiserie, and Gothic revival styles.

Chirac /ˈʃɪəræk/, Jacques (René) (born 1932), French statesman, Prime Minister 1974–6 and 1986–8 and President since 1995. He was elected mayor of Paris in 1977, a position he held for eighteen years. The founder and leader of the right-wing RPR (Rally for the Republic) Party, Chirac headed the right's coalition in the National Assembly during the socialist government of 1981–6. When his coalition was victorious in the 1986 National Assembly elections, he was appointed Prime Minister by the socialist President François Mitterrand. After an unsuccessful bid for the presidency in 1988,

Chirac was elected to succeed Mitterrand as President in 1995.

Chirico /'kɪrɪ,kəʊ/, Giorgio de (1888–1978), Greek-born Italian painter. After 1910 he started painting disconnected and unsettling dream images, a style that became known as 'metaphysical painting'. His work exerted a significant influence on surrealism and he participated in the surrealist's Paris exhibition of 1925. Major works include *The Uncertainty of the Poet* (1913), portraying a bust with bananas, an arcade, and a distant train.

Chomsky /'tʃɒmskɪ/, (Avram) Noam (born 1928), American theoretical linguist and political activist. His theory of transformational grammar is set out in *Syntactic Structures* (1957). Language is seen as a formal system possessing an underlying 'deep structure', from which the 'surface structure' is derived by a series of transformations. A grammar is seen as a set of rules capable of generating all and only the grammatical sentences of a language when applied to the lexicon of that language. A distinction is made between a speaker's linguistic competence, which is idealized, and actual performance; the theory sets out to account only for the former. Chomsky has revised the theory since 1957, most notably in *Lectures on Government and Binding* (1981). In addition, Chomsky was a leading opponent of the American involvement in the Vietnam War, and later also voiced his doubts about the American role in the Gulf War of 1991.

Chopin[1] /'ʃəʊpæn/, Frédéric (François) (Polish name Fryderyk Franciszek Szopen) (1810–49), Polish-born French composer and pianist. A concert pianist from the age of 8, he wrote almost exclusively for the piano. Inspired by Polish folk music, his mazurkas (fifty-five in all) and polonaises (some thirteen) were to become his trademarks. He is also noted for short piano pieces full of poetic intensity; good examples are his nineteen nocturnes and twenty-four preludes. As well as writing for solo piano, he wrote two piano concertos (1829; 1830). For some years Chopin was the lover of the French writer George Sand, but their affair ended two years before his death from tuberculosis.

Chopin[2] /'ʃəʊpæn/, Kate (O'Flaherty) (1851–1904), American novelist and short-story writer. In 1882 she returned to her native St Louis from Lousiana following the death of her Creole husband. There she began to write her noted interpretations of Creole and Cajun life in collections such as *Bayou Folk* (1894) and *A Night in Acidie* (1897). Her novel *The Awakening* (1899) met with a storm of criticism owing to its frank treatment of sexuality.

Chou En-lai see ZHOU ENLAI.

Chrétien /'kreɪtjen/, (Joseph-Jacques) Jean (born 1934), Canadian Liberal statesman, Prime Minister since 1993. He became an MP in 1963 and held a series of ministerial posts in the Pearson and Trudeau administrations before serving briefly as deputy Prime Minister in 1984. As leader of the Liberal Party from 1990, he led the party to victory in the 1993 elections. A Quebecker, Chrétien has always been committed to keeping Quebec within the Canadian federation.

Chrétien de Troyes /də 'trwʌ/ (12th century), French poet. The author of courtly romances, including some of the earliest on Arthurian themes, he is also thought to have written a romance about the legendary knight Tristram. Of his four extant volumes of romances, *Lancelot* (c.1177–81) is the most famous, while his unfinished *Perceval* (1181–90) contains the first reference in literature to the Holy Grail.

Christian /'krɪstɪən, 'krɪstʃən/, Fletcher (c.1764–c.1793), English seaman and mutineer. In 1787 he became master's mate under Captain William Bligh on HMS *Bounty*, a ship sailing for the West Indies. In April 1789 Christian seized the ship and cast Bligh adrift on account of his alleged tyranny. In 1790 the crew settled on Pitcairn Island, where Christian was probably killed by Tahitians.

Christie[1] /'krɪstɪ/, Dame Agatha (1890–1976), English writer of detective fiction. Many of her novels feature the Belgian Hercule Poirot or the resourceful Miss Marple, her two most famous and successful creations. Among her best-known detective stories are *Murder on the Orient Express* (1934) and *Death on the Nile* (1937). Her novels are characterized by brisk, humorous dialogue and ingenious plots. She also wrote plays; *The Mousetrap* (1952) has had a record run of more than forty years on the London stage.

Christie[2] /'krɪstɪ/, Linford (born 1960), Jamaican-born British sprinter. Having won Olympic silver medals in the 100 metres

and 4 × 100 metres relay events in 1988, Christie took the individual 100-metre title in 1992. This was followed by the world championship title at this distance in 1993, and in 1994 he took the European 100-metre championship title for the third consecutive time.

Chrysostom, St John /'krɪsəstəm/ (c.347–407), Doctor of the Church, bishop of Constantinople. His name (Greek for 'golden-mouthed') is a tribute to the eloquence of his preaching. As patriarch of Constantinople, he attempted to reform the corrupt state of the court, clergy, and people; this offended many, including the Empress Eudoxia (died 404), who banished him in 403. Feast day, 27 January.

Churchill[1] /'tʃɜːtʃɪl/, Caryl (born 1938), English dramatist. She is best known for the satire *Serious Money* (1986); written in rhyming couplets, it deals with 1980s speculators and the ethics of high finance. Her other plays include *Top Girls* (1982) and *Mad Forest* (1990).

Churchill[2] /'tʃɜːtʃɪl/, Sir Winston (Leonard Spencer) (1874–1965), British Conservative statesman, Prime Minister 1940–5 and 1951–5. He served as Home Secretary (1910–11) under the Liberals and First Lord of the Admiralty (1911–15), but lost this post after the unsuccessful Allied attack on the Turks in the Dardanelles. He was only to regain it in 1939 under Neville Chamberlain, whom he replaced as Prime Minister in May 1940. Serving as war leader of a coalition government until 1945, Churchill demonstrated rare qualities of leadership and outstanding gifts as an orator. Part of his contribution to victory was to forge and maintain the Alliance, especially with the US, which defeated the Axis Powers. After the victory he was defeated in the general election of 1945; elected Prime Minister for a second term in 1951, he retired from the premiership in 1955, but remained an MP until 1964. His writings include *The Second World War* (1948–53) and *A History of the English-Speaking Peoples* (1956–8); he was awarded the Nobel Prize for literature in 1953.

Churchward /'tʃɜːtʃwəd/, George Jackson (1857–1933), English railway engineer. He spent most of his working life at the Swindon works of the Great Western Railway, rising to take effective control of rolling stock from 1899 to 1921. Churchward made Swindon the most modern locomotive works in the country, and is particularly remembered for the standard four-cylinder 4-6-0 locomotives that he introduced in 1903–11. These formed the basis of many subsequent designs. Churchward also became the first mayor of Swindon; he was killed while crossing a railway line.

Cibber /'sɪbə(r)/, Colley (1671–1757), English actor, theatre manager, and dramatist. He excelled in comic roles and won recognition as a dramatist with his first comedy, *Love's Last Shift* (1696). He became joint manager of Drury Lane, where he spent most of his career, in 1711. After his much-ridiculed appointment as Poet Laureate in 1730 he wrote an *Apology for the Life of Mr Colley Cibber, Comedian* (1740).

Cicero /'sɪsə,rəʊ/, Marcus Tullius (106–43 BC), Roman statesman, orator, and writer. A supporter of Pompey against Julius Caesar, in the *Philippics* (43 BC) he attacked Mark Antony, who had him put to death. As an orator and writer, Cicero established a model for Latin prose; his surviving works include many speeches, treatises on rhetoric, philosophical works, and books of letters, recording his personal and political interests and activities.

Cid, El /sɪd/ (also **the Cid**) (born Rodrigo Díaz de Vivar), Count of Bivar (c.1043–99), Spanish soldier. A champion of Christianity against the Moors, he began his long fighting career in 1065; in 1094 he captured Valencia, which he went on to rule. He is immortalized in the Spanish *Poema del Cid* (12th century) and in Corneille's play *Le Cid* (1637).

Clair /kleə(r)/, René (born René Lucien Chomette) (1898–1981), French film director. He made a number of silent films, notably *Un Chapeau de paille d'Italie* (1927); his early sound films included *Sous les toits de Paris* (1930), *Le Million* (1931), and *À nous la liberté* (1931). He later achieved wider success with *Les Belles de nuit* (1952). Clair was always involved in the scriptwriting for his films, which typically contain elements of surrealism, underpinned by satire.

Clapton /'klæptən/, Eric (born 1945), English blues and rock guitarist, singer, and composer. He played in the Yardbirds and then formed his own group, Cream (1966–8), whose lengthy improvisations and experimental harmonies were influential in the development of rock music. The song 'Layla' (1972) is perhaps his best known;

since then he has developed a restrained style that displays less of his instrumental virtuosity but has brought immense commercial success.

Clare /kleə(r)/, John (1793–1864), English poet. After working as a day labourer and gardener, he published *Poems Descriptive of Rural Life and Scenery* (1820). This was followed by *The Shepherd's Calendar* (1827), which has received renewed critical attention in recent years, along with *The Rural Muse* (1835) and other later poems. Clare's poetry is a simple man's celebration of the natural world; it is notable for its use of the poet's own dialect and grammar. In 1837 he was certified insane and spent the rest of his life in an asylum.

Clarendon /'klærəndən/, Earl of (title of Edward Hyde) (1609–74), English statesman and historian, chief adviser to Charles II 1660–7. He shifted his allegiance from the Roundheads to Charles I on the outbreak of the Civil War, becoming royal adviser and accompanying the king to Oxford. He was Chancellor of Oxford University (1660–7) and author of the prestigious *History of the Rebellion and Civil Wars in England*, which he began writing in 1646, but which was published posthumously (1702–4). A number of University and public buildings in Oxford are named after him.

Clare of Assisi, St /ə'siːzɪ/ (1194–1253), Italian saint and abbess. She joined St Francis in 1212 and together they founded the order of Poor Ladies of San Damiano, more commonly known as the 'Poor Clares', of which she was appointed abbess. She was canonized two years after her death and in 1958 Pope Pius XII declared her the patron saint of television, alluding to a story of her miraculously experiencing the Christmas midnight mass being held in the Church of St Francis in Assisi when on her deathbed. Feast day, 11 (formerly 12) August.

Clark /klɑːk/, William (1770–1838), American explorer. With Meriwether Lewis, he jointly commanded the Lewis and Clark expedition (1804–6) across the North American continent. (See LEWIS[5].)

Clarke[1] /klɑːk/, Arthur C(harles) (born 1917), English writer of science fiction. Originally a scientific researcher, he conceived the idea of communications satellites. He is better known as the writer of such novels as *Earthlight* (1955) and *The Fountains of Paradise* (1979). He also co-wrote

(with Stanley Kubrick, the film's director) the screenplay for the film *2001: A Space Odyssey* (1968); Clarke and Kubrick collaborated in writing the novel of the same title, published in the year of the film's release.

Clarke[2] /klɑːk/, Marcus (Andrew Hislop) (1846–81), British-born Australian writer. In 1863 he emigrated to Australia, where he worked on a sheep station before becoming a journalist. His fame is based on his novel *For the Term of his Natural Life* (1874) about an Australian penal settlement, as well as his shorter stories of Australian life, such as *Old Tales of a Young Country* (1871).

Claude Lorraine /ˌklɔːd lə'reɪn/ (also Lorrain) (born Claude Gellée) (1600–82), French painter. By 1630 he had achieved great fame in Italy, where he served his apprenticeship as a landscape painter. His paintings were so much in demand that he recorded them in the form of sketches in his *Liber Veritatis* (*c*.1635) to guard against forgeries. Although the influence of the late mannerists is evident in his early landscapes, his mature works (such as *Ascanius and the Stag*, 1682) concentrate on the poetic power of light and atmosphere. He was particularly admired in England, where he inspired the painters J. M. W. Turner and Richard Wilson (1714–82).

Claudius /'klɔːdɪəs/ (full name Tiberius Claudius Drusus Nero Germanicus) (10 BC–AD 54), Roman emperor 41–54. He spent his early life engaged in historical study, prevented from entering public life by his physical infirmity; he was proclaimed emperor after the murder of Caligula. His reign was noted for its restoration of order after Caligula's decadence and for its expansion of the Roman Empire, in particular his invasion of Britain in the year 43, in which he personally took part. His fourth wife, Agrippina (AD 15–59), is said to have killed him with a dish of poisoned mushrooms.

Clausewitz /'klauzə,vɪts/, Karl von (1780–1831), Prussian general and military theorist. A Chief of Staff in the Prussian army (1815) and later a general (1818), he went on to write the detailed study *On War* (1833), which had a marked influence on strategic studies in the 19th and 20th centuries.

Clausius /'klauzɪəs/, Rudolf (1822–88), German physicist, one of the founders of modern thermodynamics. He was the first, in 1850, to formulate the second law of thermodynamics, thereby reconciling

apparent conflicts between the work of Nicolas Carnot and James Joule. He later developed the concept of (and coined the term) entropy, which was his greatest contribution to physics. Clausius also carried out pioneering work on the kinetic theory of gases, in which he introduced the idea of the mean path length and effective radius of a moving molecule.

Clay /kleɪ/, Cassius, see MUHAMMAD ALI².

Cleese /kliːz/, John (Marwood) (born 1939), English comic actor and writer. He began his television writing and acting career in the 1960s, gaining widespread fame with *Monty Python's Flying Circus* (1969–74). He also co-wrote and starred in the situation comedy *Fawlty Towers* (1975–9). John Cleese has also appeared in films, notably *A Fish Called Wanda* (1988), which he wrote.

Cleisthenes /'klaɪsθəˌniːz/ (c.570 BC–c.508 BC), Athenian statesman. From 525 to 524 he served as principal archon (chief magistrate) of Athens. In 508 he sought to undermine the power of the nobility by forming an alliance with the Popular Assembly, passing laws to assign political responsibility according to citizenship of a locality as opposed to membership of a clan or kinship group. His reforms consolidated the Athenian democratic process begun by Solon and later influenced the policies of Pericles.

Clemenceau /'klemənˌsəʊ/, Georges (Eugène Benjamin) (1841–1929), French statesman, Prime Minister 1906–9 and 1917–20. A radical politician and journalist, he persistently opposed the government during the early years of the First World War, before becoming Premier and seeing France through to victory in 1918. He presided at the Versailles peace talks, where he pushed hard for a punitive settlement with Germany, but failed to obtain all that he demanded (notably the River Rhine as a frontier). He founded the newspaper *L'Aurore*.

Clemens /'klemənz/, Samuel Langhorne, see TWAIN.

Clement, St /'klemənt/ (known as St Clement of Rome) (1st century AD), pope c.88–c.97. Probably the third bishop of Rome after St Peter, he was the author of an epistle written c.96 to the Church at Corinth, insisting that certain deposed presbyters be reinstated. In later tradition he became the subject of a variety of legends; one held that he was martyred. Feast day, 23 November.

Clement of Alexandria, St /'klemənt, ˌælɪg'zɑːndrɪə/ (Latin name Titus Flavius Clemens) (c.150–c.215), Greek theologian. He was head of the catechetical school at Alexandria (c.190–202), but was forced to flee from Roman imperial persecution and was succeeded by his pupil Origen. Clement's main contribution to theological scholarship was to relate the ideas of Greek philosophy to the Christian faith. Feast day, 5 December.

Cleopatra /klɪə'pætrə/ (also **Cleopatra VII**) (69–30 BC), queen of Egypt 47–30. The last Ptolemaic ruler, she was restored to the throne by Julius Caesar, having been ousted by the guardians of her father Ptolemy Auletes (died 51). After her brief liaison with Caesar she forged a longer political and romantic alliance with Mark Antony, by whom she had three children. Their ambitions for the expansion of the Egyptian empire ultimately brought them into conflict with Rome, and she and Antony were defeated by Octavian at the battle of Actium in 31. She is reputed to have committed suicide by allowing herself to be bitten by an asp.

Cleveland /'kliːvlənd/, (Stephen) Grover (1837–1908), American Democratic statesman, 22nd and 24th President of the US 1885–9 and 1893–7. His first term was marked by efforts to reverse the heavily protective import tariff, and his second by his application of the Monroe doctrine to Britain's border dispute with Venezuela (1895).

Clift /klɪft/, (Edward) Montgomery (1920–66), American actor. He performed in New York theatre for ten years before making his film début in *Red River* (1946). He went on to receive Oscar nominations for his roles in *The Search* (1948), *A Place in the Sun* (1951), *From Here to Eternity* (1953), and *Judgment at Nuremberg* (1961). By 1950 he was an alcoholic and receiving psychiatric help. In 1956 he ran his car into a tree, an accident which permanently disfigured his face.

Cline /klaɪn/, Patsy (born Virginia Petterson Hensley) (1932–63), American country singer. She was discovered in 1957 when she sang 'Walkin' After Midnight' on a television show, and later had hits with 'Crazy' (1961) and 'Sweet Dreams of You' (1963). Just as she was becoming well

known she was killed in an air crash. She was elected to the Country Music Hall of Fame in 1973.

Clinton /'klɪntən/, William Jefferson ('Bill') (born 1946), American Democratic statesman, 42nd President of the US (since 1993). He was governor of Arkansas 1979–81 and 1983–92. Problems at home during his presidency included contested allegations of financial and sexual misconduct, while the mid-term elections of November 1994 left the Republicans controlling both Congress and the Senate. In 1995 at Dayton, Ohio, leaders of the warring factions in Bosnia signed a peace agreement that was based on a plan put forward by Clinton. He was re-elected in 1996, defeating Bob Dole.

Clive /klaɪv/, Robert, 1st Baron Clive of Plassey (known as Clive of India) (1725–74), British general and colonial administrator. In 1743 he joined the East India Company in Madras, becoming governor of Fort St David in 1755. Following the Black Hole of Calcutta incident, he commanded the forces that recaptured Calcutta from Siraj-ud-Dawlah (c.1729–57), nawab of Bengal, in 1757. Clive's victory at Plassey later that year made him virtual ruler of Bengal, helping the British to gain an important foothold in Britain 1760–5, he served as governor of Bengal until 1767, restructuring the administration of the colony and restoring discipline to the East India Company, whose reputation had been called into question. Clive was subsequently implicated in the company's corruption scandals; although officially exonerated, he committed suicide.

Clouet /'kluːeɪ/, Jean (c.1485–1541) and his son François (c.1516–72), French painters. Jean worked as court painter to Francis I (1494–1547); the monarch's portrait in the Louvre is attributed to him. François succeeded his father as court painter, and is chiefly known for his undated portraits of Elizabeth of Austria and of Mary, Queen of Scots.

Clough /klʌf/, Arthur Hugh (1819–61), English poet. He is especially remembered for his longer poems: *The Bothie of Tober-na-Vuolich* (1848) is about a student reading party in Scotland; *Amours de Voyage* (1858) concerns a traveller's spiritual crisis in Rome; *Dipsychus* (1865) is a dialogue reminiscent of Faust and set in Venice.

Clovis /'kləʊvɪs/ (465–511), king of the Franks 481–511. He succeeded his father Childeric (died 481) as king of the Salian Franks at Tournai, and extended Merovingian rule to Gaul and Germany after victories at Soissons (486) and Cologne (496). After his conversion to Christianity, he championed orthodoxy against the Arian Visigoths, finally defeating them in the battle of Poitiers (507). He made Paris his capital.

Cnut see CANUTE.

Cobain /'kəʊbeɪn/, Kurt (Donald) (1967–94), American rock singer, guitarist, and songwriter. Cobain was the leader of the Seattle band Nirvana, the most successful of the 'grunge' bands that emerged in the early 1990s. Their single 'Smells Like Teen Spirit' and album *Nevermind* (both 1991) were international hits. Apparently depressed by drug and health problems, he shot himself in April 1994.

Cobbett /'kɒbɪt/, William (1763–1835), English writer and political reformer. He started his political life as a Tory, but later became a radical; the change is reflected in *Cobbett's Political Register*, a periodical that he founded in 1802 and continued for the rest of his life. Cobbett was one of the leaders of the campaign for political and social reform after 1815, although he had already spent two years in prison for his outspoken criticism of flogging in the army (1810–12). A prolific writer, he published more than forty works in his lifetime, including *Rural Rides* (1830).

Cobden /'kɒbdən/, Richard (1804–65), English political reformer. A Manchester industrialist, Cobden was one of the leading spokesmen of the free-trade movement in Britain. From 1838, together with John Bright, he led the Anti-Corn Law League in its successful campaign for the repeal of the Corn Laws (1846).

Cochran[1] /'kɒkrən/, Sir C(harles) B(lake) (1872–1951), English theatrical producer. Agent for Houdini and the French dancer Mistinguett (1874–1956), he is most famous for the musical revues which he produced from 1918 onwards at the London Pavilion, including Noël Coward's *Bitter Sweet* (1929) and *Cavalcade* (1931).

Cochran[2] /'kɒkrən/, Eddie (born Edward Cochrane) (1938–60), American rock and roll singer and songwriter. Cochran recorded several classic rock and roll an-

thems, notably 'Summertime Blues' (1958), 'C'mon Everybody' (1959), and 'Three Steps to Heaven' (1960). He was killed in a car crash during a British tour.

Cochran[3] /'kɒkrən/, Jacqueline (1910–80), American aviator. She made aviation history when she became the first woman to enter the trans-American Bendix Cup Air Race in 1935 and the first to win it in 1938. She achieved more than 200 speed, distance, and altitude records in her flying career, more than any of her contemporaries. Her achievements included becoming the first woman to break the sound barrier (1953), logging record speeds for men and women for the 15 km, 100 km, and 500 km distances (1953), and breaking the women's jet speed record (1964) when she flew at 1,429 m.p.h. (2,300 k.p.h.).

Cockcroft /'kɒkkrɒft/, Sir John Douglas (1897–1967), English physicist. He joined the Cavendish Laboratory, Cambridge, and in 1932 succeeded (with E. T. S. Walton) in splitting the atom by means of artificially accelerated protons. With their high-energy particle accelerator they bombarded lithium atoms with protons and produced alpha particles. This demonstrated the transmutation of elements and Einstein's theory of the equivalence of mass and energy, and ushered in the whole field of nuclear and particle physics, which relied on particle accelerators. The two shared the 1951 Nobel Prize for physics. After the war, Cockcroft became the first director of the Atomic Energy Research Establishment at Harwell.

Cockerell /'kɒkərəl/, Sir Christopher Sydney (born 1910), English engineer. He was a boat-designer, and in 1955 he took out the first patent on the vessel that later came to be known as the hovercraft.

Cocteau /'kɒktəʊ/, Jean (1889–1963), French dramatist, novelist, and film director. His plays, noted for their striking blend of poetry, irony, and fantasy, include *La Machine infernale* (1934), based on the Oedipus legend, and *Orphée* (1926), which he made into a film in 1950. Among his other major films are *Le Sang d'un poète* (1930) and *La Belle et la bête* (1946), both of which mingle myth and reality. Also a prolific novelist, he is best known for *Les Enfants terribles* (1929).

Cody /'kəʊdɪ/, William Frederick, see BUF-FALO BILL.

Coe /kəʊ/, Sebastian (born 1956), British middle-distance runner and Conservative politician. He won a gold medal in the 1,500 metres at the Olympic Games in 1980 and 1984. In 1981 he created new world records in the 800 metres, 1,000 metres, and the mile. On retiring from athletics, Coe became an MP (1992–7).

Coetzee /kʊt'sɪə/, J(ohn) M(axwell) (born 1940), South African novelist. In his major works, such as the two *Dusklands* novellas (1974), and the novels *In the Heart of the Country* (1977) and the Booker Prize-winning *Life and Times of Michael K* (1983), he explores the psychology and mythology of colonialism and racial domination. His recent output includes *White Writing* (1988), a collection of critical essays, and the novel *Age of Iron* (1990).

Cohn /kəʊn/, Ferdinand Julius (1828–98), German botanist, a founder of bacteriology. Noted for his studies of algae, bacteria, and other micro-organisms, Cohn was the first to devise a systematic classification of bacteria into genera and species. It was Cohn who recognized the importance of the work of Robert Koch on anthrax.

Colbert /'kɒlbeə(r)/, Jean Baptiste (1619–83), French statesman, chief minister to Louis XIV 1665–83. A vigorous reformer, he put order back into the country's finances, boosted industry and commerce, and established the French navy as one of the most formidable in Europe. His reforms, however, could not keep pace with the demands of Louis's war policies and extensive royal building programme, and by the end of Louis's reign the French economy was again experiencing severe problems.

Cole /kəʊl/, Nat King (born Nathaniel Adams Coles) (1919–65), American singer and pianist. Although Cole made his professional début as a jazz pianist, it was his mellow vocal tones that won him international recognition. In 1937 he formed the King Cole Trio (also known as the Fiddlers Three) and later became the first black man to have his own radio (1948–9) and television (1956–7) series. Cole recorded a number of major successes, including 'Mona Lisa' (1950), 'Too Young' (1951), and 'Ramblin' Rose' (1962).

Coleman /'kəʊlmən/, Ornette (born 1930), American jazz saxophonist, trumpeter, violinist, and composer. In 1958 he formed the Ornette Coleman Quartet and in 1959 moved to New York, where he helped to

establish the style of free jazz. His music, with its lack of harmony and chordal structure, attracted controversy, but gradually won acceptance in the 1960s. His compositions include both jazz and classical chamber pieces.

Coleridge /ˈkəʊləˌrɪdʒ/, Samuel Taylor (1772–1834), English poet, critic, and philosopher. His *Lyrical Ballads* (1798), written with William Wordsworth, marked the start of English romanticism. The collection included Coleridge's famous poem 'The Rime of the Ancient Mariner'. His other well-known poems include the ballad 'Christabel' (1816) and the opium fantasy 'Kubla Khan' (1816). Coleridge's opium addiction is also recorded in his pessimistic poem 'Dejection: an Ode' (1802). During the latter part of his life he wrote little poetry, but contributed significantly to critical and philosophical literature.

Colette /kɒˈlet/ (born Sidonie Gabrielle Claudine) (1873–1954), French novelist. Her *Claudine* series (1900–3) was published by her husband, the novelist Henri Gauthier-Villars (1859–1931), who caused a scandal by inserting salacious passages. Colette made her name as a serious writer with her novels *Chéri* (1920) and *La Fin de Chéri* (1926), telling of a passionate relationship between a young man and an older woman. She was awarded the Legion of Honour in 1953.

Collins[1] /ˈkɒlɪnz/, Joan (Henrietta) (born 1933), English actress. She established a reputation as a sex symbol in her nine films of the 1950s, including the romantic comedy *Our Girl Friday* (1953). She continued to act in glamorous roles throughout the 1960s, 1970s, and 1980s, including that of Alexis in the US television soap opera *Dynasty* (1981–9). She is the sister of the novelist Jackie Collins.

Collins[2] /ˈkɒlɪnz/, Michael (1890–1922), Irish nationalist leader and politician. He took part in the Easter Rising in 1916. Elected to Parliament as a member of Sinn Fein in 1919, he became Minister of Finance in the provisional government, at the same time directing the Irish Republican Army's guerrilla campaign against the British. He was one of the negotiators of the Anglo-Irish Treaty of 1921, and commanded the Irish Free State forces in the civil war that followed partition. On the death of Arthur Griffith in 1922, he became head of state, but was shot in an ambush ten days later.

Collins[3] /ˈkɒlɪnz/, (William) Wilkie (1824–89), English novelist. Although he wrote in a number of genres, he is chiefly remembered as the writer of the first full-length detective stories in English, notably *The Woman in White* (1860) and *The Moonstone* (1868). These are striking for their use of multiple narrators and the complexity of their plots.

Colt /kəʊlt/, Samuel (1814–62), American inventor. He is remembered chiefly for the automatic pistol named after him. Colt patented his invention in 1836, but had to wait ten years before its adoption by the US army after the outbreak of the war with Mexico. The revolver was highly influential in the 19th-century development of small arms.

Coltrane /kɒlˈtreɪn/, John (William) (1926–67), American jazz musician. Once established as a jazz saxophonist, he played in groups led by Dizzy Gillespie and Miles Davis. In 1960 he formed his own quartet and soon became a leading figure in avant-garde jazz, bridging the transition between the harmonically dense jazz of the 1950s and the free jazz that was evolving in the 1960s.

Columba, St /kəˈlʌmbə/ (*c*.521–97), Irish abbot and missionary. After founding several churches and monasteries in his own country, he established the monastery at Iona in *c*.563, led a number of missions to mainland Scotland from there, and converted the Picts to Christianity. He is considered one of the leading figures of the Celtic missionary tradition in the British Isles and contributed significantly to the literature of Celtic Christianity. Feast day, 9 June.

Columbus /kəˈlʌmbəs/, Christopher (Spanish name Cristóbal Colón) (1451–1506), Italian-born Spanish explorer. A Genoese by birth, Columbus persuaded the rulers of Spain, Ferdinand and Isabella, to sponsor an expedition to sail westwards across the Atlantic in search of Asia and prove that the world was round. Sailing with three small ships in 1492, he discovered the New World (in fact various Caribbean islands). He made three further voyages to the New World between 1493 and 1504, in 1498 discovering the South American mainland and finally exploring the coast of Mexico.

Comaneci /ˌkɒməˈnetʃ/, Nadia (born 1961), Romanian-born American gymnast. She became the first competitor in the history of the Olympic Games to be awarded the maximum score (10.00) when she won three gold medals for her performances at the Montreal Olympics in 1976. She emigrated to the US in 1989.

Compton[1] /ˈkɒmptən/, Arthur Holly (1892–1962), American physicist. He observed that the wavelength of X-rays increased when scattered by electrons (later known as the Compton effect). This demonstrated the dual particle and wave properties predicted by quantum theory. Compton shared the 1927 Nobel Prize for physics, and during the war he contributed to work on the atom bomb by developing plutonium production for the Manhattan Project.

Compton[2] /ˈkɒmptən/, Denis (Charles Scott) (1918–97), English cricketer. Compton's flamboyant and largely self-taught batting brought him great success with Middlesex, for whom he made 38,942 runs with 123 centuries, and England, for whom he scored 5,807 runs. He was also a fine footballer who played as a winger for Arsenal and England.

Compton-Burnett /ˌkɒmptənbɜːˈnet, -ˈbɜːnɪt/, Dame Ivy (1884–1969), English novelist. Her works include *Brothers and Sisters* (1929), *A Family and a Fortune* (1939), and *Manservant and Maidservant* (1947). Her novels typically portray life at the turn of the 19th century and are characterized by ironic wit and an emphasis on dialogue.

Comte /kɒmt/, Auguste (1798–1857), French philosopher, one of the founders of sociology. In his historical study of the progress of the human mind, he discerned three phases: the theological, the metaphysical, and the positive. He argued that only the last phase survives in mature sciences. Comte's positivist philosophy attempted to define the laws of social evolution and to found a genuine social science that could be used for social reconstruction. Major works include his *Cours de philosophie positive* (1830–42) and *Système de politique positive* (1851–4).

Conan Doyle /ˈkəʊnən/ see Doyle.

Conegliano /ˌkɒneˈljɑːnəʊ/, Emmanuele, see Da Ponte.

Confucius /kənˈfjuːʃəs/ (Latinized name of K'ung Fu-tzu = 'Kong the master') (551–479 BC), Chinese philosopher. He spent much of his life as a moral teacher of a group of disciples, at first working for the government and later taking up the role of an itinerant sage. His ideas about the importance of practical moral values formed the basis of the philosophy of Confucianism. His teachings were collected by his pupils after his death in the *Analects*; later collections of Confucianist writings are probably only loosely based on his work.

Congreve /ˈkɒŋgriːv/, William (1670–1729), English dramatist. A close associate of Jonathan Swift, Alexander Pope, and Sir Richard Steele, he wrote plays such as *Love for Love* (1695) and *The Way of the World* (1700), which epitomize the wit and satire of Restoration comedy.

Connery /ˈkɒnərɪ/, Sean (born Thomas Connery) (born 1930), Scottish actor. He is best known for his portrayal of James Bond in the films of Ian Fleming's spy thrillers. He played the part seven times from his first performance in *Dr No* (1962) to his last in *Never Say Never Again* (1984). He has since appeared in other films, such as *The Name of the Rose* (1986).

Connolly[1] /ˈkɒnəlɪ/, Billy (born 1942), Scottish comedian. A tall Glaswegian with an aggressive stage persona, he began as a folk-singer in the duo the Humblebums (with Gerry Rafferty, later a successful solo singer). He developed his earthy stand-up act in television shows such as *An Audience with Billy Connolly*, and went on to a successful career in the US with shows such as *Head of the Class* (1990–2).

Connolly[2] /ˈkɒnəlɪ/, Cyril (Vernon) (1903–74), English writer. His only novel, *The Rock Pool* (1936), is a satire describing the adventures of an artistic expatriate colony on the French Riviera. His other works include collections of essays, aphorisms, and reflections, among which are *Enemies of Promise* (1938) and *The Unquiet Grave* (1944). He co-founded and edited the literary magazine *Horizon* in 1930, and he worked for the *Sunday Times* 1951–74.

Connolly[3] /ˈkɒnəlɪ/, Maureen Catherine (known as 'Little Mo') (1934–69), American tennis player. She was 16 when she first won the US singles title and 17 when she took the Wimbledon title; she retained these titles for a further two years each. In 1953 she became the first woman to win

the grand slam. She lost a mere four matches after the age of 16, being forced to retire in 1954 after a riding accident.

Connors /'kɒnəz/, James Scott ('Jimmy') (born 1952), American tennis player. He established himself as one of the world's top players when he defeated the Australian Ken Rosewall (born 1934) in the 1974 Wimbledon and US Open championships. He won the US title again in 1976, 1978, 1982, and 1983 and Wimbledon in 1982.

Conrad /'kɒnræd/, Joseph (born Józef Teodor Konrad Korzeniowski) (1857–1924), Polish-born British novelist. Conrad's long career at sea (1874–94) inspired many of his most famous works, including his novel *Lord Jim* (1900). Much of Conrad's work, including his story *Heart of Darkness* (1902) and the novel *Nostromo* (1904), explores the darker side of human nature; however, the novel that initially brought him fame and success was *Chance* (1913), in which there is a romantic theme. Although French was his first foreign language, Conrad wrote in English and became a British citizen in 1886. His work had a significant influence on modernist fiction.

Constable /'kʌnstəb(ə)l/, John (1776–1837), English painter. Among his best-known works are early paintings like *Flatford Mill* (1817) and *The Hay Wain* (1821), both inspired by the landscape of his native Suffolk. By the late 1820s and early 1830s, Constable had become fascinated by the painting of changing weather patterns, and in works such as *Sketch for 'Hadleigh Castle'* (c.1828–9) and *The Valley Farm* (1835) he focused on the transient effects of clouds and light, so breaking new ground in landscape painting. He proved a great influence on French painters, especially Eugène Delacroix and the Barbizon School.

Constantine /'kɒnstənˌtaɪn/ (known as Constantine the Great) (c.274–337), Roman emperor. The years from 305 until Constantine became sole emperor in 324 were marked by civil wars and continuing rivalry for the imperial throne. Constantine was the first Roman emperor to be converted to Christianity; he issued a decree of toleration towards Christians in the empire in 313. In 324 he made Christianity a state religion, although paganism was also tolerated. In 330 he moved his capital from Rome to Byzantium, renaming it Constantinopolis (Constantinople). His reign was marked by increasing imperial control of the Eastern Church and much church building, especially at the holy sites in Palestine. In the Orthodox Church he is venerated as a saint.

Cook[1] /kʊk/, Captain James (1728–79), English explorer. He conducted an expedition to the Pacific (1768–71) in his ship *Endeavour*, charting the coasts of New Zealand and New Guinea as well as exploring the east coast of Australia and claiming it for Britain. He returned to the Pacific in 1772–5 to search for the fabled Antarctic continent, landing at Tahiti, the New Hebrides, and New Caledonia. Cook's final voyage (1776–9) to discover a passage round North America from the Pacific side ended in disaster when he was killed in a skirmish with native peoples in Hawaii.

Cook[2] /kʊk/, Peter (Edward) (1937–94), English comedian and actor. Cook first rose to prominence as one of the writers and performers of the revue *Beyond the Fringe* (1959–64). He invented the character E. L. Wisty, a forlorn fellow perplexed by the mysteries of life. Cook collaborated with Dudley Moore from 1964 to 1970 in the irreverent television series *Not Only . . . But Also*; he also appeared in a number of films, including *The Bed-Sitting Room* (1970), *Derek and Clive* (1981), and *Whoops Apocalypse* (1987). Cook also had a long association with the satirical magazine *Private Eye*.

Cook[3] /kʊk/, Thomas (1808–92), English founder of the travel firm Thomas Cook. In 1841 he organized the first publicly advertised excursion train in England, carrying 570 passengers from Leicester to Loughborough and back, to attend a temperance meeting, for the price of one shilling. The success of this induced him to organize further excursions both in Britain and abroad and to lay the foundations for the tourist and travel industry of the 20th century.

Cooke /kʊk/, Sir William Fothergill (1806–79), English inventor. He became interested in the application of electric telegraphy to alarm systems and railway signalling, and went into partnership with Charles Wheatstone in the 1830s. They took out a joint patent for a railway alarm system in 1837, when they set up the first practical telegraph between two stations in London, and they progressively improved the system over the next few years. The patents were

later acquired by the Electro-Telegraph Company, which Cooke formed in 1848.

Cookson /ˈkʊks(ə)n/, Dame Catherine (Anne) (born 1906), English writer. A prolific author of light romantic fiction, she is best known for the Mary Ann series (1956–67), the Mallen trilogy (1973–4), and the Tilly Trotter series (1980–2).

Coolidge /ˈkuːlɪdʒ/, (John) Calvin (1872–1933), American Republican statesman, 30th President of the US 1923–9. Highly popular personally, he was seen as an embodiment of thrift, caution, and honesty in a decade when corruption in public life was common, even in his own administration. He was committed to reducing income taxes and the national debt, and was noted for his policy of non-interference in foreign affairs, which culminated in the signing of the Kellogg Pact in 1928.

Cooper[1] /ˈkuːpə(r)/, Gary (born Frank James Cooper) (1901–61), American actor. His performance in such westerns as *The Virginian* (1929) and *High Noon* (1952) established his reputation in tough cowboy roles. He also starred in other films, including *For Whom the Bell Tolls* (1943).

Cooper[2] /ˈkuːpə(r)/, Henry (born 1934), English boxer. He won his first British heavyweight title in 1959. Two years later he beat Joe Erskine to claim his first Lonsdale belt, eventually becoming the only man to win one outright three times. He beat Muhammad Ali (then Cassius Clay) in 1963, but a bad cut inflicted by the same opponent in 1966 in his only world title fight hastened his retirement in 1971.

Cooper[3] /ˈkuːpə(r)/, James Fenimore (1789–1851), American novelist. He is renowned for his tales of American Indians and frontier life, including *The Last of the Mohicans* (1826), *The Prairie* (1827), and *The Deerslayer* (1841). He also wrote novels inspired by his early career at sea, as well as historical studies.

Cooper[4] /ˈkuːpə(r)/, Susan Vera ('Susie') (1902–95), English ceramic designer and manufacturer. She founded a decorating firm at Tunstall in Staffordshire (1929), moving in 1931 to Burslem. Her work was noted for its functional shapes and simple, vivid designs, and was exhibited at the 1951 Festival of Britain.

Copernicus /kəˈpɜːnɪkəs/, Nicolaus (Latinized name of Mikołaj Kopernik) (1473–1543), Polish astronomer. Copernicus, canon of the cathedral at Frauenberg, first published his astronomical theories in outline in 1530, and more fully in *De Revolutionibus Orbium Coelestium* (1543). In order to avoid the complex system of epicycles required to explain planetary motions in Ptolemaic theory, he proposed a simpler model in which the planets orbited in perfect circles around the sun. His work ultimately led to the overthrow of the established geocentric cosmology.

Copland /ˈkəʊplənd/, Aaron (1900–90), American composer, pianist, and conductor, of Lithuanian descent. He worked to establish a distinctive American style in music, borrowing from jazz in his *Music for the Theater* (1925), from Shaker music in *Appalachian Spring* (1944), and from other folk and traditional music in the ballet score *Rodeo* (1942). The first American composer to earn a living from music, he contributed to the professional standing of composers nationally by establishing the American Composers' Alliance (1937).

Copley /ˈkɒplɪ/, John Singleton (1738–1815), American painter. A distinguished colonial portraitist, he sailed for England in 1774 and subsequently settled there. He made his mark with such paintings as *The Death of Chatham* (1779–80) and *The Death of Major Peirson* (1783), which are among the first large-scale paintings of contemporary events.

Coppola /ˈkɒpələ/, Francis Ford (born 1939), American film director, writer, and producer. Coppola's reputation rests chiefly on *The Godfather* (1972) and its two sequels, a film trilogy charting the fortunes of a New York Mafia family over several generations; it earned him three Oscars as writer and director. Other films include *Apocalypse Now* (1979), a retelling of Joseph Conrad's story *Heart of Darkness* in the context of the Vietnam War, *The Cotton Club* (1984), and *Bram Stoker's Dracula* (1993).

Corday /kɔːˈdeɪ/, Charlotte (full name Marie Anne Charlotte Corday d'Armont) (1768–93), French political assassin. The daughter of an impoverished nobleman and royalist, she became involved with the Girondists, the moderate republican party, and in 1793 assassinated the revolutionary leader Jean Paul Marat in his bath. The Revolutionary Tribunal found her guilty of treason and she was guillotined four days later.

Corelli[1] /kə'relɪ/, Arcangelo (1653–1713), Italian violinist and composer. His best-known works are his trio and solo sonatas for the violin (1681; 1685; 1689; 1694; 1700), and his concerti grossi (published posthumously in 1714), especially the 'Christmas' concerto, with its pastorale on the Nativity. Corelli's innovative use of harmony and attention to melody had an important influence on composers abroad, particularly Purcell, J. S. Bach, and Handel.

Corelli[2] /kə'relɪ/, Marie (pseudonym of Mary Mackay) (1855–1924), English writer of romantic fiction. After the success of her first novel, *A Romance of Two Worlds* (1886), the sales of her novels *Thelma* (1887), *Barabbas* (1893), and *The Sorrows of Satan* (1895) broke all existing records for book sales. Her popular success was not matched by critical acclaim, however; although briefly championed by Oscar Wilde and William Gladstone, she had little enduring literary success.

Coriolanus /ˌkɒrɪə'leɪməs/, Gaius (or Gnaeus) Marcius (5th century BC), Roman general. He earned his name by capturing the Volscian town of Corioli. He is said to have been banished from Rome in 491 BC after opposing the distribution of corn to the starving people and being charged with tyrannical conduct. He joined forces with the Volscians; according to legend, he led a Volscian army against Rome in 491 BC, and was turned back only by the pleas of his mother Veturia and his wife Volumnia. He was subsequently put to death by the Volscians.

Corneille /kɔː'neɪ/, Pierre (1606–84), French dramatist. He worked as a magistrate 1624–30 before moving to Paris in the early 1630s. He is generally regarded as the founder of classical French tragedy; his plays in this genre include *Le Cid* (1637), *Cinna* (1641), and *Polyeucte* (1643); the newly founded Académie française criticized *Le Cid* for moral laxity and performances of it were subsequently banned. He also wrote comedies such as *Mélite* (his first play, 1629) and *Le Menteur* (1642).

Corot /'kɒrəʊ/, (Jean-Baptiste) Camille (1796–1875), French landscape painter. Trained in the neoclassical tradition, he worked in an essentially classical style despite his contact with the Barbizon School and his preference for taking preliminary studies outdoors. One of his most famous paintings is *La Danse des nymphes* (1850). Corot was a major influence on the impressionists, notably Camille Pissarro.

Correggio /kɒ'redʒɪˌəʊ/, Antonio Allegri da (born Antonio Allegri) (c.1494–1534), Italian painter. He is best known for his series of frescos in Parma churches, especially San Giovanni Evangelista (1520–3) and Parma cathedral (c.1526–30). His treatment of the cupolas shows the influence of Mantegna in its use of extreme foreshortening to give the illusion of great height. His devotional painting *The Mystic Marriage of St Catherine* (1520–6) and such mythological paintings as *Jupiter and Io* (c.1530) epitomize his soft and sensual style of painting, which influenced the rococo of the 18th century.

Cort /kɔːt/, Henry (1740–1800), English ironmaster. Initially a supplier of wrought iron for naval and ordnance use, he set up his own forge, and patented a process for producing iron bars by passing iron through grooved rollers to avoid the laborious business of hammering. He later patented the puddling process for refining molten pig-iron, which gave Britain a lead in the industry and earned Cort the nickname 'the Great Finer'.

Cortés /'kɔːtez, Spanish kor'tes/, Hernando (also **Cortez**) (1485–1547), first of the Spanish conquistadores. Cortés overthrew the Aztec empire with a comparatively small army of adventurers; he conquered its capital city, Tenochtitlán, in 1519 and deposed the emperor, Montezuma. In 1521 he destroyed Tenochtitlán completely and established Mexico City as the new capital of Mexico (then called New Spain), serving briefly as governor of the colony.

Cosimo de' Medici /'kɒzɪˌməʊ də 'medɪtʃɪ, mə'diːtʃɪ/ (known as Cosimo the Elder) (1389–1464), Italian statesman and banker. He laid the foundations for the Medici family's power in Florence, becoming the city's ruler in 1434. He used his considerable wealth to promote the arts and learning, and funded the establishment of public buildings such as the Medici Library.

Costa /'kɒstə/, Lúcio (1902–63), French-born Brazilian architect, town planner, and architectural historian. He headed the group that designed the Ministry of Education in Rio de Janeiro (1937–43) and achieved a worldwide reputation with his plan for Brazil's new capital Brasilia, which was chosen by an international jury in 1956.

Cotman /'kɒtmən/, John Sell (1782–1842), English painter. His main importance is as a watercolourist and landscape painter; he is regarded as one of the leading figures of the Norwich School. His early watercolours, including *Greta Bridge* (1805), are notable for their bold configurations of light and shade and have been compared in their flat areas of colour to Japanese painting. In the 1820s he developed a more richly coloured style, as in *The Drop Gate* (c.1826). He also completed a number of distinctive etchings, but these have not enjoyed the same popularity as his watercolours.

Coulomb /'ku:lɒm/, Charles-Augustin de (1736–1806), French military engineer. He conducted research on structural mechanics, elasticity, friction, electricity, and magnetism. He is best known for Coulomb's Law, established with a sensitive torsion balance in 1785, according to which the forces between two electrical charges are proportional to the product of the sizes of the charges and inversely proportional to the square of the distance between them. Coulomb's verification of the inverse square law of electrostatic force enabled the quantity of electric charge to be defined.

Couperin /'ku:pəˌræn/, François (1668–1733), French composer, organist, and harpsichordist. A composer at the court of Louis XIV, he is principally known for his harpsichord works, particularly those 220 pieces contained in his four books (1713; 1716–17; 1722; 1730). These pieces are characterized by extensive ornamentation and a blend of Italian and French styles; Couperin's music, as well as his treatise *L'Art de toucher le clavecin* (1716), later proved a significant influence on J. S. Bach.

Courbet /'kuəbeɪ/, Gustave (1819–77), French painter. A leader of the 19th-century realist school of painting, he favoured an unidealized choice of subject-matter that did not exclude the ugly or vulgar. Important works include *Burial at Ornans* (1850) and *Painter in His Studio* (1855).

Courrèges /kuə'reɪʒ/, André (born 1923), French fashion designer. After training with Balenciaga (1952–60), he opened a fashion house in Paris in 1961. He became known for his futuristic and youth-oriented styles, introducing the miniskirt in 1964 and promoting unisex fashion with his trouser suits for women. He briefly ceased trading in 1966 in protest at the mass-produced imitations of his designs, but reopened the following year with both ready-made and couture clothes.

Courtauld /'kɔ:təʊld/, Samuel (1876–1947), English industrialist. He was a director of his family's silk firm and one of the earliest British collectors of French impressionist and post-impressionist paintings. He presented his collection to the University of London, endowed the Courtauld Institute of Art, and bequeathed to it his house in Portman Square, London.

Cousteau /'ku:stəʊ/, Jacques-Yves (1910–97), French oceanographer and film director. A naval officer interested in underwater exploration, he began using a camera under water in 1939 and devised the scuba apparatus. Cousteau has made three feature films and several popular series for television. He turned increasingly to biological research and marine conservation issues.

Coverdale /'kʌvəˌdeɪl/, Miles (1488–1568), English biblical scholar. He translated the first complete printed English Bible (1535), published in Zurich while he was in exile for preaching against confession and images. He also edited the Great Bible, brought out in 1539 by the printer Richard Grafton (c.1513–c.1572).

Coward /'kaʊəd/, Sir Noel (Pierce) (1899–1973), English dramatist, actor, and composer. He is remembered for witty, satirical plays such as *Hay Fever* (1925) and *Private Lives* (1930), as well as revues and musicals, including *Cavalcade* (1931), *Words and Music* (1932), and *Sigh No More* (1945). Individual songs from some of these, including 'Mad Dogs and Englishmen' (1932), became famous in their own right. Coward was also active in film-making. Among his successes were the war film *In Which We Serve* (1942), of which he was producer, co-director, writer, and star, and *Brief Encounter* (1945), which he wrote and produced.

Cowper /'ku:pə(r)/, William (1731–1800), English poet. He wrote *Olney Hymns* (1779) with the evangelical minister John Newton (1725–1807), contributing 'Oh! for a Closer Walk with God' amongst other well-known hymns. His famous comic ballad *John Gilpin* appeared in 1782. Cowper is best known, however, for his long poem *The Task* (1785), notable for its intimate sketches of rural life.

Crabbe /ˈkræb/, George (1754–1832), English poet. Crabbe's name is associated with grimly realistic narrative poems, such as *The Village* (1783) and *The Borough* (1810); the latter was based on his native Aldeburgh in Suffolk, and included tales of Peter Grimes and Ellen Orford. These later provided the subject-matter for Benjamin Britten's opera *Peter Grimes* (1945).

Cranach /ˈkrænək/, Lucas (known as Cranach the Elder) (1472–1553), German painter. A member of the Danube School, he is noted for his early religious pictures, in which landscape plays a prominent part, as in *The Rest on the Flight into Egypt* (1504). He also painted portraits, including several of his friend Martin Luther, and is regarded as the originator of the full-length secular portrait as a subject in its own right. His son Lucas (known as Cranach the Younger) (1515–86) continued working in the same tradition.

Crane¹ /kreɪn/, (Harold) Hart (1899–1932), American poet. He is recognized as an outstanding poet of his era, despite having published only two books during his lifetime. The collection *White Buildings* (1926) was followed by *The Bridge* (1930), a mystical epic poem concerned with American life and the consciousness to which it gives rise. He committed suicide by jumping from a ship while returning from a voyage to Mexico.

Crane² /kreɪn/, Stephen (1871–1900), American writer. His reputation rests on his novel *The Red Badge of Courage* (1895), a study of an inexperienced soldier and his reactions to the ordeal of battle in the American Civil War. It was hailed as a masterpiece of psychological realism, even though Crane himself had no personal experience of war. In 1895 he came to England, where he developed a close friendship with Joseph Conrad, to whose work his own has been compared.

Cranmer /ˈkrænmə(r)/, Thomas (1489–1556), English Protestant cleric and martyr. After helping to negotiate Henry VIII's divorce from Catherine of Aragon, he was appointed Archbishop of Canterbury in 1532. The first Protestant to hold this position, he was largely responsible for English liturgical reform, particularly under Edward VI, and for the compilation of the Book of Common Prayer (1549). After the accession of the Catholic Mary Tudor, Cran-

mer was tried for treason and heresy and burnt at the stake in Oxford.

Crassus /ˈkræsəs/, Marcus Licinius ('Dives') (*c.*115–53 BC), Roman politician. He defeated Spartacus in 71 BC, though Pompey claimed credit for the victory. Crassus joined Caesar and Pompey in the First Triumvirate in 60. In 55 he was made consul and given a special command in Syria, where he hoped to regain a military reputation equal to that of his allies by a victory over the Parthians, but after some successes he was defeated and killed.

Crawford¹ /ˈkrɔːfəd/, Joan (born Lucille le Sueur) (1908–77), American actress. For more than forty years she ranked among Hollywood's leading film stars. A dancer in her early films, she later played the female lead in films such as *Rain* (1932) and *Mildred Pierce* (1945), as well as mature roles, such as her part in the horror film *Whatever Happened to Baby Jane?* (1962).

Crawford² /ˈkrɔːfəd/, Osbert Guy Stanhope (1886–1957), British archaeologist. He pioneered the use of aerial photography in the detection of previously unlocated or buried archaeological sites and monuments. He also made an important contribution to the cartographic representation of archaeology when he worked as the Ordnance Survey's first archaeology officer (1920–40).

Crazy Horse (Sioux name Ta-Sunko-Witko) (*c.*1849–77), Sioux chief. In 1876 he led a successful rearguard action of Sioux and Cheyenne warriors against invading US army forces in Montana. Shortly afterwards he and his men joined Sitting Bull at Little Bighorn, where Crazy Horse played an important strategic and military role in the massacre of US forces under General Custer. He surrendered in 1877 and was killed in custody in Nebraska a few months later.

Crichton /ˈkraɪt(ə)n/, James (known as 'the Admirable Crichton') (1560–*c.*1585), Scottish adventurer. Crichton was an accomplished swordsman, poet, and scholar. He travelled a great deal in Europe, serving in the French army and later making a considerable impression on French and Italian universities with his intellect and skills as a polyglot orator.

Crick /krɪk/, Francis Harry Compton (born 1916), English biophysicist. Together with J. D. Watson he proposed the double helix

structure of the DNA molecule, thus broadly explaining how genetic information is carried in living organisms and how genes replicate. He has since worked on the triplet code of bases in DNA, the processes of transcription into RNA and translation into amino acids, and the structure of other macromolecules and of viruses. He shared a Nobel Prize with Watson and M. H. F. Wilkins in 1962.

Crippen /'krɪpɪn/, Hawley Harvey (known as Doctor Crippen) (1862–1910), American-born British murderer. Crippen poisoned his wife at their London home and sailed to Canada with his former secretary. His arrest in Canada was achieved through the intervention of radio-telegraphy, the first case of its use in apprehending a criminal. Crippen was later hanged.

Croce /'krəʊtʃeɪ/, Benedetto (1866–1952), Italian philosopher. The author of some seventy books, he founded and edited the influential review *Critica* (1903), in which he sought to revitalize Italian thought. Croce presented his philosophical system in his major work *Filosofia dello spirito* (1902–17), which is notable for its denial of the physical reality of a work of art and its identification of philosophical endeavour with a methodological approach to history. Croce served as Minister of Education 1920–1, but opposed Mussolini and all forms of totalitarianism; he returned to political life and helped to rebuild democracy in Italy after the fall of Mussolini.

Crockett /'krɒkɪt/, David ('Davy') (1786–1836), American frontiersman, soldier, and politician. He was a member of the House of Representatives 1827–35 and cultivated the image of a rough backwoods legislator. On leaving politics he returned to the frontier, where he took up the cause of Texan independence and was killed at the siege of the Alamo.

Croesus /'kriːsəs/ (6th century BC), last king of Lydia c.560–546 BC. He subjugated the Greek cities on the coast of Asia Minor, and was proverbial for his great wealth. His empire, with its capital at Sardis, was overthrown by the Persian king Cyrus the Great. At this point Croesus' fate becomes the theme of legend; Cyrus is said to have cast him on a pyre from which he was saved by the miraculous intervention of the god Apollo.

Crome /krəʊm/, John (1768–1821), English painter. Founder and leading member of the Norwich School, he was influenced by Dutch artists such as Hobbema and Ruisdael. He later developed a distinctive romantic style of his own, exemplified in such landscapes as *Slate Quarries* and *Moonrise on the Marshes of the Yare* (both undated).

Crompton[1] /'krɒmptən/, Richmal (pseudonym of Richmal Crompton Lamburn) (1890–1969), English writer. A classics teacher who wrote stories for magazines, she made her name with *Just William* (1922), a collection of stories for children about a mischievous schoolboy, William Brown. She published a further thirty-seven collections based on the same character, as well as some fifty books for adults, during her writing career.

Crompton[2] /'krɒmptən/, Samuel (1753–1827), English inventor. Famed for his invention of the spinning mule, he lacked the means to obtain a patent and sold his rights to a Bolton industrialist for £67. The House of Commons subsequently gave him £5,000 in compensation.

Cromwell[1] /'krɒmwel/, Oliver (1599–1658), English general and statesman. He was the driving force in the revolutionary opposition to Charles I in the English Civil War, and was the leader of the Parliamentary forces (or Roundheads), winning decisive battles at Marston Moor and Naseby. After helping to arrange the trial and execution of Charles I, he returned to military command to suppress resistance to the Commonwealth in Ireland and Scotland, finally defeating a Scottish army at Worcester (1651). He styled himself Lord Protector of the Commonwealth (1653–8); although he called and dissolved a succession of Parliaments, he refused Parliament's offer of the crown in 1657. His rule was notable for its puritan reforms in the Church of England and for the establishment of the Commonwealth as the major Protestant power in the world.

Cromwell[2] /'krɒmwel/, Thomas (c.1485–1540), English statesman, chief minister to Henry VIII 1531–40. After serving Cardinal Wolsey from 1514, he succeeded him as the king's chief adviser. He presided over the king's divorce from Catherine of Aragon (1533) and his break with the Roman Catholic Church, as well as the dissolution of the monasteries and a series of administrative measures, such as the Act of Supremacy (1534), designed to strengthen the

Crown. He fell from favour over Henry's marriage to Anne of Cleves and was executed on a charge of treason.

Cronin /'krəʊnɪn/, A(rchibald) J(oseph) (1896–1981), Scottish novelist. His novels often reflect his early experiences as a doctor; they include *The Citadel* (1937), telling of the struggles of an idealistic young doctor, and *The Stars Look Down* (1935), about a mining community. Cronin's Scottish medical stories were successfully adapted for radio and television as *Dr Finlay's Casebook* in the 1960s and 1990s.

Crookes /krʊks/, Sir William (1832–1919), English physicist and chemist. Crookes combined private experimental research with business; he also edited several photographic and scientific journals. In 1861, shortly after the spectroscopic discoveries of Robert Bunsen and Gustav Kirchhoff, he discovered the element thallium. This led him indirectly to the invention of the radiometer in 1875. He later developed a vacuum tube (the precursor of the X-ray tube) and in 1903 invented the spinthariscope. His interest in spiritualism and psychic research led him into controversy.

Crosby /'krɒzbɪ/, Bing (born Harry Lillis Crosby) (1904–77), American singer and actor. His songs include 'Pennies from Heaven', 'Blue Skies', and in particular 'White Christmas' (from the film *Holiday Inn*, 1942), which has sold more than 30 million copies. He also starred in the series of *Road* films (1940–62) with Bob Hope and Dorothy Lamour (1914–96).

Cruft /krʌft/, Charles (1852–1939), English showman. In 1886 he initiated the first dog show in London. The Cruft's shows, held annually, have helped to raise standards in dog breeding and are now internationally known.

Cruikshank /'krʊkʃæŋk/, George (1792–1878), English painter, illustrator, and caricaturist. The most eminent political cartoonist of his day, he was known for exposing the private life of the Prince Regent. His later work includes illustrations for Charles Dickens's *Sketches by Boz* (1836), as well as a series of etchings supporting the temperance movement.

Cruyff /krɔɪf/, Johan (born 1947), Dutch footballer and football manager. An attacking midfielder, he played for the Amsterdam team Ajax (1965–73), and was a member of the team that won three con-

secutive European Cup Finals (1971–3). Cruyff's exceptional skills were recognized when he was made European Footballer of the Year in both 1973 and 1974. He later played for Barcelona (1973–8) and captained the Netherlands in their unsuccessful World Cup Final against West Germany (1974). On retiring he managed Barcelona 1988–96, winning four successive league titles (1991–4) and the European Cup in 1992 before being replaced by former England manager Bobby Robson (born 1933).

Cudlipp /'kʌdlɪp/, Hugh, Baron Cudlipp of Aldingbourne (born 1913), British newspaper editor. The features editor on the *Daily Mirror* from 1935 and (after the Second World War) its editorial director, he was a pioneer of tabloid journalism. He conceived the formula of the sensationalized presentation of sex and crime together with populist politics that later proved a basis for other tabloids; this dramatically increased the paper's circulation. He gives an account of his career in *Publish and Be Damned* (1953).

Culbertson /'kʌlbəts(ə)n/, Ely (1891–1955), American bridge player. An authority on contract bridge, he revolutionized the game by formalizing a system of bidding. This, together with his other activities in the early 1930s, such as well-publicized challenge matches with high stakes, helped to establish this form of the game in preference to auction bridge.

Culpeper /'kʌl,pepə(r)/, Nicholas (1616–54), English herbalist. He is chiefly remembered for his *Complete Herbal* (1653), which popularized herbalism and, despite embracing ideas of astrology and the doctrine of signatures (the belief that the form or colouring of a medicinal plant in some way resembled the organ or disease it was used to treat), was important in the development of botany and pharmacology. Culpeper was unpopular among his contemporaries, partly because of his unauthorized and critical translation of the London *Pharmacopoeia* (1649).

Cumberland /'kʌmbələnd/, William Augustus, Duke of (1721–65), third son of George II, English military commander. He gained great notoriety (and his nickname 'the Butcher') for the severity of his suppression of the Jacobite clans in the aftermath of his victory at the Battle of Culloden (1746).

cummings /'kʌmɪŋz/, e(dward) e(stlin) (1894–1962), American poet and novelist.

His novel *The Enormous Room* (1922), an account of his brief internment in a French detention camp in 1917, won him an international reputation and introduced many of the themes of his subsequent work. He is now chiefly remembered for his poems, which are characterized by their experimental typography (most notably in the avoidance of capital letters), technical skill, frank vocabulary, and the sharpness of his satire. His many volumes of poetry include *95 Poems* (1956).

Cunard /kjuː'nɑːd/, Sir Samuel (1787–1865), Canadian-born British shipowner. One of the pioneers of the regular transatlantic passenger service, he founded the steamship company which still bears his name with the aid of a contract to carry the mail between Britain and Canada. The first such voyage for the company was made in 1840.

Cunningham /'kʌnɪŋəm/, Merce (born 1919), American dancer and choreographer. While a dancer with the Martha Graham Dance Company (1939–45), he began to experiment with choreography, collaborating with the composer John Cage in solo performances in 1944. He formed his own company in 1953 and explored new abstract directions for modern dance. Cunningham's works include *Suite for Five* (1956) and *Travelogue* (1977).

Cunobelinus see CYMBELINE.

Curie /'kjʊərɪ/, Marie (1867–1934), Polish-born French physicist, and Pierre (1859–1906), French physicist, pioneers of radioactivity. Pierre's early researches were on piezoelectricity and on the effects of temperature on magnetism. The two scientists married in 1895. Working together on the mineral pitchblende, they discovered the elements polonium and radium, for which they shared the 1903 Nobel Prize for physics with A.-H. Becquerel. Marie succeeded to her husband's chair of physics at the Sorbonne after his accidental death, receiving another Nobel Prize (for chemistry) in 1911 for her isolation of radium. She also studied radioactive decay and the applications of radioactivity to medicine, pioneered mobile X-ray units, headed the French Radiological Service during the First World War, and afterwards worked in the new Radium Institute. She died of leukaemia, undoubtedly caused by prolonged exposure to radioactive materials.

Curry /'kʌrɪ/, John (Anthony) (1949–94), English ice-skater. Curry was British junior figure-skating champion in 1970 and went on to win a succession of championships, including the British, European, and World titles. He won the gold medal for men's figure-skating in his second Winter Olympics in 1976, setting new standards for artistic interpretation. He later turned professional, forming the John Curry Theatre of Skating and the School of Skating in 1978.

Curtin /'kɜːtɪn/, John (Joseph Ambrose) (1885–1945), Australian Labor statesman, Prime Minister 1941–5. He led the Labor party from 1935 to 1945. As Premier during the Second World War, he mobilized Australian resources to meet the danger of Japanese invasion, laid down the groundwork for the postwar economy, and introduced various welfare measures. Curtin died while in office.

Curtiss /'kɜːtɪs/, Glenn (Hammond) (1878–1930), American air pioneer and aircraft designer. He began by building and selling bicycles; from 1901 he built motorcycles, setting motorcycle speed records in 1905 and 1907. He built his first aeroplane in 1909, and invented the aileron and demonstrated the first practical seaplane two years later. In 1908 Curtiss made the first public American flight of 1.0 km (0.6 miles), and won the James Gordon Bennett Cup in 1909 for a flight in his own aeroplane at 46.6 m.p.h.

Cushing[1] /'kʊʃɪŋ/, Harvey Williams (1869–1939), American surgeon. He introduced techniques that greatly increased the likelihood of success in neurosurgical operations, and described the hormonal disorder that was later named after him.

Cushing[2] /'kʊʃɪŋ/, Peter (1913–94), English actor. Cushing was known particularly for his roles in horror films, especially those made by Hammer films; these include *Dracula* (1958) and *Frankenstein Must Be Destroyed* (1969). Making his début in 1939, he appeared in more than a hundred films; he played Sherlock Holmes in *The Hound of the Baskervilles* (1959), and also appeared in *Star Wars* (1977).

Custer /'kʌstə(r)/, George (Armstrong) (1839–76), American cavalry general. He served with distinction in the American Civil War but led his men to their deaths in a clash (popularly known as Custer's Last Stand) with the Sioux at Little Bighorn in

Montana. Controversy over his conduct in the final battle still continues.

Cuthbert, St /'kʌθbət/ (died 687), English monk. He travelled in the north of England as a missionary before living as a hermit on Farne Island and later becoming bishop of Lindisfarne. Feast day, 20 March.

Cuvier /'kuːvɪˌeɪ/, Georges Léopold Chrétien Frédéric Dagobert, Baron (1769–1832), French naturalist. Cuvier carried out a study of fossil elephants which in effect founded the science of palaeontology. Pioneering also in comparative anatomy, he was the first to classify the lower invertebrates. He realized that each species could be derived from another by small changes in structure, which proved crucial in the emergence of evolutionary theory. However, he believed resolutely in the creationist view and quarrelled publicly with the early proponents of evolution, notably Lamarck.

Cymbeline /'sɪmbəˌliːn/ (also **Cunobelinus** /ˌkjuːnəʊbə'laɪnəs/) (died c.42 AD), British chieftain. He was a powerful ruler whose tribe occupied a wide area from Northamptonshire to SE England. He made Camulodunum (Colchester) his capital, and established a mint there. He was the subject of a medieval fable used by Shakespeare for his play *Cymbeline*.

Cynewulf /'kɪnɪˌwʊlf/ (late 8th–9th centuries), Anglo-Saxon poet. Of the many poems that have been attributed to him in the past, modern scholarship restricts attribution to four: *Juliana*, *Elene*, *The Fates of the Apostles*, and *Christ II*. Each of these is inscribed with his name in runes in Anglo-Saxon collections.

Cyprian, St /'sɪprɪən/ (died 258), Carthaginian bishop and martyr. The author of a work on the nature of true unity in the Church in its relation to the episcopate, he was martyred in the reign of the Roman emperor Valerian. Feast day, 16 or 26 September.

Cyrano de Bergerac /ˌsɪrənəʊ də 'beəʒəˌræk/, Savinien (1619–55), French soldier, duellist, and writer. He wrote comedies and satire, but is now chiefly remembered for the large number of duels that he fought (many on account of his proverbially large nose); this aspect of his

life is immortalized in a play by Edmond Rostand (*Cyrano de Bergerac*, 1897).

Cyril, St /'sɪrɪl/ (826–69), Greek missionary. The invention of the Cyrillic alphabet is ascribed to him. He and his brother St Methodius (c.815–85) became known as the 'Apostles to the Slavs'. Sent to Moravia, they taught in the vernacular, which they adopted also for the liturgy, and circulated a Slavonic version of the Scriptures. Feast day (in the Eastern Church) 11 May; (in the Western Church) 14 February.

Cyril of Alexandria, St /'sɪrɪl, ˌælɪg'zɑːndrɪə/ (died 444), Doctor of the Church and patriarch of Alexandria. A champion of orthodox thought on the person of Christ, he is best known for his vehement opposition to the views of Nestorius (whose condemnation he secured at the Council of Ephesus in 431). His extensive writings include a series of theological treatises, sermons, and letters. Feast day, 9 February.

Cyrus[1] /'saɪərəs/ (known as Cyrus the Great) (died c.530 BC), father of Cambyses, king of Persia 559–530 BC and founder of the Achaemenid dynasty. He became ruler of the Median empire after the capture of King Astyages in 550 BC, and went on to conquer Asia Minor, Babylonia, Syria, Palestine, and most of the Iranian plateau. He is said to have ruled his empire with wisdom and moderation, maintaining good relations with the Jews (whom he freed from the Babylonian Captivity) and the Phoenicians.

Cyrus[2] /'saɪərəs/ (known as Cyrus the Younger) (died 401 BC), Persian prince, second son of Darius II. On the death of his father (405 BC), Cyrus led an army of mercenaries against his elder brother, who had succeeded to the throne as Artaxerxes II; his campaign is recounted by the historian Xenophon, who had enlisted in his army. Cyrus was killed in battle north of Babylon.

Czerny /'tʃeənɪ/, Karl (1791–1857), Austrian pianist, teacher, and composer. A pupil of Beethoven and the teacher of Liszt, he was active at a time when the piano was undergoing important structural developments; the bulk of his output is made up of more than 1,000 exercises and studies for this instrument.

D

Dadd /dæd/, Richard (1817–86), English painter. In 1837 Dadd entered the Royal Academy schools, and became regarded as one of the most talented students of his generation. In 1842–3 he toured Europe and the Middle East before experiencing a mental breakdown and killing his father. He was confined in asylums for the rest of his life, where he produced a series of visionary paintings over many years, including *The Fairy Feller's Master-stroke* (1855–64).

da Gama /də ˈɡɑːmə/, Vasco (*c*.1469–1524), Portuguese explorer. He led the first European expedition round the Cape of Good Hope in 1497, sighting and naming Natal on Christmas Day before crossing the Indian Ocean and arriving in Calicut in 1498. The Portuguese king Manuel I (1469–1521) ennobled him on his return and chose him to lead a second expedition to Calicut in 1502. Da Gama forced the raja of Calicut (who had massacred Portuguese settlers from an earlier expedition) to make peace, also establishing colonies on the coast of Mozambique. After twenty years in retirement he was sent east again in 1524 as a viceroy to India, but died soon after his arrival.

Daguerre /dəˈɡeə(r)/, Louis-Jacques-Mandé (1789–1851), French physicist, painter, and inventor of the first practical photographic process. While working as a painter he co-invented the diorama, and he later went into partnership with Joseph-Nicéphore Niépce (1765–1833) to improve the latter's heliography process. Daguerre greatly reduced the exposure time, and in 1839 he presented to the French Academy of Sciences his daguerreotype process, which produced positive images directly on silvered copper plates.

Dahl /dɑːl/, Roald (1916–90), British writer, of Norwegian descent. The short-story collection *Tales of the Unexpected* (1979) is characteristic of his fiction and drama, which typically include macabre plots and unexpected outcomes. Dahl is also widely known for his stories and poems for children; they include *Charlie and the Chocolate Factory* (1964), *The BFG* (1982), and *Revolting Rhymes* (1982).

Daimler /ˈdeɪmlə(r)/, Gottlieb (1834–1900), German engineer and motor manufacturer. An employee of Nikolaus Otto, he produced a small engine using the Otto cycle in 1884 and made it propel a bicycle in 1886, using petrol vapour. He founded the Daimler motor company in 1890.

Dalcroze see JAQUES-DALCROZE.

Dale /deɪl/, Sir Henry Hallett (1875–1968), English physiologist and pharmacologist. He worked first on the physiological action of ergot, going on to investigate the role of histamine in anaphylactic shock and allergy. He discovered the role of acetylcholine as a natural neurotransmitter, which led to a clearer understanding of the chemical transmission of nerve impulses. Dale later held the most senior posts in British medical research, and shared a Nobel Prize in 1936.

Dalglish /dælˈɡliːʃ/, Kenneth Mathieson ('Kenny') (born 1951), Scottish footballer and manager. He played as an attacker for Celtic (1970–7) and then Liverpool (1977–89). He was capped 102 times for Scotland and is the only player to have scored 100 goals in both English and Scottish football. He managed Liverpool from 1985, leading them to three League Championship and two FA Cup victories before moving to manage Blackburn Rovers 1991–6 (winning the League with them in 1995) and Newcastle United in 1997.

Dalhousie /dælˈhaʊzɪ/, 1st Marquess of (title of James Andrew Broun Ramsay) (1812–60), British colonial administrator. As Governor-General of India (1847–56) he was responsible for a series of reforms and innovations, notably the introduction of railways and telegraphic communications, as well as the drafting of legislation against slavery, suttee, and female infanticide. He considerably expanded British territory in India, taking Punjab and Pegu and annexing Oudh and Nagpur.

Dali /ˈdɑːlɪ/, Salvador (1904–89), Spanish painter. He joined the surrealists in 1928 and became one of the most prominent

members of the movement. Like many surrealists, he was much influenced by Sigmund Freud's writings on dreams; many of his paintings portray subconscious or dream images painted with almost photographic realism against backgrounds of arid Catalan landscapes. Expelled from the surrealist group in 1938 because of his repudiation of its Marxist politics, he settled in the US; after becoming a Roman Catholic he devoted the latter part of his life to symbolic religious paintings. His most famous pictures include The Persistence of Memory (1931) and Christ of St John of the Cross (1951). He also produced surrealist writings and collaborated with Luis Buñuel in the production of Un chien andalou (1928) and other films.

Dallapiccola /ˌdælə'pɪkələ/, Luigi (1904–75), Italian composer. Influenced by the serial technique of Schoenberg and Webern, he further developed the twelve-note system in a variety of compositions, including songs, opera, ballet music, and a piano concerto. Among his best-known works is Songs of Prison (1938–41).

Dalton /'dɔːlt(ə)n/, John (1766–1844), English chemist, the father of modern atomic theory. His study of gases led to his formulation of the law of partial pressures (Dalton's law), according to which the total pressure of a mixture of gases is equal to the sum of the pressures that each gas would exert separately. He then worked on the solubility of gases, producing fundamental work on atomic theory. He defined an atom as the smallest part of a substance that could participate in a chemical reaction, argued that elements are composed of atoms and that elements combine in definite proportions, and produced the first table of comparative atomic weights. He also gave the first detailed description of colour-blindness, based on his own inability to distinguish green from red.

Dampier /'dæmpɪə(r)/, William (1652–1715), English explorer and adventurer. He is notable for having sailed round the world twice. In 1683 he set out on a privateering expedition from Panama, crossing the Pacific to the Philippines, China, and Australia before eventually reaching England again in 1691. In 1699 he was commissioned by the British government to explore the NW coast of Australia and circumnavigated the globe again, despite being shipwrecked on Ascension Island on the way home.

Dana[1] /'deɪnə/, James Dwight (1813–95), American naturalist, geologist, and mineralogist. At the age of 24 he produced A System of Mineralogy and founded a classification of minerals based on chemistry and physics; revised editions of this still appear under his name. His view of the earth as a unit, with its physical features changing and developing progressively, was an evolutionary one, but he did not accept Darwin's theory of evolution until the last edition of his Manual of Geology, published shortly before his death.

Dana[2] /'deɪnə/, Richard Henry (1815–82), American adventurer, lawyer, and writer. He wrote a faithful and lively account of his voyage from Boston round Cape Horn to California, published anonymously as Two Years Before the Mast (1840). In professional life he was an expert in maritime law and editor of an international law journal.

d'Annunzio /dɑːˈnʊntsɪˌəʊ/, Gabriele (1863–1938), Italian novelist, dramatist, and poet. The publication of his 'Romances of the Rose' trilogy, including The Child of Pleasure (1890), established d'Annunzio as a leading Italian literary figure of the fin de siècle. His strong admiration for Nietzsche is particularly evident in the second of these novels, The Triumph of Death (1894).

Dante /'dæntɪ/ (full name Dante Alighieri) (1265–1321), Italian poet. His early work consisted mainly of courtly love poetry; his first book, Vita nuova (c.1290–4), consists of thirty-one poems linked by a prose narrative and tells of his love for Beatrice Portinari (c.1265–90). However, Dante's international renown and reputation as the founding figure of Italian literature rests on The Divine Comedy (c.1309–20), an epic poem telling of his spiritual journey, in the form of an imagined visit to Hell and Purgatory with Virgil as guide and finally to Paradise with Beatrice, now a blessed spirit, as guide. Dante also wrote scholarly treatises on a number of subjects, including philosophy, science, and politics; his political activity led to his spending part of his life in exile from his native Florence. His innovative use of Italian did much to establish a vernacular literature; his Latin treatise De Vulgari Eloquentia (c.1303) promoted vernacular Italian as a literary language fit to replace Latin.

Danton /'dæntən, French dãtɔ̃/, Georges (Jacques) (1759–94), French revolutionary. A noted orator, he won great popularity in the early days of the French Revolution. He served as Minister of Justice (1792–4) in the new republic and was a founder member of the governing body, the Committee of Public Safety (1793). Initially an ally of Robespierre and the Jacobins, he later revolted against their radicalism and the severity of the Revolutionary Tribunal, only to be arrested and executed on Robespierre's orders.

Da Ponte /dɑː 'pɒntɪ/, Lorenzo (born Emmanuele Conegliano) (1749–1838), Italian poet and librettist. He became poet to the Court Opera in Vienna in 1784 and wrote the libretti for Mozart's *Marriage of Figaro* (1786), *Don Giovanni* (1787), and *Così fan tutte* (1790).

Darius I /də'raɪəs/ (known as Darius the Great) (c.550–486 BC), king of Persia 521–486 BC. His reign divided the empire into provinces governed by satraps, allowing each province its own government while maintaining some centralizing authority. He developed commerce, building a network of roads, exploring the Indus valley, and connecting the Nile with the Red Sea by canal. After suppressing a revolt of the Greek cities in Ionia (499–494 BC), he invaded Greece to punish the mainland Greeks for their interference, but was defeated at Marathon (490 BC).

Darling /'dɑːlɪŋ/, Grace (1815–42), English heroine. The daughter of a lighthouse keeper on the Farne Islands off the coast of Northumberland, she became a national heroine when in September 1838 she and her father rowed through a storm to rescue the survivors of the wrecked *Forfarshire*.

Darnley /'dɑːnlɪ/, Lord (title of Henry Stewart or Stuart) (1545–67), Scottish nobleman, second husband of Mary, Queen of Scots, and father of James I of England. He was implicated in the murder of his wife's secretary Rizzio in 1566, and was later killed in a mysterious gunpowder explosion in Edinburgh.

Dart /dɑːt/, Raymond Arthur (1893–1988), Australian-born South African anthropologist and anatomist. While based in Johannesburg he became interested in fossil primates. He obtained the skull of a juvenile hominid from a limestone quarry at Taung near Kimberley in 1924, and a year later coined the genus name *Australopith-*

ecus for it. It was assigned to the species *A. africanus*, and was the first of many specimens of *Australopithecus* obtained in Africa.

Darwin[1] /'dɑːwɪn/, Charles (Robert) (1809–82), English natural historian and geologist, proponent of the theory of evolution by natural selection. Grandson of the physician and scientist Erasmus Darwin, he failed to complete his medical training and narrowly achieved a theological degree. Darwin took the post of unpaid naturalist on HMS *Beagle* for her voyage around the southern hemisphere (1831–6), during which he collected the material which became the basis for his ideas on natural selection. On his return he made his name as a geologist, in particular with his accounts of the formation of coral reefs and atolls. In 1858, he and A. R. Wallace agreed to publish simultaneously their similar thoughts on evolution, to the consternation of theologians. He went on to write an extensive series of books, monographs, and papers; *On the Origin of Species* (1859) and *The Descent of Man* (1871) changed our concepts of nature and of humanity's place within it.

Darwin[2] /'dɑːwɪn/, Erasmus (1731–1802), English physician, scientist, inventor, and poet. Darwin was a founder of the Lunar Society, which counted many eminent men among its members, but he is chiefly remembered for his scientific and technical writings, which often appeared in the form of long poems. These include *The Botanic Garden* (1789–91), which was later parodied to Darwin's detriment. Darwin's major work was *Zoonomia* (1794–6), which proposed a Lamarckian view of evolution. His grandsons (by different wives) included Charles Darwin and Francis Galton.

Daubigny /'dəʊbiː,njiː/, Charles François (1817–78), French landscape painter. He was a member of the Barbizon School and is often regarded as a linking figure between this group of painters and the impressionists. His landscapes frequently feature stretches of water, for example *The Banks of the Oise* (1872).

Daudet /'dəʊdeɪ/, Alphonse (1840–97), French novelist and dramatist. He is best known for his sketches of life in his native Provence, particularly the *Lettres de mon moulin* (1869), and as the creator of Tartarin, a caricature of the Frenchman of the

south of France, whose comic exploits are first related in *Tartarin de Tarascon* (1872).

Daumier /'dəʊmɪˌeɪ/, Honoré (1808–78), French painter and lithographer. From the 1830s he worked as a cartoonist for periodicals such as *Charivari*, in which he produced over 4,000 lithographs sharply satirizing French society and politics. His later oil paintings, such as *Don Quixote* (1868), deal with their subjects in a powerfully realistic and unromanticized manner.

David[1] /'deɪvɪd/ (died *c*.962 BC), king of Judah and Israel *c*.1000–*c*.962 BC. In the biblical account he was the youngest son of Jesse, and was made a military commander by Saul after slaying the Philistine Goliath. On Saul's death he became king of Judah and later of the whole of Israel, making Jerusalem his capital. He is traditionally regarded as the author of the Psalms, but it is unlikely that more than a fraction of the psalter is his work.

David[2] /'deɪvɪd/ the name of two kings of Scotland:

David I (*c*.1084–1153), sixth son of Malcolm III, reigned 1124–53. Much of his youth was spent at the English court, after his sister Matilda (1080–1118) married King Henry I of England in 1100. After succeeding his brother Alexander (*c*.1080–1124) as king of Scotland, David established a strong administration on the Norman model, bringing many retainers with him from England, encouraging the development of trade, and introducing legal reforms. In 1136, after Henry's death, David invaded England in support of his niece Matilda's claim to the throne, but was decisively defeated at the Battle of the Standard in Yorkshire in 1138.

David II (1324–71), son of Robert the Bruce, reigned 1329–71. His long reign witnessed a renewal of fighting between England and Scotland, with Edward III taking advantage of the Scottish king's minority to introduce Edward de Baliol (*c*.1283–1364) as an English puppet in his place. After returning from exile in France (1334–41), David was defeated by the English at Neville's Cross (1346) and spent eleven years in prison. His death without issue in 1371 left the throne to the Stuarts.

David[3] /'deɪvɪd/, Elizabeth (1913–92), British cookery writer. She played a leading role in introducing Mediterranean cuisine to Britain in the 1950s and 1960s. Her best-selling books include *French Provincial Cooking* (1960).

David[4] /dæ'viːd/, Jacques-Louis (1748–1825), French painter. He is famous for neoclassical paintings such as *The Oath of the Horatii* (1784) and *The Intervention of the Sabine Women* (1799). He became actively involved in the French Revolution, voting for the death of Louis XVI and supporting Robespierre. Famous works of his from the revolutionary era include *The Dead Marat* (1793), which treats contemporary events with a grandeur hitherto reserved for history painting. Imprisoned after the fall of Robespierre, he returned to prominence under Napoleon.

David, St (also **Dewi** /'dewɪ/) (6th century), Welsh monk. Since the 12th century he has been regarded as the patron saint of Wales. Little is known of his life, but it is generally accepted that he transferred the centre of Welsh ecclesiastical administration from Caerleon to Mynyw, now St David's. He also established a number of monasteries in England and Wales and many churches in South Wales. Feast day, 1 March.

Davies[1] /'deɪvɪs/, Sir Peter Maxwell (born 1934), English composer and conductor. In 1967, with Harrison Birtwistle, he co-founded the Pierrot Players (later the Fires of London ensemble), for whom he composed many of his works. These include *Taverner* (1970) and *Eight Songs for a Mad King* (1969). Davies's work is influenced particularly by serialism and early English music.

Davies[2] /'deɪvɪs/, W(illiam) H(enry) (1871–1940), English poet. He emigrated to the US and lived as a vagrant and jobbing labourer there, writing *The Autobiography of a Super-Tramp* (1908) about his experiences. His poems often focus on the natural world; collections include *The Soul's Destroyer and Other Poems* (1905), which earned him the patronage of George Bernard Shaw.

Davies[3] /'deɪvɪs/, (William) Robertson (1913–95), Canadian novelist, dramatist, and journalist. He won international recognition with his Deptford trilogy of novels. The first two of these, *Fifth Business* (1970) and *The Manticore* (1972), show the influence on Davies of Jungian psychology; the third novel, *World of Wonders* (1975), also explores psychological and spiritual issues.

da Vinci, Leonardo, see LEONARDO DA VINCI.

Davis[1] /'deɪvɪs/, Bette (born Ruth Elizabeth Davis) (1908–89), American actress. She established her Hollywood career playing a number of strong, independent female characters in such films as *Dangerous* (1935), *Jezebel* (1938), and *All About Eve* (1950). Her flair for suggesting the macabre and menacing emerged in later films, such as the melodrama *Whatever Happened to Baby Jane?* (1962) and the thriller *Murder with Mirrors* (1984).

Davis[2] /'deɪvɪs/, Joe (1901–78) and Fred (born 1913), English billiards and snooker players. Joe Davis was the dominant figure in snooker for many years, holding the world championship from 1927 until his retirement in 1946. He was also world billiards champion (1928–32). His brother Fred Davis was world snooker champion (1948–9; 1951–6) and world billiards champion (1980).

Davis[3] /'deɪvɪs/, Miles (Dewey) (1926–91), American jazz trumpeter, composer, and band-leader. In the 1950s he played and recorded arrangements by Gil Evans in a new style which became known as 'cool' jazz, heard on albums such as *Kind of Blue* (1959). For much of the time between 1955 and 1960 his quintet included John Coltrane. In the 1960s Davis pioneered the fusion of jazz and rock, on albums such as *In a Silent Way* (1969).

Davis[4] /'deɪvɪs/, Steve (born 1957), English snooker player. He won a number of national and international events in the 1980s, becoming UK Professional Champion (1980–1; 1984–7) and World Professional Champion (1981; 1983–4; 1987–9).

Davisson /'deɪvɪs(ə)n/, Clinton Joseph (1881–1958), American physicist. Following work in support of a patent suit, and after a laboratory accident, he and L. H. Germer (1896–1971) discovered electron diffraction, thus confirming de Broglie's theory of the wave nature of electrons. He shared the Nobel Prize for physics for this in 1937, and later worked on the application of electron waves to crystal physics and electron microscopy.

Davy /'deɪvɪ/, Sir Humphry (1778–1829), English chemist, a pioneer of electrochemistry. After an apprenticeship with an apothecary-surgeon, he discovered nitrous oxide (laughing gas) and was invited to join the Royal Institution. Using electrolytic decomposition, he discovered the elements sodium, potassium, magnesium, calcium, strontium, and barium. Davy identified and named the element chlorine after he had demonstrated that oxygen was not a necessary constituent of acids, determined the properties of iodine, and demonstrated that diamond was a form of carbon. He appointed Faraday as his assistant.

Dawkins /'dɔːkɪnz/, Richard (born 1941), English biologist. Dawkins's book *The Selfish Gene* (1976) did much to popularize the theory of sociobiology. In *The Blind Watchmaker* (1986), Dawkins discussed evolution by natural selection and suggested that the theory could answer the fundamental question of why life exists.

Day /deɪ/, Doris (born Doris Kappelhoff) (born 1924), American actress and singer. She became a star in the 1950s with roles in a number of films, at first musicals but later also comedies and light romances. Her films include *Calamity Jane* (1953) and *Pillow Talk* (1959).

Dayan /daɪˈæn/, Moshe (1915–81), Israeli statesman and general. He fought in the British army in the Second World War, in which he lost an eye. After commanding Israeli forces at the time of the Suez crisis he entered Parliament, originally representing the Labour Party but later forming an independent group with David Ben-Gurion. Dayan became Minister of Defence in 1967 and oversaw Israel's victory in the Six Day War, but resigned in 1974 following criticisms of the country's state of readiness at the start of the Yom Kippur War. As Foreign Minister (1977–9) he played a prominent role in negotiations towards the Israeli-Egyptian peace treaty of 1979, hosted by President Carter at Camp David in the US.

Day Lewis /deɪ ˈluːɪs/, C(ecil) (1904–72), English poet and critic. During the 1930s he was associated with a group of left-wing poets which included W. H. Auden and Stephen Spender, and his early volumes of verse, such as *Transitional Poems* (1929), reflect the influence of radical and revolutionary ideas. After 1940, however, he became increasingly a figure of the Establishment; he published several works of criticism, including *The Poetic Image* (1947), and further collections of verse, such as *The Whispering Roots* (1970). He was Poet Laureate 1968–72.

Deakin /'diːkɪn/, Alfred (1856–1919), Australian Liberal statesman, Prime Minister

1903–4, 1905–8, and 1909–10. He accompanied Sir Edmund Barton to London to steer the Commonwealth Bill through Parliament (1900) and as Attorney-General (1901–3) introduced legislation which created the Australian high court. In his second term as Prime Minister he introduced far-reaching legislation, including protectionist tariffs and commercial laws.

Dean[1] /diːn/, Christopher, see TORVILL AND DEAN.

Dean[2] /diːn/, James (born James Byron) (1931–55), American actor. He starred in only three films, *East of Eden* (1955), *Rebel Without a Cause* (1955; released posthumously), and *Giant* (1956), before dying in a car accident. However, he became a cult figure closely identified with the title role of *Rebel Without a Cause*, symbolizing for many the disaffected youth of the postwar era.

de Beauvoir /də ˈbəʊvwɑː(r)/, Simone (1908–86), French existentialist philosopher, novelist, and feminist. While studying philosophy at the Sorbonne in 1929 she began her lifelong association with Jean-Paul Sartre; they became leading exponents of existentialism and founded the review *Les Temps modernes* (1945). De Beauvoir is regarded as an important figure in the 'second wave' of feminism, bringing the ideas of psychology, myth, political theory, and history to bear on the issue in her best-known work, *The Second Sex* (1949). Her fiction includes *The Blood of Others* (1944).

Debrett /dɪˈbret/, John (c.1750–1822), English publisher. He compiled *The Peerage of England, Scotland and Ireland* (first issued in 1803 and until 1971 issued annually), which is regarded as the authority on the British nobility; it is now published every five years.

de Broglie /də ˈbrəʊglɪ, French də brɔj/, Louis-Victor, Prince (1892–1987), French physicist. He was the first to suggest that subatomic particles can also have the properties of waves, and his name is now applied to such a wave. He further developed the study of wave mechanics, which was fundamental to the subsequent development of quantum mechanics. He was awarded the Nobel Prize for physics in 1929.

Debussy /dəˈbuːsɪ, French dəbysi/, (Achille) Claude (1862–1918), French composer and critic. Debussy carried the ideas of impressionist art and symbolist poetry into music, using melodies based on the whole-tone scale and delicate harmonies exploiting overtones. His orchestral tone-poem *Prélude à l'après-midi d'un faune* (1894) and his books of piano preludes and studies are outstanding examples of the delicate, suggestive character of his music. Debussy was to have a profound influence on later composers such as Berg, Bartók, and Boulez.

Debye /dɪˈbaɪ/, Peter Joseph William (1884–1966), Dutch-born American chemical physicist. Debye made substantial contributions in several fields. He established the existence of permanent electric dipole moments in many molecules, demonstrated the use of these to determine molecular size and shape, modified Einstein's theory of specific heats as applied to solids, pioneered the use of X-ray scattering to determine crystal structure, and solved problems of electrolytic conductance. He received the Nobel Prize for chemistry in 1936.

Decius /ˈdiːsɪəs/, Gaius Messius Quintus Trajanus (c.201–51), Roman emperor 249–51. He was the first Roman emperor to promote systematic persecution of the Christians in the empire; popular protest eventually forced him to reverse this policy shortly before the end of his reign. He resisted a Gothic invasion of Moesia in 249, but was defeated and killed two years later.

Dedekind /ˈdeɪdəˌkɪnt/, Richard (1831–1916), German mathematician. One of the founders of abstract algebra and modern mathematics, Dedekind was professor at Brunswick from 1862 until his death. His analysis of the properties of real numbers solved the question of what numbers are, and supplied a satisfactory foundation on which analysis could be based. He is remembered also for his theory of rings of algebraic integers, which cast the theory of algebraic numbers into its general modern form. He introduced collections of numbers as entities of interest in their own right, whose relationships to each other may be studied by means of set theory.

de Duve /də ˈduːv/, Christian René (born 1917), British-born Belgian biochemist. He was a pioneer in the study of cell biology, and his research suggested the existence of organelles that contain and isolate a cell's digestive enzymes. In 1955, with the aid of electron microscopy, he proved the ex-

istence of lysosomes. De Duve shared a Nobel Prize in 1974.

Dee /diː/, John (1527–1608), English alchemist, mathematician, and geographer. He was a student at Cambridge and on the Continent, and became a respected academic figure. He helped in the first English translation of Euclid's works, and was Elizabeth I's astrologer. In later life he absorbed himself in alchemy, acquired notoriety as a sorceror, and died in poverty.

de Falla, Manuel, see FALLA.

Defoe /dɪˈfəʊ/, Daniel (1660–1731), English novelist and journalist. After a varied career of political journalism and secret service work, Defoe wrote *Robinson Crusoe* (1719) when he was nearly 60. Loosely based on the true story of the sailor Alexander Selkirk, it has a claim to being the first English novel. Its tale of the shipwrecked Crusoe battling for survival in virtual solitude is one of the most familiar and resonant myths of modern literature. Other major works include the novel *Moll Flanders* (1722) and the historical fiction *A Journal of the Plague Year* (1722).

De Forest /də ˈfɒrɪst/, Lee (1873–1961), American physicist and electrical engineer. His triode valve (patented in 1907) became the basic device for the large-scale amplification of signals, and was crucial to the development of radio communication, television, and computers. De Forest was one of the pioneers of radio broadcasting, successfully transmitting a live broadcast in 1910. He later developed a method of representing sound waves visually for recording and reproducing sound on cinema film.

Degas /ˈdeɪgɑː, French dəgɑ/, (Hilaire Germain) Edgar (1834–1917), French painter and sculptor. Having been a pupil of Ingres, he became associated with impressionism; he took part in most of the impressionist exhibitions, including the first in 1874. Unlike other impressionist painters, who often concentrated on landscape, Degas is best known for his paintings of ballet-dancers, such as *Dancer Lacing Her Shoe* (c.1878); in his sculpture, to which he turned in later life, he also concentrated on the human form.

de Gaulle /də ˈgəʊl/, Charles (André Joseph Marie) (1890–1970), French general and statesman, head of government 1944–6, President 1959–69. He served in the French army during the First World War, and

during the Second World War was a member of the Cabinet at the time of France's surrender in June 1940. He escaped to Britain, where he was an instigator of the resistance and organized the Free French movement. Following the war he became interim President of the new French Republic, but later resigned. Having been asked to form a government, he became President in 1959 and went on to establish the presidency as a democratically elected office (1962). He resigned in 1969 after proposed constitutional changes were rejected by the electorate. In addition to extricating France from the Algerian crisis and strengthening the French economy, he is remembered for his assertive foreign policy (including withdrawing French forces from NATO and blocking Britain's entry to the EEC) and for quelling the student uprisings and strikes of May 1968.

de Havilland /də ˈhævɪlənd/, Sir Geoffrey (1882–1965), English aircraft designer and manufacturer. Having built the BE series of fighters in the First World War, he started his own company in 1920. He designed and built many famous aircraft, including the Moth series, the Mosquito of the Second World War, and some of the first jet aircraft, and also produced the Gipsy series of aircraft engines.

de Hooch /də ˈhuːtʃ, Dutch də ˈhoːx/, Pieter (also **de Hoogh**) (c.1629–c.1684), Dutch genre painter. He is noted for his depictions of domestic interior and courtyard scenes, which he painted while living in Delft. His best works, such as *Interior with a Woman Peeling Apples* (1663), are characterized by their sensitive handling of light and tranquil atmosphere.

Deighton /ˈdeɪt(ə)n/, Leonard Cyril ('Len') (born 1929), English novelist. His reputation is based on his spy thrillers, several of which have been adapted as films and for television. The best known include his first novel *The Ipcress File* (1962) and the trilogy *Berlin Game*, *Mexico Set*, and *London Match* (1983–5).

Dekker /ˈdekə(r)/, Thomas (c.1570–1632), English dramatist and novelist. He is chiefly known for his two-part tragicomedy *The Honest Whore* (1604; 1630), the first part of which he wrote jointly with Thomas Middleton. He is also remembered for the revenge tragedy *The Witch of Edmonton*

(1623), in which he collaborated with John Ford and William Rowley (c.1585–1626).

de Klerk /də 'kleək/, F(rederik) W(illem) (born 1936), South African statesman, State President 1989–94. Becoming State President only months after assuming leadership of the National Party, he instigated significant political reforms designed to bring about the dismantling of apartheid in South Africa. After freeing Nelson Mandela and other ANC leaders in 1990 he lifted the ban on membership of the ANC and opened the negotiations with black political leaders that led to the country's first true democratic elections in 1994. After the ANC's electoral victory de Klerk was given a Cabinet post, but retired in 1997. In 1993 he shared the Nobel Peace Prize with Nelson Mandela.

de Kooning /də 'ku:nɪŋ/, Willem (1904–97), Dutch-born American painter. He and Jackson Pollock are generally regarded as the leading exponents of abstract expressionism. De Kooning's work in this genre from the late 1940s onwards usually retained figurative elements, whether represented or merely hinted at, as in *Painting* (1948). The female form became a central theme in his later work, notably in the *Women* series (1950–3).

de la Beche /ˌdə læ 'bi:tʃ/, Sir Henry Thomas (1796–1855), English geologist. He travelled extensively to study geology in the field, and produced the first geological description and map of Jamaica. Having already surveyed Devon, he was involved in the establishment of the Geological Survey of Great Britain in 1835, directing it from then until his death.

Delacroix /ˌdelə'krwʌ/, (Ferdinand Victor) Eugène (1798–1863), French painter. The chief painter of the French romantic school, he is known for his use of vivid colour, free drawing, and exotic, violent, or macabre subject-matter. *The Massacre at Chios* (1824) was an early example of his work and attracted much criticism when it was first exhibited. In his later work Delacroix experimented with complementary colours, purifying his palette to exclude black and earth colours and thus anticipating impressionist methods.

de la Mare /ˌdə læ 'meə(r)/, Walter (John) (1873–1956), English poet and novelist. Essentially a lyric poet, he had his first major success with *The Listeners* (1912). His many volumes of verse for children include *Pea-*

cock Pie (1913) and *Tom Tiddler's Ground* (1932).

de la Roche /ˌdə læ 'rɒʃ/, Mazo (1879–1961), Canadian novelist. She won acclaim for *Jalna* (1927), the first of a series of novels about the Whiteoak family. The 'Jalna' cycle was noted for its characterization and also for its evocation of rural Ontario, despite being more popular in the United States and Europe than in Canada.

Delaunay /dəˈlɔːneɪ/, Robert (1885–1941), French painter. For most of his career he experimented with the abstract qualities of colour, notably in his Eiffel Tower series (1910–12), and was one of the founder members of Orphism together with his wife, Sonia Delaunay-Terk. He was influenced by early cubism and painted some of the first purely abstract pictures, including his *Formes circulaires cosmiques* series (from 1912).

Delaunay-Terk /dəˌlɔːnerˈteək/, Sonia (1885–1979), Russian-born French painter and textile designer. She and her husband Robert Delaunay were among the founders of the movement of Orphism. She created abstract paintings based on harmonies of form and colour, her interest in the use of colour being reflected in her fabric and tapestry designs of the 1920s; her work in this field had a significant impact on international fashion.

de Lenclos, Ninon, see LENCLOS.

Delfont /ˈdelfɒnt/, Bernard, Baron Delfont of Stepney (born Boris Winogradsky) (1909–94), British impresario, born in Russia. Having emigrated to Britain with his brother (see GRADE) in 1912, he pursued a successful career in theatrical management; from the early 1940s onwards he presented more than 200 shows in London's West End.

Delibes /dəˈliːb/, (Clément Philibert) Léo (1836–91), French composer and organist. He wrote a number of light operas such as *Lakmé* (1883), but his best-known works are the ballets *Coppélia* (1870) and *Sylvia* (1876).

Delius /ˈdiːlɪəs/, Frederick (1862–1934), English composer, of German and Scandinavian descent. He is best known for pastoral works such as *Brigg Fair* (1907) and *On Hearing the First Cuckoo* (1912), but he also wrote songs, concertos, and much choral and theatre music, including operas, often showing his deep interest in German and

Scandinavian music and culture. Delius settled in France in the 1890s; blinded and paralysed by illness in 1928 he dictated his last works to an amanuensis, Eric Fenby (1906–97).

della Francesca see PIERO DELLA FRANCESCA.

della Quercia /ˌdelə ˈkwɜːʃə/, Jacopo (c.1374–1438), Italian sculptor. He is noted for his tomb of Ilaria del Carretto in Lucca cathedral (c.1406) and, above all, for the biblical reliefs on the portal of San Petronio in Bologna (1425–35), which are notable for the sense of depth they achieve. He became chief architect of the cathedral in his native Siena in 1435.

della Robbia /ˌdelə ˈrɒbɪə/, a family of Italian sculptors and ceramicists. Luca (1400–82) is the most famous, and is particularly well known for his relief panels in Florence cathedral. He invented vitreous glazes to colour terracotta figures, thus making it possible for polychromatic sculpture to be used in outdoor settings without suffering from the effects of damp. His nephew Andrea (1434–1525) carried on the family business of glazed terracotta production.

Delors /dəˈlɔː(r)/, Jacques (Lucien Jean) (born 1925), French socialist politician, president of the European Commission 1985–94. During his presidency he pressed for closer European union and oversaw the introduction of a single market within the European Community, which came into effect on 1 January 1993.

del Sarto, Andrea, see SARTO.

de Maintenon see MAINTENON.

de Maupassant, Guy, see MAUPASSANT.

de' Medici[1], Catherine, see CATHERINE DE' MEDICI.

de' Medici[2], Cosimo, see COSIMO DE' MEDICI.

de' Medici[3], Giovanni, the name of Pope Leo X (see LEO).

de' Medici[4], Lorenzo, see LORENZO DE' MEDICI.

de Médicis, Marie, see MARIE DE MÉDICIS.

de Mille /də ˈmɪl/, Cecil B(lount) (1881–1959), American film producer and director. He founded the Jesse L. Lasky Feature Play Company (later Paramount) with Samuel Goldwyn in 1913 and chose the then little-known Los Angeles suburb of Hollywood as a location for their first film, *The Squaw Man* (1914); the success of this first American feature film helped to establish Hollywood as the world's prime centre of film-making. As a film-maker de Mille is particularly known for lavish biblical spectacles such as *The Ten Commandments* (1923; remade by de Mille in 1956) and *Samson and Delilah* (1949).

Democritus /dɪˈmɒkrɪtəs/ (c.460–c.370 BC), Greek philosopher. He wrote widely on a variety of subjects and further developed the atomic theory originated by his teacher, Leucippus (5th century BC); this theory explained natural phenomena in terms of the arrangement and rearrangement of atoms moving in a void. Democritus was nicknamed 'the laughing philosopher', reputedly because he showed amusement at human nature.

de Montespan, Marquise de, see MONTESPAN.

de Montfort, Simon, see MONTFORT[2].

Demosthenes /dɪˈmɒsθəˌniːz/ (384–322 BC), Athenian orator and statesman. He is best known for his political speeches on the need to defend Athens against the pretensions of Philip II of Macedon, which are known as the *Philippics*. Demosthenes was at the forefront of the campaign to unite the Greek city-states militarily against Macedon; the Greeks were defeated at the battle of Chaeronea in 338 BC, and Demosthenes committed suicide after the failure of an Athenian revolt against Macedon.

Dempsey /ˈdempsɪ/, William Harrison ('Jack') (1895–1983), American boxer. He was world heavyweight champion 1919–26, and during this time drew extremely large audiences to boxing; his defence of the title in 1921 was the first fight at which a million dollars was taken at the gate.

Dench /dentʃ/, Dame Judi(th Olivia) (born 1934), English actress. She performed with the Old Vic Company between 1957 and 1961 before joining the Royal Shakespeare Company for a season. Returning to the RSC in 1969, she also appeared in numerous West End and television productions. Her films include *84 Charing Cross Road* (1986), *A Handful of Dust* (1987), and *Goldeneye* (1995).

Deneuve /dəˈnɜːv/, Catherine (born Catherine Dorléac) (born 1943), French actress. She is best known for her roles in such

films as *Repulsion* (1965) and Luis Buñuel's *Belle de jour* (1967).

Deng Xiaoping /ˌdeŋ ʃaʊˈpɪŋ, ˌdʌŋ/ (also **Teng Hsiao-p'ing** /ˌteŋ/) (1904–97), Chinese Communist statesman, Vice-Premier 1973–6 and 1977–80; Vice-Chairman of the Central Committee of the Chinese Communist Party 1977–80. Discredited during the Cultural Revolution, he was reinstated in 1977, becoming the most prominent exponent of economic modernization, improving relations with the West, and taking a firm stance in relation to the Soviet Union. After that, despite the announcement of his retirement in 1989, he was considered to be the effective leader of China. In 1989 his orders led to the massacre of some 2,000 pro-democracy demonstrators in Beijing's Tiananmen Square.

De Niro /də ˈnɪərəʊ/, Robert (born 1943), American actor. Since his first major film success, in *Mean Streets* (1972), he has starred in many films, often playing gangsters and other tough characters and frequently working with director Martin Scorsese. He won Oscars for *The Godfather Part II* (1974) and *Raging Bull* (1980). More recently De Niro made his début as a director with *A Bronx Tale* (1994), in which he also acted.

Denis /dəˌniː/, Maurice (1870–1943), French painter, designer, and art theorist. A founder member and leading theorist of the Nabi Group, he wrote many works on art, including *Théories* (1913) and *Nouvelles Théories* (1921). As a painter he is best known for his group portrait *Hommage à Cézanne* (1900) and his religious paintings. He founded the Ateliers d'Art Sacré in 1919 as part of a programme to revive religious painting.

Denis, St /ˈdenɪs/ (also **Denys**; Roman name Dionysius) (died *c.*250), Italian-born French bishop, patron saint of France. According to tradition he was one of a group of seven missionaries sent from Rome to convert Gaul; he became bishop of Paris, and was martyred in the reign of the emperor Valerian. He was later confused with Dionysius the Areopagite. Feast day, 9 October.

Depardieu /ˈdepɑːdjə, French dəpardjø/, Gérard (born 1948), French actor. He made his screen début in 1965. His international reputation is based on the many films he has made since the early 1980s; these include *Danton* (1982), *Jean de Florette* (1986), and *Cyrano de Bergerac* (1990).

de Pisan /də ˈpiːzæn/, Christine (also **de Pizan**) (*c.*1364–*c.*1430), Italian writer, resident in France from 1369. After the death of her husband when she was 25, she turned to writing for her living, becoming the first professional woman writer in France. She is best known for her works in defence of women's virtues and achievements; these include *Epistre au dieu d'amour* (1399), *La Cité des dames* (1405; *Book of the City of Ladies*), which celebrates the lives of famous women throughout history, and *Le Livre des trois vertus* (1406), a treatise on women's education. Other works include a biography of Charles V of France (1404).

Deprez see DES PREZ.

De Quincey /də ˈkwɪnsɪ/, Thomas (1785–1859), English essayist and critic. After first taking opium for toothache at Oxford, he became a lifelong addict. He achieved fame with his *Confessions of an English Opium Eater* (1822), a study of his addiction and its psychological effects, ranging from euphoria to nightmares. His writing had an important influence on Charles Baudelaire and Edgar Allan Poe.

Derain /dəˈræn/, André (1880–1954), French painter. He was one of the exponents of fauvism, joining with Vlaminck and Matisse in treating colour as an independent decorative and expressive element; this is particularly evident in his paintings of Hyde Park and the Thames (1906–7). He was also influenced by early cubism and the post-impressionist painting of Cézanne. In addition to painting, he designed theatre sets and costumes, notably for the Ballets Russes.

Derby /ˈdɑːbɪ/, 14th Earl of (title of Edward George Geoffrey Smith Stanley) (1799–1869), British Conservative statesman, Prime Minister 1852, 1858–9, and 1866–8. He led the protectionists in the House of Lords in their opposition to Sir Robert Peel's attempted repeal of the Corn Laws in 1846, and in his last term as Prime Minister he carried the second Reform Act (1867) through Parliament.

Derrida /ˈderɪdə/, Jacques (born 1930), French philosopher and critic. His radical critique of traditional Western philosophy and literary analysis led to the emergence of the school of deconstruction in Paris in the late 1960s. His work, which includes *Of Grammatology* (1967) and *Writing and Difference* (1967), rejects earlier structuralist assumptions about the relationship between

language and meaning and between text and the objective world, often concentrating on ambiguity and contradiction in meaning.

de Sade, Marquis, see SADE.

Descartes /'deɪkɑːt/, René (1596–1650), French philosopher, mathematician, and man of science, often called the father of modern philosophy. Aiming to reach totally secure foundations for knowledge, he began by attacking all his beliefs with sceptical doubts. What was left was the certainty of his own conscious experience, and with it of his existence: 'Cogito, ergo sum' (I think, therefore I am). From this certainty he argued for the existence of God (as the first cause) and the reality of the physical world, and developed a dualistic theory of mind (conscious experience) and matter. His approach was of fundamental importance in the development of modern philosophy, particularly epistemology. In mathematics he developed the use of coordinates to locate a point in two or three dimensions: this enabled the techniques of algebra and calculus to be used to solve geometrical problems. Descartes suppressed his heretical doctrines of the earth's rotation and the infinity of the universe; fragments of his work in this field were published after his death. From 1628 to 1649 he lived in Holland, then departed for Sweden at the invitation of Queen Christina (1626–89).

De Sica /də 'siːkə/, Vittorio (1901–74), Italian film director and actor. After acting in more than 150 films, in 1940 he turned to directing, becoming a key figure in Italian neo-realist cinema. His celebrated films in this genre include *Shoeshine* (1946) and the Oscar-winning *Bicycle Thieves* (1948). During the 1960s he made a number of successful films starring Sophia Loren, notably *Two Women* (1960), which won an Oscar.

de Spinoza, Baruch, see SPINOZA.

des Prez /deɪ 'preɪ/, Josquin (also **des Prés**, **Deprez**) (c.1440–1521), Flemish composer. Regarded as one of the leading composers of the Renaissance, he wrote eighteen complete masses, 112 motets, and some seventy songs, many of them typical examples of polyphonic song. He is perhaps best known for his Italian song 'El Grillo', with its parody of the chirrup of the cricket.

de Staël /də 'stɑːl/ Mme (née Anne Louise Germaine Necker) (1766–1817), French nov-

elist and critic. A major precursor of the French romantics, she wrote two semi-autobiographical novels, *Delphine* (1802) and *Corinne* (1807). Her best-known critical work *De l'Allemagne* (1810) introduced late 18th-century German writers and thinkers to France; it was banned on publication by Napoleon.

de Troyes, Chrétien, see CHRÉTIEN DE TROYES.

de Valera /ˌdə vəˈleərə/, Eamon (1882–1975), American-born Irish statesman. A fervent Irish nationalist, de Valera was one of the leaders of the Easter Rising in 1916 and was sentenced to death by the British, but was released a year later. He served as leader of Sinn Fein (1917–26) and President of the Irish provisional government (1919–22), and as an opponent of the Anglo-Irish Treaty headed the militant republicans in the ensuing civil war. In 1926 he founded the Fianna Fáil Party, which he led in the Dáil. In 1932 de Valera became President of the Irish Free State, and was largely responsible for the new constitution of 1937, which created the sovereign state of Eire. He served as Taoiseach (Prime Minister) 1937–48, 1951–4, and 1957–9, and President 1959–73.

de Valois /də 'vælwɑː/, Dame Ninette (born Edris Stannus) (born 1898), Irish choreographer, ballet-dancer, and teacher. A former soloist with Diaghilev's Ballets Russes, she turned to choreography in the 1920s. The success of her ballet *Job* in 1931 led to the formation of the Vic-Wells Ballet and the Sadler's Wells ballet school. De Valois was director of the company, which eventually became the Royal Ballet, from 1931 until 1963. Among the ballets she choreographed for the company were *The Rake's Progress* (1935) and *Checkmate* (1937).

Devoy /də'vɔɪ/, Susan (born 1954), New Zealand squash player. She was ranked first in the world when aged 20, the youngest player to achieve this distinction. She won the British Open Championship seven consecutive times (1984–90), and again in 1992, and was five times world champion between 1985 and 1992.

de Vries /də 'vriːs/, Hugo (1848–1935), Dutch plant physiologist and geneticist. Until about 1890 he worked largely on osmosis and water relations in plants, coining the term *plasmolysis*. He then switched abruptly to work on heredity and variation, carrying out plant-breeding experiments which gave similar results to those

of Mendel (of which he was unaware). His extensive experiments with the evening primrose, though wrongly interpreted at the time, contributed substantially to the chromosome theory of heredity.

Dewar /'dju:ə(r)/, Sir James (1842–1923), Scottish chemist and physicist. He is chiefly remembered for his work in cryogenics. He devised the vacuum flask, achieved temperatures close to absolute zero, and was the first to produce liquid oxygen and hydrogen in quantity. Dewar also worked on structural organic chemistry, spectroscopic analysis, high temperature reactions, thin films, and infrared radiation.

Dewey[1] /'dju:ɪ/, John (1859–1952), American philosopher and educationist. Working in the pragmatic tradition of William James and C. S. Pierce, he defined knowledge as successful practice, and evolved the educational theory that children would learn best by doing. He published his ideas in *The School and Society* (1899) and convinced many American educationists that it was necessary to create less structured, more pupil-centred, practical schools.

Dewey[2] /'dju:ɪ/, Melvil (1851–1931), American librarian. He devised a decimal system of classifying books, using ten main subject categories. The system was first invented for Amherst College Library in 1876.

Dewi see DAVID, ST.

Diaghilev /dɪ'ægɪˌlef/, Sergei (Pavlovich) (1872–1929), Russian ballet impresario. After the closure of his magazine *The World of Art* (1899–1904), he organized opera and ballet productions in Paris and in 1909 formed the Ballets Russes, which he directed until his death. Initially with Nijinsky as his star performer, and later with Massine, he transformed the European ballet scene into a creative centre for a large and varied array of artists, pooling the talents of leading choreographers, painters, and composers of his day.

Diana, Princess of Wales /daɪ'ænə/ (born Lady Diana Frances Spencer) (1961–97), former wife of Prince Charles. She married Charles, Prince of Wales, in 1981; the couple divorced in 1996. Her death in a car crash in Paris following pursuit by press photographers gave rise to intense national mourning.

Dias /'di:æs/, Bartolomeu (also **Diaz**) (c.1450–1500), Portuguese navigator and explorer. He was the first European to round the Cape of Good Hope (1488), thereby establishing a sea route from the Atlantic to Asia via the southernmost point of Africa; he later accompanied Vasco da Gama on the first European expedition to Asia by this route.

Díaz /'di:æs/, Porfirio (1830–1915), Mexican general and statesman, President 1877–80 and 1884–1911. He led a military coup in 1876 and was elected President the following year. During his second term of office he introduced a highly centralized government, backed by loyal mestizos and landowners, which removed powers from rural workers and American Indians. Díaz promoted the development of Mexico's infrastructure and industry, using foreign capital and engineers to build railways, bridges, and mines. Eventually the poor performance of Mexico's economy and the rise of a democratic movement under Francisco Madero (1873–1913) contributed to Díaz's forced resignation and exile in 1911.

Dickens /'dɪkɪnz/, Charles (John Huffam) (1812–70), English novelist. His early work consisted mainly of humorous sketches and short pieces for periodical publication; much of his fiction also first appeared in instalments in magazines. Dickens drew on his own childhood experiences of hardship and deprivation in his fiction, and many of his works are set in his native London. His novels are broad in scope and deal with all social classes, but they are particularly notable for their treatment of contemporary social problems, including the plight of the urban poor, corruption and inefficiency within the legal system, and general social injustices. Some of his most famous novels include *Oliver Twist* (1837–8), *Nicholas Nickleby* (1838–9), *Bleak House* (1852–3), and *Great Expectations* (1860–1). His satirical humour and varied characterizations, including such familiar caricatures as Scrooge (*A Christmas Carol*, 1843) and Mr Micawber (*David Copperfield*, 1850), contributed to the great popular appeal of his work.

Dickinson /'dɪkɪns(ə)n/, Emily (Elizabeth) (1830–86), American poet. From the age of 24 she led the life of a recluse in Amherst, Massachussets. Her withdrawal and inner struggle are reflected in her mystical

poems, expressed in her own elliptical language, with a greater emphasis on assonance and alliteration than rhyme. Although she wrote nearly 2,000 poems, only seven were published in her lifetime; the first selection appeared in 1890.

Diderot /'di:də,rəʊ/, Denis (1713–84), French philosopher, writer, and critic. He was a leading figure of the Enlightenment in France and principal editor of the *Encyclopédie* (1751–76), through which he disseminated and popularized philosophy and scientific knowledge. His major philosophical writings include *Pensées sur l'interprétation de la nature* (1754), which in some ways anticipated evolutionary ideas on the nature and origin of life. His *Salons* (1755; 1759–71; 1781) are the first examples of modern art criticism in France.

Diesel /'di:z(ə)l/, Rudolf (Christian Karl) (1858–1913), French-born German engineer, inventor of the diesel engine. He studied thermodynamics at Munich before moving to Paris in 1880 to manage a refrigeration plant. In 1892 he patented a design for a new, more efficient internal-combustion engine and developed it, exhibiting the prototype in 1897. It attracted worldwide interest, and a factory to manufacture the engine was built at Augsburg, where Diesel spent most of his life.

Dietrich /'di:trɪx/, Marlene (born Maria Magdelene von Losch) (1901–92), German-born American actress and singer. She became famous for her part as Lola in *Der Blaue Engel* (1930; *The Blue Angel*), directed by Josef von Sternberg. It was her last film before she went to the US, where she and von Sternberg made a series of films together, such as *Blonde Venus* (1932) and *The Devil is a Woman* (1935). From the 1950s she was also successful as an international cabaret star. She became increasingly reclusive towards the end of her life.

DiMaggio /dɪ'mædʒɪ,əʊ/, Joseph Paul ('Joe') (born 1914), American baseball player. Star of the New York Yankees team 1936–51, he was renowned for his outstanding batting ability and for his outfield play. He was briefly married to Marilyn Monroe in 1954.

Dimbleby /'dɪmb(ə)lbɪ/, (Frederick) Richard (1913–65), English broadcaster. He was the BBC's first news correspondent (1936) and the first broadcaster to be commemorated in Westminster Abbey. He distinguished himself in his radio and television commentaries on royal, national, and international events and in his reports on current affairs. His sons David (born 1938) and Jonathan (born 1944) have both followed their father into careers in news broadcasting.

Dinesen /'dɪnɪs(ə)n/, Isak, see BLIXEN.

Diocletian /,daɪə'kli:ʃ(ə)n/ (full name Gaius Aurelius Valerius Diocletianus) (245–313), Roman emperor 284–305. Faced with military problems on many frontiers and insurrection in the provinces, in 286 he divided the empire between himself in the east and Maximian (died 310) in the west. In 293 he further divided the empire, giving Galerius (died 311) control of Illyricum and the valley of the River Danube, with Constantius Chlorus (died 306) ruling Gaul, Spain, and Britain. An enthusiast for the old Roman religion, tradition, and discipline, Diocletian insisted on the maintenance of Roman law in the provinces and launched the final harsh persecution of the Christians (303). He abdicated in 305.

Diogenes /daɪ'ɒdʒɪ,ni:z/ (*c*.400–*c*.325 BC), Greek philosopher. He was the most famous of the Cynics and the pupil of Antisthenes (*c*.445–*c*.365 BC). He lived a life of extreme poverty and asceticism in Athens (according to legend, he lived in a tub) and was accordingly nicknamed *Kuōn* ('the dog'), from which the Cynics derived their name. He emphasized self-sufficiency and the need for natural, uninhibited behaviour, regardless of social conventions. Among the many stories told of him is that he took a lantern in daylight, saying that he was seeking an honest man.

Dionysius /,daɪə'nɪsɪəs/ the name of two rulers of Syracuse:
Dionysius I (known as Dionysius the Elder) (*c*.430–367 BC), ruled 405–367. After establishing himself as a tyrannical ruler in 405, he waged three wars against the Carthaginians for control of Sicily, the third of which (383–*c*.375) resulted in his defeat at Cronium. Nevertheless, his reign made him the principal power in Greek Italy, after the capture of Rhegium (386) and other Greek cities in southern Italy.
Dionysius II (known as Dionysius the Younger) (*c*.397–*c*.344 BC), son of Dionysius I, ruled 367–357 and 346–344. He lacked his father's military ambitions and signed a peace treaty with Carthage in 367. Despite his patronage of philosophers, he resisted the attempt by Plato to turn him

into a philosopher-king, in 366 banishing the wealthy Syracusan Dion (*c.*408–*c.*354), the proponent of the scheme. He was subsequently overthrown by Dion in 357.

Dionysius Exiguus /ˌɪgˈzɪgjʊəs/ (died *c.*556), Scythian monk and scholar. He is famous for introducing the system of dates BC and AD that is still in use today, accepting 753 AUC as the year of the Incarnation; this has since been shown to be mistaken. He is said to have given himself the nickname *Exiguus* (Latin for 'little'), as a sign of humility.

Dionysius of Halicarnassus /ˌhælɪkɑːˈnæsəs/ (1st century BC), Greek historian, literary critic, and rhetorician. He lived in Rome from 30 BC. He is best known for his detailed history of Rome, written in Greek; this covers the period from the earliest times until the outbreak of the first Punic War (264 BC).

Dionysius the Areopagite /ˌærɪˈɒpəˌgaɪt/ (1st century AD), Greek churchman. His conversion by St Paul is recorded in Acts 17:34 and according to tradition he went on to become the first bishop of Athens. He was later confused with St Denis and with a mystical theologian, Pseudo-Dionysius the Areopagite (*fl.* 500), whose Neoplatonic Christian writings exercised a profound influence on medieval theology.

Diophantus /ˌdaɪəˈfæntəs/ (*fl.* prob. *c.*250 AD), Greek mathematician, of Alexandria. Diophantus was the first to attempt an algebraical notation. In his *Arithmetica* he showed how to solve simple and quadratic equations. His work led Pierre de Fermat to take up the theory of numbers, in which he made his famous discoveries.

Dior /ˈdiːɔː(r)/, Christian (1905–57), French couturier. In 1947 he showed his first collection, featuring narrow-waisted tightly fitted bodices and full pleated skirts; this became known as the New Look and initially shocked the fashion world by its extravagance. He remained an influential figure in fashion, for example creating the first A-line garments, and built up a range of quality accessories. He discovered and trained Yves Saint Laurent.

Dirac /dɪˈræk/, Paul Adrian Maurice (1902–84), English theoretical physicist. He applied Einstein's theory of relativity to quantum mechanics in order to describe the behaviour of the electron, including its spin, and later predicted the existence of the positron. He also developed a quantum theory of radiation, and was the co-inventor of Fermi–Dirac statistics, which describe the behaviour of the particles later called fermions. Dirac shared the 1933 Nobel Prize for physics.

Disney /ˈdɪznɪ/, Walter Elias ('Walt') (1901–66), American animator and film producer. He made his name with the creation of Mortimer (later Mickey) Mouse in 1927; many other familiar cartoon characters, including Minnie Mouse, Goofy, Pluto, and Donald Duck, were invented by Disney. He produced the first full-length cartoon feature film with sound and colour, *Snow White and the Seven Dwarfs* (1937); this was followed by *Pinocchio* (1940), *Bambi* (1942), and many others. Disney also made many animal and adventure films for children; after his death the tradition of animation and film-making was continued under the Disney name. He was also immortalized by the creation of Disneyland, an amusement park in California, which was opened in 1955; the first European Disneyland was established just outside Paris in 1992.

Disraeli /dɪzˈreɪlɪ/, Benjamin, 1st Earl of Beaconsfield (1804–81), British Tory statesman, of Italian Jewish descent; Prime Minister 1868 and 1874–80. He played a dominant role in the reconstruction of the Tory Party after Sir Robert Peel, guiding it away from protectionism and generating enthusiasm for the British Empire. He was largely responsible for the introduction of the second Reform Act (1867), which doubled the electorate. In his second term as Prime Minister he ensured that Britain bought a controlling interest in the Suez Canal (1875) and also made Queen Victoria Empress of India. At home his government passed much useful social legislation, including measures to improve public health and working conditions in factories. He wrote a number of novels, including *Coningsby* (1844) and *Sybil* (1845), which drew on his experience of political life.

Di Stefano /dɪ ˈstefəˌnəʊ/, Alfredo (born 1926), Argentinian-born Spanish footballer. Considered to be one of the greatest footballers of all time, he made his début in 1944, playing as a forward in his home country and in Colombia before taking Spanish nationality and playing for the national side. With Real Madrid he won the European Cup in each of the first five seasons of the competition (1956–60), scoring in each final.

Dobell /dəʊ'bel/, Sir William (1899–1970), Australian painter. Noted for his portraits, he won the 1943 Archibald Prize, awarded by the Art Gallery of New South Wales, for his portrait of fellow artist Joshua Smith. The award was contested in court by two of the unsuccessful competitors on the grounds that it was not a portrait but a caricature, and created a *cause célèbre* for modernism in Australia.

Dodgson /'dɒdʒsən/, Charles Lutwidge, see CARROLL.

Doisneau /'dwʌnəʊ/, Robert (1912–94), French photographer. He is best known for his photos portraying the city and inhabitants of Paris, which he began taking in the 1930s; one of his most famous images is 'The Kiss at the Hôtel de Ville' (1950). His photojournalism includes pictures taken during the liberation of Paris in 1944.

Dole /dəʊl/, Robert Joseph ('Bob') (born 1923), American Republican politician. A senator since 1968, he became leader of the Republican Party in 1992, and was defeated by Bill Clinton in the presidential elections of 1996.

Dolin /'dəʊlɪn, 'dɒl-/, Sir Anton (born Sydney Francis Patrick Chippendall Healey-Kay) (1904–83), English ballet-dancer and choreographer. From 1923 until 1926, and again from 1928 to 1929, he was a principal with the Ballets Russes. With Alicia Markova he founded the Markova–Dolin Ballet in 1935; the company lasted until 1938. After a period spent abroad, Dolin returned to Britain in 1948, and in 1950 became artistic director and first soloist of the newly founded London Festival Ballet, a post he held until 1961.

D'Oliveira /ˌdɒlɪ'vɪərə/, Basil (Lewis) (born 1931), British cricketer and coach, born in South Africa. Of Cape Coloured origin, D'Oliveira was brought to England in 1960 to play professional cricket. He made his début for Worcestershire at the age of 33 and for England the following season, going on to win forty-four caps and to score five test centuries. South Africa's refusal to allow D'Oliveira into the country led to the cancellation of England's 1968–9 tour and to South Africa's subsequent banishment from test cricket.

Doll /dɒl/, Sir (William) Richard (Shaboe) (born 1912), English physician. He investigated the aetiology of lung cancer, leukaemia, and other cancers, and (with Sir A.

Bradford Hill, 1897–1991) was the first to provide a statistical link between smoking and lung cancer. They later showed that stopping smoking is immediately effective in reducing the risk of lung cancer. Doll also studied peptic ulcers, the effects of ionizing radiation, and oral contraceptives.

Dollfuss /'dɒlfʊs/, Engelbert (1892–1934), Austrian statesman, Chancellor of Austria 1932–4. He was elected leader of the Christian Socialist Party and Chancellor in 1932. From 1933 Dollfuss attempted to govern without Parliament in order better to oppose Austrian Nazi attempts to force the *Anschluss* (the union of Austria and Germany). Five months after promulgating a new Fascist constitution in 1934, he was assassinated by Austrian Nazis in an abortive coup.

Domingo /də'mɪŋgəʊ/, Placido (born 1941), Spanish-born tenor. He moved to Mexico with his family in 1950, and made his operatic début in 1957. He established his reputation as one of the world's leading operatic tenors in the 1970s; his performances in operas by Verdi and Puccini have met with particular acclaim.

Dominic, St /'dɒmɪnɪk/ (Spanish name Domingo de Guzmán) (*c*.1170–1221), Spanish priest and friar. In 1203 he began a mission to reconcile the Albigenses to the Church. Although largely unsuccessful in this aim he established a number of religious communities and undertook the training of preachers; in 1216 this led to the foundation of the Order of Friars Preachers, known as the Dominicans, at Toulouse in France. At one time St Dominic was believed to have originated the practice of saying the rosary, but this belief has now been discredited. Feast day, 8 August.

Domino /'dɒmɪˌnəʊ/, Fats (born Antoine Domino) (born 1928), American pianist, singer, and songwriter. His music represents the transition from rhythm and blues to rock and roll and shows the influence of jazz, boogie-woogie, and gospel music. He made most of his recordings in the 1950s and early 1960s; his many songs include 'Ain't That a Shame' (1955) and 'Blueberry Hill' (1956).

Domitian /də'mɪʃ(ə)n/ (full name Titus Flavius Domitianus) (AD 51–96), son of Vespasian, Roman emperor 81–96. An energetic but autocratic ruler, on succeeding his brother Titus he embarked on a

large building programme, including monumental palaces on the Palatine Hill in Rome. His wife was implicated in his assassination, which ended a period of terror that had lasted a number of years.

Donatello /ˌdɒnə'teləʊ/ (born Donato di Betto Bardi) (1386–1466), Italian sculptor. He was one of the pioneers of scientific perspective, and is especially famous for his lifelike sculptures, including the bronze *David* (probably created between 1430 and 1460), his most classical work. He was in Padua from 1443 to 1453, where he made the *Gattamelata*, the first equestrian statue to be created since antiquity. On his return to Florence he reacted somewhat against classical principles, evolving a late style in which distortion is used to convey dramatic and emotional intensity, as in his carved wooden statue *St Mary Magdalene* (c.1455).

Donatus /də'neɪtəs/, Aelius (4th century), Roman grammarian. His treatises on Latin grammar were collected in the *Ars Grammatica* (undated); it was the sole textbook used in schools in the Middle Ages.

Donizetti /ˌdɒnɪ'tsetɪ/, Gaetano (1797–1848), Italian composer. He is generally regarded as the leading Italian composer of the 1830s, bridging the gap between Verdi and Bellini. He wrote seventy-five operas, including tragedies such as *Anna Bolena* (1830) and *Lucia di Lammermoor* (1835) and the comedies *L'Elisir d'amore* (1832) and *Don Pasquale* (1843).

Donkin /'dɒŋkɪn/, Bryan (1768–1855), English engineer. He made pioneering contributions in several fields, including paper-making and printing, patenting (with Richard Mackenzie Bacon, an English writer and printer, 1775–1844) the first rotary press. In the 1830s, he successfully developed a method of food preservation by heat sterilization, sealing the food inside a container made of sheet steel, so producing the first tin can.

Donne /dʌn/, John (1572–1631), English poet and preacher. Generally regarded as the first of the metaphysical poets, he is most famous for his *Satires* (c.1590–9), *Elegies* (c.1590–9), and love poems, which appeared in the collection *Songs and Sonnets* (undated). He also wrote religious poems and, as dean of St Paul's from 1621, was one of the most celebrated preachers of his age.

Doolittle /'duːˌlɪt(ə)l/, Hilda (1886–1961), American poet. From 1911 she lived in London, where she met Ezra Pound and other imagist poets, whose style and concerns are reflected in her own work. Her many volumes of poetry (published under the pseudonym H.D.) also show the influence of classical mythology; they include *Sea Garden* (1916).

Doppler /'dɒplə(r)/, Johann Christian (1803–53), Austrian physicist. Doppler qualified in mathematics and held several professorships, mainly in Prague. He is famous for his discovery, in 1842, of what is now known as the *Doppler effect*: that the observed frequency of a wave depends on the relative motions of the source and the observer (heard in the change in the pitch of a train whistle as it passes by). Its effect on light is known as the *Doppler shift*, which causes receding galaxies to appear redder and is evidence of an expanding universe.

Doré /'dɔːreɪ/, Gustave (1832–83), French book illustrator. He was widely known for his dark, detailed woodcut illustrations of books such as Dante's *Inferno* (1861), Cervantes' *Don Quixote* (1863), and the Bible (1865–6); he produced so many of these that at one time he employed more than forty block-cutters.

Dos Passos /dɒs 'pæsɒs/, John (Roderigo) (1896–1970), American novelist. He is chiefly remembered for his collage-like portrayal of the energy and diversity of American life in the first decades of the 20th century in such novels as *Manhattan Transfer* (1925) and *U.S.A.* (1938).

Dostoevsky /ˌdɒstɔɪ'efskɪ/, Fyodor Mikhailovich (also **Dostoyevsky**) (1821–81), Russian novelist. His early socialist activism led to his being sentenced to death, but a last-minute reprieve led instead to exile in Siberia (1849–54). During this time he suffered periods of great mental and physical pain and recurring bouts of epilepsy; his experiences are recounted in *Notes from the House of the Dead* (1860–1). From the 1860s he wrote the novels on which his reputation is based, including *Crime and Punishment* (1866), *The Idiot* (1868), and *The Brothers Karamazov* (1880). These dark works reveal Dostoevsky's keen psychological insight, savage humour, and his concern with profound religious, political, and moral problems, especially that of human suffering.

Douglas /'dʌgləs/, Lord Alfred (Bruce) (1870–1945), English poet. In 1891 he

began his long intimacy with Oscar Wilde, because of which his father, the 8th Marquess of Queensberry, cut off Douglas's allowance and subsequently had Wilde imprisoned. After Wilde's death Douglas was himself imprisoned in 1923 for libel against Winston Churchill. He published two collections of sonnets, *In Excelsis* (1924) and *Sonnets and Lyrics* (1935), as well as his revealing *Autobiography* (1929).

Douglas-Home /ˌdʌɡləsˈhjuːm/, Sir Alec, Baron Home of the Hirsel of Coldstream (born Alexander Frederick Douglas-Home) (1903–95), British Conservative statesman, Prime Minister 1963–4. He served as private secretary to Neville Chamberlain in the negotiations with Hitler from 1937 to 1940. Various ministerial offices followed before his appointment as Foreign Secretary under Harold Macmillan in 1960. When Macmillan resigned in 1963, Douglas-Home became Prime Minister, relinquishing his hereditary peerage as 14th Earl of Home (to which he had succeeded in 1951), and for a time being neither a member of the House of Commons nor of the House of Lords, in an unprecedented situation for a British Prime Minister. His government was defeated by the Labour Party in the 1964 elections. Douglas-Home later served as Foreign Secretary under Edward Heath (1970–4).

Dowding /ˈdaʊdɪŋ/, Hugh (Caswall Tremenheere), Baron (1882–1970), British Marshal of the RAF. Dowding became a member of the Air Council in 1930 and was heavily involved in the development of the all-metal monoplane fighter and of radar. As Commander-in-Chief of Fighter Command (1936–40) Dowding organized the air defence that defeated the Luftwaffe during the Battle of Britain in 1940. He was relieved of his post the same year in controversial circumstances and retired in 1942.

Dowson /ˈdaʊs(ə)n/, Ernest (Christopher) (1867–1900), English poet. Associated with the 'decadent' school of Oscar Wilde and Aubrey Beardsley, he published two books of poems, *Verses* (1896) and *Decorations* (1899), which deal with themes of ennui and world-weariness. He died an alcoholic in France.

Doyle /dɔɪl/, Sir Arthur Conan (1859–1930), Scottish novelist. He is chiefly remembered for establishing the detective story as a major fictional genre with his creation of the private detective Sherlock Holmes. Holmes and his friend Dr Watson (the narrator of the stories) first appeared in *A Study in Scarlet* (1887) and continued to demonstrate their ingenuity at crime-solving in a long line of stories contained in such collections as *The Adventures of Sherlock Holmes* (1892) and *The Hound of the Baskervilles* (1902). Doyle also wrote historical and other romances.

D'Oyly Carte /ˌdɔɪlɪ ˈkɑːt/, Richard (1844–1901), English impresario and producer. He brought together the librettist Sir W. S. Gilbert and the composer Sir Arthur Sullivan, producing many of their operettas in London's Savoy Theatre, which he had established in 1881.

Drabble /ˈdræb(ə)l/, Margaret (born 1939), English novelist. Her early works, such as *The Garrick Year* (1964) and *The Millstone* (1966), deal mainly with the concerns of the individual and are characterized by their atmosphere of reflection and introspection; her later novels, including *The Ice Age* (1977) and *The Radiant Way* (1987), have a more documentary approach to social change. Drabble is also a literary critic and biographer. She is the younger sister of the novelist A. S. Byatt.

Draco /ˈdreɪkəʊ/ (7th century BC), Athenian legislator. His codification of Athenian law was notorious for its severity in that the death penalty was imposed for both serious and trivial crimes; this gave rise to the adjective *draconian* in English.

Drake /dreɪk/, Sir Francis (c.1540–96), English sailor and explorer. He spent his early career privateering in Spanish seas. He was the first Englishman to circumnavigate the globe; he set off in 1577 with five ships under the sponsorship of Elizabeth I to investigate the Strait of Magellan, tried unsuccessfully to find the North-west Passage, and finally returned to England via the Cape of Good Hope with only his own ship, the *Golden Hind*, in 1580. He was knighted the following year. Drake's raid on Cadiz in 1587 delayed the sailing of the Armada for a year by destroying its supply-ships, and the next year he played an important part in its defeat in the English Channel.

Dreiser /ˈdraɪsə(r)/, Theodore (Herman Albert) (1871–1945), American novelist. His first novel, *Sister Carrie* (1900), an account of a young working girl's rise to success, caused controversy for its frank treatment

of the heroine's sexuality and ambition. His later works, such as *America is Worth Saving* (1941), express a growing faith in socialism that replaces the pessimism of his earlier writings.

Dreyfus /'dreɪfəs/, Alfred (1859–1935), French army officer, of Jewish descent. In 1894 he was falsely accused of providing military secrets to the Germans; his trial, imprisonment, and eventual rehabilitation in 1906 caused a major political crisis in France, polarizing deep-set anti-militarist and anti-Semitic trends in a society still coming to terms with defeat and revolution in 1870–1. Notable among his supporters was the novelist Émile Zola, whose *J'accuse*, published in 1898, accused the judges at the trial of having convicted Dreyfus at the behest of the War Office.

Dryden /'draɪd(ə)n/, John (1631–1700), English poet, dramatist, and critic. One of the principal exponents of Augustan literature in England, he is remembered for his codification of verse metres and the establishment of the heroic couplet as the favoured verse form. He wrote many plays, including comedies (*Marriage à la mode*; 1673), tragedies such as the blank verse drama *All for Love* (1678), and satires, of which the best known is *Absalom and Achitophel* (1681). His prose writing style is often considered the model for modern English literature. Many of his critical works appear as prefaces to his plays; they include *Of Dramatic Poesie* (1668).

Drysdale /'draɪzdeɪl/, Sir Russell (1912–81), British-born Australian painter. His subject-matter is the harsh life of the Australian bush, as in *The Rabbiter and Family* (1938); he also deals with the plight of Aboriginals in contact with white settlement, as in *Mullaloonah Tank* (1953).

Dubček /'dʊbtʃek/, Alexander (1921–92), Czechoslovak statesman, First Secretary of the Czechoslovak Communist Party 1968–9. He is generally regarded as the driving force behind the attempted democratization of Czech political life in 1968 that became known as the Prague Spring. At this time he and other liberal members of the government made plans for a new constitution as well as legislation for civil liberties and began to pursue a foreign policy independent of the Soviet Union. In response, Warsaw Pact forces invaded Czechoslovakia in August 1968 and Dubček was removed from office the following year. After the abandonment of Communism at the end of 1989 he returned to public life and was elected speaker of the Federal Assembly in a new democratic regime.

Du Bois /duː 'bɔɪs/, W(illiam) E(dward) B(urghardt) (1868–1963), American writer and political activist. While professor of economics and sociology at Atlanta University (1897–1910), he researched the social conditions of blacks in the US and wrote his influential works *The Philadelphia Negro; A Social Study* (1899) and *The Souls of Black Folk* (1903). In the latter Du Bois launched a fierce attack on Booker T. Washington's policy of appeasement towards whites, arguing that racial equality could only be achieved by political organization and struggle. In 1905 he formed the pressure group known as the Niagara Movement to campaign against the Washington lobby. Four years later Du Bois co-founded the National Association for the Advancement of Colored People, working as the editor of its magazine *Crisis* from 1910 to 1934.

Dubuffet /djuː'buːfeɪ/, Jean (1901–85), French artist. He rejected traditional techniques, placing untrained spontaneity above professional skill. He made a collection of what he termed 'Art Brut' (raw art) – the products of children, illiterates, the mentally disturbed, and anything uninhibited and without pretensions, of which his own work is often reminiscent. His painting typically incorporates sand, plaster, and 'junk' materials, and is seen as a precursor of pop art and Dadaism.

Duccio /'duːtʃɪˌəʊ/ (full name Duccio di Buoninsegna) (c.1255–c.1320), Italian painter. The founder of the Sienese school of painting, he built on elements of the Byzantine tradition. The only fully documented surviving work by him is the *Maestà* for the high altar of Siena cathedral (completed 1311). His work conveys emotion through facial expression, sequence of colour, and arrangement of scenery, while keeping the composition within Byzantine conventions.

Duchamp /djuː'ʃɒm/, Marcel (1887–1968), French-born painter, sculptor, and art theorist. His main influence on 20th-century art has been in the area of anti-art movements: the origins of conceptual art can be traced to him, he was a leader of the Dada movement, and in 1912 he originated the ready-made art form, whereby the artist

selects a mass-produced article such as a bottle rack and displays it as a work of art. His most famous provocative gesture was adding a moustache and goatee beard to a reproduction of the *Mona Lisa* in 1920, in a bid to destroy the mystique of good taste and aesthetic beauty. He became an American citizen in 1955.

Dudley /'dʌdlɪ/, Robert, Earl of Leicester (*c.*1532–88), English nobleman. He became a favourite of Elizabeth I soon after her accession in 1558. Following the mysterious death of Dudley's wife, Amy Robsart, in 1560 it was rumoured that he would marry the queen; this did not happen, although Dudley remained in favour with Elizabeth throughout his life and in 1564 was created Earl of Leicester. He was later given the command of the military campaign in the Netherlands (1585–7) and of the forces preparing to resist the Armada (1588).

Dufay /dju:'feɪ/, Guillaume (*c.*1400–74), French composer. He was a noted teacher and made a significant contribution to the development of Renaissance polyphony. Of his works, almost 200 are extant; they include much church music (his own Requiem Mass, now lost, was sung at his funeral), motets, and eighty-four songs.

Du Fu see Tu Fu.

Dufy /dju:'fi:/, Raoul (1877–1953), French painter and textile designer. In his early work he was much influenced by fauvism but he later developed his own characteristic style using bright colours, with calligraphic outlines sketched on brilliant background washes. His chief subjects were the racecourse, boating scenes, and society life on the French Riviera and in London.

Dulles /'dʌlɪs/, John Foster (1888–1959), American Republican statesman and international lawyer. He was adviser to the US delegation at the conference which set up the United Nations in 1945 and negotiated the Peace Treaty with Japan in 1951. As Secretary of State under President Eisenhower (1953–9) he strove to improve the position of the US in the cold war, to which end he strengthened NATO and urged that the US should stockpile nuclear arms as a deterrent against Soviet aggression.

Dumas /'dju:mɑː/, Alexandre (known as Dumas *père*) (1802–70), French novelist and dramatist. A pioneer of the romantic theatre in France, he first achieved fame

with his historical dramas, such as *Henry III et sa cour* (1829). His reputation now rests on his historical adventure novels, including *The Three Musketeers* (1844–5) and *The Count of Monte Cristo* (1844–5). His son Alexandre Dumas (1824–95) (known as Dumas *fils*) wrote the novel (and play) *La Dame aux camélias* (1848), which formed the basis of Verdi's opera *La Traviata* (1853).

Du Maurier[1] /dju: 'mɒrɪ,eɪ/, Dame Daphne (1907–89), English novelist, granddaughter of George du Maurier. Many of her popular novels and period romances are set in the West Country of England, where she spent most of her life. Her works include *Jamaica Inn* (1936) and *Rebecca* (1938).

Du Maurier[2] /dju: 'mɒrɪ,eɪ/, George (Louis Palmella Busson) (1834–96), French-born cartoonist, illustrator, and novelist. He is chiefly remembered for his novel *Trilby* (1894), which included the character Svengali and gave rise to the word *Svengali* for a person who has a hypnotic influence.

Dunbar /dʌn'bɑː(r)/, William (*c.*1456–*c.*1513), Scottish poet. His first major poem, 'The Thrissill and the Rois' ('The Thistle and the Rose', 1503), is a political allegory on the marriage of James IV to Margaret Tudor (the daughter of Henry VII) and the first of his many satires. Dunbar is also remembered for his elegies, such as 'Lament for the Makaris' (on Chaucer and other fellow poets).

Duncan /'dʌnkən/, Isadora (1878–1927), American dancer and teacher. A pioneer of modern dance, she developed a form of 'free' barefoot dancing based on instinctive movements and inspired by classical Greek art. She was much admired in Europe, where she settled and founded several schools of dance; her informal style deeply influenced Diaghilev. She died through being accidentally strangled when her scarf became entangled in the wheels of a car.

Dunlop /'dʌnlɒp/, John Boyd (1840–1921), Scottish inventor. He worked in Edinburgh and Belfast as a veterinary surgeon but is best known for having invented the first successful pneumatic bicycle tyre (1888), which was manufactured by the company named after him. Though his invention was crucial to the development of the motor car, Dunlop himself received little profit from it.

Dunne /dʌn/, John William (1875–1949), English philosopher. His work is especially concerned with time and includes *An Experiment with Time* (1927) and *The Serial Universe* (1934), both of which influenced the plays of J. B. Priestley.

Duns Scotus /dʌnz 'skəʊtəs/, John (known as 'the Subtle Doctor') (*c.*1265–1308), Scottish theologian and scholar. In opposition to the teaching of St Thomas Aquinas he argued that faith was a matter of will, not dependent on logical proofs. He was also the first major theologian to defend the theory of the Immaculate Conception. His system was accepted by the Franciscans as their doctrinal basis and exercised a profound influence in the Middle Ages. In the Renaissance his followers were ridiculed for their conservatism and abused as enemies of learning, which gave rise to the word *dunce*.

Dunstable /'dʌnstəb(ə)l/, John (*c.*1390–1453), English composer. He was a significant early exponent of counterpoint; his works include secular songs, masses, and motets.

Dunstan, St /'dʌnstən/ (*c.*909–88), Anglo-Saxon prelate. During his tenure as abbot at Glastonbury the monastery became a centre of religious teaching. He was appointed Archbishop of Canterbury by King Edgar in 960, and together they carried through a reform of Church and state. He introduced the strict Benedictine rule into England and succeeded in restoring monastic life; a zealous supporter of education, he also achieved fame as a musician, illuminator, and metalworker. Feast day, 19 May.

du Pré /dju: 'preɪ/, Jacqueline (1945–87), English cellist. She made her solo début in London at the age of 16. She became famous for her interpretations of the cello concertos, especially that of Elgar. When her performing career was halted in 1972 by multiple sclerosis, she gave a notable series of master classes. She was married to the pianist and conductor Daniel Barenboim.

Duras /'djʊərɑːs/, Marguerite (pseudonym of Marguerite Donnadieu) (1914–96), French novelist, film director, and dramatist. She established her reputation as a novelist in the 1950s and won the Prix Goncourt with *L'Amant* (1984). As well as directing a number of her own films she wrote screenplays, for example *Hiroshima mon amour* (1959).

Dürer /'djʊərə(r)/, Albrecht (1471–1528), German painter and engraver. He is generally regarded as the leading German artist of the Renaissance. He was responsible for developing techniques and raising standards of craftsmanship in his favoured media of woodcut and copper engraving; examples of his work include a series of ninety-two woodcut blocks in honour of the Emperor Maximilian. He also painted detailed watercolour studies of plants and animals.

Durey /djʊə'reɪ/, Louis (1888–1979), French composer. Until 1921 he belonged to the group known as Les Six, writing mainly chamber music and songs. After 1945 he was one of a group of French composers who wrote music of a deliberate mass appeal, in accordance with Communist doctrines on art; his works from this period include the cantata *La Longue marche* (1949).

Durham /'dʌrəm/, John George Lambton, Earl of (1792–1840), British Whig statesman. A man of strong liberal views, he was Lord Privy Seal in the administration of his father-in-law, Lord Grey, and helped draft the Reform Bill of 1832. In 1838 he was appointed Governor-General of Canada and submitted the influential *Report on the Affairs of British North America*, which advocated the union of Canada.

Durkheim /'dɜːkhaɪm/, Émile (1858–1917), French sociologist. Now regarded as one of the founders of modern sociology, he wrote about the influence of social structures on the behaviour of individuals (*The Division of Labour in Society*, 1893), formalized a methodology for sociological investigation, and examined the social causes of suicide (*Suicide*, 1897).

Durrell[1] /'dʌrəl/, Gerald (Malcolm) (1925–95), English zoologist and writer. He acquired an interest in animals as a child in Corfu. From 1947 he organized a number of animal-collecting expeditions, which resulted in a popular series of broadcasts and books, including the autobiographical *My Family and Other Animals* (1956). Durrell became increasingly concerned with conservation and captive breeding, and in 1958 he founded a zoo in Jersey, Channel Islands, which later became the Jersey Wildlife Preservation Trust. He was the younger brother of the novelist Lawrence Durrell.

Durrell[2] /'dʌrəl/, Lawrence (George) (1912–90), English novelist, poet, and travel writer. He spent his childhood in India and his adolescence in Corfu, moving to France in the late 1950s. He first achieved fame with the *Alexandria Quartet* (1957–60), a series of novels set in Alexandria before the Second World War and written in an ornate, poetic style. He published several collections of poetry and a number of travel books, including *Bitter Lemons* (1957), about Cyprus. He was the elder brother of the zoologist and writer Gerald Durrell.

Duse /'duːzə/, Eleonora (1858–1924), Italian actress. She played Juliet at the age of 14 before earning a reputation throughout Europe and America as one of the world's greatest actresses. She championed the plays of her lover, Gabriele D'Annunzio, acting in his *La città morta* and *La Gioconda* (both 1898). She refused to use stage make-up, preferring not to disguise her mobile, expressive features, and was at her best in strong emotional roles.

Duvalier /dju:'væli,ei/, François (known as 'Papa Doc') (1907–71), Haitian statesman, President 1957–71. His regime was noted for being authoritarian and oppressive; many of his opponents were either assassinated or forced into exile by his security force, known as the Tontons Macoutes. He proclaimed himself President for life in 1964 and was succeeded on his death by his son Jean-Claude (known as 'Baby Doc', born 1951); the Duvalier regime ended in 1986 when a mass uprising forced Jean-Claude to flee the country.

Du Vigneaud /du: 'viːnjəʊ/, Vincent (1901–78), American biochemist. He specialized in the study of vitamins and hormones that contain sulphur, beginning with insulin. He went on to study the function of methionine, to isolate and determine the structure of biotin, and to contribute to the synthesis of penicillin G. For isolating and synthesizing the pituitary hormones oxytocin and vasopressin, Du Vigneaud was awarded the Nobel Prize for chemistry in 1955.

Dvořák /'dvɔː3æk, -3ɑːk/, Antonín (1841–1904), Czech composer. Living at a time of strong national consciousness, he combined ethnic folk elements with the Viennese musical tradition from Haydn to Brahms. He is probably best known for his ninth symphony ('From the New World', 1892–5), which he wrote while working in the US as director of the New York Conservatoire; it contains motifs from negro spirituals as well as Bohemian melodies. Dvořák also wrote chamber music, operas, and songs.

Dylan /'dɪlən/, Bob (born Robert Allen Zimmerman) (born 1941), American singer and songwriter. The leader of the urban folk-music revival in the 1960s, he became known for his political and protest songs, including 'A Hard Rain's A-Gonna Fall', 'Blowin' in the Wind' (both 1963), and 'The Times They Are A-Changin'' (1964). When on tour in 1966 he caused controversy and aroused severe criticism for using an amplified backing group. His albums include *Highway 61 Revisited* (1965) and *Blood on the Tracks* (1975).

Dzerzhinsky /dzɜː'ʒɪnskɪ/, Feliks (Edmundovich) (1877–1926), Russian Bolshevik leader, of Polish descent. He was the organizer and first head of the post-revolutionary Soviet security police (the Cheka and the OGPU).

E

Eadwig see EDWY.

Eakins /ˈiːkɪnz/, Thomas (1844–1916), American painter and photographer. Influenced by Diego Velázquez and José Ribera, he was a dominant figure in American realist painting of the 19th century. He was noted for his portraits and genre pictures of the life of his native city, Philadelphia; boating and bathing were favourite themes. His most famous picture, *The Gross Clinic* (1875), aroused controversy because of its explicit depiction of surgery.

Earhart /ˈeəhɑːt/, Amelia (1898–1937), American aviator. In 1932 she became the first woman to fly across the Atlantic solo, completing the journey from Newfoundland to Londonderry in a time of 13¹/₄ hours. The aircraft carrying Earhart and her navigator disappeared over the Pacific Ocean during a subsequent round-the-world flight.

Earp /ɜːp/, Wyatt (Berry Stapp) (1848–1929), American gambler and marshal. He went to Tombstone, Arizona, in 1878 and worked as a gambler and guard in the Oriental Saloon. His brother Virgil was marshal and a feud developed between the Earps and the Clantons, leading in 1881 to the gunfight at the OK Corral, which involved Wyatt, Virgil, their brother Morgan, and Doc Holliday, a friend of Wyatt from Dodge City. Wyatt collaborated in writing his own biography (published 1931), which presents a fictionalized portrait of him as a heroic frontiersman.

Eastman /ˈiːstmən/, George (1854–1932), American inventor and manufacturer of photographic equipment. In 1884 he established a company which in 1892 became the Eastman Kodak Company ('Kodak' was a name Eastman invented). He invented flexible roll-film coated with light-sensitive emulsion, and the Kodak camera (1888) with which to use it. These did much to popularize amateur photography, as did his subsequent development of colour photography.

Eastwood /ˈiːstwʊd/, Clint (born 1930), American film actor and director. He became a star with his role in *A Fistful of Dollars* (1964), the first cult spaghetti western. His performance as the 'dirty cop' in *Dirty Harry* (1971) proved as much of a box-office success as his many western performances. He started directing in 1971, receiving acclaim for his portrait of the saxophonist Charlie Parker in *Bird* (1988) and for his uncompromising western *Unforgiven* (1992).

Eccles /ˈek(ə)lz/, Sir John Carew (1903–97), Australian physiologist. He demonstrated the means by which nerve impulses are conducted, showing that a chemical neurotransmitter is released to initiate propagation across the synapses, followed by another that inhibits the propagation. This discovery greatly influenced the medical treatment of nervous diseases and physiological research. Eccles was awarded a Nobel Prize in 1963.

Eco /ˈekəʊ/, Umberto (born 1932), Italian novelist and semiotician. Professor of semiotics at the University of Bologna since 1971, he is known both for his extensive writings on his subject, such as *Travels in Hyperreality* (1986), and as a novelist. His best-known fictional work is *The Name of the Rose* (1981), a complex detective novel set in a medieval monastery.

Edberg /ˈedbɜːg/, Stefan (born 1966), Swedish tennis player. He turned professional in 1983 and won his first grand slam title, the Australian Open, two years later. He won Wimbledon twice, in 1990 and 1991, and was ranked first in the world during these years. He excelled on grass but his versatility brought him success on all surfaces. He announced his retirement in 1996.

Eddington /ˈedɪŋtən/, Sir Arthur Stanley (1882–1944), English astronomer, founder of the science of astrophysics. He established the fundamental principles of stellar structure, discovered the relationship between stellar mass and luminosity, and suggested possible sources of the energy within stars. He wrote one of the finest presentations of Einstein's theory of relativity, and provided some of the best evidence in support of it when his observations of star positions during the solar eclipse of 1919 demonstrated the bending of light by gravity.

Eddy /'edɪ/, Mary Baker (1821–1910), American religious leader and founder of the Christian Science movement. Long a sufferer from various ailments, she believed herself cured by a faith-healer, Phineas Quimby (1802–66). After his death she evolved her own system of spiritual healing, set out in her book *Science and Health* (1875), and established the Church of Christ, Scientist, in Boston in 1879. Members believe that God and the mind are the only ultimate reality, and that matter and evil have no existence; illness and sin, they believe, are illusions that can be overcome by prayer and faith. As a consequence they generally refuse medical treatment.

Eden /'iːd(ə)n/, (Robert) Anthony, 1st Earl of Avon (1897–1977), British Conservative statesman, Prime Minister 1955–7. He served as War Secretary under Churchill in 1940, in addition to three terms as Foreign Secretary (1935–8; 1940–5; 1951–5). His premiership was dominated by the Suez crisis of 1956. Widespread opposition to Britain's role in this, together with his own failing health, led to his resignation.

Edgar /'edgə(r)/ (944–75), king of England 959–75. He became king of Northumbria and Mercia in 957 when these regions renounced their allegiance to his elder brother Edwy, succeeding to the throne of England on Edwy's death. Edgar worked closely with St Dunstan during his reign and was renowned for his support of organized religion; he played an important role in the growth of monasticism.

Edgeworth /'edʒwəθ/, Maria (1767–1849), Irish novelist, born in England. She is best known for works such as *Castle Rackrent* (1800), a novel of Irish life, and she is considered an important figure in the development of the historical and regional novel. Other significant works include *Belinda* (1801), a portrait of contemporary English society.

Edinburgh, Duke of see PHILIP, PRINCE.

Edison /'edɪs(ə)n/, Thomas (Alva) (1847–1931), American inventor. He was employed by the age of 15 as a telegraph operator, from which he developed an interest in electricity and its applications. He took out the first of more than a thousand patents at the age of 21. His chief inventions include automatic telegraph systems, the mimeograph, the carbon microphone for telephones, the phonograph, the carbon filament lamp, and the nickel-iron accumulator. He created the precursor of the thermionic valve, and devised systems for generating and distributing electricity. Edison also established the practice of installing industrial laboratories in commercial organizations.

Edmund /'edmənd/ the name of two kings of England:

Edmund I (921–46), reigned 939–46. Soon after Edmund succeeded Athelstan, a Norse army took control of York and its dependent territories. From 941 Edmund set about recovering these northern territories, but after his death Northumbria fell again under Norse control.

Edmund II (known as Edmund Ironside) (c.980–1016), son of Ethelred the Unready, reigned 1016. Edmund led the resistance to Canute's forces in 1015 and on his father's death was proclaimed king. After some initial success he was defeated at Ashingdon in Essex (1016) and was forced to divide the kingdom with Canute, retaining only Wessex. On Edmund's death Canute became king of all England.

Edmund, St (born Edmund Rich) (c.1175–1240), English churchman and teacher. Archbishop of Canterbury 1234–40, he was the last Primate of all England and the first Oxford University teacher to be canonized. The Oxford college St Edmund Hall takes its name from him. Feast day, 16 November.

Edmund Campion, St see CAMPION, ST EDMUND.

Edmund Ironside /'aɪən,saɪd/ Edmund II of England (see EDMUND).

Edmund the Martyr, St (c.841–70), king of East Anglia 855–70. After the defeat of his army by the invading Danes in 870, tradition holds that he was captured and shot with arrows for refusing to reject the Christian faith or to share power with his pagan conqueror. His body was interred at Bury St Edmunds, Suffolk. Feast day, 20 November.

Edward /'edwəd/ the name of six kings of England since the Norman Conquest and also one of Great Britain and Ireland and one of the United Kingdom:

Edward I (known as 'the Hammer of the Scots') (1239–1307), son of Henry III, reigned 1272–1307. After coming to the throne Edward did much to improve the ineffectual central administration he had inherited; this included summoning the

Model Parliament (1295). His campaign against the Welsh Prince Llewelyn ended with the annexation of Wales in 1284. He failed to conquer Scotland, though he had a successful first campaign there in 1296, deposing the Scottish king, John de Baliol (c.1250–1313), who had made an alliance with the French against him. From 1297 to 1305 the Scots were in a state of armed insurrection, initially under the leadership of Sir William Wallace. Edward died on his way north to begin a new campaign against the Scots, who were by then led by Robert the Bruce.

Edward II (1284–1327), son of Edward I, reigned 1307–27. The first English Prince of Wales, he soon proved unequal to the problems left him by his more military father, and early trouble with his barons led to civil war. In 1314 he invaded Scotland, only to be defeated by Robert the Bruce at Bannockburn in the same year. In 1326 Edward's wife, Isabella of France, allied herself with the exiled Roger de Mortimer to invade England. Edward was deposed in favour of his son and was murdered at Berkeley Castle, Gloucestershire.

Edward III (1312–77), son of Edward II, reigned 1327–77. In 1330 Edward ended the four-year regency of his mother Isabella and her lover Roger de Mortimer by taking control of his kingdom, banishing Isabella, and executing Mortimer. He supported Edward de Baliol (c.1283–1364), the pretender to the Scottish throne, and started the Hundred Years War with France by claiming the French throne in right of his mother (1337). Towards the end of his reign effective government fell into the hands of his fourth son, John of Gaunt.

Edward IV (1442–83), son of Richard, Duke of York, reigned 1461–83. He became king after defeating the Lancastrian king Henry VI in battle in 1461. The early years of his reign were troubled by Lancastrian plots, but the most serious threat arose in 1470–1 as a result of an alliance between his old Lancastrian enemies and his disaffected former lieutenant, the Earl of Warwick. Edward was briefly forced into exile, but returned to crush his opponents at Tewkesbury (1471), thereafter ruling in relative peace until his death.

Edward V (1470–c.1483), son of Edward IV, reigned 1483, but not crowned. Following his father's death he was illegitimized on debatable evidence of the illegality of Edward IV's marriage; his throne was taken by his uncle, Richard III, who placed young Edward and his brother Richard in the Tower of London. The boys disappeared soon afterwards, and are generally assumed to have been murdered; they have become known as the Princes in the Tower.

Edward VI (1537–53), son of Henry VIII, reigned 1547–53. During his brief reign as a minor, England was effectively ruled by two protectors, the Duke of Somerset and the Duke of Northumberland. Nevertheless, the king's Protestant beliefs contributed significantly to the establishment of Protestantism as the state religion, especially with the publication of the *Book of Common Prayer* (1549). He was succeeded by his elder sister, Mary I.

Edward VII (1841–1910), son of Queen Victoria, reigned 1901–10. Edward was kept away from the conduct of royal affairs during the long reign of his mother. Although he played little part in government on finally coming to the throne, his popularity and willingness to make public appearances, both at home and abroad, helped revitalize the monarchy.

Edward VIII (1894–1972), son of George V, reigned 1936, but was not crowned. A popular Prince of Wales, Edward abdicated eleven months after coming to the throne in order to marry the American divorcee Mrs Wallis Simpson. Created Duke of Windsor, he served as Governor-General of the Bahamas during the Second World War before spending the rest of his life in France.

Edward, Prince, Edward Antony Richard Louis (born 1964), third son of Elizabeth II. He served in the Royal Marines from 1986 to 1987 after graduating from Cambridge, and has more recently worked in the theatre.

Edward, Prince of Wales see BLACK PRINCE.

Edward the Confessor, St (c.1003–66), son of Ethelred the Unready, king of England 1042–66. Famed for his piety, Edward founded Westminster Abbey, where he was eventually buried. He was dominated through much of his reign by his wife's father, Earl Godwin (died 1053). In later years Edward took less interest in affairs of state, letting effective control fall to Godwin's son, who eventually succeeded him as Harold II. He was canonized in 1161. Feast day, 13 October.

Edward the Elder (*c.*870–924), son of Alfred the Great, king of Wessex 899–924. During his reign he conquered lands previously held by the Danes, including East Anglia and the Midlands; on the death of his sister, the ruler of Mercia, in 918 he merged the kingdoms of Wessex and Mercia. His conquests made it possible for his son Athelstan to become the first king of all England in 925.

Edward the Martyr, St (*c.*963–78), son of Edgar, king of England 975–8. Shortly after his accession the youthful Edward was faced by a challenge for the throne from supporters of his half-brother Ethelred, who eventually had him murdered at Corfe Castle, Dorset (978). Canonized in 1001, he became the subject of an important medieval cult. Feast day, 18 March.

Edwards[1] /'edwədz/, Gareth (Owen) (born 1947), Welsh Rugby Union player. His international career, during which he played chiefly at half-back, lasted from 1967 to 1978. He was appointed captain of the Welsh team in 1968, the youngest person ever to hold that position.

Edwards[2] /'edwədz/, Jonathan (David) (born 1966), English athlete. Making his international début in the triple jump in 1988, he won a bronze medal in the 1989 World Cup and a gold in 1992. In the 1995 world championships he set a new triple-jump world record of 18.29 metres, becoming the first person to break the 18-metre barrier and breaking the previous record of 17.97 metres.

Edwy /'edwɪ/ (also **Eadwig** /'edwɪg/) (died 959), king of England 955–7. He was probably only 15 years old when he became king. Edwy alienated a large part of his kingdom during his short reign; after Mercia and Northumbria had renounced him in favour of his brother Edgar in 957, he ruled only over the lands south of the Thames.

Egas Moniz /ˌiːgæʒ məˈniːz/, Antonio Caetano de Abreu Freire (1874–1955), Portuguese neurologist. He developed cerebral angiography as a diagnostic technique, and pioneered the treatment of certain psychotic disorders by the use of prefrontal leucotomy. He shared a Nobel Prize for this in 1949. Egas Moniz was also an active politician and diplomat.

Egbert /'egbət/ (died 839), king of Wessex 802–39. In 825 he won a decisive victory near Swindon, bringing Mercian supremacy to an end, and annexed Kent, Essex, Surrey, and Sussex. In 829 Mercia itself fell to Egbert and Northumbria acknowledged his rule. By the time of his death, Mercia had become independent again, but his reign foreshadowed the supremacy that Wessex later secured over all England.

Ehrenburg /'eərən,bɜːg/, Ilya (Grigorevich) (1891–1967), Russian novelist and journalist. As a journalist, he became famous during the Second World War for his anti-German propaganda in *Pravda* and *Red Star.* His novels include *The Thaw* (1954), a work containing open criticism of Stalinism and dealing with the temporary period of liberalization following Stalin's death.

Ehrlich /'eəlɪx/, Paul (1854–1915), German medical scientist, one of the founders of modern immunology. He developed techniques for staining specific tissues, from which he became convinced that a disease organism could be destroyed by an appropriate magic bullet, thus pioneering the study of chemotherapy. Success in this came in 1911 when a synthetic compound of arsenic proved effective against syphilis.

Eichmann /'aɪxmən/, (Karl) Adolf (1906–62), German Nazi administrator. He was responsible for carrying out Hitler's final solution and for administering the concentration camps, to which 6 million Jews were shipped from all over Europe. After the war he went into hiding in Argentina, but in 1960 he was traced by Israeli agents, abducted, and executed after trial in Israel.

Eiffel /'aɪf(ə)l/, French ɛfɛl/, Alexandre Gustave (1832–1923), French engineer. He is best known as the designer and builder of the Eiffel Tower and as the architect of the inner structure of the Statue of Liberty.

Eijkman /'eɪkmən/, Christiaan (1858–1930), Dutch physician. Working in Indonesia, Eijkman discovered the cause of beriberi to be dietary rather than bacteriological. Although he did not correctly recognize the reason for this, his work resulted in a simple cure for the disease. It also led later to the discovery of the vitamin thiamine, a deficiency of which causes beriberi. He shared a Nobel Prize in 1929.

Einstein /'aɪnstaɪn/, Albert (1879–1955), German-born American theoretical physicist, founder of the theory of relativity, often regarded as the greatest scientist of

the 20th century. In 1905 he published outstanding papers dealing with the photoelectric effect, Brownian motion, and his special theory of relativity. In this he abandoned the idea of absolute space and time as a common framework of reference for all bodies in the universe, instead distinguishing between the viewpoint or framework of the observer and that of the object or process being observed. Among the theory's most important conclusions is that mass and energy are equivalent and interconvertible, expressed by the equation $e = mc^2$ (c being the speed of light). In 1915 Einstein published the general theory of relativity. This extended his ideas to gravitation, which he treated as a curvature of the space–time continuum. The general theory was vindicated when one of its predictions — the deflection and reddening of light rays passing through a substantial gravitational field — was confirmed by observations during the solar eclipse of 1919. He was in America when Hitler came to power in 1933 and decided to stay there, spending the remainder of his life searching without success for a unified field theory embracing electromagnetism, gravitation, relativity, and quantum mechanics. In 1939 he wrote to President Roosevelt about the military potential of nuclear energy, greatly influencing the decision to build an atom bomb. After the war he spoke out passionately against nuclear weapons.

Einthoven /'aɪntˌɦəʊv(ə)n/, Dutch /'eɪntˌhoːvə/, Willem (1860–1927), Dutch physiologist. He devised the first electrocardiograph, using a string galvanometer with an optical system to amplify the deflection of a fine wire. He was subsequently able to link the resulting electrocardiograms with specific muscular contractions in the heart, and thus begin to diagnose various heart diseases.

Eisenhower /'aɪz(ə)nˌhaʊə(r)/, Dwight David ('Ike') (1890–1969), American general and Republican statesman, 34th President of the US 1953–61. In the Second World War he was Commander-in-Chief of Allied forces in North Africa and Italy 1942–3 and Supreme Commander of Allied Expeditionary Forces in western Europe 1943–5. As President, he adopted a hard line towards Communism both in his domestic and foreign policy; in the US an extreme version of this was reflected in McCarthyism.

Eisenstein /'aɪz(ə)nˌstaɪn/, Sergei (Mikhailovich) (1898–1948), Soviet film director, born in Latvia. He made his name with *The Battleship Potemkin* (1925), a film commemorating the Russian Revolution of 1905; its innovative use of montage received international acclaim. At odds with the prevailing style of socialist realism, Eisenstein fell into disfavour in 1932 and had to wait for the release of *Alexander Nevsky* (1938) to regain his reputation. His final film was *Ivan the Terrible*; although the first part (1944) was well received, the second (1946) earned Stalin's disapproval and was not released until a decade after Eisenstein's death.

Ekman /'ekmən/, Vagn Walfrid (1874–1954), Swedish oceanographer. He recognized the importance of the Coriolis effect on ocean currents, showing that it can be responsible for surface water moving at an angle to the prevailing wind direction. He also explained why water flow at different depths can vary in both velocity and direction, and devised various instruments including a type of current meter that is still in use.

Elagabalus see HELIOGABALUS.

El Cid see CID, EL.

Eleanor of Aquitaine /'elmə(r), ˌækwɪ'teɪn/ (c.1122–1204), daughter of the Duke of Aquitaine, queen of France 1137–52 and of England 1154–89. She was married to Louis VII of France from 1137; in 1152, with the annulment of their marriage, she married the future Henry II of England. Her ten children included the monarchs Richard I (Richard the Lionheart) and John, whose accession she strove to secure. She acted as regent (1190–4) while Richard was away on the Crusades.

Elgar /'elgɑː(r)/, Sir Edward (William) (1857–1934), British composer. A self-taught musician from Worcester, he made his mark with the *Enigma Variations* (1899), a set of fourteen orchestral variations (on an undisclosed theme), thirteen of which are titled by the initials of his friends. He gained an international reputation with the oratorio *The Dream of Gerontius* (1900), the violin concerto (1910), and the cello concerto (1919). In Britain he is perhaps most famous for patriotic pieces such as the five *Pomp and Circumstance* marches (1901–30).

Elgin[1] /'elgɪn/, 7th Earl of (title of Thomas Bruce) (1766–1841), British diplomat and

art connoisseur. When envoy at Constantinople (1799–1803) he feared the destruction of Greek antiquities in the conflict between Turks and Greeks and obtained permission from the Turks to remove them. Between 1803 and 1812 he transported a number of sculptures to England, many from the Parthenon in Athens (which was under Turkish control), creating fierce controversy. The British government vindicated Elgin's actions and purchased the 'Elgin Marbles' from him in 1816.

Elgin[2] /'elgɪn/, 8th Earl of (title of James Bruce) (1811–63), British colonial statesman. After serving as governor of Jamaica (1842–6), he became Governor-General of Canada (1847–54). He commissioned Louis Hippolyte Lafontaine (1807–64) to form Canada's first Cabinet government in 1848. He maintained good relationships with subsequent administrations and successfully negotiated a reciprocity treaty between Canada and the US in 1854.

El Greco /el 'grekəʊ/ (Spanish for 'the Greek'; born Domenikos Theotokopoulos) (1541–1614), Cretan-born Spanish painter. After studying in Venice and working in Rome he settled in Toledo in 1577. His portraits and religious works are characterized by distorted perspective, elongated figures, and strident use of colour. Famous works include the altarpiece *The Assumption of the Virgin* (1577–9) and the painting *The Burial of Count Orgaz* (1586).

Elia /'iːliə/ the pseudonym adopted by Charles Lamb in his *Essays of Elia* (1823) and *Last Essays of Elia* (1833).

Eliot[1] /'elɪət/, George (pseudonym of Mary Ann Evans) (1819–80), English novelist. She is best known for her novels of provincial life, including *Adam Bede* (1859), *The Mill on the Floss* (1860), and *Middlemarch* (1871–2). Famed for her intellect, scholarly style, and moral sensibility, she is regarded as one of the great English novelists. Early influenced by evangelicalism, she later adopted agnostic views, although religious themes continued to feature prominently in her novels.

Eliot[2] /'elɪət/, T(homas) S(tearns) (1888–1965), American-born British poet, critic, and dramatist. Associated with the rise of literary modernism, he struck a new note in modern poetry with his verse collection *Prufrock and Other Observations* (1917), which combined satire with allusion and lyricism. In his newly founded literary quarterly *The Criterion*, he published *The Waste Land* (1922), which established him as the voice of a disillusioned generation. In 1927 he became an Anglo-Catholic and subsequent works, such as *Four Quartets* (1943), reveal his increasing involvement with Christianity. He was awarded the Nobel Prize for literature in 1948.

Elizabeth I /ɪˈlɪzəbəθ/ (1533–1603), daughter of Henry VIII, queen of England and Ireland 1558–1603. Succeeding her Catholic sister Mary I, Elizabeth re-established a moderate form of Protestantism as the religion of the state. None the less, her reign was dominated by the threat of a Catholic restoration (eventually leading to the execution of Mary, Queen of Scots) and by war with Spain, during which the country was saved from invasion by the defeat of the Armada in 1588. Her reign was characterized by a flowering of national culture, particularly in the field of literature, in which Shakespeare, Marlowe, and Spenser were all active. Although frequently courted, she never married.

Elizabeth II /ɪˈlɪzəbəθ/ (born Princess Elizabeth Alexandra Mary) (born 1926), daughter of George VI, queen of the United Kingdom since 1952. She has always shown a strong personal commitment to the Commonwealth, and is one of the most travelled 20th-century monarchs, having made extensive overseas tours and many public appearances at home.

Elizabeth, the Queen Mother (born Lady Elizabeth Angela Marguerite Bowes-Lyon) (born 1900), wife of George VI. She married George VI in 1923, when he was Duke of York; they had two daughters, Elizabeth II and Princess Margaret.

Ellington /'elɪŋtən/, Duke (born Edward Kennedy Ellington) (1899–1974), American jazz pianist, composer, and band-leader. His band established its fame in the early 1930s and some of its members remained with him for more than thirty years. Ellington wrote over 900 compositions and was one of the first popular musicians to write extended pieces; his first worldwide success was *Mood Indigo* (1930).

Ellis /'elɪs/, (Henry) Havelock (1859–1939), English psychologist and writer. Ellis qualified as a doctor in 1889 but is remembered as the pioneer of the scientific study of sex. His major technical work was the six-volume *Studies in the Psychology of Sex* (1897–

1910, with a seventh volume added in 1928), and he wrote several popular works on the same subject, notably *Man and Woman* (1894). As well as being a prolific scientific writer Ellis was also editor of several series, most of which were in the field of literature and the arts.

Ellsworth /'elzwəθ/, Lincoln (1880–1951), American explorer. He participated in a number of polar expeditions and was the first person to fly over both the North (1926) and South (1935) Poles. During his Antarctic explorations of 1935 and 1939 he discovered new mountain ranges and named Ellsworth Land after his father.

Elton /'elt(ə)n/, Charles Sutherland (1900–91), English zoologist. Elton pioneered the study of animal ecology and investigated the relationship between animal populations and their environment. He was a founder of the Bureau of Animal Population at Oxford in 1932 and became the first editor of the *Journal of Animal Ecology* in the same year. Elton's research into rodent populations found practical application in vermin control during the Second World War, and his book *The Control of Rats and Mice* (1954) became the standard work.

Éluard /'elʊˌɑː(r)/, Paul (pseudonym of Eugène Grindel) (1895–1952), French poet. Following the First World War he became a leading figure in the surrealist movement; his poetry from this period includes the collection *Capitale de la douleur* (1926). He broke with the surrealists in 1938 and joined the Communist Party in 1942. He then became an active figure in the French resistance movement, secretly circulating his poetry denouncing the German occupation (such as the collection *Poésie et vérité*, 1942).

Elzevir /'elzəˌvɪə(r)/ a family of Dutch printers. Fifteen members were active 1581–1712. Louis (*c*.1542–1617) founded the business at Leiden *c*.1580. His son Bonaventure (1583–1652) and grandson Abraham (1592–1652) managed the firm in its prime, when it published elegant editions of the works of classical authors (1634–6) and a series on countries called *Petites Républiques* (1625–49).

Emerson /'eməs(ə)n/, Ralph Waldo (1803–82), American philosopher and poet. While visiting England in 1832 he met Coleridge, Wordsworth, and Carlyle, through whom he became associated with German idealism. On his return to the US he evolved the concept of Transcendentalism, a philosophy based on a belief that divinity pervades the whole of nature and humankind; it found expression in his essay *Nature* (1836). He and Thoreau are regarded as the central figures of New England Transcendentalism, which, in its reverence for nature, foreshadowed the ecological movement of the 20th century.

Empedocles /em'pedəˌkliːz/ (*c*.493–*c*.433 BC), Greek philosopher, born in Sicily. His hexametric poem *On Nature* taught that the universe is composed of the four imperishable elements of fire, air, water, and earth, which mingle and separate under the influence of the opposing principles of Love and Strife. According to legend, he leapt into the crater of Mount Etna in order that he might be thought a god.

Empson /'emps(ə)n/, Sir William (1906–84), English poet and literary critic. His intricate, closely reasoned poems, published in the *Collected Poems* (1955), reflect his training as a mathematician. His influential literary criticism includes *Seven Types of Ambiguity* (1930).

Enders /'endəz/, John Franklin (1897–1985), American virologist. He devised a skin test for detecting antibodies to the mumps virus, and, with Frederick C. Robbins (1916–92) and Thomas H. Weller (1915–92), developed a method of growing viruses in tissue cultures. This led eventually to the development of vaccines against mumps, polio, and measles. The three scientists shared a Nobel Prize for this work in 1954.

Engels /'eŋg(ə)lz/, Friedrich (1820–95), German socialist and political philosopher, resident chiefly in England from 1842. The founder of modern communism with Karl Marx, he collaborated with him in the writing of the *Communist Manifesto* (1848). Engels also completed the second and third volumes of Marx's *Das Kapital* (1885; 1894). Engels's own writings include *The Condition of the Working Classes in England in 1844* (1845).

Ennius /'enɪəs/, Quintus (239–169 BC), Roman poet and dramatist. He was largely responsible for the creation of a native Roman literature based on Greek models. Of his many works (surviving only in fragments) the most important was the *Annals* (undated), a hexametric epic on the history of Rome, which was a major influence on Virgil.

Ensor /'ensɔː(r)/, James (Sydney), Baron (1860–1949), Belgian painter and engraver. An artist whose work is significant both for symbolism and for the development of 20th-century expressionism, he began to use the characteristic elements of fantasy and the macabre in his paintings in the late 1880s. Works such as *The Entry of Christ into Brussels* (1888) typically depict brightly coloured and bizarre carnival scenes crowded with skeletons or other grotesque or masked figures.

Enver Pasha /ˌenvə ˈpɑːʃə/ (1881–1922), Turkish political and military leader. A leader of the Young Turks in the revolution of 1908, he came to power as part of a ruling triumvirate following a coup d'état in 1913. He played a significant role in creating Turkey's alliance with Germany during the First World War, and served as Minister of War (1914–18).

Epictetus /ˌepɪkˈtiːtəs/ (c.55–c.135 AD), Greek philosopher. Originally a slave, he preached the common brotherhood of man and advocated a Stoic philosophy. His teachings were published posthumously in the *Enchiridion*.

Epicurus /ˌepɪˈkjʊərəs/ (341–270 BC), Greek philosopher. His physics (later expounded by the Roman writer Lucretius) is based on the theory of a materialist universe, unregulated by divine providence, composed of indestructible atoms moving in a void. From this follows his philosophy of Epicureanism, a restrained type of hedonism: mental pleasure was regarded more highly than physical and the ultimate pleasure was held to be freedom from anxiety and mental pain, especially that arising from needless fear of death and of gods.

Epstein[1] /'epstaɪn/, Brian (1934–67), English manager of the Beatles. Epstein became fascinated with the Beatles in 1961 and became their manager, replacing drummer Pete Best with Ringo Starr and arranging a contract with Parlophone. Epstein was not successful in financial negotiation, however, failing to capitalize on the US rights to Beatles merchandise. He died suddenly, probably of an accidental drugs overdose.

Epstein[2] /'epstaɪn/, Sir Jacob (1880–1959), American-born British sculptor. His first important commission was a group of eighteen figures for the British Medical Association in the Strand (1907–8); it was the first of many works to arouse violent criticism for the use of distortion and alleged obscenity. A founder member of the vorticist group, he moved towards abstract sculpture and later scored great success in his modelled portraits of the famous, in particular his *Einstein* (1933).

Erasmus /ɪˈræzməs/, Desiderius (Dutch name Gerhard Gerhards) (c.1469–1536), Dutch humanist and scholar. During his lifetime he was the most famous scholar in Europe and the first there to achieve renown through the printed word. He published his own Greek edition of the New Testament (1516), followed by a Latin translation, and paved the way for the Reformation with his satires on the Church, including the *Colloquia Familiaria* (1518). However, he opposed the violence of the Protestant Reformation and condemned Luther in *De Libero Arbitrio* (1523).

Erastus /ɪˈræstəs/ (Swiss name Thomas Lieber; also called Liebler or Lüber) (1524–83), Swiss theologian and physician. He was professor of medicine at Heidelberg University from 1558. A follower of Zwingli, he opposed the imposition of a Calvinist system of church government in Heidelberg because of the Calvinists' excessive use of excommunication. The doctrine of Erastianism (that the state should have supremacy over the Church in ecclesiastical matters) was later attributed to him, although his views were less extreme.

Eratosthenes /ˌerəˈtɒsθəˌniːz/ (c.275–194 BC), Greek scholar, geographer, and astronomer. He was a pupil of Callimachus and head of the library at Alexandria. Active in the fields of literary criticism and chronology, he was also the first systematic geographer of antiquity. He accurately calculated the circumference of the earth by measuring the angle of the sun's rays at different places at the same time, and he attempted (less successfully) to determine the magnitude of the sun and moon and their distance from the earth.

Ericsson[1] /'erɪks(ə)n/, John (1803–89), Swedish engineer. His inventions included a steam railway locomotive for the 1829 competition which was won by Stephenson's *Rocket*, and the marine screw propeller (1836). He then moved to the US, where he built the ironclad *Monitor*, which was the first ship to have a revolving armoured turret and was used in a battle on the Union side in the American Civil War.

Ericsson was also a pioneer of solar energy, constructing a steam pump supplied from a boiler heated by a concentrating mirror.

Ericsson² /ˈerɪks(ə)n/, Leif (also **Ericson, Eriksson**), Norse explorer, son of Eric the Red. He sailed westward from Greenland (c.1000) and reputedly discovered land (variously identified as Labrador, New-foundland, or New England), which he named Vinland because of the vines he claimed to have found growing there.

Eric the Red /ˈerɪk/ (c.940–c.1010), Norse explorer. He left Iceland in 982 in search of land to the west, exploring Greenland and establishing a Norse settlement there in 986.

Erlanger /ˈɜːlæŋə(r)/, Joseph (1874–1965), American physiologist. He worked mainly in cardiac physiology, designing a sphyg-momanometer to study the components of the pulse wave and examining the conduc-tion of impulses in the heart. Using an oscilloscope with H. Gasser, Erlanger found that the velocity of a nerve impulse is proportional to the diameter of the fibre. Erlanger and Gasser shared a Nobel Prize for this in 1944.

Ernst /ɜːnst/, Max (1891–1976), German art-ist. In 1919 he became leader of the Col-ogne Dada group, and was responsible for adapting the techniques of collage and photomontage to surrealist uses. He is best known, however, for the surrealist paint-ings he did after moving to Paris, including *L'Eléphant de Célèbes* (1921). In 1925 he de-veloped the technique of frottage, using such surfaces as leaves and wood grain, as in *Habit of Leaves* (1925). He spent much of the 1940s in the US but later returned to France, adopting French citizenship in 1958.

Erté /ˈeɪteɪ/ (born Romain de Tirtoff) (1892–1990), Russian-born French fashion de-signer and illustrator. From 1912 he worked in Paris as a fashion designer, and during the First World War his garments became internationally famous through his decorative magazine illustrations. In the 1920s he became a noted art deco designer, moving into the design of house-hold items and fabrics and creating elab-orate *tableaux vivants* for Broadway shows such as the *Ziegfeld Follies*.

Esaki /eˈzɑːkɪ/, Leo (born 1925), Japanese physicist. He investigated and pioneered the development of quantum-mechanical tunnelling of electrons in semiconductor devices, and designed the tunnel diode. These (also known as *Esaki diodes*), small and fast in operation, are now widespread in electronic devices. Esaki shared the Nobel Prize for physics in 1973.

Escher /ˈeʃə(r)/, M(aurits) C(orneille) (1898–1972), Dutch graphic artist. Escher's prints make sophisticated use of visual illusion, exploiting the ambiguity between figure and ground, and between flat pattern and apparent three-dimensional recession. From the 1940s his work took on a surreal-ist flavour as he made play with optical illusion to represent, for example, stair-cases that appear to lead both up and down in the same direction.

Escoffier /eˈskɒfɪˌeɪ/, Georges-Auguste (1846–1935), French chef. He gained an international reputation while working in London at the Savoy Hotel (1890–9) and later at the Carlton (1899–1919). His many culinary inventions include peach Melba, first made in 1893 in honour of the singer Dame Nellie Melba when she was staying at the Savoy.

Ethelred /ˈeθəlˌred/ the name of two kings of England:
Ethelred I (died 871), king of Wessex and Kent 865–71, elder brother of Alfred the Great. His reign was marked by the con-tinuing struggle against the invading Danes. Alfred joined Ethelred's campaigns and succeeded him on his death.
Ethelred II (known as Ethelred the Un-ready) (c.969–1016), king of England 978–1016. Ethelred's inability to confront the Danes after he succeeded his murdered half-brother St Edward the Martyr led to his payment of tribute to prevent their attacks. In 1013 he briefly lost his throne to the Danish king Sweyn I. His nickname came from an Old English word meaning 'lacking good advice; rash'.

Euclid /ˈjuːklɪd/ (c.300 BC), Greek mathem-atician. He taught at Alexandria, and is famous for his great work *Elements of Geom-etry*, which covered plane geometry, the theory of numbers, irrationals, and solid geometry. This was the standard work until other kinds of geometry were con-ceived in the 19th century.

Eugénie /juːˈʒeɪnɪ/ (born Eugénia María de Montijo de Guzmán) (1826–1920), Spanish empress of France 1853–70 and wife of Napoleon III. Throughout her husband's reign she contributed much to the bril-

liance of his court and was an important influence on his foreign policy. She acted as regent on three occasions (1859; 1865; 1870).

Euler [1] /'ɔɪlə(r)/, Leonhard (1707–83), Swiss mathematician. Euler, who worked mainly in St Petersburg and Berlin, was a prolific and original contributor to all branches of mathematics. His attempts to elucidate the nature of functions and his successful (though logically dubious) study of infinite series led his successors, notably Abel and Cauchy, to introduce ideas of convergence and rigorous argument into mathematics. One of his best-known theorems defines a connection between two of the most important constants in mathematics, expressed in the equation $e^{i\pi} = -1$.

Euler [2] /'ɔɪlə(r)/, Ulf Svante von (1905–83), Swedish physiologist, the son of Hans Euler-Chelpin. He was the first to discover a prostaglandin, which he isolated from semen. He then searched for the principal chemical neurotransmitter of the sympathetic nervous system, and identified it as noradrenalin. Euler was awarded a Nobel Prize for this in 1970.

Euler-Chelpin /ˌɔɪlə'kelpɪn/, Hans Karl August Simon von (1873–1964), German-born Swedish biochemist. He worked mainly on enzymes and vitamins, and explained the role of enzymes in the alcoholic fermentation of sugar. He shared the Nobel Prize for chemistry in 1929.

Euripides /jʊə'rɪpɪˌdiːz/ (480–c.406 BC), Greek dramatist. He was the last of the trio of important tragedians after Aeschylus and Sophocles. His nineteen surviving plays show important innovations in the handling of the traditional myths, such as their introduction of a low realism into grand subject-matter, their interest in feminine psychology, and their portrayal of abnormal and irrational states of mind. They include *Medea*, *Hippolytus*, *Electra*, *Trojan Women*, and *Bacchae*.

Eusebio /juː'sebɪəʊ/ (full name Ferraira da Silva Eusebio) (born 1942), Mozambican-born Portuguese footballer. An accomplished forward, he joined the Portuguese club Benfica in 1961 and made his international début the same year, going on to win seventy-seven caps. He was voted European Footballer of the Year in 1965, was the top scorer in the 1966 World Cup, and won the Golden Boot award for the highest

scorer in European football in 1968 and 1973.

Eusebius /juː'siːbɪəs/ (known as Eusebius of Caesaria) (c.264–c.340 AD), bishop and Church historian. His *Ecclesiastical History* is the principal source for the history of Christianity (especially in the Eastern Church) from the age of the Apostles until 324.

Evans [1] /'ev(ə)nz/, Sir Arthur (John) (1851–1941), English archaeologist. He is best known for his excavations at Knossos (1899–1935), which resulted in the discovery of the Bronze Age civilization of Crete; he called this civilization Minoan after the legendary Cretan king Minos.

Evans [2] /'ev(ə)nz/, Dame Edith (Mary) (1888–1976), English actress. Her stage repertoire encompassed a wide range of Shakespearian and contemporary roles; she acted in the first production of George Bernard Shaw's *Heartbreak House* (1921). She is particularly remembered as Lady Bracknell in Oscar Wilde's *The Importance of Being Earnest*, a role which she portrayed for the first time on stage in 1939 and on film in 1952.

Evans [3] /'ev(ə)nz/, Gil (born Ian Ernest Gilmore Green) (1912–88), Canadian jazz pianist, composer, and arranger. In 1947 he began a long association with Miles Davis, producing albums such as *Porgy and Bess* (1958) and *Sketches of Spain* (1959). From the 1970s he experimented successfully with electronic and synthesized sound, and his music became increasingly improvisational.

Evans-Pritchard /ˌev(ə)nz'prɪtʃəd/, Sir Edward (Evan) (1902–73), English anthropologist. He is noted for his studies of African tribal life and cultures, especially those based on his time spent living in Sudan with the Azande and Nuer peoples in the 1920s and 1930s. Among the important works of social anthropology he wrote are *Witchcraft, Oracles and Magic Among the Azande* (1937) and *The Nuer* (1940).

Evelyn /'iːvlɪn/, John (1620–1706), English diarist and writer. He is remembered chiefly for his *Diary* (published posthumously in 1818), which covers most of his life, describing his travels abroad, his contemporaries, and such important historical events as the Great Plague and the Great Fire of London. He was also a pioneer of

English forestry and gardening, and a founder member of the Royal Society.

Evert /'evət/, Christine Marie ('Chris') (born 1954), American tennis player. Her career began at an early age as a Wightman Cup player (1971) and included winning both the US and French Open championships six times and three Wimbledon titles (1974; 1976; 1981).

Eyre /eə(r)/, Edward John (1815–1901), British-born Australian explorer and colonial statesman. He undertook explorations in the interior deserts of Australia (1840–1) and discovered what came to be known as Lake Eyre. He later served as Lieutenant-Governor of New Zealand (1847–53) and Governor of Jamaica (1864–6).

Eysenck /'aɪseŋk/, Hans Jürgen (1916–97), German-born British psychologist. Noted for his strong criticism of conventional psychotherapy, particularly Freudian psychoanalysis, he developed an alternative treatment for mental disorders in the form of behaviour therapy. Eysenck also devised methods for assessing intelligence and personality, and published his controversial ideas in *Race, Intelligence, and Education* (1971).

F

Fabergé /ˈfæbə.ʒeɪ/, Peter Carl (1846–1920), Russian goldsmith and jeweller, of French descent. He is famous for the intricate and imaginative Easter eggs and many other ornaments that he made for the family of Tsar Alexander III and royal households in other countries.

Fabius /ˈfeɪbɪəs/ (full name Quintus Fabius Maximus Verrucosus, known as 'Fabius Cunctator') (died 203 BC), Roman general and statesman. After Hannibal's defeat of the Roman army at Cannae in 216 BC, Fabius successfully pursued a strategy of caution and delay in order to wear down the Carthaginian invaders. This earned him his nickname, which means 'delayer'.

Fabre /ˈfæbrə/, Jean Henri (1823–1915), French entomologist. Fabre worked for thirty years as a teacher, much of the time in poverty, and then left for the full-time study of entomology in his native Provence. He became well known for his meticulous observations of insect behaviour, notably the life cycles of dung beetles, oil beetles, and solitary bees and wasps. Fabre's major work was the ten-volume *Souvenirs entomologiques* (1879–1907), but he also wrote some forty popular works, including *The Sacred Beetle and Others* (translated 1918).

Fabriano, Gentile da, see GENTILE DA FABRIANO.

Fabricius /fəˈbrɪʃəs/, Johann Christian (1745–1808), Danish entomologist. Fabricius studied for two years under Linnaeus, whose work in entomology he greatly extended. He wrote extensively on the nomenclature and classification of insects, naming and describing some 10,000 new species in the process. Fabricius believed in the evolution of species by hybridization and (ahead of his time) by adaptation to the prevailing environment.

Fahrenheit /ˈfærən.haɪt/, Gabriel Daniel (1686–1736), German physicist. Becoming interested in manufacturing scientific instruments, Fahrenheit set up his own business. He improved the performance of thermometers, found that liquids have their own characteristic boiling-point, developed an instrument to determine atmospheric pressure from the boiling-point of water, and designed a hydrometer. Fahrenheit is best known, however, for his thermometer scale, which he originally planned with fixed points at the human body temperature and at the coldest temperature he could achieve by mixing ice and salt.

Fairbanks /ˈfeəbæŋks/, Douglas (Elton) (born Julius Ullman) (1883–1939), American actor. With Charlie Chaplin, Mary Pickford, and D. W. Griffith, he founded United Artists in 1919 and embarked on the series of swashbuckling films that made him a celebrity, including *The Mark of Zorro* (1920) and *The Thief of Baghdad* (1924). His son, Douglas Fairbanks Jr. (born 1909), also an actor, played roles similar to those of his father, including that of Rupert of Hentzau in *The Prisoner of Zenda* (1937).

Fairfax /ˈfeəfæks/, Thomas, 3rd Baron Fairfax of Cameron (1612–71), English Parliamentary general. He was appointed commander of the New Model Army in 1645 and led the Parliamentary forces to victory at the decisive Battle of Naseby. In 1650 he was replaced as commander by Oliver Cromwell for refusing to march against the Scots, who had proclaimed the future Charles II king. Fairfax later helped to secure the restoration of Charles II to the throne in 1660.

Faisal /ˈfaɪs(ə)l/ the name of two kings of Iraq:
Faisal I (1885–1933), reigned 1921–33. A British-sponsored ruler, he was also supported by fervent Arab nationalists. Under his rule Iraq achieved full independence in 1932.
Faisal II (1935–58), grandson of Faisal I, reigned 1939–58. After the Suez crisis he initially pledged Iraq's continuing loyalty to Egypt, but, as relations grew more strained, he united with King Hussein of Jordan against Egypt and Syria. He was assassinated in a military coup, after which a republic was established.

Faldo /ˈfældəʊ/, Nicholas Alexander ('Nick') (born 1957), English golfer. He won the British Open championship in 1987 and

1990 and the US Masters Tournament in 1989, 1990, and 1996.

Falla /'fɑːjə/, Manuel de (1876–1946), Spanish composer and pianist. While in Paris from 1907 to 1914, he became friends with Ravel and Debussy. Later he composed the ballets *Love, the Magician* (1915) and *The Three-Cornered Hat* (1919); the latter was produced by Diaghilev, with designs by Picasso. After declaring himself a pacifist during the Spanish Civil War, he emigrated to Argentina in 1939.

Fangio /'fændʒɪ,əʊ/, Juan Manuel (1911–95), Argentinian motor-racing driver. He first won the world championship in 1951, and then held the title from 1954 until 1957. He retired from racing in 1958.

Faraday /'færə,deɪ/, Michael (1791–1867), English physicist and chemist. One of the greatest experimentalists, Faraday was largely self-educated. Appointed by Sir Humphry Davy as his assistant at the Royal Institution, he initially concentrated on analytical chemistry, and discovered benzene in 1825. His most important work was in electromagnetism, in which field he demonstrated electromagnetic rotation and discovered electromagnetic induction (the key to the development of the electric dynamo and motor). Faraday's concept of magnetic lines of force formed the basis of the classical field theory of electromagnetic behaviour. He also discovered the laws of electrolysis.

Farnese [1] /fɑː'neɪsɪ/, Alessandro, see PAUL III.

Farnese [2] /fɑː'neɪsɪ/, Alessandro, Duke of Parma (1545–92), Italian general and statesman. While in the service of Philip II of Spain he acted as Governor-General of the Netherlands (1578–92). He captured Antwerp in 1585, securing the southern Netherlands for Spain.

Farouk /fə'ruːk/ (1920–65), king of Egypt, reigned 1936–52. On assuming power he dismissed Prime Minister Nahas Pasha, but was forced by the British government to reinstate him. Farouk's defeat in the Arab–Israeli conflict of 1948, together with the general corruption of his reign, led to a military coup in 1952, headed by General Neguib (1901–84) and masterminded by Nasser. Farouk was forced to abdicate in favour of his infant son, Fuad; he was sent into exile and eventually became a citizen of Monaco.

Farquhar /'fɑːkə(r)/, George (1678–1707), Irish dramatist. A principal figure in Restoration comedy, he is remembered for *The Recruiting Officer* (1706) and *The Beaux' Stratagem* (1707), plays marked by realism and genial merriment as well as by pungent satire.

Farrell [1] /'færəl/, J(ames) G(ordon) (1935–79), English novelist. He is best known for his novels *The Siege of Krishnapur* (1973), dealing with events of the Indian Mutiny, and *The Singapore Grip* (1978), describing the fall of Singapore to the Japanese.

Farrell [2] /'færəl/, J(ames) T(homas) (1904–79), American novelist. He achieved fame with his trilogy about Studs Lonigan, a young Chicago Catholic of Irish descent: *Young Lonigan* (1932), *The Young Manhood of Studs Lonigan* (1934), and *Judgement Day* (1935).

Fassbinder /'fæs,bɪndə(r)/, Rainer Werner (1946–82), German film director. Fassbinder is remembered for films such as *The Bitter Tears of Petra von Kant* (1972) and the allegorical *The Marriage of Maria Braun* (1979). Influenced by Brecht, Marx, and Freud, Fassbinder's films dealt largely with Germany during the Second World War and postwar West German society.

Fatima /'fætɪmə/ (AD c.606–32), youngest daughter of the prophet Muhammad and wife of the fourth caliph, Ali (died 661). The descendants of Muhammad trace their lineage through her; she is revered especially by Shiite Muslims as the mother of the imams Hasan (624–80) and Husayn (626–80).

Faulkner /'fɔːknə(r)/, William (1897–1962), American novelist. His works deal with the history and legends of the American South and have a strong sense of a society in decline; in the first of his major novels, *The Sound and the Fury* (1929), he was also influenced by modernist concerns of form. Other important works include *As I Lay Dying* (1930) and *Absalom! Absalom!* (1936). He was awarded the Nobel Prize for literature in 1949.

Fauré /'fɔːreɪ/, Gabriel (Urbain) (1845–1924), French composer and organist. He composed songs throughout his career, incorporating some in cycles such as *La Bonne Chanson* (1891–2). His best-known work is the *Requiem* (1887) for solo voices, choir, and orchestra; he also wrote piano pieces,

chamber music, and incidental music for the theatre.

Faust /faʊst/ (also **Faustus** /-təs/) (died c.1540), German astronomer and necromancer. Reputed to have sold his soul to the Devil, he became the subject of many legends and was the subject of a drama by Goethe, an opera by Gounod, and a novel by Thomas Mann.

Fawkes /fɔːks/, Guy (1570–1606), English conspirator. He was hanged for his part in the Gunpowder Plot of 5 November 1605. The occasion is commemorated annually with fireworks, bonfires, and the burning of a guy.

FDR the nickname of President Franklin Delano Roosevelt (see ROOSEVELT[2]).

Fechner /'fexnə(r)/, Gustav Theodor (1801–87), German physicist and psychologist. His early work was in electricity, but after a long illness he became interested in psychology. He sought to define the quantitative relationship between degrees of physical stimulation and the resulting sensations, the study of which he termed *psychophysics*. By associating sensations with numerical values, Fechner hoped to make psychology a truly objective science.

Fellini /fə'liːnɪ/, Federico (1920–93), Italian film director. He rose to international fame in the 1950s with *La Strada* (1954), which won an Oscar for best foreign film. Other major films include *La Dolce Vita* (1960) – a satire on Rome's high society and winner of the Grand Prix at Cannes – and the semi-autobiographical $8^1/_2$ (1963).

Fender /'fendə(r)/, Leo (1907–91), American guitar-maker. He pioneered the production of electric guitars, designing the Fender Broadcaster of 1948 (later called the Telecaster), which was the first solid-body electric guitar to be widely available, and the Fender Stratocaster, first marketed in 1956. These two types are still produced and sold worldwide by the Fender company. Leo Fender also pioneered the design of a number of electric bass guitars.

Ferdinand /'fɜːdɪnənd/ (known as Ferdinand of Aragon or Ferdinand the Catholic) (1452–1516), king of Castile 1474–1516 and of Aragon 1479–1516. His marriage to Isabella of Castile in 1469 ensured his accession (as Ferdinand V) to the throne of Castile with her. During this time, they instituted the Spanish Inquisition (1478). Ferdinand subsequently succeeded to the throne of Aragon (as Ferdinand II) and was joined as monarch by Isabella (as Isabella I). Together they supported Columbus's expedition in 1492. Their capture of Granada from the Moors in the same year effectively united Spain as one country. Their daughter Catherine of Aragon became the first wife of Henry VIII of England.

Ferguson /'fɜːgəs(ə)n/, Alex(ander Chapman) (born 1941), Scottish football manager and footballer. After a playing career in Scotland he managed St Mirren (1974–8) and Aberdeen (1978–86), with whom he won the European Cup Winner's Cup in 1983 and a Scottish league and cup double in 1984. He took over as manager of Manchester United in 1986, and in ten years took them to three Premier League championships (1993, 1994, 1996), three FA Cup wins (1990, 1994, 1996), including an unprecedented two league and cup doubles.

Ferlinghetti /ˌfɜːlɪŋ'getɪ/, Lawrence (Monsanto) (born Lawrence Ferling) (born 1919), American poet and publisher. From the early 1950s he lived in San Francisco, with whose beat movement he is identified. In 1952 he founded his own bookshop and publishing house, City Lights: the bookshop was the focus for many writers and artists in the late 1950s, while the publishing house produced works such as Allen Ginsberg's *Howl* (1957). His own works include the collection *A Coney Island of the Mind* (1958), the novel *Her* (1960), and a number of experimental plays.

Fermat /'fɜːmɑː/, Pierre de (1601–65), French mathematician. His work on curves led directly to the general methods of calculus introduced by Newton and Leibniz. Fermat is also recognized as the founder of the theory of numbers and is best known for his conjecture (*Fermat's last theorem*) that if n is an integer greater than 2, $x^n + y^n = 2^n$ has no positive integral solutions. A general proof of this theorem was not found until 1995.

Fermi /'fɜːmɪ/, Enrico (1901–54), Italian-born American atomic physicist. Working at first in Italy, he invented (with Paul Dirac) Fermi–Dirac statistics, a mathematical tool of great value in atomic, nuclear, and solid-state physics. He predicted the existence of the neutrino, and produced radioactive isotopes by bombarding atomic nuclei with neutrons. He was awarded the Nobel Prize for physics in 1938. Moving to the US, Fermi directed the first controlled

nuclear chain reaction in 1942, and joined the Manhattan Project to work on the atom bomb. The artificial element fermium and a class of subatomic particles, the fermions, are named after him.

Ferranti /fə'ræntɪ/, Sebastian Ziani de (1864–1930), English electrical engineer. He was one of the pioneers of electricity generation and distribution in Britain, his chief contribution being the use of high voltages for economical transmission over a distance.

Ferrari /fə'rɑːrɪ/, Enzo (1898–1988), Italian car designer and manufacturer. He became a racing driver for Alfa Romeo in 1920 and proceeded to work as one of their designers. In 1929 he founded the company named after him, launching the famous Ferrari marque in 1947 and producing a range of high-quality sports and racing cars. Since the early 1950s Ferraris have won more world championship Grands Prix than any other car.

Ferrier /'fɛrɪə(r)/, Kathleen (1912–53), English contralto. She made her operatic début as Lucretia in the first performance of Britten's *The Rape of Lucretia* (1946), and is particularly famous for her performance in 1947 of Mahler's song cycle *Das Lied von der Erde*.

Fessenden /'fɛsəndən/, Reginald Aubrey (1866–1932), Canadian-born American physicist and radio engineer. He pioneered radio-telephony, devised the amplitude modulation of radio waves for carrying audio signals, and invented the heterodyne receiver. He made the first sound broadcast at Christmas 1906 in the US. Fessenden was involved in both industrial and academic research, and obtained hundreds of patents for his inventions.

Feuerbach /'fɔɪəˌbɑːx/, Ludwig (Andreas) (1804–72), German materialist philosopher. He studied theology at Heidelberg and then philosophy under Hegel at Berlin. His best-known work, *The Essence of Christianity*, was published in 1841. He maintained that the dogmas and beliefs of Christianity are figments of human imagination, fulfilling a need inherent in human nature.

Feydeau /'feɪdəʊ/, Georges (1862–1921), French dramatist. His name has become a byword for French bedroom farce. He wrote some forty plays, including *Hotel Paradiso* (1894) and *Le Dindon* (1896).

Feynman /'feɪnmən/, Richard Phillips (1918–88), American theoretical physicist. He worked in quantum electrodynamics, and introduced important new techniques for studying the electromagnetic interactions between subatomic particles. This approach is expressed in diagrams that describe the exchange of particles (Feynman diagrams). He shared the Nobel Prize for physics in 1965.

Fibonacci /ˌfɪbə'nɑːtʃɪ/, Leonardo (known as Fibonacci of Pisa) (c.1170–c.1250), Italian mathematician. Fibonacci learnt of the 'new' Arabic numerals while in North Africa and the Middle East, and later popularized their use in Europe through such works as *Liber Abaci* (1202, revised 1228). He made many original contributions in complex calculations, algebra, and geometry, and pioneered number theory and indeterminate analysis. He is famous as the discoverer of the Fibonacci series, in which each term is the sum of its two predecessors (1, 1, 2, 3, 5, 8, etc.).

Fichte /'fɪxtə/, Johann Gottlieb (1762–1814), German philosopher. A pupil of Kant, he postulated that the ego is the only basic reality; the world around it, or the 'non-ego', is posited by the ego in defining and delimiting itself. Fichte preached moral virtues and encouraged patriotic values; his political addresses had some influence on the development of German nationalism and the overthrow of Napoleon.

Field /fiːld/, John (1782–1837), Irish composer and pianist. He is noted for the invention of the nocturne and for his twenty compositions in this form.

Fielding /'fiːldɪŋ/, Henry (1707–54), English novelist. After writing several comedies and farces, he provoked the introduction of censorship with his sharp political satire *The Historical Register for 1736*; the resultant Licensing Act of 1737 effectively ended his career as a dramatist. He turned to writing picaresque novels, including *Joseph Andrews* (1742) – which begins as a parody of Samuel Richardson's *Pamela* – and *Tom Jones* (1749). Fielding became Justice of the Peace for Westminster in 1748, and was responsible for the formation of the Bow Street Runners the following year.

Fields[1] /fiːldz/, Dame Gracie (born Grace Stansfield) (1898–1979), English singer and comedienne. During the 1930s she enjoyed great success with English music-hall audiences. She went on to star in a series of

popular films, including *Sing as We Go* (1934).

Fields[2] /ˈfiːldz/, W. C. (born William Claude Dukenfield) (1880–1946), American comedian. Having made his name as a comedy juggler he became a vaudeville star, appearing in the *Ziegfeld Follies* revues between 1915 and 1921. His films established him as an internationally famous comic; they include *The Bank Dick* (1940).

Fillmore /ˈfɪlmɔː(r)/, Millard (1800–74), American Whig statesman, 13th President of the US 1850–3. He succeeded to the presidency on the death of Zachary Taylor. Fillmore was an advocate of compromise on the slavery issue. However, his unpopular enforcement of the 1850 Fugitive Slave Act hastened the end of the Whig Party.

Finney /ˈfɪnɪ/, Thomas ('Tom') (born 1929), English footballer. He joined Preston North End on leaving school and became one of the outstanding wingers of his era. He remained loyal to Preston throughout his career, and won 76 caps for England between 1946 and 1958, scoring 30 goals. He was the first player to be voted Footballer of the Year twice, in 1954 and 1957.

Fischer[1] /ˈfɪʃə(r)/, Emil Hermann (1852–1919), German organic chemist. He studied the structure of sugars, other carbohydrates, and purines, and synthesized many of them. He also worked on peptides and proteins, and confirmed that they consist of chains of amino acids. Fischer's work was to a large extent the basis for the German drug industry, and he was awarded the Nobel Prize for chemistry in 1902.

Fischer[2] /ˈfɪʃə(r)/, Hans (1881–1945), German organic chemist. His work was largely concerned with the porphyrin group of natural pigments. He determined the complex structure of the red oxygen-carrying part of haemoglobin, the green chlorophyll pigments found in plants, and the orange bile pigment bilirubin. He also synthesized some of these, and was awarded the Nobel Prize for chemistry in 1930.

Fischer[3] /ˈfɪʃə(r)/, Robert James ('Bobby') (born 1943), American chess player. He was world champion 1972–5 after defeating Boris Spassky, whom he beat again in a 1992 rematch.

Fischer-Dieskau /ˌfɪʃəˈdiːskaʊ/, Dietrich (born 1925), German baritone. He is noted for his interpretations of German lieder, in

particular Schubert's song cycles. He has made more recordings of songs than any other recording artist and has the largest vocal repertoire of any contemporary singer (more than 1,000 songs).

Fisher /ˈfɪʃə(r)/, Sir Ronald Aylmer (1890–1962), English statistician and geneticist. Fisher made major contributions to the development of statistics, publishing influential books on statistical theory, the design of experiments, statistical methods for research workers, and the relationship between Mendelian genetics and evolutionary theory. He also carried out experimental work in agriculture and on the genetics of blood groups.

Fisher, St John /ˈfɪʃə(r)/ (1469–1535), English churchman. In 1504 he became bishop of Rochester and earned the disfavour of Henry VIII by opposing his divorce from Catherine of Aragon. When he refused to accept the king as supreme head of the Church, he was condemned to death. Feast day, 22 June.

Fittipaldi /ˌfɪtɪˈpældɪ/, Emerson (born 1946), Brazilian motor-racing driver. He started his career in Kart racing before progressing to Formula One with the Lotus team in 1970. Two years later, at the age of 25, he became the youngest-ever world champion. In 1974 he won his second world title, with McLaren. He retired in 1980, but made a successful comeback in North America, winning the Indianapolis 500 in 1989.

Fitzgerald[1] /fɪtsˈdʒerəld/, Edward (1809–83), English scholar and poet. He is remembered for his free poetic translation of *The Rubáiyát of Omar Khayyám* (1859).

Fitzgerald[2] /fɪtsˈdʒerəld/, Ella (1917–96), American jazz singer. In the 1940s she evolved a distinctive style of scat singing. Fitzgerald joined the American impresario Norman Granz (born 1918) on his world tours in 1946, appearing with Count Basie and Duke Ellington. From the mid-1950s she made a successful series of recordings of songs by George Gershwin and Cole Porter.

Fitzgerald[3] /fɪtsˈdʒerəld/, F(rancis) Scott (Key) (1896–1940), American novelist. His novels, particularly *The Great Gatsby* (1925), provide a vivid portrait of the US during the jazz era of the 1920s. From the mid-1920s Fitzgerald and his wife, the writer Zelda Sayre (1900–47), became part of an affluent and fashionable set living on the French Riviera; their lifestyle is reflected in

the semi-autobiographical novel *Tender is the Night* (1934).

FitzGerald[4] /fɪts'dʒerəld/, George Francis (1851–1901), Irish physicist. He suggested that length, time, and mass depend on the relative motion of the observer, while the speed of light is constant. This hypothesis, postulated independently by Lorentz, prepared the way for Einstein's special theory of relativity.

Flamsteed /'flæmstiːd/, John (1646–1719), English astronomer. He was appointed the first Astronomer Royal at the Royal Greenwich Observatory, with the task of accurately providing the positions of stars for use in navigation. He eventually produced the first star catalogue, which gave the positions of nearly 3,000 stars. Flamsteed also worked on the motions of the sun and moon, tidal tables, and other measurements.

Flaubert /'fləʊbeə(r)/, Gustave (1821–80), French novelist and short-story writer. A dominant figure in the French realist school, he achieved fame with his first published novel, *Madame Bovary* (1857). Its portrayal of the adulteries and suicide of a provincial doctor's wife caused Flaubert to be accused of immorality, but he was tried and acquitted. His *Trois contes* (1877) demonstrates Flaubert's versatility with different modes of narrative and anticipates Maupassant's experiments with the short story.

Flaxman /'flæksmən/, John (1755–1826), English sculptor and draughtsman. He worked for Josiah Wedgwood 1775–87, designing medallion portraits and plaques. In 1793 he published engraved illustrations to Homer, influenced by Greek vase-painting; these won him international fame. Flaxman also sculpted church monuments such as the memorial to the Earl of Mansfield in Westminster Abbey (1793–1801).

Flecker /'flekə(r)/, James (Herman) Elroy (1884–1915), English poet. His best-known works are the verse collection *The Golden Journey to Samarkand* (1913) and the poetic Eastern play *Hassan* (1922), for which Delius wrote incidental music.

Fleming[1] /'flemɪŋ/, Sir Alexander (1881–1955), Scottish bacteriologist. He worked mainly at St Mary's Hospital, London, where he investigated the body's defences against bacteriological infection. In 1928 he fortuitously discovered the effect of penicillin on bacteria, and twelve years later Florey and Chain established its therapeutic use as an antibiotic. In 1942 Fleming was officially publicized as a British scientific hero, and so achieved fame retrospectively for his work in the 1920s. He was jointly awarded a Nobel Prize in 1945.

Fleming[2] /'flemɪŋ/, Ian (Lancaster) (1908–64), English novelist. He is known for the spy novels whose hero is the secret agent James Bond. Many of these stories (of which Fleming completed one a year from 1953 until his death) were successfully turned into feature films, making the character of James Bond world famous.

Fleming[3] /'flemɪŋ/, Sir John Ambrose (1849–1945), English electrical engineer. He is chiefly remembered for his invention of the thermionic valve (1900), which was the basis for all electronic devices until the transistor began to supersede it more than fifty years later. He also worked on transformers, radio-telegraphy, and telephony.

Fletcher /'fletʃə(r)/, John (1579–1625), English dramatist. A writer of Jacobean tragicomedies, he wrote some fifteen plays with Francis Beaumont, including *The Maid's Tragedy* (1610–11). He is also believed to have collaborated with Shakespeare on such plays as *The Two Noble Kinsmen* and *Henry VIII* (both *c*.1613).

Flinders /'flɪndəz/, Matthew (1774–1814), English explorer. He explored the coast of New South Wales (1795–1800) before being commissioned by the Royal Navy to circumnavigate Australia (1801–3). During this voyage he charted much of the west coast of the continent for the first time.

Florey /'flɔːrɪ/, Howard Walter, Baron (1898–1968), Australian pathologist. In collaboration with Sir Ernst Chain he isolated and purified penicillin, developed techniques for its large-scale production, and performed the first clinical trials. Florey and Chain shared a Nobel Prize in 1945 with Sir Alexander Fleming.

Florio /'flɔːrɪˌəʊ/, John (*c*.1553–1625), English lexicographer, of Italian descent. In 1598 he produced an Italian–English dictionary entitled *A Worlde of Wordes*. His most important work was the first translation into English of Montaigne's essays (1603), on which Shakespeare drew in *The Tempest*.

Flynn /flɪn/, Errol (born Leslie Thomas Flynn) (1909–59), Australian-born American actor. His usual role was the swashbuckling hero of romantic costume dramas in films such as *Captain Blood* (1935), *The Adventures of Robin Hood* (1938), and *The Master of Ballantrae* (1953).

Fo /fəʊ/, Dario (born 1926), Italian dramatist. After many years of performing and writing revues and plays for assorted theatre groups, he made his name internationally with the political satire *Accidental Death of an Anarchist* (1970). Subsequent successes include *Trumpets and Raspberries* (1980) and the farcical *Open Couple* (1983), written with his wife, the Italian dramatist Franca Rame (born 1929).

Foch /fɒʃ/, Ferdinand (1851–1929), French general. He strongly supported the use of offensive warfare, which resulted in many of his 20th Corps being killed by German machine-guns in August 1914. He became Supreme Commander of all Allied Forces on the Western Front in early 1918, and served as the senior French representative at the Armistice negotiations.

Fokine /ˈfəʊkɪn/, Michel (born Mikhail Mikhailovich Fokin) (1880–1942), Russian-born American dancer and choreographer. He became known as a reformer of modern ballet, striving for a greater dramatic, stylistic, and directional unity. From 1909 he was Diaghilev's chief choreographer and staged the premières of Stravinsky's *The Firebird* (1910) and Ravel's *Daphnis and Chloë* (1912).

Fokker /ˈfɒkə(r)/, Anthony Herman Gerard (1890–1939), Dutch-born American pioneer aircraft designer and pilot. He built his first aircraft in 1908, the monoplane Eindecker, a type used by Germany as a fighter aircraft in the First World War. He also designed the successful Trimotor F-7 airliners, later versions of which provided the backbone of continental airlines in the 1930s.

Fonda /ˈfɒndə/ a family of American actors. Henry Fonda (1905–82) is noted for his roles in such films as *The Grapes of Wrath* (1939) and *Twelve Angry Men* (1957). He won his only Oscar for his role in his final film, *On Golden Pond* (1981). His daughter Jane (born 1937) was a model and stage actress before becoming a screen star. Her films include *Klute* (1971), for which she won an Oscar, and *The China Syndrome* (1979); she also acted alongside her father in *On Golden Pond*. In the 1980s she became known for her fitness routine, *Jane Fonda's Workout*. Her brother Peter (born 1939) is also an actor, as is his daughter Bridget (born 1964).

Fonteyn /fɒnˈteɪn/, Dame Margot (born Margaret Hookham) (1919–91), English ballet-dancer. She danced her first major role in Sir Frederick Ashton's *Le Baiser de la fée* (1935), later dancing all the classical ballerina roles and creating many new ones for the Royal Ballet. In 1962 she began a celebrated partnership with Rudolf Nureyev, dancing in *Giselle* and *Romeo and Juliet*. In 1979 she was named *prima ballerina assoluta*, a title given only three times in the history of ballet.

Ford[1] /fɔːd/, Ford Madox (born Ford Hermann Hueffer) (1873–1939), English novelist and editor. He was the grandson of the Pre-Raphaelite painter Ford Madox Brown and is chiefly remembered as the author of the novel *The Good Soldier* (1915). As founder of both the *English Review* (1908) and the *Transatlantic Review* (1924), he published works by such writers as Ernest Hemingway, James Joyce, and Ezra Pound.

Ford[2] /fɔːd/, Gerald R(udolph) (born 1913), American Republican statesman, 38th President of the US 1974–7. He became President on the resignation of Richard Nixon in the wake of the Watergate affair. The free pardon he granted Nixon two months later aroused controversy.

Ford[3] /fɔːd/, Harrison (born 1942), American actor. He made his screen début in 1966. Ford became internationally famous with his leading roles in the science-fiction film *Star Wars* (1977) and its two sequels, and in the adventure film *Raiders of the Lost Ark* (1981) and its two sequels (including *Indiana Jones and the Temple of Doom*, 1984). Other films include *The Fugitive* (1993).

Ford[4] /fɔːd/, Henry (1863–1947), American motor manufacturer. He was a pioneer of mass production and had a profound influence on the widespread use of motor vehicles. By 1903 he had evolved a reliable car and founded his own firm, the Ford Motor Company. In 1909 Ford produced his famous Model T, of which 15 million were made over the next 19 years at gradually reducing prices due to large-scale manufacture, a succession of simple assembly tasks, and the use of a conveyor belt. He went on to produce a cheap and effective farm tractor, the Fordson, which had a

great effect on agricultural mechanization. Control of the Ford Motor Company passed to his grandson, Henry Ford II (1917–87), in 1945 and today it is a huge multinational corporation. Among the first Henry Ford's philanthropic legacies is the Ford Foundation (established 1936), a major charitable trust.

Ford[5] /fɔːd/, John (1586–c.1639), English dramatist. He often collaborated with other dramatists, notably writing *The Witch of Edmonton (c.*1621) with Thomas Dekker and William Rowley. Robert Burton's *The Anatomy of Melancholy* (1621) exerted a considerable influence on Ford's own plays, which explore human delusion, melancholy, and horror. Among his best-known works are *'Tis Pity She's a Whore* (1633) and *The Broken Heart* (1633).

Ford[6] /fɔːd/, John (born Sean Aloysius O'Feeney) (1895–1973), American film director. He is chiefly known for his westerns, which depict the early pioneers and celebrate the frontier spirit. His many films starring John Wayne include *Stagecoach* (1939) and *She Wore a Yellow Ribbon* (1949). Notable films in other genres include *The Grapes of Wrath* (1940), for which he won an Oscar.

Foreman /'fɔːmən/, George (born 1948), American boxer. He won the heavyweight gold medal at the 1968 Olympic Games, and became a professional the following year. In 1973 he beat Joe Frazier to take the world heavyweight title, but lost it to Muhammad Ali in 1974. He retired in 1977, but made a comeback in 1991, losing on points to Evander Holyfield in a world title qualifier.

Forester /'fɒrɪstə(r)/, C(ecil) S(cott) (pseudonym of Cecil Lewis Troughton Smith) (1899–1966), English novelist. He is remembered for his seafaring novels set during the Napoleonic Wars, featuring Captain Horatio Hornblower. His other works include *The African Queen* (1935), later made into a celebrated film by John Huston (1951).

Forkbeard /'fɔːkbɪəd/, Sweyn, see SWEYN I.

Forman /'fɔːmən/, Milos (born 1932), Czech-born American film director. He achieved international success with two films, *The Lives of a Blonde* (1965) and *The Firemen's Ball* (1967). Having taken US citizenship in 1968 he continued to make acclaimed films, including *One Flew Over the Cuckoo's Nest* (1975), which won five Oscars, and his adaptation of Peter Shaffer's stage play *Amadeus* (1983), which won eight Oscars, including that for best director.

Formby /'fɔːmbɪ/, George (born George Booth) (1904–61), English comedian. He became famous for his numerous musical films in the 1930s, in which he projected the image of a Lancashire working lad and accompanied his songs on the ukulele.

Forrest /'fɒrɪst/, John, 1st Baron (1847–1918), Australian explorer and statesman, Premier of Western Australia 1890–1901. From 1864, as colonial surveyor, he was one of the principal explorers of Western Australia. He did much to secure the colony's self-government and became its first Premier.

Forster /'fɔːstə(r)/, E(dward) M(organ) (1879–1970), English novelist and literary critic. His novels, many of which have been made into successful films, include *A Room with a View* (1908) and *A Passage to India* (1924). Forster's novel *Maurice*, dealing with homosexual themes, was written in 1914, and appeared posthumously in 1971. He is also noted for his critical work *Aspects of the Novel* (1927).

Forsyth /fɔː'saɪθ/, Frederick (born 1938), English novelist. He is known for political thrillers such as *The Day of the Jackal* (1971), *The Odessa File* (1972), and *The Fourth Protocol* (1984).

Fosbury /'fɒzbərɪ/, Richard (born 1947), American high jumper. He originated the style of jumping known as the 'Fosbury flop', in which the jumper clears the bar head-first and backwards. In 1968 he won the Olympic gold medal using this technique.

Foster[1] /'fɒstə(r)/, Jodie (born 1962), American film actress. She appeared in *Alice Doesn't Live Here Anymore* (1974) before coming to fame with *Taxi Driver* (1976), for which she won an Oscar nomination. She went on to win Oscars for her performances in *The Accused* (1988) and *Silence of the Lambs* (1991). She founded the production company Egg Pictures, which she owns and chairs, in 1990.

Foster[2] /'fɒstə(r)/, Sir Norman (Robert) (born 1935), English architect. His work is notable for its sophisticated engineering approach and technological style. Examples of his buildings include the Hong Kong and Shanghai Bank, Hong Kong (1986), the Terminal Zone at Stansted Air-

port (1991), and the Century Tower, Tokyo (1991).

Foster[3] /'fɒstə(r)/, Stephen (Collins) (1826–64), American composer. He wrote more than 200 songs, and, though a Northerner, was best known for songs which captured the Southern plantation spirit, such as 'Oh! Susannah' (1848), 'Camptown Races' (1850), and 'Old Folks at Home' (1851).

Foucault[1] /'fu:kəʊ/, Jean Bernard Léon (1819–68), French physicist. He is chiefly remembered for the huge pendulum which he hung from the roof of the Panthéon in Paris in 1851: as the pendulum swung, the path of its oscillations slowly rotated, demonstrating the rotation of the earth. He obtained the first reasonably accurate determination of the velocity of light, invented the gyroscope, introduced the technique of silvering glass for the reflecting telescope, pioneered astronomical photography, discovered eddy currents in the cores of electrical equipment, and improved a host of devices such as the arc lamp and the induction coil.

Foucault[2] /'fu:kəʊ/, Michel (1926–84), French philosopher. A student of Louis Althusser, he was mainly concerned with exploring how society defines categories of abnormality such as insanity, sexuality, and criminality, and the manipulation of social attitudes towards such things by those in power. Major works include *Histoire de la folie* (1961; *Madness and Civilization*, 1967) and *L'Histoire de la sexualité* (three volumes 1976–84; *The History of Sexuality*, 1978–86).

Fourier /'fʊərɪˌeɪ/, Jean Baptiste Joseph (1768–1830), French mathematician. His theory of the diffusion of heat involved him in the solution of partial differential equations by the method of separation of variables and superposition. This led him to study the series and integrals that are now known by his name. His belief that a wide class of periodic phenomena could be described by means of Fourier series was substantially vindicated by later mathematicians, and this theory now provides one of the most important methods for solving many partial differential equations that occur in physics and engineering.

Fowler /'faʊlə(r)/, H(enry) W(atson) (1858–1933), English lexicographer and grammarian. With his brother F(rancis) G(eorge) Fowler (1870–1918) he compiled the first *Concise Oxford Dictionary* (1911). He is most famous for his moderately prescriptive guide to style and idiom, *Modern English Usage*, first published in 1926.

Fowles /faʊlz/, John (Robert) (born 1926), English novelist. His works include the psychological thriller *The Collector* (1963), the magic-realist novel *The Magus* (1966), and the semi-historical novel *The French Lieutenant's Woman* (1969).

Fox[1] /fɒks/, Charles James (1749–1806), British Whig statesman. At the age of 19 he entered Parliament advocating American independence, and later welcomed the French Revolution. After Lord North's resignation he became Secretary of State, collaborating with his former opponent North to form a government in 1783. The coalition was brought down the same year and Fox remained in opposition until the death of Pitt the Younger in 1806, when he took office again as Foreign Secretary and passed an anti-slavery bill through Parliament.

Fox[2] /fɒks/, George (1624–91), English preacher and founder of the Society of Friends (Quakers). He began preaching in 1647, teaching that truth is the inner voice of God speaking to the soul, and rejecting priesthood and ritual. Despite repeated imprisonment, he established a society called the 'Friends of the Truth' (*c.*1650), which later became the Society of Friends.

Foxe /fɒks/, John (1516–87), English religious writer. After fleeing to the Continent on the accession of Queen Mary I, he published his *Actes and Monuments* in Strasbourg in 1554; popularly known as *The Book of Martyrs*, it appeared in England in 1563. This passionate account of the persecution of English Protestants fuelled hostility towards Catholicism for generations.

Fox Talbot, William Henry, see TALBOT.

Fragonard /'fræɡəˈnɑː(r)/, Jean-Honoré (1732–1806), French painter. His paintings, usually landscapes, gardens, and family scenes, embody the rococo spirit. He is most famous for erotic canvases such as *The Swing* (*c.*1766) and *The Progress of Love* (1771).

Frame /freɪm/, Janet (Paterson) (born 1924), New Zealand novelist. Her novels, including *Faces in the Water* (1961), draw on her experiences of psychiatric hospitals after she suffered a severe mental breakdown. Other works include *A State of Siege* (1966), *Intensive Care* (1970), and a three-volume

autobiography (1982–5), which was made into the film *An Angel at my Table* (1990).

France /frɑːns/, Anatole (pseudonym of Jacques-Anatole-François Thibault) (1844–1924), French writer. He achieved success as a novelist with *Le Crime de Sylvestre Bonnard* (1881). His later work was more satirical, notably *L'Île des pingouins* (1908), an ironic version of the Dreyfus case, and *Les Dieux ont soif* (1912), a study of fanaticism during the French Revolution. He was awarded the Nobel Prize for literature in 1921.

Francis /'frɑːnsɪs/, Richard Stanley ('Dick') (born 1920), English jockey and writer. He was champion jockey 1953–4 and began writing after his retirement in 1957. He has written a series of thrillers, mostly set in the world of horse-racing.

Francis I /'frɑːnsɪs/ (1494–1547), king of France 1515–47. He succeeded his cousin Louis XII in 1515 and soon afterwards took the duchy of Milan. The greater part of his reign (1521–44) was spent at war with the Holy Roman emperor Charles V, with the result that Francis relinquished all claims to Italy. In the early years of his reign Francis generally practised religious toleration towards supporters of the Reformation, although his policies became harsher from the mid-1530s. A noted patron of the arts, he supported Rabelais and Cellini, and commissioned many new buildings in Paris, including the Louvre.

Francis of Assisi, St /ə'siːzɪ/ (born Giovanni di Bernardone) (c.1181–1226), Italian monk, founder of the Franciscan order. Born into a wealthy family, he renounced his inheritance in favour of a life of poverty after experiencing a personal call to rebuild the semi-derelict church of San Damiano of Assisi. He soon attracted followers, founding the Franciscan order in 1209 and drawing up its original rule (based on complete poverty). His generosity, simple faith, deep humility, and love of nature have made him one of the most cherished saints. Feast day, 4 October.

Francis of Sales, St /saːl/ (1567–1622), French bishop. One of the leaders of the Counter-Reformation, he was bishop of Geneva (1602–22) and co-founder of the Order of the Visitation, an order of nuns (1610). The Salesian order (founded in 1859) is named after him. Feast day, 24 January.

Francis Xavier, St see XAVIER, ST FRANCIS.

Franck[1] /frɒŋk/, César (Auguste) (1822–90), Belgian-born French composer. He was a noted organist, becoming organ professor at the Paris Conservatoire in 1872. His reputation rests on a few works composed late in life, particularly the *Symphonic Variations* for piano and orchestra (1885), the D minor Symphony (1886–8), and the String Quartet (1889).

Franck[2] /fræŋk/, James (1882–1964), German-born American physicist. He worked on the bombardment of atoms by electrons, and found that the atoms absorb and lose energy in discrete increments or quanta. He then studied the vibration and rotation of dissociated molecules. After moving to America in 1935 he eventually joined the Manhattan Project to develop the atom bomb: in the Franck report, completed in 1945, he and other scientists proposed the explosion of the bomb in an uninhabited area to demonstrate its power to Japan, rather than using it directly in war.

Franco /'fræŋkəʊ/, Francisco (1892–1975), Spanish general and statesman, head of state 1939–75. After commanding the Spanish Foreign Legion in Morocco, Franco was among the leaders of the military uprising against the Republican government which led to the Spanish Civil War. In 1937 he became leader of the Falange (Fascist) Party and proclaimed himself 'Caudillo' (leader) of Spain. With the surrender of Madrid and the defeat of the republic in 1939, he took control of the government and established a dictatorship. Despite pressure from Germany and Italy, Franco kept Spain neutral during the Second World War. In 1969 he named Prince Juan Carlos as his successor and heir to the reconstituted Spanish throne.

Frank /fræŋk/, Anne (1929–45), German Jewish girl. Her diary (1947; *The Diary of a Young Girl*, 1953) records the experiences of her family living for two years in hiding from the Nazis in occupied Amsterdam. They were eventually betrayed and sent to concentration camps; Anne died in Belsen from typhoid. Her diary has been translated into more than thirty languages.

Franklin[1] /'fræŋklɪn/, Aretha (born 1942), American soul and gospel singer. She made her name with the album *I Never Loved a Man (the Way I Love You)* (1967), going on to record more than thirty albums, including the live gospel set *Amazing Grace* (1972).

She is known particularly for the song 'I Say a Little Prayer' (1967).

Franklin[2] /'fræŋklɪn/, Benjamin (1706–90), American statesman, inventor, and scientist. A wealthy printer and publisher, he was one of the signatories to the peace between the US and Great Britain after the War of American Independence. His main scientific achievements were the formulation of a theory of electricity, based on the concept of an electric fluid, which introduced (and arbitrarily defined) positive and negative electricity, and a demonstration of the electrical nature of lightning, which led to the invention of the lightning conductor. His inventions include the 'Franklin stove' (a kind of free-standing cast-iron heater) and bifocal spectacles.

Franklin[3] /'fræŋklɪn/, (Stella Maria Sarah) Miles (1879–1954), Australian novelist. She is recognized as having written the first true Australian novel, her acclaimed first book *My Brilliant Career* (1901). From 1906 until 1927 she lived in the US and England. She produced a series of chronicle novels under her pseudonym 'Brent of Bin Bin' as well as writing books under her own name.

Franklin[4] /'fræŋklɪn/, Rosalind Elsie (1920–58), English physical chemist and molecular biologist. Her early work was on the structure of coals, and she went on to investigate the various forms of carbon by means of X-ray crystallography. She then used this technique on DNA, and with Maurice Wilkins contributed to the discovery of its structure. Franklin was using the technique to investigate the structure of viruses at the time of her premature death from cancer.

Franz Josef /frænts 'jəʊzef/ (1830–1916), emperor of Austria 1848–1916 and king of Hungary 1867–1916. The early part of his reign was characterized by his efforts to rule as an absolutist monarch. Later he made concessions, granting Austria a parliamentary constitution in 1861 and giving Hungary equal status with Austria (Austria–Hungary) after Austria's defeat by Prussia in 1866. His annexation of Bosnia-Herzegovina (1908) contributed to European political tensions, and the assassination in Sarajevo of his nephew and heir apparent, Archduke Franz Ferdinand (1863–1914), prompted Austria's attack on Serbia and precipitated the First World War.

Fraser[1] /'freɪzə(r)/, Dawn (born 1937), Australian swimmer. She won the Olympic gold medal for the 100-metres freestyle in 1956, 1960, and 1964, the first competitor to win the same title at three successive Olympics. She was the first woman to swim 100 metres in under one minute (1964), and set many world records.

Fraser[2] /'freɪzə(r)/, (John) Malcolm (born 1930), Australian Liberal statesman, Prime Minister 1975–83. He became the youngest-ever Australian MP in 1955 and was minister for the army, education and science, and defence before becoming leader of the Liberal Party in 1975. He was appointed Prime Minister with the dissolution of the previous administration by the Governor-General and was elected a month later. Unable to curb unemployment, his government was defeated in 1983.

Fraunhofer /'fraʊn,həʊfə(r)/, Joseph von (1787–1826), German optician and pioneer in spectroscopy. He observed and mapped a large number of fine dark lines in the solar spectrum and plotted their wavelengths. These lines, now named after him, were later used to determine the chemical elements present in the spectra of the sun and stars. He became noted for his finely ruled diffraction gratings, used to determine the wavelengths of specific colours of light and of the major spectral lines.

Frazer /'freɪzə(r)/, Sir James George (1854–1941), Scottish anthropologist. He is often regarded as the founder of British social anthropology and ethnology. In a series of essays, *The Golden Bough* (1890–1915), he proposed an evolutionary theory of the development of human thought, from the magical and religious to the scientific. The first chair in anthropology was created for him at Liverpool University in 1907.

Frazier /'freɪzɪə(r)/, Joseph ('Joe') (born 1944), American boxer. In 1964 he won the gold medal as a heavyweight at the Tokyo Olympics. He then turned professional, winning the world title in 1968, and in 1971 became the first man to beat Muhammad Ali in a professional fight. He lost his title to George Foreman in 1973 and subsequently lost to Ali twice before his retirement in 1976.

Frederick I /'fredrɪk/ (known as Frederick Barbarossa, 'Redbeard') (c.1123–90), king of Germany and Holy Roman emperor 1152–90. He made a sustained attempt to subdue Italy and the papacy, but was eventually

defeated at the battle of Legnano in 1176. He was drowned in Asia Minor while on his way to the Third Crusade.

Frederick II /'fredrɪk/ (known as Frederick the Great) (1712–86), king of Prussia 1740–86. On his succession Frederick promptly claimed Silesia, launching Europe into the War of the Austrian Succession (1740–8). During the Seven Years War (1756–63), he joined with Britain and Hanover against a coalition of France, Russia, Austria, Spain, Sweden, and Saxony, and succeeded in considerably strengthening Prussia's position. By the end of his reign he had doubled the area of his country. He was a distinguished patron of the arts.

Frederick William (known as 'the Great Elector') (1620–88), Elector of Brandenburg 1640–88. His programme of reconstruction and reorganization following the Thirty Years War, including the strengthening of the army and the development of the civil service, brought stability to his country and laid the basis for the expansion of Prussian power in the 18th century. In his foreign policy he sought to create a balance of power by the formation of shifting strategic alliances.

Frege /'freɪgə/, Gottlob (1848–1925), German philosopher and mathematician, founder of modern logic. He developed a logical system for the expression of mathematics which was a great improvement on the syllogistic logic which it replaced, and he also worked on general questions of philosophical logic and semantics. His theory of meaning, based on his use of a distinction between what a linguistic term refers to and what it expresses, is still influential. Frege tried to provide a rigorous foundation for mathematics on the basis of purely logical principles, but abandoned the attempt when Bertrand Russell, on whose work he had a profound influence, pointed out that his system was inconsistent.

Frémont /'fri:mɒnt/, John Charles (known as 'the Pathfinder') (1813–90), American explorer and politician. He was responsible for exploring several viable routes to the Pacific across the Rockies in the 1840s. He made an unsuccessful bid for the presidency in 1856, losing to James Buchanan.

Fresnel /'frem(ə)l, French frɛnɛl/, Augustin Jean (1788–1827), French physicist and civil engineer. He took up the study of polarized light and postulated that light moves in a wavelike motion, which had already been suggested by, among others, Christiaan Huygens and Thomas Young. They, however, assumed the waves to be longitudinal, while Fresnel was sure that they vibrated transversely to the direction of propagation, and he used this to explain successfully the phenomenon of double refraction. He invented the lens that is named after him.

Freud[1] /frɔɪd/, Anna (1895–1982), Austrian-born British psychoanalyst, the youngest child of Sigmund Freud. Anna continued with her father's work and introduced important innovations in method and theory, notably with regard to disturbed children. In 1938 the Freuds narrowly escaped from the Nazis to Britain; after the war Anna set up a child therapy course and clinic in London, and continued to write and lecture extensively. Her major works include The Ego and Mechanisms of Defence (1937) and Normality and Pathology in Childhood (1966).

Freud[2] /frɔɪd/, Lucian (born 1922), German-born British painter, grandson of Sigmund Freud. He came to Britain in 1931, becoming a British citizen in 1939. Since the 1950s he has established a reputation as a powerful figurative painter. His subjects, especially his portraits and nudes, are painted in a meticulously detailed style based on firm draughtsmanship, often using striking angles.

Freud[3] /frɔɪd/, Sigmund (1856–1939), Austrian neurologist and psychotherapist. He was the first to draw attention to the significance of unconscious processes in normal and neurotic behaviour, and was the founder of psychoanalysis as both a theory of personality and a therapeutic practice. He proposed the existence of an unconscious element in the mind which influences consciousness, and of conflicts in it between various sets of forces. Freud also emphasized the importance of a child's semiconsciousness of sex as a factor in mental development, and his theory of the sexual origin of neuroses aroused great controversy. His works include The Interpretation of Dreams (1899), Totem and Taboo (1913), and The Ego and the Id (1923).

Freyberg /'fraɪbɜːg/, Bernard Cyril, 1st Baron Freyberg of Wellington and of Munstead (1889–1963), British-born New Zealand general. He served in both world wars, winning the VC in France in 1917. He was

Governor-General of New Zealand 1946–52. Appointed Commander-in-Chief of the New Zealand Expeditionary Forces in 1939, Freyberg led the unsuccessful Commonwealth expedition to Greece and Crete (1941), and later took an active role in the North African and Italian campaigns.

Friedan /'fri:d(ə)n/, Betty (born 1921), American feminist and writer. After the birth of her three children she published *The Feminine Mystique* (1963), an instant best seller which presented femininity as an artificial construct and traced the ways in which American women are socialized to become mothers and housewives. In 1966 she founded the National Organization for Women, serving as its president until 1970.

Friedman /'fri:dmən/, Milton (born 1912), American economist. A principal exponent of monetarism, he was awarded the Nobel Prize for economics in 1976. He acted as a policy adviser to President Reagan from 1981 to 1989.

Friedrich /'fri:drɪx/, Caspar David (1774–1840), German painter. Noted for his romantic landscapes in which he saw a spiritual significance, he caused controversy with his altarpiece *The Cross in the Mountains* (1808), which lacked a specifically religious subject.

Frink /frɪŋk/, Dame Elisabeth (1930–93), English sculptor and graphic artist. She made her name with somewhat angular bronzes, often of birds. During the 1960s her figures — typically male nudes, horses, and riders — became smoother, although she retained a feeling for the bizarre.

Frisch[1] /frɪʃ/, Karl von (1886–1982), Austrian zoologist. He is noted for his work on the behaviour of the honey bee. He studied the vision of bees, showing that they can use polarized light for navigation and see ultraviolet. He also investigated communication between bees, and concluded that they perform an elaborate dance in the hive to show other bees the direction and distance of a source of food. Von Frisch shared a Nobel Prize in 1973 with Konrad Lorenz and Nikolaas Tinbergen.

Frisch[2] /frɪʃ/, Otto Robert (1904–79), Austrian-born British physicist. With his aunt, Lise Meitner, he recognized that Otto Hahn's experiments with uranium had produced a new type of nuclear reaction. Frisch named it nuclear fission, and indi-

cated the explosive potential of its chain reaction. During the Second World War he continued his research in England, and worked on nuclear weapons in the US at Los Alamos.

Frisch[3] /frɪʃ/, Ragnar (Anton Kittil) (1895–1973), Norwegian economist. A pioneer of econometrics, he shared the first Nobel Prize for economics with Jan Tinbergen (1969).

Frith /frɪθ/, William Powell (1819–1909), English painter. He is remembered for his panoramic paintings of Victorian life, including *Derby Day* (1858) and *The Railway Station* (1862).

Frobisher /'frəʊbɪʃə(r)/, Sir Martin (c.1535–94), English explorer. In 1576 he led an unsuccessful expedition in search of the North-west Passage, discovering Frobisher Bay (in Baffin Island) and landing in Labrador. He returned to Canada in each of the following two years in a fruitless search for gold, before serving in Sir Francis Drake's West Indies expedition of 1585–6 and playing a prominent part in the defeat of the Spanish Armada (for which he was knighted). He died from wounds received in an attack on a Spanish fort in Brittany.

Froebel /'frəʊb(ə)l, 'frɜ:b-/, Friedrich (Wilhelm August) (1782–1852), German educationist and founder of the kindergarten system. Believing that play materials, practical occupations, and songs are needed to develop a child's real nature, he opened a school for young children in 1837, later naming it the Kindergarten ('children's garden'). He also established a teacher-training school.

Fromm /frɒm/, Erich (1900–80), German-born American psychoanalyst and social philosopher. He became a US citizen in 1934, and taught at several universities before being appointed professor of psychiatry at New York in 1962. His works, which include *Escape from Freedom* (1941), *Man for Himself* (1947), and *The Sane Society* (1955), emphasize the role of culture in neurosis and strongly criticize materialist values.

Frost /frɒst/, Robert (Lee) (1874–1963), American poet. Much of his poetry reflects his affinity with New England, including the verse collections *North of Boston* (1914) and *New Hampshire* (1923). Noted for his ironic tone, conversational manner, and

simple language, he won the Pulitzer Prize on three occasions (1924; 1931; 1937).

Fry[1] /fraɪ/, Christopher (Harris) (born 1907), English dramatist. He is chiefly remembered for his comic verse dramas, especially *The Lady's Not for Burning* (1948) and *Venus Observed* (1950). He also wrote several screenplays and translated other dramatists, notably Jean Anouilh.

Fry[2] /fraɪ/, Elizabeth (1780–1845), English Quaker prison reformer. In the forefront of the early 19th-century campaign for penal reform, she concerned herself particularly with conditions in Newgate and other prisons, the plight of convicts transported to Australia, and the vagrant population in London and the south-east.

Fry[3] /fraɪ/, Roger (Eliot) (1866–1934), English art critic and painter. He was a champion of modern French painting, and of the post-impressionist movement in England. He argued for an aesthetics of pure form, regarding content as incidental. In 1913 he founded the Omega workshops for the benefit of young British artists, and he became professor of fine art at Cambridge in 1933.

Frye /fraɪ/, (Herman) Northrop (1912–91), Canadian literary critic. His first major work was *Fearful Symmetry* (1947), a study of William Blake and of the role of myth and symbol in various literary genres. He subsequently analysed the structure and mythology of the Bible in *The Great Code: The Bible and Literature* (1982).

Fuad /'fuːæd/ the name of two kings of Egypt:
Fuad I (1868–1936), reigned 1922–36. Formerly sultan of Egypt (1917–22), he became Egypt's first king after independence.
Fuad II (born 1952), grandson of Fuad I, reigned 1952–3. Named king as an infant on the forced abdication of his father, Farouk, he was deposed when Egypt became a republic.

Fuchs[1] /fʊks/, (Emil) Klaus (Julius) (1911–88), German-born British physicist. Fuchs was a Communist who came to England to escape Nazi persecution. During the 1940s he passed to the USSR secret information acquired while working in the US, where he was involved in the development of the atom bomb, and in Britain, where he held a senior post in the Atomic Energy Research Establishment at Harwell. He was

imprisoned from 1950 to 1959, and on his release he returned to East Germany.

Fuchs[2] /fʊks/, Sir Vivian (Ernest) (born 1908), English geologist and explorer. He led the Commonwealth Trans-Antarctic Expedition (1955–8). His party met Sir Edmund Hillary's New Zealand contingent, approaching from the opposite direction, at the South Pole, and went on to complete the first overland crossing of the continent.

Fuentes /'fwentes/, Carlos (born 1928), Mexican novelist and writer. His first novel, *Where the Air is Clear* (1958), took Mexico City as its theme and was an immediate success. Other novels include *Terra nostra* (1975), which explores the Spanish heritage in Mexico, and *The Old Gringo* (1984).

Fugard /'fuːɡɑːd/, Athol (born 1932), South African dramatist. His plays, including *Blood Knot* (1963) and *The Road to Mecca* (1985), are mostly set in contemporary South Africa and deal with social deprivation and other aspects of life under apartheid.

Fulbright /'fʊlbraɪt/, (James) William (1905–95), American senator. His name designates grants awarded under the Fulbright Act of 1946, which authorized funds from the sale of surplus war materials overseas to be used to finance exchange programmes of students and teachers between the US and other countries. The scheme was later supported by grants from the US government.

Fuller[1] /'fʊlə(r)/, R(ichard) Buckminster (1895–1983), American designer and architect. An advocate of the use of technology to produce efficiency in many aspects of life, he is best known for his postwar invention of the geodesic dome. These domes enable large spaces to be enclosed with great efficiency — in line with Fuller's ideals of using the world's resources with maximum purpose and least waste.

Fuller[2] /'fʊlə(r)/, Thomas (1608–61), English cleric and historian. He is chiefly remembered for *The History of the Worthies of England* (1662), a description of the counties with short biographies of local personages.

Fulton /'fʊlt(ə)n/, Robert (1765–1815), American pioneer of the steamship. During the Napoleonic Wars he spent some time in France and proposed both torpedoes and submarines, constructing a

steam-propelled 'diving-boat' called *Nautilus* in 1800 which submerged to a depth of 7.6 m (25 ft). He returned to America in 1806 and built the first successful paddle-steamer, the *Clermont*. Eighteen other steamships were subsequently built, inaugurating the era of commercial steam navigation.

Funk /fʌŋk/, Casimir (1884–1967), Polish-born American biochemist. He showed that a number of diseases, including scurvy, rickets, beriberi, and pellagra, were each caused by the deficiency of a particular dietary component. He coined the term *vitamins* for the chemicals concerned, from his belief (later shown to be inaccurate) that they were all amines. His work formed the basis of modern dietary studies.

Furtwängler /'fʊət,veŋglə(r)/, Wilhelm (1886–1954), German conductor. He was chief conductor of the Berlin Philharmonic Orchestra from 1922, and often worked at Bayreuth. He is noted particularly for his interpretations of Beethoven and Wagner.

Fuseli /'fju:z(ə)lɪ, fju:'zelɪ/, Henry (born Johann Heinrich Füssli) (1741–1825), Swiss-born British painter and art critic. In 1763 he went to England, where he became a prominent figure of the romantic movement. His work is often derived from literary themes (notably those of Shakespeare and Milton) and is inspired by a vivid imagination, tending towards the horrifying and the fantastic, as in *The Nightmare* (1781). In 1799 he was appointed professor of painting at the Royal Academy.

G

Gable /'geɪb(ə)l/, (William) Clark (1901–60), American actor. He became famous through his numerous roles in Hollywood films of the 1930s: they include *It Happened One Night* (1934), for which he won an Oscar, and *Gone with the Wind* (1939), in which he starred as Rhett Butler. His last film was *The Misfits* (1961), in which he played opposite Marilyn Monroe.

Gabo /'gɑːbəʊ/, Naum (born Naum Neemia Pevsner) (1890–1977), Russian-born American sculptor. With his brother, Antoine Pevsner, he was a founder of Russian constructivism, and was one of the first sculptors to use transparent materials. The brothers' *Realistic Manifesto* of 1920 set down their artistic principles, including the idea of introducing time and movement into sculpture; Gabo made his first kinetic sculpture, a vibrating metal rod powered by an electric motor, in 1920.

Gabor /'gɑːbɔː(r), gə'bɔː(r)/, Dennis (1900–79), Hungarian-born British electrical engineer. Having left Hungary for Britain in 1934, he became a British citizen in 1946. The following year he conceived the idea of holography, originally as a microscopic technique, greatly improving it after the invention of lasers in 1960. He was awarded the Nobel Prize for physics in 1971.

Gaddafi /gə'dɑːfɪ/, Mu'ammer Muhammad al (also **Qaddafi**) (born 1942), Libyan colonel, head of state since 1970. After leading the coup which overthrew King Idris (1890–1983) in 1969, he gained power as chairman of the revolutionary council and established the Libyan Arab Republic. As self-appointed head of state Gaddafi has pursued an anti-colonial policy at home, expelling foreigners from Libya and seeking to establish an Islamic Socialist regime. He has been accused of supporting international terrorism and has been involved in a number of conflicts with the West, as also with neighbouring Arab countries. Since 1979 he has held no formal post, although he has the ceremonial title 'leader of the revolution'.

Gagarin /gə'gɑːrɪn/, Yuri (Alekseevich) (1934–68), Russian cosmonaut. In 1961 he made the first manned space flight, completing a single orbit of the earth in 108 minutes. He was killed in a crash while testing an aeroplane.

Gainsborough /'geɪmzbərə/, Thomas (1727–88), English painter. From 1760 he worked in Bath and from 1774 in London, where he became a society portrait painter. Although he was famous for his portraits, such as *Mr and Mrs Andrews* (1748) and *The Blue Boy* (c.1770), landscape was his preferred subject; his works reflect the influence of the naturalistic approach to landscape of 17th-century Dutch painting and include *The Watering Place* (1777). He was a founder member of the Royal Academy of Arts (1768).

Gaitskell /'geɪtskɪl/, Hugh (Todd Naylor) (1906–63), British Labour statesman. Having served in the Attlee government in several ministerial posts, including Chancellor of the Exchequer (1950–1), he became leader of the Labour Party in opposition from 1955 until his death. Although his leadership covered a period of upheaval and reassessment within his party following successive election defeats, he eventually succeeded in restoring party unity. He was particularly vigorous in his opposition to the government over the Suez crisis and in resisting calls for unilateral disarmament within his own party.

Galba /'gælbə/ (full name Servius Sulpicius Galba) (c.3 BC–AD 69), Roman emperor AD 68–9. He was a governor in Spain when invited to succeed Nero as emperor in AD 68. Once in power, he aroused hostility by his severity and parsimony, as well as alienating the legions in Germany by removing their commander. In AD 69 he was murdered in a conspiracy organized by Otho.

Galbraith /gæl'breɪθ/, John Kenneth (born 1908), Canadian-born American economist. He is well known for his criticism of consumerism, the power of large multinational corporations, and a perceived preoccupation in Western society with economic growth for its own sake. His books have a broad appeal and include *The Afflu-*

ent Society (1958) and *The New Industrial State* (1967).

Galen /'geɪlən/ (129–99), Greek physician (full name Claudios Galenos; Latin name Claudius Galenus). He spent the latter part of his life in Rome, becoming court physician to the emperor Marcus Aurelius in 169. He was the author of numerous works which attempted to systematize the whole of medicine, and was especially productive as a practical anatomist and experimental physiologist. He demonstrated that the arteries carry blood not (as had been thought) air, but postulated the presence of minute pores in the wall between the ventricles of the heart, allowing blood to pass through, a theory which was accepted until medieval times. His works reached Europe in the 12th century and were widely influential.

Galileo Galilei /ˌgælɪˌleɪəʊ ˌgælɪˈleɪɪ/ (1564–1642), Italian astronomer and physicist, one of the founders of modern science. His discoveries include the constancy of a pendulum's swing, later applied to the regulation of clocks. He formulated the law of uniform acceleration of falling bodies, and described the parabolic trajectory of projectiles. Galileo applied the telescope to astronomy and observed craters on the moon, sunspots, the stars of the Milky Way, Jupiter's satellites, and the phases of Venus. His acceptance of the Copernican system was rejected by the Catholic Church, and under threat of torture from the Inquisition he publicly recanted his heretical views.

Galois /'gælwʌ/, Évariste (1811–32), French mathematician. His memoir on the conditions for solubility of polynomial equations was highly innovative but was only published posthumously, in 1846. He was imprisoned for his republican activities aged 19, and died aged 20 after a duel.

Galsworthy /'gɔːlz,wɜːðɪ/, John (1867–1933), English novelist and dramatist. He wrote several plays on social and moral themes, but is remembered chiefly for his sequence of novels known collectively as *The Forsyte Saga* (1906–28), tracing the declining fortunes of an affluent middle-class family in the years leading up to the First World War. These novels gained a wider audience through their adaptation for television in 1967. Galsworthy was awarded the Nobel Prize for literature in 1932.

Galtieri /ˌgæltɪˈeərɪ/, Leopoldo Fortunato (born 1926), Argentinian general and statesman, President 1981–2. He was one of the leaders of the right-wing junta that ordered the invasion of the Falkland Islands in 1982, precipitating the Falklands War. After the British victory in the war, Galtieri was court-martialled and, in 1986, sentenced to twelve years in prison.

Galton /'gɔːlt(ə)n/, Sir Francis (1822–1911), English scientist. A man of wide interests and a cousin of Charles Darwin, he is remembered chiefly for his founding and advocacy of eugenics. He introduced methods of measuring human mental and physical abilities, and developed statistical techniques to analyse his data. Galton also carried out important work in meteorology, especially on the theory of anticyclones, and pioneered the use of fingerprints as a means of identification.

Galvani /gæl'vɑːnɪ/, Luigi (1737–98), Italian anatomist. He studied the structure of organs and the physiology of tissues, but he is best known for his discovery of the twitching of frogs' legs in an electric field. He concluded that these convulsions were caused by 'animal electricity' found in the body. This was disputed by Alessandro Volta who, in the course of this argument, invented his electrochemical cell. The current produced by this device was for many years called *galvanic electricity*.

Gama, Vasco da, see DA GAMA.

Gamow /'geɪməʊ/, George (1904–68), Russian-born American physicist. He explained (with Ralph Asher Alpher, born 1921, and Hans Albrecht Bethe, born 1906) the abundances of chemical elements in the universe, and was a proponent of the big bang theory. He also suggested the triplet code of bases in DNA, which governs the synthesis of amino acids.

Gance /gɒns/, Abel (1889–1991), French film director. He was a notable early pioneer of technical experimentation in film; *Napoléon* (1926), for example, was significant for its use of the split-screen, hand-held camera, and wide-angle photography. His other films include *J'accuse* (1918) and *La Roue* (1921).

Gandhi[1] /'gændɪ/, Mrs Indira (1917–84), Indian stateswoman, Prime Minister 1966–77 and 1980–4. The daughter of Jawaharlal Nehru, she had already served as president of the Indian National Congress (1959–60)

and Minister of Information (1964) when she succeeded Lal Bahadur Shastri (1904–66) as Prime Minister. In her first term of office she sought to establish a secular state and to lead India out of poverty. However, in 1975 she introduced an unpopular state of emergency to deal with growing political unrest, and the Congress Party lost the 1977 election. Mrs Gandhi lost her seat and was unsuccessfully tried for corruption. Having formed a breakaway group from the Congress Party — known as the Indian National Congress (I) — in 1978, she was elected Prime Minister again in 1980. Her second period of office was marked by prolonged religious disturbance, during which she alienated many Sikhs by allowing troops to storm the Golden Temple at Amritsar; she was assassinated by her own Sikh bodyguards.

Gandhi[2] /'gændɪ/, Mahatma (born Mohandas Karamchand Gandhi) (1869–1948), Indian nationalist and spiritual leader. After early civil-rights activities as a lawyer in South Africa, in 1914 Gandhi returned to India, where he became prominent in the opposition to British rule, pursuing a policy of passive resistance and non-violent civil disobedience. The president of the Indian National Congress (1925–34), he never held government office, but was regarded as the country's supreme political and spiritual leader and the principal force in achieving India's independence. He was assassinated by a Hindu following his agreement to the creation of the state of Pakistan for the Muslim minority.

Gandhi[3] /'gændɪ/, Rajiv (1944–91), Indian statesman, Prime Minister 1984–9. The eldest son of Indira Gandhi, he entered politics following the accidental death of his brother Sanjay (1946–80), becoming Prime Minister after his mother's assassination. His premiership, at the head of the Indian National Congress (I) party, was marked by continuing unrest and he resigned in 1989; he was assassinated during the election campaign of 1991.

Garbo /'gɑːbəʊ/, Greta (born Greta Gustafsson) (1905–90), Swedish-born American actress. In 1924 her first important Swedish film led to a Hollywood contract; she gained instant recognition for her compelling screen presence and enigmatic beauty in *The Torrent* (1925). She made the transition from silent pictures to sound in *Anna Christie* (1930), later starring in *Mata Hari*

(1931) and *Anna Karenina* (1935). She also starred in two comedies; the second was less successful than the first and in 1941 she retired and lived as a recluse for the rest of her life.

Garcia /gɑːˈsɪə/, Jerry (full name Jerome John Garcia) (1942–95), American rock singer and guitarist. Garcia was the central figure of the Grateful Dead, a group formed *c*.1966 that were strongly associated with the West Coast hippy culture of the time. Mixing psychedelic rock with country and blues influences in lengthy improvisations, the band toured extensively until Garcia's death.

García Lorca see LORCA.

García Márquez /gɑːˌsɪə ˈmɑːkes/, Gabriel (born 1928), Colombian novelist. His left-wing sympathies brought him into conflict with the Colombian government and he spent the 1960s and 1970s in voluntary exile in Mexico and Spain. During this time he wrote *One Hundred Years of Solitude* (1967), which has come to be regarded as a classic example of magic realism. More recent novels include *The General in His Labyrinth* (1990). He was awarded the Nobel Prize for literature in 1982 and was formally invited back to Colombia, where he has since lived.

Gardner[1] /'gɑːdnə(r)/, Ava (Lavinia) (1922–90), American actress. Her beauty won her her first screen roles, and she came to prominence in *The Killers* (1946). She received critical praise for her performances in films such as *Bhowani Junction* (1956) and *The Night of the Iguana* (1964). She was married to Mickey Rooney, Frank Sinatra, and the jazz musician Artie Shaw.

Gardner[2] /'gɑːdnə(r)/, Erle Stanley (1899–1970), American novelist and short-story writer. He practised as a defence lawyer (1922–38) and went on to become famous for his series of novels featuring the lawyer-detective Perry Mason, many of which end with a dramatic courtroom scene..

Garfield /'gɑːfiːld/, James A(bram) (1831–81), American Republican statesman, 20th President of the US March–September 1881. A major-general who had fought for the Union side in the American Civil War, he resigned his command to enter Congress, where he served as leader of the Republican Party (1863–80). He was assassinated within months of taking presidential office.

Gatling

Garibaldi /ˌgærɪˈbɔːldɪ/, Giuseppe (1807–82), Italian patriot and military leader. He was a hero of the Risorgimento (the movement for the unification and independence of Italy), who began his political activity as a member of the Young Italy Movement. After involvement in the early struggles against Austrian rule in the 1830s and 1840s he commanded a volunteer force on the Sardinian side in 1859, and successfully led his 'Red Shirts' to victory in Sicily and southern Italy in 1860–1, thus playing a vital part in the establishment of a united kingdom of Italy. He was less successful in his attempts to conquer the papal territories around French-held Rome in 1862 and 1867.

Garland /ˈgɑːlənd/, Judy (born Frances Gumm) (1922–69), American singer and actress. The daughter of vaudeville entertainers, she became a child star and was under contract to MGM at the age of 13. Her most famous early film role was as Dorothy in *The Wizard of Oz* (1939), in which she sang 'Over the Rainbow'. Later successful films included *Meet Me in St Louis* (1944) and *A Star is Born* (1954). She apparently died of a drug overdose after suffering many personal problems. Among her children is the actress Liza Minelli (born 1946), her daughter from her marriage to the film director Vincente Minelli (1910–86).

Garrick /ˈgærɪk/, David (1717–79), English actor, manager, and dramatist. His style of acting was characterized by an easy, natural manner of speech, and he was equally successful in tragic and comic roles in both Shakespearian and contemporary plays. In 1747 he became involved in the management of the Drury Lane Theatre and later became its sole manager.

Garvey /ˈgɑːvɪ/, Marcus (Mosiah) (1887–1940), Jamaican political activist and black nationalist leader. He was the leader of the Back to Africa Movement, which advocated the establishment of an African homeland for black Americans, and founder of the Universal Negro Improvement Association (1914). He was chiefly active in the US, attracting a large following in support of his calls for black civil rights and economic independence. He died in obscurity, however, after his movement lost support during the Depression, but his thinking was later an important influence in the growth of Rastafarianism.

Gascoigne /ˈgæskɔɪn/, Paul (known as 'Gazza') (born 1967), English footballer. Gascoigne established himself as a gifted attacking midfielder and irrepressible personality after joining Tottenham Hotspur from Newcastle United in 1988, and he quickly became a member of the England team. During the 1991 FA Cup Final Gascoigne sustained a career-threatening knee injury, but after a long recovery period moved to the Italian club Lazio and then to Glasgow Rangers in 1995. At both clubs he continued to attract controversy both on and off the field.

Gaskell /ˈgæsk(ə)l/, Mrs Elizabeth (Cleghorn) (1810–65), English novelist. An active humanitarian from a Unitarian background, she is famous for *Mary Barton* (1848), *Cranford* (1853), and *North and South* (1855); all of these display her interest in social concerns. She also wrote a biography (1857) of her friend Charlotte Brontë.

Gassendi /gæˈsendɪ/, Pierre (1592–1655), French astronomer and philosopher. He is best known for his atomic theory of matter, which was based on his interpretation of the works of Epicurus, and he was an outspoken critic of Aristotle. He observed a new comet, a lunar eclipse, and a transit of Mercury (confirming Kepler's theories), and he coined the term *aurora borealis*.

Gasser /ˈgæsə(r)/, Herbert Spencer (1888–1963), American physiologist. Collaborating with Joseph Erlanger, he used an oscilloscope to show that the velocity of a nerve impulse is proportional to the diameter of the fibre. He also demonstrated the differences between sensory and motor nerves. Gasser and Erlanger shared a Nobel Prize in 1944.

Gates /geɪts/, William (Henry) ('Bill') (born 1955), American computer entrepreneur. In 1975 he co-founded Micro-Soft (later Microsoft), a private company for the manufacture and sale of computers. As its chairman and chief executive, Gates expanded the firm overseas in the early 1980s; by the end of the decade Microsoft was a leading multinational computer company and had made Gates the youngest multi-billionaire in American history. The company's success continued with the introduction of Windows 95 (1995), a successor to the original Windows system of 1985.

Gatling /ˈgætlɪŋ/, Richard Jordan (1818–1903), American inventor. Gatling was a

prolific inventor, first designing sowing machines, ploughs, and other agricultural machines and later turning to armaments. He is best known for the Gatling gun, invented in 1862, which was the first successful rapid-fire gun. It consisted of ten parallel barrels which were rotated by a hand crank and fired in turn, and was first put to use in the American Civil War.

Gaudí /'gaʊdɪ/, Antonio (full surname Gaudí y Cornet) (1853–1926), Spanish architect. A leading but idiosyncratic exponent of art nouveau, he worked chiefly in Barcelona, designing distinctive buildings such as the Parc Güell (begun 1900) and the Casa Batlló (begun 1905), notable for their use of ceramics, wrought-iron work, flowing lines, and organic forms. He began work on his most ambitious project, the church of the Sagrada Familia, in 1884; unfinished at his death, it is still under construction.

Gaudier-Brzeska /ˌgəʊdɪˌeɪˈbʒeskə/, Henri (1891–1915), French sculptor. He settled in London in 1911 and became a leading member of the vorticist movement. His stylistically varied and advanced work, such as the faceted bust of Horace Brodzky (1912) and the semi-abstract *Bird Swallowing a Fish* (1913), only achieved wide recognition after his death.

Gauguin /'gəʊgæn/, (Eugène Henri) Paul (1848–1903), French painter. He left Paris in search of an environment that would bring him closer to nature, going first to Brittany, where he painted works such as *The Vision After the Sermon* (1888), and later briefly to stay with Van Gogh at Arles. In 1891 he left France for Tahiti; he spent most of the rest of his life there, painting enigmatic works such as *Faa Iheihe* (1898). He was a post-impressionist whose painting was influenced by primitive art, freeing colour from its representational function to use it in flat contrasting areas to achieve decorative or emotional effects. His work influenced both the Nabi Group and the symbolist movement.

Gaulle, Charles de, see DE GAULLE.

Gaunt /gɔ:nt/ John of, see JOHN OF GAUNT.

Gauss /gaʊs/, Karl Friedrich (1777–1855), German mathematician, astronomer, and physicist. Regarded as the 'prince of mathematics', he laid the foundations of number theory, and in 1801 he rediscovered the lost asteroid Ceres using advanced computational techniques. He contributed to many areas of mathematics, and applied rigorous mathematical analysis to such subjects as geometry, geodesy, electrostatics, and electromagnetism. He was involved in the first worldwide survey of the earth's magnetic field. Two of Gauss's most interesting discoveries, which he did not pursue, were non-Euclidean geometry and quaternions.

Gautama /'gaʊtəmə/, Siddhartha, see BUD-DHA.

Gavaskar /gəˈvæskə(r)/, Sunil Manohar (born 1949), Indian cricketer. He made his test début in the West Indies at the age of 20, making his mark by scoring an aggregate of 774 runs. He later captained India and achieved several world batting records, in 1987 becoming the first batsman to score 10,000 runs in test cricket.

Gay /geɪ/, John (1685–1732), English poet and dramatist. He is now chiefly known for *The Beggar's Opera* (1728), a ballad opera combining burlesque and political satire and dealing with life in low society. A major success in its day, it has been revived several times this century, and was adapted by Brecht in *The Threepenny Opera* (1928).

Gaye /geɪ/, Marvin (1939–84), American soul singer and songwriter. Gaye moved to Detroit with the vocal group the Rainbows, and signed a contract with Motown in 1961. He later began recording as a solo singer and had a succession of hits, including his best-known song 'I Heard It Through the Grapevine' (1968). His albums include *Let's Get It On* (1973) and *Midnight Love* (1982). He was shot dead by his father during a quarrel.

Gay-Lussac /geɪˈluːsæk/, Joseph Louis (1778–1850), French chemist and physicist. He is best known for his work on gases, and in 1808 he formulated the law usually known by his name, that gases which combine chemically do so in volumes which are in a simple ratio to each other. He developed techniques of quantitative chemical analysis, confirmed that iodine was an element, discovered cyanogen, improved the process for manufacturing sulphuric acid, prepared potassium and boron, and made two balloon ascents to study the atmosphere and terrestrial magnetism.

Geber /'dʒiːbə(r)/ (Latinized name of Jabir ibn Hayyan, *c.*721–*c.*815), Arab chemist. He

was a member of the court of Harun ar-Rashid, the caliph of Baghdad. Although many works are attributed to him there is doubt about the authenticity of some of them, and his name was used by later writers. He was familiar with many chemicals and laboratory techniques, including distillation and sublimation.

Gehrig /'gerɪg/, Henry Louis ('Lou') (1903–41), American baseball player. He set a record of playing 2,130 major-league games for the New York Yankees from 1925 to 1939; his stamina caused him to be known as 'the Iron Horse'. He died from a form of motor neurone disease now often called *Lou Gehrig's disease*.

Geiger /'gaɪgə(r)/, Hans (Johann) Wilhelm (1882–1945), German nuclear physicist. He worked with Sir Ernest Rutherford at Manchester on radioactivity, and in 1908 developed his prototype radiation counter for detecting alpha particles. In 1925 he was appointed professor of physics at Kiel, where he improved the sensitivity of his device with Walther Müller.

Geikie /'giːkɪ/, Sir Archibald (1835–1924), Scottish geologist. He carried out most of his field work in Scotland. He specialized in Pleistocene geology, especially the geomorphological effects of glaciations and the resulting deposits. Geikie wrote several important works and was a leading figure in British geology, eventually becoming director-general of the British Geological Survey. He was also president of the Geological Society, the Royal Society, and the Classical Association.

Gell-Mann /gel'mæn/, Murray (born 1929), American theoretical physicist. He coined the word *quark*, proposed the concept of strangeness in quarks, and made major contributions on the classification and interactions of subatomic particles. He was awarded the Nobel Prize for physics in 1969.

Gemayel /dʒə'maɪəl/, Pierre (1905–84), Lebanese political leader. A Maronite Christian, he founded the right-wing Phalange Party (1936) and served as a member of parliament 1960–84; during this time he held several government posts and led the Phalange militia forces during the civil war (1975–6). His youngest son, Bashir (1947–82), was assassinated while President-elect; his eldest son, Amin (born 1942), served as President 1982–8.

Genet /ʒə'neɪ/, Jean (1910–86), French novelist, poet, and dramatist. He began to write while serving a prison sentence; much of his work portrayed life in the criminal and homosexual underworlds, of which he was a part, and his first novel *Notre-Dame des fleurs* (*Our Lady of the Flowers*) caused a sensation when it was first published in 1944. He also wrote the autobiographical *Journal du voleur* (1949, *The Thief's Journal*) and a number of plays, including *Les Bonnes* (1947, *The Maids*) and *Les Nègres* (1958).

Genghis Khan /ˌgeŋgɪs 'kaːn, ˌdʒeŋ-/ (1162–1227), the founder of the Mongol empire. Originally named Temujin, he took the name Genghis Khan (= 'ruler of all') in 1206 after uniting the nomadic Mongol tribes under his command and becoming master of both eastern and western Mongolia. He then attacked China, capturing Beijing in 1215. When he died his empire extended from the shores of the Pacific to the northern shores of the Black Sea. His grandson Kublai Khan completed the conquest of China.

Gentile da Fabriano /dʒenˌtiːleɪ daː ˌfæbrɪ'aːnəʊ/ (c.1370–1427), Italian painter. He painted a number of frescos and altarpieces and worked chiefly in Florence and Rome. Most of the work on which his contemporary reputation was based has been destroyed; his major surviving work, the altarpiece *The Adoration of the Magi* (1423), is notable for its rich detail and naturalistic treatment of light.

Geoffrey of Monmouth /'dʒefrɪ, 'mɒnməθ/ (c.1100–c.1154), Welsh chronicler. His *Historia Regum Britanniae* (c.1139; first printed in 1508), which purports to give an account of the kings of Britain, is now thought to contain little historical fact; it was, however, a major source for English literature, including stories of King Arthur and the plots of some of Shakespeare's plays.

George /dʒɔːdʒ/ the name of four kings of Great Britain and Ireland, one of Great Britain and Ireland (from 1920 of the United Kingdom), and one of the United Kingdom:

George I (1660–1727), great-grandson of James I, reigned 1714–27, Elector of Hanover 1698–1727. George succeeded to the British throne as a result of the Act of Settlement (1701). Unpopular in England as a foreigner who never learned English, he left the administration of his new kingdom to his ministers and devoted himself

to diplomacy and the interests of Hanover. However, the relatively easy suppression of the Jacobite uprisings of 1715 and 1719 demonstrated that he was generally preferred to the Catholic Old Pretender (James Stuart, see STUART[2]).

George II (1683–1760), son of George I, reigned 1727–60, Elector of Hanover 1727–60. Like his father, he depended heavily on his ministers, although he took an active part in the War of the Austrian Succession (1740–8), successfully leading a British army against the French at Dettingen in 1743, the last occasion on which a British king was present on the field of battle. In the latter years of his reign, George largely withdrew from active politics, allowing advances in the development of constitutional monarchy which his successor George III was ultimately unable to reverse.

George III (1738–1820), grandson of George II, reigned 1760–1820, Elector of Hanover 1760–1815 and king of Hanover 1815–20. He took great interest in British domestic politics and attempted to exercise royal control of government to the fullest possible extent. His determination to suppress the War of American Independence dominated British foreign policy 1775–83, but his political influence declined from 1788 after a series of bouts of mental illness. In 1811 it became clear that the king's mental health made him unfit to rule and his son was made regent.

George IV (1762–1830), son of George III, reigned 1820–30. Known as a patron of the arts and *bon viveur*, he was Prince Regent during his father's final period of mental illness. His lifestyle gained him a bad reputation which was further damaged by his attempt to divorce his estranged wife Caroline of Brunswick just after coming to the throne. His only child, Charlotte, died in 1817.

George V (1865–1936), son of Edward VII, reigned 1910–36. He won respect for his punctilious attitude towards royal duties and responsibilities, especially during the First World War. He exercised restrained but none the less important influence over British politics, playing an especially significant role in the formation of the government in 1931.

George VI (1894–1952), son of George V, reigned 1936–52. He was created Duke of York in 1920 and came to the throne on the abdication of his elder brother Edward VIII. Despite a retiring disposition he became a popular monarch, gaining respect for the staunch example he and his family set during the London Blitz.

George, St, patron saint of England. Little is known of his life, and his historical existence was once challenged but is now generally accepted. He may have been martyred near Lydda in Palestine some time before the reign of Constantine (died 337), but his cult did not become popular until the 6th century. The slaying of the dragon (possibly derived from the legend of Perseus) was not attributed to him until the 12th century. His rank as patron saint of England (in place of St Edward the Confessor) probably dates from the reign of Edward III. The latter founded the Order of the Garter (*c*.1344) under the patronage of St George, who by that time was honoured as the ideal of chivalry. Feast day, 23 April.

Gerard /ˈdʒerɑːd/, John (1545–1612), English herbalist. Gerard was qualified as a barber-surgeon in London and soon developed an interest in plants, particularly those with medicinal properties. He was superintendent of Lord Burghley's gardens for more than twenty years, became curator of the physic garden of the College of Surgeons, and cultivated his own large garden in Holborn. His famous *Herball*, with more than 1,800 woodcuts, was published in 1597, and despite its shortcomings became the best-known English herbal.

Géricault /ˈʒerɪˌkəʊ/, (Jean Louis André) Théodore (1791–1824), French painter. His rejection of the prevailing classicism of his day and use of bright colours in a bold, romantic style brought him criticism from the art world. His most famous work, *The Raft of the Medusa* (1819), depicts the survivors of a famous shipwreck of 1816, with realistic treatment of the macabre. He also painted landscapes and scenes of horse-races.

Geronimo /dʒəˈrɒnɪˌməʊ/ (*c*.1829–1909), Apache chief. He led his people in resistance to white encroachment on tribal reservations in Arizona, waging war against settlers and US troops in a series of raids, before surrendering in 1886.

Gershwin /ˈɡɜːʃwɪn/, George (born Jacob Gershovitz) (1898–1937), American composer and pianist, of Russian Jewish descent. He had no formal musical training, but gained early experience of popular music from working in New York's Tin Pan

Alley. He made his name in 1919 with the song 'Swanee' and went on to compose many successful songs and musicals. The lyrics for many of these were written by his brother Ira (Israel, 1896–1983), who was also the librettist for the opera *Porgy and Bess* (1935). In 1924 George Gershwin successfully turned to orchestral music with his jazz-influenced *Rhapsody in Blue*.

Getty /ˈgetɪ/, Jean Paul (1892–1976), American industrialist. He made a large fortune in the oil industry and was also a noted art collector. He founded the museum which bears his name in California.

Getz /gets/, Stan (born Stanley Gayetsky) (1927–91), American jazz saxophonist. He played with other prominent jazz musicians such as Stan Kenton, Benny Goodman, and Woody Herman. He was a leader of the 'cool' school of jazz and developed a distinctive style that was both emotive and attacking. His recordings include 'Early Autumn' (1948) and the highly popular 'The Girl from Ipanema' (1963).

Ghiberti /gɪˈbeətɪ/, Lorenzo (1378–1455), Italian sculptor and goldsmith. His career was dominated by his work on two successive pairs of bronze doors for the baptistery in Florence. The second, more famous, pair (1425–52) depicts episodes from the Bible laid out on carefully constructed perspective stages.

Ghirlandaio /ˌgɪəlænˈdaɪəʊ/ (born Domenico di Tommaso Bigordi) (*c.*1448–94), Italian painter. Born the son of a goldsmith, he acquired the name Ghirlandaio ('garland-maker') in recognition of his father's skill in metal garland-work. He worked mainly in Florence and is noted for his religious frescos, painted in a naturalistic style and including detailed portraits of leading contemporary citizens. His major works include the fresco *Christ Calling Peter and Andrew* (1482–4) in the Sistine Chapel, Rome.

Giacometti /ˌdʒækəˈmetɪ/, Alberto (1901–66), Swiss sculptor and painter. He experimented with both naturalistic sculpture and surrealism, but his most characteristic style, which he adopted after the Second World War, features human figures that are notable for their emaciated and extremely elongated forms, exemplified in such works as *Pointing Man* (1947).

Giap /dʒæp/, Vo Nguyen (born 1912), Vietnamese military and political leader. As North Vietnamese Vice-Premier and Defence Minister, he was responsible for the strategy leading to the withdrawal of American forces from South Vietnam in 1973 and the subsequent reunification of the country in 1975. His book, *People's War, People's Army* (1961), was an influential text for revolutionaries.

Gibbon[1] /ˈgɪb(ə)n/, Edward (1737–94), English historian. A Catholic convert at 16, he reconverted to Protestantism the following year while studying in Lausanne. While in Rome in 1764 he formed the plan for his book *The History of the Decline and Fall of the Roman Empire* (1776–88), chapters of which aroused controversy for their critical account of the spread of Christianity. The complete work, originally published in six volumes, covers a period from the age of Trajan to the fall of Constantinople in 1453; it is regarded as a contribution to literature as well as historical analysis.

Gibbon[2] /ˈgɪb(ə)n/, Lewis Grassic (pseudonym of James Leslie Mitchell) (1901–35), Scottish writer. Encouraged by H. G. Wells he began writing short stories, which from 1927 were regularly published in the *Cornhill Magazine*. In 1930 he published his first novel, *Stained Radiance*. His greatest achievement was probably the trilogy *A Scots Quair* (1932–4).

Gibbons[1] /ˈgɪb(ə)nz/, Grinling (1648–1721), Dutch-born English sculptor. From 1671 he worked in England, where he was introduced to Charles II by the writer John Evelyn, and became Master Carver in Wood to the Crown. He is famous for his decorative carvings (chiefly in wood) of fruit and flowers, small animals, and cherubs' heads; examples of his work can be seen in the choir stalls of St Paul's Cathedral, London.

Gibbons[2] /ˈgɪb(ə)nz/, Orlando (1583–1625), English composer and musician. Gibbons is regarded as one of the greatest of the early English composers. He became a chamber musician to King James I in 1619 and the organist of Westminster Abbey in 1623. He composed mainly sacred music, including anthems, motets, and madrigals, notably *The Silver Swan* (1612). His oeuvre also includes forty keyboard pieces and thirty fantasies for viols.

Gibbs[1] /gɪbz/, James (1682–1754), Scottish architect. An admirer of Sir Christopher

Wren, he developed Wren's ideas for London's city churches, especially in his masterpiece, St Martin's-in-the-Fields (1722–6). The latter's combination of steeple and portico was influential in subsequent church design.

Gibbs[2] /gɪbz/, Josiah Willard (1839–1903), American physical chemist. He was the founder of the study of chemical thermodynamics and statistical mechanics, though the importance of his theoretical work was not generally appreciated until after his death.

Gibran /dʒɪˈbrɑːn/ (also **Jubran**), Khalil (1883–1931), Lebanese-born American writer and artist. He emigrated to Boston in 1895, but in 1898 returned to his native Beirut to study. He published his first literary essays on his return to Boston in 1903, and devoted himself to writing and painting. His writings, in both Arabic and English, are deeply romantic, displaying his religious and mystical nature.

Gibson[1] /ˈgɪbs(ə)n/, Althea (born 1927), American tennis player. She was the first black player to compete successfully at the highest level of tennis, winning all the major world women's singles titles, including the French and Italian championships (1956) and the British and American titles (1957 and 1958).

Gibson[2] /ˈgɪbs(ə)n/, Mel (Columcille Gerard) (born 1956), American-born Australian actor and director. Gibson lived in Australia from the age of 12 and had his first film success there, starring in *Mad Max* (1979). Gibson won worldwide recognition with the film's sequel *Mad Max II: The Road Warrior* (1986), and his unsmiling, brooding screen presence led to a series of energetic, masculine roles in films that included the police thriller *Lethal Weapon* (1987) and its two sequels (1989, 1992). In 1993 he made his directorial début with *The Man Without a Face*; in 1995 he directed and starred in *Braveheart*, which won five Oscars, including those for best director and best film, the following year.

Gide /ʒiːd/, André (Paul Guillaume) (1869–1951), French novelist, essayist, and critic. The first of a series of visits to North Africa in 1893 caused him to rebel against his strict Protestant upbringing and to acknowledge the importance of individual expression and sexual freedom, including his own bisexuality. He was a prolific writer, completing more than fifty books

in his lifetime and coming to be regarded as the father of modern French literature. His works include *The Immoralist* (1902), *La Porte étroite* (1909, *Strait is the Gate*), *Si le grain ne meurt* (1926, *If I die . . .*), *The Counterfeiters* (1927), and his *Journal* (1939–50). He was awarded the Nobel Prize for literature in 1947.

Gielgud /ˈgiːlgʊd/, Sir (Arthur) John (born 1904), English actor and director. A notable Shakespearian actor, he is particularly remembered for his interpretation of the role of Hamlet, which he performed for the first time in 1929; he also appeared in contemporary plays, such as those by Harold Pinter. Gielgud has also appeared on television and in numerous films, taking on many roles late in his life; he won an Oscar for his role as a butler in *Arthur* (1980).

Gigli /ˈdʒiːlɪ/, Beniamino (1890–1957), Italian operatic tenor. He made his Milan début with the conductor Toscanini in 1918, and retained his singing talents to a considerable age, touring the US in 1955. Notable roles included Rodolfo in *La Bohème*, the Duke of Mantua in *Rigoletto*, and Cavaradossi in *Tosca*.

Gilbert[1] /ˈgɪlbət/, Sir Humphrey (c.1539–83), English explorer. After a distinguished career as a soldier, Gilbert led an unsuccessful attempt to colonize the New World (1578–9). On a second voyage in 1583 he claimed Newfoundland for Elizabeth I and established a colony at St John's, but was lost on the trip homewards when his ship foundered in a storm off Nova Scotia.

Gilbert[2] /ˈgɪlbət/, William (1544–1603), English physician and physicist. He worked on terrestrial magnetism, discovered how to make magnets, and was the first to use the term *magnetic pole*. His book *De Magnete* (1600) is one of the most important early works on physics published in England.

Gilbert[3] /ˈgɪlbət/, Sir W(illiam) S(chwenck) (1836–1911), English dramatist. His early writing career was chiefly devoted to humorous verse, such as his *Bab Ballads* (1866–73). However, he is best known for his collaboration with the composer Sir Arthur Sullivan; between 1871 and 1896 he wrote the libretti for fourteen light operas, including *Trial by Jury* (1875), *HMS Pinafore* (1878), *The Pirates of Penzance* (1879), *Iolanthe* (1882), *The Mikado* (1885), and *The Gondoliers* (1889).

Gill /gɪl/, (Arthur) Eric (Rowton) (1882–1940), English sculptor, engraver, and typographer. His best-known sculptures are the relief carvings *Stations of the Cross* (1914–18) at Westminster cathedral and the *Prospero and Ariel* (1931) on Broadcasting House in London. He illustrated many books for the Golden Cockerell Press, and designed printing types for the Monotype Corporation. Among his famous type designs was the first sanserif type, Gill Sans.

Gillespie /gɪˈlespɪ/, Dizzy (born John Birks Gillespie) (1917–93), American jazz trumpet player and band-leader. He was a virtuoso trumpet player and a leading exponent of the bebop style. After working with various other groups he formed his own in New York in 1944, and thereafter toured the world almost annually.

Ginsberg /ˈgɪnzbɜːg/, Allen (1926–97), American poet. A leading poet of the beat generation, and later influential in the hippy movement of the 1960s, he is notable for his *Howl and Other Poems* (1956), in which he attacked American society for its materialism and complacency. He later campaigned for civil rights, gay liberation, and the peace movement.

Giolitti /dʒɒˈlɪtɪ/, Giovanni (1842–1928), Italian statesman, Prime Minister five times between 1892 and 1921. A former lawyer, as Prime Minister he was responsible for the introduction of a wide range of social reforms, including national insurance (1911) and universal male suffrage (1912).

Giorgione /ˌdʒɔːdʒˈəʊnɪ/ (also called Giorgio Barbarelli or Giorgio da Castelfranco) (c.1478–1510), Italian painter. He was an influential figure in Renaissance art, especially for his introduction of the small easel picture in oils intended for private collectors. Although the attribution of many of his works is doubtful, paintings such as *The Tempest* typically feature enigmatic figures in pastoral settings and gave a new prominence to landscape. His pupils included Titian, who is said to have completed some of his works, such as *Sleeping Venus* (c.1510), after his death.

Giotto /ˈdʒɒtəʊ/ (full name Giotto di Bondone) (c.1267–1337), Italian painter. He is an important figure in the development of painting for his rejection of the flat, formulaic, and static images of Italo-Byzantine art in favour of a more naturalistic style showing human expression. Notable works include the frescos in the Arena Chapel,

Padua (1305–8), and those in the church of Santa Croce in Florence (c.1320).

Giovanni de' Medici /dʒɒˈvænɪ də ˈmedɪtʃɪ, məˈdiːtʃɪ/ the name of Pope Leo X (see Leo).

Giscard d'Estaing /ˌʒiːskɑː deˈstæŋ/, Valéry (born 1926), French statesman, President 1974–81. As Secretary of State for Finance (1959–62) and Finance Minister (1962–6) under President de Gaulle, he was responsible for the policies which formed the basis of France's economic growth. Dismissed following mounting opposition to his policies, he regained the finance portfolio under President Pompidou, whose death in 1974 paved the way for Giscard d'Estaing's own election to the presidency. However, French economic conditions worsened during his term of office and he was defeated by François Mitterrand. He was a member of the European Parliament 1989–93, and has been leader of the centre-right Union pour la démocratie française since 1988.

Gish /gɪʃ/, Lillian (1896–1993), American actress. She and her sister Dorothy (1898–1968) appeared in a number of D. W. Griffith's films, including *Hearts of the World* (1918) and *Orphans of the Storm* (1922).

Gissing /ˈgɪsɪŋ/, George (Robert) (1857–1903), English novelist. His own experiences of poverty and failure provided material for much of his fiction. His many novels include *New Grub Street* (1891), *Born in Exile* (1892), and *The Private Papers of Henry Ryecroft* (1903). He also wrote a notable biography of Charles Dickens (1898).

Gladstone /ˈglædstən/, William Ewart (1809–98), British Liberal statesman, Prime Minister 1868–74, 1880–5, 1886, and 1892–4. After an early career as a Conservative minister, he joined the Liberal Party, becoming its leader in 1867. His ministries were notable for the introduction of a series of social and political reforms (including the introduction of elementary education, and the passing of the Irish Land Acts and the third Reform Act) and for his campaign in favour of Home Rule for Ireland, which led to the defection of the Unionists from the Liberal Party.

Glashow /ˈglæʃaʊ/, Sheldon Lee (born 1932), American theoretical physicist. In 1967 Glashow began work at Harvard University on the interactions between subatomic particles. He independently

developed a unified theory to explain electromagnetic interactions and the weak nuclear force, and extended the quark theory of Murray Gell-Mann. Glashow shared the Nobel Prize for physics in 1979.

Glass /glɑːs/, Philip (born 1937), American composer. A leading minimalist, he studied with the Indian musician and composer Ravi Shankar; his work is influenced by Asian and North African music as well as reflecting his interest in jazz and rock. Major works include the opera *Einstein on the Beach* (1976), the ballet *Glass Pieces* (1982), and his first orchestral symphony, *Low Symphony* (1993).

Glazunov /ˈɡlæzʊˌnɒf/, Aleksandr (Konstantinovich) (1865–1936), Russian composer. He was a pupil of Rimsky-Korsakov (1880–1) and his work was influenced by Liszt and Wagner. His output includes orchestral and chamber music, songs, and the ballet *The Seasons* (1901).

Glendower /ɡlenˈdaʊə(r)/, Owen (also **Glyndwr**) (*c*.1354–*c*.1417), Welsh chief. A legendary symbol of Welsh nationalism, he was leader first of armed resistance to English overlordship and then of a national uprising against Henry IV. He proclaimed himself Prince of Wales and allied himself with Henry's English opponents, including Henry Percy ('Hotspur'); by 1404 this policy had proved sufficiently successful for Glendower to hold his own Parliament. Though suffering subsequent defeats, he continued fighting against the English until his death.

Glinka /ˈɡlɪŋkə/, Mikhail (Ivanovich) (1804–57), Russian composer. Regarded as the father of the Russian national school of music, he is best known for his operas *A Life for the Tsar* (1836), inspired by Russian folk music, and *Russlan and Ludmilla* (1842), based on a poem by Pushkin.

Gloriana /ˌɡlɔːrɪˈɑːnə/ the nickname of Elizabeth I of England and Ireland.

Gluck /ɡlʊk/, Christoph Willibald von (1714–87), German composer. From early operas in the Italian style he went on to seek a balance of music and drama in his 'reform' operas, reducing the emphasis on the star singer and attempting a continuous musical unfolding of the narrative. He spent much of his working life in Paris as a protégé of Marie Antoinette. His most notable works include *Orfeo ed Euridice* (1762) and *Iphigénie en Aulide* (1774).

Glyndwr see GLENDOWER.

Göbbels see GOEBBELS.

Gobbi /ˈɡɒbɪ/, Tito (1915–84), Italian operatic baritone. Particularly renowned for his interpretations of Verdi's baritone roles, he also gained notable successes with his performances in the title role of Berg's *Wozzeck* and as Scarpia in Puccini's *Tosca*.

Gobineau /ˈɡɒbɪˌnəʊ/, Joseph Arthur, Comte de (1816–82), French writer and anthropologist. Gobineau is best known for his theories of racial superiority; he claimed the existence of a hierarchy of races, at the top of which was the 'Aryan race' and noted that Aryan civilization and culture degenerated when its members interbred with the so-called black and yellow races, which he considered inferior. Gobineau cited 'Aryan' Germans as the sole remaining ideal of racial purity. His theories anticipated the 'master-class' philosophy of Nietzsche, and later influenced the ideology and policies of the Nazis.

Godard /ˈɡʊdɑː(r)/, Jean-Luc (born 1930), French film director. He was one of the leading figures of the *nouvelle vague*; his films frequently deal with existentialist themes and are notable for their use of improvised dialogue, disjointed narratives, and unconventional shooting and cutting techniques. In addition to his more commercial works, such as *Breathless* (1960), *Alphaville* (1965), and *Slow Motion* (1980), he has also explored the use of film for more overtly political purposes, for example in *Wind from the East* (1969).

Goddard /ˈɡʊdɑːd/, Robert Hutchings (1882–1945), American physicist. He carried out pioneering work in rocketry, and designed and built the first successful liquid-fuelled rocket (1926). NASA's Goddard Space Flight Center is named after him.

Gödel /ˈɡɜːd(ə)l/, Kurt (1906–78), Austrian-born American mathematician. He made several important contributions to mathematical logic, especially the *incompleteness theorem* (Gödel's proof): that in any sufficiently powerful, logically consistent formulation of logic or mathematics there must be true formulas which are neither provable nor disprovable. This makes such formulations essentially incomplete, and entails the corollary that the consistency of such a system cannot be proved within that system.

Godiva /gə'daɪvə/, Lady (died 1080), English noblewoman, wife of Leofric, Earl of Mercia (died 1057). According to a 13th-century legend, she agreed to her husband's proposition that he would reduce some particularly unpopular taxes only if she rode naked on horseback through the marketplace of Coventry. Later versions of the story describe how all the townspeople stayed indoors at Lady Godiva's request, except for peeping Tom, who as a result was struck blind.

Godunov /'gɒdʊˌnɒf/, Boris (1550–1605), tsar of Russia 1598–1605. He rose to prominence as a counsellor of Ivan the Terrible and eventually succeeded Ivan's son as tsar. His reign was overshadowed by famine, doubts over his involvement in the earlier death of Ivan's eldest son, and the appearance of a pretender, the so-called False Dmitri. Godunov died suddenly while his army was resisting an invasion by the pretender. He has been made famous outside Russia by Mussorgsky's opera *Boris Godunov*.

Godwin /'gɒdwɪn/, William (1756–1836), English social philosopher and novelist. At first a dissenting minister, he subsequently became an atheist and expounded theories of anarchic social organization based on a belief in the goodness of human reason and on his doctrine of extreme individualism. His ideological novel *Caleb Williams* (1794), which exposes the tyranny exercised by the ruling classes, was an early example of the crime and detection novel. In 1797 he married Mary Wollstonecraft; the couple's daughter was Mary Shelley.

Goebbels /'gɜːb(ə)lz/, (Paul) Joseph (also **Göbbels**) (1897–1945), German Nazi leader and politician. In 1933 he became Hitler's Minister of Propaganda, with control of the press, radio, and all aspects of culture, and manipulated these in order to further Nazi aims. A supporter of Hitler to the last, he committed suicide rather than surrender to the Allies.

Goering /'gɜːrɪŋ/, Hermann Wilhelm (1893–1946), German Nazi leader and politician. In 1934 he became commander of the German air force, and was responsible for the German rearmament programme. Until 1936 Goering headed the Gestapo, which he had founded; from then until 1943 he directed the German economy. In that year he fell from favour, was deprived of all authority, and was finally dismissed

in 1945 after unauthorized attempts to make peace with the Allies. Sentenced to death at the Nuremberg war trials, he committed suicide in his cell.

Goes /ɡuːs/, Hugo van der (*fl. c.*1467–82), Flemish painter, born in Ghent. He worked chiefly in his birthplace, though his best-known work is the large-scale *Portinari Altarpiece* (1475), commissioned for a church in Florence.

Goethe /'gɜːtə/, Johann Wolfgang von (1749–1832), German poet, dramatist, and scholar. In his early career he was involved with the *Sturm und Drang* movement, an early aspect of romanticism. In 1775 he moved to Weimar (later becoming a close friend of Friedrich von Schiller) and held a number of government posts 1776–86, after which he spent two years in Italy. His writing began to move away from the energy and romanticism of *Sturm und Drang* and became more measured and classical in style, as in the 'Wilhelm Meister' novels (1796–1829), which are also the prototype of the *Bildungsroman*. An important figure of the Enlightenment in Germany, he had wide-ranging interests including philosophy, physics, and biology; he wrote drama, poetry, novels, ballads, and autobiography, and was also director of the Weimar Theatre 1791–1817. His works include the epic drama *Götz von Berlichingen* (1773), the epistolary novel *The Sorrows of Young Werther* (1774), and the two-part poetic drama *Faust* (1808–32), as well as the classical dramas *Iphigenia in Tauris* (1787) and *Tasso* (1790).

Gogol /'ɡəʊɡɒl, 'ɡɒɡ(ə)l/, Nikolai (Vasilevich) (1809–52), Russian novelist, dramatist, and short-story writer, born in Ukraine. He first became famous for his play *The Inspector General* (1836), a savagely satirical picture of life in a provincial Russian town. His St Petersburg stories (including *Notes of a Madman*, 1835, and *The Greatcoat*, 1842) also display a trenchant satirical wit. Living mainly abroad from 1836 to 1848, he wrote the comic epic novel *Dead Souls* (1842), widely regarded as the foundation of the modern Russian novel, but after a spiritual crisis he burned the manuscript of the second part.

Gokhale /'ɡəʊkəˌleɪ/, Gopal Krishna (1866–1915), Indian political leader and social reformer. A member of the Indian National Congress, he became its president in 1905. He was a leading advocate of Indian self-government, favouring gradual reform

through constitutional or moderate means; he met and influenced Mahatma Gandhi. He also founded the Servants of India Society (1905), whose members pledged themselves to assisting the under-privileged.

Golding /'gəʊldɪŋ/, Sir William (Gerald) (1911–93), English novelist. He achieved literary success with his first novel *Lord of the Flies* (1954), about a group of boys who revert to savagery when stranded on a desert island. The human capacity for evil and guilt is a predominant theme in Golding's work, including *The Inheritors* (1955), which describes the extermination of Neanderthal man by modern *Homo sapiens*. Later works include *The Spire* (1964) and *Fire Down Below* (1989). He was awarded the Nobel Prize for literature in 1983.

Goldman /'gəʊldmən/, Emma (known as 'Red Emma') (1869–1940), Lithuanian-born American political activist. She emigrated to the US in 1885, where she later became involved in New York's anarchist movement. With Alexander Berkman (1870–1936) she founded and co-edited the anarchist monthly *Mother Earth* (1906–17). She was imprisoned in 1917 with Berkman for opposing US conscription; they were released after two years and deported to Russia. She eventually settled in France. Her disenchantment with and opposition to the Soviet system are related in *My Disillusionment in Russia* (1923).

Goldmark /'gəʊldmɑːk/, Peter Carl (1906–77), Hungarian-born American inventor and engineer. He made the first colour television broadcast in 1940, invented the long-playing record in 1948, and pioneered video cassette recording.

Goldschmidt /'gəʊldʃmɪt/, Victor Moritz (1888–1947), Swiss-born Norwegian chemist, the founder of modern geochemistry. He carried out fundamental work on crystal structure, suggesting a law relating it to chemical composition, and used X-ray crystallography to determine the structure of many compounds.

Goldsmith /'gəʊldsmɪθ/, Oliver (1728–74), Irish novelist, poet, essayist, and dramatist. After studying medicine and travelling in Europe, in 1756 he settled in London, where he practised as a physician and began his literary career as a journalist and essayist. He is now best known for his novel *The Vicar of Wakefield* (1766), the poem *The Deserted Village* (1770), and the comic plays *The Good-Natur'd Man* (1768) and *She Stoops to Conquer* (1773).

Goldwyn /'gəʊldwɪn/, Samuel (born Schmuel Gelbfisz; changed to Goldfish then Goldwyn) (1882–1974), Polish-born American film producer. He produced his first film in 1913; his film company, Metro-Goldwyn-Mayer (MGM), which he formed with Louis B. Mayer in 1924, soon became world famous. His successful films include an adaptation of Emily Brontë's novel *Wuthering Heights* (1939), *The Little Foxes* (1941), and the musical *Guys and Dolls* (1955). Goldwyn is also famous for introducing a number of catch-phrases (such as 'Include me out') to the English language.

Golgi /'gɒldʒɪ/, Camillo (1844–1926), Italian histologist and anatomist. He devised a method of staining nerve tissue with silver salts to reveal details of the cells and nerve fibres, classified types of nerve cell, and described a complex structure in the cytoplasm of most cells (the *Golgi body* or *apparatus*) that is now known to be involved in secretion. Golgi shared a Nobel Prize with Ramón y Cajal in 1906.

Gollancz /'gɒlænts/, Sir Victor (1893–1967), British publisher and philanthropist. In 1928 he founded his own publishing company, Victor Gollancz Ltd., concentrating on fiction, politics, music, and philosophy. A committed socialist, he was active in campaigning against the rise of Fascism, founded the Left Book Club (1936), and also contributed to the growing influence of the Labour Party in British politics. After the Second World War he organized aid for refugees, founded the charity War on Want, and also campaigned for nuclear disarmament and the abolition of capital punishment.

Goncharov /'gɒntʃəˌrɒf, Russian ˌɡəntʃɪˈrɔf/, Ivan (1812–91), Russian novelist. On graduating from Moscow University in 1834 Goncharov went into the Russian civil service, where he led an uneventful life. He is best known for his novel *Oblomov* (1857), which is regarded as one of the greatest and most representative works of Russian realism.

Goncourt /gɒnˈkʊə(r)/, Edmond de (1822–96) and Jules de (1830–70), French novelists and critics. The Goncourt brothers collaborated closely in their writing, originally producing art criticism and social history. They regarded their highly detailed realist novels, such as *Germinie Lacerteux* (1864) and *Madame Gervaisais* (1869), as a form of con-

temporary social history. They also wrote the *Journal des Goncourt*, a detailed record of cultural life in Paris between 1851 and 1896. In his will Edmond de Goncourt provided for the establishment of the Académie Goncourt, which awards the annual Prix Goncourt for a work of French literature; this continued the tradition of the literary circle that the Goncourt brothers had gathered around them during their lifetime.

Goodall /'gʊdɔːl/, Jane (born 1934), English zoologist. Goodall obtained employment in Tanzania with Louis Leakey in 1957, and has been based at the Gombe Stream Reserve by Lake Tanganyika since 1970. She has made prolonged and intimate studies of the chimpanzees of Gombe, which has become a respected centre of primate research. Her first popular work, *In the Shadow of Man* (1971), depicted a rather idealized view of chimpanzee behaviour, but her later book *Through a Window* (1990) showed that hunting, murder, war, and cannibalism are integral parts of their life.

Goodman /'gʊdmən/, Benjamin David ('Benny') (1909–86), American jazz clarinettist and band-leader. He formed his own big band in 1934, and soon gained a mass following through radio and live performances. Goodman chose players for their musicianship regardless of their colour, and his bands were the first to feature black and white musicians together. The advent of his distinctive style marked the start of a new era in the history of jazz; he soon became known as the 'King of Swing'. He also performed a wide variety of classical clarinet music; Bartók, Hindemith, and Copland all composed works for him.

Goodyear /'gʊdjɪə(r)/, Charles (1800–60), American inventor. Goodyear searched for ways in which rubber could be prevented from turning tacky when warm and hard and brittle when cold. He found the answer accidentally in 1839 when he dropped some rubber mixed with sulphur and white lead on to a hot stove, which led to the development of the process that he called vulcanization. However, Goodyear was not successful in business, and he died a pauper after his requests for patents were turned down in Britain and France.

Goossens /'guːs(ə)nz/, Sir (Aynsley) Eugene (1893–1962), English conductor, violinist, and composer, of Belgian descent. He played the violin in a number of orchestras and chamber ensembles before deciding to concentrate on a career as a conductor and composer. After conducting in the US (1923–45), in 1947 Goossens was appointed the director of the New South Wales Conservatorium and conductor of the Sydney Symphony Orchestra. His compositions include opera, ballet, and symphonies. His brother Leon (1897–1988) was a virtuoso oboist, and his sister Marie (1894–1991) a distinguished harpist.

Gorbachev /ˌgɔːbəˈtʃɒf/, Mikhail (Sergeevich) (born 1931), Soviet statesman, General Secretary of the Communist Party of the USSR 1985–91 and President 1988–91. He was born in Russia. His foreign policy was notable for bringing about an end to the cold war, largely through arms control negotiations with the West that culminated in the signing of treaties with the US in 1987 (the INF treaty) and 1991 (the START treaty). Within the USSR he introduced major political, economic, and cultural reforms, including the eventual removal of the Communist Party's monopoly of power, moves towards a market economy, and more open government (policies known as glasnost and perestroika). Opposition to his policies led to an attempted coup in 1991, and eventually his wish to retain a centrally controlled union of Soviet states conflicted with the Soviet republics' desire for autonomy. Losing his battle with his chief political opponent, Boris Yeltsin, he resigned in December 1991. He was awarded the Nobel Peace Prize in 1990.

Gordimer /'gɔːdɪmə(r)/, Nadine (born 1923), South African novelist and short-story writer. The impetus for her writing was provided by the contrast between her own wealthy background and the conditions experienced by black miners in her home town of Johannesburg. Her work avoids overt polemicism, examining the effect of apartheid on the oppressed and the privileged alike. Her novels include *The Conservationist* (1974) and *My Son's Story* (1990). She was awarded the Nobel Prize for literature in 1991.

Gordon /'gɔːd(ə)n/, Charles George (1833–85), British general and colonial administrator. He went to China in 1860 while serving with the Royal Engineers, and became known as 'Chinese Gordon' after crushing the Taiping Rebellion (1863–4). In

1884 he was sent to rescue the Egyptian garrisons in Sudan from forces led by the Mahdi (Muhammad Ahmad of Dongola, 1843–85), but was trapped at Khartoum and killed before a relieving force could reach him.

Gordy /'gɔːdɪ/, Berry Jr. (born 1929), American record producer. He founded the Motown record company in 1959, introducing Stevie Wonder, who remained one of his major performers. Among the black artistes recorded by Motown were Smokey Robinson, Diana Ross, and Marvin Gaye; their impact and popularity integrated black music into the mainstream of popular music.

Górecki /gə'retskɪ/, Henryk (Mikołaj) (born 1933), Polish composer. He studied at Katowice Conservatory and with Olivier Messiaen in Paris. His works are chiefly for orchestra and chamber ensemble; they include three symphonies and a chamber trilogy, *Genesis* (1963). In *Old Polish Music* (1969) he draws on medieval Polish religious music as his source of inspiration, while his Third Symphony (1976), also called the *Symphony of Sorrowful Songs*, is heavily influenced by church music.

Gorky[1] /'gɔːkɪ/, Arshile (1904–48), Turkish-born American painter. At first influenced by Picasso, he later gained inspiration from the surrealist techniques of artists such as Miró to develop a distinctive style of abstract expressionism. He is best known for his work of the early 1940s, which uses ambiguous biomorphic forms characterized by bright colours, fluid handling of the paint, and black sinuous outlines, and is represented by paintings such as *Waterfall* (1943).

Gorky[2] /'gɔːkɪ/, Maxim (pseudonym of Aleksei Maksimovich Peshkov) (1868–1936), Russian writer and revolutionary. He became famous for the short stories that he published between 1895 and 1900; he later turned to writing novels and plays. Among his best-known works are the play *The Lower Depths* (1901) and his autobiographical trilogy (1915–23). He was imprisoned for his involvement in the Russian Revolution of 1905 and exiled for his revolutionary activity. On his final return to the Soviet Union in 1931 after periods spent abroad, he was honoured as the founder of the new, officially sanctioned socialist realism.

Gould[1] /'guːld/, Glenn (Herbert) (1932–82), Canadian pianist and composer. He made his début as a soloist with the Toronto Symphony Orchestra at the age of 14 and gave many performances both in Canada and abroad until 1964, when he retired from the concert platform to concentrate on recording and broadcasting. He is well known for his performances of works by Beethoven, Hindemith, Schoenberg, and especially Bach.

Gould[2] /guːld/, John (1804–81), English bird artist. Gould taught himself taxidermy and was taxidermist to the Zoological Society of London for more than fifty years. He produced his first finely illustrated hand-painted book of birds following the receipt of a collection of skins from the Himalayas in 1830, and went on to produce another forty large illustrated volumes containing some 3,000 plates. It seems that many of the finest plates were actually drawn by Gould's wife and other artists that he employed.

Gould[3] /guːld/, Stephen Jay (born 1941), American palaeontologist. He has studied modifications of Darwinian evolutionary theory, proposed the concept of punctuated equilibrium, and is especially interested in the social context of scientific theory. His popular science books include *Ever Since Darwin* (1977), *Hen's Teeth and Horses' Toes* (1983), and *Bully for Brontosaurus* (1992).

Gounod /'guːnəʊ/, Charles François (1818–93), French composer, conductor, and organist. He achieved his first operatic success in 1859 with *Faust*, a grand opera in the French tradition, but with a grace and naturalism new to the genre. Gounod's later operas have not maintained their popularity to the same extent as *Faust*, but *Roméo et Juliette* (1867) and several of his songs are still performed.

Gowon /'gəʊwən/, Yakubu (born 1934), Nigerian general and statesman, head of state 1966–75. He seized power in 1966, ousting the leader of an earlier military coup. Following the Biafran civil war (1967–70), he maintained a policy of 'no victor, no vanquished' which helped to reconcile the warring factions. Gowon was himself removed in a military coup in 1975.

Goya /'gɔɪə/ (full name Francisco José de Goya y Lucientes) (1746–1828), Spanish painter and etcher. Although he painted notable portraits, such as *The Family of Charles IV* (1800), he is now chiefly famous for the works which express his reaction to

the French occupation of Spain (1808–14): the painting *The Shootings of May 3rd 1808* (1814) and the set of sixty-five etchings *The Disasters of War* (1810–14), depicting the cruelty and horror of war. His work influenced many artists, including Manet and Delacroix.

Gracchus /'grækəs/, Tiberius Sempronius (c.163–133 BC), Roman tribune. He and his brother, Gaius Sempronius Gracchus (c.153–121 BC), were responsible for radical social and economic legislation, passed against the wishes of the senatorial class. Tiberius was killed by his opponents after the passing of his agrarian bill (133 BC), which aimed at a redistribution of land to the poor. Gaius continued his brother's programme and instituted other reforms to relieve poverty, but was killed in a riot.

Grace /greɪs/, W(illiam) G(ilbert) (1848–1915), English cricketer. He began playing first-class cricket for Gloucestershire in 1864 and played in his last test match at the age of 50. During his career he made 126 centuries, scored 54,896 runs, and took 2,864 wickets. He twice captained England in test matches against Australia (1880 and 1882).

Grade /greɪd/, Lew, Baron Grade of Elstree (born Louis Winogradsky) (born 1906), British television producer and executive, born in Russia. Having emigrated to Britain with his brother (see DELFONT) in 1912, he established a reputation as one of the pioneers of British commercial television in the 1950s; he was long associated with the television company ATV (Associated Television), later serving as its president from 1977 to 1982. His nephew Michael Grade (born 1943) was chief executive of Channel Four 1988–97.

Graf /grɑːf/, Stephanie ('Steffi') (born 1969), German tennis player. She was ranked top women's player at the age of 16; in 1988 she won the Australian, French, and US Open championships, as well as the Wimbledon trophy and an Olympic gold medal. She won her seventh Wimbledon singles title in 1996.

Grafton /'grɑːftən/, Augustus Henry Fitzroy, 3rd Duke of (1735–1811), British Whig statesman, Prime Minister 1768–70.

Graham[1] /'greɪəm/, Martha (1893–1991), American dancer, teacher, and choreographer. An influential teacher of modern dance, she evolved a new dance language using more flexible movements intended to express psychological complexities and emotional power. She established her own studio in 1927, and during the 1930s produced works on the theme of American roots and values, such as *Appalachian Spring* (1931). Her later works include *Care of the Heart* (1946).

Graham[2] /'greɪəm/, Thomas (1805–69), Scottish physical chemist. He studied the diffusion of gases, and suggested a law which relates a gas's rate of diffusion to its density. He also investigated the passage of dissolved substances through porous membranes, and coined the word *osmose* (an earlier form of *osmosis*); he was also the first (in 1861) to use the word *colloid* in its modern (chemical) sense.

Graham[3] /'greɪəm/, William Franklin ('Billy') (born 1918), American evangelical preacher. A minister of the Southern Baptist Church, he became world famous as a mass evangelist; he has conducted large, theatrically staged religious meetings throughout the world, including several in Britain, as well as others in South Korea and the former Soviet Union.

Grahame /'greɪəm/, Kenneth (1859–1932), Scottish-born writer of children's stories, resident in England from 1864. He is most famous for *The Wind in the Willows* (1908), a collection of stories about animals of the river-bank, now regarded as a children's classic. The main characters (Rat, Mole, Badger, and Toad) became even more familiar to British children through A. A. Milne's musical version of the story (*Toad of Toad Hall*, 1930) and various television adaptations of Grahame's work.

Grainger /'greɪndʒə(r)/, (George) Percy (Aldridge) (1882–1961), Australian-born American composer and pianist. From 1901 he lived in London, where he gained fame as a concert pianist; he later settled in the US. He joined the English Folk Song Society in 1905 and collected, edited, and arranged English folk-songs. As a composer he is best known for his light music incorporating traditional melodies, such as *Shepherd's Hey* (1911), *Handel in the Strand* (1912), and *Country Gardens* (1919).

Gramsci /'græmʃɪ/, Antonio (1891–1937), Italian political theorist and activist. A founder of the Italian Communist Party, he became its leader and was elected to the Chamber of Deputies in 1924. He was imprisoned when the Communist Party was

banned by the Fascists in 1926, and died shortly after his release. Gramsci's most notable writings date from his imprisonment, and include *Letters from Prison* (1947). His work on the dictatorship of the proletariat remains an important influence on left-wing thought and cultural theory.

Grant[1] /grɑːnt/, Cary (born Alexander Archibald Leach) (1904–86), British-born American actor. He made his Hollywood screen début in *This is the Night* (1932) after appearing in Broadway musicals. He acted in more than seventy films, including *Holiday* (1938) and *The Philadelphia Story* (1940).

Grant[2] /grɑːnt/, Duncan (James Corrow) (1885–1978), Scottish painter and designer. He was a cousin of Lytton Strachey and a member of the Bloomsbury Group. He exhibited in the second post-impressionist exhibition (1912), and became a pioneer of abstract art in Britain. He was a gifted designer, working for Roger Fry's Omega workshops and producing a variety of work that included textiles, pottery, and murals. He also worked in collaboration with Vanessa Bell, with whom he lived from 1914.

Grant[3] /grɑːnt/, Ulysses S(impson) (born Hiram Ulysses Grant) (1822–85), American general and 18th President of the US 1869–77. Having made his reputation through a series of victories on the Union side in the American Civil War (most notably the capture of Vicksburg in 1863), Grant was made supreme commander of the Unionist armies. His policy of attrition against the Confederate army eventually proved successful in ending the war. He became President in 1869, but was unable to check widespread political corruption and inefficiency.

Granville-Barker /ˌgrænvɪl'bɑːkə(r)/, Harley (1877–1946), English dramatist, critic, theatre director, and actor. As co-manager of the Royal Court Theatre, London (1904–7), he presented plays incorporating social comment and realism, including works by Ibsen and Shaw. His own plays, such as *The Voysey Inheritance* (1905), also dealt naturalistically with social and moral issues. His Shakespearian productions and his *Prefaces to Shakespeare* (1927–46) were influential for subsequent interpretation and staging of Shakespeare's work.

Grappelli /grə'pelɪ/, Stephane (1908–97), French jazz violinist. After early classical training, he turned to jazz in the late 1920s; in 1934, together with the guitarist

Django Reinhardt, he formed the Quintette du Hot Club de France, becoming famous for his improvisational style of swing, and making many recordings with the group until it split up in 1939. Grappelli went on to pursue a successful international career, both as a soloist and with groups.

Grass /grɑːs/, Günter (Wilhelm) (born 1927), German novelist, poet, and dramatist. He won international acclaim with his first novel, *The Tin Drum* (1959), a picaresque tale drawing on Grass's own experiences as a youth in Nazi Germany. He is known for his outspoken socialist views, which are reflected in the play *The Plebeians Rehearse the Uprising* (1966). His other well-known novels include *Dog Years* (1965).

Graves /greɪvz/, Robert (Ranke) (1895–1985), English poet, novelist, and critic. His early poetry was written during the First World War, but he is better known for his later work, which is individualistic and cannot be associated with any school or movement. He was professor of poetry at Oxford University 1961–6. His prose includes autobiography (*Good-bye to All That*, 1929; *Occupation Writer*, 1950), historical fiction (*I, Claudius*, 1934; *Claudius the God*, 1934), and non-fiction (*The White Goddess*, 1948). All of his writing reflects his keen interest in classics and mythology.

Gray[1] /greɪ/, Asa (1810–88), American botanist. He was the author of many textbooks which greatly popularized botany. Finding no conflict between evolution and his view of divine design in nature, he supported Darwin's theories at a time when they were anathema to many.

Gray[2] /greɪ/, Thomas (1716–71), English poet. He first gained recognition with the poem 'Elegy Written in a Country Churchyard' (1751) and this remains his best-known work. His other poems include two Pindaric odes, 'The Bard' (1757) and 'The Progress of Poesy' (1757); these mark a clear transition from neoclassical lucidity towards the obscure and the sublime and are regarded as precursors of romanticism.

Greaves /griːvz/, James ('Jimmy') (born 1940), English footballer. He made his début as a striker for Chelsea in 1957, going on to join AC Milan, Tottenham Hotspur, and West Ham United and scoring 357 goals in 517 league matches. He also won 57 international caps (from 1959), scoring

44 goals. After his retirement he became a television football presenter.

Greco, El see EL GRECO.

Greenaway[1] /ˈgriːnəˌweɪ/, Catherine ('Kate') (1846–1901), English artist. She is known especially for her illustrations of children's books such as *Under the Windows* (1879) and *Mother Goose* (1881). An annual award for the best children's book illustration in Britain is named after her.

Greenaway[2] /ˈgriːnəˌweɪ/, Peter (born 1942), English film director. Greenaway first won substantial critical recognition with *The Draughtsman's Contract* (1982). His often contrived and controversial works are concerned with sex, human mutability, and gamesmanship; among his later films are *The Cook, The Thief, His Wife, and Her Lover* (1989), *Prospero's Books* (1991), and *The Baby of Mâcon* (1993).

Greene /griːn/, (Henry) Graham (1904–91), English novelist. He became a Roman Catholic in 1926; the moral paradoxes of his faith underlie much of his work. Well-known works which explore religious themes include *Brighton Rock* (1938), *The Power and the Glory* (1940), and *Travels with My Aunt* (1969). Among his other novels are thrillers, which Greene classed as 'entertainments', such as his first successful novel, *Stamboul Train* (1932), and *The Third Man* (1950); the latter was originally written as a screenplay and filmed in 1949.

Greer /grɪə(r)/, Germaine (born 1939), Australian feminist and writer. She first achieved recognition with her influential book *The Female Eunuch* (1970), an analysis of women's subordination in a male-dominated society. She has since become a high-profile figure in the women's movement; other books include *The Change* (1991), about social attitudes to female ageing.

Gregory, St /ˈgregərɪ/, (known as St Gregory the Great) (*c*.540–604), pope (as Gregory I) 590–604 and Doctor of the Church. He made peace with the Lombards after their invasions of Italy and appointed governors to the Italian cities, thus establishing the temporal power of the papacy. He sent St Augustine to England to lead the country's conversion to Christianity. He is also credited with the introduction of Gregorian chant. Feast day, 12 March.

Gregory of Nazianzus, St /ˈgregərɪ, ˌnæzɪˈænzəs/ (329–89), Doctor of the Church, bishop of Constantinople. With St Basil and St Gregory of Nyssa he was an upholder of Orthodoxy against the Arian and Apollinarian heresies, and influential in restoring adherence to the Nicene Creed. Feast day, (in the Eastern Church) 25 and 30 January; (in the Western Church) 2 January (formerly 9 May).

Gregory of Nyssa, St /ˈgregərɪ, ˈnɪsə/ (*c*.330–*c*.395), Doctor of the Eastern Church, bishop of Nyssa in Cappadocia. The brother of St Basil, he was an Orthodox follower of Origen and joined with St Basil and St Gregory of Nazianzus in opposing the heresy of Arianism. Feast day, 9 March.

Gregory of Tours, St /ˈgregərɪ, tʊə(r)/ (*c*.540–94), Frankish bishop and historian. He was elected bishop of Tours in 573; his writings provide the chief authority for the early Merovingian period of French history. Feast day, 17 November.

Grenfell /ˈgrenf(ə)l/, Joyce (Irene Phipps) (1910–79), English entertainer and writer. She specialized in portraying gauche and toothy females, often spinsters or schoolteachers, and appeared in revues and several one-woman shows, such as *Joyce Grenfell Requests the Pleasure* (1954). She also appeared in many films, notably Ealing comedies and the St Trinian's series, and was often seen on television.

Grenville /ˈgrenvɪl/, George (1712–70), British Whig statesman, Prime Minister 1763–5. The American Stamp Act (1765), which aroused great opposition in the North American colonies, was passed during his term of office.

Gresham /ˈgreʃəm/, Sir Thomas (*c*.1519–79), English financier. He founded the Royal Exchange in 1566 and served as the chief financial adviser to the Elizabethan government.

Gresley /ˈgrezlɪ/, Sir (Herbert) Nigel (1876–1941), British railway engineer. He became locomotive engineer of the Great Northern Railway in 1911, continuing as chief mechanical engineer on the newly formed London and North Eastern Railway from 1923. He is most famous for designing express steam locomotives, such as the A3 class exemplified by *Flying Scotsman*. His A4 pacifics hauled the first British streamlined train service in 1935, and in 1938 one of these engines, *Mallard*, achieved a world speed record of 126 m.p.h., never surpassed by a steam locomotive.

Gretzky /'gretskɪ/, Wayne (born 1961), Canadian ice-hockey player. He made his professional début in 1978 with the Indianapolis Racers, soon moving to the Edmonton Oilers. A prolific scorer, from 1980 to 1987 he was voted Most Valuable Player (MVP) in the National Hockey League.

Greuze /grɜːz/, Jean-Baptiste (1725–1805), French painter. He first gained recognition with his narrative genre painting *A Father Reading the Bible to his Children* (1755). Much of his later work, such as *The Broken Pitcher* (c.1773), consisted of pictures of young women, often in *décolleté* dress.

Grey[1] /greɪ/, Charles, 2nd Earl (1764–1845), British statesman, Prime Minister 1830–4. He was an advocate of electoral reform and his government passed the first Reform Act (1832) as well as important factory legislation and the Act abolishing slavery throughout the British Empire.

Grey[2] /greɪ/, Sir George (1812–98), British statesman and colonial administrator, Prime Minister of New Zealand 1877–9. He was appointed as governor in South Australia (1840), New Zealand (1845; 1861), and Cape Colony (1854), in each case at a time of conflict between the native peoples and European settlers. As Prime Minister of New Zealand he brought peace to the country and established good relations with the Maoris, learning their language and studying their mythology and culture.

Grey[3] /greɪ/, Lady Jane (1537–54), queen of England 9–19 July 1553. In 1553 Jane, the granddaughter of Henry VIII's sister, was forced by the Duke of Northumberland to marry his son to ensure a Protestant succession. Northumberland then persuaded the dying Edward VI to name Jane as his successor, but she was deposed after nine days on the throne by forces loyal to Edward's elder sister Mary. Jane was executed in the following year because she was seen as a potential focal point for Protestant opposition to Mary's Catholic regime.

Grey[4] /greɪ/, Zane (born Pearl Grey) (1872–1939), American writer. He wrote fifty-four westerns, which sold more than 13 million copies during his lifetime. His stories, the best known of which is *Riders of the Purple Sage* (1912), deal with cowboy life in a somewhat romanticized and formulaic style.

Grieg /griːg/, Edvard (1843–1907), Norwegian composer, conductor, and violinist. He took much of his inspiration from Norwegian folk music, as in many of his songs and the incidental music to Ibsen's play *Peer Gynt* (1876). He avoided the larger forms of opera and symphony in favour of songs, orchestral suites, and violin sonatas. Other famous works include the Piano Concerto in A minor (1869).

Grierson /'grɪəs(ə)n/, John (1898–1972), Scottish film director and producer. His pioneering work in British documentary film-making is represented by films for the Empire Marketing Board (1928–33) and the GPO Film Unit (1933–6); his work for the latter includes *Night Mail* (1936), with a verse commentary by W. H. Auden. Grierson is also notable for establishing the National Film Board of Canada (1939) and for his television series *This Wonderful World* (1957–68).

Griffith[1] /'grɪfɪθ/, Arthur (1872–1922), Irish nationalist leader and statesman, President of the Irish Free State 1922. In 1905 he founded and became president of Sinn Fein. Griffith was among those who established the unofficial Irish Parliament in 1919, becoming Vice-President of the newly declared republic in the same year. He led the Irish delegation during negotiations over the Anglo-Irish Treaty (1921), and was elected President of the Irish Free State in 1922, only to die in office several months later.

Griffith[2] /'grɪfɪθ/, D(avid) W(ark) (1875–1948), American film director. A significant figure in the history of film, he began to discover the elements of cinematic expression in his early one-reel films, and is responsible for introducing the techniques of flashback and fade-out. Notable films include his epic of the American Civil War *The Birth of a Nation* (1915), *Intolerance* (1916), and *Broken Blossoms* (1919). He made only two sound films, in 1930 and 1931, and then retired.

Grimaldi[1] /grɪ'mældɪ/, Francesco Maria (1618–63), Italian Jesuit physicist and astronomer, discoverer of the diffraction of light. He verified Galileo's law of the uniform acceleration of falling bodies, drew a detailed map of the moon, and began the practice of naming lunar features after astronomers and physicists.

Grimaldi[2] /grɪ'mældɪ/, Joseph (1779–1837), English circus entertainer. He created the role of the clown in the circus; it was in his honour that later clowns were nicknamed

Joey. From 1806 until his retirement in 1823 he performed at Covent Garden, where he became famous for his acrobatic skills.

Grimm /grɪm/, Jacob (Ludwig Carl) (1785–1863) and Wilhelm (Carl) (1786–1859), German philologists and folklorists. Jacob produced a historical German grammar (1819, 1822) and in 1852 the brothers jointly inaugurated a dictionary of German on historical principles; it was continued by other scholars and completed in 1960. The brothers are also remembered for the anthology of German fairy tales which they compiled; this appeared in three volumes between 1812 and 1822.

Grimond /'grɪmənd/, Joseph ('Jo'), Baron (1913–93), British Liberal politician. As leader of the Liberal Party (1956–67), he advocated British membership of the European Economic Community and sought to make the Liberal Party the only radical alternative to Conservatism.

Gris /griːs/, Juan (born José Victoriano Gonzales) (1887–1927), Spanish painter. His association with Braque and Picasso in Paris during their early cubist period influenced his approach, although his chief concern was not the analytical treatment of form. His main contribution was to the development of the later phase of synthetic cubism. His work, such as The Sunblind (1914), uses collage and paint in simple fragmented shapes which are arranged to create interplays and contrasts of textures, colours, and forms.

Grivas /'griːvəs/, George (Theodorou) (1898–1974), Greek-Cypriot patriot and soldier. A lifelong supporter of the union of Cyprus with Greece, he led the guerrilla campaign against British rule in Cyprus during the 1950s, which culminated in the country's independence in 1959. Grivas was rewarded for his role in this by promotion to general in the Greek army. He returned to Cyprus in 1971 to organize guerrilla opposition to President Makarios and died a fugitive.

Gromyko /grə'miːkəʊ/, Andrei (Andreevich) (1909–89), Soviet statesman, President of the USSR 1985–8. Born in Russia, he pursued a career in the Soviet diplomatic service. He was appointed Foreign Minister in 1957, a post which he held until becoming President in 1985. As Foreign Minister he represented the Soviet Union abroad throughout most of the cold war. His ap-

pointment to the presidency (at that time largely a formal position) by Mikhail Gorbachev was widely interpreted as a manoeuvre to reduce Gromyko's influence and make possible an ending of the cold war.

Gropius /'grəʊpɪəs/, Walter (1883–1969), German-born American architect. He was the first director of the Bauhaus School of Design (1919–28) and a pioneer of the international style; his intention was to relate architecture more closely to social needs and to the industrial techniques and modern construction materials on which it increasingly relied. He left Germany in 1934 and eventually settled in the US in 1938; he was professor of architecture at Harvard University until 1952 and designed the Harvard Graduate Center (1949).

Grosseteste /'grəʊstest/, Robert (c.1175–1253), English churchman, philosopher, and scholar. He taught theology at Oxford before becoming bishop of Lincoln in 1235. His interests were wide-ranging and his experimental approach to science, especially in optics and mathematics, inspired his pupil Roger Bacon. His writings include translations of Aristotle, philosophical treatises, and devotional works.

Grosz /grəʊs/, George (1893–1959), German painter and draughtsman. His revulsion at contemporary bourgeois society was strengthened by his experiences during the First World War. He became prominent in the Neue Sachlichkeit (New Objectivity) movement of the 1920s; his satirical drawings and paintings characteristically depicted a decaying society in which gluttony and depraved sensuality are juxtaposed with poverty and disease. Major works include the paintings Suicide (1916) and Metropolis (1917). In 1932 he emigrated to the United States and became an American citizen in 1938.

Grotius /'grəʊtɪəs/, Hugo (Latinized name of Huig de Groot) (1583–1645), Dutch jurist and diplomat. His fame rests on the legal treatise De Jure Belli et Pacis, written in exile in Paris and published in 1625, which established the basis of modern international law.

Grove /grəʊv/, Sir George (1820–1900), English musicologist. He is chiefly remembered as the founder and first editor of the multi-volume Dictionary of Music and Musicians (1879–89). He was also instrumental

in establishing the Royal College of Music (1883–95) and served as its first director (1883–94).

Grünewald /'gru:nə,vælt/, Mathias (born Mathis Nithardt; also called Mathis Gothardt) (c.1460–1528), German painter. His most famous work, the nine-panel *Isenheim Altar* (completed 1516), exemplifies his style: figures with twisted limbs, contorted postures, and expressive faces, painted in glowing colour against a dark background.

Guardi /'gwɑ:dɪ/, Francesco (1712–93), Italian painter. He came from a family of artists working in Venice and was a pupil of Canaletto. His paintings of Venice are notable for their free handling of light and atmosphere. His works include *View of S. Giorgio Maggiore* (1775–80).

Guarneri /gwɑ:'neərɪ/ Giuseppe ('del Gesù') (1687–1744), Italian violin-maker. The most famous of a family of three generations of violin-makers based in Cremona, he is noted for the attention he gave to the tone quality of his instruments, which do not conform to any standard shape or dimensions.

Guericke /'gerɪkə/, Otto von (1602–86), German engineer and physicist. He invented an air pump, using it to produce a partial vacuum. He was the first to investigate the properties of a vacuum, and devised the Magdeburg hemispheres to demonstrate atmospheric pressure. Guericke also built the first known electrostatic machine.

Guevara /gə'vɑ:rə/, Che (full name Ernesto Guevara de la Serna) (1928–67), Argentinian revolutionary and guerrilla leader. He played a significant part in the Cuban revolution (1956–9) and as a government minister under Fidel Castro was instrumental in the transfer of Cuba's traditional economic ties from the US to the Communist bloc. In 1967 he was captured and executed while training guerrillas for a planned uprising against the Bolivian government. He became a hero figure among radical students in the West during the 1960s and early 1970s.

Guggenheim /'gʊgən,haɪm/, Meyer (1828–1905), Swiss-born American industrialist. With his seven sons he established large mining and metal-processing companies. His children established several foundations providing support for the arts, including the Guggenheim Foundation,

established in 1925 to provide financial support for scholars, artists, and writers. In 1937 Guggenheim's son Solomon (1861–1949) established a foundation for the advancement of art; it now operates the Guggenheim Museum in New York and directs the Guggenheim Collection in Venice.

Guinness /'gɪnɪs/, Sir Alec (born 1914), English actor. His stage career ranges from Shakespeare to contemporary drama and includes a notable interpretation of Hamlet. He made his film début in *Great Expectations* (1946); other films include *Kind Hearts and Coronets* (1949), *Bridge on the River Kwai* (1957), and *Star Wars* (1977). He is also known for his portrayal of the espionage chief George Smiley in television versions of John Le Carré's *Tinker, Tailor, Soldier, Spy* (1979) and *Smiley's People* (1981–2).

Gulbenkian /gʊl'beŋkɪən/, Calouste Sarkis (1869–1955), Turkish-born British oil magnate and philanthropist, of Armenian descent. He was a pioneer in the development of the oil industry in the Middle East and his company (established in 1911) was the first to exploit the Iraqi oilfields. He bequeathed his large fortune and valuable art collection to the Calouste Gulbenkian Foundation (based in Lisbon); this disburses funds for the advancement of social and cultural projects in Portugal and elsewhere.

Gunn /gʌn/, Thomson William ('Thom') (born 1929), English poet. His first volume of poems, *Fighting Terms*, was published in 1954; shortly afterwards he moved to California, where he has lived ever since. Subsequent volumes of verse include *The Sense of Movement* (1959) and *My Sad Captains* (1961). His poetry is written in a predominantly low-key, laconic, and colloquial style.

Gunnell /'gʌn(ə)l/, Sally (Jane Janet) (born 1966), English athlete. Gunnell made her British début as a sprinter in 1984 but quickly became a hurdles specialist, concentrating especially on the 400-metres hurdles. After winning a silver medal at the world championships in this event in 1991, Gunnell went on to take the Olympic title in 1992 and the world championship title the following year.

Gurdjieff /'gɜ:djef/, George (Ivanovich) (1877–1949), Russian spiritual leader and occultist. After travels in India, Tibet, and the Middle East, he founded the Institute

for the Harmonious Development of Man in Paris (1922). Those who attended the Institute were taught to attain a higher level of consciousness through a programme of lectures, dance, and physical labour. His ideas were published posthumously in *All and Everything* (1950) and *Meetings with Remarkable Men* (1963).

Gurney /'gɜːnɪ/, Ivor (Bertie) (1890–1937), English poet and composer. He fought on the Western Front during the First World War, and wrote the verse collections *Severn and Somme* (1917) and *War's Embers* (1919). Gurney also wrote nearly 300 songs, many of which were influenced by Elizabethan music. He suffered a breakdown and spent the last fifteen years of his life in a mental hospital.

Gustavus Adolphus /ɡʊˌstɑːvəs əˈdɒlfəs/ (1594–1632), king of Sweden 1611–32. He raised Sweden to the status of a European power by his victories against Denmark, Poland, and Russia in the first part of his reign. In 1630 he intervened on the Protestant side in the Thirty Years War, revitalizing the anti-imperialist cause with several victories and earning himself the title of 'Lion of the North'. At home he instituted reforms in administration, economic development, and education, laying the foundation of the modern state.

Gutenberg /'ɡuːt(ə)nˌbɜːɡ/, Johannes (c.1400–68), German printer. He is remembered as the first in the West to print using movable type; he introduced typecasting using a matrix, and was the first to use a press. By c.1455 he had produced what later became known as the Gutenberg Bible, the first book to be printed from movable type and the oldest book still extant in the West.

Guthrie /'ɡʌθrɪ/, Woody (born Woodrow Wilson Guthrie) (1912–67), American folksinger and songwriter. His radical political stance and commitment to causes such as the hardships of the rural poor during the Depression inspired many of his best-known songs, such as 'This Land is Your Land' (1944). His work was responsible for a revival of interest in folk music and influenced later singers and songwriters such as Bob Dylan.

Gutiérrez /ˌɡʊtɪˈeərəz/, Gustavo (born 1928), Peruvian theologian. He was an important figure in the emergence of liberation theology in Latin America, outlining its principles in *A Theology of Liberation* (1971). Gutiérrez argued that the theologian should be concerned with liberating the poor and oppressed, and that this entailed responding to local needs rather than applying alien ideas and solutions.

Gwynn /ɡwɪn/, Eleanor ('Nell') (1650–87), English actress. Originally an orange-seller, she became famous as a comedienne at the Theatre Royal, Drury Lane, London. She was a mistress of Charles II; one of her sons was later created Duke of St Albans.

H

Habermas /ˈhɑːbəˌmæs/, Jürgen (born 1929), German social philosopher. He was a principal figure of the Frankfurt School, and was heavily involved in its reappraisal of Marxism in terms of the cultural and aesthetic dimensions of modern industrial society. His publications include *Theory of Communicative Action* (1981).

Hadlee /ˈhædlɪ/, Sir Richard (John) (born 1951), New Zealand cricketer. An all-round cricketer, he made his test début in 1973; in 1989 he became the first bowler to take more than 400 test wickets, finishing his career with a total of 431. He was knighted in 1990 and was the first cricketer to receive this honour while still playing in test matches.

Hadrian /ˈheɪdrɪən/ (full name Publius Aelius Hadrianus) (AD 76–138), Roman emperor 117–38. He became emperor as the adopted successor of Trajan, and spent much of his reign touring the provinces of the Empire, promoting good government and loyalty to Rome, and securing the frontiers. The building of Hadrian's Wall was begun after his visit to Britain in 122.

Haeckel /ˈhek(ə)l/, Ernst Heinrich (1834–1919), German biologist and philosopher. His popularization of Darwin's theories introduced them to many readers for the first time. Haeckel saw evolution as providing a framework for describing the world; he rejected religion as superstition and believed that the German Empire represented the highest evolved form of civilized nation. He upheld the essential unity of mind, organic life, and inorganic matter, and developed the recapitulation theory of ontogenesis, now discredited. He is said to have coined the word *ecology* in 1869.

Haggard /ˈhægəd/, Sir H(enry) Rider (1856–1925), English novelist. He is famous for his adventure novels, many of which have an African setting and are based on the time he spent in South Africa in the mid-1870s. Among the best known of his books are *King Solomon's Mines* (1885) and *She* (1889).

Hahn /hɑːn/, Otto (1879–1968), German chemist, co-discoverer of nuclear fission. He pioneered the study of radiochemistry in England, first with Sir William Ramsay in London and then with Sir Ernest Rutherford in Manchester, identifying various radioactive isotopes of thorium. His fruitful partnership with Lise Meitner began shortly after his return to Germany and ended when she fled from the Nazis in 1938. They discovered the new element protactinium in 1917, but the culmination of their collaboration occurred in 1938 when, with Fritz Strassmann (1902–80), they discovered nuclear fission. Hahn was awarded the Nobel Prize for chemistry in 1944.

Haig /heɪg/, Douglas, 1st Earl Haig of Bemersyde (1861–1928), British Field Marshal. During the First World War he served as Commander-in-Chief of British forces in France (1915–18). He believed that the war could be won only by defeating the German army on the Western Front and maintained a strategy of attrition throughout his period of command. The strength of the main German army was eventually broken by this means, albeit with a very high cost in lives. In 1921 Haig helped to establish the Royal British Legion to improve the welfare of ex-servicemen.

Haile Selassie /ˌhaɪlɪ səˈlæsɪ/ (born Tafari Makonnen) (1892–1975), emperor of Ethiopia 1930–74. He lived in exile in Britain during the Italian occupation of Ethiopia (1936–41), but was restored to the throne by the Allies and ruled until deposed in a Communist military coup. As a statesman, he made his country a prominent force in Africa and helped establish the Organization of African Unity in the early 1960s. He is revered by the Rastafarian religious sect, which is named after him.

Hailwood /ˈheɪlwʊd/, Mike (full name Stanley Michael Bailey Hailwood) (1940–81), English racing motorcyclist. He achieved a record fourteen wins in the Isle of Man TT races between 1961 and 1979, and was world champion nine times in three different classes between 1961 and 1967.

Haitink /ˈhaɪtɪŋk/, Bernard (born 1929), Dutch conductor. He was artistic director and principal conductor with the Amster-

dam Concertgebouw, with whom he made notable recordings of all of Mahler's and Bruckner's symphonies, between 1964 and 1987. Haitink fulfilled a similar role with the London Philharmonic Orchestra (1967–79) and was musical director of Glyndebourne (1977–87) before becoming musical director at Covent Garden in 1987.

Hakluyt /'hækluːt/, Richard (c.1552–1616), English geographer and historian. He compiled *Principal Navigations, Voyages, and Discoveries of the English Nation* (1589), a collection of accounts of famous voyages of discovery, which brought to light the hitherto obscure achievements of English navigators and gave great impetus to discovery and colonization.

Haldane /'hɔːldeɪn/, J(ohn) B(urdon) S(anderson) (1892–1964), Scottish mathematical biologist. Haldane helped to lay the foundations of population genetics. He also worked in biochemistry, and on the effects of diving on human physiology. Haldane became well known as a popularizer of science and for his outspoken Marxist views.

Hale /heɪl/, George Ellery (1868–1938), American astronomer. He discovered that sunspots are associated with strong magnetic fields, and invented the spectroheliograph. He initiated the construction of several large telescopes, culminating in the 5-metre (200-inch) reflector at Mount Palomar in California, named the Hale reflector in his honour.

Haley /'heɪlɪ/, William John Clifton ('Bill') (1925–81), American rock and roll singer. He was the first to popularize rock and roll with the release of his song 'Rock Around the Clock' (1954), recorded with his group The Comets.

Halifax /'hælɪˌfæks/, George Montagu Dunk, 2nd Earl of (1716–71), British Tory statesman. In 1748 he became president of the Board of Trade and was active in colonial development, founding and giving his name to Halifax, Nova Scotia. He held other positions of state, including Lord Lieutenant of Ireland (1761–3), Lord Privy Seal (1770), and Secretary of State for the Northern Department (1762–3, 1771).

Hall[1] /hɔːl/, Charles Martin (1863–1914), American industrial chemist. He investigated different processes for producing aluminium from bauxite, and settled on electrolysis, obtaining the best results with alumina dissolved in molten cryolite. This remains the usual commercial method.

Hall[2] /hɔːl/, (Marguerite) Radclyffe (1883–1943), English novelist and poet. Her novels attracted both acclaim and outrage; while *Adam's Breed* (1926) was awarded the James Tait Black Memorial Prize, *The Well of Loneliness* (1928), with its exploration of a lesbian relationship, was banned for obscenity (in Britain though not in the US), despite the support of writers such as Virginia Woolf, E. M. Forster, and Arnold Bennett. The ban was overturned after Hall's death.

Hallé /'hæleɪ/, Sir Charles (German name Karl Halle) (1819–95), German-born pianist and conductor. He went to Manchester from Paris in 1848 to escape the revolution and remained there for the rest of his life. He founded his own orchestra (still known as the Hallé Orchestra and based in Manchester) and inaugurated a series of orchestral concerts (the Hallé Concerts) in 1858.

Haller /'hælə(r)/, Albrecht von (1708–77), Swiss anatomist and physiologist. He pioneered the study of neurology and experimental physiology, and wrote the first textbook of physiology.

Halley /'hælɪ, 'hɔːlɪ/, Edmond (1656–1742), English astronomer and mathematician. Halley became an influential Fellow of the Royal Society and friend of Newton, the publication of whose *Principia* was due largely to him. He became professor of geometry at Oxford and was later appointed Astronomer Royal. He realized that nebulae were clouds of luminous gas among the stars, and that the aurora was a phenomenon connected with the earth's magnetism. Halley is best known for recognizing that a bright comet (later named after him) had appeared several times, and for successfully predicting its return.

Hallowes /'hæləʊz/, Odette (born Marie Céline) (1912–95), French heroine of the Second World War. She entered occupied France in 1942 and worked secretly as a British agent until captured by the Gestapo in 1943. Imprisoned until 1945, she refused to betray her associates despite being tortured. For her work and her courage she was awarded the George Cross (1946).

Hals /hæls/, Frans (c.1580–1666), Dutch portrait and genre painter. His use of bold brushwork to capture the character, mood,

and facial expressions of his subjects gave a vitality to his portraits and represented a departure from conventional portraiture. His best-known portraits include groups, such as *The Banquet of the Officers of the St George Militia Company* (1616), and single figures, such as *The Laughing Cavalier* (1624). His genre pictures, painted during the 1620s, reflect the influence of the Dutch followers of Caravaggio.

Hamada /'hæmədə/, Shoji (1894–1978), Japanese potter. He visited England in 1920 and collaborated with his friend Bernard Leach before returning to Japan in 1923 to set up his own kiln at Mashiko. He worked mainly in stoneware, producing utilitarian items of unpretentious simplicity; he was a firm believer in the beauty and individuality of the handmade object as opposed to the uniformity of the products of industrialization.

Hamilcar /hæ'mɪlkɑː(r), 'hæmɪl,kɑː(r)/ (c.270–229 BC), Carthaginian general and father of Hannibal. He fought Rome in the first Punic War and negotiated terms of peace after the Carthaginian defeat of 241, which led to the loss of Sicily to the Romans. From 237 he and Hannibal were engaged in the conquest of Spain.

Hamilton[1] /'hæmɪlt(ə)n/, Alexander (c.1757–1804), American Federalist politician. As First Secretary of the Treasury under George Washington (1789–95), he established the US central banking system. Hamilton was a prime mover behind the Federalist Party's commitment to strong central government in the aftermath of American independence. He died from a gunshot wound after a duel with Aaron Burr.

Hamilton[2] /'hæmɪlt(ə)n/, Sir Charles (1900–78), New Zealand inventor and motor-racing driver. He is best known for his development of the jet boat, being knighted in 1974 for his services to manufacturing. Hamilton was also a successful motor-racing driver and was the first New Zealander to exceed 100 m.p.h.

Hamilton[3] /'hæmɪlt(ə)n/, Lady Emma (born Amy Lyon) (c.1765–1815), English beauty and mistress of Lord Nelson. In 1791 she married Sir William Hamilton (1730–1803), the British ambassador to Naples, after living with him there for five years. She first met Lord Nelson in Naples in 1793; they became lovers after his second visit in 1799. She had a daughter by him in 1801

and lived with him after her husband's death.

Hamilton[4] /'hæmɪlt(ə)n/, Sir William Rowan (1806–65), Irish mathematician and theoretical physicist. Hamilton made influential contributions to optics and in the foundations of algebra. He invented quaternions while investigating the subject of complex numbers. Hamilton's formulation of mechanics was incorporated into the equations of quantum mechanics.

Hammarskjöld /'hæmə,ʃʊld/, Dag (Hjalmar Agne Carl) (1905–61), Swedish diplomat and politician. He was chairman of the Bank of Sweden (1941–8) before becoming Swedish foreign affairs minister (1951–3). As Secretary-General of the United Nations (1953–61) he was influential in the establishment of the UN emergency force in Sinai and Gaza (1956), and also initiated peace moves in the Middle East (1957–8). He was posthumously awarded the 1961 Nobel Peace Prize after his death in an air crash in Zambia.

Hammerstein /'hæmə,staɪn/, Oscar (full name Oscar Hammerstein II) (1895–1960), American librettist. He collaborated with the composers Jerome Kern (for example in *Showboat*, 1927), Sigmund Romberg, and most notably with Richard Rodgers. He also wrote the libretto for the musical *Carmen Jones* (1943), an adaptation of Bizet's opera *Carmen*.

Hammett /'hæmɪt/, (Samuel) Dashiell (1894–1961), American novelist. His detective fiction, based in part on his own experiences as a detective, is characterized by a hard-boiled style and influenced Raymond Chandler and other writers in the genre. Many of Hammett's stories, including *The Maltese Falcon* (1930) and *The Thin Man* (1932), were made into successful films. He lived for many years with the dramatist Lillian Hellman; they were both persecuted for their left-wing views during the McCarthy era.

Hammond /'hæmənd/, Dame Joan (1912–96), Australian operatic soprano, born in New Zealand. She made her operatic début in Sydney in 1929 and went on to an international career with a wide repertoire. Her operatic successes included Puccini's *Madame Butterfly* and *Turandot*; she also performed in choral works and oratorios, such as Handel's *Messiah*.

Hammurabi /ˌhæmʊˈrɑːbɪ/ (died 1750 BC), the sixth king of the first dynasty of Babylonia, reigned 1792–1750 BC. He made Babylon the capital of Babylonia and extended the Babylonian empire. He instituted one of the earliest known legal codes, which took the form of 282 case laws dealing with the economy and with family, criminal, and civil law.

Hamnett /ˈhæmnɪt/, Katharine (born 1952), English fashion designer. After working as a freelance designer she established her own company in 1979. Her designs are characterized by their loose, simple lines and use of utilitarian fabrics. She also made a name for herself as a feminist and supporter of CND.

Hamsun /ˈhæmsʊn/, Knut (pseudonym of Knut Pedersen) (1859–1952), Norwegian novelist. He worked in a variety of manual jobs before the publication of his first novel, *Hunger* (1890), a semi-autobiographical account of the mental and physical hardships he experienced during this period. This successful novel was followed by further works exploring the human psyche and written in a similar fragmentary, vivid style, including *Growth of the Soil* (1917). He was awarded the Nobel Prize for literature in 1920.

Hancock /ˈhæŋkɒk/, Tony (full name Anthony John Hancock) (1924–68), English comedian. He made his name in 1954 with the radio series *Hancock's Half Hour*, in which he played a materialistic, lonely misfit and was noted for his sardonic wit. The series readily adapted to television (1956–61); Hancock later turned to writing his own material and starred in other comedy shows, as well as appearing in several films, but failed to repeat his earlier success. He committed suicide in 1968.

Handel /ˈhænd(ə)l/, George Frederick (born Georg Friedrich Händel) (1685–1759), German-born composer, resident in England from 1712. He was a major baroque composer whose prolific output included choral works, chamber music, operas, concerti grossi, and orchestral pieces. He is now chiefly remembered for his oratorios, the most famous of which is *Messiah* (1742); other choral works include *Samson* (1743) and *Judas Maccabaeus* (1747). Of his many other works, perhaps the best known is the *Water Music* suite for orchestra (c.1717), written for George I's procession down the River Thames. Handel was also a noted organist and invented the organ concerto, which he intended to be performed between the acts of his own oratorios.

Handley Page, Frederick, see PAGE.

Handy /ˈhændɪ/, W(illiam) C(hristopher) (1873–1958), American blues musician. As a cornettist he became leader of the band the Mahara Minstrels (1896–1903). He then began to write pieces for his own band and set up a music publishing house in 1914. His transcriptions of traditional blues, such as the 'St Louis Blues' (1914), were influential in establishing the accepted pattern of the modern twelve-bar blues.

Hanks /hæŋks/, Thomas J. ('Tom') (born 1956), American actor. Hanks built a reputation as a deft comedian in light-hearted films such as *Splash!* (1984), and won major international success with *Big* (1988). He went on to win Oscars for his performances in *Philadelphia* (1993) and *Forrest Gump* (1994).

Hannibal /ˈhænɪb(ə)l/ (247–182 BC), Carthaginian general. He precipitated the second Punic War by attacking the town of Saguntum in Spain, an ally of Rome. In 218, in a pre-emptive move, he led an army of about 30,000 over the Alps into Italy. There he inflicted a series of defeats on the Romans, campaigning for sixteen years undefeated but failing to take Rome itself. After being recalled to Africa he was defeated at Zama by Scipio Africanus in 202.

Hardie /ˈhɑːdɪ/, (James) Keir (1856–1915), Scottish Labour politician. He worked as a miner before entering Parliament in 1892, becoming the first leader of the Independent Labour Party the next year. In 1906 he became a co-founder and first leader of the Labour Party. His pacifist views prompted his withdrawal from Labour politics when the majority of his party's MPs declared their support for British participation in the First World War, although he remained an MP until his death.

Harding /ˈhɑːdɪŋ/, Warren (Gamaliel) (1865–1923), American Republican statesman, 29th President of the US 1921–3.

Hardy[1], Oliver, see LAUREL AND HARDY.

Hardy[2] /ˈhɑːdɪ/, Thomas (1840–1928), English novelist and poet. He spent most of his life in his native Dorset (the 'Wessex' of his novels). A recurrent theme in Hardy's work is the struggle of human beings against the

indifferent force that inflicts the sufferings and ironies of life. Major novels include *The Mayor of Casterbridge* (1886), *Tess of the D'Urbervilles* (1891), and *Jude the Obscure* (1896). He turned to writing poetry in the late 1890s and published eight volumes of poems, as well as a drama in blank verse, *The Dynasts* (1904–8).

Hare /heə(r)/, William, see BURKE[4].

Harefoot /'heəfʊt/, Harold, Harold I of England (see HAROLD).

Hargreaves /'hɑːgriːvz/, James (1720–78), English inventor. A pioneer of the Lancashire cotton industry, he invented *c*.1760 an improved carding-machine, which used a roller with multiple pins to comb out the cotton fibres. In 1770 he patented his most famous invention, the spinning-jenny, an early form of spinning-machine which was the first to use multiple spindles. His success in speeding up the spinning process caused opposition: spinners on the old-fashioned wheels were alarmed at the threat to their employment and in 1768 his house and machinery were destroyed by a mob.

Harlow /'hɑːləʊ/, Jean (born Harlean Carpenter) (1911–37), American film actress. She led a tempestuous life, becoming a film extra in Hollywood after eloping from Kansas when she was 16. Her breakthrough came with Howard Hughes's *Hell's Angels* (1930), and her platinum blonde hair and sex appeal brought immediate success. She made six films with Clark Gable, including *Red Dust* (1932) and *Saratoga* (1937), before her death from uraemic poisoning.

Harmsworth /'hɑːmzwɜːθ/, Alfred Charles William, see NORTHCLIFFE.

Harold /'hærəld/ the name of two kings of England:
Harold I (known as Harold Harefoot) (died 1040), reigned 1035–40. Harold was an illegitimate son of Canute and first came to the throne when his half-brother Hardecanute (Canute's legitimate heir) was king of Denmark and thus absent at the time of his father's death. When a third royal claimant was murdered a year later, Harold was formally recognized as king, although Hardecanute returned to the kingdom when Harold himself died.
Harold II (*c*.1019–66), reigned 1066, the last Anglo-Saxon king of England. He succeeded Edward the Confessor, having dominated the latter's court in the last years of

his reign, but was faced with two invasions within months of his accession. He resisted his half-brother Tostig and the Norse king Harald Hardrada at Stamford Bridge, but was killed and his army defeated at the Battle of Hastings; the victor, William of Normandy, took the throne as William I.

Haroun-al-Raschid see HARUN AR-RASHID.

Harris[1] /'hærɪs/, Sir Arthur (Travers), 1st Baronet (known as 'Bomber Harris') (1892–1984), British Marshal of the RAF. After joining the Royal Flying Corps in the First World War, Harris served as Commander-in-Chief of Bomber Command in the Second World War from 1942 to 1945. He organized mass bombing raids against German towns and cities which, as well as inflicting major economic damage, resulted in large-scale civilian casualties. As this became known throughout Britain, the morality of Harris's policy was repeatedly questioned, but he and Churchill remained committed.

Harris[2] /'hærɪs/, Frank (born James Thomas Harris) (1856–1931), Irish writer. He spent much of his life in England, where he gained a reputation as a fearless journalist, editing several journals including the *Saturday Review* (1894–8). His autobiography, the three-volume *My Life and Loves* (1923–7), became notorious for its unreliability and sexual frankness. He also wrote biographies of Oscar Wilde and Bernard Shaw.

Harrison[1] /'hærɪs(ə)n/, Benjamin (1833–1901), American Republican statesman, 23rd President of the US 1889–93. He was the grandson of William Henry Harrison.

Harrison[2] /'hærɪs(ə)n/, George (born 1943), English rock and pop guitarist. Harrison was the lead guitarist of the Beatles, to whom he contributed occasional songs (one of the best known being 'Something', 1969). His fascination with India (he sometimes played sitar on Beatles records) was reflected in the solo career that he pursued after the group's breakup in 1970; latterly he has concentrated on running a film production company.

Harrison[3] /'hærɪs(ə)n/, Sir Rex (born Reginald Carey Harrison) (1908–90), English actor. He first appeared on the stage in 1924 and made his film début in 1930 with *The Great Game*. His most famous role was as Professor Higgins in the stage and film

musical *My Fair Lady* (1956, 1964). His other films include *Blithe Spirit* (1944) and *Cleopatra* (1962).

Harrison[4] /'hærɪs(ə)n/, William Henry (1773–1841), American Whig statesman, 9th President of the US, 1841. He died of pneumonia one month after his inauguration. He was the grandfather of Benjamin Harrison.

Harrod /'hærəd/, Charles Henry (1800–85), English grocer and tea merchant. In 1853 he took over a shop in Knightsbridge, London, which, after expansion by his son Charles Digby Harrod (1841–1905), became a prestigious department store.

Harte /hɑːt/, (Francis) Bret (1836–1902), American short-story writer and poet. He is chiefly remembered for his stories about life in a gold-mining settlement, which were inspired by his own brief experience of mining and collected in works such as *The Luck of Roaring Camp* (1870).

Hartley /'hɑːtlɪ/, L(eslie) P(oles) (1895–1972), English novelist. Much of his work deals with memory and the effects of childhood experience on adult life and character, as in his trilogy *The Shrimp and the Anemone* (1944), *The Sixth Heaven* (1946), and *Eustace and Hilda* (1947), as well as the novel *The Go-Between* (1953).

Hartnell /'hɑːtn(ə)l/, Sir Norman (1901–79), English couturier. He is remembered as the dressmaker to Queen Elizabeth II (whose coronation gown he designed) and the Queen Mother.

Harun ar-Rashid /hæˌruːn ɑːræˈʃiːd/ (also **Haroun-al-Raschid** /-ælræˈʃiːd/) (763–809), fifth Abbasid caliph of Baghdad 786–809. He was the most powerful and vigorous of the Abbasid caliphs; he and his court were made famous by their portrayal in the *Arabian Nights*.

Harvey /'hɑːvɪ/, William (1578–1657), English discoverer of the mechanism of blood circulation and physician to James I and Charles I. Harvey set out to provide a satisfactory account of the motion of the heart, and in *De Motu Cordis* (1628) concluded that it forcibly expelled blood in contraction. He drew attention to the quantity of blood emerging from the heart into the arteries, and deduced that it must pass through the flesh and enter the veins,

returning once more to the heart. Harvey also studied embryology and animal locomotion.

Hasdrubal[1] /'hæzdrʊb(ə)l/ (died 221 BC), Carthaginian general. He was the son-in-law of Hamilcar, whom he accompanied to Spain in 237. Hasdrubal advanced to the Ebro, which became recognized as the boundary between Carthaginian and Roman spheres of influence.

Hasdrubal[2] /'hæzdrʊb(ə)l/ (died 207 BC), Carthaginian general. He was the son of Hamilcar and younger brother of Hannibal. At the start of the second Punic War in 218 he was left in command of Carthaginian forces in Spain after Hannibal had departed for Italy. After a defeat, Hasdrubal campaigned with only moderate success before crossing the Alps with the aim of joining Hannibal, but was intercepted and killed in battle.

Hašek /'hæʃek/, Jaroslav (1883–1923), Czech novelist and short-story writer. He is chiefly known as the author of an unfinished four-volume work published in Czechoslovakia between 1921 and 1923; it first appeared in Britain in a bowdlerized form as *The Good Soldier Schweik* (1930). The book is a comic novel satirizing military life and bureaucracy; its central character is the archetypal 'little man' fighting against the system.

Hastings /'heɪstɪŋz/, Warren (1732–1818), British colonial administrator. In 1774 he became India's first Governor-General and during his term of office introduced many of the administrative reforms vital to the successful maintenance of British rule in India. On his return to England in 1785 he was impeached for corruption; he was eventually acquitted in 1795 after a seven-year trial before the House of Lords.

Hathaway /'hæθəˌweɪ/, Anne (*c.*1557–1623), the wife of Shakespeare, whom she married in 1582. They had three children, a daughter (Susannah) and a twin daughter and son (Judith and Hamnet).

Hatshepsut /hæt'ʃepsʊt/ (died 1482 BC), Egyptian queen of the 18th dynasty, reigned *c.*1503–1482 BC. She was the wife of her half-brother Tuthmosis II, on whose death she became regent for her nephew Tuthmosis III. She then proclaimed herself co-ruler, and dominated the partnership until her death; she called herself pharaoh and was often portrayed as male. Her reign

was predominantly peaceful and she promoted Egypt's cultural life.

Hauptmann /ˈhaʊptmən/, Gerhart (1862–1946), German dramatist. He was an early pioneer of naturalism in the German theatre; his plays, such as *Before Sunrise* (1889) and *The Weavers* (1892), treat social and moral issues with directness and realism. He also wrote plays which combined naturalism with symbolism, such as *The Ascension of Joan* (1893). He was awarded the Nobel Prize for literature in 1912.

Havel /ˈhɑːv(ə)l/, Václav (born 1936), Czech dramatist and statesman, President of Czechoslovakia 1989–92 and of the Czech Republic since 1993. Having written plays, such as *The Garden Party* (1963), which were critical of totalitarianism, in the 1970s he became the leading spokesman for Charter 77 and other human rights groups and was twice imprisoned as a dissident. Shortly after his release in 1989 he founded the opposition group Civic Forum and led a renewed campaign for political change; in December of that year he was elected President following the peaceful overthrow of Communism (the velvet revolution). He remained as President of the Czech Republic after the partition of Czechoslovakia on 1 January 1993.

Hawke /hɔːk/, Robert James Lee ('Bob') (born 1929), Australian Labor statesman, Prime Minister 1983–91. He was elected leader of the Australian Labor Party in 1983, becoming Prime Minister a month later following his party's election victory over the Liberal government. During his premiership he pursued an economic programme based on free-market policies and tax reform. In 1990 he won a record fourth election victory but lost a leadership challenge the following year to Paul Keating.

Hawking /ˈhɔːkɪŋ/, Stephen William (born 1942), English theoretical physicist. His main work has been on space–time, quantum mechanics, and black holes, which he deduced can emit thermal radiation at a steady rate. While still a student he developed a progressive disabling neuromuscular disease: confined to a wheelchair, unable to write, and with severely impaired speech, he carries out his mathematical calculations mentally and communicates them in a developed form. Hawking's life and work are a triumph over severe physical disability, and his book *A Brief History of Time* (1988) has proved a popular best seller.

Hawkins[1] /ˈhɔːkɪnz/, Coleman Randolph (1904–69), American jazz saxophonist. During the 1920s and 1930s he was influential in making the tenor saxophone popular as a jazz instrument; playing with the Fletcher Henderson band (1923–34), he used a stiff reed which enabled him to be heard as a soloist over the band. His playing was characterized by its deep and rich expressive tone.

Hawkins[2] /ˈhɔːkɪnz/, Sir John (also **Hawkyns**) (1532–95), English sailor. In the 1560s and early 1570s he became involved in the slave trade and participated in early privateering raids in the Spanish West Indies. He was appointed treasurer of the Elizabethan navy in 1573 and played an important part in building up the fleet which defeated the Spanish Armada in 1588. He died at sea during an unsuccessful expedition to the West Indies.

Hawks /hɔːks/, Howard (1896–1977), American film director, producer, and screenwriter. He entered the film industry in 1922, directing and writing the screenplay for his first film in 1926. Over the next forty years he directed some of the most famous stars in comedies, westerns, musicals, and gangster films. His best-known films include *Scarface* (1931), *The Big Sleep* (1946), *Gentlemen Prefer Blondes* (1953), and *Rio Bravo* (1959).

Hawksmoor /ˈhɔːksmʊə(r), -mɔː(r)/, Nicholas (1661–1736), English architect. He began his career at the age of 18 as a clerk to Sir Christopher Wren, and from 1690 worked with Vanbrugh at Castle Howard and Blenheim Palace. In 1711 he was commissioned to design six London churches; notable examples include St Mary Woolnooth (1716–24) and St George's, Bloomsbury (1716–30).

Hawkyns see Hawkins[2].

Haworth /ˈhaʊwəθ/, Sir Walter Norman (1883–1950), English organic chemist. He was a pioneer in carbohydrate chemistry, making major contributions to understanding the structure and classification of sugars and polysaccharides. His book *The Constitution of the Sugars* (1929) became a standard work. Haworth also determined the structure of vitamin C and later synthesized it, the first person to make a vitamin

artificially. He shared the Nobel Prize for chemistry in 1937.

Hawthorne /ˈhɔːθɔːn/, Nathaniel (1804–64), American novelist and short-story writer. Hawthorne's New England Puritan background is evident in much of his fiction, which uses allegory and symbolism to explore themes of hereditary guilt, sin, and morality. His works include collections of short stories, such as *Twice-Told Tales* (1837), and the novels *The Scarlet Letter* (1850) and *The House of Seven Gables* (1851). He also wrote a number of books for children, including *Tanglewood Tales* (1853).

Hay /heɪ/, Will(iam Thomson) (1888–1949), English actor and comedian. Regarded as a master of comic timing, he is remembered for his screen characterizations of grudging and inadequate authority, especially that of the seedy, blustering, and ineffectual schoolmaster. His seventeen films include *Oh, Mr Porter!* (1937), *The Goose Steps Out* (1942), and his last, *My Learned Friend* (1944).

Haydn /ˈhaɪd(ə)n/, Franz Joseph (1732–1809), Austrian composer. He was a major exponent of the classical style and a teacher of Mozart and Beethoven. In 1761 he joined the household of the Hungarian Prince Esterházy as musical director, a post which he held for nearly thirty years and which was conducive to his prolific output and his development of musical forms. His work comprises more than 100 symphonies and many string quartets and keyboard sonatas, and he played a significant role in the development of the symphony and the string quartet in their classical four-movement forms. His choral music includes twelve masses and the oratorios *The Creation* (1796–8) and *The Seasons* (1799–1801).

Hayek /ˈhaɪjek/, Friedrich August von (1899–1992), Austrian-born economist. He is known as a leading advocate of the free market and a critic of government intervention and Keynesian economics. His book *The Road to Serfdom* (1944) linked state economic control with the loss of individual liberty, a topic he became increasingly concerned with in his later writings. He held various academic posts in Austria, the UK, and the US, and became a British citizen in 1938. He shared the Nobel Prize for economics in 1974.

Hayes /heɪz/, Rutherford B(irchard) (1822–93), American Republican statesman, 19th President of the US 1877–81. His administration brought the Reconstruction era in the South to an end; power returned from Federal government to white southern leaders, who then introduced a policy of racial segregation.

Hayworth /ˈheɪwəθ/, Rita (born Margarita Carmen Cansino) (1918–87), American actress and dancer. She began her career as a dancer at the age of 12 and made her screen début in 1935. Hayworth achieved stardom with a succession of film musicals including *Cover Girl* (1944). She also played leading roles in several films of the *film noir* genre, notably *Gilda* (1946) and *The Lady from Shanghai* (1948), in which she co-starred with her second husband Orson Welles.

Hazlitt /ˈhæzlɪt, ˈheɪz-/, William (1778–1830), English essayist and critic. From about 1812 he wrote many articles on diverse subjects for several periodicals, including the *Edinburgh Review* and the *Morning Chronicle*; his essays were collected in *Table Talk* (1821–2) and *The Plain Speaker* (1826). Among his critical works are *Lectures on the English Poets* (1818) and *The Spirit of the Age* (1825). His style, marked by clarity and conviction, brought a new vigour to English prose writing.

H.D. the pseudonym used by Hilda Doolittle.

Head /hed/, Edith (born 1907), American costume designer. She joined Paramount studios in 1923, and worked on films ranging from westerns to musicals and comedies. She was awarded Oscars for costume design in several films, including *All About Eve* (1950). Head later worked for Universal, where she won a further Oscar for the costumes in *The Sting* (1973).

Heaney /ˈhiːnɪ/, Seamus (Justin) (born 1939), Irish poet. He was born in Northern Ireland and his early poetry, such as *Death of a Naturalist* (1966), reflects the rural life of his youth. In 1972 he took Irish citizenship; the same year saw a marked change in his poetry, which began to deal with wider social and cultural themes. Later collections include *North* (1975), which deals with the conflict in Northern Ireland, and *The Haw Lantern* (1987). He was awarded the Nobel Prize for literature in 1995.

Hearst /hɜːst/, William Randolph (1863–1951), American newspaper publisher and tycoon. He is noted for his introduction of

large headlines, sensational crime reporting, and other features designed to increase circulation; his innovations revolutionized American journalism. At the peak of his fortunes in the mid-1930s he had acquired a number of newspapers and magazines, radio stations, and two film companies. He was the model for the central character of Orson Welles's film *Citizen Kane* (1941).

Heath /hi:θ/, Sir Edward (Richard George) (born 1916), British Conservative statesman, Prime Minister 1970–4. In 1973 his long-standing commitment to European unity was realized when Britain joined the European Economic Community. His premiership was marked by problems of inflation and balance of payments (exacerbated by a marked increase in oil prices in 1973); attempts to restrain wage rises led to widespread strikes. After a second national coal strike Heath called an election to strengthen his position, but was defeated.

Heaviside /'hevɪ,saɪd/, Oliver (1850–1925), English physicist and electrical engineer. His theoretical contributions improved long-distance telephone communication and had significance to both cable and wireless telegraphy. He studied inductance, introduced the concept of impedance, and pioneered the use of calculus for dealing with the properties of electrical networks. In 1902 he suggested (independently of A. E. Kennelly) the existence of a layer in the atmosphere responsible for reflecting radio waves back to earth. It is now known as the Heaviside or Kennelly–Heaviside layer, or the E region of the ionosphere.

Hegel /'heɪg(ə)l/, Georg Wilhelm Friedrich (1770–1831), German philosopher. His philosophy represents a complex system of thought with far-reaching influences and diverse applications. He is especially known for his three-stage process of dialectical reasoning (set out in his *Science of Logic*, 1812–16), which underlies his idealist concepts of historical development and the evolution of ideas; Marx based his theory of dialectical materialism on this aspect of Hegel's work. Other major works include *The Phenomenology of Mind* (1807), which describes the progression of the human mind from consciousness through self-consciousness, reason, spirit, and religion to absolute knowledge.

Heidegger /'haɪ,degə(r)/, Martin (1889–1976), German philosopher. In *Being and Time* (1927) he examines the setting of human existence in the world. He regards *Angst* (dread) as a fundamental part of human consciousness, a symptom of the gravity of the human situation with its radical freedom of choice and awareness of death. Consequently human beings are continually attempting to escape their destiny, either by disguising it or by distracting their attention from its inevitability. Although he did not consider himself an existentialist, his work had a significant influence on existentialist philosophers such as Jean-Paul Sartre.

Heine /'haɪnə/, (Christian Johann) Heinrich (born Harry Heine) (1797–1856), German poet. His reputation rests on his lyric poetry, particularly that in *Das Buch der Lieder* (1827), much of which was set to music by Schumann and Schubert. In 1830 Heine emigrated to Paris, where his works became more political; they include *Zur Geschichte der Religion und Philosophie in Deutschland* (1834), a witty and savage attack on German thought and literature, and his two verse satires *Atta Troll* (1843) and *Deutschland* (1844).

Heinz /haɪnz/, Henry John (1844–1919), American food manufacturer. In 1869 he established a family firm for the manufacture and sale of processed foods. Heinz devised the marketing slogan '57 Varieties' in 1896 and erected New York's first electric sign to promote his company's pickles in 1900. By the turn of the century, his firm was one of the largest in the US; since his death, it has become a major multinational company.

Heisenberg /'haɪz(ə)n,bɜ:g/, Werner Karl (1901–76), German mathematical physicist and philosopher, who developed a system of quantum mechanics based on matrix algebra. For this and his discovery of the allotropic forms of hydrogen he was awarded the 1932 Nobel Prize for physics. He stated his famous uncertainty principle (that the momentum and position of a particle cannot both be precisely determined at the same time) in 1927.

Helena, St /'helɪnə/ (AD c.255–c.330), Roman empress and mother of Constantine the Great. She was a convert to Christianity and in 326 visited the Holy Land, where she founded basilicas on the Mount of Olives and at Bethlehem. Later tradition ascribes to her the finding of the cross on which Christ was crucified. Feast day (in

the Eastern Church) 21 May; (in the Western Church) 18 August.

Heliogabalus /ˌhiːliəˈgæbələs/ (also **Elagabalus** /ˌelə-/) (born Varius Avitus Bassianus) (AD 204–22), Roman emperor 218–22. He took his name from the Syro-Phoenician sun-god Elah-Gabal, whose hereditary priest he was. During his reign he became notorious for his dissipated lifestyle and neglect of state affairs; he and his mother were both murdered.

Heller /ˈhelə(r)/, Joseph (born 1923), American novelist. His experiences in the US air force during the Second World War inspired his best-known novel *Catch-22* (1961), an absurdist black comedy satirizing war. The book's hero tries to avoid combat duty by pleading insanity, only to be told that anyone wishing to avoid combat must be sane and therefore fit to fight; the novel's title has passed into the language as a name for a dilemma that is inescapable because of two mutually incompatible but necessary conditions.

Hellman /ˈhelmən/, Lillian (Florence) (1907–84), American dramatist. She gained her first success with *The Children's Hour* (1934), which was followed by plays such as *The Little Foxes* (1939) and the anti-Fascist *Watch on the Rhine* (1941). Hellman was a socialist and a feminist, and her plays frequently reflect her political concerns. For more than thirty years she lived with the detective-story writer Dashiell Hammett; both were blacklisted during the McCarthy era.

Helmholtz /ˈhelmhɒlts/, Hermann Ludwig Ferdinand von (1821–94), German physiologist and physicist. His investigation of animal heat led to his formulation of the principle of the conservation of energy in 1847. He produced two studies on sense perception: first with physiological optics (in the course of which he invented the ophthalmoscope), and then with physiological acoustics. Other achievements include his attempts to measure the speed of nerve impulses, and his studies of vortex motion in hydrodynamics and the properties of oscillating electric currents. He also contributed to non-Euclidean geometry.

Helmont /ˈhelmɒnt/, Joannes Baptista van (1577–1644), Belgian chemist and physician. He made early studies on the conservation of matter, was the first to distinguish gases, and coined the word *gas*. Having failed to realize that green plants take in carbon dioxide, he concluded that they are composed entirely of water.

Héloïse /ˌeləʊˈiːz/ (1098–1164), French abbess. She is chiefly remembered for her passionate but tragic love affair with Abelard, which began after she became his pupil (at the instigation of her uncle, Fulbert) c.1118. She gave birth to a son, after which the two were secretly married; when the affair came to light relatives of Héloïse castrated Abelard, while Héloïse was forced to enter a convent. She later became abbess of Paraclete. (See also ABELARD.)

Helpmann /ˈhelpmən/, Sir Robert (Murray) (1909–86), Australian ballet-dancer, choreographer, director, and actor. Coming to England in 1933, he joined the Vic-Wells Ballet and in 1935 began a long partnership with Margot Fonteyn. Helpmann was noted for his dramatic ability and for his strongly theatrical choreography; his own ballets include *Comus* and *Hamlet* (both 1942).

Hemingway /ˈhemɪŋˌweɪ/, Ernest (Miller) (1899–1961), American writer. After the First World War he lived in Paris, where he came into contact with writers such as Ezra Pound and worked as a journalist before publishing short stories and then novels. His early novels reflect the disillusionment of the postwar 'lost generation'; they include *The Sun Also Rises* (1926) and *A Farewell to Arms* (1929). During the Second World War he joined in the D-Day landings as a war correspondent. In Hemingway's later works there is a developing theme of the strength and dignity of the human spirit; the most famous are *For Whom the Bell Tolls* (1940) and *The Old Man and the Sea* (1952). He was awarded the Nobel Prize for literature in 1954.

Hendrix /ˈhendrɪks/, Jimi (born James Marshall Hendrix) (1942–70), American rock guitarist and singer. Remembered for the flamboyance and originality of his improvisations, he greatly widened the scope of the electric guitar. He gave notable live performances with his groups, playing with the Jimi Hendrix Experience at the Monterey pop festival (1967) and with the Band of Gypsies at the Woodstock festival (1969). His best-known singles include 'Purple Haze' (1967) and 'All Along the Watchtower' (1968).

Hendry /ˈhendrɪ/, Stephen (Gordon) (born 1969), Scottish snooker player. He made his professional début in 1985, becoming the

youngest world snooker champion in 1990. He regained the title in 1992 and held it until 1996, when he won his sixth championship. He was the first player to win all nine world-ranking tournaments and in 1996 held the record for the most breaks over 100.

Hengist /'heŋgɪst/ (died 488), semi-mythological Jutish leader. He and his brother Horsa (died 455) are said by Bede to have been invited to Britain by the British king Vortigern in 449 to assist in defeating the Picts, and later to have established an independent Anglo-Saxon kingdom in Kent. The historicity of the brothers has been questioned, and they may have been mythological figures (their names mean 'gelding' and 'horse').

Henri /'henrɪ/, Robert (1865–1929), American painter. He was an advocate of realism and believed that the artist must be a social force; as a teacher at the New York School of Art (1898–1928), he encouraged his students to turn away from academicism and towards a realistic depiction of everyday life. The Ashcan School of painters was formed largely as a result of his influence.

Henrietta Maria /ˌhenrɪˌetə məˈriːə/ (1609–69), daughter of Henry IV of France, queen consort of Charles I of England 1625–49. Her Roman Catholicism heightened public anxieties about the court's religious sympathies and was a contributory cause of the English Civil War. From 1644 she lived mainly in France.

Henry[1] /'henrɪ/ the name of eight kings of England:
Henry I (1068–1135), youngest son of William I, reigned 1100–35. On the death of his brother, William II, Henry seized the throne in the absence of his other brother, Robert of Normandy; Henry conquered Normandy in 1105. After his only son was drowned in 1120 there were problems with the succession, and although Henry extracted an oath of loyalty to his daughter Matilda from the barons in 1127, his death was followed almost immediately by the outbreak of civil war.
Henry II (1133–89), son of Matilda, reigned 1154–89. The first Plantagenet king, Henry restored order after the reigns of Stephen and Matilda, added Anjou and Aquitaine to the English possessions in France, established his rule in Ireland, and forced the king of Scotland to acknowledge him as

overlord of that kingdom. Henry was less successful in reducing the power of the Church; opposition to his policies was led by Thomas à Becket, who was eventually murdered by four of Henry's knights.
Henry III (1207–72), son of John, reigned 1216–72. Until Henry declared himself of age to rule personally in 1227, his regent the Earl of Pembroke kept the rebellious barons in check, but afterwards the king's ineffectual government caused widespread discontent, ending in Simon de Montfort's defeat and capture of the king in 1264. Although Henry was restored after the defeat of the rebels a year later, real power resided with his son, who eventually succeeded him as Edward I.
Henry IV (known as Henry Bolingbroke) (1367–1413), son of John of Gaunt, reigned 1399–1413. He returned from exile in 1399 to overthrow Richard II and establish the Lancastrian dynasty. His reign was scarred by rebellion, both in Wales and in the north, where the Percy family raised several uprisings. Although Henry defeated Sir Henry Percy ('Hotspur') in 1403, the Percy threat did not abate until the head of the family was killed in 1408.
Henry V (1387–1422), son of Henry IV, reigned 1413–22. He renewed the Hundred Years War soon after coming to the throne and defeated the French at Agincourt in 1415. By the Treaty of Troyes (1420) Henry was named successor to Charles VI of France and betrothed to his daughter Catherine of Valois. When the Dauphin repudiated the treaty, Henry returned to France but fell ill and died, leaving his infant son to inherit the throne.
Henry VI (1421–71), son of Henry V, reigned 1422–61 and 1470–1. Succeeding his father while still an infant, Henry VI proved to have a recurrent mental illness which made him unfit to rule effectively on his own. During his reign the Hundred Years War with France was finally lost, and government by the monarchy, in the hands of a series of regents and noble favourites, became increasingly unpopular. In the 1450s opposition coalesced round the House of York, and, after intermittent civil war between the followers of that House and those of the House of Lancaster (the Wars of the Roses), Henry was deposed in 1461 by Edward IV. In 1470 Henry briefly regained his throne following a Lancastrian uprising, but was deposed again and murdered soon after.
Henry VII (known as Henry Tudor) (1457–

1509), the first Tudor king, son of Edmund Tudor, Earl of Richmond, reigned 1485–1509. Although he was the grandson of Owen Tudor, it was through his mother, a great-granddaughter of John of Gaunt, that he inherited the Lancastrian claim to the throne. Having grown up in exile in France, Henry returned to England in 1485 and ascended the throne after defeating Richard III at Bosworth Field. Threatened in the early years of his reign by a series of Yorkist plots, Henry eventually established an unchallenged Tudor dynasty, dealing ruthlessly with other claimants to the throne. As king he continued the strengthening of royal government commenced by his Yorkist predecessors.

Henry VIII (1491–1547), son of Henry VII, reigned 1509–47. Henry had six wives (Catherine of Aragon, Anne Boleyn, Jane Seymour, Anne of Cleves, Catherine Howard, Katherine Parr), two of whom he had executed and two of whom he divorced. His efforts to divorce his first wife, Catherine of Aragon, which were opposed by the pope, led to England's break with the Roman Catholic Church and indirectly to the establishment of Protestantism. Henry's ensuing dissolution of the monasteries not only destroyed most of the remaining vestiges of the old religious Establishment but also changed the pattern of land ownership. The final years of Henry's reign were marked by wars and rebellion.

Henry[2] /ˈhenrɪ/ (known as Henry the Navigator) (1394–1460), Portuguese prince. The third son of John I of Portugal, he was a leading patron of voyages of exploration, from which he earned his title. He established a school of navigation at Cape St Vincent and organized and funded many voyages of discovery, most notably south along the African coast. The efforts of his captains, who reached as far south as Cape Verde and the Azores, laid the groundwork for later Portuguese imperial expansion south-east round Africa to the Far East.

Henry[3] /ˈhenrɪ/ the name of seven kings of the Germans, six of whom were also Holy Roman emperors:
Henry I (known as Henry the Fowler) (c.876–936), reigned 919–36. As duke of Saxony, he was elected king by the nobles of Saxony and Franconia following the death of Conrad I (903–18). He waged war successfully against the Slavs in Brandenburg, the Magyars, and the Danes, from

whom he gained the territory of Schleswig in 934.
Henry II (known as Saint Henry) (973–1024), reigned 1002–24, Holy Roman emperor 1014–24.
Henry III (1017–56), reigned 1039–56, Holy Roman emperor 1046–56. He brought stability and prosperity to the empire, defeating the Czechs in 1041 and fixing the frontier between Austria and Hungary in 1043. A devout Christian, he introduced religious reforms, attacked corruption in the Church, and strengthened the papacy, securing the appointment of four successive German popes.
Henry IV (1050–1106), son of Henry III, reigned 1056–1105, Holy Roman emperor 1084–1105. Following the end of his regency in 1065 he came into increasing conflict with Pope Gregory VII (c.1020–85), which culminated in 1076 when Henry called a council to depose the Pope. Gregory retaliated by excommunicating Henry and absolving his subjects from their oaths of loyalty to him. In 1077 Henry obtained absolution by doing penance before Gregory at Canossa in Italy, and spent the next three years waging war on his rebellious subjects. He finally managed to depose Gregory in 1084, being crowned emperor by his successor in the same year.
Henry V (1086–1125), reigned 1099–1125, Holy Roman emperor 1111–25.
Henry VI (1165–97), reigned 1169–97, Holy Roman emperor 1191–7.
Henry VII (c.1269/74–1313), reigned 1308–13, Holy Roman emperor 1312–13.

Henry[4] /ˈhenrɪ/, O. (pseudonym of William Sydney Porter) (1862–1910), American short-story writer. He was jailed for embezzlement in 1898 and started writing short stories in prison under his pseudonym. After his release in 1902 he published his first volume, *Cabbages and Kings* (1904). He was a prolific and popular writer whose humorous, ironic stories of everyday life depend on coincidence and twists. His other collections include *The Voice of the City* (1908) and *Waifs and Strays* (published posthumously in 1917).

Henry IV /ˈhenrɪ, French ɑ̃ri/ (known as Henry of Navarre) (1553–1610), king of France 1589–1610. As king of Navarre, Henry was the leader of Huguenot forces in the latter stages of the French Wars of Religion, but on succeeding the Catholic Henry III he became Catholic himself in order to guarantee peace. He founded the

Bourbon dynasty, established religious freedom with the Edict of Nantes (1598), and restored order after prolonged civil war. He was assassinated by a Catholic fanatic.

Henry Bolingbroke, Henry IV of England (see HENRY¹).

Henry the Fowler, Henry I, king of the Germans (see HENRY³).

Henry Tudor, Henry VII of England (see HENRY¹).

Henze /'hentsə/, Hans Werner (born 1926), German composer and conductor. His musical style is diverse, displaying a respect for classical forms such as the sonata and influenced by both Italian opera and serialism. His many works include *The Raft of the Medusa* (1968, a requiem for Che Guevara), the operas *We Come to the River* (1974–6) and *The English Cat* (1982), seven symphonies, and ballet and chamber music.

Hepburn¹ /'hepbɜːn/, Audrey (1929–93), British actress, born in Belgium. After pursuing a career as a stage and film actress in England, she moved to Hollywood, where she starred in such films as *Roman Holiday* (1953), for which she won an Oscar, and *War and Peace* (1956). She is perhaps best known for her performance as Eliza Doolittle in the film musical *My Fair Lady* (1964).

Hepburn² /'hepbɜːn/, Katharine (born 1909), American actress. After her screen début in 1932 she went on to star in a wide range of films, including many in which she formed a partnership with Spencer Tracy. Her films include *The Philadelphia Story* (1940), *Woman of the Year* (1942), *The African Queen* (1951), and *On Golden Pond* (1981), for which she won her fourth Oscar.

Hepplewhite /'hep(ə)lˌwaɪt/, George (died 1786), English cabinet-maker and furniture designer. None of his furniture has been identified, and his fame depends on the posthumously published book of his designs, *The Cabinet-Maker and Upholsterer's Guide* (1788). This contains almost 300 designs which sum up the neoclassical taste of the period in pieces that are characterized by their light and elegant lines.

Hepworth /'hepwəθ/, Dame (Jocelyn) Barbara (1903–75), English sculptor. A pioneer of abstraction in British sculpture, in the 1930s she worked chiefly in wood and

stone, using forms suggested by the inherent qualities of these materials and assimilating them to organic forms or to the human figure. From the 1950s onwards she also worked in bronze, producing simple monumental works for landscape and architectural settings. Her works include the nine-piece group *The Family of Man* (1972).

Heraclitus /ˌherəˈklaɪtəs/ (*c.*500 BC), Greek philosopher. He regarded the universe as a ceaselessly changing conflict of opposites, all things being in a harmonious process of constant change, and held that fire, the type of this constant change, is their origin. He believed that the mind derives a false idea of the permanence of the external world from the passing impressions of experience.

Herbert¹ /'hɜːbət/, Sir A(lan) P(atrick) (1890–1970), English writer and politician. He was a writer of versatility and humour who contributed to the magazine *Punch* for many years, wrote libretti for a number of comic operas, and published a number of novels. He also campaigned for several causes, most notably the reform of the divorce laws; as Independent MP for Oxford University (1935–50) he was responsible for introducing the Matrimonial Causes Act (1937), which radically amended the legislation.

Herbert² /'hɜːbət/, George (1593–1633), English metaphysical poet. In 1630 he became the vicar of Bemerton, near Salisbury, after a brief time spent as MP for Montgomery (1624–5). His devout religious verse is pervaded by simple piety and reflects the spiritual conflicts he experienced before submitting his will to God. His poems are marked by metrical versatility and homely imagery; most were published just after his death in *The Temple: Sacred Poems and Private Ejaculations*.

Hereward the Wake /'herɪwəd, weɪk/ (11th century), semi-legendary Anglo-Saxon rebel leader. Although little is known of Hereward's life beyond what can be found in literary accounts of dubious reliability, he is remembered as a leader of Anglo-Saxon resistance to William I's new Norman regime, and was apparently responsible for an uprising centred on the Isle of Ely in 1070.

Hero /'hɪərəʊ/ (known as Hero of Alexandria) (1st century), Greek mathematician and inventor. His surviving works are im-

portant as a source for ancient practical mathematics and mechanics. He described a number of hydraulic, pneumatic, and other mechanical devices designed both for utility and amusement, including elementary applications of the power of steam.

Herod /'herəd/ the name of four rulers of ancient Palestine:

Herod the Great (c.74–4 BC), ruled 37–4 BC. He built the palace of Masada and rebuilt the Temple in Jerusalem. Jesus is thought to have been born during his reign; according to the New Testament (Matt. 2:16), he ordered the massacre of the innocents.

Herod Antipas (22 BC–AD c.40), son of Herod the Great, tetrarch of Galilee and Peraea 4 BC–AD 40. He married Herodias and was responsible for the beheading of John the Baptist. According to the New Testament (Luke 23:7), Pilate sent Jesus to be questioned by him before the Crucifixion.

Herod Agrippa I (10 BC–AD 44), grandson of Herod the Great, king of Judaea AD 41–4. He imprisoned St Peter and put St James the Great to death.

Herod Agrippa II (AD 27–c.93), son of Herod Agrippa I, king of various territories in northern Palestine 50–c.93. He presided over the trial of St Paul (Acts 25:13 ff.).

Herodotus /hɪ'rɒdətəs/ (known as 'the Father of History') (5th century BC), Greek historian. His *History* tells of the Persian Wars of the early 5th century BC, with an account of the earlier history of the Persian empire and its relations with the Greeks to explain the origins of the conflict. He was the first historian to collect his materials systematically, test their accuracy to a certain extent, and arrange them in a well-constructed and vivid narrative.

Herophilus /hɪə'rɒfiləs/ (4th–3rd centuries BC), Greek anatomist, regarded as the father of human anatomy. Based in Alexandria, he made fundamental discoveries concerning the anatomy of the brain, eye, and reproductive organs, and some of his terms are still in use. Herophilus distinguished nerves from tendons, recognizing that nerves are connected to the brain and that they can be either sensory or motor in function. He also distinguished between veins and arteries, showing that they contain blood, and carried out the first systematic study of the pulse. None of his works survive.

Herrick /'herɪk/, Robert (1591–1674), English poet. He is best known for *Hesperides*, a collection of poems published in 1648, which contained a section of religious poems, *Noble Numbers*. His secular poems, which deal chiefly with country rituals, folklore, and love, show a clear debt to the classical poets, particularly Horace and Catullus; notable examples include 'To the Virgins, To Make Much of Time' and 'Cherry Ripe'.

Herriot /'herɪət/, James (pseudonym of James Alfred Wight) (1916–95), English short-story writer and veterinary surgeon. His experiences at work as a vet in North Yorkshire inspired a series of stories, collected in *If Only They Could Talk* (1970), *All Creatures Great and Small* (1972), and *The Lord God Made Them All* (1981), which were made into a British television series as well as a number of films.

Herschel[1] /'hɜːʃ(ə)l/, Sir (Frederick) William (1738–1822), German-born British astronomer, the father of stellar astronomy. He was a skilful telescope maker whose painstaking cataloguing of the skies resulted in the discovery of the planet Uranus. His unsuccessful attempts to measure the distances of the stars from the earth convinced him of their remoteness, while his mapping of stellar distributions suggested to him that the sun was a member of a great star system forming the disc of the Milky Way. He was elected first president of the Royal Astronomical Society in 1820.

Herschel[2] /'hɜːʃ(ə)l/, Sir John (Frederick William) (1792–1871), British astronomer and physicist, son of William Herschel. He extended the sky survey to the southern hemisphere, cataloguing many new clusters and nebulae. He carried out pioneering work in photography, to which he introduced the words *positive* and *negative*, and also made contributions to meteorology and geophysics.

Hertz /hɜːts/, Heinrich Rudolf (1857–94), German physicist and pioneer of radio communication. He worked for a time as Hermann Helmholtz's assistant in Berlin, and in 1886 began studying the electromagnetic waves that James Maxwell had predicted. He demonstrated them experimentally, and also showed that they behaved like light and radiant heat, thus proving that these phenomena, too, were electromagnetic. In 1889 he was appointed

professor of physics at Bonn; he died of blood-poisoning at the early age of 37.

Herzl /'hɜːts(ə)l/, Theodor (1860–1904), Hungarian-born journalist, dramatist, and Zionist leader. He worked for most of his life as a writer and journalist in Vienna, advocating the establishment of a Jewish state in Palestine; in 1897 he founded the Zionist movement, of which he was the most influential statesman.

Herzog /'hɜːtsʊg/, Werner (born Werner Stipetic) (born 1942), German film director. He occupied a leading position in German cinema in the 1970s. His first feature, *Signs of Life* (1967), displays themes of remoteness in time and space that remained dominant elements throughout his films. Among his other films are *Aguirre, Wrath of God* (1973), *The Enigma of Kaspar Hauser* (1974), and *Fitzcarraldo* (1982).

Hesiod /'hiːsɪəd/ (c.700 BC), Greek poet. He is one of the earliest known Greek poets and is often linked or contrasted with Homer as the other leading writer of early epic verse. His hexametric poem the *Theogony* deals with the origin and genealogies of the gods; his *Works and Days* contains moral and practical advice for living an honest life of (chiefly agricultural) work, and was the chief model for later ancient didactic poetry.

Hess[1] /hes/, Dame Myra (1890–1965), English pianist. She was noted for her performances of the music of Schumann, Beethoven, Mozart, and Bach. Her many piano transcriptions of baroque music include 'Jesu, Joy of Man's Desiring' from Bach's Cantata No. 147.

Hess[2] /hes/, (Walther Richard) Rudolf (1894–1987), German Nazi politician. He was deputy leader of the Nazi Party (1934–41) and a close friend of Hitler. In 1941, secretly and on his own initiative, he parachuted into Scotland to negotiate peace with Britain. He was imprisoned for the duration of the war, and after his conviction at the Nuremberg war trials was sentenced to life imprisonment in Spandau prison, where he died.

Hess[3] /hes/, Victor Francis (born Victor Franz Hess) (1883–1964), Austrian-born American physicist. He worked on atmospheric electricity and radioactivity. After making several balloon flights he was able to show that some ionizing radiation was extraterrestrial in origin, but did not come from the sun. The high-energy particles responsible were later termed *cosmic rays*, and their study led to the discovery of the positron by C. D. Anderson. They shared the Nobel Prize for physics in 1936.

Hesse /hes, 'hesə/, Hermann (1877–1962), German-born Swiss novelist and poet. In 1911 he visited India, where he became interested in Indian mysticism; this experience, together with his involvement with Jungian analysis in 1916–17, had a marked effect on his work, which emphasizes spiritual values as expressed in Eastern religion. His novels — titles include *Siddhartha* (1922), *Der Steppenwolf* (1927), and *The Glass Bead Game* (1943) — met with renewed interest in the 1960s and 1970s. Hesse was awarded the Nobel Prize for literature in 1946.

Hevesy /'hevəʃɪ/, George Charles de (1885–1966), Hungarian-born radiochemist. He worked in seven different European countries, and made fundamental contributions to the study of radioisotopes, an interest he acquired while working with Sir Ernest Rutherford in Manchester. He invented the technique of labelling with isotopic tracers, for which he was awarded the Nobel Prize for chemistry in 1943. Hevesy was also co-discoverer of the element hafnium (1923).

Heyer /'heɪə(r)/, Georgette (1902–74), English novelist. She is noted especially for her historical novels, which include numerous Regency romances, such as *Regency Buck* (1935) and *Faro's Daughter* (1941). She also wrote detective stories, including *Envious Casca* (1941) and *Detection Unlimited* (1953).

Heyerdahl /'heɪəˌdɑːl/, Thor (born 1914), Norwegian anthropologist. He is noted for his ocean voyages in primitive craft to demonstrate his theories of cultural diffusion. His first such voyage, in 1947, was an attempt to show that Polynesian peoples could originally have been migrants from South America. His raft (the *Kon-Tiki*) successfully made the journey from Peru to the islands east of Tahiti. Later journeys included a transatlantic crossing in 1969 from Morocco towards Central America in the *Ra*, a raft made according to an ancient Egyptian design.

Heyhoe-Flint /ˌheɪhəʊˈflɪnt/, Rachel (born 1939), English cricketer. Between 1966 and 1977 she was the captain of the England women's cricket team, leading England to victory in the first Women's World Cup in

1972. She combined her long playing career for England (1960–83) with journalism, and in 1972 became the first woman sports reporter on Independent Television.

Hickok /'hɪkɒk/, James Butler (known as 'Wild Bill Hickok') (1837–76), American frontiersman and marshal. He became a US marshal in the West after the Civil War. The legend of his invincibility in his encounters with frontier desperadoes became something of a challenge to gunmen, and he was murdered at Deadwood, South Dakota.

Hicks /hɪks/, Sir John Richard (1904–89), English economist. He is chiefly remembered for his pioneering work on general economic equilibrium (the theory that economic forces tend to balance one another rather than simply reflect cyclical trends), for which he shared a Nobel Prize with K. J. Arrow in 1972.

Highsmith /'haɪsmɪθ/, Patricia (born Patricia Plangman) (1921–95), American writer of detective fiction. Many of her novels have been made into films, most famously her first novel *Strangers on a Train* (1949), filmed by Alfred Hitchcock in 1951. Her works featuring her psychotic hero Tom Ripley are considered her best. Examples include *The Talented Mr Ripley* (1956) and *Ripley Under Water* (1991).

Hilary, St /'hɪlərɪ/ (*c*.315–*c*.367), French bishop. In *c*.350 he was appointed bishop of Poitiers, in which position he became a leading opponent of the heresy of Arianism. Feast day, 13 January (in the Roman Catholic Church, 14 January).

Hilbert /'hɪlbət/, David (1862–1943), German mathematician. He proved fundamental theorems about rings, collected, systematized, and extended all that was then known about algebraic numbers, and reorganized the axiomatic foundations of geometry. He set potential theory and the theory of integral equations on its modern course with his invention of *Hilbert space* (an infinite-dimensional analogue of Euclidean space), and formulated the formalist philosophy of mathematics and mathematical logic. In 1900 Hilbert proposed twenty-three problems which crystallized mathematical thinking for the next few decades.

Hilda, St /'hɪldə/ (614–80), English abbess. Related to the Saxon kings of Northumbria, around 658 she founded a monastery for both men and women at Whitby. She was one of the leaders of the Celtic Church delegation at the Synod of Whitby, but accepted the eventual decision in favour of Roman rather than Celtic customs. Feast day, 17 November.

Hildegard of Bingen, St /'hɪldə,gɑːd, 'bɪŋən/ (1098–1179), German abbess, scholar, composer, and mystic. A nun of the Benedictine order, she became Abbess of Diessem in 1136, later moving her community to Bingen. She described and illustrated her mystical experiences in *Scivias*, and also wrote poetry and composed sacred music. Her scientific writings covered a range of subjects, including the circulation of the blood and aspects of natural history.

Hill[1] /hɪl/, Benny (born Alfred Hawthorne) (1925–92), English comedian. After working in clubs and seaside shows he made an early and successful transition to television in 1949, being named TV Personality of the Year in 1954. His risqué humour, as seen in the series of programmes *The Benny Hill Show*, had an international appeal.

Hill[2] /hɪl/, Damon (born 1960), English motor-racing driver, son of Graham Hill. He was Formula One world champion in 1996, having been runner-up in 1994.

Hill[3] /hɪl/, (Norman) Graham (1929–75), English motor-racing driver. He won the Formula One world championship in 1962 with the BRM team before returning to his original team, Lotus, and becoming world champion again in 1975. He was killed when his plane crashed in north London.

Hill[4] /hɪl/, Octavia (1838–1912), English housing reformer. An active campaigner for the improvement of housing for the poor, she met John Ruskin while working for a Christian Socialist association. In 1864 Ruskin provided financial assistance for Hill to fund the first of several housing projects, the purchase and refurbishment of three London slum houses.

Hill[5] /hɪl/, Sir Rowland (1795–1879), British educationist, administrator, and inventor. He was initially a teacher who introduced a system of self-government at his school in Birmingham and wrote on the challenges of mass education. In the 1830s he invented a rotary printing-press. Hill is chiefly remembered for his introduction of the penny postage-stamp system in 1840;

he later became Secretary to the Post Office (1854–64).

Hillary /'hɪlərɪ/, Sir Edmund (Percival) (born 1919), New Zealand mountaineer and explorer. In 1953 Hillary and Tenzing Norgay were the first people to reach the summit of Mount Everest, as members of a British expedition. Hillary later led the New Zealand contingent of the Commonwealth Trans-Antarctic Expedition (1955–8), organized by Sir Vivian Fuchs.

Himmler /'hɪmlə(r)/, Heinrich (1900–45), German Nazi leader, chief of the SS (1929–45) and of the Gestapo (1936–45). He established and oversaw the programme of systematic genocide of more than 6 million Jews and other disfavoured groups between 1941 and 1945. He was captured by British forces in 1945, and committed suicide by swallowing a cyanide capsule.

Hinault /iːˈnəʊ/, Bernard (born 1954), French racing cyclist. During his professional career he won the Tour de France five times between 1978 and 1985; he also achieved three wins in the Tour of Italy between 1980 and 1985.

Hindemith /'hɪndə,mɪt/, Paul (1895–1963), German composer. His music forms part of the neoclassical trend which began in the 1920s. Hindemith believed that music should have a social purpose and that audiences should participate as well as listen; his *Gebrauchsmusik* ('utility music') compositions are intended for performance by amateurs. A prolific composer, he wrote operas (such as *Mathis der Maler*, 1938), concertos, and orchestral and chamber music. He left Germany in the 1930s after Nazi hostility to his work, eventually settling in the US.

Hindenburg /'hɪndən,bɜːg/, Paul Ludwig von Beneckendorff und von (1847–1934), German Field Marshal and statesman, President of the Weimar Republic 1925–34. He was recalled from retirement at the outbreak of the First World War and appointed Commander-in-Chief of German forces from 1916, directing the war effort in partnership with Erich Ludendorff. He was elected President in 1925 and re-elected in 1932, and was reluctantly persuaded to appoint Hitler as Chancellor in 1933.

Hinshelwood /'hɪnʃ(ə)l,wʊd/, Sir Cyril Norman (1897–1967), English physical chemist. He made fundamental contributions to reaction kinetics in gases and liquids. He later applied the laws of kinetics to bacterial growth, and suggested the role of nucleic acids in protein synthesis. Hinshelwood was simultaneously president of both the Royal Society and the Classical Association. He shared the Nobel Prize for chemistry in 1956.

Hipparchus /hɪˈpɑːkəs/ (*c.*170–after 126 BC) Greek astronomer and geographer, working in Rhodes. His major works are lost, but his astronomical observations were developed by Ptolemy. He constructed the celestial coordinates of 800 stars, indicating their relative brightness, but rejected Aristarchus' hypothesis that the sun is the centre of the planetary system. Hipparchus is best known for his discovery of the precession of the equinoxes. He suggested improved methods of determining latitude and longitude, and is credited with the invention of trigonometry.

Hippocrates /hɪˈpɒkrə,tiːz/ (*c.*460–377 BC), the most famous of all physicians, of whom, paradoxically, almost nothing is known. Referred to briefly by Plato, his name was later attached to a body of ancient Greek medical writings of which probably none was written by him. This collection is so varied that all subsequent physicians have been able to find within it notions that agreed with their own ideas of what medicine and doctors should be. If there are common features of an agreed Hippocratic philosophy, they might be that nature has an innate power of healing, and that diseases are closely linked to the physical environment.

Hirohito /,hɪrəˈhiːtəʊ/ (born Michinomiya Hirohito) (1901–89), emperor of Japan 1926–89. Regarded as the 124th direct descendant of Jimmu, he ruled as a divinity and generally refrained from involvement in politics. In 1945, however, he was instrumental in obtaining his government's agreement to the unconditional surrender which ended the Second World War. He was obliged to renounce his divinity and become a constitutional monarch by the terms of the constitution established in 1946.

Hiss /hɪs/, Alger (1904–96), American public servant. In 1948 he was accused of copying and passing on State Department documents to a Communist. Having protested his innocence before the House Committee on Un-American Activities, Hiss was

charged with perjury, and controversial trials followed. The first resulted in a hung jury, but he was then convicted, and the case led to an upsurge of anti-Communist feeling and the rise of Senator Joseph McCarthy. Hiss was released in 1954.

Hitchcock /'hɪtʃkɒk/, Sir Alfred (Joseph) (1899–1980), English film director. Having established his reputation in Britain in the 1930s with films such as *The Thirty-Nine Steps* (1935) and *The Lady Vanishes* (1938), in 1939 he moved to Hollywood, where his first film was *Rebecca* (1940). Outstanding among his numerous later works are the thrillers *Strangers on a Train* (1951), *Psycho* (1960), with its famous shower murder, and *The Birds* (1963). His films are notable for their ability to generate suspense and for their technical ingenuity.

Hitchens /'hɪtʃɪnz/, Ivon (1893–1979), English painter. His main interest was in landscape, which he represented in an almost abstract style using broad fluid areas of vibrant colour, usually on a long rectangular canvas, as in *Winter Stage* (1936).

Hite /haɪt/, Shere (born 1942), American feminist. She published her research into sex, gender definition, and private life in the groundbreaking work *The Hite Report on Female Sexuality* (1976), which she followed with *The Hite Report on Men and Male Sexuality* (1981), *Women and Love* (1987), and *Hite on the Family* (1994), all based on the anonymous responses of thousands of people to questionnaires.

Hitler /'hɪtlə(r)/, Adolf (1889–1945), Austrian-born Nazi leader, Chancellor of Germany 1933–45. A co-founder of the National Socialist German Workers' Party (which later became known as the Nazi Party) after the First World War, Hitler was imprisoned in 1923 as one of the organizers of an unsuccessful putsch in Munich. While in prison he wrote *Mein Kampf*, an exposition of his political ideas. After his release his powers as an orator soon won prominence for him and the Nazi Party; following his appointment as Chancellor in 1933 he was able to overthrow the Weimar Republic and establish the totalitarian Third Reich, proclaiming himself *Führer*. His expansionist foreign policy precipitated the Second World War, while his fanatical anti-Semitism and desire to create an Aryan German state led to the deaths of millions of Jews. Hitler committed suicide in his Berlin headquarters

as Soviet Allied forces were attacking the city.

Hobbema /'hɒbɪmə/, Meindert (1638–1709), Dutch landscape painter. He was a pupil of Jacob van Ruisdael and was one of the last 17th-century Dutch landscape painters, since demand for such work was diminishing in the late 1660s. His work features a narrow range of favourite subject-matter, often including a water-mill and trees round a pool. Among his best-known paintings is *Avenue at Middelharnis* (1689).

Hobbes /hɒbz/, Thomas (1588–1679), English philosopher. There were two key components in Hobbes's conception of humankind: he was a materialist, claiming that there was no more to the mind than the physical motions discovered by science, and a cynic, holding that human action was motivated entirely by selfish concerns, notably fear of death. His view of society was expressed in his most famous work, *Leviathan* (1651), in which he argued, by means of a version of a social contract theory, that simple rationality made social institutions and even absolute monarchy inevitable.

Hobbs /hɒbz/, Sir John Berry ('Jack') (1882–1963), English cricketer. His career as a batsman in first-class cricket extended from 1905 to 1934, during which time he scored a total of 61,237 runs and 197 centuries. He first played for England in 1907 and went on to make 61 test appearances.

Ho Chi Minh /ˌhəʊ tʃi: 'mɪn/ (born Nguyen That Thanh) (1890–1969), Vietnamese Communist statesman, President of North Vietnam 1954–69. He was a committed nationalist who was instrumental in gaining his country's independence from French rule. He founded the Indo-Chinese Communist Party in 1930, and led the Vietminh in guerrilla warfare against the Japanese during the Second World War. He then fought the French for eight years until their defeat in 1954, when Vietnam was divided into North Vietnam, of which he became President, and South Vietnam. Committed to the creation of a united Communist country, Ho Chi Minh then deployed his forces in the guerrilla struggle that became the Vietnam War.

Hockney /'hɒknɪ/, David (born 1937), English painter and draughtsman. His work of

the early 1960s was associated with the pop art movement; deliberately naive and characterized by an ironic humour, it reflected the influence of graffiti and children's art. While in California in the mid-1960s he produced perhaps his best--known work: a series of paintings, such as *A Bigger Splash* (1967), which depict flat, almost shadowless architecture, lawns, and swimming-pools.

Hodgkin[1] /ˈhɒdʒkɪn/, Sir Alan Lloyd (born 1914), English physiologist. Hodgkin worked mainly at Cambridge University, where he was a research professor from 1952 to 1970. He collaborated with Andrew Huxley on the physiology of nerve transmission, studying chiefly the giant nerve fibres of squid. Hodgkin and Huxley demonstrated that the passage of a nerve impulse involves a movement of sodium and potassium ions associated with a change in the electrical potential of the cell membrane. They were awarded a Nobel Prize in 1963.

Hodgkin[2] /ˈhɒdʒkɪn/, Dorothy (Crowfoot) (1910–94), British chemist. She worked mainly at Oxford, where she developed Sir Lawrence Bragg's X-ray diffraction technique for investigating the structure of crystals and applied it to complex organic compounds. Using this method Hodgkin determined the structures of penicillin (1945), vitamin B_{12} (1956), and (after many years work) the large insulin molecule (1969). She was awarded the Nobel Prize for chemistry in 1964.

Hoe /həʊ/, Richard March (1812–86), American inventor and industrialist. In 1846 he became the first printer to develop a successful rotary press. This greatly increased the speed of printing compared with the use of a flat plate; by 1857 *The Times* had a Hoe press printing 20,000 impressions an hour. This machine had still to be fed with individual cut sheets, but by 1871 Hoe had developed a machine fed from a continuous roll.

Hoffa /ˈhɒfə/, James Riddle ('Jimmy') (1913–c.1975), American trade union leader. He joined the Teamsters union in 1931 and became president in 1957. After investigations for corruption he was imprisoned in 1967 for attempted bribery of a federal court judge, fraud, and looting pension funds. His sentence was commuted by President Nixon and he was given parole in 1971 on condition that he resigned as president of the union. He disappeared in 1975, and is thought to have been murdered.

Hoffman /ˈhɒfmən/, Dustin (Lee) (born 1937), American actor. His first major film was *The Graduate* (1967); he has since appeared in a wide variety of roles, including that of a man pretending to be a woman in the comedy *Tootsie* (1983). Other films include *Midnight Cowboy* (1969) and *Rain Man* (1989), for which he received his second Oscar.

Hoffmann /ˈhɒfmən/, E(rnst) T(heodor) A(madeus) (1776–1822), German novelist, short-story writer, and music critic. He is best known for his extravagantly fantastic stories; his shorter tales appear in collections such as *Phantasiestücke* (1814–15), while longer works include *Elixire des Teufels* (1815–16). His stories provided the inspiration for Offenbach's opera *Tales of Hoffmann* (1881).

Hofmannsthal /ˈhɒfmənsˌtɑːl/, Hugo von (1874–1929), Austrian poet and dramatist. He wrote the libretti for Richard Strauss's operas *Elektra* (1909), *Der Rosenkavalier* (1911), *Ariadne auf Naxos* (1912), and *Arabella* (1933). With Strauss and Max Reinhardt he helped found the Salzburg Festival. His *Jedermann* (1912), a modernized form of a morality play, was first performed at the opening of the festival in 1920.

Hogarth /ˈhəʊgɑːθ/, William (1697–1764), English painter and engraver. He contributed to the development of an English school of painting, both by his criticism of the contemporary taste for foreign artists and by encouraging the establishment of art institutions in England, a process which later culminated in the foundation of the Royal Academy (1768). Notable works include his series of engravings on 'modern moral subjects', such as *A Rake's Progress* (1735) and *Marriage à la Mode* (1743–5), which satirized the vices of both high and low life in 18th-century England.

Hogg /hɒg/, James (1770–1835), Scottish poet. He was a shepherd in the Ettrick Forest whose poetic talent was discovered by Sir Walter Scott; he gained the nickname 'the Ettrick Shepherd'. He made his reputation as a poet with *The Queen's Wake* (1813), but is better known today for his

prose work *The Confessions of a Justified Sinner* (1824).

Hokusai /'həʊkʊˌsaɪ, ˌhəʊkʊ'saɪ/, Katsushika (1760–1849), Japanese painter and wood-engraver. He was a leading artist of the ukiyo-e school who vividly represented many aspects of Japanese everyday life in his woodcuts. His best-known pictures are contained in the ten-volume *Mangwa* (1814–19) and the *Hundred Views of Mount Fuji* (1835). His prints were a significant stylistic influence on the work of impressionist and post-impressionist artists such as Van Gogh.

Holbein /'hɒlbaɪn/, Hans (known as Holbein the Younger) (1497–1543), German painter. He worked in Basle, where he produced the series of woodcuts the *Dance of Death* (c.1523–6), and in England, which he first visited in 1526. In England he became a well-known portraitist, depicting Sir Thomas Cromwell and other prominent courtiers, and painting group portraits such as *The Ambassadors* (1533). In 1536 he was appointed painter to Henry VIII; his commissions included portraits of the king's prospective brides, such as the miniatures *Christina, Duchess of Milan* (1538) and *Anne of Cleves* (1539).

Hölderlin /'hɜːldəˌlɪn/, (Johann Christian) Friedrich (1770–1843), German poet. His early poetry was full of political idealism fostered by the French Revolution, but most of his poems express a romantic yearning for ancient Greek harmony with nature and beauty. While working as a tutor he fell in love with his employer's wife, who is portrayed in his novel *Hyperion* (1797–9). Her death in 1802 exacerbated his already advanced schizophrenic condition.

Holiday /'hɒlɪˌdeɪ/, Billie (born Eleanora Fagan) (1915–59), American jazz singer. Following an early life of poverty and work in a brothel, she became a singer in the clubs of Harlem; in 1933 she began her recording career with Benny Goodman's band and went on to perform with many small jazz groups. Her style was characterized by dramatic intensity and vocal agility, as of a jazz musician playing a solo. Her autobiography *Lady Sings the Blues* (1956) was made into a film in 1972.

Holinshed /'hɒlɪnˌʃed/, Raphael (died c.1580), English chronicler. Although the named compiler of *The Chronicles of England, Scotland and Ireland* (1577), Holinshed in fact wrote only the *Historie of England* and had help with the remainder. In 1587 the work was revised and reissued, and this edition was widely used by Shakespeare and other dramatists.

Hollerith /'hɒlərɪθ/, Herman (1860–1929), American engineer. He invented a tabulating machine using punched cards for computation, an important precursor of the electronic computer. He founded a company in 1896 that later expanded to become the IBM Corporation.

Holly /'hɒlɪ/, Buddy (born Charles Hardin Holley) (1936–59), American rock and roll singer, guitarist, and songwriter. Initially a hillbilly singer, Holly went on to become an important figure in early rock and roll, helping to shape rock guitar styling and being among the first to use a line-up of two guitars, bass, and drums. In 1955 Holly and some friends formed the band known as the Crickets, recording such hits as 'That'll be the Day' and 'Oh Boy' in 1957. The group toured Britain in 1958 (inspiring the name of the Beatles), before Holly left to go solo later the same year. He was killed in a plane crash.

Holmes[1] /həʊmz/, Arthur (1890–1965), English geologist and geophysicist. He pioneered the dating of rocks using isotopic decay, and he was the first to use it to provide absolute dates for the geological time-scale. He was one of the first supporters of the theory of continental drift. His book *Principles of Physical Geology* (1944) became a standard text.

Holmes[2] /həʊmz/, Oliver Wendell (1809–94), American physician and writer. He was professor of anatomy and physiology at Dartmouth College, New Hampshire, where he discovered that puerperal fever was contagious, and then professor of anatomy at Harvard University 1847–82. His humorous writings, both verse and prose, include 'Old Ironsides' (1830) and his 'Breakfast Table' essays. These witty conversational pieces appeared in the *Atlantic Monthly* from 1857 onwards and were collected in four volumes.

Holst /həʊlst/, Gustav (Theodore) (1874–1934), English composer, of Swedish and Russian descent. He made his reputation with the orchestral suite *The Planets* (1914–16), which was an instant success when first performed in 1919. He took inspiration for his music from a range of sources: the *St Paul's Suite* for strings (1913) reflects

his interest in English folk-song, while his enthusiasm for Sanskrit literature resulted in works such as the four sets of *Choral Hymns from the Rig Veda* (1908–12).

Holyoake /ˈhəʊlɪˌəʊk/, Sir Keith (Jacka) (1904–83), New Zealand National Party statesman, Prime Minister 1957 and 1960–72. One of New Zealand's longest-serving statesmen, Holyoake first entered politics in 1932 as the youngest member in the House of Representatives; after two terms as Prime Minister he went on to serve as Governor-General 1977–80.

Home of the Hirsel of Coldstream /ˈhɜːs(ə)l, ˈkəʊldstriːm/, Baron, see DOUGLAS-HOME.

Homer[1] /ˈhəʊmə(r)/ (8th century BC), Greek epic poet. He is traditionally held to be the author of the *Iliad* and the *Odyssey*. Various cities in Ionia claim to be his birthplace, and he is said to have been blind. Modern scholarship has revealed the place of the Homeric poems in a pre-literate oral tradition, in which a succession of bards elaborated the traditional stories of the heroic age; questions of authorship are thus very difficult to answer. In later antiquity Homer was regarded as the greatest and unsurpassable poet, and his poems were constantly used as a model and source by others.

Homer[2] /ˈhəʊmə(r)/, Winslow (1836–1910), American painter. He illustrated magazines such as *Harper's Weekly* (1859–67) before recording scenes from life at the front in the Civil War (for example *Prisoners from the Front*, 1866). He is now best known for his seascapes, such as *Cannon Rock* (1895). His naturalistic style combines imagination and strength, and is considered to express the American pioneering spirit.

Honda /ˈhɒndə/, Soichiro (1906–92), Japanese motor manufacturer. In 1928 he opened his own garage; his first factory, producing piston-rings, was established in 1934. He began motorcycle manufacture in 1948, becoming the world's largest producer. During the 1960s he successfully expanded his operations into car production; the Honda Corporation has since become involved in joint ventures with firms such as the British car manufacturer Rover.

Honecker /ˈhɒnɪkə(r)/, Erich (1912–94), East German Communist statesman, head of state 1976–89. He was appointed First Sec-

retary of the Socialist Unity Party in 1971, becoming effective leader of East Germany in 1973, and head of state (Chairman of the Council of State) three years later. His repressive regime was marked by a close allegiance to the Soviet Union. Honecker was ousted in 1989 after a series of pro-democracy demonstrations. In 1992 he was arrested but proceedings against him for manslaughter and embezzlement were later dropped because of his ill health.

Honegger /ˈhɒnɪgə(r)/, Arthur (1892–1955), French composer, of Swiss descent. He lived and worked chiefly in Paris, where he became a member of the anti-romantic group Les Six. His orchestral work *Pacific 231* (1924), a musical representation of a steam locomotive, brought him his first major success; his work also includes five symphonies (1930–51) and the dramatic oratorio *Joan of Arc at the Stake* (1935).

Hooch, Pieter de, see DE HOOCH.

Hood /hʊd/, Thomas (1799–1845), English poet and humorist. He was the editor of a number of literary magazines and a friend of Charles Lamb, William Hazlitt, and Thomas De Quincey. He wrote much humorous verse but is now chiefly remembered for serious poems such as 'The Song of the Shirt' (1843) and 'The Bridge of Sighs' (1844).

Hooke /hʊk/, Robert (1635–1703), English scientist. He began as Boyle's assistant, and soon became curator of experiments for the new Royal Society. After the Fire of London he was made a surveyor to the City, and designed several of London's prominent buildings. His scientific achievements were many and varied: he proposed an undulating theory of light, formulated the law of elasticity (*Hooke's law*), introduced the term *cell* to biology, postulated elliptical orbits for the earth and moon, and proposed the inverse square law of gravitational attraction. He improved the compound microscope and reflecting telescope, and invented many scientific instruments and mechanical devices.

Hooker /ˈhʊkə(r)/, Sir Joseph Dalton (1817–1911), English botanist and pioneer in plant geography. Following a voyage to the Antarctic he proposed an ancient joining of land between Australia and South America, and from NE India he sent rhododendrons home and later introduced their cultivation. Hooker firmly supported Dar-

win's theories and applied them to plants. His many works include *Genera Plantarum* (1862–83), a classification of plants devised jointly with George Bentham (1800–84). He became director of Kew Gardens on the death of his father Sir William Jackson Hooker (1785–1865), who had greatly extended the royal gardens there, opened them to the public, and founded a museum.

Hoover[1] /'hu:və(r)/, Herbert C(lark) (1874–1964), American Republican statesman, 31st President of the US 1929–33. He first gained prominence for his work in organizing food production and distribution in the US and Europe during and after the First World War. As President he was faced with the long-term problems of the Depression which followed the stock market crash of 1929. He returned to relief work after the Second World War as coordinator of food supplies to avert the threat of postwar famine.

Hoover[2] /'hu:və(r)/, J(ohn) Edgar (1895–1972), American lawyer and director of the FBI 1924–72. Beginning his term of office with the fight against organized crime in the 1920s and 1930s, he went on to be instrumental in reorganizing the FBI into an efficient, scientific law-enforcement agency. However, he came under criticism for the organization's role during the McCarthy era and for its reactionary political stance in the 1960s.

Hoover[3] /'hu:və(r)/, William (Henry) (1849–1932), American industrialist. In 1908 he bought the patent of a lightweight electric cleaning machine from James Murray Spangler, a janitor, and formed the Electric Suction Sweeper Company to manufacture it. The machine proved an international success and in 1910 the company was renamed Hoover.

Hope /həʊp/, Bob (born Leslie Townes Hope) (born 1903), British-born American comedian. His dry allusive style gave him the character of a humorously cowardly incompetent, always cheerfully failing in his attempts to become a romantic hero, particularly in *Road to Singapore* (1940) and the rest of the series of *Road* films (1940–62), in which he starred with Bing Crosby and Dorothy Lamour (1914–96).

Hopkins[1] /'hɒpkɪnz/, Sir Anthony (Philip) (born 1937), Welsh actor. His acting career began on the stage in 1961, with his screen début following in 1967. His films include

The Elephant Man (1980), *The Bounty* (1984), and *The Remains of the Day* (1993). He won an Oscar for his performance in *The Silence of the Lambs* (1991).

Hopkins[2] /'hɒpkɪnz/ Sir Frederick Gowland (1861–1947), English biochemist, considered the father of British biochemistry. He carried out pioneering work on 'accessory food factors' essential to the diet, later called vitamins. Hopkins shared a Nobel Prize in 1929.

Hopkins[3] /'hɒpkɪnz/, Gerard Manley (1844–89), English poet. Influenced at Oxford by John Henry Newman, Hopkins converted to Roman Catholicism in 1866 and became a Jesuit two years later. He wrote little poetry until 1876, when the shipwreck of a vessel carrying nuns and other emigrants to America the previous year inspired him to write 'The Wreck of the Deutschland'. The poem makes bold use of Hopkins's 'sprung rhythm' technique (whereby each foot has one stressed syllable followed by a varying number of unstressed), as do his best-known poems 'Windhover' and 'Pied Beauty', both written in 1877. His work, collected in *Poems* (1918), was published posthumously by his friend Robert Bridges.

Hopper /'hɒpə(r)/, Edward (1882–1967), American realist painter. He supported himself as a commercial illustrator before gaining recognition for his paintings in the 1920s. He is best known for his mature works, such as *Early Sunday Morning* (1930) and *Nighthawks* (1942), depicting scenes from everyday American urban life in which still figures appear in introspective isolation, often in bleak or shabby settings.

Horace /'hɒrɪs/ (full name Quintus Horatius Flaccus) (65–8 BC), Roman poet of the Augustan period. His two books of *Satires* departed from earlier convention with their realism and irony directed at both the satirist and his targets. His *Odes*, displaying a mastery of poetic form in the style of earlier Greek lyric poets, celebrate friendship, love, good wine, and the contentment of a peaceful rural life in contrast to the turmoil of politics and civil war. (Horace had fought with Brutus and Cassius at Philippi in 42.) They were much imitated by later ages, especially by 17th and 18th-century English poets. Horace was also a notable literary critic; his

Ars Poetica influenced John Dryden and his fellow Augustans in their critical writing.

Hordern /'hɔːd(ə)n/, Sir Michael (Murray) (1911–95), English actor. He built a strong reputation in the classical theatre, playing King Lear (1960) and Prospero in the 1978 Stratford production of *The Tempest*. He displayed versatility with acclaimed performances in modern plays such as Tom Stoppard's *Jumpers* (1972) and made a succession of film and television appearances.

Horkheimer /'hɔːkˌhaɪmə(r)/, Max (1895–1973), German philosopher and sociologist. He was director of the Frankfurt Institute for Social Research from 1930 to 1958 and a principal figure in the Frankfurt School of philosophy. His reputation is based on a series of articles written in the 1930s expounding the school's Marxist analysis of modern industrial society and culture; these were collected into the two-volume *Critical Theory* (1968). Other works include *Dialectic of the Enlightenment* (1947), written with his colleague Theodor Adorno.

Hornung /'hɔːnəŋ/, Ernest William (1866–1921), English novelist. He is remembered as the creator of the gentleman burglar Raffles, who first featured in *The Amateur Cracksman* (1899). Hornung was the brother-in-law of Sir Arthur Conan Doyle.

Horowitz /'hɒrəvɪts/, Vladimir (1904–89), Russian pianist. He first toured the US in 1928, and settled there soon afterwards. He was a leading international virtuoso and was best known for his performances of Scarlatti, Liszt, Scriabin, and Prokofiev. His concert career was interrupted by periodic bouts of illness.

Horsa /'hɔːsə/ see HENGIST.

Horta /'ɔːtə/, Victor (1861–1947), Belgian architect. He was a leading figure in art nouveau architecture and worked chiefly in Brussels. His buildings include the Hôtel Tassel (1892), notable for its decorative iron staircase with a slender exposed iron support, and the Maison du Peuple (1896–9), with an innovative curved façade of iron and glass.

Hotspur /'hɒtspɜː(r)/ the nickname of Sir Henry Percy (see PERCY).

Houdini /huːˈdiːnɪ/, Harry (born Erik Weisz) (1874–1926), Hungarian-born American magician and escape artist. In the early 1900s he became famous for his ability to escape from all kinds of bonds and containers, from prison cells to aerially suspended straitjackets.

Housman /'haʊsmən/, A(lfred) E(dward) (1859–1936), English poet and classical scholar. Having failed his final examinations at Oxford University, he worked as a clerk and studied Greek and Latin in his spare time. In 1892 he was appointed professor of Latin at University College, London, on the strength of his classical publications. He is now chiefly remembered for the poems collected in *A Shropshire Lad* (1896), a series of nostalgic verses largely based on ballad forms.

Howard[1] /'haʊəd/, Catherine (c.1521–42), fifth wife of Henry VIII. She married Henry soon after his divorce from Anne of Cleves in 1540, probably at the instigation of her ambitious Howard relatives. She was accused of infidelity, confessed, and was beheaded in 1542.

Howard[2] /'haʊəd/, John (1726–90), English philanthropist and prison reformer. In 1773 his sense of horror at conditions in Bedford jail led him to undertake a tour of British prisons; this culminated the following year in two Acts of Parliament setting down sanitary standards. His work *The State of Prisons in England and Wales* (1777) gave further impetus to the movement for improvements in the design and management of prisons.

Howard[3] /'haʊəd/, John (Winston) (born 1939), Australian Liberal statesman, Prime Minister from 1996. He was elected an MP in 1974 and held several posts in the Cabinet, including Federal Treasurer (1977–83). He was leader of the Liberal Party in opposition 1985–9 and from 1995 before becoming Prime Minister of a coalition government.

Howard[4] /'haʊəd/, Leslie (born Leslie Howard Stainer) (1893–1943), English actor. After making his film début in *Outward Bound* (1930) he played the archetypal English gentleman in a series of films such as *The Scarlet Pimpernel* (1935) and *Pygmalion* (1938), which he also directed. Other films include *Gone with the Wind* (1939) and the patriotic *The First of the Few* (1942), which he also directed and produced. He died returning from Lisbon to London when his plane was shot down by German aircraft.

Howard[5] /'haʊəd/, Trevor (Wallace) (1916–88), English actor. Howard was a versatile film actor who starred in the highly successful *Brief Encounter* (1945) and *The Third Man* (1949) and had a distinguished career in film and television. In the 1970s and 1980s he made many appearances in character roles, often eccentric ones, in films such as *Gandhi* (1982) and *White Mischief* (1987).

Howe /haʊ/, Elias (1819–67), American inventor. In 1846 he patented a sewing machine with an eyed needle to carry the upper thread and a holder resembling a shuttle for the lower thread. The machine's principles were adapted by Isaac Merrit Singer and others, in violation of Howe's patent rights, and it took a seven-year litigation battle to secure the royalties.

Hoxha /'hɒdʒə/, Enver (1908–85), Albanian statesman, Prime Minister 1944–54 and First Secretary of the Albanian Communist Party 1954–85. In 1941 he founded the Albanian Communist Party and led the fight for national independence. As Prime Minister and thereafter First Secretary of the Communist Party's Central Committee, he rigorously isolated Albania from Western influences and implemented a Stalinist programme of nationalization and collectivization.

Hoyle /hɔɪl/, Sir Fred (born 1915), English astrophysicist, one of the proponents of the steady-state theory of cosmology. He also formulated theories about the origins of stars, and of the processes by which atoms of the heavier chemical elements are built up within the stars, writing a seminal paper on the subject in 1956 with the American physicist William A. Fowler (1911–95). His later theories have been controversial, including the suggestions that life on earth has an extraterrestrial origin, and that viruses arrived from space. His publications include works of popular science and science fiction.

Hubble /'hʌb(ə)l/, Edwin Powell (1889–1953), American astronomer. In 1929 he demonstrated that the distance of a galaxy from the earth is directly proportional to its observed velocity of recession from us (*Hubble's law*), a natural consequence of a uniformly expanding universe. It implies that the age of the universe is inversely proportional to a constant of proportionality (*Hubble's constant*) in the mathematical expression of the law. Current estimates of this constant are still uncertain to a factor of at least two, but suggest an age for the universe of between ten and twenty thousand million years.

Hudson[1] /'hʌds(ə)n/, Henry (c.1565–1611), English explorer. He discovered the North American bay, river, and strait which bear his name. In 1607 and 1608 he conducted two voyages in search of the North-east Passage to Asia, reaching Greenland and Spitzbergen on the first and Novaya Zemlya on the second. In 1609 he explored the NE coast of America, sailing up the Hudson River to Albany. During his final voyage in 1610 he attempted to winter in Hudson Bay, but his crew mutinied and set Hudson and a few companions adrift, never to be seen again.

Hudson[2] /'hʌds(ə)n/, William Henry (1841–1922), British naturalist and writer, born in Argentina. Hudson was brought up by his American parents in Argentina, moving to England in 1869. After he had spent some thirty years in London he received a pension which enabled him to spend periods elsewhere, and he became a prolific author. Hudson was an astute observer and lover of nature, his works ranging from the exotic (*The Naturalist in La Plata*, 1892) to the familiar (*Nature in Downland*, 1900).

Huggins /'hʌgmz/, Sir William (1824–1910), British astronomer. He pioneered spectroscopic analysis in astronomy, showing that nebulae are composed of luminous gas, and that some comets contain hydrocarbon molecules. He discovered the red shift in stellar spectra, correctly interpreting it as being due to the Doppler effect and using it to measure recessional velocities.

Hughes[1] /hjuːz/, Edward James ('Ted') (born 1930), English poet. His work is pervaded by his vision of the natural world as a place of violence, terror, and beauty, as can be seen in his first volume of poetry, *The Hawk in the Rain* (1957). This vision is continued in later works; *Crow* (1970) explores the legends surrounding creation and birth through the character of the sinister and mocking crow. Hughes was appointed Poet Laureate in 1984. From 1956 to 1963 he was married to the American poet Sylvia Plath.

Hughes[2] /hjuːz/, Howard (Robard) (1905–76), American industrialist, film producer, and aviator. When his father died in 1924 he took control of the Hughes Tool Company; this formed the basis of his large

fortune. He made his début as a film director in 1926; notable titles include *Hell's Angels* (1930) and *The Outlaw* (1941). From 1935 to 1938 he broke many world aviation records, sometimes while flying an aircraft of his own design. For the last twenty-five years of his life he lived as a recluse.

Hughes[3] /hjuːz/, (James Mercer) Langston (1902–67), American writer. He began a prolific literary career with *The Weary Blues* (1926), a series of poems on black themes using blues and jazz rhythms. He is best known for his poetry, which includes the collections *The Negro Mother* (1931) and *Shakespeare in Harlem* (1941). Among his other writings are two novels, collections of stories, and a number of plays.

Hugo /'hjuːgəʊ/ Victor(-Marie) (1802–85), French poet, novelist, and dramatist. He was a leading figure of French romanticism, and brought a new freedom of diction, subject, and versification to French poetry; his many collections include *Les Feuilles d'automne* (1831). He set out his ideas on drama in the preface to his play *Cromwell* (1827); this included the view that the theatre should express both the grotesque and the sublime of human existence and became a manifesto of the romantic movement. The success of his drama *Hernani* (1830) signalled the triumph of romanticism over the conventions which had prevailed in French theatre since the time of Racine and Corneille. *Notre Dame de Paris* (1831) and *Les Misérables* (1862) are among his best-known novels and demonstrate Hugo's concern for social and political issues. Between 1851 and 1870 he lived in exile in Guernsey, where he wrote his satire against Napoleon III (*Les Châtiments*, 1853).

Humboldt /'hʌmbəʊlt/, Friedrich Heinrich Alexander, Baron von (1769–1859), German explorer and scientist. Humboldt travelled in Central and South America (1799–1804) and wrote extensively on natural history, meteorology, and physical geography. He proved that the Amazon and Orinoco river systems are connected, and ascended to 5,877 m (19,280 ft) in the Andes, the highest ascent ever made at that time, researching the relation of temperature and altitude. He spent the next twenty years in Paris writing up his results, returning later to Berlin, where he served as the Prussian court. He wrote a popular work in several volumes, *Kosmos* (1845–62), describing the

structure of the universe as it was then known.

Hume /hjuːm/, David (1711–76), Scottish philosopher, economist, and historian. His philosophy rejected the possibility of certainty in knowledge, and he agreed with John Locke that there are no innate ideas, only a series of subjective sensations, and that all the data of reason stem from experience. His philosophical legacy is particularly evident in the work of 20th-century empiricist philosophers. In economics, he attacked mercantilism and anticipated the views of economists such as Adam Smith. Among his chief works are *A Treatise of Human Nature* (1739–40) and a five-volume *History of England* (1754–62).

Humperdinck /'hʌmpə,dɪŋk, 'hʊm-/, Engelbert (1854–1921), German composer. He was influenced by Wagner, whose opera *Parsifal* he helped to prepare for performance. He is chiefly remembered as the composer of the opera *Hänsel und Gretel* (1893).

Humphries /'hʌmfrɪz/, (John) Barry (born 1934), Australian comedian. He became widely known with his creation and impersonation of the female celebrity 'Dame Edna Everage', which was first shown on British television in the late 1970s.

Hunt /hʌnt/, (William) Holman (1827–1910), English painter. In 1848 he co-founded the Pre-Raphaelite Brotherhood and was the only member of the group to remain true to its aims. He made several visits to Egypt and the Holy Land to ensure that his biblical scenes accurately reflected local settings, as in *The Scapegoat* (1855). Much of his painting has a didactic or moral purpose which is reinforced by his extensive use of symbolism, as in *The Light of the World* (1854).

Hunter /'hʌntə(r)/, John (1728–93), Scottish anatomist. Hunter is regarded as a founder of scientific surgery and made valuable investigations in pathology, physiology, dentistry, and biology. His large museum collection of comparative anatomy was eventually passed to the Royal College of Surgeons in London.

Huntingdon /'hʌntɪŋdən/, Selina, Countess of (title of Selina Hastings, née Shirley) (1707–91), English religious leader. On her husband's death in 1746 she devoted herself to religious and social work and was instrumental in introducing Methodism to

the upper classes. Following the expulsion of six theological students from Oxford University on allegations of Methodism, she established Trevecca House in mid-Wales as a college for the training of evangelical clergymen in 1768. She was a follower of the English evangelical preacher George Whitefield (1714–70) and made him her chaplain. The Calvinistic Methodist chapels which she helped to establish are still known as 'Countess of Huntingdon chapels'.

Hurston /'hɜːstən/, Zora Neale (1901–60), American novelist. In 1928 she graduated in cultural anthropology and continued her studies into the folklore of the Deep South until 1932. Her novels, which include *Jonah's Gourd Vine* (1934), *Moses, Man of the Mountain* (1938), and *Seraph on the Suwanee* (1948), reflect her continuing interest in folklore. Her work was largely ignored after her death until the novelist Alice Walker instigated a revival of interest in her writings, many of which, including her autobiography *Dust Tracks on a Road* (1942), have since been reprinted.

Husain see HUSSEIN², HUSSEIN³.

Husák /'huːsæk/, Gustáv (1913–91), Czechoslovak statesman, leader of the Communist Party of Czechoslovakia 1969–87 and President 1975–89. He succeeded Alexander Dubček as leader of the Communist Party; the latter had been removed in the wake of the Soviet military invasion which suppressed the Prague Spring, the attempted democratization of Czech politics in 1968. Husák's objectives were to re-establish order, to purge the party of its reformist element, and to implement a new federalist constitution. He was ousted during the velvet revolution of 1989.

Huss /hʌs/, John (Czech name Jan Hus) (*c.*1372–1415), Bohemian religious reformer. He was a preacher in Prague and a rector of Prague University; his support for the views of John Wyclif and his attacks on ecclesiastical abuses aroused the hostility of the Church and he was excommunicated in 1411. He was later tried (1414) and burnt at the stake. After his execution his followers, the Hussites, eventually succeeded in gaining their more moderate demands (1436), and a Church was established that remained independent of the Roman Catholic Church until 1620.

Hussein¹, Abdullah ibn, see ABDULLAH IBN HUSSEIN.

Hussein² /huˈseɪn/, Saddam (also **Husain**) (full name Saddam bin Hussein at-Takriti) (born 1937), Iraqi President, Prime Minister, and head of the armed forces since 1979. In 1968 he played a leading role in the coup which returned the Baath Socialist Party to power. As President he suppressed opposing parties, built up the army and its weaponry, and made himself the object of an extensive personality cult. During his presidency Iraq fought a war with Iran (1980–8) and invaded Kuwait (1990), from which Iraqi forces were expelled in the Gulf War of 1991. He also ordered punitive attacks on Kurdish rebels in the north of Iraq and on the Marsh Arabs in the south.

Hussein³ /huˈseɪn/, ibn Talal (also **Husain**) (born 1935), king of Jordan since 1953. Throughout his reign Hussein has steered a middle course in his policies, seeking to maintain good relations both with the West and with other Arab nations. His moderate policies led to conflict with the Palestinians who had entered Jordan after the Six Day War of 1967, and after a short civil war in 1970 the Palestinians were expelled. In 1990 he acted as a mediator between the opposing sides following the Iraqi invasion of Kuwait, but in the subsequent Gulf War Jordan was the only Middle Eastern country to give open support to Iraq. In 1994 Hussein signed a treaty normalizing relations with Israel.

Husserl /'hʊsɜːl/, Edmund (Gustav Albrecht) (1859–1938), German philosopher. His work forms the basis of the school of phenomenology; having originally trained as a mathematician he turned to philosophy, seeking in his work the clarity and certainty he found in mathematics and science. He rejected metaphysical assumptions about what actually exists, and explanations of why it exists, in favour of pure subjective consciousness as the condition for all experience, with the world as the object of this consciousness. He taught at the University of Freiberg, where Martin Heidegger was among his pupils.

Huston /'hjuːstən/, John (1906–87), American-born film director. After a varied background as a boxer, cavalryman, journalist, and actor, he made his début as a film director in 1941 with *The Maltese Falcon*. A number of successful adventure films followed, including *The Asphalt Jungle* (1950), *The African Queen* (1951), and *Moby Dick*

(1956); more recent successes include *Prizzi's Honour* (1985). He became an Irish citizen in 1964.

Hutton[1] /ˈhʌt(ə)n/, James (1726–97), Scottish geologist. Hutton's views, controversial at the time, became accepted tenets of modern geology. In opposition to Abraham Werner's Neptunian theory, he emphasized heat as the principal agent in the formation of land masses, and held that rocks such as granite were igneous in origin. He described the processes of deposition and denudation and proposed that such phenomena, operating over millions of years, would account for the present configuration of the earth's surface; it therefore followed that the earth was very much older than was believed. Hutton's views were not widely known until a concise account was published in 1802.

Hutton[2] /ˈhʌt(ə)n/ Sir Leonard ('Len') (1916–90), English cricketer. In his long career he played for Yorkshire (1934–55) and for England (1937–55). He scored a record 364 in the 1938 test against Australia and became the first professional captain of the England team in 1953.

Huxley[1] /ˈhʌkslɪ/, Aldous (Leonard) (1894–1963), English novelist and essayist. During the 1920s and 1930s he lived in Italy and France; his fiction during this period included *Antic Hay* (1923) and the futuristic *Brave New World* (1932), probably his best-known work. In 1937 he left for California, where he remained for the rest of his life and pursued his interests in Eastern mysticism and parapsychology. In 1953 he experimented with psychedelic drugs, writing of his experiences with mescalin in *The Doors of Perception* (1954).

Huxley[2] /ˈhʌkslɪ/, Andrew Fielding (born 1917), English physiologist and grandson of Thomas Henry Huxley. He worked with Sir Alan Hodgkin on the physiology of nerve transmission (see HODGKIN[1]).

Huxley[3] /ˈhʌkslɪ/, Sir Julian (1887–1975), English biologist. He contributed to the early development of the study of animal behaviour, was a notable interpreter of science to the public through writing and broadcasting, and became the first director-general of UNESCO (1946–8). He was the grandson of Thomas Henry Huxley.

Huxley[4] /ˈhʌkslɪ/, Thomas Henry (1825–95), English biologist. A qualified surgeon, Huxley made his reputation as a marine biologist during service as a ship's surgeon off the coast of northern Australia. Later he turned to the study of fossils, especially of fishes and reptiles, and became a leading supporter of Darwinism in opposition to Richard Owen. On the basis of a detailed study in anthropology he wrote *Man's Place in Nature* (1863), and coined the word *agnostic* to describe his own beliefs. Huxley was a supporter of education for the less privileged and argued for the inclusion of science in the school curriculum. He was the grandfather of Sir Julian Huxley.

Huygens /ˈhaɪɡənz/, Christiaan (1629–95), Dutch physicist, mathematician, and astronomer. He is probably best known for his pendulum-regulated clock, which he patented in 1657; this was a great advance on previous clocks because a swinging pendulum is free from the friction to which the earlier weighted arm was subject. However, his work covered a number of fields. He improved the lenses of his telescope, discovered a satellite of Saturn, and also that planet's rings, whose nature had eluded Galileo. In dynamics he studied centrifugal force and the problem of colliding bodies, but his greatest contribution was his wave theory of light. He formulated the principle that every point on a wave front is the centre of a new wave, and this allowed him to explain reflection and refraction, including the double refraction of light in some minerals.

Hyde /haɪd/, Edward, see CLARENDON.

Hypatia /haɪˈpeɪʃɪə/ (c.370–415), Greek philosopher, astronomer, and mathematician. She taught geometry, algebra, and astronomy at Alexandria, and was head of the Neoplatonist school there. Hypatia wrote several learned treatises as well as devising instruments such as an astrolabe. She was murdered by a Christian mob opposed to the scientific rationalism advocated by her Neoplatonist philosophy.

barruri Gomez /ɪˌbɑːˈruːrɪ ˈɡəʊmez/, Dolores (known as 'La Pasionaria') (1895–1989), Spanish Communist politician. A founder of the Spanish Communist Party (1920), she was elected to Parliament in 1936. During the Spanish Civil War (1936–9) she became famous as an inspirational leader of the Republicans. She left Spain after the Nationalist victory and did not return until 1977, when she won re-election to the National Assembly at the age of 81.

on Batuta /ˌɪb(ə)n bɑːˈtuːtɑː/ (c.1304–68), Arab explorer. From 1325 to 1354 he journeyed through North and West Africa, India, and China, writing a vivid account of his travels in the *Rihlah* (undated).

on Hussein, Abdullah, see ABDULLAH IBN HUSSEIN.

osen /ˈɪbs(ə)n/, Henrik (1828–1906), Norwegian dramatist. After the success of his verse drama *Peer Gynt* (1867), he turned to writing prose plays on social issues, including *A Doll's House* (1879) and *Ghosts* (1881). He is credited with being the first major dramatist to write tragedy about ordinary people in prose, and was an important influence on George Bernard Shaw. Ibsen's later works, such as *The Master Builder* (1892), deal increasingly with the forces of the unconscious and were admired by Sigmund Freud.

ctinus /ɪkˈtaməs/ (5th century BC), Greek architect. His most famous building was the Parthenon in Athens, which he is said to have designed with the architect Callicrates and the sculptor Phidias between 448 and 437 BC.

lesias /ɪˈɡleɪzɪˌæs/, Julio (born 1943), Spanish singer. He has recorded more than sixty albums since the start of his singing career in 1970 and is famous for love songs and ballads; his many hits include 'Begin the Beguine' (1981) and 'Yours' (1982).

gnatius Loyola, St /ɪɡˌneɪʃəs ˈlɔɪələ, lɔɪˈəʊlə/ (1491–1556), Spanish theologian and founder of the Jesuits. After sustaining a leg wound as a soldier, he renounced military life and turned to prayer and mortification. In 1534 he founded the Society of Jesus and became its first general. His *Spiritual Exercises* (1548), an ordered scheme of meditations on the life of Christ and the truths of the Christian faith, is still used in the training of Jesuits. Feast day, 31 July.

Ikhnaton see AKHENATEN.

Illich /ˈɪlɪtʃ/, Ivan (born 1926), Austrian-born American educationist and writer. He is chiefly known as a critic of the centralized nature of Western industrial society and as an advocate of the deinstitutionalization of education, religion, and medicine. His books include *Deschooling Society* (1971) and *Limits to Medicine* (1978).

Imhotep /ɪmˈhəʊtep/ (fl. 27th century BC), Egyptian architect and scholar. He is usually credited with designing the step pyramid built at Saqqara for the 3rd-dynasty pharaoh Djoser (c.2686–c.2613 BC) and, through this, with pioneering the use of hewn stone in building. He was later deified; in Egypt, he was worshipped as the patron of architects, scribes, and doctors, while in Greece he was identified with the god Asclepius.

Indurain /ˈændjʊˌræn/, Miguel (born 1964), Spanish cyclist. He was the first person to win the Tour de France five consecutive times, from 1991 onwards, setting the record for the fastest average speed in 1992.

Ine /ˈiːnə/ king of Wessex 688–726. He extended the prestige and power of the throne, developing an extensive legal code.

Ingenhousz /ˈɪŋənˌhuːs/, Jan (1730–99), Dutch scientist. His early work was in medicine, and he popularized the inoculation of live smallpox vaccine as a protection against the disease. He is best known, however, for his work on photosynthesis, discovering that sunlit green plants take in carbon dioxide, fix the carbon, and 'restore' the air (oxygen) required by animals for respiration. Ingenhousz investigated Brownian motion, and introduced the use of cover slips for microscopy. He also worked in physics.

Ingres /ˈæŋɡrə/, Jean Auguste Dominique (1780–1867), French painter. He was a pupil

of David and a vigorous opponent of Delacroix's romanticism, upholding neoclassicism in paintings such as *Ambassadors of Agamemnon* (1801). Ingres's many nudes, including the *Bather* (1808), reflect his skills as a draughtsman. In his feeling for pure form, he was admired by Degas.

Ionesco /ˌiːəˈneskəʊ/, Eugène (1912–94), Romanian-born French dramatist. A leading exponent of the Theatre of the Absurd, he achieved fame with his first play *The Bald Prima Donna* (1950), which blended a dialogue of platitudes with absurd logic and surrealist effects. In *Rhinoceros* (1960), he depicted a totalitarian society whose members eventually conform by turning into rhinoceroses.

Ipatieff /ɪˈpætɪˌef/, Vladimir Nikolaievich (1867–1952), Russian-born American chemist. He worked mainly on the catalysis of hydrocarbons, particularly the use of high-pressure catalysis and of metallic oxides as catalysts. These techniques became vitally important to the petrochemical industry, which he helped to establish in both pre- and post-revolutionary Russia. Ipatieff continued his research on catalysis after moving to the US in 1930.

Iqbal /ˈɪkbæl/, Sir Muhammad (1875–1938), Indian poet and philosopher, generally regarded as the father of Pakistan. Writing in both Persian and Urdu, he became a champion of an international Islamic community, eventually concluding that it could only find expression in the free association of Muslim states. As president of the Muslim League in 1930, he advocated the creation of a separate Muslim state in NW India; the demands of the Muslim League led ultimately to the establishment of Pakistan in 1947.

Irenaeus, St /ˌaɪərɪˈniːəs/ (AD c.130–c.200), Greek theologian. He became bishop of Lyons in Gaul in 177, and was the author of *Against Heresies* (c.180), a detailed attack on Gnosticism. Feast day (in the Eastern Church) 23 Aug.; (in the Western Church) 28 June.

Iron Chancellor the nickname of Bismarck after he used the phrase 'blood and iron' in a speech in 1862, referring to war as an instrument of foreign policy.

Iron Duke the nickname of Wellington, said to have been first used by the magazine *Punch* in 1845.

Iron Lady the nickname first given by Soviet journalists to Margaret Thatcher while she was British Prime Minister.

Irving[1] /ˈɜːvɪŋ/, Sir Henry (born Henry Brodribb) (1838–1905), English actor-manager. In 1874 he first played Hamlet at the Lyceum Theatre, and proceeded to manage the theatre from 1878 to 1902. During this period he entered into a celebrated acting partnership with Ellen Terry; they were particularly noted for their performances in Irving's productions of Shakespeare.

Irving[2] /ˈɜːvɪŋ/, Washington (1783–1859), American writer. His first publication was a series of satirical essays (1807–8) entitled *Salmagundi*. He travelled extensively in Europe and also served as US ambassador to Spain 1842–6; he is best known for *The Sketch Book of Geoffrey Crayon, Gent* (1819–20), which contains such tales as 'Rip Van Winkle' and 'The Legend of Sleepy Hollow'. He also wrote the burlesque *History of New York* (1809), under the pretended name of Diedrich Knickerbocker; the word *knickerbocker* derives from this.

Isabella I /ˌɪzəˈbelə/ (known as Isabella of Castile or Isabella the Catholic) (1451–1504), queen of Castile 1474–1504 and of Aragon 1479–1504. Her marriage to Ferdinand of Aragon in 1469 helped to join together the Christian kingdoms of Castile and Aragon, marking the beginning of the unification of Spain. As joint monarchs of Castile, they instituted the Spanish Inquisition (1478). Later, as rulers of Aragon as well as Castile, they supported Columbus's expedition in which he discovered the New World (1492). (See also FERDINAND.)

Isabella of France /ˌɪzəˈbelə/ (1292–1358), daughter of Philip IV of France. She was queen consort of Edward II of England from 1308, but returned to France in 1325. She and her lover Roger de Mortimer organized an invasion of England in 1326, forcing Edward to abdicate in favour of his son, who was crowned Edward III after his father's murder in 1327. Isabella and Mortimer acted as regents for Edward III until 1330, after which Edward took control of the kingdom and Isabella was banished.

Isherwood /ˈɪʃəˌwʊd/, Christopher (William Bradshaw) (1904–86), British-born American novelist. His novels *Mr Norris Changes Trains* (1935) and *Goodbye to Berlin* (1939; filmed as *Cabaret*, 1972) vividly portray Germany on the eve of Hitler's rise to power and reflect Isherwood's experiences in Ber-

lin from 1929 to 1933. He collaborated with W. H. Auden on three verse plays and emigrated with him to the US in 1939.

Ishiguro /ˌɪʃɪˈɡʊərəʊ/, Kazuo (born 1954), Japanese-born British novelist. In 1960 he moved with his family to Great Britain. He gained recognition with his novel *An Artist of the Floating World* (1986); his next novel, *The Remains of the Day* (1989), won the Booker Prize.

Isidore of Seville, St /ˈɪzɪˌdɔː(r), səˈvɪl/ (also called Isidorus Hispalensis) (*c*.560–636), Spanish archbishop and Doctor of the Church. He is noted for his *Etymologies*, an encyclopedic work used by many medieval authors. Feast day, 4 April.

Isocrates /aɪˈsɒkrəˌtiːz/ (436–338 BC), Athenian orator. His written speeches are amongst the earliest political pamphlets; they advocate the union of Greeks under Philip II of Macedon and a pan-Hellenic crusade against Persia.

Issigonis /ˌɪsɪˈɡəʊnɪs/, Sir Alec (Arnold Constantine) (1906–88), Turkish-born British car designer. His most famous designs were the Morris Minor (1948), produced until 1971, and the Mini (1959).

Ito /ˈiːtəʊ/, Prince Hirobumi (1841–1909), Japanese statesman, Premier four times between 1884 and 1901. In 1889 he was prominent in drafting the Japanese constitution, and the following year helped to establish a bicameral national diet. He was assassinated by a member of the Korean independence movement.

Ivan /ˈaɪv(ə)n/ the name of six rulers of Russia:

Ivan I (*c*.1304–41), grand duke of Muscovy 1328–40. He strengthened and enlarged the duchy, making Moscow the ecclesiastical capital in 1326.

Ivan II (known as Ivan the Red) (1326–59), grand duke of Muscovy 1353–9.

Ivan III (known as Ivan the Great) (1440–1505), grand duke of Muscovy 1462–1505. He consolidated and enlarged his territory, defending it against a Tartar invasion in 1480, and adopting the title of 'Ruler of all Russia' in 1472.

Ivan IV (known as Ivan the Terrible) (1530–84), grand duke of Muscovy 1533–47 and first tsar of Russia 1547–84. His expansionist foreign policy resulted in the capture of Kazan (1552), Astrakhan (1556), and Siberia (1581). However, the Tartar siege of Moscow (1572) and Ivan's defeat by the Poles in the Livonian War (1558–82) left Russia weak and divided. He grew increasingly unpredictable and tyrannical; in 1581 he killed his eldest son Ivan in a fit of rage, the succession passing to his retarded second son Fyodor.

Ivan V (1666–96), nominal tsar of Russia 1682–96.

Ivan VI (1740–64), infant tsar of Russia 1740–1.

Ives /aɪvz/, Charles (Edward) (1874–1954), American composer. Influenced by popular music and the sounds of everyday life, he developed the use of polyrhythms, polytonality, quarter-tones, note-clusters, and aleatoric techniques. He is noted for his second piano sonata *Concord* (1915), and his chamber work *The Unanswered Question* (1906), scored for two unsynchronized orchestras.

Ivory /ˈaɪvərɪ/, James (born 1928), American film director. He has made a number of films in partnership with the producer Ismail Merchant, including *Heat and Dust* (1983), *A Room with a View* (1986), *Maurice* (1987), *Howard's End* (1992), and *The Remains of the Day* (1993).

J

Jacklin /ˈdʒæklɪn/, Antony ('Tony') (born 1944), English golfer. In 1969 he won the British Open and the following year won the US Open, the first British player to do so for fifty years. He played in the Ryder Cup (1967–80) and was non-playing captain of the European team from 1983 to 1989.

Jackson¹ /ˈdʒæks(ə)n/, Andrew (1767–1845), American general and Democratic statesman, 7th President of the US 1829–37. After waging several campaigns against American Indians, he defeated a British army at New Orleans (1815) and successfully invaded Florida (1818). As President, he replaced an estimated twenty per cent of those in public office with Democrat supporters, a practice that became known as the spoils system. His reputation for toughness gave rise to the nickname 'Old Hickory' (in reference to the tough wood of the hickory tree).

Jackson² /ˈdʒæks(ə)n/, Glenda (born 1936), English actress and politician. Throughout her acting career she appeared on stage and television, but is best known for her film work. She won Oscars for her performances in *Women in Love* (1969) and *A Touch of Class* (1973); other films include *Sunday Bloody Sunday* (1971) and *Turtle Diary* (1985). In 1992 she became Labour MP for the London constituency of Hampstead and Highgate.

Jackson³ /ˈdʒæks(ə)n/, Jesse (Louis) (born 1941), American politician and clergyman. After working with Martin Luther King in the civil-rights struggle, he competed for but failed to win the Democratic Party's 1984 and 1988 presidential nominations.

Jackson⁴ /ˈdʒæks(ə)n/, Michael (Joe) (born 1958), American singer and songwriter. In the 1970s he performed with his four older brothers in the pop group the Jackson Five. His full-time solo career began in 1979, when *Off the Wall* became the best-selling album to date by a black artist. Subsequent albums, including *Bad* (1987), confirmed him as the most commercially successful American star of the 1980s. His career suffered a setback in 1993 after allegations of child molestation concerning young boys. In 1994 he married Lisa Marie Presley (born 1968), the daughter of Elvis Presley; the couple divorced in 1996.

Jackson⁵ /ˈdʒæks(ə)n/, Thomas Jonathan (known as 'Stonewall Jackson') (1824–63), American general. During the American Civil War he made his mark as a commander at the first battle of Bull Run in 1861; a successful defensive stand there earned him his nickname. As the deputy of Robert E. Lee, he played an important part in the Confederate victories in Virginia in the first two years of the war.

Jack the Ripper (19th century), unidentified English murderer. From August to November 1888 at least six prostitutes were brutally killed in the East End of London, the bodies being mutilated in a way that indicated a knowledge of anatomy. The authorities received taunting notes from a person calling himself Jack the Ripper and claiming to be the murderer, but the cases remain unsolved.

Jacobi /dʒæˈkəʊbɪ/, Karl Gustav Jacob (1804–51), German mathematician. He worked on the theory of elliptic functions, in competition with Niels Abel. Jacobi also investigated number theory, mathematical analysis, geometry, and differential equations, and his work on determinants is important in dynamics and quantum mechanics.

Jacobs /ˈdʒeɪkəbz/, William Wymark (1863–1943), English short-story writer. He is noted for his tales of the macabre, such as 'The Monkey's Paw' (1902).

Jacopo della Quercia /ˈjækə,pəʊ/ see DELLA QUERCIA.

Jagger /ˈdʒægə(r)/, Michael Philip ('Mick') (born 1943), English rock singer and songwriter. He formed the Rolling Stones *c*.1962 with guitarist Keith Richards (born 1943), a childhood friend. Originally a rhythm and blues band, the Rolling Stones became successful with a much-imitated rebel image and Jagger–Richards songs such as 'Satisfaction' (1965) and 'Jumping Jack Flash' (1968). In the 1970s they evolved a simple, derivative, yet distinctive style, heard on albums such as *Exile on Main Street*

(1972) and *Some Girls* (1978), which they retained almost unchanged into the 1990s.

Jakobson /ˈjækəbs(ə)n/, Roman (Osipovich) (1896–1982), Russian-born American linguist. In 1941 he emigrated to the US and from 1949 to 1967 was professor of Slavic languages and literature and general linguistics at Harvard University. In *Child Language, Aphasia, and Phonological Universals* (1941) he developed the hypothesis that there may be a universal sequence according to which speech sounds are learned. His *Fundamentals of Language* (1956) postulates a phonological system of twelve binary oppositions to cover all the permutations of sounds in the world's languages.

Jalal ad-Din ar-Rumi /dʒɑˌlæl æd,dɪn ɑːˈruːmɪ/ (also called Mawlana) (1207–73), Persian poet and Sufi mystic. He was born in Balkh (in modern Afghanistan), but lived for most of his life at Konya in Anatolia, where he founded the order of whirling dervishes, a sect noted for their ecstatic rituals and use of hypnotic trance-states. He wrote much lyrical poetry and an influential epic on Sufi mystical doctrine.

James[1] /dʒeɪmz/ the name of seven Stuart kings of Scotland:
James I (1394–1437), son of Robert III, reigned 1406–37. Captured by the English while a child, James remained a captive until 1424. He returned to a country divided by baronial feuds, but managed to restore some measure of royal authority. He was murdered in Perth by rebel nobles.
James II (1430–60), son of James I, reigned 1437–60. After ascending the throne as a minor, he eventually overthrew his regents and considerably strengthened the position of the Crown by crushing the powerful Douglas family (1452–5). He was killed during the siege of Roxburgh Castle.
James III (1451–88), son of James II, reigned 1460–88. He proved increasingly unable to control his nobles, who eventually raised an army against him in 1488, using his son, the future James IV, as a figurehead. The king was defeated and killed in battle at Sauchieburn, near Stirling.
James IV (1473–1513), son of James III, reigned 1488–1513. He re-established royal power throughout the realm, notably in the Highlands. He took an active part in European alliance politics, forging a dynastic link with England through his marriage to Margaret Tudor, the daughter of Henry VII, and revitalizing the traditional pact with France. When England and France went to war in 1513, he supported the latter and invaded England at the head of a large army. He died along with many of his nobles when his army was defeated at Flodden.
James V (1512–42), son of James IV, reigned 1513–42. Both during his long minority and after his marriage to the French noblewoman Mary of Guise, Scotland was dominated by French interests. Relations with England deteriorated in the later years of his reign, culminating in an invasion by Henry VIII's army and the defeat of James's troops near the border at Solway Moss in 1542.
James VI the Scottish title of James I of England: see JAMES[2].
James VII the Scottish title of James II of England: see JAMES[2].

James[2] /dʒeɪmz/ the name of two kings of England, Ireland, and Scotland:
James I (1566–1625), son of Mary, Queen of Scots, king of Scotland (as James VI) 1567–1625, and of England and Ireland 1603–25. After his minority ended in 1583, he was largely successful in restoring royal authority in Scotland. He inherited the throne of England on the death of Elizabeth I, as great-grandson of Margaret Tudor, daughter of Henry VII. His declaration of the divine right of kings, his favouritism towards the Duke of Buckingham, and his intended alliance with Spain made him unpopular with Parliament. He was succeeded by his second son, Charles I.
James II (1633–1701), son of Charles I, king of England, Ireland, and (as James VII) Scotland 1685–8. His Catholic beliefs led to the rebellion of the Duke of Monmouth in 1685 and to his deposition in favour of William of Orange and Mary II three years later. Attempts to regain the throne resulted in James's defeat at the Battle of the Boyne in 1690. He died in exile in France, leaving the Jacobite claim to the throne in the hands of his son, James Stuart.

James[3] /dʒeɪmz/, Clive (Vivian Leopold) (born 1939), Australian television personality, writer, and critic. James became known as a journalist and writer in Britain, publishing books of criticism and comment as well as a volume of poetry and the autobiographical books *Unreliable Memoirs I, II,* and *III* (1980, 1985, 1990). His popular

television shows mix chat, humour, commentary, and documentary.

James⁴ /dʒeɪmz/, C(yril) L(ionel) R(obert) (1901–89), Trinidadian historian, journalist, political theorist, and novelist. After working as a cricket columnist, he established a reputation as a historian with his study of the Haitian revolution, *Black Jacobins* (1938). A Trotskyist from 1934, he wrote a number of political works, including *World Revolution: 1917–1936* (published in 1937). He is also noted for *Beyond a Boundary* (1963), an analysis of cricket and anticolonialism.

James⁵ /dʒeɪmz/, Henry (1843–1916), American-born British novelist and critic. He settled in England in 1876, and in his early novels dealt with the relationship between European civilization and American life, notably in *The Portrait of a Lady* (1881). In *The Bostonians* (1886) he portrayed American society in its own right, before producing many novels of English life. He is also remembered for his ghost story *The Turn of the Screw* (1898), the subject of Benjamin Britten's opera by the same name (1954). He was the brother of William James.

James⁶ /dʒeɪmz/, Jesse (Woodson) (1847–82), American outlaw. He joined with his brother Frank (1843–1915) and others to form a notorious band of outlaws which specialized in bank and train robberies and inspired many westerns.

James⁷ /dʒeɪmz/, Dame P(hyllis) D(orothy) (born 1920), English writer of detective fiction. She is noted for her novels featuring the poet-detective Adam Dalgleish, including *Death of an Expert Witness* (1977) and *A Taste for Death* (1986).

James⁸ /dʒeɪmz/, William (1842–1910), American philosopher and psychologist. Influenced by C. S. Peirce, James was a leading exponent of pragmatism, who sought a functional definition of truth rather than a depiction of a structural relation between ideas and reality. Major works include *The Will to Believe* (1897) and *Essays in Radical Empiricism* (1912). In psychology he published the definitive and innovative *The Principles of Psychology* (1890), and he is credited with introducing the concept of the stream of consciousness. He was the brother of Henry James.

James, St¹ (known as St James the Great), an Apostle, son of Zebedee and brother of John. He was put to death by Herod

Agrippa I; afterwards, according to a Spanish tradition, his body was taken to Santiago de Compostela. Feast day, 25 July.

James, St² (known as St James the Less), an Apostle. Feast day (in the Eastern Church) 9 October; (in the Western Church) 1 May.

James, St³ (known as St James the Just or 'the Lord's brother'), leader of the early Christian Church at Jerusalem. He was put to death by the Sanhedrin, the highest Jewish council in Jerusalem. Feast day, 1 May.

Janáček /ˈjænəˌtʃek/, Leoš (1854–1928), Czech composer. Influenced at first by Dvořák, from 1885 he began to collect the Moravian folk-songs whose pitch inflections and rhythmic speech patterns pervade his music. His works include nine operas, notably *Jenůfa* (1904) and *The Cunning Little Vixen* (1924), the *Sinfonietta* (1926), and the *Glagolitic Mass* (1927).

Jansen /ˈdʒæns(ə)n/, Cornelius Otto (1585–1638), Flemish Roman Catholic theologian and founder of Jansenism. A strong opponent of the Jesuits, he proposed a reform of Christianity through a return to St Augustine. To this end he produced his major work, *Augustinus* (1640), which was published by his followers after his death. The four-volume study followed St Augustine's teachings on grace, predestination, and free will, and formed the basis of Jansenism.

Jansens, Cornelius, see JOHNSON³.

Jaques-Dalcroze /ˌʒækdælˈkrəʊz/, Émile (1865–1950), Austrian-born Swiss music teacher and composer. While professor of harmony at the Geneva Conservatory he evolved the eurhythmics method of teaching music and dance. He first used the method with elementary pupils in 1905, before establishing a school for eurhythmics instruction in 1910.

Jarman /ˈdʒɑːmən/, Derek (1942–94), English film director. Jarman worked in costume and set design for the Royal Ballet and was a production designer for Ken Russell's *The Devils* (1970). His controversial first feature film, *Sebastiane* (1976), heralded a succession of rich, extravagant films informed by gay sensibilities, such as *Jubilee* (1977), *Caravaggio* (1985), and *The Last of England* (1987). He published a number of books, including the autobiographical *Dancing Ledge* (1984).

Jarry /'dʒærɪ, 'ʒærɪ/, Alfred (1873–1907), French dramatist. His satirical farce *Ubu Roi* (1896) is widely claimed to have anticipated surrealism and the Theatre of the Absurd.

Jaruzelski /ˌjærʊ'zelskɪ/, Wojciech (born 1923), Polish general and Communist statesman, Prime Minister 1981–5, head of state 1985–9, and President 1989–90. After becoming Premier in 1981 he responded to Poland's economic crisis and the rise of the independent trade-union movement Solidarity by imposing martial law and banning union operation. Following the victory of Solidarity in the 1989 free elections, Jaruzelski supervised Poland's transition to a novel 'socialist pluralist' democracy.

Jean Paul /ʒɒn 'pɔːl/ (pseudonym of Johann Paul Friedrich Richter) (1763–1825), German novelist. He is noted for his romantic novels, including *Hesperus* (1795), and for comic works such as *Titan* (1800–3).

Jeans /dʒiːnz/, Sir James Hopwood (1877–1946), English physicist and astronomer. He began as a mathematician, but his major contributions were in molecular physics and astrophysics. Jeans proposed a theory for the formation of the solar system, according to which the planets were formed from natural material pulled out of the sun by the gravity of a passing star. He was the first to propose that matter is continuously created throughout the universe, one of the tenets of the steady-state theory. He also became a popularizer of science, especially as a radio lecturer.

Jefferies /'dʒefrɪz/, (John) Richard (1848–87), English writer and naturalist. He is renowned for his observation of English rural life. Important works include *Bevis* (1882), an evocation of his country childhood in Wiltshire, and his autobiography *The Story of My Heart* (1883).

Jefferson /'dʒefəs(ə)n/, Thomas (1743–1826), American Democratic Republican statesman, 3rd President of the US 1801–9. Jefferson was the principal drafter of the Declaration of Independence (1776) and played a key role in the American leadership during the War of Independence. He advocated decentralization and the restrained use of presidential power, in defiance of Alexander Hamilton. While President, Jefferson secured the Louisiana Purchase (1803), by which the western part of the Mississippi valley was sold to the US by France.

Jeffreys /'dʒefrɪz/, George, 1st Baron (c.1645–89), Welsh judge. In 1683 he was made Chief Justice of the King's Bench and took part in the Popish Plot prosecutions, sitting at the trial of the plot's fabricator, Titus Oates. He later became infamous for his brutal sentencing at the Bloody Assizes (1685), the trials of the Duke of Monmouth's supporters after their defeat at the Battle of Sedgemoor.

Jehu /'dʒiːhjuː/ (842–815 BC), king of Israel. He was famous for driving his chariot furiously (2 Kings 9).

Jekyll /'dʒiːk(ə)l/, Gertrude (1843–1932), English horticulturalist and garden designer. Forced to abandon painting because of her failing eyesight, Jekyll turned to garden design. She met the architect Edwin Lutyens in 1889 and had a long association with him, designing more than 300 gardens for his buildings. Influenced by the French impressionist painters, Jekyll was responsible for many innovations, such as the promotion of colour design in garden planning and 'wild' gardens.

Jellicoe /'dʒelɪˌkəʊ/, John Rushworth, 1st Earl (1859–1935), British admiral. He was commander of the Grand Fleet at the Battle of Jutland (1916), after which the German fleet never again sought a full-scale engagement. After the war he was appointed Governor-General of New Zealand (1920–4).

Jenkins /'dʒeŋkɪnz/, Roy (Harris), Baron Jenkins of Hillhead (born 1920), English Labour and Social Democrat MP and scholar. He was a Labour MP between 1948 and 1976, rising to deputy leader of the Labour Party (1970–2). He was president of the European Commission 1977–81 and co-founded the Social Democratic Party in 1981, representing Glasgow Hillhead between 1982 and 1987. He then became Chancellor of Oxford University. Among his works are numerous biographies of political figures, including *Mr Attlee* (1948), *Asquith* (1964), *Truman* (1986), and *Gladstone* (1995).

Jenner /'dʒenə(r)/, Edward (1749–1823), English physician, the pioneer of vaccination. A local belief that dairymaids who had had cowpox did not catch smallpox led Jenner to the idea of deliberately infecting people with cowpox in order to protect them from the more serious disease. The practice was eventually accepted throughout the world,

leading to the widespread use of vaccination for other diseases and eventually to the eradication of smallpox in the late 20th century. In intervals between medical practice he indulged his keen interest in natural history, and wrote a paper on the habits of the cuckoo.

Jerome /dʒəˈrəʊm/, Jerome K(lapka) (1859–1927), English novelist and dramatist. He is chiefly remembered for his humorous novel *Three Men in a Boat* (1889).

Jerome, St (c.342–420), Doctor of the Church. Born in Dalmatia, he acted as secretary to Pope Damasus in Rome (382–5) before settling in Bethlehem, where he ruled a newly founded monastery and devoted his life to study. He is chiefly known for his compilation of the Latin version of the Bible, the Vulgate. Feast day, 30 September.

Jervis /ˈdʒɑːvɪs/, John, Earl St Vincent (1735–1823), British admiral. In 1795 he was put in command of the British fleet, and in 1797, with Nelson as his commodore, led his forces to victory over a Spanish fleet off Cape St Vincent; Jervis was created Earl St Vincent in recognition of this achievement.

Jespersen /ˈjespəs(ə)n/ (Jens) Otto (Harry) (1860–1943), Danish philologist, grammarian, and educationist. He promoted the use of the 'direct method' in language teaching with the publication of his theoretical work *How to Teach a Foreign Language* (1904). Other books include his seven-volume *Modern English Grammar* (1909–49).

Jesus /ˈdʒiːzəs/ (also **Jesus Christ** or **Jesus of Nazareth**) the central figure of the Christian religion. A Jew, the son of Mary, he lived in Palestine at the beginning of the 1st century AD. In about AD 28–30 he conducted a mission of preaching and healing (with reported miracles) which is described in the New Testament, as are his arrest and death by crucifixion. His followers considered him to be the Christ or Messiah and the Son of the living God, and belief in his Resurrection from the dead, as recorded in the Gospels, became a central tenet of Christianity.

Jewison /ˈdʒuːɪs(ə)n/, Norman (born 1926), Canadian film director and producer. Jewison achieved recognition with the dramas *The Cincinnati Kid* (1965) and *In the Heat of the Night* (1967), which won five Oscars. Later films include the musical *Fiddler on the Roof*

(1971) and the romantic comedy *Moonstruck* (1987).

Jiang Jie Shi see CHIANG KAI-SHEK.

Jiménez de Cisneros /hɪˌmenez deɪ sɪsˈneərʊs/ (also **Ximenes de Cisneros**), Francisco (1436–1517), Spanish statesman, regent of Spain 1516–17. He was made Cardinal in 1507 and served as Grand Inquisitor for Castile and Léon from 1507 to 1517, during which time he undertook a massive campaign against heresy, having some 2,500 alleged heretics put to death.

Jinnah /ˈdʒɪnə/, Muhammad Ali (1876–1948), Indian statesman and founder of Pakistan. He headed the Muslim League in its struggle with the Hindu-oriented Indian National Congress, and from 1928 onwards championed the rights of the Muslim minority at conferences on Indian independence. After 1937, when self-governing Hindu provinces began to be formed, his fear that Muslims would be excluded from office led him to campaign for a separate Muslim state. With the establishment of Pakistan in 1947 he became its first Governor-General.

Joan of Arc, St /dʒəʊn, ɑːk/ (known as 'the Maid of Orleans') (c.1412–31), French national heroine. Inspired by 'voices' of St Catherine and St Margaret, she led the French armies against the English in the Hundred Years War, relieving besieged Orleans (1429) and ensuring that Charles VII could be crowned in previously occupied Reims. Captured by the Burgundians in 1430, she was handed over to the English, convicted of heresy, and burnt at the stake in Rouen. She was canonized in 1920. Feast day, 30 May.

Jobs /dʒʊbz/, Steven (Paul) (born 1955), American computer entrepreneur. Jobs produced the first Apple computer in 1976, setting up the Apple computer company later that year with Steve Wozniak (born 1950). He became famous as a youthful entrepreneur, remaining chairman of the company until 1985, when he resigned at the age of 30 following internal disagreements.

Joffre /ˈʒɒfrə/, Joseph Jacques Césaire (1852–1931), French Marshal. During the First World War he was Commander-in-Chief of the French army on the Western Front (1914–16). Joffre was chiefly responsible for the Allied victory in the first battle

of the Marne, but resigned after the costly Battle of Verdun (1916).

John[1] /dʒɒn/ (known as John Lackland) (1165–1216), son of Henry II, king of England 1199–1216. He lost Normandy and most of his French possessions to Philip II of France by 1205. His refusal to accept Stephen Langton as Archbishop of Canterbury caused an interdict to be placed on England in 1208, and led to his own excommunication the following year. In 1215 John was forced to sign Magna Carta by his barons. When he ignored its provisions, civil war broke out and he died on campaign.

John[2] /dʒɒn/ the name of six kings of Portugal:
John I (known as John the Great) (1357–1433), reigned 1385–1433. Reinforced by an English army, he won independence for Portugal with his victory over the Castilians at Aljubarrota (1385). He established an Anglo-Portuguese alliance (1386), married a daughter of John of Gaunt (1387), and presided over a long period of peace and prosperity which was notable for his encouragement of voyages of discovery.
John II (1455–95), reigned 1481–95.
John III (1502–57), reigned 1521–57.
John IV (known as John the Fortunate) (1604–56), reigned 1640–56. The founder of the Braganza dynasty, he expelled a Spanish usurper and proclaimed himself king. He defeated the Spanish at Montijo (1644) and drove the Dutch out of Brazil (1654).
John V (1689–1750), reigned 1706–50.
John VI (1767–1826), reigned 1816–26.

John[3] /dʒɒn/, Augustus (Edwin) (1878–1961), Welsh painter. He is perhaps best known for *The Smiling Woman* (1908), a portrait of his second wife Dorelia, which portrayed a robust gypsy type of beauty; the gypsies of Wales were frequent subjects of his work. He was subsequently noted for his portraits of the wealthy and famous, particularly prominent writers such as Thomas Hardy, George Bernard Shaw, W. B. Yeats, James Joyce, and Dylan Thomas. He was the brother of Gwen John.

John[4] /dʒɒn/, Barry (born 1945), Welsh Rugby Union player. His international career, during which he played at half-back and scored a record ninety points for his country, lasted from 1966 until his retirement in 1972. He played a prominent part in the British Lions' victorious tour of New Zealand in 1971.

John[5] /dʒɒn/, Elton (Hercules) (born Reginald Kenneth Dwight) (born 1947), English pop and rock singer, pianist, and songwriter. He has written many hit songs, the majority of them with lyricist Bernie Taupin (born 1950); they include 'Your Song' (1970) and 'Nikita' (1985). He is noted for good-humoured flamboyance and outrageous costumes. In 1997 his tribute to Diana, Princess of Wales, a new version of 'Candle in the Wind', became the highest-selling single in history.

John[6] /dʒɒn/, Gwen (1876–1939), Welsh painter. After studying with Whistler in Paris (1898), she settled in France and worked as Rodin's model (1904), becoming his devoted friend and mistress. She converted to Catholicism in 1913; her paintings, mainly watercolours, often depict nuns or girls in interior settings and are noted for their grey tonality. She was the sister of Augustus John.

John III (known as John Sobieski) (1624–96), king of Poland 1674–96. He was elected king of Poland after a distinguished early career as a soldier. In 1683 he relieved Vienna when it was besieged by the Turks, thereby becoming the hero of the Christian world.

John, St (known as St John the Evangelist or St John the Divine) an Apostle, son of Zebedee and brother of James. He has traditionally been credited with the authorship of the fourth Gospel, Revelation, and three epistles of the New Testament. Feast day, 27 December.

John Chrysostom, St see CHRYSOSTOM, ST JOHN.

John of Damascus, St /də'mɑːskəs, -'mæskəs/ (c.675–c.749), Syrian theologian and Doctor of the Church. After championing image worship against the iconoclasts, he wrote his encyclopedic work on Christian theology, *The Fount of Wisdom*. Its last section summarized the teachings of the Greek Fathers of the Church on the principal mysteries of the Christian faith and was influential for centuries in both Eastern and Western Churches. Feast day, 4 December.

John of Gaunt /ɡɔːnt/ (1340–99), son of Edward III. Born in Ghent, he was created Duke of Lancaster in 1362. John of Gaunt headed the government during the final years of his father's reign and the minority

of Richard II, and was effective ruler of England in this period. His son Henry Bolingbroke later became King Henry IV.

John of the Cross, St (born Juan de Yepis y Alvarez) (1542–91), Spanish mystic and poet. A Carmelite monk and priest, he joined with St Teresa of Ávila in trying to reassert the original Carmelite observance of austerity, and in 1568 founded the 'discalced' or barefoot Carmelite order for monks. He also wrote mystical poems including 'The Dark Night of the Soul', describing the soul's purgation. Feast day, 14 December.

John Paul II (born Karol Jozef Wojtyla) (born 1920), Polish cleric, pope since 1978. The first non-Italian pope since 1522, he has travelled abroad extensively during his papacy, especially in Central and South America. He has upheld the Church's traditional opposition to artificial means of contraception and abortion, as well as condemning homosexuality, the ordination of women, and the relaxation of the rule of celibacy for priests. He has also discouraged priests from taking part in political activity.

Johns /dʒɒnz/, Jasper (born 1930), American painter, sculptor, and printmaker. A key figure in the development of pop art, he rebelled against abstract expressionism and depicted commonplace and universally recognized images such as the US flag. He is best known for his *Flags, Targets,* and *Numbers* series produced in the mid-1950s; in these, he was noted for his use of encaustic (wax-based) paint. In the late 1950s he produced sculptures of such objects as beer cans and light bulbs cast in bronze.

John Sobieski /sɒˈbjeskɪ/ see JOHN III.

Johnson[1] /ˈdʒɒns(ə)n/, Amy (1903–41), English aviator. In 1930 she became the first woman to fly solo to Australia, although her time of 19½ days was three days short of the record. She later set a record with her solo flight to Tokyo (1931) and broke the solo-flight record to Cape Town (1932). She joined the Auxiliary Air Force in 1939, but was lost when her plane disappeared in a flight over the Thames estuary.

Johnson[2] /ˈdʒɒns(ə)n/, Andrew (1808–75), American Democratic statesman, 17th President of the US 1865–9. His lenient policy towards the southern states after the American Civil War brought him into bitter conflict with the Republican majority in Congress, who impeached him (1868); he was acquitted by a single vote.

Johnson[3] /ˈdʒɒns(ə)n/, Cornelius (also **Jansens** /ˈdʒæns(ə)nz/ or **Janssen van Ceulen** /ˌdʒæns(ə)n væn ˈkɜːlən/) (1593–c.1661), English-born Dutch portrait painter. He painted for the court of Charles I, where he was influenced by Van Dyck and became noted for his individual portrait heads. After the outbreak of the English Civil War he emigrated to Holland (1643).

Johnson[4] /ˈdʒɒns(ə)n/, Earvin (known as 'Magic Johnson') (born 1959), American basketball player. He played for the Los Angeles Lakers from 1979 to 1991, winning the National Basketball Association's Most Valuable Player award three times. After being diagnosed HIV-positive he made a comeback in 1992 and won a gold medal at the 1992 Olympics. He announced his retirement in 1996.

Johnson[5] /ˈdʒɒns(ə)n/, Jack (1878–1946), American boxer. In 1908 he took the world heavyweight title, becoming the first black holder of the title; he retained it until 1915.

Johnson[6] /ˈdʒɒns(ə)n/, Lyndon Baines (known as 'LBJ') (1908–73), American Democratic statesman, 36th President of the US 1963–9. His administration continued the programme of social and economic reform initiated by John F. Kennedy, passing the 1964 and 1965 Civil Rights Acts and legislating to reduce taxation. However, the increasing involvement of the US in the Vietnam War undermined his popularity and he refused to seek re-election.

Johnson[7] /ˈdʒɒns(ə)n/, Robert (1911–38), American blues singer and guitarist. Despite his mysterious early death and small recording output, he was very influential on the 1960s blues movement. His intense, haunting singing and piercing guitar style are displayed in songs such as 'I Was Standing at the Crossroads', 'Love In Vain', and 'I Believe I'll Dust My Broom'.

Johnson[8] /ˈdʒɒns(ə)n/, Samuel (known as Dr Johnson) (1709–84), English lexicographer, writer, critic, and conversationalist. His principal works include his *Dictionary of the English Language* (1755), one of the first to use illustrative quotations, his edition of Shakespeare (1765), and *The Lives of the English Poets* (1777). A leading figure in the literary London of his day, he formed the Literary Club (1764), which

numbered Edmund Burke, Oliver Goldsmith, Sir Joshua Reynolds, David Garrick,
and Johnson's biographer James Boswell
among its members.

John the Baptist, St, Jewish preacher and
prophet, a contemporary of Jesus. In AD
c.27 he preached on the banks of the River
Jordan, demanding repentance and bap-
tism from his hearers in view of the approach of God's judgement. Among those
whom he baptized was Christ. He was
imprisoned by Herod Antipas after denouncing the latter's marriage to Herodias,
the wife of Herod's brother Philip; Herodias' daughter Salome, offered a reward
by Herod for her dancing, asked for the
head of John the Baptist and thus caused
him to be beheaded (Matt. 14:1–12). Feast
day, 24 June.

John the Evangelist, St see JOHN, ST.

John the Fortunate, John IV of Portugal
(see JOHN²).

John the Great, John I of Portugal (see
JOHN²).

Joliot /'ʒɒlɪ,əʊ/, Jean-Frédéric (1900–58),
French nuclear physicist. He gave up engineering to study radioactivity and became
Madame Curie's assistant at the Radium
Institute. There he worked with her daughter Irène (1897–1956), whom he married,
taking the name Joliot-Curie; their joint
discovery of artificial radioactivity earned
them the 1935 Nobel Prize for chemistry.
Shortly before the war Joliot demonstrated
that a nuclear chain reaction was possible,
and later he and his wife became involved
with the establishment of the French
atomic energy commission, only to be removed because of their adherence to
Communism.

Jolson /'dʒəʊls(ə)n/, Al (born Asa Yoelson)
(1886–1950), Russian-born American singer, film actor, and comedian. He made the
Gershwin song 'Swanee' his trademark,
and appeared in the first full-length talking film *The Jazz Singer* (1927).

Jones¹ /dʒəʊnz/, Daniel (1881–1967), British
linguist and phonetician. From 1907 he
developed the recently invented International Phonetic Alphabet at the first
British department of phonetics, at University College, London. He went on to
invent a system of cardinal vowels, used as
reference points for transcribing all vowel
sounds. In his *English Pronouncing Dictionary*
(1917), he described the influential system
of received pronunciation.

Jones² /dʒəʊnz/, Inigo (1573–1652), English
architect and stage designer. He introduced the Palladian style to England and is
best known as the architect of the Queen's
House at Greenwich (1616) and the Banqueting Hall at Whitehall (1619). He also
pioneered the use of the proscenium arch
and movable stage scenery in England, and
was for many years involved with costume
design for court masques.

Jones³ /dʒəʊnz/, John Paul (born John Paul)
(1747–92), Scottish-born American naval officer. In 1775 he joined the American Continental Navy and carried out a daring
series of attacks on shipping in British
waters, his best-known exploit being his
engagement and sinking of the naval frig-
ate *Serapis* while in command of the *Bon-
homme Richard* (1779). In 1788 he joined the
Russian navy as a rear-admiral.

Jones⁴ /dʒəʊnz/, Robert Tyre ('Bobby')
(1902–71), American golfer. In a short com-
petitive career (1923–30), and as an amateur, he won thirteen major competitions
out of twenty-seven, including four American and three British Open championships.

Jones⁵ /dʒəʊnz/, Tom (born Thomas Jones
Woodward) (born 1940), Welsh pop singer.
He was heard in 1963 by the songwriter
Gordon Mills, who advised him to change
his name to Tom Jones and promoted his
powerful voice and masculine image. The
song 'It's Not Unusual' (1965) reached number one within two weeks and eventually
sold 3 million copies. Jones's other hits
include 'The Green, Green Grass of Home'
(1966) and 'Delilah' (1968).

Jong /jʊŋ/, Erica (Mann) (born 1942), American poet and novelist. She made her name
with the award-winning poetry collection
Fruits and Vegetables (1971). Her international reputation is based on the picaresque
novels *Fear of Flying* (1973), recounting
the sexual exploits of its heroine Isadora
Wing, and *Fanny* (1980), written in a
pseudo-18th-century style.

Jonson /'dʒɒns(ə)n/, Benjamin ('Ben') (1572–
1637), English dramatist and poet. With his
play *Every Man in His Humour* (1598) he
established his 'comedy of humours',
whereby each character is dominated by a
particular obsession. His vigorous and
often savage wit is evident in his comedies
Volpone (1606), *The Alchemist* (1610), and *Bartholomew Fair* (1614). During the reign of
James I his prestige and influence were

unrivalled, and he became the first Poet Laureate in the modern sense.

Joplin[1] /'dʒɒplɪn/, Janis (1943–70), American singer. At the age of 17 Joplin left Port Arthur, Texas, to hitchhike across America. She drifted into the hippy subculture of San Francisco, where she became vocalist with Big Brother and the Holding Company, and gave a raw, powerful performance with them at the Monterey pop festival in 1967. Joplin's most successful album, *Pearl*, and her number-one single 'Me and Bobby McGee' were released posthumously, shortly after her death from a heroin overdose.

Joplin[2] /'dʒɒplɪn/, Scott (1868–1917), American pianist and composer. One of the creators of ragtime, he was the first to write down his compositions. Two of Joplin's best-known rags, 'Original Rags' and 'Maple Leaf Rag', were written in 1899. The latter was so successful that a million copies of the sheet music were sold. Joplin's music, including the rag 'The Entertainer', was featured in the film *The Sting* (1973).

Jordaens /jɔː'dɑːns/, Jacob (1593–1678), Flemish painter. Influenced by Rubens, he painted in warm colours and is noted for his boisterous peasant scenes. His major works include *The King Drinks* (1638).

Jordan /'dʒɔːd(ə)n/, Michael (Jeffrey) (born 1963), American basketball player. Playing for the Chicago Bulls from 1984, he was the National Basketball Association's Most Valuable Player five times (1988, 1991, 1992, 1996, 1997) and the leading points scorer between 1987 and 1992. A member of the US Olympic gold-medal-winning teams in 1984 and 1992, he retired in 1993, but returned in 1995.

Joseph, St, carpenter of Nazareth, husband of the Virgin Mary. At the time of the Annunciation, he was betrothed to Mary. Feast day, 19 March.

Josephine /'dʒəʊzɪˌfiːn/, (born Marie Joséphine Rose Tascher de la Pagerie) (1763–1814), Empress of France 1804–09. Born in the West Indies, she was married to the Viscount de Beauharnais before marrying Napoleon in 1796. Their marriage proved childless and Josephine was divorced by Napoleon in 1809.

Josephus /dʒəʊ'siːfəs/, Flavius (born Joseph ben Matthias) (c.37–c.100), Jewish historian, general, and Pharisee. A leader of the Jewish revolt against the Romans from 66, he was captured in 67; his life was spared when he prophesied that Vespasian would become emperor. He subsequently received Roman citizenship and a pension, and is remembered as the author of the *Jewish War*, an eyewitness account of the events leading up to the revolt, and of *Antiquities of the Jews*, a history running from the Creation to 66.

Josquin des Prez /'ʒɒskæn/ see DES PREZ.

Joule /dʒuːl/, James Prescott (1818–89), English physicist. Experimenting in his private laboratory and at the family's brewery, he established that all forms of energy were basically the same and interchangeable — the basic principle of what is now called the first law of thermodynamics. Among other things, he measured the thermal effects of an electric current due to the resistance of the wire, establishing the law governing this. In 1852 he and William Thomson, later Lord Kelvin, discovered the fall in temperature when gases expand (the Joule–Thomson effect), which led to the development of the refrigerator and to the science of cryogenics.

Joyce /dʒɔɪs/, James (Augustine Aloysius) (1882–1941), Irish writer. He left Ireland in 1904 and thereafter lived in Trieste, Zurich, and Paris, becoming one of the most important writers of the modernist movement. His first major publication was *Dubliners* (1914), a collection of short stories depicting his native Dublin, which was followed by the semi-autobiographical novel *A Portrait of the Artist as a Young Man* (1914–15). His novel *Ulysses* (published in Paris in 1922 but banned in the UK and the US until 1936) revolutionized the form and structure of the modern novel and influenced the development of the stream of consciousness technique. *Finnegans Wake* (1939) pushed linguistic experimentation to the extreme.

Juan Carlos /hwɑːn 'kɑːlɒs/ (born 1938) (full name Juan Carlos Victor María de Borbón y Borbón), grandson of Alfonso XIII, king of Spain since 1975. He was nominated by Franco as his successor and became king when Franco died. His reign has seen Spain's increasing liberalization and its entry into NATO and the European Community.

Juárez /'hwɑːrez/, Benito Pablo (1806–72), Mexican statesman, President 1861–4 and 1867–72. His refusal to repay Mexico's for-

eign debts led to the occupation of Mexico by Napoleon III and the establishment of Maximilian as emperor of Mexico in 1864. The withdrawal of the occupying French forces in 1867 prompted the execution of Maximilian and the rehabilitation of Juárez in the same year.

Jubran, Khalil, see GIBRAN.

Judas /'dʒuːdəs/, see JUDE, ST.

Judas Maccabaeus /,mækə'biːəs/ (died c.161 BC), Jewish leader. He led a Jewish revolt in Judaea against the Seleucid king Antiochus IV Epiphanes from around 167, and succeeded in recovering Jerusalem, dedicating the Temple anew, and protecting Judaism from Hellenization. He also features in the Apocrypha as the hero of the Maccabees.

Jude, St /dʒuːd/ (known as Judas) an Apostle, supposed brother of James. Thaddaeus (mentioned in St Matthew's Gospel) is traditionally identified with him. According to tradition he was martyred in Persia with St Simon. Feast day (with St Simon), 28 October.

Jugurtha /dʒə'ɡɜːθə/ (died 104 BC), joint king of Numidia c.118–104. His attacks on his royal partners prompted intervention by Rome and led to the outbreak of the Jugurthine War (112–105). He was eventually captured by the Roman general Marius and executed in Rome.

Julian /'dʒuːlɪən/ (known as the Apostate) (full name Flavius Claudius Julianus) (AD c.331–63), Roman emperor 360–3, nephew of Constantine. He restored paganism as the state cult in place of Christianity, but this move was reversed after his death on campaign against the Persians.

Julian of Norwich /'nɒrɪdʒ, -rɪtʃ/ (c.1342–c.1413), English mystic. Her name probably derives from St Julian's Church, Norwich, outside which she is said to have lived as a religious recluse. She is chiefly associated with the *Revelations of Divine Love* (c.1393), which describe a series of visions she had at the end of a serious illness in 1373. In her account, she affirms the love of God and depicts the Holy Trinity as Father, Mother, and Lord.

Julius Caesar /,dʒuːlɪəs 'siːzə(r)/, Gaius (100–44 BC), Roman general and statesman. He established the First Triumvirate with Pompey and Crassus (60), and became consul in 59, obtaining command of the prov-

inces of Illyricum, Cisalpine Gaul, and Transalpine Gaul. Between 58 and 51 he fought the Gallic Wars, subjugating Transalpine Gaul, invading Britain (55–54), and acquiring immense power. Resentment at this on the part of Pompey and other powerful Romans led to civil war, which resulted in Pompey's defeat at Pharsalus (48). Julius Caesar was made dictator of the Roman Empire and initiated a series of reforms, including the introduction of the Julian calendar. Hostility to Caesar's autocracy culminated in his murder on the Ides (15th) of March in a conspiracy led by Brutus and Cassius.

Jung /jʊŋ/, Carl (Gustav) (1875–1961), Swiss psychologist. He collaborated with Sigmund Freud in the development of the psychoanalytic theory of personality, though he later divorced himself from Freud's viewpoint because of its preoccupation with sexuality as the determinant of personality. Jung originated the concept of introvert and extrovert personality, and of the four psychological functions of sensation, intuition, thinking, and feeling. In his major work, *The Psychology of the Unconscious* (1912), he proposed the existence of a collective unconscious, which he combined with a theory of archetypes for studying the history and psychology of religion.

Jussieu /ʒuː'sjɜː/, Antoine Laurent de (1748–1836), French botanist. Jussieu came from a family of botanists whose home was a centre for plant collection and research. From extensive observation he grouped plants into families on the basis of common essential properties and, in *Genera Plantarum* (1789), developed the system on which modern plant classification is based.

Justin, St /'dʒʌstɪn/ (known as St Justin the Martyr) (c.100–165), Christian philosopher. Born in Samaria, he became a Christian convert at Ephesus (c.130). He is remembered for his *Apologia* (c.150), a defence of Christianity. Tradition holds that he was martyred in Rome together with some of his followers. Feast day, 1 June.

Justinian /dʒʌ'stɪnɪən/ (Latin name Flavius Petrus Sabbatius Justinianus) (483–565), Byzantine emperor 527–65. He set out to recover the lost provinces of the Western Empire, and through his general Belisarius (c.505–65) succeeded in reclaiming North

Africa from the Vandals, Italy from the Ostrogoths, and Spain from the Visigoths. Justinian's codification of Roman law in 529 had a significant impact on the development of law in European countries. He carried out an active building programme throughout the Empire and commissioned the construction of St Sophia at Constantinople in 532.

Juvenal /ˈdʒuːvɪn(ə)l/ (Latin name Decimus Junius Juvenalis) (c.60–c.140), Roman satirist. His sixteen verse satires present a savage attack on the vice and folly of Roman society, chiefly in the reign of the emperor Domitian. They deal variously with the hardship of poverty, the profligacy of the rich, and the futility of ambition.

K

Kádár /ˈkɑːdɑː(r)/, János (1912–89), Hungarian statesman, First Secretary of the Hungarian Socialist Workers' Party 1956–88 and Prime Minister 1956–8 and 1961–5. He replaced Imre Nagy as Premier after crushing the Hungarian uprising of 1956. Kádár consistently supported the Soviet Union, involving Hungarian troops in the 1968 invasion of Czechoslovakia, while retaining a degree of decentralization for the economy. His policy of 'consumer socialism' made Hungary the most affluent state in eastern Europe. He was removed as First Secretary following his resistance to the political reforms of the 1980s.

Kafka /ˈkæfkə/, Franz (1883–1924), Czech novelist, who wrote in German. A sense of guilt haunts Kafka's stories, and his work is characterized by its lack of scenic description and its portrayal of an enigmatic and nightmarish reality where the individual is perceived as lonely, perplexed, and threatened. *The Metamorphosis* (1917) was one of the few works published in Kafka's lifetime: his novels *The Trial* (1925) and *The Castle* (1926) were published posthumously by his friend the writer Max Brod (1884–1968), against the directions of his will.

Kaiser /ˈkaɪzə(r)/, Georg (1878–1945), German dramatist. Author of some sixty plays, he is best known for his expressionist plays *The Burghers of Calais* (1914), and *Gas I* (1918) and *Gas II* (1920); the last two provide a gruesome interpretation of futuristic science ending with the extinction of all life by poisonous gas.

Kaiser Wilhelm, Wilhelm II of Germany (see WILHELM II).

Kalidasa /ˌkælɪˈdɑːsə/, Indian poet and dramatist. He is best known for his drama *Sakuntala*, the love story of King Dushyanta and the maiden Sakuntala. Kalidasa probably lived in the 5th century AD, although there is some diversity of opinion on this point.

Kalinin /kəˈliːnɪn/, Mikhail Ivanovich (1875–1946), Soviet statesman, head of state of the USSR 1919–46. Born in Russia, he was a founder of the newspaper *Pravda* in 1912.

Kamerlingh Onnes /ˌkæmənlɪŋ ˈɒnɪs/, Heike (1853–1926), Dutch physicist, who studied cryogenic phenomena. Using the Joule–Thomson effect, by which a gas changes temperature when it is allowed to expand without doing any external work, he succeeded in liquefying helium in 1908, and achieved a temperature of less than one degree above absolute zero. Onnes discovered the phenomenon of superconductivity in 1911, and was awarded the Nobel Prize for his work on low-temperature physics two years later.

Kandinsky /kænˈdɪnskɪ/, Wassily (1866–1944), Russian painter and theorist. He was a pioneer of abstract art, producing non-representational works as early as 1910. His treatise *On the Spiritual in Art* (1912) urged the expression of inner and essential feelings in art rather than the representation of surface appearances of the natural world. In 1911 he co-founded the Munich-based *Blaue Reiter* group of artists; he later taught at the Bauhaus (1922–33). His paintings from this time became almost wholly abstract, with their energy and movement being conveyed purely by colour, line, and shape.

Kant /kænt/, Immanuel (1724–1804), German philosopher. In the *Critique of Pure Reason* (1781) he countered Hume's empiricism by arguing that the human mind can neither confirm, deny, nor scientifically demonstrate the ultimate nature of reality. He claimed, however, that it can know the objects of experience, which it interprets with notions of space and time and orders according to twelve categories of thought, grouped under the classes of quantity, quality, reason, and modality. Kant's *Critique of Practical Reason* (1788) deals with ethics and affirms the existence of an absolute moral law — the categorical imperative — whose motivation is reason. His idealism left an important legacy for the philosophy of Hegel and Fichte.

Kapil Dev /ˌkæpɪl ˈdev/ (full name Kapil Dev Nikhanj) (born 1959), Indian cricketer. He made his début for India in 1978 as a medium-pace bowler, soon developing into

an all-rounder. He had two spells as captain, in one of which he led India to victory in the 1983 World Cup. In 1994 he passed Richard Hadlee's world record of 431 test match wickets.

Kapoor /kæˈpʊə(r)/, (Prithvi) Raj (1924–88), Indian actor and director. In 1944 he founded the Prithvi Theatres in Bombay, a company notable for the realism it brought to Hindi drama. Kapoor went on to direct a large number of films for the Indian market. Productions, in which Kapoor often played the lead, include *Pathan* (1946).

Karadžić /ˈkærəˌdʒɪtʃ/, Vuk Stefanović (1787–1864), Serbian writer, grammarian, lexicographer, and folklorist. He modified the Cyrillic alphabet for Serbian written usage and compiled a Serbian dictionary in 1818. Widely claimed to be the father of modern Serbian literature, he undertook the task of collecting and publishing national folk stories and poems (1821–33).

Karajan /ˈkærəˌjæn/, Herbert von (1908–89), Austrian conductor. He is chiefly remembered as the principal conductor of the Berlin Philharmonic Orchestra (1955–89), although he was also associated with the Vienna State Opera (1957–64). Karajan was artistic director of the Salzburg Festival (1956–60; 1964) and founded the Salzburg Easter Festival of operas in 1967.

Karl XII see CHARLES XII.

Karloff /ˈkɑːlɒf/, Boris (born William Henry Pratt) (1887–1969), British-born American actor. His name is chiefly linked with horror films, such as *Frankenstein* (1931) and *The Body Snatcher* (1945).

Karpov /ˈkɑːpɒf/, Anatoli (born 1951), Russian chess player. He was world champion from 1975 until defeated by Gary Kasparov in 1985.

Kasparov /ˈkæspəˌrɒf/, Gary (born Gary Weinstein) (born 1963), Azerbaijani chess player, of Armenian Jewish descent. At the age of 22 he became the youngest-ever world champion, defeating Anatoli Karpov in 1985. He has retained the title ever since, defending it against challenges from Karpov in 1986, 1987, and 1990. In 1997 he took on IBM'S Deeper Blue computer and was defeated 3.5–2.5.

Kauffmann /ˈkaʊfmən/, Angelica (also **Kauffman**) (1740–1807), Swiss painter. She made her name in Rome with her portrait of Johann Winckelmann (1764). In London

from 1766, she became well known for her neoclassical and allegorical paintings (for example *Self-Portrait Hesitating Between the Arts of Music and Painting*, 1791), and for her decorative wall-paintings in houses designed by Robert Adam and his brothers. She was a founder member of the Royal Academy of Arts (1768).

Kaunda /kɑːˈʊndə/, Kenneth (David) (born 1924), Zambian statesman, President 1964–91. He led the United National Independence Party to electoral victory in 1964, becoming Prime Minister and the first President of independent Zambia. As chairman of the Organization of African Unity (1970–1; 1987–8), he played a key role in the negotiations leading to Namibian independence in 1990.

Kawabata /ˌkɑːwəˈbɑːtə/, Yasunari (1899–1972), Japanese novelist. Known as an experimental writer in the 1920s, he reverted to traditional Japanese novel forms in the mid-1930s. His novels include *The Izu Dancer* (1925), *Snow Country* (1935–47), and *The Sound of the Mountain* (1949–54). He won the Nobel Prize for literature in 1968, the first Japanese writer to do so.

Kaye /keɪ/, Danny (born David Daniel Kominski) (1913–87), American actor and comedian. After a successful Broadway career he made his first feature film in 1944, and went on to take a number of roles in which he became known for his mimicry, comic songs, and slapstick humour. His films include *The Secret Life of Walter Mitty* (1947), *Hans Christian Andersen* (1952), and *The Court Jester* (1956).

Kazan /kəˈzæn/, Elia (born Elia Kazanjoglous) (born 1909), Turkish-born American film and theatre director. In 1947 he co-founded the Actors' Studio, one of the leading centres of method acting. Kazan's stage productions include *A Streetcar Named Desire* (1947), which he made into a film four years later; both starred Marlon Brando. Other films include *On the Waterfront* (1954), again with Marlon Brando, and *East of Eden* (1955), starring James Dean.

Kean /kiːn/, Edmund (1787–1833), English actor. He achieved fame with his performance as Shylock at London's Drury Lane theatre in 1814, and became particularly renowned for his interpretations of Shakespearian tragic roles, notably those of Macbeth and Iago.

Keating /'ki:tɪŋ/, Paul (John) (born 1944), Australian Labor statesman, Prime Minister 1991–6. He entered politics in 1969 when he became a member of the House of Representatives. He served as federal treasurer (1983–91) and deputy Prime Minister (1990–1) under Bob Hawke, whom he replaced as Premier in 1991. His term of office was notable for a vociferous republican campaign as well as for measures to combat high unemployment.

Keaton /'ki:t(ə)n/, Buster (born Joseph Francis Keaton) (1895–1966), American actor and director. His deadpan face and acrobatic skills made him one of the biggest comedy stars of the silent-film era. Major films include *Our Hospitality* (1923), *The Navigator* (1924), and *The General* (1926).

Keats /ki:ts/, John (1795–1821), English poet. In 1818 he wrote his best-known poems, including 'Hyperion', 'The Eve of St Agnes', 'La Belle Dame sans Merci', 'Ode to a Nightingale', 'Ode on a Grecian Urn', and 'Ode to Autumn', all published in 1820. A principal figure of the romantic movement, Keats was noted for his spiritual and intellectual contemplation of beauty. He died in Rome of tuberculosis.

Keble /'ki:b(ə)l/, John (1792–1866), English churchman. His sermon on national apostasy (1833) is generally held to mark the beginning of the Oxford Movement. Politically, it failed to win support for its idea that the law of the land need not coincide with the Church's teaching; theologically, however, the work of Keble's followers did much to revive traditional Catholic teaching, as well as to define and mould the Church of England.

Keegan /'ki:gən/, (Joseph) Kevin (born 1951), English footballer and manager. He played as an attacker for clubs which included Liverpool (1971–7), Hamburg (1977–80), and Newcastle United (1982–4), and won sixty-three caps for England (1972–82). He was voted European Footballer of the Year in 1978 and 1979. He managed Newcastle United 1992–7, leading them into the Premier League as First Division champions, and joined Fulham in 1997.

Keeler /'ki:lə(r)/, Christine (born 1942), English model and showgirl. She achieved notoriety in 1963 through her affair with the Conservative Cabinet minister John Profumo at a time when she was also mistress of a Soviet attaché. Profumo resigned and Keeler's patron, Stephen Ward, committed suicide after being charged with living off the immoral earnings of Keeler and her friend Mandy Rice-Davies. Keeler was imprisoned on related charges, but her trial was called into question after the publication of her autobiography and the release of the film *Scandal* (1989).

Keene /ki:n/, Charles Samuel (1823–91), English illustrator and caricaturist. He is remembered for his work in the weekly journal *Punch* from 1851.

Kekulé /'kekjʊˌleɪ/, Friedrich August (full name Friedrich August Kekulé von Stradonitz) (1829–96), German chemist. He was one of the founders of structural organic chemistry, in which he was perhaps helped by his early training as an architect. He suggested in 1858 that carbon was tetravalent, and that carbon atoms could combine with others to form complex chains. Kekulé is best known for discovering the ring structure of benzene, the key to understanding many organic compounds.

Keller /'kelə(r)/, Helen (Adams) (1880–1968), American writer, social reformer, and academic. Blind and deaf from the age of nineteen months, she learned how to read, type, and speak and went on to champion the cause of blind, deaf, and dumb people throughout the world. She is particularly remembered for her campaigning in aid of the American Foundation for the Blind.

Kellogg /'kelɒg/, Will Keith (1860–1951), American food manufacturer. He collaborated with his brother, a doctor, to develop a process of manufacturing a breakfast cereal for sanatorium patients that consisted of crisp flakes of rolled and toasted wheat and corn. The product's success led to the establishment of the W. K. Kellogg company in 1906 and a subsequent revolution in Western eating habits.

Kelly[1] /'kelɪ/, Edward ('Ned') (1855–80), Australian outlaw. He was the leader of a band of horse and cattle thieves and bank raiders operating in Victoria. A bushranger from 1878, Kelly was eventually hanged in Melbourne.

Kelly[2] /'kelɪ/, Gene (born Eugene Curran Kelly) (1912–96), American dancer and choreographer. He began his career on Broadway in 1938 and made a successful transition to film with *For Me and My Girl* (1942). He went on to perform in and

choreograph many film musicals, including *Anchors Aweigh* (1945), *An American in Paris* (1951), and *Singin' in the Rain* (1952).

Kelly[3] /'kelɪ/, Grace (Patricia) (also called (from 1956) Princess Grace of Monaco) (1928–82), American film actress. Her first starring role came in the classic western *High Noon* (1952). She won an Oscar for her performance in *The Country Girl* (1954) and also made three Hitchcock films, including *Rear Window* (1954). Kelly retired from films in 1956 on her marriage to Prince Rainier III of Monaco (born 1923). She died in a car accident.

Kelly[4] /'kelɪ/, Petra (Karin) (1947–92), German political leader. Formerly a member of the German Social Democratic Party, she became disillusioned with their policies and in 1979 co-founded the Green Party, a broad alliance of environmentalists, feminists, and anti-nuclear activists. She became the Party's leading spokesperson and in 1983 was one of seventeen Green Party members elected to the West German Parliament. The cause of her death remains a subject of controversy.

Kelvin /'kelvɪn/, William Thomson, 1st Baron (1824–1907), British physicist, professor of natural philosophy at Glasgow 1846–95. He restated the second law of thermodynamics in 1850, and introduced the absolute scale of temperature. His concept of an electromagnetic field influenced Maxwell's electromagnetic theory of light, which Kelvin never accepted. He was involved in the laying of the first Atlantic cable, for which he invented several instruments, and he devised many scientific instruments for other purposes. Kelvin's calculation of an age for the earth, although a gross underestimate, showed that physics could be useful in helping to establish a geological time-scale.

Kemal Pasha /ke'mɑ:l ˌpɑ:ʃə/ see ATATÜRK.

Kemble[1] /'kemb(ə)l/, Frances Anne ('Fanny') (1809–93), English actress. The daughter of Charles Kemble and the niece of Sarah Siddons, she was a success in both Shakespearian comedy and tragedy, playing such parts as Portia, Beatrice, Juliet, and Lady Macbeth.

Kemble[2] /'kemb(ə)l/, John Philip (1757–1823), English actor-manager, brother of Sarah Siddons. He was noted for his performances in Shakespearian tragedy, notably as Hamlet and Coriolanus, and for his

interpretations of historical roles such as Brutus in *Julius Caesar*. He was manager of the Drury Lane (1788–1803) and Covent Garden (1803–17) theatres. His younger brother Charles (1775–1854) was also a successful actor-manager.

Kempe /kemp/, Margery (c.1373–c.1440), English mystic. From about 1432 to 1436 she dictated one of the first autobiographies in English, *The Book of Margery Kempe*. This account of her spiritual life describes in a vernacular style her series of pilgrimages to Jerusalem, Rome, Germany, and Spain, as well as details of her ecstatic visions.

Kempis, Thomas à, see THOMAS À KEMPIS.

Kendall /'kend(ə)l/, Edward Calvin (1886–1972), American biochemist. He was the first to isolate crystalline thyroxine from the thyroid gland. From the adrenal cortex he obtained a number of steroid hormones, one of which was later named cortisone, and several of which are now of great value in the treatment of rheumatic, allergic, and inflammatory diseases. He shared a Nobel Prize in 1950.

Keneally /kə'nælɪ, -'ni:lɪ/, Thomas (Michael) (born 1935), Australian novelist. He first gained notice for *The Chant of Jimmy Blacksmith* (1972). Later works include war novels such as *Confederates* (1979), and the Booker Prize-winning *Schindler's Ark* (1982), the true story of the German industrialist Oskar Schindler, who helped more than 1,200 Jews to escape death in Nazi concentration camps; the book was filmed by Steven Spielberg in 1993 as *Schindler's List*.

Kennedy[1] /'kenədɪ/, Edward Moore ('Teddy') (born 1932), American Democratic politician. The brother of John F. Kennedy and Robert F. Kennedy, he was elected to the Senate in 1962. His subsequent political career was overshadowed by his involvement in a mysterious fatal car accident at Chappaquiddick Island (1969), although he remains a prominent Democratic spokesman.

Kennedy[2] /'kenədɪ/, John F(itzgerald) (known as 'JFK') (1917–63), American Democratic statesman, 35th President of the US 1961–3. A national war hero during the Second World War, Kennedy became, at 43, the youngest man ever to be elected President, as well as the first Catholic. He gained a popular reputation as an advocate of civil rights, although reforms were de-

layed by Congress until 1964. In foreign affairs he recovered from the fiasco of the Bay of Pigs invasion of Cuba to demand successfully the withdrawal of Soviet missiles from the country, and negotiated the Test-Ban Treaty of 1963 with the USSR and the UK. Kennedy was assassinated while riding in a motorcade through Dallas, Texas, in November 1963; Lee Harvey Oswald was charged with his murder, but was himself shot before he could stand trial. Oswald was said to be the sole gunman by the Warren Commission (1964), but the House of Representatives Assassinations Committee (1979) concluded that more than one gunman had been involved; the affair remains the focus for a number of conspiracy theories.

Kennedy[3] /'kenədɪ/, Robert F(rancis) (1925–68), American Democratic statesman. The brother of John F. Kennedy and Edward Kennedy, he closely assisted his brother John in domestic policy, serving as Attorney-General (1961–4), and was a champion of the civil-rights movement. Robert Kennedy stood as a prospective presidential candidate in 1968, but was assassinated during his campaign.

Kennelly /'kenəlɪ/, Arthur Edwin (1861–1939), American electrical engineer. His principal work was on the theory of alternating currents, and he also worked on the practical problems of electrical transmission. Kennelly independently discovered the layer in the atmosphere responsible for reflecting radio waves back to earth (see HEAVISIDE). He helped to develop electrical units and standards, and promoted the adoption of the metric system.

Kenneth I /'kenɪθ/ (known as Kenneth MacAlpin) (died 858), king of Scotland c.844–58. He is traditionally viewed as the founder of the kingdom of Scotland, which was established following Kenneth's defeat of the Picts in about 844.

Kent /kent/, William (c.1685–1748), English architect and landscape gardener. He promoted the Palladian style of architecture in England and is renowned for such works as the Treasury (1733–7) and Whitehall (1734–6). Holkham Hall, begun in 1734, was one of the first English buildings to feature interiors and furniture designed by the architect. Kent is chiefly remembered, however, for his landscape gardens at Stowe House in Buckinghamshire (c.1730). His design principles overturned the formal taste

of the time and anticipated the innovations of Capability Brown.

Kenton /'kentən/, Stan (born Stanley Newcomb) (1912–79), American band-leader, composer, and arranger. Kenton began his professional career in 1934 as a pianist and arranger and formed his own orchestra in 1940. He had early hits with 'Artistry in Rhythm' (1941) and 'Eager Beaver' (1943), but is particularly associated with the big-band jazz style of the 1950s.

Kenyatta /ken'jætə/, Jomo (c.1891–1978), Kenyan statesman, Prime Minister of Kenya 1963 and President 1964–78. He was imprisoned from 1952 to 1961 for alleged complicity in the Mau Mau uprising. On his release he was elected president of the Kenya African National Union and led his country to independence in 1963, subsequently serving as independent Kenya's first President.

Kepler /'keplə(r)/, Johannes (1571–1630), German astronomer. He settled in Prague in 1599, becoming Tycho Brahe's assistant and later court mathematician to the emperor. His analysis of Brahe's planetary observations enabled him to discover the laws governing planetary motion, and foreshadowed the general application of scientific method to astronomy. The first two laws recognized the elliptical orbits of the planets; in *Harmonices Mundi* (1620) he expounded the third law of planetary dynamics, relating the distances of the planets from the sun to their orbital periods. Despite these advances, Kepler's approach remained medieval in spirit; he believed in the music of the spheres and sought an inner relationship between the planets that would express it.

Kern /kɜːn/, Jerome (David) (1885–1945), American composer. He wrote several musical comedies, including *Showboat* (1927), which proved a major influence in the development of the musical. It also featured the song 'Ol' Man River', first sung by Paul Robeson.

Kerouac /'keruˌæk/, Jack (born Jean-Louis Lebris de Kérouac) (1922–69), American novelist and poet, of French-Canadian descent. A leading figure of the beat generation, he is best known for his semi-autobiographical novel *On the Road* (1957). Other works include *Big Sur* (1962).

Kesey /'kiːzɪ/, Ken (Elton) (born 1935), American novelist. His best-known novel,

One Flew Over the Cuckoo's Nest (1962), is based on his experiences as a ward attendant in a mental hospital. Kesey's adventures with the Merry Pranksters, a group who pioneered the use of psychedelic drugs, are described in *The Electric Kool-Aid Acid Test* (1967) by Tom Wolfe.

Kettering /'ketərɪŋ/, Charles Franklin (1876–1958), American automobile engineer. His first significant development was the electric starter (1912). He was leader of research at General Motors until 1947, discovering with his team tetraethyl lead as an antiknock agent and defining the octane rating of fuels. He did important work on two-stroke diesel engines, which came into widespread use for railway locomotives and road coaches, and was also responsible for the development of synchromesh gearboxes, automatic transmissions, and power steering.

Keynes /keɪnz/, John Maynard, 1st Baron (1883–1946), English economist. Keynes served as an adviser to the Treasury during both world wars and was its representative at the Versailles peace conference (1919), subsequently becoming one of the most influential critics of the Treaty of Versailles. He laid the foundations of modern macroeconomics with *The General Theory of Employment, Interest and Money* (1936). In this he argued that full employment is not a natural condition but is determined by effective demand, requiring government spending on public works to stimulate this. His theories influenced Roosevelt's decision to introduce the American New Deal.

Khachaturian /ˌkætʃə'tʊərɪən/, Aram (Ilich) (1903–78), Soviet composer, born in Georgia. In his First Symphony (1934) he first displayed his lifelong interest in the folk-music traditions of Armenia, Georgia, and Russia. His Second Symphony (1943) and the ballet *Gayane* (1942, including the well-known 'Sabre Dance') were written to celebrate the twenty-fifth anniversary of the Bolshevik revolution. His other works include his Piano Concerto (1936) and the ballet *Spartacus* (1956).

Khama /'kɑːmə/, Sir Seretse (1921–80), Botswanan statesman, Prime Minister of Bechuanaland 1965 and President of Botswana 1966–80. An heir to the chieftainship of the ruling tribe in Bechuanaland, he was banished because of opposition to his marriage to an Englishwoman in 1948.

He returned with his wife in 1956 and formed the Democratic Party in 1962, leading the party to a landslide victory in the elections of 1965; he became Botswana's first President the following year. A strong believer in multiracial democracy, he achieved nationwide free education.

Khan [1], Ayub, see AYUB KHAN.

Khan [2] /kɑːn/, Imran (full name Imran Ahmad Khan Niazi) (born 1952), Pakistani cricketer. He made his test début in 1970 and served as captain of his country in four periods between 1982 and 1992. A batsman and fast bowler, he also played county cricket for Worcestershire (1971–6) and Sussex (1977–88). After retiring from cricket in 1992, he entered politics in Pakistan.

Khan [3] /kɑːn/, Jahangir (born 1963), Pakistani squash player. In 1979 he became world amateur champion at the age of 15; after turning professional he was world squash champion five consecutive times (1981–5), and again in 1988.

Khomeini /xɒ'meɪnɪ/, Ruhollah (known as Ayatollah Khomeini) (1900–89), Iranian Shiite Muslim leader. After sixteen years in exile he returned to Iran in 1979 to lead an Islamic revolution which overthrew the shah. He established a fundamentalist Islamic republic, supported the seizure of the US embassy (1979) by Iranian students and relentlessly pursued the Iran–Iraq War 1980–8. In 1989 he issued a fatwa condemning Salman Rushdie, author of *The Satanic Verses*, provoking criticism from the West.

Khrushchev /'krʊʃtʃɒf/, Nikita (Sergeevich) (1894–1971), Soviet statesman, Premier of the USSR 1958–64. Born in Ukraine, Khrushchev became First Secretary of the Communist Party of the USSR (1953–64) after the death of Stalin. He played a prominent part in the 'de-Stalinization' programme that began in 1956, denouncing the former leader in a historic speech, and went on to succeed Bulganin as Premier (Chairman of the Council of Ministers) in 1958. He came close to war with the US over the Cuban Missile Crisis in 1962 and clashed with China over economic aid and borders. He was ousted two years later by Brezhnev and Kosygin, largely because of his antagonism to China.

Khufu /'kuːfuː/ see CHEOPS.

Kidd /kɪd/, William (known as Captain Kidd) (1645–1701), Scottish pirate. Sent to the Indian Ocean in 1695 in command of an anti-pirate expedition, Kidd became a pirate himself. In 1699 he went to Boston in the hope of obtaining a pardon, but was arrested in the same year and hanged in London.

Kierkegaard /ˈkɪəkəˌɡɑːd/, Søren (Aabye) (1813–55), Danish philosopher. Viewed as one of the founders of existentialism, he opposed the prevailing Hegelian philosophy of the time by affirming the importance of individual experience and choice. Accordingly, he refused to subscribe to the possibility of an objective system of Christian doctrinal truths, and held that one could know God only through a 'leap of faith'. His philosophical works include *Either-Or* (1843); he is also noted for his religious writings, including *The Concept of Dread* (1844) and *The Sickness Unto Death* (1849).

Kieslowski /kɪˈslɒfskɪ/, Krzysztof (1941–96), Polish film director. Kieslowski's films are noted for their mannered style and their artistic, philosophical nature. In 1988 he made the film series *Dekalog*, each film being a visual interpretation of one of the Ten Commandments. His other works include *The Double Life of Véronique* (1991) and the trilogy *Three Colours* (1993–4).

Kim Il Sung /ˌkɪm ɪl ˈsʊŋ/ (born Kim Song Ju) (1912–94), Korean Communist statesman, first Premier of North Korea 1948–72 and President 1972–94. In the 1930s and 1940s he led the armed resistance to the Japanese domination of Korea; following the country's partition at the end of the Second World War he became Premier of the Democratic People's Republic of Korea (1948). He ordered his forces to invade South Korea in 1950, precipitating the Korean War (1950–3), and remained committed to the reunification of the country. He maintained a one-party state and created a personality cult around himself and his family; on his death he was quickly replaced in power by his son Kim Jong Il (born 1942).

King[1] /kɪŋ/, B. B. (born Riley B King) (born 1925), American blues singer and guitarist. He became an established blues performer in the 1950s and early 1960s, but only came to the notice of a wider audience in the late 1960s, when his style of guitar playing was imitated by rock musicians.

King[2] /kɪŋ/, Billie Jean (born 1943), American tennis player. She won a record twenty Wimbledon titles, including six singles titles (1966–8; 1972–3; 1975), ten doubles titles, and four mixed doubles titles. King retired in 1983.

King[3] /kɪŋ/, Martin Luther (1929–68), American Baptist minister and civil-rights leader. King opposed discrimination against blacks by organizing non-violent resistance and peaceful mass demonstrations, notably the year-long black boycott of the local bus company in Montgomery, Alabama, in 1955 and the march on Washington involving 200,000 demonstrators in 1963. At the latter, King delivered his celebrated speech beginning 'I have a dream . . .'. He was awarded the Nobel Peace Prize in 1964. King was assassinated in Memphis in 1968.

King[4] /kɪŋ/, William Lyon Mackenzie (1874–1950), Canadian Liberal statesman, Prime Minister 1921–6, 1926–30, and 1935–48. The grandson of William Lyon Mackenzie, he represented Canada at the imperial conferences in London (1923; 1926; 1927), where he played an important role in establishing the status of the self-governing nations of the Commonwealth. He went on to strengthen ties with the UK and the US and introduced a number of social reforms, including unemployment insurance (1940).

Kingsley /ˈkɪŋzlɪ/, Charles (1819–75), English novelist and clergyman. He is remembered for his historical novel *Westward Ho!* (1855) and for his classic children's story *The Water-Babies* (1863).

Kinsey /ˈkɪnzɪ/, Alfred Charles (1894–1956), American zoologist and sex researcher. He co-founded and directed the Institute for Sex Research at Indiana University, carrying out pioneering studies by interviewing large numbers of people. His best-known work, *Sexual Behaviour in the Human Male* (1948) (often referred to as the *Kinsey Report*), was controversial but highly influential. It was followed five years later by a companion volume, *Sexual Behaviour in the Human Female*.

Kipling /ˈkɪplɪŋ/, (Joseph) Rudyard (1865–1936), English novelist, short-story writer, and poet. He was born in India, where he worked as a journalist 1882–9, and set many of his writings in the India of the Raj. His best-known poems, such as 'The White Man's Burden', 'If', and 'Gunga Din', came

to be regarded as epitomizing the British colonial spirit. Of his vast and varied output, Kipling is perhaps now primarily known for his tales for children, notably *The Jungle Book* (1894) and the *Just So Stories* (1902). In 1907 he became the first English writer to be awarded the Nobel Prize for literature.

Kirchhoff /ˈkɪəxhɒf/, Gustav Robert (1824–87), German physicist, a pioneer in spectroscopy. Working with Bunsen, he developed a spectroscope which used the flame of Bunsen's gas burner in conjunction with a prism which he had designed. Using this, he discovered that solar absorption lines are specific to certain elements, developed the concept of black-body radiation, and discovered the elements caesium and rubidium. He also worked on electrical circuits and the flow of currents.

Kirchner /ˈkɪəxnə(r)/, Ernst Ludwig (1880–1938), German expressionist painter. In 1905 he was a founder of the first group of German expressionists, who sought inspiration from medieval German and primitive art and were influenced by Van Gogh and Gauguin. His paintings, such as *Five Women in the Street* (1913), are characterized by the use of bright contrasting colours and angular outlines, and often depict claustrophobic street scenes. He committed suicide in 1938 after condemnation of his work by the Nazis.

Kissinger /ˈkɪsɪndʒə(r)/, Henry (Alfred) (born 1923), German-born American statesman and diplomat, Secretary of State 1973–7. As presidential assistant to Richard Nixon for national security affairs (1968–73), he helped to improve relations with both China and the Soviet Union. His role in negotiating the withdrawal of US troops from South Vietnam in 1973 was recognized when he was jointly awarded the Nobel Peace Prize that year. Later in 1973 he restored US diplomatic relations with Egypt in the wake of the Yom Kippur War and became known for his 'shuttle diplomacy' while subsequently mediating between Israel and Syria.

Kitchener /ˈkɪtʃɪnə(r)/, (Horatio) Herbert, 1st Earl Kitchener of Khartoum (1850–1916), British soldier and statesman. After defeating the Mahdist forces at Omdurman and reconquering Sudan in 1898, he served as Chief of Staff (1900–2) in the Second Boer War and Commander-in-Chief (1902–9) in India. At the outbreak of the First World War he was made Secretary of State for War, in which capacity he was responsible for organizing the large volunteer army which eventually fought the war on the Western Front. His commanding image appeared on recruiting posters urging 'Your country needs you!' He died when the ship taking him to Russia was sunk by a mine.

Kitzinger /ˈkɪtsɪŋə(r)/, Sheila (Helena Elizabeth) (born 1929), English childbirth educator. As a member of the advisory board of the National Childbirth Trust, and as one of the Trust's teachers, she has been a pioneer of natural childbirth and a leading advocate of breastfeeding. Her many books include *The Experience of Childbirth* (1962).

Klaproth /ˈklæprəʊt/, Martin Heinrich (1743–1817), German chemist, one of the founders of analytical chemistry. He discovered three new elements (zirconium, uranium, and titanium) in certain minerals, and contributed to the identification of others. A follower of Lavoisier, he helped to introduce the latter's new system of chemistry into Germany.

Klee /kleɪ/, Paul (1879–1940), Swiss painter, resident in Germany from 1906. He began as a graphic artist and exhibited with Kandinsky, whose *Blaue Reiter* group he joined in 1912. He later concentrated on painting and developed an art of free fantasy, describing his drawing method as 'taking a line for a walk'. His paintings often have a childlike quality, as in *A Tiny Tale of a Tiny Dwarf* (1925). He taught at the Bauhaus (1920–33), after which he returned to Switzerland. Seventeen of his works appeared in the 'degenerate art' exhibition mounted by the Nazi regime in Munich in 1937.

Klein[1] /klaɪn/, Calvin (Richard) (born 1942), American fashion designer. In 1968 he formed his own company, since when he has gained a reputation for his understated fashions for both men and women, including designer jeans. He is also known for his ranges of cosmetics and household linen.

Klein[2] /klaɪn/, Melanie (1882–1960), Austrian-born psychoanalyst. Klein was the first psychologist to specialize in the psychoanalysis of small children: she discovered surprising levels of aggression and sadism in young infants, and made an important contribution to the understanding of the more severe mental disorders found in children. She moved to London in

1926, becoming an influential member of the British Psychoanalytical Society.

Klemperer /'klempərə(r)/, Otto (1885–1973), German-born conductor and composer. While conductor at the Kroll Theatre in Berlin (1927–31), he was noted as a champion of new work and opera; his premières included Janáček's opera *From the House of the Dead*. He left Germany in 1933 and became an American citizen in 1937. Klemperer subsequently established a reputation as a conductor of symphonies by Beethoven, Brahms, and Mahler, and received particular acclaim for his Beethoven recordings in London during the 1950s. He adopted Israeli citizenship in 1970.

Klerk, F. W. de, see DE KLERK.

Klimt /klɪmt/, Gustav (1862–1918), Austrian painter and designer. In 1897 he co-founded and became the first president of the avant-garde group the Vienna Secession. His work combines stylized human forms with decorative and ornate clothing or backgrounds in elaborate mosaic patterns, often using gold leaf. He depicted mythological and allegorical subjects, and painted a number of portraits, chiefly of women; his works include *Judith I* (1901) and *The Kiss* (1908).

Knox[1] /nɒks/, John (c.1505–72), Scottish Protestant reformer. After early involvement in the Scottish Reformation he spent more than a decade preaching in Europe, during which time he stayed in Geneva and was influenced by Calvin. In 1559 he returned to Scotland and played a central part in the establishment of the Church of Scotland within a Scottish Protestant state. A fiery orator, he became the spokesman of the religious interests opposed to the Catholic Mary, Queen of Scots when she returned to rule in her own right in 1561.

Knox[2] /nɒks/, Ronald Arbuthnott (1888–1957), English theologian and writer. In 1917 he converted to Roman Catholicism and later served as Catholic chaplain at Oxford University (1926–39). His translation of the Bible from the Vulgate (1945–9) was accepted for use in the Roman Catholic Church. His literary output was varied and included detective fiction and humour.

Knut see CANUTE.

Koch /kɒx/, Robert (1843–1910), German bacteriologist. He successfully identified and cultured the bacillus causing anthrax in cattle, devised better methods for obtaining pure cultures, and identified the organisms causing tuberculosis and cholera. He also studied typhoid fever, malaria, and other tropical diseases, and formulated the conditions to be satisfied before a disease can be ascribed to a specific microorganism. The techniques that Koch devised are the basis of modern bacteriological methods. He was awarded a Nobel Prize in 1905.

Kodály /'kəʊdaɪ/, Zoltán (1882–1967), Hungarian composer. He was influenced by Debussy's music while studying in Paris (1910), but his main source of inspiration was his native land; he was much involved in the collection and publication of Hungarian folk-songs. His best-known compositions include the choral work *Psalmus Hungaricus* (1923), the opera *Háry János* (1925–7), and the *Marosszék Dances* (1930).

Koestler /'kɜːstlə(r)/, Arthur (1905–83), Hungarian-born British novelist and essayist. In 1940 he settled in Britain and published his best-known novel, *Darkness at Noon*, which exposed the Stalinist purges of the 1930s. In later works such as *The Sleepwalkers* (1959), a study of the Copernican revolution in astronomy, he questioned some of the common assumptions of science. He became increasingly interested in parapsychology and left money in his will for a university chair in the subject, subsequently founded at Edinburgh. He and his wife committed suicide together.

Kohl /kəʊl/, Helmut (born 1930), German statesman, Chancellor of the Federal Republic of Germany 1982–90, and of Germany since 1990. He became chairman of the Christian Democratic Party in 1973, and was leader of the opposition until 1982, becoming Chancellor of the Federal Republic of Germany when the ruling coalition collapsed. As Chancellor he showed a strong commitment to NATO and to closer European union within the European Community. In 1990 he presided over the reunification of East and West Germany and was elected Chancellor of the united country later the same year. The longest-serving postwar German leader, he won a fourth term in 1996.

Kooning, Willem de, see DE KOONING.

Korbut /'kɔːbət/, Olga (born 1955), Soviet gymnast, born in Belarus. Her performances (especially at the 1972 Olympic

Games, where she won two individual gold medals) greatly increased the popularity of the sport.

Korchnoi /'kɔːtʃnɔɪ/, Viktor (Lvovich) (born 1931), Russian chess player. From about 1960 he was one of the world's leading players for about thirty years, ranking third (c.1967–75) and second (c.1975–80). In 1976 he left the USSR, feeling that his career was in jeopardy, and moved first to the Netherlands, then Switzerland, for whom he played in the 1978 Olympics.

Korda /'kɔːdə/, Sir Alexander (born Sándor Kellner) (1893–1956), Hungarian-born British film producer and director. He settled in Britain in 1930 and founded London Film Productions two years later. His productions included *The Private Life of Henry VIII* (1933), which he also directed, *Sanders of the River* (1935), *Things to Come* (1936), and *The Third Man* (1949).

Kosciusko /ˌkɒsɪˈʌskəʊ/, Thaddeus (or Tadeusz) (1746–1817), Polish soldier and patriot. A trained soldier, he fought for the American colonists during the War of American Independence, returning to Poland in 1784. Ten years later he led a nationalist uprising, defeating a large Russian force at Racławice. Captured and imprisoned by the Russians (1794–6), he eventually moved to France, where he devoted the rest of his life to the cause of Polish independence.

Kossuth /'kɒsuːθ, 'kɒʃuːt/, Lajos (1802–94), Hungarian statesman and patriot. Long an opponent of Habsburg domination of Hungary, he led the 1848 insurrection and was appointed governor of the country during the brief period of independence which followed. In 1849 he began a lifelong period of exile when the uprising was crushed, although he continued to strive for Hungarian independence.

Kosygin /kɒˈsiːgɪn/, Aleksei Nikolaevich (1904–80), Soviet statesman, Premier of the USSR 1964–80. Born in Russia, he became a Central Committee member in 1939 and held a series of ministerial posts, mostly concerned with finance and industry. He succeeded Khrushchev as Premier (Chairman of the Council of Ministers) in 1964, but devoted most of his attention to internal economic affairs, being gradually eased out of the leadership by Brezhnev. He resigned owing to ill health in 1980.

Kotzebue /'kɒtsəˌbjuː, -ˌbuː/, August von (1761–1819), German dramatist. His many plays were popular in both Germany an England; the tragedy *Menschenhass und Reu* (1789) was produced by Richard Sherida as *The Stranger*, and *Das Kind der Liebe* (179 was adapted in England as *Lovers' Vows*. H was a political informant to Tsar Alexande I and was assassinated by the Germans. Hi son, Otto von Kotzebue (1787–1846), was navigator and explorer; he discovered a inlet of NW Alaska (Kotzebue Sound) no named after him.

Krafft-Ebing /kræft'ebɪŋ/, Richard vo (1840–1902), German physician and ps chologist. He is best known for establishin the relationship between syphilis and ge eral paralysis, and for his *Psychopath Sexualis* (1886), which pioneered the sy tematic study of aberrant sexual beha iour.

Krebs /krebz/, Sir Hans Adolf (1900–81 German-born British biochemist. Whil still in Germany he discovered the cycle reactions by which urea is synthesized b the liver as a nitrogenous waste produc After moving to Britain he discovered th biochemical cycle that is now named aft him, for which he shared a Nobel Prize i 1953.

Kreisler /'kraɪslə(r)/, Fritz (1875–1962), Au trian-born American violinist and con poser. He made his first public appearance in the US in 1889 and became an America citizen in 1943. A noted interpreter of th standard classics, in 1910 he gave the fir performance of Elgar's violin concert which was dedicated to him.

Krishnamurti /ˌkrɪʃnəˈmʊətɪ/, Jiddu (1895 1986), Indian spiritual leader. He was o ginally associated with the Theosophic Society and was declared a World Teache by Annie Besant. In 1929 he broke awa from the society, advocating his own spi tual philosophy based on a rejection organized religion and the attainment self-realization by introspection. His teac ings enjoyed a revival of interest in th 1960s and he settled in California 1969.

Kropotkin /krə'pɒtkɪn/, Prince Peter (184 1921), Russian anarchist. He was a geo rapher who carried out explorations Siberia, Finland, and Manchuria before d voting his life to political activities. became an influential exponent of ana chism and was imprisoned in 1874. escaped abroad two years later and on

returned to Russia after the Russian Revolution in 1917. His works include *Modern Science and Anarchism* (1903).

Kruger /'kru:gə(r)/, Stephanus Johannes Paulus (known as 'Oom (= uncle) Paul') (1825–1904), South African soldier and statesman. He led the Afrikaners to victory in the First Boer War in 1881 and afterwards served as President of Transvaal from 1883 to 1899. His refusal to allow equal rights to non-Boer immigrants was one of the causes of the Second Boer War, during which Kruger was forced to flee the country. He died in exile in Switzerland.

Krupp /krʊp/, Alfred (1812–87), German arms manufacturer. In the 1840s he began to manufacture ordnance at the ironworks founded in Essen by his father, and built up the company to become the largest such manufacturer in Europe. Under the management of successive members of the family the Krupp Works played a pre-eminent part in German arms production through to the end of the Second World War.

Kublai Khan /ˌkuːblaɪ ˈkɑːn/ (1216–94), Mongol emperor of China, grandson of Genghis Khan. Between 1252 and 1259 he conquered southern China with his brother Mangu (then Mongol Khan). On Mangu's death in 1259 he was elected Khan himself, completing the conquest of China and founding the Yuan dynasty; he established his capital on the site of the modern Beijing. He successfully invaded Korea and Burma, but failed in attacks on Java and Japan.

Kubrick /'kjuːbrɪk/, Stanley (born 1928), American film director, producer, and writer. He first gained acclaim as a director with the thriller *The Killing* (1956). The coldly enigmatic science-fiction epic *2001: A Space Odyssey* (1968) set new standards for special effects. Other notable films include *Lolita* (1962), *Dr Strangelove* (1964), *A Clockwork Orange* (1971), and *The Shining* (1980).

Kundera /'kʊndərə/, Milan (born 1929), Czech novelist. His books were proscribed in Czechoslovakia following the Soviet military invasion of 1968. He emigrated to France (1975), was stripped of his Czech citizenship in 1979, and became a French citizen two years later. Major novels include *Life is Elsewhere* (1973), *The Book of Laughter and Forgetting* (1979), and *The Unbearable Lightness of Being* (1984).

Kung Fu-tzu /ˌkʊŋ fuːˈtsuː/ see CONFUCIUS.

Kurosawa /ˌkʊərəˈsɑːwə/, Akira (born 1910), Japanese film director. He first gained international acclaim with *Rashomon* (1950), and later became known for his samurai films, such as *The Seven Samurai* (1954) and *Ran* (1985), a Japanese version of Shakespeare's *King Lear*. He also treats modern themes, mainly of social injustice, in films such as *Living* (1952), and has made adaptations of Dostoevsky (*The Idiot*, 1951) and Maxim Gorky (*The Lower Depths*, 1957).

Kyd /kɪd/, Thomas (1558–94), English dramatist. His anonymously published *The Spanish Tragedy* (1592), an early example of revenge tragedy, was very popular on the Elizabethan stage. The only work published under his name was a translation of Robert Garnier's *Cornelia* (1594; reissued as *Pompey the Great*, 1595). Other works attributed to Kyd are *The Tragedy of Solyman and Perseda* (1592) and a lost pre-Shakespearian play on Hamlet.

L

Laban /'lɑːb(ə)n/, Rudolf von (1879–1958), Hungarian choreographer and dancer. He was a pioneer of the central European school of modern dance and is especially significant for his contribution to the theory of dance. In 1920 he published the first of several volumes outlining his system of dance notation (known as *Labanotation*). In 1938 he moved to England, where he concentrated on modern educational dance.

la Barca, Pedro Calderón de, see CALDERÓN DE LA BARCA.

La Bruyère /,læ bruː'jeə(r)/, Jean de (1645–96), French writer and moralist. He is known for his *Caractères* (1688), a book consisting of two parts, one being a translation of the *Characters* of Theophrastus and the other a collection of portrait sketches modelled on this work. These often portray contemporary French figures with disguised names and expose the vanity and corruption of human behaviour by satirizing Parisian society. La Bruyère was a leading figure in the 'Ancient and Modern' dispute, which preoccupied the Académie française in his day; he spoke on behalf of the Ancients.

Lacan /læ'kɒn/, Jacques (1901–81), French psychoanalyst and writer. He founded the Freudian School in Paris (1964) and carried out influential work in reinterpreting Freudian psychoanalysis in the light of developments in structural linguistics and anthropology. His most significant contributions to the field concern his theory of the unconscious, which he saw as being structured like, and developing simultaneously with, language. His theories formed an element in the development of poststructuralism. A number of Lacan's articles and lectures are collected in *Écrits* (1966).

Laclos /læ'kləʊ/, Pierre (-Ambroise-François) Choderlos de (1741–1803), French novelist. He is remembered for his epistolary novel *Les Liaisons dangereuses* (1782), which caused a scandal with its depiction of the corrupt, erotic schemes of an aristocratic couple.

Ladislaus I /'lædɪs,lɔːs/ (canonized as St Ladislaus) (c.1040–95), king of Hungary 1077–95. He conquered Croatia and Bosnia and extended Hungarian power into Transylvania, as well as establishing order in his kingdom and advancing the spread of Christianity. He was canonized in 1192. Feast day, 27 June.

Ladislaus II /'lædɪs,laʊs/ (Polish name Władysław /vwad'iswaf/) (c.1351–1434), king of Poland 1386–1434. He was grand duke of Lithuania from 1377 to 1401, during which time he was known as Jogaila, and acceded to the Polish throne on his marriage to the Polish monarch, Queen Jadwiga (1374–99), thus uniting Lithuania and Poland. He converted Lithuania to Christianity and was the founder of the Jagiellon dynasty, which ruled the two states until 1572.

Lafayette /,læfɑr'et/ (also **La Fayette**), Marie Joseph Paul Yves Roch Gilbert du Motier, Marquis de (1757–1834), French soldier and statesman. In 1777 he went to America and became one of the leaders of the French Expeditionary Force, which fought alongside the American colonists in the War of Independence. On his return he played a crucial part in the early phase of the French Revolution, commanding the National Guard (1789–91) and advocating moderate policies. He became an opposition leader in the Chamber of Deputies (1825–30) and participated in the Revolution of 1830.

La Fontaine /,læ fɒn'tem/, Jean de (1621–95), French poet. He is chiefly remembered for his *Fables* (1668–94), drawn from oriental, classical, and contemporary sources; they include such tales as 'The Cicada and the Ant' and 'The Crow and the Fox'. He also wrote *Contes et nouvelles* (1664–74), a collection of bawdy verse tales drawn from Ariosto, Boccaccio, and others.

Lagerlöf /'lɑːgə,lɜːf/, Selma (Ottiliana Lovisa) (1858–1940), Swedish novelist. She made her name with *Gösta Berlings Saga* (1891), a book inspired by local legends and traditions, as were many of her later novels. She was awarded the Nobel Prize for literature in 1909, the first woman to be the sole winner of a Nobel Prize (Marie Curie shared one in 1903).

Lagrange /læ'grɒnʒ/, Joseph Louis, Comte de (1736–1813), Italian-born French mathematician. He is remembered for his proof that every positive integer can be expressed as a sum of at most four squares, and for his study of the solution of algebraic equations, which later provided the inspiration for the founding of the theory of groups and Galois theory. His most influential work, however, was the *Traité de mécanique analytique* (1788), which was the culmination of his extensive work on mechanics and its application to the description of planetary and lunar motion.

Laing /læŋ/, R(onald) D(avid) (1927–89), Scottish psychiatrist. He became famous for his controversial views on madness and in particular on schizophrenia, in which he proposed that what society calls insanity is in fact a defensive façade in response to the tensions of the close-knit nuclear family. Major works include *The Divided Self* (1960) and *Sanity, Madness, and the Family* (1965).

Lalique /læ'liːk/, René (1860–1945), French jeweller. He achieved fame with his display of art nouveau brooches and combs at the International Exhibition in Paris in 1900. He became interested in glass and, stimulated by demand for perfume bottles, developed a personal style of moulded glass with iced surfaces and patterns in relief. His display at the Paris Exhibition of 1925 further enhanced his reputation.

Lamarck /læ'mɑːk/, Jean Baptiste de (1744–1829), French naturalist, an early proponent of organic evolution. He suggested that species could have evolved from each other by small changes in their structure, and that the mechanism of such change was that characteristics acquired in order to survive could be passed on to offspring. His theory found little favour in his lifetime (it was criticized notably by Georges Cuvier), but the concept of inheritance of acquired characteristics was revived by those who did not accept Darwin's later theory of natural selection. Lamarck's theory is not usually accepted today.

Lamartine /ˌlæmɑː'tiːn/, Alphonse Marie Louis de (1790–1869), French poet, statesman, and historian. His first volume of poems, *Méditations poétiques* (1820), brought a fresh lyricism to French poetry and established him as a leading figure of French romanticism. During the 1830s he devoted more time to politics and spoke out on behalf of the working classes. He served as Minister of Foreign Affairs in the provisional government following the Revolution of February 1848, but was deposed in June. His writings include *Histoire des Girondins* (1847).

Lamb /læm/, Charles (1775–1834), English essayist and critic. He devoted much of his life to caring for his sister Mary, who suffered from a recurrent mental illness; together they wrote *Tales from Shakespeare* (1807). He also compiled *Specimens of English Dramatic Poets* (1808), an anthology of scenes and speeches from Elizabethan and Jacobean dramatists, with accompanying critical comments. His essays were published in leading periodicals; the best known are the semi-autobiographical *Essays of Elia* (published in a collected edition in 1823).

Lambert /'læmbət/, (Leonard) Constant (1905–51), English composer, conductor, and critic. While still a student he was commissioned by Diaghilev to write the music for the ballet *Romeo and Juliet* (1926). Thereafter he took a leading part in the establishment of British ballet as musical director of Sadler's Wells (1930–47). His other works include *The Rio Grande* (1929), a work in a jazz idiom for orchestra, piano, and voices.

Lampedusa /ˌlæmpɪ'duːzə/, Giuseppe Tomasi de (1896–1957), Italian novelist. After a nervous breakdown he devoted himself to a life of intellectual activity. In 1955 he began writing his only novel, *Il Gattopardo* (*The Leopard*), which was originally rejected by publishers but won worldwide acclaim on its posthumous publication in 1958.

Lancaster /'læŋˌkæstə(r)/, Burt(on Stephen) (1913–94), American film actor. He made his film début in *The Killers* (1946) and was often cast in 'tough guy' roles. He took more dramatic parts in films such as *From Here to Eternity* (1953), *Elmer Gantry* (1960), for which he won an Oscar, and *Birdman of Alcatraz* (1962). Later films include *Atlantic City* (1980) and *Field of Dreams* (1989).

Landau /'lændɔː, Russian lan'daʊ/, Lev (Davidovich) (1908–68), Soviet theoretical physicist, born in Russia. He created an influential school of theoretical physics at Moscow State University, studying a wide range of problems. He contributed to thermodynamics, particle physics,

quantum mechanics and electrodynamics, astrophysics, condensed matter physics, and several other areas. Landau was awarded the Nobel Prize for physics in 1962 for his work on the superfluidity and thermal conductivity of liquid helium.

Landor /'lændɔ:(r)/, Walter Savage (1775–1864), English poet and essayist. Among his poems is the exotic oriental epic *Gebir* (1798), which won him the admiration and friendship of the poet Robert Southey. During his long residence in Italy (1815–35) he wrote his best-known prose work, *Imaginary Conversations of Literary Men and Statesmen* (1824–8). In verse and prose his style shows a clear debt to classical forms and themes.

Landseer /'lændsɪə(r)/, Sir Edwin Henry (1802–73), English painter and sculptor. He was Queen Victoria's favourite painter and his works enjoyed great popular appeal. He is best known for his animal subjects, including scenes set in the Scottish Highlands (such as *The Monarch of the Glen*, 1851) and sentimental pictures of domestic pets. As a sculptor he is chiefly remembered for the bronze lions which he modelled in 1867 for the base of Nelson's Column in Trafalgar Square, London.

Landsteiner /'lænd,staɪnə(r)/, Karl (1868–1943), Austrian-born American physician. His main interest was immunology, and he devised the system of classifying blood into four main immunological groups (A, B, AB, and O), which made it possible for blood transfusions to be carried out successfully. Landsteiner was awarded a Nobel Prize for this in 1930, and in 1940 he was the first to describe the rhesus factor in blood.

Lang /læŋ/, Fritz (1890–1976), Austrian-born film director. A pioneer of German cinema, during the 1920s he directed such notable silent films as the dystopian *Metropolis* (1927), making the transition to sound in 1931 with the thriller *M*. When *The Testament of Dr Mabuse* (1933) was banned by the Nazis, Lang left Germany. He eventually settled in the US and made a range of films, including westerns (such as *Rancho Notorious*, 1952) and *films noirs* (such as *The Big Heat*, 1953).

Langland /'læŋlənd/, William (c.1330–c.1400), English poet. A minor friar, he devoted much of his life to writing and rewriting *Piers Plowman* (c.1367–70), a long allegorical poem in alliterative verse; it takes the form of a spiritual pilgrimage,

through which the narrator is guided ┃ the Plowman and experiences a series visions, with vivid vignettes of conte┃ porary life, on his journey in search Truth.

Langley /'læŋlɪ/, Samuel Pierpoint (183- 1906), American astronomer and aviati┃ pioneer. He invented the bolometer (187┃ 81) and used it to study the radiant ener┃ of the sun. His work on aerodynami┃ contributed to the design of early ae┃ planes.

Langmuir /'læŋmjʊə(r)/, Irving (1881–195┃ American chemist and physicist. His pri┃ cipal work was in surface chemistry, es┃ cially the phenomenon of adsorption a┃ the application of this to catalysis. ┃ worked on high-temperature electrical d┃ charges in gases, introducing the use inert gas in the tungsten lamp, developi┃ an atomic-hydrogen welding torch capab┃ of reaching temperatures up to 3,000°┃ and first using the term *plasma*. Whi┃ studying atomic structure he introduc┃ the terms *covalence* and *electrovalence*.

Langton /'læŋtən/, Stephen (c.1150–122┃ English prelate. His reputation re┃ mainly on his promotion of the interests the English Church in the face of confli┃ ing pressures from the papacy and t┃ English throne. As Archbishop of Cant┃ bury he defended the Church's intere┃ against King John, was intermediary d┃ ing the negotiations leading to the signi┃ of Magna Carta, and protected the you┃ Henry III against baronial domination.

Langtry /'læŋtrɪ/, Lillie (born Emilie Ch┃ lotte le Breton) (1853–1929), British actre┃ Born in Jersey and the daughter of t┃ dean of the island, she was noted for h┃ beauty and became known as 'the Jers┃ Lily' from the title of a portrait of h┃ painted by Sir John Millais. She made h┃ stage début in 1881 and was one of the fi┃ actresses from an aristocratic backgrou┃ She became the mistress of the Prince Wales, later Edward VII.

Laplace /læ'plɑ:s/, Pierre Simon, Marquis (1749–1827), French applied mathem┃ ician and theoretical physicist. He devot┃ his greatest treatise, *Mécanique céleste* (179┃ 1825), to an extensive mathematical ana┃ sis of geophysical matters and of planeta┃ and lunar motion. He demonstrated t┃ long-term stability of planetary orbits, a┃ added considerably to the earlier work

Newton. Laplace is also known for his innovative work on partial differential equations, for his contributions to probability theory, and for other mathematical discoveries.

Lara /'lɑːrə/, Brian (Charles) (born 1969), West Indian cricketer. Born in Trinidad, he first played for the West Indies in 1990. Two years later Lara made his mark on international cricket with an innings of 277 against Australia in Sydney. In 1994 he scored 375 against England in Antigua, breaking the record test score previously set by Gary Sobers in 1957. A few weeks later, playing for Warwickshire against Durham, he scored 501 not out, a world record in first-class cricket.

Larkin /'lɑːkɪn/, Philip (Arthur) (1922–85), English poet. His distinctive poetic voice first became apparent in *The Less Deceived* (1955), and was further developed in *The Whitsun Weddings* (1964) and *High Windows* (1974). His style is notable for its adaptation of contemporary speech rhythms and colloquial vocabulary to poetic metre; many poems are set in urban and suburban landscapes and are pervaded by an air of melancholy, bitterness, and stoic wit.

La Rochefoucauld /læ 'rɒʃfuːˌkəʊ/, François de Marsillac, Duc de (1613–80), French writer and moralist. He was a supporter of Marie de Médicis in plotting against Richelieu and later joined the uprising of the nobles (known as the Fronde, 1648–53) against Mazarin and the court when Louis XIV was a minor. He returned to court on Mazarin's death in 1661. His chief work, *Réflexions, ou sentences et maximes morales* (1665), consists of 504 epigrammatic reflections analysing human conduct, and finding self-interest to be its driving force.

Larousse /læˈruːs/, Pierre (1817–75), French lexicographer and encyclopedist. He edited the fifteen-volume *Grand dictionnaire universel du XIXᵉ siècle* (1866–76), which aimed to treat every area of human knowledge. In 1852 he co-founded the publishing house of Larousse, which continues to issue the dictionaries and reference works that bear its name.

Larwood /'lɑːwʊd/, Harold (1904–95), English cricketer. He built a reputation as a fearsome fast bowler with Nottinghamshire. In the 1932-3 MCC tour of Australia he bowled fast short-pitched 'bodyline' deliveries, and was involved in controversy when several of the home batsmen were injured. He retired from test cricket after that tour, and his cricketing career was cut short by an injury to his left foot.

La Salle /læ 'sæl/, René-Robert Cavelier, Sieur de (1643–87), French explorer. A settler in French Canada, he sailed down the Ohio and Mississippi rivers to the sea in 1682, naming the Mississippi basin Louisiana in honour of Louis XIV. In 1684 he led an expedition to establish a French colony on the Gulf of Mexico; over two years were wasted in fruitless searches for the Mississippi delta. La Salle eventually landed in Texas by mistake and was murdered when his followers mutinied.

Lassus /'læsəs/, Orlande de (Italian name Orlando di Lasso) (c.1532–94), Flemish composer. He was a notable composer of polyphonic music and wrote more than 2,000 secular and sacred works, including masses, motets, madrigals, and settings of psalms.

Latimer /'lætɪmə(r)/, Hugh (c.1485–1555), English Protestant prelate and martyr. He became one of Henry VIII's chief advisers when the king formally broke with the papacy in 1534, and was made bishop of Worcester in 1535. Latimer's opposition to Henry's moves to restrict the spread of Reformation doctrines and practices led to his resignation in 1539. Under Mary I he was imprisoned for heresy and burnt at the stake with Nicholas Ridley at Oxford.

La Tour /læ 'tʊə(r)/, Georges de (1593–1652), French painter. He was largely forgotten until his rediscovery in the 20th century, when he was hailed as the most inspired of the painters in the style of Caravaggio. He is best known for his nocturnal religious scenes, with their subtle portrayal of candlelight and sombre mood. His works include *St Joseph the Carpenter* (1645) and *The Denial of St Peter* (1650).

Laud /lɔːd/, William (1573–1645), English prelate. In 1633 he was appointed Archbishop of Canterbury and set about the suppression of the prevailing Calvinism in England and Presbyterianism in Scotland. His moves to impose liturgical uniformity by restoring pre-Reformation practices aroused great hostility; they led to war in Scotland and were a contributory cause of the English Civil War. In 1640 Laud was impeached and imprisoned; he was later executed for treason.

Lauda /'laʊdə/. Nikolaus Andreas ('Niki') (born 1949), Austrian motor-racing driver. He was world champion in 1975 and went on to win two more championships (1977 and 1984), despite suffering severe injuries in a crash in the 1976 German Grand Prix. He retired in 1985.

Lauder /'lɔːdə(r)/, Sir Harry (born Hugh MacLennan Lauder) (1870–1950), Scottish music-hall performer. In 1900 he made his London début and became highly popular there singing songs such as his compositions 'I Love a Lassie' and 'Roamin' in the Gloamin''. He entertained troops at home and abroad in both world wars and made many successful tours of the US and the Commonwealth countries.

Laughton /'lɔːt(ə)n/, Charles (1899–1962), British-born American actor. He began his acting career on the English stage, turning to film in 1932. His appearance suited him for character roles such as Henry VIII (*The Private Life of Henry VIII*, 1933) and Captain Bligh (*Mutiny on the Bounty*, 1935); he also played Quasimodo in *The Hunchback of Notre Dame* (1939). He became an American citizen in 1950.

Laurel and Hardy /'lɒrəl, 'hɑːdɪ/, Stan Laurel (born Arthur Stanley Jefferson) (1890–1965) and Oliver Hardy (1892–1957), American comedy duo. British-born Stan Laurel played the scatterbrained and often tearful innocent, Oliver Hardy ('Ollie') his pompous, overbearing, and frequently exasperated friend. They brought their distinctive slapstick comedy to many films from 1927 onwards.

Laurence /'lɒrəns/, (Jean) Margaret (1926–87), Canadian novelist. She lived in Somalia and Ghana 1950–7, a period which influenced her early work, including her first novel, *This Side Jordan* (1960). In 1962 she moved to England, where she wrote her *Manawaka* series. This draws on the harsh Scots Presbyterianism of her small home town in Manitoba, and includes *The Stone Angel* (1964) and *The Diviners* (1974).

Laurier /'lɔːrɪˌeɪ/, Sir Wilfrid (1841–1919), Canadian Liberal statesman, Prime Minister 1896–1911. He became the leader of the Liberal Party in 1891 and five years later was elected Canada's first French-Canadian and Roman Catholic Prime Minister. While in office he worked to achieve national unity in the face of cultural conflict; he also oversaw the building of a second trans-continental railway and the creation of the provinces of Alberta and Saskatchewan.

Laver /'leɪvə(r)/, Rodney George ('Rod') (born 1938), Australian tennis player. In 1962 he became the second man (after Don Budge in 1938) to win the four major singles championships (British, American, French, and Australian) in one year; in 1969 he was the first to repeat this.

Lavoisier /læ'vwʌzɪˌeɪ/, Antoine Laurent (1743–94), French scientist, regarded as the father of modern chemistry. He caused a revolution in chemistry by his description of the true nature of combustion, his rigorous methods of analysis, and his development of a new rational chemical nomenclature. He realized that it was Joseph Priestley's 'dephlogisticated air' that combined with substances during burning, and (believing it to be a constituent of acids) he renamed the gas *oxygen*. He held a number of important public offices, and his involvement in the collection of indirect taxes led to his death by guillotine in the French Revolution.

Law[1] /lɔː/, (Andrew) Bonar (1858–1923), Canadian-born British Conservative statesman, Prime Minister 1922–3. Brought up in Scotland, he was a successful businessman before entering Parliament in 1900. He was leader of the Conservative Party (1911–21; 1922–3) and held several ministerial posts from 1915 until retiring in 1921. In October 1922 he returned from retirement to become Prime Minister following Lloyd George's resignation, but himself resigned six months later because of ill health.

Law[2] /lɔː/, Denis (born 1940), Scottish footballer. At the age of 18 he made his international début and went on to win forty caps as a striker for Scotland. He signed for Manchester City in 1960 and spent most of his playing career in England, apart from a short period with the Italian club Turin. In 1962 he joined Manchester United, with whom he had great success, although he missed their 1968 European Cup victory through injury.

Lawrence[1] /'lɒrəns/, D(avid) H(erbert) (1885–1930), English novelist, poet, and essayist. Although he gained acclaim for *Sons and Lovers* (1913), his subsequent work met with hostile reactions; he left England permanently in 1919 and thereafter lived chiefly in Italy and Mexico. A moralist who believed that industrial society was caus-

ing humankind to become divorced from its basic instincts, he is chiefly remembered for his frank exploration of sexual relationships, as in *The Rainbow* (1915) and *Women in Love* (1921); *Lady Chatterley's Lover* (published in Italy, 1928) was only published in Britain in an unexpurgated form after an unsuccessful prosecution for obscenity in 1960.

Lawrence[2] /'lɒrəns/, Ernest Orlando (1901–58), American physicist. He developed the first circular particle accelerator, later called a cyclotron, capable of achieving very high electron voltages. This opened the way for the new science of high-energy physics, with the production of many new isotopes and elements, and Lawrence and his team investigated some of the subatomic particles generated. He also worked on providing fissionable material for the atom bomb. He received the Nobel Prize for physics in 1939.

Lawrence[3] /'lɒrəns/, Sir Thomas (1769–1830), English painter. He first achieved success with his full-length portrait (1789) of Queen Charlotte, the wife of King George III. Many portrait commissions followed and by 1810 he was recognized as the leading portrait painter of his time. In 1818 he was sent by the Prince Regent (later George IV) to paint the portraits of heads of state and military leaders after the allied victory over Napoleon.

Lawrence[4] /'lɒrəns/, T(homas) E(dward) (known as Lawrence of Arabia) (1888–1935), British soldier and writer. From 1916 onwards he helped to organize and lead the Arab revolt against the Turks in the Middle East. His campaign of guerrilla raids contributed to General Allenby's eventual victory in Palestine in 1918; Lawrence described this period in *The Seven Pillars of Wisdom* (1926). In 1922 he enlisted in the RAF under an assumed name to avoid attention and remained in the ranks of that service for most of the rest of his life. He was killed in a motorcycle accident.

Lawrence, St (Latin name Laurentius) (died 258), Roman martyr and deacon of Rome. According to tradition Lawrence was ordered by the prefect of Rome to deliver up the treasure of the Church; when in response to this order he presented the poor people of Rome to the prefect, he was roasted to death on a gridiron. Feast day, 10 August.

Layamon /'laɪəmən/ (late 12th century), English poet and priest. He wrote the verse chronicle known as the *Brut*, a history of England from the period of the legendary Brutus to that of the 7th-century king Cadwalader. One of the earliest major works in Middle English, the poem introduces for the first time in English the story of King Arthur and other figures prominent in later English literature.

Leach /liːtʃ/, Bernard (Howell) (1887–1979), British potter, born in Hong Kong. After studying in Japan he settled in Britain in 1920 and, with the Japanese potter Shoji Hamada, founded his pottery at St Ives in Cornwall. He practised and taught for more than fifty years, becoming a key figure in British 20th-century ceramics. His work amalgamated the ideas, methods, and traditions of Japanese and English pottery and his products were designed to combine beauty with functionality.

Leacock /'liːkɒk/, Stephen (Butler) (1869–1949), Canadian humorist and economist. He was the head of the department of economics and political science at McGill University (1908–36) and published a number of books on these subjects. However, he is chiefly remembered for his many humorous short stories, parodies, and essays, among which are *Sunshine Sketches of a Little Town* (1912), an affectionate account of Canadian small-town life, and *Arcadian Adventures with the Idle Rich* (1914), a sharper and more satirical portrayal of an American city.

Leakey /'liːkɪ/, Louis (Seymour Bazett) (1903–72), British-born Kenyan archaeologist and anthropologist. Leakey is noted for his work on human origins in East Africa, where after the Second World War his excavations brought to light the remains of early hominids and their implements at Olduvai Gorge. His wife Mary (Douglas) Leakey (1913–96) was also an anthropologist, discovering *Australopithecus* (or *Zinjanthropus*) *boisei* at Olduvai in 1959 and initiating work at the nearby Laetoli site in the mid-1970s. Their son Richard (Erskine) Leakey (born 1944) has continued his parents' work on early hominids; he was appointed director of the new Kenya Wildlife Service in 1989, but resigned in 1994 following a controversial political campaign to remove him.

Lean /liːn/, Sir David (1908–91), English film director. He made his début as a director in

1942 and went on to make many notable films, including *Brief Encounter* (1945), *Great Expectations* (1946), *The Bridge on the River Kwai* (1957), *Lawrence of Arabia* (1962), *Dr Zhivago* (1965) and *A Passage to India* (1984).

Lear /lɪə(r)/, Edward (1812–88), English humorist and illustrator. He worked as a zoological draughtsman, and was especially noted as a bird artist; his *Illustrations of the Family of the Psittacidae* was published in 1832. He later came under the patronage of the 13th Earl of Derby, for whose grandchildren he wrote *A Book of Nonsense* (1845), incorporating his own limericks and illustrations; subsequent collections of nonsense verses include *Laughable Lyrics* (1877). He also published illustrated accounts of his travels in Italy, Greece, and the Holy Land.

Leary /ˈlɪərɪ/, Timothy (Francis) (1920–96), American psychologist and drug pioneer. In 1963 Leary was dismissed from his teaching post at Harvard University after he began to experiment with consciousness-altering drugs. He became a figurehead for the hippy drug culture in the mid-1960s when he continually praised the qualities of LSD. Leary was imprisoned for possession of marijuana in 1970, but resumed his lecturing and writing on his release in 1976.

Leavis /ˈliːvɪs/, F(rank) R(aymond) (1895–1978), English literary critic. As a teacher of English at Cambridge from the 1920s and founder and editor of the quarterly *Scrutiny* (1932–53), he exerted a considerable influence on literary criticism. He regarded the rigorous critical study of English literature as central to preserving cultural continuity, which he considered to be under threat from technology and the mass media. He was a champion of D. H. Lawrence and led the way for a more serious appreciation of Charles Dickens. His books include *The Great Tradition* (1948) and *The Common Pursuit* (1952).

Leblanc /ləˈblɒŋk/, Nicolas (1742–1806), French surgeon and chemist. Leblanc became interested in the large-scale manufacture of soda because of the offer of a prize. He developed a process for making soda ash (sodium carbonate) from common salt, making possible the large-scale manufacture of glass, soap, paper, and other chemicals. The factory he set up with others was confiscated during the French Revolution, and he later committed suicide.

Lebrun /ləˈbrɜːn/, Charles (1619–90), French painter, designer, and decorator. He was prominent in the development and institutionalization of French art. In 1648 he helped to found the Royal Academy of Painting and Sculpture, becoming its director in 1663; from this position he sought to impose orthodoxy in artistic matters, laying the basis of academicism. His work for Louis XIV at Versailles (1661–83), which included painting, furniture, and tapestry design, established him as a leading exponent of 17th-century French classicism.

Le Carré /lə ˈkæreɪ/, John (pseudonym of David John Moore Cornwell) (born 1931), English novelist. His spy novels are characterized by their unromanticized view of espionage and frequently explore the moral dilemmas inherent in such work; they often feature the British agent George Smiley and include *The Spy Who Came in from the Cold* (1963) and *Tinker, Tailor, Soldier, Spy* (1974).

Leconte de Lisle /ləˌkɒnt də ˈliːl/ Charles Marie René (1818–94), French poet. He was leader of the Parnassians, a group that emphasized strictness of form. He published a number of collections of poetry, including *Poèmes antiques* (1852) and *Poèmes barbares* (1862); his work often draws inspiration from mythology, biblical history, and exotic Eastern landscape.

Le Corbusier /ˌlə kɔːˈbjuːzɪˌeɪ/ (born Charles Édouard Jeanneret) (1887–1965), French architect and town planner, born in Switzerland. Influential both as an architect and as a theorist, he was a pioneer of the international style, a style characterized by new building materials (especially steel and reinforced concrete), wide windows, uninterrupted interior spaces, simple lines, and strict geometric forms. In 1918 he set out his aesthetic manifesto with the launch of Purism; he later developed his theories on functionalism, the use of industrial techniques in architecture, and the Modulor, a modular system of standard-sized units, in books such as *Towards a New Architecture* (1923) and *Le Modulor I* (1948). His buildings include the block of flats in Marseilles known as the *unité d'habitation* ('living unit', 1945–50); he also planned the city of Chandigarh in India.

Lee[1] /liː/, Bruce (born Lee Yuen Kam) (1941–73), American actor. He was an expert in kung fu and starred in a number of martial arts films featuring elaborately staged fight

scenes, such as *Fists of Fury* (1972) and *Enter the Dragon* (1973).

Lee[2] /liː/, Christopher (Frank Carandini) (born 1922), English actor. Since the late 1940s he has made a variety of films, including thrillers and adventure films, but his reputation is chiefly based on the horror films that he made for the British film company Hammer. These include *Dracula* (1958) and seven sequels (the last in 1973), and *The Mummy* (1959).

Lee[3] /liː/, Gypsy Rose (born Rose Louise Hovick) (1914–70), American striptease artist. In the 1930s she became famous on Broadway for her sophisticated striptease act, imbuing what was previously considered vulgar entertainment with a new artistic content and style.

Lee[4] /liː/, (Nelle) Harper (born 1926), American novelist. She won a Pulitzer Prize with her novel, *To Kill a Mockingbird* (1960). The plot turns on the sensational trial of a black man falsely charged with raping a white woman, as seen through the eyes of the daughter of the white defence lawyer.

Lee[5] /liː/, Laurie (born 1914), English writer. He is best known for his autobiographical novels *Cider With Rosie* (1959) and *As I Walked Out One Midsummer Morning* (1969), evocative accounts of his rural childhood in Gloucestershire and his travelling experiences in pre-war Europe. Lee's volumes of poetry, including *The Sun My Monument* (1944) and *My Many-Coated Man* (1955), display a rich, sensuous apprehension of the natural world.

Lee[6] /liː/, Robert E(dward) (1807–70), American general. He was the commander of the Confederate army of Northern Virginia, leading it for most of the American Civil War. Although he did much to prolong Confederate resistance against the Union's greater manpower and resources, his invasion of the North was repulsed by General Meade at the Battle of Gettysburg (1863) and he eventually surrendered to General Grant in 1865.

Lee[7] /liː/, Spike (born Shelton Jackson Lee) (born 1957), American film director. Lee's declared intention is to express the richness of African-American culture: he first won recognition for the comedy *She's Gotta Have It* (1986), while later films, such as *School Daze* (1988), *Do the Right Thing* (1989), and *Malcolm X* (1992), sparked controversy with their treatment of racism. Lee aided

Jesse Jackson in his presidential campaign of 1988.

Leeuwenhoek /ˈleɪv(ə)n,huːk/, Antoni van (1632–1723), Dutch naturalist. Apprenticed to a Delft cloth-merchant, he developed a lens for scientific purposes from those used to inspect cloth, and was the first to observe bacteria, protozoa, and yeast. He accurately described red blood cells, capillaries, striated muscle fibres, spermatozoa, and the crystalline lens of the eye. Being without Latin he was out of touch with the scientific community, and his original work on micro-organisms only became known through the Royal Society's translation and publication of his letters (1673–1723).

Le Fanu /ˈlefə,njuː:, lə ˈfɑːnuː/, Joseph Sheridan (1814–73), Irish novelist. He is best known for his stories of mystery, suspense, and the supernatural; notable works include *The House by the Churchyard* (1861), *Uncle Silas* (1864), and the collection of ghost stories *In a Glass Darkly* (1872).

Léger /ˈleɪʒeɪ/, Fernand (1881–1955), French painter. From about 1909 he was associated with the cubist movement, but then began to develop a distinctive style inspired by the beauty of machinery and celebrating modern technology; works include the *Contrast of Forms* series (1913). He was also involved with theatre decor and cinema, and made the experimental film *Ballet mécanique* (1924).

Leghari /legˈhɑːrɪ/, Farooq Ahmed (born 1940), Pakistani statesman, President since 1993.

Lehár /ˈleɪhɑː(r)/, Franz (Ferencz) (1870–1948), Hungarian composer. He is chiefly known for his operettas, of which the most famous is *The Merry Widow* (1905).

Leibniz /ˈlaɪbnɪts/, Gottfried Wilhelm (1646–1716), German rationalist philosopher, mathematician, and logician. He spent his life in the diplomatic and political service and in 1700 was appointed first president of the Academy of Sciences in Berlin. Leibniz is chiefly known as an exponent of optimism; he believed that the world is fundamentally harmonious and good, being composed of single units (monads), each of which is self-contained but acts in harmony with every other; these form an ascending hierarchy culminating in God. Their harmony is ordained by God, who never acts except for a reason

that requires it, and so this world is the best of all possible worlds (a view satirized in Voltaire's *Candide*). Leibniz made the important distinction between necessary (logical) truths and contingent (factual) truths, and proposed a universal logical language which would eliminate ambiguity. He also devised a method of calculus independently of Newton.

Leibovitz /'li:bə,vɪts/, Annie (born 1950), American photographer. She was chief photographer of *Rolling Stone* magazine from 1973 until 1983, when she moved to *Vanity Fair*. She has had numerous exhibitions, including those at the Smithsonian National Portrait Gallery, Washington, DC (1991), and produced portraits of celebrities such as John Lennon, Ella Fitzgerald, and Arnold Schwarzenegger.

Leicester /'lestə(r)/, Earl of, see DUDLEY.

Leichhardt /'laɪkhɑːt/, (Friedrich Wilhelm) Ludwig (1813–48), Australian explorer, born in Prussia. After emigrating to Australia in 1841, he began a series of geological surveys, crossing from Moreton Bay near Brisbane to Port Essington on the coast of Arnhem Land (1843–5); he disappeared without trace during another attempt at a transcontinental crossing in 1848.

Leif Ericsson see ERICSSON[2].

Leigh /li:/, Vivien (born Vivian Mary Hartley) (1913–67), British actress, born in India. She made her screen début in 1934; major film roles include her Oscar-winning performances as Scarlett O'Hara in *Gone with the Wind* (1939) and Blanche du Bois in *A Streetcar Named Desire* (1951). From 1935 Leigh also pursued a successful career on stage, often playing opposite Laurence Olivier, to whom she was married from 1940 to 1961.

Leighton /'leɪt(ə)n/, Frederic, 1st Baron Leighton of Stretton (1830–96), English painter and sculptor. He was a leading exponent of Victorian neoclassicism and chiefly painted large-scale mythological and genre scenes; he first gained renown with the picture *Cimabue's Madonna Carried in Procession Through the Streets of Florence* (1855), although perhaps his best-known painting today is *Flaming June* (c.1895). His sculptures include *Athlete Struggling with a Python* (1874–7).

Lely /'li:lɪ/, Sir Peter (Dutch name Pieter van der Faes) (1618–80), Dutch portrait painter,

resident in England from 1641. He became principal court painter to Charles II and consolidated the tradition of society portrait painting. By 1650 he had a large studio and produced hundreds of portraits of court figures in a baroque style. Notable works include his series of *Windsor Beauties*, painted during the 1660s.

Lemmon /'lemən/, Jack (born John Uhler) (born 1925), American actor. He made his name in comedy films such as *Some Like It Hot* (1959); he later played serious dramatic parts in such films as *Save the Tiger* (1973), for which he won an Oscar, *The China Syndrome* (1979), and *Missing* (1981).

Lenclos /lɒŋ'kləʊ/, Ninon de (born Anne de Lenclos) (1620–1705), French courtesan. She was a famous wit and beauty and numbered many prominent writers and nobles among her lovers. She advocated a form of Epicureanism and defended her philosophy and lifestyle in her book *La Coquette vengée* (1659). In later life she presided over one of the most distinguished literary salons of the age.

Lendl /'lend(ə)l/, Ivan (born 1960), Czech-born tennis player. He won many singles titles in the 1980s and early 1990s, including the US, Australian, and the French Open championships. He became an American citizen in 1992.

Lenin /'lenɪn/, Vladimir Ilich (born Vladimir Ilich Ulyanov) (1870–1924), the principal figure in the Russian Revolution and first Premier (Chairman of the Council of People's Commissars) of the Soviet Union 1918–24. Lenin was the first political leader to attempt to put Marxist principles into practice, though, like Marx, he saw the need for a transitional period to full communism, during which there would be a 'dictatorship of the proletariat'. The policies that he pursued led ultimately to the establishment of Marxism-Leninism in the Soviet Union and, later, in China. Born in Russia, he lived in Switzerland from 1900, but was instrumental in the split between the Bolsheviks and Mensheviks in 1903, when he became leader of the more radical Bolsheviks. He returned to Russia in 1917, established Bolshevik control after the overthrow of the tsar, and in 1918 became head of state; he founded the Third International (or Comintern) the following year to further the cause of world revolution. With Trotsky's help he defeated counter-revolutionary forces in the Russian Civil

War, but was forced to moderate his socio-economic policies to allow the country to recover from the effects of war and revolution. During the last years of his life he denounced, but was unable to prevent, the concentration of power in the hands of Stalin.

Lennon /'lenən/, John (1940–80), English pop and rock singer, guitarist, and songwriter. He was a founder member of the Beatles, and with Paul McCartney wrote most of their songs; at first they worked together, later apart, although the songs were still credited to Lennon–McCartney. Their first single, 'Love Me Do' (1962), was followed by many more, including 'She Loves You' (1963) and 'Help' (1965), before the group retired from live performance to work with producer George Martin on the more sophisticated and experimental albums *Revolver* (1966) and *Sergeant Pepper's Lonely Hearts Club Band* (1967). In 1969 Lennon announced his intention to leave the group, and the Beatles split up acrimoniously the following year. A more controversial and acerbic figure than McCartney, Lennon frequently collaborated with his second wife Yoko Ono in his subsequent recording career, producing avant-garde works as well as the popular album and single *Imagine* (1971). He took up residency in the US and was shot dead outside his home in New York.

Le Nôtre /lə 'nəʊtrə/, André (1613–1700), French landscape gardener. He designed many formal gardens, including the parks of Vaux-le-Vicomte and Versailles, begun in 1655 and 1662 respectively. These incorporated his ideas on architecturally conceived garden schemes: geometric formality and perfect equilibrium of all the individual elements — sculpture, fountains, parterres, and open spaces. His influence spread throughout the Continent and to England, where his style was imitated.

Leo /'li:əʊ/ the name of thirteen popes, notably:
Leo I (known as Leo the Great; canonized as St Leo I) (died 461), pope from 440 and Doctor of the Church. His statement of the doctrine of the Incarnation was accepted at the Council of Chalcedon (451). He extended and consolidated the power of the Roman see, claiming jurisdiction in Africa, Spain, and Gaul. He persuaded the Huns to retire beyond the Danube and secured concessions from the Vandals when they cap-

tured Rome. Feast day (in the Eastern Church) 18 February; (in the Western Church) 11 April.
Leo X (born Giovanni de' Medici) (1475–1521), pope from 1513. He excommunicated Martin Luther and bestowed on Henry VIII of England the title of Defender of the Faith. He was a noted patron of learning and the arts.

Leo III /'li:əʊ/ (*c*.680–741), Byzantine emperor 717–41. He repulsed several Muslim invasions and carried out an extensive series of financial, legal, administrative, and military reforms. In 726 he forbade the use of images in public worship; this policy, enforced by teams of iconoclasts, met with much popular opposition and a split with Rome.

Leo I, St Pope Leo I (see LEO).

Leonard /'lenəd/, Elmore (John) (born 1925), American writer of thrillers. He worked as an advertising copywriter in the 1950s and 1960s before concentrating on writing and becoming acknowledged as one of the leading crime writers in America. His books, notable for their pace and understated, credible style, include *Unknown Man No. 89* (1977), *Freaky Deaky* (1988), and *Get Shorty* (1990).

Leonardo da Vinci /lɪə,nɑ:dəʊ də 'vɪntʃɪ/ (1452–1519), Italian painter, scientist, and engineer. He spent his early life in Florence; thereafter he worked also in Milan, Rome, and France. Although Leonardo's paintings are relatively few in number, they are notable for their use of the technique of *sfumato* and reflect his studies of nature; they include *The Virgin of the Rocks* (1483–5), *The Last Supper* (1498), a tempera painting on the wall of the refectory at Santa Maria delle Grazie in Milan, and *Mona Lisa* (1504–5), his most famous easel painting, showing a woman with an enigmatic smile. In addition to painting, he devoted his mental energy to a wide range of subjects, from anatomy and biology to mechanics and hydraulics. His nineteen notebooks contain meticulously observed drawings of plants, clouds, skeletons, etc., studies of the human circulatory system, and plans for a helicopter-like flying machine, an armoured tank, and a submarine.

Leopold I /'li:ə,pəʊld/ (1790–1865), first king of Belgium 1831–65. The fourth son of the Duke of Saxe-Coburg-Saalfield, Leopold was

an uncle of Queen Victoria, whom he advised during the early part of her reign. In 1830 he refused the throne of Greece, but a year later accepted that of the newly independent Belgium, reigning peacefully thereafter.

Leo the Great Pope Leo I (see LEO).

Lepidus /'lepɪdəs/, Marcus Aemilius (died c.13 BC), Roman statesman and triumvir. After supporting Julius Caesar in the civil war against Pompey, Lepidus was elected consul in 46. He was appointed one of the Second Triumvirate with Octavian and Antony in 43 as well as consul again in 42. Lepidus was given control over Africa after losing the provinces of Gaul and Spain to his two more powerful partners. He retired from public life following a failed revolt in Sicily against Octavian in 36.

Lerner /'lɜːnə(r)/, Alan J(ay) (1918–86), American lyricist and dramatist. His collaboration with composer Frederick Loewe (1904–88) produced a series of musicals which were also filmed, including *Paint Your Wagon* (1951; filmed 1969) and *My Fair Lady* (1956; filmed 1964). He won Oscars for the films *An American in Paris* (1951) and *Gigi* (1958).

Lesage /lə'sɑːʒ/, Alain-René (1668–1747), French novelist and dramatist. He is best known for the picaresque novel *Gil Blas* (1715–35).

Lesseps /'lesəps/, Ferdinand Marie, Vicomte de (1805–94), French diplomat. While in the consular service in Egypt he became aware of plans to link the Mediterranean and the Red Sea by means of a canal, and from 1854 onwards devoted himself to the project. Work began in 1859 and the Suez Canal was opened ten years later. In 1881 he embarked on the building of the Panama Canal, but had not anticipated the difficulties of this very different enterprise; the project was abandoned in 1889.

Lessing[1] /'lesɪŋ/, Doris (May) (born 1919), British novelist and short-story writer, brought up in Rhodesia. An active Communist in her youth, she frequently deals with social and political conflicts in her fiction, especially as they affect women; *The Golden Notebook* (1962) was hailed as a landmark by the women's movement. Other works include *The Grass is Singing* (1950), about interracial relationships in Africa, and a quintet of science-fiction novels collectively entitled *Canopus in Argus: Archives* (1979–83).

Lessing[2] /'lesɪŋ/, Gotthold Ephraim (1729–81), German dramatist and critic. He wrote tragedies such as *Miss Sara Sampson* (1755) and *Emilia Galotti* (1772), the former considered to be the first significant domestic tragedy in German; a comedy, *Minna von Barnhelm* (1767); and the dramatic poem *Nathan der Weise* (1779), a plea for religious toleration. In his critical works, such as *Laokoon* (1766), he criticized the reliance of German literature on the conventions of the French classical school and suggested that German writers should look to Shakespeare and English literature instead.

Leverhulme /'liːvə,hjuːm/, 1st Viscount (born William Hesketh Lever) (1851–1925), English industrialist and philanthropist. He and his brother started the manufacture of soap from vegetable oil (instead of tallow) under the trade name Sunlight. In the 1880s they founded and built the industrial new town and factory complex of Port Sunlight in Cheshire (now in Merseyside); workers were accommodated in model housing and were entitled to medical care, pensions, and a form of profit-sharing. In the 20th century Leverhulme's company, Lever Bros., came to form the basis of the international corporation Unilever.

Le Verrier /lə 'verɪ,eɪ/, Urbain (1811–77), French mathematician. His analysis of the motions of the planets suggested that an unknown body was disrupting the orbit of Uranus, the same conclusion being reached almost simultaneously by John Couch Adams. Under the prompting of Le Verrier, the German astronomer Johann Galle (1812–1910) searched the region of the sky in which the mysterious object was predicted to lie, and discovered the planet Neptune on 23 September 1846.

Levi /'leɪvɪ/, Primo (1919–87), Italian novelist and poet, of Jewish descent. His experiences as a survivor of Auschwitz are recounted in his first book *If This is a Man* (1947); other books include *The Periodic Table* (1985), a collection of memoirs.

Lévi-Strauss /,levɪ'straʊs/, Claude (born 1908), French social anthropologist. He was an influential pioneer in the use of a structuralist analysis to study cultural systems; he regarded language as an essential common denominator underlying cultural phenomena, a view which forms the basis for his theories concerning the relationships of such societal elements as religion,

myth, and kinship. His books include the two-volume *Structural Anthropology* (1958; 1973).

Lewis [1] /'luːɪs/, Cecil Day, see DAY LEWIS.

Lewis [2] /'luːɪs/, C(live) S(taples) (1898–1963), British novelist, religious writer, and literary scholar. A convert to Christianity from atheism, Lewis wrote and broadcast widely on religious and moral issues, producing books such as *The Screwtape Letters* (1942). He also wrote a trilogy of allegorical science-fiction novels, and a series of fantasies for children set in the imagined land of 'Narnia' which began with *The Lion, the Witch, and the Wardrobe* (1950). His works on medieval and Renaissance literature include *The Allegory of Love* (1936). In 1957 he married an American writer, Joy Davidman (1915–60), who was then discovered to be dying of cancer; their relationship was the subject of the popular film *Shadowlands* (1993).

Lewis [3] /'luːɪs/, Frederick Carleton ('Carl') (born 1961), American athlete. He has won a total of nine gold medals in the Olympic Games of 1984, 1988, 1992, and 1996 (in the 100 and 200 metres, long jump, and 4 × 100 metre relay). He won four consecutive Olympic long-jump titles, and broke the world record for the 100 metres on several occasions.

Lewis [4] /'luːɪs/, Jerry Lee (born 1935), American rock and roll singer and pianist. In 1957 he joined Sun Records in Memphis, and with his second release, 'Whole Lotta Shakin' Going On' (1957), earned a gold disc. This was followed by a succession of hits, including 'Great Balls of Fire' (1957), but his career was interrupted when his marriage to his 14-year-old cousin caused a public outcry. He made a comeback in 1961, and despite a series of scandals and health problems continued to perform into the 1990s.

Lewis [5] /'luːɪs/, Meriwether (1774–1809), American explorer. He was the joint leader, with William Clark, of an expedition to explore the newly acquired Louisiana Purchase. The Lewis and Clark expedition started out from St Louis in 1804 and crossed America, reaching the mouth of the Columbia river on the Pacific coast in 1805; they returned to St Louis in 1806.

Lewis [6] /'luːɪs/, (Harry) Sinclair (1885–1951), American novelist. He gained recognition with *Main Street* (1920), a social satire on small-town life in the Midwest. His later novels, such as *Babbitt* (1922), *Elmer Gantry* (1927), and *Dodsworth* (1929), continued in a similar vein, using satire and caricature to attack targets such as the urban middle class and the Church. He was awarded the Nobel Prize for literature in 1930, the first American writer to achieve this.

Lewis [7] /'luːɪs/, (Percy) Wyndham (1882–1957), British novelist, critic, and painter, born in Canada. He was a leader of the vorticist movement, and with Ezra Pound edited the magazine *Blast* (1914–15). His satirical novels and polemical works include *The Apes of God* (1930) and the trilogy *The Human Age* (1928–55); he expounds his philosophical ideas in *Time and Western Man* (1927). He later aroused hostility for his Fascist sympathies and his satirical attacks on his contemporaries (especially the Bloomsbury Group).

Liberace /ˌlɪbəˈrɑːtʃɪ/ (full name Wladziu Valentino Liberace) (1919–87), American pianist and entertainer. He was known for his romantic arrangements of popular piano classics and for his flamboyant costumes. His television show ran for five years (1952–7) and he gave a great many spectacular live performances.

Li Bo see LI PO.

Lichtenstein /'lɪktənˌstaɪn/, Roy (born 1923), American painter and sculptor. A leading exponent of pop art, he chiefly based his work on images from commercial art or made parodies of the work of other painters. He became known in the 1960s for paintings inspired by comic strips; these paintings are made up of thick black outlines enclosing areas of dots in imitation of the half-tones used to print blocks of colour in comics. One of the best-known examples of this style is *Whaam!* (1963).

Liddell /'lɪd(ə)l/, Eric (1902–45), British athlete and missionary, born in China. In the 1924 Olympic Games the heats of his own event (the 100 metres) were held on a Sunday and he withdrew on religious grounds; he ran in the 400 metres instead, winning the race in a world record time. His exploits were celebrated in the film *Chariots of Fire* (1981). Liddell went on to serve as a missionary in China and died there in a Japanese prisoner-of-war camp.

Liddell Hart /ˌlɪd(ə)l 'hɑːt/, Sir Basil Henry (1895–1970), British military historian and

theorist. Appalled at the slaughter produced by trench warfare in the First World War, he formulated a strategy using an indirect approach, in which attacks would be made with tanks and aircraft to destroy enemy command centres, communications, and supply lines. His theories were particularly influential in Germany, where the idea of strategic penetration by tank divisions was successfully adopted in the Second World War.

Lie /liː/, Trygve Halvdan (1896–1968), Norwegian Labour politician, first Secretary-General of the United Nations 1946–53.

Liebig /'liːbɪx/, Justus von, Baron (1803–73), German chemist and teacher. With Friedrich Wöhler he discovered the benzoyl radical, and demonstrated that such radicals were groups of atoms that remained unchanged in many chemical reactions. He applied chemistry to physiology and to agriculture, stressed the importance of artificial fertilizers, and developed techniques for quantitative organic analysis.

Ligeti /'lɪɡətɪ/, György Sándor (born 1923), Hungarian composer. His early works employ electronic instruments, but he made his name when he returned to the traditional orchestra with *Apparitions* (1958–9) and *Atmosphères* (1961). These compositions are remarkable for their use of slowly evolving complexes of polyphonic sound, dispensing with the formal elements of melody, harmony, and rhythm. His many other compositions include choral works, such as the *Requiem* (1963–5), string quartets, and pieces satirizing the work of other composers.

Lilienthal /'liːlɪənˌtɑːl/, Otto (1848–96), German pioneer in the design and flying of gliders. Trained as an engineer, he invented a light steam motor and worked on marine signals. In his flying experiments he constructed wings connected to a tail, made of osier wands and covered with shirt fabric, fitted them to his shoulders, and took off by running downhill into the wind. In 1896 he experimented with a small motor to flap the wings. Working with his brother he made more than 2,000 flights in various gliders before being killed in a crash. He also studied the science of bird flight, demonstrating the superiority of a curved over a flat wing.

Lillee /'lɪlɪ/, Dennis (Keith) (born 1949), Australian cricketer. He was a notable fast bowler who took 355 wickets in seventy matches during his career in test cricket (1971–84).

Linacre /'lɪnəkə(r)/, Thomas (c.1460–1524), English physician and classical scholar. In 1518 he founded the College of Physicians in London, and became its first president. He wrote textbooks on Latin grammar, and his students of Greek included Thomas More and probably Erasmus. Linacre's translations of Galen's Greek works on medicine and philosophy into Latin brought about a revival of studies in anatomy, botany, and clinical medicine in Britain.

Lin Biao /lɪn 'bjaʊ/ (also **Lin Piao** /'pjaʊ/) (1908–71), Chinese Communist statesman and general. After joining the Communists (1927) he became a commander of Mao Zedong's Red Army in the fight against the Kuomintang. He was appointed Minister of Defence (1959) and then Vice-Chairman under Mao (1966), later being nominated to become Mao's successor (1969). Having staged an unsuccessful coup in 1971, Lin Biao was reported to have been killed in an aeroplane crash while fleeing to the Soviet Union.

Lincoln /'lɪŋkən/, Abraham (1809–65), American Republican statesman, 16th President of the US 1861–5. His election as President on an anti-slavery platform antipathetic to the interests of the southern states helped precipitate the American Civil War. He eventually managed to unite the Union side behind the anti-slavery cause and emancipation was formally proclaimed on New Year's Day, 1864. Lincoln won re-election in 1864, but was assassinated shortly after the surrender of the main Confederate army had ended the war. During his lifetime Lincoln was noted for his succinct, eloquent speeches, including the Gettysburg address of 1863.

Lind[1] /lɪnd/, James (1716–94), Scottish physician. After a period as a naval surgeon he performed some famous experiments which demonstrated that sailors could be cured of scurvy by supplementing their diet with citrus fruit. It was not until just after his death that the Royal Navy officially adopted the practice of giving lime juice to sailors. His work was a major step towards the discovery of vitamins.

Lind[2] /lɪnd/, Jenny (born Johanna Maria Lind Goldschmidt) (1820–87), Swedish soprano. Known as 'the Swedish nightingale' for the purity and agility of her voice, she

achieved international success with her performances in opera, oratorio, and concerts. She funded musical scholarships and other charitable causes in England and Sweden.

Lindbergh /'lɪndbɜːg/, Charles (Augustus) (1902–74), American aviator. In 1927 he made the first solo transatlantic flight, taking 33½ hours to fly from New York to Paris, in a single-engined monoplane, *Spirit of St Louis*. Lindbergh moved to Europe with his wife to escape the publicity surrounding the kidnap and murder of his two-year-old son in 1932.

Lindemann /'lɪndəmən/, Frederick Alexander, see CHERWELL.

Lindsay /'lɪndzɪ/ a family of Australian artists. The most prominent members include Sir Lionel Lindsay (1874–1961), art critic, watercolour painter, and graphic artist, who did much to generate Australian interest in the collection of original prints, and his brother, Norman Lindsay (1879–1969), a graphic artist, painter, critic, and novelist.

Lineker /'lɪnɪkə(r)/, Gary (Winston) (born 1960), English footballer. A fast, alert striker, Lineker started his career with Leicester City (1976–85) before going on to play for Everton (1985–6), Barcelona (1986–9), and Tottenham Hotspur (1989–92). He played for England 80 times (1984–92), scoring 48 goals, one short of Bobby Charlton's England record. After a spell in Japan he retired in 1994 and became a television sports broadcaster.

Linnaeus /lɪ'niːəs, -'neɪəs/, Carolus (Latinized name of Carl von Linné) (1707–78), Swedish botanist, founder of modern systematic botany and zoology. He devised a classification system for flowering plants based on stamen type and number of pistils, and became the authority to whom collectors all over the world sent specimens. He described over 7,000 plants, introducing binomial Latin names, although his classification was later superseded by that of Antoine Jussieu. His classification of animals was less satisfactory, as he paid little attention to internal anatomy. He set out his system in *Systema Naturae* (1735) and other works. The tenth edition of this (1758) and *Species Plantarum* (1753) are internationally recognized as the starting-points for zoological and botanical nomenclature respectively. Linnaeus also carried out early experiments in biological pest control.

Lin Piao see LIN BIAO.

Lipchitz /'lɪpʃɪts/, Jacques (born Chaim Jacob Lipchitz) (1891–1973), Lithuanian-born French sculptor. In 1909 he moved to Paris, where he produced cubist works such as *Sailor with a Guitar* (1914). During the 1920s he produced his influential series of 'transparent' sculptures, which explore the interpenetration of solids and voids, and by the time he moved to the US in 1941 he had become internationally recognized. His later works include the massive *Prometheus Strangling the Vulture II* (1944–53).

Li Po /liː 'pəʊ/ (also **Li Bo** /'bəʊ/, **Li T'ai Po** /ˌliː taɪ 'pəʊ/) (AD 701–62), Chinese poet. He had a bohemian lifestyle at the emperor's court, alternating with long periods of wandering. Typical themes in his poetry are wine, women, and the beauties of nature.

Lippi[1] /'lɪpɪ/, Filippino (c.1457–1504), Italian painter, son of Fra Filippo Lippi. Having trained with his father and Botticelli he completed the fresco cycle on the life of St Peter in the Brancacci Chapel, Florence (c.1481–3), a project begun by Masaccio. His other works include the series of frescos in the Carafa Chapel in Rome (1488–93) and the painting *The Vision of St Bernard* (c.1486).

Lippi[2] /'lɪpɪ/, Fra Filippo (c.1406–69), Italian painter. He joined a Carmelite order, but later renounced his vows in order to marry; he was the father of the painter Filippino Lippi. In the early 1420s he became a pupil of Masaccio, whose influence can be seen in the fresco *The Relaxation of the Carmelite Rule* (c.1432). His characteristic later style is more decorative and less monumental than his early work; typical works depict the Madonna as the central feature, stressing the human aspect of the theme. His paintings influenced the Pre-Raphaelites.

Lippmann /'lɪpmən/, Gabriel Jonas (1845–1921), French physicist. He is best known today for his production of the first fully orthochromatic colour photograph, in 1893. His earlier research was on the effect of electricity on capillary tubing, using it to develop an electrometer that was sensitive to potential changes of a thousandth

of a volt. Lippmann also designed a number of other instruments, notably a coelostat, and devised methods for the precise measurement of various units.

Lister /'lɪstə(r)/, Joseph, 1st Baron (1827–1912), English surgeon, inventor of antiseptic techniques in surgery. In 1865 he became acquainted with Louis Pasteur's theory that putrefaction is due to microorganisms, and realized its significance in connection with sepsis in wounds, a major cause of deaths in patients who had undergone surgery. In the same year Lister first used carbolic acid dressings, and later he used a carbolic spray in the operating theatre. After about 1883 aseptic rather than antiseptic techniques became popular, though Lister believed in the use of both.

Liston /'lɪstən/, Sonny (born Charles Liston) (1932–70), American boxer. He was encouraged to box at Missouri State penitentiary while serving a sentence for robbery, and launched a professional career in 1953. In 1962 he became world heavyweight champion by defeating Floyd Patterson, but in 1964 lost his title to Muhammad Ali (then Cassius Clay).

Liszt /lɪst/, Franz (1811–86), Hungarian composer and pianist. He was a key figure in the romantic movement and a virtuoso pianist; many of his piano compositions combine lyricism with great technical complexity. His orchestral works include the Faust and Dante Symphonies (1854–7; 1855–6); his twelve symphonic poems (1848–58) created a new musical form. He also composed masses, and oratorios such as *Christus* (1862–7). Apart from his own influence as a composer and teacher, Liszt was also significant as a champion of Wagner's work.

Li T'ai Po see LI PO.

Littlewood /'lɪt(ə)l,wʊd/, (Maud) Joan (1914–91), English theatre director. She is best known for co-founding the Theatre Workshop (1945), which set out to present established plays in radical productions and to stage plays with contemporary working-class themes. Memorable productions included Brendan Behan's *The Quare Fellow* (1956). Littlewood's name is most closely associated with the direction of the musical *Oh, What a Lovely War* (1963).

Littré /'lɪtreɪ/, Émile (1801–81), French lexicographer and philosopher. He was the

author of the major *Dictionnaire de la langue française* (1863–77) and also wrote a history of the French language (1862). He was a follower of Auguste Comte, and became the leading exponent of positivism after Comte's death.

Liverpool /'lɪvə,puːl/, 2nd Earl of (title of Robert Banks Jenkinson) (1770–1828), British Tory statesman, Prime Minister 1812–27. His government opposed both parliamentary reform and Catholic Emancipation, and took repressive measures to deal with popular discontent at the time of the Peterloo massacre. Lord Liverpool was later influenced by more liberal figures such as Sir Robert Peel to introduce some important reforms.

Livingstone /'lɪvɪŋstən/, David (1813–73), Scottish missionary and explorer. He first went to Bechuanaland as a missionary in 1841; on his extensive travels in the interior he discovered Lake Ngami (1849), the Zambezi river (1851), and the Victoria Falls (1855). In 1866 he led an expedition into central Africa in search of the source of the Nile; after many hardships he was eventually found in poor health by the explorer Sir Henry Morton Stanley on the eastern shore of Lake Tanganyika in 1871.

Livy /'lɪvɪ/ (Latin name Titus Livius) (59 BC–AD 17), Roman historian. His history of Rome from its foundation to his own time contained 142 books, of which thirty-five survive (including the earliest history of the war with Hannibal). Livy is notable for his power of vivid historical reconstruction as he sought to give Rome a history that in conception and style might be worthy of her imperial rise and greatness.

Llewelyn /luːˈelm, hluː-/ (also **Llywelyn ap Gruffydd** /æp ˈgrɪfɪð/) (died 1282), prince of Gwynedd in North Wales. In 1258 he proclaimed himself prince of all Wales and four years later formed an alliance with Simon de Montfort, leader of the baronial opposition to Henry III. He later signed a treaty with Henry, which made him chief of the other Welsh princes but recognized Henry as his overlord (1265). His refusal to pay homage to Edward I led the latter to invade and subjugate Wales (1277–84); Llewelyn died in battle after raising a rebellion against Edward's rule.

Llosa, Mario Vargas, see VARGAS LLOSA.

Lloyd[1] /lɔɪd/, Harold (Clayton) (1893–1971), American film comedian. With the devel-

opment of his bespectacled, white-faced screen character he became one of the most popular cinema personalities of the 1920s. He performed his own hair-raising stunts, using physical danger as a source of comedy in silent movies such as *High and Dizzy* (1920), *Safety Last* (1923), and *The Freshman* (1925). He was presented with an honorary Academy Award in 1952.

Lloyd[2] /lɔɪd/, Marie (born Matilda Alice Victoria Wood) (1870–1922), English musichall entertainer. She made her first stage appearance in 1885 and soon achieved fame for her risqué songs and extravagant costumes; she later took her act to the US, South Africa, and Australia.

Lloyd George /lɔɪd 'dʒɔːdʒ/, David, 1st Earl Lloyd George of Dwyfor (1863–1945), British Liberal statesman, Prime Minister 1916–22. As Chancellor of the Exchequer (1908–15) he introduced old-age pensions (1908) and national insurance (1911). His 'People's Budget' (1909), intended to finance reform by raised death duties and other taxes, was rejected by the Lords and led to a constitutional crisis which was eventually resolved by the Parliament Act of 1911. Supported by the Conservatives, he took over from Asquith as Prime Minister at the end of 1916 and led the coalition government for the remainder of the First World War. In the postwar period his administration was threatened by increasing economic problems and trouble in Ireland; he resigned in 1922 after the Conservatives withdrew their support.

Lloyd Webber /lɔɪd 'webə(r)/, Sir Andrew (born 1948), English composer. He has written many successful musicals, several of them in collaboration with the lyricist Sir Tim Rice; they include *Jesus Christ Superstar* (1970), *Evita* (1976), *Cats* (1981), *The Phantom of the Opera* (1986), *Aspects of Love* (1989), and *Sunset Boulevard* (1993).

Llywelyn ap Gruffydd see LLEWELYN.

Loach /ləʊtʃ/, Ken(neth) (born 1936), English film director. He started in television, highlighting social problems with films such as *Cathy Come Home* (1966), which dealt with homelessness. He continued to explore social and political issues, for example in his first feature film *Poor Cow* (1967), in his best-known work *Kes* (1969), and in his TV documentary *Questions of Leadership* (1983), which was banned on political grounds. Other films include *Land and Freedom* (1995).

Lobachevski /ˌlɒbə'tʃefskɪ/ Nikolai Ivanovich (1792–1856), Russian mathematician. At about the same time as Gauss in Germany and János Bolyai (1802–60) in Hungary, he independently discovered non-Euclidean geometry. His work was not widely recognized until the non-Euclidean nature of space–time was revealed by the general theory of relativity.

Locke[1] /lɒk/, John (1632–1704), English philosopher, a founder of empiricism and political liberalism. Both his major works were published in 1690. In *Two Treatises of Government* he justified the Revolution of 1688 by arguing that, contrary to the theory of the divine right of kings, the authority of rulers has a human origin and is limited. In *An Essay Concerning Human Understanding* he denied that any ideas are innate, and argued instead for a central empiricist tenet that all knowledge is derived from sense-experience. He concluded that it is not possible to know everything of the world and that our limited knowledge must be reinforced by faith.

Locke[2] /lɒk/, Joseph (1805–60), English civil engineer. A major railway pioneer, he enjoyed a lifelong association with Thomas Brassey, during which time he built important lines in England, Scotland, and France.

Lockyer /'lɒkjə(r)/, Sir (Joseph) Norman (1836–1920), English astronomer. Following the first observation of solar prominences (streams of incandescent gas issuing from the sun) during an eclipse, Lockyer demonstrated that they could be seen at other times with suitable equipment. His spectroscopic analysis of the sun led to his discovery of a new element, which he named *helium*. Lockyer also studied possible astronomical alignments in ancient monuments such as Stonehenge. He is perhaps best known today for founding both the Science Museum in London and the scientific journal *Nature*, which he edited for fifty years.

Lodge[1] /lɒdʒ/, David (John) (born 1935), English novelist and academic. He became honorary professor of Modern English Literature at the University of Birmingham in 1976. His novels are generally satires on academia and literary criticism, and include *Changing Places* (1975) and *Small World* (1984); *Nice Work* (1989) contrasted industry and academic life. He has done much to introduce and explain continental literary

theory in Britain; his critical works include *The Language of Fiction* (1966) and *Write On* (1986).

Lodge[2] /lɒdʒ/, Sir Oliver (Joseph) (1851–1940), English physicist. He made important contributions to the study of electromagnetic radiation, and was a pioneer of radio-telegraphy. He also devised an ingenious experiment which demonstrated that the hypothetical ether did not exist, and he carried out intensive studies of psychic phenomena.

Loewi /'ləʊɪ/, Otto (1873–1961), American pharmacologist and physiologist, born in Germany. He is chiefly remembered today for his contributions in the field of chemical transmission of nerve impulses. By means of experiments using a pair of isolated frog hearts he was the first to show that a chemical neurotransmitter is produced at the junction between a parasympathetic nerve and a muscle; he later identified it as the substance acetylcholine. Loewi shared a Nobel Prize with Sir Henry Dale in 1936.

London /'lʌndən/, Jack (pseudonym of John Griffith Chaney) (1876–1916), American novelist. He grew up in poverty, scratching a living in various ways and taking part in the Klondike gold rush of 1897–8; his experiences provided the material for his works and also made him a socialist. His most famous novels are *The Call of the Wild* (1903) and *White Fang* (1906).

Longfellow /'lɒŋ,feləʊ/, Henry Wadsworth (1807–82), American poet. His *Ballads and Other Poems* (1841) contains such well-known pieces as 'The Wreck of the Hesperus' and 'The Village Blacksmith'. Longfellow's popularity increased with subsequent volumes, especially his narrative poems. His best-known work is *The Song of Hiawatha* (1855), which tells in romantic style of the life and legendary exploits of the American Indian chieftain Hiawatha. The poem's repetitive metre, derived from the Finnish *Kalevala*, attracted both imitators and parodists.

Longinus /lɒn'dʒaɪnəs/ (fl. 1st century AD), Greek scholar. He is the supposed author of a Greek literary treatise *On the Sublime*, a critical analysis of literary greatness showing concern with the moral function of literature and impatience with pedantry. After its translation into French in 1674 it became a very influential work with Augustan writers such as Dryden and Pope.

Lorca /'lɔːkə/, Federico García (1898–1936), Spanish poet and dramatist. His volumes of verse include *Gypsy Ballads* (1928), strongly influenced by the folk poetry of his native Andalusia. However, he is particularly known for intense, poetic tragedies evoking the passionate emotions of Spanish life; they include *Blood Wedding* (1933), *Yerma* (1934), and *The House of Bernarda Alba* (published posthumously in 1945). He was murdered by Nationalist partisans after the outbreak of the Spanish Civil War.

Loren /lə'ren/, Sophia (born Sophia Scicolone) (born 1934), Italian actress. She has starred in many Italian and American films, ranging from the romantic melodrama *The Black Orchid* (1959) and the slapstick comedy *The Millionairess* (1960) to the wartime drama *La Ciociara* (1961), for which she won an Oscar. She received an honorary Academy Award in 1991.

Lorentz /'lɒrənts/, Hendrik Antoon (1853–1928), Dutch theoretical physicist. He worked on the forces affecting electrons, making substantial advances on the work of Maxwell and realizing that electrons and cathode rays were the same thing. Lorentz's name is applied to various concepts and phenomena which he described. For their work on electromagnetic theory, he and his pupil Pieter Zeeman (1865–1943) shared the 1902 Nobel Prize for physics.

Lorenz /'lɒrənts/, Konrad (Zacharias) (1903–89), Austrian zoologist. He pioneered the science of ethology, emphasizing innate rather than learned behaviour or conditioned reflexes. His major studies were in ornithology, especially with geese (in which he discovered the phenomenon of imprinting), and with jackdaws. Lorenz extrapolated these studies to human behaviour patterns, and compared the ill effects of the domestication of animals to human civilizing processes. His popular books include *King Solomon's Ring* (1952) and *On Aggression* (1966); he shared a Nobel Prize in 1973 with Karl von Frisch and Nikolaas Tinbergen.

Lorenzo de' Medici /lə'renzəʊ, də 'medɪtʃɪ, mə'diːtʃɪ/ (known as Lorenzo the Magnificent) (1449–92), Italian statesman and scholar. The grandson of Cosimo de' Medici, he came to power in Florence in 1469 following his father's death. He was a patron of the arts, promoted humanist learning and Neoplatonic philosophy, and was a

noted poet and scholar in his own right; Botticelli, Leonardo da Vinci, and Michelangelo were among the artists who enjoyed his patronage.

Lorrain, Claude see CLAUDE LORRAIN.

Lorre /'lɒrɪ/, Peter (born Laszlo Lowenstein) (1904–64), Hungarian-born American actor. He achieved international recognition as the child murderer in the German film M (1931), and went on to play the Japanese detective Mr Moto in eight Hollywood films (1937–9). He was cast in other sinister roles in The Maltese Falcon (1941), Casablanca (1942), and The Raven (1963).

Loti /lɒ'ti:/, Pierre (pseudonym of Louis Marie Julien Viaud) (1850–1923), French novelist. His novels were written while he served as a naval officer and his voyages provided the background for his work. His fame chiefly rests on three novels: Mon frère Yves (1883), Pêcheur d'Islande (1886), and Matelot (1893). These tell of the struggles of sailors who leave Brittany to fish in the waters around Iceland and the heartbreak of those left behind.

Lotto /'lɒtəʊ/, Lorenzo (c.1480–1556), Italian painter. His early art reflects the influence of his training in the studio of Giovanni Bellini in Venice, while his more mature work incorporates a wide range of influences, from the art of northern Europe to Raphael and Titian. Although chiefly a painter of religious subjects, he also produced a number of notable portraits, such as A Lady as Lucretia (c.1533).

Louis[1] /'lu:ɪ/ the name of eighteen kings of France:
Louis I (778–840), son of Charlemagne, king of the West Franks and Holy Roman emperor 814–40.
Louis II (846–79), reigned 877–9.
Louis III (863–82), son of Louis II, reigned 879–82.
Louis IV (921–54), reigned 936–54.
Louis V (967–87), reigned 979–87.
Louis VI (1081–1137), reigned 1108–37.
Louis VII (1120–80), reigned 1137–80.
Louis VIII (1187–1226), reigned 1223–6.
Louis IX (canonized as St Louis) (1214–70), son of Louis VIII, reigned 1226–70. His reign was dominated by his two crusades to the Holy Land, neither of which proved successful: the first (1248–54) ended in disaster with his capture by the Egyptians, the second (1270–1) in his own death from plague in Tunis. Feast day, 25 August.

Louis X (1289–1316), reigned 1314–16.
Louis XI (1423–83), son of Charles VII, reigned 1461–83. He continued his father's work in laying the foundations of a united France ruled by an absolute monarchy. His reign was dominated by his struggle with Charles the Rash, Duke of Burgundy. This ended with Charles's death in battle in 1477 and France's absorption of much of Burgundy's former territory along her border.
Louis XII (1462–1515), reigned 1498–1515.
Louis XIII (1601–43), son of Henry IV of France, reigned 1610–43. During his minority, the country was ruled by his mother Marie de Médicis. Louis asserted his right to rule in 1617, but from 1624 he was heavily influenced in policy-making by his chief minister Cardinal Richelieu.
Louis XIV (1638–1715), son of Louis XIII, reigned 1643–1715. He is known as the 'Sun King' from the magnificence of his reign, which represented the high point of the Bourbon dynasty and of French power in Europe, and during which French art and literature flourished. However, his almost constant wars of expansion united Europe against him, and, despite the reforms of Colbert, gravely weakened France's financial position. The Peace of Utrecht (1713–14), which ended the War of the Spanish Succession, represented the ultimate failure of Louis's attempt at European hegemony, preventing as it did the union of the French and Spanish crowns.
Louis XV (1710–74), great-grandson and successor of Louis XIV, reigned 1715–74. He led France into the Seven Years War (1756–63).
Louis XVI (1754–93), grandson and successor of Louis XV, reigned 1774–92. He inherited a situation of growing political discontent and severe problems of debt in the state finances. When the French Revolution broke out, he took refuge in a series of half measures, such as constitutional reforms and concessions to the republicans, which proved disastrous to his cause. After Louis's unsuccessful attempt to flee the country (1791), the Revolution became progressively more extreme and, with foreign invaders massing on the borders, the monarchy was abolished and Louis and his wife Marie Antoinette were executed.
Louis XVII (1785–95), son of Louis XVI, titular king who died in prison during the Revolution.

Louis XVIII (1755–1824), brother of Louis XVI, reigned 1814–24. Following the outbreak of the French Revolution he went into exile in 1791; two years later he pronounced himself regent for his nephew Louis XVII. After his nephew's death Louis XVIII became titular king until the fall of Napoleon in 1814, when he returned to Paris on the summons of Talleyrand and was officially restored to the throne. Louis introduced a constitutional monarchy in the same year, but was forced to flee the capital when Napoleon regained power briefly in 1815. After the latter's defeat at Waterloo, Louis returned to Paris and inaugurated parliamentary government.

Louis² /'luːɪs/, Joe (born Joseph Louis Barrow) (1914–81), American boxer. Known as 'the Brown Bomber', he was heavyweight champion of the world 1937–49, defending his title twenty-five times during that period.

Louis I /'luːɪ/ (known as Louis the Great) (1326–82), king of Hungary 1342–82 and of Poland 1370–82. He fought two successful wars against Venice (1357–8; 1378–81), and the rulers of Serbia, Wallachia, Moldavia, and Bulgaria became his vassals. Under his rule Hungary became a powerful state, though Poland was troubled by revolts.

Louis, St, Louis IX of France (see LOUIS ¹).

Louis-Napoleon /ˌluːməˈpəʊlɪən/, Napoleon III of France (see NAPOLEON).

Louis Philippe /ˌluːɪ friˈliːp/ (1773–1850), king of France 1830–48. As the Duc d'Orléans, Louis Philippe participated in the early, liberal phase of the French Revolution, but later went into exile abroad. Returning to France after the restoration of the Bourbons that followed Napoleon's fall, he became the focus for liberal discontent, and after the overthrow of Charles X in 1830 was made king. His bourgeois-style regime was popular at first but it was gradually undermined by radical discontent and overthrown in a brief uprising in 1848, with Louis once more going into exile.

Louis the Great, Louis I of Hungary (see LOUIS I).

Lovelace¹ /'lʌvleɪs/, Countess of (title of Augusta Ada King) (1815–52), English mathematician. The daughter of Lord Byron, she was brought up by her mother, who encouraged her studies in mathematics and astronomy. In 1833 Lovelace met the mathematician and computer pioneer Charles Babbage, subsequently becoming his assistant. In 1843 she made a translation of an Italian paper on Babbage's computer or 'difference engine', to which she added significant and detailed notations as to how the machine could be programmed. The high-level computer programming language *Ada* is named after her.

Lovelace² /'lʌvleɪs/, Richard (1618–57), English poet. A Royalist, in 1642 he was committed to prison, where he probably wrote the poem 'To Althea from Prison'. He rejoined Charles I in 1645 and was again imprisoned in 1648; during this time he prepared his collection of poetry *Lucasta*, which includes the lyric 'On going to the wars'.

Lovell /'lʌv(ə)l/, Sir (Alfred Charles) Bernard (born 1913), English astronomer and physicist, and pioneer of radio astronomy. He became professor of radio astronomy at Manchester University in 1951, and founded the university's radio observatory at Jodrell Bank. He directed the construction of the large radio telescope there, now named after him.

Lovelock /'lʌvlɒk/, James (Ephraim) (born 1919), English scientist. Lovelock was the first (in 1966) to detect CFCs, released from aerosols and coolants and now known to damage the ozone layer, in the atmosphere. He is best known for the *Gaia hypothesis* — first presented by him in 1972 and named after the Greek earth goddess — that the living and non-living components of earth collectively define and regulate the material conditions necessary for the continuance of life. The earth is thus likened to a vast self-regulating organism, modifying the biosphere to suit its needs. Lovelock discussed the hypothesis in the popular book *Gaia* (1979) and in several sequels.

Low /ləʊ/, Sir David (Alexander Cecil) (1891–1963), British cartoonist, born in New Zealand. He came to England in 1919 and worked for newspapers, joining the *Evening Standard* in 1927. Here he earned a worldwide reputation for his political cartoons, inventing the character Colonel Blimp and producing a series of anti-Nazi cartoons during the Second World War. In 1953 he joined the *Manchester Guardian*. He published more than thirty collections of cartoons, including *Low's Company* (1952).

Lowell[1] /ˈləʊəl/, Amy (Lawrence) (1874–1925), American poet. After producing her first volume of relatively conventional poetry she became influenced by the imagist movement, and while visiting England in 1913 and 1914 met Ezra Pound and other imagists. Her subsequent volumes, including *Men, Women and Ghosts* (1916), show her increasing allegiance to the imagist movement and her experiments in 'polyphonic prose'. Her love of New England is expressed in 'Lilacs' and 'Purple Grackles' (in the Pulitzer Prize-winning *What's O'Clock*, 1925). She was the sister of the astronomer Percival Lowell.

Lowell[2] /ˈləʊəl/, James Russell (1819–91), American poet and critic. His works include volumes of verse, the satirical *Biglow Papers* (1848 and 1867; prose and verse), memorial odes after the Civil War, and various volumes of essays, including *Among My Books* (1870) and *My Study Window* (1871).

Lowell[3] /ˈləʊəl/, Percival (1855–1916), American astronomer. Lowell founded an observatory in Flagstaff, Arizona, which now bears his name. He inferred the existence of a ninth planet beyond Neptune, and when it was eventually discovered in 1930 it was given the name Pluto, with a symbol that also included Lowell's initials. He claimed to have seen the supposed canals on Mars, and was a devout believer in the existence of intelligent life on the planet. He was the brother of poet Amy Lowell.

Lowell[4] /ˈləʊəl/, Robert (Traill Spence) (1917–77), American poet. In 1940 he married and was converted to Roman Catholicism. His first volume, *Land of Unlikeness* (1944), reflects his conflicts with Catholicism and his Boston ancestry. His personal life was marked by recurring bouts of manic illness, alcoholism, and marital discord; his poetry is notable for its intense confessional nature and for its ambiguous complex imagery, as in the volumes *Life Studies* (1959), *For the Union Dead* (1964), and *The Dolphin* (1973).

Lowry[1] /ˈlaʊərɪ/, L(aurence) S(tephen) (1887–1976), English painter. He spent most of his life in Salford, near Manchester, which provided the characteristic industrial setting of his pictures. Deliberately adopting a childlike manner of visualization, he painted small matchstick figures set against the iron and brick expanse of urban and industrial landscapes, providing a wry perspective on life in the industrial North.

Lowry[2] /ˈlaʊərɪ/, (Clarence) Malcolm (1909–57), English novelist. He lived in Mexico in the 1930s and his experiences provided the background for his symbolic semi-autobiographical novel *Under the Volcano* (1947); set in a Mexican town, it uses a complex narrative structure with many shifts of time sequence to trace the decline of an alcoholic British ex-consul.

Lucan /ˈluːkən/ (Latin name Marcus Annaeus Lucanus) (AD 39–65), Roman poet, born in Spain. At first held in esteem by Nero, he was forced to commit suicide after joining a conspiracy against the emperor. His major work, a hexameter epic in ten books known as the *Pharsalia*, deals with the civil war between Julius Caesar and Pompey; Lucan's republican and Stoic ideals find expression in his description of Cato the Younger.

Lucas /ˈluːkəs/, George (born 1944), American film director, producer, and screenwriter. He is chiefly known as the director and writer of the science-fiction adventure film *Star Wars* (1977). He produced and wrote the screenplays for two further episodes in the saga, namely *The Empire Strikes Back* (1980) and *Return of the Jedi* (1983), as well as for Steven Spielberg's *Raiders of the Lost Ark* (1981) and its two sequels.

Lucas van Leyden /ˌluːkəs væn ˈlaɪd(ə)n/ (c.1494–1533), Dutch painter and engraver. He produced his most significant work as an engraver and was active in this field from an early age; his *Muhammad and the Murdered Monk* dates from 1508 and *Ecce Homo* from 1510. His later work was influenced by that of Dürer, whom he met in 1521. His paintings include portraits, genre scenes, and religious subjects, such as the triptych *The Last Judgement* (1526–7).

Lucretius /luːˈkriːʃəs/ (full name Titus Lucretius Carus) (c.94–c.55 BC), Roman poet and philosopher. His didactic hexameter poem *On the Nature of Things* is an exposition of the atomist physics of Epicurus; it is based on a firmly materialistic view of the universe which is directed to the goal of giving humans peace of mind by showing that fear of the gods and of death is without foundation.

Ludendorff /ˈluːd(ə)n,dɔːf/, Erich (1865–1937), German general. Shortly after the outbreak of the First World War he was

appointed Chief of Staff to General von Hindenburg and they jointly directed the war effort until the final offensive failed (September 1918). Ludendorff later joined the Nazi Party and served as an MP (1924–8).

Ludwig /'lʊdvɪg/ the name of three kings of Bavaria:

Ludwig I (1786–1868), reigned 1825–48. His reactionary policies and lavish expenditure were the cause of radical protests in 1830; his domination by the dancer Lola Montez led to further unrest and he was forced to abdicate in favour of his son.

Ludwig II (1845–86), reigned 1864–86. He came increasingly under Prussian influence and his country eventually joined the new German Empire in 1871. A patron of the arts, in particular of Wagner, he later became a recluse and concentrated on building a series of elaborate castles. He was declared insane and deposed in 1886.

Ludwig III (1845–1921), reigned 1913–18.

Lugosi /lə'gəʊsɪ/, Bela (born Béla Ferenc Blasko) (1884–1956), Hungarian-born American actor. From 1904 he pursued a successful career as a classical actor in the Hungarian theatre, before emigrating to the US in 1921. Lugosi became famous with his performance in the title role of *Dracula* (1927) on Broadway; in 1931 he recreated the role for Hollywood in the first Dracula film. He subsequently appeared in a succession of horror films, including *Mark of the Vampire* (1935) and *The Wolf Man* (1940).

Lukács /'luːkætʃ/, György (1885–1971), Hungarian philosopher, literary critic, and politician. A major figure in Western Marxism, he is best known for his philosophical work *History and Class Consciousness* (1923), in which he stresses the central role of alienation in Marxist thought. His literary criticism is noted for its realist standpoint, notably in *The Theory of the Novel* (1916) and *The Historical Novel* (1955).

Luke, St /luːk/ an evangelist, closely associated with St Paul and traditionally the author of the third Gospel and the Acts of the Apostles. A physician, he was possibly the son of a Greek freedman of Rome. Feast day, 18 October.

Lully /'luːlɪ/, Jean-Baptiste (Italian name Giovanni Battista Lulli) (1632–87), French composer, born in Italy. He lived in France from the age of 14 and entered the service of Louis XIV in 1653. From 1664 he collaborated with Molière, writing incidental music for a series of comedies, including *Le Bourgeois Gentilhomme* (1670). In 1673 he turned to composing operas; his works, which include *Alceste* (1674) and *Armide* (1686), mark the beginning of the French operatic tradition.

Lumière /'luːmɪˌeə(r)/, Auguste Marie Louis Nicholas (1862–1954) and Louis Jean (1864–1948), French inventors and pioneers of cinema. In 1895 the brothers patented their 'Cinématographe', a cine-camera and projector in one; it had its first public demonstration later the same year. They also invented an improved process of colour photography.

Luther /'luːθə(r)/, Martin (1483–1546), German Protestant theologian, the principal figure of the German Reformation. From 1508 he taught at the University of Wittenberg, latterly as professor of scripture (1512–46). He began to preach the doctrine of justification by faith rather than by works; his attack on the sale of indulgences with his ninety-five theses (1517) was followed by further attacks on papal authority, and in 1521 Luther was condemned and excommunicated at the Diet of Worms. At a meeting with Swiss theologians at Marburg (1529) he opposed Zwingli and gave a defence of the doctrine of consubstantiation (the presence in the Eucharist of the real substances of the body and blood of Christ); the next year he gave his approval to Melanchthons' Augsburg Confession, which laid down the Lutheran position. His translation of the Bible into High German (1522–34) contributed significantly to the spread of this form of the language and to the development of German literature in the vernacular.

Luthuli /luː'tuːlɪ/, Albert John (also **Lutuli**) (c.1898–1967), South African political leader. He inherited a Zulu chieftaincy in 1935 and was president of the African National Congress from 1952 to 1960. Luthuli's presidency was marked by the Defiance Campaign, his programme of civil disobedience. He was awarded the Nobel Peace Prize in 1960 for his commitment to non-violence as a means of opposing apartheid.

Lutosławski /ˌluːtə'swɑːfskɪ/, Witold (1913–94), Polish composer. He is noted for his orchestral music, including three symphonies (1947; 1967; 1983), *Mi-parti* (1976), and *Chain 3* (1986). From the early 1960s,

his works have been characterized by a blend of notational composition and aleatoric sections.

Lutyens[1] /'lʌtjənz/, Sir Edwin (Landseer) (1869–1944), English architect. He established his reputation designing country houses, moving from a romantic red-brick style to Palladian-influenced formal designs. Lutyens is perhaps best known for his plans for New Delhi (1912), where he introduced an open garden-city layout; his Viceroy's House (1915–30) combined classical features with decoration in the Indian idiom. He is also remembered for the Cenotaph in London (1919–21) and his unfulfilled design for the Roman Catholic cathedral in Liverpool (1929).

Lutyens[2] /'lʌtjənz/, (Agnes) Elizabeth (1906–83), English composer. She was one of the first English composers to use the serialist twelve-note system (in which the notes are used on an equal basis without dependence on a key system); the Chamber Concerto No. 1 (1939) is an example of her interpretation of this technique. Her works include operas, orchestral and choral works, and chamber music; she also wrote many scores for films and radio, as well as incidental music for plays. She was the daughter of Sir Edwin Lutyens.

Luxemburg /'lʌksəm,bɜːg/, Rosa (1871–1919), Polish-born German revolutionary leader. She co-founded what became the Polish Communist Party (1893), before obtaining German citizenship in 1898. Imprisoned in 1915 for opposing the First World War, she co-founded the revolutionary and pacifist group known as the Spartacus League (the Spartacists) in 1916 with the German socialist Karl Liebknecht (1871–1919). After her release from prison in 1918 she co-founded the German Communist Party; the following year she and Liebknecht were assassinated after organizing an abortive Communist uprising in Berlin.

Lycurgus /laɪˈkɜːgəs/ (9th century BC), Spartan lawgiver. He is traditionally held to have been the founder of the constitution and military regime of ancient Sparta.

Lydgate /'lɪdɡeɪt/, John (c.1370–c.1450), English poet and monk. He is noted for his copious output of verse, often in Chaucerian style, and for translations. Of the latter the best known are the *Troy Book* (1412–20), written at the request of Prince Henry (later Henry V), and *The Fall of Princes*

(1431–8), based on a French version of a book on tragedy by Boccaccio.

Lyell /'laɪəl/, Sir Charles (1797–1875), Scottish geologist. His textbook *Principles of Geology* (1830–3) influenced a generation of geologists. He held that the earth's features were shaped over a long period of time by natural processes, and not during short periodic upheavals as proposed by the catastrophist school of thought. In this he revived the theories of James Hutton, but his influence on geological opinion was much greater. Lyell's views cleared the way for Darwin's theory of evolution, which he accepted after some hesitation.

Lyly /'lɪlɪ/, John (c.1554–1606), English prose writer and dramatist. He is remembered for his prose romance in two parts: *Euphues, The Anatomy of Wit* (1578) and *Euphues and his England* (1580). Both were written in an elaborate style that became known as *euphuism*.

Lynn /lɪn/, Dame Vera (born Vera Margaret Lewis) (born 1917), English singer. During the Second World War she sang to the troops and became known as 'the Forces' Sweetheart'. She is mainly remembered for her rendering of such songs as 'We'll Meet Again' and 'White Cliffs of Dover'. She had a number of postwar successes, including 'Auf Wiederseh'n, Sweetheart' (1952).

Lyotard /'ljɒtɑː(r)/, Jean-François (born 1924), French philosopher and literary critic. At first a Marxist, he abandoned this position in *L'Économie libidinale* (1974), where he outlined his 'philosophy of desire', based on the politics of Nietzsche. He came to international prominence with his book *La Condition postmoderne* (1979). By the time of *La Différend* (1983) he had adopted a quasi-Wittgensteinian linguistic philosophy which was connected with postmodernism.

Lysander /laɪˈsændə(r)/ (died 395 BC) Spartan general. He commanded the Spartan fleet that defeated the Athenian navy in 405. Lysander captured Athens in 404, so bringing the Peloponnesian War to an end.

Lysenko /lɪˈsɛŋkəʊ/, Trofim Denisovich (1898–1976), Soviet biologist and geneticist. He was an adherent of Lamarck's theory of evolution by the inheritance of acquired characteristics. Since his ideas harmonized with Marxist ideology he was favoured by

Stalin and dominated Soviet genetics for many years. Among other false claims, he stated that the process of vernalization — growing a plant, especially a food crop, in a cold climate — will adapt the plant genetically to resist low temperatures.

Lysippus /laɪˈsɪpəs/ (4th century BC), Greek sculptor. His name is associated with a series of bronze athletes, notably the Apoxyomenos (c.320–315), which represents a young male athlete scraping and cleaning his oil-covered skin. With such works Lysippus is said to have introduced a naturalistic scheme of proportions for the human body into Greek sculpture.

Lytton /ˈlɪt(ə)n/, 1st Baron (born Edward George Earle Bulwer-Lytton) (1803–73), British novelist, dramatist, and statesman. His prolific literary output includes *Pelham* (1828), a novel of fashionable society with which he had his first success, many historical romances (such as *The Last Days of Pompeii*, 1834), and plays. He entered Parliament as an MP in 1831 and later served as Colonial Secretary in Lord Derby's government (1858–9).

M

Mabuse /məˈbjuːz/ Jan (Flemish name Jan Gossaert) (c.1478–c.1533), Flemish painter. In 1508 he visited Italy, where the art of the High Renaissance made a lasting impression on him; he subsequently became one of the first artists to disseminate the Italian style in the Netherlands. His works are largely nudes, studies of the Virgin and Child, and commissioned portraits.

MacAlpin /məˈkælpm/, Kenneth, see KENNETH I.

MacArthur /məˈkɑːθə(r)/, Douglas (1880–1964), American general. He was in command of US (later Allied) forces in the SW Pacific during the Second World War. He formally accepted Japan's surrender in 1945, and administered that country during the Allied occupation that followed. In 1950 he was put in charge of UN forces in Korea, but was relieved of his command the following year.

Macaulay[1] /məˈkɔːlɪ/, Dame (Emilie) Rose (1881–1958), English novelist and essayist. After works such as *Dangerous Ages* (1921) and *They Were Defeated* (1932) she wrote no fiction for over a decade. Her return to the Anglican Church, from which she had long been estranged, was followed by her best-known novels *The World My Wilderness* (1950) and *The Towers of Trebizond* (1956).

Macaulay[2] /məˈkɔːlɪ/, Thomas Babington, 1st Baron (1800–59), English historian, essayist, and philanthropist. As a civil servant in India (1834–8) he established an English system of education and devised a new criminal code, before returning to Britain and devoting himself to literature and politics. Among his best-known works are *The Lays of Ancient Rome* (1842) and his *History of England* (1849–61), which covers the period from the accession of James II to the death of William III from a Whig standpoint.

Macbeth /məkˈbeθ/ (c.1005–57), king of Scotland 1040–57. He came to the throne after killing his cousin Duncan I in battle, and was himself defeated and killed by Malcolm III. He is chiefly remembered as the subject of Shakespeare's tragedy *Mac-*beth, in which the historical events are considerably embroidered.

Maccabaeus, Judas, see JUDAS MACCABAEUS.

McCarthy[1] /məˈkɑːθɪ/, Joseph R(aymond) (1909–57), American Republican politician. Between 1950 and 1954, latterly as chairman of a government committee, he was the instigator of widespread investigations into alleged Communist infiltration in US public life. Although most of those accused during the period of 'McCarthyism' were not in fact members of the Communist Party, many of them were blacklisted, lost their jobs, or were otherwise discriminated against in a mood of hysteria which abated only after the public censure of McCarthy in December 1954.

McCarthy[2] /məˈkɑːθɪ/, Mary (Therese) (1912–89), American novelist and critic. Her novels are satirical social commentaries that draw on her experience of intellectual circles and academic life; they include *The Groves of Academe* (1952), which describes political persecution under McCarthyism, and *The Group* (1963), tracing the lives and careers of eight college girls.

McCartney /məˈkɑːtnɪ/, Sir (James) Paul (born 1942), English pop and rock singer, songwriter, and bass guitarist. He was a founder member of the Beatles, and with John Lennon wrote most of their songs (see LENNON); McCartney is known particularly for melodic, accessible songs such as 'Yesterday' (1965) and 'Penny Lane' (1967). After the group broke up in 1970 he formed the band Wings, with whom he recorded hit singles such as 'Mull of Kintyre' (1977). Thereafter his musical career has included solo albums, film scores, and a classical composition, the *Liverpool Oratorio* (1991), written with the American composer Carl Davis (born 1936).

McCullers /məˈkʌləz/, (Lula) Carson (1917–67), American writer. Born in Georgia, McCullers spent most of her adult life in New York. Paralysis of one side confined her permanently to a wheelchair at the age of 29. Her work deals sensitively with loneliness and the plight of the eccentric; her

first book, *The Heart is a Lonely Hunter* (1940), won instant acclaim. Other works include the novella *The Ballad of the Sad Café* (1951), which was dramatized by Edward Albee in 1963.

MacDiarmid /mək'dɜːmɪd/, Hugh (pseudonym of Christopher Murray Grieve) (1892–1978), Scottish poet and nationalist. As a poet, he is chiefly remembered for his lyrics in a synthetic Scots that drew on the language of various regions and historical periods, such as the poems in the volume *A Drunk Man Looks at the Thistle* (1926). In the 1930s he wrote political poetry, including *First Hymn to Lenin and Other Poems* (1931). He was a founder member (1928) of the National Party of Scotland (later the Scottish National Party).

MacDonald[1] /mək'dɒn(ə)ld/, Flora (1722–90), Scottish Jacobite heroine. She aided Charles Edward Stuart's escape from Scotland, after his defeat at Culloden in 1746, by smuggling him over to the Isle of Skye in a small boat under the eyes of government forces.

Macdonald[2] /mək'dɒn(ə)ld/, Sir John Alexander (1815–91), Scottish-born Canadian statesman, Prime Minister 1867–73 and 1878–91. Entering politics in the 1840s, he became leader of the Conservatives and joint Premier (with George-Étienne Cartier) in 1856. Thereafter he played a leading role in the confederation of the Canadian provinces, and was appointed first Prime Minister of the Dominion of Canada in 1867.

MacDonald[3] /mək'dɒn(ə)ld/, (James) Ramsay (1866–1937), British Labour statesman, Prime Minister 1924, 1929–31, and 1931–5. In 1922 he became leader of the Labour Party, and served as Britain's first Labour Prime Minister in the short-lived Labour government of 1924; he was elected Prime Minister again in 1929, but without an overall majority. Faced with economic crisis, and weakened by splits in his own party, he formed a national government with some Conservatives and Liberals; this led to his being expelled from the Labour Party.

McEnroe /'mækɪn.rəʊ/, John (Patrick) (born 1959), American tennis player. A temperamental player, he dominated the game in the early 1980s; among his many titles are seven Wimbledon titles, three for the singles (1981, 1983–4) and four for the doubles (1979–84), six victories in the US Masters doubles (1978–83), and four US Open singles championships (1979–84).

McGonagall /mə'gɒnəg(ə)l/, William (1830–1902), Scottish poet. He became a popular figure when travelling around Scotland, giving public readings of his own poetry and selling it in broadsheets. His verse, including 'The Tay Bridge Disaster' (1880), is naive yet entertaining doggerel which has won him a reputation as one of the worst poets in the world.

Mach /mɑːk, mæk/, Ernst (1838–1916), Austrian physicist and philosopher of science. His belief that all knowledge of the physical world comes from sensations, and that science should be solely concerned with observables, inspired the logical positivist philosophers of the Vienna Circle in the 1920s. Mach also influenced scientists such as Einstein in the formulation of his theory of relativity, and Niels Bohr in quantum mechanics. In commemoration of his work on aerodynamics, his name has been preserved in the Mach number.

Machiavelli /,mækɪə'velɪ/, Niccolò di Bernardo dei (1469–1527), Italian statesman and political philosopher. After holding high office in Florence he was exiled by the Medicis on suspicion of conspiracy, but was subsequently restored to some degree of favour. His best-known work is *The Prince* (1532), a treatise on statecraft which advises rulers that the acquisition and effective use of power may necessitate unethical methods that are not in themselves desirable. He is thus often regarded as the originator of a political pragmatism in which 'the end justifies the means'.

Mackenzie[1] /mə'kenzɪ/, Sir Alexander (1764–1820), Scottish explorer of Canada. He entered the service of the North-West Company in 1779, undertaking explorations throughout NW Canada. He discovered the Mackenzie River in 1789 and in 1793 became the first European to reach the Pacific Ocean by land along a northern route.

Mackenzie[2] /mə'kenzɪ/, Sir (Edward Montague) Compton (1883–1972), English novelist, essayist, and poet. He produced essays, memoirs, poems, and biographies, but is best known as a novelist. His works include the semi-autobiographical *Sinister Street* (1913–14) and the comic novel *Whisky Galore* (1947).

Mackenzie[3] /məˈkenzɪ/, William Lyon (1795–1861), Scottish-born Canadian politician and journalist. Having emigrated to Canada in 1820, he became involved with the movement for political reform, at first as a radical journalist and later as a member of the provincial Parliament and mayor of Toronto (1834–6). In 1837 he led a short-lived rebellion, unsuccessfully attempting to set up a new government in Toronto. He fled to New York, returning to Canada in 1849.

McKinlay /məˈkɪnlɪ/, John (1819–72), Scottish-born explorer. Having emigrated to New South Wales in 1836, he was appointed in 1861 to lead an expedition to search for the missing explorers Burke and Wills. Although he found only traces of part of the Burke and Wills party, he carried out valuable exploratory work in the Australian interior and brought his entire party back safely despite tremendous hardships.

McKinley /məˈkɪnlɪ/, William (1843–1901), American Republican statesman, 25th President of the US 1897–1901. He supported US expansion into the Pacific, fighting the Spanish–American War of 1898 which resulted in the acquisition of Puerto Rico, Cuba, and the Philippines as well as the annexation of Hawaii. He was assassinated by an anarchist.

Mackintosh /ˈmækɪnˌtɒʃ/, Charles Rennie (1868–1928), Scottish architect and designer. He was a leading exponent of art nouveau and a precursor of several trends in 20th-century architecture. In particular, he pioneered the new concept of functionalism in architecture and interior design. His influence was very great abroad, especially in Austria and Germany, but less so in Britain. His fame chiefly rests on his Glasgow School of Art (1898–1909) and four Glasgow tearooms (1897–1912), designed with all their furniture and equipment.

Maclean[1] /məˈkleɪn/, Alistair (1922–87), Scottish novelist. His numerous thrillers and adventure stories, many of which were made into films, include *The Guns of Navarone* (1957), *Where Eagles Dare* (1967), and *Bear Island* (1971).

Maclean[2] /məˈkleɪn/, Donald Duart (1913–83), British Foreign Office official and Soviet spy. After acting as a Soviet agent from the late 1930s he fled to the USSR with Guy Burgess in 1951, following a warning from

Kim Philby of impending proceedings against him.

Macleod /məˈklaʊd/, John James Rickard (1876–1935), Scottish physiologist. He specialized in carbohydrate metabolism and held various chairs in physiology, notably at the University of Toronto. He provided facilities there for the research on pancreatic extracts by F. G. Banting and C. H. Best, much of which was directed by Macleod personally, and which led to the discovery and isolation of insulin. Macleod shared a Nobel Prize with Banting in 1923.

McLuhan /məˈkluːən/, (Herbert) Marshall (1911–80), Canadian writer and thinker. He became famous in the 1960s for his theories on the role of the media and technology in society. He is particularly known for claiming that the world had become 'a global village' in its electronic interdependence, and that 'the medium is the message', because it is the characteristics of a particular medium rather than the information it disseminates which influence and control society. His books include *Understanding Media: The Extensions of Man* (1964).

Macmillan /məkˈmɪlən/, (Maurice) Harold, 1st Earl of Stockton (1894–1986), British Conservative statesman, Prime Minister 1957–63. His term of office saw the signing of the Test-Ban Treaty (1963) with the US and the USSR. He advocated the granting of independence to British colonies but his attempt to take Britain into the European Economic Community was blocked by the French President de Gaulle (1963). Macmillan resigned on grounds of ill health shortly after the scandal surrounding the Secretary of State for War, John Profumo.

MacNeice /məkˈniːs/, (Frederick) Louis (1907–63), Northern Irish poet. He was part of W. H. Auden's circle at Oxford, where he published his first volume of poetry in 1929; later volumes include *Collected Poems* (1966). His work is characterized by the use of assonance, internal rhythms, and ballad-like repetitions absorbed from the Irish background of his youth. He also wrote documentaries and plays for radio, notably the fantasy *The Dark Tower* (1947).

Macquarie /məˈkwɒrɪ/, Lachlan (1762–1824), Scottish-born Australian colonial administrator. He served as governor of New South Wales 1809–21; the colony was chiefly populated by convicts, but during

his term of office he improved its prosperity, expanded opportunities for former convicts, and promoted public works, further settlement, and exploration.

Madison /'mædɪs(ə)n/, James (1751–1836), American Democratic Republican statesman, 4th President of the US 1809–17. Before taking office, he played a leading part in drawing up the US Constitution (1787) and proposed the Bill of Rights (1791). His presidency saw the US emerge successfully from the War of 1812 against Britain.

Madonna /mə'dɒnə/ (born Madonna Louise Ciccone) (born 1958), American pop singer and actress. She rose to international stardom in the mid-1980s through her records and accompanying videos, cultivating her image as a sex symbol and frequently courting controversy. Among her singles are 'Holiday' (1983), while her albums include *Like a Virgin* (1984) and *Erotica* (1992). Probably her best-known film is *Desperately Seeking Susan* (1985).

Maecenas /mar'si:nəs/, Gaius (c.70–8 BC), Roman statesman. He was a trusted adviser of Augustus but shunned official position. Himself a writer, he was a notable patron of poets such as Virgil and Horace (a role for which his name became a byword).

Maeterlinck /'meɪtə,lɪŋk/, Count Maurice (1862–1949), Belgian poet, dramatist, and essayist. He published a collection of symbolist poems in 1889, and became established as a leading figure in the symbolist movement with his prose dramas *La Princesse Maleine* (1889) and *Pelléas et Mélisande* (1892), the source of Debussy's opera of that name (1902). He also achieved great popularity in his day with the play *L'Oiseau bleu* (1908; *The Blue Bird*). His work draws on traditions of fairy tale and romance, and is characterized by an air of mystery and melancholy. He was awarded the Nobel Prize for literature in 1911.

Magellan /mə'gelən/, Ferdinand (Portuguese name Fernão Magalhães) (c.1480–1521), Portuguese explorer. In 1519, while in the service of Spain, he commanded five vessels on a voyage from Spain to the East Indies by the western route. He reached South America later that year, rounding the continent through the strait which now bears his name and emerging to become the first European to navigate the Pacific. He reached the Philippines in 1521, but soon after was killed in a skirmish on

Cebu. The survivors, in the one remaining ship, sailed back to Spain round Africa, thereby completing the first circumnavigation of the globe (1522).

Magritte /mə'gri:t/, René (François Ghislain) (1898–1967), Belgian painter. His paintings are typical examples of surrealism; they display startling or amusing juxtapositions of the ordinary, the strange, and the erotic, all depicted in a realist manner. He had a repertory of images which appear in incongruous settings, for example in *Threatening Weather* (1928), in which a chair, a table, and a torso hover like clouds over the sea.

Mahdi /'mɑːdɪ/ (in popular Muslim belief) a spiritual and temporal leader who will rule before the end of the world and restore religion and justice. The title has been claimed by various leaders; the most widely known of these was Muhammad Ahmad of Dongola in Sudan (1843–85), who proclaimed himself Mahdi in 1881 and launched a political and revolutionary movement which captured Khartoum and overthrew the Egyptian regime. For Shiite Muslims the title *Mahdi* refers to the twelfth imam.

Mahfouz /mɑː'fuːz/, Naguib (born 1911), Egyptian novelist and short-story writer. His novels include the Cairo Trilogy (1956–7), which monitors the stages of Egyptian nationalism up to the revolution of 1952, and *Miramar* (1967), an attack on President Nasser's subsequent policies; his short stories of the late 1960s examine the aftermath of the 1967 war with Israel. In 1988 he became the first writer in Arabic to be awarded the Nobel Prize for literature.

Mahler /'mɑːlə(r)/, Gustav (1860–1911), Austrian composer, conductor, and pianist. He was director (1897–1907) of the Vienna State Opera. His large-scale works include nine complete symphonies (1888–1910) and the symphonic song-cycle *Das Lied von der Erde* (1908). His music forms a link between the romantic tradition of the 19th century and the experimentalism of 20th-century composers such as Schoenberg; there has been a significant revival of interest in his work in the second half of the 20th century.

Mailer /'meɪlə(r)/, Norman (born 1923), American novelist and essayist. He gained recognition with his first novel, *The Naked and the Dead* (1948), which drew on his experiences in the Second World War. The

effect of war and violence on human relationships is a recurrent theme in his work, which frequently also includes an element of social criticism. His later novels, such as *The Presidential Papers* (1963) and *The Armies of the Night* (1968), combine journalism, autobiography, political commentary, and fictional passages in a wide range of styles.

Maimonides /mar'mɒnɪˌdiːz/ (born Moses ben Maimon) (1135–1204), Jewish philosopher and Rabbinic scholar, born in Spain. He eventually settled in Cairo, where he became head of the Jewish community. His writings include the *Guide for the Perplexed* (1190), which endeavoured to reconcile Talmudic scripture with the philosophy of Aristotle. His work had a great influence on medieval Christian thought.

Maintenon /'mæntəˌnɒn/ Marquise de (title of Françoise d'Aubigné) (1635–1719), mistress and later second wife of the French king Louis XIV. Already a widow, in 1669 she became the governess of Louis's children by his previous mistress, Madame de Montespan. In 1674, with the king's assistance, she bought the marquisate of Maintenon. She was married to Louis after his first wife's death in 1683.

Major /'meɪdʒ(ə)r/, John (born 1943), British Conservative statesman, Prime Minister 1990–7. He became Prime Minister following the resignation of Margaret Thatcher, and in 1992 he was returned for a further term of office. His premiership saw the joint 'Downing Street Declaration' of the UK and Irish governments, intended as the basis of a peace initiative in Northern Ireland, and the negotiations leading to the signing of the Maastricht Treaty. Major survived a leadership challenge in 1995, and was faced with divisions within the Conservative Party over the degree to which Britain should integrate with Europe.

Makarios III /məˈkɑːrɪˌɒs/ (born Mikhail Christodolou Mouskos) (1913–77), Greek Cypriot archbishop and statesman, President of the republic of Cyprus 1960–77. He was primate and archbishop of the Greek Orthodox Church in Cyprus from 1950, and combined this position with a vigorous political role. He reorganized the movement for enosis (union of Cyprus with Greece) and was exiled (1956–9) by the British for allegedly supporting the EOKA terrorist campaign. He was elected first President of an independent Cyprus and, although forced briefly into exile by a Greek military coup (1974), continued in office until his death.

Malamud /'mæləməd/, Bernard (1914–86), American novelist and short-story writer. The son of Russian Jewish immigrants, he is perhaps best known for his novel *The Fixer* (1967), the story of a Jewish handyman or 'fixer' in tsarist Russia just before the First World War who is falsely accused of murder and turned into a scapegoat for anti-Semitic feeling.

Malcolm /'mælkəm/ the name of four kings of Scotland:
Malcolm I (died 954), reigned 943–54.
Malcolm II (*c*.954–1034), reigned 1005–34.
Malcolm III (known as Malcolm Canmore, from Gaelic *Ceann-mor* 'great head') (*c*.1031–93), son of Duncan I, reigned 1058–93. He came to the throne after killing Macbeth in battle (1057). One of the monarchs most responsible for welding Scotland into an organized kingdom, Malcolm spent a large part of his reign involved in intermittent border warfare with the new Norman regime in England, eventually being killed in battle near Alnwick.
Malcolm IV (known as Malcolm the Maiden) (1141–65), grandson of David I, reigned 1153–65. His reign witnessed a progressive loss of power to Henry II of England; he died young and without an heir.

Malcolm X /ˌmælkəm 'eks/ (born Malcolm Little) (1925–65), American political activist. He joined the Black Muslims (Nation of Islam) in 1946 and during the 1950s and early 1960s became a vigorous campaigner against the exploitation of blacks. He advocated the use of violence for self-protection and was opposed to the cooperative approach that characterized the rest of the civil-rights movement. In 1964, after converting to orthodox Islam, he broke away from the Black Muslims and moderated his views on black separatism; he was assassinated the following year.

Malenkov /'mælɪnˌkɒf/, Georgy (Maksimilianovich) (1902–88), Soviet statesman, born in Russia. In 1930 he became secretary of the Moscow section of the Soviet Communist Party (CPSU). He was promoted through the party ranks, being appointed deputy Prime Minister and a full member

of the Politburo in 1946. Following the death of Stalin he became Prime Minister and First Secretary of the CPSU in 1953 but resigned two years later over his inability to resolve problems of agriculture and industrialization.

Malevich /'mælɪ,vɪtʃ/, Kazimir (Severinovich) (1878–1935), Russian painter and designer. He founded the suprematist movement (1915). His abstract works used only basic geometrical shapes and a severely restricted range of colour, culminating in the *White on White* series (1918). After the Soviet government suppressed modern art he died in poverty and obscurity, but later had immense influence on western European art.

Malherbe /mæ'leəb/ François de (1555–1628), French poet. An architect of classicism in poetic form and grammar, he sternly criticized excess of emotion and ornamentation and the use of Latin and dialectal forms.

Malinowski /,mælɪ'nɒfskɪ/, Bronisław Kaspar (1884–1942), Polish anthropologist. An influential teacher, from 1916 onwards he was chiefly based in England and the US. He initiated the technique of 'participant observation', where the anthropologist spends a period living with a community; he first applied this in his study of the people of the Trobriand Islands, conducted from 1915 to 1918. He also developed the functionalist approach to anthropology, especially in his studies of the Pueblo Indians in Mexico and Bantu-speaking peoples in Africa.

Mallarmé /,mælɑ:'meɪ/, Stéphane (1842–98), French poet. His best-known poems include 'Hérodiade' (c.1871) and 'L'Après-midi d'un faune' (1876). He was a symbolist, who made use of elaborate symbols and metaphors in his work and experimented with rhythm and syntax by transposing words and omitting grammatical elements. These tendencies culminated in the poem 'Un Coup de dés jamais n'abolira le hasard' (1897), which makes revolutionary use of typographical possibilities to suggest a musical score.

Malle /mæl/, Louis (1932–95), French film director. He won recognition with *Ascenseur pour l'échafaud* (1958) and the erotic *Les Amants* (1959), which are considered seminal examples of the French *nouvelle vague*. He gained international acclaim with a series of successful films such as *Pretty Baby*

(1978), *Au Revoir les enfants* (1987), and *Damage* (1992).

Malory /'mælərɪ/, Sir Thomas (d.1471), English writer. Although his exact identity is uncertain, it is probable that he was Sir Thomas Malory of Newbold Revel, Warwickshire. His major work, *Le Morte d'Arthur* (printed 1483), is a prose translation of a collection of the legends of King Arthur, selected from French and other sources. It was one of the earliest works to be printed by Caxton, and is the standard source for later versions in English of the Arthurian romances.

Malpighi /mæl'pi:gɪ/, Marcello (c.1628–94), Italian microscopist. Seeking a mechanical interpretation of animal bodies, he looked for and found visible structures underlying physiological functions. He discovered the alveoli and capillaries in the lungs and the fibres and red cells of clotted blood, and demonstrated the pathway of blood from arteries to veins. Malpighi began the study of embryology, and also investigated the structures of the kidney and the skin, the anatomy of the silkworm, the structure of plant cells, and the breathing system of animals.

Malraux /mæl'rəʊ/, André (1901–76), French novelist, politician, and art critic. Malraux was involved in the Chinese communist uprising of 1927 and fought in the Spanish Civil War and the Second World War. He then became a Gaullist, and was appointed the first Minister of Cultural Affairs (1959–69). He is best known for novels such as *La Condition humaine* (1933) and *L'Espoir* (1937), which in several respects anticipate the existentialism of Jean-Paul Sartre.

Malthus /'mælθəs/, Thomas Robert (1766–1834), English economist and clergyman. He was a pioneer of the science of political economy and is known for his theory, as expressed in *Essay on Population* (1798), that the rate of increase of the population tends to be out of proportion to the increase of its means of subsistence; controls on population (by sexual abstinence or birth control) are therefore necessary to prevent catastrophe.

Mamet /'mæmɪt/, David (born 1947), American dramatist, director, and screenwriter. In 1974 he co-founded the Chicago-based St Nicholas Theater Company, for whom he wrote and directed a succession of plays noted for their approach to social issues,

including *Glengarry Glen Ross* (1984), which won the Pulitzer Prize. Other works include the film *House of Games* (1986), which he wrote and directed, and the play *Oleanna* (1992), whose portrayal of a case involving false accusations of sexual harassment caused much controversy.

Mandela /mæn'delə/, Nelson (Rolihlahla) (born 1918), South African statesman, President since 1994. From his twenties he was an activist for the African National Congress (ANC); he was first jailed in 1962 and was sentenced to life imprisonment in 1964. His authority as a moderate leader of black South Africans did not diminish while he was in detention, and he became a symbol of the struggle against apartheid. On his release in 1990 Mandela resumed his leadership of the ANC, and engaged in talks with President F. W. de Klerk on the introduction of majority rule. He shared the Nobel Peace Prize with President de Klerk in 1993, and in the country's first democratic elections was elected President the following year.

Mandelbrot /'mænd(ə)l,brɒt/, Benoit (born 1924), Polish-born French mathematician. Mandelbrot moved to the US in 1958, working at the IBM Research Center and at Harvard and Yale universities. He is known as the pioneer of fractal geometry, which is concerned with the construction of apparently irregular shapes from forms that are endlessly repeated with increasing magnification, as in a snowflake. This is exemplified by the *Mandelbrot set*, which is constructed from a mathematical formula and visualized graphically by computer.

Mandelstam /'mænd(ə)l,ʃtæm/, Osip (Emilevich) (also **Mandelshtam**) (1891–1938), Russian poet. As one of the Acmeist group of poets (with Anna Akhmatova), Mandelstam favoured concrete detail, clarity, and precision of language as a reaction against the mysticism of contemporary Russian symbolist poetry. During the 1920s his poetry met with increasing official criticism; Mandelstam was sent into internal exile (1934–7) and eventually died in a prison camp. Major works include *Stone* (1913) and *Tristia* (1922).

Mandeville /'mændə,vɪl/, Sir John (14th century), English nobleman. He is remembered as the reputed author of a book of travels and travellers' tales which takes the reader to Turkey, Tartary, Persia, Egypt, and India. Written in French and much

translated, it was actually compiled by an unknown hand from the works of several writers.

Manet /'mæneɪ/, Édouard (1832–83), French painter. He adopted a realist approach which greatly influenced the impressionists, and abandoned half-tones and shadings in favour of pure colour to give a direct unsentimental effect. Several of his paintings aroused outrage because of the frank and unidealized treatment of their subject-matter; *Olympia* (1865) depicted a nude woman with clear indications that she was a prostitute. Among other notable works are *Déjeuner sur l'herbe* (1863) and *A Bar at the Folies-Bergère* (1882).

Manetho /'mæ'neθəʊ/ (3rd century BC), Egyptian priest. He wrote a history of Egypt (*c.*280) from mythical times to 323. He arbitrarily divided the succession of rulers known to him into thirty dynasties, an arrangement which is still followed.

Man in the Iron Mask a mysterious prisoner held in the Bastille and other prisons in 17th-century France. According to the novel of the same name by Alexandre Dumas the man was the twin brother of Louis XIV, and was considered a threat to Louis's position on the throne; his face was concealed by a mask so that he could not be recognized. Various other theories as to the identity of the prisoner have been advanced, but it is now considered most likely that he was an Italian agent, Count Matthioli, who had angered the king by his betrayal of secret negotiations for France to acquire the stronghold of Casale from the Duke of Mantua.

Manley /'mænlɪ/, Michael (Norman) (1923–97), Jamaican statesman, Prime Minister 1972–80 and 1989–92. He became the island's first Vice-President in 1955 and leader of the People's National Party in 1969. Elected Prime Minister on a socialist platform, he introduced policies to strengthen Jamaica's economy through the expansion of public works and the encouragement of local industry; he also introduced a system of free education.

Mann /mæn/, Thomas (1875–1955), German novelist and essayist. He achieved recognition with his first novel *Buddenbrooks* (1901), which describes the decline of a merchant family and has strongly autobiographical features. The role and character of the artist in relation to society is a constant theme in his works, and is linked with the

rise of Nazism in *Dr Faustus* (1947). Other notable works include the novella *Death in Venice* (1912). When Hitler came to power Mann was forced into exile; he became a US citizen in 1944 but later settled in Switzerland. He was awarded the Nobel Prize for literature in 1929.

Manning /'mænɪŋ/, Olivia (Mary) (1908–80), English novelist. Manning published her first novel, *The Wind Changes*, in 1937, before marrying and going abroad with her husband in 1939. Returning to London in 1946, she became an acclaimed and prolific novelist, publishing eleven novels between 1949 and 1980. Her experiences in Bucharest, Athens, and Egypt formed the basis for her Balkan trilogy (1960–5) and her Levant trilogy (1977–80), the two together forming a single narrative, *Fortunes of War*.

Man Ray see RAY².

Mansart /'mɒnsɑː(r)/, François (1598–1666), French architect. His first major work was the rebuilding of part of the château of Blois, which incorporated the type of roof now named after him, the mansard: this has four sloping sides, each of which becomes steeper halfway down. Other buildings include a number of town houses in Paris, the château of Maisons (1642–6), and the church of Val-de-Grâce (1645).

Mansell /'mæns(ə)l/, Nigel (born 1954), English motor-racing driver. He won the Formula One world championship in 1992 and the Indy car championship in 1993, only the second driver to win both titles.

Mansfield /'mænsfiːld/, Katherine (pseudonym of Kathleen Mansfield Beauchamp) (1888–1923), New Zealand short-story writer. Her stories show the influence of Chekhov and range from extended impressionistic evocations of family life to short sketches. Collections include *In a German Pension* (1911) and *Bliss* (1920). She married the English writer and critic John Middleton Murry (1889–1957) in 1918 and spent much of the remainder of her short life travelling in Europe in search of a cure for the tuberculosis from which she eventually died.

Manson¹ /'mæns(ə)n/, Charles (born 1934), American cult leader. In 1967 he founded a commune based on free love and complete subordination to him. Two years later its members carried out a series of murders, including that of the American actress

Sharon Tate (1943–69), for which he and a number of his followers received the death sentence. They later escaped this owing to a Supreme Court ruling against capital punishment.

Manson² /'mæns(ə)n/, Sir Patrick (1844–1922), Scottish physician, pioneer of tropical medicine. Working for many years in China, he discovered the organism responsible for elephantiasis and established that it was spread by the bite of a mosquito. After returning to London he suggested a similar role for the mosquito in spreading malaria, and studied a number of tropical parasites and infections. He was the chief founder of the London School of Tropical Medicine.

Mantegna /mæn'tenjə/, Andrea (1431–1506), Italian painter and engraver. He is noted especially for his frescos, which include those painted for the bridal chamber of the ducal family in Mantua, with both the ceiling and walls painted in an illusionistic style which extends the interior space and gives the impression that the room is open to the sky. His work reveals his knowledge of the artefacts and architecture of classical antiquity, as can be seen in his nine paintings depicting the *Triumph of Caesar* (begun 1486).

Mantell /mæn'tel/, Gideon Algernon (1790–1852), English geologist. Mantell worked mainly as a surgeon in Sussex, though fossil-hunting was his major interest. He is best known as the first person to recognize dinosaur remains as reptilian, and in 1825 he published a description of the teeth of a 'giant fossil lizard' which he named *Iguanodon*. Mantell accumulated a large collection of fossils, which he eventually sold to the British Museum.

Manutius, Aldus, see ALDUS MANUTIUS.

Manzoni /mæn'zəʊnɪ/, Alessandro (1785–1873), Italian novelist, dramatist, and poet. He is remembered chiefly as the author of the historical novel *I Promessi sposi* (1825–42). The novel is a powerfully characterized historical reconstruction of 17th-century Lombardy during the period of Spanish administration; it had great patriotic appeal at a time when Italy was seeking independence from Austrian rule.

Mao Zedong /ˌmaʊ dziːˈdʊŋ/ (also **Mao Tse-tung** /tseɪˈtʊŋ/) (1893–1976), Chinese statesman, chairman of the Communist Party of the Chinese People's Republic 1949–76 and

head of state 1949–59. After studying Marxism as a student he was among the founders of the Chinese Communist Party in 1921, becoming its effective leader following the Long March (the withdrawal of the Communists from SE to NW China, 1934–5). He eventually defeated both the occupying Japanese and rival Kuomintang nationalist forces to form the People's Republic of China, becoming its first head of state (1949). Although he initially adopted the Soviet Communist model, following Khrushchev's denunciation of Stalin (1956) Mao began to introduce his own measures, central to which were the concepts of permanent revolution, the importance of the peasantry, and agricultural collectivization. A brief period of freedom of expression (the Hundred Flowers) ended with the introduction of the economically disastrous Great Leap Forward (1958–60). Mao resigned as head of state in 1959 but retained his position as chairman of the Communist Party, and as such remained China's most powerful politician. He was the instigator of the Cultural Revolution (1966–8), which was intended to effect a return to revolutionary Maoist beliefs; during this time he became the focus of a powerful personality cult which lasted until his death.

Maradona /ˌmærəˈdɒnə/, Diego (Armando) (born 1960), Argentinian footballer. He was captain of the victorious Argentinian team in the 1986 World Cup, but aroused controversy with his apparent handball when scoring a goal in Argentina's quarter-final match against England. In 1984 he joined the Italian club Napoli, and subsequently contributed to that team's victories in the Italian championship (1987) and the UEFA Cup (1989). However, clashes with authority culminated in Maradona being suspended from football for fifteen months in 1991 for cocaine use, and then sent home from the 1994 World Cup after failing a drugs test.

Marat /ˈmærɑː/, Jean Paul (1743–93), French revolutionary and journalist. The founder of a radical newspaper, he became prominent during the French Revolution as a virulent critic of the moderate Girondists and was instrumental (with Danton and Robespierre) in their fall from power in 1793. Suffering from a skin disease, he spent much of his time in later life in his bath, where he was murdered by the Girondist Charlotte Corday. This was used as a pretext by Robespierre and the Jacobins to purge their Girondist rivals.

Marceau /mɑːˈsəʊ/, Marcel (born 1923), French mime artist. He is known for the mimes in which he appears as the white-faced Bip, a character he developed from the traditional Pierrot character. He directed his own company between 1948 and 1964 and made many stage and television appearances. He also created a number of mime-dramas, including *Don Juan* (1964).

Marciano /ˌmɑːsɪˈɑːnəʊ/, Rocky (born Rocco Francis Marchegiano) (1923–69), American boxer. In 1952 he became world heavyweight champion and successfully defended his title six times until he retired, undefeated, in 1956.

Marconi /mɑːˈkəʊnɪ/, Guglielmo (1874–1937), Italian electrical engineer, the father of radio. He appreciated the potential of earlier work on electric waves and their detection, and made a radio transmission over a distance of a mile at Bologna in 1895. He later transmitted a signal across the Atlantic from Cornwall to Newfoundland, and in 1912 produced a continuously oscillating wave, essential for the transmission of sound. Marconi went on to develop short-wave transmission over long distances, especially valuable to shipping, and set up successful companies to exploit his work. In 1909 he was awarded the Nobel Prize for physics.

Marco Polo /ˌmɑːkəʊ ˈpəʊləʊ/ (c.1254–c.1324), Italian traveller. Between 1271 and 1275 he accompanied his father and uncle on a journey east from Acre into central Asia, eventually reaching China and the court of Kublai Khan. After service with the emperor and travelling widely in the empire for a decade and a half, Polo returned home (1292–5) via Sumatra, India, and Persia. His book recounting his travels gave considerable impetus to the European quest for the riches of the East.

Marcus Aurelius see AURELIUS.

Marcuse /mɑːˈkuːzə/, Herbert (1898–1979), German-born American philosopher. He was an associate at the Frankfurt Institute of Social Research and a leading figure in the Frankfurt School (the school of philosophy involved in reappraising Marx) until 1933, when he left Germany and eventually settled in the US. His works include *Eros and Civilization* (1955), *Soviet Marxism*

(1958), a rejection of bureaucratic Communism which argues that revolutionary change can come only from alienated élites such as students, and *One-Dimensional Man* (1964).

Mare, Walter de la, see DE LA MARE.

Margaret, Princess /'mɑːgrɪt/, Margaret Rose (born 1930), only sister of Elizabeth II. In 1960 she married Antony Armstrong-Jones (born 1930), who was later created Earl of Snowdon; the marriage was dissolved in 1978. Their two children are David, Viscount Linley (born 1961) and Lady Sarah Armstrong-Jones (born 1964).

Margaret, St /'mɑːgrɪt/ (c.1046–93), Scottish queen, wife of Malcolm III. She exerted a strong influence over royal policy during her husband's reign, and was instrumental in the reform of the Scottish Church. Feast day, 16 November.

Maria de' Medici /məˈriːə/ see MARIE DE MÉDICIS.

Maria Theresa /məˌriːə təˈreɪzə/ (1717–80), Archduchess of Austria, queen of Hungary and Bohemia 1740–80. The daughter of the Emperor Charles VI, Maria Theresa married the future Emperor Francis I in 1736 and succeeded to the Habsburg dominions in 1740 by virtue of the Pragmatic Sanction (by which her father made provision for her to succeed him). Her accession triggered the War of the Austrian Succession (1740–8), during which Silesia was lost to Prussia. She attempted but failed to regain Silesia from the Prussians in the Seven Years War (1756–63). After the death of Francis I in 1765 she ruled in conjunction with her son, the Emperor Joseph II.

Marie Antoinette /ˌmærɪ ˌæntwəˈnet, French mari ɑ̃twanɛt/ (1755–93), French queen, wife of Louis XVI. A daughter of Maria Theresa and the Emperor Francis I, she married the future Louis XVI of France in 1770, becoming queen four years later. She became a focus for opposition to reform and won widespread unpopularity through her extravagant lifestyle. Like her husband she was imprisoned during the French Revolution and eventually executed.

Marie de Médicis /mɑːˌriː də ˌmeɪdiːˈsiːs/ (Italian name Maria de' Medici) (1573–1642), queen of France. The second wife of Henry IV of France, she ruled as regent during the minority of her son Louis XIII (1610–17). She continued to exert a significant influence after her son came to power, and plotted against Cardinal Richelieu, her former protégé, but was eventually exiled in 1631.

Marinetti /ˌmærɪˈneti/, Filippo Tommaso (1876–1944), Italian poet and dramatist. He launched the futurist movement with a manifesto published in the magazine *Le Figaro* (1909), which exalted technology, glorified war, and demanded revolution and innovation in the arts. In his poems he abandoned syntax and grammar; in the theatre he renounced verisimilitude and traditional methods of plot development and characterization and introduced the simultaneous staging of unrelated actions.

Marius /'mæriəs/, Gaius (c.157–86 BC), Roman general and politician. Consul for the first time in 107, he established his dominance by victories over Jugurtha and invading Germanic tribes. He was subsequently involved in a struggle for power with Sulla and was expelled from Italy, only to return and take Rome by force in 87. He was again elected consul in 86 but died soon afterwards.

Mark, St /mɑːk/ an Apostle, companion of St Peter and St Paul, traditional author of the second Gospel. Feast day, 25 April.

Mark Antony see ANTONY.

Markova /mɑːˈkəʊvə, 'mɑːkəvə/, Dame Alicia (born Lilian Alicia Marks) (born 1910), English ballet-dancer. In 1931 she joined the Vic-Wells Ballet, where she was the first English dancer to take the lead in *Giselle* and *Swan Lake*; she also created roles in new ballets such as Sir Frederick Ashton's *Façade* (1931). She founded the Markova-Dolin Ballet with Anton Dolin in 1935; they later both joined the emergent London Festival Ballet (1950), with which Markova was prima ballerina until 1952.

Marks /mɑːks/, Simon, 1st Baron Marks of Broughton (1888–1964), English businessman. In 1907 he inherited the Marks and Spencer Penny Bazaars established by his father and Thomas Spencer (1851–1905). These became the nucleus of the successful company created in 1926 as Marks & Spencer, a chain of retail stores selling clothes, food, and household goods under the brand name 'St Michael'.

Marlborough /'mɔːlbərə/, 1st Duke of (title of John Churchill) (1650–1722), British general. He was appointed commander of British and Dutch troops in the War of the

Spanish Succession and won a series of victories over the French armies of Louis XIV, most notably Blenheim (1704), Ramillies (1706), Oudenarde (1708), and Malplaquet (1709), which effectively ended Louis's attempts to dominate Europe. The building of Blenheim Palace, Marlborough's seat at Woodstock in Oxfordshire, was funded by Queen Anne as a token of the nation's gratitude for his victory.

Marley /'mɑːlɪ/, Robert Nesta ('Bob') (1945–81), Jamaican reggae singer, guitarist, and songwriter. In 1965 he formed the trio the Wailers, with whom he went on to become the first internationally acclaimed reggae musician. Bob Marley was a devout Rastafarian and supporter of black power whose lyrics frequently reflect his religious and political beliefs; by the 1970s he had gained the status of a cult hero. Among his albums are *Burnin'* (1973) and *Exodus* (1977).

Marlowe /'mɑːləʊ/, Christopher (1564–93), English dramatist and poet. As a dramatist he brought a new strength and vitality to blank verse; major works include *Tamburlaine the Great* (1587–8), *Doctor Faustus* (c.1590), *Edward II* (1592), and *The Jew of Malta* (1592). His poems include 'Come live with me and be my love' (published in *The Passionate Pilgrim*, 1599) and the unfinished *Hero and Leander* (1598; completed by George Chapman). His work had a significant influence on Shakespeare's early historical plays. Marlowe was killed during a brawl in a tavern.

Marquette /mɑːˈket/, Jacques (1637–75), French Jesuit missionary and explorer. He travelled to North America in 1666 and played a prominent part in the attempt to Christianize the American Indians there, especially during his mission among the Ottawa tribe. In 1673 he was a member of an expedition which explored the Wisconsin and Mississippi rivers as far as the mouth of the Arkansas.

Márquez, Gabriel García, see GARCÍA MÁRQUEZ.

Marquis de Sade see SADE.

Marryat /'mærɪət/, Frederick (known as Captain Marryat) (1792–1848), English novelist. In 1830 he resigned his commission in the navy to concentrate on writing. He produced a number of novels dealing with life at sea, such as *Peter Simple* (1833) and *Mr Midshipman Easy* (1836), while his books for children include the historical story *The Children of the New Forest* (1847).

Marsh /mɑːʃ/, Dame Ngaio (Edith) (1899–1982), New Zealand writer of detective fiction. Her works include *Vintage Murder* (1937), *Surfeit of Lampreys* (1941), and *Final Curtain* (1947); many of the novels feature Chief Detective Inspector Roderick Alleyn.

Marshall /'mɑːʃ(ə)l/, George C(atlett) (1880–1959), American general and statesman. As US Secretary of State (1947–9) he initiated the programme of economic aid to European countries known as the Marshall Plan. He was awarded the Nobel Peace Prize in 1953.

Martel, Charles, see CHARLES MARTEL.

Martial /'mɑːʃ(ə)l/ (Latin name Marcus Valerius Martialis) (AD c.40–c.104), Roman epigrammatist, born in Spain. His fifteen books of epigrams, in a variety of metres, reflect all facets of Roman life; they are witty, mostly satirical, and often coarse.

Martin[1] /'mɑːtɪn/, Dean (born Dino Paul Crocetti) (1917–95), American singer and actor. He became known originally for his comedy and singing act with Jerry Lewis (born 1925). In 1948 they first appeared on television, going on to make a series of comedy films that began with *My Friend Irma* (1949). They parted in 1956 and Martin joined with Frank Sinatra and Sammy Davis Jr. (1925–90) — forming the 'Rat Pack' — in a number of films including *Bells are Ringing* (1960). Martin also had his own television show from 1965 until the 1970s.

Martin[2] /'mɑːtɪn/, Sir George (Leonard) (born 1926), English record producer. He joined EMI Records in 1950 and later managed the Parlophone label, signing the Beatles in 1962. He became very much part of their creative activities, recording the acclaimed and revolutionary albums *Revolver* (1966) and *Sergeant Pepper's Lonely Hearts Club Band* (1967) with them. After their split he continued as a major figure in the British pop music scene.

Martin[3] /'mɑːtɪn/, Steve (born 1945), American actor and comedian. He successfully moved from zany stand-up comedy to farcical film comedies with *The Jerk* (1979), which he co-wrote. He went on to star in films such as *Parenthood* (1989) and *Sgt Bilko* (1996) and wrote, produced, and starred in *Roxanne* (1987) and *LA Story* (1991).

Martin, St /'mɑːtɪn/ (died 397), French bishop, a patron saint of France. While serving in the Roman army he gave half his cloak to a beggar and received a vision of Christ, after which he was baptized. He joined St Hilary at Poitiers and founded the first monastery in Gaul. On becoming bishop of Tours (371) he pioneered the evangelization of the rural areas. Feast day, 11 November.

Martineau /'mɑːtɪˌnəʊ/, Harriet (1802–76), English writer. She overcame deafness and heart disease to become one of the foremost English intellectuals of her day. She wrote mainly on social, economic, and historical subjects, achieving recognition with works such as her twenty-five-volume series *Illustrations of Political Economy* (1832–4). Her other works include her acclaimed two-volume translation of Auguste Comte's *Philosophie positive* (1853). Her candid *Autobiography* was published posthumously in 1877.

Martini /mɑː'tiːnɪ/, Simone (c.1284–1344), Italian painter. His work is characterized by strong outlines and the use of rich colour. He worked in Siena and Assisi in Italy, and for the papal court at Avignon in France (c.1339–44). Notable works include *The Annunciation* (1333).

Marvell /'mɑːv(ə)l, mɑː'vel/, Andrew (1621–78), English poet. He served as an MP (1659–78) and was best known during his lifetime for his verse satires and pamphlets attacking Charles II and his ministers, particularly for corruption at court and in Parliament. Most of his poetry was published posthumously (1681) and did not achieve recognition until the early 20th century, when it was reappraised along with the work of other metaphysical poets such as John Donne. His best-known poems include 'To His Coy Mistress', 'Bermudas', and 'An Horatian Ode upon Cromwell's Return from Ireland'.

Marx /mɑːks/, Karl (Heinrich) (1818–83), German political philosopher and economist, resident in England from 1849. The founder of modern communism with Engels, he collaborated with him in the writing of the *Communist Manifesto* (1848). Thereafter Marx spent much of his time enlarging the theory of this pamphlet into a series of books, the most important being the three-volume *Das Kapital*. The first volume of this appeared in 1867 and the remainder was completed by Engels and published after Marx's death (1885; 1894). At the centre of Marxist theory is an explanation of past and present societies and social change in terms of economic factors, in which labour and the means of production provide the economic base which influences or determines the political and ideological superstructure. The history of society shows progressive stages (ancient, feudal, capitalist) in the control and ownership of the means of production; in a projected future stage the imbalances inherent in these systems lead to change, and eventually to a class struggle in which the working classes overturn the capitalist class and capitalism. How an alternative society is then established was not detailed by Marx; it was assumed that a necessary interim period called the 'dictatorship of the proletariat' would be followed by the establishment of communism and the eventual 'withering away' of the state.

Marx Brothers /mɑːks/ a family of American comedians, consisting of the brothers 'Chico' (Leonard, 1886–1961), 'Harpo' (Adolph Arthur, 1888–1964), 'Groucho' (Julius Henry, 1890–1977), and 'Zeppo' (Herbert, 1901–79). Their films, which are characterized by their anarchic humour, include *Horse Feathers* (1932), *Duck Soup* (1933), and *A Night at the Opera* (1935).

Mary[1] /'meərɪ/ (known as the (Blessed) Virgin Mary, or St Mary, or Our Lady), mother of Jesus. According to the Gospels she was a virgin, betrothed to Joseph at the time of the Annunciation, who conceived Jesus by the power of the Holy Spirit. She has been venerated by Catholic and Orthodox Churches from the earliest Christian times. The doctrines of her Immaculate Conception and Assumption are taught by some Churches. Feast days, 1 January (RC Ch.), 25 March (Annunciation), 15 August (Assumption), 8 September (Immaculate Conception).

Mary[2] /'meərɪ/ the name of two queens of England:
Mary I (known as Mary Tudor) (1516–58), daughter of Henry VIII, reigned 1553–8. Having regained the throne after the brief attempt to install Lady Jane Grey in her place, Mary attempted to reverse the country's turn towards Protestantism, which had begun to gain momentum during the reign of her brother, Edward VI. She married Philip II of Spain, and after putting down several revolts began the series of

religious persecutions which earned her the name of 'Bloody Mary'. She died childless and the throne passed to her Protestant sister, Elizabeth I.

Mary II (1662–94), daughter of James II, reigned 1689–94. Although her father was converted to Catholicism, Mary remained a Protestant, and was invited to replace him on the throne after his deposition in 1689. She insisted that her husband, William of Orange (William III; see WILLIAM), be crowned along with her and afterwards left most of the business of the kingdom to him, although she frequently had to act as sole head of state because of her husband's absence on campaigns abroad.

Mary, Queen of Scots (known as Mary Stuart) (1542–87), daughter of James V, queen of Scotland 1542–67. Mary was sent to France as an infant and was married briefly to Francis II, but after his death returned to Scotland in 1561 to resume personal rule. A devout Catholic, she was unable to control her Protestant lords; her position was made more difficult by her marriages to Lord Darnley and the Earl of Bothwell, and after the defeat of her supporters she fled to England in 1567. There she was imprisoned and became the focus of several Catholic plots against Elizabeth I; she was eventually beheaded.

Mary, St see MARY¹.

Mary Magdalene, St /ˈmægdə,liːn/ (in the New Testament) a woman of Magdala in Galilee. She was a follower of Jesus, who cured her of evil spirits (Luke 8:2); she is also traditionally identified with the 'sinner' of Luke 7:37. Feast day, 22 July.

Mary Stuart see MARY, QUEEN OF SCOTS.

Mary Tudor, Mary I of England (see MARY²).

Masaccio /mæˈsætʃɪ,əʊ/ (born Tommaso Giovanni di Simone Guidi) (1401–28), Italian painter. He was based chiefly in Florence and is remembered particularly for his frescos in the Brancacci Chapel (1424–7). He was the first artist to develop the laws of perspective (which he learned from Brunelleschi) and apply them to painting. His work is also notable for the use of light to define the construction of the body and its draperies and to unify a whole composition.

Masaryk /ˈmæsərɪk/, Tomáš (Garrigue) (1850–1937), Czechoslovak statesman, President 1918–35. A founder of modern Czechoslovakia, during the First World War he was in London, where he founded the Czechoslovakian National Council with Edvard Beneš and promoted the cause of his country's independence. When this was achieved in 1918 he became Czechoslovakia's first President. In 1935 he retired in favour of Beneš.

Mascagni /mæˈskænjɪ/, Pietro (1863–1945), Italian composer and conductor. His compositions include operas and choral works; he is especially remembered for the opera *Cavalleria Rusticana* (1890).

Masefield /ˈmeɪsfiːld/, John (Edward) (1878–1967), English poet and novelist. His fascination with the sea is reflected in his first published book of poetry, *Salt-Water Ballads* (which contained 'I must go down to the sea again', 1902). His other works include several narrative poems and novels, and the children's story *The Midnight Folk* (1927). He was appointed Poet Laureate in 1930.

Mason¹ /ˈmeɪs(ə)n/, A(lfred) E(dward) W(oodley) (1865–1948), English novelist. His work includes adventure stories (*The Four Feathers*, 1902), historical novels (*Musk and Amber*, 1942), detective novels featuring Inspector Hanaud, and several plays.

Mason² /ˈmeɪs(ə)n/, James (Neville) (1909–84), English actor. He became an established stage actor after making his début in 1931. He made his first film appearance in 1935 and went on to act in more than one hundred films. Notable examples include *Odd Man Out* (1947) and *Lolita* (1962); he received Oscar nominations for his performances in *A Star is Born* (1954), *Georgy Girl* (1966), and *The Verdict* (1982).

Massine /mæˈsiːn/, Léonide Fëdorovich (born Leonid Fëdorovich Myassin) (1895–1979), Russian-born choreographer and ballet-dancer. In 1914 he joined Diaghilev's Ballets Russes as a dancer; he took up choreography the following year and went on to create ballets such as *Le Tricorne* (1919). He was the originator of the symphonic ballet, including *Les Présages* (1933), which uses Tchaikovsky's Fifth Symphony. He also danced in and choreographed the film *The Red Shoes* (1948). He settled in Europe and became a French citizen in 1944.

Massinger /ˈmæsɪndʒə(r)/, Philip (1583–1640), English dramatist. He wrote many of his works in collaboration with other

dramatists, most notably John Fletcher. His plays include tragedies (for example *The Duke of Milan*, 1621–2) and the social comedies *A New Way to Pay Old Debts* (1625–6) and *The City Madam* (1632).

Masson /'mæsɒn/, André (1896–1987), French painter and graphic artist. He joined the surrealists in the mid-1920s; his early works pioneered the use of 'automatic' drawing, a form of fluid, spontaneous composition intended to express images emerging from the unconscious. His later works are characterized by themes of psychic pain, violence, and eroticism, with near-abstract biomorphic forms; they include the painting *Iroquois Landscape* (1942).

Mata Hari /ˌmɑːtə 'hɑːrɪ/ (born Margaretha Geertruida Zelle) (1876–1917), Dutch dancer and secret agent. She became a professional dancer in Paris in 1905 and probably worked for both French and German intelligence services before being executed by the French in 1917. Her name derives from Malay *mata* eye and *hari* day.

Matilda /mə'tɪldə/ (known as 'the Empress Maud') (1102–67), English princess, daughter of Henry I. She was Henry's only legitimate child and was named his heir in 1127. In 1135 her father died and Matilda was forced to flee when his nephew Stephen seized the throne. Her claim was supported by King David I of Scotland, and she and her half-brother Robert, Earl of Gloucester (died 1147) invaded England in 1139. She waged an unsuccessful civil war against Stephen and eventually left England in 1148. Her son became Henry II.

Matisse /mæ'tiːs/, Henri (Émile Benoît) (1869–1954), French painter and sculptor. He was influenced by the impressionists, Gauguin, and oriental art. His use of non-naturalistic colour in works such as *Open Window Collioure* (1905) led him to be regarded as a leader of the fauvists. Large figure compositions, such as *The Dance* (1909), heralded a new style based on simple reductive line, giving a rhythmic decorative pattern on a flat ground of rich colour. Later works include abstracts made of cut-out coloured paper, such as *The Snail* (1953). His sculpture displays a similar trend towards formal simplification and abstraction.

Matthew, St /'mæθjuː/ an Apostle, a tax-gatherer from Capernaum in Galilee, trad-

itional author of the first Gospel. Feast day, 21 September.

Matthew Paris /ˌmæθjuː 'pærɪs/ (c.1199–1259), English chronicler and Benedictine monk. His *Chronica Majora*, a history of the world from the Creation to the mid-13th century, is a valuable source for contemporary events.

Matthews /'mæθjuːz/, Sir Stanley (born 1915), English footballer. He played on the right wing for Stoke City and Blackpool, and was famous for his dribbling skill. His career in professional football lasted until he was 50, during which time he played for England fifty-four times.

Matthias, St /mə'θaɪəs/ an Apostle, chosen by lot after the Ascension to take the place left by Judas. Feast day (in the Western Church) 14 May; (in the Eastern Church) 9 August.

Maugham /mɔːm/, (William) Somerset (1874–1965), British novelist, short-story writer, and dramatist. He was born in France, where he spent his childhood, returning to live on the Riviera in 1926. His life and wide travels often provide the background to his writing; his work for British intelligence during the First World War is reflected in the *Ashenden* short stories (1928), while a visit to Tahiti gave the setting for the novel *The Moon and Sixpence* (1919). Other works include the novels *Of Human Bondage* (1915) and *Cakes and Ale* (1930), and the play *East of Suez* (1922).

Maupassant /'məʊpæˌsɒn/, (Henri René Albert) Guy de (1850–93), French novelist and short-story writer. He embarked on a literary career after encouragement from Flaubert, joining Zola's circle of naturalist writers. He contributed the story 'Boule de Suif' to their collection *Les Soirées de Médan* (1880) and became an immediate celebrity. He wrote about 300 short stories and six novels, portraying a broad spectrum of society and embracing themes of war, mystery, hallucination, and horror; these are written in a simple direct narrative style. His best-known novels include *Une Vie* (1883) and *Bel-Ami* (1885).

Mauriac /'mɒrɪˌæk/, François (1885–1970), French novelist, dramatist, and critic. His works include the novels *Thérèse Desqueyroux* (1927) and *Le Noeud de vipères* (1932), and the play *Asmodée* (1938). His stories, usually set in the country round Bordeaux, show the conflicts suffered by prosperous

bourgeois people pulled in different directions by convention, religion, and human passions. He was awarded the Nobel Prize for literature in 1952.

Maury /'mɔːrɪ/, Matthew Fontaine (1806–73), American oceanographer. He conducted the first systematic survey of oceanic winds and currents, publishing charts which were of great value to merchant shipping. Maury also produced the first bathymetric charts, including a transatlantic profile, and pilot charts which enabled voyages to be considerably shortened. His work on physical oceanography was flawed in the eyes of many scientists by the religious tone of his writing.

Mawlana /mɔː'lɑːnə/ see JALAL AD-DIN AR-RUMI.

Maximilian /ˌmæksɪ'mɪlɪən/ (full name Ferdinand Maximilian Joseph) (1832–67), emperor of Mexico 1864–7. Brother of the Austro-Hungarian emperor Franz Josef and Archduke of Austria, Maximilian was established as emperor of Mexico under French auspices in 1864. In 1867, however, Napoleon III was forced to withdraw his support as a result of American pressure, and Maximilian was confronted by a popular uprising led by Benito Juárez. His forces proved unable to resist the rebels and he was captured and executed.

Maxwell[1] /'mækswel/, James Clerk (1831–79), Scottish physicist. Maxwell contributed to thermodynamics, the kinetic theory of gases (showing the importance of the statistical approach), and colour vision (demonstrating one of the earliest colour photographs in 1861). His greatest achievement was to extend the ideas of Faraday and Kelvin into his field equations of electromagnetism, thus unifying the phenomena of electricity and magnetism, identifying the electromagnetic nature of light, and postulating the existence of other electromagnetic radiation.

Maxwell[2] /'mækswel/, (Ian) Robert (born Jan Ludvik Hoch) (1923–91), Czech-born British publisher and media entrepreneur. In 1940 he came to Britain, founding Pergamon Press, the basis of his publishing empire, in 1951. His business interests expanded during the 1980s and he became the proprietor of Mirror Group Newspapers in 1984; he also moved into cable television and became chairman of two football clubs. He died in obscure circumstances while yachting off Tenerife;

it subsequently emerged that he had misappropriated company pension funds.

Mayakovsky /ˌmaɪə'kɒfskɪ/, Vladimir (Vladimirovich) (1893–1930), Soviet poet and dramatist, born in Georgia. From 1910 he aligned himself with the Russian futurists, signing the futurist manifesto 'A Slap in the Face for Public Taste' in 1912. His early poems are declamatory in tone and employ an aggressive avant-garde style. After 1917, Mayakovsky saw a clear political role for futurism in the Bolshevik revolution and the new society, altering his style to have a comic mass appeal. He fell from official favour by the end of the 1920s, and committed suicide in 1930; five years later his reputation was restored by Stalin.

Mayer /'meɪə(r)/, Louis B(urt) (born Eliezer Mayer) (1885–1957), Russian-born American film executive. In 1907 he acquired a chain of cinemas, moving into production with Metro Films in 1915. He joined with Samuel Goldwyn to form Metro-Goldwyn-Mayer (MGM) in 1924; he was head of MGM until 1951 and the company was responsible for many successful films. He also helped establish the Academy of Motion Picture Arts and Sciences (1927), and received an honorary award from the Academy in 1950.

Mayr /'maɪə(r), 'meɪə(r)/, Ernst Walter (born 1904), German-born American zoologist. Although responsible for several surveys and books on the birds of Pacific countries, Mayr is best known for his work in the field of evolution, speciation, and population genetics. His classic *Animal Species and Evolution* (1963) independently presented a neo-Darwinian approach to evolution which is still mostly accepted by the majority of zoologists.

Mazarin /'mæzəˌrɪn/, Jules (Italian name Giulio Mazzarino) (1602–61), Italian-born French statesman. In 1634 he was sent to Paris as the Italian papal legate; he became a naturalized Frenchman and entered the service of Louis XIII in 1639. He was made a cardinal in 1641 and the following year succeeded Cardinal Richelieu as chief minister of France, which he governed during the minority of Louis XIV. His administration aroused such opposition as to provoke the civil wars of the Fronde (1648–53).

Mazzini /mæt'siːnɪ/, Giuseppe (1805–72), Italian nationalist leader. While in exile in Marseilles he founded the patriotic movement Young Italy (1831) and thereafter

worked for the independence and unification of Italy, becoming one of the Risorgimento's most committed leaders and planning attempted insurrections in a number of Italian cities during the 1850s. He continued to campaign for a republican Italy following the country's unification as a monarchy in 1861.

Mead /miːd/, Margaret (1901–78), American anthropologist and social psychologist. She worked in Samoa and the New Guinea area and wrote a number of specialized studies of primitive cultures, but was also concerned to relate her findings to current American life and its problems; her writings made anthropology accessible to a wide readership and demonstrated its relevance to Western society. Her books include *Male and Female* (1949), an examination of the extent to which male and female roles are shaped by social factors rather than heredity.

Medawar /ˈmedəwə(r)/, Sir Peter (Brian) (1915–87), English immunologist and author. He studied the biology of tissue transplantation, and his early work showed that the rejection of grafts was the result of an immune mechanism. His subsequent discovery of the acquired tolerance of grafts encouraged the early attempts at human organ transplantation. In later life he wrote a number of popular books on the philosophy of science, notably *The Limits of Science* (1985). Medawar shared a Nobel Prize in 1960.

Médicis, Marie de, see MARIE DE MÉDICIS.

Meiji Tenno /ˌmeɪdʒiː ˈtenəʊ/ (born Mutsuhito) (1852–1912), emperor of Japan 1868–1912. He took the name Meiji Tenno when he became emperor. His accession saw the restoration of imperial power after centuries of control by the shoguns. During his reign he encouraged Japan's rapid process of modernization and political reform and laid the foundations for the country's emergence as a major world power; the feudal system was abolished, Cabinet government introduced, and a new army and navy were established.

Meir /meɪˈɪə(r)/, Golda (born Goldie Mabovich) (1898–1978), Israeli stateswoman, Prime Minister 1969–74. Born in Ukraine, she emigrated to the US in 1907 and in 1921 moved to Palestine, where she became active in the Labour movement. Following Israel's independence she served in ministerial posts (1949–66); having left government in 1966 to build up the Labour Party from disparate socialist factions, she was elected Prime Minister in 1969, retaining her position through coalition rule until her retirement in 1974.

Meitner /ˈmaɪtnə(r)/, Lise (1878–1968), Austrian-born Swedish physicist. She was the second woman to obtain a doctorate from Vienna University, and became interested in radiochemistry. She worked in Germany with Otto Hahn, discovering the element protactinium with him in 1917, but fled the Nazis in 1938 to continue her research in Sweden. Meitner formulated the concept of nuclear fission with her nephew Otto Frisch, but, unlike him, refused to work on nuclear weapons.

Melanchthon /məˈlæŋkθɒn/, Philipp (born Philipp Schwarzerd) (1497–1560), German Protestant reformer. In 1521 he succeeded Luther as leader of the Reformation movement in Germany. Professor of Greek at Wittenberg, he helped to systematize Martin Luther's teachings in the *Loci Communes* (1521) and drew up the Augsburg Confession (1530).

Melba /ˈmelbə/, Dame Nellie (born Helen Porter Mitchell) (1861–1931), Australian operatic soprano. She was born near Melbourne, from which city she took her professional name. Melba gained worldwide fame with her coloratura singing.

Melbourne /ˈmelbən, -bɔːn/, William Lamb, 2nd Viscount (1779–1848), British Whig statesman, Prime Minister 1834 and 1835–41. He was appointed Home Secretary under Lord Grey in 1830, before becoming Premier in 1834. Out of office briefly that year, he subsequently became chief political adviser to Queen Victoria after her accession in 1837. His term was marked by Chartist and anti-Corn Laws agitation.

Meleager /ˌmelɪˈeɪɡə(r)/ (fl. 1st century BC), Greek poet. He is best known as the compiler of *Stephanos*, one of the first large anthologies of epigrams. Meleager was also the author of many epigrams of his own and of short poems on love and death.

Mellon /ˈmelən/, Andrew W(illiam) (1855–1937), American financier and philanthropist. He donated his considerable art collection, together with funds, to establish the National Gallery of Art in Washington, DC in 1941.

Melville /ˈmelvɪl/, Herman (1819–91), American novelist and short-story writer.

After first going to sea in 1839, Melville made a voyage on a whaler to the South Seas in 1841; this experience formed the basis of several novels, including *Moby Dick* (1851). He is also remembered for his novella *Billy Budd* (first published in 1924), a symbolic tale of a mutiny, which inspired Benjamin Britten's opera of the same name (1951).

Menander /məˈnændə(r)/ (*c.*342–292 BC), Greek dramatist. He is noted as the originator of New Comedy, a genre in which young lovers typically undergo endless vicissitudes in the company of various stock characters; his plays, set in contemporary Greece, deal with domestic situations and capture colloquial speech patterns. The *Dyskolos* is his sole complete extant play; others were adapted by the Roman dramatists Terence and Plautus.

Mencius /ˈmenʃɪəs/ (Latinized name of Meng-tzu or Mengzi, 'Meng the Master') (*c.*371–*c.*289 BC), Chinese philosopher. He is noted for developing Confucianism; two of his central doctrines were that rulers should provide for the welfare of the people and that human nature is intrinsically good. His teachings, contained in one of the Four Books of Confucianism, formed the basis of primary and secondary education in imperial China from the 14th century.

Mencken /ˈmeŋkən/, H(enry) L(ouis) (1880–1956), American journalist and literary critic. From 1908 he boldly attacked the political and literary Establishment, championing such diverse writers as George Bernard Shaw, Nietzsche, and Mark Twain. He strongly opposed the dominance of European culture in America, and in his book *The American Language* (1919) defended the vigour and versatility of colloquial American usage.

Mendel /ˈmend(ə)l/, Gregor Johann (1822–84), Moravian monk, the father of genetics. From his experiments with peas, he demonstrated that parent plants showing different characters produced hybrids exhibiting the dominant parental character, and that the hybrids themselves produced offspring in which the parental characters re-emerged unchanged and in precise ratios. After the rediscovery of Mendel's work in 1900, Mendelism was often thought, wrongly, to be the antithesis of the Darwinian theory of natural selection; in fact, Mendel had demonstrated the primary source of variability in plants and animals, on which natural selection could then operate.

Mendeleev /ˌmendəˈleɪef/, Dmitri (Ivanovich) (1834–1907), Russian chemist. He developed the periodic table, in which the chemical elements are classified according to their atomic weights in groups with similar properties. This allowed him to systematize much chemical knowledge, pinpoint elements with incorrectly assigned atomic weights, and successfully predict the discovery of several new elements. His study of gases and liquids led him to the concept of critical temperature, independently of Thomas Andrews.

Mendelssohn /ˈmend(ə)ls(ə)n/, Felix (full name Jakob Ludwig Felix Mendelssohn-Bartholdy) (1809–47), German composer and pianist. As a child prodigy, Mendelssohn first performed in public at the age of 9, proceeding to compose a String Octet at 16 and the overture to *A Midsummer Night's Dream* at 17. His romantic music is known for its elegance and lightness, as well as its melodic inventiveness. Other works include the overture *Fingal's Cave* (also called *The Hebrides*; 1830–2), his Violin Concerto (1844), and the oratorio *Elijah* (1846).

Mendoza /menˈdəʊzə/, Antonio de (*c.*1490–1552), Spanish colonial administrator. He served as the first viceroy of New Spain (which centred on present-day Mexico City) from 1535 to 1550, and did much to improve relations between Spaniards and American Indians, fostering economic development (especially in mining) and educational opportunities for both groups. From 1551 he was viceroy of Peru.

Menes /ˈmiːniːz/, Egyptian pharaoh, reigned *c.*3100 BC. He founded the first dynasty that ruled ancient Egypt and is traditionally held to have united Upper and Lower Egypt with Memphis as its capital.

Meng-tzu /meŋˈtsuː/ see MENCIUS.

Mengzi /meŋˈziː/ see MENCIUS.

Menuhin /ˈmenjuɪn/, Sir Yehudi (born 1916), American-born British violinist. His career began as a child prodigy in 1924, when he performed the Mendelssohn Violin Concerto. Menuhin received critical acclaim for his interpretations of Bach, Beethoven, and Mozart, as well as for his 1932 performance of Elgar's violin concerto, conducted by the composer. He also

became a noted performer of contemporary music, including Bartók's solo violin sonata (1942). Having settled in England, he founded a school of music, named after him, in Surrey in 1962.

Menzies /'menzɪz/, Sir Robert Gordon (1894–1978), Australian Liberal statesman, Prime Minister 1939–41 and 1949–66. Australia's longest-serving Prime Minister, he implemented policies resulting in fast industrial growth in the 1950s and gave impetus to the development of Australian universities. Menzies was noted for his anti-Communism, making an abortive attempt to abolish the Australian Communist Party in 1951 and actively supporting the US in the Vietnam War.

Mercator /mɜː'keɪtə(r)/, Gerardus (Latinized name of Gerhard Kremer) (1512–94), Flemish geographer and cartographer, resident in Germany from 1552. He is best known for inventing the system of map projection that is named after him. His world map of 1569 showed a navigable North-west Passage between Asia and America, and a large southern continent. Mercator is also credited with introducing the term *atlas* to refer to a book of maps, following the publication of his *Atlas* of part of Europe (1585).

Merchant /'mɜːtʃənt/, Ismail (born 1936), Indian film producer. In 1961 he became a partner with James Ivory in Merchant Ivory Productions and is noted for a number of films made in collaboration with Ivory, including *Shakespeare Wallah* (1965), *The Europeans* (1979), *The Bostonians* (1984), and *Howard's End* (1992).

Merckx /mɜːks/, Eddy (born 1945), Belgian racing cyclist. During his professional career he won the Tour de France five times (1969–72 and 1974). He also gained five victories in the Tour of Italy between 1968 and 1974.

Mercouri /mɜː'kʊərɪ/, Melina (born Anna Amalia Mercouri) (1925–94), Greek actress and politician. She came to international prominence with her roles in films such as *Never on Sunday* (1960) and *Phaedra* (1962). She was exiled and deprived of her nationality owing to her active opposition to the military junta which took power in Greece in 1967, but was elected to Parliament in the socialist government of 1978, becoming Minister of Culture in 1985.

Mercury /'mɜːkjʊrɪ/, Freddy (born Frederick Bulsara) (1946–91), British rock singer, born in Zanzibar. He was the camp, outrageous vocalist of the band Queen, which formed in 1971. Queen initially played heavy rock but soon added extravagant, almost operatic elements to their sound, as exemplified by the hugely successful 'Bohemian Rhapsody' (1975). Their appearance at the international event Live Aid (1985) brought them still further acclaim. Mercury died of Aids in November 1991, and the group disbanded.

Meredith /'merə,dɪθ/, George (1828–1909), English novelist and poet. His semi-autobiographical verse collection *Modern Love* (1862) describes the disillusionment of married love. Meredith's reputation rests chiefly on his novels, particularly *The Egoist* (1879). He is noted for his control of narrative, sharp psychological characterization, and deliberately intricate style.

Mesmer /'mezmə(r)/, Franz Anton (1734–1815), Austrian physician. He had a successful practice in Vienna, where he used a number of novel treatments. Mesmer is chiefly remembered for introducing hypnotism — formerly known as *animal magnetism* or *mesmerism* — as a therapeutic technique. However, it was much steeped in archaic ideas, mysticism, and sensationalism, and Mesmer effectively retired following the critical report of a royal commission in 1784.

Messalina /,mesə'liːnə/, Valeria (also **Messallina**) (AD *c*.22–48), Roman empress, third wife of Claudius. She married her second cousin Claudius in about 39, and became notorious in Rome for the murders she instigated in court and for her extramarital affairs. She was executed on Claudius' orders, after the disclosure of her secret marriage to one of his political opponents.

Messerschmidt /'mesə,ʃmɪt/, Wilhelm Emil ('Willy') (1898–1978), German aircraft designer and industrialist. Messerschmidt designed and constructed his first glider in 1915 and set up a company in 1923, while still a student. The Nazi authorities encouraged the development of aircraft in the 1930s, resulting in the Messerschmidt 109, which became the standard fighter of the Luftwaffe during the Second World War. Messerschmidt continued to be active in aerospace companies until his death.

Messiaen /'mesjɒn/, Olivier (Eugène Prosper Charles) (1908–92), French composer. Messiaen was organist of the church of La Trinité in Paris for more than forty years. His music shows many influences, including Greek and Indian rhythms, birdsong, the music of Stravinsky and Debussy, and the composer's Roman Catholic faith. His *Quartet for the End of Time* for violin, clarinet, cello, and piano (1941) was written and first performed in a prison camp in Silesia during the Second World War. Other major works include *La Nativité du Seigneur* for organ (1935), the *Turangalîla Symphony* for large orchestra (1946–8), *Catalogues d'oiseaux* for piano (1956–8), and *La Transfiguration de Notre Seigneur Jésus-Christ* (1969) for chorus and orchestra.

Messier /'mesɪˌeɪ/, Charles (1730–1817), French astronomer. Without any technical training, Messier became a clerical assistant at the Paris Observatory and soon began a search for new comets that was to be his lifelong obsession. While doing so he came across a number of nebulae, galaxies, and star clusters, which he designated by M numbers and made into a list that had reached a total of 103 items by 1784. Almost all of these designations, such as M1 (the Crab Nebula), are still in use today, though the list of such objects has been greatly extended.

Methodius, St /mɪ'θəʊdɪəs/, the brother of St Cyril (see CYRIL, ST).

Metternich /'metənɪx/, Klemens Wenzel Nepomuk Lothar, Prince of Metternich-Winneburg-Beilstein (1773–1859), Austrian statesman. As Foreign Minister (1809–48), he was one of the organizers of the Congress of Vienna (1814–15), which devised the settlement of Europe after the Napoleonic Wars. He pursued policies which reflected his reactionary conservatism at home and abroad until forced to resign during the revolutions of 1848.

Meyerbeer /'maɪəˌbɪə(r)/, Giacomo (born Jakob Liebmann Beer) (1791–1864), German composer. He made his mark as a pianist before achieving success as an opera composer during a stay in Italy (1816–24). He then settled in Paris, establishing himself as a leading exponent of French grand opera with a series of works including *Robert le diable* (1831), *Les Huguenots* (1836), and *L'Africaine* (1865).

Meyerhof /'maɪəˌhɒf/, Otto Fritz (1884–1951), German-born American biochemist.

He worked in Germany on the biochemical processes involved in muscle action, including the production of lactic acid and heat as by-products, and provided the basis for understanding the process by which glucose is broken down to provide energy. He shared a Nobel Prize in 1922, and fled the Nazis in 1938 to continue his work in America.

Michelangelo /ˌmaɪk(ə)l'ændʒəˌləʊ/ (full name Michelangelo Buonarroti) (1475–1564), Italian sculptor, painter, architect, and poet. A leading figure during the High Renaissance, Michelangelo established his reputation in Rome with statues such as the *Pietà* (c.1497–1500) and then in Florence with his marble *David* (1501–4). Under papal patronage Michangelo decorated the ceiling of the Sistine Chapel in Rome (1508–12) and painted the fresco *The Last Judgement* (1536–41), both important works in the development of the mannerist style. His architectural achievements include the design of the Laurentian Library in Florence (1524–34), as well as the completion of St Peter's in Rome, including the design of its great dome (1546–64).

Michelin /'mɪtʃəlɪn, French miʃlɛ̃/, André (1853–1931) and Édouard (1859–1940), French industrialists. In 1888 they founded the Michelin Tyre Company, and they pioneered the use of pneumatic tyres on motor vehicles in the 1890s. The company also introduced steel-belted radial tyres in 1948.

Michelozzo /ˌmi:ke'lɒtsəʊ/ (full name Michelozzo di Bartolommeo) (1396–1472), Italian architect and sculptor. In partnership with Ghiberti and Donatello he led a revival of interest in classical Roman architecture. His most famous building is the Palazzo Medici-Riccardi in Florence (1444–59), one of the most influential palace designs of the early Renaissance.

Michelson /'maɪk(ə)ls(ə)n/, Albert Abraham (1852–1931), American physicist. He specialized in precision measurement in experimental physics, and became in 1907 the first American to be awarded a Nobel Prize. He performed a number of accurate determinations of the velocity of light. His crucial experiment demonstrating that the hypothetical ether did not exist was repeated in 1887 with E. W. Morley, using improved apparatus. The Michelson-Morley result contradicted Newtonian

physics, and was eventually resolved by Einstein's special theory of relativity.

Middleton /ˈmɪd(ə)lt(ə)n/, Thomas (c.1570–1627), English dramatist. After collaborating with Thomas Dekker on the first part of *The Honest Whore* (1604), Middleton wrote the two tragedies for which he is best known, namely *The Changeling* (1622), written with William Rowley (c.1585–1626), and *Women Beware Women* (1620–7).

Mies van der Rohe /ˌmiːz væn də ˈrəʊə/, Ludwig (1886–1969), German-born architect and designer. In the 1920s he produced unexecuted designs for glass skyscrapers and designed the German pavilion at the 1929 International Exhibition at Barcelona; the latter is regarded as a classic example of pure geometrical architecture. He is also noted for his design of tubular steel furniture, notably the 'Barcelona Chair'. He succeeded Walter Gropius as director of the Bauhaus 1930–3. He emigrated to the US in 1937; his most celebrated American design is probably the Seagram Building in New York (1954–8).

Mihailović /mɪˈhaɪləˌvɪtʃ/, Dragoljub ('Draža') (1893–1946), Yugoslav soldier. Born in Serbia, he was leader of the Chetniks during the Second World War, resisting the German occupation of Yugoslavia. In 1941 he became Minister of War for the Yugoslav government in exile, but as Chetnik relations with Tito's Communist partisans grew more strained, Allied support went to Tito and Mihailović was forced to go into hiding. After the war he was tried and shot for war crimes and collaboration with the Germans.

Milhaud /ˈmiːjəʊ/, Darius (1892–1974), French composer. After travelling in Brazil, he became a member of the group known as Les Six. Milhaud composed the music to Jean Cocteau's ballet *Le Boeuf sur le toit* (1919), and his contact with Latin American music formed the inspiration for his two dance suites *Saudades do Brasil* (1920–1). Much of his music was polytonal, and, after 1920, influenced by jazz.

Mill /mɪl/, John Stuart (1806–73), English philosopher and economist. He won recognition as a philosopher with his defence of empiricism in *System of Logic* (1843). Mill is best known, however, for his political and moral works, especially *On Liberty* (1859), which argued for the importance of individuality, and *Utilitarianism* (1861), which developed Jeremy Bentham's theory, considering explicitly the relation between utilitarianism and justice. In other works he advocated representative democracy, criticized the contemporary treatment of married women, and claimed that an end to economic growth was desirable as well as inevitable.

Millais /ˈmɪleɪ/, Sir John Everett (1829–96), English painter. A founder member of the Pre-Raphaelite Brotherhood, he initially adhered to a pure vision of nature with unidealized figures in such paintings as *Christ in the House of his Parents* (1850). However, with the success of *The Blind Girl* (1856) and other paintings, he gradually departed from the moral and aesthetic rigour of the early Pre-Raphaelites, going on to produce lavishly painted portraits, landscapes, and sentimental genre pictures, notably *Bubbles* (1886).

Mille, Cecil B. de, see DE MILLE.

Miller[1] /ˈmɪlə(r)/, Arthur (born 1915), American dramatist. He established his reputation with *Death of a Salesman* (1949), before writing *The Crucible* (1953), which used the Salem witch trials of 1692 as an allegory for McCarthyism in America in the 1950s. Miller was married to Marilyn Monroe from 1955 to 1961.

Miller[2] /ˈmɪlə(r)/, (Alton) Glenn (1904–44), American jazz trombonist and band-leader. From 1938 he led his celebrated swing big band, with whom he recorded his signature tune 'Moonlight Serenade'. He joined the US army in 1942 and died when his aircraft disappeared on a routine flight across the English Channel.

Miller[3] /ˈmɪlə(r)/, Henry (Valentine) (1891–1980), American novelist. From 1930 to 1940 he lived in France, where he published the autobiographical novels *Tropic of Cancer* (1934), about his life in Paris, and *Tropic of Capricorn* (1939), dealing with his youth in New York. Their frank depiction of sex and use of obscenities caused them to be banned in the US until the 1960s. Other works include *The Air-Conditioned Nightmare* (1945), reflections on a return to the US.

Millet /ˈmiːeɪ/, Jean (François) (1814–75), French painter. He studied art in Cherbourg, and then in 1837 travelled to Paris to work with Paul Delaroche (1797–1859), the professor of painting at the École Nationale Supérieure des Beaux-Arts. From 1850 he concentrated on the peasant sub-

jects, such as *Sower* (1850) and *The Gleaners* (1857), for which he became famous, achieving popularity and recognition after the Great Exhibition in Paris (1867).

Millett /'mɪlɪt/, Katherine ('Kate') (born 1934), American feminist. She became involved in the civil-rights movement of the 1960s, and in 1970 she published her influential book *Sexual Politics*, in which she advocated a radical feminism. *Going to Iran* (1981) tells of her experiences in and expulsion from that country in 1979 while campaigning for women's rights.

Milligan /'mɪlɪgən/, Spike (born Terence Alan Milligan) (born 1918), British comedian and writer, born in India. His work is characterized by his sense of the absurd. He came to prominence in the cult radio programme *The Goon Show* (1951–9), and thereafter appeared regularly on stage and television, and in minor film roles. He also wrote children's books, poetry, and autobiographical novels such as *Adolf Hitler, My Part in His Downfall* (1971).

Millikan /'mɪlɪkən/, Robert Andrews (1868–1953), American physicist. He was the first to give an accurate figure for the electric charge on an electron. Progressing from this to study the photoelectric effect, he confirmed the validity of Einstein's equation and gave an accurate figure for Planck's constant. Millikan also worked on the spectrometry of the lighter elements, and investigated cosmic rays. He was awarded the 1923 Nobel Prize for physics, and did much to establish the scientific reputation of the California Institute of Technology.

Mills /mɪlz/, Sir John (Lewis Ernest Watts) (born 1908), English actor. He is well known for his appearances in war films such as *This Happy Breed* (1944), in classics such as *Great Expectations* (1946), where he played the adult Pip, and in adventure films such as *Scott of the Antarctic* (1948) and *Ice Cold in Alex* (1958). Mills won an Oscar for his portrayal of a village idiot in *Ryan's Daughter* (1971). His daughters Juliet Mills (born 1941) and Hayley Mills (born 1946) have also had acting careers.

Milne /mɪln/, A(lan) A(lexander) (1882–1956), English writer of stories and poems for children. He is remembered for his series of nursery stories written for his son Christopher Robin (1920–96), namely *Winnie-the-Pooh* (1926) and *The House at Pooh Corner* (1928). He also wrote two collections

of verse for children: *When We Were Very Young* (1924) and *Now We Are Six* (1927).

Milton /'mɪlt(ə)n/, John (1608–74), English poet. Milton's prolific early writings include the masque *Comus* (1637) and the elegy 'Lycidas' (1638). He became politically active during the Civil War, publishing the *Areopagitica* (1644), which demanded a free press, and writing a defence of republicanism on the eve of the Restoration (1660). His three major poems, all completed after he had gone blind (1652), have biblical subjects and show his skilful use of blank verse: they are *Paradise Lost* (1667, revised 1674), an epic on the fall of man, *Paradise Regained* (1671), on Christ's temptations, and *Samson Agonistes* (1671), on Samson's final years.

Mingus /'mɪŋgəs/, Charles (1922–79), American jazz bassist and composer. After studying the double bass in Los Angeles with Louis Armstrong, he became part of the 1940s jazz scene alongside Dizzy Gillespie, Thelonious Monk, and Charlie Parker. Well-known compositions of that time included 'Goodbye Porkpie Hat' and 'The Black Saint and the Sinner Lady'. Mingus's music reflects his experiments with atonality, as well as the influence of gospel and blues.

Minkowski /mɪŋ'kɒfskɪ/, Hermann (1864–1909), Russian-born German mathematician. He studied the theory of quadratic forms, and contributed to the understanding of the geometrical properties of sets in multidimensional space. Minkowski was the first to suggest the concept of four-dimensional space–time, which was the basis for Einstein's later work on the general theory of relativity.

Minton /'mɪntən/, Thomas (1765–1836), English pottery and china manufacturer. He was an engraver with Josiah Spode before founding his own business in Stoke-on-Trent (1789). Four years later he built a pottery works in Stoke, where he popularized the willow pattern, and in 1820 started producing bone china. During the 19th century the Minton factory became the best-known source of made-to-order tableware in the country.

Mirabeau /'mɪrəˌbəʊ/, Honoré Gabriel Riqueti, Comte de (1749–91), French revolutionary politician. Mirabeau rose to prominence in the early days of the French Revolution, when he became deputy of the Third Estate in the States General. His moderate political stance led him to press

for a form of constitutional monarchy; he was made President of the National Assembly in 1791, but died shortly afterwards.

Miró /mɪˈrəʊ/, Joan (1893–1983), Spanish painter. From 1919 he spent much of his time in Paris, returning to live in Spain in 1940. One of the most prominent figures of surrealism, he painted a brightly coloured fantasy world of variously spiky and amoebic calligraphic forms against plain backgrounds. Major works include *Harlequinade* (1924–5).

Mishima /ˈmɪʃɪmə/, Yukio (pseudonym of Hiraoka Kimitake) (1925–70), Japanese writer. He won acclaim for his first novel, *Confessions of a Mask* (1949), in which he describes coming to terms with his homosexuality. His best-known work, the four-volume *The Sea of Fertility* (1965–70), deals with themes of reincarnation and the sterility of modern life. He was an avowed imperialist, who committed suicide by disembowelling himself in public after a failed attempt to incite soldiers against the postwar regime.

Mitchell[1] /ˈmɪtʃəl/, Joni (born Roberta Joan Anderson) (born 1943), Canadian singer and songwriter. After making her name as a singer and guitarist in Toronto clubs, she became known as a songwriter in the late 1960s. Mitchell's career as a recording artist began in 1968; her many albums, often highly personal in their lyrics, reflect her move from a folk style to a fusion of folk, jazz, and rock. They include *Blue* (1971), *Mingus* (1979), and *Dog Eat Dog* (1986).

Mitchell[2] /ˈmɪtʃəl/, Margaret (1900–49), American novelist. She is famous as the author of the best-selling novel *Gone with the Wind* (1936), set during the American Civil War. It was awarded the Pulitzer Prize, as well as being made into a successful film (1939).

Mitchell[3] /ˈmɪtʃəl/, R(eginald) J(oseph) (1895–1937), English aeronautical engineer. He is best known for designing the Spitfire fighter aircraft; 19,000 aeroplanes based on his 1936 prototype were used by the RAF during the Second World War.

Mitchum /ˈmɪtʃəm/, Robert (1917–97), American actor. He was a workman and professional boxer before going to Hollywood in 1943 and becoming a film extra. He rose to stardom in films such as *Out of the Past* (1947), *Night of the Hunter* (1955), and *Farewell My Lovely* (1975), in which he developed a brooding screen persona.

Mitford /ˈmɪtfəd/, Nancy (Freeman) (1904–73) and her sister Jessica (Lucy) (1917–96), English writers. They were born into an aristocratic family; their sisters included Unity (1914–48), who was an admirer of Hitler, and Diana (born 1910), who married Sir Oswald Mosley in 1936. Nancy achieved fame with her comic novels, including *The Pursuit of Love* (1945) and *Love in a Cold Climate* (1949). She was also the editor of *Noblesse Oblige* (1956), which popularized the terms U and Non-U, used by the British linguist Alan Ross to categorize the speech and behaviour of the upper class as opposed to other social classes. Jessica became an American citizen in 1944 and was a member of the American Communist Party in the 1940s and 1950s. She is best known for her works on American culture, notably *The American Way of Death* (1963) and *The American Way of Birth* (1992).

Mithridates VI /ˌmɪθrɪˈdeɪtiːz/ (also **Mithradates VI**; known as Mithridates the Great) (*c.*132–63 BC), king of Pontus 120–63. His expansionist policies led to a war with Rome (88–85), during which he occupied most of Asia Minor and much of Greece, until driven back by Sulla. Two further wars followed (83–82, 74–66); he was defeated by the Roman general Lucullus (*c.*110–*c.*57) and finally by Pompey.

Mitterrand /ˈmiːtəˌrɒn/, François (Maurice Marie) (1916–96), French statesman, President 1981–95. After working to strengthen the Left alliance, Mitterrand became First Secretary of the new Socialist Party in 1971. As President he initially moved to raise basic wages, increase social benefits, nationalize key industries, and decentralize government. After the Socialist Party lost its majority vote in the 1986 general election, Mitterrand asked the right-wing politician Jacques Chirac to serve as Prime Minister. Mitterrand was re-elected as President in 1988.

Mobutu /məˈbuːtuː/, Sese Seko (full name Mobutu Sese Seko Kuku Ngbendu Wa Za Banga) (1930–97), Zairean statesman, President 1965–97. After seizing power in a military coup, he changed his original name (Joseph-Désiré Mobutu) and that of his country (then known as the Belgian Congo) as part of his policy of Africanizing names. He remained in power despite much opposition from tribal groups and

small farmers, but was finally overthrown in 1997.

Modigliani /ˌmɒdrˈljɑːnɪ/, Amedeo (1884–1920), Italian painter and sculptor, resident in France from 1906. Influenced by Botticelli and other 14th-century artists, his portraits and nudes are noted for their elongated forms, linear qualities, and earthy colours. Modigliani's works include the sculpture *Head of a Woman* (1910–13) and the portrait *Jeanne Hébuterne* (1919).

Mohammed see MUHAMMAD [1].

Moholy-Nagy /ˌməʊhɔɪˈnɒdʒ/, László (1895–1946), Hungarian-born American painter, sculptor, and photographer. Based in Berlin from 1920, he became identified with the constructivist school, pioneering the experimental use of plastic materials, light, photography, and film. Moholy-Nagy taught with Walter Gropius at the Bauhaus (1923–9), later heading the new Bauhaus school in Chicago from 1937.

Moissan /ˈmwʌsɒn/, Ferdinand Frédéric Henri (1852–1907), French chemist. In 1886 he succeeded in isolating the very reactive element fluorine. In 1892 he invented the electric arc furnace that bears his name, in which he claimed to have synthesized diamonds. This is now in doubt, but the very high temperatures achieved in the furnace made it possible to reduce some uncommon metals from their ores. An influential teacher, he was appointed professor of inorganic chemistry at the Sorbonne in 1900. Moissan was awarded the Nobel Prize for chemistry in 1906.

Molière /ˈmɒlɪˌeə(r)/ (pseudonym of Jean-Baptiste Poquelin) (1622–73), French dramatist. In 1658 he established himself in Paris as an actor, dramatist, and manager of his own troupe. His high reputation as a writer of French comedy is based on more than twenty plays, which took the vices and follies of contemporary France as their subject, simultaneously adopting and developing stock characters from Italian *commedia dell'arte*. Major works include *Tartuffe* (1664), *Don Juan* (1665), *Le Misanthrope* (1666), and *Le Malade imaginaire* (1673). Molière also collaborated with the composer Lully for *Le Bourgeois Gentilhomme* (1670).

Molotov /ˈmɒləˌtɒf/, Vyacheslav (Mikhailovich) (born Vyacheslav Mikhailovich Skryabin) (1890–1986), Soviet statesman. Born in Russia, he was an early member of the Bolsheviks and a staunch supporter of

Stalin after Lenin's death. As Commissar (later Minister) for Foreign Affairs (1939–49; 1953–6), he negotiated the non-aggression pact with Nazi Germany (1939) and after 1945 represented the Soviet Union at meetings of the United Nations, where his frequent exercise of the veto helped to prolong the cold war. He was expelled from his party posts in 1956 after quarrelling with Khrushchev.

Mommsen /ˈmɒmz(ə)n/, Theodor (1817–1903), German historian. He is noted for his three-volume *History of Rome* (1854–6; 1885) and his treatises on Roman constitutional law (1871–88). Mommsen was also editor of the *Corpus Inscriptionum Latinarum* (1863) for the Berlin Academy. He was awarded the Nobel Prize for literature in 1902.

Monash /ˈmɒnæʃ/, Sir John (1865–1931), Australian general. After commanding the 4th Australian Brigade at Gallipoli (1915), he served with distinction as commander of the 3rd Australian Division in France (1916).

Monck /mʌŋk/, George, 1st Duke of Albemarle (1608–70), English general. Although initially a Royalist in the Civil War, he became a supporter of Oliver Cromwell, and later completed the suppression of the Royalists in Scotland (1651). He subsequently campaigned against the Dutch at sea (1652–4), and from 1654 to 1660 he was Commander-in-Chief in Scotland. Concerned at the growing unrest following the death of Cromwell in 1658, Monck eventually marched his army south to London, persuaded his fellow generals that the only alternative to anarchy was the restoration of the monarchy, and negotiated the return of Charles II (1660).

Mondrian /ˈmɒndrɪˌɑːn/, Piet (born Pieter Cornelis Mondriaan) (1872–1944), Dutch painter. He was a co-founder of the De Stijl movement and the originator of neo-plasticism, one of the earliest and strictest forms of geometrical abstract painting. His use of vertical and horizontal lines, rectangular shapes, and primary colours is typified by such paintings as *Composition with Red, Yellow, and Blue* (1921).

Monet /ˈmɒneɪ/, Claude (1840–1926), French painter. He was a founder member of the impressionists; his early painting *Impression: soleil levant* (1874) gave the movement its name. Of all the group, Monet

remained the most faithful to the impressionist principles of painting directly from the subject (often out of doors) and giving primacy to transient visual perception. His fascination with the play of light on objects led to a series of paintings of single subjects painted at different times of day and under different weather conditions, notably the *Haystacks* series (1890–1), *Rouen Cathedral* (1892–5), and the *Water-lilies* sequence (1899–1906; 1916 onwards).

Monica, St /'mɒnɪkə/ (332–c.387), mother of St Augustine of Hippo. Born in North Africa, she is often seen as the model of Christian mothers for her patience with her son's spiritual crises, ending with his conversion in 386. She became the object of a cult in the late Middle Ages and is frequently chosen as the patron of associations of Christian mothers. Feast day, 27 August (formerly 4 May).

Monk /mʌŋk/, Thelonious (Sphere) (1917–82), American jazz pianist and composer. In the early 1940s he played alongside Dizzy Gillespie and Charlie Parker in Harlem, becoming one of the founders of the bebop style. He achieved popularity in the late 1950s, as the new style of 'cool' jazz reached a wider audience. Memorable compositions include 'Round Midnight', 'Straight, No Chaser', and 'Well, You Needn't'.

Monmouth /'mɒnməθ/, Duke of (title of James Scott) (1649–85), English claimant to the throne of England. The illegitimate son of Charles II, he became the focus for Whig supporters of a Protestant succession. In 1685 he led a rebellion against the Catholic James II; he proclaimed himself king at Taunton in Somerset, but his force was defeated at the Battle of Sedgemoor and he was executed.

Monod /'mɒnəʊ/, Jacques Lucien (1910–76), French biochemist. Monod joined the Pasteur Institute after the Second World War and became its director in 1971. He worked on bacterial genetics in collaboration with his fellow French biochemist François Jacob (born 1920), and they formulated a theory to explain how genes are activated. In 1960 they coined the term *operon* for a gene which regulates others, and a year later proposed the existence of messenger RNA, which transmits the information from genes to the site of protein synthesis. Monod and Jacob were awarded a Nobel Prize in 1965, and in 1971 Monod pub-lished his wide-ranging popular work *Chance and Necessity*.

Monroe[1] /mən'rəʊ/, James (1758–1831), American Democratic Republican statesman, 5th President of the US 1817–25. In 1803, while minister to France under President Jefferson, he negotiated and ratified the Louisiana Purchase, by which territory formerly owned by France was sold to the US. He is chiefly remembered, however, as the originator of the Monroe doctrine, a principle of US foreign policy that any intervention by external powers in the politics of the Americas is a potentially hostile act against the US. It was first expressed in Monroe's address to Congress in 1823 against a background of continued involvement and threat of expansion from European colonial powers in South America.

Monroe[2] /mən'rəʊ/, Marilyn (born Norma Jean Mortenson, later Baker) (1926–62), American actress. After a career as a photographer's model, she starred in a series of comedy films, including *Gentlemen Prefer Blondes* (1953) and *Some Like it Hot* (1959), emerging as the definitive Hollywood sex symbol. Her last film was *The Misfits* (1961), written for her by her third husband, the dramatist Arthur Miller. She is thought to have died of an overdose of sleeping-pills, although there is continuing controversy over the cause of her death.

Montagna /mɒn'taːnjə/, Bartolommeo Cincani (c.1450–1523), Italian painter. He settled in Vicenza and helped establish it as a centre of art. He is noted for his altarpiece *Sacra Conversazione* (1499).

Montaigne /mɒn'tein/, Michel (Eyquem) de (1533–92), French essayist. Often regarded as the originator of the modern essay, he wrote about prominent personalities and ideas of his age in his sceptical *Essays* (1580; 1588). Translated by John Florio in 1603, they were an influence on Shakespeare, Francis Bacon, and others.

Montana /mɒn'temə/, Joe (known as 'Cool Joe') (born 1956), American football player. He joined the San Francisco 49ers as quarterback in 1980 and played in four winning Super Bowls (1982; 1985; 1989; 1990). He retired in 1995 after two seasons with the Kansas City Chiefs.

Montcalm /mɒn'kɑːm/, Louis Joseph de Montcalm-Gozon, Marquis de (1712–59), French general. He defended Quebec

against British troops under General Wolfe, but was defeated and mortally wounded in the battle on the Plains of Abraham.

Montespan /'mɒntɪˌspɒn/, Marquise de (title of Françoise-Athénaïs de Rochechouart) (1641–1707), French noblewoman. She was mistress of Louis XIV from 1667 to 1679, and had seven illegitimate children by him. She subsequently fell from favour when the king became attracted to their governess, Madame de Maintenon.

Montesquieu /'mɒntəˌskjɜː, -ˌskjuː/, Baron de La Brède et de (title of Charles Louis de Secondat) (1689–1755), French political philosopher. A former advocate, he became known with the publication of his *Lettres Persanes* (1721), a satire of French society from the perspective of two Persian travellers visiting Paris. Montesquieu's reputation rests chiefly on *L'Esprit des lois* (1748), a comparative study of political systems in which he championed the separation of judicial, legislative, and executive powers as being most conducive to individual liberty, holding up the English state as a model. His theories were highly influential in Europe in the late 18th century, as they were in the drafting of the American Constitution.

Montessori /ˌmɒntɪ'sɔːrɪ/, Maria (1870–1952), Italian educationist. Her success with mentally retarded children led her, in 1907, to apply similar methods to younger children of normal intelligence. Montessori's system, set out in her book *The Montessori Method* (1909), advocates a child-centred approach, in which the pace is largely set by the child and play is free but guided, using a variety of sensory materials. Her ideas have since become an integral part of modern nursery and infant-school education.

Monteverdi /ˌmɒntɪ'veədɪ/, Claudio (1567–1643), Italian composer. From the 1580s he published many books of madrigals, noted for their use of harmonic dissonance. Monteverdi is chiefly remembered for his opera *Orfeo* (1607), which introduced a sustained dramatic focus and more fully defined characters, interweaving the instrumental accompaniment and the singing with the drama. His other baroque operas include *The Return of Ulysses* (1641) and *The Coronation of Poppea* (1642). As a composer of sacred music, he is particularly associated with the *Vespers* (1610).

Montez /'mɒntez/, Lola (born Marie Dolores Eliza Rosanna Gilbert) (1818–61), Irish dancer. While performing in Munich in 1846 she came to the notice of Ludwig I of Bavaria; she became his mistress and exercised great influence on his ruling of the country until banished the following year.

Montezuma II /ˌmɒntɪ'zuːmə/ (1466–1520), Aztec emperor 1502–20. The last ruler of the Aztec empire in Mexico, he was defeated and imprisoned by the Spanish conquistadors under Cortés in 1519. Montezuma was killed while trying to pacify some of his former subjects during the Aztec uprising against his captors.

Montfort[1] /'mɒntfət/, Simon de (c.1165–1218), French soldier. From 1209 he was leader of the Albigensian Crusade against the Cathars in southern France. He died while besieging the city of Toulouse. He was the father of Simon de Montfort, Earl of Leicester.

Montfort[2] /'mɒntfət/, Simon de, Earl of Leicester (c.1208–65), English soldier, born in Normandy. He was the son of the French soldier Simon de Montfort. As leader of the baronial opposition to Henry III, he campaigned against royal encroachment on the privileges gained through Magna Carta, and defeated the king at Lewes, Sussex, in 1264. The following year he summoned a Parliament which included not only barons, knights, and clergymen, but also two citizens from every borough in England. He was defeated and killed by reorganized royal forces under Henry's son (later Edward I) at Evesham.

Montgolfier /mɒn'gɒlfɪˌeɪ, -fɪə(r)/, Joseph Michel (1740–1810) and Jacques Étienne (1745–99), French inventors. Sons of a paper manufacturer, they pioneered experiments in hot-air ballooning. In 1782 they built a large balloon from linen and paper, lit a fire on the ground, and with the rising hot air successfully lifted a number of animals; the first human ascents followed in 1783.

Montgomery[1] /mɒnt'gʌmərɪ, -'gɒmərɪ/, Bernard Law, 1st Viscount Montgomery of Alamein ('Monty') (1887–1976), British Field Marshal. In 1942 he commanded the 8th Army in the Western Desert, where his victory at El Alamein proved the first significant Allied success in the Second World War. He was later given command of the Allied ground forces in the invasion of

Normandy in 1944 and accepted the German surrender on 7 May 1945.

Montgomery[2] /mɒntˈɡʌmərɪ, -ˈɡʊmərɪ/, Lucy Maud (1874–1942), Canadian novelist. She is chiefly remembered for her first novel *Anne of Green Gables* (1908), the story of a spirited orphan girl brought up by an elderly couple. It became an instant best seller and was followed by seven sequels.

Montrose /mɒnˈtrəʊz/, James Graham, 1st Marquess of (1612–50), Scottish general. Montrose supported Charles I when Scotland entered the English Civil War and, commanding a small army of Irish and Scottish irregulars, inflicted a dramatic series of defeats on the stronger Covenanter forces in the north (1644–5) before being defeated at Philiphaugh. After several years in exile, he returned to Scotland in 1650 in a bid to restore the new king Charles II, but was betrayed to the Covenanters and hanged.

Moog /muːɡ, məʊɡ/, Robert (born 1934), American inventor. Qualified in physics and engineering, Moog set up a company to develop a keyboard instrument capable of producing electronically synthesized music. The first synthesizer was unveiled in 1964 and quickly became standard equipment in popular music, with *Moog* and *synthesizer* becoming effectively synonymous for a time.

Moon /muːn/, Sun Myung (born 1920), Korean industrialist and religious leader. In 1954 he founded the Holy Spirit Association for the Unification of World Christianity, which became known as the Unification Church; his followers are popularly known as 'Moonies'.

Moore[1] /mʊə(r), mɔː(r)/, Dudley (Stuart John) (born 1935), English actor, comedian, and musician. Moore appeared in the highly successful television show *Beyond the Fringe* (1959–64), for which he also wrote the music. He then joined Peter Cook in what was to become a noted partnership for the TV series *Not Only . . . But Also* (1964–70). Moore starred in several films, including *Arthur* (1981) and *Crazy People* (1990), and regularly performed and recorded with the Dudley Moore Trio as an accomplished jazz pianist.

Moore[2] /mʊə(r), mɔː(r)/, Francis (1657–*c.*1715), English physician, astrologer, and schoolmaster. In 1699 he published an almanac containing weather predictions in order to promote the sale of his pills, and in 1700 one with astrological observations. There are now several almanacs called 'Old Moore', and predictions range far beyond the weather.

Moore[3] /mʊə(r), mɔː(r)/, George (Augustus) (1852–1933), Irish novelist. From about 1870 he lived in Paris, where he studied painting and gained a knowledge of the works of writers such as Balzac and Zola. On his return to London (1880) Moore embarked on a career as a novelist; influenced by Zola, he experimented with naturalistic techniques in works such as *A Mummer's Wife* (1885), set in the Potteries in North Staffordshire, and *Esther Waters* (1894). He became involved in the Irish literary revival and collaborated in the planning of the Irish National Theatre, established in 1899.

Moore[4] /mʊə(r), mɔː(r)/, G(eorge) E(dward) (1873–1958), English philosopher. He led the revolt against the Hegelianism prevalent at the turn of the century, objecting that it was inapplicable to the familiar world of 'tables and chairs'. In his best-known work, *Principia Ethica* (1903), he argued that good was a simple, indefinable, unanalysable, and non-natural property, but that it was still possible to identify certain things as pre-eminently good. These he declared to be 'personal affection and aesthetic enjoyments', values seized upon by several of his associates in the Bloomsbury Group.

Moore[5] /mʊə(r), mɔː(r)/, Henry (Spencer) (1898–1986), English sculptor and draughtsman. In the 1920s he rejected modelling in favour of direct carving in stone and wood, and allowed natural qualities such as texture and grain to influence form. Moore subsequently received major commissions for architectural sculpture, including large reclining figures for the UNESCO building in Paris (1957–8). Prominent themes for the postwar period were upright figures, family groups, and two and three-piece semi-abstract reclining forms; Moore was keen that these sculptures should be viewed in the open air.

Moore[6] /mʊə(r), mɔː(r)/, Sir John (1761–1809), British general. From 1808 he commanded the British army during the Peninsular War, conducting a successful 250-mile retreat to Corunna in mid-winter before being mortally wounded by his French pursuers. His burial was the subject

of a famous poem by the Irish poet Charles Wolfe (1791–1823).

Moore[7] /mʊə(r), mɔː(r)/, Robert Frederick ('Bobby') (1941–93), English footballer. He is chiefly remembered as the captain of the English team that won the World Cup in 1966.

Moore[8] /mʊə(r), mɔː(r)/, Thomas (1779–1852), Irish poet and musician. He wrote patriotic and nostalgic songs, which he set to Irish tunes, and collected in *Irish Melodies* (1807–34). His most famous songs include The Harp that once through Tara's Halls' and 'The Minstrel Boy'. He is also noted for his oriental romance *Lalla Rookh* (1817).

More /mɔː(r)/, Sir Thomas (canonized as St Thomas More) (1478–1535), English scholar and statesman, Lord Chancellor 1529–32. From the time of the accession of Henry VIII (1509), More held a series of public offices, but was forced to resign as Lord Chancellor when he opposed the king's divorce from Catherine of Aragon. He was imprisoned in 1534 after refusing to take the oath on the Act of Succession, sanctioning Henry's marriage to Anne Boleyn. After opposing the Act of Supremacy in the same year, More was beheaded. Regarded as one of the leading humanists of the Renaissance, he owed his reputation largely to his *Utopia* (1516), describing an ideal city-state. Feast day, 22 June.

Moreau /mɒˈrəʊ/, Jeanne (born 1928), French actress. She was acclaimed for her portrayals of isolated and autonomous women in films such as *Ascenseur pour l'échafaud* (1958), *Les Liaisons dangereuses* (1959), and *Jules et Jim* (1961). Later she had some success as a director, especially with *L'Adolescente* (1978), and she also continued to act, her more recent films including *Nikita* (1990).

Morecambe /ˈmɔːkəm/, Eric (born John Eric Bartholomew) (1926–84), English comedian. In 1941 he formed a double act with comedian Ernie Wise (born 1925) that led to the immensely popular *The Morecambe and Wise Show*, which ran on television from 1961. In 1968 Morecambe suffered a heart attack but recovered to continue his TV work, appear in three films, and write a number of books, including the children's book *The Reluctant Vampire* (1982). He carried on performing until his death from another heart attack.

Morgan[1] /ˈmɔːgən/, J(ohn) P(ierpont) (1837–1913), American financier, philanthropist, and art collector. From 1871 he was a partner in a New York banking firm (which became J. P. Morgan and Company in 1895); during the 1870s and 1880s he became a powerful financier, acquiring interests in a number of US railways and instigating their reorganization. Morgan created General Electric (1891) from two smaller concerns, and, in 1901, merged several companies to form the United States Steel Corporation. In 1893 and 1907 his personal influence was sufficient to stabilize critically unbalanced financial markets. He built up one of the leading art collections of his day, bequeathing it to the Museum of Modern Art in New York.

Morgan[2] /ˈmɔːgən/, Thomas Hunt (1866–1945), American zoologist. He is best known for demonstrating the mechanism in the animal cell responsible for inheritance. His studies with the rapidly reproducing fruit fly *Drosophila* showed that the genetic information was carried by genes arranged along the length of the chromosomes. Though this work was not widely accepted initially, Morgan was awarded a Nobel Prize in 1933.

Morisot /ˈmɒriˌzəʊ/, Berthe (Marie Pauline) (1841–95), French painter. A pupil of Corot, she was the first woman to join the impressionists, exhibiting with them from 1874. Her works typically depicted women and children, as in *The Cradle* (1872), and waterside scenes, notably *A Summer's Day* (1879).

Morland /ˈmɔːlənd/, George (1763–1804), English painter. Although indebted to Dutch and Flemish genre painters such as David Teniers the Younger, he drew his inspiration for his pictures of taverns, cottages, and farmyards from local scenes, as with *Inside a Stable* (1791). His art achieved widespread popularity through the engravings of William Ward (1766–1826).

Morley /ˈmɔːlɪ/, Edward Williams (1838–1923), American chemist. He specialized in accurate quantitative measurements, such as those of the combining weights of hydrogen and oxygen. He is best known, however, for his collaboration with Albert Michelson in their 1887 experiment to determine the speed of light (see MICHELSON).

Morris[1] /ˈmɒrɪs/, William (1834–96), English designer, craftsman, poet, and socialist

writer. He was a leading figure in the Arts and Crafts Movement, and in 1861 he established Morris & Company, an association of craftsmen whose members included Edward Burne-Jones and Dante Gabriel Rossetti, to produce hand-crafted goods for the home. Morris's Kelmscott Press, founded in 1890, printed limited editions of fine books using his own type designs and ornamental borders, and was an important influence on English book design. He is also noted for his poetry and many prose romances, especially *News from Nowhere* (1891), which portrays a socialist Utopia.

Morris[2] /'mɒrɪs/, William Richard, see NUFFIELD.

Morrison[1] /'mɒrɪs(ə)n/, James Douglas ('Jim') (1943–71), American rock singer. Morrison was the flamboyant lead singer of the Doors, a group formed in 1965. Associated with the psychedelia of the late 1960s, the group is remembered for dramatic songs such as 'Light My Fire' (1967) and 'Riders on the Storm' (1971). Morrison died in Paris, of a heart attack in his bath. His poetry was published in two volumes, *The Lords* and *The New Creatures* (first printed privately, 1969).

Morrison[2] /'mɒrɪs(ə)n/, Toni (full name Chloe Anthony Morrison) (born 1931), American novelist. She is noted for her novels depicting the black American experience and heritage, often focusing on rural life in the South, as in *The Bluest Eye* (1970). Other works include *Song of Solomon* (1976), *Tar Baby* (1979), and the Pulitzer Prize-winning *Beloved* (1987), a tale of a runaway slave who commits infanticide in mid-19th-century Kentucky. Morrison was awarded the Nobel Prize for literature in 1993, becoming the first black woman writer to receive the prize.

Morrison[3] /'mɒrɪs(ə)n/, Van (full name George Ivan Morrison) (born 1945), Northern Irish singer, songwriter, and musician. Van Morrison has developed a distinctive personal style from a background of blues, soul, folk music, and rock. Among his albums are *Astral Weeks* (1968), *Moondance* (1970), and *Irish Heartbeat* (1989). He started his career as lead singer of the sixties band Them.

Morse /mɔːs/, Samuel F(inley) B(reese) (1791–1872), American inventor. His early career was as a painter, but he became interested in electricity and from 1832 pioneered the development of the electric telegraph. In 1837 he extended the range and capabilities of his working model by means of electromagnetic relays, at a time when similar work was being done concurrently in England by Charles Wheatstone and William Cooke. The US Congress gave financial support for an experimental line from Washington, DC to Baltimore, over which Morse sent the famous message 'What hath God wrought' in his new code, Morse code, on 24 May 1844.

Mortimer /'mɔːtɪmə(r)/, Roger de, 8th Baron of Wigmore and 1st Earl of March (*c*.1287–1330), English noble. In 1326 he invaded England with his lover Isabella of France, forcing her husband Edward II to abdicate in favour of her son, the future Edward III. Mortimer and Isabella acted as regents for the young Edward until 1330, when the monarch assumed royal power and had Mortimer executed.

Morton[1] /'mɔːt(ə)n/, Jelly Roll (born Ferdinand Joseph La Menthe Morton) (1885–1941), American jazz pianist, composer, and band-leader. He was one of the principal links between ragtime and New Orleans jazz, and formed his own band, the Red Hot Peppers, in 1926. For the next four years he and his band made a series of notable jazz recordings, but Morton's popularity waned during the 1930s.

Morton[2] /'mɔːt(ə)n/, John (*c*.1420–1500), English prelate and statesman. He rose to become Henry VII's chief adviser, being appointed Archbishop of Canterbury in 1486 and Chancellor a year later. He is traditionally associated with the Crown's stringent taxation policies, which made the regime in general and Morton in particular widely unpopular.

Mosander /mɒ'sændə(r)/, Carl Gustaf (1797–1858), Swedish chemist. He succeeded Berzelius in Stockholm and continued his work on the rare-earth elements, isolating new elements successively from preparations that turned out to be mixtures. In 1839 Mosander discovered and named the element lanthanum, which was present as the oxide in a mineral that had also yielded cerium. Four years later he announced the discovery of the new elements erbium and terbium, and of the supposed element didymium.

Moseley /'məʊzlɪ/, Henry Gwyn Jeffreys (1887–1915), English physicist. While working under Sir Ernest Rutherford he discovered that there is a relationship

between the atomic numbers of elements and the wavelengths of the X-rays they emit. He demonstrated experimentally that nuclear charge and atomic number are connected, that the element's chemical properties are determined by this number, and that there are only 92 naturally occurring elements. He was killed in action in the First World War.

Moses[1] /'məʊzɪz/ (*fl. c.*14th–13th centuries BC), Hebrew prophet and lawgiver. According to the biblical account, he was born in Egypt and led the Israelites away from servitude there, across the desert towards the Promised Land. During the journey he was inspired by God on Mount Sinai to write down the Ten Commandments on tablets of stone (Exod. 20). He was the brother of Aaron.

Moses[2] /'məʊzɪz/, Anna Mary (known as Grandma Moses) (1860–1961), American painter. She lived as a farmer's wife until widowed in 1927, when she took up painting as a hobby; her work began to appear in exhibitions from the late 1930s. Grandma Moses produced more than a thousand naive paintings, principally colourful scenes of American rural life.

Moses[3] /'məʊzɪz/, Ed(win Corley) (born 1955), American athlete. The outstanding 400-metres hurdler of his generation, he won gold medals in the 1976 and 1984 Olympics. He finished first in 122 consecutive races between 1977 and 1987 and set four successive world records. He combined this with his profession as an engineer, having received a degree in physics in 1978.

Mosley /'məʊzlɪ/, Sir Oswald (Ernald), 6th Baronet (1896–1980), English Fascist leader. Mosley sat successively as a Conservative, Independent, and Labour MP before founding and leading the British Union of Fascists (1932), also known as the Blackshirts. The party was effectively destroyed by the Public Order Act of 1936 and Mosley was interned from 1940 to 1943. In 1948 he founded the right-wing Union Movement.

Moss /mɒs/, Stirling (born 1929), English motor-racing driver. He was especially successful in the 1950s, winning various Grands Prix and other competitions, though the world championship always eluded him.

Mother Teresa see TERESA, MOTHER.

Mountbatten /maʊnt'bæt(ə)n/, Louis (Francis Albert Victor Nicholas), 1st Earl Mountbatten of Burma (1900–79), British admiral and administrator. A great-grandson of Queen Victoria, Mountbatten served in the Royal Navy before rising to become supreme Allied commander in SE Asia (1943–5). As the last viceroy (1947) and first Governor-General of India (1947–8), he oversaw the independence of India and Pakistan. He was killed by an IRA bomb while on his yacht in Ireland.

Moussorgsky see MUSSORGSKY.

Mozart /'məʊtsɑːt/, (Johann Chrysostom) Wolfgang Amadeus (1756–91), Austrian composer. A child prodigy as a harpsichordist, pianist, and composer, he was taken on tours of western Europe by his father Leopold (1719–87). While in Vienna he collaborated with the librettist Da Ponte in the composition of his three comic operas, *The Marriage of Figaro* (1786), *Don Giovanni* (1787), and *Così fan tutte* (1790). His use of music to aid characterization in these works marked an important advance in the development of opera. Early influenced by Haydn, Mozart's work came to epitomize classical music in its purity of form and melody. A prolific composer, he wrote forty-one symphonies, twenty-seven piano concertos, twenty-five string quartets, sixteen operas, and a vast quantity of other instrumental and orchestral music.

Mubarak /muːˈbɑːræk/, (Muhammad) Hosni (Said) (born 1928), Egyptian statesman, President since 1981. Appointed head of the Egyptian air force in 1972, Mubarak became Vice-President in 1975 and succeeded President Sadat following the latter's assassination. Although he did much to establish closer links between Egypt and other Arab nations, including distancing himself from Israel when it invaded Lebanon in 1982, he risked division by aligning Egypt against Saddam Hussein in the Gulf War of 1991. After the resurgence of militant Islamic fundamentalism in Egypt in 1992, Mubarak's National Democratic Party government adopted harsh measures to suppress activists.

Mucha /'muːkə/, Alphonse (born Alfons Maria) (1860–1939), Czech painter and designer. Based in Paris from 1889, he was a leading figure in the art nouveau movement. He is noted for his flowing poster designs, often featuring the actress Sarah Bernhardt, as in *Gismonda* (1894); with the

success of this poster, Mucha was given a six-year commission to design further posters, sets, costumes, and jewellery for the actress.

Mugabe /mʊˈɡɑːbɪ/, Robert (Gabriel) (born 1924), Zimbabwean statesman, Prime Minister 1980-7 and President since 1987. In 1963 he co-founded the Zimbabwe African National Union (ZANU) and in 1975 became its leader; the following year he formed the Patriotic Front with the leader of the Zimbabwe African People's Union (ZAPU), Joshua Nkomo. Mugabe was declared Prime Minister in 1980 after ZANU won a landslide victory in the country's first post-independence elections. In 1982 he ousted Nkomo from his Cabinet; ZANU and ZAPU agreed to merge in 1987 and Mugabe became President.

Muhammad[1] /məˈhæmɪd/ (also **Mohammed**) (c.570-632), Arab prophet and founder of Islam. He was born in Mecca, where in c.610 he received the first of a series of revelations which became the doctrinal and legislative basis of Islam and which were written down c.610-32 as the Koran. His sayings (the Hadith) and the accounts of his daily practice (the Sunna) constitute the other major sources of guidance for most Muslims. In the face of opposition to his preaching he and his small group of supporters were forced to flee to Medina in 622; this flight, known as the Hegira, is of great significance in Islam, and the Islamic calendar (which is based on lunar months) is dated from AD 622 (= 1 AH). After consolidation of the community in Medina Muhammad led his followers into a series of battles which resulted in the capitulation of Mecca in 630. He died two years later, having successfully united tribal factions of the Hejaz region into a force which would expand the frontiers of Islam. He was buried in Medina. Islam is now the professed faith of some 1,000 million people worldwide.

Muhammad[2] /məˈhæmɪd/, Mahathir (born 1925), Malaysian statesman, Prime Minister since 1981.

Muhammad Ahmad /ˈɑːmæd/ see MAHDI.

Muhammad Ali[1] /məˌhæmɪd ˈɑːlɪ, ɑːˈliː/ (1769-1849), Ottoman viceroy and pasha of Egypt 1805-49, possibly of Albanian descent. As a commander in the Ottoman army he had overthrown the Mamelukes, Egypt's ruling military caste, by 1811. Although technically the viceroy of the Ottoman sultan, he was effectively an independent ruler and modernized Egypt's infrastructure, making it the leading power in the eastern Mediterranean. In 1841 he and his family were given the right to become hereditary rulers of Egypt, and the dynasty survived until 1952.

Muhammad Ali[2] /məˌhæmɪd ˈɑːlɪ, ɑːˈliː/ (born Cassius Marcellus Clay) (born 1942), American boxer. He first won the world heavyweight title in 1964 and regained it in 1974 and 1978, becoming the only boxer to be world champion three times. He changed his name in 1964 after converting to Islam. After his retirement in 1981 it was confirmed that he was suffering from Parkinson's disease.

Muir[1] /mjʊə(r)/, Edwin (1887-1959), Scottish poet and translator. His collections of poems include *The Labyrinth* (1949). He is also remembered for his translations of Franz Kafka's works, done in collaboration with his wife, the novelist Willa Anderson (1890-1970); these appeared in the 1930s and established Kafka's reputation in Britain.

Muir[2] /mjʊə(r)/, Jean (Elizabeth) (1933-95), English fashion designer. In 1961 she started producing her own clothing under the name Jane & Jane, establishing her own company, Jean Muir, in 1966, which built an international reputation for women's fashion. Her designs are noted for their classic nature and their subtle, restrained, and fluid styles.

Muir[3] /mjʊə(r)/, John (1838-1914), Scottish-born American naturalist, a pioneer of environmental conservation. Devoting himself to nature after being injured in an industrial accident, Muir campaigned vigorously for the protection of unspoilt wilderness areas and was largely responsible for the establishment of Yosemite and Sequoia National Parks in California (1890). He wrote several books about the American wilderness, such as *The Mountains of California* (1894).

Mujibur Rahman /mʊˌdʒiːbʊə rəˈmɑːn/ (known as Sheikh Mujib) (1920-75), Bangladeshi statesman, Prime Minister 1972-5 and President 1975. In 1949 he co-founded the Awami (People's) League, which advocated autonomy for East Pakistan. He led the party to victory in the 1970 elections, but was imprisoned in 1971 when civil war broke out. Released in 1972, he became the first Prime Minister of independent Bangla-

desh. After his failure to establish parliamentary democracy, he assumed dictatorial powers in 1975. He and his family were assassinated in a military coup.

Muldoon /mʌl'duːn/, Sir Robert (David) (1921–92), New Zealand statesman, Prime Minister 1975–84. He became a National Party MP in 1960, serving as deputy Prime Minister for a brief period in 1972 and as leader of the opposition from 1973 to 1974 before becoming Premier the following year. He was chairman of the board of governors for the IMF and World Bank (1979–80) and chairman of the ministerial council for the OECD (1982). His term of office was marked by domestic measures to tackle low economic growth and high inflation.

Muller /'mʌlə(r)/, Hermann Joseph (1890–1967), American geneticist. Realizing that natural mutations were both rare and detrimental, he discovered that he could use X-rays to induce mutations in the genetic material of the fruit fly *Drosophila*, enabling him to carry out many more genetic studies with it. He also recognized the danger of X-radiation to living things, and was concerned about the build-up of genetic mutations in the human population. Muller was awarded a Nobel Prize in 1946.

Müller[1] /'mʊlə(r)/, Johannes Peter (1801–58), German anatomist and zoologist. He was a pioneer of comparative and microscopical methods in biology. His investigations in physiology included respiration in the foetus, the nervous and sensory systems, the glandular system, and locomotion. Müller also studied the classification of marine animals.

Müller[2] /'mʊlə(r)/, (Friedrich) Max (1823–1900), German-born British philologist. He is remembered for his edition of the sacred early Sanskrit text the Rig-veda (1849–75); he also promoted the comparative study of Indo-European languages, as well as exploring comparative mythology and religion.

Müller[3] /'mʊlə(r)/, Paul Hermann (1899–1965), Swiss chemist. Searching for an effective chemical for use in pest control, he synthesized DDT in 1939 and soon patented it as an insecticide. It was immediately successful, especially in controlling lice and mosquitoes, but was withdrawn by most countries in the 1970s when its environmental persistence and toxicity in

higher animals was realized. He was awarded a Nobel Prize in 1948.

Mulroney /mʌl'ruːnɪ/, (Martin) Brian (born 1939), Canadian Progressive Conservative statesman, Prime Minister 1984–93. After becoming leader of the Progressive Conservative Party in 1983, he won a landslide victory in the 1984 election. He was re-elected in 1988 on a ticket of free trade with the US, but stood down in 1993 after the Canadian recession caused his popularity to slump in the opinion polls.

Munch /mʊŋk/, Edvard (1863–1944), Norwegian painter and engraver. One of the chief sources of German expressionism, he infused his subjects with an intense emotionalism and explored the use of violent colour and linear distortion to express feelings about life and death. Major works include his *Frieze of Life* sequence, incorporating *The Scream* (1893).

Munro /mən'rəʊ/, H(ector) H(ugh), see SAKI.

Murat /mjʊə'rɑː/, Joachim (*c*.1767–1815), French general, king of Naples 1808–15. One of Napoleon's marshals, Murat made his name as a cavalry commander in the Italian campaign (1800). After he was made king of Naples by Napoleon, he made a bid to become king of all Italy in 1815, but was captured in Calabria and executed.

Murdoch[1] /'mɜːdɒk/, Dame (Jean) Iris (born 1919), British novelist and philosopher, born in Ireland. The author of several philosophical works, Murdoch is primarily known for her novels; many of these portray complex sexual relationships, as in *The Sandcastle* (1957) and *The Red and the Green* (1965). Others simultaneously explore the quest for the spiritual life, particularly *The Sea, The Sea* (1978), which won the Booker Prize. More recent novels include *The Good Apprentice* (1985) and *The Message to the Planet* (1989).

Murdoch[2] /'mɜːdɒk/, (Keith) Rupert (born 1931), Australian-born American publisher and media entrepreneur. As the founder and head of the News International Communications empire, he owns major newspapers in Australia, Britain, and the US, together with film and television companies and the publishing firm Harper-Collins.

Murillo /mjʊə'rɪləʊ/, Bartolomé Esteban (*c*.1618–82), Spanish painter. He is noted both for his genre scenes of urchins and

peasants and for his devotional pictures, which are characterized by delicate colour and ethereal form. Major works include *Two Boys Eating a Pie* (c.1665–75) and the *Soult Immaculate Conception* (1678).

Murnau /ˈmʊənaʊ/, F. W. (born Frederick Wilhelm Plumpe) (1888–1931), German film director. His revolutionary use of the camera to record and interpret human emotion resulted in films such as *Nosferatu* (1922), where he used technical effects to produce macabre results. *Der Letzte Mann* (1924) helped establish him as Germany's leading director. Other films include the Hollywood-made *Sunrise* (1927), which won three of the newly founded Oscar awards.

Murray[1] /ˈmʌri/, (George) Gilbert (Aimé) (1866–1957), Australian-born British classical scholar. He is remembered for his rhymed verse translations of Greek dramatists, particularly Euripides. His translations of the latter's *Medea*, *Bacchae*, and *Electra* were staged in London from 1902, and helped to revive contemporary interest in Greek drama. Murray was also a founder of the League of Nations and later a joint president of the United Nations.

Murray[2] /ˈmʌri/, Sir James (Augustus Henry) (1837–1915), Scottish lexicographer. He was chief editor of the largest of all dictionaries in English, the *Oxford English Dictionary*. Murray did not live to see the dictionary completed; he died after finishing a section of the letter T, two years short of his 80th birthday. Originally issued in instalments between 1884 and 1928 under the title *A New English Dictionary on Historical Principles* (NED), the dictionary was not completed until 1928.

Musil /ˈmuːzɪl/, Robert (1880–1942), Austrian novelist. He is best known for his unfinished novel *The Man Without Qualities* (1930–43), a complex experimental work without a conventional plot, depicting the disintegration of traditional Austrian society and culture just before the outbreak of the First World War.

Mussolini /ˌmʊsəˈliːni/, Benito (Amilcaro Andrea) (known as 'Il Duce' = the leader) (1883–1945), Italian Fascist statesman, Prime Minister 1922–43. Originally a socialist, Mussolini founded the Italian Fascist Party in 1919. Three years later he orchestrated the march on Rome by the Blackshirts and was created Prime Minister, proceeding to organize his government along dictatorial lines. He annexed Abyssinia in 1936 and entered the Second World War on Germany's side in 1940. Mussolini was forced to resign after the Allied invasion of Sicily in 1943; he was rescued from imprisonment by German paratroopers, but was captured and executed by Italian Communist partisans in 1945, a few weeks before the end of the war.

Mussorgsky /məˈsɔːgskɪ/, Modest (Petrovich) (also **Moussorgsky**) (1839–81), Russian composer. Most of his best-known works are vocal, his interest in speech rhythms combining with the lyricism of his songs. They include the opera *Boris Godunov* (1874) and *Songs and Dances of Death* (1875–7). He is also noted for the piano suite *Pictures at an Exhibition* (1874). After his death many of his works were completed and altered by Rimsky-Korsakov and others, but recently there has been a tendency to return to Mussorgsky's original scoring.

Mutsuhito /ˌmʊtsuˈhiːtəʊ/ see Meiji Tenno.

Myron /ˈmaɪərən/ (fl. c.480–440 BC), Greek sculptor. Only two certain copies of his work survive, the best known being the *Discobolus* (c.450 BC), a figure of a man throwing the discus, which demonstrates a remarkable interest in symmetry and movement.

N

Nabokov /'næbəˌkɒf, nəˈbəʊkɒf/, Vladimir (Vladimorovich) (1899–1977), Russian-born American novelist and poet. After writing a number of novels in Russian, Nabokov turned to writing in English in 1941. He is best known for *Lolita* (1958), his novel about a middle-aged European man's obsession with a twelve-year-old American girl. Other works include *Pale Fire* (1962) and *Ada: A Family Chronicle* (1969). He was also a keen lepidopterist and wrote a number of papers on the subject.

Nader /'neɪdə(r)/, Ralph (born 1934), American lawyer and reformer. He initiated a campaign on behalf of public safety that gave impetus to the consumer rights movement of the 1960s onwards. His views on defective car design, set out in *Unsafe at Any Speed* (1965), led to Federal legislation on safety standards. Nader was also a moving force behind legislation concerning radiation hazards, food packaging, and the use of insecticides.

Nagy /nɒdʒ/, Imre (1896–1958), Hungarian Communist statesman, Prime Minister 1953–5 and 1956. During his first term in office he introduced liberal policies, pushing for greater availability of consumer goods and less collectivization, but was forced to resign. Back in power in 1956, he announced Hungary's withdrawal from the Warsaw Pact and sought a neutral status for his country. When the Red Army moved in later that year to crush the uprising Nagy was removed from office and executed by the new regime under János Kádár.

Naipaul /'naɪpɔːl/, V(idiadhar) S(urajprasad) (born 1932), Trinidadian novelist and travel writer of Indian descent, resident in Britain since 1950. He is best known for his satirical novels, mostly set in Trinidad, such as *A House for Mr Biswas* (1961). Naipaul's *In a Free State* (1971) won the Booker Prize for its sharp analysis of issues of nationality and identity. His travel books include *An Area of Darkness* (1964), about a visit to India.

Nanak /'nɑːnək/ (known as Guru Nanak) (1469–1539), Indian religious leader and founder of Sikhism. He was born into a Hindu family in a village near Lahore. Many Sikhs believe that he was in a state of enlightenment at birth and that he was destined from then to be God's messenger. He learned about both Hinduism and Islam as a child, and at the age of 30 he underwent a religious experience which prompted him to become a wandering preacher. He eventually settled in Kartarpur, in what is now Punjab province, Pakistan; there he built the first Sikh temple. Nanak sought neither to unite the Hindu and Muslim faiths nor to create a new religion, preaching rather that spiritual liberation could be achieved through practising an inward and disciplined meditation on the name of God. His teachings are contained in a number of hymns which form part of the principal sacred scripture of Sikhism, the Adi Granth.

Nansen /'næns(ə)n/, Fridtjof (1861–1930), Norwegian Arctic explorer. In 1888 he led the first expedition to cross the Greenland ice-fields. Five years later he sailed north of Siberia on board the *Fram*, intending to reach the North Pole by allowing the ship to become frozen in the ice and letting the current carry it towards Greenland. By 1895, it had drifted as far north as 84° 4′; Nansen then made for the Pole on foot, reaching a latitude of 86° 14′, the furthest north anyone had been at that time. Nansen became increasingly involved in affairs of state, serving as Norwegian minister in London (1906–8). In 1922 he was awarded the Nobel Peace Prize for organizing relief work among victims of the Russian famine.

Napier /'neɪpɪə(r)/, John (1550–1617), Scottish mathematician. Napier was the inventor (independently of the German mathematician Joost Bürgi (1552–1632)) of logarithms. His tables, modified and republished by Henry Briggs, had an immediate and lasting influence on mathematics.

Napoleon /nəˈpəʊlɪən/ the name of three rulers of France:

Napoleon I (known as Napoleon; full name Napoleon Bonaparte) (1769–1821),

emperor 1804–14 and 1815. Born in Corsica, he was appointed general of the French Army in Italy in 1796, where he led successful campaigns against Sardinia and Austria to establish a French-controlled republic in northern Italy. Thwarted in his attempt (1798) to create a French empire overseas by Nelson, who defeated the French fleet at the Battle of Aboukir Bay, Napoleon returned to France (1799) and joined a conspiracy which overthrew the Directory. As First Consul he became the supreme ruler of France and over the next four years began his reorganization of the French legal and education systems. He declared himself emperor in 1804, embarking on a series of campaigns known as the Napoleonic Wars, winning such battles as those at Austerlitz (1805) and Jena (1806), and establishing a French empire stretching from Spain to Poland. However, his plans to invade England resulted in the destruction of the French fleet at Trafalgar (1805); then, after the failure of his attack on Russia in 1812, his conquests were gradually lost to a coalition of all his major opponents. Forced into exile in 1814 (to the island of Elba), he returned briefly to power a year later, but, after his defeat at Waterloo (1815), he was once again exiled, this time to the island of St Helena.

Napoleon II (full name Napoleon François Charles Joseph Bonaparte) (1811–32), son of Napoleon I and Empress Marie-Louise. In 1814 Napoleon I abdicated on behalf of himself and Napoleon II. The Empress took Napoleon II to the court of her father, Austrian emperor Francis I. In 1818 the title Herzog von (duke of) Reichstadt was conferred on Napoleon, but he was given no active political role.

Napoleon III (full name Charles Louis Napoleon Bonaparte; known as Louis-Napoleon) (1808–73), emperor 1852–70. A nephew of Napoleon I, Napoleon III came to power after the 1848 revolution, when he was elected President of the Second Republic. In late 1851 he staged a coup, dissolving the Legislative Assembly and establishing a new constitution which was approved by plebiscite, after which the empire was restored and he was confirmed emperor. As emperor, he was noted for his aggressive foreign policy, which included intervention in Mexico, participation in the Crimean War, and war against Austria in Italy. He abdicated in 1870 after the defeat at Sedan in the Franco-Prussian War.

Narayan /nəˈrɑːjən/, R(asipuram) K(rishnaswamy) (born 1906), Indian novelist and short-story writer. His best-known novels are set in the imaginary small Indian town of Malgudi, and portray its inhabitants in an affectionate yet ironic manner; they include *Swami and Friends* (1935), *The Man-Eater of Malgudi* (1961), and *The Painter of Signs* (1977). His short stories include *Under the Banyan Tree and Other Stories* (1985).

Nash[1] /næʃ/, John (1752–1835), English town planner and architect. Under the patronage of the Prince Regent (later George IV), he planned the layout of Regent's Park (1811–25), Regent Street (1826–c.1835; subsequently rebuilt), Trafalgar Square (1826–c.1835), and many other parts of London. He also began the reconstruction of Buckingham Palace (c.1821–30), for which he designed the Marble Arch, again for George IV.

Nash[2] /næʃ/, (Frederic) Ogden (1902–71), American poet. He is noted for his sophisticated light verse, comprising puns, epigrams, highly asymmetrical lines, and other verbal eccentricities. His verse appeared in many collections from 1931 onwards.

Nash[3] /næʃ/, Paul (1889–1946), English painter and designer. He won renown for his paintings as an official war artist in the First World War; these recorded scenes of devastation in a modernist style. From 1928 the influence of surrealism resulted in a number of enigmatic pictures based on dreams or suggestive landscape motifs, as in *Equivalents for the Megaliths* (1935). A war artist again in the Second World War, he depicted the Battle of Britain, notably in *Totes Meer* (1940–1).

Nash[4] /næʃ/, Richard (known as Beau Nash) (1674–1762), Welsh dandy. Master of Ceremonies in Bath from 1704, he established the city as the centre of fashionable society and was an arbiter of fashion and etiquette in the early Georgian age.

Nashe /næʃ/, Thomas (1567–1601), English pamphleteer, prose writer, and dramatist. After writing several anti-Puritan pamphlets, he wrote his best-known work *The Unfortunate Traveller* (1594), a medley of picaresque narrative and pseudo-historical fantasy.

Nasmyth /ˈneɪsmɪθ/, James (1808–90), British engineer. He designed and built a number of steam-driven machines, and went on

to manufacture railway locomotives. He is best known, however, for his invention of the steam hammer (1839), a major innovation for the forging industry. Nasmyth also became interested in astronomy, particularly the moon, producing a map of it in 1851 and a book twenty-three years later.

Nasser /ˈnɑːsə(r), ˈnæs-/, Gamal Abdel (1918–70), Egyptian colonel and statesman, Prime Minister 1954–6 and President 1956–70. He was the leader of a successful military coup to depose King Farouk in 1952, after which a republic was declared with Muhammad Neguib (1901–84) as its President. Nasser deposed Neguib in 1954, declaring himself Prime Minister; two years later he announced a new one-party constitution, becoming President shortly afterwards. His nationalization of the Suez Canal brought armed conflict with Britain, France, and Israel in 1956; he also led Egypt in two unsuccessful wars against Israel (1956 and 1967). With considerable Soviet aid he launched a programme of domestic modernization, including the building of the High Dam at Aswan.

Navratilova /ˌnævrætɪˈlʌvə/, Martina (born 1956), Czech-born American tennis player. Her major successes include nine Wimbledon singles titles (1978–9; 1982–7; 1990), and eight successive grand slam doubles titles.

Nebuchadnezzar /ˌnebjʊkədˈnezə(r)/ (c.630–562 BC), king of Babylon 605–562 BC. He rebuilt the city with massive fortification walls, a huge temple, and a ziggurat, and extended his rule over ancient Palestine and neighbouring countries. In 586 BC he captured and destroyed Jerusalem and deported many Israelites from Palestine to Babylon (the Babylonian Captivity, which lasted until 539 BC).

Necker /ˈnekə(r)/, Jacques (1732–1804), Swiss-born banker. He began work as a bank clerk in Switzerland, moving to his firm's headquarters in Paris in 1750. He rose to hold the office of director-general of French finances on two occasions. During Necker's first term (1777–81), his social and administrative reform programmes aroused the hostility of the court and led to his forced resignation. While in office for a second time (1788–9), he recommended summoning the States General, resulting in his dismissal on 11 July 1789. News of this angered the people and was

one of the factors which resulted in the storming of the Bastille three days later.

Needham /ˈniːdəm/, Joseph (1900–95), English scientist and historian. He studied biochemistry and published an influential *History of Embryology* (1934), but had a diverse range of interests, especially that of scientific achievement in China. He is best known for his seven-volume *Science and Civilization in China* (1954). In 1924 he was appointed fellow of Gonville and Caius College, Cambridge, and was Master there 1966–76.

Nefertiti /ˌnefəˈtiːtɪ/ (also **Nofretete** /ˌnɒfrə-/) (fl. 14th century BC), Egyptian queen, wife of Akhenaten. She initially supported her husband's religious reforms, although it is a matter of dispute whether she persisted in her support or withdrew it in favour of the new religion promoted by her half-brother Tutankhamen. Nefertiti is frequently represented beside Akhenaten, with their six daughters, on reliefs from Tell el-Amarna; however, she is best known from the painted limestone bust of her, now in Berlin (c.1350).

Nehemiah /nɪəˈmaɪə/ a Hebrew leader (5th century BC) who supervised the rebuilding of the walls of Jerusalem (c.444) and introduced moral and religious reforms (c.432). His work was continued by Ezra.

Nehru /ˈneəruː/, Jawaharlal (known as Pandit Nehru) (1889–1964), Indian statesman, Prime Minister 1947–64. An early associate of Mahatma Gandhi, Nehru was elected leader of the Indian National Congress, succeeding his father Pandit Motilal Nehru (1861–1931), in 1929. Imprisoned nine times by the British for his nationalist campaigns during the 1930s and 1940s, he eventually played a major part in the negotiations preceding independence. Nehru subsequently became the first Prime Minister of independent India. He was the father of Indira Gandhi.

Neill[1] /niːl/, A(lexander) S(utherland) (1883–1973), Scottish teacher and educationist. He is best known as the founder of the progressive school Summerhill, established in Dorset in 1924 and based in Suffolk from 1927. Since its inception, the school has attracted both admiration and hostility for its anti-authoritarian ethos.

Neill[2] /niːl/, Sam (born Nigel John Dermot) (born 1947), New Zealand actor. After working for the New Zealand National Film Unit for six years as a writer and director, he

made his feature-film début in *Sleeping Dogs* (1977), going on to star in *The Final Conflict* (1981) and the British TV series *Reilly: The Ace of Spies* (1983). He achieved international recognition with *Jurassic Park* and *The Piano* (both 1993).

Nelson[1] /'nels(ə)n/, Horatio, Viscount Nelson, Duke of Bronte (1758–1805), British admiral. Nelson's victories at sea during the early years of the Napoleonic Wars made him a national hero. His unorthodox independent tactics (as a commodore under Admiral Jervis) led to the defeat of a Spanish fleet off Cape St Vincent in 1797. In 1798 Nelson virtually destroyed the French fleet in the Battle of Aboukir Bay; he began his notorious affair with Lady Hamilton shortly afterwards. He proceeded to rout the Danes at Copenhagen in 1801, but is best known for his decisive victory over a combined French and Spanish fleet at the Battle of Trafalgar in 1805; Nelson was mortally wounded in the conflict.

Nelson[2] /'nels(ə)n/, Willie (born 1933), American country singer and songwriter. He built a reputation in Nashville as a prolific and successful songwriter, writing the hit 'Crazy' for Patsy Cline in 1961. An influential stylist with a spare, intense sound, he was one of the original country 'outlaws', leaving Nashville for Texas in 1971 and taking control of his recording career with a move to CBS records; albums such as *Red Headed Stranger* (1975) established him as one of the most successful country singers in the world.

Nennius /'nenɪəs/ (fl. c.800), Welsh chronicler. He is traditionally credited with the compilation or revision of the *Historia Britonum*, a collection of historical and geographical information about Britain, including one of the earliest known accounts of King Arthur.

Nepia /'niːpɪə/, George (1905–86), New Zealand Rugby Union player. While playing for the All Blacks 1929–30, he created a New Zealand record by playing thirty-eight consecutive matches for the country.

Nernst /neənst/, Hermann Walther (1864–1941), German physical chemist. He made a number of contributions to physical chemistry, chiefly in electrochemistry and thermodynamics. He is best known for his discovery of the third law of thermodynamics (also called *Nernst's heat theorem*, that it is impossible to reduce the temperature of a system to absolute zero in a finite number of operations), and devoted many years of low-temperature research to verify it. Nernst also investigated photochemistry, the diffusion of electrolytic ions, and the distribution of solutes in immiscible liquids, and devised an electric lamp. He was awarded the Nobel Prize for chemistry in 1920.

Nero /'nɪərəʊ/ (full name Nero Claudius Caesar Augustus Germanicus) (AD 37–68), Roman emperor 54–68. The adopted son and successor of Claudius, he became infamous for his cruelty following his ordering of the murder of his mother Agrippina in 59. His reign was marked by wanton executions of leading Romans and witnessed a fire which destroyed half of Rome in 64. A wave of uprisings in 68 led to his flight from Rome and his eventual suicide.

Neruda /nəˈruːdə/, Pablo (born Ricardo Eliezer Neftalí Reyes) (1904–73), Chilean poet and diplomat. He adopted the name Neruda as his pseudonym in 1920 after the Czech poet Jan Neruda (1834–91), later changing his name by deed poll (1946). From 1927 to 1952 he spent much of his life abroad, either serving in diplomatic posts or as a result of his membership of the Chilean Communist party, which was outlawed in 1948. His major work, *Canto General* (completed 1950), was originally conceived as an epic on Chile and was later expanded to cover the history of all the Americas from their ancient civilizations to their modern wars of liberation. He was awarded the Nobel Prize for literature in 1971.

Nerva /'nɜːvə/, Marcus Cocceius (AD c.30–98), Roman emperor 96–8. Appointed emperor by the Senate after the murder of the autocratic Domitian, he returned to a liberal and constitutional form of rule.

Nervi /'neəvɪ/, Pier Luigi (1891–1979), Italian engineer and architect. He is noted as a pioneer of new technology and materials, especially reinforced concrete. Nervi co-designed the UNESCO building in Paris (1953), as well as designing the Pirelli skyscraper in Milan (1958) and San Francisco cathedral (1970).

Nesbit /'nezbɪt/, E(dith) (1858–1924), English novelist. She is best known for her children's books, including *The Story of the Treasure Seekers* (1899), *Five Children and It* (1902), and *The Railway Children* (1906). Nes-

bit was also a founder member of the Fabian Society.

Netanyahu /ˌnet(ə)nˈjɑːhuː/, Benjamin (born 1949), Israeli Likud statesman, Prime Minister since 1996. Leader of the right-wing Likud coalition since 1993, he narrowly defeated Shimon Peres in the elections of 1996.

Neumann /ˈnɔɪmən/, John von (1903–57), Hungarian-born American mathematician and computer pioneer. His contributions ranged from pure logic and set theory to the most practical areas of application. He analysed the mathematics of quantum mechanics, founding a new area of mathematical research (algebras of operators in Hilbert space), and also established the branch of mathematics known as game theory, which has become influential in economics, business, and many other fields. Neumann also helped to develop the US hydrogen bomb, but perhaps his most influential contribution was in the design and operation of electronic computers.

Neville /ˈnevɪl/, Richard, see WARWICK.

Nevsky see ALEXANDER NEVSKY.

Newby /ˈnjuːbɪ/, (George) Eric (born 1919), English travel writer. In 1956 he made the first of a number of expeditions in Central Asia, describing his experiences in *A Short Walk in the Hindu Kush* (1958) and *Slowly Down the Ganges* (1966). His later books include *A Traveller's Life* (1982) and *A Small Place in Italy* (1994). He was travel editor of the *Observer* from 1964 to 1973.

Newcastle /ˈnjuːˌkɑːs(ə)l/, 1st Duke of (title of Thomas Pelham-Holles) (1693–1768), British Whig statesman, Prime Minister 1754–6 and 1757–62. Newcastle succeeded his brother Henry Pelham as Prime Minister on the latter's death in 1754. During his second term in office, he headed a coalition with William Pitt the Elder, until Pitt's resignation in 1761.

Newcomen /ˈnjuːˌkʌmən/, Thomas (1663–1729), English engineer, developer of the first practical steam engine. He designed a beam engine to operate a pump for the removal of water from mines; the first such steam engine was erected in Worcestershire in 1712. To avoid infringing a patent held by Thomas Savery for his pumping engine, Newcomen went into partnership with him. Newcomen's engine was later greatly improved by James Watt.

Ne Win /neɪ ˈwɪn/ (born 1911), Burmese general and socialist statesman, Prime Minister 1958–60, head of state 1962–74, and President 1974–81. An active nationalist in the 1930s, Ne Win was appointed Chief of Staff in Aung San's Burma National Army in 1943. He led a military coup in 1962, after which he established a military dictatorship and formed a one-party state, governed by the Burma Socialist Programme Party (BSPP). He stepped down from the presidency in 1981 and retired as leader of the BSPP after riots in Rangoon in 1988.

Newlands /ˈnjuːləndz/, John Alexander Reina (1837–98), English industrial chemist. He proposed a periodic table shortly before Dmitri Mendeleev, based on his *law of octaves*. Newlands observed that if elements were arranged in order of atomic weight, similar chemical properties appeared in every eighth element, a pattern he likened to the musical scale. The significance of his idea was not understood until Mendeleev's periodic table had been accepted. Newlands claimed priority, but his rigid scheme had a number of inadequacies.

Newman[1] /ˈnjuːmən/, Barnett (1905–70), American painter. A seminal figure in colour-field painting from the late 1940s, he is noted for his vast canvases, which achieve dramatic effects from their juxtaposition of large blocks of uniform colour with narrow marginal strips of contrasting colours. His paintings include *Who's Afraid of Red, Yellow, and Blue III* (1966–7).

Newman[2] /ˈnjuːmən/, John Henry (1801–90), English prelate and theologian. In 1833, while vicar of St Mary's Church in Oxford, he founded the Oxford Movement together with John Keble and Edward Pusey. The Oxford Movement aimed to restore traditional Catholic teaching within the Church of England. Newman was a leading influence within the Movement and wrote twenty-four of its series of pamphlets *Tracts for the Times*. However, his Tract 90 (1841) on the compatibility of the Church of England's Thirty-nine Articles with Roman Catholic theology aroused much hostility and he withdrew from the Movement. In 1845 he was received into the Roman Catholic Church, becoming a cardinal in 1879. His works include *Apologia pro Vita Sua* (1864) and the poem *The Dream of Gerontius* (1865), describing the soul's journey to God.

Newman[3] /'nju:mən/, Paul (born 1925), American actor and film director. Among his many films are *Butch Cassidy and the Sundance Kid* (1969), *The Sting* (1973), and *The Color of Money* (1987), for which he won an Oscar. He has also directed several films, including *Rachel, Rachel* (1968) and *The Glass Menagerie* (1987).

Newton /'nju:t(ə)n/, Sir Isaac (1642–1727), English mathematician and physicist. He was the greatest single influence on theoretical physics until Einstein. His most productive period was in 1665–7, when he retreated temporarily from Cambridge to his isolated home in Lincolnshire during the Great Plague. He discovered the binomial theorem, and made several other contributions to mathematics, notably differential calculus and its relationship with integration. A bitter quarrel with Leibniz ensued as to which of them had discovered calculus first. In his major treatise, *Principia Mathematica* (1687), Newton gave a mathematical description of the laws of mechanics and gravitation, and applied these to planetary and lunar motion. For most purposes Newtonian mechanics has survived even the introduction of relativity theory and quantum mechanics, to both of which it stands as a good approximation. Another influential work was *Opticks* (1704), which gave an account of Newton's optical experiments and theories, including the discovery that white light is made up of a mixture of colours. In 1699 Newton was appointed Master of the Mint; he entered Parliament as MP for Cambridge University in 1701, and in 1703 was elected president of the Royal Society.

Ney /neɪ/, Michel (1768–1815), French marshal. He was one of Napoleon's leading generals, and after the Battle of Borodino (1812) became known as 'the bravest of the brave'. He commanded the French cavalry at Waterloo (1815), but after Napoleon's defeat and final overthrow he was executed by the Bourbons despite attempts by Wellington and other allied leaders to intervene on his behalf.

Ngata /'nɑːtə/, Sir Apirana Turupa (1874–1950), New Zealand Maori leader and politician. As Minister for Native Affairs he devoted much time to Maori resettlement. Believing firmly in the continuing individuality of the Maori people, he sought to preserve the characteristic elements of their life and culture, including tribal customs and folklore, and emphasized pride in Maori traditions and history.

Nicholas /'nɪkələs/ the name of two tsars of Russia:

Nicholas I (1796–1855), brother of Alexander I, reigned 1825–55. He pursued rigidly conservative policies, maintaining serfdom and building up a large secret police force to suppress radical reformers. He was largely concerned with keeping the peace in Europe, but his expansionist policies in the Near East led to the Crimean War, during which he died.

Nicholas II (1868–1918), son of Alexander III, reigned 1894–1917. He proved incapable of coping with the dangerous political legacy left by his father and was criticized for allowing his wife Alexandra (and her favourites such as Rasputin) too much influence. Previously resistant to reform, after the disastrous war with Japan (1904–5) the tsar pursued a less reactionary line, but the programme of reforms which was introduced was not sufficient to prevent the disintegration of the tsarist regime under the strain of fresh military disasters during the First World War. Nicholas was forced to abdicate after the Russian Revolution in 1917 and was shot along with his family a year later.

Nicholas, St (4th century), Christian prelate. Little is known of his life, but he is said to have been bishop of Myra in Lycia; his supposed remains were taken to Bari in SE Italy in 1087. He became the subject of many legends and is patron saint of children, sailors, and the countries of Greece and Russia. In late medieval Europe he became identified with Father Christmas; the cult of Santa Claus (a corruption of his name) arose in North America in the 17th century from the Dutch custom of giving gifts to children on his feast day (6 December), a practice now usually transferred to Christmas.

Nicholson[1] /'nɪk(ə)ls(ə)n/, Ben (1894–1982), English painter. A pioneer of British abstract art, he met Piet Mondrian in 1933 and from that time produced painted reliefs with circular and rectangular motifs. These became his main output, together with purely geometrical paintings and still lifes.

Nicholson[2] /'nɪk(ə)ls(ə)n/, Jack (born 1937), American actor. He made his film début in 1958, but it was not until he appeared in *Easy Rider* (1969) that he gained wide recog-

nition. He went on to act in such diverse films as *Five Easy Pieces* (1970), *The Shining* (1980), and *A Few Good Men* (1992), and won Oscars for *One Flew Over the Cuckoo's Nest* (1975) and *Terms of Endearment* (1983).

Nicklaus /'nɪklaʊs, -ləs/, Jack (William) (born 1940), American golfer. Since the start of his professional career in 1962, he has won more than eighty tournaments: major titles include six wins in the PGA championship, four in the US Open, and three in the British Open.

Nielsen /'niːls(ə)n/, Carl August (1865–1931), Danish composer. A major figure in the development of modern Scandinavian music, he gained his first success in 1888 with his *Little Suite* for string orchestra. His six symphonies (1890–1925) form the core of his achievement; other major works include the opera *Maskerade* (1906), concertos, and the organ work *Commotio* (1931).

Niemeyer /'niː,maɪə(r)/, Oscar (born 1907), Brazilian architect. He was an early exponent of modernist architecture in Latin America and was influenced by Le Corbusier, with whom he worked as part of the group which designed the Ministry of Education in Rio de Janeiro (1937–43). His most significant individual achievement was the design of the main public buildings of Brasília (1950–60) within the master plan drawn up by Lúcio Costa.

Niemöller /'niː,mɜːlə(r)/, Martin (1892–1984), German Lutheran pastor. He was ordained in 1924 after serving as a U-boat commander in the First World War. During the 1930s he was an outspoken opponent of Nazism and organized resistance to Hitler's attempts to control the German Church. Despite a prohibition he continued to preach and was eventually imprisoned in Sachsenhausen and Dachau concentration camps (1937–45). In the postwar period he became known as an advocate of a united neutral Germany and nuclear disarmament.

Nietzsche /'niːtʃə/, Friedrich Wilhelm (1844–1900), German philosopher. His main period of creativity began in 1872 with the publication of his first book *The Birth of Tragedy* and lasted until 1889, when his mental instability developed into permanent insanity; other major works include *Thus Spake Zarathustra* (1883–5) and *Beyond Good and Evil* (1886). His work is open to different interpretations, but his influence can be seen in existentialism and in the work of such varied figures as Michel Foucault, Martin Heidegger, and George Bernard Shaw. The principal features of his writings are contempt for Christianity, with its compassion for the weak, and exaltation of the 'will to power' and of the *Übermensch* (superman), superior to ordinary morality, who will replace the Christian ideal. He divided humankind into a small, dominant 'master-class' and a large, dominated 'herd' – a thesis which was taken up in a debased form by the Nazis after Nietzsche's death.

Nightingale /'naɪtɪŋ,geɪl/, Florence (1820–1910), English nurse and medical reformer. She became famous during the Crimean War for her attempts to publicize the state of the army's medical arrangements and improve the standard of care. In 1854 she took a party of nurses to the army hospital at Scutari, where she improved sanitation and medical procedures, thereby achieving a dramatic reduction in the mortality rate; she became known as 'the Lady of the Lamp' for her nightly rounds. She returned to England in 1856 and devoted the rest of her life to attempts to improve public health and hospital care.

Nijinsky /nɪ'dʒɪnskɪ/, Vaslav (Fomich) (1890–1950), Russian ballet-dancer and choreographer. From 1909 he was the leading dancer with Diaghilev's Ballets Russes, giving celebrated performances in the classics and Fokine's ballets, including *Le Spectre de la rose* (1911). He was encouraged by Diaghilev to take up choreography, resulting in productions of Debussy's *L'Après-midi d'un faune* (1912) and *Jeux* (1913) and Stravinsky's *The Rite of Spring* (1913). These ballets foreshadowed many developments of later avant-garde choreography. Nijinsky's career declined when he stopped working with Diaghilev and was brought to a premature end by schizophrenia.

Nilsson /'nɪls(ə)n/, (Märta) Birgit (born 1918), Swedish operatic soprano. She made her Swedish début in 1946, gaining international success in the 1950s. She was particularly noted for her interpretation of Wagnerian roles, and sang at the Bayreuth Festivals between 1953 and 1970. Her repertoire also included the operas of Richard Strauss and Verdi.

Nin /nɪn/, Anaïs (1903–77), American writer. Born in Paris, she lived in the US between 1914 and 1920, after which she returned to Europe and studied psychoanalysis. She started writing in 1932, publishing her first novel *House of Incest* in 1936. She returned to the US in 1940 and produced collections of short stories, essays, novels, and erotica. She is perhaps best known for her ceaselessly introspective *Diaries* (1966–81).

Ninian, St /'nɪnɪən/ (c.360–c.432), Scottish bishop and missionary. According to Bede he founded a church at Whithorn in SW Scotland (c.400) and from there evangelized the southern Picts.

Niro, Robert De, see DE NIRO.

Nixon /'nɪks(ə)n/, Richard (Milhous) (1913–94), American Republican statesman, 37th President of the US 1969–74. He served as Vice-President under Eisenhower (1953–61), narrowly losing to John F. Kennedy in the 1960 presidential election. In his first term of office he sought to resolve the Vietnam War; the negotiations were brought to a successful conclusion by his Secretary of State, Henry Kissinger, in 1973. Nixon also restored Sino-American diplomatic relations by his visit to China in 1972. He was elected for a second term in November of that year, but it soon became clear that he was implicated in the Watergate scandal, and in 1974 he became the first President to resign from office, taking this action shortly before impeachment proceedings began.

Nkomo /əŋ'kəʊməʊ/, Joshua (Mqabuko Nyongolo) (born 1917), Zimbabwean statesman. In 1961 he became the leader of ZAPU; in 1976 he formed the Patriotic Front with Robert Mugabe, leader of ZANU, and was appointed to a Cabinet post in Mugabe's government of 1980. Dismissed from his post in 1982, he returned to the Cabinet in 1988, when ZANU and ZAPU agreed to merge, and became Vice-President in 1990.

Nkrumah /əŋ'kruːmə/, Kwame (1909–72), Ghanaian statesman, Prime Minister 1957–60, President 1960–6. The leader of the non-violent struggle for the Gold Coast's independence, he became first Prime Minister of the country when it gained independence as Ghana in 1957. He declared Ghana a republic in 1960 and proclaimed himself President for life in 1964, banning all opposition parties; Nkrumah's dictatorial methods seriously damaged Ghana's economy and eventually led to his overthrow in a military coup.

Nobel /nəʊ'bel/, Alfred Bernhard (1833–96), Swedish chemist and engineer. He was interested in the use of high explosives, and after accidents with nitroglycerine he invented the much safer dynamite (1866), followed by other new explosives. He took out a large number of patents in a variety of disciplines, making a large fortune which enabled him to endow the prizes that bear his name (from 1901 onwards).

Noether /'nɜːtə(r)/, Emmy (1882–1935), German mathematician. She simplified and extended the work of her predecessors, particularly Hilbert and Dedekind, on the properties of rings. She lacked status in what was then a man's world, and her position at Göttingen remained insecure and unsalaried until terminated by the anti-Semitic laws of 1933. Nevertheless, she exercised an enormous influence, and inaugurated the modern period in algebraic geometry and abstract algebra.

Nofretete see NEFERTITI.

Nolan /'nəʊlən/, Sir Sidney Robert (1917–93), Australian painter. He is chiefly known for his paintings of famous characters and events from Australian history, especially his 'Ned Kelly' series (begun in 1946). He has also painted landscapes and themes from classical mythology, such as his 'Leda and the Swan' series of 1960.

Noriega /ˌnɒrɪ'eɪgə/, Manuel (Antonio Morena) (born 1940), Panamanian statesman and general, head of state 1983–9. He was Panama's head of intelligence (1970), becoming Chief of Staff and de facto head of state in 1983. He was charged with drug trafficking by a US grand jury in 1988; US support for his regime was withdrawn, relations worsened, and a year later President George Bush sent US troops into the country to arrest Noriega. He eventually surrendered and was brought to trial and convicted in 1992.

Norman[1] /'nɔːmən/, Gregory John ('Greg') (born 1955), Australian golfer. He turned professional in 1976 and subsequently won the world match-play championship three

times (1980; 1983; 1986) and the British Open twice (1986; 1993).

Norman[2] /'nɔːmən/, Jessye (born 1945), American operatic soprano. She made her début in Berlin (1969) and subsequently performed in the major European opera houses, appearing in New York for the first time in 1973. Her repertoire includes both opera and concert music and she has given notable interpretations of the works of Wagner, Schubert, and Mahler.

North /nɔːθ/, Frederick, Lord (1732–92), British Tory statesman, Prime Minister 1770–82. He sought to prevent the War of American Independence, but was regarded as responsible for the loss of the American colonies. This, together with allegations that his ministry was dominated by the influence of George III, led to his resignation in 1782.

Northcliffe /'nɔːθklɪf/, 1st Viscount (title of Alfred Charles William Harmsworth) (1865–1922), British newspaper proprietor. With his younger brother Harold (later Lord Rothermere, 1868–1940), Northcliffe built up a large newspaper empire in the years preceding the First World War, including *The Times*, the *Daily Mail*, and the *Daily Mirror*. During the war he used his press empire to exercise a strong influence over British war policy; despite his criticism of Lloyd George and Lord Kitchener, he worked for the British government in charge of propaganda in enemy countries from 1917 to 1918.

Nostradamus /ˌnɒstrə'dɑːməs, -'deɪməs/ (Latinized name of Michel de Nostredame) (1503–66), French astrologer and physician. His predictions, in the form of rhymed quatrains, appeared in two collections (1555; 1558). Cryptic and apocalyptic in tone, they were given extensive credence at the French court, where Nostradamus was for a time personal physician to Charles IX. Their interpretation has continued to be the subject of controversy into the 20th century.

Novello /nə'veləʊ/, Ivor (born David Ivor Davies) (1893–1951), Welsh composer, actor, and dramatist. In 1914 he wrote 'Keep the Home Fires Burning', which became one of the most popular songs of the First World War. Later he composed and acted in a series of musicals, including

Glamorous Night (1935), *The Dancing Years* (1939), and *King's Rhapsody* (1949).

Noverre /nɒ'veə(r)/, Jean-Georges (1727–1810), French choreographer and dance theorist. A great reformer, he stressed the importance of dramatic motivation in ballet and was critical of the overemphasis hitherto placed on technical virtuosity. His work, especially as set out in *Lettres sur la danse et sur les ballets* (1760), had a significant influence on the development of ballet.

Novotný /'nɒvɒtniː/, Antonín (1904–75), Czechoslovak Communist statesman, President 1957–68. In 1921 he became a founder member of the Czechoslovak Communist Party, rising to prominence when he played a major part in the Communist seizure of power in 1948. He was appointed First Secretary of the Czechoslovak Communist Party in 1953, and became President four years later. A committed Stalinist whose policies caused much resentment, he was ousted by the reform movement in 1968.

Nuffield /'nʌfiːld/, 1st Viscount (title of William Richard Morris) (1877–1963), British motor manufacturer and philanthropist. Working in Oxford, he started by building bicycles. In 1912 he opened the first Morris automobile factory there and launched his first car the following year. Morris Motors Limited was formed in 1926, the year of the first MG (Morris Garage) models. In later life he devoted his considerable fortune to philanthropic purposes; these include the endowment of Nuffield College, Oxford (1937), and the creation of the Nuffield Foundation (1943) for medical, social, and scientific research.

Nureyev /nə'reɪef, 'njʊərɪˌef/, Rudolf (1939–93), Russian-born ballet-dancer and choreographer. He defected to the West in 1961, joining the Royal Ballet in London the following year; it was there he began his noted partnership with Margot Fonteyn. Thereafter he danced the leading roles of the classical and standard modern repertory and choreographed many others, including *La Bayadère* (1963). He became a naturalized Austrian citizen in 1982, and was artistic director of the Paris Opéra Ballet 1983–9.

Nyerere /nje'reərɪ/, Julius Kambarage (born 1922), Tanzanian statesman, President of Tanganyika 1962–4 and of Tanzania

1964–85. He was an active campaigner for the nationalist movement in the 1950s, forming the Tanganyika African National Union (1954). He served as Prime Minister of Tanganyika following its independence in 1961 and became President a year later. In 1964 he successfully negotiated a union with Zanzibar and remained President of the new state of Tanzania until his retirement.

Nyman /ˈnaɪmən/, Michael (born 1944), English composer. His collaborations with the film director Peter Greenaway established him as a leading film composer and he went on to write the scores for films such as Jane Campion's *The Piano* (1993). His works, such as *I'll Stake My Cremona to a Jew's Trump* (1983), have a distinctive minimalist style that synthesizes strands from many periods.

O

Oakley /'əʊklɪ/, Annie (full name Phoebe Anne Oakley Mozee) (1860–1926), American markswoman. In 1885 she joined Buffalo Bill's Wild West Show, of which she became a star attraction for the next seventeen years, often working with her husband, the marksman Frank E. Butler. The musical *Annie Get Your Gun* (1946), with music by Irving Berlin, was based on her life.

Oates /əʊts/, Titus (1649–1705), English clergyman and conspirator. He is remembered as the fabricator of the Popish Plot, a fictitious Jesuit plot which supposedly involved a plan to kill Charles II, massacre Protestants, and put the Catholic Duke of York on the English throne. Convicted of perjury in 1685, Oates was imprisoned in the same year, but was subsequently released and granted a pension.

Obote /ə'bəʊtɪ/, (Apollo) Milton (born 1924), Ugandan statesman, Prime Minister 1962–6, President 1966–71 and 1980–5. After founding the Uganda People's Congress in 1960, he became the first Prime Minister of independent Uganda. Overthrown by Idi Amin in 1971, he returned from exile nine years later and was re-elected President. Obote established a multi-party democracy, but was removed in a second military coup in 1985.

O'Brien[1] /əʊ'braɪən/, Edna (born 1932), Irish novelist and short-story writer. Her novels include the trilogy *The Country Girls* (1960), *The Lonely Girl* (1962), and *Girls in Their Married Bliss* (1964), which follows the fortunes of two Irish girls from their rural, convent-educated early years to new lives in Dublin and later in London. Among her collections of short stories is *Lantern Slides* (1990).

O'Brien[2] /əʊ'braɪən/, Flann (pseudonym of Brian O'Nolan) (1911–66), Irish novelist and journalist. He gained recognition as a novelist with his first book *At Swim-Two-Birds* (1939), an exploration of Irish life combining naturalism and farce which employed an experimental narrative structure much influenced by James Joyce. Writing under the name of Myles na Gopaleen, O'Brien

contributed a satirical column to the *Irish Times* for nearly twenty years.

O'Casey /əʊ'keɪsɪ/, Sean (1880–1964), Irish dramatist. Encouraged by W. B. Yeats, he wrote a number of plays, including *The Shadow of a Gunman* (1923) and *Juno and the Paycock* (1924), which were successfully staged at the Abbey Theatre, Dublin. They deal with the lives of the Irish poor before and during the civil war that followed the establishment of the Irish Free State.

Occam, William of see WILLIAM OF OCCAM.

Ockham, William of see WILLIAM OF OCCAM.

O'Connell /əʊ'kɒn(ə)l/, Daniel (known as 'the Liberator') (1775–1847), Irish nationalist leader and social reformer. His election to Parliament in 1828 forced the British government to grant Catholic Emancipation in order to enable him to take his seat in the House of Commons, for which Roman Catholics were previously ineligible. In 1839 he established the Repeal Association to abolish the union with Britain; O'Connell was arrested and briefly imprisoned for sedition in 1844.

O'Connor /əʊ'kɒnə(r)/, (Mary) Flannery (1925–64), American novelist and short-story writer. She drew on her deeply Catholic upbringing in her two Gothic novels, *Wise Blood* (1952) and *The Violent Bear It Away* (1960). She also won acclaim for short stories notable for their dark humour and grotesque characters; they are published in collections such as *A Good Man Is Hard to Find, and Other Stories* (1955).

Octavian /ɒk'teɪvɪən/ see AUGUSTUS.

Odets /əʊ'dets/, Clifford (1906–63), American dramatist. He was a founder member in 1931 of the avant-garde Group Theatre, which followed the naturalistic methods of the Moscow Art Theatre and staged his best-known play, *Waiting for Lefty* (1935). His plays of the 1930s (especially *The Golden Boy*, 1937) reflect the experiences of the Depression, often displaying a strong sense of social issues.

Oersted /'ɜːsted/, Hans Christian (1777–1851), Danish physicist, discoverer of the magnetic effect of an electric current. He had postulated the existence of electromagnetism earlier, but it was not demonstrated until 1820, when he carried out an experiment during a lecture and noticed the deflection of a compass needle placed below a wire carrying a current. He also worked on the compressibility of gases and liquids, and on diamagnetism.

Offa /'ɒfə/ (died 796), king of Mercia 757–96. After seizing power in Mercia in 757, he expanded his territory to become overlord of most of England south of the Humber. Offa is chiefly remembered for constructing the frontier earthworks called Offa's Dyke.

Offenbach /'ɒf(ə)n,bɑːx/, Jacques (born Jacob Offenbach) (1819–80), German composer, resident in France from 1833. Offenbach is associated with the rise of the operetta, whose style was typified by his *Orpheus in the Underworld* (1858). He is also noted for his opera *The Tales of Hoffmann* (1881), based on the stories of E. T. A. Hoffmann and first produced after Offenbach's death.

O'Higgins /əʊ'hɪgɪnz/, Bernardo (c.1778–1842), Chilean revolutionary leader and statesman, head of state 1817–23. The son of a Spanish officer of Irish origin, he was educated in England, where he first became involved in nationalist politics. On his return to Chile he led the independence movement and, with the help of José de San Martín, liberator of Argentina, led the army which triumphed over Spanish forces in 1817, paving the way for Chilean independence the following year. For the next six years he was head of state (supreme director) of Chile, but then fell from power and lived in exile in Peru for the remainder of his life.

Ohm /əʊm/, Georg Simon (1789–1854), German physicist. He published two major papers in 1826, which between them contained the law that is named after him. This states that the electric current flowing in a conductor is directly proportional to the potential difference (voltage), and inversely proportional to the resistance. Applying this to a wire of known diameter and conductivity, the current is inversely proportional to length. The units *ohm* and *mho* are also named after him.

O'Keeffe /əʊ'kiːf/, Georgia (1887–1986), American painter. She was a pioneer of modernism in America and her early work is largely abstract. In 1916 her work was exhibited by the photographer Alfred Stieglitz, whose circle in New York she then joined; she married him in 1924. In the 1920s she adopted a more figurative style, producing her best-known paintings; they depict enlarged studies, particularly of flowers, and are often regarded as being sexually symbolic (for example *Black Iris*, 1926). She also painted notable landscapes of New Mexico, where she settled after her husband's death in 1946.

Olaf /'əʊlæf/ the name of five kings of Norway:
  Olaf I Tryggvason (969–1000), reigned 995–1000. According to legend he was brought up in Russia, being converted to Christianity and carrying out extensive Viking raids before returning to Norway to be accepted as king. He jumped overboard and was lost after his fleet was defeated by the combined forces of Denmark and Sweden at the battle of Svöld, but his exploits as a warrior and his popularity as sovereign made him a national legend.
  Olaf II Haraldsson (canonized as St Olaf) (c.995–1030), reigned 1016–30. Notable for his attempts to spread Christianity in his kingdom, Olaf was forced into exile by a rebellion in 1028 and killed in battle at Stiklestad while attempting to return. He is the patron saint of Norway. Feast day, 29 July.
  Olaf III Haraldsson (died 1093), reigned 1066–93.
  Olaf IV Haakonson (1370–87), reigned 1380–7.
  Olaf V (full name Olaf Alexander Edmund Christian Frederik) (1903–91), reigned 1957–91.

Oldfield /'əʊldfiːld/, Bruce (born 1950), English fashion designer. In 1973 he became a freelance fashion designer, working for the New York department store Bendel's and sketching for Yves St Laurent. He displayed his first collection in London in 1975 and gained an international reputation for his ready-to-wear designs and his lavish evening dresses.

Old Hickory a nickname given to Andrew Jackson (see JACKSON¹).

Old Pretender, the James Stuart, son of James II of England and Ireland (James VII of Scotland) (see STUART²).

Olivier /ə'lɪvɪˌeɪ/, Laurence (Kerr), Baron Olivier of Brighton (1907–89), English actor and director. He made his professional début in 1924 and subsequently performed all the major Shakespearian roles; he was also director of the National Theatre 1963–73. His films include *Wuthering Heights* (1939) and *Rebecca* (1940), as well as adaptations of Shakespeare; he produced, co-directed, and starred in *Henry V* (1944) and directed and starred in *Hamlet* (1948) and *Richard III* (1955). The Olivier Theatre, part of the National Theatre, is named in his honour. He was married to Vivien Leigh from 1940 to 1961 and to Joan Plowright (born 1929) from 1961 until his death.

Omar I /'əʊmɑː(r)/ (*c.*581–644), Muslim caliph 634–44. In early life an opponent of Muhammad, Omar was converted to Islam in 617. After becoming caliph he began an extensive series of conquests, adding Syria, Palestine, and Egypt to his empire. He was assassinated by a Persian slave.

Omar Khayyám /ˌəʊmɑː kaɪ'ɑːm/ (died 1123), Persian poet, mathematician, and astronomer. He is remembered for his *rubáiyát* (quatrains), translated and adapted by Edward Fitzgerald in *The Rubáiyát of Omar Khayyám* (1859); the work contains meditations on the mysteries of existence, expressing scepticism regarding divine providence and a consequent celebration of the sensuous and fleeting pleasures of the earthly world.

Onassis[1] /əʊ'næsɪs/, Aristotle (Socrates) (1906–75), Greek shipping magnate and international businessman. The owner of a substantial shipping empire, he was also the founder of the Greek national airline, Olympic Airways (1957). In 1968 he married Jacqueline Bouvier Kennedy, the widow of John F. Kennedy.

Onassis[2] /əʊ'næsɪs/, Jacqueline Lee Bouvier Kennedy (known as 'Jackie O') (1929–94), American First Lady. She worked as a photographer before marrying John F. Kennedy in 1953. Her term as First Lady, which began in 1961, was cut short by the President's assassination in 1963. She married Aristotle Onassis in 1968 and after being widowed for a second time in 1975 pursued a career in publishing.

Ondaatje /ɒn'dɑːtjə/, (Philip) Michael (born 1943), Canadian writer, born in Sri Lanka. He emigrated to Canada in 1962, and in 1967 became a university lecturer. In his works, which include poetry, novels, and an autobiography *Running in the Family* (1982), he compels the reader to see reality as transient and uncertain by his use of unusual settings and thematic and stylistic shifts. In 1992 his novel *The English Patient* was awarded the Booker Prize.

O'Neill /əʊ'niːl/, Eugene (Gladstone) (1888–1953), American dramatist. He achieved recognition with his first full-length play, *Beyond the Horizon* (1920), which won a Pulitzer Prize. Among his many other plays are the trilogy *Mourning Becomes Electra* (1931), in which he adapted the theme of Aeschylus' *Oresteia* to portray the aftermath of the American Civil War; *The Iceman Cometh* (1946), a tragedy about a collection of bar-room derelicts; and *Long Day's Journey into Night* (performed and published posthumously in 1956), a semi-autobiographical tragedy portraying mutually destructive family relationships. He was awarded the Nobel Prize for literature in 1936.

Ono /'əʊnəʊ/, Yoko (born 1933), American musician and artist, born in Japan. She was an established avant-garde performance artist when she met John Lennon, whom she married in 1969. They collaborated on experimental recordings such as *Unfinished Music No. 1: Two Virgins* (1969) and performed together in the Plastic Ono Band; Ono also recorded her own albums, starting with *Approximately Infinite Universe* (1973). After Lennon's murder in 1980 she continued her solo career with 1981's *Season of Glass*.

Oort /ɔːt/, Jan Hendrik (1900–92), Dutch astronomer. His early measurements of the proper motion of stars enabled him to prove that the Galaxy is rotating, and to determine the position and orbital period of the sun within it. Oort was director of the observatory at Leiden for twenty-five years, during which time he was involved in the discovery of the wavelength of radio emission from interstellar hydrogen, and noted the strong polarization of light from the Crab Nebula. He also proposed the existence of a cloud of incipient comets beyond the orbit of Pluto, now named after him (the Oort cloud).

Opel /'əʊp(ə)l/, Wilhelm von (1871–1948), German motor manufacturer. In 1898 he and his brothers converted their grandfather's bicycle and sewing-machine factory to car production, launching their first original model in 1902. After the First

World War the company became the first in Germany to introduce assembly-line production and manufactured more than a million cars. Opel sold control of the company to the US manufacturer General Motors in 1929.

Opie /ˈəʊpɪ/, John (1761–1807), English painter. His work includes portraits of contemporary figures such as Mary Wollstonecraft and history paintings such as *The Murder of Rizzio* (1787).

Oppenheimer /ˈɒp(ə)n͵haɪmə(r)/, Julius Robert (1904–67), American theoretical physicist. He showed in 1928 that the positron should exist. Fourteen years later he was appointed director of the laboratory at Los Alamos which designed and built the first atom bomb. After the Second World War he opposed development of the hydrogen bomb and — like many intellectuals of the McCarthy era — was investigated for alleged un-American activities. His security clearance was withdrawn in 1953 and his advisory activities stopped; with the passing of the McCarthy era his public standing was restored.

Orange, William of William III of Great Britain and Ireland (see WILLIAM).

Orbison /ˈɔːbɪs(ə)n/, Roy (1936–88), American singer and composer. He began by writing country-music songs for other artists, establishing himself as a singer with the ballad 'Only the Lonely' (1960). Further hits followed, including 'Crying' (1961), 'Blue Bayou' (1963), and 'Oh, Pretty Woman' (1964), which was one of the best-selling singles of the 1960s.

Orcagna /ɔːˈkɑːnjə/ (born Andrea di Cione) (c.1308–68), Italian painter, sculptor, and architect. His painting represents a return to a devotional, brightly coloured style in opposition to Giotto's naturalism; his work includes frescos and an altarpiece in the church of Santa Maria Novella, Florence (1357). His only known sculpture is the tabernacle in the church of Or San Michele, Florence, notable for its reliefs depicting scenes from the life and the Assumption of the Virgin (1359).

Orczy /ˈɔːtsɪ/, Baroness Emmusca (1865–1947), Hungarian-born British novelist. Her best-known novel is *The Scarlet Pimpernel* (1905), telling of the adventures of an English nobleman smuggling aristocrats out of France during the French Revolution.

Orff /ɔːf/, Carl (1895–1982), German composer. Orff is best known for his secular cantata *Carmina Burana* (1937), based on a collection of medieval Latin poems; although originally conceived as a dramatic work, it is more often performed on the concert platform. His early career was devoted to evolving a system of musical education for children, beginners, and amateurs based on the Jaques-Dalcroze eurhythmics method of teaching. He set out his theory in *Schulwerk* (1930–3), stressing the value of simplicity and controlled improvisation in music. Among his other musical works is an operatic trilogy which includes *Antigone* (1949).

Origen /ˈɒrɪdʒən/ (c.185–c.254), Christian scholar and theologian, probably born in Alexandria. Of his numerous works the most famous was the *Hexapla*, an edition of the Old Testament with six or more parallel versions. He recognized literal, moral, and allegorical interpretations of Scripture, preferring the last. His teachings are important for their introduction of Neoplatonist elements into Christianity but were later rejected by Church orthodoxy.

Ortega /ɔːˈteɪɡə/, Daniel (full surname Ortega Saavedra) (born 1945), Nicaraguan statesman, President 1985–90. He joined the Sandinista National Liberation Front (FSLN) in 1963, becoming its leader in 1966. After a period of imprisonment he played a major role in the revolution which overthrew Anastasio Somoza in 1979. He headed a provisional socialist government from this date, later gaining the presidency after the Sandinista victory in the 1984 elections, but his regime was constantly under attack from the US-backed Contras. He lost power to an opposition coalition following elections in 1990.

Ortega y Gasset /ɔː͵teɪɡə i: ɡæˈset/, José (1883–1955), Spanish philosopher. In 1910 he was appointed to the chair of metaphysics at Madrid University. An existentialist thinker, he became one of the most influential figures in 20th-century Spanish thought, and in 1923 he founded the magazine *Revista de occidente*, which introduced northern European ideas to Spanish intellectuals. His many academic works include *The Revolt of the Masses* (1930), in which he proposed leadership by an intellectual élite.

Orton[1] /ˈɔːt(ə)n/, Arthur (known as 'the Tichborne claimant') (1834–98), English

butcher. In 1852 he emigrated to Australia, but returned to England in 1866 claiming to be the heir to the wealthy Tichborne estate; he asserted that he was the eldest son of the 10th baronet, who was presumed lost at sea, and convinced the lost heir's mother that he was her son. After a long trial he lost his claim and was tried and imprisoned for perjury.

Orton[2] /'ɔːt(ə)n/, Joe (born John Kingsley Orton) (1933–67), English dramatist. He wrote a number of unconventional black comedies, notable for their examination of corruption, sexuality, and violence; they include *Entertaining Mr Sloane* (1964), *Loot* (1965), and the posthumously performed *What the Butler Saw* (1969). Orton was murdered by his homosexual lover, who then committed suicide.

Orwell /'ɔːwel/, George (pseudonym of Eric Arthur Blair) (1903–50), British novelist and essayist. Born in Bengal, he returned to Europe in 1928. His work is characterized by his concern with social injustice; after living as a vagrant in London, he described his experiences in *Down and Out in Paris and London* (1933); he also wrote about the plight of the unemployed in *The Road to Wigan Pier* (1937), and fought for the Republicans in the Spanish Civil War. His most famous works are *Animal Farm* (1945), a satire on Communism as it developed under Stalin, and *Nineteen Eighty-Four* (1949), a dystopian account of a future state in which every aspect of life is controlled by Big Brother.

Osborne /'ɒzbɔːn/, John (James) (1929–94), English dramatist. His first play, *Look Back in Anger* (1956), ushered in a new era of kitchen-sink drama; its hero Jimmy Porter was seen as the archetype of contemporary disillusioned youth, the so-called 'angry young man'. Later plays include *The Entertainer* (1957), *A Patriot for Me* (1965), and *Déjà vu* (1991).

Osler /'əʊzlə(r), 'əʊslə(r)/, Sir William (1849–1919), Canadian-born physician and classical scholar. He was professor of medicine at four universities, and his *Principles and Practice of Medicine* (1892) became the chosen clinical textbook for medical students. At Johns Hopkins University, Baltimore, he instituted a model teaching unit in which clinical observation was combined with laboratory research.

Osman I /'ɒzmən/ (also **Othman** /'ɒθmən/) (1259–1326), Turkish conqueror, founder of the Ottoman (Osmanli) dynasty and empire. After succeeding his father as leader of the Seljuk Turks in 1288, Osman reigned as sultan, conquering NW Asia Minor. He assumed the title of emir in 1299.

Ostade /ɒ'staːdə/, Adriaen van (1610–85), Dutch painter and engraver. He is thought to have been a pupil of Frans Hals, and his work chiefly depicts lively genre scenes of peasants carousing or brawling in crowded taverns or barns. His brother and pupil, Isack (1621–49), was also a painter, particularly of winter landscapes and genre scenes of peasants outside cottages or taverns.

Ostwald /'ɒstvælt/, Friedrich Wilhelm (1853–1932), German physical chemist. He did much to establish physical chemistry as a separate discipline, and is particularly remembered for his pioneering work on catalysis. He also worked on chemical affinities, the hydrolysis of esters, and electrolytic conductivity and dissociation. After retiring Ostwald studied colour science, and developed a new quantitative colour theory. He was awarded the Nobel Prize for chemistry in 1909.

Oswald /'ɒzwəld/, Lee Harvey (1939–63), American alleged assassin of John F. Kennedy. In November 1963 he was arrested in Dallas, Texas, shortly after the assassination of President Kennedy and charged with his murder. He denied the charge, but was murdered by Jack Ruby (1911–67), a Dallas nightclub owner, before he could be brought to trial. Oswald was said to be the sole gunman by the Warren Commission (1964), but the House of Representatives Assassinations Committee (1979) concluded that more than one gunman had been involved; the affair remains the focus of a number of conspiracy theories.

Oswald of York, St /'ɒzwəld, jɔːk/ (died 992), English prelate and Benedictine monk. He rose first to become bishop of Worcester and then Archbishop of York. He founded several Benedictine monasteries and, along with St Dunstan, was responsible for the revival of the Church and of learning in 10th-century England. Feast day, 28 February.

Othman see OSMAN I.

Otho /'əʊθəʊ/, Marcus Salvius (AD 32–69), Roman emperor January–April 69. He was proclaimed emperor after he had procured the death of Galba in a conspiracy of the

praetorian guard. Otho was not recognized as emperor by the German legions; led by their candidate, Vitellius, they defeated his troops and Otho committed suicide.

Otis /'əʊtɪs/, Elisha Graves (1811–61), American inventor and manufacturer. He produced the first efficient elevator with a safety device in 1852; it consisted of a mechanical hoist for carrying machinery to the upper floors of a factory, with a device to prevent it from falling even if the lifting cable broke. In 1857 he installed the first public elevator for passengers in a New York department store.

O'Toole /əʊ'tuːl/, (Seamus) Peter (born 1932), Irish-born British actor. He began his career at the Bristol Old Vic Theatre (1955–8), and after a season with the Royal Shakespeare Company came to international prominence as a film star in *Lawrence of Arabia* (1962). His other films include *Goodbye Mr Chips* (1969), *The Stunt Man* (1980), and *The Last Emperor* (1987); he is especially noted for his polished portrayals of unpredictable or eccentric characters.

Otto /'ɒtəʊ/, Nikolaus August (1832–91), German engineer. Otto's name is given to the four-stroke cycle on which most internal-combustion engines work. His patent of 1876 was invalidated ten years later when it was found that Alphonse-Eugène Beau de Rochas (1815–93) had described the successful cycle earlier, so enabling other manufacturers to adopt it.

Otto I /'ɒtəʊ/ (known as Otto the Great) (912–73), king of the Germans 936–73, Holy Roman emperor 962–73. As king of the Germans he carried out a policy of eastward expansion from his Saxon homeland and defeated the invading Hungarians in 955. He was crowned Holy Roman emperor in 962 and began to establish a strong imperial presence in Italy to rival that of the papacy.

Otway /'ɒtweɪ/, Thomas (1652–85), English dramatist. After failing as an actor he wrote for the stage and achieved success with his second play, *Don Carlos* (1676), a tragedy in rhymed verse. He is now chiefly remembered for his two blank verse tragedies, *The Orphan* (1680) and *Venice Preserved* (1682).

Ouida /'wiːdə/ (pseudonym of Marie Louise de la Ramée) (1839–1908), English novelist. She lived mostly in Italy, and wrote forty-five novels often set in a fashionable world far removed from reality and showing a spirit of rebellion against the moral ideals that were prevalent in much of the fiction of the time. Her books include *Under Two Flags* (1867), *Folle-Farine* (1871), and *Two Little Wooden Shoes* (1874).

Overbury /'əʊvəbərɪ/, Sir Thomas (1581–1613), English poet and courtier. He is remembered for his 'Characters', portrait sketches on the model of those of Theophrastus, published posthumously in 1614. On the pretext of his refusal of a diplomatic post he was sent to the Tower of London. There he was fatally poisoned by the agents of Frances Howard, Lady Essex, whose marriage to his patron Robert Carr (afterwards Earl of Somerset) he had opposed.

Ovid /'ɒvɪd/ (full name Publius Ovidius Naso) (43 BC–AD c. 17), Roman poet. He was a major poet of the Augustan period, particularly known for his elegiac love-poems (such as the *Amores* and the *Ars Amatoria*) and for the *Metamorphoses*, a hexametric epic which retells Greek and Roman myths in roughly chronological order. His irreverent attitudes offended Augustus and in AD 8 he was exiled to Tomis (modern Constanţa), on the Black Sea, where he continued to write elegiac poems describing his plight; these are collected in the *Tristia*.

Owen[1] /'əʊɪn/, David (Anthony Llewellyn), Baron Owen of the City of Plymouth (born 1938), British politician. After serving as Foreign Secretary (1977–9) in the Labour government he became increasingly dissatisfied with the Labour Party's policies, and in 1981 broke away to become a founding member of the Social Democratic Party (SDP). He led the SDP from 1983 to 1987, resigning to form a breakaway SDP when the main party decided to merge with the Liberals; he eventually disbanded this party in 1990. In 1992 he was appointed the EC's chief mediator in attempts to solve the crisis in the former Yugoslavia.

Owen[2] /'əʊɪn/, Sir Richard (1804–92), English anatomist and palaeontologist. A qualified surgeon, Owen was superintendent of natural history at the British Museum for twenty-eight years and planned the new Natural History Museum in South Kensington. He made important contributions to the taxonomy and understanding of the evolution of monotremes and marsupials, flightless birds, and fossil reptiles,

and coined the word *dinosaur* in 1841. Owen is chiefly remembered for his opposition to Darwinism and to its defender T. H. Huxley, because he did not accept that natural selection was sufficient to explain evolution.

Owen[3] /ˈəʊm/, Robert (1771–1858), Welsh social reformer and industrialist. A pioneer socialist thinker, he believed that character is a product of the social environment. He founded a model industrial community centred on his cotton mills at New Lanark in Scotland; this was organized on principles of mutual cooperation, with improved working conditions and housing together with educational institutions provided for workers and their families. He went on to found a series of other cooperative communities; although these did not always succeed, his ideas had an important long-term effect on the development of British socialist thought and on the practice of industrial relations.

Owen[4] /ˈəʊm/, Wilfred (1893–1918), English poet. He fought in the First World War and his experiences inspired his best-known works, most of which he wrote after a meeting with Siegfried Sassoon in 1917. Only five of Owen's poems appeared in his lifetime and his reputation has grown following publication of editions of his poems by Sassoon in 1920 and Edmund Blunden in 1931; among the most famous are 'Strange Meeting' and 'Anthem for Doomed Youth'. Owen's poetry is characterized by its bleak realism, its indignation at the horrors of war, and its pity for the victims — of whom he became one, killed in action in the last hours of the war.

Owens /ˈəʊnz/, Jesse (born James Cleveland Owens) (1913–80), American athlete. In 1935 he equalled or broke six world records in 45 minutes, and in 1936 won four gold medals (100 and 200 metres, long jump, and 4 × 100 metres relay) at the Olympic Games in Berlin. The success in Berlin of Owens, as a black man, outraged Hitler, who was conspicuously absent when Owens's medals were presented.

Ozawa /əˈzɑːwə/, Seiji (born 1935), Japanese conductor. In 1959 he won an international conducting competition and since then has been based chiefly in North America; he was the conductor of the Toronto Symphony Orchestra (1965–70) and in 1973 became music director and conductor of the Boston Symphony Orchestra.

P

Pachelbel /ˈpæx(ə)lˌbel/, Johann (1653–1706), German composer and organist. In 1695 he became organist of St Sebald's church in his native Nuremberg, a post he held until his death. His compositions, which influenced Bach, include seventy-eight chorale preludes, thirteen settings of the Magnificat, and his best-known work, Canon and Gigue in D for three violins and continuo.

Pacino /pəˈtʃiːnəʊ/, Al(fred) (born 1940), American film actor. Nominated for an Oscar eight times, he first achieved recognition with *The Godfather* (1972) and *The Godfather Part II* (1974). Other films include *Scarface* (1983), *Dick Tracy* (1990), and *Scent of a Woman* (1992), for which he won an Oscar.

Packer /ˈpækə(r)/, Kerry (Francis Bullmore) (born 1937), Australian media entrepreneur. He launched a number of Australian sport initiatives, notably the 'World Series Cricket' tournaments (1977–9), for which he claimed exclusive television coverage rights. As part of these tournaments Packer engaged many of the world's leading cricketers in defiance of the wishes of cricket's ruling bodies, precipitating a two-year schism in international cricket.

Paderewski /ˌpædəˈrefskɪ/, Ignacy Jan (1860–1941), Polish pianist, composer, and statesman, Prime Minister 1919. He became one of the most famous international pianists of his time and also received acclaim for his compositions, which include the opera *Manru* (1901). He was the first Prime Minister of independent Poland, but resigned after only ten months in office and resumed his musical career. In 1939 he served briefly as head of the Polish government in Paris, before emigrating to the US in 1940 when France surrendered to Germany.

Paganini /ˌpægəˈniːnɪ/, Niccolò (1782–1840), Italian violinist and composer. His virtuoso violin recitals established him as an almost legendary figure of the romantic movement and radically changed the violin technique of the day. Paganini's technical innovations, such as widespread use of pizzicato and harmonics as well as new styles of fingering, were exhibited in his best-known composition, the twenty-four *Capricci* (1820). His technical innovations had a major influence on the work of Liszt.

Page /peɪdʒ/, Sir Frederick Handley (1885–1962), English aircraft designer. In 1909 he founded Handley Page Ltd., the first British aircraft manufacturing company. He is noted for designing the first twin-engined bomber (1915), as well as the Halifax heavy bombers of the Second World War.

Paglia /ˈpɑːlɪə/, Camille (Anna) (born 1947), American cultural critic. Her first book, *Sexual Personae* (1990), brought her to public attention, with its controversial pro-capitalist and anti-feminist examination of art and decadence through the ages. She has remained in the public eye through her active self-promotion and the publication of subsequent essay collections, *Sex, Art, and American Culture* (1992) and *Vamps and Tramps* (1994). She became professor of humanities at the University of the Arts, Philadelphia, in 1995.

Pagnol /pæˈnjɒl/, Marcel (1895–1974), French dramatist, film director, and writer. As a director Pagnol is best known for the film trilogy comprising *Marius* (1931), *Fanny* (1932), and *César* (1936), cinematic adaptations of his own plays. Enormously popular for their humour and the affectionate depiction of their Marseilles characters, they were remade in other languages and also transformed into a Broadway musical. In 1946 Pagnol became the first film-maker to be elected to the Académie française. His novels include *La Gloire de mon père* (1957) and *Le Chateau de ma mère* (1958); the films *Jean de Florette* and *Manon des Sources* (both 1986) were based on Pagnol's *L'Eau des collines* (1963).

Pahlavi[1] /ˈpɑːləvɪ/, Muhammad Reza (also known as Reza Shah) (1919–80), shah of Iran 1941–79. His early years as shah were dominated by conflict with the nationalist Prime Minister Muhammad Mosaddeq (1880–1967). From 1953 he assumed direct control over all aspects of Iranian life and, with US support, embarked on a national development plan promoting public

works, industrial development, and social and land reform. Opposition to his regime culminated in the Islamic revolution of 1979 under Ayatollah Khomeini; Reza Shah was forced into exile and died in Egypt.

Pahlavi[2] /'pɑːləvɪ/, Reza (born Reza Khan) (1878–1944), shah of Iran 1925–41. An army officer, he took control of the Persian government after a coup in 1921. In the absence of the reigning monarch, Reza Khan was elected shah by the National Assembly in 1925. He abdicated in 1941, following the occupation of Iran by British and Soviet forces, passing the throne to his son Muhammad Reza Pahlavi.

Paine /pein/, Thomas (1737–1809), English political writer. After emigrating to the US in 1774, he wrote the pamphlet *Common Sense* (1776), which called for American independence and laid the ground for the Declaration of Independence. On returning to England in 1787, he published *The Rights of Man* (1791), defending the French Revolution in response to Burke's *Reflections on the Revolution in France* (1790). His radical views prompted the British government to indict him for treason and he fled to France. There he supported the Revolution but opposed the execution of Louis XVI. He was imprisoned for a year, during which time he wrote *The Age of Reason* (1794), an attack on orthodox Christianity.

Paisley /'peɪzlɪ/, Ian (Richard Kyle) (born 1926), Northern Irish clergyman and politician. He was ordained as a minister of the Free Presbyterian Church in 1946, becoming its leader in 1951. Paisley first became politically active in the 1960s and was elected MP for North Antrim in 1970. A co-founder of the Ulster Democratic Unionist Party (1972), he has been a vociferous and outspoken defender of the Protestant Unionist position in Northern Ireland. Paisley became a Member of the European Parliament in 1979.

Palestrina /ˌpælə'striːnə/, Giovanni Pierluigi da (c.1525–94), Italian composer. He composed several madrigals, but is chiefly known for his sacred music, notably 105 masses and more than 250 motets. His music is characterized by its control of counterpoint; major works include the *Missa Papae Marcelli* (1567).

Palgrave /'pælgreɪv, 'pɔːl-/, Francis Turner (1824–97), English critic and poet. He is best known for his anthology *The Golden Treasury of Songs and Lyrical Poems in the English Language* (1861). The work is a reflection of the tastes of the age, originally containing no work by living poets. He compiled other anthologies, wrote several volumes of verse, and was professor of poetry at Oxford from 1886 to 1895.

Palissy /'pælɪsɪ/, Bernard (c.1510–90), French potter. From the late 1550s he became famous for richly coloured earthenware decorated with reliefs of plants and animals. From about 1565 he enjoyed royal patronage and was employed by the court.

Palladio /pə'lɑːdɪˌəʊ/, Andrea (1508–80), Italian architect. He led a revival of classical architecture in 16th-century Italy, in particular promoting the Roman ideals of harmonic proportions and symmetrical planning. He designed many villas, palaces, and churches; major buildings include the church of San Giorgio Maggiore in Venice (1566 onwards). His theoretical work *Four Books on Architecture* (1570) was the main source of inspiration for the English Palladian movement.

Palme /'pɑːlmə/, (Sven) Olof (Joachim) (1927–86), Swedish statesman, Prime Minister 1969–76 and 1982–6. He became leader of the Social Democratic Socialist Workers' Party in 1969. During his first term of prime-ministerial office Palme was a critic of US intervention in the Vietnam War and granted asylum to US army deserters. His electoral defeat in 1976 marked the end of forty-four continuous years in power for the Social Democratic Party. He was killed by an unknown assassin during his second term of office.

Palmer[1] /'pɑːmə(r)/, Arnold (Daniel) (born 1929), American golfer. His many championship victories include the US Masters (1958; 1960; 1962; 1964), the US Open (1960), and the British Open (1961–2).

Palmer[2] /'pɑːmə(r)/, Samuel (1805–91), English painter and etcher. By the age of 14 he was exhibiting his landscape paintings at the Royal Academy. From 1824 his friendship with William Blake resulted in the mystical, visionary landscape paintings, such as *Repose of the Holy Family* (1824), for which he is best known. He was leader of The Ancients (a group of artists so called because of their love of the medieval), who were inspired by Blake's mysticism. Later, after a visit to Italy (1837–9), he devoted himself to more conventional pastoral works.

Palmerston /'pɑ:məstən/, Henry John Temple, 3rd Viscount (1784–1865), British Whig statesman, Prime Minister 1855–8 and 1859–65. He left the Tory Party in 1830 to serve with the Whigs as Foreign Secretary (1830–4; 1835–41; 1846–51). In his foreign policy Palmerston was single-minded in his promotion of British interests, declaring the second Opium War against China in 1856, and overseeing the successful conclusion of the Crimean War in 1856 and the suppression of the Indian Mutiny in 1858. He maintained British neutrality during the American Civil War.

Pandit /'pʌndɪt/, Vijaya (Lakshmi) (1900–90), Indian politician and diplomat. After joining the Indian National Congress, led by her brother Jawaharlal Nehru, she was imprisoned three times by the British (1932; 1941; 1942) for nationalist activities. Following independence she led the Indian delegation to the United Nations (1946–8; 1952–3) and was the first woman to serve as president of the United Nations General Assembly (1953–4).

Panini /'pɑ:nɪnɪ/, Indian grammarian. Little is known about his life; sources vary as to when he lived, with dates ranging from the 4th to the 7th century BC. He is noted as the author of the *Eight Lectures*, a grammar of Sanskrit, outlining rules for the derivation of grammatical forms.

Pankhurst /'pæŋkhɜːst/, Mrs Emmeline (1858–1928), Christabel (1880–1958), and (Estelle) Sylvia (1882–1960), English suffragettes. In 1903 Emmeline and her daughters Christabel and Sylvia founded the Women's Social and Political Union, with the motto 'Votes for Women'. Following the imprisonment of Christabel in 1905, Emmeline initiated the militant suffragette campaign and was responsible for keeping the suffragette cause in the public eye until the outbreak of the First World War.

Paolozzi /pau'lɒtsɪ/, Eduardo (Luigi) (born 1924), Scottish artist and sculptor, of Italian descent. He was a key figure in the development of pop art in Britain in the 1950s. His work is typified by mechanistic sculptures in a figurative style, often surfaced with cog wheels and machine parts, as in *Japanese War God* (1958).

Papineau /'pæpɪˌnəu/, Louis Joseph (1786–1871), French-Canadian politician. The leader of the French-Canadian party in Lower Canada (later Quebec province), he served as speaker of the House of Assembly for Lower Canada from 1815 to 1837. During this time he campaigned against British proposals for the union of Lower and Upper Canada (later Ontario), and pressed for greater French-Canadian autonomy in government. He was forced to flee the country after leading an abortive French rebellion against British rule in Lower Canada in 1837.

Pappus /'pæpəs/ (known as Pappus of Alexandria) (*fl. c.*300–350 AD), Greek mathematician. Little is known of his life, but his *Collection* of six books (another two are missing) is the principal source of knowledge of the mathematics of his predecessors. They are particularly strong on geometry, to which Pappus himself made major contributions. Fragments of other works survive.

Paracelsus /ˌpærə'selsəs/ (born Theophrastus Phillipus Aureolus Bombastus von Hohenheim) (*c.*1493–1541), Swiss physician. He developed a new approach to medicine and philosophy condemning medical teaching that was not based on observation and experience. He introduced chemical remedies to replace traditional herbal ones, and gave alchemy a wider perspective. Paracelsus saw illness as having a specific external cause rather than being caused by an imbalance of the humours in the body, although this progressive view was offset by his overall occultist perspective. His study of a disease of miners was one of the first accounts of an occupational disease.

Paris, Matthew, see MATTHEW PARIS.

Park[1] /pɑːk/, Mungo (1771–1806), Scottish explorer. He undertook a series of explorations in West Africa (1795–7), among them being the navigation of the Niger. His experiences were recorded in his *Travels in the Interior of Africa* (1799). He drowned on a second expedition to the Niger (1805–6).

Park[2] /pɑːk/, Nick (born 1958), English animator. Nick Park has won Oscars for three films which he wrote, directed, and animated using clay models. The films are *Creature Comforts* (1990), a humorous look at what zoo animals might think of their surroundings, and *The Wrong Trousers* (1993) and *A Close Shave* (1995), which star part-time inventor Wallace and his dog Gromit. The first Wallace and Gromit film was *A Grand Day Out* (1992).

Park Chung Hee /ˌpɑːk tʃʊŋ ˈhiː/ (1917–79), South Korean statesman, President 1963–79. In 1961 he staged a military coup that ousted the country's democratic government. Two years later he was elected President, assuming dictatorial powers in 1971. Under Park's presidency South Korea emerged as a leading industrial nation, with one of the world's highest rates of economic growth. He was assassinated by Kim Jae Kyu (1926–80), the head of the Korean Central Intelligence Agency.

Parker[1] /ˈpɑːkə(r)/, Charles Christopher ('Charlie'; known as 'Bird' or 'Yardbird') (1920–55), American saxophonist. From 1944 he was based in New York, where he played with Thelonious Monk and Dizzy Gillespie and became one of the key figures of the bebop movement. He is noted especially for his recordings with Miles Davis in 1945.

Parker[2] /ˈpɑːkə(r)/, Dorothy (Rothschild) (1893–1967), American humorist, literary critic, short-story writer, and poet. She was a leading member of the Algonquin Round Table, a circle of writers and humorists that met in the 1920s and included James Thurber. From 1927 Parker wrote book reviews and short stories for the *New Yorker* magazine, becoming one of its legendary wits. As a poet, she made her name with the best-selling verse collection *Enough Rope* (1927).

Parmenides /pɑːˈmenɪˌdiːz/ (fl. 5th century BC), Greek philosopher. Born in Elea in SW Italy, he founded the Eleatic school of philosophers and was noted for the philosophical work *On Nature*, written in hexameter verse. In this he maintained that the apparent motion and changing forms of the universe are in fact manifestations of an unchanging and indivisible reality.

Parmigianino /ˌpɑːmɪdʒɑːˈniːnəʊ/ (also **Parmigiano** /-ˈdʒɑːnəʊ/) (born Girolamo Francesco Maria Mazzola) (1503–40), Italian painter. A follower of Correggio, he made an important contribution to early mannerism with the graceful figure style of his frescos and portraits. His works include *Self-Portrait in a Convex Mirror* (1524) and *Madonna with the Long Neck* (1534).

Parnell /pɑːˈnel/, Charles Stewart (1846–91), Irish nationalist leader. Elected to Parliament in 1875, Parnell became leader of the Irish Home Rule faction in 1880, and, through his obstructive parliamentary tactics, successfully raised the profile of Irish

affairs. In 1886 he supported Gladstone's Home Rule bill, following the latter's conversion to the cause. He was forced to retire from public life in 1890 after the public exposure of his adultery with Mrs Katherine ('Kitty') O'Shea (1840–1905).

Parr /pɑː(r)/, Katherine (1512–48), sixth and last wife of Henry VIII. Having married the king in 1543, she influenced his decision to restore the succession to his daughters Mary and Elizabeth (later Mary I and Elizabeth I).

Parry /ˈpærɪ/, Sir (Charles) Hubert (Hastings) (1848–1918), English composer. He is noted for his choral music, including the cantata *Blest Pair of Sirens* (1887). Parry's best-known work, however, is his setting of William Blake's poem 'Jerusalem' (1916), which has acquired the status of an English national song.

Parsons /ˈpɑːs(ə)nz/, Sir Charles (Algernon) (1854–1931), British engineer, scientist, and manufacturer. He patented and built the first practical steam turbine in 1884, a 7.5-kW engine designed to drive electricity generators. Many such machines were installed in power stations, and their output was later increased by adding a condenser and using superheated steam. Parsons also developed steam turbines for marine propulsion, the experimental vessel *Turbinia* creating a sensation by its unscheduled appearance at a British naval review in 1897. He was also interested in optics, manufacturing searchlight reflectors, large reflecting telescopes, and optical glass.

Parton /ˈpɑːt(ə)n/, Dolly (Rebecca) (born 1946), American singer and songwriter. She is best known as a country-music singer; in the mid-1960s she moved to Nashville and had her first hit in 1967 with 'Dumb Blonde'. Her other hits include 'Joshua' (1971) and 'Jolene' (1974). She has also had a number of film roles.

Pascal /ˈpæˈskɑːl/, Blaise (1623–62), French mathematician, physicist, and religious philosopher. A child prodigy, before the age of 16 he had proved an important theorem in the projective geometry of conics, and at 19 constructed the first mechanical calculator to be offered for sale. He discovered that air has weight, confirmed that vacuum could exist, and derived the principle that the pressure of a fluid at rest is transmitted equally in all directions. He also founded the theory of probabilities, and developed a forerunner

of integral calculus. He later entered a Jansenist convent, where he wrote two classics of French devotional thought, the *Lettres provinciales* (1656–7), directed against the casuistry of the Jesuits, and *Pensées* (1670), a defence of Christianity.

Pašić /'pæʃɪtʃ/, Nikola (1845–1926), Serbian statesman, Prime Minister of Serbia five times between 1891 and 1918, and of the Kingdom of Serbs, Croats, and Slovenes 1921–4 and 1924–6. As Prime Minister of the Serbian government in exile during the First World War, he signed the Corfu Declaration (1917), which set down a blueprint for a postwar unified Yugoslavia. Although Pašić was reluctant for the Serbs to share power with the South Slavs of Austria–Hungary, he was a party to the formation of the Kingdom of Serbs, Croats, and Slovenes (called Yugoslavia from 1929) in 1918.

Pasolini /,pæsə'liːnɪ/, Pier Paolo (1922–75), Italian film director and novelist. Following the Second World War Pasolini became a Marxist and moved to Rome, where he lived in the city's slums. He drew on his experiences there first for his novels and then his films, including his directorial début, *Accattone!* (1961). Pasolini became recognized for his controversial, bawdy literary adaptations, such as *The Gospel According to St Matthew* (1964) and *The Canterbury Tales* (1973). He was murdered in a Rome suburb.

Passos, John Dos, see Dos Passos.

Pasternak /'pæstə,næk/, Boris (Leonidovich) (1890–1960), Russian poet, novelist, and translator. On the eve of the Russian Revolution in 1917 he wrote the lyric poems *My Sister, Life* (1922), which established his reputation when published. In the 1930s he started work on the novel *Doctor Zhivago* (1957), a testament to the experience of the Russian intelligentsia before, during, and after the Revolution. It was banned in the Soviet Union and first published in Italian and then, with equal success, in other languages; in 1958 Pasternak was awarded the Nobel Prize for literature, but was forced to turn it down under pressure from the Soviet authorities.

Pasteur /pæ'stɜː(r)/, Louis (1822–95), French chemist and bacteriologist. His early work, in which he discovered the existence of dextrorotatory and laevorotatory forms of sugars, was of fundamental importance in chemistry, but he is popularly remembered for his 'germ theory' (1865) — that each fermentation process could be traced to a specific living micro-organism. Following the success of his introduction of pasteurization, he developed an interest in diseases. Pasteur isolated bacteria infecting silkworms, finding methods of preventing the disease from spreading. He then isolated the bacteria causing anthrax and chicken cholera, made vaccines against them, and pioneered vaccination against rabies using attenuated virus.

Pater /'peɪtə(r)/, Walter (Horatio) (1839–94), English essayist and critic. He came to fame with *Studies in the History of the Renaissance* (1873), which incorporated his essays on the then neglected Botticelli and on Leonardo da Vinci's *Mona Lisa*; it had a major impact on the development of the Aesthetic Movement. Pater's other works include *Marius the Epicurean* (1885), which develops his ideas on 'art for art's sake'.

Pathé /'pæθeɪ/, Charles (1863–1957), French film pioneer. In 1896 he and his brothers founded a company which dominated the production and distribution of films in the early 20th century, and which initiated the system of leasing (rather than selling) copies of films. The firm also became internationally known for its newsreels, the first of which were introduced in France in 1909. After Charles Pathé's retirement in 1929 the company continued to produce Pathé newsreels until the mid-1950s.

Patmore /'pætmɔː(r)/, Coventry (Kersey Dighton) (1823–96), English poet. His most important work is *The Angel in the House* (1854–63), a sequence of poems in praise of married love.

Paton /'peɪt(ə)n/, Alan (Stewart) (1903–88), South African writer and politician. He is best known for his novel *Cry, the Beloved Country* (1948), a passionate indictment of the apartheid system. Paton helped found the South African Liberal Party in 1953, later becoming its president until it was banned in 1968.

Patrick, St /'pætrɪk/ (5th century), Apostle and patron saint of Ireland. His *Confession* is the chief source for the events of his life. Of Romano-British parentage, he was captured at the age of 16 by raiders and shipped to Ireland as a slave; there he experienced a religious conversion. Escaping after six years, probably to Gaul, he was ordained and returned to Ireland in about 432. Many of the details of his mission are

uncertain but it is known that he founded the archiepiscopal see of Armagh in about 454. Feast day, 17 March.

Paul /pɔːl/, Les (born Lester Polfus) (born 1915), American jazz guitarist. In 1946 he invented the solid-body electric guitar for which he is best known; it was first promoted in 1952 as the Gibson Les Paul guitar, and is still sold under that name. Paul was also among the first to use such recording techniques as overdubbing. In the 1950s he wrote and recorded a number of hit songs with his wife, Mary Ford (1928–77), such as 'Mockin' Bird Hill' (1951).

Paul III /pɔːl/ (born Alessandro Farnese) (1468–1549), Italian pope 1534–49. He excommunicated Henry VIII of England in 1538, instituted the order of the Jesuits in 1540, and initiated the Council of Trent in 1545. Paul III was also a keen patron of the arts, commissioning Michelangelo to paint the fresco of the *Last Judgement* for the Sistine Chapel and to design the dome of St Peter's in Rome.

Paul, St (known as Paul the Apostle, or Saul of Tarsus, or 'the Apostle of the Gentiles') (died *c*.64), missionary of Jewish descent. He was brought up as a Pharisee and at first opposed the followers of Jesus, assisting at the martyrdom of St Stephen. On a mission to Damascus, he was converted to Christianity after a vision and became one of the first major Christian missionaries and theologians. His missionary journeys are described in the Acts of the Apostles, and his epistles form part of the New Testament. He was martyred in Rome. Feast day, 29 June.

Pauli /'paʊlɪ/, Wolfgang (1900–58), Austrian-born American physicist who worked chiefly in Switzerland. He is best known for the *exclusion principle*, according to which only two electrons in an atom could occupy the same quantum level, provided they had opposite spins. This made it easier to understand the structure of the atom and the chemical properties of the elements, and was later extended to a whole class of subatomic particles, the fermions, which includes the electron. In 1931 he postulated the existence of the neutrino, later discovered by Enrico Fermi. He was awarded the 1945 Nobel Prize for physics.

Pauling /'pɔːlɪŋ/, Linus Carl (1901–94), American chemist. He is particularly renowned for his study of molecular structure and chemical bonding, especially of complex biological macromolecules, for which he received the 1954 Nobel Prize for chemistry. His suggestion of the helix as a possible structure for proteins formed the foundation for the later elucidation of the structure of DNA. Pauling also proved that sickle-cell anaemia is caused by a defect in haemoglobin at the molecular level. After the war he became increasingly involved with attempts to ban nuclear weapons, for which he was awarded the Nobel Peace Prize in 1962.

Pausanias /pɔːˈseɪnɪəs/ (2nd century), Greek geographer and historian. His *Description of Greece* (also called the *Itinerary of Greece*) is a guide to the topography and remains of ancient Greece and is still considered an invaluable source of information.

Pavarotti /ˌpævəˈrɒtɪ/, Luciano (born 1935), Italian operatic tenor. He made his début as Rudolfo in Puccini's *La Bohème* in 1961, and achieved rapid success in this and a succession of other leading roles, including Edgardo in Donizetti's *Lucia di Lammermoor* and the Duke in Verdi's *Rigoletto* (both 1965). Widely acclaimed for his bel canto singing, Pavarotti has appeared in concerts and on TV throughout the world, and has made many recordings.

Pavese /pæˈveɪsɪ/, Cesare (1908–50), Italian novelist, poet, and translator. He is best known for his last novel *La Luna e i falò* (1950), in which he portrays isolation and the failure of communication as a general human predicament. Pavese also made many important translations of works written in English, including novels by Herman Melville, James Joyce, and William Faulkner. He committed suicide in 1950.

Pavlov /'pævlɒf/, Ivan (Petrovich) (1849–1936), Russian physiologist. He was awarded a Nobel Prize in 1904 for his work on digestion, but is best known for his later studies on the conditioned reflex. He showed by experiment with dogs how the secretion of saliva can be stimulated not only by food but also by the sound of a bell associated with the presentation of food, and that this sound comes to elicit salivation when presented alone. Pavlov applied his findings to show the importance of such reflexes in human and animal behaviour. His experiments form the basis for much current research in the field of conditioning.

Pavlova /'pævləvə, pæv'ləʊvə/ Anna (Pavlovna) (1881–1931), Russian dancer, resident in Britain from 1912. As the prima ballerina of the Russian Imperial Ballet she toured Russia and northern Europe in 1907 and 1908. Her highly acclaimed solo dance *The Dying Swan* was created for her by Michel Fokine in 1905. After brief appearances with the Ballets Russes in 1909, Pavlova made her New York and London débuts the following year. On settling in Britain, she formed her own company and embarked on numerous tours which made her a pioneer of classical ballet all over the world.

Paxton /'pækstən/, Sir Joseph (1801–65), English gardener and architect. He became head gardener to the Duke of Devonshire at Chatsworth House in Derbyshire in 1826, and designed a series of glass-and-iron greenhouses. He later reworked these, making the first known use of prefabricated materials, in his design for the Crystal Palace (1851).

Paz /pæz/, Octavio (born 1914), Mexican poet and essayist. His poems are noted for their preoccupation with Aztec mythology, as in *Sun Stone* (1957). He is also known for his essays, particularly *The Labyrinth of Solitude* (1950), a critique of Mexican culture, and *Postscript* (1970), a response to Mexico's brutal suppression of student demonstrators in 1968. Paz was awarded the Nobel Prize for literature in 1990.

Peacock /'pi:kɒk/, Thomas Love (1785–1866), English novelist and poet. He is chiefly remembered for his prose satires, including *Nightmare Abbey* (1818) and *Crotchet Castle* (1831), lampooning the romantic poets.

Peake /pi:k/, Mervyn (Laurence) (1911–68), British novelist, poet, and artist, born in China. He is principally remembered for the trilogy comprising *Titus Groan* (1946), *Gormenghast* (1950), and *Titus Alone* (1959), set in the surreal world of Gormenghast Castle. Peake was also a notable book illustrator.

Pears /pɪəz/, Sir Peter (1910–86), English operatic tenor. Pears was celebrated in his own right as a singer of oratorio, lieder, and opera, but it is for his lifelong partnership with Benjamin Britten that he is particularly known. Pears created the title roles in most of Britten's operas, notably *Peter Grimes* (1945). With Britten he founded and organized the Aldeburgh Festival in 1948.

Pearson[1] /'pɪəs(ə)n/, Karl (1857–1936), English mathematician, the principal founder of 20th-century statistics. He realized from Francis Galton's work on the measurement of human variation that such data are amenable to mathematical treatment. The fields of heredity and evolution were the first to receive statistical analysis. Pearson defined the concept of standard deviation, and devised the chi-square test. He wrote numerous articles, and was the principal editor of the journal *Biometrika* for many years.

Pearson[2] /'pɪəs(ə)n/, Lester Bowles (1897–1972), Canadian diplomat and Liberal statesman, Prime Minister 1963–8. As Secretary of State for External Affairs (1948–57) he headed the Canadian delegation to the United Nations, served as chairman of NATO (1951), and acted as a mediator in the resolution of the Suez crisis (1956), for which he received the Nobel Peace Prize in 1957. Pearson became leader of the Liberal Party in 1958; he resigned as Prime Minister and Liberal Party leader in 1968.

Peary /'pɪərɪ/, Robert Edwin (1856–1920), American explorer. He made eight Arctic voyages before becoming the first person to reach the North Pole, on 6 April 1909.

Peck /pek/, (Eldred) Gregory (born 1916), American actor. He made his screen début in 1944. His many films range from the thriller *Spellbound* (1945) to the western *The Big Country* (1958). Peck won an Oscar for his role as the lawyer Atticus in the literary adaptation *To Kill a Mockingbird* (1962). More recent films include *The Omen* (1976) and *The Old Gringo* (1989).

Peel /pi:l/, Sir Robert (1788–1850), British Conservative statesman, Prime Minister 1834–5 and 1841–6. During his second term as Home Secretary (1828–30) Peel established the Metropolitan Police (and gave his name to the nicknames *bobby* and *peeler*). As leader of the new Conservative Party he affirmed his belief in moderate electoral reform in the Tamworth Manifesto (1834). His repeal of the Corn Laws in 1846, however, split the Conservatives and forced his resignation. In the last years of his career he came to support the Whig policies of free trade.

Pei /peɪ/, I(eoh) M(ing) (born 1917), American architect, born in China. His name is associated with monumental public buildings, in which simple geometric forms are placed in dramatic juxtaposition. Major

works include the John F. Kennedy Memorial Library at Harvard University (1964), the east wing of the National Gallery of Art, Washington, DC (1971–8), and the controversial glass and steel pyramid in the forecourt of the Louvre, Paris (1989).

Peirce /pɪəs/, Charles Sanders (1839–1914), American philosopher and logician. One of the founders of American pragmatism, he proposed a theory of meaning in which the meaning of a belief or an idea is to be understood by the actions, uses, and habits to which it gives rise. Logic was central to Peirce's philosophic concerns; his work on logical atomism and the distinction between arbitrary and non-arbitrary signs was highly influential in the development of modern semantics and semiotics. He also pioneered the logic of relations, in which he argued that induction is an indispensable correlative of deduction, and, as a formal logician, discovered the quantifier shortly after Gottlob Frege.

Peisistratus see PISISTRATUS.

Pelagius /prˈleɪdʒɪəs/ (c.360–c.420), British or Irish monk. He denied the doctrines of original sin and predestination, defending innate human goodness and free will. His beliefs were opposed by St Augustine of Hippo and condemned as heretical by the Synod of Carthage in about 418.

Pelé /ˈpeleɪ/ (born Edson Arantes do Nascimento) (born 1940), Brazilian footballer. He played for Brazil at the age of 17, scoring twice in his country's victory in the World Cup Final of 1958. In all he appeared 111 times for Brazil, scoring 97 goals, including one in the 1970 World Cup Final victory. Regarded as one of the greatest footballers of all time, he ended his career with New York Cosmos (1975–7) and is credited with over 1,200 goals in first-class soccer.

Pelham /ˈpeləm/, Henry (1696–1754), British Whig statesman, Prime Minister 1743–54. After serving in Sir Robert Walpole's Cabinet from 1721 onwards, he replaced him as Premier, and introduced a period of peace and prosperity by bringing to an end the War of the Austrian Succession (1740–8). His term also saw the adoption of the Gregorian calendar.

Pelletier /pəˈletɪˌeɪ/, Pierre-Joseph (1788–1842), French chemist. He specialized in plant products, and began with a study of gum resins and pigments. He is best known

as the founder of alkaloid chemistry, having isolated a number of alkaloids for the first time with his friend Joseph-Bienaimé Caventou (1795–1877). Pelletier and Caventou also isolated the green pigment of leaves and gave it the name *chlorophyll*.

Penderecki /ˌpendəˈretskɪ/, Krzysztof (born 1933), Polish composer. His music frequently uses unorthodox effects, including sounds drawn from extra-musical sources and note clusters, as in his *Threnody for the Victims of Hiroshima* (1960) for fifty-two strings. Penderecki's many religious works include *Stabat Mater* (1962), a fusion of conventional and avant-garde elements, and the *Polish Requiem* (1980–4).

Penn /pen/, William (1644–1718), English Quaker, founder of Pennsylvania. He was imprisoned in the Tower of London in 1668 for writing in defence of Quaker practices. Acquitted in 1670, he was granted a charter to land in North America by Charles II (1682), using it to found the colony of Pennsylvania as a sanctuary for Quakers and other Nonconformists in the same year. Penn also co-founded the city of Philadelphia.

Pepys /piːps/, Samuel (1633–1703), English diarist and naval administrator. He is particularly remembered for his *Diary* (1660–9), which remains an important document of contemporary events such as the Great Plague (1665–6), the Fire of London (1666), and the sailing of the Dutch fleet up the Thames (1665–7). The *Diary* was written in code and was first deciphered in 1825. Pepys became secretary of the Admiralty in 1672 but was deprived of his post in 1679 and committed to the Tower for his alleged complicity in Titus Oates's fabricated Popish Plot, being reappointed in 1684.

Perceval /ˈpɜːsɪv(ə)l/, Spencer (1762–1812), British Tory statesman, Prime Minister 1809–12. He was shot dead in the lobby of the House of Commons by a bankrupt merchant who blamed the government for his insolvency.

Percy /ˈpɜːsɪ/, Sir Henry (known as 'Hotspur' and 'Harry Hotspur') (1364–1403), English soldier. Son of the 1st Earl of Northumberland (1342–1408), he was killed at the battle of Shrewsbury during his father's revolt against Henry IV.

Perelman /ˈperəlmən/, S(idney) J(oseph) (1904–79), American humorist and writer. In the early 1930s he worked in Hollywood

as a scriptwriter, notably on some of the Marx Brothers' films. From 1934 his name is linked with the *New Yorker* magazine, for whom he wrote most of his short stories and sketches.

Peres /'perez/, Shimon (Polish name Szymon Perski) (born 1923), Israeli statesman, Prime Minister 1984–6 and 1995–6. Born in Poland, he emigrated to Palestine in 1934. Labour Party leader since 1977, Peres became head of a coalition government with the Likud Party in 1984, later serving as deputy to Yitzhak Shamir. As Foreign Minister from 1992 he played a major role in negotiating the PLO–Israeli peace accord (1993), and shared the 1994 Nobel Peace Prize with Yitzhak Rabin and Yasser Arafat. He replaced Rabin as Prime Minister after the latter's assassination, only to be narrowly defeated in the elections of 1996 by Benjamin Netanyahu.

Pérez de Cuéllar /ˌperez də 'kwe:jɑ:(r)/, Javier (born 1920), Peruvian diplomat. He served as Secretary-General of the United Nations from 1982 to 1991, and played a key role in the diplomatic aftermath of the Falklands War (1982) and in ending the Iran–Iraq War (1980–8). His efforts to avert the Gulf War in 1990 raised his international standing, as did his part in negotiating the release of Western hostages held in the Middle East.

Pericles /'perɪˌkliːz/ (*c.*495–429 BC), Athenian statesman and general. A champion of Athenian democracy, he pursued an imperialist policy and masterminded Athenian strategy in the Peloponnesian War. He commissioned the building of the Parthenon in 447 and promoted the culture of Athens in a golden age that produced such figures as Aeschylus, Socrates, and Phidias.

Perkin /'pɜːkɪn/, Sir William Henry (1838–1907), English chemist and pioneer of the synthetic organic chemical industry. At the age of 18 he prepared the first synthetic dyestuff, mauve, which is made from aniline. The discovery was made by accident when he was trying to synthesize the drug quinine. He and his father then set up a factory to make mauve, which was used for textiles and postage stamps, and other synthetic dyes.

Perón[1] /pe'rɒn/, Eva (full name María Eva Duarte de Perón; known as 'Evita') (1919–52), Argentinian politician. After pursuing a successful career as a radio actress in the

1930s and 1940s, she married Juan Perón and became de facto Minister of Health and of Labour. Idolized by the poor, she organized female workers, secured the vote for women, and earmarked substantial government funds for social welfare. She was nominated for the vice-presidency in 1951, but was forced by the army to withdraw. She died the following year from cancer.

Perón[2] /pe'rɒn/, Juan Domingo (1895–1974), Argentinian soldier and statesman, President 1946–55 and 1973–4. He participated in the military coup organized by pro-Fascist army officers in 1943, and was elected President in 1946, when he assumed dictatorial powers. He won popular support with his programme of social reform, but, after the death of his second wife, Evita, the faltering economy and his conflict with the Roman Catholic Church led to his removal and exile in 1955. Following a resurgence by the Peronist Party in the early 1970s, Perón returned to power in 1973, but died in office.

Perrault /pe'rəʊ/, Charles (1628–1703), French writer. He is remembered for his *Mother Goose Tales* (1697), containing such fairy tales as 'Sleeping Beauty', 'Little Red Riding Hood', 'Puss in Boots', 'Bluebeard', and 'Cinderella'. They were translated into English by Robert Samber in 1729.

Perrin /pe'ræn/, Jean Baptiste (1870–1942), French physical chemist. He proved that cathode rays are negatively charged, and went on to investigate Brownian motion (the erratic random movement of microscopic particles in a fluid, as a result of continuous bombardment from molecules of the surrounding medium). The latter studies led to a number of mathematical proofs and determinations, and it was accepted that Perrin had provided the definitive proof of the existence of atoms. He was awarded the Nobel Prize for physics in 1926.

Perry /'perɪ/, Frederick John ('Fred') (1909–95), British-born American tennis player. He began his career as a table-tennis player, winning the world singles championship in 1929. In tennis, his record of winning three consecutive singles titles at Wimbledon (1934–6) was unequalled until the success of Björn Borg. Perry subsequently pursued a career as a commentator for radio and television. In 1950 he founded a successful sportswear company.

Perthes, Jacques Boucher de, see BOUCHER DE PERTHES.

Pestalozzi /ˌpestə'lɒtsɪ/, Johann Heinrich (1746–1827), Swiss educational reformer. He pioneered education for poor children and had a major impact on the development of primary education. Influenced by Jean-Jacques Rousseau, Pestalozzi believed in the morally improving effects of a rural environment, and held that education should allow for individual differences in ability and pace of development, as well as acknowledge the role of family life and the importance of moral teaching. His theory and method are set out in *How Gertrude Teaches Her Children* (1801). Pestalozzi's work is commemorated in the International Children's Villages named after him; the first, for war orphans, was established at Trogen in Switzerland in 1946.

Pétain /per'tæn/, (Henri) Philippe (Omer) (1856–1951), French general and statesman, head of state 1940–2. He became a national hero in the First World War for halting the German advance at Verdun (1916) and later became Commander-in-Chief of French forces (1917). In the Second World War he concluded an armistice with Nazi Germany after the collapse of French forces in 1940 and established the French government at Vichy (effectively a puppet regime for the Third Reich) until German occupation in 1942. After the war Pétain received a death sentence for collaboration, but this was commuted to life imprisonment.

Peter I /'piːtə(r)/ (known as Peter the Great) (1672–1725), tsar of Russia 1682–1725. After the death of his half-brother Ivan in 1696 Peter I assumed sole authority and launched a policy of expansion along the Baltic coast. Modernizing his armed forces he waged the Great Northern War (1700–21) against Charles XII of Sweden, and went on to annex Estonia and Latvia, as well as parts of Finland, following the defeat of the Swedish monarch. Peter I's introduction of extensive government and administration reforms were instrumental in transforming Russia into a significant European power. In 1703 he made St Petersburg his capital.

Peter, St (born Simon) an Apostle. 'Peter' (from *petros*, 'stone') is the Greek form of the name given him by Jesus, signifying the rock on which he would establish his church. He is regarded by Roman Catholics as the founder and first bishop of the Church at Rome, where he is said to have been martyred in about AD 67. He is often represented as the keeper of the door of heaven; his attribute is a set of keys. Feast day, 29 June.

Peterson[1] /'piːtəs(ə)n/, Oscar (Emmanuel) (born 1925), Canadian jazz pianist and composer. He toured with the American impresario Norman Granz (born 1918) from 1949, becoming internationally famous in the 1960s, when he often appeared with Ella Fitzgerald. During this period he usually led a trio with a bass and guitar. In the 1970s he frequently played the piano solo, recording the album *My Favourite Instrument* (1973).

Peterson[2] /'piːtəs(ə)n/, Roger Tory (1908–96), American ornithologist and artist. Peterson produced his first book for identifying birds in the field in 1934, introducing the concept of illustrating similar birds in similar postures with their differences highlighted. The book was the forerunner of his *Field Guide to the Birds* (1947), the first of the famous Peterson field guides, which were published in America and elsewhere. Their format has become standard in field guides for all groups of animals and plants.

Peter the Great see PETER I.

Peter the Hermit (c.1050–1115), French monk. His preaching on the First Crusade was a rallying cry for thousands of peasants throughout Europe to journey to the Holy Land; most were massacred by the Turks in Asia Minor. Peter later became prior of an Augustinian monastery in Flanders.

Petipa /ˌpətr'pɑː/, Marius (Ivanovich) (1818–1910), French ballet-dancer and choreographer, resident in Russia from 1847. He became principal dancer for the Russian Imperial Ballet in St Petersburg in 1847 and first ballet master in 1869. Petipa choreographed more than fifty ballets, collaborating closely with Tchaikovsky on the premières of *Sleeping Beauty* (1890) and *The Nutcracker* (1892), works which were to have an important influence on modern classical ballet in Russia.

Petrarch /'petrɑːk/ (Italian name Francesco Petrarca) (1304–74), Italian poet. His reputation is chiefly based on his lyrical poetry, in particular the *Canzoniere* (c.1351–3), a sonnet sequence in praise of a woman he

calls Laura; this was to be a major source of inspiration for the English sonnet writers such as Thomas Wyatt and Philip Sidney. Petrarch was also an important figure in the rediscovery of classical antiquity, together with his friend Boccaccio, initiating the revived study of Greek and Latin literature and writing most of his works in Latin. In 1341 Petrarch was crowned Poet Laureate in Rome.

Petrie /'pi:trɪ/, Sir (William Matthew) Flinders (1853–1942), English archaeologist and Egyptologist. After fieldwork at Stonehenge in the 1870s he began excavating the Great Pyramid at Giza in 1880, pioneering the use of mathematical calculation and precise measurement in field archaeology. In his excavations in Egypt and Palestine Petrie also became the first to establish the system of sequence dating, now standard archaeological practice, by which sites are excavated layer by layer and historical chronology determined by the dating of artefacts found *in situ*.

Petronius /pɪ'trəʊnɪəs/, Gaius (known as Petronius Arbiter) (died AD 66), Roman writer. Petronius is generally accepted as the author of the *Satyricon*, a work in prose and verse satirizing the excesses of Roman society. Only fragments of the *Satyricon* survive, most notably that recounting a tastelessly extravagant banquet held by Trimalchio, a character bearing some resemblance to Nero. According to Tacitus, Petronius was 'arbiter of taste' at Nero's court. Petronius committed suicide after being accused of treason by Nero.

Pevsner /'pevznə(r)/, Antoine (1886–1962), Russian-born French sculptor and painter. He was a founder of Russian constructivism, together with his brother, Naum Gabo. In 1920 the theoretical basis of the movement was put forward in their *Realistic Manifesto*; this advanced the notion of incorporating time and movement in sculpture. Pevsner settled in Paris in 1923, becoming a French citizen in 1930. His first sculptures were mainly in plastic, and he later worked in welded metal.

Pheidippides /faɪ'dɪpɪˌdiːz/ (5th century BC), Athenian messenger. He was sent to Sparta to ask for help after the Persian landing at Marathon in 490 and is said to have covered the 250 km (150 miles) in two days on foot.

Phidias /'fɪdɪˌæs, 'faɪd-/ (5th century BC), Athenian sculptor. In about 447 he was appointed by Pericles to plan and supervise public building on the Acropolis in Athens. His own contributions to the project included a colossal gold-and-ivory statue of Athene Parthenos for the Parthenon (*c*.438), which has not survived, and the Elgin Marbles. He is also noted for his vast statue of Zeus at Olympia (*c*.430), which was one of the Seven Wonders of the World.

Philby /'fɪlbɪ/, Harold Adrian Russell ('Kim') (1912–88), British Foreign Office official and spy. While chief liaison officer at the British Embassy in Washington, DC (1949–51) he was suspected of being a Soviet agent and interrogated, but in the absence of firm evidence against him Philby was merely asked to resign. He defected to the USSR in 1963, and in the same year it was officially revealed that he had spied for the Soviets from 1933. He became a Soviet citizen in 1963 and was appointed a general in the KGB.

Philip[1] /'fɪlɪp/ the name of five kings of ancient Macedonia, notably:
Philip II (known as Philip II of Macedon) (382–336 BC), father of Alexander the Great, reigned 359–336. He unified and expanded ancient Macedonia, as well as carrying out a number of army reforms, such as the introduction of the phalanx formation. His victory over Athens and Thebes at the battle of Chaeronea in 338 established his hegemony over Greece. He was assassinated as he was about to lead an expedition against Persia.
Philip V (238–179 BC), reigned 221–179. His expansionist policies led to a series of confrontations with Rome, culminating in his defeat in Thessaly in 197 and his resultant loss of control over Greece.

Philip[2] /'fɪlɪp/ the name of six kings of France:
Philip I (1052–1108), reigned 1059–1108.
Philip II (known as Philip Augustus) (1165–1223), son of Louis VII, reigned 1180–1223. His reign was marked by a dramatic expansion of Capetian influence, at the expense of the English Plantagenet empire in France. After mounting a series of military campaigns against the English kings Henry II, Richard I, and John, Philip succeeded in regaining Normandy (1204), Anjou (1204), and most of Poitou (1204–5). Towards the end of his reign, after success in the crusade (1209–31) against the Albigensian her-

etics, he also managed to add fresh territories in the south to his kingdom.

Philip III (known as Philip the Bold) (1245–85), reigned 1270–85.

Philip IV (known as Philip the Fair) (1268–1314), son of Philip III, reigned 1285–1314. He continued the Capetian policy of extending French dominions, waging wars of expansion with England (1294–1303) and Flanders (1302–5). His reign, however, was dominated by his struggle with the papacy; in 1303 he imprisoned Pope Boniface VIII (c.1228–1303), and, in 1305, his influence secured the appointment of the French Clement V (c.1260–1314) as pope. Philip's domination of the papacy was further consolidated when Clement moved the papal seat to Avignon (1309), where it remained until 1377. Philip also persuaded Clement to dissolve the powerful and wealthy order of the Knights Templars; its leaders were executed and its property divided between the Crown and the Knights Hospitallers.

Philip V (known as Philip the Tall) (1293–1322), reigned 1316–22.

Philip VI (known as Philip of Valois) (1293–1350), reigned 1328–50. The founder of the Valois dynasty, Philip came to the throne on the death of his cousin Charles IV (1294–1328), whose only child was a girl and barred from ruling by law. His claim was disputed by Edward III of England, who could trace a claim through his mother Isabella of France. War between the two countries, which was to develop into the Hundred Years War, ensued. Philip was defeated by Edward at the Battle of Crécy (1346).

Philip[3] /ˈfɪlɪp/ the name of five kings of Spain:

Philip I (known as Philip the Handsome) (1478–1506), reigned 1504–6. Son of the Holy Roman emperor Maximilian I of Habsburg (1459–1519), Philip married the infanta Joanna, daughter of Ferdinand of Aragon and Isabella of Castile, in 1496. After Isabella's death he ruled Castile jointly with Joanna, establishing the Habsburgs as the ruling dynasty in Spain.

Philip II (1527–98), son of Charles I, reigned 1556–98. Philip married the second of his four wives, Mary I of England, in 1554, and came to the throne following his father's abdication two years later. His reign came to be dominated by an anti-Protestant crusade which exhausted the Spanish economy. He failed to suppress

revolt in the Netherlands (1567–79), and although he conquered Portugal in 1580, his war against England also proved a failure, an attempted Spanish invasion being thwarted by the defeat of the Armada in 1588.

Philip III (1578–1621), reigned 1598–1621.

Philip IV (1605–65), reigned 1621–65.

Philip V (1683–1746), grandson of Louis XIV, reigned 1700–24 and 1724–46. The selection of Philip, a Bourbon, as successor to Charles II, and Louis XIV's insistence that Philip remain an heir to the French throne, gave rise to the threat of the union of the French and Spanish thrones and led to the War of the Spanish Succession (1701–14). Internationally recognized as king of Spain by the Peace of Utrecht (1713–14), Philip reigned until 1724, when he abdicated in favour of his son Louis I (1707–24), but returned to the throne following Louis's death in the same year.

Philip, Prince, Duke of Edinburgh (born 1921), husband of Elizabeth II. The son of Prince Andrew of Greece and Denmark (1882–1944), he married Princess Elizabeth in 1947; on the eve of his marriage he was created Duke of Edinburgh. He served in the Royal Navy until Elizabeth's accession in 1952.

Philip, St[1] an Apostle. He is commemorated with St James the Less on 1 May.

Philip, St[2] (known as St Philip the Evangelist) one of seven deacons appointed to superintend the secular business of the Church at Jerusalem (Acts 6:5–6). Feast day, 6 June.

Philip II of Macedon /ˈmæsɪˌdɒn, -d(ə)n/, Philip II of Macedonia (see PHILIP[1]).

Philip Augustus /ɔːˈɡʌstəs/, Philip II of France (see PHILIP[2]).

Philip of Valois /ˈvælwʌ/, Philip VI of France (see PHILIP[2]).

Philip the Bold, Philip III of France (see PHILIP[2]).

Philip the Fair, Philip IV of France (see PHILIP[2]).

Philip the Handsome, Philip I of Spain (see PHILIP[3]).

Philip the Tall, Philip V of France (see PHILIP[2]).

Philo Judaeus /ˌfaɪləʊ dʒuːˈdiːəs/ (also known as Philo of Alexandria) (c.15 BC–AD c.50), Jewish philosopher of Alexandria. His

numerous works (written in Greek) trace many links between Jewish Scripture and Greek philosophy. He is particularly known for his commentaries on the Pentateuch, which he interpreted allegorically in the light of Platonic and Aristotelian philosophy.

Phiz /fɪz/, (pseudonym of Hablot Knight Browne) (1815–82), English illustrator. He was apprenticed to an engraver, but turned to etching and watercolour painting. In 1836 he was chosen to illustrate Dickens's *Pickwick Papers*, and took his pseudonym to complement Dickens's 'Boz'. He illustrated many of Dickens's works, including *Martin Chuzzlewit* and *Bleak House*.

Photius /'fəʊtɪəs/ (*c*.820–*c*.891), Byzantine scholar and patriarch of Constantinople. His most important work is the *Bibliotheca*, a critical account of 280 earlier prose works and an invaluable source of information about many works now lost.

Piaf /'piːæf/, Edith (born Edith Giovanna Gassion) (1915–63), French singer. She acquired her name in 1935, when a cabaret impresario called her *la môme piaf* (= little sparrow), referring to her small size. She became known as a cabaret and music-hall singer in the late 1930s, touring Europe and America in the 1940s. She is especially remembered for her defiant and nostalgic songs, some of which she wrote herself, including 'La Vie en rose'. Other songs include 'Je ne regrette rien'.

Piaget /pɪ'æʒeɪ/, Jean (1896–1980), Swiss psychologist. Piaget's work provided the single biggest impact on the study of the development of thought processes. His central thesis is that children initially lack intellectual and logical abilities, which they acquire through experience and interaction with the world around them. They then proceed through a series of fixed stages of cognitive development, each being a prerequisite for the next.

Picasso /pɪ'kæsəʊ/, Pablo (1881–1973), Spanish painter, sculptor, and graphic artist, resident in France from 1904. His prolific inventiveness and technical versatility assured his position as the dominant figure in avant-garde art in the first half of the 20th century. The paintings of Picasso's Blue Period (1901–4) used melancholy blue tones to depict social outsiders. These gave way to his Rose Period (1905–6), in which circus performers were represented in pinks and greys. *Les Demoiselles d'Avignon*

(1907), with its rejection of naturalism and focus on the analysis of form, signalled the emergence of cubism, which he developed with Georges Braque and others from 1908 to 1914. The 1920s and 1930s saw the evolution of a neoclassical figurative style, designs for Diaghilev's Ballets Russes, and the evolution of semi-surrealist paintings using increasingly violent imagery, notably *The Three Dancers* (1935) and *Guernica* (1937), his response to the destruction of the Basque capital by German bombers.

Pickering /'pɪkərɪŋ/, William Hayward (born 1910), New Zealand-born American engineer. He spent most of his career at the California Institute of Technology at Pasadena, becoming director of the Jet Propulsion Laboratory there in 1954. Pickering carried out early work on the telemetry, guidance, and communications systems of rockets, and went on to develop America's first satellite, Explorer I, which was launched in 1958. Several unmanned probes to the moon and planets were launched by the JPL during his directorship, notably the Ranger, Surveyor, and Mariner missions.

Pickford /'pɪkfəd/, Mary (born Gladys Mary Smith) (1893–1979), Canadian-born American actress. She was a star of silent films, usually playing the innocent young heroine, as in *Rebecca of Sunnybrook Farm* (1917) and *Pollyanna* (1920). In 1919 she co-founded the film production company United Artists; she was married to one of the other founders, Douglas Fairbanks, between 1919 and 1936.

Pierce /pɪəs/, Franklin (1804–69), American Democratic statesman, 14th President of the US 1853–7. His presidency saw the rise of divisions within the country over slavery and the encouragement of settlement in the north-west.

Piero della Francesca /ˌpjeərəʊ ˌdelə fræn'tʃeskə/ (1416–92), Italian painter. He worked in a number of cities, including Florence and Arezzo, and was influenced by the work of Masaccio and Uccello. He used perspective, proportion, and geometrical relationships to create ordered and harmonious pictures in which the figures appear to inhabit real space. He is best known as a fresco painter, and among his major works is a fresco cycle in Arezzo depicting the story of the True Cross (begun 1452). After a long period of neglect

his work was regarded more favourably in the 20th century.

Piggott /ˈpɪɡət/, Lester (Keith) (born 1935), English jockey. He was champion jockey nine times between 1960 and 1971 and again in 1981 and 1982; he won the Derby a record nine times. He made a comeback as a jockey in 1990 after a period of imprisonment for tax irregularities (1987–8).

Pilate /ˈpaɪlət/, Pontius (died AD c.36), Roman procurator of Judaea c.26–c.36. Little is known of his life; he is chiefly remembered for presiding at the trial of Jesus Christ and sentencing him to death by crucifixion, as recorded in the New Testament. Pilate was later recalled to Rome to stand trial on charges of cruelty, having ordered a massacre of the Samaritans in 36. According to one tradition he subsequently committed suicide.

Pindar /ˈpɪndə(r)/ (c.518–c.438 BC), Greek lyric poet. His surviving works include four books of odes (the *Epinikia*) celebrating victories won in athletic contests at Olympia and elsewhere. The odes are often in the form of choral hymns, written in an elevated style and imbued with religious significance.

Pinero /pɪˈnɪərəʊ/, Sir Arthur Wing (1855–1934), English dramatist and actor. He began writing for the stage in 1877, creating a series of comedies and farces, such as *Dandy Dick* (1887). From 1889 he embarked on a number of serious plays dealing with social issues, especially the double standards of morality for men and women (for example *The Second Mrs Tanqueray*, 1893).

Pinkerton /ˈpɪŋkət(ə)n/, Allan (1819–84), Scottish-born American detective. He emigrated to the US in 1842, and in 1850 he established the first American private detective agency (in Chicago), becoming famous after solving a series of train robberies. In the early years of the American Civil War (1861–2) he served as chief of the secret service for the Union side. His agency was later involved in anti-trade union activity, particularly in the coal industry (1877).

Pinochet /ˈpɪnəˌʃeɪ/, Augusto (full name Augusto Pinochet Ugarte) (born 1915), Chilean general and statesman, President 1974–90. He became Commander-in-Chief of Chile's armed forces in 1973 and in the same year masterminded the military coup which overthrew President Allende. He imposed a repressive military dictatorship until forced to call elections (December 1989), giving way to a democratically elected President in 1990.

Pinter /ˈpɪntə(r)/, Harold (born 1930), English dramatist, actor, and director. His plays are associated with the Theatre of the Absurd and are often marked by a sense of brooding menace; they include *The Birthday Party* (1958), *The Caretaker* (1960), and *Party Time* (1991). He has also written screenplays, including the film version of John Fowles's *The French Lieutenant's Woman* (1981).

Piper /ˈpaɪpə(r)/, John (1903–92), English painter and decorative designer. His early paintings were abstract, but in the 1930s he turned to a romantic naturalism. During the Second World War he was one of the artists commissioned to depict the results of air raids on Britain. He is best known for watercolours and aquatints of buildings (such as those depicting Windsor Castle, 1941–2) and stained glass for Coventry and Llandaff cathedrals.

Pirandello /ˌpɪrənˈdeləʊ/, Luigi (1867–1936), Italian dramatist and novelist. His plays challenged the conventions of naturalism and had a significant influence on the development of European drama, anticipating the anti-illusionist theatre of Brecht. Of his ten plays the best known include *Six Characters in Search of an Author* (1921) and *Henry IV* (1922). Among his novels are *The Outcast* (1901) and *The Late Mattia Pascal* (1904). He was awarded the Nobel Prize for literature in 1934.

Piranesi /ˌpɪrəˈneɪzɪ/, Giovanni Battista (1720–78), Italian engraver. His interest in classical Roman architecture is reflected in his prints, in which he relied on atypical viewpoints and dramatic chiaroscuro to aggrandize its power and scale. His *Prisons* (1745–61) extended this imagery into the realms of fantasy, producing a nightmare vision of claustrophobic space and endless dimensions that prefigured later romantic concerns.

Pisan, Christine de, see DE PISAN.

Pisano[1] /pɪˈsɑːnəʊ/, Andrea (c.1290–c.1348) and Nino, his son (died c.1368), Italian sculptors. Andrea is notable as the creator of the earliest pair of bronze doors for the baptistery at Florence (completed 1336). Nino was one of the earliest to specialize in free-standing life-size figures.

Pisano[2] /pɪˈsɑːnəʊ/, Nicola (c.1220–c.1278) and Giovanni, his son (c.1250–c.1314), Italian sculptors. Nicola's work departed from medieval conventions and signalled a revival of interest in classical sculpture. He brought human expression and dramatic power to his works, the best known of which are the pulpits in the baptistery at Pisa (c.1255–60) and in Siena cathedral (1265–8). Giovanni's works carried this process further and foreshadow the sculptural renaissance which followed. His works include a pulpit in the church of Santa Andrea in Pistoia (completed 1301), and the richly decorated façade of Siena cathedral (completed in 1284).

Pisistratus /paɪˈsɪstrətəs/ (also **Peisistratus**) (c.600–c.527 BC), tyrant of Athens. He seized power in 561 and after twice being expelled ruled continuously from 546 until his death. As ruler he reduced aristocratic power in rural Attica and promoted the financial prosperity and cultural pre-eminence of Athens.

Pissarro /pɪˈsɑːrəʊ/, Camille (1830–1903), French painter and graphic artist. Born in the West Indies, he moved to France in the 1850s and studied in Paris with Monet. At first influenced by Corot, he later began to paint out of doors and to develop a spontaneous style typical of other impressionist painters; he participated in all eight of the impressionist exhibitions. He also experimented with pointillism in the 1880s as well as encouraging Cézanne and Gauguin in their attempts to depart from an impressionist style of painting. Works include *Red Roofs* (1877) and *Boulevard Montmartre* (1897).

Pitman /ˈpɪtmən/, Sir Isaac (1813–97), English inventor of a shorthand system. Inspired by the phonetic shorthand system designed in 1786 by Samuel Taylor (1749–1811), Pitman devised his own system, published as *Stenographic Sound Hand* (1837). Pitman shorthand, first adopted (in the US) in 1852, is still widely used in the UK and elsewhere.

Pitt[1] /pɪt/, William (known as Pitt the Elder), 1st Earl of Chatham (1708–78), British Whig statesman. He became Secretary of State (effectively Prime Minister) in 1756 and headed coalition governments 1756–61 and 1766–8. He brought the Seven Years War to an end in 1763 by using a successful maritime strategy to defeat France. He also masterminded the conquest of French pos-

sessions overseas, particularly in Canada and India. He was the father of Pitt the Younger.

Pitt[2] /pɪt/, William (known as Pitt the Younger) (1759–1806), British statesman, Prime Minister 1783–1801 and 1804–6. The son of Pitt the Elder, he became Prime Minister at the age of 24, the youngest ever to hold this office. He restored the authority of Parliament, introduced financial reforms, reduced the enormous national debt he had inherited, and reformed the administration of India. With Britain's entry into war against France (1793), Pitt became almost entirely occupied with the conduct of the war and with uniting European opposition to France. Having secured the Union of Great Britain and Ireland in 1800, he resigned in 1801 over the issue of Catholic Emancipation (which George III refused to accept). He returned as Premier in 1804 after hostilities with France had been resumed, and died in office.

Pitt-Rivers /ˈpɪtˈrɪvəz/, Augustus Henry Lane Fox (1827–1900), English archaeologist and anthropologist. In 1882 he retired from the army and began a series of excavations of the prehistoric, Roman, and Saxon sites on his Wiltshire estate. His scientific approach and emphasis on the importance of everyday objects greatly influenced the development of modern archaeological techniques. He also carried out pioneering work in establishing typological sequences of artefacts from different cultures. He donated his collection of weapons and artefacts to found the ethnological museum in Oxford which bears his name.

Pius XII /ˈpaɪəs/ (born Eugenio Pacelli) (1876–1958), pope 1939–58. He upheld the neutrality of the Roman Catholic Church during the Second World War, maintaining diplomatic relations with both Allied and Axis governments. After the war there was criticism of his failure to condemn Nazi atrocities and of his apparent ambivalence towards anti-Semitism. Pius XII took steps to counter the rise of Communism in postwar Italy, threatening to excommunicate its supporters.

Pizan, Christine de, see DE PISAN.

Pizarro /pɪˈzɑːrəʊ/, Francisco (c.1478–1541), Spanish conquistador. In 1531 he set out from Panama to conquer the Inca empire in Peru. Crossing the mountains, he defeated the Incas and in 1533 executed their emperor Atahualpa (born 1502), setting up an Inca puppet monarchy at Cuzco and

building his own capital at Lima (1535). He was assassinated in Lima by supporters of his rival Diego de Almagro (1475–1538).

Planck /plæŋk/, Max (Karl Ernst Ludwig) (1858–1947), German theoretical physicist, who founded the quantum theory. He published fundamental papers on thermodynamics before taking up the problem of black-body radiation. In 1900 he announced his radiation law, according to which electromagnetic radiation from heated bodies was not emitted as a continuous flow but was made up of discrete units or quanta of energy, the size of which involved a fundamental physical constant (Planck's constant). The quantum concept was immediately used to explain atomic structure and the photoelectric effect. Planck was awarded the 1918 Nobel Prize for physics.

Plath /plæθ/, Sylvia (1932–63), American poet. She married Ted Hughes in 1956 and first published her poetry in 1960. Her life was marked by periods of severe depression and her work is notable for its controlled and intense treatment of extreme and painful states of mind. In 1963 she committed suicide; it was only after the posthumous publication of *Ariel* (1965) that she gained wide recognition. She also wrote a novel, *The Bell Jar* (1963).

Plato /'pleɪtəʊ/ (*c.*429–*c.*347 BC), Greek philosopher. He was a disciple of Socrates and the teacher of Aristotle, and he founded the Academy in Athens. His system of thought had a profound influence on Christian theology and Western philosophy. His philosophical writings, which cover metaphysics, politics, and ethics, are presented in the form of dialogues, with Socrates as the principal speaker; they include the *Symposium* and the *Phaedo*. An integral part of his thought is the theory of 'ideas' or 'forms', in which abstract entities or *universals* are contrasted with their objects or *particulars* in the material world. Plato's political theories appear in the *Republic*, in which he explored the nature and structure of a just society. He proposed a political system based on the division of the population into three classes, determined by education rather than birth or wealth: rulers, police and armed forces, and civilians.

Plautus /'plɔːtəs/, Titus Maccius (*c.*250–184 BC), Roman comic dramatist. His plays, of which twenty-one survive, are modelled on the New Comedy of Greek dramatists such as Menander, but with a few important differences. Fantasy and imagination are more important than realism in the development of the plots, for example; his stock characters, which follow Greek types, are often larger than life and their language is correspondingly exuberant.

Player /'pleɪə(r)/, Gary (born 1936), South African golfer. He has won numerous championships including the British Open (1959; 1968; 1974), the US Masters (1961; 1974; 1978), the PGA (1962; 1972), and the US Open (1965).

Playfair /'pleɪfeə(r)/, John (1748–1819), Scottish mathematician and geologist. A friend of James Hutton, he is chiefly remembered for his *Illustrations of the Huttonian Theory of the Earth* (1802), which presented Hutton's views on geology — and some of his own — in a concise and readable form, enabling them to reach a far wider audience than Hutton's own writings.

Pliny[1] /'plɪnɪ/ (known as Pliny the Elder; Latin name Gaius Plinius Secundus) (23–79), Roman statesman and scholar. He combined a busy life in public affairs with prodigious activity in reading and writing. His *Natural History* (77) is a vast encyclopedia of the natural and human worlds, and is one of the earliest known works of its kind. He died while observing the eruption of Vesuvius in 79, an event which was described by his nephew Pliny the Younger.

Pliny[2] /'plɪnɪ/ (known as Pliny the Younger; Latin name Gaius Plinius Caecilius Secundus) (*c.*61–*c.*112), Roman senator and writer. He was the nephew of Pliny the Elder. His books of letters deal with both public and private affairs; they include a description of the eruption of Vesuvius in 79 which destroyed the town of Pompeii and in which his uncle died. The letters also include Pliny's correspondence with the Emperor Trajan, which contains one of the earliest descriptions of non-Christian attitudes towards Christians.

Plotinus /plə'taɪnəs/ (*c.*205–70), philosopher, probably of Roman descent, the founder and leading exponent of Neoplatonism. Neoplatonism was a religious and philosophical system based on elements from Plato, Pythagoras, Aristotle, and the Stoics, with overtones of Eastern mysticism. It was the dominant philosophy

of the pagan world from the mid-3rd century AD until the closing of the pagan schools by Justinian in 529, and also strongly influenced medieval and Renaissance thought. Plotinus studied in Alexandria and later Persia before finally settling in Rome in 244 and setting up a school of philosophy. His writings were published after his death by his pupil Porphyry.

Plutarch /'pluːtɑːk/ (Latin name Lucius Mestrius Plutarchus) (c.46–c.120), Greek biographer and philosopher. He is chiefly known for his *Parallel Lives*, a collection of biographies of prominent Greeks and Romans in which the moral character of his subjects is illustrated by a series of anecdotes. The work was an important source for Shakespeare's Roman plays, and was used as a model by biographers such as Izaak Walton.

Pocahontas /ˌpɒkə'hɒntəs/ (c.1595–1617), American Indian princess, daughter of Powhatan (died 1618), an Algonquian chief in Virginia. According to the story of an English colonist, Captain John Smith (1580–1631), she rescued him from death at the hands of her father. In 1613 she was seized as a hostage by the English, and she later married a colonist, John Rolfe (1585–1622). In 1616 she and her husband visited England, where she died.

Poe /pəʊ/, Edgar Allan (1809–49), American short-story writer, poet, and critic. He spent most of his life in poverty and ill health. His fiction and poetry are Gothic in style and characterized by their exploration of the macabre, the fantastic, and the grotesque. His most famous short stories include the Gothic romance 'The Fall of the House of Usher' (which appeared in *Tales of the Grotesque and Arabesque*, 1840) and 'The Pit and the Pendulum' (1843), while his poems include 'The Raven' (1845) and 'Annabel Lee' (1849). His story 'The Murders in the Rue Morgue' (1841) is often regarded as the first detective story in English literature. His critical writings include 'The Poetic Principle' (1850), which anticipated many of the concerns of the Aesthetic Movement ('art for art's sake').

Poincaré /ˌpwʌŋkæ'reɪ/, Jules-Henri (1854–1912), French mathematician and philosopher of science. Poincaré made far-reaching contributions to pure and applied mathematics. He worked extensively on differential equations which allowed him to transform celestial mechanics, and was one of the pioneers of algebraic topology. By 1900 he was proposing a relativistic philosophy, suggesting that it implied the absolute velocity of light, which nothing could exceed.

Poisson /'pwʌsɒn/, Siméon-Denis (1781–1840), French mathematical physicist. Early in his career he began applying the integration of differential equations to problems in physics, an approach which he used for many years with great effect. He added to the work of Laplace and Lagrange on planetary motions, and went on to study electrostatics, heat, elasticity, and magnetism. Perhaps his major contributions were in probability theory, in which he greatly improved Laplace's work and developed several concepts that are now named after him.

Poitier /'pwɑːtɪˌeɪ/, Sidney (born 1924), American actor and film director. He appeared with the American Negro Theater in New York before making his Hollywood début in 1950. He won an Oscar for his performance in *Lilies of the Field* (1963) and became the first African-American superstar actor. In the 1970s he began directing films such as *Uptown Saturday Night* (1974), and after ten years away from acting he reappeared in *Little Nikita* in 1988.

Polanski /pə'lænskɪ/, Roman (born 1933), French film director, of Polish descent. Born in France, he grew up in Poland, where he pursued a career as an actor from the age of 14 and directed the film *Knife in the Water* (1962), which established his international reputation. He subsequently worked in Hollywood, having success with films such as *Rosemary's Baby* (1968) and *Chinatown* (1974). He left the US for France in 1977 under threat of prosecution for drug and sex offences. His later films, including *Tess* (1979) and *Frantic* (1988), have not had the success of his earlier titles. His second wife, Hollywood actress Sharon Tate (1943–69), was one of the victims of a multiple murder by followers of the cult leader Charles Manson.

Polk /pəʊk/, James Knox (1795–1849), American Democratic statesman, 11th President of the US 1845–9. His term of office resulted in major territorial additions to the US: Texas was admitted to the Union in 1845, and the successful outcome of the conflict with Mexico resulted in the annexation of California and the south-west two years later.

Pollaiuolo /ˌpɒlaɪˈwəʊləʊ/, Antonio (c.1432–98) and Piero (1443–96), Italian sculptors, painters, and engravers. Antonio assisted Ghiberti with the doors for the baptistery of Florence (1452) and both brothers worked on the monuments to the popes Sixtus IV and Innocent VIII in St Peter's, Rome; other joint works include the painting the *Martyrdom of St Sebastian* (1475). Antonio is particularly known for his realistic depiction of the human form, which reflects his studies of anatomy; his works include the engraving *Battle of the Naked Men* (c.1470) and the bronze statuette *Hercules and Antaeus* (c.1475).

Pollock /ˈpɒlək/, (Paul) Jackson (1912–56), American painter. His earlier work shows the influence of surrealist painters such as Joan Miró, but he later became a leading figure of abstract expressionism and from 1947 onwards developed the style known as action painting. Fixing the canvas to the floor or wall, he poured, splashed, or dripped paint on it, covering the whole canvas and avoiding any point of emphasis in the picture. He often used sticks, trowels, and knives instead of brushes and occasionally mixed the paint with sand or broken glass. He was killed in a car accident; he had earlier been treated for alcoholism and in 1938 suffered a mental breakdown.

Polo, Marco, see MARCO POLO.

Pol Pot /pɒl ˈpɒt/ (born Saloth Sar) (born c.1925), Cambodian Communist leader, Prime Minister 1976–9. From 1968 he led the Khmer Rouge, becoming Prime Minister soon after its seizure of power in 1975. During his regime the Khmer Rouge embarked on a brutal reconstruction programme in which more than 2 million Cambodians died. Overthrown in 1979, Pol Pot led the Khmer Rouge in a guerrilla war against the new Vietnamese-backed government until his official retirement from the leadership in 1985.

Polybius /pəˈlɪbɪəs/ (c.200–c.118 BC), Greek historian. After an early political career in Greece, he was deported to Rome. His forty books of *Histories* (only partially extant) chronicled the rise of the Roman Empire from 220 to 146 BC.

Polycarp, St /ˈpɒlɪˌkɑːp/ (c.69–c.155), Greek bishop of Smyrna in Asia Minor. His dates are uncertain but he was probably the leading Christian figure in Smyrna in the mid-2nd century. He was arrested during a pagan festival, refused to recant his faith, and was burnt to death. His followers buried his remains and wrote an account of his martyrdom which provides one of the oldest such records to survive. Feast day, 23 February.

Polyclitus /ˌpɒlɪˈklaɪtəs/ (5th century BC), Greek sculptor. He is known for his statues of idealized male athletes. Two Roman copies of his works survive, the *Doryphoros* (spear-bearer) and the *Diadumenos* (youth fastening a band round his head). His other works include a large gold and ivory statue of the goddess Hera.

Pompadour /ˈpɒmpəˌdʊə(r)/, Marquise de (title of Jeanne Antoinette Poisson; known as Madame de Pompadour) (1721–64), French noblewoman. In 1744 she became the mistress and lifelong confidante of Louis XV; although she did not remain his only mistress, she retained her influence and place at court. She was a notable patron of the arts and founded the porcelain factory at Sèvres. She became unpopular through her interference in political affairs, particularly when obtaining ministerial appointments for her favourites.

Pompey /ˈpɒmpɪ/ (known as Pompey the Great; Latin name Gnaeus Pompeius Magnus) (106–48 BC), Roman general and statesman. His greatest achievements were the suppression of the Mediterranean pirates (66), and the defeat of Mithridates in the east (63). He formed the First Triumvirate with Caesar and Crassus in 60, but disagreement with Caesar resulted in civil war. Pompey was defeated at the battle of Pharsalus, after which he fled to Egypt, where he was murdered.

Pompidou /ˈpɒmpɪˌduː/, Georges (Jean Raymond) (1911–74), French statesman, Prime Minister 1962–8 and President 1969–74. In 1944 he became an adviser of Charles de Gaulle; when the latter was returned to power in 1959, Pompidou assisted in the drafting of the new constitution. He was instrumental in ending the conflict in Algeria between French forces and nationalist guerrillas. He resigned after criticism of his handling of the strikes and riots of 1968. Pompidou was elected President the following year, following de Gaulle's resignation; he died in office.

Ponce de León /ˌpɒns də ˈliːɒn, ˌpɒnseɪ də leɪˈɒn/, Juan (c.1460–1521), Spanish explorer. He accompanied Columbus on his

second voyage to the New World in 1493 and later became governor of Puerto Rico (1510–12). He landed on the coast of Florida in 1513, claiming the area for Spain and becoming its governor the following year.

Ponte, Lorenzo Da, see DA PONTE.

Pontormo /pɒnˈtɔːməʊ/, Jacopo da (1494–1557), Italian painter. He was a pupil of Andrea del Sarto and was influenced by the work of Leonardo da Vinci and later by Michelangelo. From about 1518 onwards he began to develop a style characterized by dynamic composition, anatomical exaggeration, and bright colours, which placed him at the forefront of early mannerism. His works include the *Deposition* (c.1525), an altarpiece in the chapel of Santa Felicità in Florence.

Pope /pəʊp/, Alexander (1688–1744), English poet. He was a major figure of the Augustan period in England, famous for his caustic wit and metrical skill, in particular his use of the heroic couplet. His *Essay on Criticism* (1711), a poem on the art of writing, drew him to the attention of Addison's literary circle; he later associated with Jonathan Swift, John Gay, and others. Among Pope's other major works are the mock-heroic *The Rape of the Lock* (1712; enlarged 1714), the philosophical poem *An Essay on Man* (1733–4), and the *Epistle to Dr Arbuthnot* (1735), a fierce and ironic attack on his critics. He published an edition of Shakespeare's plays (1725) which was criticized for inaccuracies by the scholar Lewis Theobald (1688–1744); Pope retaliated by making Theobald the hero of his satire attacking 'Dulness', *The Dunciad* (1728). Pope also made notable translations of the *Iliad* (1715–20) and the *Odyssey* (1726).

Popper /ˈpɒpə(r)/, Sir Karl Raimund (1902–94), Austrian-born British philosopher. He was originally associated with the logical positivist group the Vienna Circle, but was highly critical of the emphasis placed by logical positivism on verification. In *The Logic of Scientific Discovery* (1934) he posits instead that scientific hypotheses can never be finally confirmed as true and are acceptable only in so far as they manage to survive frequent attempts to falsify them. He is also known for his criticism of the historicist social theories of Plato, Hegel, and Marx, as, for example, in *The Open Society and its Enemies* (1945). He left Vienna on Hitler's rise to power and eventually settled in England, where he was a pro-

fessor at the London School of Economics (1949–69).

Porphyry /ˈpɔːfɪrɪ/ (born Malchus) (c.232–303), Neoplatonist philosopher. Born in Tyre, he studied first at Athens. He then moved to Rome, where he became a pupil of Plotinus, whose works he edited after the latter's death. Porphyry's own works include *Against the Christians*, of which only fragments survive.

Porsche /pɔːʃ, German ˈpɔrʃə/, Ferdinand (1875–1952), Austrian car designer. In 1934, with backing from the Nazi government, he designed the Volkswagen ('people's car'), a small economical car with a rear engine, developed and produced in great numbers by the Volkswagen company after the Second World War. Porsche's name has since become famous for the high-performance sports and racing cars produced by his company, originally to his designs.

Porsenna /pɔːˈsenə/, Lars (also **Porsena** /ˈpɔːsmə/) (6th century BC), a legendary Etruscan chieftain, king of the town of Clusium. He was summoned by Tarquinius Superbus after the latter's overthrow and exile from Rome and as a result laid siege to Rome but was ultimately unsuccessful in capturing the city.

Porter[1] /ˈpɔːtə(r)/, Cole (1892–1964), American songwriter. He made his name with a series of Broadway musicals during and after the 1930s; these include *Anything Goes* (1934) and *Kiss me, Kate* (1948). He also wrote songs for films, including *Rosalie* (1937) and *High Society* (1956). Among his best-known songs are 'Let's Do It', 'Night and Day', and 'Begin the Beguine'.

Porter[2] /ˈpɔːtə(r)/, Katherine Anne (1890–1980), American short-story writer and novelist. Her collections of short stories include *Pale Horse, Pale Rider* (1939) and *Collected Short Stories* (1965), for which she won a Pulitzer Prize. Her novel *Ship of Fools* (1962) is an allegorical treatment of a voyage from Mexico to Germany during the period of the rise of Nazism.

Porter[3] /ˈpɔːtə(r)/, Peter (Neville Frederick) (born 1929), Australian poet, resident chiefly in England since 1951. His early collections, such as *Poems, Ancient and Modern* (1964), provide a sharply satiric portrait of London in the 1960s. His later work became increasingly meditative, complex, and allusive. Other collections include *Eng-*

lish *Subtitles* (1981) and *The Automatic Oracle* (1987).

Potter[1] /'pɒtə(r)/, (Helen) Beatrix (1866–1943), English writer of children's stories. She is known for her series of animal stories, illustrated with her own delicate watercolours, which began with *The Tale of Peter Rabbit* (first published privately in 1900).

Potter[2] /'pɒtə(r)/, Dennis (Christopher George) (1935–94), English television dramatist. He began suffering from a crippling form of psoriasis in the 1960s, after which he wrote his most acclaimed works, the series *Pennies from Heaven* (1978) and *The Singing Detective* (1986). Both use popular songs of the 1920s, 1930s, and 1940s to contrast the humdrum or painful realities of everyday life with the imagination's capacity for hope and self-delusion. Other plays include *Blue Remembered Hills* (1979), in which adults played the parts of children, and the controversial *Brimstone and Treacle* (1976). In 1996, after Potter's death, his last works *Karaoke* and *Cold Lazarus* were screened jointly by two otherwise competing TV stations, BBC1 and Channel Four, in tribute to the writer.

Poulenc /'puːlæŋk/, Francis (Jean Marcel) (1899–1963), French composer. He was a member of the group Les Six. The influence of Satie and Cocteau can be seen particularly in his adoption of the idioms of popular music such as jazz. His work is also characterized by a lyricism heard especially in his many songs and in such instrumental works as the sonatas for flute (1957) and oboe (1962). He also wrote a series of lyrical and contrapuntal sacred choral pieces, while his works for the theatre include the opera *Dialogues des Carmélites* (1957) and the ballet *Les Biches* (1923).

Pound /paʊnd/, Ezra (Weston Loomis) (1885–1972), American poet and critic. He came to Europe in 1908 and co-founded the imagist movement, rejecting romanticism and seeking clarity of expression through the use of precise images. Collections of poetry from this period include *Ripostes* (1912). He also co-edited the magazine of the vorticist movement, *Blast*, from 1914 to 1915. After this he gradually moved away from imagism and began to develop a highly eclectic poetic voice, drawing on a vast range of classical and other references, which ensured his reputation as one of the foremost modernist poets. Work from this later period includes *Hugh Selwyn Mauberley*

(1920) and the long (unfinished) series of *Cantos* (1917–70). In 1925 he settled in Italy; he was charged with treason in 1945 following his pro-Fascist radio broadcasts during the Second World War, but was adjudged insane and committed to a mental institution until 1958.

Poussin /puː'sæn, French pusɛ̃/, Nicolas (1594–1665), French painter. Regarded as the chief representative of French classicism in art and a master of the grand manner, he was extremely influential in the development of French art. From 1624 he lived mostly in Rome and was influenced by the work of Italian painters, particularly Titian and Raphael. In the 1630s and 1640s he developed in his painting a harmony and sense of order suffused with a rich colour sense. His subject-matter included biblical scenes (*The Adoration of the Golden Calf*, *c.*1635), classical mythology (*Et in Arcadia Ego*, *c.*1655), and historical landscapes.

Powell[1] /'pəʊəl/, Anthony (Dymoke) (born 1905), English novelist. He is best known for his sequence of twelve novels, *A Dance to the Music of Time*, beginning with *A Question of Upbringing* (1951) and ending with *Hearing Secret Harmonies* (1975). These novels are a satirical and panoramic portrayal of the fortunes of the English upper middle classes between the First and Second World Wars.

Powell[2] /'paʊəl/, (John) Enoch (born 1912), British politician. He was a classical scholar before the Second World War, joining the Conservative Party in 1946. After serving as Minister of Health (1960–3), he attracted public attention in 1968 with his frank condemnation of multiracial immigration into Britain; as a result he was dismissed from the shadow Cabinet. Powell also opposed British entry into the Common Market, resigning from the Conservative Party in 1974 on this issue. He later served as an Ulster Unionist MP (1974–87).

Powell[3] /'paʊəl/, Michael (Latham) (1905–90), English film director, producer, and screenwriter. Having made his directing début in 1931, he co-founded the Archers Company in 1942 with the Hungarian scriptwriter Emeric Pressburger (1902–88). Their films are visually striking and often fantastic, and include *The Tales of Hoffman* (1951), *The Red Shoes* (1948), and the controversial *Peeping Tom* (1960).

Prandtl /'prænt(ə)l/, Ludwig (1875–1953), German physicist. Prandtl is remembered

for his studies of both aerodynamics and hydrodynamics. He established the existence of the boundary layer (a layer of more or less stationary fluid immediately surrounding an immersed and moving object), and made important studies on streamlining. The design of an efficient shape, weight, and mass for aircraft and ships owes much to his work.

Praxiteles /præk'sɪtəˌliːz/ (mid-4th century BC), Athenian sculptor. Although only one of his works, *Hermes Carrying the Infant Dionysus*, survives, he is regarded as one of the greatest Greek sculptors of his day. Other examples of his work survive in Roman copies or are known from their descriptions by writers; they include a statue of Aphrodite, which represents the first important female nude in sculpture.

Preminger /'premɪndʒə(r)/, Otto (Ludwig) (1906–86), Austrian-born American film director. He was a theatre and film director in Vienna before moving to New York, where he was a director on Broadway and with Twentieth Century Fox (1941–51). He then made a series of independent productions, including the influential films *The Moon is Blue* (1953), *The Man with the Golden Arm* (1955), and *Bonjour Tristesse* (1959).

Presley /'prezlɪ/, Elvis (Aaron) (1935–77), American rock-and-roll and pop singer. He was the dominant personality of early rock and roll, known particularly for the vigour and frank sexuality of his style. He first gained fame in 1956 with the success of such records as 'Heartbreak Hotel' and 'Blue Suede Shoes', attracting a worldwide following. After doing his national service in the army he made a number of films during the 1960s, resuming his personal appearances at the end of the decade, mostly in Las Vegas. He lived much of his life in his Memphis mansion Graceland.

Previn /'prevɪn/, André (George) (born 1929), German-born American conductor, pianist, and composer. He is most famous as a conductor, notably with the London Symphony Orchestra (1968–79), the Pittsburgh Symphony Orchestra (1976–86), and the Royal Philharmonic Orchestra (1987–91). He has also composed musicals, film scores, and orchestral and chamber works, and is a noted jazz and classical pianist.

Prévost d'Exiles /ˌpreɪvəʊ deg'ziːl/, Antoine-François (known as Abbé Prévost) (1696–1763), French novelist. He became a Benedictine monk in 1721 and was or-

dained as a priest five years later. He is remembered for his novel *Manon Lescaut* (1731), the story of a mutually destructive passion between a nobleman and a *demimondaine*, which inspired operas by Jules Massenet (1842–1912) and Puccini.

Prez, Josquin des, see DES PREZ.

Price /praɪs/, Vincent (1911–93), American actor. An enduringly popular performer associated particularly with horror films, he made his début in the genre with *House of Wax* (1953), although his first film appearance was in 1939 (*Tower of London*). He is perhaps best known for his performances in a series of low-budget but imaginative adaptations of Edgar Allan Poe stories directed by Roger Corman (born 1926); these included *Fall of the House of Usher* (1960) and *The Pit and the Pendulum* (1961).

Priestley[1] /'priːstlɪ/, J(ohn) B(oynton) (1894–1984), English novelist, dramatist, and critic. His first major success came with the picaresque novel *The Good Companions* (1929); this was followed by many other novels, including the more sombre *Angel Pavement* (1930). His plays include *Time and the Conways* (1937) and the mystery drama *An Inspector Calls* (1947). During and after the Second World War he was a popular radio broadcaster on current affairs.

Priestley[2] /'priːstlɪ/, Joseph (1733–1804), English scientist and theologian. Priestley was the author of about 150 books, mostly theological or educational. His chief work was on the chemistry of gases, a number of which he managed to isolate, including ammonia, sulphur dioxide, nitrous oxide, and nitrogen dioxide. Priestley's most significant discovery was of 'dephlogisticated air' (oxygen) in 1774; he demonstrated that it was important to animal life, and that plants give off this gas in sunlight. In his theological writings he maintained a Unitarian position. His support of the French Revolution provoked so much hostility that he settled in America in 1794.

Primo de Rivera /ˌpriːməʊ deɪ rɪ'veərə/, Miguel (1870–1930), Spanish general and statesman, head of state 1923–30. He came to power after leading a military coup in 1923, when he assumed dictatorial powers with the consent of Alfonso XIII. The decline of the economy contributed to his forced resignation in 1930. His son, José Antonio Primo de Rivera (1903–36), founded the Falange in 1933 and was exe-

cuted by Republicans in the Spanish Civil War.

Prince /prɪns/ (full name Prince Rogers Nelson) (born 1958), American rock, pop, and funk singer, songwriter, and musician. An eccentric, prolific performer, Prince has been responsible for an extremely varied output since the release of his first album in 1978, much of it overtly sexual but also frequently humorous. He is perhaps best known for the album and film *Purple Rain* (1984). In 1993 he announced that he was no longer to be known as Prince, but rather by an unpronounceable symbol.

Prince Albert, Prince Charles, etc. see ALBERT, PRINCE; CHARLES, PRINCE, etc.

Prince of Wales see CHARLES, PRINCE.

Princes in the Tower the young sons of Edward IV, namely Edward, Prince of Wales (born 1470), and Richard, Duke of York (born 1472), supposedly murdered in the Tower of London in or shortly after 1483. In 1483 Edward reigned briefly as Edward V on the death of his father but was not crowned; he and his brother were taken to the Tower of London by their uncle (the future Richard III). Richard was appointed Protector and the princes disappeared soon afterwards. They are generally assumed to have been murdered, but whether at the instigation of Richard III (as Tudor propagandists claimed) or of another is not known; two skeletons discovered in 1674 are thought to have been those of the princes.

Princess Anne, Princess Diana, etc. see ANNE, PRINCESS; DIANA, PRINCESS, etc.

Priscian /'prɪʃɪən/ (full name Priscianus Caesariensis) (6th century AD), Byzantine grammarian. He taught Latin in Constantinople and his *Grammatical Institutions* became one of the standard Latin grammatical works in the Middle Ages.

Pritchett /'prɪtʃɪt/, Sir V(ictor) S(awdon) (1900–97), English writer and critic. He is chiefly remembered as a writer of short stories; collections include *The Spanish Virgin and Other Stories* (1930). Among his critical works are *The Living Novel* (1946) and *Lasting Impressions* (1990). He is also noted for his novels and for two volumes of autobiography, *A Cab at the Door* (1968) and *Midnight Oil* (1971).

Procopius /prə'kəʊpɪəs/ (c.500–c.562), Byzantine historian, born in Caesarea in Palestine. He accompanied Justinian's general Belisarius (c.505–65) on his campaigns between 527 and 540. His principal works are the *History of the Wars of Justinian* and *On Justinian's Buildings*. The authenticity of another work, the *Secret History*, has often been doubted but is now generally accepted; it is a virulent attack on Justinian, his policy, and his officials, and also contains comments on the dubious morals of the Empress Theodora.

Profumo /prə'fju:məʊ/, John (Dennis) (born 1915), British Conservative politician. In 1960 he was appointed Secretary of State for War under Harold Macmillan. Three years later news broke of his relationship with the mistress of a Soviet diplomat, Christine Keeler, raising fears of a security breach and precipitating his resignation.

Prokofiev /prə'kɒfɪˌef/, Sergei (Sergeevich) (1891–1953), Russian composer. By the age of 13 he had already written operas, sonatas, and piano pieces. In 1918 Prokofiev emigrated to the US; he lived there and in Paris before returning to the Soviet Union in 1933. Notable works include seven symphonies, the operas *The Love for Three Oranges* (1919) and *War and Peace* (1941–3), the *Lieutenant Kijé* suite (1934), and the ballet music for *Romeo and Juliet* (1935–6). He also wrote *Peter and the Wolf* (1936), a young person's guide to the orchestra in the form of a fairy tale.

Propertius /prə'pɜ:ʃəs/, Sextus (c.50–c.16 BC), Roman poet. His four books of elegies are largely concerned with his love affair with a woman whom he called Cynthia, though the later poems also deal with mythological and historical themes.

Prost /prɒst/, Alain (born 1955), French motor-racing driver. He was the first Frenchman to win the Formula One world championship (1985); he won the championship again in 1986, 1989, and 1993, after which he retired from racing. Since 1987 Prost has held the record for the most Grand Prix victories.

Proudhon /'pru:dɒn/, Pierre Joseph (1809–65), French social philosopher and journalist. His criticism of Napoleon III (Louis-Napoleon) and the Second Republic led to his imprisonment from 1849 to 1852; he later spent a period (1858–62) in exile in Belgium. His writings exercised considerable influence on the development of anarchism and socialism in Europe. He is chiefly remembered for his pamphlet *What*

is Property? (1840), which argued that property, in the sense of the exploitation of one person's labour by another, is theft. His theories were developed by his disciple Bakunin.

Proust[1] /pruːst/, Joseph Louis (1754–1826), French analytical chemist. He is remembered mainly for proposing the law of constant proportions, demonstrating that any pure sample of a chemical compound (such as an oxide of a metal) always contains the same elements in fixed proportions. Berzelius later established the connection between this and John Dalton's atomic theory, giving Proust full credit, though some exceptions to the law were found many years later.

Proust[2] /pruːst/, Marcel (1871–1922), French novelist, essayist, and critic. Although he moved in fashionable Paris society during the 1890s, he was severely incapacitated by asthma and became a virtual recluse after his mother's death in 1905. He devoted the remainder of his life to writing his novel *À la recherche du temps perdu* (published in seven sections between 1913 and 1927). Influenced by the philosophy of Henri Bergson, the work traces the life of the narrator from childhood to middle age; its central theme is the recovery of the lost past and the releasing of its creative energies through the stimulation of unconscious memory.

Prout /praʊt/, William (1785–1850), English chemist and biochemist. He was trained as a physician, and carried out analyses of urine, gastric juices, and foodstuffs. In theoretical chemistry he developed the hypothesis that hydrogen is the primary substance from which all other elements are formed, and if the atomic weight of hydrogen is regarded as unity the weights of all other elements are exact multiples of it. Although this hypothesis was later found to be incorrect, it stimulated research in atomic theory, and in modern particle physics the hydrogen nucleus (proton) is indeed considered a fundamental particle.

Ptolemy /'tɒlɪmɪ/ (2nd century) Greek astronomer and geographer. His major work, known by its Arabic title (*Almagest*), was a textbook of astronomy based on the geocentric system of Hipparchus. Ptolemy's teachings had enormous influence on medieval thought, the geocentric view of the cosmos being adopted as Christian doctrine until the late Renaissance. The *Almagest* included detailed tables of lunar and solar motion with eclipse predictions, and a catalogue giving the positions and magnitudes of 1,022 stars. Ptolemy's *Geography*, giving lists of places with their longitudes and latitudes, was also a standard work for centuries, despite its inaccuracies.

Puccini /pʊ'tʃiːnɪ/, Giacomo (1858–1924), Italian composer. He established his reputation with his third opera, *Manon Lescaut* (1893). Puccini's sense of the dramatic, gift for melody, and skilful use of the orchestra have ensured that his works remain among the most popular in the repertoire. Several others followed, including *La Bohème* (1896), *Tosca* (1900), *Madama Butterfly* (1904), and *Turandot*, which was completed by a pupil after his death and produced in 1926.

Pugin /'pjuːdʒɪn/, Augustus Welby Northmore (1812–52), English architect, theorist, and designer. He converted to Roman Catholicism in 1835 and became the main champion of the Gothic revival; he believed that the Gothic style was the only proper architectural style because of its origins in medieval Christian society. Among his chief contributions to architecture and design is his work on the external detail and internal fittings for the Houses of Parliament designed by Sir Charles Barry. Pugin's views, set out in works such as *Contrasts* (1836), influenced John Ruskin and ultimately the Arts and Crafts Movement.

Pulitzer /'pʊlɪtsə(r)/, Joseph (1847–1911), Hungarian-born American newspaper proprietor and editor. A pioneer of campaigning popular journalism, he owned a number of newspapers, including the *New York World*. Through his journalism he aimed to remedy abuses and reform social and economic inequalities by the exposure of striking instances and by the vigorous expression of popular opinion. He made provisions in his will for the establishment of the annual Pulitzer Prizes.

Pulu /'puːluː/ Tiglath-pileser III, king of Assyria (see TIGLATH-PILESER).

Purcell /pɜːˈsel, 'pɜːs(ə)l/, Henry (1659–95), English composer. He enjoyed royal patronage and was organist for Westminster Abbey (1679–95) and the Chapel Royal (1682–95). He composed many choral odes and songs for royal occasions as well as sacred anthems for the Chapel Royal. His main interest was in music for the theatre;

he composed the first English opera, *Dido and Aeneas* (1689), moving away from the tradition of the masque, breaking new dramatic ground and accommodating a wide emotional range. He also composed the incidental music for many plays, while his instrumental music includes a series of *Fantasias* for the viol (1680).

Pusey /'pju:zɪ/, Edward Bouverie (1800–82), English theologian. In 1833, while professor of Hebrew at Oxford, he founded the Oxford Movement together with John Henry Newman and John Keble; he became leader of the Movement after the withdrawal of Newman (1841). His many writings include a series of *Tracts for the Times* and a statement of his doctrinal views *The Doctrine of the Real Presence* (1856–7).

Pushkin /'pʊʃkɪn/, Aleksandr (Sergeevich) (1799–1837), Russian poet, novelist, and dramatist. His revolutionary beliefs and atheistic writings led to his dismissal from the civil service and eventual internal exile; he was rehabilitated in 1826 after the accession of Nicholas I. A leading figure in Russian literature, he wrote prolifically in many genres; his first success was the romantic narrative poem *Ruslan and Ludmilla* (1820). Other notable works include the verse novel *Eugene Onegin* (1833), and the blank-verse historical drama *Boris Godunov* (1831). He was fatally wounded in a duel with his wife's admirer.

Puskas /'pʊʃkəs/, Ferenc (born 1927), Hungarian footballer. A striker, he came to prominence in the celebrated Hungarian national team of the early 1950s. In 1956 he left Hungary to play for Real Madrid, scoring four goals in their 1960 European Cup Final victory and a hat trick in the corresponding 1962 final, in which Real Madrid lost.

Puttnam /'pʌtnəm/, Sir David (Terence) (born 1941), English film director. After a series of polished low-budget features Puttnam directed the internationally acclaimed *Chariots of Fire* (1981), which won four Oscars. Its success enabled him to explore human and moral dilemmas on a larger scale in films such as *The Killing Fields* (1984) and *The Mission* (1986). He became

chairman and chief executive of Columbia Pictures in 1986, but returned to Britain a year later. Later films include *Memphis Belle* (1990).

Pym /pɪm/, Barbara (Mary Crampton) (1913–80), English novelist. During the 1950s she wrote a number of novels dealing satirically with English middle-class village life, including *Excellent Women* (1952) and *Less than Angels* (1955). Having endured a period of unfashionability in the 1960s and 1970s, she published more novels, including *Quartet in Autumn* (1977), which gained her fresh recognition.

Pynchon /'pɪntʃən/, Thomas (Ruggles) (born 1937), American novelist. He is an elusive author who shuns public attention, while his works, experimental and often esoteric, abandon the normal conventions of the novel. They include *V* (1963), *The Crying of Lot 49* (1966), *Gravity's Rainbow* (1972), and the collection of short stories *Slow Learner* (1984).

Pyrrho /'pɪrəʊ/ (*c.*365–*c.*270 BC), Greek philosopher. Regarded as the founder of scepticism, he established the Pyrrhonic school of philosophy at Elis. He held that certainty of knowledge is impossible and that true happiness must therefore come from suspending judgement.

Pyrrhus /'pɪrəs/ (*c.*318–272 BC), king of Epirus *c.*307–272. After invading Italy in 280, he defeated the Romans at Asculum in 279, but sustained heavy losses; the term *pyrrhic victory* is named in allusion to this.

Pythagoras /paɪ'θægərəs/ (known as Pythagoras of Samos) (*c.*580–500 BC), Greek philosopher. Pythagoras is said to have discovered the numerical ratios determining the intervals of the musical scale, leading to his attempt at interpreting the entire physical world in terms of numbers, and founding their systematic (and mystical) study. In astronomy, his analysis of the courses of the sun, moon, and stars into circular motions was not set aside until the 17th century. Pythagoras also founded a secret religious, political, and scientific sect in Italy: the Pythagoreans held that the soul is condemned to a cycle of reincarnation, from which it may escape by attaining a state of purity.

Q

Qaddafi see GADDAFI.

Quant /kwɒnt/, Mary (born 1934), English fashion designer. She was a principal creator of the '1960s look', launching the miniskirt in 1966 and promoting bold colours and geometric designs. She was one of the first to design for the ready-to-wear market, and her styles, created especially for the young, did much to make London a leading fashion centre at the time. Since the 1970s she has concentrated on marketing a range of cosmetics.

Quasimodo /kwɑː'zɪmə,dəʊ/, Salvatore (1901–68), Italian poet. His early work was influenced by French symbolism. Major collections include *Water and Land* (1930) and *And It's Suddenly Evening* (1942). His later work is more extrovert and concerned with political and social issues. He was awarded the Nobel Prize for literature in 1959.

Queen /kwiːn/, Ellery (pseudonym of Frederic Dannay, 1905–82, and Manfred Lee, 1905–71), American writers of detective fiction. Their many detective novels, featuring the detective also called Ellery Queen, include *The French Powder Mystery* (1930). They went on to found and edit *Ellery Queen's Mystery Magazine* (1941).

Quercia, Jacopo della, see DELLA QUERCIA.

Quincey, Thomas De, see DE QUINCEY.

Quine /kwaɪn/, Willard Van Orman (born 1908), American philosopher and logician. A radical critic of modern empiricism, Quine took issue with the philosophy of language proposed by Rudolf Carnap, arguing that 'no statement is immune from revision' and that even the principles of logic themselves can be questioned and replaced. In *Word and Object* (1961), he held that there is no such thing as satisfactory translation. He also developed the work on the foundations of mathematics begun by Frege and Russell, specializing in the theory of sets, published in *Set Theory and Its Logic* (1963).

Quintilian /kwɪn'tɪlɪən/ (Latin name Marcus Fabius Quintilianus) (AD *c*.35–*c*.96), Roman rhetorician. A famous teacher, he is best known for his *Education of an Orator*, a comprehensive treatment of the art of rhetoric and the training of an orator; the work was highly influential in the Middle Ages and the Renaissance.

R

Rabelais /'ræbə,leɪ/, François (c.1494–1553), French satirist. He spent a period in his early life as a Franciscan monk, although his works were later condemned by the Church; he also later worked as a physician. He is remembered for his sequence of allegorical works parodying medieval learning and literature, attacking asceticism, and affirming humanist values. These are marked by coarse humour and an imaginative and exuberant use of language, and include *Pantagruel* (c.1532) and *Gargantua* (1534). The English translations of his work that appeared from 1653 were to exert a marked influence on writers such as Jonathan Swift and Laurence Sterne.

Rabin /rə'biːn/, Yitzhak (1922–95), Israeli statesman and military leader, Prime Minister 1974–7 and 1992–5. As Chief of Staff (1964–8), he led Israel's armed forces to victory during the Six Day War of 1967. During his first term as Prime Minister he supported Henry Kissinger's moves to bring peace to the Middle East and negotiated Israel's partial withdrawal from Sinai. Rabin resigned as Prime Minister in 1977. He was re-elected to the premiership in 1992 and negotiated a PLO–Israeli peace accord with Yasser Arafat which allowed for limited Palestinian autonomy in the West Bank and Gaza Strip (from 1994). The same year he was awarded the Nobel Peace Prize, together with Arafat and Shimon Peres. He was assassinated by a Jewish extremist.

Rachmaninov /ræk'mænɪ,nɒf/, Sergei (Vasilevich) (1873–1943), Russian composer and pianist, resident in the US from 1917. Rachmaninov belongs to the Russian romantic tradition, and was particularly influenced by Tchaikovsky. He was a celebrated pianist and is primarily known for his compositions for piano, in particular the Prelude in C sharp minor (1892), the Second Piano Concerto (1901), and the *Rhapsody on a Theme of Paganini* (1934) for piano and orchestra. He also wrote three other piano concertos, as well as three symphonies and three operas.

Racine /ræ'siːn/, Jean (1639–99), French dramatist. The principal tragedian of the French classical period, he drew on many different sources, including Greek and Roman literature (*Andromaque*, 1667; *Iphigénie*, 1674; *Phèdre*, 1677) and the Bible (*Athalie*, 1691). Central to the majority of his tragedies is a perception of the blind folly of human passion, continually enslaved to the pursuit of its object and destined always to be unsatisfied. Like his contemporary Corneille he wrote within the constraints of the rules governing tragic composition that were derived from Aristotle, in particular observance of the three unities of time, place, and action.

Rackham /'rækəm/, Arthur (1867–1939), English illustrator. He established his reputation as an artist of high imagination and Gothic invention with his edition of the Grimm brothers' *Fairy Tales* (1900). Rackham's best-known pictures appear in books such as *Rip Van Winkle* (1905) and *Peter Pan* (1906), and were displayed in many galleries worldwide.

Radcliffe /'rædklɪf/, Mrs Ann (1764–1823), English novelist. She was a leading exponent of the Gothic novel and influenced the work of other writers, including Byron, Shelley, and Charlotte Brontë. Her five novels include *The Mysteries of Udolpho* (1794) and *The Italian* (1797).

Radhakrishnan /,rɑːdə'krɪʃnən/, Sir Sarvepalli (1888–1975), Indian philosopher and statesman, President 1962–7. A teacher of philosophy at Mysore, Calcutta, and Oxford universities, he introduced some of the main ideas of classical Indian philosophy to the West. Major works include *Indian Philosophy* (1923–7) and *Eastern Religions and Western Thought* (1939). Radhakrishnan was Indian ambassador to the Soviet Union (1949–52) before returning to India in 1952 to become Vice-President under Nehru; he was elected President ten years later.

Raeburn /'reɪbɜːn/, Sir Henry (1756–1823), Scottish portrait painter. Influenced by Sir Joshua Reynolds, he became the leading Scottish portraitist of his day, depicting the

local intelligentsia and Highland chieftains in a bold and distinctive style. Raeburn was famed for painting directly on to the canvas, dispensing with preliminary drawings. Major works include *The Reverend Robert Walker Skating* (c.1784) and *The MacNab* (1803–13).

Raffles /'ræf(ə)lz/, Sir (Thomas) Stamford (1781–1826), British colonial administrator. Born in Jamaica, he joined the East India Company in 1795, becoming Lieutenant General of Java in 1811. He later served as Lieutenant General of Sumatra (1818–23), during which time he persuaded the company to purchase the undeveloped island of Singapore (1819) and undertook much of the preliminary work for transforming it into an international port and centre of commerce. He was also a keen botanical collector.

Rafsanjani /ˌræfsæn'dʒɑːnɪ/, Ali Akbar Hashemi (born 1934), Iranian statesman and religious leader, President 1989–97. A supporter and former pupil of Ayatollah Khomeini, in 1978 he helped organize the mass demonstrations that led to the shah's overthrow the following year. In 1988 he helped to bring an end to the Iran–Iraq War, having persuaded Khomeini to accept the UN's peace terms. When Khomeini died in 1989 Rafsanjani emerged from the ensuing power struggle as Iran's leader. He sought to improve Iran's relations with the West, and kept his country neutral during the Gulf War of 1991.

Rahman see ABDUL RAHMAN, MUJIBUR RAHMAN.

Rajneesh /rɑːdʒ'niːʃ/, Bhagwan Shree (born Chandra Mohan Jain; known as 'the Bhagwan' from a Sanskrit word meaning 'lord') (1931–90), Indian guru. After founding an ashram in Poona, India, he moved to the US in 1981 and founded a commune in Oregon. He became notorious for his doctrine of communal therapy, in particular for his preaching of salvation through free love. Rajneesh was deported in 1985 for immigration violations and the Oregon commune broke up shortly afterwards.

Rákosi /'rɑːkɒʃɪ/, Mátyás (1892–1971), Hungarian Communist statesman, First Secretary of the Hungarian Socialist Workers' Party 1945–56 and Prime Minister 1952–3 and 1955–6. After the Communist seizure of power at the end of the Second World War he did much to establish a firmly Stalinist regime. Ousted as Premier by the

more liberal Imre Nagy in 1953, Rákosi retained his party leadership and briefly returned to power in 1955, but in 1956 was dismissed, fleeing to the USSR during the Hungarian uprising later that year.

Raleigh /'rɑːlɪ, 'rɔːlɪ/, Sir Walter (also **Ralegh**) (c.1552–1618), English explorer, courtier, and writer. A favourite of Elizabeth I, he organized several voyages of exploration and colonization to the Americas, including an unsuccessful attempt to settle Virginia (1584–9) and a journey up the Orinoco river in search of gold (1595); from his travels he brought back potato and tobacco plants to England. Raleigh was imprisoned in 1603 by James I on a charge of conspiracy, but released in 1616 to lead a second expedition up the Orinoco in search of the fabled land of El Dorado. He returned empty-handed after a clash with some Spanish settlers, and was subsequently executed on the original charge.

Ramakrishna /ˌrɑːmə'krɪʃnə/ (born Gadadhar Chatterjee) (1836–86), Indian yogi and mystic. In his teachings he condemned lust, money, and the caste system, and preached that all religions leading to the attainment of mystical experience are equally good and true. His doctrines were spread widely in the US and Europe by his disciple Vivekananda.

Raman /'rɑːmən/, Sir Chandrasekhara Venkata (1888–1970), Indian physicist. He discovered the optical effect that is named after him (a change of wavelength exhibited by some of the light scattered in a medium), which was one of the most important proofs of the quantum theory of light. He also studied vibrations and sound, and the theory of musical instruments. In optics he went on to investigate the properties of crystals and minerals and the physiology of colour vision. Raman was awarded the 1930 Nobel Prize for physics.

Ramanujan /rɑː'mɑːnʊdʒən/, Srinivasa Aaiyangar (1887–1920), Indian mathematician. Largely self-taught, he was a mathematical genius who produced a number of original discoveries in number theory and power series. Collaborating with G. H. Hardy (1877–1947) in Cambridge, he made what is probably his most important contribution — a theorem concerning the partition of numbers into a sum of smaller integers. He was elected to the Royal Society in 1918.

Rambert /'rɒmbeə(r)/, Dame Marie (born Cyvia Rambam) (1888–1982), British ballet-dancer, teacher, and director, born in Poland. In 1913 she joined Diaghilev's Ballets Russes as a teacher of eurhythmics, moving to London in 1917. Rambert later formed the Ballet Club (1930), which became known as the Ballet Rambert (1935). For over fifty years the company, under her direction, promoted new British ballets and young choreographers and dancers such as her pupil Frederick Ashton.

Rameau /rɑːˈməʊ/, Jean-Philippe (1683–1764), French composer, musical theorist, and organist. In 1722 he published his influential *Treatise on Harmony*. He is best known for his four volumes of harpsichord pieces (1706–41); noted for their bold harmonies and textural diversity, these consist largely of genre pieces with descriptive titles, such as 'La Poule'. Rameau also wrote many operas, including *Castor and Pollux* (1737).

Rameses see RAMSES.

Ramón y Cajal /rəˌmɒn iː kəˈhɑːl/, Santiago (1852–1934), Spanish physician and histologist. He is best known for his research on nerve cells and the brain, and was a founder of the science of neurology. He identified the neuron as the fundamental unit of the nervous system, but argued (incorrectly) that the axons end only in the brain and do not join up with other axons or neurons. Ramón y Cajal shared a Nobel Prize with Camillo Golgi in 1906.

Ramsay[1] /ˈræmzɪ/, Allan (1713–84), Scottish portrait painter. From the late 1730s he was based in London, where he became much in demand as a portraitist in the 1750s. His style is noted for its French rococo grace and sensitivity, particularly in his portraits of women; major works of this period include *The Artist's Wife* (1755). In 1767 he was appointed painter to George III.

Ramsay[2] /ˈræmzɪ/, Sir William (1852–1916), Scottish chemist, discoverer of the noble gases. Investigating the reason why laboratory-prepared nitrogen was less dense than that isolated from air, he decided that the latter must be contaminated by a heavier gas. He went on to discover five chemically inert gases — argon, helium, and (with the help of M. W. Travers, 1872–1961) neon, krypton, and xenon — and determined their atomic weights and places in the periodic table. In 1910, with Frederick Soddy and Sir Robert Whytlaw-Gray (1877–1958), he identified the last noble gas, radon. He was awarded the Nobel Prize for chemistry in 1904.

Ramses /ˈræmsiːz/ (also **Rameses** /ˈræmɪˌsiːz/) the name of eleven Egyptian pharaohs, notably:

Ramses II (known as Ramses the Great) (died *c*.1225 BC), reigned *c*.1292–*c*.1225 BC. The third pharaoh of the 19th dynasty, he is famed for the vast monuments and statues that he built, including the two rock temples at Abu Simbel. He launched a major offensive against the Hittites, leading his troops in person and winning a military victory at the Hittite stronghold of Kadesh, but failing to capture the city; the battle is celebrated in a long poem and carvings on temple walls in Egypt and Nubia.

Ramses III (died *c*.1167 BC), reigned *c*.1198–*c*.1167 BC. The second pharaoh of the 20th dynasty, he fought decisive battles against the Libyans and the Sea Peoples, who attempted invasions. After his death the power of Egypt declined steadily.

Ramsey /ˈræmzɪ/, Sir Alf(red Ernest) (born 1920), English footballer and manager. He played as a defender for Southampton before moving to Tottenham Hotspur in 1949. He also played for England, winning thirty-one caps. As a manager he took Ipswich Town from the third division to the first division championship (1962). He then managed England (1963–74), winning the World Cup in 1966.

Rand /rænd/, Ayn (born Alissa Rosenbaum) (1905–82), American writer and philosopher, born in Russia. Emigrating to the US in 1926, she became known for her novels *The Fountainhead* (1943) and *Atlas Shrugged* (1957). She developed her philosophy of 'objectivism' in *For the New Intellectual* (1961), arguing for 'rational self-interest', individualism, and laissez-faire capitalism.

Ranjit Singh /ˌrʌndʒɪt ˈsɪŋ/ (known as 'the Lion of the Punjab') (1780–1839), Indian maharaja, founder of the Sikh state of Punjab. After succeeding his father as a Sikh ruler at the age of 12, he seized Lahore from the Afghans in 1799 and proclaimed himself maharaja of Punjab in 1801. He proceeded to make the state the most powerful in India, securing the holy city of Amritsar (1802) and expanding his control north-west with the capture of Peshawar (1818) and Kashmir (1819). At the end of the

Sikh Wars which followed his death most of his territory was annexed by Britain.

Ranjitsinhji Vibhaji /ˌrʌndʒɪt‚sɪndʒɪ vɪˈbɑːdʒɪ/, Kumar Shri, Maharaja Jam Sahib of Navanagar (1872–1933), Indian cricketer and statesman. He made his cricketing début for Sussex in 1895, going on to score a total of 72 centuries as a batsman for Sussex and England (when he was popularly known as 'Ranji'). In 1907 he succeeded his cousin as maharaja of the state of Navanagar and promoted a number of modernization schemes to improve the state's infrastructure. He was knighted in 1917.

Rank /ræŋk/, J(oseph) Arthur, 1st Baron (1888–1972), English industrialist and film executive, founder of the Rank Organization. In the 1930s he became interested in films when, as a Methodist Sunday school teacher, he realized that they could be an ideal medium for spreading the Gospel. He founded the film production and distribution company known as the Rank Organization in 1941. Under his chairmanship it went on to own or control the leading British studios and cinema chains in the 1940s and 1950s.

Ransom /ˈrænsəm/, John Crowe (1888–1974), American poet and critic. He studied at Oxford University and then taught at Vanderbilt University 1914–38, during which time he published *Poems About God* (1919). With the book *The New Criticism* (1941) he started a school of criticism which rejected the Victorian emphasis on literature as a moral force and advocated a close analysis of textual structure in isolation from the social background of the text.

Ransome /ˈrænsəm/, Arthur (Michell) (1884–1967), English novelist. Ransome is best known for his children's classics, such as *Swallows and Amazons* (1930) and *Great Northern?* (1947), which depict the imaginative world of children while reflecting a keen interest in sailing, fishing, and the countryside. Before writing these books, however, Ransome covered the Russian Revolution as a journalist and published a successful collection of Russian legends and fairy stories.

Rao /raʊ/, P(amulaparti) V(enkata) Narasimha (born 1921), Indian statesman, Prime Minister 1991–6.

Raphael /ˈræfeɪəl/ (Italian name Raffaello Sanzio) (1483–1520), Italian painter and architect. He was a leading figure of the High Renaissance in Italy. In 1505 he went to Florence, where he painted a series of small madonnas distinguished by a serenity of expression. On moving to Rome he was commissioned to paint the frescos in one of the papal rooms in the Vatican (1509). At this time he worked on further madonnas, including his best-known altarpiece the *Sistine Madonna* (*c*.1513), in which Mother and Child appear among the clouds, simultaneously human and divine, in a significant departure from the naturalism characteristic of previous paintings of the Madonna. He was also an important architect and was put in charge of the work on St Peter's Basilica in Rome (1514).

Rasputin /ræˈspjuːtɪn/, Grigori (Efimovich) (1871–1916), Russian monk. He came to exert great influence over Tsar Nicholas II and his family during the First World War by claiming miraculous powers to heal the heir to the throne, who suffered from haemophilia. His appropriation of ecclesiastical, political, and military powers, combined with a reputation for debauchery, steadily discredited the imperial family. Rasputin was eventually assassinated by a group loyal to the tsar.

Ratana /ˈrɑːtənə/, Tahupotiki Wiremu (1873–1939), Maori political and religious leader. A Methodist farmer, he founded the Ratana Church (1920), an interdenominational movement whose aim was to unite Maoris of all tribes. Its doctrine of faith-healing and many unorthodox rituals led to a rift with other Christian denominations in 1925. Politically Ratana struggled for Maori rights by pressing for full implementation of the Treaty of Waitangi.

Rattigan /ˈrætɪgən/, Sir Terence (Mervyn) (1911–77), English dramatist. His plays include *The Winslow Boy* (1946), concerning a father's fight to clear the name of his accused son, *The Browning Version* (1948), about a repressed and unpopular schoolmaster, and *Ross* (1960), based on the life of T. E. Lawrence. He also wrote screenplays for several films, including *The Yellow Rolls Royce* (1965).

Rattle /ˈræt(ə)l/, Sir Simon (Denis) (born 1955), English conductor. He made his reputation as principal conductor with the City of Birmingham Symphony Orchestra, a post which he held from 1980 until 1991,

when he became the orchestra's music director (until 1996). He is noted particularly for his interpretation of works by early 20th-century composers such as Mahler and as a champion of new music.

Rauschenberg /'rauʃ(ə)n‚bɜːg/, Robert (born 1925), American artist. During the 1950s and 1960s he produced a series of 'combine' paintings, such as *Charlene* (1954) and *Rebus* (1955), which incorporate three-dimensional objects such as nails, rags, and bottles. His work has also included theatre design and choreography, and he combined art with new technology in pieces such as *Soundings* (1968).

Ravel /ræ'vel/, Maurice (Joseph) (1875–1937), French composer. His early music was influenced by impressionism and the piano music of Liszt, but his mature works have a distinctive tone colour as well as an ironic flavour derived from the use of unresolved dissonances. Major works include the ballet *Daphnis and Chloë* (1912), staged by Diaghilev's Ballets Russes, the opera *L'Enfant et les sortilèges* (1925), and the orchestral works *La Valse* (1920) and *Boléro* (1928).

Rawls /rɔːlz/, John (born 1921), American philosopher. He is the author of *A Theory of Justice* (1972), which invokes the philosophical concept of social contract and attacks the utilitarian doctrine of subjugating individual needs to the more pressing claims of the general good, arguing for principles to be formulated that guarantee basic liberties.

Ray[1] /reɪ/, John (1627–1705), English naturalist. His principal interest was botany, and his major work was the three-volume *Historia Plantarum* (1686–1704). He toured Europe with F. Willoughby (1635–72) in search of specimens of flora and fauna. Ray was the first to classify flowering plants into monocotyledons and dicotyledons, he established the species as the basic taxonomic unit, and his systematic scheme was not improved upon until the advent of Linnaeus's system. The Ray Society of London is named in his honour.

Ray[2] /reɪ/, Man (born Emmanuel Rudnitsky) (1890–1976), American photographer, painter, and film-maker. He helped to found the New York Dada movement before moving to Paris in 1921 and becoming a leading figure in the European Dada and surrealist movements. Ray pioneered the photogram or 'rayograph', placing objects on sensitized paper and exposing them to light; he later applied the technique to film-making. He is perhaps best known for his photograph the *Violin d'Ingres* (1924), which achieved the effect of making the back of a female nude resemble a violin.

Ray[3] /raɪ/, Satyajit (1921–92), Indian film director. His first film, *Pather Panchali* (1955), won a prize at Cannes and brought Indian films to the attention of Western audiences. Filmed in neo-realist style and set in his native Bengal, it formed part of a trilogy completed by *Aparijito* (1956) and *Apur Sansar* (1959). His other films include *Kanchenjunga* (1962), for which he also wrote the music, and *The Home and the World* (1984).

Rayleigh /'reɪlɪ/, John William Strutt, 3rd Baron (1842–1919), English physicist. He published a major work on acoustics, *The Theory of Sound*, and carried out pioneering work on atmospheric airglow and black-body radiation. He was director of the Cavendish Laboratory after James Maxwell, his researches including the establishment of electrical units of resistance, current, and electromotive force. He worked with William Ramsay from 1894, and their accurate measurement of the constituents of the atmosphere led to the discovery of argon and other inert gases. In 1904 Rayleigh was awarded the Nobel Prize for physics.

Reade /riːd/, Charles (1814–84), English novelist and dramatist. He is remembered for his historical romance *The Cloister and the Hearth* (1861); set in the 15th century, it relates the adventures of Gerard, father of Erasmus.

Reagan /'reɪgən/, Ronald (Wilson) (born 1911), American Republican statesman, 40th President of the US 1981–9. He was a Hollywood actor before entering politics and becoming governor of California (1966–74). In 1981, at the age of 69, he became the oldest-ever President of the US. During his presidency military expenditure was increased, the Strategic Defense Initiative was launched, taxes and spending on social services were reduced, and the national budget deficit rose to record levels. An intermediate nuclear forces non-proliferation treaty with the USSR was signed in 1987.

Réaumur /'reɪə‚mjʊə(r)/, René Antoine Ferchault de (1683–1757), French scientist.

He compiled a list of France's arts, industries, and professions, and, as a consequence, suggested improvements in several manufacturing processes. He is chiefly remembered for his thermometer scale, now obsolete, which set the melting-point of ice at 0° and the boiling-point of water at 80°. Réaumur also carried out pioneering work on insects and other invertebrates.

Red Baron, the see RICHTHOFEN.

Redding /'redɪŋ/, Otis (1941–67), American soul singer. Despite never achieving a major US pop success until after his death, Redding was one of the most influential soul singers of the late 1960s. It was not until an appearance at the Monterey pop festival in 1967 that he gained widespread recognition; he died in a plane crash the following December, and the posthumously released 'Dock of the Bay' became a number-one US hit in 1968.

Redford /'redfəd/, (Charles) Robert (born 1936), American film actor and director. He made his name playing opposite Paul Newman in *Butch Cassidy and the Sundance Kid* (1969), co-starring again with him in *The Sting* (1973). Other notable films include *The Great Gatsby* (1974), *All the President's Men* (1976), and *Out of Africa* (1986). Redford won an Oscar as the director of *Ordinary People* (1980), and was nominated for one for *Quiz Show* (1994).

Redgrave /'redɡreɪv/ a family of English actors. Sir Michael (Scudamore) (1908–85) was a well-known stage actor, who played numerous Shakespearian roles as well as appearing in other plays, notably in the title role of *Uncle Vanya* (1963). He also starred in films such as *The Browning Version* (1951) and *The Importance of Being Earnest* (1952). His elder daughter Vanessa (born 1937) has had a successful career in the theatre and cinema: her films include *Mary Queen of Scots* (1972), *Julia* (1976), for which she won an Oscar, and *Howard's End* (1992). His son Corin (born 1939) is also an actor, as is his younger daughter Lynn (born 1944), who has made a number of stage and screen performances, and is best known for such films as *Georgy Girl* (1966). Vanessa's two daughters Joely (born 1958) and Natasha Richardson (born 1963) are both actresses.

Redmond /'redmənd/, John (Edward) (1856–1918), Irish politician. He succeeded Charles Parnell as leader of the Irish Na-

tionalist Party in the House of Commons (1891–1918). The Home Rule Bill of 1912 was introduced with his support, although it was never implemented because of the First World War.

Redon /rə'dɒn/, Odilon (1840–1916), French painter and graphic artist. He was a leading exponent of symbolism, and an important forerunner of the surrealists, especially in his early work, which chiefly consisted of charcoal drawings of fantastic, often nightmarish, subjects. He began to use colour from about 1890 onwards, becoming known for his richly coloured pastels depicting flowers, mythological subjects, and portraits.

Reed[1] /ri:d/, Sir Carol (1906–76), English film director. He made a succession of celebrated films in the postwar years, including *Odd Man Out* (1947) and *The Third Man* (1949), starring Orson Welles. Among his notable later films are the *Outcast of the Islands* (1952) and the musical *Oliver!* (1968), for which he won an Oscar.

Reed[2] /ri:d/, Lou (full name Lewis Allan Reed) (born 1942), American rock singer, guitarist, and songwriter. Reed led the Velvet Underground, an influential group probably best known for their first album, *The Velvet Underground and Nico* (1967), produced in association with Andy Warhol. Reed's literate songs dealt with hitherto taboo subjects such as heroin addiction and sado-masochism, to a backing that combined avant-garde classical influences with stripped-down, basic rock. His best-known solo recordings are the song 'Walk on the Wild Side' and the album *Transformer* (both 1972).

Reed[3] /ri:d/, Walter (1851–1902), American physician. He worked mainly in the US Army Medical Corps, and finally headed the Yellow Fever Board (1900–1), based in Cuba. His group proved that the disease was transmitted by the mosquito *Aedes aegypti*, and then showed that the agent responsible was a virus — the first to be recognized as the cause of a human disease. The mosquito's breeding places were successfully attacked, and a vaccine was developed some years later.

Regiomontanus /,redʒiəʊmɒn'tɑːnəs/, Johannes (born Johannes Müller) (1436–76), German astronomer and mathematician. He was probably the most important astronomer of the 15th century, and worked in Venice, Buda (Hungary), Nuremberg,

and finally Rome. Regiomontanus completed a translation of Ptolemy's *Mathematical Syntaxis*, with revisions and comments, and wrote four monumental works on mathematics (especially trigonometry) and astronomy.

Rehoboam /ˌriːəˈbəʊəm/, son of Solomon, king of ancient Israel *c*.930–*c*.915 BC. His reign witnessed the secession of the northern tribes and their establishment of a new kingdom under Jeroboam, leaving Rehoboam as the first king of Judah (1 Kings 11–14).

Reich /raɪx/, Steve (born 1936), American composer. He established himself as a leading minimalist in the mid-1960s; his work is influenced by his study of drumming as well as by Balinese and West African music, and he uses both traditional and electronic instruments. His musical style is based on the repetition of short phrases within a simple harmonic field. Major works include *Drumming* (1971), for percussion and two voices, and *The Desert Music* (1984), for chorus and orchestra.

Reinhardt[1] /ˈramhɑːt/, Django (born Jean Baptiste Reinhardt) (1910–53), Belgian jazz guitarist. He became famous in Paris in the 1930s for his original improvisational style, blending swing with influences from his gypsy background. In 1934, together with violinist Stephane Grappelli, he formed the Quintette du Hot Club de France and went on to make many recordings with the group until they disbanded in 1939. Reinhardt also toured the US with Duke Ellington in 1946.

Reinhardt[2] /ˈramhɑːt/, Max (born Max Goldmann) (1873–1943), Austrian theatre director and impresario. He dominated the theatre in Berlin during the first two decades of the 20th century with his large-scale productions of such works as Sophocles' *Oedipus Rex* (1910) and Vollmöller's *The Miracle* (1911). Reinhardt also helped establish the Salzburg Festival, with Richard Strauss and Hugo von Hofmannsthal, in 1920.

Reith /riːθ/, John (Charles Walsham), 1st Baron (1889–1971), Scottish administrator and politician, first general manager (1922–7) and first director-general (1927–38) of the BBC. He played a major part in the growth and developing ethos of the BBC, refusing to treat broadcasting simply as a means of entertainment and championing its moral and intellectual role in the community. Reith later served in various Cabinet posts during the Second World War. In 1948 the BBC established the Reith Lectures, broadcast annually, in his honour.

Remarque /rɪˈmɑːk/, Erich Maria (1898–1970), German-born American novelist. His first novel, *All Quiet on the Western Front* (1929), was a huge international success and was made into a film in 1930. The book and its sequel *The Road Back* (1931) were banned by the Nazis in 1933 and he emigrated to the US in 1939, becoming an American citizen in 1947. Remarque's other novels, all dealing with the horror of war and its aftermath, include *Spark of Life* (1952) and *A Time to Live and a Time to Die* (1956).

Rembrandt /ˈrembrænt/ (full name Rembrandt Harmensz van Rijn) (1606–69), Dutch painter. After working at first in his native Leiden, he moved to Amsterdam, where he made his name as a portrait painter with the *Anatomy Lesson of Dr Tulp* (1632), a strongly lit group portrait in the manner of Caravaggio. With his most celebrated painting, the *Night Watch* (1642), he used chiaroscuro to give his subjects a more spiritual and introspective quality, a departure which was to transform the Dutch portrait tradition. Rembrandt is especially identified with the series of more than sixty self-portraits painted from 1629 to 1669, a sustained exercise in self-analysis. His prolific output also included many religious, genre, and landscape paintings, drawings, and etchings. Although his name remained well known after his death, it was not until the romantic period that Rembrandt was recognized as a supreme artist.

Renan /rəˈnɒn/, (Joseph) Ernest (1823–92), French historian, theologian, and philosopher. A major figure in 19th-century French theology and philosophy, he provoked a controversy with the publication of his *Vie de Jésus* (1863), which rejected the supernatural element in the life of Jesus. His belief that the future of the world lay in the progress of science found expression in *L'Avenir de la science* (1890).

Renault[1] /ˈrenəʊ/, Louis (1877–1944), French engineer and motor manufacturer. Together with his brothers he established the original Renault company in 1898 and became known for designing and manufacturing a series of racing cars. In 1918 the

company produced its first tank; Renault subsequently expanded the firm's range to incorporate industrial and agricultural machinery, as well as further military technology. In 1944 Renault was imprisoned, accused of collaborating with the Germans; he died before the trial began. His company was nationalized in 1945 and subsequently became one of France's leading manufacturers of motor cars.

Renault[2] /'renəʊ/, Mary (pseudonym of Mary Challans) (1905–83), British novelist, resident in South Africa from 1948. Her reputation is based on her historical novels set in ancient Greece and Asia Minor. They include two trilogies, one recalling the legend of Theseus (*The Last of the Wine*, 1956; *The King Must Die*, 1958; *The Bull from the Sea*, 1962) and the other the story of Alexander the Great (*Fire from Heaven*, 1970; *The Persian Boy*, 1972; *Funeral Games*, 1981).

Rendell /'rend(ə)l/, Ruth (Barbara) (born 1930), English writer of detective fiction and thrillers. She is known as the creator of Chief Inspector Wexford, who appears in a series of detective novels starting with *From Doon with Death* (1964). Rendell is also noted for her psychological crime novels, including *A Judgement in Stone* (1977) and — under the pseudonym of Barbara Vine — *A Dark-Adapted Eye* (1986).

Rennie /'renɪ/, John (1761–1821), Scottish civil engineer. He is best known as the designer of the London and East India Docks (built *c.*1800), the Inchcape Rock lighthouse (1807–*c.*1811), and Waterloo Bridge, Southwark Bridge, and London Bridge (1811–31).

Renoir[1] /rə'nwɑ:(r), 'renwɑ:(r)/, (Pierre) Auguste (1841–1919), French painter. One of the early impressionists, he developed a style characterized by light, fresh colours and indistinct, subtle outlines. In his later work he concentrated on the human, especially female, form. His best-known paintings include *Le Moulin de la galette* (1876), *Les Grandes Baigneuses* (1884–7), and *The Judgement of Paris* (*c.*1914).

Renoir[2] /rə'nwɑ:(r), 'renwɑ:(r)/, Jean (1894–1979), French film director, son of Auguste Renoir. His fame is based chiefly on the films he made in France in the 1930s, including *La Grande Illusion* (1937), concerning prisoners of war in the First World War, and *La Règle du jeu* (1939), a black comedy about a weekend shooting-party. After spending the Second World War in the US,

he returned to Europe, where he had an important influence on the *nouvelle vague* film directors of the 1960s.

Repton /'reptən/, Humphry (1752–1818), English landscape gardener. Repton's reconstructions of estates often used regular bedding and straight paths close to the house, but his parks were carefully informal after the model of Capability Brown. Important designs include the park at Cobham in Kent (*c.*1789–*c.*1793) and the house and grounds at Sheringham Hall in Norfolk (1812).

Resnais /rə'neɪ/, Alain (born 1922), French film director. He was one of the foremost directors of the *nouvelle vague*; his films are noted for their use of experimental techniques to explore memory and time, and often focus on the theme of a loss of touch with humanity. Throughout his career Resnais has collaborated with writers such as Marguerite Duras, notably in *Hiroshima mon amour* (1959), and Alain Robbe-Grillet, in *L'Année dernière à Marienbad* (1961). More recent films include *Mon oncle d'Amérique* (1980) and *L'Amour à mort* (1984).

Respighi /re'spi:gɪ/, Ottorino (1879–1936), Italian composer. He is best known for his suites the *Fountains of Rome* (1917) and the *Pines of Rome* (1924), based on the poems of Gabriele d'Annunzio and influenced by Rimsky-Korsakov, his former composition teacher, in their orchestration. In addition to writing nine operas he arranged Diaghilev's ballet *La Boutique fantasque* (1919) from Rossini's original music.

Reuter /'rɔɪtə(r)/, Paul Julius, Baron von (born Israel Beer Josaphat) (1816–99), German pioneer of telegraphy and news reporting. After establishing a service for sending commercial telegrams in Aachen (1849), he moved his headquarters to London, where he founded the news agency Reuters.

Revere /rɪ'vɪə(r)/, Paul (1735–1818), American patriot. He was one of the demonstrators involved in the Boston Tea Party of 1773, the protest at the imposition of tax on tea by Britain. Two years later he made his famous midnight ride from Boston to Lexington to warn fellow American revolutionaries of the approach of British troops; the journey is immortalized in Longfellow's poem 'Paul Revere's Ride' (1863).

Reynolds[1] /'ren(ə)ldz/, Albert (born 1933), Irish Fianna Fáil statesman, Taoiseach

(Prime Minister) 1992–4. He was involved with John Major in drafting the 'Downing Street Declaration' (1993), intended as the basis of a peace initiative in Northern Ireland.

Reynolds[2] /'ren(ə)ldz/, Sir Joshua (1723–92), English painter. He became the first president of the Royal Academy (1768), and through his professional and social prestige succeeded in raising the status of painting in Britain. He insisted on the intellectual basis of painting and became a respected figure in literary circles. Reynolds sought to raise portraiture to the status of history painting by adapting poses and settings from classical statues and Renaissance paintings (as in *Mrs Siddons as the Tragic Muse*, 1784). His theories were presented in the *Discourses* delivered annually at the Royal Academy (1769–90).

Reza Shah /ˌreɪzə 'ʃɑː/ see PAHLAVI[1].

Rhodes[1] /rəʊdz/, Cecil (John) (1853–1902), British-born South African statesman, Prime Minister of Cape Colony 1890–6. He went to South Africa in 1870, where he became a successful diamond prospector, and twenty years later owned 90 per cent of the world's production of diamonds. Entering politics in 1881, he expanded British territory in southern Africa, annexing Bechuanaland (now Botswana) in 1884 and developing Rhodesia from 1889 onwards through the British South Africa Company, which he founded. While Premier, Rhodes was implicated in the Jameson Raid into Boer territory (1895) and forced to resign. In his will he established the system of Rhodes Scholarships to allow students from the British Empire (now the Commonwealth), the US, and Germany to study at Oxford University.

Rhodes[2] /rəʊdz/, Wilfred (1877–1973), English cricketer. An all-rounder, he played for Yorkshire (1898–1930) and for England (1899–1926), scoring almost 40,000 runs during this time and taking 4,187 first-class wickets, more than any other player.

Rhys /riːs/, Jean (pseudonym of Ella Gwendolen Rees Williams) (1890–1979), British novelist and short-story writer, born in Dominica. Her novels include *Good Morning, Midnight* (1939) and *Wide Sargasso Sea* (1966); the latter, set in Dominica and Jamaica in the 1830s, recreates Charlotte Brontë's *Jane Eyre* from the point of view of Mrs Rochester, the 'mad woman in the attic'.

Ribbentrop /'rɪb(ə)n,trɒp/, Joachim von (1893–1946), German Nazi politician. A close associate of Hitler, Ribbentrop served as Foreign Minister from 1938 to 1945. During his ministry, he signed the non-aggression pact with the Soviet Union (1939). He was convicted as a war criminal at the Nuremberg trials and hanged.

Ribera /rɪ'beərə/, José (or Jusepe) de (known as 'Lo Spagnoletto', 'the little Spaniard') (c.1591–1652), Spanish painter and etcher, resident in Italy from 1616. He is best known for his paintings of religious subjects and for his genre scenes; these are noted for their dramatic chiaroscuro effects and for their realistic depiction of torture and martyrdom. Important works include the *Martyrdom of St Bartholomew* (c.1630).

Rice /raɪs/, Sir Tim(othy Miles Bindon) (born 1944), English lyricist and entertainer. He came to public attention as the co-writer, with Andrew Lloyd Webber, of a number of hit musicals, including *Joseph and the Amazing Technicolor Dreamcoat* (1968), *Jesus Christ Superstar* (1970), and *Evita* (1976). He later moved into new partnerships with lyrics for productions such as *Chess* (1984), and in 1994 won the second of his two Oscars for best original film song with 'Can You Feel the Love Tonight', a collaboration with Elton John, from *The Lion King*.

Rich /rɪtʃ/, Buddy (born Bernard Rich) (1917–87), American jazz drummer and band-leader. He was a child prodigy, having a solo drum act when only 6 years old. At the age of 16 he joined the band of clarinettist Joe Marsala, and subsequently played for band-leaders such as Artie Shaw and Tommy Dorsey. He formed his own band in 1946, which he reduced to a smaller group in 1951, but fronted another large band in 1966 and toured extensively until his death.

Richard[1] /'rɪtʃəd/ the name of three kings of England:
Richard I (known as Richard Coeur de Lion or Richard the Lionheart) (1157–99), son of Henry II, reigned 1189–99. Richard's military exploits made him a medieval legend, but meant that he spent most of his reign absent from his kingdom, leading to a growth in the power of the barons. Soon after succeeding his father he left to lead the Third Crusade, defeating Saladin at Arsuf (1191), but failing to capture Jerusalem. He was taken prisoner on his way

home in 1192 by Duke Leopold of Austria (1157–94) and subsequently held hostage by the Holy Roman emperor Henry VI (1165–97), only being released in 1194 following the payment of a huge ransom. After later embarking on a campaign against Philip II of France, Richard was fatally wounded during the siege of the castle of Châlus.

Richard II (1367–1400), son of the Black Prince, reigned 1377–99. On his accession as a minor the government was placed in the hands of selected nobles, dominated by his uncle John of Gaunt. During this time Richard helped to put down the Peasants' Revolt, but was soon facing a threat to his power from rebel nobles; in 1389 he asserted his right to rule independently of his protectors and later executed or banished most of his former opponents (1397–8). However, his confiscation of John of Gaunt's estate on the latter's death provoked Henry Bolingbroke's return from exile to overthrow him.

Richard III (1452–85), brother of Edward IV, reigned 1483–5. During the Wars of the Roses he served as a commander in the battle of Tewkesbury (1471), which restored Edward IV to the throne. After his brother's death he served as Protector to his nephew Edward V, who, two months later, was declared illegitimate on dubious grounds and subsequently disappeared (see PRINCES IN THE TOWER). As king, Richard ruled with some success for a brief period, before being defeated and killed at Bosworth Field (1485) by Henry Tudor (later Henry VII). Historical opinion on the popular picture of Richard as a hunchbacked cutthroat usurper is still divided; many modern historians argue that he was demonized as part of Tudor propaganda.

Richard[2] /'rɪtʃəd/, Cliff (born Harry Roger Webb) (born 1940), British pop singer, born in India. Influenced by rock and roll, he formed his own group the Drifters (later called the Shadows) in 1958, recording such songs as 'Living Doll' (1959) and 'Bachelor Boy' (1961) with them. Richard went on to act in several films, mainly musicals such as *Expresso Bongo* (1960) and *Summer Holiday* (1962). He left the Shadows in 1968, and in the 1970s became a born-again Christian; he has since combined a successful pop career with evangelism.

Richard Coeur de Lion /,kɜː də 'liːɒn/, Richard I of England (see RICHARD[1]).

Richards[1] /'rɪtʃədz/, Sir Gordon (1904–86), English jockey. He was champion jockey twenty-six times between 1925 and 1953.

Richards[2] /'rɪtʃədz/, I(vor) A(rmstrong) (1893–1979), English literary critic and poet. In 1929 he became a fellow of Magdalene College, Cambridge, and was appointed professor of English at Harvard in 1944. He is best known for his emphasis on the importance of close textual study and his praise of irony, ambiguity, and allusiveness. His works include *Principles of Literary Criticism* (1924) and *Practical Criticism* (1929).

Richards[3] /'rɪtʃədz/, Viv (full name Isaac Vivian Alexander Richards) (born 1952), West Indian cricketer. Born in Antigua, he made his début for the West Indies in 1974, and captained the team from 1985 until 1991, a period during which his country dominated international cricket. He scored more than 6,000 runs during his test career; his century against England in Antigua in 1986 remains the fastest ever in test cricket (in terms of the number of balls received). He also played county cricket in England for Somerset (1974–86) and Glamorgan (1990–3).

Richardson[1] /'rɪtʃəds(ə)n/, Sir Ralph (David) (1902–83), English actor. He established himself as a leading actor with the Old Vic in London in the early 1930s. He played many Shakespearian roles, as well as leading parts in plays such as Harold Pinter's *No Man's Land* (1975) and films such as *Oh! What a Lovely War* (1969).

Richardson[2] /'rɪtʃəds(ə)n/, Samuel (1689–1761), English novelist. His first novel, *Pamela* (1740–1), was entirely in the form of letters and journals and was responsible for popularizing the epistolary novel. He experimented further with the genre in *Clarissa Harlowe* (1747–8), which explored moral issues in a detailed social context with psychological intensity.

Richard the Lionheart /'laɪən,hɑːt/, Richard I of England (see RICHARD[1]).

Richelieu /'riːʃljɜː/ Armand Jean du Plessis (1585–1642), French cardinal and statesman. From 1624 to 1642 he was chief minister of Louis XIII, dominating French government. He destroyed the power base of the Huguenots in the late 1620s and set out to undermine the Habsburg empire by supporting the Swedish king Gustavus Adolphus in the Thirty Years War, involv-

ing France from 1635. In the same year, Richelieu was also responsible for establishing the Académie française.

Richler /'rɪtʃlə(r)/, Mordecai (born 1931), Canadian novelist. Much of his work reflects his Jewish upbringing in Montreal. His best-known novel is probably his fourth, *The Apprenticeship of Duddy Kravitz* (1959); other works include the satirical *The Incomparable Atuk* (1963), *St Urbain's Horseman* (1971), and *Solomon Gursky was Here* (1989).

Richter /'rɪktə(r)/, 'rɪxt-/, Charles Francis (1900–85), American geologist. Richter worked mainly in California, becoming professor of seismology at the California Institute of Technology in 1952. He devised the *Richter scale* for measuring the strength of earthquakes in 1935, basing it on the amplitude of the waves produced. The scale is logarithmic, so that an increase of one point represents a tenfold increase in amplitude, with the release of about thirty times more energy.

Richthofen /'rɪxt,həʊv(ə)n/, Manfred, Freiherr von (known as 'the Red Baron') (1882–1918), German fighter pilot. In the First World War he initially fought in the cavalry, but transferred to the flying corps, joining a fighter squadron in 1915 and flying a distinctive bright red aircraft. He was eventually shot down, probably by Allied infantrymen, after destroying eighty enemy planes.

Ridley /'rɪdlɪ/, Nicholas (c.1500–55), English Protestant bishop and martyr. He became one of Thomas Cranmer's chaplains in 1537 and, during the reign of Edward VI, was appointed bishop of Rochester (1547) and then of London (1550). During this period, he emerged as one of the leaders of the Reformation, opposing the Catholic policies of Edward's sister and successor Mary I, for which he was later imprisoned (1553) and burnt at the stake in Oxford.

Rie /riː/, Lucie (1902–95), British potter, born in Austria. In 1938 she came to England as a refugee. The following year she established a studio, and went on to influence a generation of British potters. Her pottery and stoneware are much admired for their precise, simple shapes and varied, subtle glazes, and are found in collections worldwide. She was made a Doctor of the Royal Academy of Arts in 1969.

Riefenstahl /'riːf(ə)n,ʃtɑːl/, Leni (full name Bertha Helene Amalie Riefenstahl) (born 1902), German film-maker and photographer. She is chiefly known for two films which she made during the 1930s; *Triumph of the Will* (1934), a powerful depiction of the 1934 Nuremberg Nazi Party rallies, and *Olympia* (1938), a two-part documentary of the 1936 Berlin Olympic Games. She was not a Nazi Party member and insisted on full control over these films, but outside Germany her work was regarded as Nazi propaganda and her postwar reputation suffered as a result.

Riel /riː'el/, Louis (1844–85), Canadian political leader. He headed the rebellion of the Metis at Red River Settlement (now in Manitoba) in 1869 to protest against the planned transfer of the territorial holdings of the Hudson's Bay Company to Canadian jurisdiction, a move which the Metis feared would result in the loss of some of their land to Anglo-Protestant settlers. Having formed a provisional government with himself at its head, Riel oversaw negotiations for acceptable terms for union with Canada, including the establishment of the province of Manitoba. He was executed for treason after leading a further rebellion of the Metis in the Saskatchewan valley (1884–5).

Riemann /'riːmən/, (Georg Friedrich) Bernhard (1826–66), German mathematician. He studied under Karl Gauss at Göttingen and became professor there. He founded Riemannian geometry, which is of fundamental importance to both mathematics and physics. The *Riemann hypothesis*, about the complex numbers which are roots of a certain transcendental equation, remains one of the unsolved problems of mathematics.

Riley /'raɪlɪ/, Bridget (Louise) (born 1931), English painter. A leading exponent of op art, she worked with flat patterns of lines, dots, and squares, initially in black and white and later in colour, to create optical illusions of light and movement. Notable paintings include *Movement in Squares* (1961) and *Fall* (1963).

Rilke /'rɪlkə/, Rainer Maria (pseudonym of René Karl Wilhelm Josef Maria Rilke) (1875–1926), Austrian poet, born in Bohemia. Two trips to Russia (1899–1900) inspired him to write the *Book of Hours* (1905), written from the perspective of a Russian monk. Rilke's conception of art as a quasi-

religious vocation culminated in the hymnic lyrics for which he is best known: the *Duino Elegies* and *Sonnets to Orpheus* (both 1923). In these he sought to define a poet's spiritual role in the face of transience and death.

Rimbaud /'ræmbəʊ/, (Jean Nicholas) Arthur (1854–91), French poet. Rimbaud wrote his most famous poem, 'Le Bateau ivre', at the age of 17. In the same year he began a passionate relationship with the poet Paul Verlaine, which partly inspired his collection of symbolist prose poems *Une Saison en enfer* (1873). In this and *Les Illuminations* (*c.*1872; published 1884), he explored the visionary possibilities of systematically 'disorientating the senses'. He stopped writing at about the age of 20 and spent the rest of his life travelling.

Rimsky-Korsakov /ˌrɪmskɪ'kɔːsəˌkɒf/, Nikolai (Andreevich) (1844–1908), Russian composer. He achieved fame with his orchestral suite *Scheherazade* (1888) and his many operas drawing on Russian and Slavonic folk tales, notably *The Golden Cockerel* (1906–7); the latter was based on Pushkin's poem lampooning autocracy and was banned in Russia until 1909. Rimsky-Korsakov was also a noted orchestrator, completing works by composers such as Borodin and Mussorgsky.

Rivera /rɪ'veərə/, Diego (1886–1957), Mexican painter. His monumental frescos of the 1920s and 1930s gave rise to a revival of fresco painting in Latin America and the US. Rivera's largest and most ambitious mural was a history of Mexico for the National Palace in Mexico City; begun in 1929 and unfinished at his death, it explicitly sought to construct a sense of nationalist and socialist identity.

Robbe-Grillet /rɒb'griːeɪ/, Alain (born 1922), French novelist. He established himself as a leading exponent of the avant-garde *nouveau roman* in the 1950s; his first novel *The Erasers* (1953) was an early example of the form, which rejected the plot, characters, and omniscient narrator central to the traditional novel. Among his later fictional works are *The Voyeur* (1955) and *Jealousy* (1957). His theories on fiction appeared in his collection of essays *Towards a New Novel* (1963). He also wrote screenplays in which he explored the visual potential of his fictional techniques, most notably that for *L'Année dernière à Marienbad* (1961).

Robbia see DELLA ROBBIA.

Robbins /'rɒbɪnz/, Jerome (born 1918), American ballet-dancer and choreographer. He choreographed a long series of successful musicals including *The King and I* (1951), *West Side Story* (1957), and *Fiddler on the Roof* (1964). Although chiefly inspired by jazz and modern dance, he has also created a number of ballets with music by classical composers.

Robert /'rɒbət/ the name of three kings of Scotland:
   Robert I (known as Robert the Bruce) (1274–1329), reigned 1306–29. He led the Scottish campaign against Edward I after the death of Sir William Wallace. His subsequent campaign against Edward II culminated in victory at Bannockburn (1314). He then went on to re-establish Scotland as a separate kingdom, negotiating the Treaty of Northampton (1328), which committed the Plantagenets to recognizing his title as king of Scotland and relinquishing their claims to overlordship.
   Robert II (1316–90), grandson of Robert the Bruce, reigned 1371–90. He was steward of Scotland from 1326 to 1371, and the first of the Stuart line.
   Robert III (born John) (*c.*1337–1406), son of Robert II, reigned 1390–1406. Before ascending the throne, he was involved in an accident in which the kick of a horse made him physically disabled. As a result, his reign was marked by a power struggle amongst members of his family and Scotland was chiefly ruled by his brother Robert, Duke of Albany (*c.*1340–1420).

Roberts /'rɒbəts/, Frederick Sleigh, 1st Earl Roberts of Kandahar (1832–1914), British Field Marshal. He won a Victoria Cross in 1858 for his part in suppressing the Indian Mutiny and commanded the British army in its victory at Kandahar (1880), which ended the Second Afghan War (1878–80). As Commander-in-Chief (1899–90) during the Second Boer War, he planned the successful march on the Boer capital of Pretoria (1900).

Robert the Bruce, Robert I of Scotland (see ROBERT).

Robeson /'rəʊbs(ə)n/, Paul (Bustill) (1898–1976), American singer and actor. His singing of 'Ol' Man River' in Jerome Kern's musical *Showboat* (1927) established his international reputation. Noted for his rich and resonant bass voice, he gave many recitals of spirituals. As an actor, Robeson

was particularly identified with the title role of *Othello*, which he performed to great acclaim in London (1930) and on Broadway (1943). He was a prominent black activist, and had his passport revoked in 1950 because of his Communist affiliations.

Robespierre /'rəʊbzpjeə(r)/, Maximilien François Marie Isidore de (1758–94), French revolutionary. Robespierre was the leader of the radical Jacobins in the National Assembly and, as such, backed the execution of Louis XVI and implemented a successful purge of the moderate Girondists (both 1793). Later the same year he consolidated his power with his election to the Committee of Public Safety (the revolutionary governing body 1793–4) and his appointment as president of the National Assembly. Robespierre was guillotined for his role in the Terror, although he had objected to the scale of the executions.

Robey /'rəʊbɪ/, Sir George (born George Edward Wade) (1869–1954), British comedian and actor. From the 1890s, he performed in music-halls and was billed as the 'Prime Minister of Mirth'. He later appeared in films such as Laurence Olivier's *Henry V* (1944).

Robinson[1] /'rɒbɪns(ə)n/, Edward G. (born Emanuel Goldenberg) (1893–1972), Romanian-born American actor. After playing the part of Rico Bandello in the gangster film *Little Caesar* (1930), he went on to appear in a string of similar films in the 1930s. He later played a wider range of screen roles, such as the father in Arthur Miller's *All My Sons* (1948). Robinson was also a noted art collector.

Robinson[2] /'rɒbɪns(ə)n/, (William) Heath (1872–1944), English cartoonist and illustrator. He is best known for his humorous drawings, through which he achieved worldwide fame. He lampooned the machine age by inventing absurdly complicated, jerry-built 'Heath Robinson contraptions' to perform elementary or ridiculous actions such as serving peas to diners or putting mites into green cheese. He also provided more conventional illustrations for editions of *Don Quixote* (1897) and *Twelfth Night* (1908).

Robinson[3] /'rɒbɪns(ə)n/, Mary (Terese Winifred) (born 1944), Irish Labour stateswoman, President 1990–97. She was called to the bar in 1967 and entered politics in 1969, when she became a member of the Irish Senate. In 1990 she became Ireland's first woman President. She was noted for her platform of religious toleration and for her liberal attitude to abortion, divorce, and homosexuality.

Robinson[4] /'rɒbɪns(ə)n/, Smokey (born William Robinson) (born 1940), American soul singer and songwriter. His group the Miracles were one of the first signings to the Motown label. They had a series of successes with songs written by Robinson such as 'Tracks of my Tears' (1965) and 'Tears of a Clown' (1970). Robinson also wrote many songs for other Motown artistes, for example 'My Guy' (1964) for Mary Wells. He left the Miracles in 1972 to embark on a solo career and to work for Motown.

Robinson[5] /'rɒbɪns(ə)n/, Sugar Ray (born Walker Smith) (1920–89), American boxer. He was world welterweight champion (1946–51) and five times middleweight champion (1951, twice; 1955; 1957; 1958–60).

Rob Roy /rɒb 'rɔɪ/ (born Robert Macgregor) (1671–1734), Scottish outlaw. His escapades as a highland cattle thief and opponent of the government's agents on the eve of the Jacobite uprising of 1715 were popularized in Sir Walter Scott's novel of the same name (1817).

Robsart /'rɒbsɑːt/, Amy (1532–60), English noblewoman, wife of Robert Dudley, Earl of Leicester. Her mysterious death at a country house near Oxford aroused suspicions that her husband (the favourite of Queen Elizabeth I) had had her killed so that he could be free to marry the queen. Sir Walter Scott's novel *Kenilworth* (1821) follows this version of her fate.

Robson /'rɒbs(ə)n/, Dame Flora (1902–84), English actress. She is noted for her screen performances of historical parts such as the Empress Elizabeth in *Catherine the Great* (1934) and Queen Elizabeth I in *Fire Over England* (1937). Her many acclaimed stage roles included Mrs Alving in Ibsen's *Ghosts* (1959).

Rochester /'rɒtʃɪstə(r)/, 2nd Earl of (title of John Wilmot) (1647–80), English poet and courtier. Infamous for his dissolute life at the court of Charles II, he wrote many sexually explicit love poems and, with his social and literary verse satires, is regarded as one of the first Augustans. Famous works include his *Satire Against Mankind* (1675).

Rockefeller /'rɒkə,felə(r)/, John D(avison) (1839–1937), American industrialist and philanthropist. One of the first to recognize the industrial possibilities of oil, Rockefeller established the Standard Oil Company (1870) and by the end of the decade exercised a virtual monopoly over oil refining in the US. Early in the 20th century he handed over his business interests to his son, John D(avison) Rockefeller Jr. (1874–1960), and devoted his private fortune to numerous philanthropic projects, such as the establishment of the Rockefeller Foundation (1913). His son's many philanthropic institutions include the Rockefeller Center in New York (1939).

Rockwell /'rɒkwel/, Norman (Percevel) (1894–1978), American illustrator. Rockwell's often sentimental depictions of small-town American life made him one of the most popular artists in the US. He was an illustrator for several major periodicals, including *Life* and the *Saturday Evening Post*, for whom he created 317 covers (1916–63).

Roddenberry /'rɒd(ə)n,berɪ/, Gene (full name Eugene Wesley Roddenberry) (1921–91), American television producer and scriptwriter. He is best-known as the creator of the TV science-fiction drama series *Star Trek*, first broadcast 1966–9. Roddenberry wrote many scripts for the series, which attracted an international cult following. He later worked on feature films and launched a successful follow-up series, *Star Trek: The Next Generation*, in 1987.

Roddick /'rɒdɪk/, Anita (Lucia) (born 1943), English businesswoman. In 1976 she opened her first shop, selling cosmetics with an emphasis on environmentally conscious products made from natural ingredients and not tested on animals. This developed into the Body Shop chain, which by the late 1980s comprised several hundred outlets in the UK and abroad.

Rodgers /'rɒdʒəz/, Richard (Charles) (1902–79), American composer. Together with librettist Lorenz Hart (1895–1943), he created musicals such as *On Your Toes* (1936). After Hart's death, Rodgers collaborated with Oscar Hammerstein II on a succession of popular musicals, including *Oklahoma!* (1943), *Carousel* (1945), *South Pacific* (1949), and *The Sound of Music* (1959).

Rodin /'rəʊdæn/, Auguste (1840–1917), French sculptor. Influenced by Michelangelo, Rodin was chiefly concerned with the human form in his work, and developed a naturalistic style that made him a controversial figure in his day. His first major work, *The Age of Bronze* (1875–6), was considered so lifelike that Rodin was alleged to have taken a cast from a live model. By 1880 he had been publicly commissioned to create *The Gate of Hell* for the Musée des arts décoratifs; it remained unfinished at his death and its many figures inspired such independent statues as *The Thinker* (1880) and *The Kiss* (1886).

Roe /rəʊ/, Sir (Edwin) Alliott Verdon (1877–1958), English engineer and aircraft designer. He built the first British seaplane to take off from the water and (in 1912) the first aircraft with an enclosed cabin. With his brother H. V. Roe he founded the Avro Company and built a number of planes, of which the Avro 504 trainer biplane was the most successful; in 1928 he formed the Saunders-Roe Company to design and manufacture flying boats. Roe also invented anti-dazzle car headlights.

Roeg /rəʊg/, Nicholas (Jack) (born 1928), English film director. His work is often unsettling and impressionistic, and uses cutting techniques to create disjointed narratives. His films include *Performance* (1970), *Walkabout* (1970), *Don't Look Now* (1972), *The Man Who Fell to Earth* (1975), and *Castaway* (1986).

Rogers[1] /'rɒdʒəz/, Ginger (born Virginia Katherine McMath) (1911–95), American actress and dancer. She is best known for her dancing partnership with Fred Astaire; from 1933 they appeared in a number of film musicals, including *Top Hat* (1935), *Swing Time* (1936), and *Shall We Dance?* (1937). Rogers's solo acting career included the film *Kitty Foyle* (1940), for which she won an Oscar.

Rogers[2] /'rɒdʒəz/, Sir Richard (George) (born 1933), British architect, born in Italy. He was a leading exponent of high-tech architecture and founded his own practice, Team 4, in 1963. He gained international recognition in the 1970s for the Pompidou Centre in Paris (1971–7), which he designed in partnership with the Italian architect Renzo Piano (born 1937) and which featured ducts and pipes on the outside of the building. Rogers's other major work, the Lloyd's Building in London (1986), followed a similarly original high-tech design.

Roget /'rɒʒeɪ/, Peter Mark (1779–1869), English scholar. He worked as a physician but is remembered as the compiler of *Roget's Thesaurus of English Words and Phrases*, which he completed after his retirement and which was first published in 1852. The work, which has been revised many times since, is important for its innovative classification of words according to underlying concept or meaning.

Rolland /'rɒlɒn/, Romain (1866–1944), French novelist, dramatist, and essayist. His interest in genius led to biographies of Beethoven (1903), Michelangelo (1905), and Tolstoy (1911), and ultimately to *Jean-Christophe* (1904–12), a cycle of ten novels about a German composer. These epitomize the literary form known as the *roman-fleuve* and in their portrayal of the composer's friendship with a Frenchman symbolized Rolland's desire for harmony between nations. He was awarded the Nobel Prize for literature in 1915.

Rolls /rəʊlz/, Charles Stewart (1877–1910), English motoring and aviation pioneer. He was one of the founder members of the Royal Automobile Club (RAC) in 1897 and the Royal Aero Club (1903). In 1906 he and Henry Royce formed the company Rolls-Royce Ltd., with Royce as chief engineer and Rolls as demonstrator-salesman. The company became a major producer of aircraft engines and luxury motor cars; after becoming bankrupt in 1971 it was formed into two separate companies. Rolls was the first Englishman to fly across the English Channel, and made the first double crossing in 1910 shortly before he was killed in an air crash, the first English casualty of aviation.

Romberg /'rɒmbɜːg/, Sigmund (1887–1951), Hungarian-born American composer. He wrote a succession of popular operettas, including *The Student Prince* (1924), *The Desert Song* (1926), and *New Moon* (1928).

Rommel /'rɒm(ə)l/, Erwin (known as 'the Desert Fox') (1891–1944), German Field Marshal. Rommel was posted to North Africa in 1941 after the collapse of the Italian offensive, and, as commander of the Afrika Korps, he deployed a series of surprise manoeuvres and succeeded in capturing Tobruk (1942). After being defeated by Montgomery at El Alamein (1942), he was ordered home the following year to serve as Inspector of Coastal Defences. He was forced to commit suicide after being implicated in the officers' conspiracy against Hitler in 1944.

Romney /'rɒmnɪ, 'rʌm-/, George (1734–1802), English portrait painter. Based in London from 1762, he rivalled Thomas Gainsborough and Sir Joshua Reynolds for popularity in the late 18th century. From the early 1780s he produced more than fifty portraits of Lady Hamilton in historical poses.

Röntgen /'rʌntjən, 'rɒntgən, German 'rœntg(ə)n/, Wilhelm Conrad (1845–1923), German physicist, the discoverer of X-rays. He was a skilful experimenter and worked on a variety of topics. In 1888 he demonstrated the existence of a magnetic field caused by the motion of electrostatic charges, predicted by James Clerk Maxwell and important for future electrical theory. In 1895 Röntgen observed that a nearby fluorescent screen glowed when a current was passed through a Crookes' vacuum tube. He investigated the properties of the radiation responsible, which he called 'X-rays', and produced the first X-ray photograph (of his wife's hand). He was awarded the first Nobel Prize for physics in 1901.

Rooney /'ruːnɪ/, Mickey (born Joseph Yule Jr.) (born 1920), American actor. From childhood he appeared in a great many films, starting with *Not to Be Trusted* (1926). He played Andy Hardy in a series of sixteen comedy drama films over twenty years about the Hardy family, America's favourite fictional characters during the Second World War. Other films include the musical *Babes in Arms* (1939), the comedy *The Human Comedy* (1943), for both of which he received Oscar nominations, and *The Black Stallion* (1979).

Roosevelt[1] /'rəʊzə‚velt/, (Anna) Eleanor (1884–1962), American humanitarian and diplomat. She was the niece of Theodore Roosevelt, and married Franklin D. Roosevelt in 1905. She was involved in a wide range of liberal causes, including civil and women's rights. After Roosevelt died in 1945 she became a delegate to the United Nations, and, as chair of the UN Commission on Human Rights, played a major role in drafting the Declaration of Human Rights (1948).

Roosevelt[2] /'rəʊzə‚velt/, Franklin D(elano) (known as FDR) (1882–1945), American Democratic statesman, 32nd President of the US 1933–45. Roosevelt's early political career was curtailed by his contraction of polio in 1921; in spite of the disease, he

resumed public life in 1928 and received the Democratic presidential nomination in 1932. His New Deal package of economic measures (1933) helped to lift the US out of the Great Depression, and after the American entry into the Second World War he played an important part in the coordination of the Allied war effort. In 1940 Roosevelt became the first American President to be elected for a third term in office, and he subsequently secured a fourth term. He was the joint author, with Winston Churchill, of the Atlantic Charter (1941), a declaration of eight common principles in international relations that was intended to guide a postwar peace settlement.

Roosevelt[3] /'rəʊzə,velt/, Theodore ('Teddy') (1858–1919), American Republican statesman, 26th President of the US 1901–9. He was elected Vice-President in 1900, succeeding William McKinley in 1901 following the latter's assassination. At home Roosevelt was noted for his antitrust laws, while abroad he successfully engineered the American bid to build the Panama Canal (1904–14) and won the Nobel Peace Prize in 1906 for negotiating the end of the Russo-Japanese War. The teddy bear is named after Roosevelt, with reference to his bear-hunting.

Rosa /'rəʊzə/, Salvator (1615–73), Italian painter and etcher. His reputation is chiefly based on his landscapes, often peopled with bandits and containing scenes of violence in wild natural settings; their picturesque and 'sublime' qualities were an important influence on the romantic art of the 18th and 19th centuries.

Roscius /'rɒsɪəs, 'rɒʃɪ-/ (full name Quintus Roscius Gallus) (died 62 BC), Roman actor. He achieved phenomenal success as a comic actor during his lifetime and later became identified with all that was considered best in acting; many notable English actors from the 16th century onwards were nicknamed in reference to him.

Rosebery /'rəʊzbərɪ/, 5th Earl of (title of Archibald Philip Primrose) (1847–1929), British Liberal statesman, Prime Minister 1894–5. He succeeded Gladstone as Premier after the latter's retirement and subsequently alienated Liberal supporters as a result of his imperialist loyalties during the Second Boer War (1899–1902).

Ross[1] /rɒs/, Diana (born 1944), American pop and soul singer. She made her name as the lead singer of the Supremes, with whom she recorded many hit singles. She left the group in 1969 and became a successful solo artist, recording songs such as 'Remember Me' (1971). She has also appeared in several films, including *Lady Sings the Blues* (1973), for which she received an Oscar for her role as the jazz singer Billie Holiday.

Ross[2] /rɒs/, Sir James Clark (1800–62), British explorer. He discovered the north magnetic pole in 1831, and headed an expedition to the Antarctic from 1839 to 1843, in the course of which he discovered Ross Island, Ross Dependency, and the Ross Sea, all named after him. He was the nephew of Sir John Ross.

Ross[3] /rɒs/, Sir John (1777–1856), British explorer. He led an expedition to Baffin Bay in 1818 and another in search of the Northwest Passage between 1829 and 1833, during which he surveyed King William Land, the Boothia Peninsula, and the Gulf of Boothia. He was the uncle of Sir James Clark Ross.

Ross[4] /rɒs/, Sir Ronald (1857–1932), British physician. He worked in the Indian Medical Service and became interested in malaria, and while on a visit to England met Patrick Manson, who suggested that it was transmitted by a mosquito. Ross confirmed that the *Anopheles* mosquito was indeed the vector, and went on to elucidate the stages in the malarial parasite's life cycle. He was awarded a Nobel Prize in 1902.

Rossellini /,rɒsə'li:nɪ/, Roberto (1906–77), Italian film director. He is known for his neo-realist films, particularly his quasi-documentary trilogy about the Second World War, filmed using a mainly non-professional cast; this comprises *Open City* (1945), *Paisà* (1946), and *Germany, Year Zero* (1947).

Rossetti[1] /rə'zetɪ/, Christina (Georgina) (1830–94), English poet. She contributed several poems to the Pre-Raphaelite journal *The Germ* in 1850. Influenced by the Oxford Movement, Rossetti wrote much religious poetry reflecting her High Anglican faith, although she also wrote love poetry and children's verse. Marked by technical virtuosity, a sense of melancholy, and recurrent themes of frustrated love and premature resignation, her work includes the verse collection *Goblin Market and Other Poems* (1862). She was the sister of Dante Gabriel Rossetti.

Rossetti[2] /rəˈzetɪ/, Dante Gabriel (full name Gabriel Charles Dante Rossetti) (1828–82), English painter and poet. He was a founder member of the Pre-Raphaelite Brotherhood (1848), and encouraged the movement to make links between painting and literature, basing many of his paintings on the work of the Italian poet Dante. Rossetti is best known for his dreamy and idealized images of women including *Beata Beatrix* (c.1863) and *The Blessed Damozel* (1871–9); the latter took its subject from his poem of 1850. From 1861 Rossetti was associated with William Morris's firm Morris & Company. He was the brother of Christina Rossetti.

Rossini /rɒˈsiːnɪ/, Gioacchino Antonio (1792–1868), Italian composer. He wrote more than thirty operas, of which the best known are the comic opera *The Barber of Seville* (1816) and the grand opera *William Tell* (1829). He was one of the creators of the Italian bel canto style of singing, along with Bellini and Donizetti.

Rostand /ˈrɒstɒn/, Edmond (1868–1918), French dramatist and poet. His reputation is chiefly based on his poetic drama *Cyrano de Bergerac* (1897), which romanticized the life of the 17th-century soldier, duellist, and writer Cyrano de Bergerac.

Roth /rɒθ/, Philip (Milton) (born 1933), American novelist and short-story writer. The complexity and diversity of contemporary American Jewish life is the subject of many of his works, to which he often brings both irony and humour. His best-known novel, *Portnoy's Complaint* (1969), records the intimate, often sexually explicit, confessions of an adolescent boy, Alexander Portnoy, to his psychiatrist.

Rothko /ˈrɒθkəʊ/, Mark (born Marcus Rothkovich) (1903–70), American painter, born in Latvia. In the late 1940s he became a leading figure in colour-field painting, creating canvases consisting of hazy and apparently floating rectangles of colour, usually arranged vertically and in parallel, with the intention of absorbing the spectator in an act of contemplation. Famous works include his series of nine paintings for the Seagram Building in New York, notably *Black on Maroon* (1958).

Rothschild /ˈrɒθʃaɪld, ˈrɒtʃaɪld/, Meyer Amschel (1743–1812), German financier. He was the founder of the Rothschild banking-house in Frankfurt and financial adviser to the landgrave of Hesse. By the time of his death, his firm had already conducted significant financial transactions for a number of European governments. He had five sons, all of whom entered banking, setting up branches of the organization across western Europe. Notable among them were Nathan Meyer, Baron de Rothschild (1777–1836), who founded a bank in London (1804) and became a British citizen; Nathan's son, Lionel Nathan, Baron de Rothschild (1808–79), was Britain's first Jewish MP.

Rouault /ˈruːəʊ, French rwo/, Georges (Henri) (1871–1958), French painter and engraver. Although he exhibited with the fauves in 1905, he is chiefly associated with expressionism. His best-known paintings are characterized by the use of vivid colours and simplified forms enclosed in thick black outlines, reflecting the influence of his apprenticeship to a stained-glass window-maker (1885–90). A devout Roman Catholic, from the 1930s he turned increasingly towards religious subject-matter; notable among such works is *Christ Mocked by Soldiers* (1932).

Rousseau[1] /ˈruːsəʊ/, Henri (Julien) (known as 'le Douanier', 'the customs officer') (1844–1910), French painter. After retiring as a customs official in 1893, he devoted himself fully to painting, although it was only after his death that he was recognized as a notable naive artist. Fantastic dreams and exotic jungle landscapes often form the subjects of his bold and colourful paintings. Famous works include the *Sleeping Gypsy* (1897) and *Tropical Storm with Tiger* (1891).

Rousseau[2] /ˈruːsəʊ/, Jean-Jacques (1712–78), French philosopher and writer, born in Switzerland. From 1750 he came to fame with a series of works highly critical of the existing social order; his philosophy is underpinned by a belief in the fundamental goodness of human nature, encapsulated in the concept of the 'noble savage', and the warping effects of civilization. In his novel *Émile* (1762) Rousseau formulated new educational principles giving the child full scope for individual development in natural surroundings, shielded from the corrupting influences of civilization. His *Social Contract* (1762) anticipated much of the thinking of the French Revolution. Rousseau is also noted for his *Confessions*

(1782), one of the earliest autobiographies.

Rousseau[3] /'ru:səʊ/, (Pierre Étienne) Théodore (1812–67), French painter. He was a leading landscapist of the Barbizon School and placed great importance on making preliminary studies for studio paintings out of doors, directly from nature. His works typically depict the scenery and changing light effects of the forest of Fontainebleau, and include *Under the Birches, Evening* (1842–4).

Rowe /rəʊ/, Nicholas (1674–1718), English dramatist. He is best known for his tragedies *Tamerlane* (1701) and *The Fair Penitent* (1703). The latter, marked by pathos and suffering, provided Mrs Siddons with one of her most celebrated roles.

Rowlandson /'rəʊlənds(ə)n/, Thomas (1756–1827), English painter, draughtsman, and caricaturist. He is remembered for his many watercolours and drawings satirizing Georgian manners, morals, and occupations. His best-known illustrations feature in a series of books known as *The Tours of Dr Syntax* (1812–21).

Rowntree /'raʊntri:/, a family of English business entrepreneurs and philanthropists. Joseph (1801–59), a grocer, established several Quaker schools. His son Henry Isaac Rowntree (1838–83) founded the family cocoa and chocolate manufacturing firm in York; Henry's brother Joseph Rowntree (1836–1925) became a partner in 1869 and subsequently founded three Rowntree trusts (1904) to support research into social welfare and policy. The latter's son B(enjamin) Seebohm Rowntree (1871–1954), chairman of the firm from 1925 to 1941, conducted surveys of poverty in York (1897–8; 1936).

Royce /rɔɪs/, Sir (Frederick) Henry (1863–1933), English engine designer. He founded the company of Rolls-Royce Ltd. with Charles Stewart Rolls in 1906, previously having established his own successful electrical manufacturing business and designing and building his own car and engine. He became famous as the designer of the Rolls-Royce Silver Ghost motor car and later also became known for his aircraft engines, which were used to power planes in the First and Second World Wars and beyond.

Rubbra /'rʌbrə/, (Charles) Edmund (1901–86), English composer and pianist. He wrote eleven symphonies, of which the fifth (1947–8) is the most frequently performed; the ninth, the *Sinfonia Sacra* (1971–2), is in the nature of a choral passion. He also wrote two masses (1945; 1949) and many songs.

Rubens /'ru:bmz/, Sir Peter Paul (1577–1640), Flemish painter. The foremost exponent of northern baroque, he spent a period of time in Italy (1600–8), where he studied the work of artists such as Titian and Raphael, before settling in Antwerp and becoming court portraitist in 1609. He quickly gained fame as a religious painter with altarpieces such as *Descent from the Cross* (1611–14). He built up a prestigious workshop that executed numerous commissions from across Europe ranging from decorative ceilings to landscapes; its more famous assistants included Anthony Van Dyck and Jacob Jordaens. On a visit to England (1629–30) he was knighted by Charles I and executed several commissions for him, including a series of decorative ceilings at the Banqueting Hall in Whitehall. In addition to his portraits, Rubens is perhaps best known for mythological paintings featuring voluptuous female nudes, as in *Venus and Adonis* (c.1635).

Rubinstein[1] /'ru:bm,staɪn/, Anton (Grigorevich) (1829–94), Russian composer and pianist. In 1862 he founded the St Petersburg Conservatory and was its director 1862–7 and 1887–91; Tchaikovsky was among his pupils. Rubinstein composed symphonies, operas, songs, and piano music, including *Melody in F* (1852). His brother Nikolai (1835–81) was also a pianist and composer; he was prominent in Moscow's musical life and founded the Moscow Conservatory.

Rubinstein[2] /'ru:bm,staɪn/, Artur (1888–1982), Polish-born American pianist. He first came to public attention with his Berlin début in 1900 at the age of 12, when he played the Mozart Concerto in A major. Thereafter he toured extensively in Europe as well as the US and made many recordings, including the complete works of Chopin. He became an American citizen in 1946.

Rubinstein[3] /'ru:bm,staɪn/, Helena (1882–1965), American beautician and businesswoman. Born in Poland, she trained in medicine there before going to Australia in 1902, where she opened her first beauty

salon. Her success enabled her to return to Europe and open salons in London (1908) and Paris (1912), and later to go to the US and open salons in New York (1915) and elsewhere. After the First World War her organization expanded to become an international cosmetics manufacturer and distributor.

Ruisdael /'riːzdɑːl, 'rɔɪz-, -deɪl/, Jacob van (also **Ruysdael**) (c.1628–82), Dutch landscape painter. Born in Haarlem, he painted the surrounding landscape from the mid-1640s until his move to Amsterdam in 1657, where he spent the rest of his life. His typical subject-matter was forest scenes, seascapes, and cloudscapes, and his work demonstrated the possibilities of investing landscape with subtle intimations of mood. Meindert Hobbema was his most famous pupil, while among those influenced by his work were Thomas Gainsborough, John Constable, and the Barbizon School.

Ruiz de Alarcón y Mendoza /ruːˌiːz deɪ ˌælɑːˌkɒn iː menˈdəʊzə/, Juan (1580–1639), Spanish dramatist, born in Mexico City. His most famous play, the moral comedy *La Verdad sospechosa*, was the basis of Corneille's *Le Menteur* (1642).

Runyon /'rʌnjən/, (Alfred) Damon (1884–1946), American author and journalist. He is best known for his short stories about New York's Broadway and underworld characters, written in a highly individual style with much use of colourful slang. His collections include *Guys and Dolls* (1932), which formed the basis for the musical of the same name (1950).

Rupert, Prince /'ruːpət/ (1619–82), English Royalist general, son of Frederick V, elector of the Palatinate, and nephew of Charles I. Born in Bohemia, he went to England and joined the Royalist side just before the outbreak of the Civil War in 1642. He made his name in the early years of the war as a leader of cavalry, but after a series of victorious engagements was defeated by Parliamentarian forces at Marston Moor (1644) and Naseby (1645). He later lived chiefly in France until the Restoration (1660), when he returned to England and commanded naval operations against the Dutch (1665–7 and 1672–4). In 1670 Rupert became the first governor of the Hudson's Bay Company in Canada. He was also responsible for the introduction of mezzotint engraving into England.

Rushdie /'rʌʃdɪ, 'rʊʃ-/, (Ahmed) Salman (born 1947), Indian-born British novelist. He was educated in England and became a British citizen in 1964. His work is chiefly associated with magic realism; his Booker Prize-winning novel *Midnight's Children* (1981) views the development of India since independence through the eyes of a telepathic child. His later novel *The Satanic Verses* (1988), with its portrayal of a figure that many identified with Muhammad, was regarded by Muslims as blasphemous; in 1989 Ayatollah Khomeini issued a fatwa condemning Rushdie to death and he has since lived in hiding with a permanent police guard.

Ruskin /'rʌskɪn/, John (1819–1900), English art and social critic. His prolific writings profoundly influenced 19th-century opinion and the development of the Labour movement. He was a champion of the painter J. M. W. Turner (at that time a controversial figure), the Pre-Raphaelite Brotherhood, and of Gothic architecture, which (following Pugin) he saw as a religious expression of medieval piety. *The Stones of Venice* (1851–3), attacking Renaissance art, led on to later attacks on capitalism in his lectures 'The Political Economy of Art' (1857), and on utilitarianism in *Unto This Last* (1860). His *Fors Clavigera* (1871–8) or 'Letters to the Workmen and Labourers of Great Britain' was an attempt to spread his notions of social justice, coupled with aesthetic improvement. His religious and philanthropic instincts also expressed themselves in the founding of the Guild of St George in 1871, a major contribution to the Arts and Crafts Movement.

Russell[1] /'rʌs(ə)l/, Bertrand (Arthur William), 3rd Earl Russell (1872–1970), British philosopher, mathematician, and social reformer. His work on mathematical logic had great influence on symbolic logic and on set theory in mathematics; his major work in this field is *Principia Mathematica* (1910–13), written with A. N. Whitehead. His philosophical views underwent continual development and revision; however, he wrote several books in the empiricist tradition (such as *Our Knowledge of the External World*, 1914) and was a principal proponent of neutral monism (a denial of the duality of matter and mind) and of logical atomism (the theory that all statements or propositions can be analysed into simple independent or atomic statements which correspond directly to facts about

our experience of the world). During the First World War Russell became widely known as a conscientious objector; he also campaigned for women's suffrage and later took a leading role in CND. He was awarded the Nobel Prize for literature in 1950.

Russell[2] /ˈrʌs(ə)l/, George William (1867–1935), Irish poet. He met W. B. Yeats in 1886 and became interested in theosophy and mysticism; the first of several volumes of verse (published under the pseudonym AE) appeared in 1894. After the performance of his poetic drama *Deirdre* (1902) Russell became a leading figure in the Irish literary revival. His interests extended to public affairs and he edited *The Irish Homestead* (1905–23) and *The Irish Statesman* (1923–30).

Russell[3] /ˈrʌs(ə)l/, Henry Norris (1877–1957), American astronomer. He worked mainly in astrophysics and spectroscopy, and is best known for his discovery of the relationship between stellar magnitude and spectral type. Russell and Ejnar Hertzsprung (1873–1967) independently devised a two-dimensional graph (the Hertzsprung–Russell diagram) in which the absolute magnitudes of stars are plotted against their spectral types; stars are found to occupy only certain regions of this diagram, depending on their mass and the stage of their life cycle. Russell believed that this diagram represented a sequence of stellar evolution, a view no longer accepted. He carried out spectroscopic analyses to determine the constituent elements of stars, and he discovered that the sun contained much more hydrogen than had been expected.

Russell[4] /ˈrʌs(ə)l/, John, 1st Earl Russell (1792–1878), British Whig statesman, Prime Minister 1846–52 and 1865–6. As a member of Lord Grey's government (1830–4), he was responsible for introducing the Reform Bill of 1832 into Parliament. He became Prime Minister when Sir Robert Peel was defeated (1846) and later served as Foreign Secretary in Lord Aberdeen's coalition government (1852–4); Russell's second premiership ended with his resignation when his attempt to extend the franchise again in a further Reform Bill was unsuccessful.

Russell[5] /ˈrʌs(ə)l/, Ken (born Henry Kenneth Alfred Russell) (born 1927), English film director. After making a series of in-creasingly unconventional biographical films on composers for the BBC he gained an international reputation with a lavish screen adaptation of D. H. Lawrence's *Women in Love* (1969). His films are characterized by their extravagant and extreme imagery, and have often attracted controversy for their depiction of sex and violence. His prolific output includes *The Devils* (1971), *The Rainbow* (1989), and the television film *Lady Chatterley* (1993).

Ruth /ruːθ/, Babe (born George Herman Ruth) (1895–1948), American baseball player. He played for the Boston Red Sox (1914–19) and the New York Yankees (1919–35); during his career he set the record for the most home runs (714), which remained unbroken until 1974.

Rutherford[1] /ˈrʌðəfəd/, Sir Ernest, 1st Baron Rutherford of Nelson (1871–1937), New Zealand physicist. He is regarded as the founder of nuclear physics, and worked mainly in Britain. He established the nature of alpha and beta particles, and (with Frederick Soddy) proposed the laws of radioactive decay. He later concluded that the positive charge in an atom, and virtually all its mass, is concentrated in a central nucleus, with negatively charged electrons in orbit round it. In 1919 Rutherford announced the first artificial transmutation of matter — he had changed nitrogen atoms into oxygen by bombarding them with alpha particles. He was awarded the Nobel Prize for chemistry in 1908.

Rutherford[2] /ˈrʌðəfəd/, Dame Margaret (1892–1972), English actress. She is chiefly remembered for her roles as a formidable but jovial eccentric; they include Miss Prism in *The Importance of Being Earnest*, which she played on stage in 1939 and on film in 1952. Among her other films are *Passport to Pimlico* (1949), several film versions of Agatha Christie novels in which she played Miss Marple, and *The VIPs* (1963), for which she won an Oscar.

Ruysdael see RUISDAEL.

Ryder /ˈraɪdə(r)/, Sue, Baroness Ryder of Warsaw and Cavendish (born 1923), English philanthropist. After the Second World War she co-founded an organization to care for former inmates of concentration camps; later known as the Sue Ryder Foundation for the Sick and the Disabled, it expanded to provide homes for the men-

tally and physically disabled in the UK and elsewhere in Europe. Ryder married the philanthropist Leonard Cheshire in 1959, and is a trustee of the Cheshire Foundation.

Ryle[1] /raɪl/, Gilbert (1900–76), English philosopher. He was professor of metaphysical philosophy at Oxford (1945–68) and did much to make Oxford a leading centre for philosophical research. He was a prominent figure in the linguistic school of philosophy and held that philosophy should identify 'the sources in linguistic idioms of recurrent misconstructions and absurd theories'. His most famous work, *The Concept of Mind* (1949), is a strong attack on the mind-and-body dualism of Descartes. He was a cousin of the astronomer Sir Martin Ryle.

Ryle[2] /raɪl/, Sir Martin (1918–84), English astronomer. He carried out pioneering work in radio astronomy in the 1950s, when he produced the first detailed sky map of radio sources. His demonstration that remote objects appeared to be different from closer ones helped to establish the big bang as opposed to the steady-state theory of the universe. Ryle was Astronomer Royal 1972–82 and was awarded the Nobel Prize for physics in 1974, the first astronomer to be so honoured. He was a cousin of the philosopher Gilbert Ryle.

S

Saadi see SADI.

Sachs /sæks, zæks/, Hans (1494–1576), German poet and dramatist. A shoemaker by trade, he was a renowned member of the Guild of Meistersingers in Nuremberg, as well as the prolific author of verse and some 200 plays. Some of his poetry celebrated Martin Luther and furthered the Protestant cause, while other pieces were comic verse dramas. Forgotten after his death, he was restored to fame in a poem by Goethe, and Wagner made him the hero of his opera *Die Meistersinger von Nürnberg* (1868).

Sackville-West /ˌsækvɪlˈwest/, Victoria Mary ('Vita') (1892–1962), English novelist and poet. Her works include the long poem *The Land* (1927), notable for its evocation of the English countryside, and the novel *All Passion Spent* (1931). She is also known for the garden which she created at Sissinghurst in Kent and for her friendship with Virginia Woolf; the central character of Woolf's novel *Orlando* (1928) is said to have been based on her.

Sadat /sæˈdæt/, (Muhammad) Anwar al- (1918–81), Egyptian statesman, President 1970–81. He broke with the foreign policies of his predecessor President Nasser, for example by dismissing the Soviet military mission to Egypt, removing the ban on political parties, and introducing measures to decentralize Egypt's political structure and diversify the economy. He later worked to achieve peace in the Middle East, visiting Israel (1977), and attending talks with Prime Minister Begin at Camp David in 1978, the year they shared the Nobel Peace Prize. Also in that year he founded the National Democratic Party, with himself as leader. He was assassinated by members of the Islamic Jihad.

Saddam Hussein /səˈdæm/ see HUSSEIN[2].

Sade /saːd/, Donatien Alphonse François, Comte de (known as the Marquis de Sade) (1740–1814), French writer and soldier. His career as a cavalry officer was interrupted by prolonged periods of imprisonment for cruelty and debauchery. While in prison he wrote a number of sexually explicit works, which include *Les 120 Journées de Sodome* (1784), *Justine* (1791), and *La Philosophie dans le boudoir* (1795). The word *sadism* owes its origin to his name, referring to the sexual practices which he described.

Sadi /ˈsɑːdɪ/ (also **Saadi**) (born Sheikh Muslih Addin) (c.1213–c.1291), Persian poet. His principal works were the collections known as the *Bustan* (1257) and the *Gulistan* (1258); the former is a series of poems on religious themes, while the latter is a mixture of poems, prose, and maxims concerning moral issues.

Sagan[1] /ˈseɪɡən/, Carl (Edward) (1934–96), American astronomer. He specialized in studies of the planets Mars and Venus, and in 1968 became director of the Laboratory of Planetary Studies at Cornell, dealing with information from space probes to those planets. Sagan showed that amino acids can be synthesized in an artificial primordial soup irradiated by ultraviolet light — a possible explanation for the origin of life on earth. In 1983 he and several other scientists put forward the concept of a nuclear winter as a likely consequence of global nuclear war. He wrote several popular science books, and was co-producer and narrator of the television series *Cosmos* (1980).

Sagan[2] /sæˈɡɒn/, Françoise (pseudonym of Françoise Quoirez) (born 1935), French novelist, dramatist, and short-story writer. She rose to fame with her first novel *Bonjour Tristesse* (1954); in this and subsequent novels, she examined the transitory nature of love as experienced in brief liaisons. Other novels include *Un Certain sourire* (1956) and *Aimez-vous Brahms?* (1959).

Saha /səˈhɑː/, Meghnad (1894–1956), Indian physicist. He worked on thermal ionization in stars, using both thermodynamics and quantum theory, and laid the foundations for modern astrophysics. He showed that the ionization of metal atoms increases with temperature, leading to a reduction in the absorption lines visible in stellar spectra. Saha devised an equation, now named after him, expressing the relationship between ionization and temperature.

Said /sæ'i:d/, Edward W(adi) (born 1935), American critic, born in Palestine. A professor of English and comparative literature at the University of Columbia, he came to public notice with *Orientalism* (1978), a study of Western attitudes towards Eastern culture. In *The Question of Palestine* (1985), Said defended the Palestinian struggle for political autonomy and has since played an active role in moves to form a Palestinian state. Other works include *Culture and Imperialism* (1993), a critique of Western culture.

Sainsbury /'seɪnzbərɪ/, John James (1844–1928), English grocer. He opened his first grocery store in London in 1875. After his death the business was continued by members of his family, developing into the large supermarket chain bearing the Sainsbury name.

St Agnes, St Barnabas, etc. see AGNES, ST; BARNABAS, ST; etc.

Sainte-Beuve /sænt'bɜ:v/, Charles Augustin (1804–69), French critic and writer. He is chiefly known for his contribution to 19th-century literary criticism, in which he concentrated on the influence of social and other factors in the development of authors' characters; his critical essays were published in collected form as *Causeries du lundi* (1851–62) and *Nouveaux lundis* (1863–70). He also wrote a study of Jansenism (*Port-Royal*, 1840–59) and was an early champion of French romanticism.

Saint-Exupéry /ˌsæntɪg'zu:peɪrɪ/, Antoine (Marie Roger de) (1900–44), French writer and aviator. His best-known work is probably the fable *The Little Prince* (1943). He drew on his experiences as a commercial and air-force pilot in novels such as *Night Flight* (1931). He was shot down and killed while on active service in North Africa during the Second World War.

Saint Laurent /ˌsæn lɔ:'rɒn/, Yves (Mathieu) (born 1936), French couturier. He was Christian Dior's assistant from 1953 and after Dior's death in 1957 succeeded him as head designer. His fashions at this time reflected youth culture, and included a 'beatnik' look of turtle-neck sweaters and black leather jackets. He opened his own fashion house in 1962; four years later, he launched the first of a worldwide chain of Rive Gauche boutiques to sell ready-to-wear garments. From the 1970s he expanded the business to include perfumes and household fabrics.

Saint-Saëns /'sænsɒn, French sɛ̃sɑ̃s/, (Charles) Camille (1835–1921), French composer, pianist, and organist. He was organist at the church of the Madeleine in Paris (1858–77) and played an important role in the city's musical life. His works include operas (notably *Samson et Dalila*, 1877) and oratorios, but he is probably now best known for his Third Symphony (1886), the symphonic poem *Danse macabre* (1874), which was the first orchestral piece to use a xylophone, and the *Carnaval des animaux* (1886).

Saint-Simon[1] /ˌsænsi:'mɒn/, Claude-Henri de Rouvroy, Comte de (1760–1825), French social reformer and philosopher. In reaction to the chaos engendered by the French Revolution he developed a new theory of social organization and was later claimed to be the founder of French socialism. His central theory was that society should be organized in an industrial order, controlled by leaders of industry, and given spiritual direction by scientists. His works, which greatly influenced figures such as John Stuart Mill and Friedrich Engels, include *Du système industriel* (1821) and *Nouveau Christianisme* (1825).

Saint-Simon[2] /ˌsænsi:'mɒn/, Louis de Rouvroy, Duc de (1675–1755), French writer. He is best known for his *Mémoires*, a detailed record of court life between 1694 and 1723, in the reigns of Louis XIV and XV.

Sakharov /'sækərɒf/, Andrei (Dmitrievich) (1921–89), Russian nuclear physicist. Having helped to develop the Soviet hydrogen bomb, he campaigned against nuclear proliferation and called for Soviet–American cooperation. He fought courageously for reform and human rights in the USSR, for which he was awarded the Nobel Peace Prize in 1975. His international reputation as a scientist kept him out of jail, but in 1980 he was banished to Gorky (Nizhni Novgorod) and kept under police surveillance. He was freed (1986) in the new spirit of glasnost, and at his death he was honoured in his own country as well as in the West.

Saki /'sɑːkɪ/ (pseudonym of Hector Hugh Munro) (1870–1916), British short-story writer, born in Burma. His stories include the satiric, comic, macabre, and supernatural, and frequently depict animals as agents seeking revenge upon humankind; collections include *Reginald* (1904). He was

killed in France during the First World War.

Saladin /'sælədɪn/ (Arabic name Salah-ad-Din Yusuf ibn-Ayyub) (1137–93), sultan of Egypt and Syria 1174–93. He invaded the Holy Land and reconquered Jerusalem from the Christians (1187), and, for a period, resisted the Third Crusade, the leaders of which included Richard the Lionheart. He was later defeated by Richard at Arsuf (1191) and withdrew to Damascus, where he died. Saladin earned a reputation not only for military skill but also for honesty and chivalry.

Salam /sə'lɑːm/, Abdus (1926–96), Pakistani theoretical physicist. He worked on the interaction of subatomic particles, and independently developed a unified theory to explain electromagnetic interactions and the weak nuclear force. In 1979 he shared the Nobel Prize for physics, the first Nobel laureate from his country.

Salazar /ˌsælə'zɑː(r)/, Antonio de Oliveira (1889–1970), Portuguese statesman, Prime Minister 1932–68. While Finance Minister (1928–40), he formulated austere fiscal policies to effect Portugal's economic recovery. During his long premiership, he ruled the country as a virtual dictator, firmly suppressing opposition and enacting a new authoritarian constitution along Fascist lines. Salazar maintained Portugal's neutrality throughout the Spanish Civil War and the Second World War.

Salieri /ˌsælɪ'eərɪ/, Antonio (1750–1825), Italian composer. His output includes more than forty operas, four oratorios, and much church music. He lived in Vienna for many years and taught Beethoven, Schubert, and Liszt. Salieri was hostile to Mozart and a story arose that he poisoned him, though the story is apparently without foundation.

Salinger /'sælɪndʒə(r)/, J(erome) D(avid) (born 1919), American novelist and short-story writer. He is best known for his colloquial novel of adolescence *The Catcher in the Rye* (1951). His other works include *Franny and Zooey* (1961).

Salisbury /'sɔːlzbərɪ/, Robert Arthur Talbot Gascoigne-Cecil, 3rd Marquess of (1830–1903), British Conservative statesman, Prime Minister 1885–6, 1886–92, and 1895–1902. His main area of concern was foreign affairs; he was a firm defender of British imperial interests and supported the policies which resulted in the Second Boer War (1899–1902).

Salk /sɔːlk/, Jonas Edward (1914–95), American microbiologist. Salk worked at various universities before becoming the director of the institute in San Diego that now bears his name. He worked in the early 1950s on developing a safe vaccine for polio, first having to devise a method of growing the virus in chick embryos and then treating the virus to make it harmless to the patient. After initial trials and improvements in 1954, the vaccine was widely promoted and successfully used on millions of people without causing any disease.

Sallust /'sæləst/ (Latin name Gaius Sallustius Crispus) (86–35 BC), Roman historian and politician. As a historian he was concerned with the political decline of Rome after the fall of Carthage in 146 BC, to which he accorded a simultaneous moral decline. His chief surviving works deal with the Catiline conspiracy and the Jugurthine War.

Sand /sɒnd/, George (pseudonym of Amandine-Aurore Lucille Dupin, Baronne Dudevant) (1804–76), French novelist. In 1831 she left her husband to lead an independent literary life in Paris. Her earlier romantic novels, including *Lélia* (1833), portray women's struggles against conventional morals; she later wrote a number of pastoral novels (for example *La Mare au diable*, 1846). Among her other works are *Elle et lui* (1859), a fictionalized account of her affair with the poet Alfred de Musset (1810–57), and *Un Hiver à Majorque* (1841), describing an episode during her ten-year relationship with Chopin.

Sanger[1] /'sæŋə(r)/, Frederick (born 1918), English biochemist. Sanger worked mainly for the Medical Research Council, becoming a divisional head of the Molecular Biology Laboratory at Cambridge in 1961. He worked first on the structure of proteins, determining the complete amino-acid sequence of insulin in 1955, and later on the structure of nucleic acids, establishing the complete nucleotide sequence of a viral DNA in 1977. Sanger twice received the Nobel Prize for chemistry, in 1958 and 1980.

Sanger[2] /'sæŋə(r)/, Margaret (Higgins) (1883–1966), American birth-control campaigner. Her experiences as a nurse from 1912 prompted her two years later to dis-

tribute the pamphlet *Family Limitation* in defence of birth control. Legal proceedings were initiated against her for disseminating 'obscene' literature, but these were dropped in 1916. In the same year she founded the first American birth-control clinic in Brooklyn, serving as its president for seven years. She also set up the first World Population Conference in Geneva in 1927 and became the first president of the International Planned Parenthood Federation in 1953.

San Martín /ˌsæn mɑːˈtiːn/, José de (1778–1850), Argentinian soldier and statesman. Having assisted in the liberation of his country from Spanish rule (1812–13) he went on to aid Bernardo O'Higgins in the liberation of Chile (1817–18). He was also involved in gaining Peruvian independence, becoming Protector of Peru in 1821; he resigned a year later after differences with the other great liberator Simón Bolívar.

Sansovino /ˌsænsəˈviːnəʊ/, Jacopo Tatti (1486–1570), Italian sculptor and architect. He was city architect of Venice from 1529, where his buildings include the Palazzo Corner (1533) and St Mark's Library (begun 1536), all of which show the influence of his early training in Rome and the development of classical architectural style for contemporary use. His sculpture includes the colossal statues *Mars* and *Neptune* (1554–6) for the staircase of the Doges' Palace.

Santayana /ˌsæntɪˈjɑːnə/, George (born Jorge Augustin Nicolás Ruiz de Santayana) (1863–1952), Spanish philosopher and writer. He was educated at Harvard, where he became professor of philosophy in 1907. He then moved to England in 1912, before settling in Rome in 1924. He wrote a number of philosophical works, including *The Realms of Being* (1924), and was also known for his poetry and his best-selling novel *The Last Puritan* (1935).

Sapir /səˈpɪə(r)/, Edward (1884–1939), German-born American linguistics scholar and anthropologist. One of the founders of American structural linguistics, he carried out important work on American Indian languages and linguistic theory. His book *Language* (1921) presents his thesis that language should be studied within its social and cultural context.

Sappho /ˈsæfəʊ/ (early 7th century BC) Greek lyric poet. She was renowned in her own day and became the centre of a circle of women and young girls on her native island of Lesbos. The surviving fragments of her poetry, written in her local dialect, are mainly love poems, dealing with subjects such as passion, jealousy, and enmity. Many of her poems express her affection and love for women, and have given rise to her association with female homosexuality, from which the words *lesbian* and *Sapphic* derive.

Sargent[1] /ˈsɑːdʒənt/, John Singer (1856–1925), American painter. Born in Florence, he travelled and studied widely in Europe in his youth. In the 1870s he painted some impressionist landscapes, but it was in portraiture that he developed the bold brushwork typical of his style, which reflects the influence of Manet, Hals, and Velázquez. He was much in demand in Parisian circles, but following a scandal over the supposed eroticism of *Madame Gautreau* (1884) he moved to London, where he dominated society portraiture for more than twenty years. In the First World War he worked as an official war artist.

Sargent[2] /ˈsɑːdʒənt/, Sir (Henry) Malcolm (Watts) (1895–1967), English conductor and composer. He is remembered particularly for his involvement with the BBC Promenade Concerts, for which he was responsible from 1948 until his death. He made an acclaimed début at a promenade concert conducting his own *Impressions of a Windy Day* in 1921. Sargent conducted a number of ensembles, including the Liverpool Philharmonic Orchestra (1942–8), and in 1950 was appointed conductor of the BBC Symphony Orchestra.

Sargon II (died 705 BC), king of Assyria 721–705. He was probably a son of Tiglathpileser III, and is thought to have been named after the semi-legendary King Sargon. He is famous for his conquest of a number of cities in Syria and Palestine; he also took ten of the tribes of Israel into a captivity from which they are believed never to have returned, becoming known as the Lost Tribes of Israel (2 Kings 17:6).

Sarto /ˈsɑːtəʊ/, Andrea del (born Andrea d'Agnolo) (1486–1531), Italian painter. He worked chiefly in Florence, where among his works are fresco cycles in the church of Santa Annunziata (such as *Nativity of the Virgin*, 1514) and the series of grisailles in the cloister of the Scalzi (1511–26) depicting the story of St John the Baptist. His

work displays a feeling for tone and harmonies of colour, while the gracefulness of his figures influenced the mannerist style of his pupils Pontormo and Vasari.

Sartre /'sɑːtrə/, Jean-Paul (1905–80), French philosopher, novelist, dramatist, and critic. While studying at the Sorbonne in 1929 he began his lifelong association with Simone de Beauvoir; they founded the review *Les Temps modernes* in 1945. A leading exponent of existentialism, he was originally influenced by the work of Martin Heidegger; his later philosophy deals with the social responsibility of freedom, and attempts to synthesize existentialism with Marxist sociology. His works include the treatise *Being and Nothingness* (1943), the novel *Nausée* (1938), the trilogy *Les Chemins de la liberté* (1945–9), and the plays *Les Mouches* (1943) and *Huis clos* (1944). In 1964 he was offered but refused the Nobel Prize for literature.

Sassoon[1] /sə'suːn/, Siegfried (Lorraine) (1886–1967), English poet and writer. He is known for his starkly realistic poems written while serving in the First World War, expressing his contempt for war leaders and what he regarded as patriotic cant, as well as compassion for his comrades; collections include *The Old Huntsman* (1917). While in hospital in 1917 he met and gave encouragement to the poet Wilfred Owen; he published Owen's poems in 1920. After the war he also wrote a number of semi-autobiographical novels, including *Memoirs of a Fox-Hunting Man* (1928).

Sassoon[2] /sə'suːn/, Vidal (born 1928), English hairstylist. After opening a London salon in 1953, he introduced the cut and blow-dry. Ten years later he created a hairstyle that was short at the back and long at the sides; first modelled at a Mary Quant fashion show, it became known as the 'Sassoon Cut'.

Satie /'sɑːti/, Erik (Alfred Leslie) (1866–1925), French composer. He formed the centre of an irreverent avant-garde artistic set, associated not only with the composers of Les Six, but also with Jean Cocteau, Dadaism, and surrealism. Many of his works are short and have facetious titles: *Three Pieces in the Shape of a Pear* (1903), for example, is in fact a set of six pieces. One of his few large-scale works is the symphonic drama *Socrate* (1918) for four sopranos and chamber orchestra to a libretto based on the writings of Plato. His work influenced

Debussy and the development of minimalism.

Saul[1] /sɔːl/ (also **Saul of Tarsus** /'tɑːsəs/) the original name of St Paul.

Saul[2] /sɔːl/ (in the Bible) the first king of Israel (11th century BC).

Saussure /səʊ'sjʊə(r)/, Ferdinand de (1857–1913), Swiss linguistics scholar. He is one of the founders of modern linguistics and his work is fundamental to the development of structuralism. Departing from traditional diachronic studies of language, he emphasized the importance of a synchronic approach, treating language as a system of mutually dependent and interacting signs. He also made a distinction between *langue* (the total system of language) and *parole* (individual speech acts), and stressed that linguistic study should focus on the former. In his lifetime he published works of fundamental importance for Indo-European studies, but his most influential work, *Cours de linguistique générale* (1916), was compiled from lecture-notes and published posthumously.

Savage /'sævɪdʒ/, Michael Joseph (1872–1940), New Zealand Labour statesman, Prime Minister 1935–40. He was born in Australia and, after working as a trade union organizer, moved to New Zealand in 1907 and joined the New Zealand Labour Party on its formation in 1916, becoming party leader in 1933. Two years later his party won the general election and Savage became New Zealand's first Labour Prime Minister, a position he held until his death. He introduced many reforms, including social security legislation which he dubbed 'applied Christianity'.

Savery /'seɪvərɪ/, Thomas (known as 'Captain Savery') (c.1650–1715), English engineer. He took out a number of patents, notably one for an engine to raise water 'by the Impellent Force of Fire' (1698). It was described as being suitable for raising water from mines, supplying towns with water, and operating mills. In fact its use of high-pressure steam made it dangerous, and only a few were actually used (at low pressure) in water mills. However, Savery's patent covered the type of engine developed by Thomas Newcomen, who was therefore obliged to join him in its exploitation.

Savonarola /ˌsævənə'rəʊlə/, Girolamo (1452–98), Italian preacher and religious

reformer. A Dominican monk and strict ascetic, in 1482 he moved to Florence, where he attracted great attention for his passionate preaching denouncing immorality, vanity, and corruption within the Church, and for his apocalyptic prophecies. He became virtual ruler of Florence (1494–5), but made many enemies, and in 1495 the pope forbade him to preach and summoned him to Rome. His refusal to comply with these orders led to his excommunication in 1497; he was hanged and burned as a schismatic and heretic.

Sayers /'seɪəz/, Dorothy L(eigh) (1893–1957), English novelist and dramatist. She is chiefly known for her detective fiction featuring the amateur detective Lord Peter Wimsey; titles include *Murder Must Advertise* (1933) and *The Nine Tailors* (1934). She also wrote religious plays (such as *The Devil to Pay*, 1939), which gained her recognition as a Christian polemicist.

Scaliger [1] /'skælɪdʒə(r)/, Joseph Justus (1540–1609), French scholar. The son of Julius Caesar Scaliger, he was a leading Renaissance scholar, often regarded as the founder of historical criticism. His edition of Manilius (1579) and his *De Emendatione Temporum* (1583) revolutionized understanding of ancient chronology and gave it a more scientific foundation by comparing and revising the computations of time made by different civilizations, including those of the Babylonians and Egyptians.

Scaliger [2] /'skælɪdʒə(r)/, Julius Caesar (1484–1558), Italian-born French classical scholar and physician. Appointed physician to the bishop of Agen, he settled in France and became a French citizen in 1528. Besides polemical works directed against Erasmus (1531, 1536), he wrote a long Latin treatise on poetics, a number of commentaries on botanical works, and a philosophical treatise. He was the father of Joseph Scaliger.

Scarlatti [1] /skɑː'lætɪ/, (Pietro) Alessandro (Gaspare) (1660–1725), Italian composer. He was an important and prolific composer of operas, more than seventy of which survive; in them can be found the elements which carried Italian opera through the baroque period and into the classical. He also established the three-part form of the opera overture which was a precursor of the classical symphony. His many other works include cantatas, masses, and ora-

torios. He was the father of Domenico Scarlatti.

Scarlatti [2] /skɑː'lætɪ/, (Giuseppe) Domenico (1685–1757), Italian composer. He was a prolific composer of keyboard music, writing more than 550 sonatas for the harpsichord. His work made an important contribution to the development of the sonata form and did much to expand the range of the instrument. He was the son of Alessandro Scarlatti.

Scheele /'ʃiːlə, 'ʃeɪlə/, Carl Wilhelm (1742–86), Swedish chemist. He was a keen experimenter, working in difficult and often hazardous conditions; he discovered a number of substances including glycerol and a green gas that was later named chlorine. He is also noted for his discovery of oxygen in 1773, which he named 'fire air', although he did not publish his findings until after the publication of Joseph Priestley's work in 1774. He also discovered a process resembling pasteurization.

Schiaparelli [1] /ˌskjæpə'relɪ/, Elsa (1896–1973), Italian-born French fashion designer. She settled in Paris and opened her own establishment in the late 1920s. She introduced padded shoulders to her garments in 1932, and the vivid shade now known as 'shocking pink' in 1947. Her fashions also included touches of the surreal, drawing inspiration from artists such as Salvador Dali. She later expanded her interests into ready-to-wear fashions and ranges of perfume and cosmetics.

Schiaparelli [2] /ˌskjæpə'relɪ/, Giovanni Virginio (1835–1910), Italian astronomer. He studied the nature of cometary tails, and showed that many meteors are derived from comets and follow similar orbits. He observed Mars in detail, identifying the southern polar ice cap and features which he termed 'seas', 'continents', and 'channels' (*canali*). The last was mistranslated by Percival Lowell as 'canals', beginning a long-running controversy about intelligent life on Mars.

Schiele /'ʃiːlə/, Egon (1890–1918), Austrian painter and draughtsman. He joined the Vienna Academy of Fine Arts in 1906 but left in 1909 because his teacher disapproved of his paintings, which were influenced by Gustav Klimt and art nouveau. From 1910 onwards he evolved a distinctive expressionist style, characterized by an aggressive linear energy and a neurotic intensity, reflecting his interest in the work

of Sigmund Freud; his paintings and drawings (often self-portraits) depicted distorted, frequently emaciated bodies with an explicit erotic content, which resulted in him being imprisoned for a month in 1911. His pictures received international acclaim at the exhibition of the Vienna Secession in 1918; Schiele died in the same year of Spanish influenza.

Schiller /ˈʃɪlə(r)/, (Johann Christoph) Friedrich von (1759–1805), German dramatist, poet, historian, and critic. His early work was influenced by the *Sturm und Drang* movement; his mature work established him as a major figure, with Goethe (with whom he formed a long-standing friendship from 1794 until his death), of the Enlightenment in Germany. His first major work was the historical drama in blank verse *Don Carlos* (1787). His other historical plays include the trilogy *Wallenstein* (1800), which drew on his historical studies of the Thirty Years War, *Mary Stuart* (1800), and *William Tell* (1804). These works are concerned with freedom and responsibility, whether political, personal, or moral. Among his best-known poems are 'Ode to Joy', which Beethoven set to music in his Ninth Symphony, and 'The Artists' (both written *c*.1787). His many essays on aesthetics include *On Naive and Reflective Poetry* (1795–6), in which he contrasts his poetry with that of Goethe.

Schindler /ˈʃɪndlə(r)/, Oskar (1908–74), German industrialist. In 1940 he established a lucrative enamelware factory in Cracow, Poland, employing Jewish workers from the city's ghetto. After the Nazi evacuation of the ghetto in 1943, Schindler exercised his financial and political influence to protect his employees from being sent to Plaszów, a nearby labour camp. In 1944 he compiled a list of more than 1,200 Jews from Plaszów and his own factory to be relocated at a new armaments factory in Czechoslovakia, thereby saving them from certain death in concentration camps. Schindler's life and role in rescuing Polish Jews are celebrated in the novel *Schindler's Ark* (1982), by Thomas Keneally, and the film *Schindler's List* (1993), directed by Steven Spielberg.

Schlegel /ˈʃleɪɡ(ə)l/, August Wilhelm von (1767–1845), German poet and critic. In 1798 he became professor of literature and fine art at Jena, before periods in Berlin (1801–4) and Bonn (1818), where he was professor of literature until his death. He was prominent in the romantic movement and stands at the beginning of art history and comparative philology. His translations of Shakespeare are still used on the German stage.

Schlick /ʃlɪk/, Moritz (1882–1936), German philosopher and physicist. From 1922 he was professor of inductive sciences at Vienna. In the late 1920s he formed the Vienna Circle, a group of young empiricist thinkers who laid the foundations of logical positivism. He had a relatively modest output, his major works including *General Theory of Knowledge* (1918). He was murdered by one of his graduate students.

Schliemann /ˈʃliːmən/, Heinrich (1822–90), German archaeologist. A former businessman with an amateur interest in archaeology, he was determined to discover the location of the ancient city of Troy, and in 1871 began excavating the mound of Hissarlik on the NE Aegean coast of Turkey. He discovered the remains of a succession of nine cities on the site, identifying the second oldest as Homer's Troy (and romantically naming a hoard of jewellery 'Priam's Treasure'), although he had in fact uncovered a pre-Homeric site. He subsequently undertook significant excavations at Mycenae (1876) and at other sites in mainland Greece.

Schoenberg /ˈʃɜːnbɜːɡ/, Arnold (1874–1951), Austrian-born American composer and music theorist. His major contribution to modernism is his development of the concepts of atonality and serialism. He introduced atonality into the final movement of his second string quartet (1907–8) and abolished the distinction between consonance and dissonance in his *Three Piano Pieces* (1909). From these experiments he evolved a serial system of composition, in which a fixed series of notes, especially the twelve notes of the chromatic scale, are used to generate the harmonic and melodic basis of a piece and are subject to change only in specific ways: the third and fourth movements of the *Serenade* (1923) for seven instruments and bass voice are the first clear examples of this technique. He was a professor of music in Vienna and in Berlin until 1933 when, after condemnation of his music by Hitler, he emigrated to the US. He continued to develop his serial techniques and his work influenced com-

posers such as his pupils Berg and Webern.

Schopenhauer /'ʃəʊp(ə)n,haʊə(r), 'ʃɒp-/, Arthur (1788–1860), German philosopher. His pessimistic philosophy is based on studies of Kant, Plato, and the Hindu Vedas, and is embodied in his principal work *The World as Will and Idea* (1819). According to this, the will (self-consciousness in man and the unconscious forces of nature) is the only reality; the material world is an illusion created by the will. This will is a malignant thing, which deceives us into reproducing and perpetuating life. Asceticism and chastity are the duty of humankind, with a view to terminating the evil; egoism, which manifests itself principally as 'the will to live', must be overcome. His theory of the predominance of the will influenced the development of Freudian psychoanalysis and, via Nietzsche, existentialism.

Schreiner /'ʃraɪnə(r)/, Olive (Emilie Albertina) (1855–1920), South African novelist and feminist. She worked as a governess, in 1881 moving to England, where she published her best-known novel *The Story of an African Farm* (1883), initially under the pseudonym Ralph Iron. The novel was both acclaimed and condemned for its heroine's unconventional approach to religion and marriage. Schreiner returned to South Africa in 1889, later becoming an active supporter of the women's suffrage movement and writing the influential study *Woman and Labour* (1911).

Schrödinger /'ʃrɜːdɪŋə(r)/, Erwin (1887–1961), Austrian theoretical physicist. In the 1920s he founded the study of wave mechanics, deriving the equation whose roots define the energy levels of atoms. Professor of physics at Berlin from 1927, Schrödinger left Germany after the Nazis came to power in 1933, returning to Austria in 1936 but fleeing again after the *Anschluss* of 1938 and finally settling in Dublin. He wrote a number of general works, including *What is Life?* (1944), which proved influential among scientists of all disciplines. He shared the Nobel Prize for physics in 1933.

Schubert /'ʃuːbət/, Franz (1797–1828), Austrian composer. While his music is associated with the romantic movement for its lyricism and emotional intensity, it belongs in formal terms to the classical age of Haydn and Mozart. During his brief life he produced more than 600 songs, nine symphonies, fifteen string quartets, and twenty-one piano sonatas, as well as operas and church music. One of his most important contributions to music was as the foremost composer of German lieder; works include the songs 'Gretchen am Spinnrade' (1814) and 'Erlkönig' (1815; 'Erl-King'), in addition to such song cycles as *Die Schöne Müllerin* (1823) and *Winterreise* (1827). Among his other significant works are the String Quintet in C major (1828), the 'Trout' piano quintet, and the Ninth Symphony ('the Great C Major').

Schulz /ʃʊlts/, Charles (born 1922), American cartoonist. He is the creator of the 'Peanuts' comic strip (originally entitled 'Li'l Folks') featuring a range of characters including the boy Charlie Brown and the dog Snoopy. The comic strip was first published in 1950 after Schulz sold the rights to United Features Syndicate, and it later appeared in many publications around the world.

Schumacher /'ʃuː,mæxə(r)/, E(rnst) F(riedrich) (1911–77), German economist and conservationist. His reputation is chiefly based on his book *Small is Beautiful: Economics as if People Mattered* (1973), which argues that economic growth is a false god of Western governments and industrialists, and that mass production needs to be replaced by smaller, more energy-efficient enterprises. Schumacher also worked to encourage conservation of natural resources and supported the development of intermediate technology in developing countries.

Schumann /'ʃuːmən/, Robert (Alexander) (1810–56), German composer. He was a leading romantic composer and is particularly noted for his songs and piano music. He drew much of his inspiration from literature, writing incidental music for Byron's *Manfred* (1849) and setting to music poems by Heinrich Heine and Robert Burns. Notable among his piano pieces are the miniatures *Papillons* (1829–31), *Carnaval* (1834–5), and *Waldszenen* (1848–9), the Fantasy in C major (1836), and the Piano Concerto in A minor (1845). His other works include four symphonies and much chamber music. He spent the last two years of his life in a mental asylum.

Schütz /ʃʊts/, Heinrich (1585–1672), German composer and organist. He is regarded as the first German baroque composer and his work reflects the influence of periods spent in Italy, for example in the settings of

Psalms of David (1619). He composed much church music and what is thought to have been the first German opera (*Dafne*, 1627; now lost). His three settings of the Passion story represent a turning towards a simple meditative style, eschewing instrumental accompaniment and relying on voices alone.

Schwann /ʃvæn, ʃwɒn/, Theodor Ambrose Hubert (1810–82), German physiologist. He is chiefly remembered for his support of cell theory, showing that animals (as well as plants) are made up of individual cells, and that the egg begins life as a single cell. He also isolated the first animal enzyme, pepsin, recognized that fermentation is caused by processes in the yeast cells, and discovered the cells forming the myelin sheaths of nerve fibres (*Schwann cells*). Schwann became disillusioned following criticism of his work by chemists, emigrated to Belgium at the age of 28, and withdrew from scientific work.

Schwarzenegger /'ʃwɔːtsə,negə(r)/, Arnold (born 1947), Austrian-born American actor. Schwarzenegger won several bodybuilding titles before retiring to concentrate on acting and appearing in the highly successful *Conan the Barbarian* (1982). He went on to play a number of action roles, such as that of *The Terminator* (1984), before attempting to diversify in films such as the comedy *Kindergarten Cop* (1990) and the spy thriller *True Lies* (1994).

Schwarzkopf /'ʃvɑːtskɒpf/, Dame (Olga Maria) Elisabeth (Friederike) (born 1915), German operatic soprano. She made her début in Berlin in 1942, and went on to become especially famous for her recitals of German lieder and for her roles in works by Richard Strauss such as *Der Rosenkavalier*.

Schweitzer /'ʃwaɪtsə(r), 'ʃvaɪ-/, Albert (1875–1965), German theologian, musician, and medical missionary, born in Alsace. He decided to devote the first thirty years of his life to learning and music and the remainder to the service of others. His main contribution to theology was his book *The Quest for the Historical Jesus* (1906), which emphasized the importance of understanding Jesus within the context of the Jewish apocalyptic thought of his day. In 1913 he qualified as a doctor and went as a missionary to Lambaréné in French Equatorial Africa (now Gabon), where he established a hospital and lived for most of the rest of his life. He was awarded the Nobel Peace Prize in 1952.

Scipio Aemilianus /,sɪpɪəʊ iː,mɪlɪ'ɑːnəs/ (full name Publius Cornelius Scipio Aemilianus Africanus Minor) (*c.*185–129 BC), Roman general and politician. He achieved distinction in the third Punic War, and blockaded and destroyed Carthage in 146. His successful campaign in Spain (133) ended organized resistance in that country. Returning to Rome in triumph, he initiated moves against the reforms introduced by his brother-in-law Tiberius Gracchus. Scipio's sudden death at the height of the crisis gave rise to the rumour that he had been murdered.

Scipio Africanus /,sɪpɪəʊ ,æfrɪ'kɑːnəs/ (full name Publius Cornelius Scipio Africanus Major) (236–*c.*184 BC), Roman general and politician. His aggressive tactics were successful in concluding the second Punic War, firstly by the defeat of the Carthaginians in Spain in 206 and then by the defeat of Hannibal in Africa in 202; his victories pointed the way to Roman hegemony in the Mediterranean. His son was the adoptive father of Scipio Aemilianus.

Scorsese /skɔː'seɪzɪ/, Martin (born 1942), American film director. He made his directorial début in 1968, but first gained recognition five years later with *Mean Streets*, a realistic study of New York's Italian community, focusing on the plight of a group of friends entangled in a web of crime and violence. The film marked the beginning of Scorsese's long collaboration with the actor Robert De Niro, which continued in such films as *Taxi Driver* (1976), *Raging Bull* (1980), *GoodFellas* (1990), and *Casino* (1995). Other films include the controversial *The Last Temptation of Christ* (1988).

Scott[1] /skɒt/, Sir George Gilbert (1811–78), English architect. Influenced by Pugin, he was a prolific Gothic revivalist, designing or restoring many churches, cathedrals, and other buildings. He attracted controversy for his restoration of medieval churches and in 1858 came into conflict with Palmerston over the design for the new Foreign Office, for which Scott was ultimately compelled to adopt an Italianate style; his Albert Memorial in London (1863–72) reflects more accurately his preferred aesthetic. His grandson Sir Giles Gilbert Scott (1880–1960) also worked as a revivalist architect and is best known for

the Gothic Anglican cathedral in Liverpool (begun in 1904, completed in 1978).

Scott[2] /skɒt/, Sir Peter (Markham) (1909–89), English naturalist and artist. He was particularly interested in wildfowl and their conservation, and in 1946 founded the Wildfowl Trust at Slimbridge in Gloucestershire. He was well known as a wildfowl artist and a presenter of natural history programmes on television, and he became increasingly involved in conservation worldwide. He was also an accomplished yachtsman, and maintained an interest in the search for a monster at Loch Ness. He was the son of the explorer Robert Falcon Scott.

Scott[3] /skɒt/, Ridley (born 1939), English film director. With films such as *Alien* (1979) Scott established himself as one of modern cinema's foremost visual stylists. In the influential *Blade Runner* (1982) he fused the medieval with the technological to create the image of a dirty, overcrowded, and run-down future. His later films include *Thelma and Louise* (1991). His brother Tony (born 1944) is also a successful film director, responsible for such works as *Top Gun* (1986) and *True Romance* (1993).

Scott[4] /skɒt/, Sir Robert Falcon (1868–1912), English explorer and naval officer. As commander of the ship *Discovery* he led the National Antarctic Expedition (1900–4), surveying the interior of the continent and charting the Ross Sea. On a second expedition (1910–12) Scott and four companions made a journey to the South Pole by sled, arriving there in January 1912 to discover that the Norwegian explorer Amundsen had beaten them to their goal by a month. Scott and his companions died on the journey back to base, and their bodies and diaries were discovered by a search party eight months later. Scott, a national hero, was posthumously knighted. He was the father of the naturalist and artist Sir Peter Scott.

Scott[5] /skɒt/, Sir Walter (1771–1832), Scottish novelist and poet. He established the form of the historical novel in Britain, and was also influential in his treatment of rural themes and use of regional speech. Among his novels are *Waverley* (1814), *Old Mortality* (1816), *Ivanhoe* (1819), and *Kenilworth* (1821). His poetry was influenced by medieval French and Italian poetry, and by contemporary German poets; he collected and imitated old Borders tales and ballads,

while among his original works are the romantic narrative poems *The Lay of the Last Minstrel* (1805) and *The Lady of the Lake* (1810).

Scriabin /skrɪˈɑːbɪn/, Aleksandr (Nikolaevich) (also **Skryabin**) (1872–1915), Russian composer and pianist. He wrote symphonies, symphonic poems, and numerous pieces for the piano, including sonatas and preludes. Much of his later music reflects his interest in mysticism and theosophy, especially his third symphony *The Divine Poem* (1903) and the symphonic poem *Prometheus: The Poem of Fire* (1909–10), which is scored for orchestra, piano, optional choir, and 'keyboard of light' (projecting colours on to a screen).

Seaborg /ˈsiːbɔːɡ/, Glenn (Theodore) (born 1912), American nuclear chemist. During 1940–58 Seaborg and his colleagues at the University of California, Berkeley, produced nine of the transuranic elements (plutonium to nobelium) by bombarding uranium and other elements with nuclei in a cyclotron, and he coined the term *actinide* for the elements in this series. Seaborg and his early collaborator Edwin McMillan (1907–91) shared the Nobel Prize for chemistry in 1951, and Seaborg was chairman of the US Atomic Energy Commission 1962–71.

Searle /sɜːl/, Ronald (William Fordham) (born 1920), English artist and cartoonist. He is best known for his humorous drawings, his most famous creations being the schoolgirls of St Trinian's, who became the subjects of four films (starting with *The Belles of St Trinians*, 1954) and a number of books. He was a contributor to *Punch* magazine from 1949.

Sedgwick /ˈsedʒwɪk/, Adam (1785–1873), English geologist. He was based in Cambridge and specialized in the fossil record of rocks from North Wales, assigning the oldest of these to a period that he named the Cambrian. Sedgwick also amassed one of the greatest geological collections.

Seeger /ˈsiːɡə(r)/, Pete (born 1919), American folk musician and songwriter. In 1949 he formed the folk group the Weavers, with whom he recorded a series of bestselling protest songs. From the early 1950s he followed a solo career and was prominent in the American folk revival. Among his most famous songs are 'If I Had a Hammer' (c.1949) and 'Where Have All the Flowers Gone?' (1956). Seeger fell under

suspicion during the McCarthy era and was not cleared of all charges until 1962.

Segovia /sɪˈɡəʊvɪə/, Andrés (1893–1987), Spanish guitarist and composer. He was largely responsible for the revival of interest in the classical guitar, elevating it to the status of a major concert instrument. He made a large number of transcriptions of classical music, including Bach, to increase the repertoire of the instrument, and also commissioned works from contemporary composers such as Manuel de Falla.

Selcraig /ˈselkreɪɡ/ see SELKIRK.

Seles /ˈseles/, Monica (born 1973), American tennis player, born in Yugoslavia. She became the youngest woman to win a grand slam singles title with her victory in the French Open in 1990, and in 1991 she was the youngest woman to win the Australian Open. Her career was interrupted in 1993 when she was stabbed on court by a fan of Steffi Graf, but she returned to play in 1995, winning the Australian Open in 1996.

Selfridge /ˈselfrɪdʒ/, Harry Gordon (1858–1947), American-born British businessman. In 1906 he came to England and began to build the department store in Oxford Street, London, that bears his name; it opened in 1909.

Selkirk /ˈselkɜːk/, Alexander (also called Alexander Selcraig) (1676–1721), Scottish sailor. While on a privateering expedition in 1704, Selkirk quarrelled with his captain and was put ashore, at his own request, on one of the uninhabited Juan Fernandez Islands in the Pacific, where he remained until he was rescued in 1709. His experiences later formed the basis of Daniel Defoe's novel *Robinson Crusoe* (1719).

Sellers /ˈseləz/, Peter (1925–80), English comic actor. He made his name in *The Goon Show*, a British radio series of the 1950s, with Spike Milligan and Harry Secombe (born 1921). Sellers then turned to films, starring in many comedies such as *The Lady Killers* (1955), *I'm All Right Jack* (1959), and *Dr Strangelove* (1964). In the 'Pink Panther' series of films of the 1960s and 1970s, he played the role of the French detective Inspector Clouseau, for which he is best known.

Selous /səˈluː/, Frederick Courteney (1851–1917), English explorer, naturalist, and soldier. He first visited South Africa in 1871 and spent the following ten years in exploration and big-game hunting in south central Africa. From 1890 he was involved in the British South Africa Company, negotiating mineral and land rights for the British (see also RHODES[1]). The Selous Game Reserve in Tanzania is named after him.

Selye /ˈseljeɪ/, Hans Hugo Bruno (1907–82), Austrian-born Canadian physician. After working in several European countries, he moved to Montreal and later became director of the University of Montreal's Institute of Experimental Medicine and Surgery. He showed that environmental stress and anxiety could result in the release of hormones that, over a long period, could produce many of the biochemical and physiological disorders characteristic of the 20th century. Selye's theory had a profound effect on modern medicine, and he became a popularizer of research on stress.

Selznick /ˈselznɪk/, David O(liver) (1902–65), American film producer. Based in Hollywood from 1926, he produced such films as *King Kong* (1933) for RKO and *Anna Karenina* (1935) for MGM. In 1936 he established his own production company, Selznick International, with whom he produced such screen classics as *Gone with the Wind* (1939) and *Rebecca* (1940).

Semmelweis /ˈzem(ə)l̩ˌvaɪs/, Ignaz Philipp (born Ignác Fülöp Semmelweis) (1818–65), Hungarian obstetrician who spent most of his working life in Vienna. He discovered the infectious character of puerperal fever, at the time a major cause of death following childbirth. Semmelweis demonstrated that the infection was transmitted by the hands of doctors who examined patients after working in the dissecting room, and advocated rigorous cleanliness and the use of antiseptics. Despite the spectacular results obtained by Semmelweis, R. K. Virchow and other senior figures opposed his views for many years, and his involvement in events in Vienna during the 1848 revolution hindered his career.

Senanayake /ˌsenəˈnaɪəkə/, Don Stephen (1884–1952), Sinhalese statesman, Prime Minister of Ceylon 1947–52. In 1919 he co-founded the Ceylon National Congress, and during the 1920s and 1930s held ministerial positions on Ceylon's legislative and state councils. He became Prime Minister in 1947, and the following year presided over Ceylon's achievement of full dominion status within the Commonwealth.

Seneca[1] /'senɪkə/, Lucius Annaeus (known as Seneca the Younger) (c.4 BC–AD 65), Roman statesman, philosopher, and dramatist. Born in Spain, he was the son of Seneca the Elder. He was banished to Corsica by Claudius in 41, charged with adultery; in 49 his sentence was repealed and he became tutor to Nero, through the influence of Nero's mother and Claudius' wife, Agrippina. Seneca was a dominant figure in the early years of Nero's reign and was appointed consul in 57; he retired in 62. His subsequent implication in a plot on Nero's life led to his forced suicide. As a philosopher, he expounded the ethics of Stoicism in such works as *Epistulae Morales*. Seneca wrote nine plays, whose lurid violence and use of rhetoric later influenced Elizabethan and Jacobean tragedy.

Seneca[2] /'senɪkə/, Marcus (or Lucius) Annaeus (known as Seneca the Elder) (c.55 BC–c. AD 39), Roman rhetorician, born in Spain. He was the father of Seneca the Younger. Seneca is best known for his works on rhetoric, only parts of which survive, including *Oratorum Sententiae Divisiones Colores* and *Suasoriae*.

Senna /'senə/, Ayrton (1960–94), Brazilian motor-racing driver. He won the Formula One world championship in 1988, 1990, and 1991. He died from injuries sustained in a crash during the Italian Grand Prix in 1994.

Sennacherib /sɪ'nækərɪb/ (died 681 BC) king of Assyria 705–681. The son of Sargon II, he devoted much of his reign to suppressing revolts in various parts of his empire, including Babylon, which he sacked in 689. In 701 he put down a Jewish rebellion, laying siege to Jerusalem but sparing it from destruction (according to 2 Kings 19:35) after an epidemic of illness amongst his forces. He rebuilt and extended the city of Nineveh and made it his capital, and also initiated irrigation schemes and other civil engineering projects.

Seraphic Doctor the nickname of St Bonaventura.

Sergius, St /'sɜːdʒɪəs/ (Russian name Svyatoi Sergi Radonezhsky) (1314–92), Russian monastic reformer and mystic. He founded the monastery of the Holy Trinity near Moscow, and thereby re-established monasticism, which had been lost in Russia as a result of the Tartar invasion; altogether he founded forty monasteries. His political influence was also considerable: he stopped four civil wars between Russian princes, and inspired the resistance which saved Russia from the Tartars in 1380. Feast day, 25 September.

Seurat /'sɜːrɑ/, Georges Pierre (1859–91), French painter. The founder of neo-impressionism, he is chiefly associated with pointillism, which he developed during the 1880s. The technique involved the application of small dots of unmixed colour, which, though separate on the canvas, would blend when viewed from a distance; the aim was to produce a greater degree of luminosity and brilliance of colour. Among his major paintings using this technique is *Sunday Afternoon on the Island of La Grande Jatte* (1884–6).

Severus /sɪ'vɪərəs/, Septimius (full name Lucius Septimius Severus Pertinax) (146–211), Roman emperor 193–211. He was active in reforms of the imperial administration and of the army, which he recognized as the real basis of imperial power. In 208 he took an army to Britain to suppress a rebellion in the north of the country, and later died at York.

Seymour[1] /'siːmɔː(r)/, Jane (c.1509–37), third wife of Henry VIII and mother of Edward VI. She married Henry in 1536 and finally provided the king with the male heir he wanted, although she died twelve days afterwards.

Seymour[2] /'siːmɔː(r)/, Lynn (born 1939), Canadian ballet-dancer. From 1957 she danced for the Royal Ballet in London, performing principal roles in ballets choreographed by Kenneth MacMillan (1929–92) and Frederick Ashton. Her most acclaimed roles came in Ashton's *Five Brahms Waltzes in the Manner of Isadora Duncan* and *A Month in the Country* (both 1976). Seymour later worked as artistic director of the Bavarian State Opera in Munich (1978–80).

Shabaka /'ʃæbəkə/ (known as Sabacon) (died 698 BC), Egyptian pharaoh of the 25th dynasty, reigned 712–698 BC. He succeeded his brother Piankhi as king of Cush in about 716; four years later he conquered Egypt and founded its 25th dynasty. A conservative ruler, he promoted the cult of Amun and revived the custom of pyramid burial in his own death arrangements.

Shackleton /'ʃæk(ə)lt(ə)n/, Sir Ernest Henry (1874–1922), British explorer. A junior officer on Robert Falcon Scott's National Antarctic Expedition (1900–4), he commanded his own expedition in 1909, getting within 155 km (97 miles) of the South Pole (the farthest south anyone had reached at that time). On a second Antarctic expedition (1914–16), Shackleton's ship *Endurance* was crushed in the ice. He and his crew eventually reached an island, from where he and five others set out in an open boat on a 1,300-km (800-mile) voyage to South Georgia to get help. In 1920 he led a fourth expedition to the Antarctic, but died on South Georgia.

Shaftesbury /'ʃɑːftsbərɪ/, Anthony Ashley Cooper, 7th Earl of (1801–85), English philanthropist and social reformer. He was a dominant figure of the 19th-century social reform movement, inspiring much of the legislation designed to improve conditions for the large working class created as a result of the Industrial Revolution. His reforms included the introduction of the ten-hour working day (1847); he was also actively involved in improving housing and education for the poor.

Shah¹ /ʃɑː/, Karim Al-Hussain, see AGA KHAN.

Shah² /ʃɑː/, Reza, see PAHLAVI¹.

Shaka /'ʃækə/ (also **Chaka**) (c.1787–1828), Zulu chief. After seizing the Zulu chieftaincy from his half-brother in 1816, he reorganized his forces and waged war against the Nguni clans in SE Africa, subjugating them and forming a Zulu empire in the region. Shaka's military campaigns led to a huge displacement of people and a lengthy spell of clan warfare in the early 1820s. He was subsequently assassinated by his two half-brothers.

Shakespeare /'ʃeɪkspɪə(r)/, William (also known as 'the Bard (of Avon)') (1564–1616), English dramatist. He was born a merchant's son in Stratford-upon-Avon in Warwickshire and married Anne Hathaway in about 1582. Some time thereafter he went to London, where he pursued a career as an actor, poet, and dramatist. He probably began to write for the stage in the late 1580s; although his plays were widely performed in his lifetime, many were not printed until the First Folio of 1623. His plays are written mostly in blank verse and include comedies (such as *A Midsummer Night's Dream* and *As You Like It*); historical plays, including *Richard III* and *Henry V*; the Greek and Roman plays, which include *Julius Caesar* and *Antony and Cleopatra*; the so-called 'problem plays', enigmatic comedies which include *All's Well that Ends Well* and *Measure for Measure*; the great tragedies, *Hamlet*, *Othello*, *King Lear*, and *Macbeth*; and the group of tragicomedies with which he ended his career, such as *The Winter's Tale* and *The Tempest*. He also wrote more than 150 sonnets, published in 1609, as well as narrative poems such as *The Rape of Lucrece* (1594).

Shalmaneser III /ˌʃælməˈniːzə(r)/ (died 824 BC), king of Assyria 859–824. Most of his reign was devoted to the expansion of his kingdom and the conquest of neighbouring lands. According to Assyrian records (though it is not mentioned in the Bible) he defeated an alliance of Syrian kings and Ahab, king of Israel, in a battle at Qarqar on the Orontes in 853 BC. His other military achievements included the invasion of Cilicia and the capture of Tarsus.

Shamir /ʃæˈmɪə(r)/, Yitzhak (Polish name Yitzhak Jazernicki) (born 1915), Israeli statesman, Prime Minister 1983–4 and 1986–92. Born in Poland, he emigrated to Palestine in 1935. On Menachem Begin's retirement in 1983, Shamir became Premier, but his Likud party was narrowly defeated in elections a year later. As Prime Minister of a coalition government with Labour, he sacked Shimon Peres in 1990 and formed a new government with a policy of conceding no land to a Palestinian state. Under his leadership Israel did not retaliate when attacked by Iraqi missiles during the Gulf War of 1991, thereby possibly averting the formation of a pro-Saddam Hussein Arab coalition.

Shankar¹ /'ʃæŋkə(r)/, Ravi (born 1920), Indian sitar player and composer. Already an established musician in his own country, from the mid-1950s he embarked on tours of Europe and the US giving sitar recitals, doing much to stimulate contemporary Western interest in Indian music. He founded schools of Indian music in Bombay (1962) and Los Angeles (1967).

Shankar² /'ʃæŋkə(r)/, Uday (1900–77), Indian dancer. He collaborated with Anna Pavlova, introducing her to Indian dance and performing with her in his ballet *Krishna and Radha* (1923). He toured the world with his own company, continuing to perform until the late 1960s, and was

mainly responsible for introducing the art of Indian dance to European audiences. He was the brother of Ravi Shankar.

Shankly /'ʃæŋklɪ/, William ('Bill') (1913–81), Scottish-born football manager and footballer. Shankly played as a wing-half for Carlisle United and Preston North End, with whom he won the FA Cup in 1938, and won five international caps. He managed a number of clubs, including Carlisle, before becoming manager of Liverpool (1960–74). There he created a strong and stylish team which had outstanding success in Britain and Europe, and became a legend in British football. The success of Shankly's Liverpool team continued under his successor, Bob Paisley (1919–96).

Shannon /'ʃænən/, Claude Elwood (born 1916), American engineer. He was a pioneer of information theory, which has become vital to the design of both communication and electronic equipment. He also investigated digital circuits, and was the first to use the term *bit* to denote a unit of information.

Shapley /'ʃæplɪ/, Harlow (1885–1972), American astronomer. He studied globular star clusters, using cepheid variables within them to determine their distance. He then used their distribution to locate the likely centre of the Galaxy and infer its structure and dimensions. For 31 years Shapley was director of the Harvard Observatory, where he studied the distribution of stars of different spectral types, investigated the Magellanic Clouds, and carried out an extensive survey of galaxies.

Sharma /'ʃɑːmə/, Shankar Dayal (born 1918), Indian statesman, President 1992–7. A member of the Congress party, Sharma served as Vice-President 1987–92.

Sharp /ʃɑːp/, Cecil (James) (1859–1924), English collector of folk-songs and folk-dances. His work was responsible for a revival of interest in English folk music; from 1904 onwards he published a number of collections of songs and dances, including morris dances. He founded the English Folk Dance Society in 1911 and helped establish the teaching of this music in schools.

Shaw /ʃɔː/, (George) Bernard (1856–1950), Irish dramatist and writer. He moved to London in 1876 and began his literary career as a critic and unsuccessful novelist. His first play was performed in 1892. His best-known plays combine comedy with intellectual debate in challenging conventional morality and thought; they include *Man and Superman* (1903), *Major Barbara* (1907), *Pygmalion* (1913), *Heartbreak House* (1919), and *St Joan* (1923). He wrote lengthy prefaces for most of his plays, in which he expanded his philosophy and ideas. A socialist, he joined the Fabian Society in 1884 and was an active member during its early period, championing many progressive causes, including feminism. He was awarded the Nobel Prize for literature in 1925.

Shearer /'ʃɪərə(r)/, Moira (full name Moira Shearer King) (born 1926), Scottish balletdancer and actress. As a ballerina with Sadler's Wells ballet from 1942 she created roles in a number of works by Sir Frederick Ashton. She is perhaps best known for her portrayal of a dedicated ballerina in the film *The Red Shoes* (1948). Her later acting career included roles in plays by Shaw and Chekhov.

Sheene /ʃiːn/, Barry (born Stephen Frank Sheene) (born 1950), English racing motorcyclist. He won the 500 cc. world championship in 1976 and 1977.

Shelley[1] /'ʃelɪ/, Mary (Wollstonecraft) (1797–1851), English writer. The daughter of William Godwin and Mary Wollstonecraft, she eloped with the poet Shelley in 1814 and married him in 1816. She is chiefly remembered as the author of the Gothic novel *Frankenstein, or the Modern Prometheus* (1818). Her other works include further novels, short stories (some with science-fiction elements, others Gothic or historical), and an edition of her husband's poems (1830).

Shelley[2] /'ʃelɪ/, Percy Bysshe (1792–1822), English poet. He was a leading figure of the romantic movement, with radical political views which are often reflected in his work. After the collapse of his first marriage in 1814 he eloped abroad with Mary Godwin and her stepsister, marrying Mary in 1816; they settled permanently in Italy two years later. Major works include the political poems *Queen Mab* (1813) and *The Mask of Anarchy* (1819), *Prometheus Unbound* (1820), a lyrical drama on his aspirations and contradictions as a poet and radical, lyric poetry (for example 'Ode to the West Wind', 1820), the essay *The Defence of Poetry* (1821), vindicating the role of poetry in an increasingly industrial society, and *Adonais*

(1821), an elegy on the death of Keats. Shelley was drowned in a boating accident.

Sheridan /'ʃerɪd(ə)n/, Richard Brinsley (1751–1816), Irish dramatist and Whig politician. He settled in London in 1773 and became principal director of Drury Lane Theatre in 1776 and sole proprietor in 1779. His plays are comedies of manners and include *The Rivals* (1775) — whose character Mrs Malaprop gave her name to the word *malapropism* — and *The School for Scandal* (1777). He became the friend and supporter of the Whig politician Charles James Fox and entered Parliament in 1780, where he became a celebrated orator, held senior government posts, and became a friend and adviser of the Prince Regent.

Sherman /'ʃɜːmən/, William Tecumseh (1820–91), American general. He held various commands in the American Civil War from its outset in 1861, and in March 1864 succeeded Ulysses S. Grant as chief Union commander in the west. He set out with 60,000 men on a march through Georgia, during which he crushed Confederate forces and broke civilian morale with his policy of deliberate destruction of the South's sources of supply. In 1869 he was appointed commander of the US army, a post he held until his retirement in 1884.

Sherrington /'ʃerɪŋtən/, Sir Charles Scott (1857–1952), English physiologist. His researches contributed greatly to understanding of the nervous system, particularly concerning motor pathways, sensory nerves in muscles, and the areas innervated by spinal nerves. He introduced the concept of reflex actions and the reflex arc and was the first to apply the term *synapsis* (later *synapse*) to the junction of two nerve cells. Sherrington shared a Nobel Prize in 1932.

Shevardnadze /ˌʃevɑːdˈnɑːdzɪ/, Eduard (Amvrosievich) (born 1928), Soviet statesman and head of state of Georgia since 1992. He became a candidate member of the Soviet Politburo in 1978 and a full member in 1985. In the same year Shevardnadze was appointed Minister of Foreign Affairs under Mikhail Gorbachev, a position he retained until his resignation in 1990. While in office, Shevardnadze supported Gorbachev's commitment to détente and played a key role in arms control negotiations with the West. In 1992 Shevardnadze was elected head of state of his native Georgia, following the toppling of President Zviad Gamsakhurdia (1939–94).

Shilton /'ʃɪlt(ə)n/, Peter (born 1949), English footballer. He played in goal for Leicester City, Stoke City, Nottingham Forest (with whom he won the League Championship in 1978 and successive European Cups in 1979 and 1980), Southampton, and Derby, and made a UK record 1,000th league appearance in 1996. With England he won a record 125 caps (1970–90) and was regarded by many as the finest goalkeeper in the world.

Shivaji /ʃɪˈvɑːdʒɪ/ (also **Sivaji**) (1627–80), Indian raja of the Marathas 1674–80. In 1659 he raised a Hindu revolt against Muslim rule in Bijapur, southern India, inflicting a crushing defeat on the army of the sultan of Bijapur. Shivaji was later captured by the Mogul emperor Aurangzeb, but escaped in 1666 and proceeded to expand Maratha territory. He had himself crowned raja in 1674; during his reign he enforced religious toleration throughout the Maratha empire and blocked Mogul expansionism by forming an alliance with the sultans in the south.

Shockley /'ʃɒklɪ/, William (Bradford) (1910–89), American physicist. He worked mainly at the Bell Telephone Laboratories, where he organized a group to research into solid-state physics. By 1948 they had developed the transistor, which was eventually to replace the thermionic valve, and Shockley shared with his co-workers the Nobel Prize for physics in 1958. He was appointed professor of engineering science at Stanford in 1963, and later became a controversial figure because of his views on a supposed connection between race and intelligence.

Shostakovich /ˌʃɒstəˈkɒvɪtʃ/, Dmitri (Dmitrievich) (1906–75), Russian composer. He was a prolific composer whose works include fifteen symphonies, operas, and many chamber works, although it is for the symphonies that he is most renowned. Shostakovich developed a highly personal style and, although he experimented with atonality and twelve-note techniques, his music always returned to a basic tonality. The failure of his music to conform to Soviet artistic ideology earned him official condemnation, especially during the Stalinist period. His later work, particularly the last symphonies, written after Stalin's death when the strictures on artistic free-

dom were less tight, became increasingly sombre and intense.

Shute /ʃuːt/, Nevil (pseudonym of Nevil Shute Norway) (1899–1960), English novelist. After the Second World War he settled in Australia, which provides the setting for his later novels; among the best known are *A Town Like Alice* (1950) and *On the Beach* (1957), which depicts a community facing gradual destruction in the aftermath of a nuclear war.

Sibelius /sɪˈbeɪlɪəs/, Jean (born Johan Julius Christian Sibelius) (1865–1957), Finnish composer. He is best known for the series of seven symphonies spanning the years 1898 to 1924. His affinity for his country's landscape and legends, especially the epic *Kalevala*, expressed themselves in a series of symphonic poems including *The Swan of Tuonela* (1893), *Finlandia* (1899), and *Tapiola* (1925); he also wrote a violin concerto (1903) and more than 100 songs.

Sickert /ˈsɪkət/, Walter Richard (1860–1942), British painter, of Danish and Anglo-Irish descent. He was a pupil of Whistler and also worked with Degas. His subjects were mainly urban scenes and figure compositions, particularly pictures of the theatre and music-hall and drab domestic interiors, avoiding the conventionally picturesque. His best-known painting, *Ennui* (1913), portrays a stagnant marriage.

Siddons /ˈsɪd(ə)nz/, Mrs Sarah (née Kemble) (1755–1831), English actress. The sister of John Kemble, she made her first, unsuccessful, London appearance in 1775; she then toured the provinces and made a successful return to the London stage in 1782, where she became an acclaimed tragic actress, noted particularly for her role as Lady Macbeth. She retained her pre-eminence until her retirement in 1812.

Sidney /ˈsɪdnɪ/, Sir Philip (1554–86), English poet and soldier. Generally considered to represent the apotheosis of the Elizabethan courtier, he was a leading poet and patron of poets, including Edmund Spenser. His best-known work is *Arcadia* (published posthumously in 1590), a prose romance including poems and pastoral eclogues in a wide variety of verse forms.

Siemens /ˈsiːmənz/, Ernst Werner von (1816–92), German electrical engineer. He developed electroplating and an electric generator which used an electromagnet, and set up a factory which manufactured telegraph systems and electric cables and pioneered electrical traction. His brother Karl Wilhelm (Sir Charles William, 1823–83) moved to England, where he developed the open-hearth steel furnace and designed the cable-laying steamship *Faraday*, and also designed the electric railway at Portrush in Northern Ireland. A third brother Friedrich (1826–1904) worked both with Werner in Germany and with Charles in England; he applied the principles of the open-hearth furnace to glassmaking.

Signac /siːˈnjæk/, Paul (1863–1935), French neo-impressionist painter. He was an ardent disciple of Seurat, although his own technique was freer than Seurat's and was characterized by the use of small dashes and patches of pure colour rather than dots; his subject-matter included landscapes, seascapes, and city scenes. He also wrote *D'Eugène Delacroix aux néo-impressionisme* (1899), a manifesto defending the movement.

Sihanouk /ˈsɪənʊk/, Norodom (born 1922), Cambodian king 1941–55 and since 1993, Prime Minister 1955–60, and head of state 1960–70 and 1975–6. Two years after Cambodian independence (1953), Sihanouk abdicated in order to become Premier, passing the throne to his father Prince Norodom Suramarit (died 1960). On his father's death, Prince Sihanouk proclaimed himself head of state, a position he retained until a US-backed military coup ten years later. Sihanouk was reinstated by the Khmer Rouge in 1975, only to be removed the following year. After serving as President of the government-in-exile (1982–9), he was appointed head of state by the provisional government and subsequently crowned for the second time (1993).

Sikorsky /sɪˈkɔːskɪ/, Igor (Ivanovich) (1889–1972), Russian-born American aircraft designer. He studied aeronautics in Paris before returning to Russia to build the first large four-engined aircraft, the Grand, in 1913. After experimenting unsuccessfully with helicopters he emigrated to New York, where he established the Sikorsky Aero Engineering Co. and produced many famous amphibious aircraft and flying boats. Sikorsky again turned his attention to helicopters, personally flying the prototype of the first mass-produced helicopter in 1939,

and was closely associated with their sub-sequent development.

Sillitoe /'sɪlɪˌtəʊ/, Alan (born 1928), English writer. His fiction is notable for its depiction of working-class provincial life; his first novel *Saturday Night and Sunday Morning* (1958) describes the life of a dissatisfied young Nottingham factory worker, while the title story in *The Loneliness of the Long-Distance Runner* (1959) portrays a rebellious Borstal boy. He has also published volumes of poetry, short stories, and plays.

Simenon /'siːməˌnɒn/, Georges (Joseph Christian) (1903–89), Belgian-born French novelist. He is best known for his series of detective novels featuring Commissaire Maigret, who was introduced in 1931. Maigret relies on his understanding of the criminal's motives rather than scientific deduction to solve crimes and the novels show considerable insight into human psychology.

Simeon Stylites, St /ˌsɪmɪən staɪˈlaɪtiːz/ (c.390–459), Syrian monk. After living in a monastic community he became the first to practise an extreme form of asceticism which involved living on top of a pillar; this became a site of pilgrimage.

Simnel /'sɪmn(ə)l/, Lambert (c.1475–1525), English pretender and rebel. The son of a baker, he was trained by Yorkists to impersonate firstly one of the sons of Edward IV, both of whom had been imprisoned in the Tower of London (see PRINCES IN THE TOWER), and subsequently the Earl of Warwick (also imprisoned in the Tower of London), in an attempt to overthrow Henry VII. He was crowned in Dublin in 1487 as Edward VI but captured when the Yorkist uprising was defeated. He was not executed, but was given a menial post in the royal household.

Simon[1] /'saɪmən/, (Marvin) Neil (born 1927), American dramatist. Most of his plays are wry comedies portraying aspects of middle-class life; they include *Barefoot in the Park* (1963), *The Odd Couple* (1965), and *Brighton Beach Memoirs* (1983). Among his musicals are *Sweet Charity* (1966) and *They're Playing Our Song* (1979).

Simon[2] /'saɪmən/, Paul (born 1942), American singer and songwriter. He formed a folk-rock partnership with his school friend Art Garfunkel (born 1941), which first made its mark with the album *Sounds of Silence* (1966). Further achievements were

the soundtrack music to the film *The Graduate* (1968) and the song 'Bridge Over Troubled Water' (1970) from the album of the same name. The duo split up in 1970 and Simon went on to pursue a successful solo career, recording albums such as *Graceland* (1986), which featured many black South African musicians. He has also acted in films, including Woody Allen's *Annie Hall* (1977).

Simon, St (known as Simon the Zealot), an Apostle. According to one tradition he preached and was martyred in Persia along with St Jude. Feast day (with St Jude), 28 October.

Simonides /saɪˈmɒnɪˌdiːz/ (c.556–468 BC), Greek lyric poet. He wrote for the rulers of Athens, Thessaly, and Syracuse; much of his poetry, which includes elegies, odes, and epigrams, celebrates the heroes of the Persian Wars, and includes verse commemorating those killed at Marathon and Thermopylae.

Simpson[1] /'sɪmps(ə)n/, Sir James Young (1811–71), Scottish surgeon and obstetrician. He discovered the usefulness of chloroform as an anaesthetic by experimentation on himself and his colleagues shortly after the first use of ether, and he was active in the debate over which of the two was the best agent to use in surgery. Simpson was also a distinguished antiquarian and historian, publishing monographs on archaeology and the history of medicine.

Simpson[2] /'sɪmps(ə)n/, O(renthal) J(ames) (born 1947), American football player, actor, and celebrity. He was arrested in 1994, accused of murdering his wife and her male companion, but was acquitted after a lengthy, high-profile trial. An outstanding player of American football, he joined the Buffalo Bills in 1968 as a running back and rushed the most yards four years in a row (1972–6). In 1975 he scored a record twenty-three touchdowns in one season. As an actor he has appeared in numerous films including the *Naked Gun* series (1988, 1991, and 1994).

Simpson[3] /'sɪmps(ə)n/, Wallis (née Wallis Warfield) (1896–1986), American wife of Edward, Duke of Windsor (Edward VIII). Her relationship with the king caused a national scandal in 1936, especially in view of her impending second divorce, and forced the king's abdication. The couple were married shortly afterwards and she

became the Duchess of Windsor. She remained in France after her husband died and lived as a recluse until her death.

Sinatra /sɪˈnɑːtrə/, Frank (full name Francis Albert Sinatra) (born 1915), American singer and actor. He began his long career as a singer in 1938 performing with big bands on the radio, becoming a solo star in the 1940s with a large teenage following; his many hits include 'Night and Day' and 'My Way'. Among his numerous films are *From Here to Eternity* (1953), for which he won an Oscar.

Sinclair[1] /ˈsɪŋkleə(r)/, Sir Clive (Marles) (born 1940), English electronics engineer and entrepreneur. Sinclair founded a research and development company and launched a range of innovative products including pocket calculators, wrist-watch televisions, and personal computers. A three-wheeled electric car, the C5, powered by a washing-machine motor, failed to achieve commercial success.

Sinclair[2] /ˈsɪŋkleə(r)/, Upton (Beall) (1878–1968), American novelist and social reformer. Sinclair first came to prominence with *The Jungle* (1906), his graphic exposure of the conditions in Chicago's meatpacking industry. Sinclair became a socialist as a young man and in 1907 attempted to found an experimental Utopian commune in New Jersey, which was destroyed by fire. He agitated for social justice in seventy-nine books, including the eleven-volume 'Lanny Budd' series (1940–53).

Singer[1] /ˈsɪŋə(r)/, Isaac Bashevis (1904–91), Polish-born American novelist and short-story writer. His work, written in Yiddish but chiefly known from English translations, blends realistic detail and elements of fantasy, mysticism, and magic to portray the lives of Polish Jews from many periods. Notable titles include the novels *The Magician of Lublin* (1955) and *The Slave* (1962) and the short-story collection *The Spinoza of Market Street* (1961). He was awarded the Nobel Prize for literature in 1978.

Singer[2] /ˈsɪŋə(r)/, Isaac Merritt (1811–75), American inventor. In 1851 he designed and built the first commercially successful sewing machine, which included features already developed by Elias Howe. Although he was successfully sued by Howe for infringement of patent, Singer founded his own company, gained patents for improvements to the machine, and became the world's largest sewing machine manufac-

turer; his success was partly based on his pioneering use of hire-purchase agreements.

Sisley /ˈsɪslɪ, ˈsɪzlɪ/, Alfred (1839–99), French impressionist painter, of English descent. His development towards impressionism from his early Corot-influenced landscapes was gradual and greatly indebted to Monet. He is chiefly remembered for his paintings of the countryside around Paris in the 1870s, with their concentration on reflecting surfaces and fluid brushwork; like Monet, he also painted the same scenes under different weather conditions.

Sitting Bull (Sioux name Tatanka Iyotake) (*c.*1831–90), Sioux chief. As the main chief of the Sioux peoples from about 1867, he resisted the US government order of 1875 forcibly resettling the Sioux on reservations; when the US army opened hostilities in 1876, Sitting Bull led the Sioux in the fight to retain their lands, which resulted in the massacre of General Custer and his men at Little Bighorn. In 1885 he appeared in Buffalo Bill's Wild West Show, but continued to lead his people; becoming an advocate of the Ghost Dance cult, he was killed in an uprising.

Sitwell /ˈsɪtwel/, Dame Edith (Louisa) (1887–1964), English poet and critic. Light-hearted and experimental, her early verse, like that of her brothers Osbert (1892–1969) and Sacheverell (1897–1988), marked a revolt against the prevailing Georgian style of the day. In 1923 she attracted attention with *Façade*, a group of poems in notated rhythm recited to music by William Walton. Her later verse is graver and makes increasing use of Christian symbolism.

Sivaji see SHIVAJI.

Skelton /ˈskelt(ə)n/, John (*c.*1460–1529), English poet. He was court poet to Henry VIII, to whom he had acted as tutor. Skelton's principal works include *The Bowge of Courte* (*c.*1498), a satire on the court of Henry VII, *Magnificence* (1516), a morality play, and *Collyn Cloute* (1522), which contained an attack on Cardinal Wolsey. His characteristic verse consisted of short irregular rhyming lines with rhythms based on colloquial speech, giving rise to the word *Skeltonic* to describe this type of verse or metre.

Skinner /ˈskɪnə(r)/, Burrhus Frederic (1904–90), American psychologist. He promoted

the view that the proper aim of psychology should be to predict, and hence be able to control, behaviour. He demonstrated that arbitrary responses in animals could be obtained by using reinforcements — rewards and punishments. He applied similar techniques in both clinical and educational practice, devising one of the first teaching machines, and was involved in the development of programmed learning. Skinner also attempted to account for the nature and development of language as a response to conditioning.

Skryabin see SCRIABIN.

Sloane /sləʊn/, Sir Hans (1660–1753), Irish physician and naturalist. He purchased the manor of Chelsea and endowed the Chelsea Physic Garden. His collections, which included a large number of books and manuscripts, were purchased by the nation and placed in Montague House, which afterwards became the British Museum. Sloane's geological and zoological specimens formed the basis of the Natural History Museum in South Kensington.

Smetana /'smetənə/, Bedřich (1824–84), Czech composer. Regarded as the founder of Czech music, he was dedicated to the cause of Czech nationalism, as is apparent in his operas (for example *The Bartered Bride*, 1866) and in the cycle of symphonic poems *My Country* (1874–9). He also contributed to the cause through his work as conductor of the National Theatre in Prague. He died in an asylum after suffering ten years of deteriorating health as a result of syphilis, which had left him completely deaf in 1874.

Smith[1] /smɪθ/, Adam (1723–90), Scottish economist and philosopher. He is regarded by many as the founder of modern economics, and his work marks a significant turning-point in the breakdown of mercantilism and the spread of laissez-faire ideas. Smith retired from academic life to write his *Inquiry into the Nature and Causes of the Wealth of Nations* (1776), establishing theories of labour, distribution, wages, prices, and money, and advocating free trade and minimal state interference in economic matters. His work was highly influential in terms not only of economic but also of political theory in the following century.

Smith[2] /smɪθ/, Bessie (1894–1937), American blues singer. She became a leading artist in the 1920s and made more than 150 recordings, including some with Benny Goodman and Louis Armstrong. She was involved in a car accident and died after being refused admission to a 'whites only' hospital.

Smith[3] /smɪθ/, David (Roland) (1906–65), American sculptor. He allied his metal-working skills with an enthusiasm for cubism, and in particular the work of Picasso, to produce his first steel sculpture in 1933. The recurring motifs of human violence and greed characterize his early work, including *Pillars of Sunday* (1945). In the late 1950s and 1960s these give way to a calmer, more monumental style, reflected in works such as the *Cubi* series.

Smith[4] /smɪθ/, Ian (Douglas) (born 1919), Rhodesian statesman, Prime Minister 1964–79. He founded the white supremacist Rhodesian Front (renamed the Republican Front in 1981) in 1962, becoming Prime Minister and head of the white minority government two years later. In 1965 he issued a unilateral declaration of independence (UDI) after Britain stipulated that it would only grant the country independence if Smith undertook to prepare for black majority rule. He eventually conceded in 1979 and resigned to make way for majority rule; after the country became the independent state of Zimbabwe he remained active in politics, leading the Republican Front until 1987.

Smith[5] /smɪθ/, Joseph (1805–44), American religious leader and founder of the Church of Jesus Christ of Latter-Day Saints (the Mormons). In 1827, according to his own account, he was led by divine revelation to find the sacred texts written by the prophet Mormon, which he later translated and published as the Book of Mormon in 1830. He founded the Mormon Church in the same year and established a large community in Illinois, of which he became mayor. He was murdered by a mob while in prison awaiting trial for conspiracy.

Smith[6] /smɪθ/, Stevie (pseudonym of Florence Margaret Smith) (1902–71), English poet and novelist. Although she first attracted notice with her novel *Novel on Yellow Paper* (1936), she is now mainly remembered for her witty, caustic, and enigmatic verse, often illustrated by her own comic drawings. Collections include *A Good Time Was Had by All* (1937), *Not Waving But Drowning* (1957), and the posthumous *Collected Poems* (1975).

Smith[7] /smɪθ/, Sydney (1771–1845), English Anglican churchman, essayist, and wit. He is notable for his witty contributions to the periodical the *Edinburgh Review* and as the author of the *Letters of Peter Plymley* (1807), which defended Catholic Emancipation.

Smith[8] /smɪθ/, William (1769–1839), English land-surveyor and geologist. Despite being self-taught, he became known as the father of English geology. Working initially in the area around Bath, he discovered that rock strata could be distinguished on the basis of their characteristic assemblages of fossils, and that strata in different places could be identified by these. Smith later travelled extensively in Britain, accumulating data which enabled him to produce the first geological map of England and Wales. Many of the names he devised for particular strata are still in use.

Smollett /'smɒlɪt/, Tobias (George) (1721–71), Scottish novelist. His novels are picaresque tales characterized by fast-moving narrative and humorous caricature; they include *The Adventures of Roderick Random* (1748), *The Adventures of Peregrine Pickle* (1751), and the epistolary work *The Expedition of Humphry Clinker* (1771). Among his other works are *A Complete History of England* (1757–8) and translations of Voltaire and Cervantes.

Smuts /smʌts/, Jan Christiaan (1870–1950), South African statesman and soldier, Prime Minister 1919–24 and 1939–48. He led Boer forces during the Second Boer War, but afterwards supported Louis Botha's policy of Anglo-Boer cooperation and was one of the founders of the Union of South Africa. During the First World War he led Allied troops against the Germans in East Africa (1916); he later attended the peace conference at Versailles in 1919 and helped to found the League of Nations. He then succeeded Botha as Prime Minister, a post he held again between 1939 and 1948. After the Second World War Smuts played a leading role in the formation of the United Nations and drafted the preamble to the UN charter.

Snorri Sturluson /ˌsnɔːrɪ 'stɜːləs(ə)n/ (1178–1241), Icelandic historian and poet. A leading figure of medieval Icelandic literature, he wrote the *Younger* or *Prose Edda* (a handbook to Icelandic poetry, with prosodic and grammatical treatises, quotations, and prose paraphrases from old poems) and the

Heimskringla, a history of the kings of Norway from mythical times to the year 1177.

Snow /snəʊ/, C(harles) P(ercy), 1st Baron Snow of Leicester (1905–80), English novelist and scientist. The title novel of his sequence of eleven novels *Strangers and Brothers* appeared in 1940; the series, which also includes *The Masters* (1951) and *The Corridors of Power* (1964), deals with moral dilemmas and power-struggles in the academic world. He is also known for his lecture *Two Cultures*, delivered in 1959, in which he discussed the deleterious effects of the division between science and the humanities, which provoked an acerbic and controversial response from the critic F. R. Leavis.

Soane /səʊn/, Sir John (1753–1837), English architect. After initial training in England and Italy he was appointed architect of the Bank of England in 1788, where he developed a characteristic neoclassical style. By 1810 his style had become more severe, avoiding unnecessary ornament and adopting structural necessity as the basis of design. His collection of pictures is housed in the house he designed for himself in London, the Sir John Soane Museum.

Sobers /'səʊbəz/, Sir Garfield St Aubrun ('Gary') (born 1936), West Indian cricketer. Born in Barbados, he first played for the West Indies in 1953. Four years later he hit a record test score of 365 not out, which stood until beaten by Brian Lara in 1994. He was captain of the West Indies (1965–72) and of Nottinghamshire (1968–74). During his test career he scored more than 8,000 runs and took 235 wickets, bowling in three different styles; he was also a fine fielder. In 1968 Sobers became the first batsman in first-class cricket to hit all six balls of an over for six.

Sobieski /sɒ'bjeskɪ/, John, see JOHN III.

Socrates /'sɒkrəˌtiːz/ (469–399 BC), Greek philosopher. His interests lay not in the speculation about the natural world engaged in by earlier philosophers but in pursuing questions of ethics. He was the centre of a circle of friends and disciples in Athens and his method of inquiry (the *Socratic method*) was based on discourse with those around him; his careful questioning was designed to reveal truth and to expose error. Although he wrote nothing himself, he was immensely influential; he is known chiefly through his disciple Plato, who recorded Socrates' dialogues and

teachings in, for example, the *Symposium* and the *Phaedo*. Charged with introducing strange gods and corrupting the young, Socrates was sentenced to death and condemned to take hemlock, which he did, spurning offers to help him escape into exile.

Soddy /'sɒdɪ/, Frederick (1877–1956), English physicist. He worked with Ernest Rutherford in Canada on radioactive decay and formulated a theory of isotopes, the word *isotope* being coined by him in 1913. He also assisted William Ramsay in London in the discovery of helium. Soddy wrote on economics, and later concentrated on creating an awareness of the social relevance of science. He was awarded the Nobel Prize for chemistry in 1921.

Soliman see SULEIMAN I.

Solomon /'sɒləmən/, son of David, king of ancient Israel *c*.970–*c*.930 BC. During his reign he extended the kingdom of Israel to the border with Egypt and the Euphrates, and became famous both for his wisdom and for the magnificence of his palaces. In 957 he built the Temple of Jerusalem, with which his name is associated; this, together with his other building schemes and the fortifying of strategic cities, led to a system of levies and enforced labour. The resulting discontent culminated in the secession of the northern tribes, who formed a separate kingdom (*c*.930–721 BC) but were carried away to captivity in Babylon. In the Bible Solomon is traditionally associated with the Song of Solomon, Ecclesiastes, and Proverbs; the Wisdom of Solomon in the Apocrypha is also ascribed to him.

Solon /'səʊlɒn/ (*c*.630–*c*.560 BC), Athenian statesman and lawgiver. One of the Seven Sages listed by Plato, he is notable for his economic, constitutional, and legal reforms, begun in about 594. He revised the existing code of laws established by Draco, making them less severe; for example, he abolished the punishment of slavery for debt and freed those already enslaved for this, and reserved the death penalty for murder. His division of the citizens into four classes based on wealth rather than birth with a corresponding division of political responsibility laid the foundations of Athenian democracy.

Solti /'ʃɒltɪ/, Sir Georg (1912–97), Hungarian-born British conductor. From 1961 to 1971 Solti revivified Covent Garden as musical director, and took British nationality

in 1972. Solti commenced a long association with the London Philharmonic Orchestra in 1973, but his appointment as conductor of the Chicago Symphony Orchestra (1969–91) brought him his greatest fame. He became artistic director of the Salzburg Easter Festival in 1992.

Solyman see SULEIMAN I.

Solzhenitsyn /ˌsɒlʒə'nɪtsɪn/, Alexander (Russian name Aleksandr Isaevich Solzhenitsyn) (born 1918), Russian novelist. In 1945 he was imprisoned for eight years in a labour camp for criticizing Stalin and spent another three years in internal exile before being rehabilitated. After his release he was allowed to publish his first novel *One Day in the Life of Ivan Denisovich* (1962), describing conditions in a labour camp. In 1963, however, he was again in conflict with the authorities and thereafter was unable to have his books published in the Soviet Union. He was deported to West Germany in 1974 following the publication abroad of the first part of his trilogy *The Gulag Archipelago* in 1973; the first Russian-language edition appeared in 1989. Solzhenitsyn lived in the US until returning to Russia in 1994. He was awarded the Nobel Prize for literature in 1970.

Somoza /sə'məʊzə/, Anastasio (full surname Somoza García) (1896–1956), Nicaraguan soldier and statesman, President 1937–47 and 1951–6. After becoming Commander-in-Chief of the Nicaraguan army in 1933, he organized a military coup in 1936 and took presidential office the following year. From this time he ruled Nicaragua as a virtual dictator, exiling the majority of his political opponents and building up a fortune from land and business ventures. He was assassinated in 1956, after which his eldest son Luis Somoza Debayle (1922–67) succeeded him as President, serving from 1957 to 1963. Luis's younger brother Anastasio Somoza Debayle (1925–80) became President in 1967, after winning the general election that year. His dictatorial regime was overthrown by the Sandinistas in 1979, and he was assassinated while in exile in Paraguay.

Sondheim /'sɒndhaɪm/, Stephen (Joshua) (born 1930), American composer and lyricist. He became famous with his lyrics for Leonard Bernstein's *West Side Story* (1957), and later wrote both words and music for a number of musicals, including *A Funny Thing Happened on the Way to the Forum*

(1962), *A Little Night Music* (1973), and *Sweeney Todd* (1979).

Sontag /'sɒntæg/, Susan (born 1933), American writer and critic. She established her reputation as a radical intellectual with a series of essays which were collected in *Against Interpretation* (1966). In the 1970s Sontag made two films and won critical acclaim for her study *On Photography* (1976) and her collection of essays *Illness as Metaphor* (1979); the latter was prompted by her experiences as a cancer patient.

Sophocles /'sɒfəˌkliːz/ (*c*.496–406 BC), Greek dramatist. He is one of the trio of major Greek tragedians, with Aeschylus and Euripides. His seven surviving plays are notable for their addition of a third actor to the previous two (in addition to the chorus), thus allowing a greater complexity of plot and fuller depiction of character, and for their examination of the relationship between mortals and the divine order. The plays include *Antigone*, *Electra*, and *Oedipus Rex* (also called *Oedipus Tyrannus*).

Sopwith /'sɒpwɪθ/, Sir Thomas (Octave Murdoch) (1888–1989), English aircraft designer. During the First World War he designed a number of planes, including the famous fighter biplane the Sopwith Camel, which were built by his Sopwith Aviation Company (founded 1912). During the Second World War, as chairman of the Hawker Siddeley company, he was responsible for the production of aircraft such as the Hurricane fighter.

Sousa /'suːzə/, John Philip (1854–1932), American composer and conductor. He became director of the US Marine Band in 1880, and then formed his own band in 1892. His works include more than 100 marches, for example *The Stars and Stripes*, *King Cotton*, and *Hands Across the Sea*. The sousaphone, invented in 1898, was named in his honour.

Southey /'saʊðɪ, 'saʊðɪ/, Robert (1774–1843), English poet. Associated with the Lake Poets, he wrote a number of long narrative poems including *Madoc* (1805), but is best known for his shorter poems such as the anti-militarist ballad the 'Battle of Blenheim' (1798), and for his biography the *Life of Nelson* (1813). Southey was made Poet Laureate in 1813.

Soutine /suːˈtiːn/, Chaim (1893–1943), French painter, born in Lithuania. After emigrating to Paris in 1913, he was closely associated with a group of painters that included Chagall and Modigliani. A major exponent of expressionism, Soutine evolved a style distinguished by bright colours, vigorous brushstrokes, and impasto, imbued with a feverish emotional content. During the 1920s he produced pictures of grotesque figures, with twisted faces and deformed bodies. From 1925 he increasingly painted still lifes, including plucked fowl and flayed carcasses.

Soyinka /ʃɔɪˈɪŋkə/, Wole (born 1934), Nigerian dramatist, novelist, and critic. He made his name in 1959 with the play *The Lion and the Jewel*. His writing often uses satire and humour to explore the contrast between traditional and modern society in Africa, and combines elements of both African and European aesthetics. His works include the novel *The Interpreters* (1965), the play *Kongi's Harvest* (1964), and the collection of poems and other writings *The Man Died* (1972), a record of his time spent serving a sentence as a political prisoner 1967–9. In 1986 Soyinka became the first African to receive the Nobel Prize for literature.

Spallanzani /ˌspælənˈzɑːnɪ/, Lazzaro (1729–99), Italian physiologist and biologist. A priest as well as a keen traveller and collector, he is known today for his meticulous experiments on a wide variety of subjects. He explained the circulation of the blood and the digestive system of animals, showed that fertilization can result only from contact between egg and seminal fluid, demonstrated that protozoa do not appear as a result of spontaneous generation, and studied regeneration in invertebrates. Spallanzani also worked on various problems in the physical and earth sciences.

Spark /spɑːk/, Dame Muriel (born 1918), Scottish novelist. Her novels include *Memento Mori* (1959), a comic and macabre study of old age, and *The Prime of Miss Jean Brodie* (1961), a sardonic portrait of an emancipated Edinburgh schoolmistress and her favourite pupils. In 1954 Spark converted to Roman Catholicism; her awareness of the paradoxes and ironies of the faith informs much of her work, particularly her novel *The Mandelbaum Gate* (1965).

Spartacus /'spɑːtəkəs/ (died *c*.71 BC), Thracian slave and gladiator. He led a revolt against Rome in 73, increasing his army

from some seventy gladiators at the outset to several thousand rebels. He was eventually defeated by Crassus in 71 and crucified.

Spassky /'spæskɪ/, Boris (Vasilyevich) (born 1937), Russian chess player. He became both international grandmaster and junior world champion in 1953. In 1969 he won the world championship, but was faced with hostility in his homeland after losing his title to the American Bobby Fischer in 1972. He lived in Paris from 1975, and played for France in the 1984 Olympics. In a rematch with Fischer in 1992 he was again defeated.

Spector /'spektə(r)/, Phil (born 1940), American record producer. In 1961 he formed a record company and pioneered a 'wall of sound' style, using echo and tape loops. He had a succession of hit recordings in the 1960s with girl groups such as the Ronettes and the Crystals, produced 'River Deep — Mountain High' for Ike and Tina Turner (1966), and worked on the last Beatles album, *Let it Be* (1970).

Speer /spɪə(r)/, Albert (1905–81), German architect and Nazi government official. He joined the Nazi Party in 1931 and as head of government construction designed the Berlin chancellery and the Nuremberg stadium for the 1934 Nazi Party congress. He was also Minister for Armaments and Munitions 1942–5 and was the only Nazi leader to admit responsibility at the Nuremberg trials for the regime's actions. He served twenty years in Spandau prison (1946–66).

Speke /spiːk/, John Hanning (1827–64), English explorer. From 1854 to 1858 he accompanied Sir Richard Burton on expeditions to trace the source of the Nile. They became the first Europeans to discover Lake Tanganyika (1858), after which Speke went on to reach a great lake which he identified as the 'source reservoir' of the Nile; he called it Lake Victoria in honour of the queen.

Spence /spens/, Sir Basil (Urwin) (1907–76), British architect, born in India. He designed the new Coventry cathedral (1962), embellished with the works of Jacob Epstein, John Piper, and Graham Sutherland. In the 1950s and 1960s he was much in demand for the designs of new British universities.

Spencer[1] /'spensə(r)/, Herbert (1820–1903), English philosopher and sociologist. He was an early adherent of evolutionary theory, which he set down in his *Principles of Psychology* (1855). Spencer embraced Darwin's theory of natural selection proposed four years later, coined the phrase the 'survival of the fittest' (1864), and advocated social and economic laissez-faire. He later sought to synthesize the natural and social sciences in the *Programme of a System of Synthetic Philosophy* (1862–96).

Spencer[2] /'spensə(r)/, Sir Stanley (1891–1959), English painter. He is best known for his religious and visionary works in the modern setting of his native village of Cookham in Berkshire. Famous works include the painting *Resurrection: Cookham* (1926), the series of military murals for the Sandham Memorial Chapel at Burghclere in Hampshire (1927–32), and the sequence of panels portraying the Clyde shipyards during the Second World War when he was an official war artist.

Spender /'spendə(r)/, Sir Stephen (1909–95), English poet and critic. His *Poems* (1933) contained both personal and political poems including 'The Pylons', which lent its name to the group of young left-wing poets of the 1930s known as the 'Pylon School'; its members used industrial imagery in their work and included W. H. Auden, C. Day Lewis, and Louis MacNeice. In his critical work *The Destructive Element* (1935), Spender defended the importance of political subject-matter in literature. He later wrote the autobiography *World Within World* (1951), giving an account of his association with the Communist Party.

Spengler /'spenglə(r)/, Oswald (1880–1936), German philosopher. His fame rests on his book *The Decline of the West* (1918–22), in which he argues that civilizations undergo a seasonal cycle of about a thousand years and are subject to growth, flowering, and decay analogous to biological species.

Spenser /'spensə(r)/, Edmund (c.1552–99), English poet. His first major poem was the *Shepheardes Calendar* (1579) in twelve eclogues. He is best known for his allegorical romance the *Faerie Queene* (1590; 1596), celebrating Queen Elizabeth I. The poem is written in the stanza invented by Spenser (later used by Keats, Shelley, and Byron) with eight iambic pentameters and an alexandrine, rhyming *ababbcbcc*. He also

wrote the marriage poem *Epithalamion* (1594).

Spielberg /'spiːlbɜːg/, Steven (born 1947), American film director and producer. He established a wide popular appeal with films concentrating on sensational and fantastic themes, such as *Jaws* (1975), *Close Encounters of the Third Kind* (1977), and *ET* (1982), which he also produced. He later directed a series of adventure films, notably *Raiders of the Lost Ark* (1981) and *Indiana Jones and the Temple of Doom* (1984). Other films include *Jurassic Park* (1993), which like his earlier film *ET* broke box-office records in the US and Britain, and *Schindler's List* (1993), which won seven Oscars, including that for best director and best picture.

Spillane /spɪ'leɪn/, Mickey (pseudonym of Frank Morrison Spillane) (born 1918), American writer. He wrote a series of enormously popular detective novels during the late 1940s and early 1950s which emphasized sadistic violence rather more than mystery. He wrote the screenplay and starred in the film of his book *The Girl Hunters* (1962). His other books include *My Gun Is Quick* (1950) and *The Big Kill* (1951).

Spinoza /spɪ'nəʊzə/, Baruch (or Benedict) de (1632–77), Dutch philosopher, of Portuguese Jewish descent. His unorthodox views led to his expulsion from the Amsterdam synagogue in 1656. Spinoza rejected the Cartesian dualism of spirit and matter in favour of a pantheistic system, seeing God as the single infinite substance, the immanent cause of the universe and not a ruler outside it. His *Ethics* (1677) sought to formulate a metaphysical system that was mathematically deduced from theorems and hypotheses; its rationalist method broke new ground in biblical analysis. Spinoza espoused a determinist political doctrine, arguing that the individual surrenders his or her natural rights to the state in order to obtain security.

Spitz /spɪts/, Mark (Andrew) (born 1950), American swimmer. He won seven gold medals in the 1972 Olympic Games at Munich and set twenty-seven world records for free style and butterfly (1967–72).

Spock /spɒk/, Benjamin McLane (known as Dr Spock) (born 1903), American paediatrician and writer. His manual *The Common Sense Book of Baby and Child Care* (1946) challenged traditional ideas of discipline and rigid routine in child rearing in favour of a psychological approach and influ-

enced a generation of parents after the Second World War. He was sent to prison in 1968 for helping draft-dodgers.

Spode /spəʊd/, Josiah (1755–1827), English potter. Having inherited the pottery founded by his father in Stoke-on-Trent, he invented what became standard English bone china by combining china clay with bone ash. Much of his characteristic work done around the turn of the 19th century consisted of elaborate services and large vases, ornately decorated and gilded.

Springsteen /'sprɪŋstiːn/, Bruce (born 1949), American rock singer, songwriter, and guitarist. He is noted for his songs about working-class life in the US and for his energetic stage performances. Major albums include *Born to Run* (1975) and *Born in the USA* (1984).

Staël, Mme de, see DE STAËL.

Stainer /'steɪnə(r)/, Sir John (1840–1901), English composer. He is remembered for his church music, including hymns, cantatas, and the oratorio *Crucifixion* (1887).

Stalin /'stɑːlɪn/, Joseph (born Iosif Vissarionovich Dzhugashvili) (1879–1953), Soviet statesman, General Secretary of the Communist Party of the USSR 1922–53. Born in Georgia, he joined the Bolsheviks under Lenin in 1903 and co-founded the party's newspaper *Pravda* in 1912, adopting the name 'Stalin' (Russian, 'man of steel') by 1913; in the same year he was exiled to Siberia until just after the Russian Revolution. Following Lenin's death he became chairman of the Politburo and secured enough support within the party to eliminate Trotsky, who disagreed with his theory of building socialism in the Soviet Union as a base from which Communism could spread. By 1927 he was the uncontested leader of the party, and in the following year he launched a succession of five-year plans for the industrialization and collectivization of agriculture; as a result of this process, some 10 million peasants are thought to have died, either of famine, or, in the case of those who resisted Stalin's policies, of hard labour or by execution. His large-scale purges of the intelligentsia in the 1930s along similarly punitive and ruthless lines removed all opposition, while his direction of the armed forces led to victory over Hitler 1941–5. After 1945 he played a large part in the restructuring of postwar Europe and attempted to maintain a firm grip on other Communist states; he

was later denounced by Khrushchev and the Eastern bloc countries.

Stanford /'stænfəd/, Sir Charles (Villiers) (1852–1924), British composer, born in Ireland. As professor of composition at the Royal College of Music, London (1883–1924), and professor of music at Cambridge University (1887–1924), he was a highly influential teacher and played a significant role in the revival of English music at the turn of the century; his pupils included Gustav Holst and Ralph Vaughan Williams. A prolific composer in many genres, he is now known mainly through his Anglican church music and numerous choral works.

Stanhope /'stænəp/, Lady Hester Lucy (1776–1839), English traveller. She kept house for her uncle William Pitt the Younger from 1803 to 1806, becoming a distinguished political hostess. Stanhope was granted a pension on Pitt's death and later set out for the Middle East (1810), settling in a ruined convent in the Lebanon Mountains four years later. She participated in Middle Eastern politics for several years, but eventually died in poverty after her pension was stopped by Lord Palmerston.

Stanier /'stæniə(r)/, Sir William (Arthur) (1876–1965), English railway engineer. After working for the Great Western Railway he became chief mechanical engineer of the London Midland and Scottish Railway in 1932. Stanier was given the task of modernizing the company's entire locomotive stock, and he is chiefly remembered for his new standard locomotive designs of the 1930s — especially large engines of 4-6-0 and pacific type. He was elected to the Royal Society in 1944.

Stanislaus, St /'stænɪsˌlɔːs/ (known as St Stanislaus of Cracow; Polish name Stanisław /sta'niswaf/ (1030–79), patron saint of Poland. He became bishop of Cracow in 1072 and, as such, excommunicated King Boleslaus II (1039–81). According to tradition, Stanislaus was murdered by Boleslaus while taking Mass. Feast day, 11 April (formerly 7 May).

Stanislavsky /ˌstænɪs'læfskɪ/, Konstantin (Sergeevich) (born Konstantin Sergeevich Alekseev) (1863–1938), Russian theatre director and actor. In 1898 he founded the Moscow Art Theatre and became known for his innovative productions of works by Chekhov and Maxim Gorky. He trained his

actors to take a psychological approach and use latent powers of self-expression when taking on roles; his theory and technique of acting were later adopted in the US and developed into the system known as method acting.

Stanley /'stænlɪ/, Sir Henry Morton (born John Rowlands) (1841–1904), Welsh explorer. As a newspaper correspondent he was sent in 1869 to central Africa to find the Scottish missionary and explorer David Livingstone; two years later he found him on the eastern shore of Lake Tanganyika. After Livingstone's death, Stanley continued his exploration, charting Lake Victoria (1874), tracing the course of the Congo (1874–7), mapping Lake Albert (1889), and becoming the first European to discover Lake Edward (1889). Stanley also helped establish the Congo Free State (now Zaire), with Belgian support, from 1879 to 1885.

Starling /'stɑːlɪŋ/, Ernest Henry (1866–1927), English physiologist. Studying the digestive system, he demonstrated the existence of peristalsis, and showed that a substance secreted by the pancreas passes via the blood to the duodenal wall, where it stimulates the secretion of digestive juices. He coined the term *hormone* for such substances, and founded the science of endocrinology. Starling also studied the theory of circulation, the functioning of heart muscle, and fluid exchange at capillary level.

Starr /stɑː(r)/, Ringo (born Richard Starkey) (born 1940), English rock and pop drummer. He replaced Pete Best in the Beatles in 1962, by which time he was already an experienced professional drummer. In 1966 he sang the hit 'Yellow Submarine', which later formed the basis of a cartoon film (1969). After the band's split (1970) he pursued a solo career and narrated the Rev. W. V. Awdry's *Thomas the Tank Engine* stories for television (1984).

Statius /'steɪʃəs/, Publius Papinius (AD c.45–96), Roman poet. He flourished at the court of Domitian and is best known for the *Silvae*, a miscellany of poems addressed to friends, and the *Thebais*, an epic concerning the bloody quarrel between the sons of Oedipus. His work, which often uses mythological or fantastical images, was much admired in the Middle Ages.

Steele /stiːl/, Sir Richard (1672–1729), Irish essayist and dramatist. He founded and wrote for the periodicals the *Tatler* (1709–

11) and the *Spectator* (1711–12), the latter in collaboration with Joseph Addison; both had an important influence on the manners, morals, and literature of the time. Steele also launched the short-lived periodical the *Guardian* (1713), to which Addison contributed.

Stein /staɪn/, Gertrude (1874–1946), American writer. From 1903 she lived mainly in Paris, where during the 1920s and 1930s her home became a focus for the avant-garde, including writers such as Ernest Hemingway and Ford Madox Ford and artists such as Matisse. In her writing, Stein developed an esoteric stream-of-consciousness style, whose hallmarks include use of repetition and lack of punctuation. Her best-known work is *The Autobiography of Alice B. Toklas* (1933), in which her long-standing American companion Alice B. Toklas (1877–1967) is made the ostensible author of her own memoir.

Steinbeck /'staɪnbek/, John (Ernst) (1902–68), American novelist. His work is noted for its sympathetic and realistic portrayal of the migrant agricultural workers of California, as in *Of Mice and Men* (1937) and *The Grapes of Wrath* (1939). His later novels include *East of Eden* (1952). Steinbeck was awarded the Nobel Prize for literature in 1962.

Steiner /'staɪnə(r)/, Rudolf (1861–1925), Austrian philosopher, founder of anthroposophy. He joined Annie Besant's theosophical movement in 1902, but ten years later broke away to found his own Anthroposophical Society. Steiner proposed that the spiritual development of humankind had been stunted by over-attention to the material world and that to reverse this process it was necessary to nurture the faculty of cognition. His society is noted for its contribution to child-centred education, and particularly for its Steiner schools for children with learning difficulties, operating in many parts of the Western world.

Steinway /'staɪnweɪ/, Henry (Engelhard) (born Heinrich Engelhard Steinweg) (1797–1871), German piano-builder, resident in the US from 1849. His name is used to designate pianos manufactured by the firm which he founded in New York in 1853.

Stella /'stelə/, Frank (Philip) (born 1936), American painter. In the late 1950s he reacted against the subjectivity of abstract expressionism and became an important figure in minimalism, painting a series of all-black paintings. He later experimented with shaped canvases and cut-out shapes in relief.

Steller /'stelə(r)/, Georg Wilhelm (1709–46), German naturalist and geographer. Working for a period as a physician with the Russian army, Steller became a research member of Vitus Bering's ill-fated second expedition to Kamchatka and Alaska. Following their shipwreck on Bering Island (1741) he made a large collection of specimens but had to abandon it; however, he later described many new birds and mammals, several of which (including the extinct giant sea cow) now bear his name. Steller later died of fever in Siberia at the age of 37.

Stendhal /'stɒndɑːl/ (pseudonym of Marie Henri Beyle) (1783–1842), French novelist. His two best-known novels are *Le Rouge et le noir* (1830), relating the rise and fall of a young man from the provinces in the France of the Restoration (1814), and *La Chartreuse de Parme* (1839), set in a small Italian court in the same period. Both are notable for their psychological realism and political analysis.

Steno /'stiːnəʊ/, Nicolaus (Danish name Niels Steensen) (1638–86), Danish anatomist and geologist. He proposed several ideas that are now regarded as fundamental to geology — that fossils are the petrified remains of living organisms, that many rocks arise from consolidation of sediments, and that such rocks occur in layers in the order in which they were laid down, thereby constituting a record of the geological history of the earth. Steno also recognized the constancy of crystal form in particular minerals. He later became a bishop.

Stephen /'stiːv(ə)n/ (*c.*1097–1154), grandson of William the Conqueror, king of England 1135–54. Stephen seized the throne of England from Matilda a few months after the death of her father Henry I. Having forced Matilda to flee the kingdom, Stephen was confronted with civil war following her invasion in 1139; although captured at Lincoln (1141) and temporarily deposed, he ultimately forced Matilda to withdraw from England in 1148. However, the year before he died Stephen was obliged to recognize Matilda's son, the future Henry II, as heir to the throne.

Stephen, St[1] (died *c*.35), Christian martyr. He was one of the original seven deacons in Jerusalem appointed by the Apostles. He incurred the hostility of the Jews and was charged with blasphemy before the Sanhedrin and stoned, so becoming the first Christian martyr. Saul (the future St Paul) was present at his execution. Feast day (in the Western Church) 26 December; (in the Eastern Church) 27 December.

Stephen, St[2] (*c*.977–1038), king and patron saint of Hungary, reigned 1000–38. The first king of Hungary, he united Pannonia and Dacia as one kingdom, and took steps to Christianize the country. Feast day, 2 September or (in Hungary) 20 August.

Stephenson /ˈstiːvəns(ə)n/, George (1781–1848), English engineer, the father of railways. He started as a colliery engineman, applied steam power to the haulage of coal wagons by cable, and built his first locomotive in 1814. He became engineer to the Stockton and Darlington Railway, and in 1825 drove the first train on it using a steam locomotive of his own design. George's son Robert (1803–59) assisted him in the building of engines and of the Liverpool to Manchester railway, for which they built the famous *Rocket* (1829) – the prototype for all future steam locomotives. Robert became famous also as a bridge designer, notably major bridges at Menai Strait and Conwy in Wales, Berwick and Newcastle in northern England, Montreal in Canada, and in Egypt.

Sterne /stɜːn/, Laurence (1713–68), Irish novelist. He worked as a clergyman in the north of England before publishing the first two volumes of his best-known work *The Life and Opinions of Tristram Shandy* in 1759. Seven subsequent volumes appeared between 1761 and 1767. Both praised for its humour and condemned for its indecency at the time, *Tristram Shandy* parodied the developing conventions of the novel form and used devices – including a distinctive fluid narrative – which anticipated many of the stylistic concerns of modernist and later writers. He suffered from tuberculosis and after 1762 spent much of his time in France and Italy, later writing *A Sentimental Journey Through France and Italy* (1768).

Stevens /ˈstiːv(ə)nz/, Wallace (1879–1955), American poet. He spent most of his working life as a lawyer for an insurance firm, writing poetry privately and mostly in isolation from the literary community, developing an original and colourful style. Collections of his work include *Harmonium* (1923), *Man with the Blue Guitar and Other Poems* (1937), and *Collected Poems* (1954), which won a Pulitzer Prize.

Stevenson /ˈstiːv(ə)ns(ə)n/, Robert Louis (Balfour) (1850–94), Scottish novelist, poet, and travel writer. He suffered from a chronic bronchial condition and spent much of his life abroad, notably in the South Seas. Stevenson made his name with the adventure story *Treasure Island* (1883). His other works include the novel *The Strange Case of Dr Jekyll and Mr Hyde* (1886) and a series of Scottish romances including *Kidnapped* (1886) and *The Master of Ballantrae* (1889). He is also known for *A Child's Garden of Verses*, a collection of poetry first published as *Penny Whistles* in 1885.

Stewart[1] /ˈstjuːət/, Jackie (born John Young Stewart) (born 1939), British motor-racing driver. He was three times world champion (1969; 1971; 1973).

Stewart[2] /ˈstjuːət/, James (Maitland) (1908–97), American actor. He made his screen début in 1935. Notable films include *The Philadelphia Story* (1940), which earned him an Oscar, Alfred Hitchcock's *Rear Window* (1954) and *Vertigo* (1958), and westerns such as *The Man from Laramie* (1955).

Stewart[3] /ˈstjuːət/, Rod(erick David) (born 1945), English rock singer and songwriter. A recognized figure of London's rhythm and blues community in the mid-1960s, Stewart began a solo recording career in 1969 while also singing with the band the Faces. In 1971 his single 'Maggie May' and album *Every Picture Tells a Story* topped the singles and album charts in both Britain and America. His later hits include 'Sailing' (1976) and 'Do You Think I'm Sexy?' (1978).

Stieglitz /ˈstiːɡlɪts/, Alfred (1864–1946), American photographer. He was important in his pioneering attempt to establish photography as a fine art in the US, which he achieved through his galleries and publications, as well as through his own work. Stieglitz gained an international reputation in the 1890s when he experimented with such innovations as night-time photography. He opened the first of three galleries in New York in 1905; known as '291', the gallery exhibited not only photographs but also modern paintings and sculpture, with work by Picasso, Matisse, and Rodin, as well as by contemporary

American painters such as Georgia O'Keeffe, whom Stieglitz married in 1924.

Stirling[1] /'stɜ:lɪŋ/, James (1692–1770), Scottish mathematician. He proved Newton's work on cubic curves, thus earning Newton's support. His main work, *Methodus Differentialis* (1730), was concerned with summation and interpolation. A formula named after him, giving the approximate value of the factorial of a large number, was actually first worked out by the French-born mathematician Abraham De Moivre (1667–1754).

Stirling[2] /'stɜ:lɪŋ/, Sir James (Frazer) (1926–92), Scottish architect. He came to prominence with brutalist designs such as that for the Engineering Department at Leicester University (1959–63). Later work is more playful and postmodern, for example the Neuestaatsgalerie in Stuttgart (1977), which is often regarded as his most accomplished work. Other designs include the controversial Number 1 Poultry, Mansion House Square, London (1985).

Stirling[3] /'stɜ:lɪŋ/, Robert (1790–1878), Scottish engineer and Presbyterian minister. In 1816 he was co-inventor (with his brother) of a type of external-combustion engine using heated air, and both the engine and the heat cycle that it uses are named after him. This engine achieved a modest success in the 1890s but development lapsed until 1938, and it has not achieved commercial success despite postwar efforts using pressurized helium.

Stockhausen /'stɒk,haʊz(ə)n/, Karlheinz (born 1928), German composer. After studying with Olivier Messiaen (1952) he co-founded the new electronic music studio of West German Radio, creating works such as *Gesang der Jünglinge* (1956), in which the human voice is combined with electronic sound. Later works include the serialist *Gruppen* (1955–7) for three orchestras, influenced by Anton Webern, and *Momente* (1962). With *Donnerstag* (1980), Stockhausen embarked on his *Licht* cycle of musical ceremonies, meant to be performed on each evening of a week; four further parts of the cycle had been completed by 1994.

Stoker /'stəʊkə(r)/, Abraham ('Bram') (1847–1912), Irish novelist and theatre manager. He was secretary and touring manager for the actor Henry Irving from 1878 to 1905, but is chiefly remembered as the author of the vampire story *Dracula* (1897).

Stokowski /stɒ'kɒfskɪ/, Leopold (1882–1977), British-born American conductor, of Polish descent. He is best known for arranging and conducting the music for Walt Disney's film *Fantasia* (1940), which sought to bring classical music to cinema audiences by means of cartoons.

Stone /stəʊn/, Oliver (born 1946), American film director, screenwriter, and producer. His adaptation of the novel *Midnight Express* (1978) for the screen won him his first Oscar. He became known for his political films indicting recent American history, such as *JFK* (1991), and especially those about the Vietnam War: examples are *Platoon* (1986) and *Born on the Fourth of July* (1989), for both of which he won an Oscar for best director.

Stopes /stəʊps/, Marie (Charlotte Carmichael) (1880–1958), Scottish birth-control campaigner. After establishing an academic reputation as a botanist, she published the best seller *Married Love* (1918), a frank treatment of sexuality within marriage. In 1921 she founded the Mothers' Clinic for Birth Control in Holloway, London, thus pioneering the establishment of birth-control clinics in Britain. Her study *Contraception: Its Theory, History, and Practice* (1923) was one of the first comprehensive works on the subject.

Stoppard /'stɒpɑ:d/, Sir Tom (born Thomas Straussler) (born 1937), British dramatist, born in Czechoslovakia. His best-known plays are comedies, which often deal with metaphysical and ethical questions and are characterized by verbal wit and the use of pastiche. His most famous play is *Rosencrantz and Guildenstern are Dead* (1966), based on the characters in *Hamlet*; other works include *Jumpers* (1972) and *The Real Thing* (1982).

Stowe /stəʊ/, Harriet (Elizabeth) Beecher (1811–96), American novelist. She won fame with her anti-slavery novel *Uncle Tom's Cabin* (1852), which was successfully serialized 1851–2, and strengthened the contemporary abolitionist cause with its descriptions of the sufferings caused by slavery. Other works include the controversial *Lady Byron Vindicated* (1870), which charged the poet Byron with incestuous relations with his half-sister.

Strabo /'streɪbəʊ/ (*c.*63 BC–AD *c.*23), historian and geographer of Greek descent. His only extant work, *Geographica*, in seventeen volumes, provides a detailed physical and

historical geography of the ancient world during the reign of Augustus.

Strachey /'streɪtʃɪ/, (Giles) Lytton (1880–1932), English biographer. A prominent member of the Bloomsbury Group, he achieved recognition with *Eminent Victorians* (1918), which attacked the literary Establishment through satirical biographies of Florence Nightingale, General Gordon, and others. His irreverence and independence were influential in the development of biography. Other works include a biography of Queen Victoria (1921) and *Elizabeth and Essex* (1928).

Stradivari /ˌstrædɪ'vɑːrɪ/, Antonio (c.1644–1737), Italian violin-maker. He devised the proportions of the modern violin, altering the bridge and reducing the depth of the body to produce a more powerful and rounded sound than earlier instruments. About 650 of his celebrated violins, violas, and violoncellos are still in existence.

Strasberg /'stræzbɜːg/, Lee (born Israel Strassberg) (1901–82), American actor, director, and drama teacher, born in Austria. As artistic director of the Actors' Studio in New York City (1948–82), he was the leading figure in the development of method acting in the US. Among his pupils were Marlon Brando, James Dean, Jane Fonda, and Dustin Hoffman.

Strauss[1] /straʊs/, Johann (known as Strauss the Elder) (1804–49), Austrian composer. He was a leading composer of waltzes from the 1830s, although probably his best-known work is the *Radetzky March* (1838).

Strauss[2] /straʊs/, Johann (known as Strauss the Younger) (1825–99), Austrian composer. The son of Strauss the Elder, he became known as 'the waltz king', composing many famous waltzes such as *The Blue Danube* (1867) and *Tales from the Vienna Woods* (1868). He is also noted for the operetta *Die Fledermaus* (1874).

Strauss[3] /straʊs/, Richard (1864–1949), German composer. From the mid-1880s he composed a succession of symphonic poems, including *Till Eulenspiegels Lustige Streiche* (1895) and *Also Sprach Zarathustra* (1896). His reputation grew as he turned to opera, exploring polytonality in *Salome* (1905) and *Elektra* (1905). The latter marked the beginning of his collaboration with the librettist Hugo von Hofmannsthal; together they produced such popular operas as *Der Rosenkavalier* (1911). Often regarded as

the last of the 19th-century romantic composers, Strauss retained his romanticism to the end of his long career, notably in *Four Last Songs* (1948) for soprano and orchestra.

Stravinsky /strə'vɪnskɪ/, Igor (Fyodorovich) (1882–1971), Russian-born composer. He made his name as a composer for Diaghilev's Ballets Russes, writing the music for the ballets *The Firebird* (1910) and *The Rite of Spring* (1913); both shocked Paris audiences with their irregular rhythms and frequent dissonances. Stravinsky later developed a neoclassical style, typified by the ballet *Pulcinella* (1920) and, ultimately, the opera *The Rake's Progress* (1948–51), based on William Hogarth's paintings. In the 1950s he experimented with serialism in such works as the cantata *Threni* (1957–8). Resident in the US from the outbreak of the Second World War, Stravinsky became an American citizen in 1945.

Streep /striːp/, Meryl (born Mary Louise Streep) (born 1949), American actress. After her screen début in 1977 she became a leading star in the 1980s. She won an Oscar for her part as a divorcee in *Kramer vs. Kramer* (1980). Her other films include *The French Lieutenant's Woman* (1981), *Sophie's Choice* (1982), for which she won a second Oscar, and *Out of Africa* (1986).

Streisand /'straɪs(ə)nd, -sænd/, Barbra (Joan) (born 1942), American singer, actress, and film director. She became a star in 1964 in the Broadway musical *Funny Girl*, winning an Oscar in 1968 for her performance in the film of the same name. She later played the lead in *A Star is Born* (1976), which she also produced; the film's song 'Evergreen', composed by Streisand, won an Oscar. She took other starring roles in films such as *Yentl* (1983), which she also produced and directed.

Strindberg /'strɪndbɜːg/, (Johan) August (1849–1912), Swedish dramatist and novelist. Although best known outside Scandinavia as a dramatist and precursor of expressionism in the theatre, Strindberg was also a leading figure in the naturalist movement in literature; his satire *The Red Room* (1879) is regarded as Sweden's first modern novel. His earlier plays, also naturalistic in style, depict a bitter power struggle between the sexes, notably in *The Father* (1887) and *Miss Julie* (1888). His later plays are typically tense, symbolic, psychic dramas; the trilogy *To Damascus* (1898–

1904) and, more particularly, *A Dream Play* (1902) introduced expressionist techniques and are of major importance for the development of modern drama.

Struve /'stru:və/, Otto (1897–1963), Russian-born American astronomer. He belonged to the fourth generation of a line of distinguished astronomers that began with the German-born Friedrich Georg Wilhelm Struve (1793–1864). Otto Struve was successively director of four observatories in the US, including the McDonald Observatory in Texas, which he was instrumental in founding. He was mainly interested in spectroscopic investigations into the composition, evolution, and rotation of stars, but his most important contribution was his discovery of the presence of ionized hydrogen in interstellar space (1938).

Stuart[1] /'stju:ət/, Charles Edward (known as 'the Young Pretender' or 'Bonnie Prince Charlie') (1720–88), pretender to the British throne, son of James Stuart. He led the Jacobite uprising of 1745–6, gaining the support of the Highlanders, with whom he invaded England and advanced as far as Derby. However, he was driven back to Scotland by the Duke of Cumberland and defeated at the Battle of Culloden (1746). He later died in exile in Rome.

Stuart[2] /'stju:ət/, James (Francis Edward) (known as 'the Old Pretender') (1688–1766), pretender to the British throne, son of James II (James VII of Scotland). He arrived in Scotland too late to alter the outcome of the 1715 Jacobite uprising and left the leadership of the 1745–6 uprising to his son Charles Edward Stuart.

Stuart[3] /'stju:ət/, John McDouall (1815–66), Scottish explorer. He was a member of Charles Sturt's third expedition to Australia (1844–6), and subsequently crossed Australia from south to north and back again, at his sixth attempt (1860–2).

Stuart[4] /'stju:ət/, Mary, see MARY, QUEEN OF SCOTS.

Stubbs[1] /stʌbz/, George (1724–1806), English painter and engraver. Known for the anatomical accuracy of his depictions of animals, he established his reputation with the book *Anatomy of the Horse* (1766), illustrated with his own engravings. He is particularly noted for his sporting scenes and paintings of horses and lions, for example, the *Mares and Foals in a Landscape* series (c.1760–70).

Stubbs[2] /stʌbz/, William (1825–1901), English historian and ecclesiastic. He wrote the influential *Constitutional History of England* (three volumes 1874–8), which charted the history of English institutions from the Germanic invasion to 1485. He was also bishop of Chester (1884–8) and of Oxford (1888–1901).

Sturt /stɜːt/, Charles (1795–1869), English explorer. He led three expeditions into the Australian interior, becoming the first European to discover the Darling River (1828) and the source of the Murray (1830). He wrote about his travels in *Two Expeditions into the Interior of Southern Australia, 1828–31* (1833). Sturt went blind during his third expedition into central Australia (1844–6) and later returned to England.

Suckling /'sʌklɪŋ/, Sir John (1609–42), English poet, dramatist, and Royalist leader. He lived at court from 1632 and was a leader of the Cavaliers during the English Civil War. His poems include 'Ballad upon a Wedding', published in the posthumous collection *Fragmenta Aurea* (1646). According to John Aubrey, Suckling invented the game of cribbage.

Sucre /'su:kreɪ/, Antonio José de (1795–1830), Venezuelan revolutionary and statesman, President of Bolivia 1826–8. Sucre served as Simón Bolívar's Chief of Staff, liberating Ecuador (1822), Peru (1824), and Bolivia (1825) from the Spanish. The first President of Bolivia, Sucre resigned following a Peruvian invasion in 1828; he was later assassinated. The Bolivian judicial capital Sucre is named after him.

Suetonius /swiːˈtəʊnɪəs/ (full name Gaius Suetonius Tranquillus) (AD c.69–c.150), Roman biographer and historian. His surviving works include *Lives of the Caesars*, covering Julius Caesar and the Roman emperors who followed him, up to Domitian.

Sukarno /suːˈkɑːnəʊ/, Achmad (1901–70), Indonesian statesman, President 1945–67. One of the founders of the Indonesian National Party (1927), he was Indonesian leader during the Japanese occupation (1942–5) and led the struggle for independence, which was formally granted by the Netherlands in 1949. From the mid-1950s his dictatorial tendencies aroused opposition. He was alleged to have taken part in the abortive Communist coup of 1965, after which he steadily lost power to the army, being finally ousted two years later.

Suleiman I /'suːlɪmən, ˌsuːleɪ'mɑːn/ (also **Soliman** /'sɒlɪmən/ or **Solyman**) (c.1494–1566), sultan of the Ottoman Empire 1520–66. The Ottoman Empire reached its fullest extent under his rule; his conquests included Belgrade (1521), Rhodes (1522), and Tripoli (1551), in addition to those in Iraq (1534) and Hungary (1562). This and the cultural achievements of the time earned him the nickname in Europe of 'Suleiman the Magnificent'. He was also a noted administrator, known to his subjects as 'Suleiman the Lawgiver'.

Sulla /'sʌlə/ (full name Lucius Cornelius Sulla Felix) (138–78 BC), Roman general and politician. Having come to prominence as a result of military successes in Africa, Sulla became involved in a power struggle with Marius, and in 88 marched on Rome. After a victorious campaign against Mithridates VI Sulla invaded Italy in 83, ruthlessly suppressing his opponents. He was elected dictator in 82, after which he implemented constitutional reforms in favour of the Senate, resigning in 79.

Sullivan /'sʌlɪv(ə)n/, Sir Arthur (Seymour) (1842–1900), English composer. Although he composed much 'serious' music, his fame rests on the fourteen light operas which he wrote in collaboration with the librettist W. S. Gilbert (see GILBERT³), many for Richard D'Oyly Carte's company at the Savoy Theatre.

Sun King the nickname of Louis XIV of France (see LOUIS¹).

Sun Yat-sen /ˌsʊn jæt'sen/ (also **Sun Yixian** /ˌsʊn jiːʃiː'æn/) (1866–1925), Chinese Kuomintang statesman, provisional President of the Republic of China 1911–12 and President of the Southern Chinese Republic 1923–5. Generally regarded in the West as the father of the modern Chinese state, he spent the period 1895–1911 in exile after an abortive attempt to overthrow the Manchus. During this time he issued an early version of his influential 'Three Principles of the People' (nationalism, democracy, and the people's livelihood) and set up a revolutionary society which became the nucleus of the Kuomintang. He returned to China to play a vital part in the revolution of 1911 in which the Manchu dynasty was overthrown. After being elected provisional President, Sun Yat-sen resigned in 1912 in response to opposition from conservative members of the government and established a secessionist government at

Guangzhou. He reorganized the Kuomintang along the lines of the Soviet Communist Party and began a period of uneasy cooperation with the Chinese Communists before dying in office.

Surtees /'sɜːtiːz/, Robert Smith (1805–64), English journalist and novelist. He is remembered for his comic sketches of Mr Jorrocks, the sporting Cockney grocer, collected in *Jorrocks's Jaunts and Jollities* (1838); its style, format, and illustrations by 'Phiz' were to influence Dickens's *Pickwick Papers*. Other famous caricatures, all set against a background of English fox-hunting society, include Mr Soapy Sponge in *Mr Sponge's Sporting Tour* (1849; 1853).

Sutherland¹ /'sʌðələnd/, Graham (Vivian) (1903–80), English painter. During the Second World War he was an official war artist, who concentrated on depicting the devastation caused by bombing. Among his portraits are those of Somerset Maugham (1949) and Sir Winston Churchill (1954); the latter was considered unflattering and was destroyed by Churchill's family. His postwar work included the tapestry *Christ in Majesty* (1962), designed for the rebuilt Coventry cathedral.

Sutherland² /'sʌðələnd/, Dame Joan (born 1926), Australian operatic soprano. Noted for her dramatic coloratura roles, she is best known for her performance of the title role in Donizetti's *Lucia di Lammermoor* in 1959.

Suyin /suː'jɪn/, Han (pseudonym of Elizabeth Comber) (born 1917), Chinese-born British writer and doctor. Born to a Chinese father and Belgian mother, she came to England in 1939 and trained as a doctor. Her autobiographical novel *A Many Splendoured Thing* (1952) brought her to public attention. She has written an acclaimed five-volume series of autobiography and Chinese history, the first volume of which was *The Crippled Tree* (1965).

Suzman /'sʊzmən/, Helen (born 1917), South African politician, of Lithuanian Jewish descent. In 1953 she became an MP for the opposition United Party, before becoming one of the founders of the anti-apartheid Progressive Party in 1959. In the elections two years later she was the only Progressive candidate to be returned to parliament, and from this time until 1974 she was the sole MP opposed to apartheid. Suzman was awarded the UN Human

Rights Award in 1978; she retired in 1989.

Sven see SWEYN I.

Swammerdam /'swɑ:məˌdæm/, Jan (1637–80), Dutch naturalist and microscopist. Qualified in medicine, he preferred to commit himself to research. He worked extensively on insects, describing their anatomy and life history and classifying them into four groups. A pioneer in the use of lenses, Swammerdam was the first to observe red blood cells. He also provided an elegant demonstration of the fact that muscles do not change in volume during motion.

Swan /swɒn/, Sir Joseph Wilson (1828–1914), English physicist and chemist. He was a pioneer of electric lighting, devising in 1860 an electric light bulb consisting of a carbon filament inside a glass bulb; he worked for nearly twenty years to perfect it. In 1883 he formed a partnership with Thomas Edison to manufacture the bulbs. Swan also devised a dry photographic plate, and bromide paper for the printing of negatives.

Swanson /'swɒns(ə)n/, Gloria (born Gloria May Josephine Svensson) (1899–1983), American actress. She was the most highly paid star of silent films in the 1920s; with her own production company, Swanson Productions, she made such films as *Sadie Thompson* (1928) and *Queen Kelly* (1928). Swanson is perhaps now chiefly known for her performance as the fading movie star Norma Desmond in *Sunset Boulevard* (1950).

Swedenborg /'swi:d(ə)nˌbɔ:g/, Emanuel (1688–1772), Swedish scientist, philosopher, and mystic. As a scientist he concerned himself with many subjects, anticipating in his speculative and inventive work later developments such as the nebular theory, crystallography, and flying machines. He became increasingly concerned to show by scientific means the spiritual structure of the universe. However, a series of mystical experiences (1743–5) prompted him to devote the rest of his life to expounding his spiritual beliefs. His doctrines, which blended Christianity with elements of both pantheism and theosophy, were taken up by a group of followers, who founded the New Jerusalem Church in 1787.

Sweyn I /swem/ (also **Sven** /sven/; known as Sweyn Forkbeard) (died 1014), king of Denmark *c.*985–1014. From 1003 he launched a series of attacks on England, finally driving the English king Ethelred the Unready to flee to Normandy at the end of 1013. Sweyn then became king of England until his death five weeks later. His son Canute was later king of England, Denmark, and Norway.

Swift /swɪft/, Jonathan (known as Dean Swift) (1667–1745), Irish satirist, poet, and Anglican cleric. He was born in Dublin, a cousin of John Dryden, and divided his life between London and Ireland. His *Journal to Stella* (1710–13) gives a vivid account of life in London, where he was close to Tory ministers. In 1713 he was made Dean of St Patrick's in Dublin, where he wrote his greatest work, *Gulliver's Travels* (1726), a satire on human society and institutions in the form of a fantastic tale of travels in imaginary lands. He also involved himself in Irish affairs and wrote many political pamphlets, such as *A Modest Proposal* (1729), ironically urging that the children of the poor should be fattened to feed the rich. His poems include the *Verses on the Death of Dr Swift* (1739), in which he reviews his life with pathos and humour.

Swinburne /'swɪnbɜ:n/, Algernon Charles (1837–1909), English poet and critic. Associated with Dante Gabriel Rossetti and the Pre-Raphaelites, he came to fame with *Atalanta in Calydon* (1865), a drama in classical Greek form which was praised for its metrical finesse. In *Songs Before Sunrise* (1871), Swinburne expressed his hatred of authority and his support for Mazzini's struggle for Italian independence. As a critic he contributed to the revival of contemporary interest in Elizabethan and Jacobean drama and produced influential studies of William Blake and the Brontës.

Swithin, St /'swɪðɪn/ (also **Swithun** /-ðən/) (died 862), English ecclesiastic. He was chaplain to Egbert, the king of Wessex, and bishop of Winchester from 852. The tradition that if it rains on St Swithin's day it will do so for the next forty days may have its origin in the heavy rain said to have occurred when his relics were to be transferred to a shrine in Winchester cathedral. Feast day, 15 July.

Sydenham /'sɪd(ə)nəm/, Thomas (*c.*1624–89), English physician. He was known as 'the English Hippocrates', because of his

contemporary reputation as a physician and his scepticism towards theoretical medicine. He emphasized the healing power of nature, made a study of epidemics, wrote a treatise on gout (from which he suffered), and explained the nature of the type of chorea that is named after him (one found especially in children as one of the manifestations of rheumatic fever).

Symons /'saɪmənz/, Julian (Gustave) (born 1912), English writer of detective fiction. He is an important exponent of psychological crime fiction whose many novels include *The Colour of Murder* (1957) and *The Progress of a Crime* (1960).

Synge /sɪŋ/, (Edmund) J(ohn) M(illington) (1871–1909), Irish dramatist. Between 1898 and 1902 he lived with the peasant community on the Aran Islands, an experience that inspired his plays *Riders to the Sea* (1905) and *The Playboy of the Western World* (1907). The latter caused outrage and riots at the Abbey Theatre, Dublin, with its explicit language and its implication that Irish peasants would condone a brutal murder.

Szent-Györgyi /sent'dʒɔːdʒɪ/, Albert von (1893–1986), American biochemist, born in Hungary. After working in various countries Szent-Györgyi returned to Hungary in 1930 and then emigrated to the US in 1947. He isolated a substance from both adrenal glands and plant material that became known as ascorbic acid, which was later identified with vitamin C. He later worked on the biochemistry of muscle, in particular the mechanisms of cellular respiration and fibre contraction. Szent-Györgyi was awarded a Nobel Prize in 1937.

Szilard /'sɪlɑːd/, Leo (1898–1964), Hungarian-born American physicist and molecular biologist. Working in Germany before the Second World War, he developed an electromagnetic pump that is now used for refrigerants in nuclear reactors. He fled the Nazis, first to Britain, where he suggested the idea of nuclear chain reactions, and then to the US, where he became a central figure in the Manhattan Project to develop the atom bomb. After the war Szilard turned to experimental and theoretical studies in molecular biology and biochemistry.

T

Tacitus /'tæsɪtəs/ (full name Publius, or Gaius, Cornelius Tacitus) (AD c.56–c.120), Roman historian. His major works on the history of the Roman Empire, only partially preserved, are the *Annals* (covering the years 14–68) and the *Histories* (69–96). They are written in an elevated and concise style, pervaded by a deep pessimism about the course of Roman history since the end of the Republic.

Taft /tæft/, William Howard (1857–1930), American Republican statesman, 27th President of the US 1909–13. His presidency is remembered for its dollar diplomacy in foreign affairs and for its tariff laws, which were criticized as being too favourable to big business. Taft later served as Chief Justice of the Supreme Court (1921–30).

Tagore /tə'gɔː(r)/, Rabindranath (1861–1941), Indian writer and philosopher. His poetry pioneered the use of colloquial Bengali instead of the archaic literary idiom then approved for verse; his own translations established his reputation in the West, and he won the Nobel Prize for literature in 1913 for *Gitanjali* (1912), a set of poems modelled on medieval Indian devotional lyrics. He also wrote philosophical plays, novels such as *Gora* (1929), and short fiction which often commented on Indian national and social concerns. He was knighted in 1915, an honour which he renounced after the Amritsar massacre (1919).

Tailleferre /taɪ'feə(r)/, Germaine (1892–1983), French composer and pianist. She was a pupil of Ravel and later became a member of the group Les Six. Her works include concertos for unusual combinations of instruments, including one for baritone, piano, and orchestra.

Talbot /'tɔːlbət, 'tɒl-/, (William Henry) Fox (1800–77), English pioneer of photography. Working at the family seat of Lacock Abbey in Wiltshire, he produced the first photograph on paper in 1835. Five years later he discovered a process for producing a negative from which multiple positive prints could be made, though the independently developed daguerreotype proved to be superior. Apart from patenting a number of other photographic processes and publishing two of the earliest books illustrated with photographs, he also made contributions to mathematics and deciphered cuneiform scripts.

Talleyrand /'tælɪˌrænd, French talɛrɑ̃/ (full surname Talleyrand-Périgord), Charles Maurice de (1754–1838), French statesman. Foreign Minister under the Directory (the revolutionary government of 1795–9) from 1797, he was involved in the coup that brought Napoleon to power, and held the same position under the new leader (1799–1807); he then resigned office and engaged in secret negotiations to have Napoleon deposed. Talleyrand became head of the new government after the fall of Napoleon (1814) and recalled Louis XVIII to the throne. He was later instrumental in the overthrow of Charles X and the accession of Louis Philippe (1830).

Tallis /'tælɪs/, Thomas (c.1505–85), English composer. Organist of the Chapel Royal jointly with William Byrd, he served under Henry VIII, Edward VI, Mary, and Elizabeth I. In 1575 he and Byrd were given a twenty-one-year monopoly in printing music, and in that year published *Cantiones Sacrae*, a collection of thirty-four of their motets. Tallis is known particularly for his church music, especially the forty-part motet *Spem in Alium*.

Tambo /'tæmbəʊ/, Oliver (1917–93), South African politician. He joined the African National Congress in 1944, and when the organization was banned by the South African government (1960) he left the country in order to organize activities elsewhere; he returned in 1990 when the ban on the ANC was lifted. During Nelson Mandela's long imprisonment he became acting president of the ANC (1967) and president (1977), a position he held until 1991, when he gave it up in favour of the recently released Mandela. Tambo remained as ANC national chairman until his death.

Tamerlane /'tæməˌleɪn/ (also **Tamburlaine** /'tæmbə-/) (born Timur Lenk, 'lame Timur') (1336–1405), Mongol ruler of Samarkand 1369–1405. Leading a force of Mongols and

Turks, between about 1364 and 1405 he conquered a large area including Persia, northern India, and Syria and established his capital at Samarkand; he defeated the Ottomans near Ankara in 1402, but died during an invasion of China. He was an ancestor of the Mogul dynasty in India.

Tange /'tæŋgeɪ/, Kenzo (born 1913), Japanese architect. His work reflects the influence of Le Corbusier and is characterized by the use of modern materials, while retaining a feeling for traditional Japanese architecture. During the 1950s he built a number of civic buildings in Brutalist style, including the Peace Centre at Hiroshima (1955). Later buildings, such as the National Gymnasium in Tokyo (built for the 1964 Olympics), make use of dynamic, sweeping curves.

Tannhäuser /'tæn.hɔɪzə(r)/, (c.1200–c.1270), German poet. In reality a Minnesinger (an aristocratic poet-musician who performed songs of courtly love), he became a legendary figure as a knight who visited Venus' grotto and spent seven years in debauchery, then repented and sought absolution from the pope; he is the subject of Wagner's opera *Tannhäuser* (1845). The real Tannhäuser's surviving works include lyrics and love poetry.

Tansen /'tænsen/ (c.1500–89), Indian musician and singer. He is regarded as the leading exponent of northern Indian classical music. A native of Gwalior, he became an honoured member of the court of Akbar the Great, and was noted both for his skill as an instrumentalist and as a singer. Many legends arose about his life and musical achievements.

Tarantino /ˌtærən'tiːnəʊ/, Quentin (Jerome) (born 1963), American film director, screenwriter, and actor. Tarantino came to sudden prominence with the gangster thriller *Reservoir Dogs* (1992), which he followed in 1994 with *Pulp Fiction*. Both aroused controversy for their amorality and violence, but also won much admiration for their wit, style, and structure. Tarantino also wrote the script for the similarly violent film *True Romance* (1993).

Tarkovsky /tɑːˈkɒfskɪ/, Andrei (Arsenevich) (1932–86), Russian film director. He rejected the constraints of socialist realism in the post-Stalin era in favour of a poetic, impressionistic, and personal style that brought his works criticism from the So-

viet authorities. He won critical acclaim with *Ivan's Childhood* (1962), *Andrei Rublev* (1966), *Solaris* (1972), and *Stalker* (1979). His final film, *The Sacrifice* (1986), won the special grand prize at Cannes.

Tarquinius /tɑːˈkwɪnɪəs/ (anglicized name Tarquin) the name of two semi-legendary Etruscan kings of ancient Rome:
Tarquinius Priscus (full name Lucius Tarquinius Priscus), reigned c.616–c.578 BC. According to tradition, he was murdered by the sons of the previous king.
Tarquinius Superbus (full name Lucius Tarquinius Superbus; known as Tarquin the Proud), reigned c.534–c.510 BC. Traditionally, he was the son or grandson of Tarquinius Priscus and the seventh and last king of Rome. His reign was noted for its cruelty, and he was ultimately expelled from the city after the rape of a woman called Lucretia by his son; following his expulsion the Republic was founded. He was later engaged in a number of unsuccessful attacks on Rome, assisted by Lars Porsenna.

Tasman /'tæzmən/, Abel (Janszoon) (1603–c.1659), Dutch navigator. In 1642 he was sent by Anthony van Diemen (1593–1645, the Governor-General of the Dutch East Indies) to explore Australian waters; that year he reached Tasmania (which he named Van Diemen's Land) and New Zealand, and in 1643 arrived at Tonga and Fiji. On a second voyage in 1644 he also reached the Gulf of Carpentaria on the north coast of Australia.

Tate /teɪt/, Nahum (1652–1715), Irish dramatist and poet, resident in London from the 1670s. He wrote a number of plays, chiefly adaptations from earlier writers; he is especially known for his version of Shakespeare's *King Lear*, in which he substituted a happy ending. He also wrote the libretto for Purcell's *Dido and Aeneas* (1689) and (with John Dryden) the second part of *Absalom and Achitophel* (1682). He was appointed Poet Laureate in 1692.

Tati /'tætɪ/ Jacques (born Jacques Tatischeff) (1908–82), French film director and actor. Although he made only five full-length films, he became internationally known as a comic actor with his performances as Monsieur Hulot, a character which he introduced in his second film *Monsieur Hulot's Holiday* (1953). Subsequent films fea-

turing the character include the Oscar-winning *Mon oncle* (1958).

Tatum /'teɪtəm/, Arthur ('Art') (1910–56), American jazz pianist. He was born with cataracts in both eyes and as a result was almost completely blind throughout his life. He first became famous in the 1930s as a musician of great technical accomplishment; he performed chiefly in a trio with bass and guitar or as a soloist.

Taylor[1] /'teɪlə(r)/, Elizabeth (born 1932), American actress, born in England. She began her career as a child star in films such as *National Velvet* (1944). She went on to star in many films, including *Cat on a Hot Tin Roof* (1958), *Who's Afraid of Virginia Woolf?* (1966), for which she won an Oscar, and *The Mirror Crack'd* (1980). She has been married eight times, including twice to the actor Richard Burton, with whom she starred in a number of films, notably *Cleopatra* (1963).

Taylor[2] /'teɪlə(r)/, Jeremy (1613–67), English Anglican churchman and writer. He was chaplain to Charles I during the English Civil War and lived chiefly in Wales until the Restoration, when he was appointed bishop of Down and Connor (1660). Although a celebrated preacher in his day, he is now remembered chiefly for his devotional writings, especially *The Rule and Exercises of Holy Living* (1650) and *The Rule and Exercises of Holy Dying* (1651).

Taylor[3] /'teɪlə(r)/, Zachary (1784–1850), American Whig statesman, 12th President of the US 1849–50. He became a national hero after his victories in the war with Mexico (1846–8). As President, he came into conflict with Congress over his desire to admit California to the Union as a free state (without slavery). He died in office before the problem could be resolved.

Tchaikovsky /tʃaɪ'kɒfskɪ/, Pyotr (Ilich) (1840–93), Russian composer. He is especially known as a composer of the ballets *Swan Lake* (1877), *Sleeping Beauty* (1890), and *The Nutcracker* (1892), the First Piano Concerto (1875), and the overture *1812* (1880); other notable works include the operas *Eugene Onegin* (1879) and *The Queen of Spades* (1890). His music is characterized by melodiousness, depth of expression, and, especially in his later symphonies (including his sixth symphony, the 'Pathétique', 1893), melancholy. His death was officially

attributed to cholera, but there is now a theory that he took poison because of a potential scandal arising from an alleged homosexual relationship with a member of the royal family.

Teilhard de Chardin /ˌteɪɑː də 'ʃɑːdæn/, Pierre (1881–1955), French Jesuit philosopher and palaeontologist. He is best known for his theory, blending science and Christianity, that man is evolving mentally and socially towards a perfect spiritual state. His views were held to be unorthodox by the Roman Catholic Church and his major works (such as *The Phenomenon of Man*, 1955) were published posthumously.

Te Kanawa /te 'kɑːnəwə/, Dame Kiri (Janette) (born 1944), New Zealand operatic soprano, resident in Britain since 1966. She made her début in London in 1970 and since then has sung in the world's leading opera houses, especially in works by Mozart, Richard Strauss, and Verdi.

Telemann /'teɪləˌmæn/, Georg Philipp (1681–1767), German composer and organist. His prolific output includes 600 overtures, 44 Passions, 12 complete services, and 40 operas; his work reflects a variety of influences, particularly French composers such as Lully. In his lifetime his reputation was far greater than that of his friend and contemporary J. S. Bach.

Telford /'telfəd/, Thomas (1757–1834), Scottish civil engineer. He built hundreds of miles of roads, especially in Scotland, more than a thousand bridges, and a number of canals. Among his most important achievements are the London to Holyhead road, including the suspension bridge crossing the Menai Strait (1819–26), the Caledonian Canal across Scotland (opened 1822), and the Göta Canal in Sweden. He was the first president of the Institution of Civil Engineers (founded 1818).

Teller /'telə(r)/, Edward (born 1908), Hungarian-born American physicist. After moving to America in the 1930s he worked on the first atomic reactor, later working on the first atom bombs at Los Alamos. Teller studied the feasibility of producing a fusion bomb, and work under his guidance after the Second World War led to the detonation of the first hydrogen bomb in 1952. His own studies on fusion were mainly theoretical and later concerned with its peaceful use, though he was a

forceful advocate of the nuclear deterrent.

Tempest /'tempɪst/, Dame Marie (born Mary Susan Etherington) (1864–1942), English actress. Though trained as a singer she made her name in comedy, becoming noted for her playing of elegant middle-aged women; the role of Judith Bliss in *Hay Fever* (1925) was created for her by Noel Coward.

Temple /'temp(ə)l/, Shirley (latterly Shirley Temple Black) (born 1928), American child star. In the 1930s she appeared in a succession of films, often adapted from children's classics (such as *Rebecca of Sunnybrook Farm*, 1938). She later became active in Republican politics, represented the US at the United Nations, and served as ambassador in various countries.

Teng Hsiao-p'ing see DENG XIAOPING.

Teniers /'tenɪəz/, David (known as David Teniers the Younger) (1610–90), Flemish painter. The son of the painter David Teniers the Elder (1582–1649), he worked chiefly in Antwerp and Brussels, and from 1651 was court painter to successive regents of the Netherlands. His many works include peasant genre scenes in the style of Brouwer, religious subjects, landscapes, and portraits.

Tenniel /'tenɪəl/, Sir John (1820–1914), English illustrator and cartoonist. He is known chiefly for his illustrations for Lewis Carroll's *Alice's Adventures in Wonderland* (1865) and *Through the Looking Glass* (1871). He also worked as a cartoonist for the magazine *Punch* between 1851 and 1901.

Tennyson /'tenɪs(ə)n/, Alfred, 1st Baron Tennyson of Aldworth and Freshwater (1809–92), English poet. His first poems, published in the early 1830s, include 'Mariana', 'The Lotos-Eaters', and 'The Lady of Shalott'; a later collection (1842) included 'Morte d'Arthur', the germ of *Idylls of the King* (1859). His reputation was established by *In Memoriam*, a long poem concerned with immortality, change, and evolution, written in memory of his friend Arthur Hallam (1811–33); although begun in about 1833, it was not published until 1850. The same year he was made Poet Laureate; thereafter he enjoyed considerable celebrity and was one of the most popular poets of his day, publishing 'The Charge of the Light Brigade' in 1854 and *Maud* in 1855. His later works include the

collection *Tiresias and Other Poems* (1885) and several dramas.

Tenzing Norgay /ˌtensɪŋ 'nɔːgeɪ/ (1914–86), Sherpa mountaineer. In 1953, as members of the British Expedition, he and Sir Edmund Hillary were the first to reach the summit of Mount Everest.

Terence /'terəns/ (Latin name Publius Terentius Afer) (*c*.190–159 BC), Roman comic dramatist. His six surviving comedies are based on the Greek New Comedy; set in Athens, they use the same stock characters as are found in Plautus, but are marked by a more realistic treatment of character and language, and a greater consistency of plot. Terence's work had an influence on the development of Renaissance and Restoration comedy.

Teresa, Mother /tə'reɪzə, -'riːzə/ (also **Theresa**) (born Agnes Gonxha Bojaxhiu) (1910–97), Roman Catholic nun and missionary, born in what is now Macedonia of Albanian parentage. In 1928 she went to India, where she devoted herself to helping the destitute. In 1948 she became an Indian citizen and founded the Order of Missionaries of Charity, which became noted for its work among the poor and the dying in Calcutta. Her organization now operates in many other parts of the world. Mother Teresa was awarded the Nobel Peace Prize in 1979.

Teresa of Ávila, St /'ævɪlə/ (1515–82), Spanish Carmelite nun and mystic. She combined vigorous activity as a reformer with mysticism and religious contemplation. Seeking to return the Carmelite Order to its original discipline and observances, she instituted the 'discalced' reform movement, establishing the first of a number of convents in 1562 and encouraging St John of the Cross to found a similar monastic order. Her spiritual writings include *The Way of Perfection* (1583) and *The Interior Castle* (1588). Feast day, 15 October.

Teresa of Lisieux, St /liː'zjɜː/ (also **Thérèse** /te'rez/) (born Marie-Françoise Thérèse Martin) (1873–97), French Carmelite nun. After her death from tuberculosis her cult grew through the publication of her autobiography *L'Histoire d'une âme* (1898), teaching that sanctity can be attained through continual renunciation in small matters, and not only through extreme self-mortification. Feast day, 3 October.

Tereshkova /ˌterɪʃˈkəʊvə/, Valentina (Vladimirovna) (born 1937), Russian cosmonaut. In June 1963 she became the first woman in space; her spacecraft returned to earth after three days in orbit.

Terry /ˈterɪ/, Dame (Alice) Ellen (1847–1928), English actress. She was already well known when in 1878 Henry Irving engaged her as his leading lady at the Lyceum Theatre in London. For the next twenty-four years she played in many of his Shakespearian productions, notably in the roles of Desdemona, Portia, and Beatrice. She also acted in plays by George Bernard Shaw, with whom she conducted a long correspondence; the part of Lady Cicely Waynflete in *Captain Brassbound's Conversion* (1905) was among a number of roles Shaw created for her. She was married to the painter George Frederick Watts from 1864 to 1877.

Tertullian /tɜːˈtʌlɪən/ (Latin name Quintus Septimius Florens Tertullianus) (c.160–c.240), early Christian theologian. Born in Carthage after the Roman conquest, he converted to Christianity c.195. His writings (in Latin) include Christian apologetics and attacks on pagan idolatry and Gnosticism. He later joined the millenarian heretics the Montanists, urging asceticism and venerating martyrs.

Tesla /ˈteslə/, Nikola (1856–1943), American electrical engineer and inventor, born in what is now Croatia of Serbian descent. He emigrated to the US in 1884 and worked briefly on motors and direct-current generators with Thomas Edison before joining the Westinghouse company, where he developed the first alternating-current induction motor (1888) and made contributions to long-distance electrical power transmission. Tesla also studied high-frequency current, developing several forms of oscillators and the tesla coil, and developed a wireless guidance system for ships. Although his inventions revolutionized the electrical industry, he died in poverty.

Thackeray /ˈθækərɪ/, William Makepeace (1811–63), British novelist, born in Calcutta. He worked in London as a journalist and illustrator after leaving Cambridge University without a degree. All of his novels originally appeared in serial form; he established his reputation with *Vanity Fair* (1847–8), a vivid portrayal of early 19th-century society, satirizing upper-middle class pretensions through its central character Becky Sharp. Later novels include *Pendennis* (1848–50), *The History of Henry Esmond* (1852), and *The Virginians* (1857–9). In 1860 Thackeray became the first editor of the *Cornhill Magazine*, in which much of his later work was published.

Thaddaeus /ˈθædɪəs/ an apostle named in St Matthew's Gospel, traditionally identified with St Jude.

Thales /ˈθeɪliːz/ (c.624–c.545 BC), Greek philosopher, mathematician, and astronomer, of Miletus. He was one of the Seven Sages listed by Plato and was held by Aristotle to be the founder of physical science; he is also credited with founding geometry. He proposed that water was the primary substance from which all things were derived, and represented the earth as floating on an underlying ocean; his cosmology had Egyptian and Semitic affinities.

Thatcher /ˈθætʃə(r)/, Margaret (Hilda), Baroness Thatcher of Kesteven (born 1925), British Conservative stateswoman, Prime Minister 1979–90. She became Conservative Party leader in 1975 and in 1979 was elected the country's first woman Prime Minister; she went on to become the longest-serving British Prime Minister of the 20th century. Her period in office was marked by an emphasis on monetarist policies and free enterprise, privatization of nationalized industries, and legislation to restrict the powers of trade unions. In international affairs she was a strong supporter of the policies of President Reagan. She was well known for determination and resolve (she had been dubbed 'the Iron Lady' as early as 1976), especially in her handling of the Falklands War of 1982. She resigned after a leadership challenge and was created a life peer in 1992.

Themistocles /θɪˈmɪstəˌkliːz/ (c.528–462 BC) Athenian statesman. He was instrumental in building up the Athenian fleet, which under his command defeated the Persian fleet at Salamis in 480. In the following years he lost influence, was ostracized in 470, and eventually fled to the Persians in Asia Minor, where he died.

Theocritus /θɪˈɒkrɪtəs/ (c.310–c.250 BC), Greek poet, born in Sicily. Little is known of his life but he is thought to have lived on the island of Kos and in Alexandria as well as Sicily. He is chiefly known for his bucolic idylls, hexameter poems presenting the song-contests and love-songs of imaginary shepherds. These poems were the model

for Virgil's *Eclogues* and for subsequent pastoral poetry.

Theodora /θɪəˈdɔːrə/ (*c*.500–48), Byzantine empress, wife of Justinian. She is reputed (according to Procopius) to have led a dissolute life in her early years. She later became noted for her intellect and learning and, as Justinian's closest adviser, exercised a considerable influence on political affairs and the theological questions of the time.

Theodorakis /ˌθɪədəˈrɑːkɪs/, Mikis (born 1925), Greek composer. His prolific output includes the ballet *Antigone* (1958) and the well-known score for the film *Zorba the Greek* (1965). In 1964 he was elected as a member of the Greek Parliament, but in 1967 was imprisoned by the new military government for his left-wing political activities. He was released in 1970 after worldwide protests and re-elected to Parliament in 1981. His later work includes the opera *Kostas Kariotakis* (1985).

Theodoric /θɪˈɒdərɪk/ (known as Theodoric the Great) (*c*.454–526), king of the Ostrogoths 471–526. He invaded Italy in 488 and completed its conquest in 493, establishing a kingdom with the capital at Ravenna. At its greatest extent his empire included not only the Italian mainland, but Sicily, Dalmatia, and parts of Germany.

Theodosius I /θɪəˈdəʊsɪəs/ (known as Theodosius the Great; full name Flavius Theodosius) (*c*.346–95), Roman emperor 379–95. In 379 he was proclaimed co-emperor by the emperor Gratian (359–83) and took control of the eastern Empire. During his reign he brought an end to war with the Visigoths by a treaty in 382. He later defeated two usurpers of the western throne, on which he installed his son in 393. A pious Christian and rigid upholder of the Nicene Creed (a formal statement of Christian belief), in 391 he banned all forms of pagan worship, probably under the influence of St Ambrose.

Theophrastus /θɪəˈfræstəs/ (*c*.370–*c*.287 BC), Greek philosopher and scientist. He was the pupil and successor of Aristotle, whose method and researches he continued, with a particular emphasis on empirical observation. The few surviving works of Theophrastus include treatises on botany and other scientific subjects, and the *Characters*, a collection of sketches of psychological types, which in post-classical times was the most influential of his works.

Theresa, Mother see TERESA, MOTHER.

Thérèse of Lisieux, St see TERESA OF LISIEUX, ST.

Thesiger /ˈθesɪdʒə(r)/, Wilfred (Patrick) (born 1910), English explorer. He made his first expedition at the age of 23, living with the Ethiopian Danakil tribe. In 1935 he joined the Sudan Political Service, and he fought in Africa during the Second World War. He explored Saudi Arabia and Oman from 1945 to 1950, and from 1960 onwards travelled and lived in East Africa. He described his adventures in a number of books, including *Arabian Sands* (1959) and *The Marsh Arabs* (1964).

Thespis /ˈθespɪs/ (6th century BC), Greek dramatic poet. He is regarded as the founder of Greek tragedy, having been named by Aristotle as the originator of the role of the actor in addition to the traditional chorus.

Thom /tɒm/, Alexander (1894–1985), Scottish expert on prehistoric stone circles. Thom was a qualified engineer and was employed first at Glasgow University and later (as professor) at Oxford. In the 1930s he began a detailed survey of the stone circles of Britain and Brittany, drawing some surprising and controversial conclusions: most of the 'circles' are complex ellipses rather than true circles, many indicate a knowledge of the complex lunar cycle, and they were constructed using units of measurement which he dubbed the 'megalithic yard' and 'megalithic inch'. His chief books are *Megalithic Sites in Britain* (1967) and *Megalithic Lunar Observatories* (1971).

Thomas[1] /ˈtɒməs/, Dylan (Marlais) (1914–53), Welsh poet. He moved to London in 1934 and worked in journalism and broadcasting while continuing to write poetry. He won recognition with *Deaths and Entrances* (1946), and continued his success with works such as *Portrait of the Artist as a Young Dog* (1940; prose); *Adventures in the Skin Trade*, an unfinished novel, was published posthumously in 1955. Shortly before his death in New York of alcohol poisoning, he narrated on radio his best-known work, *Under Milk Wood*, a portrait of a small Welsh town, interspersing poetic alliterative prose with songs and ballads.

Thomas[2] /ˈtɒməs/, (Philip) Edward (1878–1917), English poet. He wrote mostly journalistic prose and reviews before being

encouraged by Robert Frost in 1914 to concentrate on writing poetry; most of his work was written while serving in the First World War and was published posthumously after he was killed at Arras in 1917. His work offers a sympathetic but un-idealized depiction of rural English life, adapting colloquial speech rhythms to poetic metre.

Thomas, St an Apostle. He said that he would not believe that Christ had risen again until he had seen and touched his wounds (John 20:24–9); the story is the origin of the nickname 'doubting Thomas'. According to tradition he preached in SW India. Feast day, 21 December.

Thomas à Kempis /ə 'kempɪs/ (born Thomas Hemerken) (c.1380–1471), German theologian. Born at Kempen, near Cologne (from where he gets his name), he became an Augustinian canon in Holland. He wrote a number of ascetic treatises and is the probable author of *On the Imitation of Christ* (c.1415–24), a manual of spiritual devotion.

Thomas Aquinas, St see AQUINAS, ST THOMAS.

Thomas More, St see MORE.

Thompson[1] /'tɒmps(ə)n/, Daley (born 1958), English athlete. He won a number of major decathlon titles in the 1980s, including gold medals in the Olympic Games of 1980 and 1984.

Thompson[2] /'tɒmps(ə)n/, Emma (born 1959), English actress and screenwriter. Although noted at first for her versatile comic talent, she later built a reputation as a serious actress. In 1989 she appeared in Kenneth Branagh's film of *Henry V*, and married Branagh the same year; the couple separated in 1995. Her other films include *Howard's End* (1992), for which she won an Oscar for best actress, *Carrington* (1995), and *Sense and Sensibility* (1995), for which she also wrote the Oscar-winning screenplay.

Thompson[3] /'tɒmps(ə)n/, Flora (Jane) (1876–1947), English writer. She is remembered for her semi-autobiographical trilogy *Lark Rise to Candleford* (1945), which evokes through the childhood memories and youth of 'Laura' a vanished world of rural customs and culture. It was originally published in three parts as *Lark Rise* (1939), *Over to Candleford* (1941), and *Candleford Green* (1943).

Thompson[4] /'tɒmps(ə)n/, Francis (1859–1907), English poet. His best-known work uses powerful imagery to convey intense religious experience, and includes the poems 'The Hound of Heaven' and 'The Kingdom of God'. He published three volumes of verse (1893–7) and much literary criticism in periodicals. He died from the combined effects of opium addiction and tuberculosis.

Thomson[1] /'tɒms(ə)n/, James (1700–48), Scottish poet. His poem in four books *The Seasons* (1726–30) anticipated the romantic movement in its treatment of nature; the text was adapted for Haydn's oratorio of that name (1799–1801). He also co-wrote the masque *Alfred* (1740) with David Mallet (c.1705–65); it contains the song 'Rule, Britannia', whose words have been attributed to him.

Thomson[2] /'tɒms(ə)n/, James (1834–82), Scottish poet. He is chiefly remembered for the poem 'The City of Dreadful Night' (1874), a powerful evocation of a half-ruined city where the narrator encounters tormented shades wandering in a Dantesque living hell, presided over by Melancolia.

Thomson[3] /'tɒms(ə)n/, Sir Joseph John (1856–1940), English physicist, discoverer of the electron. While professor of physics at Cambridge (1884–1918) he consolidated the reputation of the Cavendish Laboratory. From his experiments on the deflection of cathode rays in magnetic and electric fields, Thomson deduced that he was dealing with particles smaller than the atom. These he initially called *corpuscles* and later *electrons*, a word coined by the Irish mathematical physicist George Johnstone Stoney (1826–1911). Thomson received the 1906 Nobel Prize for physics for his researches into the electrical conductivity of gases. His son Sir George Paget Thomson (1892–1975) shared the 1937 Nobel Prize for physics for his discovery of electron diffraction by crystals.

Thomson[4] /'tɒms(ə)n/, Roy Herbert, 1st Baron Thomson of Fleet (1894–1976), Canadian-born British newspaper proprietor and media entrepreneur. In 1931 he opened his own radio station in northern Ontario. He then built up his North American press and radio holdings before acquiring his first British newspaper, the *Scotsman*, in 1952, the year he settled in Britain. He subsequently added the *Sunday*

Times (1959) and *The Times* (1966) to his acquisitions, by which time the Thomson Organization had become an international corporation, with interests in publishing, printing, television, and travel.

Thomson[5] /'tɒms(ə)n/, Tom (full name Thomas John Thomson) (1877–1917), Canadian painter. A pioneering artist of Canada's wilderness, he began sketching in Algonquin Park, Ontario, in the spring of 1912, returning there in subsequent summers. Major paintings include *Northern Lake* (1913), *The West Wind* (1917), and *The Jack Pine* (1917). Thomson's premature death at Canoe Lake, Algonquin Park, remains a mystery.

Thomson[6] /'tɒms(ə)n/, Sir William, see KELVIN.

Thoreau /'θɔːrəʊ/, Henry David (1817–62), American essayist and poet. Together with his friend and mentor Ralph Waldo Emerson he is regarded as a key figure of the philosophical, religious, and social movement Transcendentalism. He is best known for his book *Walden, or Life in the Woods* (1854), an account of a two-year experiment in self-sufficiency when he built a wooden hut by Walden Pond, near his home town of Concord, Massachusetts, and sought to live according to his ideals of simplicity and closeness to nature. His essay on civil disobedience (1849), in which he argues the right of the individual to refuse to pay taxes when conscience dictates, influenced Mahatma Gandhi's policy of passive resistance.

Thorndike /'θɔːndaɪk/, Dame (Agnes) Sybil (1882–1976), English actress. She gave notable performances in a wide range of Shakespearian and other roles; she was particularly memorable in the title part of the first London production of George Bernard Shaw's *St Joan* (1924). From the 1920s she appeared in a number of films, including *Nicholas Nickleby* (1947).

Thorvaldsen /'tɔːvæls(ə)n/, Bertel (also **Thorwaldsen**) (c.1770–1844), Danish neoclassical sculptor. From 1797 he lived and worked chiefly in Rome, where he made his name with a statue of Jason (1803); other major works include the tomb of Pius VII at St Peter's in Rome (1824–31) and a monument to Byron in Cambridge (1829).

Thrale /θreɪl/, Mrs Hester Lynch (latterly Hester Lynch Piozzi) (1741–1821), English writer. She and her husband became great friends of Dr Johnson, who lived for several years at their house in Streatham Place in London. Three years after her husband's death in 1781 she married the Italian musician Gabriel Piozzi amid much opposition from family and friends, especially Johnson, who ended their intimacy. Among her writings are her *Anecdotes of Dr Johnson* (1786), and a number of poems.

Thucydides /θjuː'sɪdɪˌdiːz/ (c.455–c.400 BC), Greek historian. He is remembered for his *History of the Peloponnesian War*, an account of a conflict in which he fought on the Athenian side. The work covers events up to about 411 and presents an analysis of the origins and course of the war, based on painstaking inquiry into what actually happened and including the reconstruction of political speeches of figures such as Pericles, whom he greatly admired.

Thurber /'θɜːbə(r)/, James (Grover) (1894–1961), American humorist and cartoonist. In 1927 he began his lifelong association with the *New Yorker* magazine, in which he published many of his essays, stories, and sketches. Among his many collections are *My Life and Hard Times* (1933) and *My World — and Welcome to It* (1942), which contains the story 'The Secret Life of Walter Mitty'.

Tiberius /taɪ'bɪərɪəs/ (full name Tiberius Julius Caesar Augustus) (42 BC–AD 37), Roman emperor AD 14–37. He was the adopted successor of his stepfather and father-in-law Augustus, under whom he had pursued a distinguished military career. As emperor he sought to continue his stepfather's policies but became increasingly tyrannical and his reign was marked by a growing number of treason trials and executions. In 26 he retired to Capri, never returning to Rome.

Tibullus /tɪ'bʌləs/, Albius (c.50–19 BC), Roman poet. He is known for his elegiac love poetry and for his celebration of peaceful rural life in preference to the harsh realities of military campaigning.

Tichborne claimant /'tɪtʃbɔːn/ see ORTON[1].

Tiepolo /'tjepəˌləʊ/, Giovanni Battista (1696–1770), Italian painter. One of the leading artists of the rococo style, he painted numerous frescos and altarpieces in Italy, Germany, and Spain, assisted on many commissions by his two sons. His painting is characterized by dramatic foreshorten-

ing, translucent colour, and settings of theatrical splendour. His works include the *Antony and Cleopatra* frescos in the Palazzo Labia, Venice (*c*.1750), and the decoration of the residence of the Prince-Bishop at Würzburg (1751–3). In 1762, at the request of Charles III, he moved to Madrid where he spent the rest of his life, working on the ceilings of the Royal Palace and the royal chapel at Aranjuez.

Tiffany /'tɪfənɪ/, Louis Comfort (1848–1933), American glass-maker and interior decorator. He was the son of Charles Louis Tiffany (1812–1902), who founded the New York jewellers Tiffany and Company. A leading exponent of American art nouveau, he established an interior decorating firm in New York in 1881 which produced stained glass and mosaic in a distinctive style, as well as iridescent glass vases and lamps.

Tiglath-pileser /ˌtɪglæθpaɪˈliːzə(r)/ the name of three kings of Assyria, notably: **Tiglath-pileser I**, reigned *c*.1115–*c*.1077 BC. He extended Assyrian territory further into Asia Minor, taking Cappadocia and reaching Syria, as well as expanding his kingdom to the upper Euphrates and defeating the king of Babylonia. **Tiglath-pileser III** (known as Pulu), reigned *c*.745–727 BC. He brought the Assyrian empire to the height of its power, subduing large parts of Syria and Palestine, and, towards the end of his reign, conquering Babylonia and ascending the Babylonian throne under the name of Pulu.

Tillich /'tɪlɪk/, Paul (Johannes) (1886–1965), German-born American theologian and philosopher. He proposed a form of Christian existentialism, outlining a reconciliation of religion and secular society, as expounded in *Systematic Theology* (1951–63).

Timothy, St (1st century AD), convert and disciple of St Paul. Traditionally he was the first bishop of Ephesus and was martyred in the reign of the Roman emperor Nerva. Feast day, January 22 or 26.

Timur /tiːˈmʊə(r)/ see TAMERLANE.

Tinbergen[1] /'tɪnˌbɜːgən/, Jan (1903–94), Dutch economist. In 1969 he shared with Ragnar Frisch the first Nobel Prize for economics, awarded for his pioneering work on econometrics. He was the brother of the zoologist Nikolaas Tinbergen.

Tinbergen[2] /'tɪnˌbɜːgən/, Nikolaas (1907–88), Dutch zoologist. After the Second World War he moved to Oxford where he helped to establish ethology as a distinct discipline, with relevance also to human psychology and sociology. From his classical studies on herring gulls, sticklebacks, and digger wasps, he found that much animal behaviour was innate and stereotyped, and he introduced the concept of displacement activity. Tinbergen shared a Nobel Prize in 1973 with Karl von Frisch and Konrad Lorenz. He was the brother of the economist Jan Tinbergen.

Tintoretto /ˌtɪntəˈretəʊ/ (born Jacopo Robusti) (1518–94), Italian painter. He acquired his name because his father was a dyer (Italian *tintore*). Based in Venice, Tintoretto gained fame with the painting *St Mark Rescuing a Slave* (1548), whose bright colours were influenced by Titian. From this time, his work was typified by a mannerist style, including unusual viewpoints, striking juxtapositions in scale, and bold chiaroscuro effects. Primarily a religious painter, he is best known for the huge canvas *Paradiso* (after 1577) in the main hall of the Doges' Palace in Venice, and for his paintings of the life of the Virgin, the life of Christ, and the Passion (1576–88) in the halls of the Scuola di San Rocco, also in Venice.

Tippett /'tɪpɪt/, Sir Michael (Kemp) (born 1905), English composer. He established his reputation with the oratorio *A Child of Our Time* (1941), which drew on jazz, madrigals, and spirituals besides classical sources. He is also noted for five operas, for all of which he also wrote the libretti; these include *The Midsummer Marriage* (1955). Among his other works are the oratorio *The Mask of Time* (1983), four symphonies, and several song cycles.

Titian /'tɪʃ(ə)n/ (Italian name Tiziano Vecellio) (*c*.1488–1576), Italian painter. The most important painter of the Venetian school, he was first a pupil of Bellini and Giorgione, and completed a number of the latter's unfinished paintings after his death in 1510. Titian subsequently experimented with vivid colours and often broke conventions of composition; his *Madonna with Saints and Members of the Pesaro Family* (1519–*c*.1528) was innovative in not having the Madonna in the centre of the picture. He also painted many sensual mythological works, including *Bacchus and Ariadne* (*c*.1518–23). He was much in demand throughout Europe for his portraits, which

were notable for the characterization of their sitters; he was appointed court painter by the Holy Roman emperor Charles V in 1533.

Tito /'tiːtəʊ/ (born Josip Broz) (1892–1980), Yugoslav Marshal and statesman, Prime Minister 1945–53 and President 1953–80. Born in Croatia, he served in the Austro-Hungarian army during the First World War and was captured by the Russians in 1915. After escaping, he fought with the Bolsheviks in the Russian Revolution and became an active Communist organizer on returning to his country in 1920. Tito responded to the German invasion of Yugoslavia (1941) by organizing a Communist resistance movement using guerrilla tactics. His success in resisting the Germans earned him Allied support and he emerged as head of the new government at the end of the war. Tito defied Stalin over policy in the Balkans in 1948, proceeding to establish Yugoslavia as a non-aligned Communist state with a federal constitution. He was made President for life in 1974.

Titus /'taɪtəs/ (full name Titus Vespasianus Augustus; born Titus Flavius Vespasianus) (AD 39–81), Roman emperor 79–81, son of Vespasian. In 70 he ended a revolt in Judaea with the conquest of Jerusalem. Titus also helped to complete the Colosseum and provided relief for the survivors of the eruption of Vesuvius in 79.

Titus, St (1st century AD), Greek churchman. A convert and helper of St Paul, he was traditionally the first bishop of Crete. Feast day (in the Eastern Church) 23 August; (in the Western Church) 6 February.

Todd /tɒd/, Mark James (born 1956), New Zealand equestrian. He won individual gold medals for three-day eventing in the Olympic Games of 1984 and 1988, and was ranked number one in the world in 1984, 1988, and 1989.

Tojo /'təʊdʒəʊ/, Hideki (1884–1948), Japanese military leader and statesman, Prime Minister 1941–4. By 1937 he had risen to Chief of Staff of the Japanese army of occupation in Manchuria, and was appointed Minister of War in 1940. Shortly after becoming Premier in 1941 he initiated the Japanese attack on the US base at Pearl Harbor. By 1944 Tojo had assumed virtual control of all political and military decision-making, but was forced to resign later that year following a number of Japanese military defeats. After Japan's surrender in 1945 he was tried and hanged as a war criminal.

Tolkien /'tɒlkiːn/, J(ohn) R(onald) R(euel) (1892–1973), British novelist and academic, born in South Africa. Professor of Anglo-Saxon and later of English language and literature at Oxford University, Tolkien is famous for the fantasy adventures *The Hobbit* (1937) and *The Lord of the Rings* (1954–5). These were set in Middle Earth, an imaginary land peopled by hobbits and other mythical beings, and for which he devised languages with considerable thoroughness. *The Silmarillion*, an account of the mythology and early history of Middle Earth, was published posthumously (1977).

Tolstoy /'tɒlstɔɪ/, Leo (Russian name Count Lev Nikolaevich Tolstoi) (1828–1910), Russian writer. He is best known for the novels *War and Peace* (1863–9) and *Anna Karenina* (1873–7). The former is an epic tale of the Napoleonic invasion and the lives of three aristocratic families; the latter describes a married woman's passion for a young officer and her tragic fate. Tolstoy subsequently underwent a spiritual crisis, espousing a moral code based on self-sufficiency, non-resistance to evil, belief in God, love of humankind, renouncing property, and repudiating government and organized religion. This provoked his excommunication from the Russian Orthodox Church in 1901 and the banning of many of his works.

Tombaugh /'tɒmbɔː/, Clyde William (1906–97), American astronomer. His chief interest was in the search for undiscovered planets, which he carried out mainly at the Lowell Observatory in Arizona. His extensive examination of photographic plates led to his discovery of the planet Pluto on 13 March 1930. Tombaugh subsequently discovered numerous asteroids.

Tompion /'tɒmpɪən/, Thomas (c.1639–1713), English clock and watchmaker. He made one of the first balance-spring watches to the design of Robert Hooke, and for the Royal Greenwich Observatory he made two large pendulum clocks which needed winding only once a year. Tompion also collaborated with Edward Barlow (1636–1716) in patenting the horizontal-wheel cylinder escapement needed to produce flat watches.

Tone /təʊn/, (Theobald) Wolfe (1763–98), Irish nationalist. In 1791 he helped found

the Society of United Irishmen, which lobbied for parliamentary reform. In 1794 he went to France to induce a French invasion of Ireland to overthrow English rule. The invasion failed, and during the Irish insurrection in 1798 Tone obtained only limited French support. He was captured by the British and committed suicide in prison.

Torquemada /ˌtɔːkɪˈmɑːdə/, Tomás de (c.1420–98), Spanish cleric and Grand Inquisitor. A Dominican monk, he became confessor to Ferdinand and Isabella, whom he persuaded to institute the Inquisition in 1478. Torquemada was appointed Inquisitor-General of Spain in 1483, and earned a reputation for ruthlessness and ferocious suppression of heresy. He was also the prime mover behind the expulsion of the Jews from Spain in and after 1492.

Torricelli /ˌtɒrɪˈtʃelɪ/, Evangelista (1608–47), Italian mathematician and physicist. He was a disciple of Galileo, whom he succeeded as mathematician to the court of Tuscany. He proposed a physical law governing the velocity of liquids flowing under the force of gravity from orifices. Torricelli's most important invention, however, was the mercury barometer, with which he demonstrated that the atmosphere exerts a pressure sufficient to support a column of mercury in an inverted closed tube. He was also the first person to produce a sustained vacuum.

Tortelier /tɔːˈtelɪˌeɪ/, Paul (1914–90), French cellist. He made his concert début as a cellist in 1931, achieving international recognition after the Second World War. He was noted for his interpretations of Bach and Elgar, and also gave recitals with his wife and children, all musicians. Tortelier was appointed professor at the Paris Conservatoire in 1957, where Jacqueline du Pré was among his pupils.

Torvill and Dean /ˈtɔːvɪl, diːn/, Jayne Torvill (born 1957) and Christopher (Colin) Dean (born 1958), English ice-skaters. In partnership they won the European ice-dancing championship (1981–2), the world championships (1981–3), and the gold medal in the 1984 Winter Olympics (with a famous routine to Ravel's Boléro). After a spell as professionals they returned to amateur competition in 1994, winning the European championship again and then a bronze medal in the 1994 Winter Olympics.

Toscanini /ˌtɒskəˈniːnɪ/, Arturo (1867–1957), Italian conductor. Making his conducting début in 1886, he was musical director at La Scala in Milan (1898–1903; 1906–8) before becoming a conductor at the Metropolitan Opera, New York (1908–21). Toscanini later returned to La Scala (1921–9). Among the works he premièred were Puccini's La Bohème (1896) and Turandot (1926).

Toulouse-Lautrec /tuːˌluːz ləʊˈtrek/, Henri (Marie Raymond) de (1864–1901), French painter and lithographer. Toulouse-Lautrec's reputation is based on his colour lithographs from the 1890s, depicting actors, music-hall singers, prostitutes, and waitresses in Montmartre: particularly well known is the Moulin Rouge series (1894). His work is noted for its calligraphic line and flatness, influenced by Japanese prints.

Toussaint L'Ouverture /ˌtuːsæn ˌluːvəˈtjʊə(r)/, Pierre Dominique (c.1743–1803), Haitian revolutionary leader. Brought up a slave in the western part of Hispaniola (now Haiti), in 1791 he became one of the leaders of a rebellion that succeeded in emancipating the island's slaves by 1793. In 1797 he was appointed Governor-General by the revolutionary government of France, and led the drive to expel the British and Spanish from western Hispaniola. In 1801 he took control of the whole island, establishing his own constitution, but the following year Napoleon (wishing to restore slavery) ordered his forces to regain the island; Toussaint was eventually taken to France, where he died in prison.

Townes /taʊnz/, Charles Hard (born 1915), American physicist. Following work on radar in the Second World War he investigated the quantum electronic effects associated with microwave radiation. His development of microwave oscillators and amplifiers led to his invention of the maser in 1954. Townes later showed that an optical maser (a laser) was possible, though the first working laser was constructed by others. He shared the Nobel Prize for physics in 1964.

Toynbee[1] /ˈtɔɪnbɪ/, Arnold (1852–83), English economist and social reformer. He became an economist at Oxford, subsequently lecturing both to undergraduates and workers' adult education classes and working with the poor in London's East

End. He is best known for his pioneering work *The Industrial Revolution*, published posthumously in 1884.

Toynbee[2] /'tɔɪnbɪ/, Arnold (Joseph) (1889–1975), English historian. He is best known for his twelve-volume *Study of History* (1934–61), in which he surveyed the history of different civilizations, tracing in them a pattern of growth, maturity, and decay and concluding that contemporary Western civilization is in the last of these stages.

Tracy /'treɪsɪ/, Spencer (1900–67), American actor. After his screen début in 1930, he won his first Oscar seven years later for his performance in *Captain Courageous*. Tracy formed a successful film partnership with Katharine Hepburn, co-starring with her in films such as *Adam's Rib* (1949) and *Guess Who's Coming to Dinner* (1967).

Tradescant /'trædɪˌskænt/, John (1570–1638), English botanist and horticulturalist. He was the earliest known collector of plants and other natural history specimens, and took part in a number of collecting trips to Western Europe, Russia, and North Africa. Tradescant was later employed as gardener to Charles I and set up his own garden and museum in Lambeth, London. His son John (1608–62) had similar interests and added many plants to his father's collection, which was eventually bequeathed to Elias Ashmole.

Traherne /trə'hɜːn/, Thomas (1637–74), English prose writer and poet. His major prose work *Centuries*, originally published in 1699, faded into obscurity until it was rediscovered on a London bookstall along with some poems in manuscript form in 1896; it was republished as *Centuries of Meditation* (1908). Its account of his early intuitions constitutes an important contribution to the portrayal of childhood experience in English literature. His poems were republished as *Poetical Works* (1903).

Trajan /'treɪdʒən/ (Latin name Marcus Ulpius Traianus) (AD c.53–117), Roman emperor 98–117. Born in Spain, he was adopted by Nerva as his successor. Trajan's reign is noted for the Dacian wars (101–6), which ended in the annexation of Dacia as a province; the campaigns are illustrated on Trajan's Column in Rome. He was also an efficient administrator and many public works were undertaken during his reign.

Trenchard /'trenʃəd/, Hugh Montague, 1st Viscount of Wolfeton (1873–1956), British

Marshal of the RAF. He served in the army 1893–1912 before training as a pilot and becoming head of the Royal Flying Corps during the First World War. As Chief of Staff (1918) then First Marshal (1927) of the RAF he built the force into the third major element of the British armed services. He was also Metropolitan Police Commissioner from 1931 to 1935.

Trevino /trə'viːnəʊ/, Lee (Buck) (known as 'Supermex') (born 1939), American golfer. After first winning the US Open in 1968, in 1971 he became the first man to win all three Open championships (Canadian, US, and British) in the same year. After winning the 1974 US PGA championship he was struck by lightning and had to undergo back surgery, but he rallied to win the same championship ten years later.

Trevithick /trə'vɪθɪk/, Richard (1771–1833), English engineer. Known as 'the Cornish Giant', he was the most notable engineer from the Cornish mining industry, where steam engines were first widely used. His chief contribution was in the use of high-pressure steam to drive a double-acting engine, which could then be both compact and portable. Trevithick built many stationary engines and a few that were self-propelled – including the world's first railway locomotive (1804), designed for an ironworks in South Wales. He also applied the principle in other enterprises, though his attempt to introduce steam power to silver mines in Peru proved financially disastrous.

Trevor /'trevə(r)/, William (pseudonym of William Trevor Cox) (born 1928), Irish novelist and short-story writer. His works deal insightfully with the elderly, the lonely, and the unsuccessful, and show an increasing preoccupation with the effects of terrorism on Northern Ireland. They include the novels *The Old Boys* (1964) and *Fools of Fortune* (1983), and several acclaimed collections of short stories, such as *The Day We Got Drunk on Cake* (1967) and *Beyond the Pale* (1981).

Trollope /'trɒləp/, Anthony (1815–82), English novelist. He worked for the General Post Office in London, Ireland, and other parts of the world from 1834 to 1867, during which time he introduced the pillar-box to Britain. Trollope established his reputation as a writer with his fourth novel *The Warden* (1855), the first of the six

'Barsetshire' novels, which also include *Barchester Towers* (1857) and *The Last Chronicle of Barset* (1867). Set in an imaginary English West Country and with recurring characters, they portray a solid rural society of curates and landed gentry. Another novel sequence, the six political 'Palliser' novels, was published 1864–80. Trollope was a prolific writer, publishing travel books, biographies, and short stories as well as forty-seven novels.

Trotsky /'trɒtskɪ/, Leon (born Lev Davidovich Bronstein) (1879–1940), Russian revolutionary. Joining the Bolsheviks in 1917, he helped to organize the October Revolution with Lenin, and built up the Red Army that eventually defeated the White Russian forces in the Russian Civil War. After Lenin's death he alienated Stalin and others with his view that socialism within the Soviet Union could not come about until revolution had occurred in western Europe and worldwide. Trotsky was eventually defeated by Stalin in the struggle for power, being expelled from the party in 1927 and exiled in 1929. After settling in Mexico in 1937, he was murdered three years later by a Stalinist assassin.

Troyes, Chrétien de, see CHRÉTIEN DE TROYES.

Trudeau /'tru:dəʊ/, Pierre (Elliott) (born 1919), Canadian Liberal statesman, Prime Minister of Canada 1968–79 and 1980–4. A committed federalist, Trudeau made both English and French official languages of the Canadian government (1969). During his second term, in 1980, a provincial referendum rejected independence for Quebec; Trudeau also presided over the transfer of residual constitutional powers from Britain to Canada in 1982.

Trueman /'tru:mən/, Frederick Sewards ('Fred') (born 1931), English cricketer. A fast bowler, he played for England from 1952 until 1965, during which time he became the first bowler to take 300 test wickets (1964) and took 307 wickets overall. He also played for his home county, Yorkshire (1949–68), taking a total of 2,304 wickets in first-class games. After retiring from the sport he became a cricket commentator and journalist.

Truffaut /'tru:fəʊ/, François (1932–84), French film director. He was an influential film critic in the 1950s and originated the idea of the director as 'auteur'. In 1959 he directed his first feature film, *Les Quatre Cents Coups*, a work which established him as a leading director of the *nouvelle vague*. He acted and collaborated in the scriptwriting of this and many of his other films, among which are *Jules et Jim* (1961), *La Nuit américaine* (1973; *Day for Night*), which won an Oscar for best foreign film, and *The Last Metro* (1980).

Trujillo /tru:'hi:əʊ/, Rafael (born Rafael Leónidas Trujillo Molina; known as 'Generalissimo') (1891–1961), Dominican statesman, President of the Dominican Republic 1930–8 and 1942–52. Although he was formally President for only two periods, he wielded dictatorial powers from 1930 until his death. His dictatorship was marked by some improvement in social services and material benefits for the people, but also by the deployment of a strong and ruthless police force to crush all opposition. He was assassinated in 1961.

Truman /'tru:mən/, Harry S (1884–1972), American Democratic statesman, 33rd President of the US 1945–53. As Vice-President, he automatically took office on Franklin Roosevelt's death in 1945. One of his first actions was to authorize the use of the atom bomb against Hiroshima and Nagasaki in 1945 to end the war with Japan. At home Truman put forward an extensive social programme which was largely blocked by Congress, although racial segregation in the armed forces and in federally funded schools was ended. His expression in 1947 of what became known as the Truman Doctrine (the principle that the US should give support to countries or peoples threatened by Soviet forces or Communist insurrection) was seen by the Communists as an open declaration of the cold war. In 1948 his administration introduced the Marshall Plan of emergency aid to war-shattered European countries and helped to establish NATO the following year. He later involved the US in the Korean War.

Truth /tru:θ/, Sojourner (previously Isabella Van Wagener) (*c*.1797–1883), American evangelist and reformer. Born into slavery, she was sold to a man named Isaac Van Wagener, who set her free in 1827. She became a zealous evangelist and in 1843 changed her name and travelled across the US. Her preaching in favour of black rights and women's suffrage drew large crowds,

her fame grew, and in 1864 she was received at the White House by Abraham Lincoln.

Tsiolkovsky /ˌtsiːɒlˈkɒfskɪ/, Konstantin (Eduardovich) (1857–1935), Russian aeronautical engineer. His early ideas for aircraft and rockets were not officially recognized until after the Russian Revolution, though his proposal for the use of liquid fuel in rockets predated Robert Goddard's successful rocket flight by nearly forty years. During the 1920s Tsiolkovsky carried out pioneering theoretical work on multi-stage rockets, jet engines, and space flight.

Tudor[1] /ˈtjuːdə(r)/, Henry, Henry VII of England (see HENRY[1]).

Tudor[2] /ˈtjuːdə(r)/, Mary, Mary I of England (see MARY[2]).

Tu Fu /tuː ˈfuː/ (also **Du Fu** /duː/) (AD 712–70), Chinese poet. He is noted for his bitter satiric poems attacking social injustice and corruption at court. The finest of these were written during the turbulent 750s, in which he suffered much personal hardship.

Tull /tʌl/, Jethro (1674–1741), English agriculturalist. He had a profound effect on agricultural practice with his invention of the seed drill (1701), which could sow seeds in accurately spaced rows at a controlled rate. This made possible the control of weeds by horse-drawn hoe, reducing the need for farm labourers.

Tulsidas /ˈtʊlsɪˌdɑːs/ (c.1543–1623), Indian poet. He was a leading Hindu devotional poet who is chiefly remembered for the *Ramcaritmanas* (c.1574–7), a work consisting of seven cantos and based on the Sanskrit epic the Ramayana. The poet's expression of worship or bhakti for Rama led to the cult of Rama (rather than that of Krishna) dominating the Hindu culture of northern India.

Turgenev /tɜːˈɡeɪnjef, tʊəˈɡenjef/, Ivan (Sergeevich) (1818–83), Russian novelist, dramatist, and short-story writer. From the 1850s he spent much of his life abroad, especially in Paris and Baden-Baden. His play *A Month in the Country* (1850) was followed by the prose work *A Sportsman's Sketches* (1852), which condemned the institution of serfdom. He subsequently wrote a series of novels examining individual lives to illuminate the social, political, and philosophical issues of the day, as in *Rudin* (1856) and *Fathers and Sons* (1862); in the latter, Turgenev depicted the rise of nihilism in Russia through his hero Bazarov.

Turing /ˈtjʊərɪŋ/, Alan (Mathison) (1912–54), English mathematician. He developed the concept of a theoretical computing machine in 1937, a key step in the development of the first computer. Turing carried out important work on code-breaking during the Second World War, after which he worked on early computers at the National Physical Laboratory and the University of Manchester. He also investigated artificial intelligence and suggested criteria for a machine which would respond like a human being. Turing committed suicide after being prosecuted for homosexuality and forced to undergo hormone treatment.

Turner[1] /ˈtɜːnə(r)/, J(oseph) M(allord) W(illiam) (1775–1851), English painter. The originality of his work and the extent to which it anticipated later styles such as impressionism and abstract art made him a highly controversial figure in his day. He made his name with stormy seascapes such as *The Shipwreck* (1805) and landscapes painted in the grand Italian style of Claude Lorrain, as in *Crossing the Brook* (1815). From 1819 Turner made several visits to Italy and became increasingly concerned with depicting the power of light, using primary colours — especially yellow — often arranged in a swirling vortex. In the 1830s and 1840s he adopted watercolour techniques for his 'colour beginnings' in oil, which he later worked up to finished paintings, notably in *Norham Castle* (c.1845). He is perhaps best known for *Rain, Steam, Speed* (1844) and for the seascape *The Fighting Téméraire* (1838).

Turner[2] /ˈtɜːnə(r)/, Tina (born Anna Mae Bullock) (born 1939), American rock and soul singer. In 1958 she married musician Ike Turner (born 1931) and started singing with his band. They had hits such as 'River Deep — Mountain High' (1966), but despite Tina's dynamic vocals and stage presence her husband maintained rigorous control over the group's act. Tina Turner divorced her husband in 1976 and built her own career, becoming an international superstar with the release of the album *Private Dancer* (1984).

Turpin /'tɜ:pɪn/, Dick (1706–39), English highwayman. He was a cattle and deer thief in Essex before entering into partnership with Tom King, a notorious highwayman. Turpin eventually fled north and was hanged at York for horse-stealing. His escapades were celebrated in the popular literature of the day.

Tussaud /təˈsɔːd, French tyso/, Madame (née Marie Grosholtz) (1761–1850), French founder of Madame Tussaud's waxworks, resident in Britain from 1802. After taking death masks in wax of prominent victims of the French Revolution, she toured Britain with her wax models, which came to include other famous and topical people. In 1835 she founded a permanent waxworks exhibition in Baker Street, London.

Tutankhamen /ˌtuːt(ə)nˈkɑːm(ə)n/ (also **Tutankhamun** /-kɑːˈmuːn/) (died c.1352 BC), Egyptian pharaoh of the 18th dynasty, reigned c.1361–c.1352 BC. Ascending the throne while still a boy, he abandoned the worship of the sun-god instituted by Akhenaten, reinstating the worship of Amun and making Thebes the capital city once again. Although not important in the history of Egypt, he became world famous because of the rich and varied contents of his tomb, discovered virtually intact by Howard Carter in 1922.

Tuthmosis III /tʌθˈməʊsɪs/ (died c.1450 BC), son of Tuthmosis II, Egyptian pharaoh of the 18th dynasty c.1504–c.1450. He was initially joint ruler with his aunt Hatshepsut until her death in 1482. His reign was marked by the conquest of all of Syria and the annexation of part of Nubia, as well as by extensive building; the monuments he erected included Cleopatra's Needles (c.1475).

Tutu /'tuːtuː/, Desmond (Mpilo) (born 1931), South African clergyman. He served as General Secretary of the South African Council of Churches (1979–84), during which time he became a leading voice in the struggle against apartheid, calling for economic sanctions against South Africa and emphasizing non-violent action. He was awarded the Nobel Peace Prize in 1984, and in the following year he became Johannesburg's first black Anglican bishop. He was archbishop of Cape Town 1986–96.

Twain /tweɪn/, Mark (pseudonym of Samuel Langhorne Clemens) (1835–1910), Ameri-

can novelist and humorist. After working as a river pilot on the Mississippi he established a reputation as a humorist with early work including *The Innocents Abroad* (1869), a satirical account of an American cruise to the Mediterranean. He is best known for the novels *The Adventures of Tom Sawyer* (1876) and *The Adventures of Huckleberry Finn* (1885); both works give a vivid evocation of Mississippi frontier life, faithfully capturing Southern speech patterns and combining picaresque adventure with moral commentary.

Tycho Brahe see BRAHE.

Tyler[1] /'taɪlə(r)/, John (1790–1862), American Whig statesman, 10th President of the US 1841–5. Successor to William Henry Harrison as President, he was noted for securing the annexation of Texas (1845). Throughout his political career Tyler advocated states' rights, and his alliance with Southern Democrats on this issue helped to accentuate the divide between North and South in the years leading up to the American Civil War.

Tyler[2] /'taɪlə(r)/, Wat (died 1381), English leader of the Peasants' Revolt of 1381. After capturing Canterbury, he led the rebels to Blackheath and took London. During a conference with the young king Richard II he put forward the rebels' demands (including the lifting of the newly imposed poll tax), to which Richard consented. At a later conference in Smithfield he was killed by the Lord Mayor of London and several other royal supporters.

Tyndale /'tɪnd(ə)l/, William (c.1494–1536), English translator and Protestant martyr. Faced with ecclesiastical opposition to his project for translating the Bible into English, Tyndale went abroad in 1524, never to return to his own country; his translation of the New Testament (c.1525–6) was published in Germany. He then translated the Pentateuch (1530) and Jonah (1531), both of which were printed in Antwerp. Tyndale's translations later formed the basis of the Authorized Version. In 1535 he was arrested in Antwerp on a charge of heresy, and subsequently strangled and burnt at the stake.

Tyndall /'tɪnd(ə)l/, John (1820–93), Irish physicist. He is best known for his work on heat, studying such aspects as the absorbance and transmission of heat by gases

and liquids, the thermal conductivity of solids, and the use of discontinuous heating as a sterilization technique. Tyndall also worked on diamagnetism, glaciers, the transmission of sound, and the scattering of light by suspended particles, becoming the first person to explain the blue colour of the sky. He was a prolific and popular lecturer and writer.

Tyson /'taɪs(ə)n/, Michael Gerald ('Mike') (born 1966), American boxer. He became undisputed world heavyweight champion in 1987, winning the WBA, WBC, and IBF titles, and successfully defended his position until 1990. He was imprisoned in 1992 for rape; after his release in 1995 he came back to defeat Frank Bruno and reclaim the WBC and WBA titles in 1996.

Tzara /'zɑːrə/, Tristan (born Samuel Rosenstock) (1896–1963), Romanian-born French poet. Emigrating to France at the age of 19, in 1916 he became one of the founders of the Dada movement; he edited the periodical *Dada* (1917–21) and wrote the movement's manifestos. His poetry, with its continuous flow of unconnected images, and his suggestion that poems should be composed from words cut from a newspaper and selected at random, helped form the basis for surrealism, a movement he became involved with from about 1930 onwards.

U

Uccello /uːˈtʃeləʊ/, Paolo (born Paolo di Dono) (c.1397–1475), Italian painter. His nickname (*uccello*, 'bird') is said to refer to his love of animals, especially birds. He was based largely in Florence and is associated with the early use of perspective in painting. His surviving works include *The Rout of San Romano* (one of a series of three panels, c.1454–7) and *The Hunt*, one of the earliest known paintings on canvas, noted for its atmosphere of fairy-tale romance.

Ulanova /uːˈlɑːnəvə/, Galina (Sergeevna) (born 1910), Russian ballet-dancer. In 1928 she joined the Kirov Ballet, transferring to the Bolshoi company in 1944. She gave notable interpretations of 19th-century ballets, such as *Swan Lake* and *Giselle*, and also danced the leading roles, composed especially for her, in all three of Prokofiev's ballets. During the 1950s she became well known in the West through touring with the Bolshoi Ballet. After her retirement as a dancer in 1962 she remained with the company as a teacher.

Ulfilas /ˈʊlfɪˌlæs/ (also **Wulfila** /ˈwʊlfɪlə/) (c.311–c.381), bishop and translator. Believed to be of Cappadocian descent, he became bishop of the Visigoths in 341. Ulfilas is best known for his translation of the Bible from Greek into Gothic (of which fragments survive), the earliest known translation of the Bible into a Germanic language. The translation uses the Gothic alphabet, based on Latin and Greek characters, which Ulfilas is traditionally held to have invented.

Ulpian /ˈʌlpɪən/ (Latin name Domitius Ulpianus) (died c.228), Roman jurist, born in Phoenicia. His numerous legal writings provided one of the chief sources for Justinian's *Digest* of 533.

Ulyanov /uːˈljɑːnɒf/, Vladimir Ilich, see LENIN.

Updike /ˈʌpdaɪk/, John (Hoyer) (born 1932), American novelist, poet, and short-story writer. He is noted for his quartet of novels *Rabbit, Run* (1960), *Rabbit Redux* (1971), *Rabbit is Rich* (1981), and *Rabbit at Rest* (1990), a small-town tragicomedy tracing the career of an ex-basketball player; the latter two novels were awarded Pulitzer Prizes. Other novels include *Couples* (1968) and *The Witches of Eastwick* (1984).

Urey /ˈjʊərɪ/, Harold Clayton (1893–1981), American chemist. He searched for a heavy isotope of hydrogen, discovering deuterium in 1932, and developing a technique for obtaining heavy water. Because of his work on isotope separation he was made director of the atom bomb project at Columbia University during the Second World War. Urey pioneered the use of isotope labelling; he also developed theories on the formation of the planets and of the possible synthesis of organic compounds in earth's primitive atmosphere. He was awarded the Nobel Prize for chemistry in 1934.

Ustinov /ˈjuːstɪˌnɒf/, Sir Peter (Alexander) (born 1921), British actor, director, and dramatist, of Russian descent. He has written and acted in a number of plays including *Romanoff and Juliet* (1956), and his many films include *Spartacus* (1960) and *Death on the Nile* (1978). Ustinov is also well known as a mimic, raconteur, broadcaster, and novelist.

Utamaro /ˌuːtəˈmɑːrəʊ/, Kitagawa (born Kitagawa Nebsuyoshi) (1753–1806), Japanese painter and printmaker. A leading exponent of the ukiyo-e school, he created many books of woodblock prints and was noted for his sensual depictions of women. His technique of portraying his subjects seemingly cut off by the margin of a print was admired by the impressionists.

Utrillo /juːˈtrɪləʊ, French ytrijo/, Maurice (1883–1955), French painter. The son of the French painter Susan Valadon (1867–1938), he was adopted by the Spanish architect and writer Miguel Utrillo in 1891. Utrillo is chiefly known for his depictions of Paris street scenes, especially the Montmartre district; the works of his 'white period' (1909–14), when he made extensive use of white pigment, are considered particularly notable.

Uttley /ˈʌtlɪ/, Alison (1884–1976), English writer. She is remembered for her children's books, particularly the 'Little Grey Rabbit' series (1929 onwards) and the 'Sam Pig' stories (1940 onwards).

V

Valentino /ˌvælənˈtiːnəʊ/, Rudolph (born Rodolfo Guglielmi di Valentina d'Antonguolla) (1895–1926), Italian-born American actor. He became a leading star of silent films in the 1920s, playing the romantic hero in films such as *The Sheikh* (1921) and *Blood and Sand* (1922). After his death from a perforated ulcer thousands of women attended his funeral, at which there were scenes of mass hysteria and reports of several suicides.

Valera, Eamon de, see DE VALERA.

Valerian /vəˈlɪərɪən/ (Latin name Publius Licinius Valerianus) (died 260), Roman emperor 253–60. He became emperor following the murder of Gallus (reigned 251–3), and appointed his son Gallienus as joint ruler. During his reign Valerian renewed the persecution of the Christians initiated by Decius. He was captured while campaigning against the Persians of the Sassanian dynasty and died in captivity. Gallienus continued to rule as sole emperor until 268.

Valéry /ˈvæleɪrɪ/, (Ambroise) Paul (Toussaint Jules) (1871–1945), French poet, essayist, and critic. His poetry, influenced by symbolist poets such as Mallarmé and blending lyricism, rich imagery, and intellectual eloquence, includes *La Jeune parque* (1917) and 'Le Cimetière marin' (1922). He later concentrated on prose, publishing essays on a variety of literary, philosophical, and aesthetic subjects. He is also known for his notebooks, published posthumously as *Cahiers* (1958–62).

Valois, Dame Ninette de, see DE VALOIS.

Van Allen /væn ˈælən/, James Alfred (born 1914), American physicist. Van Allen was head of physics at Iowa University for thirty-four years. Expertise in missile technology and electronics led him to use balloons and rockets to study cosmic radiation in the upper atmosphere. The first orbiting satellites encountered zones of high radiation, which Van Allen showed were the result of charged particles from the solar wind being trapped in two belts around the earth, later known as Van Allen belts.

Vanbrugh /ˈvænbrə/, Sir John (1664–1726), English architect and dramatist. In his early life he gained success as a dramatist with his comedies, including *The Relapse* (1696) and *The Provok'd Wife* (1697). After 1699 he became known as an architect and as one of the chief exponents of the English baroque; major works include Castle Howard in Yorkshire (1702) and Blenheim Palace in Oxfordshire (1705), both produced in collaboration with Nicholas Hawksmoor, and Seaton Delaval Hall in Northumberland (1720).

Van Buren /væn ˈbjʊərən/, Martin (1782–1862), American Democratic statesman, 8th President of the US 1837–41. He was appointed Andrew Jackson's Vice-President in 1832 and became President five years later. His measure of placing government funds, previously held in private banks, in an independent treasury caused many Democrats to join the Whig party.

Vancouver /vænˈkuːvə(r)/, George (1757–98), English navigator. After accompanying Captain James Cook on his second and third voyages, he took command of a naval expedition exploring the coasts of Australia, New Zealand, and Hawaii (1791–2). He later charted much of the west coast of North America between southern Alaska and California. Vancouver Island and the city of Vancouver are named after him.

Van de Graaf /ˌvæn də ˈɡrɑːf/, Robert Jemison (1901–67), American physicist. Van de Graaf worked in various countries before he returned to the US in 1929, moving to the Massachusetts Institute of Technology two years later. He invented the high-voltage *Van de Graaf generator* in about 1929, using a hollow sphere to store up a large electrostatic charge. This device was improved in later years, being adapted for use as a particle accelerator and as a high-energy X-ray generator for medical treatment and industrial use.

Vanderbilt /ˈvændəˌbɪlt/, Cornelius (1794–1877), American businessman and philanthropist. Vanderbilt amassed a fortune from shipping and railroads, and from this made an endowment to found Vanderbilt University in Nashville, Tennessee (1873).

Subsequent generations of his family, including his son William Henry Vanderbilt (1821–85), increased the family wealth and continued his philanthropy.

Van der Post /ˌvæn də ˈpɒst/, Sir Laurens (Jan) (1906–96), South African explorer and writer. In 1949 Van der Post was sent to explore Nyasaland (now Malawi) for the British; his book of the journey, *Venture to the Interior* (1952), was the first of several works combining travel writing and descriptions of fauna with philosophical speculation based on his Jungian ideas of the necessary balance between 'unconscious, feminine' Africa, and 'conscious, masculine' Europe. He developed this theme after travels among the Bushmen of the Kalahari Desert, described in books such as *The Lost World of the Kalahari* (1958).

van de Velde[1] /ˌvæn də ˈvelt, ˈveldə/, a family of Dutch painters. Willem (known as Willem van de Velde the Elder) (1611–93) painted marine subjects and was for a time official artist to the Dutch fleet. He also worked for Charles II. His sons were Willem (known as Willem van de Velde the Younger) (1633–1707) and Adriaen (1636–72). Like his father, Willem the Younger was a notable marine artist who painted for Charles II, while Adriaen's works included landscapes, portraits, and biblical and genre scenes.

van de Velde[2] /ˌvæn də ˈvelt, ˈveldə/, Henri (Clemens) (1863–1957), Belgian architect, designer, and teacher. He was influenced by the Arts and Crafts Movement and pioneered the development of art nouveau design and architecture in Europe. In 1906 he became head of the Weimar School of Arts and Crafts (which developed into the Bauhaus), Walter Gropius being among his pupils. Van de Velde's buildings include the Werkbund Theatre in Cologne (1914) and his own house near Brussels (1895). He also designed furniture, ceramics, and graphics.

Van Dyck /væn ˈdaɪk/, Sir Anthony (also **Vandyke**) (1599–1641), Flemish painter. Having worked as an assistant in Rubens's workshop in Antwerp (1618–20), he visited Italy, where he based himself in Genoa and studied Titian and other Venetian painters. While in Genoa he painted a number of portraits which marked the onset of his artistic maturity. Thereafter he received commissions from several royal clients,

including Charles I, who invited Van Dyck to England and knighted him in 1632. His subsequent portraits of members of the English court, noted for their refinement of style and elegant composition, determined the course of portraiture in England for more than 200 years.

Van Eyck /væn ˈaɪk/, Jan (*c*.1370–1441), Flemish painter. He is said by Vasari to have invented oil-painting, and though it is known that oils were used before his time there is no doubt that he made an innovative contribution to the technique of their use, bringing greater flexibility, richer and denser colour, and a wider range from light to dark. His best-known works include the altarpiece *The Adoration of the Lamb* (known as the Ghent Altarpiece, 1432) in the church of St Bavon in Ghent and the portrait *The Arnolfini Marriage* (1434).

Van Gogh /væn ˈɡɒx, ˈɡɒf, ˈɡəʊ/, Vincent (Willem) (1853–90), Dutch painter. Although he is most closely identified with post-impressionism, his early paintings, such as *The Potato Eaters* (1885), were often of peasants and are characterized by the use of dark colours. A move to Paris in 1886 brought him into contact with the works of the impressionists and with Japanese woodcuts, instigating a change in his technique. He began to use brighter colours and adopted broad, vigorous, swirling brushstrokes. In 1888 he settled at Arles, where he was briefly joined by Gauguin, but they quarrelled, and Van Gogh, suffering from depression, cut off part of his own ear. After a year spent in an asylum he entered into a period of intense creative activity but continued to suffer from severe depression, and eventually committed suicide. Among his best-known works are several studies of sunflowers and *A Starry Night* (1889).

van Leyden, Lucas, see LUCAS VAN LEYDEN.

Varah /ˈvɑːrə/, (Edward) Chad (1911–93), English clergyman, founder of the Samaritans. He founded the Samaritans in 1953 after recognizing a widespread need for an anonymous counselling service; the organization offers help, particularly via the telephone, to the suicidal and despairing. He was president of Befrienders International (Samaritans Worldwide) from 1983 to 1986 and travelled widely abroad to spread the organization's principles.

Varèse /væ'rez/, Edgar(d) (1883–1965), French-born American composer. Varèse emigrated to the US in 1915, and most of his works from before this date have been lost. His compositions were predominantly orchestral in nature until the 1950s, when he began to experiment with electronic instruments and tape-recordings of natural sounds, becoming a prominent figure in the development of *musique concrète*. His works are known for their use of dissonance and for their experimentation with unusual sounds and instrument combinations; they include *Ionisation* (1931), for percussion, piano, and two sirens, and *Poème électronique* (1958).

Vargas /'vɑ:ɡəs/, Getúlio Dornelles (1883–1954), Brazilian statesman, President 1930–45 and 1951–4. Although defeated in the presidential elections of 1930, Vargas seized power in the ensuing revolution, overthrowing the republic and ruling as a virtual dictator for the next fifteen years. He furthered Brazil's modernization by the introduction of fiscal, educational, electoral, and land reforms, but his regime was totalitarian and repressive. He was overthrown in a coup in 1945. He was returned to power after elections in 1951, but his government was unpopular and he committed suicide after widespread calls for his resignation.

Vargas Llosa /,vɑ:ɡəs 'jəʊsə/, (Jorge) Mario (Pedro) (born 1936), Peruvian novelist, dramatist, and essayist. His fiction often contains elements of myth and fantasy and has been associated with magic realism; it is frequently critical of the political situation in Peru. Novels include *The Time of the Hero* (1963), satirizing Peruvian society via the microcosm of a corrupt military academy, *Aunt Julia and the Scriptwriter* (1977), and *The War of the End of the World* (1982). He returned to Peru in 1974, after living abroad for many years, and stood unsuccessfully for the presidency in 1990.

Varro /'værəʊ/, Marcus Terentius (116–27 BC), Roman scholar and satirist. He was a prolific author and although most of his writings are now lost, his prose works are known to have covered many subjects, including philosophy, agriculture, the Latin language, and education. His satires (*Saturae Menippeae*) presented critical sketches of Roman life in a mixture of verse and prose.

Vasarely /,væsə'relɪ/, Viktor (1908–97), Hungarian-born French painter. He settled in Paris in 1930 after studying art in Budapest. A pioneer of op art, he began experimenting with the use of optical illusion during the 1930s, although the style of geometric abstraction for which he is best known dates from the late 1940s. His paintings are characterized by their repeated geometric forms and interacting vibrant colours which create a visually disorientating effect of movement.

Vasari /və'sɑːrɪ/, Giorgio (1511–74), Italian painter, architect, and biographer. He wrote *Lives of the Most Excellent Painters, Sculptors, and Architects* (1550, enlarged 1568), a work which laid the basis for later study of art history in the West; the book traces the development of Renaissance painting from the work of painters such as Giotto to that of Leonardo da Vinci, Raphael, and particularly Michelangelo, whose work he regarded as the pinnacle of achievement. His own work was mannerist in style and includes the vast frescos depicting the history of Florence and the Medici family in the Palazzo Vecchio in Florence, as well as the design of the Uffizi palace.

Vasco da Gama /'væskəʊ/ see DA GAMA.

Vaughan[1] /vɔ:n/, Henry (1621–95), Welsh poet. One of the group of metaphysical poets, his poems have a distinctive ethereal quality, which has led him to be described as a mystic. His volumes of religious poetry include *Silex Scintillans* (1650, 1655), in which he acknowledges his debt to George Herbert. Among his prose works is *The Mount of Olives, or Solitary Devotions* (1652).

Vaughan[2] /vɔ:n/, Sarah (Lois) (1924–90), American jazz singer and pianist. She began singing with jazz bands in the early 1940s and was chiefly associated with bebop. She performed as a soloist from 1945, and became internationally famous in the early 1950s, being renowned for her vocal range, her use of vibrato, and her improvisational skills.

Vaughan Williams /vɔ:n 'wɪljəmz/, Ralph (1872–1958), English composer. He composed strongly melodic music in almost every genre, including nine symphonies, operas, choral works, and many songs. His compositions frequently reflect his interest in Tudor composers and English folk-songs, which he collected and arranged from about 1903 onwards. Among his most not-

able works are the *Fantasia on a Theme by Thomas Tallis* (1910), *A London Symphony* (1914), and the Mass in G minor (1922).

Vavilov /'vævɪˌlɒf/, Nikolai (Ivanovich) (1887–*c*.1943), Soviet plant geneticist. He travelled extensively on botanical expeditions and amassed a considerable collection of new plants, with the aim of utilizing their genetic resources for crop improvement. He did much to improve the yields of Soviet agriculture, and located the centres of origin of many cultivated plants. However, Vavilov's views conflicted with official Soviet ideology (dominated by the theories of T. D. Lysenko) and he was arrested in 1940, dying later in a labour camp. His reputation was subsequently restored, a research institute being named after him.

Veblen /'veblən/, Thorstein (Bunde) (1857–1929), American economist and social scientist. He is best known as the author of *The Theory of the Leisure Class* (1899), a critique of capitalism in which he coined the phrase 'conspicuous consumption'. This and subsequent works, such as *The Theory of Business Enterprise* (1904), had a significant influence on later economists such as J. K. Galbraith.

Vega /ˌveɪɡə/, Lope de (full name Lope Felix de Vega Carpio) (1562–1635), Spanish dramatist and poet. He is regarded as the founder of Spanish drama and is said to have written 1,500 plays, of which several hundred survive. His dramas cover a wide range of genres from the historical and sacred to contemporary plays of intrigue and chivalry. His other works include epic poems and pastoral romances.

Velázquez /vɪ'læskwɪz/, Diego Rodríguez de Silva y (1599–1660), Spanish painter. His early paintings consisted chiefly of naturalistic religious works and domestic genre scenes. After his appointment as court painter to Philip IV in 1623, he painted many notable portraits, paintings which humanized the stiff and formal Spanish tradition of idealized figures and tended towards naturalness and simplicity. Among the best known are *Pope Innocent X* (1650) and *Las Meninas* (*c*.1656). Other notable works include *The Toilet of Venus* (known as The Rokeby Venus, *c*.1651).

Velázquez de Cuéllar /deɪ 'kweɪjɑ:(r)/, Diego (*c*.1465–1524), Spanish conquistador. After sailing with Columbus to the New World in 1493, he began the conquest of Cuba in 1511; he founded a number of settlements including Havana (1515), and later initiated expeditions to conquer Mexico.

Velde, van de[1], Henri, see VAN DE VELDE[2].

Velde, van de[2], Willem and sons, see VAN DE VELDE[1].

Velleius Paterculus /veˌleɪəs pə'tɜːkjʊləs/ (*c*.19 BC–AD *c*.30), Roman historian and soldier. His *Roman History* in two volumes, covering the period from the early history of Rome to AD 30, is notable for its rhetorical manner and for its eulogistic depiction of Tiberius, with whom Velleius had served in Germany before Tiberius became emperor.

Vening Meinesz /ˌvenɪŋ 'maɪneʃ/, Felix Andries (1887–1966), Dutch geophysicist. He devised a technique for making accurate gravity measurements with the aid of a pendulum, using it first for a gravity survey of the Netherlands. He then pioneered the use of submarines for marine gravity surveys, locating negative gravity anomalies in the deep trenches near island arcs in the Pacific and interpreting them as being due to the downward buckling of the oceanic crust. This was eventually confirmed; Vening Meinesz, however, never supported the idea of continental drift.

Venturi /ven'tjʊərɪ/, Robert (Charles) (born 1925), American architect. He reacted against the prevailing international style of the 1960s and pioneered the development of post-modernist architecture. His work is eclectic, making use of historical references and sometimes of kitsch. Among his buildings are the Humanities Classroom Building of the State University of New York (1973) and the Sainsbury Wing of the National Gallery in London (1991). His writings include *Complexity and Contradiction in Architecture* (1966).

Verdi /'veədɪ/, Giuseppe (Fortunino Francesco) (1813–1901), Italian composer. He is chiefly remembered for his many operas, which are notable for strong characterization, original orchestration, and memorable tunes. Verdi was a supporter of the movement for Italian unity, and several of his early works were identified with the nationalist cause, including *Nabucco* (1842), with which he established his reputation. Other operas include *Rigoletto* (1851), *La Traviata* (1853), and *Otello* (1887); *Aida*, commissioned to be staged in Cairo to celebrate

the opening of the Suez Canal, was delayed due to the Franco-Prussian War and eventually first performed there in 1871. Among his other compositions are sacred choral works such as the Requiem Mass of 1874.

Verdon Roe, Sir Edwin Alliott, see ROE.

Vergil see VIRGIL.

Verlaine /veə'leɪn/, Paul (1844–96), French poet. Initially a member of the Parnassian group of poets, he later became prominent among the symbolists, especially with the publication of his influential essay 'Art poétique' (1882). Notable collections of poetry include *Poèmes saturniens* (1867), *Fêtes galantes* (1869), and *Romances sans paroles* (1874), a work characterized by an intense musicality and metrical inventiveness. The last was written in prison, where Verlaine was serving a two-year sentence for wounding his lover, the poet Arthur Rimbaud, during a quarrel.

Vermeer /vɜː'mɪə(r)/, Jan (1632–75), Dutch painter. He spent his life in his native town of Delft, where he generally painted domestic genre scenes, often depicting a single figure engaged in an ordinary task (for example *The Kitchen-Maid, c.*1658). His work is distinguished by its clear design and simple form, and by its harmonious balance of predominant yellows, blues, and greys. His other works include two views of Delft and a self-portrait, the *Allegory of Painting* (c.1665). His paintings were long neglected and only began to receive full recognition in the later 19th century.

Verne /vɜːn/, Jules (1828–1905), French novelist. Regarded as one of the first writers of science fiction, in his adventure stories he often anticipated later scientific and technological developments. He explored the possibilities of space travel in *From the Earth to the Moon* (1865) and the use of submarines in *Twenty Thousand Leagues Under the Sea* (1870). Other novels include *Journey to the Centre of the Earth* (1864) and *Around the World in Eighty Days* (1873).

Veronese /ˌverə'neɪzɪ/, Paolo (born Paolo Caliari) (c.1528–88), Italian painter. Born in Verona, by about 1553 he had established himself in Venice, where he gained many commissions, including the painting of frescos in a number of churches and in the Doges' Palace. Assisted by the staff of a large workshop, he produced numerous paintings, mainly dealing with religious,

allegorical, and historical subjects; he is particularly known for his richly coloured feast-scenes (such as *The Marriage at Cana*, 1562). Other notable works include his series of frescos in Palladio's villa at Maser near Treviso (1561).

Verwoerd /fə'vʊət/, Hendrik (Frensch) (1901–66), South African statesman, Prime Minister 1958–66. Born in the Netherlands, he was active in Afrikaner groups during the Second World War. He joined the National Party and served as Minister of Bantu Affairs from 1950 to 1958, developing the segregation policy of apartheid. As Premier, Verwoerd banned the ANC and the Pan-Africanist Congress in 1960, following the Sharpeville massacre. He withdrew South Africa from the Commonwealth and declared it a republic in 1961. Verwoerd was assassinated by a parliamentary messenger.

Vesalius /vɪ'seɪlɪəs/, Andreas (1514–64), Flemish anatomist, the founder of modern anatomy. He challenged traditional theories of anatomy, holding them to be seriously flawed in being based on the bodies of apes — a view borne out by later studies. His major work, *De Humani Corporis Fabrica* (1543), contained accurate descriptions of human anatomy; it owed much of its great historical impact, however, to the woodcuts of his dissections, which were drawn and engraved by others. He became unofficial physician to the emperor Charles V, followed by a period with Philip II of Spain. The medical profession there still supported Galen, whose works he had strongly criticized, and Vesalius died while returning to his old post at Padua.

Vespasian /ve'speɪʒ(ə)n/ (Latin name Titus Flavius Vespasianus) (AD 9–79), Roman emperor 69–79 and founder of the Flavian dynasty. A distinguished general, he was acclaimed emperor by the legions in Egypt during the civil wars that followed the death of Nero and gained control of Italy after the defeat of Vitellius. His reign saw the restoration of financial and military order and the initiation of a public building programme which included the rebuilding of the Capitol and the beginning of the construction of the Colosseum (75).

Vespucci /ve'spuːtʃɪ/, Amerigo (1451–1512), Italian merchant and explorer. He is said to have made a number of voyages to the New World, although only two have been authenticated. His first such voyage, for the

Spanish, was probably made between 1499 and 1500 and saw the explorer reach the coast of Venezuela. Having entered Portuguese service, he embarked on another voyage (1501–2), during which he explored the Brazilian coastline and sailed at least as far south as the River Plate. The Latin form of his first name is believed to have given rise to the name of America.

Vicente /vɪˈsentɪ/, Gil (c.1465–c.1536), Portuguese dramatist and poet. Vicente is regarded as Portugal's most important dramatist. He enjoyed royal patronage for much of his life, and many of his poems and plays were written to commemorate national or court events. His works (some written in Portuguese, some in Spanish) include dramas on religious themes, farces, pastoral plays, and comedies satirizing the nobility and clergy.

Vico /ˈviːkəʊ/, Giambattista (1668–1744), Italian philosopher. His work championed the philosophy of history rather than the mathematical and scientific philosophy favoured by his contemporaries. In *Scienza Nuova* (1725) he proposed that civilizations are subject to recurring cycles of barbarism, heroism, and reason. Vico argued that these cycles are accompanied by corresponding cultural, linguistic, and political modes. He claimed that in literature, for example, poetry flourishes in the heroic age, while prose enters in the age of reason. His historicist philosophy made an impression on later philosophers such as Marx and semioticians such as Umberto Eco.

Victor Emmanuel II /ˌvɪktər ɪˈmænjʊəl/ (1820–78), ruler of the kingdom of Sardinia 1849–61 and king of Italy 1861–78. His appointment of Cavour as Premier in 1852 hastened the drive towards Italian unification. In 1859 Victor Emmanuel led his Piedmontese army to victory against the Austrians at the battles of Magenta and Solferino, and in 1860 entered the papal territories around French-held Rome to join his forces with those of Garibaldi. After being crowned first king of a united Italy in Turin in 1861, Victor Emmanuel continued to add to his kingdom, acquiring Venetia in 1866 and Rome in 1870.

Victor Emmanuel III /ˌvɪktər ɪˈmænjʊəl/ (1869–1947), king of Italy 1900–46. He succeeded to the throne after his father's assassination. Under Mussolini, whom he had invited to form a government in 1922

in order to forestall civil war, Victor Emmanuel lost all political power. However, during the Second World War, after the loss of Sicily to the Allies (1943), he acted to dismiss Mussolini and conclude an armistice. Victor Emmanuel abdicated in favour of his son in 1946, but a republic was established the same year by popular vote and both he and his son went into exile.

Victoria[1] /vɪkˈtɔːrɪə/ (1819–1901), queen of Great Britain and Ireland 1837–1901 and empress of India 1876–1901. She succeeded to the throne on the death of her uncle, William IV, and married her cousin Prince Albert in 1840; they had nine children. As queen she took an active interest in the policies of her ministers, although she did not align the Crown with any one political party. She largely retired from public life and went into seclusion after Albert's death in 1861, but lived to achieve the longest reign in British history, a time during which Britain became a powerful and prosperous imperial nation. Her golden jubilee (1887) and diamond jubilee (1897) were marked with popular celebration.

Victoria[2] /vɪkˈtɔːrɪə/, Tomás Luis de (1548–1611), Spanish composer. In 1565 he went to Rome, where he may have studied with Palestrina; he eventually returned to Spain, settling in Madrid in 1594. His music, all of it religious, is characterized by its dramatic vigour and colour and resembles that of Palestrina in its contrapuntal nature; it includes motets, masses, and hymns.

Vidal /vɪˈdɑːl/, Gore (born Eugene Luther Vidal) (born 1925), American novelist, dramatist, and essayist. His first novel *Williwaw* (1946) was based on his wartime experiences. His other novels, usually satirical comedies, include *Myra Breckenridge* (1968) and *Creation* (1981). Among his plays are *Suddenly Last Summer* (1958). His essays, published in a number of collections, form a satirical commentary on American political and cultural life.

Vigée-Lebrun /ˌviːʒeɪləˈbrɜːn/, (Marie Louise) Élisabeth (1755–1842), French painter. In 1779 she was commissioned to paint Marie Antoinette, whom she painted about twenty-five times over the next ten years. Vigée-Lebrun became a member of the Royal Academy of Painting and Sculpture in Paris in 1783. On the outbreak of the French Revolution in 1789 she fled to Italy,

where she was acclaimed for her portraits of Lady Hamilton. Vigée-Lebrun worked in many countries throughout Europe, chiefly as a portraitist of women and children, before returning to France in 1810.

Vignola /vɪˈnjəʊlə/, Giacomo Barozzi da (1507–73), Italian architect. His designs were mannerist in style and include a number of churches in Rome as well as private residences such as the Palazzo Farnese near Viterbo (1559–73). One of his most influential designs was that for the church of Il Gesù in Rome (begun 1568), the headquarters of the Jesuit order; based on Alberti's church of San Andrea, Mantua, it has a Latin cross plan, with the nave broadened and the dome area increased, in accordance with Counter-Reformation ideas and the new importance attached to preaching. He also wrote a significant treatise on the five orders of architecture.

Vigny /ˈviːnjɪ/, Alfred Victor, Comte de (1797–1863), French poet, novelist, and dramatist. From 1822 he published several volumes of verse which reveal his philosophy of stoic resignation; later poems, published posthumously in 1863, assert his faith in 'man's unconquerable mind'. Other works include his historical novel *Cinq-Mars* (1826) and the play *Chatterton* (1835), whose hero epitomizes the romantic notion of the poet as an isolated genius.

Vigo /ˈviːgəʊ/, Jean (1905–34), French film director. He is noted for his experimental films, which combine lyrical, surrealist, and realist elements. These include two short films and the two feature films *Zéro de conduite* (1933) and *L'Atalante* (1934). The former's indictment of repressive authority in a French boarding-school caused it to be banned in France until 1945.

Villa /ˈviːjə/, Pancho (born Doroteo Arango) (1878–1923), Mexican revolutionary. He played a prominent role in the revolution of 1910–11 led by Francisco Madero (1873–1913), and together with Venustiano Carranza (1859–1920) overthrew the dictatorial regime of General Victoriano Huerta (1854–1916) in 1914. Later that year, however, he and Emiliano Zapata rebelled against Carranza and fled to the north of the country after suffering a series of defeats. Villa invaded the US in 1916 but was forced back into Mexico by the American army. He continued to oppose Carranza's

regime until the latter's overthrow in 1920. Villa was eventually assassinated.

Villa-Lobos /ˌvɪləˈləʊbɒs/, Heitor (1887–1959), Brazilian composer. At the age of 18 he journeyed into the Brazilian interior collecting folk music. He later wove this music into many of his instrumental compositions, notably the series of fourteen *Chôros* (1920–9), scored in the style of Puccini, and the nine *Bachianas brasileiras* (1930–45), arranged in counterpoint after the manner of Bach. Villa-Lobos was a prolific composer, writing at least two thousand works; he was also a major force in music education in Brazil, founding the Academy of Music in Rio de Janeiro in 1945 and serving as its president until his death.

Villon /ˈviːjɒn, French vijɔ̃/, François (born François de Montcorbier or François des Loges) (*fl.c.*1460), French poet. He is one of the greatest French lyric poets, best known for *Le Lais* or *Le Petit testament* (1456) and the longer, more serious *Le Grand testament* (1461). He was notorious for his life of criminal excess and spent much time in prison. In 1462 he received the death sentence in Paris; when it was commuted to banishment he left the capital and subsequently disappeared.

Vincent de Paul, St /ˌvɪns(ə)nt də ˈpɔːl/ (1581–1660), French priest. He devoted his life to work among the poor and the sick and established a number of institutions to continue his work. In 1625 he established the Congregation of the Mission, an organization (also known as the Lazarists) that now has foundations worldwide. In 1633 Vincent de Paul was one of the founders of the Daughters of Charity (Sisters of Charity of St Vincent de Paul), an unenclosed women's order devoted to the care of the poor and the sick. Feast day, 19 July.

Vinci, Leonardo da, see LEONARDO DA VINCI.

Vine[1] /vaɪn/, Barbara, the pseudonym used by Ruth Rendell.

Vine[2] /vaɪn/, Frederick John (born 1939), English geologist. Vine worked at Princeton before returning to Britain as reader in environmental science at the University of East Anglia. Developing the hypothesis of sea-floor spreading, Vine and his colleague Drummond H. Matthews (1931–97) reasoned that new rock formed at a mid-ocean ridge should be magnetized according to

the prevailing polarity of the earth, and that successively older rocks further from the ridge should provide a record of changing polarities. Their demonstration (1963) that magnetic data from the Atlantic Ocean supported this hypothesis was a decisive step in establishing the theory of plate tectonics.

Virchow /'vɜːkəʊ, German 'fɪrço/, Rudolf Karl (1821–1902), German physician and pathologist, founder of cellular pathology. He saw the cell as the basis of life, and believed that diseases were reflected in specific cellular abnormalities. He set these views out in *Die Cellularpathologie* (1858), thus giving a scientific basis to pathology. Virchow also worked on improving sanitary conditions in Berlin, and believed that environmental factors such as poor living conditions could be as much a cause of disease as germs. He helped to make Berlin a European centre of medicine.

Virgil /'vɜːdʒɪl/ (also **Vergil**) (Latin name Publius Vergilius Maro) (70–19 BC), Roman poet. Virgil is one of the most important poets of the Augustan period. His first major work was the *Eclogues*, ten pastoral poems, modelled on those of Theocritus, in which the traditional themes of Greek bucolic poetry are blended with contemporary political and literary themes. His next work, the *Georgics*, is a didactic poem on farming, which also treats the wider themes of the relationship of human beings to nature and outlines an ideal of national revival after civil war. His last work was the *Aeneid*, an epic poem modelled on Homer which relates the wanderings of the Trojan hero Aeneas after the fall of Troy. Virgil's works quickly established themselves as classics of Latin poetry and exerted great influence on later classical and post-classical literature.

Virgin Mary, the mother of Jesus (see MARY[1]).

Visconti /vɪsˈkɒntɪ/, Luchino (full name Don Luchino Visconti, Conte di Modrone) (1906–76), Italian film and theatre director. Born into an aristocratic family, he became a Marxist and his films reflect his commitment to social issues. He worked for a time with Jean Renoir, the influence of whose naturalistic technique is seen in his first film *Obsession* (1942), which was later regarded as the forerunner of neo-realism. Other notable films include *The Leopard* (1963) and *Death in Venice* (1971). In the

theatre Visconti directed many successful dramatic and operatic productions, including works by Jean-Paul Sartre, Jean Cocteau, and Verdi.

Vitellius /vɪˈteliəs/, Aulus (15–69), Roman emperor. He was acclaimed emperor in January 69 by the legions in Germany during the civil wars that followed the death of Nero. Vitellius defeated his main rival Otho and briefly reigned as emperor but was in turn defeated and killed by the supporters of Vespasian in December of the same year.

Vitruvius /vɪˈtruːvɪəs/ (full name Marcus Vitruvius Pollio) (*fl.* 1st century BC), Roman architect and military engineer. He wrote a comprehensive ten-volume treatise on architecture, largely based on Greek sources. This deals with all aspects of building, including matters such as acoustics and water supply as well as the more obvious aspects of architectural design, decoration, and building. His influence was considerable, both during his own time and in the Renaissance.

Vitus, St /'vaɪtəs/ (died *c.*300), Christian martyr. Little is known of his life, but he is said to have been martyred during the reign of Diocletian. He was invoked against rabies and as the patron of those who suffered from epilepsy and certain nervous disorders, including St Vitus's dance (Sydenham's chorea). Feast day, 15 June.

Vivaldi /vɪˈvældɪ/, Antonio (Lucio) (1678–1741), Italian composer and violinist. Throughout his life he worked in an orphanage in Venice as violin teacher and composer, and he composed many of his works for performance there. He emerged as one of the most important baroque composers; his feeling for texture and melody is evident not only in his best-known works, such as *The Four Seasons* (1725), but also in his surviving operas and solo motets. His other numerous compositions include hundreds of concertos (several of which were later arranged by J. S. Bach) and seventy-three sonatas. His work has enjoyed a re-evaluation during the 20th century, especially since the revival of interest in authentic methods of performing baroque music.

Vivekananda /ˌvɪveɪkɑːˈnʌndə/, Swami (born Narendranath Datta) (1863–1902), Indian spiritual leader and reformer. He was

a disciple of the Indian mystic Rama-krishna and did much to spread his teach-ings; during his extensive travels he was also responsible for introducing Vedantic philosophy to the US and Europe. On his return to India in 1897 he founded the Ramakrishna Mission near Calcutta, de-voted to charitable work among the poor.

Vladimir I /'vlædɪˌmɪə(r)/ (known as Vlad-imir the Great; canonized as St Vladimir) (956–1015), grand prince of Kiev 980–1015. By 980 he had seized Kiev from his elder brother and had extended his rule from Ukraine to the Baltic Sea. After marrying a sister of the Byzantine emperor Basil II (c.987) he converted to Christianity, a move which resulted in Christianity in Russia developing in close association with the Orthodox rather than the Western Church. Feast day, 15 July.

Vlaminck /vlæ'mæŋk/, Maurice de (1876–1958), French painter and writer. Largely self-taught, he met Derain and Matisse in the early 1900s and with them became a leading exponent of fauvism, painting mainly landscapes. He was later influenced by Cézanne and from about 1908 his col-our and brushwork became more subdued. He also wrote novels and memoirs and was a pioneer collector of African art.

Volta /'vɒltə/, Alessandro Giuseppe Antonio Anastasio, Count (1745–1827), Italian physi-cist. Volta was the inventor of a number of important electrical instruments, includ-ing the electrophorus and the condensing electroscope, but is best known for the voltaic pile or electrochemical battery (1800) — the first device to produce a con-tinuous electric current. The impetus for this was Luigi Galvani's claim to have dis-covered a new kind of electricity produced in animal tissue, which Volta ascribed to normal electricity produced by the contact of two dissimilar metals.

Voltaire /vɒl'teə(r)/ (pseudonym of François-Marie Arouet) (1694–1778), French writer, dramatist, and poet. He was a lead-ing figure of the Enlightenment, and fre-quently came into conflict with the Establishment as a result of his radical political and religious views and satirical writings. He spent a period in exile in England (1726–9) and was introduced there to the theories of Isaac Newton and the empiricist philosophy of John Locke. He also became acquainted with British political institutions, and extolled them as against the royal autocracy of France. Vol-taire lived in Switzerland from 1754, only returning to Paris just before his death. Major works include *Lettres philosophiques* (1734) and *Candide* (1758), a satirical tale attacking Leibniz's optimism; he also wrote plays, poetry, and historical works, and was a contributor to the great French *Encyclopédie* (1751–76).

von Braun /braʊn/, Werner Magnus Max-imilian, see BRAUN[2].

Vonnegut /'vɒnɪɡət/, Kurt (born 1922), Am-erican novelist and short-story writer. His works are experimental in nature and blend elements of realism, science fiction, fantasy, and satire. They include *Cat's Cradle* (1963) and *Slaughterhouse-Five, or The Child-ren's Crusade* (1969), based on the fire-bombing of Dresden in 1945, which Vonnegut himself experienced as a pris-oner of war. Among his notable recent writings is the novel *Galapagos* (1985).

von Neumann see NEUMANN.

von Sternberg /fɒn 'stɜːnbɜːɡ/, Josef (1894–1969), Austrian-born American film dir-ector. After emigrating to the US in his childhood, he made a series of silent films about the criminal underworld in the 1920s, before directing his best-known film *Der Blaue Engel* (1930; *The Blue Angel*), star-ring Marlene Dietrich in Germany. Captur-ing the decadence of Berlin in the 1920s, the film made Dietrich an international star; von Sternberg proceeded to collab-orate with her on a series of Hollywood films, including *Dishonored* (1931) and *Shanghai Express* (1932).

Vuillard /'viːɑː(r)/, (Jean) Édouard (1868–1940), French painter and graphic artist. A member of the Nabi Group, he produced decorative panels, murals, paintings, and lithographs; domestic interiors and por-traits were his most typical subjects. His early work in particular, with its flat areas of colour, reflects the influence of Japanese prints.

W

Wade[1] /weɪd/, George (1673–1748), English soldier. After serving with distinction in the British army in Spain 1704–10, he was posted to the Scottish Highlands in 1724. There he was responsible for the construction of a network of roads and bridges to facilitate government control of the Jacobite clans after the 1715 uprising.

Wade[2] /weɪd/, (Sarah) Virginia (born 1945), English tennis player. She won many singles titles, including the US Open (1968), the Italian championship (1971), the Australian Open (1972), and Wimbledon (1977).

Wagner /ˈvɑːgnə(r)/, (Wilhelm) Richard (1813–83), German composer. He developed an operatic genre which he called music drama, synthesizing music, drama, verse, legend, and spectacle. In the late 1840s and early 1850s Wagner propounded his theories in a series of essays which polarized European musical opinion for decades. *The Flying Dutchman* (1841) was innovative in using scenes rather than numbers to form the structure. Wagner was forced into exile after supporting the German nationalist uprising in Dresden in 1848; in the same year he began writing the text of *Der Ring des Nibelungen* (*The Ring of the Nibelungs*), a cycle of four operas (*Das Rheingold, Die Walküre, Siegfried,* and *Götterdämmerung*) based loosely on ancient Germanic sagas. He wrote the accompanying music from 1854 to 1874, during which time he returned to Germany (1860). The *Ring* cycle is notable for its use of leitmotifs and orchestral colour to unify the music, dramatic narrative, and characterization. It was first staged in 1876 at Wagner's new Bayreuth theatre. Other works include the music drama *Tristan and Isolde* (1859) and the *Siegfried Idyll* (1870) for orchestra.

Wain /weɪn/, John (Barrington) (1925–94), English writer and critic. Wain was one of the Angry Young Men of the early 1950s. His first novels, including *Hurry on Down* (1953), are satirical portraits of young people trapped in a stifling middle-class society. He also wrote books of literary criticism, notably *Preliminary Essays* (1957), and poetry characterized by its wit and verbal dexterity. Wain was professor of poetry at Oxford from 1973 to 1978. His later novels include *Young Shoulders* (1982) and *Comedies* (1990).

Wajda /ˈvaɪdə/, Andrzej (born 1929), Polish film director. He came to prominence in the 1950s with a trilogy (including *Ashes and Diamonds,* 1958) about the disaffected younger generation in Poland during and after the Second World War. A recurrent theme in his work is the conflict between individual choice and the march of political events, as in *Man of Iron* (1981), which draws on the early history of the trade-union movement Solidarity, and *Danton* (1983), which traces developments in the French Revolution leading up to the Reign of Terror.

Waksman /ˈwæksmən/, Selman Abraham (1888–1973), Russian-born American microbiologist. He searched for potential antibiotics in soil micro-organisms, discovering the bacterium *Streptomyces griseus* in 1915 and isolating streptomycin from it in 1943. This was developed into the first effective drug against tuberculosis, which became a much less serious public health problem through its use. Waksman was awarded a Nobel Prize in 1952.

Waldheim /ˈvælthaɪm/, Kurt (born 1918), Austrian diplomat and statesman, President 1986–92. He was Secretary-General of the United Nations (1972–81), and, five years later, he stood as the right-wing People's Party candidate for the presidency of Austria; this he secured after a run-off election. During the campaign he denied allegations that as an army intelligence officer he had direct knowledge of Nazi atrocities during the Second World War; he was subsequently cleared in court of charges relating to his war record.

Wales, Prince of see CHARLES, PRINCE.

Wałęsa /vəˈwensə, -ˈlensə/, Lech (born 1943), Polish trade unionist and statesman, President 1990–5. A former electrician at the Lenin Shipyards in Gdańsk, he emerged as a strike leader at the port in 1980, founding the trade-union movement Solidarity

later the same year. Following the banning of Solidarity in 1981, Wałęsa was imprisoned from 1981 to 1982. He was awarded the Nobel Peace Prize in 1983. Wałęsa led Solidarity to a landslide victory in the 1989 free elections and successfully contested the 1990 presidential elections, but suffered a narrow defeat in the 1995 elections.

Walker[1] /'wɔːkə(r)/, Alice (Malsenior) (born 1944), American writer and critic. She won international acclaim for *The Color Purple* (1982), an epistolary novel about a young black woman faced with recreating her life after being raped by her supposed father. It won her the Pulitzer Prize and was made into a successful film by Steven Spielberg (1985). Other works include *In Search of Our Mothers' Gardens: Womanist Prose* (1983), a collection of her critical essays, and the novel *Possessing the Secret of Joy* (1992), an indictment of female circumcision.

Walker[2] /'wɔːkə(r)/, John (born 1952), New Zealand athlete. He was the first athlete to run a mile in less than 3 minutes 50 seconds (1975) and was also the first to run one hundred sub-four-minute miles.

Wallace[1] /'wɒlɪs/, Alfred Russel (1823–1913), English naturalist, a founder of zoogeography. He independently formulated a theory of the origin of species that was very similar to that of Charles Darwin, to whom he communicated his conclusions. He travelled extensively in South America and the East Indies, collecting specimens and studying the geographical distribution of animals. In 1858 a summary of the joint views of Wallace and Darwin concerning natural selection was read to the Linnaean Society in London, but credit for the theory has been attached somewhat arbitrarily to Darwin.

Wallace[2] /'wɒlɪs/, (Richard Horatio) Edgar (1875–1932), English novelist, screenwriter, and dramatist. He is noted for his crime novels, including *The Four Just Men* (1905) and *The Crimson Circle* (1922). Based in Hollywood from 1931, he wrote the screenplay for the film *King Kong*, which was made shortly after his death.

Wallace[3] /'wɒlɪs/, Sir William (c.1270–1305), Scottish national hero. He was a leader of Scottish resistance to Edward I, defeating the English army at Stirling in 1297. In the same year he mounted military campaigns against the north of England and was appointed Guardian of the Realm of Scot-

land. After Edward's second invasion of Scotland in 1298, Wallace was defeated at the battle of Falkirk; he was subsequently captured and executed by the English.

Wallenberg /'vɑːlən,bɜːg/, Raoul (1912–?), Swedish diplomat. While working as a businessman in Budapest in 1944, he was entrusted by the Swedish government with the protection of Hungarian Jews from the Nazis. Wallenberg helped many thousands of Jews (according to estimates, as many as 95,000) to escape death by issuing them with Swedish passports, but when Soviet forces took control of Budapest in 1945 he was arrested, taken to Moscow, and imprisoned. Although the Soviet authorities stated that Wallenberg had died in prison in 1947, his fate remains uncertain and there were claims that he was still alive in the 1970s.

Waller /'wɒlə(r)/, Fats (born Thomas Wright Waller) (1904–43), American jazz pianist, songwriter, band-leader, and singer. He composed the songs 'Ain't Misbehavin'' (1928) and 'Honeysuckle Rose' (1929), and was the foremost exponent of the New York 'stride school' of piano playing, which used tenths in the left hand to give a strong bass line. From 1934 onwards Waller achieved popular success as the leader of the group Fats Waller and His Rhythm.

Wallis /'wɒlɪs/, Sir Barnes Neville (1887–1979), English inventor. Working for the Vickers company, he pioneered geodetic construction in his designs for the R100 airship (1930) and the Wellington bomber used in the Second World War. During the war he designed more effective bombs, including the bouncing bomb used against the Ruhr dams in Germany in 1943. His main postwar work was on guided missiles and supersonic aircraft: he pioneered variable geometry (swing-wing) designs, although these were not fully developed at the time. Altogether he patented more than 140 designs.

Walpole[1] /'wɔːlpəʊl/, Horace, 4th Earl of Orford (1717–97), English writer and Whig politician, son of Sir Robert Walpole. He wrote *The Castle of Otranto* (1764), which is regarded as one of the first Gothic novels. Walpole is also noted for his contribution to the Gothic revival in architecture, converting his Strawberry Hill home at Twickenham, near London, into a Gothic castle (c.1753–76). He served as an MP from 1741 to 1767.

Walpole[2] /'wɔːlpəʊl/, Sir Hugh (Seymour) (1884–1941), British novelist, born in New Zealand. His third novel *Mr Perrin and Mr Traill* (1911) reflects his experiences as a schoolmaster. He is best known for *The Herries Chronicle* (1930–3), a historical sequence set in the Lake District.

Walpole[3] /'wɔːlpəʊl/, Sir Robert, 1st Earl of Orford (1676–1745), British Whig statesman, First Lord of the Treasury and Chancellor of the Exchequer 1715–17 and 1721–42. Walpole is generally regarded as the first British Prime Minister in the modern sense, having presided over the Cabinet for George I and George II during his second term as First Lord of the Treasury and Chancellor. His period of office was marked by considerable peace and prosperity, although Walpole failed to prevent war with Spain in 1739. He was the father of Horace Walpole.

Walsingham /'wɔːlsɪŋəm, 'wɒl-/, Sir Francis (c.1530–90), English politician. From 1573 to 1590 he served as Secretary of State to Queen Elizabeth I. He developed a domestic and foreign spy network that led to the detection of numerous Catholic plots against Elizabeth I and the gathering of intelligence about the Spanish Armada. In 1586 Walsingham uncovered a plot against Elizabeth involving Mary, Queen of Scots; he subsequently exerted his judicial power to have Mary executed.

Walton[1] /'wɔːlt(ə)n, 'wɒl-/, Ernest Thomas Sinton (1903–95), Irish physicist. In 1932 he succeeded, with Sir John Cockcroft, in splitting the atom (see COCKCROFT).

Walton[2] /'wɔːlt(ə)n, 'wɒl-/, Izaak (1593–1683), English writer. He is chiefly known for *The Compleat Angler* (1653; largely rewritten, 1655), which combines practical information on fishing with folklore, interspersed with pastoral songs and ballads. He also wrote biographies of John Donne (1640) and George Herbert (1670).

Walton[3] /'wɔːlt(ə)n, 'wɒl-/, Sir William (Turner) (1902–83), English composer. He lived for a time with the Sitwells, and gained fame with *Façade* (1921–3), a setting of poems by Edith Sitwell for recitation. The work of Stravinsky and Hindemith strongly influenced his Viola Concerto (1928–9). Other works include two symphonies, two operas, the oratorio *Belshazzar's Feast* (1930–1), and film scores for adaptations of three Shakespeare plays and for *The Battle of Britain* (1969).

Warbeck /'wɔːbek/, Perkin (1474–99), Flemish claimant to the English throne. Encouraged by Yorkists in England and on the Continent, he claimed to be Edward II's son Richard, Duke of York (who had disappeared in 1483 — see PRINCES IN THE TOWER), in an attempt to overthrow Henry VII. After a series of attempts to enter the country and begin a revolt he was captured and imprisoned in the Tower of London in 1497; he was later executed.

Warburg[1] /'wɔːbɜːg/, Aby (Moritz) (1866–1929), German art historian. From 1905 he built up a library in Hamburg dedicated to preserving the classical heritage of Western culture. It became part of the new University of Hamburg in 1919; four years after his death it was transferred to England and housed in the Warburg Institute (part of the University of London).

Warburg[2] /'wɔːbɜːg/, Otto Heinrich (1883–1970), German biochemist. He pioneered the use of the techniques of chemistry for biochemical investigations, especially for his chief work on intracellular respiration. He devised a manometer for this research, enabling him to study the action of respiratory enzymes and poisons in detail. Warburg was awarded a Nobel Prize in 1931, but the Hitler regime prevented him from accepting a second one in 1944 because of his Jewish ancestry.

Ward /wɔːd/, Mrs Humphry (née Mary Augusta Arnold) (1851–1920), English writer and anti-suffrage campaigner. The niece of Matthew Arnold, she is best known for several novels dealing with social and religious themes, especially *Robert Elsmere* (1888). Although she supported higher education for women, she was an active opponent of the women's suffrage movement, becoming the first president of the Anti-Suffrage League in 1908.

Warhol /'wɔːhəʊl/ Andy (born Andrew Warhola) (c.1928–87), American painter, graphic artist, and film-maker. His work played a major role in New York pop art of the 1960s. Warhol's background in commercial art and advertising illustration was central to pop art's concern with the imagery of the mass media; his famous statement 'I like boring things' was expressed in the standardized, consciously banal nature of his work. In the early 1960s he achieved fame for a series of silk-screen prints and acrylic paintings of familiar objects (such as Campbell's soup tins), car

accidents, and Marilyn Monroe, treated with objectivity and precision. From 1965 Warhol increasingly devoted himself to film, playing an important part in the emergence of the new American underground cinema. He also managed the rock group the Velvet Underground.

Warren[1] /'wɒrən/, Earl (1891–1974), American judge. During his time as Chief Justice of the US Supreme Court (1953–69) he did much to promote civil liberties, achieving the prohibition of segregation in US schools in 1954. He is also remembered for heading the commission of inquiry (known as the Warren Commission) held in 1964 into the assassination of President Kennedy; the commission found that Lee Harvey Oswald was the sole gunman, a decision that has since been much disputed.

Warren[2] /'wɒrən/, Robert Penn (1905–89), American poet, novelist, and critic. An advocate of New Criticism, he collaborated with the American critic Cleanth Brooks in writing such critical works as *Understanding Poetry* (1938) and *Understanding Fiction* (1943). Warren also wrote several novels, including *All the King's Men* (1946), and many volumes of poetry; he became the first to win Pulitzer Prizes in both fiction and poetry categories and in 1986 he was made the first American Poet Laureate.

Warwick /'wɒrɪk/, Earl of (title of Richard Neville; known as 'the Kingmaker') (1428–71), English statesman. During the Wars of the Roses he fought first on the Yorkist side, helping Edward IV to gain the throne in 1461. Having lost influence at court he then fought on the Lancastrian side, briefly restoring Henry VI to the throne in 1470. Warwick was killed at the battle of Barnet.

Washington[1] /'wɒʃɪŋtən/, Booker T(aliaferro) (1856–1915), American educationist. An emancipated slave, he pursued a career in teaching and was appointed head in 1881 of the newly founded Tuskegee Institute in Alabama for the training of black teachers. Washington emerged as a leading commentator for black Americans at the turn of the century and published his influential autobiography, *Up from Slavery*, in 1901. His emphasis on vocational skills and financial independence for blacks rather than on intellectual development or political rights, combined with his support for segregation, brought harsh criticism

from other black leaders such as W. E. B. Du Bois, and from civil-rights activists of the 20th century.

Washington[2] /'wɒʃɪŋtən/, George (1732–99), American soldier and statesman, 1st President of the US 1789–97. After serving as a soldier 1754–9 in the war against the French, Washington took part in two of the three Continental Congresses held by the American colonies in revolt against British rule (1774 and 1775), and in 1775 was chosen as commander of the army raised by the colonists, the Continental Army. He served in that capacity throughout the War of Independence, bringing about the eventual American victory by keeping the army together through the bitter winter of 1777–8 at Valley Forge and winning a decisive battle at Yorktown (1781). Washington chaired the convention at Philadelphia (1787) that drew up the American Constitution, and two years later he was unanimously elected President, initially remaining unaligned to any of the newly emerging political parties but later joining the Federalist Party. He served two terms, following a policy of neutrality in international affairs, before declining a third term and retiring to private life.

Waterhouse /'wɔːtə,haʊs/, Alfred (1830–1905), English architect. He designed the Manchester Assize courts (1859) and Town Hall (1869–77) before moving to London, where he designed the Romanesque Natural History Museum (1873–81). His work includes a number of educational buildings, such as Caius College, Cambridge (1868 onwards), and his use of red brick gave rise to the term 'redbrick university'.

Waters /'wɔːtəz/, Muddy (born McKinley Morganfield) (1915–83), American blues singer and guitarist. Based in Chicago from 1943, he became famous with his song 'Rollin' Stone' (1950). In the same year he formed a band, with which he recorded such hits as 'Got My Mojo Working' (1957). Waters impressed new rhythm and blues bands such as the Rolling Stones, who took their name from his 1950 song.

Watson[1] /'wɒts(ə)n/, James Dewey (born 1928), American biologist. Together with Francis Crick he proposed a model for the structure of the DNA molecule (see CRICK), later recounting the discovery in *The Double Helix* (1968). He shared a Nobel Prize with Crick and Maurice Wilkins in 1962. He

became director of the molecular biology laboratory at Cold Spring Harbor on Long Island in 1968, concentrating efforts on cancer research; he also served as director of the National Center for Human Genome Research (1989–92).

Watson[2] /'wɒts(ə)n/, John Broadus (1878–1958), American psychologist, founder of the school of behaviourism. He viewed behaviour as determined by an interplay between genetic endowment and environmental influences, and held that the role of the psychologist was to discern, through observation and experimentation, which behaviour was innate and which was acquired. In seeking an objective study of psychology, he set the stage for the empirical study of animal and human behaviour which was to dominate 20th-century psychology, particularly in the US.

Watson-Watt /ˌwɒts(ə)n'wɒt/, Sir Robert Alexander (1892–1973), Scottish physicist. He produced a system for locating thunderstorms by means of their radio emissions, and went on to lead a team that developed radar into a practical system for locating aircraft. This was improved and rapidly deployed in Britain for use in the Second World War, in which it was to play a vital role.

Watt /wɒt/, James (1736–1819), Scottish engineer. He greatly improved the efficiency of Thomas Newcomen's beam engine by condensing the spent steam in a separate chamber, allowing the cylinder to remain hot. The improved engines were adopted for a variety of purposes, especially after Watt entered into a business partnership with the engineer Matthew Boulton. Watt continued inventing until the end of his life, introducing rotatory engines, controlled by a centrifugal governor, and devising a chemical method of copying documents. He also introduced the term *horsepower*.

Watteau /'wɒtəʊ/, Jean Antoine (1684–1721), French painter, of Flemish descent. An initiator of the rococo style in painting, he is also known for his invention of the pastoral genre known as the *fête galante*. Watteau deliberately created an imaginary and rather theatrical world; the lighthearted imagery of his painting contrasted with the serious religious and classical subject-matter approved by the Royal Academy of Painting and Sculpture. His best-

known painting is *L'Embarquement pour l'île de Cythère* (1717).

Watts[1] /wɒts/, George Frederick (1817–1904), English painter and sculptor. His work reflects his view of art as a vehicle for moral purpose; this is most evident in his allegorical paintings such as *Hope* (1886). He is best known for his portraits of public figures, including Gladstone, Tennyson, and John Stuart Mill. He married the actress Ellen Terry in 1864, but the marriage lasted less than a year and the couple were finally divorced in 1877.

Watts[2] /wɒts/, Isaac (1674–1748), English hymn-writer and poet. His songs for children, which included 'How Doth the Little Busy Bee' (1715), anticipated those of William Blake. Watts is also remembered for hymns such as 'O God, Our Help in Ages Past' (1719).

Waugh /wɔ:/, Evelyn (Arthur St John) (1903–66), English novelist. His first novel *Decline and Fall*, a satire on life in a boys' preparatory school, was published in 1928 and was immensely successful. Waugh's other early novels, all social satires, include *Vile Bodies* (1930), *A Handful of Dust* (1934), and *Scoop* (1938). His work was profoundly influenced by his conversion to Roman Catholicism in 1930. *Brideshead Revisited* (1945), a complex story of an aristocratic Roman Catholic family, was more sombre in tone. Later works include *The Loved One* (1948) and his trilogy (based on his wartime experiences) *Men at Arms* (1952), *Officers and Gentlemen* (1955), and *Unconditional Surrender* (1961).

Wayne /weɪn/, John (born Marion Michael Morrison; known as 'the Duke') (1907–79), American actor. Associated with the film director John Ford from 1930, Wayne became a Hollywood star with his performance in Ford's western *Stagecoach* (1939). Remembered as the archetypal cowboy hero, he appeared in many other classic westerns, notably *Red River* (1948) and *True Grit* (1969), for which he won an Oscar. Wayne's fierce patriotism was reflected in his other main roles, for example as a US marine in Ford's *Sands of Iwo Jima* (1949) and as Davy Crockett in *The Alamo* (1960), which he also produced and directed.

Webb[1] /web/, (Gladys) Mary (1881–1927), English novelist. Her novels, representative of much regional English fiction popular at the beginning of the century, include *Gone to Earth* (1917) and *Precious Bane* (1924).

The earthy subject-matter and purple prose typical of her writing were satirized in *Cold Comfort Farm* (1933) by the English novelist Stella Gibbons (1902–89).

Webb[2] /web/, (Martha) Beatrice (née Potter) (1858–1943) and Sidney (James), Baron Passfield (1859–1947), English socialists, economists, and historians. After their marriage in 1892, they were prominent members of the Fabian Society, and helped to establish the London School of Economics (1895). Together they wrote several important books on socio-political theory and history, including *The History of Trade Unionism* (1894) and *Industrial Democracy* (1897), as well as founding the weekly magazine the *New Statesman* (1913). Sidney Webb became a Labour MP in 1922 and served in the first two Labour governments.

Weber[1] /'veɪbə(r)/, Carl Maria (Friedrich Ernst) von (1786–1826), German composer. He is regarded as the founder of the German romantic school of opera. In contrast to the prevailing classical school, his opera *Der Freischütz* (1817–21) turned to German folklore for its subject-matter, and was immediately successful. His German grand opera *Euryanthe* (1822–3) gave prominence to the orchestration and made use of leitmotifs; both operas were to influence Wagner.

Weber[2] /'veɪbə(r)/, Max (1864–1920), German economist and sociologist. His writings on the relationship between economy and society established him as one of the founders of modern sociology. In his celebrated book *The Protestant Ethic and the Spirit of Capitalism* (1904), Weber argued that there was a direct relationship between the Protestant work ethic and the rise of Western capitalism. Throughout his work he stressed that the bureaucratization of political and economic society was the most significant development in the modernization of Western civilization. Other works include *Economy and Society* (1922).

Weber[3] /'veɪb(ə)r/, Wilhelm Eduard (1804–91), German physicist. His early researches were in acoustics and animal locomotion, but he is chiefly remembered for his contributions in the fields of electricity and magnetism. Weber proposed a unified system for electrical units, determined the ratio between the units of electrostatic and electromagnetic charge, and devised a law of electrical force (later replaced by Maxwell's field theory). He went on to investigate electrodynamics and the nature and role of the electric charge.

Webern /'veɪb(ə)n/, Anton (Friedrich Ernst) von (1883–1945), Austrian composer. He followed the development of the work of his teacher Schoenberg from tonality to atonality; this departure is evident in his 1908–9 setting of songs by the German poet Stefan George (1868–1933). His music is marked by its brevity; the atonal *Five Pieces for Orchestra* (1911–13) lasts under a minute. Together with Berg, Webern became the leading exponent of the serialism developed by Schoenberg. Important serial works include the *Symphony* (1928) and the *Variations for Orchestra* (1940). During the Second World War his work was denounced by the Nazis. He was shot, accidentally, by an American soldier during the postwar occupation of Austria.

Webster[1] /'webstə(r)/, John (c.1580–c.1625), English dramatist. He wrote several plays in collaboration with other dramatists but his reputation rests chiefly on two revenge tragedies, *The White Devil* (1612) and *The Duchess of Malfi* (1623). His plays were not popular in his own day; Charles Lamb, in particular, was responsible for his revival in the 19th century.

Webster[2] /'webstə(r)/, Noah (1758–1843), American lexicographer. His *American Dictionary of the English Language* (1828) in two volumes was the first dictionary to give comprehensive coverage of American usage, and his name survives in the many dictionaries produced by the American publishing house Merriam–Webster. These include the collegiate dictionaries, published since 1898, and *Webster's Third New International Dictionary of the English Language* (1961).

Wedekind /'veɪdə,kɪnt/, Frank (1864–1918), German dramatist. He was a key figure in the emergence of expressionist drama. His play *The Awakening of Spring* (1891) scandalized contemporary German society with its explicit and sardonic portrayal of sexual awakening. Wedekind later attacked the bourgeois sexual code at the turn of the century in his two tragedies *Earth Spirit* (1895) and *Pandora's Box* (1904), both featuring the femme fatale Lulu. The plays form the basis of Berg's opera *Lulu*.

Wedgwood /'wedʒwʊd/ Josiah (1730–95), English potter. He earned an international reputation with the pottery factories that he established in Staffordshire in the

1760s. These produced both practical and ornamental ware, maintaining high standards of quality despite large-scale production. Wedgwood's designs, and those of his chief designer John Flaxman, were often based on antique relief sculptures and contributed to the rise of neoclassical taste in England. His name is perhaps most associated with the powder-blue stoneware pieces with white embossed cameos that first appeared in 1775.

Wegener /'veɪɡənə(r)/, Alfred Lothar (1880–1930), German meteorologist and geologist. He was the first serious proponent of the theory of continental drift, but this was not accepted by most geologists during his lifetime, partly because he could not suggest a convincing motive force to account for continental movements. It is, however, now accepted as correct in principle. Wegener also wrote a standard textbook of meteorology. He died on the Greenland ice-cap in 1930 during an expedition.

Weil /vaɪl, French vɛj/, Simone (1909–43), French essayist, philosopher, and mystic. Weil deliberately chose to work in a Renault car factory (1934–5) and to serve in the Spanish Civil War on the Republican side (1936). Two years later she had the first in a series of mystical experiences which were to have a profound influence on her writing; she did not, however, affiliate herself to any established religion. During the Second World War Weil joined the resistance movement in England, where she died from tuberculosis. Her reputation is based on such autobiographical works as *Waiting for God* (1949) and *Notebooks* (1951–6), both published posthumously.

Weill /vaɪl/, Kurt (1900–50), German composer, resident in the US from 1935. In 1926 Weill married the Austrian singer Lotte Lenya (1900–81), for whom many of his songs were written. He was based in Berlin until 1933 and is best known for the operas he wrote in collaboration with Bertolt Brecht, political satires which evoke the harsh decadence of the pre-war period in Germany and which are marked by his direct and harmonically simple style of composition. These include *The Rise and Fall of the City of Mahagonny* (1927) and *The Threepenny Opera* (1928).

Weinberg /'waɪmbɜːɡ/, Steven (born 1933), American theoretical physicist. Weinberg worked at several universities before being appointed as professor of physics at the University of Texas. He devised a theory to unify electromagnetic interactions and the weak forces within the nucleus of an atom, for which he shared the Nobel Prize for physics in 1979. Weinberg's popular work *The First Three Minutes* (1977) is an account of the processes occurring immediately after the big bang.

Weismann /'vaɪsmən/, August Friedrich Leopold (1834–1914), German biologist, one of the founders of modern genetics. He expounded the theory of germ plasm, a substance which he postulated bore the factors that determine the transmission of characters from parent to offspring. The theory ruled out the transmission of acquired characteristics. Weismann realized that reproduction involved the halving and later reuniting of chromosomes, and suggested that variability came from their recombination.

Weissmuller /'vaɪs,mʊlə(r)/, John Peter ('Johnny') (1904–84), American swimmer and actor. He won three Olympic gold medals in 1924 and two in 1928. He was the first man to swim 100 metres in under a minute and set twenty-eight world records in freestyle events. He later achieved wider recognition as the star of the Tarzan films of the 1930s and 1940s.

Weizmann /'vaɪtsmən, 'waɪzmən/, Chaim (Azriel) (1874–1952), Israeli statesman, President 1949–52. Born in Russia, he became a British citizen in 1910. A supporter of Zionism from the early 1900s, Weizmann participated in the negotiations that led to the Balfour Declaration (1917), which outlined British support for a Jewish homeland in Palestine. He later served as president of the World Zionist Organization (1920–31; 1935–46), facilitating Jewish immigration into Palestine in the 1930s. Weizmann also played an important role in persuading the US government to recognize the new state of Israel (1948) and became its first President in 1949.

Welles /welz/, (George) Orson (1915–85), American film director and actor. Welles formed his own Mercury Theatre company and caused a public sensation in 1938 with a radio dramatization of H. G. Wells's *The War of the Worlds*, whose realism and contemporary American setting persuaded many listeners that a Martian invasion was really happening. Turning to films, he produced, directed, wrote, and acted in the

critically acclaimed *Citizen Kane* (1941), based on the life of the newspaper tycoon William Randolph Hearst. Welles was an important figure in the *film noir* genre as shown by such films as *The Lady from Shanghai* (1948), in which he co-starred with his second wife Rita Hayworth. His best-known film performance was as Harry Lime in *The Third Man* (1949).

Wellington /'welɪŋtən/, 1st Duke of (title of Arthur Wellesley; also known as 'the Iron Duke') (1769–1852), British soldier and Tory statesman, Prime Minister 1828–30 and 1834. Born in Ireland, he served as commander of British forces in the Peninsular War, winning a series of victories against the French and finally driving them across the Pyrenees into southern France (1814). The following year Wellington defeated Napoleon at the Battle of Waterloo, so ending the Napoleonic Wars. During his first term as Prime Minister he granted Catholic Emancipation under pressure from Daniel O'Connell.

Wells /welz/, H(erbert) G(eorge) (1866–1946), English novelist. After studying biology with T. H. Huxley he wrote some of the earliest science-fiction novels, such as *The Time Machine* (1895) and *The War of the Worlds* (1898). These combined political satire, warnings about the dangerous new powers of science, and a hope for the future. In 1903 Wells joined the Fabian Society; his socialism was reflected in several comic novels about lower-middle-class life, including *Kipps* (1905) and *The History of Mr Polly* (1910). He is also noted for much speculative writing about the future of society, particularly in *The Shape of Things to Come* (1933).

Welsbach /'welzbæk/, Carl Auer von, see AUER.

Welty /'weltɪ/, Eudora (born 1909), American novelist, short-story writer, and critic. During the Depression of the mid-1930s she worked in her native Mississippi as an official photographer for the US government. She published her first short-story collection in 1941; several collections followed including *The Golden Apples* (1949), about three generations of Mississippi families. Welty's novels chiefly focus on life in the South and contain Gothic elements; they include *Delta Wedding* (1946) and *The Optimist's Daughter* (1972), which won the Pulitzer Prize.

Wenceslas /'wensɪsləs/ (also Wenceslaus) (1361–1419), king of Bohemia (as Wenceslas IV) 1378–1419. He became king of Germany and Holy Roman emperor in the same year as he succeeded to the throne of Bohemia, but was deposed by the German Electors in 1400. As king of Bohemia, Wenceslas supported the growth of the Hussite movement, but could not prevent the execution of John Huss in 1415.

Wenceslas, St (also Wenceslaus; known as 'Good King Wenceslas') (c.907–29), Duke of Bohemia and patron saint of the Czech Republic. He worked to Christianize the people of Bohemia but was murdered by his brother Boleslaus; he later became venerated as a martyr and hero of Bohemia. The story told in the Christmas carol 'Good King Wenceslas', by J. M. Neale (1818–66), appears to have no basis in fact. Feast day, 28 September.

Werner[1] /'vɜːnə(r)/, Abraham Gottlob (1749–1817), German geologist. He was the chief exponent of the Neptunian theory, which included the belief that rocks such as granites (now known to be of igneous origin) were formed as crystalline precipitates from a primeval ocean. Although this theory was invalid, the controversy that it stimulated prompted a rapid increase in geological research, and Werner's was probably the first attempt to establish a universal stratigraphic sequence.

Werner[2] /'vɜːnə(r)/, Alfred (1866–1919), French-born Swiss chemist, founder of co-ordination chemistry. He demonstrated that the three-dimensional structure of molecules was important not just for organic compounds but for the whole of chemistry. In 1893 he announced his theory of chemical coordination, proposing a secondary or residual form of valency to explain the structures of coordination compounds. He was awarded the Nobel Prize for chemistry in 1913.

Wesker /'weskə(r)/, Arnold (born 1932), English dramatist. His writing is associated with British kitchen-sink drama of the 1950s and his plays, reflecting his commitment to socialism, often deal with the working-class search for cultural identity, as in *Roots* (1959). He is also noted for *Chips with Everything* (1962), a study of class attitudes in the RAF during national service, and *The Merchant* (1977), which reworks the story of Shylock in an indictment of anti-Semitism.

Wesley /'wezlɪ/, John (1703–91), English preacher and co-founder of Methodism. He became the leader of a small group in Oxford which had been formed in 1729 by his brother Charles (1707–88); its members were nicknamed the 'Methodists'. In 1738 John Wesley experienced a spiritual conversion as a result of a reading in London of Luther's preface to the Epistle to the Romans. He resolved to devote his life to evangelistic work; however, when Anglican opposition caused the churches to be closed to him, he and his followers began preaching out of doors. Wesley subsequently travelled throughout Britain winning many working-class converts and widespread support of the Anglican clergy. Despite his wish for Methodism to remain within the Church of England, his practice of ordaining his missionaries himself (since the Church refused to do so) brought him increasing opposition from the Anglican establishment and eventual exclusion; the Methodists formally separated from the Church of England in 1791.

West[1] /west/, Benjamin (1738–1820), American painter, resident in Britain from 1763. He was appointed historical painter to George III in 1769 and became the second president of the Royal Academy on Joshua Reynolds's death in 1792. His portrait *The Death of General Wolfe* (1771) depicted its subject in contemporary rather than classical dress, signifying a new departure in English historical painting.

West[2] /west/, Mae (1892–1980), American actress and dramatist. She made her name on Broadway appearing in her own comedies *Sex* (1926) and *Diamond Lil* (1928), which were memorable for their frank and spirited approach to sexual matters; the former resulted in a short period of imprisonment for alleged obscenity. In the early 1930s West began her long and successful Hollywood career; major films included *She Done Him Wrong* (1933) and *Klondike Annie* (1936). She is also noted for the autobiography *Goodness Had Nothing to Do with It* (1959). The inflatable life-jacket used by the RAF in the Second World War was nicknamed the Mae West in tribute to her curvaceous figure.

West[3] /west/, Dame Rebecca (born Cicily Isabel Fairfield) (1892–1983), British writer and feminist, born in Ireland. From 1911 she wrote journalistic articles in support of women's suffrage, adopting 'Rebecca West'

as her pseudonym after one of Ibsen's heroines. She was sent to report on Yugoslavia in 1937, publishing her observations in the *Black Lamb and Grey Falcon* (1942) in two volumes. Her other works include *The Meaning of Treason* (1949), a study of the psychology of traitors, and *A Train of Power* (1955), a critique of the Nuremberg war trials. West's many novels include *The Fountain Overflows* (1957).

Westinghouse /'westɪŋˌhaʊs/, George (1846–1914), American engineer. His achievements were wide and he held over 400 patents, but he is best known for developing vacuum-operated safety brakes and electrically controlled railway signals. He was concerned with the generation and transmission of electric power; he championed the use of alternating current (making use of the work of Nikola Tesla), and built up a huge company to manufacture his products. Westinghouse also pioneered the use of natural gas and compressed air, and installed water turbines to generate electric power at Niagara Falls.

Weyden /'vaɪd(ə)n/, Rogier van der (French name Rogier de la Pasture) (c.1400–64), Flemish painter. He was based in Brussels from about 1435, when he was appointed official painter to the city. His work, mostly portraits and religious paintings, became widely known in Europe during his lifetime; he was particularly influential in the development of Dutch portrait painting. Major works include *The Last Judgement* and *The Deposition in the Tomb* (both c.1450).

Wharton /'wɔːt(ə)n/, Edith (Newbold) (1862–1937), American novelist and short-story writer, resident in France from 1907. She established her reputation with the novel *The House of Mirth* (1905). Her novels, many of them set in New York high society, show the influence of Henry James and are chiefly preoccupied with the often tragic conflict between social and individual fulfilment. They include *Ethan Frome* (1911) and *The Age of Innocence* (1920), which won a Pulitzer Prize.

Wheatstone /'wiːtstən/, Sir Charles (1802–75), English physicist and inventor. He was a member of a family of musical instrument-makers and his interests included acoustics, optics, electricity, and telegraphy. He invented the stereoscope and concertina, but is best known for his electrical inventions, which included an

electric clock. In the 1830s Wheatstone collaborated with Sir W. F. Cooke to develop the electric telegraph, and he later devised the rheostat and the Wheatstone bridge (an apparatus for measuring electrical resistances by equalizing the potential at two points of a circuit, based on an idea of the mathematician Samuel Christie).

Wheeler /'wiːlə(r)/, John Archibald (born 1911), American theoretical physicist. Wheeler was involved in early work with Niels Bohr on nuclear fission, and joined the team to develop the hydrogen bomb at Los Alamos in 1949–50. He became professor of physics at Princeton in 1947 and at Texas in 1976. Wheeler worked on the search for a unified field theory, and collaborated with Richard Feynman on problems concerning the retarded effects of action at a distance. He was the first to use the term *black hole*, in 1968.

Whistler /'wɪslə(r)/, James (Abbott) McNeill (1834–1903), American painter and etcher. In 1855 he went to Paris, where he was influenced by the realist painter Gustave Courbet. Based mainly in London from 1859, Whistler retained his contact with Paris and shared the admiration of contemporary French painters for Japanese prints; his work reflected this in the attention he gave to the composition of subtle patterns of light. Whistler mainly painted in one or two colours, and sought to achieve harmony of colour and tone, as in the portrait *Arrangement in Grey and Black: The Artist's Mother* (1872) and the landscape *Old Battersea Bridge: Nocturne — Blue and Gold* (c.1872–5).

White[1] /waɪt/, Gilbert (1720–93), English clergyman and naturalist. He spent most of his life in his native village of Selborne, Hampshire, becoming curate there in 1784. White is best known for the many letters he wrote to friends, sharing his acute observations on all aspects of natural history, especially ornithology; these were published in 1789 as *The Natural History and Antiquities of Selborne*, which has remained in print ever since. He was the first to identify the harvest mouse and the noctule bat, and the first to recognize the chiffchaff, willow warbler, and wood warbler as different species.

White[2] /waɪt/, Patrick (Victor Martindale) (1912–90), Australian novelist, born in Britain. White's international reputation is based on his two novels *The Tree of Man*

(1955) and *Voss* (1957); the latter relates the doomed attempt made in 1845 by a German explorer to cross the Australian continent. He was awarded the Nobel Prize for literature in 1973.

White[3] /waɪt/, T(erence) H(anbury) (1906–64), British novelist, born in India. White first won recognition with *England Have My Bones* (1936). He is best known for the tetralogy *The Once and Future King*, his highly original reworking of the Arthurian legend that began with *The Sword in the Stone* (1937). This was adapted as the Broadway musical *Camelot* (1959), which brought him considerable fame and financial success.

Whitehead /'waɪthed/, A(lfred) N(orth) (1861–1947), English philosopher and mathematician. Whitehead is remembered chiefly for *Principia Mathematica* (1910–13), in which he and his pupil Bertrand Russell attempted to express all of mathematics in formal logical terms. He was also concerned to explain more generally the connections between mathematics, theoretical science, and ordinary experience. Whitehead's work on geometry led to an interest in the philosophy of science; he proposed an alternative to Einstein's theories of relativity, and later developed a general and systematic metaphysical view.

Whitlam /'wɪtləm/, (Edward) Gough (born 1916), Australian Labor statesman, Prime Minister 1972–5. While in office he ended compulsory military service in Australia and relaxed the laws for Asian and African immigrants. When, in 1975, the opposition blocked finance bills in the Senate, he refused to call a general election and was dismissed by the Governor-General Sir John Kerr, the first occasion in 200 years that the British Crown had removed an elected Prime Minister. Whitlam remained leader of the Labor Party until 1977.

Whitman /'wɪtmən/, Walt (1819–92), American poet. His philosophical outlook was profoundly influenced by his experience of frontier life in his travels to Chicago and St Louis in 1848, as well as by transcendentalist ideas, in particular the work of Ralph Waldo Emerson. He published the first edition of *Leaves of Grass*, incorporating 'I Sing the Body Electric' and 'Song of Myself', in 1855; eight further editions followed in Whitman's lifetime, the work enlarging as the poet developed. Written in free verse, the collection celebrates democracy, sexuality, the self, and the liberated

American spirit in union with nature. It was criticized as immoral during his lifetime and later formed the basis of the claims that he was homosexual. In *Drum-Taps* (1865) Whitman recorded his impressions as a hospital visitor during the American Civil War. The *Sequel* (1865) to these poems included his elegy on Abraham Lincoln, 'When Lilacs Last in the Dooryard Bloom'd'.

Whitney /'wɪtnɪ/, Eli (1765–1825), American inventor. He devised the mechanical cotton-gin (patented 1794), as well as conceiving the idea of mass-producing interchangeable parts. This he applied in his fulfilment of a US government contract (1797) to supply muskets; Whitney manufactured these in standardized parts for reassembly, meaning that for the first time worn parts could be replaced by spares rather than requiring special replacements to be made.

Whittier /'wɪtɪə(r)/, John Greenleaf (1807–92), American poet and abolitionist. From the early 1840s he edited various periodicals and wrote poetry for the abolitionist cause. He is best known for his poems on rural themes, especially 'Snow-Bound' (1866).

Whittington /'wɪtɪŋtən/, Sir Richard ('Dick') (died 1423), English merchant and Lord Mayor of London. Whittington was a London mercer who became Lord Mayor three times (1397–8; 1406–7; 1419–20). He left legacies for rebuilding Newgate Prison and for establishing a city library. The popular legend of Dick Whittington's early life as an orphan from a lowly background, his only possession a cat, is first recorded in 1605.

Whittle /'wɪt(ə)l/, Sir Frank (1907–96), English aeronautical engineer, test pilot, and inventor of the jet aircraft engine. He took out the first patent for a turbojet engine in 1930, while still a student. A Gloster aircraft made the first British flight using Whittle's jet engine in May 1941 (two years after the first German jet aircraft), and similar machines later entered service with the RAF. He took up a post at the US Naval Academy in Maryland in 1977.

Whymper /'wɪmpə(r)/, Edward (1840–1911), English mountaineer. In 1860 he was commissioned to make drawings of the Alps, and in the following year he returned to attempt to climb the Matterhorn. After seven attempts he finally succeeded in 1865, at the age of 25. On the way down four of his fellow climbers fell to their deaths, raising contemporary public doubts about the sport.

Wiener /'wiːnə(r)/, Norbert (1894–1964), American mathematician. He is best known for establishing the science of cybernetics in the late 1940s. Wiener spent most of his working life at the Massachusetts Institute of Technology, making major contributions to the study of stochastic processes, integral equations, harmonic analysis, and related fields.

Wiesel /'wiːz(ə)l/, Elie (full name Eliezer Wiesel) (born 1928), Romanian-born American human-rights campaigner, novelist, and academic. A survivor of Auschwitz and Buchenwald concentration camps, he emigrated to the US in 1956 and subsequently pursued a career as a humanities lecturer. Wiesel emerged as a leading authority on the Holocaust, documenting and publicizing Nazi war crimes perpetrated against Jews and others during the Second World War. Genocide, violence, and racism were also the subjects of several acclaimed novels and short-story collections. Wiesel was awarded the Nobel Peace Prize in 1986.

Wiesenthal /'viːz(ə)n,taːl/, Simon (born 1908), Austrian Jewish investigator of Nazi war crimes. After spending 1942 to 1945 in Nazi labour and concentration camps he began his long campaign to bring Nazi war criminals to justice. Enlisting the help of West German, Israeli, and other government agents, he traced some 1,000 unprosecuted criminals, including Adolf Eichmann. In 1961 he opened the Jewish Documentation Centre, also known as the Wiesenthal Centre, in Vienna and continued to track down Nazi criminals when other countries had ceased to pursue their cases.

Wilberforce /'wɪlbə,fɔːs/, William (1759–1833), English politician and social reformer. An MP and close associate of Pitt the Younger, he was a prominent campaigner for the abolition of the slave trade, successfully promoting a bill outlawing its practice in the British West Indies (1807). Later he pushed for the abolition of slavery throughout the British Empire, his efforts resulting in the 1833 Slavery Abolition Act.

Wilcox /'wɪlkɒks/, Ella Wheeler (1850–1919), American poet, novelist, and short-story writer. She wrote many volumes of

romantic verse, the most successful one being *Poems of Passion* (1883).

Wilde /waɪld/, Oscar (Fingal O'Flahertie Wills) (1854–1900), Irish dramatist, novelist, poet, and wit. He was born in Dublin but from the early 1880s spent most of his time in London. He became known for his flamboyant aestheticism and his advocacy of 'art for art's sake' regardless of moral stance; this is particularly evident in his only novel *The Picture of Dorian Gray*, published in 1890. As a dramatist he achieved considerable success with a series of comedies noted for their epigrammatic wit and sharp social observation, including *Lady Windermere's Fan* (1892) and *The Importance of Being Earnest* (1895). However, Wilde's drama *Salomé* (1893), written in French, was refused a performing licence; it was published in English in 1894 and first performed in Paris in 1896. Wilde's relationship with Lord Alfred Douglas resulted in his imprisonment for homosexual offences (1895–7); he died in exile in Paris.

Wilder[1] /'waɪldə(r)/, Billy (born Samuel Wilder) (born 1906), American film director and screenwriter, born in Austria. After emigrating to the US in 1934, he wrote screenplays for a number of Hollywood films before earning recognition as a writer-director with *Double Indemnity* (1944); written with Raymond Chandler, it is regarded as a *film noir* classic. He subsequently co-wrote and directed *Sunset Boulevard* (1950), *Some Like It Hot* (1959), and *The Apartment* (1960); the latter won Oscars for best script, director, and picture.

Wilder[2] /'waɪldə(r)/, Thornton (Niven) (1897–1975), American novelist and dramatist. His work is especially concerned with the universality of human experience, irrespective of time or place. He established his reputation as a novelist with *The Bridge of San Luis Rey* (1927), for which he won a Pulitzer Prize. His plays, often experimental in form, include *Our Town* (1938) and *The Skin of Our Teeth* (1942), both of which received Pulitzer Prizes. His comic drama *The Matchmaker* (1954) provided the basis for the musical *Hello, Dolly!* (1964).

Wilhelm I /'vɪlhelm/ (1797–1888), king of Prussia 1861–88 and emperor of Germany 1871–88. His reign saw the unification of Germany, the driving force behind which was Bismarck, his chief minister. He became the first emperor of Germany after Prussia's victory against France in 1871. The latter part of his reign was marked by the rise of German socialism, to which he responded with harsh repressive measures.

Wilhelm II /'vɪlhelm/ (known as Kaiser Wilhelm) (1859–1941), emperor of Germany 1888–1918, grandson of Queen Victoria. After forcing his chief minister, Bismarck, to resign in 1890 he proved unable to exercise a strong or consistent influence over German policies, which became increasingly militaristic in foreign affairs. He was unable to prevent the outbreak of the First World War (1914), and was vilified by Allied propaganda as the author of the conflict. In 1918 he went into exile in Holland and abdicated his throne.

Wilhelmina /ˌwɪlə'miːnə/, (1880–1962), queen of the Netherlands 1890–1948. She became queen as a child, with her mother as regent until 1898. During the Second World War she maintained a government in exile in London, and through frequent radio broadcasts became a symbol of resistance to the Dutch people. She returned to the Netherlands in 1945, but three years later abdicated in favour of her daughter Juliana.

Wilkie /'wɪlkɪ/, Sir David (1785–1841), Scottish painter. He made his name with the painting *Village Politicians* (1806); influenced by 17th-century Dutch and Flemish genre painters, it defined Wilkie's style for the next twenty years. Wilkie's paintings were popular and contributed to the growing prestige of genre painting in Britain.

Wilkins /'wɪlkɪnz/, Maurice Hugh Frederick (born 1916), New Zealand-born British biochemist and molecular biologist. Studying the structure of the DNA molecule by means of X-ray diffraction analysis, he and his colleague Rosalind Franklin provided the evidence for and confirmed the double helix structure proposed by Francis Crick and James Watson in 1953. Wilkins, Crick, and Watson shared a Nobel Prize for their work on DNA in 1962.

Willard /'wɪlɑːd/, Emma (1787–1870), American educational reformer. A pioneer of women's education, she founded a boarding-school in Vermont (1814) to teach subjects not then available to women (such as mathematics and philosophy). Willard moved the school to Troy, New York (1821), where it became known as the Troy Female Seminary; the college education that it

offered served as a model for subsequent women's colleges in the US and Europe.

William /'wɪljəm/ the name of two kings of England, and two of Great Britain and Ireland:

William I (known as William the Conqueror) (*c*.1027–87), reigned 1066–87, the first Norman king of England. He was the illegitimate son of Robert, Duke of Normandy, and claimed the English throne on the death of Edward the Confessor, stating that Edward had promised it to him. He landed in England at the head of an invasion force, defeated Harold II at the Battle of Hastings (1066), and was crowned king. Having repressed a series of uprisings, he imposed his rule on England, introducing Norman institutions and customs (including feudalism and administrative and legal practices). He also instigated the property survey of England known as the Domesday Book.

William II (known as William Rufus, 'redfaced') (*c*.1060–1100), son of William I, reigned 1087–1100. His succession was challenged by a group of Norman barons in England who wanted William's elder brother Robert Curthose (*c*.1054–1134), Duke of Normandy, to rule England instead. However, William's forces crushed their rebellions in 1088 and 1095. William also campaigned against his brother Robert in Normandy (1089–96), ultimately acquiring the duchy in 1096 when Robert mortgaged it to William before leaving to go on the First Crusade. In the north of England William secured the frontier against the Scots along a line from the Solway Firth to the Tweed. He was killed by an arrow while out hunting; whether he was assassinated or whether his death was an accident remains unclear.

William III (known as William of Orange) (1650–1702), grandson of Charles I, reigned 1689–1702. Son of the Prince of Orange and Mary, daughter of Charles I, William was stadtholder (chief magistrate) of the Netherlands from 1672 and married Mary, daughter of the future James II, in 1677. In 1688 he landed in England at the invitation of disaffected politicians, deposed James II, and, having accepted the Declaration of Rights (which was designed to ensure that the Crown would not act without Parliament's consent), was crowned along with his wife the following year. He defeated James's supporters in Scotland and Ireland (1689–90), and thereafter devoted most of his energies towards opposing the territorial ambitions of Louis XIV of France.

William IV (known as 'the Sailor King') (1765–1837), son of George III, reigned 1830–7. He served in the Royal Navy from 1779, rising to Lord High Admiral in 1827, and came to the throne after the death of his brother George IV. Although an opponent of the first Reform Bill (1832), William reluctantly agreed to create fifty new peers to overcome opposition to it in the House of Lords. In 1834 he intervened in political affairs by imposing his own choice of Prime Minister (the Conservative Robert Peel), despite a Whig majority in Parliament.

William I (known as William the Lion) (1143–1214), grandson of David I, king of Scotland 1165–1214. He attempted to reassert Scottish independence but was forced to pay homage to Henry II of England after being captured by him in 1174.

William of Occam /'ɒkəm/ (also **Ockham**) (*c*.1285–1349), English philosopher and Franciscan friar. He studied and taught philosophy at Oxford until 1324; in the later part of his life (1333–47) he lived in Munich and was active in writing antipapal pamphlets. He was the last of the major scholastic philosophers; his form of nominalist philosophy saw God as beyond human powers of reasoning, and things as provable only by experience or by scriptural authority – hence his maxim, known as *Occam's razor*, that in explaining something entities are not to be multiplied beyond necessity, i.e. the fewest possible assumptions are to be made. Occam distinguished between faith and reason, advocated a radical separation of the Church from the world, denied the pope all temporal authority, and conceded large powers to the laity and their representatives. He was also a firm supporter of the Franciscan doctrine of poverty; this brought strong papal opposition and he was excommunicated in 1328. His ideas had a significant influence on Luther.

William of Orange, William III of Great Britain and Ireland (see WILLIAM).

William Rufus, William II of England (see WILLIAM).

Williams[1] /'wɪljəmz/, Hank (born Hiram King Williams) (1923–53), American country singer and songwriter. A performer since boyhood, Williams had the first of

many country hits, 'Lovesick Blues', in 1949, and that year joined the *Grand Ole Opry* TV programme. He soon began to cross over into the mainstream pop market, many of his songs being successfully recorded by other artists. Probably his most famous song, 'Your Cheatin' Heart' (recorded 1952), was released after his sudden death.

Williams[2] /'wɪljəmz/, John (Christopher) (born 1941), Australian guitarist and composer. He studied with Andrés Segovia before making his London début in 1958. Based in Britain, he became much in demand as a recitalist, noted for an eclectic repertoire that includes both classical and popular music. In 1979 he founded the pop group Sky, playing with them until 1984.

Williams[3] /'wɪljəmz/, J(ohn) P(eter) R(hys) (born 1949), Welsh Rugby Union player. A former junior Wimbledon tennis champion (1966), he made his rugby début for Wales in 1969 and became one of the leading full-backs of the 1970s. Williams played sixty-three times for his country (1969–81), as well as for the British Lions (1971–7). In 1981 he retired from rugby to pursue a career in orthopaedic medicine.

Williams[4] /'wɪljəmz/, Tennessee (born Thomas Lanier Williams) (1911–83), American dramatist. He was brought up in the South, the setting for many of his plays. He achieved success with the semi-autobiographical *The Glass Menagerie* (1944) and *A Streetcar Named Desire* (1947), plays which deal with the tragedy of vulnerable heroines living in fragile fantasy worlds shattered by brutal reality. Williams's later plays, while still dealing with strong passions and family tensions, increasingly feature Gothic and macabre elements; they include *Cat on a Hot Tin Roof* (1955), *Suddenly Last Summer* (1958), and *The Night of the Iguana* (1962).

Williams[5] /'wɪljəmz/, William Carlos (1883–1963), American poet, essayist, novelist, and short-story writer. He worked throughout his life as a paediatrician in his native New Jersey. His poetry illuminates the ordinary by vivid, direct observation; it is characterized by avoidance of emotional content and the use of the American vernacular. Collections of his poetry include *Spring and All* (1923) and *Pictures from Brueghel* (1963). His long poem *Paterson* (1946–58), written in free verse, draws on and explores the cultural, historical, and mythic resonances associated with the industrial New Jersey city of Paterson. Nonfiction works include *In the American Grain* (1925), essays exploring the nature of American literature and the influence of Puritanism in American culture.

Williamson /'wɪljəms(ə)n/, Henry (1895–1977), English novelist. After serving in the First World War Williamson moved in 1921 to North Devon, where he wrote his best-known work, *Tarka the Otter* (1927). His pro-Hitler views in the 1930s led to a brief internment at the outbreak of the Second World War. Williamson continued to write and produced his most ambitious work, the fifteen-volume semi-autobiographical sequence *A Chronicle of Ancient Sunlight*, between 1951 and 1969.

William the Conqueror, William I of England (see WILLIAM).

Wills /wɪlz/, William John (1834–61), English explorer. Having emigrated to Australia, in 1860 he was a member, with two others, of Robert Burke's expedition to cross the continent from south to north. They became the first white people to make this journey, but Wills, Burke, and one of their companions died of starvation on the return journey.

Wilson[1] /'wɪls(ə)n/, Sir Angus (Frank Johnstone) (1913–91), English novelist and short-story writer. His works include the novels *Anglo-Saxon Attitudes* (1956), *The Old Men at the Zoo* (1961), and *Setting the World on Fire* (1980). These, together with several volumes of short stories, display his satiric wit, acute social observation, and love of the macabre and the farcical. He also wrote studies of Zola, Dickens, and Kipling.

Wilson[2] /'wɪls(ə)n/, Charles Thomson Rees (1869–1959), Scottish physicist. He is chiefly remembered for inventing the cloud chamber, building his first one in 1895 in an attempt to reproduce the conditions in which clouds are formed in nature. He later improved the design and by 1911 had developed a chamber in which the track of an ion could be made visible. This became a major tool of particle physicists in subsequent years, and Wilson shared a Nobel Prize for physics in 1927. He also investigated atmospheric electricity and thundercloud formation, and predicted the discovery of cosmic rays.

Wilson[3] /'wɪls(ə)n/, Edmund (1895–1972), American critic, essayist, and short-story

writer. He is remembered chiefly for works of literary and social criticism, which include *Axel's Castle* (1931), a study of symbolist literature, *To the Finland Station* (1940), tracing socialist and revolutionary theory, and *Patriotic Gore: Studies in the Literature of the American Civil War* (1962). He was a friend of F. Scott Fitzgerald, and edited the latter's unfinished novel *The Last Tycoon* (published posthumously in 1941). Wilson's third wife was the novelist Mary McCarthy.

Wilson[4] /'wɪls(ə)n/, Edward Osborne (born 1929), American social biologist. He worked principally on social insects, notably ants and termites, extrapolating his findings to the social behaviour of other animals including humans. His book *Sociobiology: the New Synthesis* (1975) integrated these ideas and effectively launched the science of sociobiology. Wilson also studied the colonization of islands by insects, showing that the number of species reaches a dynamic equilibrium for any given island.

Wilson[5] /'wɪls(ə)n/, (James) Harold, Baron Wilson of Rievaulx (1916–95), British Labour statesman, Prime Minister 1964–70 and 1974–6. His administrations were pragmatic in outlook rather than rigidly socialist. In both terms of office he faced severe economic problems; repeated sterling crises led to devaluation in 1967, while he attempted unsuccessfully to deal with high inflation in 1974–6 by seeking an agreement with trade unions over limiting pay increases. His government introduced a number of social reforms, including reducing the voting age to 18, liberalizing the laws on divorce, homosexuality, and abortion, and introducing comprehensive schooling. Overseas, he was unable to persuade the regime of Ian Smith in Rhodesia (Zimbabwe) to back down over its declaration of independence (1965), and therefore introduced economic sanctions against Rhodesia. In 1974 Wilson renegotiated Britain's terms of entry into the European Economic Community, confirming British membership after a referendum in 1975. He resigned as leader of the Labour Party the following year and was replaced as Prime Minister by James Callaghan.

Wilson[6] /'wɪls(ə)n/, John Tuzo (1908–93), Canadian geophysicist. Wilson was professor of geophysics at Toronto for twenty-eight years. He was a pioneer in the study of what is now known as plate tectonics, introducing the term *plate* in this context in the early 1960s and providing evidence in support of the hypothesis of sea-floor spreading. In 1965 Wilson identified *transform faults*, which occur at the boundaries of plates which merely slide past each other.

Wilson[7] /'wɪls(ə)n/, (Thomas) Woodrow (1856–1924), American Democratic statesman, 28th President of the US 1913–21. He was a prominent academic in the field of law and political economy prior to his election victory. As President he carried out a series of successful administrative and fiscal reforms. He initially kept America out of the First World War, but, following the German reintroduction of unrestricted submarine warfare, entered the war on the Allied side in April 1917. Wilson's conditions for a peace treaty, as set out in his 'Fourteen Points' speech (1918), and his plan for the formation of the League of Nations were crucial in the international negotiations surrounding the end of the war, and he was awarded the Nobel Peace Prize in 1919. However, he was unable to obtain the Senate's ratification of the Treaty of Versailles, his health collapsed, and he lost the presidential election.

Winckelmann /'vɪŋk(ə)lmən/, Johann (Joachim) (1717–68), German archaeologist and art historian, born in Prussia. In 1755 he was appointed librarian to a cardinal in Rome; there he took part in the excavations at Pompeii and Herculaneum and was instrumental in enforcing professional archaeological standards. Winckelmann became superintendent of Roman antiquities in 1763. His best-known work, *History of the Art of Antiquity* (1764), was a seminal text in the neoclassical movement; it was particularly influential in popularizing the art and culture of ancient Greece.

Windaus /'vɪndaʊs/, Adolf (1876–1959), German organic chemist. He did pioneering work on the chemistry and structure of steroids and their derivatives, notably cholesterol. He also investigated the D vitamins and vitamin B_1, and discovered the important substance histamine. Windaus was awarded the Nobel Prize for chemistry in 1928.

Windsor, Duke of the title conferred on Edward VIII on his abdication in 1936.

Winterhalter /'vɪntə,hæltə(r)/, Franz Xavier (1806–73), German painter. He painted many portraits of European royalty and aristocracy. His subjects included Napoleon III, the emperor Franz Josef, and Queen Victoria and her family.

Wisden /'wɪzdən/, John (1826–84), English cricketer. He is remembered as the publisher of *Wisden Cricketers' Almanack*, an annual publication which first appeared in 1864.

Wittgenstein /'vɪtgən,staɪn/, Ludwig (Josef Johann) (1889–1951), Austrian-born philosopher. He came to England in 1911 and studied mathematical logic at Cambridge under Bertrand Russell (1912–13). He then turned to the study of language and its relationship to the world, and in the *Tractatus Logico-philosophicus* (1921) contended that language achieves meaning by 'picturing' things by established conventions. He also pointed out that logical truths are tautologous because they are necessarily true within their own system and argued that metaphysical speculation is meaningless, theories which influenced the development of logical positivism. He returned to Cambridge in 1929, where he was professor of philosophy (1939–47); he became a British citizen in 1938. Principal among his later works (all published posthumously) is *Philosophical Investigations* (1953). In this he argues that words take on different roles according to the different human activities in which they are used, and that they do not have definite intrinsic meanings. He showed that some philosophical problems are simply a result of a misunderstanding of the nature of language, as for example the assumption by some earlier philosophers that individual human beings have a private language in which their thoughts as well as their utterances are composed.

Władysław II see LADISLAUS II.

Wodehouse /'wʊdhaʊs/, Sir P(elham) G(renville) (1881–1975), British-born writer. He was a prolific writer of humorous novels and short stories and his writing career spanned more than seventy years. His best-known works are those set in the leisured English upper-class world of Bertie Wooster and his valet, Jeeves, the first of which appeared in 1917. During the Second World War Wodehouse was interned by the Germans; when released in 1941 he made five radio broadcasts from Berlin, which, although they were comic and non-political in nature, led to accusations in Britain that he was a traitor. He eventually settled in the US, becoming an American citizen in 1955; he was knighted a few weeks before his death.

Wöhler /'vɜːlə(r)/, Friedrich (1800–82), German chemist. With his synthesis of urea from ammonium cyanate in 1828, he demonstrated that organic compounds could be made from inorganic compounds, ending for many scientists their belief in the doctrine of vitalism (that life originates in a vital principle distinct from chemical and other physical forces). He went on to make a number of new inorganic and organic compounds, and was the first to isolate the elements aluminium and beryllium. Wöhler and Justus von Liebig discovered the existence of chemical radicals (see LIEBIG).

Wolf /vɒlf/, Hugo (Philipp Jakob) (1860–1903), Austrian composer. He is chiefly known as a composer of lieder and from about 1883 onwards produced some 300 songs. His early songs are settings of German poets, especially Goethe and Heinrich Heine. He turned to translations of Spanish and Italian verse for the three volumes of his *Spanish Songbook* (1891) and the two volumes of his *Italian Songbook* (1892–6). He also wrote an opera, *Der Corregidor* (1895). His career was cut short by mental illness resulting from syphilis, and his last years were spent in an asylum.

Wolfe[1] /wʊlf/, James (1727–59), British general. As one of the leaders of the expedition sent to seize French Canada, he played a vital role in the capture of Louisbourg on Cape Breton Island in 1758. The following year he commanded the attack on the French capital, the city of Quebec. He was fatally wounded while leading his troops to victory on the Plains of Abraham, the scene of the battle which was to lead to British control of Canada.

Wolfe[2] /wʊlf/, Thomas (Clayton) (1900–38), American novelist. He gave up his teaching post at New York University after the success of his first, autobiographical novel *Look Homeward Angel* (1929). His intense, romantic works dwell idealistically on America. Many, including the short-story collection *The Hills Beyond* (1941), were published posthumously, following his death from a brain tumour.

Wolfe[3] /wʊlf/, Tom (full name Thomas Kennerley Wolfe Jr.) (born 1931), American writer. He was a news reporter for the *Washington Post* (1959–62) and the *Herald Tribune* (1962–6), and became known for his advocacy of the New Journalism and his treatment of contemporary American culture in books such as *The Electric Kool-Aid Acid Test* (1968). His novel *The Bonfire of the Vanities* (1988) was immensely successful.

Wolfson /'wʊlfs(ə)n/, Sir Isaac (1897–1991), Scottish businessman and philanthropist. He was appointed managing director of Great Universal Stores in 1934, later becoming its chairman (1946) and honorary life president (1987). In 1955 he established the Wolfson Foundation for promoting and funding medical research and education. In 1966 Wolfson endowed the Oxford college that now bears his name; University College, Cambridge, changed its name to Wolfson College in 1973 in recognition of grants received from the foundation.

Wollaston /'wʊləstən/, William Hyde (1766–1828), English chemist and physicist. He pioneered powder metallurgy, developed while he was attempting to produce malleable platinum; in the course of this work he discovered palladium and rhodium. The income he derived from his platinum process allowed him to devote himself to scientific research. Wollaston demonstrated that static and current electricity were the same, and was the first to observe the dark lines in the solar spectrum. He also invented a kind of slide-rule for use in chemistry, and several optical instruments. He supported John Dalton's atomic theory and the wave theory of light.

Wollstonecraft /'wʊlstən,krɑːft/, Mary (1759–97), English writer and feminist, of Irish descent. She was associated with a radical circle known as the 'English Jacobins', whose members included Thomas Paine and William Godwin. In 1790 she published *A Vindication of the Rights of Man* in reply to Edmund Burke's *Reflections on the Revolution in France*. Her best-known work, *A Vindication of the Rights of Woman* (1792), defied Jean-Jacques Rousseau's assumptions about male supremacy and championed educational equality for women. In 1797 she married Godwin and died shortly after giving birth to their daughter Mary Shelley.

Wolsey /'wʊlzɪ/, Thomas (known as Cardinal Wolsey) (c.1474–1530), English prelate and statesman. Favoured by Henry VIII, he dominated foreign and domestic policy in the early part of Henry's reign and served to foster the development of royal absolutism in politics and Church affairs; he held positions as Archbishop of York (1514–30), cardinal (1515–30), and Lord Chancellor (1515–29). His main interest was foreign politics, in which he sought to increase England's influence in European affairs by holding the balance of power between the Holy Roman Empire and France. Wolsey incurred royal displeasure through his failure to secure the papal dispensation necessary for Henry's divorce from Catherine of Aragon; he was arrested on a charge of treason and died on his way to trial in London.

Wonder /'wʌndə(r)/, Stevie (born Steveland Judkins Morris) (born 1950), American singer, songwriter, and musician. He was blind from birth, but his musical gifts were recognized at an early age and he became a recording artist with Motown in 1961. Although he was at first a soul singer, from the 1970s his repertoire has broadened to include rock, funk, and romantic ballads. Among his albums are *Innervisions* (1973) and *Songs in the Key of Life* (1976).

Wood[1] /wʊd/, Mrs Henry (née Ellen Price) (1814–87), English novelist. She had immense success with her first novel *East Lynne* (1861) and went on to write nearly forty books. Her ingenious and sensational plots about murders, thefts, and forgeries, in works such as *Elster's Folly* (1866) and *Roland Yorke* (1869), make her one of the forerunners of the modern detective novelist.

Wood[2] /wʊd/, Sir Henry (Joseph) (1869–1944), English conductor. In 1895 he instituted the first of the Promenade Concerts at the Queen's Hall in London, and conducted these every year until he died. During this time he introduced music by composers such as Schoenberg, Janáček, and Scriabin to British audiences. He made many orchestral transcriptions and arranged the *Fantasia on British Sea Songs* (including 'Rule, Britannia'), which has become a regular feature of the last night of each year's promenade concert season.

Wood[3] /wʊd/, Natalie (1938–81), American actress. On joining Warner Brothers in 1955 Wood immediately attracted serious

attention as the vulnerable adolescent heroine of *Rebel Without A Cause* (1955). She continued to play similar film roles in productions such as *Cry in the Night* (1956), *West Side Story* (1961), and *Inside Daisy Clover* (1966). She drowned in an accident in 1981.

Woodward /'wʊdwəd/, Robert Burns (1917–79), American organic chemist. He was the first to synthesize a wide range of complex organic compounds, including quinine, cholesterol, cortisone, strychnine, chlorophyll, and vitamin B$_{12}$. In 1965, with the Polish-born American chemist Roald Hoffmann (born 1937), he devised the symmetry-based rules which govern the course of concerted rearrangement reactions involving cyclic intermediates. He was awarded the Nobel Prize for chemistry in 1965.

Woolf /wʊlf/, (Adeline) Virginia (née Stephen) (1882–1941), English novelist, essayist, and critic. From 1904 her family's London house became the centre of the Bloomsbury Group, among whose members was Leonard Woolf (1880–1969), whom she married in 1912. She and her husband founded the Hogarth Press in 1917. She gained recognition with her third novel, *Jacob's Room* (1922); subsequent novels, such as *Mrs Dalloway* (1925), *To the Lighthouse* (1927), and *The Waves* (1931), characterized by their stream-of-consciousness technique and poetic impressionism, established her as a principal exponent of modernism. Her non-fiction includes *A Room of One's Own* (1929), a major work of the women's movement, and collections of essays and letters. She suffered from severe depression throughout her life, and drowned herself shortly after completing her final and most experimental novel, *Between the Acts* (published posthumously in 1941).

Woolley /'wʊlɪ/, Sir (Charles) Leonard (1880–1960), English archaeologist. Between 1922 and 1934 he was director of a joint British–American archaeological expedition to excavate the Sumerian city of Ur (in what is now southern Iraq). His discoveries included rich royal tombs and thousands of clay tablets providing valuable information on everyday life of the period.

Woolworth /'wʊlwəθ/, Frank Winfield (1852–1919), American businessman. He opened his first shop selling low-priced

goods in 1879. He gradually built up a large chain of US stores selling a wide variety of items, and the business later became an international retail organization.

Wordsworth[1] /'wɜːdzwəθ/, Dorothy (1771–1855), English diarist. She was William Wordsworth's sister and devoted companion. Her detailed diaries (such as her *Grasmere Journal*, 1800–3), in addition to providing a biographical perspective on her brother, document her intense response to nature and mingle the sublime with the matter-of-fact. In 1835 she began to suffer from a form of dementia from which she never recovered.

Wordsworth[2] /'wɜːdzwəθ/, William (1770–1850), English poet. He was born in the Lake District and much of his work was inspired by the landscape of this region. He spent some time in France (1790–1) and became an enthusiastic supporter of the French Revolution, although he later became disillusioned by the excesses of the Terror and in later life assumed a more conservative stance. From 1795 to 1799 he lived in Somerset, where, with Coleridge, he composed the *Lyrical Ballads* (1798), a landmark in the history of English romantic poetry, containing in particular his poem 'Tintern Abbey'. In 1799 he returned to the Lake District, settling in Grasmere with his sister Dorothy; his wife joined them after their marriage in 1802. Among his many poems are the ode 'Intimations of Immortality' (1807), sonnets, such as 'Surprised by Joy' and 'I Wandered Lonely as a Cloud' (both 1815), and the posthumously published, autobiographical *The Prelude* (1850). He was appointed Poet Laureate in 1843.

Worth /wɜːθ/, Charles Frederick (1825–95), English couturier, resident in France from 1845. He opened his own establishment in Paris in 1858, and soon gained the patronage of the Empress Eugénie, wife of Napoleon III. Regarded as the founder of Parisian *haute couture*, he is noted for designing gowns with crinolines, making extensive use of rich fabrics, and for introducing the bustle.

Wren[1] /ren/, Sir Christopher (1632–1723), English architect. He turned to architecture in the 1660s after an academic career as a scientist. Following the Great Fire of London (1666) he submitted plans for the rebuilding of the city; although these were never realized, Wren was appointed Surveyor-General of the King's Works in 1669

and was responsible for the design of the new St Paul's Cathedral (1675–1711) and many of the city's churches. The influence of the baroque, seen in elements of St Paul's, is particularly apparent in his Greenwich Hospital (begun 1696). Among Wren's other works are Greenwich Observatory (1675) and a partial rebuilding of Hampton Court (1689–94). He was a founder member and later president of the Royal Society (1680–2).

Wren[2] /ren/, P(ercival) C(hristopher) (1885–1941), English novelist. He is best known for his romantic adventure stories dealing with life in the French Foreign Legion, the first of which was *Beau Geste* (1924).

Wright[1] /raɪt/, Frank Lloyd (1869–1959), American architect. His early work, with its use of new building materials and cubic forms, was particularly significant for the development of modernist architecture, in particular the international style. His 'prairie-style' houses in Chicago revolutionized American domestic architecture in the first decade of the 20th century with their long low horizontal lines and intercommunicating interior spaces. He advocated an 'organic' architecture, characterized by a close relationship between building and landscape and the nature of the materials used, as can be seen in the Kaufmann House (known as 'Falling Water') in Pennsylvania (1935–9), which incorporates natural features such as a waterfall into its design. Other notable buildings include the Johnson Wax office block in Racine, Wisconsin (1936), and the Guggenheim Museum of Art in New York (1956–9).

Wright[2] /raɪt/, Orville (1871–1948) and Wilbur (1867–1912), American aviation pioneers. In 1903 at Kitty Hawk, North Carolina, the Wright brothers were the first to make a brief powered, sustained, and controlled flight, in an aeroplane which they had designed and built themselves; they had first experimented with gliders. They were also the first to make and fly a fully practical powered aeroplane (1905) and passenger-carrying aeroplane (1908).

Wright[3] /raɪt/, William Ambrose ('Billy') (1924–94), English footballer. A wing-half and latterly a defender, Wright spent his entire professional career with Wolverhampton Wanderers, with whom he won three league championships. He won 105 England caps (ninety as captain), and was

the first player to make more than a hundred appearances for his country. After his retirement in 1959 he managed Arsenal 1962–6 and then worked as an executive in television sport.

Wulfila see ULFILAS.

Wundt /vʊnt/, Wilhelm (1832–1920), German psychologist. Working in Leipzig, he was the founder of psychology as a separate discipline, establishing a laboratory devoted to its study. He felt that the major task of the psychologist was to analyse human consciousness, which could be broken down into simpler fundamental units. Wundt required subjects to report their sensory impressions under controlled conditions, and although this method of inquiry was later rejected, his legacy includes the rigorous methodology upon which he insisted.

Wyatt[1] /'waɪət/, James (1746–1813), English architect. Following a six-year stay in Italy he returned to England, where he built the neoclassical Pantheon in London (1772), later destroyed by fire. Although he continued to build in a neoclassical style Wyatt became a leading figure in the Gothic revival, most notably with his design for Fonthill Abbey in Wiltshire (1796–1807). He was also involved in the restoration of several English medieval cathedrals, work which was later strongly criticized by Pugin.

Wyatt[2] /'waɪət/, Sir Thomas (1503–42), English poet. He held various diplomatic posts in the service of Henry VIII, one of which took him to Italy (1527), a visit which probably stimulated him to translate and imitate the poems of Petrarch. His work includes sonnets, rondeaux, songs for the lute, and satires. His son, also named Sir Thomas Wyatt (c.1521–54), was executed after leading an unsuccessful rebellion against the proposed marriage of Mary I to the future Philip II of Spain.

Wycherley /'wɪtʃəlɪ/, William (c.1640–1716), English dramatist. His Restoration comedies are characterized by their acute social criticism, particularly of sexual morality and marriage conventions. They include *The Gentleman Dancing-Master* (1672), *The Country Wife* (1675), and *The Plain-Dealer* (1676).

Wyclif /'wɪklɪf/, John (also **Wycliffe**) (c.1330–84), English religious reformer. He

was a lecturer at Oxford (1361–82) and a prolific writer, whose attacks on medieval theocracy are regarded as precursors of the Reformation. He criticized the wealth and power of the Church, upheld the Bible as the sole guide for doctrine, and questioned the scriptural basis of the papacy; his teachings were disseminated by itinerant preachers. In accordance with his belief that such texts should be accessible to ordinary people, he instituted the first English translation of the complete Bible. He was compelled to retire from Oxford after his attack on the doctrine of transubstantiation and after the Peasants' Revolt (1381), which was blamed on his teaching. The followers of Wyclif were known as Lollards.

Wyndham /'wɪndəm/, John (pseudonym of John Wyndham Parkes Lucas Beynon Har-ris) (1903–69), English writer of science fiction. He is noted for several novels, including *The Day of the Triffids* (1951), *The Chrysalids* (1955), and *The Midwich Cuckoos* (1957). His fiction often deals with a sudden invasion of catastrophe, usually fantastic rather than technological in nature, and analyses its psychological impact.

Wynette /wɪ'net/, Tammy (born Tammy Wynette Pugh) (born 1942), American country singer. She started singing to pay the medical bills for her last child, who suffered from spinal meningitis. Her first success came in 1966 with 'Apartment No. 9' and continued with songs such as 'Stand by Your Man' (1968). Her unique lamenting voice made her one of the most popular country singers, her *Greatest Hits* album (1969) remaining in the best-seller charts for more than a year.

X

Xanthippe /zæn'θɪpɪ/ (also **Xantippe** /-'tɪpɪ/) (5th century BC), wife of the philosopher Socrates. Her bad-tempered behaviour towards her husband has made her proverbial as a shrew.

Xavier, St Francis /'zævɪə(r), 'zeɪv-/ (known as 'the Apostle of the Indies') (1506–52), Spanish missionary. While studying in Paris in 1529 he met St Ignatius Loyola and five years later became with him one of the original seven Jesuits. He was ordained in 1537, and from 1540 onwards made a series of missionary journeys to southern India, Malacca, the Moluccas, Sri Lanka, and Japan, during which he made many thousands of converts. He died while on his way to China. Feast day, 3 December.

Xenakis /ze'nɑːkɪs/, Iannis (born 1922), French composer and architect, of Greek descent. Born in Romania, he later moved to Greece, where he studied engineering, and settled in Paris in 1947. He became a French citizen and worked for twelve years for the architect Le Corbusier, during which time he began to compose music. He evolved a stochastic style of composition, in which a random sequence of notes is produced according to mathematical probabilities, as in *Pithoprakta* (1955–6). His music also makes use of computer-aided calculations and electronic instruments.

Xenophanes /ze'nɒfə,niːz/ (*c.*570–*c.*480 BC), Greek philosopher. He was a member of the Eleatic school of philosophers and a critic of the belief that the gods resembled human beings, whether in conduct, physical appearance, or understanding. He was a proponent of a form of monotheism, arguing that there is a single eternal self-sufficient Consciousness which influences the universe (with which it is identical) through thought.

Xenophon /'zenəf(ə)n/ (*c.*435–*c.*354 BC), Greek historian, writer, and military leader. He was born in Athens and became a disciple and friend of Socrates. In 401 he joined the campaign of the Persian prince Cyrus the Younger (see Cyrus²) against Artaxerxes II; when Cyrus was killed north of Babylon, Xenophon led an army of 10,000 Greek mercenaries in their retreat to the Black Sea, a journey of about 1,500 km (900 miles). His historical works include the *Anabasis*, an account of the campaign with Cyrus and its aftermath, and the *Hellenica*, a history of Greece. Among his other writings are three works concerning the life and teachings of Socrates, and the *Cyropaedia*, a historical romance about the education of Cyrus the Younger.

Xerxes I /'zɜːksiːz/ (*c.*519–465 BC), son of Darius I, king of Persia 486–465. When his father died he inherited the task of taking revenge on the Greeks for their support of the Ionian cities that had revolted against Persian rule. His invasion force crossed the Hellespont with a bridge of boats, and in 480 won victories at sea at Artemisium and on land at Thermopylae. However, he was subsequently forced to withdraw his forces from Greece after suffering defeat at sea at Salamis (480) and on land at Plataea (479). Xerxes was later murdered, together with his eldest son.

Ximenes de Cisneros see JIMÉNEZ DE CISNEROS.

Y

Yamamoto /ˌjæməˈməʊtəʊ/, Isoroku (1884–1943), Japanese admiral. Although he initially opposed his country's involvement in the Second World War, as Commander-in-Chief of the Combined Fleet (air and naval forces) from 1939, he was responsible for planning the successful Japanese attack on the US naval base at Pearl Harbor (1941). He then directed his forces in Japanese operations to gain control of the Pacific, but was thwarted by the defeat of his fleet at the Battle of Midway (1942). He was killed when the Allies shot down his plane over the Solomon Islands.

Yamasaki /ˌjæməˈsɑːkɪ/, Minoru (1912–86), American architect. He designed the St Louis Municipal Airport Terminal (1956), a barrel-vaulted building which influenced much subsequent American air-terminal design. Other notable designs include the World Trade Center in New York (1972), a skyscraper consisting of twin towers 110 storeys high.

Yeager /ˈjeɪgə(r)/, Charles E(lwood) ('Chuck') (born 1923), American pilot. Yeager was a veteran Second World War pilot who, in 1947, became the first person to break the sound barrier when he piloted the Bell X-1 rocket research aircraft to a level-flight speed of 670 m.p.h. He also set a world speed record in 1953 when he flew the Bell X-1A rocket plane at 1,650 m.p.h.

Yeats /jeɪts/, W(illiam) B(utler) (1865–1939), Irish poet and dramatist. He spent a large part of his life in London, although his interest in Irish cultural and political life remained constant. He was a co-founder of the Irish National Theatre Company (later based at the Abbey Theatre in Dublin) and his play *The Countess Cathleen* (1892) began the Irish theatrical revival. He was also prominent in Ireland's cultural and literary revival, which takes its name from his collection of stories *The Celtic Twilight* (1893). In his poetry, the elaborate style of his earlier work was influenced by the Pre-Raphaelites, while his later work used a sparser, more lyrical, style and was influenced by symbolism, as well as by his interest in mysticism and the occult. His best-known collections from this later period are *The Tower* (1928), including the poems 'Sailing to Byzantium' and 'Leda and the Swan', and *The Winding Stair* (1929). Yeats served as a senator of the Irish Free State (1922–8) and was awarded the Nobel Prize for literature in 1923.

Yeltsin /ˈjeltsɪn/, Boris (Nikolaevich) (born 1931), Russian statesman, President of the Russian Federation since 1991. At first a supporter of Mikhail Gorbachev's reform programme, he soon became its leading radical opponent. In 1990 Yeltsin was elected President of the Russian Soviet Federative Socialist Republic; shortly afterwards he and his supporters resigned from the Communist Party. He emerged with new stature after an attempted coup in 1991, during which he rallied support for Gorbachev; on the breakup of the USSR at the end of that year he became President of the independent Russian Federation. He survived another attempted coup in 1993, and despite criticism over his handling of the conflict in Chechnya he was re-elected in the presidential elections of 1996.

Yevtushenko /ˌjeftəˈʃeŋkəʊ/, Yevgeni (Aleksandrovich) (born 1933), Russian poet. He gained recognition in the 1950s with works such as *Third Snow* (1955) and *Zima Junction* (1956), which were regarded as encapsulating the feelings and aspirations of the post-Stalin generation. He also wrote love poetry and personal lyrics, which had been out of favour during the Stalin era. A champion of greater artistic freedom, he incurred official hostility because of the outspokenness of some of his poetry, notably *Babi Yar* (1961), which strongly criticized Russian anti-Semitism.

Young[1] /jʌŋ/, Brigham (1801–77), American Mormon leader. He became a Mormon in 1832 and succeeded Joseph Smith as the movement's leader in 1844, establishing its headquarters at Salt Lake City, Utah, three years later. He served as governor of the territory of Utah from 1850 until 1857, and retained his position as leader of the Mormons until his death.

Young[2] /jʌŋ/, Neil (Percival) (born 1945), Canadian singer, songwriter, and guitarist. After early success with the group Buffalo

Springfield (1966–8) Young embarked on a long and productive solo career, in which he has combined plaintive country-influenced acoustic material with his distinctively distorted electric-guitar playing. Young's greatest commercial success remains *Harvest* (1972); later albums include *Sleeps with Angels* (1994).

Young[3] /jʌŋ/, Thomas (1773–1829), English physicist, physician, and Egyptologist. Young learned thirteen languages while still a child, and pursued diverse interests in his career. His major work in physics concerned the wave theory of light, which he supported with the help of advanced experiments in optical interference. Young also devised a modulus of elasticity derived from Hooke's Law, investigated the optics of the human eye, and played a major part in the deciphering of the Rosetta Stone.

Young Pretender, the see STUART[1].

Yourcenar /'jʊəsə,nɑː(r)/, Marguerite (née Marguerite de Crayencoeur) (1903–87), French writer. She travelled widely, and wrote a series of novels, plays, poems, and essays. Her work reflects her interest in male homosexuality, notably in the novel *Alexis ou le traité du vain combat* (1929). Many of her novels are meticulous historical reconstructions, including *Mémoires d'Hadrian* (1951). Yourcenar emigrated to the US in 1939 and in 1980 became the first woman to be elected to the Académie française.

Z

Zanuck /ˈzænək/, Darryl F(rancis) (1902–79), American film producer. In 1933 Zanuck co-founded Twentieth Century pictures. After the company's merger with the Fox Company two years later Zanuck remained controlling executive of Twentieth Century Fox, and was president from 1965 until his retirement in 1971. Among his many successful productions are *The Grapes of Wrath* (1940), *The Longest Day* (1962), and *The Sound of Music* (1965).

Zapata /zəˈpɑːtə/, Emiliano (1879–1919), Mexican revolutionary. In 1911 he participated in the revolution led by Francisco Madero (1873–1913); when Madero failed to redistribute land to the peasants, Zapata intitiated his own programme of agrarian reform and attempted to implement this by means of guerrilla warfare. He later joined forces with Pancho Villa and others, overthrowing General Huerta (1854–1916) in 1914; from 1914 to 1919 he and Villa fought against the regime of Venustiano Carranza (1859–1920). Zapata was ambushed and killed by Carranza's soldiers in 1919.

Zappa /ˈzæpə/, Frank (1940–93), American rock singer, musician, and songwriter. In 1965 he formed the Mothers of Invention, who released their first album, *Freak-Out!*, in 1966. They played psychedelic rock with elements of jazz, satire, and parodies of 1950s pop, while their stage performances set out to shock. Zappa later pursued a solo career, in which he frequently combined flowing guitar improvisations with scatological humour; he also became a respected composer of avant-garde orchestral and electronic music.

Zarathustra /ˌzærəˈθʊstrə/ the Avestan name for the Persian prophet Zoroaster.

Zatopek /ˈzætəˌpek/, Emil (born 1922), Czech long-distance runner. During his career he set world records for nine different distances and in the 1952 Olympic Games won gold medals in the 5,000 metres, 10,000 metres, and the marathon.

Zeffirelli /ˌzefəˈrelɪ/, Franco (born Gianfranco Corsi) (born 1923), Italian film and theatre director. He began to direct his own operatic productions in the early 1950s, becoming known for the opulence of his sets and costumes, and working in many of the world's leading opera houses. He began his film career working as Visconti's assistant, and made his directorial début in the late 1960s. Among his films are *Romeo and Juliet* (1968), *Brother Sun, Sister Moon* (1973), and a film version of the opera *La Traviata* (1983).

Zeiss /zaɪs/, Carl (1816–88), German optical instrument-maker. He established a workshop in Jena for the production of precision optical instruments in 1846, quickly establishing a reputation for products of the highest quality. Twenty years later he went into partnership with Ernst Abbe, who further enhanced the reputation of the company and eventually became its sole owner. After the Second World War a separate Zeiss company was formed in West Germany, producing microscopes, lenses, binoculars, and cameras; following German reunification, the two companies merged and the original site at Jena was closed down.

Zeno[1] /ˈziːnəʊ/ (*fl.* 5th century BC), Greek philosopher. Born in Elea in SW Italy, he was a member of the Eleatic school of philosophers and a pupil of Parmenides. He defended Parmenides' theories by formulating paradoxes which set out to demonstrate that motion and plurality are illusions. One of the best known of these is the paradox of Achilles and the tortoise, apparently refuting the existence of motion; it shows that once Achilles has given the tortoise a start he can never overtake it, since by the time he arrives where it was it has already moved on.

Zeno[2] /ˈziːnəʊ/ (known as Zeno of Citium) (*c.*335–*c.*263 BC), Greek philosopher, founder of Stoicism. Based in Athens from about 312, he was a pupil of Cynic philosophers before founding the school of Stoic philosophy in about 300. The school taught that virtue, the highest good, is based on knowledge, and that only the wise are truly virtuous; the wise live in harmony with the divine Reason that governs nature, and are indifferent to the

vicissitudes of fortune and to pleasure and pain (and hence 'stoic' in the popular sense). Zeno's influence on the development of Stoicism was considerable, particularly in the field of ethics, although all that remains of his treatises are fragments of quotations.

Zenobia /ze'nəʊbɪə/ (3rd century AD), queen of Palmyra *c.*267-272. She succeeded her murdered husband as ruler and then conquered Egypt and much of Asia Minor. When she proclaimed her son emperor, the Roman emperor Aurelian marched against her and eventually defeated and captured her. She was later given a pension and a villa in Italy.

Zeppelin /'zepəlm/, Ferdinand (Adolf August Heinrich), Count von (1838-1917), German aviation pioneer. An army officer until his retirement in 1890, he devoted the rest of his life to the development of the dirigible airship for which he is known, the Zeppelin. After his airship's maiden flight in 1900, Zeppelin continued to develop and produce airships at his factory at Friedrichshafen; one of his craft achieved the first 24-hour flight in 1906.

Zeuxis /'zju:ksɪs/ (*fl.* late 5th century BC), Greek painter, born at Heraclea in southern Italy. His works (none of which survive) are only known through the records of ancient writers, who make reference to monochrome techniques and his use of shading to create an illusion of depth. His verisimilitude is the subject of many anecdotes; his paintings of grapes are said to have deceived the birds.

Zhou Enlai /ˌdʒəʊ en'laɪ/ (also **Chou En-lai** /tʃəʊ/) (1898-1976), Chinese Communist statesman, Prime Minister of China 1949-76. One of the founders of the Chinese Communist Party, he joined Sun Yat-sen in 1924. In 1927 he organized a Communist workers' revolt in Shanghai in support of the Kuomintang forces surrounding the city. In the early 1930s he formed a partnership with Mao Zedong, supporting his rise to power within the Communist Party in 1935. On the formation of the People's Republic of China in 1949 Zhou became Premier and also served as Foreign Minister (1949-58). During the 1960s he continued to keep open communication channels with the US, and he presided over the moves towards détente in 1972-3. He was also a moderating influence during the Cultural Revolution.

Zhukov /'ʒu:kɒf/, Georgi (Konstantinovich) (1896-1974), Soviet military leader, born in Russia. He was responsible for much of the planning of the Soviet Union's campaigns in the Second World War. He defeated the Germans at Stalingrad (1943), lifted the siege of Leningrad (1944), led the final assault on Germany and the capture of Berlin (1945), and became commander of the Soviet zone in occupied Germany after the war.

Zia ul-Haq /ˌzɪə ʊl'hæk/, Muhammad (1924-88), Pakistani general and statesman, President 1978-88. As Chief of Staff he led the bloodless coup which deposed President Zulfikar Bhutto in 1977. After being sworn in as President in 1978, he banned all political parties and began to introduce strict Islamic laws. Re-appointed President in 1984, Zia ul-Haq lifted martial law but continued to maintain strict political control. He died in an air crash, possibly as the result of sabotage.

Ziegfeld /'zi:ɡfeld/, Florenz (1869-1932), American theatre manager. In 1907 he produced the first of a series of revues in New York, based on those of the Folies-Bergère, entitled the *Ziegfeld Follies*. These continued annually until his death, being staged intermittently thereafter until 1957. Among the many famous performers promoted by Ziegfeld were W. C. Fields and Fred Astaire.

Zinnemann /'zɪnəmən/, Fred (1907-97), Austrian-born American film director. He studied law in Vienna before becoming a cinematographer and then emigrating to the US in 1929. In 1937 he joined MGM as a director of shorts, winning an Oscar for *That Mothers Might Live* (1938). His features, which are noted for their meticulous realism, include *High Noon* (1952) and the Oscar-winning films *From Here to Eternity* (1953) and *A Man for All Seasons* (1966).

Zoffany /'zɒfənɪ/, Johann (*c.*1733-1810), German-born painter, resident in England from 1758. Many of his earlier paintings depict scenes from the contemporary theatre, and feature the actor David Garrick (for example *The Farmer's Return*, 1762). Zoffany received the patronage of George III and painted several portraits of the royal family. The king also paid for Zoffany to visit Italy (1772-9), where he painted one of his best-known works, *The Tribuna of the Uffizi* (1772-80).

Zog I /zɒg/ (full name Ahmed Bey Zogu) (1895–1961), Albanian statesman and ruler, Prime Minister 1922–4, President 1925–8, and king 1928–39. A leader of the reformist Popular Party, he headed a republican government as Premier and later President, ultimately proclaiming himself king in 1928. Zog's autocratic rule resulted in a period of relative political stability, but the close links which he had cultivated with Italy from 1925 onwards led to increasing Italian domination of Albania, and when the country was invaded by Italy in 1939, Zog went into exile. He abdicated in 1946 after Albania became a Communist state, and died in France.

Zola /'zəʊlə/, Émile (Édouard Charles Antoine) (1840–1902), French novelist and critic. Between 1871 and 1893 he published a series of twenty novels collectively entitled *Les Rougon-Macquart*; it includes *Nana* (1880), *Germinal* (1885), and *La Terre* (1887). The series chronicles in great detail the lives of the Rougon and Macquart families over several generations, and sets out to show how human behaviour is determined by environment and heredity. His collection of essays *Le Roman expérimental* (1880), which establishes an analogy between the novelist's aims and practices and those of the scientist, is regarded as the manifesto of naturalism. Zola is also remembered for his outspoken support of Alfred Dreyfus, most notably for his pamphlet *J'accuse* (1898).

Zoroaster /ˌzɒrəʊ'æstə(r)/ (Avestan name Zarathustra) (*c*.628–*c*.551 BC), Persian prophet and founder of Zoroastrianism. Little is known of his life, but according to tradition he was born in Persia, and began to preach the tenets of what was later called Zoroastrianism after receiving a vision from Ahura Mazda. After his death he became the subject of many legends and was variously believed to have been a magician, an astrologer, a mathematician, and a philosopher.

Zsigmondy /'ʃɪgmɒndɪ/, Richard Adolph (1865–1929), Austrian-born German chemist. His research began with a study of the colours of glass, which developed into his main work on colloids. He investigated the properties of various colloidal solutions, especially of gold in glass or water, and invented the ultramicroscope for counting colloidal particles. Zsigmondy was awarded the Nobel Prize for chemistry in 1925.

Zurbarán /ˌzʊəbə'rɑːn/, Francisco de (1598–1664), Spanish painter. In 1628 he became official painter to the town of Seville, where he spent much of his life; he also carried out commissions for many churches and for Philip IV, for whom he painted a series of mythological pictures *The Labours of Hercules* (1634) and a historical scene *The Defence of Cadiz* (1634). His work reflects the influence of Caravaggio and much of his subject-matter is religious; his other works include narrative series of scenes from the lives of the saints, painted with simple colour and form in a realistic style.

Zwingli /'tsvɪŋlɪ/, Ulrich (1484–1531), Swiss Protestant reformer, the principal figure of the Swiss Reformation. He was minister of Zurich from 1518, where he sought to carry through his political and religious reforms and met with strong local support. From 1522 he published articles advocating the liberation of believers from the control of the papacy and bishops, and upholding the Gospel as the sole basis of truth. He attacked the idea of purgatory, the invocation of saints, monasticism, and other orthodox doctrines. His beliefs differed most markedly from Martin Luther's in his rejection of the latter's doctrine of consubstantiation: at a conference in Marburg in 1529, he upheld his belief that the significance of the Eucharist was purely symbolic. The spread of Zwingli's ideas in Switzerland met with fierce resistance in some regions, and Zwingli was killed in the resulting civil war.

Zworykin /'zwɔːrɪkɪn, zvə'riːkɪn/, Vladimir (Kuzmich) (1889–1982), Russian-born American physicist and television pioneer. He invented an electronic television input device, which incorporated a screen scanned by an electron beam and sent an electric signal to a cathode-ray tube adapted to reproduce the image. This had been developed into the first practical television camera by about 1929. Zworykin continued to be involved in television development, introducing photomultipliers to make cameras more sensitive.

Appendices

Kings and Queens of England and the United Kingdom

802–839	Egbert (King of Wessex)
839–856	Ethelwulf
856–860	Ethelbald
860–866	Ethelbert
865–871	Ethelred I
871–899	Alfred the Great
899–924	Edward the Elder
925–939	Athelstan (first monarch of all England)
939–946	Edmund I
946–955	Edred
955–957	Edwy
959–975	Edgar
975–978	Edward the Martyr
978–1016	Ethelred II the Unready
1016	Edmund II (Ironside)
1017–1035	Canute I
1035–1040	Harold I (Harefoot)
1040–1042	Canute II (Hardecanute)
1042–1066	Edward the Confessor
1066	Harold II
1066–1087	William I the Conqueror
1087–1100	William II (Rufus)
1100–1135	Henry I
1135–1154	Stephen
1154–1189	Henry II
1189–1199	Richard I (the Lionheart)
1199–1216	John (Lackland)
1216–1272	Henry III
1272–1307	Edward I
1307–1327	Edward II
1327–1377	Edward III
1377–1399	Richard II
1399–1413	Henry IV (Bolingbroke)
1413–1422	Henry V
1422–1461 / 1470–1471	Henry VI
1461–1470 / 1471–1483	Edward IV
1483	Edward V (never crowned)
1483–1485	Richard III
1485–1509	Henry VII (Henry Tudor)
1509–1547	Henry VIII
1547–1553	Edward VI
1553–1558	Mary I (Mary Tudor)
1558–1603	Elizabeth I
1603–1625	James I (James VI of Scotland)
1625–1649	Charles I
1660–1685	Charles II
1685–1688	James II (James VII of Scotland)
1689–1694	Mary II
1689–1702	William III (reigned alone from 1694)
1702–1714	Anne
1714–1727	George I
1727–1760	George II
1760–1820	George III
1820–1830	George IV
1830–1837	William IV
1837–1901	Victoria
1901–1910	Edward VII
1910–1936	George V
1936	Edward VIII (never crowned)
1936–1952	George VI
1952–	Elizabeth II

Prime Ministers of Great Britain and the United Kingdom

[1721]–1742	Sir Robert Walpole	Whig
1742–1743	Earl of Wilmington	„
1743–1754	Henry Pelham	„
1754–1756	Duke of Newcastle	„
1756–1757	Duke of Devonshire	„
1757–1762	Duke of Newcastle	„
1762–1763	Earl of Bute	Tory
1763–1765	George Grenville	Whig
1765–1766	Marquess of Rockingham	„
1766–1768	William Pitt the Elder	„
1768–1770	Duke of Grafton	„
1770–1782	Lord North	Tory
1782	Marquess of Rockingham	Whig
1782–1783	Earl of Shelburne	„
1783	Duke of Portland	coalition
1783–1801	William Pitt the Younger	Tory
1801–1804	Henry Addington	„
1804–1806	William Pitt the Younger	„
1806–1807	Lord William Grenville	Whig
1807–1809	Duke of Portland	Tory
1809–1812	Spencer Perceval	„
1812–1827	Earl of Liverpool	„
1827	George Canning	„
1827–1828	Viscount Goderich	„
1828–1830	Duke of Wellington	„
1830–1834	Earl Grey	Whig
1834	Viscount Melbourne	„
1834	Duke of Wellington	Tory
1834–1835	Sir Robert Peel	Conservative
1835–1841	Viscount Melbourne	Whig
1841–1846	Sir Robert Peel	Conservative
1846–1852	Lord John Russell	Whig
1852	Earl of Derby	Conservative
1852–1855	Earl of Aberdeen	coalition
1855–1858	Viscount Palmerston	Whig
1858–1859	Earl of Derby	Conservative

1859–1865	Viscount Palmerston	Liberal
1865–1866	Earl Russell	"
1866–1868	Earl of Derby	Conservative
1868	Benjamin Disraeli	"
1868–1874	William Ewart Gladstone	Liberal
1874–1880	Benjamin Disraeli	Conservative
1880–1885	William Ewart Gladstone	Liberal
1885–1886	Marquess of Salisbury	Conservative
1886	William Ewart Gladstone	Liberal
1886–1892	Marquess of Salisbury	Conservative
1892–1894	William Ewart Gladstone	Liberal
1894–1895	Earl of Rosebery	"
1895–1902	Marquess of Salisbury	Conservative
1902–1905	Arthur James Balfour	"
1905–1908	Sir Henry Campbell-Bannerman	Liberal
1908–1916	Herbert Henry Asquith	"
1916–1922	David Lloyd George	coalition
1922–1923	Andrew Bonar Law	Conservative
1923–1924	Stanley Baldwin	"
1924	James Ramsay MacDonald	Labour
1924–1929	Stanley Baldwin	Conservative
1929–1935	James Ramsay MacDonald	coalition
1935–1937	Stanley Baldwin	"
1937–1940	Neville Chamberlain	"
1940–1945	Winston Spencer Churchill	"
1945–1951	Clement Richard Attlee	Labour
1951–1955	Sir Winston Spencer Churchill	Conservative
1955–1957	Sir Anthony Eden	"
1957–1963	Harold Macmillan	"
1963–1964	Sir Alec Douglas-Home	"
1964–1970	Harold Wilson	Labour
1970–1974	Edward Heath	Conservative
1974–1976	Harold Wilson	Labour
1976–1979	James Callaghan	"
1979–1990	Margaret Thatcher	Conservative
1990–	John Major	"

Prime Ministers of Canada

1867–1873	John A. Macdonald	Conservative
1873–1878	Alexander Mackenzie	Liberal/Reform
1878–1891	John A. Macdonald	Conservative
1891–1892	John J. C. Abbott	Liberal-Conservative
1892–1894	John S. D. Thompson	Conservative
1894–1896	Mackenzie Bowell	„
1896	Charles Tupper	„
1896–1911	Wilfrid Laurier	Liberal
1911–1920	Robert L. Borden	Conservative
1920–1921	Arthur Meighen	„
1921–1926	W. L. Mackenzie King	Liberal
1926	Arthur Meighen	Conservative
1926–1930	W. L. Mackenzie King	Liberal
1930–1935	Richard B. Bennett	Conservative
1935–1948	W. L. Mackenzie King	Liberal
1948–1957	Louis Stephen St Laurent	„
1957–1963	John George Diefenbaker	Progressive Conservative
1963–1968	Lester B. Pearson	Liberal
1968–1979	Pierre Elliott Trudeau	„
1979–1980	Joseph Clark	Progressive Conservative
1980–1984	Pierre Elliott Trudeau	Liberal
1984	John Turner	„
1984–1993	Brian Mulroney	Progressive Conservative
1993	Kim Campbell	„
1993–	Jean Chrétien	Liberal

Prime Ministers of Australia

1901–1903	Edmund Barton	—
1903–1904	Alfred Deakin	Liberal
1904	John C. Watson	Labor
1904–1905	George Houstoun Reid	Free Trade
1905–1908	Alfred Deakin	Liberal
1908–1909	Andrew Fisher	Labor
1909–1910	Alfred Deakin	Liberal
1910–1913	Andrew Fisher	Labor
1913–1914	Joseph Cook	Liberal
1914–1915	Andrew Fisher	Labor
1915–1923	William M. Hughes	Nationalist
1923–1929	Stanley M. Bruce	„
1929–1931	James H. Scullin	Labor
1932–1939	Joseph A. Lyons	United Australia Party
1939–1941	Robert Gordon Menzies	Liberal
1941	Arthur William Fadden	Country Party
1941–1945	John Curtin	Labor
1945–1949	Joseph Benedict Chifley	„
1949–1966	Robert Gordon Menzies	Liberal
1966–1967	Harold Edward Holt	Liberal
1967–1968 (Dec.–Jan.)	John McEwen	„
1968–1971	John Grey Gorton	„
1971–1972	William McMahon	„
1972–1975	Gough Whitlam	Labor
1975–1983	J. Malcolm Fraser	Liberal
1983–1991	Robert J. L. Hawke	Labor
1991–1996	Paul Keating	„
1996–	John Howard	Liberal

Prime Ministers of New Zealand

(since the emergence of party government in 1891)

1891–1893	John Ballance	Liberal
1893–1906	Richard John Seddon	„
1906	William Hall-Jones	„
1906–1912	Joseph George Ward	„
1912	Thomas Mackenzie	„
1912–1925	William Ferguson Massey	Reform
1925	Francis Henry Dillon Bell	„
1925–1928	Joseph Gordon Coates	„
1928–1930	Joseph George Ward	Liberal
1930–1935	George William Forbes	„
1935–1940	Michael J. Savage	Labour
1940–1949	Peter Fraser	„
1949–1957	Sidney G. Holland	National Party
1957 (Aug.–Nov.)	Keith J. Holyoake	„
1957–1960	Walter Nash	Labour
1960–1972	Keith J. Holyoake	National Party
1972	John R. Marshall	„
1972–1974	Norman Kirk	Labour
1974–1975	Wallace Rowling	„
1975–1984	Robert D. Muldoon	National Party
1984–1989	David Lange	Labour
1989–1990	Geoffrey Palmer	„
1990 (Sept.–Oct.)	Mike Moore	Labour
1990–	James B. Bolger	National Party

Presidents of the United States of America

1789–1797	1. George Washington	Federalist
1797–1801	2. John Adams	„
1801–1809	3. Thomas Jefferson	Democratic Republican
1809–1817	4. James Madison	„
1817–1825	5. James Monroe	„
1825–1829	6. John Quincy Adams	Independent
1829–1837	7. Andrew Jackson	Democrat
1837–1841	8. Martin Van Buren	„
1841	9. William H. Harrison	Whig
1841–1845	10. John Tyler	Whig, then Democrat
1845–1849	11. James K. Polk	Democrat
1849–1850	12. Zachary Taylor	Whig
1850–1853	13. Millard Fillmore	„
1853–1857	14. Franklin Pierce	Democrat
1857–1861	15. James Buchanan	„
1861–1865	16. Abraham Lincoln	Republican
1865–1869	17. Andrew Johnson	Democrat
1869–1877	18. Ulysses S. Grant	Republican
1877–1881	19. Rutherford B. Hayes	„
1881	20. James A. Garfield	„
1881–1885	21. Chester A. Arthur	„
1885–1889	22. Grover Cleveland	Democrat
1889–1893	23. Benjamin Harrison	Republican
1893–1897	24. Grover Cleveland	Democrat
1897–1901	25. William McKinley	Republican
1901–1909	26. Theodore Roosevelt	„
1909–1913	27. William H. Taft	„
1913–1921	28. Woodrow Wilson	Democrat
1921–1923	29. Warren G. Harding	Republican
1923–1929	30. Calvin Coolidge	„
1929–1933	31. Herbert Hoover	„
1933–1945	32. Franklin D. Roosevelt	Democrat
1945–1953	33. Harry S Truman	„
1953–1961	34. Dwight D. Eisenhower	Republican
1961–1963	35. John F. Kennedy	Democrat
1963–1969	36. Lyndon B. Johnson	„
1969–1974	37. Richard M. Nixon	Republican
1974–1977	38. Gerald R. Ford	„
1977–1981	39. James Earl Carter	Democrat
1981–1989	40. Ronald W. Reagan	Republican
1989–1993	41. George H. W. Bush	„
1993–	42. William J. Clinton	Democrat